D1526602

Proceedings of the

# 1995 International Gas Research Conference

Cannes, France
6-9 November, 1995

Dan A. Dolenc, Editor
Gas Research Institute
Chicago, Illinois, U.S.A.

## Volume I

*Sponsored by*
Gas Research Institute
International Gas Union
American Gas Association
U.S. Department of Energy

## PUBLISHER'S NOTE

The specialized nature and timeliness of this material demands prompt publication. Therefore, to expedite publication, the text has been reproduced directly from a reduction of the original typed copy. This format eliminates the considerable time and expense of detailed text composition often required of publication processes, while conserving both paper and energy.

Readers will find the text satisfactorily edited for completeness and comprehensibility, although no special effort has been made to achieve the standard of consistency in minor detail that is typical of typeset books.

The publisher in reproducing the papers as received disclaims any and all responsibilities for the contents of individual papers.

February 1996

Published by
Government Institutes, Inc.
4 Research Place, Suite 200
Rockville, MD 20850

Copyright © 1996 by Government Institutes, Inc.

ISSN: 0736-5721
ISBN: 0-86587-498-0

Printed and bound in the United States of America

# PREFACE

The proceedings of the International Gas Research Conference series represent a continuing permanent record of some of the most important world-wide research and development activities to improve the technologies used in the production, transport, storage, and utilization of natural gas, as well as related environmental considerations.  Since the first IGRC was held in Chicago in 1980, the proceedings of each succeeding conference have provided an impressive record of significant accomplishment--from a preponderance of papers in the earlier conferences reporting on R&D plans to the present papers reporting on a wide range of major R&D results in all of the key business areas.

The increasingly high regard in which these conferences are held by the gas industry and research community is attested to by the 675 delegates representing 31 countries that attended the Cannes conference.  The 295 presentations at the conference were contributed from 24 countries.  They included 90 papers in parallel oral sessions and 205 papers in two poster sessions.  The success of the poster session format, starting with the single such session in Washington, D.C. in 1984, was evident in the outstanding response to the two poster sessions in Cannes.  These sessions provide a unique opportunity for extensive interactions between authors and delegates and are a highlight of the conference.  All presentations, both oral and poster, are included in these proceedings.

The proceedings also include the keynote presentations made at the Opening and Closing Plenary Sessions.  The two presentations, Mr. Gerard Brachet's on "Observation Satellites for the Management of Earth's Resources" and Professor Richard A. Catlow's on "Computer Modeling in Materials and Molecular Science and its Potential for the Gas Industry," were especially timely and of importance for the gas industry.  Those presentations complement the detailed technical papers presented during the remainder of the conference.

Particular thanks are owed to the conference sponsors--the International Gas Union, the American Gas Association, the U.S. Department of Energy, and the Gas Research Institute.  Gratitude must also be expressed to others who made major contributions to the success of the conference:  the IGRC Policy Committee, chaired by Dr. Hans Jørgen Rasmusen, Dansk Olie & Naturgas A/S; the Technical Program Committee, chaired by Dr. Bernard S. Lee, Institute of Gas Technology; the Organization Committee, chaired by Mr. Eric Thornton, Gas Research Institute; and the National Organization Committee of France, chaired by Mr. Pierre Henry, Association technique de l'industrie du gaz en France.

We look forward with confidence to the next equally successful International Gas Research Conference to be held in San Diego, California in 1998.

> Robert B. Rosenberg
> Vice President, International
>   and Industrial Relations
> Gas Research Institute

# 1995 INTERNATIONAL GAS RESEARCH CONFERENCE

TABLE OF CONTENTS

I. EXPLORATION AND PRODUCTION

## TECHNOLOGICAL CHALLENGES ASSOCIATED WITH THE DEVELOPMENT OF HP/HT GAS FIELDS IN THE NORTH SEA

### DEFIS TECHNIQUES LIES AU DEVELOPPEMENT DES CHAMPS DE GAZ HP/HT EN MER DU NORD

Alain GUENOT, Ted HULL,
Elf Aquitaine Production, Elf Enterprise Caledonia

**RESUME**

En relation avec le développement potentiel des champs Elgin et Franklin en Mer du Nord, Elf Aquitaine a entrepris un programme de travail important, visant à réduire les incertitudeset à répondre aux défis liés au caractères haute pression et haute température de ces champs. A partir d'une liste exhaustive des paramètres rendant ces champs exceptionnels, on a établi une liste des difficultés potentielles par spécialité, et défini un programme de travail. Quelques exemples des réalisations sont fournis.

**ABSTRACT**

In the context of the potential development of the Elgin and Franklin fields in the North sea, Elf Aquitaine has undertaken a large programme, aiming at solving the uncertainties and challenges created by High pressure high temperature fields. Through an exhaustive analysis of the criteria by which the field are unusual, a list of potential difficulties in different disciplines has been established, and a programme defined. A few examples of solutions are given.

INTRODUCTION

Elf Exploration UK are presently planning the development of the Elgin and Franklin HP/HT fields in the North Sea. These two fields are about 160 km east of Aberdeen in a geological area known as the Central Graben area. The fields are in close proximity to each other and will be jointly developed. Elf is operator of the two different licences which contain the bulk of the two fields.

Major technological challenges associated with these extreme conditions will need to be overcome for a successful development. However the development offers Elf and its partners significant potential economic reward and important strategic opportunities as it will open up for exploitation an undeveloped area of the North Sea that is rich in gas and gas condensate accumulations.

Elgin and Franklin are deep HP/HT gas condensate reservoirs. The actual conditions are unusual and as a result reservoir performance cannot be confidently predicted from analogous experience, but must instead rely more heavily on experimental and theoretical analysis. In addition, new equipment and operational methods must be developed to ensure that the extreme operational conditions are safely and efficiently handled. The Elf Exploration (UK) subsidiary, operated by Elf Enterprise Caledonia in Aberdeen, is working closely with Elf Aquitaine Production in France, to develop the necessary expertise and to apply it to the field development planning.

This paper will address the extreme conditions met in an HP/HT field, the practical consequences for the different aspects of the development and will describe several practical achievements from the ongoing Elgin/ Franklin development preparation.

An HP/HT reservoir features a series of parameters on the high side of normal experience. Although those parameters are related to each other like for instance reservoir pressure and pressure gradient, they have different consequences on the design of wells and field facilities and the potential problems associated with it. For instance two reservoirs may be qualified as HPHT because of their high reservoir pressure. As such this will impose the same criteria for the qualification of the equipment to be used at bottomhole, for the fluid and reservoir characterisation. However, if located at a different depth, this will yield considerably different values with respect to the pressure gradient and the well-head shut-in pressure. This is for instance the case for the Mary Ann field as reported for instance by Mc Dermott et al [10], where the high pressure of the reservoir around 10000 psi (76 MPa), is located below 6000 m., yielding a fairly normal pressure gradient .

It is therefore interesting when presenting an HPHT reservoir and associated problems to envisage a list of parameters. As far as the fields of the Central Graben Area are concerned and more specially with respect to the Elgin and Franklin fields, the following typical values of the parameters can be used.

| | |
|---|---|
| Reservoir pressure : | 110 MPa |
| reservoir pressure gradient : | 2.11 SG |
| In situ effective stress | 15 MPa |
| Well-head shut-in pressure : | 83 MPa |
| Total depletion : | 90 MPa |
| reservoir temperature : | 190 °C |
| surface flowing temperature : | 180 °C |

It can be seen that most of those parameters are on the high side, even if for each of the parameter individually, worst conditions have been encountered in the past.

## THE TECHNOLOGICAL CHALLENGES

For each discipline the development of these high pressure high temperature gas condensate fields will represent a challenge.

### Drilling

Drilling HPHT wells in the North Sea is not so much of a problem today. The real challenge in drilling will be to make development wells at acceptable cost levels. Development wells have more severe specifications than exploration wells. It is necessary to add to the already critical HPHT problem, the drilling problem generated by deviated production wells. This will include for instance mud losses exposure [6,9], casing design and metallurgy [8], and more specific problems such as in field drilling after some reservoir depletion has occurred.

Furthermore and not the least it is essential for the overall project economy and even sometimes for the viability of the development to cut the cost of those HPHT wells, while maintaining an acceptable level of safety and awareness on the rig. It is recognized that the human factor is responsible for a large part of the drilling blowouts which occurred historically on HPHT wells. The necessary improvement has been obtained, not only from the design of the wells, but also by the imposition of specific procedures, and from training and information to personnel. On development wells, the awareness should absolutely survive the routine and an optimum should be found for improving the procedures both from the safety and economics aspects.

### Completion

The main specification of an HPHT completion design should be simplicity. This is of course driven by the necessity to have an enhanced reliability considering the extreme conditions : high temperature and high pressure but also potentially corrosive fluids [1,2].

The completion string should be designed both for the high pressure at the beginning of the field life, but also for any production problems, such as sand production, scale or salt deposit, which might occur at a later stage.

### Reservoir

Fluid characterisation at reservoir conditions is a challenge, as it requires the use of a specific laboratory equipment, to measure rock and fluid parameters. Another challenge of reservoir engineering is the assessment of well productivity and field deliverability, and its variation with time and reservoir depletion [7].

### Production

The problems which may be anticipated during production could result from the extreme values of the surface parameters such as the flowing temperature, the well-head shut in pressure, and the fluid velocity near well-head.

The surface equipment: well-head, Christmas tree and choke will have to be qualified for such a service. An example of the work on choke testing is given by Birchennough et al.[3] Other items such as platform layout, equipment for accommodating the expected temperature variations, and operational procedures such as simultaneous operations, will have to be worked out.

The evacuation lines will have to bc designed to cope with the high initial flowing temperature and the wax content of the produced fluids, particularly later in field life when flowing temperatures will have reduced.

## EXAMPLES

### Introduction

As described above, the development of high pressure, high temperature fields in the Central Graben is a technological challenge. In the context of the possible development of the Elgin and Franklin fields, Elf Aquitaine has initiated a few years ago a large investigation programme, based on engineering studies and research. As much as possible, licence partners, but also operators of the nearby licences where other HPHT fields are located, and their partners, have been associated with this effort. The objective is to address the questions mentioned in the previous sections of this paper, and to provide the project with feasible and economical solutions.

In order to illustrate the type of work which has been done, a few examples, covering different types of activities, will be briefly described :

- Loss and gain phenomenon during drilling
- Determination of the reservoir Biot's coefficient.
- Qualification of a retrievable packer
- Development of an HPHT PVT cell.
- Qualification of a choke.

In the first two examples, fundamental research work in rock physics and rock mechanics, with practical implications in drilling and HP reservoir management, is described. The third example deals with a qualification programme, for the harsh bottomhole environment. The development of a specific laboratory equipment is described in the next example. Finally the last example deals with a surface problem: the choke. Other examples of the work performed in this programme are presented by Avignon [1],or Jelinek et al,[8] .

### Example 1: The loss and gain phenomenon during drilling in the HP zone.

One of the specific features of the drilling activities in the HPHT deep part of the well has been the occurrence of a phenomenon known as "gain and loss". Typically this occurs for mud weight values larger than 2. It starts with an increasing gas reading leading to a mud weight increase. Then the well starts to become unstable, with possible losses while drilling, and gains when the mud circulation is interrupted. When the kick is circulated, no gas is observed at surface. Another typical feature is that the situation worsens whenever the mud weight is further increased. This phenomenon has been reported several times by companies operating HPHT wells in the North Sea. Such a problem has been experienced on the exploration phase of Elgin and has been described in detail by Maury et al [9]. In the same paper, a mechanism has been proposed, and practical solutions suggested which has been applied successfully in a later well.

The basic principle is based on the hypothesis that fractures are created at the wellbore wall in the shaly section of the overburden, where mud is injected during drilling, and from which mud is expelled when mud circulation is interrupted. Incidentally, these fractures increase the contact surface with the formation and this may explain the increase in background gas observed at surface. The higher the mud weight, the larger are those fractures, and the more pronounced the phenomenon: gain, loss, background gas.

Furthermore such a phenomenon, related to a fracture opening is influenced by the thermal regime of the well. For instance an excessive cooling of the hole may enhance the creation or the extension of a fracture and may trigger or expand the phenomenon. One of the conclusion is therefore to avoid any excessive cooling at bottom while drilling, at least in the high pressure zone where this phenomenon may occur. This has been done on a later well where the mud heat exchanger used to deepen the operating zone of the MWD tool has been deliberately stopped while drilling the critical zone. Even if this is based on the experience of one well, no problem has been observed.

Example 2: Determination of the Biot coefficient in the laboratory

The driving force during production is the decrease in the reservoir pore pressure. This pore pressure decrease will result in an increase in the stress effectively applied to the rock matrix. In turn this stress increase will generate strain and deformation of the rock matrix with the possible consequences for well and field performance: loss of productivity, compaction, subsidence.

For a given decrease in pore pressure, the effective stress will be increased by a fraction of this pore pressure variation. This fraction is known as the Biot's coefficient. It varies theoretically from 1 (full transmission) to 0 (no pore pressure effect). For an ideal rock matrix, built from perfect identical spheres, it has been shown that this coefficient is equal to 1. By analogy to this calculation, the value of 1 is also usually given to the Biot's coefficient for sand or sandstone formations. If such a value is used, and assuming a vertical stress of 125 Mpa on the reservoir, the initial effective stress is then equal to 15 MPa. To the anticipated depletion value of 90 MPa will be then associated an increase on the rock matrix of a similar value, which is very important.

In order to investigate this problem in detail, cores from the reservoir have been used in an experimental and theoretical research programme undertaken jointly by Elf Aquitaine and Institut Français du Pétrole (IFP).[4]. They have shown that the value of the coefficient is a direct function of the difference between the mean stress and the pore pressure. While the coefficient is close to 1 when this stress difference is equal to 0, it drops quickly toward a value of 0.8, when the pressure difference increases. Therefore it is valid to use 80% as a reference value of the Biot's coefficient. This has consequences on the initial stress value (37 MPa), and the total variation of the effective stress during depletion (72 MPa).

An algorithm was also developed to allow for an appropriate interpretation of tests performed by increasing external stress with ambient pore pressure. This simplifies the experimental procedure, as it allows to limit the number of tests with actual high pore pressure. Tests are still proceeding within Elf Aquitaine to gather more experimental data on this problem.

Example 3 : Qualification of a retrievable production packer.

The design of the completion of existing HPHT wells , mainly in the USA, is often made by using the sealing capability of a PBR (polish bore receptacle) connecting directly the tubing and a liner hanger. Even if technical solutions have been found, the drawback of such a completion is the use of a sealing assembly, which have to be compatible with the high temperature, the possible harsh environment such as oil based mud, and the possible displacement resulting from the temperature variations whether the well is on or off production.

An alternative solution is the use of a production packer. This is particularly suited to avoid moving seals, in order to potentially improve long term reliability. To fulfil requirements for operability, the packer should be easily retrievable, compatible with the pressure, temperature and fluid conditions, and with a fixed tubing to packer connection. Such a packer has been developed and qualified through a joint project between Elf Aquitaine and Baker oil tools. This work has been described by Fennel et al.[5]. This is an hydraulic set retrievable packer, with an innovative slip system design. The packing element has also been designed in order to be compatible with the pressure conditions, a temperature from 121°C to 204°C, and an oil based mud environment. This latter condition was imposed on by the possible selection of oil based mud to be used as a packer fluid. This has created a selection problem for the proper elastomer, as many elastomers, suited to the pressure and temperature conditions, were exhibiting swelling in oil based mud. The seal assembly consists of a metal-to-metal seal stack with a non elastomeric seal stack as a debris barrier.

Each element of the packing system has been tested individually, and then the whole system has been tested in the laboratory to a combination of parameters: differential pressure and/or tension in a mud environment. Eventually it was verified that the packer could be retrieved successfully after the test.

A full scale field test, using a CRA packer is to be performed to achieve the qualification programme.

### Example 4 : Development of an HPHT PVT cell

In order to gather the necessary information on the hydrocarbons under reservoir conditions, it has been necessary to have access to a PVT cell, able to operate safely in the required range. It was decided by Elf Aquitaine to develop such a piece of equipment. It was done in close cooperation with a manufacturer in France (ROP).

The classical PVT equipment makes use of mercury to apply and maintain the cell pressure. At the HP/HT range of pressure and temperature, this system cannot be used anymore as the interaction between mercury and the hydrocarbon to be analyzed is not negligible, with regard to the expected accuracy of the measurement. Moreover mercury, as such, is a fluid to be avoided as much as possible in the laboratory, and it was thus decided to design a mercury-free apparatus. Pressure is now applied by pistons driven by electric motors. In order to further improve safety and accuracy, sapphire windows usually needed for the determination of phases, have been replaced by an infrared system. The whole system is operating in a nitrogen pressurized chamber and is fully remote operated. After one year of tests, this PVT cell known as "Belenos", is now operational. It is designed for 150 MPa and 220°C.

Based on the same principle, two other cells have been built and are operated in IFP in Paris and Rogaland's Forkning Institute in Stavanger. The first one is specifically designed for fundamental research activities. The second one will be used in the near future for a research project aiming at a better understanding of the PVT behaviour of a mud/hydrocarbon mixture, in order to improve the accuracy of kick control models.

### Example 5 : Testing a production choke for HPHT conditions

The high values of the pressure at well-head, either the shut-in pressure or the flowing pressure, indicate that production chokes will be subjected to a high differential pressure and consequently to substantial fluid velocity when the pressure is released. Moreover the flowing temperature is expected to be high as well, which will make the working conditions even more difficult.

In order to guarantee production, and particularly, in a not normally manned satellite, it is necessary to ascertain that the choke will sustain the wearing effect of the produced fluid for a period of time long enough to be acceptable for normal production conditions. For this reason a choke design has been adapted for those extreme conditions and tested in the laboratory and in the field during a well testing operation. The choke is of the internal sleeve/ external cage type, and the particularity of the design involved mainly the use of specific material, surface coating or surface treatment.[3]

One of the difficulty in the interpretation is in the accurate determination of material wastage during the test of limited duration, in order to have a good extrapolation to long production period. For this reason the thin layer activation technique (TLA) was used. In this technique, the surface to be studied is exposed to a beam of high energy protons, which convert a thin surface layer to an unstable material isotope. When material is removed during the test, this will affect the measured radioactivity of the system, and thus allow for an accurate determination of material wastage.

In field tests, this technique has allowed for the determination of a material loss in the order of a few microns. It was shown also that wear was independent of the flow rate, as sonic velocity is reached most of the time at the nozzle. In a first field test, the limits of the design have been pointed out, and corrected mainly by action on the sealing elements and on the nature of the surface treatment of the internals. Most recently another test has been performed where the choke was subjected to a 30 MPa differential pressure for about 100 hours, with a peak differential pressure of 60 MPa. The flowing temperature was in the range of 150°C. Noise measurements have also been performed which did not show any unacceptable levels. No leak was detected. The erosion effect on the choke, is presently being appraised.

CONCLUSION

The development of the HP/HT fields of the North Sea Central Graben Area presents unique challenges. Similar pressures and temperatures have been encountered in other areas, but the particular set of conditions, not only of temperature and pressure, but also considering reservoir rock parameters, fluid properties, reservoir size, well deliverability and fields location, have not yet been encountered and successfully developed. An intensive programme of research, equipment development and qualification has been incorporated with the application of existing technologies to focus on assessing and demonstrating the means for a reliable, safe and economic development.

The experience gained in drilling, and testing the exploration and appraisal wells to date, the preparatory studies and the equipment development conducted during the last 2-3 years have demonstrated not only that development is feasible, but that reservoir performance can be predicted with sufficient confidence and that an economic development is achievable.

Equipment development and qualification will need to continue to progress in parallel with detailed field development planning, but practicable solutions have been identified for a safe and reliable operation. The remaining challenges are to select field development methods that offer the best balance of cost and reliability and to prepare the procedures to ensure safe and effective operations.

REFERENCES

1.   B. Avignon,
     "High temperature High pressure completion".
     6th Northern European Drilling conference - Kristiansand - 1993

2.   LJ Bacarreza, RJ Van Melsen, G. Jantschy
     "Completion Design for HPHT surface development wells".
     European Petroleum Conference - SPE 28893 - London.-1994

3    PM.Birchennough, D. Cornally, SGB Dawson, P.McCarthy,S. Susden
     "Assessment of Choke Valve Erosion in a High-Pressure High Temperature Gas condensate
     Well using TLA."
     European Petroleum Conference. SPE 28887 - London - 1994

4    M. Bouteca, D. Bary, JM Piau,N. Kessler,M. Boisson, D. Fourmaintraux
     "Contribution of poroelasticity to reservoir engineering: Lab experiments, application to core
     decompression and implication in HP/HT reservoirs depletion"
     Eurock 94, Rotterdam,Balkema Ed. - 1994

5    B. Fennel, B. Avignon, D. Henderson,
     "Qualification of an HP/HT Retrievable Production Packer Prototype for Elgin/Franklin UKCS"
     European Petroleum Conference SPE 28895. - London - 1994

6    FR.French, MR. Mc Lean, M.R
     "Development drilling problems in High pressure reservoirs"
     Journal of Petroleum Technology, August 1993, pp 772-777.1993

7    HH. Hsu,
     "Compositional Simulation for HP/HT Rich Gas Condensate Reservoirs"
     Advances in Reservoir technology 3rd annual PSTI Conference - London - 1993.

8    J. Jelinek, S. D'Agata, M. Bonis, MF Louge, JL. Crolet
     "Selection of a C110 casing grade for midly sour service"
     EUROCORR 94 - Bournemouth, UK - 1994.

9    V. Maury, JL. Idelovici,
     "Safe Drilling in HP-HT conditions: The role of thermal regime in the loss and gain
     phenomenon"
     SPE/IADC conference, SPE 29428 - Amsterdam,- 1995.

10   JR. Mc Dermott, BL. Martin,BL.
     "Completion design for Deep sour Norphlet gas wells offshore Mobile, Alabama"
     67th SPE Annual and Technical conference SPE 24772 - Washington DC - 1992.

DISTRIBUTION OF PERMAFROST-ASSOCIATED
NATURAL GAS HYDRATE ACCUMULATIONS WITHIN
THE CIRCUMARCTIC OF THE NORTHERN HEMISPHERE

DISTRIBUTION DES ACCUMULATIONS DES HYDRATES
DE GAZ NATUREL ASSOCIÉS AU PERGÉLISOL DANS
LES RÉGIONS CIRCUMARCTIQUES DE L'HÉMISPHÈRE NORD

Timothy S. Collett
U.S. Geological Survey, USA

## ABSTRACT

Natural gas hydrates are known to be present in the West Siberian Basin and are believed to occur in other permafrost areas of northern Russia, including the Lena-Tunguska province. Permafrost-associated gas hydrates are also present in the North American Arctic. Direct evidence for gas hydrates on the North Slope of Alaska comes from a core-test, and indirect evidence comes from drilling and open-hole industry well logs which suggest the presence of numerous gas hydrate layers in the area of the Prudhoe Bay and Kuparuk River oil fields. Well-log responses attributed to the presence of gas hydrates have been obtained in about one-fifth of the wells drilled in the Mackenzie Delta of Canada, and more than half of the wells in the Sverdrup Basin are inferred to contain gas hydrates. The combined information from Arctic gas-hydrate studies shows that, in permafrost regions, gas hydrates may exist at subsurface depths ranging from about 130 to 2,000 m.

## RÉSUMÉ

Les hydrates de gaz naturel ont été identifiés dans leBassin Occidental de la Sibérie et on croit qu'ils sont présents dans d'autres régions pergélisolées du nord de la Russie, incluant le province de Lean-Tunguska. Les hydrates de gaz associés au pergélisol existent également dans l'Artique nor-américain. L'évidence directe d'hydrates de gaz sur la Pente Septentrionalle de l'Alaska provient d'un trou de forage d'essai, et l'évidence indirecte provient de forages et de régistres industriels qui suggèrent la présence de nombreuses couches d'hydrates de gaz dans la région des champs pétrolifères de Prudhoe Bay et de Kuparuk River. Les réactions, inscrites dans les régistres de puits, attribuées à la présence des hydrates de gaz ont été obtenues dans approximativement un cinquième des puits forés dans le Delta du Mackenzie au Canada, et on a déduit que plus de la moitié des puits du Bassin Sverdrup contiennent des hydrates de gaz. L'information combinée des études des hydrates de gaz arctiques indiquent que, dans les régions pergélisolées, les hydrates de gaz peuvent exister à des profondeurs s'étalant entre 130 et 2,000 mèters sous la surface.

INTRODUCTION

Gas hydrates are crystalline substances composed of water and gas, in which a solid water-lattice accommodates gas molecules in a cage-like structure, or clathrate. Gas hydrates are widespread in permafrost regions and beneath the sea in sediment of outer continental margins. While methane, propane, and other gases can be included in the clathrate structure, methane hydrates appear to be the most common in nature (1). The amount of methane sequestered in gas hydrates is probably enormous, but estimates of the amounts are speculative and range over three orders-of-magnitude, from about 3,000 to 8,000,000 trillion cubic meters (1). The production history of the Russian Messoyakha gas hydrate field demonstrates that gas hydrates are an immediate source of natural gas that can be produced by conventional methods (2). Gas hydrates also represent a significant drilling and production hazard. Russian, Canadian, and American researchers have described numerous problems associated with gas hydrates, including blowouts and casing failures (3).

Even though gas hydrates are known to occur in numerous arctic sedimentary basins, little is known about the geologic parameters controlling their distribution. The primary objectives of this paper are to assess the geologic parameters that control the stability of gas hydrates and to document the potential distribution of permafrost-associated gas hydrates within the circumarctic of the northern hemisphere. This paper begins with a discussion of the geologic parameters that affect the stability of gas hydrates in permafrost environments. The main body of the paper deals with the description of known and potential Arctic gas hydrate accumulations in northern Alaska, Canada, and Russia.

GEOLOGIC CONTROLS ON GAS HYDRATE STABILITY

A review of previous gas hydrate studies indicates that the stability of gas hydrates is controlled by formation temperature, formation pore-pressure, gas chemistry, and pore-water salinity. In the following section, these geologic controls on the stability of gas hydrates will be reviewed and assessed.

Gas hydrates exist under a limited range of temperature and pressure conditions; such that the depth and thickness of the zone of potential gas-hydrate stability can be calculated. Depicted in the temperature/depth plots of figures 1A, 1B, and 1C are a series subsurface temperature profiles from an onshore permafrost area and two laboratory-derived gas-hydrate stability curves for different natural gases (4). These gas-hydrate phase-diagrams (Figures 1A, 1B, and 1C) illustrate how variations in formation-temperature, pore-pressure, and gas composition can affect the thickness of the gas-hydrate stability zone. In each phase-diagram, the mean-annual surface temperature is assumed to be -10°C; however, the depth to the base of permafrost (0°C isotherm) is varied for each temperature profile (assumed permafrost depths of 305 m, 610 m, and 914 m). Below permafrost, three different geothermal gradients (4.0°C/100 m, 3.2°C/100 m, and 2.0°C/100 m) are used to project the sub-permafrost temperature profiles. The two gas-hydrate stability curves represent gas hydrates with different gas chemistries. One of the stability curves is for a 100 percent methane hydrate, and the other is for a hydrate that contains 98 percent methane, 1.5 percent ethane, and 0.5 percent propane. The only difference among the three phase-diagrams (Figuress 1A, 1B, and 1C) is the assumed pore-pressure gradient. Each phase diagram is constructed assuming different pore-pressure gradient; 9.048 kPa/m [0.400 psi/ft] (Figure 1A), 9.795 kPa/m [0.433 psi/ft] (Figure 1B), and 11.311 kPa/m [0.500 psi/ft] (Figure 1C).

The zone of potential gas-hydrate stability in each phase-diagram (Figuress 1A, 1B, and 1C) lies in the area between the intersections of the temperature profile and the gas-hydrate stability curve. For example, in figure 1B, which assumes a hydrostatic pore-pressure gradient, the temperature profile projected to an assumed permafrost base of 610 m intersects the 100 percent methane-hydrate stability curve at about 200 m, thus marking the upper boundary of the methane-hydrate stability zone. A geothermal gradient of 4.0°C/100 m projected from the base of permafrost at 610 m intersects the 100 percent methane-hydrate stability curve at about 1,100 m; thus, the zone of potential methane-hydrate stability is approximately 900 m thick. However, if permafrost extended to a depth of 914 m and if the geothermal gradient below permafrost is 2.0°C/100 m, the zone of potential methane-hydrate stability would be approximately 2,100 m thick.

Most gas-hydrate stability studies assume that the pore-pressure gradient is hydrostatic (9.795 kPa/m; 0.433 psi/ft). Pore-pressure gradients greater than hydrostatic will correspond to higher pore-pressures with depth and a thicker gas-hydrate stability zone. A pore-pressure gradient less than hydrostatic will correspond to a thinner gas-hydrate stability zone. The affect of pore-pressure variations on the thickness of the gas-hydrate stability zone can be quantified by comparing each of the phase diagrams in figures 1A, 1B, and 1C. For example, in figure 1A, which assumes a 9.048 kPa/m (0.400 psi/ft) pore-pressure gradient, the thickness of the 100 percent methane-hydrate stability zone with a 610 m permafrost depth and a sub-permafrost geothermal gradient of 2.0°C/100 m would be about 1,600 m. However, if a pore-pressure gradient of 11.311 kPa/m (0.500 psi/ft) is assumed (Figure 1C) the thickness of the methane-hydrate stability zone would be increased to about 1,850 m.

The gas-hydrate stability curves in figures 1A, 1B, and 1C were obtained from laboratory data published in Holder and others (4). The addition of 1.5 percent ethane and 0.5 percent propane to the pure methane gas system shifts the stability curve to the right, thus deepening the zone of potential gas-hydrate stability. For example, assuming a hydrostatic pore-pressure gradient (Figure 1B), a permafrost depth of 610 m, and a sub-permafrost geothermal gradient of 4.0°C/100 m, the zone of potential methane (100 percent methane) hydrate stability would be about 900 m thick; however, the addition of ethane (1.5 percent) and propane (0.5 percent) would thicken the gas-hydrate stability zone to 1,100 m.

Salt, such as NaCl, when added to a gas-hydrate system, lowers the temperature at which gas hydrates form. Pore-water salts in contact with the gas during gas hydrate formation can reduce the crystallization temperature by about 0.06°C for each part per thousand of salt (4). Therefore, a pore-water salinity similar to that of seawater (32 ppt) would shift the gas-hydrate stability curves in figures 1A, 1B, and 1C to the left about 2°C and reduce the thickness of the gas-hydrate stability zone.

## CIRCUMARCTIC GAS HYDRATE ACCUMULATIONS

The following section contains descriptions of confirmed and inferred permafrost-associated gas hydrate accumulations within the circumarctic of the northern hemisphere. Regions examined (Figure 2) include northern Alaska, the Mackenzie Delta-Beaufort Sea region and Sverdrup Basin of Canada, and two physiographic provinces of the Russian Federation: West Siberian Basin and Lena-Tunguska. Each description contains a brief discussion of the regional geology and a comprehensive review of the geologic parameters controlling the stability (formation temperature, pore-pressure, gas chemistry, and pore-water salinity) of gas hydrate accumulations. When available, each regional review contains a description of the confirmed or inferred in-situ gas hydrate occurrences.

### Northern Alaska, United States

The North Slope of Alaska, encompasses all of the land north of the Brooks Range drainage divide and is generally subdivided into three physiographic provinces, from south to north: the Brooks Range, the foothills, and the coastal plain. Oriented in a subparallel east-west direction, these provinces reflect underlying geologic trends. The three main structural elements that compose the North Slope are the Brooks Range orogen, the Colville trough, and the Barrow arch, all of which correspond generally to the respective physiographic provinces.

The sedimentary rocks of the North Slope can be conveniently grouped into three sequences that indicate major episodes in the tectonic development of the region and, to a degree, its lithologic character. Defined on the basis of source area, these sequences, proposed by Lerand (5) and applied to northern Alaska by Grantz and others (6) are, in ascending order, the Franklinian (Cambrian through Devonian), the Ellesmerian (Mississippian through Jurassic), and the Brookian (Cretaceous to Holocene).

The only confirmation of natural gas hydrates on the North Slope was obtained in 1972 when an oil company successfully recovered a core containing gas hydrates (7). Well-log data from an additional 445 North Slope wells were examined for possible gas-hydrate occurrences (7). This review of all available data revealed that gas hydrates occur in 50 of the surveyed wells. Many of these wells have multiple gas-hydrate-bearing units, and individual occurrences range from 3- to 31-m-thick. The well-log inferred gas hydrates occur in six laterally continuous sandstone and conglomerate units and are geographically restricted to the east end of the Kuparuk River production area and the west end of the Prudhoe Bay production area. Open-hole logs from wells in the west end of the Prudhoe Bay field also indicate the presence of a large free-gas accumulation trapped stratigraphically downdip below four of the log-inferred gas hydrates. The potential volume of gas within the identified gas hydrates (exclusive of the associated free-gas) of the Prudhoe Bay-Kuparuk River area is approximately $1.0 \times 10^{12}$ to $1.2 \times 10^{12}$ cubic meters of gas (7).

Formation Temperature. On the North Slope, subsurface temperature data come from high-resolution, equilibrated well-bore surveys in 46 wells and from estimates based on identification of the base of ice-bearing permafrost in 102 other wells (7). A comparison of geothermal gradients calculated from the high-resolution temperature surveys and projected from known ice-bearing permafrost depths are similar over most of the North Slope, with gradient values in the ice-bearing sequence ranging from about 1.5°C/100 m in the Prudhoe Bay area to about 4.5°C/100 m in the National Petroleum Reserve in

Alaska (NPRA). The calculated and projected geothermal gradients from below the ice-bearing sequence range from about $1.6\,^{\circ}$C/100 m to about 5.2°C/100 m.

Formation Pore-Pressure. On the North Slope, pressure data from petroleum drill-stem testing in 17 wells, and log evaluation of discontinuities in overburden compaction profiles (pore-pressure profiles) in 22 wells have been used to evaluate pore-pressures within the near-surface sediments (0-1,500 m). Pore-pressure gradients calculated from shut-in pressures recorded during drill-stem testing in wells from the North Slope range from 9.3 to 11.2 kPa/m, with an average gradient of 9.7 kPa/m (0.43 psi/ft), near hydrostatic. Pore-pressures in the wells we have examined are a product of a hydrostatic pore-pressure gradient; therefore, the gas-hydrate stability determinations for northern Alaska in this paper assume a hydrostatic pore-pressure gradient (9.795 kPa/m; 0.433 psi/ft).

Gas Chemistry. The analysis of mud-log gas-chromatographic data from 320 wells indicates that methane is the dominant hydrocarbon gas in the near-surface (0-1,500 m) sedimentary rocks of the North Slope (7). Analysis of gas evolved from recovered gas hydrate samples in the Prudhoe Bay area suggests that the in-situ gas hydrates are composed mostly of methane (87 to 99 percent). Therefore, the gas-hydrate stability calculations in this paper for northern Alaska have been made assuming a pure methane chemistry.

Pore-Water Salinity. Salinity data within the near-surface sediments of the North Slope are available from petroleum drill-stem and production tests, water samples from cores within the permafrost sequence, and spontaneous potential well-log calculations (7). Available data indicates that the (bulk) pore-water salinities are low, ranging from 0.5 to 19.0 ppt. The gas-hydrate stability calculations for northern Alaska in this paper have been made assuming a pore-water salinity of 19 ppt.

Gas-Hydrate Stability Calculations. The methane-hydrate stability curve used for this study was based on a stability model and experimental results published in Holder and others (4). The stability curve has been simplified as a function of temperature into two equations:

$$P(kPa)=\exp[14.7170\text{-}1886.79/T^{\circ}K] \quad \text{(from 248 to 273 }^{\circ}K \text{ or -25 to 0}^{\circ}C)$$

$$P(kPa)=\exp[38.9803\text{-}8533.80/T^{\circ}K] \quad \text{(from 273 to 298 }^{\circ}K \text{ or 0 to 25}^{\circ}C)$$

The P(kPa) represents the dissociation or formation pressure of a methane hydrate at a given temperature T ($^{\circ}K$). For the purpose of calculating subsurface gas-hydrate stability conditions, the variable T ($^{\circ}K$) represents the equilibrium temperature in Kelvins at any given depth. The depth values of the stability curve can be calculated by means of the equation by converting the derived pressure P(kPa) using the local pore-pressure gradient. As previously noted, the regional pore-pressure gradient on the North Slope is assumed to be hydrostatic (9.795 kPa/m or 0.433 psi/ft). A computer program was written to facilitate calculations of the limits of the gas-hydrate stability field. The program requires as input the mean annual surface temperature, the depth to the base of ice-bearing permafrost, the temperature at the base of ice-bearing permafrost, and the ratio between the geothermal gradient from above to below the base of the ice-bearing permafrost. The program will also allow the user to input temperature data from other sources, such as the high-resolution equilibrated wellbore temperature surveys. The program will project the geothermal gradient above and below the base of the ice-bearing permafrost and calculate the depths of the upper and lower boundaries of the zone of methane-hydrate stability.

The calculated thickness of the methane-hydrate stability zone in northern Alaska is isopached in figure 3; this map reveals that the methane-hydrate stability zone on the North Slope is thickest in the Prudhoe Bay area, with calculated values slightly greater than 1,000 m. The offshore extent of the gas-hydrate stability zone is not well established; however, "relic" permafrost and gas hydrates may exist on the Beaufort Sea continental shelf to a present water depth of 50 m (7).

Mackenzie Delta - Beaufort Sea Region, Canada

The Mackenzie Delta-Beaufort Sea region, as described by Procter and others (8), is composed in part of modern deltaic sediments and older fluvial deposits of Richards Island and the Tuktoyaktuk Peninsula, it also consists of the offshore area extending to the continental shelf at a water depth of about 200 m. This region is underlain by deltaic sandstones and shales of Mesozoic and Cenozoic age that thicken to more than 12 km over a short distance seaward from the present shoreline. This sedimentary section overlies faulted Paleozoic rocks stepping down beneath the Mesozoic and Cenozoic section.

Natural gas hydrates have been inferred to occur in 25 Mackenzie Delta-Beaufort Sea industry exploratory wells (9). All of these inferred gas hydrates occur in clastic sedimentary rocks of the Tertiary Kugmallit, Mackenzie Bay, and Iperk sequences (8,9). The most extensively studied inferred gas hydrate occurrences in the Mackenzie Delta-Beaufort Sea region are those drilled in the onshore Mallik L-38 and Ivik J-26 wells (10) and those in the offshore Nerlerk M-98, Koakoak O-22, Ukalerk C-50, and Kopanoar M-13 wells (11). On the bases of open-hole well log evaluation, it is estimated that

Mallik L-38 encountered about 100 m of gas-hydrate-bearing sandstone units, and Ivik J-26 penetrated about 25 m of gas hydrates. The well-log inferred gas-hydrate-bearing sandstone units in the Mallik L-38 well occur within the depth interval from 820 to 1,103 meters, which is below the base of ice-bearing permafrost. The inferred gas hydrates in Ivik J-26 occupy a series of fine-grained sandstone and conglomeratic rock units within the depth interval from 980 to 1,020 meters, which is below the base of ice-bearing permafrost. Analyses of open-hole well logs and mud-gas logs, indicate that the offshore Nerlerk M-98 well penetrated about 170 m of gas-hydrate-bearing sedimentary units, while the Koakoak O-22, Ukalerk C-50, and Kopanoar M-13 wells drilled approximately 40 m, 100 m, and 250 m of gas hydrates respectively (11). In all four cases the well-log inferred gas hydrates occur in fine-grained sandstone rock units, and exhibited significant gas flows during drilling. Recently, Smith and Judge (9) have determined that the Mackenzie Delta-Beaufort sea region may contain $16 \times 10^{12}$ m$^3$ of natural gas in hydrate form.

Formation Temperature. In the Mackenzie Delta-Beaufort Sea region, subsurface temperature data come from industry-acquired production drill-stem tests, bottom-hole well log surveys, and from approximately 50 industry wells that have been preserved for precise temperature studies (12). Within 1-km of the surface the thermal regime is highly complex due to widely varying surface temperature histories and significant variations in subsurface lithologies. Deep (>1-km) geothermal gradients calculated from precise industry temperature surveys in the Mackenzie Delta-Beaufort Sea region range from about 1.0°C/100 m to 4.0°C/100 m (12). Reported geothermal gradients immediately below permafrost range from 2.3°C/100 m to 3.3°C/100 m, and average about 3.0°C/100 m (12).

Formation Pore-Pressure. Data from four wells drilled on the Beaufort Sea continental shelf indicate that the pore-pressures are approximately hydrostatic within the permafrost sequence, and over pressured below permafrost. Weaver and Stewart (11) indicated that the elevated sub-permafrost pore-pressures may be due to disassociating "relic" gas hydrates, however, drilling data collected elsewhere on the continental shelf appears to refute this hypothesis. Because the anomalous sub-permafrost pore-pressure conditions reported by Weaver and Stewart (11) are not continuous across the continental shelf, the gas hydrate stability determinations for the Mackenzie Delta-Beaufort Sea region have been made assuming a hydrostatic pore-pressure gradient (9.795 kPa/m; 0.433 psi/ft).

Gas Chemistry. Analyses of gas samples and mud-log gas-chromatographic data from industry wells reveal that the formation gases within the upper 2,000 m of sediment in the Mackenzie Delta-Beaufort Sea region consist of mostly methane (99.5 %) (11). Four drill-stem production tests of suspected gas hydrate occurrences in two wells drilled on Richards Island in the Mackenzie Delta yielded gas composed principally of methane (99.19 to 99.53 %) (10). Since only methane has been detected in significant quantities, methane-hydrate stability conditions are assumed for the Mackenzie Delta-Beaufort Sea gas hydrate stability calculations in this paper.

Pore-Water Salinity. The pore-water salinity of the formation waters in the Mackenzie Delta-Beaufort Sea region, within the depth range from 200 to 2,000 m is approximately 10 ppm (11), which would have little affect on gas hydrate stability. Therefore, it is assumed that dissolved pore-water salts have no affect on gas hydrate stability in the Mackenzie Delta-Beaufort Sea region.

Gas-Hydrate Stability Calculations. Gas hydrate studies in Alaska have shown that well-log derived ice-bearing permafrost depths can be used to evaluate subsurface temperatures and assess gas-hydrate stability conditions (7). By combining the ice-bearing permafrost depths from Judge (12) with the gas-hydrate stability phase diagrams in figures 1A, 1B, and 1C, it is possible to predict the distribution of the methane-hydrate stability zone. The gas-hydrate stability map in figure 4, extrapolated from well-log derived ice-bearing permafrost depths, depicts the thickness of the methane-hydrate stability zone in the Mackenzie Delta-Beaufort Sea region. This map shows that the methane-hydrate stability zone is more than 1,000 m thick on Richards Island and is areally extensive beneath most of the continental shelf.

In a recent review of the geothermal conditions controlling gas hydrate stability, Smith and Judge (9) mapped the depth to the base of the methane-hydrate stability zone in the Mackenzie Delta-Beaufort Sea region. The Smith and Judge (9) methane-hydrate stability map compares favorably with the stability map extrapolated from well-log derived ice-bearing permafrost data (Figure 4).

Sverdrup Basin, Canada

The Sverdrup Basin is a structural depression near the northern margin of the North American Craton (Figure 2), it is about 1,300 km long and as wide as 400 km in the north-central portion of the basin and is bordered to the northwest by the Sverdrup Rime and to the south and east by the Franklin Foldbelt. The Sverdrup Basin contains up to 13 km of Lower Carboniferous to upper Tertiary marine and nonmarine terrigenous clastics, carbonates, evaporates, basalt flows, and gabbro dikes and sills.

The Sverdrup Basin was developed on older deformed strata of the late Proterozoic Franklinian basin and evolved in five phases: [1] late Paleozoic deposition of evaporites and marine muds in the axes of the basin, with sands and carbonates being deposited along the margin; [2] early Mesozoic deposition of deep water silts and clays within the axes of the basin; [3] middle Mesozoic accumulation of terrigenous clastics; [4] late Mesozoic clastic deposition overstepping the former basin margins; and [5] the late Mesozoic-Cenozoic Eurekan Orogeny imprinted the major structural characteristics of the basin.

Most studies dealing with the occurrence of gas hydrates in the Sverdrup Basin have been concerned with gas hydrate induced drilling and production hazards (13). The review of limited information obtained from reports on drilling in the Sverdrup Basin infer the possible occurrence of gas hydrates on or near King Christian, Ellef Ringnes, and Mellville Islands. In 1971, during drilling of the King Christian Island N-06 well, gas leaked into the rig around the outside of the surface casing which was set at 160 m. A well drilled on Ellef Ringnes Island also experienced significant gas flow from behind casing (405 m) while drilling at 2,560 m. Similar gas leaks have been reported throughout the basin, which may be the result of drilling activity thermally disturbing bypassed gas hydrate occurrences. Drilling on Mellville Island has also revealed the possible occurrence of gas hydrates. For example, while drilling a well at Hearne Point several significant gas flows where encountered, one at a depth of 356 m and a second at 895 m. Hydrocarbon production tests of both zones yielded classical gas hydrate test results, with low gas flow rates and shut-in pressures that slowly increased beyond hydrostatic during testing. While drilling the Jackson G-16 well off the southwestern coast of Ellef Ringnes Island gas was detected at a depth of 453 m and again at 567 m, which significantly complicated wellbore casing operations. A nearby re-drill of this well also encountered gas within the same depth interval (523 m), indicating possible gas hydrate occurrences. Based on drilling reports, it appears that gas hydrates likely exist in the Sverdrup Basin; however, no direct evidence of gas hydrates, such as recovered core material, have been obtained.

Formation Temperature. Precise temperature surveys have been obtained from 32 petroleum wells drilled in and around the Sverdrup Basin (14). Temperature logs from the Cape Allison C-47 well drilled in 244 m of water off the southern coast of Ellef Ringnes Island indicates that thick permafrost does not occur beneath the deeper parts of the inter-island channels. In coastal regions, however, permafrost is present and further inland beyond the marine limit, permafrost has been measured to depths as great as 700 m (14); thus, indicating that gas hydrates may exist on or near exposed islands in the Sverdrup Basin.

Temperature data from five onshore wells drilled on Ellef Ringnes Island show substantial variations due to effects of permafrost dynamics, recent marine regressions, and variable paleoclimatic histories. In contrast, analysis of the offshore temperature profile from the Cape Allison C-47 well suggests that the subsurface thermal regime is in equilibrium with the present marine environment. Geothermal gradients calculated from the temperature surveys in the Cape Allison C-47 well average about 1.3°C/100 m in the Lower Cretaceous Isachesen Formation and about 2.5°C/100 m in the Middle to Upper Jurassic Deer Bay Formation (14). Geothermal gradients calculated from the temperature profiles for the five onshore wells drilled on Ellef Ringnes Island range from about 4°C/100 m to 8°C/100 m within the permafrost sequence and from 3°C/100 m to 6°C/100 m below permafrost (14). Judge (12) reported that high geothermal gradients (>5°C/100 m) are typical of young tectonic regions such as the Sverdrup Basin.

Formation Pore-Pressure. A review of all known technical sources has yielded no information on formation pore-pressures within the Sverdrup Basin. Due to the lack of data, the gas hydrate stability calculations in this paper for the Sverdrup Basin have been made assuming a hydrostatic pore-pressure gradient (9.795 kPa/m; 0.433 psi/ft).

Gas Chemistry. All of the known conventional gas fields in the Sverdrup Basin contain dry gas composed almost exclusively of methane; therefore, the gas hydrate stability determination for the Sverdrup Basin in this paper assumes a pure methane chemistry.

Pore-Water Salinity. A review of available data sources uncovered no information on pore-water salinities within the Sverdrup Basin. Due to the lack of data, the gas hydrate stability calculations for the Sverdrup Basin have been made assuming no effect from dissolved pore-water salts.

Gas-Hydrate Stability Calculations. As in the Mackenzie Delta-Beaufort Sea region (this report) and on the North Slope of Alaska (7) it is possible to use information on permafrost distribution to assess gas-hydrate stability conditions in the Sverdrup Basin. The computer program described in the Alaskan section of this report has been used to calculate the limit of the gas-hydrate stability zone in 31 wells in the Sverdrup Basin (Figure 5). As previously discussed, the gas-hydrate stability program requires the following input: [1] mean annual surface temperature which is assumed to be -20°C in the Sverdrup Basin (14), [2] depth to base of ice-bearing permafrost or permafrost (14), [3] temperature at the base of ice-bearing permafrost which in this case is assumed to be 0°C since only temperature derived permafrost data are available, and [4] the ratio between the geothermal gradient from above to below the base of the ice-bearing permafrost which is assumed to be 1 in this case due to the lack of data and the complex nature of the regional subsurface thermal regime. When present, the thickness of the methane-hydrate stability zone in the Sverdrup Basin (Figure 5), extrapolated from available permafrost data, ranges from about 36 to 1,138 m. Thermal conditions preclude the occurrence of gas hydrates in five of the wells assessed. Due to the highly variable nature of the gas hydrate stability zone, no attempt has been made to contour the stability data in figure 5.

West Siberian Basin, Russian Federation

Petroleum production in the northern part of the West Siberian Basin is principally from the Neocomian reservoirs of the Vartov and Megion "Suites" (average depth of 2,800 m) and the Cenomanian reservoirs of the Pokur "Suite" (average depth 1,100 m); about two-thirds of the region's gas production is from the Cenomanian reservoirs (2). The Pokur "Suite" is a 700- to 800-m-thick complex of interbedded marine and nonmarine sandstone and shale that was deposited during an Aptian to Coniacian marine regression. The Pokur "Suite" is overlain by the shale sequence of the Kuznetsov "Suite," which forms a regional seal for most of the underlying sandstone reservoirs.

The Messoyakha field was discovered in 1968 and it was the first producing field in the northern part of the West Siberian Basin. The Messoyakha gas accumulation is confined to the Dolgan Formation of the Pokur "Suite," and production has been from the depth interval between 720 and 820 m. The upper part (about 40 m) of the Messoyakha field lies within the zone of predicted methane-hydrate stability (Figure 6). By assuming a reservoir pressure of 78 kg/cm$^2$, the 10°C isotherm defines the lower limit of the in-situ gas hydrates, thus separating the Messoyakha field into an upper gas-hydrate accumulation and a lower free-gas accumulation.

Unusually low gas yields from production tests in the upper part of the Messoyakha reservoir were the first physical evidence of possible in-situ gas-hydrate occurrences. Analysis of well logs from 62 wells drilled in the Messoyakha field reveals the presence of apparently "frozen" rock intervals within the Dolgan Formation (2). Because these "frozen" layers are more than 250 to 350 m below the zone of permafrost and are at equilibrium formation temperatures near 10°C, they have been interpreted to contain in-situ gas hydrates rather then ice. Prior to production, the calculated total gas reserves within the gas-hydrate and free-gas parts of the Messoyakha accumulation were estimated to be about 80 x 10$^9$ cubic meters, with about one-third of the reserves within the gas hydrates (2).

Formation Temperature. In the West Siberian Basin, permafrost thickness increases gradually from areas of discontinuous permafrost in the south to 580-m-thick in the northern part of the basin. Measured geothermal gradients range from 4.0°C/100 m to 5.0°C/100 m in the central and southwest portion of the basin and geothermal gradients as low as 2.0°C/100 m to 3.0°C/100 m are reported from the northern part of the basin (15).

Formation Pore-Pressure. A review of available data uncovered no evidence of significant pore-pressure anomalies in the near-surface (0-1,500 m) sedimentary section of the West Siberian Basin. Therefore, a hydrostatic pore-pressure gradient (9.795 kPa/m; 0.433 psi/ft) can be assumed for the gas-hydrate stability calculations in the West Siberian Basin.

Gas Chemistry. The Cenomanian reservoirs of the Pokur "Suite" in northern West Siberia contain mostly methane (92.5 to 99.0 percent) (2). Because methane appears to be the dominant hydrocarbon gas within the Cenomanian reservoirs of the basin, a pure methane gas chemistry can be assumed for the gas-hydrate stability calculations in the West Siberian Basin.

Pore-Water Salinity. Analyses of water samples collected during petroleum formation testing in Cenomanian reservoirs from below the permafrost sequence indicate that the (bulk) pore-water salinities are low (5 to 14 ppt) and would have little effect on gas hydrate stability.

Gas-Hydrate Stability Calculations. Cherskiy and others (15) have calculated the depth to the top and base of the methane-hydrate stability zone at 230 locations in the West Siberian Basin. They determined the thickness of the methane-hydrate stability zone in the West Siberian Basin ranges from zero along the Oba River to the south and reaches a maximum thickness of about 1,000 m along the northeastern margin of the basin (Figure 6).

Lena-Tunguska, Russian Federation

In this paper, the Vilyuy and Anabar-Khatanga basins are included in the Lena-Tunguska province. The geologic setting of the northern oil and gas provinces of Russia indicates that the Vilyuy Basin is the most promising region for the occurrence of gas hydrates. The Vilyuy Basin covers an area of about 250,000 square kilometers and it is superimposed on the margin of the early Paleozoic Siberian

Platform. The Vilyuy Basin opens to the east into the Pre-Verkhoiansk marginal trough, which together with the Vilyuy Basin forms the Lena-Vilyuy Basin. The sedimentary fill of the Vilyuy Basin is divided into three distinct rock sequences: [1] a basinal Proterozoic-Paleozoic carbonate, [2] an upper Paleozoic marine clastic section, and [3] a terrigenous Mesozoic-Cenozoic sequence. Gas production is limited to the Mesozoic-Cenozoic sequence which contains numerous Lower Triassic to Lower Jurassic terrigenous reservoirs. The Lower Triassic-Lower Jurassic reservoir rock sequences are individually capped by interbedded shale units--the Lower Triassic Nejelin series (90- to 125-m-thick), Lower Triassic Manom series (129- to 170-m-thick), and the Lower Jurassic Suntar series (50- to 60-m-thick). These seals control all of the commercial gas accumulations within the Vilyuy Basin, with over 90% of the gas reserves within the Lower Triassic terrigenous reservoirs.

The Middle to Upper Jurassic and Cretaceous continentally derived sandstone units overlying the uppermost regional Suntar shale seal are generally regarded as non-productive. However, analyses of available geologic, geochemical, and hydrogeologic data indicate that these deposits may contain significant accumulations of gas. Numerous gas shows have been reported within the Jurassic-Cretaceous sequence, which may be interpreted as evidence of in-situ gas hydrates (15). Mud logs from the first 1,000 to 1,200 m of the Vilyuy Basin often show evidence of significant gas flows in the zone of predicted gas-hydrate stability. The Jurassic-Cretaceous sequence within the Vilyuy Basin is virtually barren of conventional reservoir seals, however, permafrost which is believed to be an impermeable barrier to gas, may be an effective reservoir seal in the Vilyuy Basin which inturn may contribute to the formation of in-situ gas hydrate accumulations. Based on the occurrence of near-surface gas accumulations (0-1,000 m), it is likely that gas hydrates exist in the Vilyuy Basin, however, no direct evidence of gas hydrates has been obtained.

Formation Temperature. Most of the Lena-Tunguska province is underlain by continuous permafrost, with thicknesses greater than 1,400 m in the north-central portion of the province (15). In general, the permafrost thins toward the margins of the province and is absent to the southwest along the Yenisey River. Locally within the Vilyuy Basin permafrost is about 300 to 750 meters thick and the geothermal gradient below permafrost averages approximately 2°C/100 m. Subsurface temperature data required to determine the distribution and thickness of the gas hydrate stability zone have been obtained by projecting a regional geothermal gradient (2°C/100 m) from the known base of permafrost.

Formation Pore-Pressure. Formation under-pressuring has been observed within the Lena-Tunguska province, with calculated pore-pressures being 1.5 to 3.0 MPa lower than normal hydrostatic pore-pressures. The origin of the abnormally low formation pore pressures is unknown, however, it is possible that the frozen pore-waters within the permafrost sequence may not be contributing to the hydrostatic pore-pressure gradient. Gas hydrate stability calculations in the Lena-Tunguska province need to take into account the effect of the low pore-pressure gradient.

Gas Chemistry. Relatively few gas samples have been collected from the Lena-Tunguska province mainly due to the lack of drilling. Analysis of mud-log data from wells drilled in the sandstone units overlying the Suntar shale seal indicates that methane is the dominant hydrocarbon gas in the near-surface (0-1,000 m) sedimentary rocks of the Lena-Tunguska province. Therefore, gas hydrate stability calculations in the Lena-Tunguska province should assume a pure methane chemistry.

Pore-Water Salinity. Formation pore-waters within the Middle Jurassic-Cretaceous sedimentary section of the Lena-Tunguska province have low dissolved salt content; ranging from 1 to 10 ppt. Therefore, gas hydrate stability is not affected by pore-water salts in the Lena-Tunguska province.

Gas-Hydrate Stability Calculations. Assuming low pore-pressure gradients, methane gas chemistry, and no pore-water salts, Cherskiy and others (15) have determined that the zone of methane hydrate stability is about 2,000-m-thick within the west-central portion of the Lena-Tunguska province and in the Vilyuy Basin the methane hydrate stability zone is about 800- to 1,000-m-thick (Figure 7).

CONCLUSION

The primary objectives of this paper are to assess the geologic parameters that control the stability of gas hydrates and to document the potential distribution of permafrost-associated gas hydrates within the circumarctic of the northern hemisphere.

Two primary factors affect the distribution of the gas-hydrate stability zone--geothermal gradient and gas composition. Other factors, which are difficult to quantify and often have little effect, are pore-fluid salinity and formation pore-pressures.

Geologic studies and thermal modeling indicate that permafrost and gas hydrates may exist in all of the five regions examined in this study. However, gas hydrates have only been conclusively identified on the North Slope of Alaska and are inferred to occur in the Mackenzie Delta-Beaufort Sea region, Sverdrup Basin, West Siberian Basin, and in the Lena-Tunguska province.

REFERENCES

1.  Kvenvolden, K.A., 1988, Methane hydrate--a major reservoir of carbon in the shallow geosphere?: Chemical Geology, v. 71, p. 41-51.

2.  Collett, T.S., 1993, Natural gas production from Arctic gas hydrates, in Howell, D.G., ed., The Future of Energy Gases: U.S. Geological Survey Professional Paper 1570, p. 299-312.

3.  Yakushev, V.S., and Collett, T.S., 1992, Gas hydrates in Arctic regions: risk to drilling and production: Second International Offshore and Polar Engineering Conference, June 14-19, 1992, San Francisco, California, Proceedings, p. 669-673.

4.  Holder, G.D., Malone, R.D., Lawson, W.F., 1987, Effects of gas composition and geothermal properties on the thickness and depth of natural-gas-hydrate zone: Journal of Petroleum Technology, September, p.1147-1152.

5.  Lerand, M., 1973, Beaufort Sea, in McCrossan, R.G., ed., Future petroleum provinces of Canada--Their geology and potential: Canadian Society of Petroleum Geologists Memoir 1, p. 315-386.

6.  Grantz, Arthur, Holmes, M.L., and Kososki, B.A., 1975, Geologic framework of the Alaskan continental terrace in the Chukchi and Beaufort Seas, in Yorath, C.J., Parker, E.R., and Glass, D.J., eds., Canada's continental margins and offshore petroleum exploration: Canadian Society of Petroleum Geologists Memoir 4, p. 669-700.

7.  Collett, T.S., 1993, Natural gas hydrates of the Prudhoe Bay and Kuparuk River area, North Slope, Alaska: American Association of Petroleum Geologists Bulletin, v. 77, no. 5, p. 793-812.

8.  Procter, R.M., Taylor, G.C., and Wade, J.A., 1984, Oil and natural gas resources of Canada 1983: Geological Survey of Canada Paper 83-31, 59 p.

9.  Smith, S.L., and Judge, A.S., 1995, Estimates of methane hydrate volumes in the Beaufort-Mackenzie region, Northwest Territories: Geological Survey of Canada, Current Research 1995-B, p. 81-88.

10. Bily, C., and Dick, J.W.L., 1974, Natural occurring gas hydrates in the Mackenzie Delta, Northwest Territories: Bulletin of Canadian Petroleum Geology, v. 22, no. 3, p. 340-352.

11. Weaver, J.S., and Stewart, J.M., 1982, In situ hydrates under the Beaufort shelf, in French, M.H. ed., Proceedings of the Fourth Canadian Permafrost Conference, 1981: National Research Council of Canada, The Roger J.E. Brown Memorial Volume, p. 312-319.

12. Judge, A.S., 1986, Permafrost distribution and the Quaternary history of the Mackenzie-Beaufort region: a geothermal perspective, in Heginbottom, J.A., and Vincent, J.S., eds., Correlation of Quaternary Deposits and Events around the Margin of the Beaufort Sea: Geological Survey of Canada Open File Report 1237, p. 41-45.

13. Franklin, L.J., 1981, Hydrates in Arctic Islands, in Bowsher, A.L., Proceedings of a Workshop on Clathrates (gas Hydrates) in the National Petroleum Reserve in Alaska, July 16-17, 1979, Menlo Park, California: U.S. Geological Survey Open-File Report 81-1298, p. 18-21.

14. Taylor, A.E., 1988, A constraint to the Wisconsinan glacial history, Canadian Arctic Archipelago: Journal of Quaternary Science, v. 3, no. 1, p. 15-18.

15. Cherskiy, N.V., Tsarev, V.P., and Nikitin, S.P., 1985, Investigation and prediction of conditions of accumulation of gas resources in gas-hydrate pools: Petroleum Geology, v. 21, p. 65-89.

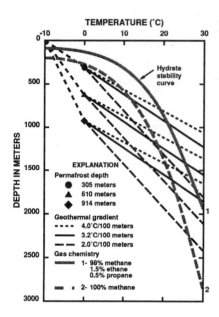

Figure 1A. Graph showing the depth-temperature zone in which gas hydrates are stable in a permafrost region [assuming a 9.048 kPa/m pore-pressure gradient] (4).

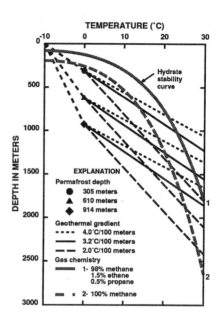

Figure 1B. Graph showing the depth-temperature zone in which gas hydrates are stable in a permafrost region [assuming a 9.795 kPa/m pore-pressure gradient] (4).

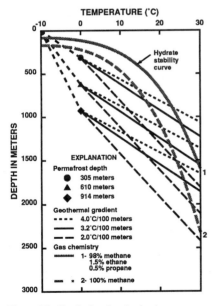

Figure 1C. Graph showing the depth-temperature zone in which gas hydrates are stable in a permafrost region [assuming a 11.311 kPa/m pore-pressure gradient] (4).

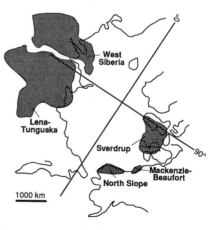

Figure 2. Location of sedimentary basins in the Northern Hemisphere that may contain in-situ natural gas hydrates.

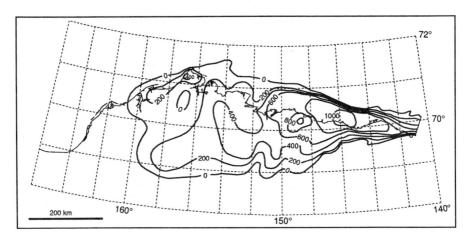

Figure 3. Isopach map of northern Alaska showing the thickness (in meters) of the methane-hydrate stability zone (7).

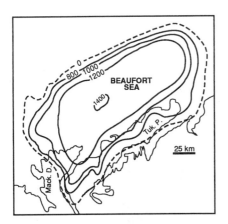

Figure 4. Isopach map of the Mackenzie Delta-Beaufort Sea region showing the thickness (in meters) of the methane-hydrate stability zone.

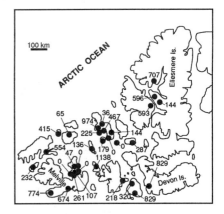

Figure 5. Map of the Sverdrup Basin showing the location of 31 petroleum wells. Also shown is the thickness of the methane-hydrate stability zone (in meters) in each well.

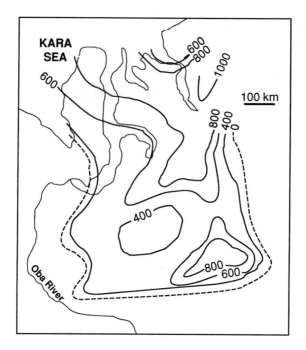

Figure 6.  Isopach map of the West Siberian Basin showing the
thickness (in meters) of the methane-hydrate stability zone (15).

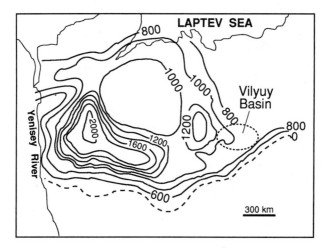

Figure 7.  Isopach map of the Lena-Tunguska province showing the
thickness (in meters) of the methane-hydrate stability zone (15).

# ORIGIN OF GASES IN RESERVOIRS

## ORIGINE DU GAZ DANS LES RESERVOIRS

J. Connan and G. Lacrampe-Couloume
Elf Aquitaine, CSTJF, 64018-Pau Cedex, France

M. Magot
Sanofi Recherches, 31676-Labège Cedex, France

ABSTRACT

Natural gases, accumulated in reservoirs, comprise hydrocarbons (methane, ethane, propane, etc.) and non-hydrocarbons (nitrogen, carbon dioxide, hydrogen sulphide, etc.). Large volume of gases are produced with oils and condensates.

Methods in organic geochemistry are currently applied to determine the most likely origin of gas and gas-oil mixtures. To approach the understanding of the possible origin of gas mixtures in which the various components are not necessarily cogenetic, one can only refer to gas compositions and isotope values ($\delta^{13}C$, $\delta D$, $\delta^{34}S$, $\delta^{18}O$, etc.) of individual moieties namely hydrocarbons, nitrogen, hydrogen sulphide, carbon dioxide, etc.

The understanding of the origin of gaseous compounds, and especially of non-hydrocarbons, may be key information to conduct exploration in some new prospective areas. For instance, the prediction of the nitrogen risk in the Netherlands and in offshore Germany plays a leading role in the selection of the most favourable area for drilling. The nitrogen risk increases in reservoirs with higher maturities, as increasing amounts of nitrogen are released from clay ammonium ions for lower amounts of methane. Similarly the discovery of guides to predict hydrogen sulphide or carbon dioxide concentrations in a basin, helps in choosing the best traps to be explored. In carbonate-rich provinces, occurrences of hydrogen sulphide and carbon dioxide, are very frequent.

Distribution of hydrogen sulphide in reservoirs is not only related to maturity but is also tightly bound to the lithology of the hosting sedimentary sequence. Under identical catagenetic conditions, hydrogen sulphide is more likely to occur in a series dominated by carbonates and anhydrite than in a series where marls predominate. In addition, in such a type of sedimentary series, secondary reactions among hydrocarbons and anhydrite may take place. These reactions, call thermo-sulphato reductions, lead to enhanced concentrations of hydrogen sulphide and carbon dioxide. Evidence of these phenomena is recorded by significant shifts in carbon isotope values of individual hydrocarbons from the gasoline produced with the gas phase. A demonstration of that type has been studied in the Aquitaine Basin in France.

Gaseous components have two major origins: thermogenic and biogenic. However primary thermogenic gas-oil accumulations may be subsequently reworked by bacteria. New tools of modern organic geochemistry are now allowing to get access to these more complex geological histories and to recognise the last reworking phase of the pristine thermogenic fluid by bacteria. A case history, studied in detail on the Emeraude field in Congo, has been chosen to illustrate how a reasonable explanation can be obtained in a complex situation.

The Emeraude field is a large sulphur-poor biodegraded oil accumulation in which associated gases contain hydrogen sulphide and carbon dioxide. Methane displays carbon isotope values reflecting the dilution of the primary thermogenic methane by a newly formed biogenic one. Hydrogen sulphide, occurring with carbon dioxide in some reservoir strata, has also been suspected to be bacterially derived. Bacteria from the corresponding reservoirs were isolated. They comprise only anaerobic strains, namely methanogens, sulphate reducers and fermentative bacteria. Sulphate reducers and methanogens have been cultivated in-vitro with an unbiodegraded Congo crude oil under close-to-reservoir conditions (35°C). Under such laboratory conditions, they generate both methane and hydrogen sulphide as was expected on the basis of isotope data. The sulphate reducers found in the Congo are unknown species. Their capability to generate hydrogen sulphide has been studied in the laboratory by referring to other sulphate reducers from International Collections. The

Emeraude example provides a demonstrative study illustrating how, both field and laboratory data may be used today to pierce a complex in-reservoir evolution of a gas-oil mixture.

## RÉSUMÉ

Les gaz naturels, accumulés dans les réservoirs, contiennent des hydrocarbures (méthane, éthane, propane, etc.) et d'autres constituants (azote, gaz carbonique, hydrogène sulfuré, etc.). De grand volume de gaz sont produits avec de l'huile et des condensats.

La géochimie organique est couramment utilisée pour déterminer l'origine des hydrocarbures gazeux et celle des mélanges huile-gaz. Afin d'approcher l'origine des mélanges de gaz dans lesquels les différents composés ne sont pas obligatoirement cogénétiques, il est nécessaire d'utiliser la composition du gaz et les valeurs isotopiques ($\delta^{13}C$, $\delta D$, $\delta^{34}S$, $\delta^{18}O$, etc.) de chacun des constituants gazeux à savoir les hydrocarbures, l'azote, l'hydrogène sulfuré, le gaz carbonique, etc. La compréhension de la formation et de l'origine des composés gazeux, et plus particulièrement celle des composés non hydrocarbonés, peut fournir des informations clés pour orienter l'exploration vers les régions les plus attrayantes à prospecter. Par exemple, la prédiction du risque azote en Hollande et dans les permis de l'offshore allemand, joue un rôle de premier plan pour sélectionner les régions qui paraissent les plus attractives pour l'exploration pétrolière. Le risque azote augmente dans les réservoirs avec l'accroissement de la maturité des sédiments car ceux-ci libèrent de plus en plus d'azote à partir des ions ammonium et corrélativement de moins en moins de méthane. De la même manière, la mise au point de guides pour prédire la concentration en hydrogène sulfuré ou en gaz carbonique dans un bassin, donne une base de référence pour choisir les pièges à forer en priorité. Dans les provinces carbonatées, la présence d'hydrogène sulfuré et de gaz carbonique est un phénomène fréquent. La distribution de l'hydrogène sulfuré dans les réservoirs n'est pas seulement fonction de l'état de maturité des séries sédimentaires concernées mais est aussi étroitement dépendante de la lithologie des séries qui renferment les horizons réservoirs. Dans des conditions catagénétiques identiques, la présence d'hydrogène sulfuré dans les réservoirs sera plus probable dans une série évaporitique dominée par des carbonates et des anhydrites que dans une série à lithologie essentiellement marneuse. De plus dans de telles séries sédimentaires, des réactions secondaires peuvent intervenir entre les hydrocarbures et l'anhydrite. Ces réactions, appelées thermosulfato-réductions, conduisent à des concentrations accrues en hydrogène sulfuré et en gaz carbonique. Des preuves de l'existence d'un tel phénomène sont discernables dans les valeurs isotopiques ($\delta^{13}C$) des composés chimiques de la fraction gazoline produite avec les gaz. En effet ces valeurs se trouvent profondément modifiées par comparaison à celle des fluides originaux. Un exemple démonstratif de ce type de phénomène a été étudié dans le bassin d'Aquitaine en France.

Les composés gazeux ont deux origines majeures : thermogénique ou biogénique. Cependant les accumulations de mélanges gaz-huiles d'origine thermogénique peuvent être ultérieurement remaniées par des bactéries. Les nouveaux outils de la géochimie organique moderne permettent d'identifier des étapes de l'histoire de ces hydrocarbures accumulés et notamment les toutes dernières c'est-à-dire le remaniement des fluides thermogéniques par les bactéries du gisement. Un exemple type a été étudié en détails sur le champ d'Emeraude au Congo où ces phénomènes bactériens ont été clairement identifiés.

Le gisement d'Emeraude est une accumulation de 800 millions de tonnes d'huile biodégradée non soufrée qui est produite avec un gaz contenant de l'hydrogène sulfuré et du gaz carbonique. L'isotopie du méthane reflète la dilution du méthane originel thermogénique par un méthane biogénique, nouvellement formé par les bactéries du gisement. L'hydrogène sulfuré qui accompagne le gaz carbonique dans certains niveaux réservoirs, a été suspecté d'origine bactérienne. Les bactéries des réservoirs correspondants ont été isolées. Ce sont essentiellement des bactéries anaérobies, à savoir des méthanogènes, des sulfato-réductrices et des bactéries fermentaires. Les sulfato-réductrices et les méthanogènes ont été cultivées en laboratoire en présence de l'huile de Likouala, une huile non biodégradée du Congo. Dans les conditions des expériences de laboratoire (30°C), proches des conditions des gisements (30-45°C), ces bactéries génèrent du méthane et de l'hydrogène sulfuré, conformément à ce qui était attendu au vu des données isotopiques en conditions géologiques. Les sulfato-réductrices, trouvées au Congo sont des espèces inconnues. Leur capacité à générer de l'hydrogène sulfuré a été étudiée au laboratoire par comparaison à celle de bactéries sulfato-réductrices de collections internationales. Le gisement d'Emeraude fournit un exemple démonstratif pour illustrer comment des études de laboratoire contribuent à mieux comprendre la composition des hydrocarbures gazeux et la présence d'hydrogène sulfuré et de gaz carbonique.

## INTRODUCTION: GASES IN RESERVOIRS

Natural reservoired gases display a wide range of compositions which reflect the diversity and complexity of processes involved in gas accumulation. Sequential genesis of gases, not necessarily cogenetic, may take place in the reservoirs. The primary thermogenic gas, accumulated during the migration of oil-gas mixtures, may subsequently be modified by various in-reservoir processes: partial diffusion through caprocks and dysmigration through faults, invasion of deep non-hydrocarbon gases ($H_2S$, $N_2$ and $CO_2$), bacterial reworking of oils and gases, thermochemical sulphate reduction. Reservoired gases may be found with or without liquid hydrocarbons. They may also comprise abnormal compositions which drastically reduce their economic value. In that case, gases are extremely enriched in non-hydrocarbons namely $CO_2$, $H_2S$ and $N_2$. Some particular gases, e.g those found in Germany[1], are unusually enriched in Hg, the origin of which is not understood yet.

The aim of the paper is:
-to provide a summary review of our present knowledge about $CO_2$ and $H_2S$ which are frequent non-hydrocarbon components in natural gases,
-to present two unpublished case histories to illustrate how to approach the understanding of the origin of natural gases in reservoirs containing oils, condensates, gaseous hydrocarbons, $CO_2$ and $H_2S$.

To study gases, present tools are limited to the gas composition ($\%CO_2$, $\%H_2S$, $\%H_2$, $\%N_2$, $\%CH_4$, $\%C_2H_6$, %propane, etc.) and the isotope values on individual components ($\delta^{13}C$ and $\delta D$ on methane and ethane, $\delta^{13}C$ on propane, i-$C_4$, n-$C_4$, i-$C_5$ and n-$C_5$, $\delta^{13}C$ and $\delta^{18}O$ on $CO_2$, $\delta^{34}S$ on $H_2S$, $\delta^{15}N$ on $N_2$)

## I-ORIGIN OF $CO_2$

Papers reviewing the present state-of-the-art on the origin of the $CO_2$ have been presented recently(2,3) and we have largely integrated their results in the following part of this chapter. $CO_2$ may be released through bacterial and thermal degradation of organic matter as well as by breakdown of carbonates and degassing of the mantle or metamorphic fluids.

$CO_2$ is a by-product of the bacterial alteration of organic matter, petroleum and gas. Aerobic or anaerobic heterotrophic, denitrifying, sulphate-reducing and methanogenic bacteria generate $CO_2$ in their metabolic pathways. In natural environments, this generation scheme takes place at a temperature lower than 70°C. In recent sediments, early $CO_2$ is generally lost for it largely contributes to precipitation of biogenic carbonates. Late biogenic $CO_2$ results from interlinked complex simultaneous processes (neogenesis of $CO_2$ by BSR, methanogens and probably fermentative bacteria; reworking of $CO_2$ by methanogens). The $\delta^{13}C$ values , registered in biological reactions, cover a wide range from -25‰/PDB for early $CO_2$ in recent sediments to +15‰/PDB in $CO_2$ released by methanogenic activity. Reservoirs of fossilised bacterial gases containing $CO_2$ in moderate amounts (<5%) are known in the Carpathian foredeep and the Carpathian Flysh, the Po valley in northern Italy, the Gulf coast.

Thermal degradation of kerogen involving decarboxylation of $CO_2$-containing moities, occurs at low to moderate temperatures (<100°C) within the immature zone and at the top of the liquid oil window. $\delta^{13}C$ of $CO_2$ depends on both maturity and isotopic values of the precursor carboxyl group. $\delta^{13}C$ values tend to become heavier with increasing maturity within the -25 /-10‰/PDB range. A typical example of such $CO_2$ is depicted in Mahakam delta coals of Figure 1. Expulsion efficiency of Mahakam delta coals has been studied in laboratory experiments using isothermal conditions at 330°C, at a pressure of 170 bars. Expelled gas and oil mixtures were collected through time. $\delta^{13}C$ values of $CO_2$ do not significantly change with time, whereas $\delta^{13}C$

values of $CH_4$ become increasingly lighter. $\delta^{13}C$ values, around -25‰/PDB, are typical of organically-derived $CO_2$ as expected.

$CO_2$ may also have a deep source. Its genesis results from degassing of the mantle and hydrothermal fluids or decomposition of carbonates, mainly limestones at high temperatures (>180°C). Isotopic fractionation effects are small at high temperature and the $\delta^{13}C$ values fall within a narrow range (-5 to -7‰/PDB). This type of $CO_2$ is economically the most important one for deep $CO_2$ is obviously responsible of high amount of $CO_2$ in natural reservoirs. A plot of $\delta^{13}C$ of $CO_2$ vs. % $CO_2$ (Figure 2), built with the Thrasher and Fleet (3) and elf aquitaine databases, clearly shows that natural gases with % $CO_2$ higher than 20% possess $\delta^{13}C$ values around -10 and 0‰/PDB. This means that when % $CO_2$ is high, the $CO_2$ is predominantly of mineral origin (carbonates, volcanic activity, etc.). Formation of mineral-derived $CO_2$ does not require extremely high temperatures (>600°C), as quoted when referring to extensive limestone decomposition. In fact, heating experiments with shaly source rocks (Toarcian shales, type II kerogen; Mahakam delta shales, type III kerogen) at 285 and 330°C, reveals $\delta^{13}C$ for $CO_2$ values ranging between -2 and 0‰/PDB, i.e. suggesting $CO_2$ genesis through carbonate decomposition. Comparison of $CO_2$ data in Mahakam delta coals and shales experiments (Figure 1), illustrates the clear influence of the carbonate mineral matrix. One should observe that the two Mahakam delta samples have the same kerogen as cross-checked by the identity of their activation energy curves. Consequently, differences in expelled $CO_2$ cannot be ascribed to changes in organic matter quality but should be related to the absence (coals) or occurrences of mineral matter.

The elf aquitaine database has been programmed to extract $\delta^{13}C$ of $CO_2$ vs. $\delta^{13}C$ of the associated $CH_4$. The diagram of the plotted data(Figure 3), providing guidelines of interpretation (3), reveals:
                    1- no correlation between $\delta^{13}C$ of $CO_2$ and $\delta^{13}C$ of $CH_4$. $CO_2$ and $CH_4$ are currently not genetically related.
                    2- occurrences of strong interference in $\delta^{13}C$ values of $CO_2$ from various sources. Consequently isotopic data will not be allowing unambiguous interpretation of the origin of $CO_2$.

Utilisation of $\delta^{18}O$ of $CO_2$ was attempted using the elf aquitaine database. No useful information have been obtained as these isotope values are less discriminatory than the $\delta^{13}C$ values. This new data set confirms the conclusions put forth by Clayton(2), who states that $\delta^{18}O$ was not an efficient tool to trace the source of $CO_2$.

## II-ORIGIN OF $H_2S$

$H_2S$ forms through three main pathways: bacteria, thermal desulphurisation of sulphur-rich sedimentary organic matter or sulphur-rich petroleum, thermochemical sulphate reduction of hydrocarbons in carbonate-evaporite petroleum systems(4,5).

Bacterial $H_2S$ is currently produced through dissimilatory sulphate reduction by sulphate-reducing bacteria, the most important species of which belong to the Desulfovibrio and Desulfotomaculum genera (6,7,8). If microbial sulphate reduction is generally considered as the major biogeochemical process for $H_2S$ formation, other pathways are also possible. Non sulphate-reducing bacteria use thiosulphates instead of sulphates are to produce $H_2S$ in reservoirs. They have been identified very recently in natural waters of Congo reservoirs(9,10) in association with active sulphate reducers. The bacterial genesis of $H_2S$ requires conditions which are compatible with the growth of these bacterial strains, i.e. temperatures generally lower than 70-75°C. Sulphate-reducing bacteria are said to be able to grow under high pressures at temperatures as high as 104°C. Nevertheless, the screening carried out in the last three years on natural waters from various reservoirs(11) indicates that the number of indigenous bacteria decreases drastically when reservoir temperatures are higher than 70°C. Living sulphate-reducers have been identified in natural environments in sediments located as deeply high as 1000 m(12) and in various petroleum reservoirs(7,8,10,13,14) with temperatures lower than 75°C.

As the second most important process of $H_2S$ generation, one should mention the thermal decomposition of sulphur moities bound in the kerogen network of type I-S and II-S or in its polar fractions including sulphur-bearing aromatics. Le Tran (15) has studied a type II-S case history in the Aquitaine basin where the sharp increase of $H_2S$ yield starts in sediments where temperatures exceed 80°C. In cases of abnormal sulphur-rich kerogen with labile sulphur bonds as sulphides and disulphides, one should expect to have even thermal $H_2S$ at the top of the liquid oil window, at temperatures lower than 70°C.

Lastly, the third mechanism which was reported earlier by Orr(5) and later by a number of workers, refers to the so-called thermochemical sulphate-reduction of hydrocarbons in reservoirs. This mechanism affects hydrocarbons in reservoirs containing carbonate-evaporite series. It has been described in various petroleum provinces in the world: the Aquitaine basin (16,17), the Smackover petroleum systems of Mississippi and Alabama (18), the Pre-Caspian provinces (19,20), the Devonian of Alberta (21), the Permian-Triassic Khuff Formation of Abu Dhabi(22), Zechstein gas reservoirs of East Netherlands(23). According to most authors, the thermochemical sulphate reduction is a thermal process occurring at elevated temperatures: >120°C after Orr, >120°C after Rooney, >110°C after Hutcheon et al., >140°C after Worden, >120°C after Ganz and Bruijn. Dakhnova et al.(20) concluded that the TSR occurs at temperatures between 50 and 80°C, however they have not provided convincing geochemical proof to substantiate such a conclusion. In our opinion, the $H_2S$ produced within this temperature range originates from the thermal decomposition of a sulphur-rich organic matter.

## III-GENESIS OF $H_2S$, SULPHUR, AND $CO_2$ BY THERMOCHEMICAL SULPHATE REDUCTION OF HYDROCARBONS IN THE AQUITAINE BASIN (SW FRANCE): MOLECULAR AND ISOTOPIC EFFECTS.

The Aquitaine basin (SW France) is the second most important oil-producing area, after the Paris basin, and the first gas producing zone in France.

The Adour sub-basin (Figure 4), located in the south-western part of the Aquitaine Basin, close to the Pyrenees mountains, contains oil accumulations in Barremo-Jurassic (Pecorade, Vic Bihl) and Senonian reservoirs (Lagrave). Giant sour gas fields (Deep Lacq, Meillon) and some other minor gas accumulations (Ucha, Rousse) are pooled in Jurassic reservoirs, close to the Tertiary Pyrenean overthrust belt.

Samples of oils, gasolines and gases have been analysed in detail using isotopic and molecular techniques. Main results have been reported elsewhere(16,17), consequently we intend herein to mainly focuse on aspects related to the origin of gases.

Although most gases fall within the reference zones proposed by Schoell (24) for dry gases or gases associated with oils (e.g. Pecorade and Vic Bilh), the deep gases of "Lacq inférieur", containing more than 15% $H_2S$, cluster within the so-called mixed zone (Figure 5). Obviously this interpretation is not valid as the fossilisation of biogenic gas is unlikely in the corresponding geological context. The sedimentary column which contains the deep gas reservoirs is presently placed within the gas window where intensive genesis of both hydrocarbons and $H_2S$ has been demonstrated(25). Therefore one should refer to another interpretation to explain the observed isotopic gas properties.

This interpretation has been elaborated after a carefull screening of all the geochemical data gathered from $H_2S$, $CO_2$, gaseous hydrocarbons and condensates.

Gas chromatograms of condensates (Figure 6) display different patterns. The Ucha 1 condensate (4517-4522 m, from a reservoir at a Ro equivalent of 1.8%), produced with a gas containing only 0.3% $H_2S$, shows a classical pattern in which the n-alkanes prevail within the $C_7$-$C_{16}$ range. The Andoins 2D and the Deep Lacq condensates, found in association with $H_2S$-rich gases (11.1 and 15.2% respectively), exhibit very unusual fingerprints marked by strong dominance of C1- and C2-benzenes (especially toluene and meta-xylene). $\delta^{13}C$ values, measured by GC-IRMS on individual compounds from $C_1(CH_4)$ to $C_{12}$ as well as $\delta^{13}C$ values on bulk fractions (whole oils, distillation residue, $C_{15+}$saturates and $C_{15+}$aromatics, Figure 7), show step-by-step isotopic shifts when comparing oils (e.g. Pecorade and Vic Bihl), a classical condensate (Ucha 1), and several abnormal ones (St Faust 5 and 4, Andoins 2D, Deep Lacq). If the differences between the oils and the Ucha condensate are predictable as related to increasing maturity, the significant shifts in the two condensate families are more surprising. In fact these shifts document isotopic effects of secondary processes which take place in anhydritic reservoirs and which were initially described as thermochemical sulphate reductions of hydrocarbons by Orr(5) and Krouse et al.(26).

Krouse et al.(26) mentioned that ethane and propane $\delta^{13}C$ values are shifted by -10 ‰/PDB due to thermosulphato-reduction. This tendency is effectively recorded in the Aquitaine Basin where ethane and propane $\delta^{13}C$ are respectively shifted of -2 and -10 ‰/PDB. Shifts in isotope values of the gasoline range compounds, as shown in Figure 7, have been recently reported by Rooney (18) in the Smackover Petroleum System of Mississippi and Alabama (i.e. the Mississippi salt basin, the Conecuh and Manila embayments and the Wiggins Arch). In that case history studied in the US, the temperatures of reservoirs containing the TSR altered oils range from 127°C to 151°C. As shown in Figure 7, the larger isotopic shifts are observed for n-alkanes whereas much smaller ones are recorded in cycloalkanes and monoaromatics (toluene, xylenes).

According to the net reaction proposed by Orr(5), the thermochemical sulphate reduction of hydrocarbons generates $CO_2$ and $H_2S$. A plot of the percent $H_2S$ vs. $\delta^{34}SH_2S$ (‰/CDT) reveals large variations in $\delta^{34}S$ values of $H_2S$ (Figure 8). In gases produced from Pecorade and Vic Bihl oils, $\delta^{34}S$ values of $H_2S$ range from 0 to +9 ‰/CDT (Figure 8) and are therefore comparable to $\delta^{34}S$ values of whole oils (Figure 8 and 9). This $H_2S$ has an organic origin through thermal desulphurisation of the Barremo-Jurassic type II-S kerogen and its related polar by-products. In $H_2S$-enriched gases, $\delta^{34}S$ values range from +14 to +18 ‰/CDT (Figure 8). These values are comparable to those of anhydrites and free sulphur from the Deep Lacq reservoirs. In addition, condensates do show converging results. The $\delta^{34}S$ values of the condensates also matches the anhydrite and the free sulphur values (Figure 9).

A plot of $\delta^{13}C_{CO_2}$ vs. %$CO_2$ and %$H_2S$ provides complementary data which confirm the tight linkage between the neogenesis of $CO_2$ and $H_2S$ in the thermochemical sulphate reduction process (Figure 10). First, the %$CO_2$ increases with the %$H_2S$, as expected from the net reaction suggested by Orr(5). Secondly, the $\delta^{13}C_{CO_2}$ values, ranging from -15 to 0 ‰/PDB as in $CO_2$ derived from the thermal carbonate decomposition, are shifted within the 0 to +5‰/PDB interval. These $\delta^{13}C_{CO_2}$ values are quite different from those given by Thrasher and Fleet(3), who report that $CO_2$ formed by thermochemical sulphate reduction covers the -15 to -5 ‰/PDB range.

To summarise, this case history clearly demonstrates that the understanding of the origin of gases, comprising hydrocarbons, $CO_2$ and $H_2S$, cannot be achieved without referring to other geochemical information. In that particular case, $\delta^{13}C$ values from individual compounds of the gasoline range of oils and condensates, coupled with $\delta^{34}S$ data on anhydrites and free sulphur, have provided key information to the understanding of the particular properties of $H_2S$, $CO_2$, $CH_4$ and $C_2H_6$ in the Deep Lacq accumulation. In addition, the example illustrates a complex geochemical history in which the pristine gas-condensate mixture interacts with minerals from the reservoirs to newly formed $CO_2$ and $H_2S$ and deeply modifying the chemical and isotopic properties of the residual condensates.

## IV-GENESIS OF $H_2S$, $CO_2$ AND $CH_4$ BY ANAEROBIC BACTERIA IN THE EMERAUDE RESERVOIRS (OFFSHORE CONGO)

In 1969, elf aquitaine discovered the Emeraude Marine oil field in Congo, i.e. the largest oil accumulation in the offshore Gulf of Guinea. The oil, accumulated in shallow reservoirs (< 500 m/sea level), has been estimated at 840 millions tons in place. However after 20 years of production, 25 millions tons of oil only have been recovered. The low oil recovery is due to the fact that the oil is fairly heavy and biodegraded.

In the Emeraude North and South oilfields, the oils from various reservoir layers, are currently devoid of n-alkanes and isoprenoids (e.g. Q 234, Emeraude North, Figure 11). The absence of both n-alkanes and isoprenoids are well known criteria used to recognise the biodegradation of a crude oil(27). However, this biodegradation has been of limited extent, as testified by the complete preservation of the most resistant biomarkers namely steranes and terpanes. According to Peters and Moldowan's classification (28), the Emeraude crude oils may be considered as moderately biodegraded. In other oilfields in the vicinity, slightly different situations have been observed. For instance in the Tchibouela oilfield, one may notice the selective and complete removal of the n-alkanes in the TBM 111 crude oil and the incipient attack of the same n-alkanes in the TBM 106 crude oil (Figure 11). Both crudes of Tchibouela are considered less biodegraded than those of the Emeraude oilfield for they have not reached the stage of isoprenoid degradation.

Some reservoir layers from Emeraude North, South and Tchibouela oilfields produce gases with $H_2S$ (maximum 1%, Table 1). This $H_2S$ has been suspected to indirectly increasing the bacterial corrosion risk of the 16" pipe linking the Emeraude production platform to the onshore Djeno treatment plant (7). The origin of the $H_2S$ has been a subject of controversy however a bacterial origin was very likely for the crude oils and the sedimentary organic matter of source rocks in that area are sulphur-poor (29).

In order to demonstrate the bacterial origin of the $H_2S$ and to get some insight into possible relationships between the gas/oil properties and the present day bacteria still alive in the associated aquifers, a detailed geochemical study of gas, gasoline and liquid hydrocarbon fractions has been combined to a microbiological study. Several reservoir layers have been produced in order to isolate crude oil and water for geochemical and microbial studies.

Preliminary results have been reported in a paper by Bernard et al. (11) and we intend herein mainly to concentrate on the topic of the Conference, i.e. the origin of the gas phases. As reference for the unaltered thermogenic gas-oil mixture in the area, we have selected the Likouala oilfield, which deeper crudes (reservoirs around 1300m) of which do show a full n-alkane pattern (Figure 11). The Likouala hydrocarbons are the unbiodegraded counterparts of those from Emeraude-Tchibouela. All hydrocarbons originate from the pre-salt "Grès de Djeno formation" (30) but at slightly different maturities: 0.6-0.8 % vitrinite equivalence for Emeraude/Tchibouela and 0.9% vitrinite equivalence for Likouala.

**a-Genesis of biogenic methane in Congo reservoirs**

The gross composition of the gas mixture and isotope data on the various constituents are listed in Table 1. Although the Likouala gases contain mainly hydrocarbons (<0.3% $CO_2$, <5% $N_2$, no $H_2S$), other gases, produced with biodegraded oils, are enriched in non-hydrocarbons ($CO_2$, $N_2$ with sometime $H_2S$). The $\delta^{13}C$ values of the $CO_2$, found in reservoirs producing biodegraded oils, range from +9 to +20 o/oo/PDB instead of -3.1/-2.6 o/oo/PDB. Such heavy values may be ascribed to a bacterial activity. Values up to +15 o/oo/PDB and even heavier are recorded in $CO_2$ associated with methanogenesis by $CO_2$-reduction (31,32). Sulphate reduction which takes place along with methanogenesis, releases carbon dioxide with an isotopic ratio ($\delta^{13}C$ of -20 to -30 0/00/PDB) similar to the source of organic matter(31).

A plot of $\delta^{13}C$ isotope values on methane and ethane in a Schoell's diagram (24), locates the Likouala gases close to the reference thermogenic zone whereas all other gases fall within the so-called thermogenic/biogenic zone (Figure 12). Similar situations have been found in other gas/condensate and oil fields, for instance in offshore Cameroon and in the Gulf of Mexico (33). These examples correspond to shallow reservoirs (e.g. 900-1400 m in the Gulf of Mexico case history) with biodegraded oils or condensates. In the case of High Island 511A, 17 to 34 % of the produced methane has been determined to be of biogenic origin. In the Congo case history, the suspected in-reservoir methanogenesis has been confirmed by laboratory experiments under anaerobic conditions, using the Likouala oil, a reconstituted consortium of bacteria from the E153 well in Emeraude South and reconstituted waters. Biogenic methane with a $\delta^{13}C$ of -92/-94 0/00/PDB, has been produced with $H_2S$ after a 6-month experimental period (Table 2). Taking into account this reference value for biogenic methane, the calculation of the dilution coefficient of a pristine thermogenic methane with a $\delta^{13}C$ value of -44 0/00/PDB by this biogenic methane has given values ranging between 4 and 14% (Table 1).

The above-mentioned laboratory experiment was undertaken after the detailed study of the indigenous bacteria of the Congo reservoirs (Table 3). Although no bacteria were identified in the Likouala aquifers, as expected on the basis of the high temperature (>80 C°) and the high salinity of these reservoir waters, the two reservoirs in E153 and BB325 wells contained a bacterial population composed of various anaerobes: oligotrophic, fermentative, sulphate-reducing, thiosulphate-reducing (9,10) and methanogenic bacteria (Table 3). Although some bacterial strains were common to both reservoirs, the two populations were shown to be clearly different, indicating that these reservoirs were not connected. The physiology of the indigenous bacteria seem to be closely adapted to the physical and chemical conditions of their related reservoir. In fact, these bacterial populations are mainly composed of unknown bacterial species (8,10), most of them still under study.

**b-Genesis of $H_2S$ and $CO_2$ by sulphate-reducing bacteria**

To complete the understanding of the reworking of the thermally formed gas/oil accumulation by bacteria, in-vitro experiments have also been carried out to document the $H_2S$ genesis. Desulfovibrio strains from International Collections have been compared to isolated sulphate-reducing bacteria from either the 16" and 20" pipe or from the Emeraude reservoirs. The 16" and 20" pipes are respectively used to tranfer the Emeraude and the Yanga-Sendji-DoukDaka production to the onshore Djeno treatment station. The incubations have been carried out under $N_2$ (98.6-99.8%) and $CO_2$ (1.4-0.2%). Genesis of $H_2S$ have been recorded with $CO_2$ (Table 4), after 2 days of experimention. In some cases the reaction reached completion as all the available sulphate was totally consumed. The changes recorded in $\delta^{13}C$ of $CO_2$ and the values of $\delta^{34}S$ in generated $H_2S$ are consistent with those found in the Congo reservoirs (Table 5). Therefore one can reasonably consider that the $H_2S$, discovered in some reservoirs of the Emeraude area, is of bacterial origin. Similarly the pristine $CO_2$, has been extensively reworked and diluted by biogenic $CO_2$, originating from the various biological processes involved in the reservoir (Sulphate reduction by sulphate-reducing and thiosulphate-reducing bacteria, methanogenesis, bacterial degradation of crude oil under anaerobic conditions, etc.).

## c-Anaerobic biodegradation of $C_7$-$C_{10}$ hydrocarbons by reservoir bacteria

In order to demonstrate the possible biodegradation of hydrocarbons under anaerobic conditions, in-vitro experiments have been undertaken using the non-degraded Likouala oil, the natural consortium of bacteria and the natural waters of the E153 well from Emeraude. One experiment was carried using thiosulphate in an attempt to stimulate the thiosulphate-reducing bacteria.

Preferential biodegradation of low molecular weight aromatics without any attack of alkanes has been recorded after 6 months of experiment without thiosulphate. Following a 14-month period, a more extensive uptake of both $C_7$-$C_{10}$ alkanes and aromatics by bacteria has been confirmed (Figure 13) Apparently, the addition of thiosulphate is a limiting factor as aromatic degradation is then much less complete (Figure 13). These analytical results have been obtained owing to the utilisation of the automated on-line HPLC-GC device(34). $C_2$- to $C_4$-alkylated benzenes were identified according to the Hartgers' paper(35).

In the total alkanes (not shown), the most easily recognisable feature is the selective removal of n-$C_8$ and n-$C_9$,along with some other unidentified structures. In the low molecular weight aromatics, profound changes are recorded with a particular specificity for meta-(1,3) and para-(1,4) disubstitutions in C2-, C3- and C4-alkylbenzenes (Figure 13). Our laboratory results agree with those published by Rueter et al.(36) and Wilkes et al. (37) with sulphate-reducing bacteria, however the specificity of their organisms is slightly different. Wilkes et al. (37) have recently reported that toluene, m- and o-xylene, m- and o-ethyltoluene, m-propyltoluene and m-cymene are degradable by a mesophilic culture (30°C) isolated from a North sea oil tank, but that benzene, ethylbenzene, p-xylene and p-ethyltoluene are unaffected. In our case, the presence of a methyl group also favours the anaerobic oxidation of either alkylbenzenes and alkylnaphthalenes (2-methyl-naphthalene has been completely biodegraded) but less removal is observed when the alkylated benzenes have ortho-disubstitutions.

Both set of experiments confirm that the anaerobic biodegradation of $C_7$-$C_9$ alkanes and aromatics is possible by anaerobic bacteria and more specifically by sulphate-reducing ones. These natural consortia, originating from an oil tank or a natural reservoir in offshore Congo, are selectively degrading alkylbenzenes with either meta-para or ortho-meta disubtitutions, dependent upon the bacterial species.

Our experiments with reservoir bacteria do prove that the anaerobic biodegradation of petroleum should be now accepted. To establish whether such a phenomenon might have taken place in natural reservoirs of Congo, results of our 14 months in-vitro experiments have been compared to data gathered from moderately biodegraded crudes of the Tchibouela oilfield (Figure 11 and 14). Good agreement between both data sets has been obtained (Figure 15) as similar changes are seen in the $C_7$-$C_9$ aromatics of the Likouala oil, biodegraded by anaerobic bacteria from Emeraude and of Tchibouela oils biodegraded naturally in two different reservoirs (Figure 15). This is the first time that a paper reports results showing that the anaerobic biodegradation of oil by in-reservoir bacteria reproduces biodegradation effects which have been recorded under natural conditions.

To conclude, the study of the Congo area has shown that the Emeraude and the Tchibouela reservoirs contain anaerobic bacteria today. These anaerobic bacteria, including sulphate and thiosulphate-reducing species as well as methanogens, are responsible of the reworking of the reservoired fluids. This alteration generates $H_2S$, $CO_2$ and $CH_4$. Biogenic methane, presently observed in the reservoirs has been estimated at 4 and 14%/total gas. This anaerobic activity also seems to have concerned the liquid hydrocarbons as the specific low molecular weight properties of the oil from one Tchibouela reservoir have been reproduced in laboratory experiments using anaerobic bacteria from well Emeraude E153 and the unbiodegraded Likouala oil.

## CONCLUSIONS

In natural reservoirs, gaseous constituents and the associated oil or condensate, are not necessarily cogenetic. Each fraction may have its own geochemical and geological history.

Secondary in-reservoir alteration processes (e.g. biodegradation, oil segregation, gas invasion) may significantly rework the pristine fluid.

The geochemical and isotopic tools (e.g. $\delta^{13}C$ for methane and $CO_2$), used to characterise gaseous hydrocarbons and non-hydrocarbons in reservoirs, do not provide unambiguous conclusions about their origin.

To reasonably approach the real origin of gases in reservoirs, we recommend integrating information from various sources:

1-geochemical data on gaseous constituents but also on the associated oil or condensate,

2-laboratory experiments (e.g. biodegradation with in-reservoir bacteria or thermal experiments) to validate hypotheses,

3-geological background (volcanism, lithological column, metamorphism, regional maturity, type of organic matter, etc.) on the area under study.

## REFERENCES

1.    W.Philipp, K.M.Reinicke "Zur Entstehung und Erschliessung der Gasprovinz Osthannover" Erdöl-Erdgas-Zeitschrift 98, 85-90, 1982.

2.    C.Clayton "Controls on the Isotope ratio of Carbon Dioxide in Oil and Gas fields" In Organic Geochemistry : Developments and applications to energy, climate, environment and human history, (Ed. J. O. Grimalt), 1073-1074, A.I.G.O.A., San Sebastian, 1995.
3.    J.Thrasher, A.J.Fleet "Predicting the risk of carbon dioxide pollution in petroleum reservoirs" In Organic Geochemistry : Developments and applications to energy, climate, environment and human history, (Ed. J. O. Grimalt), 1086-1088, A.I.G.O.A., San Sebastian, 1995.
4.    H.G.Machel "Low-temperature and high-temperature origins of elemental sulfur in diagenetic environments" In Native sulfur, Developments in geology and exploration, (eds. G.R.Wessel and B.H.Wimberly), Society of Mining, Metallurgy, and Exploration, Inc., Littleton, Colorado, 3-22, 1992.
5.    W.Orr "Changes in sulfur content and isotopic ratios of sulfur during petroleum maturation-Study of Big Horn Basin Paleozoic oils" Am.Assoc.Petrol.Geol.Bull. 50, 11, 2295-2318, 1974.
6.    W.Orr "Sulfur" In Handbook of Geochemistry, 16-L1-16-L23, Springer-Verlag, Berlin, 1974.
7.    M.Magot, C.Tardy, P.Caumette, C.Hurtevent, J.L.Crolet "Identification of sulphate-reducing bacteria from production water of various oil fields" In Progress in the understanding and prevention of corrosion , 576-580, Institute of Materials, London, 1993.
8.    C.Tardy-Jacquenod, P.Caumette, R.Matheron, C.Lanau, O.Arnaud, M.Magot "Characterization of sulfate-reducing bacteria isolated from oilfield waters" Canadian Journal of Microbiology (in press).
9.    J.L.Crolet , M.Magot " Observations of non SRB sulfidogenic bacteria from oilfield production facilities" Corrosion 95. Paper n°188, NACE, Houston, 1995.
10.    M.Magot, G.Ravot, B.Ollivier, B.K.O.Patel, J.L.Garcia "Characterization of a new anaerobic halophilic thiosulfate-reducing bacterium from an oil field: Dithiosulfovibrio peptidovorans gen.nov.,sp.nov." Int.J.System.Bacteriol. (submitted).
11.    F.P.Bernard, J.Connan, M.Magot "Indigenous Microorganisms in connate water of many oil fields : a new tool in exploration and production techniques" Society of Petroleum Engineers paper 24811, October 4-7, 1992
12.    R.J.Parkes, B.A.Cragg, S.J.Bale, J.M.Getliff, K.Goodman, P.A.Rochelle, J.C.Fry, A.J.Weightman, S.M.Harvey "Deep bacterial biosphere in Pacific Ocean sediments" Nature, 371, 410-413, 1994.

13. K.O.Stetter, R.Huber, E.Blöchl, M.Kurr, R.D.Eden, M.Fielder, H.Cash, I.Vance "Hyperthermophilic archaea are thriving in deep North Sea and Alaskan oil reservoirs" Nature, 365, 743-745, 1993.

14. S.L'Haridon, A.L.Reysenbach, P.Glénat, D.Prieur, C.Jeanthon "Hot subterranean biosphere in a continental oil reservoir" Nature, 377, 223-224, 1995.

15. K.Le Tran "Geochemical study of hydrogen sulphide sorbed in sediments" In Advances in Organic Geochemistry 1971, (Eds. H.R.v.Gaertner and H.Wehner), 717-726, Pergamon Press, Oxford, 1972.

16. G.Lacrampe-Couloume, J.Connan, Y.Poirier "Use of GC-IRMS to characterize thermal maturity and origin of gas and gasoline in the Aquitaine basin" In Organic Geochemistry : Developments and applications to energy, climate, environment and human history, (Ed. J.O.Grimalt), 19-22, A.I.G.O.A., San Sebastian, 1995.

17. J.Connan, G.Lacrampe-Couloume "The origin of the Lacq Supérieur heavy oil accumulation and the giant Lacq Inférieur gas field (Aquitaine Basin, SW France). In Applied Petroleum Geochemistry, (Ed. M.L.Bordenave), 465-488, Technip, Paris, 1993.

18. M.A.Rooney "Carbon isotopic ratios of light hydrocarbons as indicators of thermochemical sulfate reduction" In Organic Geochemistry : applications to energy, climate, environment and human history, (Ed. J.O.Grimalt), 523-525, A.I.G.O.A., San Sebastian, 1995.

19. M.V.Dakhnova, S.M.Gurieva, E.N.Shkutnik "Distribution of hydrogen sulphide in carbonate oil- and gas-bearing complexes of Russian plate. Preprint of the 3rd Conference of the European Association of Petroleum Geoscientists, Florence, 26-30, 1991.

20. M.V.Dakhnova, A.A.Ivlev, E.N.Shkutnik "The evidence for moderate temperature thermochemical sulphate reduction" In Organic Geochemistry : Developments and applications to energy, climate, environment and human history, (Ed. J.O.Grimalt),1112-1113, A.I.G.O.A., San Sebastian, 1995.

21. H.G.Machel "Saddle dolomite as a by-product of chemical compaction and thermochemical sulfate reduction" Geology, 15, 936-940, 1987.

22. R.H.Worden, P.C.Smalley, N.H.Oxtoby "Gas souring by thermochemical sulfate reduction at 140°C" Am.Assoc.Pet.Geol.Bull. , 79, 6, 854-863, 1995.

23. H.H.Ganz, A.N.Bruijn "Prediction of $H_2S$ distribution in Zechstein gas reservoirs of East Netherlands" Abstract submitted for the 17th International Meeting of Organic Geochemistry , San Sebastian, 4th-8th september 1995, unpublished.

24.    M.Schoell "Genetic characterization of natural gases" Am.Assoc.Petrol.Geol.Bull. 67, 12, 2225-2238.

25.    K.Le Tran, J.Connan, B.van der Weide "Problèmes relatifs à la formation d'hydrocarbures et d'hydrogène sulfuré dans le bassin d'Aquitaine" In Advances in Organic Geochemistry 1973, (Eds B.Tissot and F.Bienner), 761-789, Technip, Paris, 1975.

26.    H.R.Krouse, C.A.Viau, L.S.Eliuk, A.Ueda, S.Halas "Chemical and isotopic evidence of thermochemical sulphate reduction by light hydrocarbon gases in deep carbonate reservoirs" Nature, 333, 415-419, 1988.

27.    J.Connan " Biodegradation of crude oils in reservoirs" In Advances in Petroleum Geochemistry, (Ed. J.Brooks and D.Welte) , 299-335, Academic Press, London, 1984.

28.    K.E.Peters, J.M.Moldowan "Biodegradation". In The Biomarker Guide (Ed.J. Lapidus) ,252-265, Prentice-Hall, London, 1993.

29.    J.Claret, J.B.Tchikaya, B.Tissot, G.Deroo, A.Van Dorsselaer "Un exemple d'huile biodégradée à basse teneur en soufre : Le gisement d'Emeraude (Congo)" In Advances in Organic Geochemistry 1975, (Eds. R.Campos and J.Goñi) , 509-522, ENADIMSA, Madrid, 1977.

30.    D.Levaché "Origine et maturité des huiles du bassin congolais" elf aquitaine internal report, 1994.

31.    C.Clayton "Source volumetrics of biogenic gas generation",(Ed. R.Vially), 191-203, Edition Technip, Paris 1992.

32.    M.J.Whiticar, E.Faber, M.Schoell "Biogenic methane formation in marine and freshwater environments : CO2 reduction vs. acetate fermentation-isotope evidence" Geochim. et Cosmochim. Acta 50, 693-709, 1986.

33.    C.C.Walters "Organic geochemistry of gases and condensates from Block 511A High Island South Addition offshore Texas, Gulf of Mexico" Proceedings of the Ninth Annual Research Conference Society of Economic Paleontologists and Mineralogists Foundation, (Ed. Schumacher D. and Perkins B.F.), 185-198, Earth Enterprises Inc., 1990.

34.    D.Dessort, J.P.Winstel, J.B.Berrut, J.Connan "Automated on Line HPLC-GC / A powerfull technique for the analysis of trace amounts of C7+saturated and aromatic hydrocarbons" In Organic Geochemistry : Developments and applications to energy, climate, environment and human history, (Ed.J.O.Grimalt), 801-804, A.I.G.O.A., San Sebastian.

35.    W.A.Hartgres, J.S.Sinninghe Damsté, J.de Leeuw "Identification of C2-C4 alkylated benzenes in flash pyrolysates of kerogens, coals and asphaltenes" Journal of Chromatography 606, 211-220, 1992.

36.    P.Rueter, R.Rabus, H.Wilkes, F.Aeckerberg, F.A.Rainey, H.W.Jannasch, F.Widdel "Anaeorobic oxidation of hydrocarbons in crude oils by new types of sulphate-reducing bacteria" Nature 372, 455-458.

37.    H.Wilkes, H.Willsch, R.Rabus, F.Aeckersberg, P.Rueter, F.Widdel "Compositioal changes of crude oils upon anaeorobic degradation by sulphate-reducing bacteria" In Organic Geochemistry : Developments and applications to energy, climate, environment and human history, (Ed. J.O.Grimalt), 321-323, 1995.

Acknowledgements-We wish to thanks elf aquitaine which gave permission to publish these results. Thanks are also due to Mrs. O.Arnauld and C.Lanau for their technical assistance in microbiology.

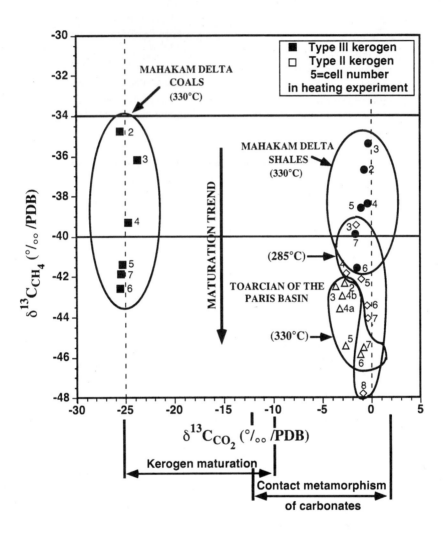

Figure 1- $\delta^{13}C$ of $CO_2$ and $CH_4$ expelled from three source rocks in laboratory experiments simulating gas/oil genesis and expulsion (experimental conditions : 285-330°C, 170 bars).

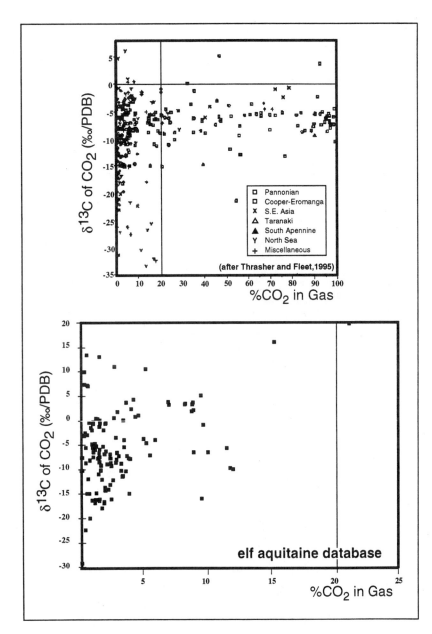

Figure 2- %CO$_2$ vs. δ$^{13}$C of CO$_2$ in petroleum reservoirs : results compiled from Thrasher and Fleet (3) and elf aquitaine database.

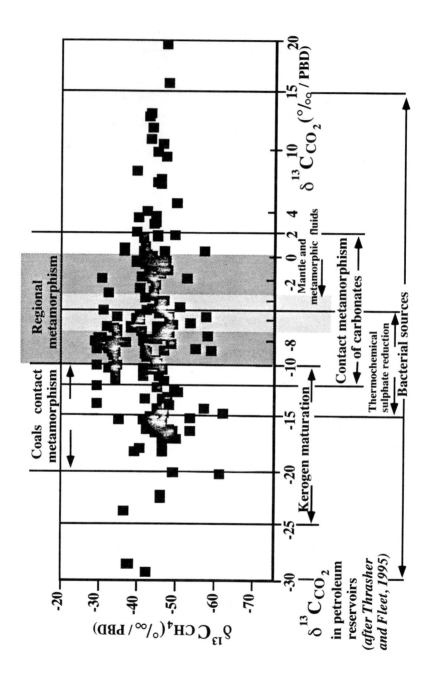

Figure 3- Plot of δ13C of methane vs. δ13C of CO2 (elf aquitaine database).

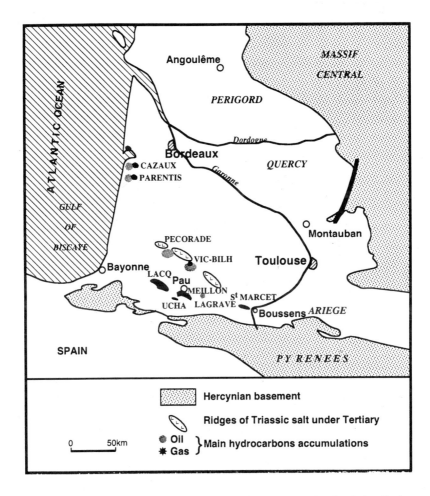

Figure 4- Location map of oil and gas accumulations in the Aquitaine Basin (SW France).

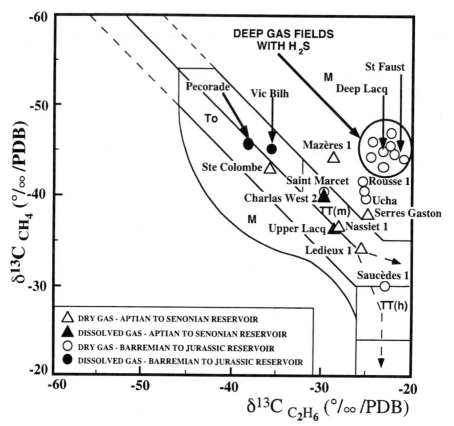

**Significance of abbreviations in Schoell's diagram (1983)**

To = Thermogenic gas associated with crude oils

TT = Dry or deep dry gas generated beyond the principal stage of oil formation
    TT(m) = From sapropelic-liptinic Organic matter
    TT(h) = From humic Organic matter

M = Mixed gas

Tc = Thermogenic gas associated with condensate

Figure 5- Genetic characterisation of natural gases from the Aquitaine basin by isotopic data on methane and ethane.

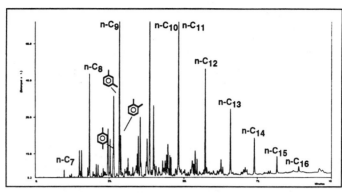

**UCHA 1** - 4517-4522 m-Production - Meillon formation

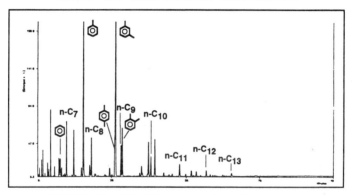

**ANDOINS 2D** - 5576-5940 m-Production - Mano formation

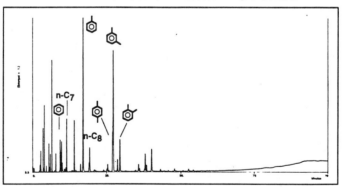

**DEEP LACQ** - 4000 m-Production

Figure 6- Gas chromatograms of three whole condensates of the Aquitaine Basin (SW France).

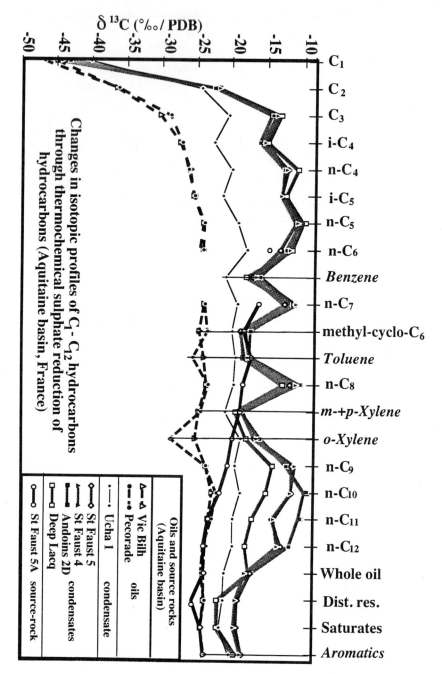

Figure 7- Changes in isotopic profiles of $C_1$-$C_{12}$ hydrocarbons through thermochemical sulphate reduction of hydrocarbons (Aquitaine basin).

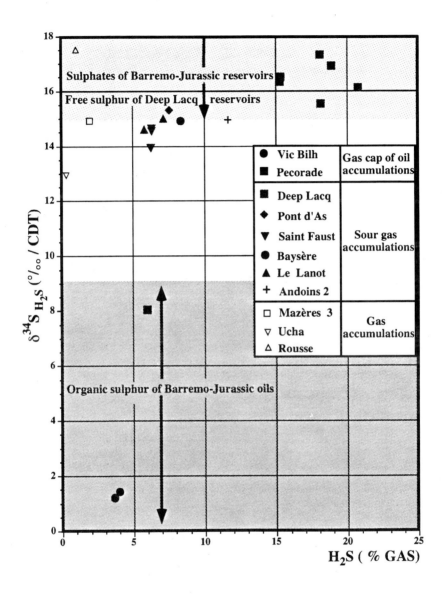

Figure 8- Plot of δ³⁴S of H₂S vs. %H₂S in samples from the Aquitaine Basin.

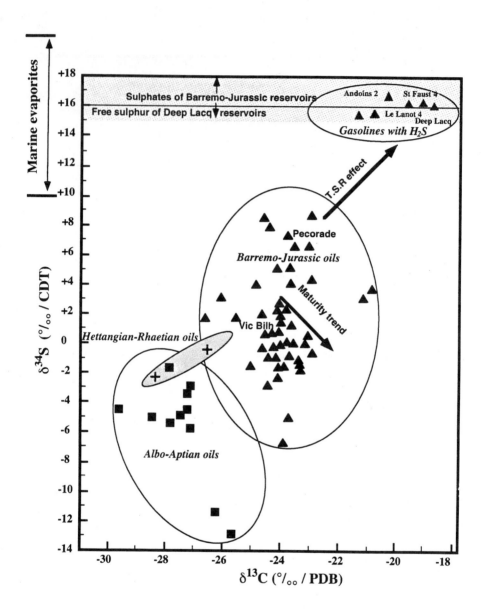

Figure 9- Plot of δ³⁴S vs. δ¹³C in oils and condensates of the Aquitaine Basin (SW France).

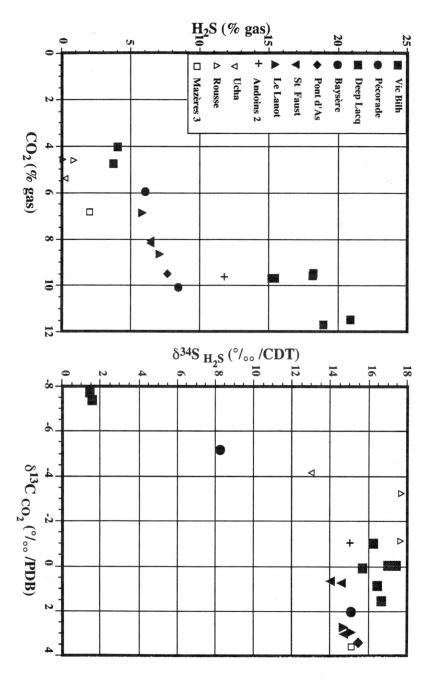

Figure 10- Plot of %H₂S vs. %CO₂ and of δ³⁴S of H₂S vs. δ¹³C of CO₂ in gas/oils and gas/condensates of the Aquitaine Basin.

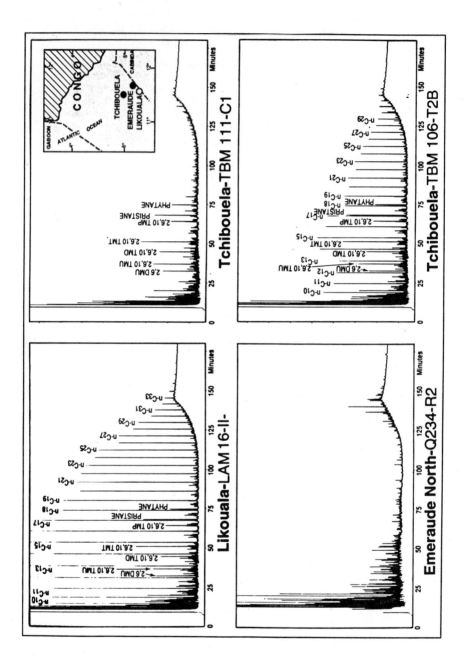

Figure 11- Gas chromatograms of $C_{6+}$alkanes showing different degrees of biodegradation in oils of offshore Congo.

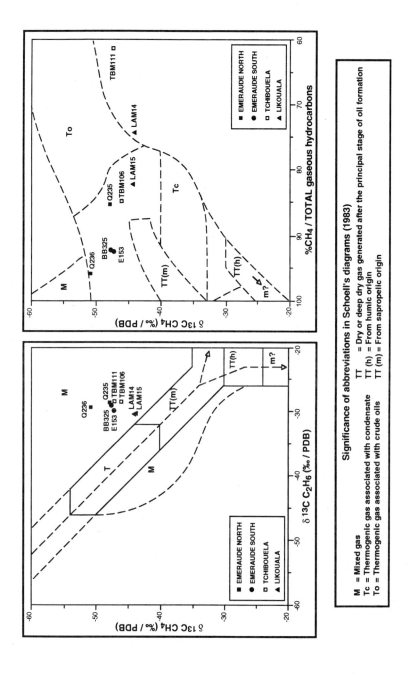

Figure 12- Genetic characterisation of natural gases from Congo reservoirs using compositional and isotopic variations on methane and ethane.

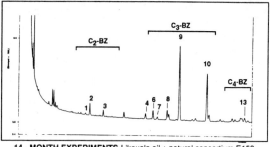

**14 - MONTH EXPERIMENTS-**Likouala oil + natural consortium E153
+ natural waters E153

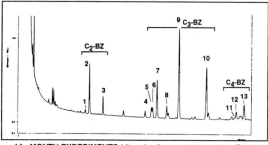

**14 - MONTH EXPERIMENTS-**Likouala oil + natural consortium E153
+ natural waters E153 + thiosulphates

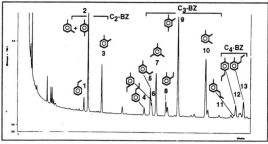

**BLANK-**Likouala oil + thiosulphates

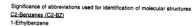

Significance of abbreviations used for identification of molecular structures

C2-Benzenes (C2-BZ)
1-Ethylbenzene
2-1,3-Dimethylbenzene +1,4-Dimethylbenzene
3-1,2-Dimethylbenzene

C3-Benzenes(C3-BZ)
4-n-Propylbenzene
5-1-Methyl-3-ethylbenzene
6-1-Methyl-4-ethylbenzene
7-1,3,5-Trimethylbenzene
8-1-Methyl-2-ethylbenzene
9-1,2,4-Trimethylbenzene
10-1,2,3-Trimethylbenzene

C4-Benzenes(C4-BZ)
11-1-Methyl-3-propylbenzene
12-1,4-Diethylbenzene
+1-Methyl-4-propylbenzene
+n-Butylbenzene
13-1-Methyl-2-propylbenzene

Figure 13- Gas chromatograms of C2- to C4-benzenes of the Likouala oil,
biodegraded under anaerobic conditions with the natural water and the
natural consortium of the E153 well from the Emeraude oilfield.

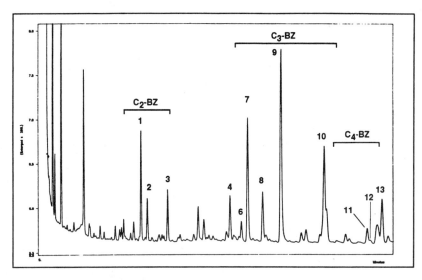

**TCHIBOUELA OIL FIELD-** TBM 111 well -T2B reservoir- Cenomanian - 45°C

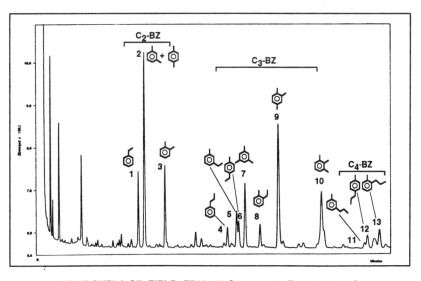

**TCHIBOUELA OIL FIELD-** TBM 106-C1 reservoir- Turonian - 45°C

Figure 14- Gas chromatograms of C2- to C4-benzenes from two reservoirs of the Tchibouela oilfield, showing a selective biodegradation of meta-and para-disubstituted isomers as seen in laboratory experiments (Figure 13). Abbreviations as in Figure 13.

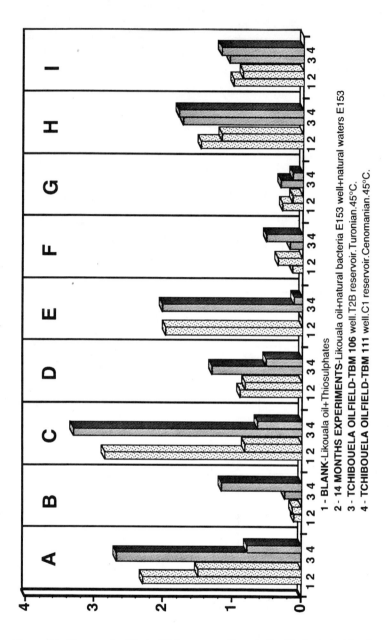

Figure 15- Changes in C2- to C4-benzene ratios of oils, biodegraded in-vitro and biodegraded in natural oil reservoirs.

Significance of ratios (see list of chemical structures in Figure 13)

A=2/3

B=1/2+3

| Laboratory | | GROSS COMPOSITION OF GASES | | | | | | | | | | d13C OF GASEOUS HYDROCARBONS | | | | | | | dD of Hydr. | | CO2 | | H2S | Whole oil | Topped oil | Estimated biogenic methane |
|---|---|---|---|---|---|---|---|---|---|---|---|---|---|---|---|---|---|---|---|---|---|---|---|---|---|---|
| Well | Number | C1 | C2 | C3 | i-C4 | n-C4 | i-C5 | n-C5 | N2 | CO2 | H2S | C1 | C2 | C3 | i-C4 | n-C4 | i-C5 | n-C5 | C1 | C2 | d13C | d18O | d34S | d13C | d13C | %/gas |
| Q235 | B39125 | 70.5 | 1.4 | 3.4 | 1.6 | 3.4 | 1.2 | 1.2 | 2.2 | 14.7 | 0.3 | -47.7 | -28.7 | -28.4 | -31.0 | -27.4 | -28.0 | -26.1 | -215 | -144 | 16.3 | 35.0 | | | | 7.4 |
| Q236 | | 65.8 | 0.5 | 1.0 | 0.3 | 0.5 | 0.3 | 0.2 | 23.7 | 7.8 | 0 | -50.8 | -29.4 | -27.7 | -30.7 | -26.5 | -27.6 | -25.2 | -206 | | 12.1 | 35.0 | | | | 13.6 |
| E153 | B39129 | 71.9 | 1.0 | 2.1 | 0.6 | 1.3 | 0.5 | 0.4 | 0.4 | 21.1 | 0.5 | -47.1 | -29.9 | -26.2 | -31.0 | -27.3 | -28.0 | -26.2 | -225 | -200 | 19.7 | 33.1 | 17.9 | | | 6.2 |
| BB325 | B39132 | 75.9 | 1.5 | 2.3 | 0.6 | 1.1 | 0.5 | 0.3 | 2.8 | 15.2 | 0 | -47.6 | -29.0 | -27.3 | -31.0 | -26.5 | -28.2 | -25.0 | -200 | -175 | 16.1 | 31.8 | | -27.6 | -27.7 | 7.2 |
| TBM 111 | B39133 | 38.4 | 10.9 | 7.8 | 2.4 | 2.3 | 1.0 | 0.1 | 31.7 | 4.3 | 0.9 | -47.1 | -28.5 | -24.8 | -26.4 | -23.2 | -25.6 | | -220 | | 9.3 | 37.5 | 21.6 | -26.3 | -26.3 | 6.2 |
| TBM106 | B39134 | 79.3 | 8.3 | 3.4 | 0.8 | 1.1 | 0.6 | 0.1 | 0.5 | 5.0 | 0.7 | -46.0 | -28.6 | -26.0 | -28.1 | -23.4 | -26.3 | -21.0 | -202 | -144 | 10.5 | 39.0 | 21.5 | -27 | -27.3 | 4 |
| LAM 14 | B43023 | 70.8 | 12.8 | 7.5 | 1.6 | 2.2 | 0.3 | 0.4 | 4.1 | 0.2 | 0 | -44.0 | -30.4 | -28.5 | -29.3 | -27.7 | -27.1 | -26.7 | -202 | -152 | -3.1 | 41.3 | | -27 | -27.5 | 0 |
| LAM 15 | B43024 | 80.5 | 10.7 | 4.8 | 0.5 | 1.0 | 0.2 | 0.3 | 1.8 | 0.3 | 0 | -44.2 | -30.5 | -28.3 | -29.4 | -27.2 | -27.1 | -26.8 | -203 | -150 | -2.6 | 42.1 | | | | 0 |

Table 1- Gross composition and isotopic data on gases and oils from offshore Congo.

dD of Hydr.=$\delta D$ ‰/SMOW of $C_{15+}$ hydrocarbons

d13C=$\delta^{13}C$ ‰/PDB

d18O=$\delta^{18}O$ ‰/SMOW

d34S=$\delta^{34}S$‰/CDT

C1=methane, C2=ethane, C3=propane, i-C4=isobutane, etc.

| Molecular compounds | Likouala oil without bacteria | | | | Likouala oil+E153 bacteria (1) | | | | Likouala oil+E153 bacteria (2) | | | |
|---|---|---|---|---|---|---|---|---|---|---|---|---|
| | %/volume | d13C 0/00/PDB | d18O 0/00/SMOW | d34S 0/00/CDT | %/volume | d13C 0/00/PDB | d18O 0/00/SMOW | d34S 0/00/CDT | %/volume | d13C 0/00/PDB | d18O 0/00/SMOW | d34S 0/00/CDT |
| methane | 0 | -27.8 | | | N.M. | -92 | | | N.M. | -96 | | |
| ethane | 0.51 | -27.7 | | | 0.2 | -28.5 | | | 0.3 | -27.6 | | |
| propane | 1.14 | -27.7 | | | 1.1 | -27.4 | | | 1.4 | -28 | | |
| i-C4 | 0.48 | -28 | | | 0.6 | -27.2 | | | 0.6 | -26.6 | | |
| n-C4 | 1.39 | -27.1 | | | 1.6 | -26.7 | | | 1.9 | -26.1 | | |
| i-C5 | 0.92 | -26.4 | | | 0.6 | -26.5 | | | 0.8 | | | |
| n-C5 | N.M. | -26.2 | | | 0.9 | -25.2 | | | 1.1 | | | |
| CO2 | 3.3 | -39.8 | 34 | | 3.4 | -34.9 | 32 | | 3.7 | -36.9 | 31.2 | |
| N2 | 92.2 | | | | 90.7 | | | | 89.3 | | | |
| H2S | 0 | | | | 0.9 | | | -3.1 | 0.8 | | | -5.7 |
| SO4 | | | | -0.2 | | | | 9.6 | | | | 7.5 |

(1)-Likouala oil+reconstituted bacterial consortium of E153 well+reconstituted waters

(2)-Likouala oil+reconstituted bacterial consortium of E153 well+reconstituted waters+vitamins+(NH4)2SO4 after 3 months of incubation.

Table 2-Genesis of $CH_4$ and $H_2S$ in laboratory experiments with the natural Emeraude bacteria grown on Likouala oils.

| Oilfield | Well | Laboratory Number(1st series) | Laboratory Number(2nd series) | Reservoir | Age/Formation | Depth (m/sea) | Temperature (°C) | Salinity (g/l) | Total bacterial count/ml | Cultivable aerobes/ml | Cultivable fermentative anaerobes/ml | Cultivable sulfate reducers/ml | Cultivable methanogens/m |
|---|---|---|---|---|---|---|---|---|---|---|---|---|---|
| Emeraude Marine North | Q 235 | B39125 | | R 1 | Senonian | | 26 | | 2.7X100000 | | | | |
| | Q 234 | B39126 | | R 2 | Senonian | | 31 | | 1.7x100000 | | | | |
| | R 222 | B39127 | | R 3 | Turonian | | 30 | 52 | 2.6x1000000 | | | | |
| | J 215 | B39128 | | R 4 | Turonian | | 32 | | 1.6x100000 | | | | |
| | Q 236 | ? | | R 5 | Turonian | | 34 | 35 | 1.4x10000 | | | | |
| Emeraude Marine South | E 153 | B39129 | B43019 | R 1 | Senonian | 227*-280* | 28 | 27 | 2.5x100000 | 0 | 4.5x10000 | 1.1x10000 | 1.0x100 |
| | B 122 | B39130 | | R 2 | Senonian | | 28 | 40 | 2.2x10000 | | | | |
| | AA 321 | B39131 | | R 3 | Turonian | | 35 | 25 | 2.2x10000 | | | | |
| | BB 325 | B39132 | B43020 | R 4 | Turonian | 398*-415* | 33 | 45 | 2.5x1000 | 2.5 | 1.5x1000 | 9.5x100 | 1.0x1000 |
| Tchibouela Marine | TBM 106 | B39134 | B43021 | T 2B | Cenomanian | 535-539 | 45 | 94 | no water | | | | |
| | TBM 111 | B39133 | B43022 | C 1 | Cenomanian | 585-620 | 45 | 94 | | | | | |
| Likouala Marine | LAM 14 | | B43023 | Level I | Aptian/Chela | 1304 | >80 | 100? | 0 | | | | |
| | LAM 15 | | B43024 | Level II | Aptian/Chela | 1315 | >80 | | 0 | | | | |
| | LAM 16 | | B43025 | Level II | Aptian/Chela | 1316 | >80 | | 0 | | | | |

Table 3-Summary of the results of the bacteriological study of the Congo oilfields production waters.

| Experimental references | Microorganisms SEBR References | Bacterial strains | GAS COMPOSITION | | | GAS | | | WATERS | | FORMED CO2 | | |
|---|---|---|---|---|---|---|---|---|---|---|---|---|---|
| | | | N2 % | CO2 % | H2S % | d13C/CO2/PDB | d18O/CO2/SMOW | d34S/H2S/CDT | BaSO4 (g) | d34S/SO4/CDT | %CO2/Gas mixture | d13C/CO2 | d18O/CO2 |
| BLANK 1 | no bacteria | no bacteria | 99.8 | 0.2 | | -41.1 | 32.4 | | 1.34 | 10 | | | |
| 1 | SEBR 2882 | Desulfovibrio Desulfuricans (Intern.Ref.) | 88.9 | 7.2 | 3.9 | -31.3 | 33.6 | 17 | 0 | | 7 | -31 | 34.5 |
| 2 | SEBR 3705 | Desulfovibrio Desulfuricans (Intern. Ref.) | 90.9 | 5.8 | 3.3 | -32 | 34 | 16 | 0 | | 3.1 | -31.7 | 34 |
| 3 | SEBR 3831 | Desulfovibrio Desulfuricans Emeraude 16" pipe | 92.6 | 4.9 | 2.5 | -28.8 | 33.8 | 13.4 | 0 | | 4.7 | -28.1 | 33.7 |
| 4 | SEBR 3849 | Desulfomicrobium Congo 20" pipe | 98.9 | 1.1 | 0.1< | -40.5 | 33.2 | 22.7 | 1.18 | 8.8 | 0.9 | -40.4 | 33.4 |
| 5 | SEBR 3851 | Desulfovibrium Emeraude 16" pipe | 90 | 7.7 | 2.3 | -28.4 | 32.4 | 12.2 | 0 | | 7.5 | -28 | |
| BLANK 2 | no bacteria | no bacteria | 98.6 | 1.4 | | -32 | | | 1.4 | 9.3 | | | |
| 6 | SEBR 4196 | Desulfovibrio Desulfuricans from BB325 well | 90.4 | 7 | 2.6 | -29.4 | | 15.9 | 0 | | 5.7 | -28.8 | |
| 7 | SEBR 4225 | SRB not identified E153 well | 90.3 | 7.1 | 2.6 | -29.3 | 32.4 | 17.2 | 0 | | 5.8 | -28.7 | |

Table 4- Results of in-vitro experiments using various bacterial strains.

| WELL/Sample(1) | OIL FIELD | | WATERS | | GAS |
|---|---|---|---|---|---|
| | H2S(% V/V water) | d34S/H2S | SO4= mg/l | d34S/SO4 | d34S/H2S |
| E153/2 | 5.4 | 13.4 | 2278 | 24.1 | 17.9 |
| E153/1 | 14.4 | 11.5 | 1000 | 35.2 | 17.9 |
| BB325/1 | 5 | 21 | 0 | | |
| BB325/2 | 9.9 | 21 | 46 | 31.3 | |
| TBM111/1 | 8.9 | 21.8 | 1285 | 25 | 21.6 |
| TBM111/2 | 16.6 | 22 | 1421 | 24.7 | 21.6 |
| LAM14/2 | 0 | | 950 | 22 | |
| LAM15/2 | 0 | | 375 | 17.9 | |
| LAM16/2 | 0 | | 1145 | 20 | |

(1)-Set of sampling = 1 or 2

Table 5- Isotopic data of sulphates and $H_2S$ from waters and gases.
d13C=$\delta^{13}$C ‰/PDB
d18O=$\delta^{18}$O ‰/SMOW
d34S=$\delta^{34}$S‰/CDT

EXPERIENCES WITH HORIZONTAL WELLS IN
A NATURALLY FRACTURED RESERVOIR

PUITS HORIZONTAUX DANS DES GISEMENTS
NATURELLEMENT FRACTURES

E.J. Schell, D.N. Meehan and D.W. Bossert
Union Pacific Resources Company, USA

ABSTRACT

Horizontal wells represent a major advancement in our approach
to developing and exploiting hydrocarbon reservoirs.  The myriad
technologies associated with horizontal wells have grown at a
startling rate in less than a decade.  Initial technical issues
of borehole stability and drilling concerns have largely given
way to current issues in completions, stimulations, reservoir
characterization and geosteering.  While much has been written
regarding the technical aspects associated with horizontal
drilling, the management of large scale efforts in horizontal
drilling has been poorly documented.

In this paper, the activities of Union Pacific Resources (UPRC)
are described during a drilling program covering more than 1,000
horizontal wells.  During the most active three years of this
campaign, UPRC was the leading driller in North America in terms
of rig count.  Critical success factors for UPRC are described,
concentrating on organizational issues, strategy, and the
development and ultra-rapid deployment of evolving technologies.
A combination of persistent efforts, a willingness to challenge
long-held assumptions and some good fortune have resulted in the
development of more than 250 million barrels of oil equivalent
(BOE) in an area on the verge of economic extinction.

RÉSUMÉ

Les puits horizontaux representent un progrés considerable pour
le développement des champs pétroliers.  Les technologies
associées aux puits horizontaux se sont développées de façon
surprenante dans la dernière décennie.  Les considérations de
stabilité des puits, ainsi que les techniques de forage ont amené
de nouvelles idées pour la completion, la stimulation, la
caractérisation de gisement ou sur la geosteering.  Même si
l'aspect technique du  forage horizontal est pleinement développé
dans la littérature, le management a` grande échelle du forage
horizontal est peu documenté.

Dans ce papier, les activités de l' "Union Pacific Resources"
(UPRC) sont  reportées pour le forage de plus de 1.000 puits
horizontaux.  Pendant les trois années les plus actives de ce
projet, UPRC était le premier foreur en Amerique du Nord en terme
de "rig count".

Les facteurs critiques du succès de UPRC sont decrits; les
problèmes d'organisation, les stratégies, et le développement
et déploiement de  nouvelles technologies sont accentués.  Un
mélange d'efforts persistants, de désir de remettre en question
les hypothèses généralement acceptées et de bonne chances, a
amené le  développement de plus de 250 millions de barrils
d'huile (BOE) dans une région au bord de l'arrêt économique.

INTRODUCTION

The first modern horizontal wells were drilled by Elf-Aquitane in the early 1980's in the Lacq Field in France and the Rospe Mare Field of Offshore Italy. Since then, more than 8000 horizontal wells have been drilled in the U.S. and Canada (Figure 1). The earliest jump in horizontal activity in the U.S. was concentrated in the Austin Chalk formation in Texas.

The Austin Chalk formation occurs along a fairway extending from Mexico through Louisiana ranging in thickness from 100 feet to 700 feet. Figure 2. This dense carbonate reservoir has low matrix permeabilities ranging from less than 0.005 to 0.02 md. The low permeability matrix is often enhanced by sparse to abundant vertical fracturing. Fracture orientations are sub-vertical and essentially parallel; horizontal wells are drilled perpendicular to fracture orientation to intersect more fractures than a vertical well.

The Austin Chalk trend went through several "boom" like development periods. More than two thousand vertical wells were drilled by Jan. 1, 1987. By January 1, 1995, more than 2000 horizontal wells have been drilled in the Austin Chalk. UPRC has drilled more than one thousand of these horizontal wells and continues to operate more than 15 rigs drilling horizontal wells. Figure 3 shows the production history of the Austin Chalk, illustrating the impact of horizontal drilling since 1987. This paper focuses on UPRC's experiences conducting this horizontal drilling program.

UPRC's net cumulative investment in wells, pipelines, facilities, land, for the Austin Chalk alone is more than 1,400 million $US. The full cycle ROI (return on investment)with this investment is estimated to exceed 20%. Figure 4 illustrates UPRC's growth in Austin Chalk production from the horizontal drilling. The reserve additions are more than 250 million gross BOE's (barrels of oil equivalent based on 6 Mscf = 1BOE). UPRC attributes their success to early testing and aggressive entry, organizing to empower, and encouraging new technology.

UPRC's ENTRY

UPRC was fortunate to have a significant HBP (held by production) land position in the Giddings Austin Chalk field as a result of the vertical well activity in the early 1980's. This acreage was quickly reaching the end of its economic life and in 1987 UPRC drilled its first horizontal well.

Although the first well was an economic failure, UPRC drilled 11 more wells over the next two years. By early 1989, the results of these wells were encouraging. Reserves averaged 240 thousand BOE and well costs averaged $1.5 million $US. The production was characterized by high initial rates with steep declines. The ROI was above 20%, mostly due to the high initial production rates. Some early observations of this play were;

1) the Austin Chalk was productive over a huge area, in excess of 500,000 acres,
2) each well produces a relatively small profit; many wells were needed,
3) controlling costs would be critical to success since well margins are small.

The Austin Chalk horizontal play was viewed as primarily a land play. Direct detection of fractured intervals is very difficult. Thin intervals of extensive fracturing are rarely obvious from conventional seismic analysis. In this sense, the Austin Chalk is a "statistical play," in that many wells must be drilled to identify the best areas.

After the first group of wells, UPRC leased 60,000 acres in the lowest risk areas, expanding their early position far beyond the HBP properties. "Low risk areas" were initially defined as having vertical wells with cumulative recoveries greater than 20,000 BOE. After high success rates in these areas, UPRC expanded to more risky areas through stepout development wells. Controlling vast quantities of land was critical to capturing opportunities. The ability to react quickly to discoveries was also important. Testing and development within the lease terms required an aggressive increase in rig count. High activity levels of leasing, farm-ins, acquisitions, and complex deal structures required a flexible and capable land management organization that interfaced very effectively with the geoscientists and engineers. This was easier to say than to accomplish. Our systems and procedures were all stressed, and some opportunities were missed. Continued growth would require increased flexibility.

Organizing to empower

The Austin Chalk group's initial organization followed the existing paradigm of the company. People were organized by function (geology, engineers, landmen, etc.). Multiple levels of management were in place and most decisions were approved through each level. This worked well with a small, 2-10 rig program operating in low risk areas.

As activity level and technology requirements increased, people had less time to communicate with multiple levels of management. The direction of each functional group was often different, leading to inefficiencies. The organization changed numerous times, evolving into multi-disciplinary, leaderless, geographically based teams. This organization eliminated 1-2 days per week that the petrotech's (geologist, landmen and engineers) spent presenting AFE's, budgets, etc. through multiple level of management. Common goals were shared by each team members, requiring the team to budget capital and production and to test and expand their areas with leasing and drilling.

Even the most successful teams have conflicts. A company-wide commitment to re-engineering helped provide resources to address some of these conflicts. One primary goal was to encourage employees to take risks that have the potential to lower costs and increase recoveries. These ideas did not all work. However, the successful ideas more than paid for numerous failures. New ideas often challenged existing paradigms and long-held opinions. Many paradigms existed because they were successful in predicting and explaining results in vertical wells. Many were replaced as we pushed the envelope of horizontal well applications.

Encouraging new technology

Applying new technology was essential to lowering costs and improving recoveries. By 1987, the service companies (drilling, cement, wireline, etc.) had already lowered prices after the precipitous decline in rig count from 1982. Reducing well costs could only be achieved through efficiencies in the drilling and completion processes.

Other than "Please lower costs!", UPRC's management gave little direction on ideas to pursue. Rather, they encouraged ideas at every opportunity even if their ultimate value was unclear or if the proposal was potentially costly if it failed. Management did not persecute failed attempts. In other words, the people were set free to follow whatever ideas they deemed appropriate.

With this company culture, ideas were quickly tested and implemented when successful. With the high activity level (up to 33 rigs) multiple experiments were conducted simultaneously. Each rig became a field laboratory. In many cases, ideas were built upon each other. Information was quickly exchanged between teams members and positive results were quickly copied throughout the program. Well cost reductions are shown by Figure 5 and overall development cost reductions are shown in Figure 6.

The technology discussion that follows focuses on the developments of drilling, stimulation and reservoir characterization. The items covered include:

· Drilling with lost returns,
· mud caps,
· mud issues,
· bit selection,
· dual power section mud motors,
· multiple laterals,
· Retrievable whipstocks,
· water fracs,

·   formation evaluation,
·   geosteering,
·   geostatistical modeling.

Drilling with lost returns. This is unheard of in vertical well drilling as
it usually results in an expensive fishing job, typically 300,000 $US. The
typical horizontal well has intermediate casing set in the top of the Austin
Chalk. The horizontal portion is drilled with mud motors and MWD's.  Early
in the program,  wells started losing returns completely while drilling.
These were located in areas with depleted vertical wells.  On the first well
that lost returns during drilling, instead of pumping lost circulation
material, the well was drilled ahead with water for another week, never
gaining back returns. Several wells have lost more than 100,000 barrels of
water. No unusual sticking problems or stuck pipe resulted. Cuttings
apparently were ground to a fine enough size to pass into the fractures.

Mud Cap. Activity expanded from areas with normal pressures and a true
vertical depth of 7500 ft. to depths greater than 14,000 ft with pore
pressures in excess of 13 ppg mud. In these deeper, gas prone areas, gas
kicks may be taken while intersecting fractures. Vertical wells encountering
such kicks show immediate pit gains and are dealt with conventionally. These
kicks may not be apparent for horizontal wells until the accumulated gas
volumes are quite large.  Small kicks are routinely circulated out without
ceasing drilling.  A rotating head is employed to control the annular
pressure.  Drilling with 500 psi and greater at the surface became common.
If the annular pressure exceeded the rotating head's design, drilling
stopped, the pipe rams were closed and the kick was circulated out. This
slowed the drilling progress and was risky.  An unconventional approach to
this circumstance was the use of mud caps. The back side was shut in and the
wells were drilled without returns. Water was pumped down the drill pipe and
lost to the natural fracture system along with the cuttings. Mud on the
annulus provided pressure control.

On one example application at 14,000 ft TVD, we drilled two laterals in a
13.5 ppg environment. The stand pipe pressures required to pump water in
such a system approached 5,000 psi. This nears the limit of 1600 hp mud
pumps. However, these laterals were successfully drilled with a total mud
cost of 500,000 $US. A nearby well was drilled conventionally with returns
with a total mud bill of 1,200,000 $US with only one lateral.

Mud Issues. UPRC's experience with horizontal wells includes drilling in
areas of substantial depletion up to high pressure gradient (>14 ppg) gas
areas. Mud issues often dominate the economics of drilling in such areas.
Lost circulation is common in drilling horizontal wells in naturally
fractured reservoirs. It is preferable to avoid extensive skin damage. The
loss of large quantities of fluids is clearly undesirable. Many of the wells
we drilled required weighted mud or brine to be drilled successfully. Figure
7 shows the estimated ultimate recovery (EUR) for six similar wells
requiring drilling fluids of 10-11 ppg. Lost circulation was much less in
the wells drilled with mud and the resulting EURs for the wells drilled with
mud were significantly greater than those of the wells drilled with brine.
The average cost of the "brine" wells in this study was 1.5 million $US, or
200,000 $US greater than the "mud" wells. For marginal wells, the Net
Present Value is often less than 200,000 $US.

This has not been obvious to other operators including our partners. On
several occasions, we have had drilling competitions with another operator
using brine while we drilled with mud. Invariably, we won these competitions
and were usually halfway through our second well before the first brine well
was completed.

Bit Selection. UPRC cooperated extensively with bit manufacturers in the
design and experimental testing of numerous bits, resulting in dramatic
performance improvements. Specifically, the use of PDC bits has been
outstanding. Often, we combine PDC bits with mud motors in the shallower,
vertical wellbore to improve penetration rates. An additional benefit of
this approach is a significant decrease in drill pipe washouts.

Dual Power Section Mud Motors. Another example of how UPRC has pushed
horizontal drilling technology forward is the development of the dual power

section mud motor and the subsequent development of extended motors[11]. The
ability to increase penetration rates (typically 50% or greater) with this
technology has lead to its uses in virtually every horizontal well we drill.
In 1992, a 500 ft per day drilling rate in the lateral was considered good.
This benchmark now has essentially doubled.

One early concern was the potential for increased bit wear. In reality, the
smoother torque provided by the extended length motors enables us to use
larger cutters and greater weight with less breakage of cutters. The net
effect has been improved bit life. Dramatically higher penetration rates
accelerate steering errors, so the necessity of a team effort in geosteering
is increased. Figure 8 shows a typical days-depth chart for a multiple
lateral well drilled with a dual power section mud motor vs. a dual lateral
with a standard motor and rock bits.

Retrievable Whipstocks. It is possible to drill multiple laterals with all
laterals open. Operational and safety concerns make it preferable to be able
to isolate previously drilled horizontal laterals while drilling and testing
subsequent laterals. The development of retrievable whipstocks is a further
example of how we leveraged our technology development. We provided a
manufacturer a small amount of seed money to develop a working retrievable
whipstock. We tested this tool and provided feedback and optimization
assistance. Similar efforts by others lead to multiple product developments.

Our primary applications for retrievable whipstocks are when lateral
isolation is required. Other applications include when liners must be run
in multiple laterals, when reentering cased vertical wells with multiple
laterals, and when casing problems require isolation during drilling.

Multiple laterals. Multiple laterals are now routine at UPRC. These include
stacked lateral (SL) to access multiple horizons or poorly communicated
layers within a formation and opposing laterals (OL) drilled in the same
intervals in opposite directions. Arbitrary combinations of these approaches
have enabled us to routinely drill multi-laterals with four or more
horizontal laterals.

Drilling very long horizontal laterals is readily achievable for distances
of 8,000 feet or more. However, the ability to steer the horizontal lateral
is severely diminished as the lateral exceeds 3,000 to 4,000 feet. Torque
and drag issues and solids transport problems also complicate ultra-long
medium radius wells. The use of OLs minimizes these problems while providing
two conventional length horizontal wells with only one surface location,
wellhead, vertical hole, etc. OL technology is most attractive for deep
wells with significant costs to reach the target formation, when
surface/location costs are large, and when steering is crucial.

Geosteering of the second lateral is generally improved because of the
improved reservoir characterization provided by the first
lateral. Risks in multiple lateral technology include potential damage to
open laterals while drilling subsequent laterals and potential difficulties
in logging, reentering, selectively stimulating or shutting off water
production, and production logging.

Water Fracs So called "water fracs" have obtained excellent results in the
Austin Chalk formation with mixed results elsewhere. This inexpensive
treatment uses high volumes of water but no proppant. Potential mechanisms
include imbibition, gravity drainage, skin damage removal, and
repressurization of the reservoir to enhance recovery. UPRC has treated
about 270 vertical and 190 horizontal wells. Incremental recoveries from
horizontal well water fracs alone exceed six million BOE.

Begun as a vertical well stimulation, these high rate treatments (70 bbl/min
for vertical wells, 150 bbl/min for horizontal wells) allowed UPRC to
maintain significant land holdings and to acquire numerous marginal vertical
wells.

Successes with vertical wells lead to tests with horizontal wells. Improved
diversion was obtained by alternating states of fresh water, wax beads and
acid. Other diverting materials (rock salt, liquid gels, etc.) were tested
with wax beads remaining the diverter of choice. These beads are lighter

than water and are used in slugs of 1,000 to 6,000 lbs. per stage at
concentrations of 0.5 ppg. Detailed examples are provided in Ref. 7 along
with potential explanations of the mechanisms involved.

Formation Evaluation There are many misconceptions associated with
horizontal wells. One of the most surprising relates to formation
evaluation. The majority of horizontal wells have no open hole logs. The
challenges of logging horizontal wells are described in references 1-6.
Costs for such logs are higher than for vertical wells because of the
mechanics and difficulties associated with negotiating hole curvature and
conveying the tools to bottom without gravity. Horizontal wells require the
use of:

· drill-pipe conveyed logs,
· logging-while-drilling,
· pump-down logs, or
· coiled tubing conveyed logs.

In addition to higher costs, many well logs designed for vertical wells have
significant interpretation difficulties when applied to horizontal wells.
UPRC's primary formation evaluation need during the initial applications of
horizontal wells for naturally fractured reservoirs was to characterize the
natural fracture system. What was the spacing, azimuth, intensity, etc. of
the natural fractures encountered?

The various tools to evaluate natural fractures in horizontal wells are
reviewed in Refs. 3 and 4. We identified the oriented micro-resistivity
devices to be most useful in identifying small fractures, predicting well
productivity, and in identifying stimulation candidates. The actual benefits
from logging many early horizontal wells were far greater than expected

A few of the early surprises included the absolute uniformity of fracture
strike. Essentially all open natural fractures were vertical to sub-vertical
and parallel[9]. Unlike "conventional wisdom," fracture direction tended to
parallel the maximum horizontal compressive stress rather than being tied
to structure. Thus, wellbore breakouts in vertical wells could be used to
predict fracture strike and the optimal direction for horizontal wells.
Virtually no fractures were observed at directions other than the primary
direction, leading to large (>100:1) permeability anisotropies[8] and the
potential for significant interwell interference[5].

Many small fractures terminate at thin (on the order of 1cm) shale streaks,
marls, or styolites. Slightly larger fractures may be offset and may not
hydraulically connect adjacent layers. The largest faults and natural
fractures may propagate through shale intervals in excess of a few meters.
References 5, 9 and 10 review the in situ and laboratory evidence associated
with this observation.

The impact of these observations made an enormous impact on subsequent
operational decisions. Huge permeability anisotropies lead to much wider
"optimal" spacing, requiring far fewer wells. Interference between wells
more than 8,000 feet apart was not uncommon[5]. The economic benefits of being
able to drill wells on larger spacing was critical to commercial field
development and avoiding the drilling of hundreds of unnecessary wells.
Zonal isolation meant that "traverse" wells (wells that crossed the entire
Chalk interval) would be much less attractive than wells that remained in
the more intensely fractured intervals. This indicated a need to improve the
ability to stay "in zone" and to a need to drill more than one horizontal
lateral per well.

Geological Steering Original horizontal wells targeted a formation and
updated the original geological model of the reservoir infrequently. We now
steer horizontal wells while drilling using the geological and geophysical
measurements made while drilling in a process known as "geosteering."[6] This
process[12] has been extremely successful in maintaining wellbores in the
desired interval, identifying "redrill" candidates, and in multiple
laterals. It would not have been possible to develop this technique without
a critical mass of horizontal well logs.

Geostatistical Modeling It is important to model well and reservoir behavior. A primary goal in reservoir characterization and reservoir modeling was to optimize well placement, lateral length and inter-well spacing. Because the reservoir is naturally fractured, UPRC initially considered dual-porosity and dual-permeability stimulators. These models are fundamentally homogenous; actual well tests from vertical and horizontal wells do not display the salient behaviors predicted by these models. Observations from the open-hole fracture logs showed extreme levels of heterogeneity.

We used these and other data[5] and public domain geostatistical models developed by the Stanford Center for Reservoir Forecasting[13] to develop credible models for conventional 3-phase simulations. These reservoir descriptions implied a high level of anisotropy, explained the unusually high level of inter-well interference, resulted in rapid history matches and predicted the degree of depletion at new locations. These models were integral in optimizing inter-well spacing and in obtaining appropriate spacing regulations. The larger spacing obtained made it possible to maintain profitabilty.

## References

1.   C. Clavier: "The Challenge of Logging Horizontal Wells," The Log Analyst, March-April 1991, pp. 63-84.

2.   D. N. Meehan: "Advances in Horizontal Well Technology," Proceedings of the Second JNOC/TRC International Symposium, JNOC, 1994, Tokyo.

3.   T. R. Svor and D. N. Meehan: "Quantifying Horizontal Well Logs in Naturally Fractured Reservoirs-Part-I," SPE 22634, presented at the 1991 Fall SPE Meeting in Dallas, TX.

4.   D. N. Meehan and T. R. Svor: "Quantifying Horizontal Well Logs in Naturally Fractured Reservoirs-Part-II," SPE 22792, presented at the 1991 Fall SPE Meeting in Dallas, TX.

5.   D. N. Meehan and S. K. Verma: "Integration of Horizontal Well Log Information in Fractured Reservoir Characterization," SPE 24697, presented at the 1992 Fall SPE Meeting in Washington, D.C.

6.   D. N. Meehan: "Geological Steering of Horizontal Wells," Technology Today Series, SPE 29242, Journal of Petroleum Technology, Oct., 1994.

7.   D. N. Meehan: "Practical and Reservoir Aspects of Austin Chalk 'Stimulations', SPE 24783, presented at the 1992 Fall SPE Meeting in Washington, D.C. Scheduled for publication in SPE Production Engineering and Facilities, May, 1995.

8.   Ehlig-Economides, M. J. Fetkovich, and D. N. Meehan: "Factoring Anisotropy into Well Design," Oil Field Review, October, 1990, v. 2, No. 2, pp. 24-33.

9.   D. N. Meehan: "Rock Mechanics Issues in Petroleum Engineering," presented at the 1st North American Rock Mechanics Symposium held in Austin, TX, June, 1994. Published in Proceedings of the 1st North American Rock Mechanics Symposium, Balkeema, 1994.

10.  M. Friedman, O. Kwon, and V. L. French: "Containment of natural fractures in brittle beds of the Austin Chalk," presented at the 1st North American Rock Mechanics Symposium held in Austin, TX, June, 1994. Published in Proceedings of the 1st North American Rock Mechanics Symposium, Balkeema, 1994.

11.  B. C. Califf, M. Johnson: "How Tandem Motors Improve Drilling Performance," World Oil, Oct., 1994, pp. 77-82.

12.  D. G. Kyte, D. N. Meehan, and T. R. Svor: "Method of Maintaining a Borehole in a Stratigraphic Interval While Drilling," U. S. Patent No. 5,311,951 issued May 17, 1994.

13.  C. V. Deutsch and A. G. Journel: GSLIB: Geostatistical Software Library and User's Guide, Oxford University Press, 1992.

14.  Messman, J. L.: "Prospering in a $1.75 World," an address to the Arthur Andersen Oil and Gas Symposium, Dec. 6, 1994, Houston, TX.

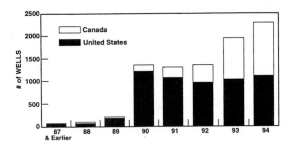

Figure 1. Horizontal wells drilled in the U.S. and Canada.

Figure 2. Austin Chalk Trend.

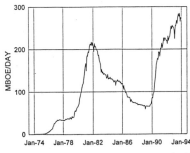

Figure 3. Total Austin Chalk Production

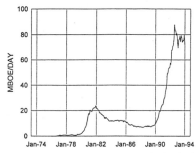

Figure 4. UPRC Austin Chalk Production

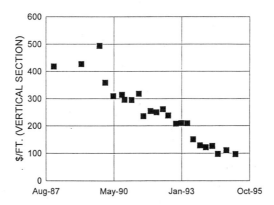

Figure 5. UPRC horizontal well drilling costs.

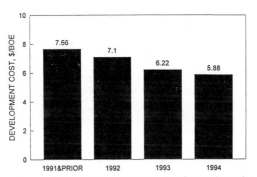

Figure 6. UPRC Austin Chalk development costs.

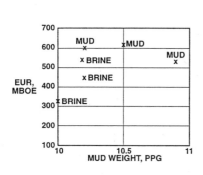

Figure 7. Drilling fluid vs. EUR

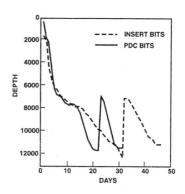

Figure 8. Days vs. Depth

# PREDICTING RESONANCE IN DRILL STRINGS

# PREVISION DE LA RESONANCE DANS LES TRAINS DE FORAGE

David Reid

British Gas plc, Research and Technology, UK.

## ABSTRACT

British Gas is currently investigating methods of reducing drilling costs by minimising rig down time due to drill string failures. Failures in drill strings have occurred despite following the industry accepted design practices. Metallurgical investigations on some of the failed drillstring components show evidence of fatigue. One of the most likely causes of fatigue is vibration - particularly at a critical rotary drilling speed where resonance occurs and the amplitude of vibration is amplified. Also, there is no industry accepted method of calculating critical speeds. Consequently, British Gas initiated a research programme to investigate practical methods of calculating drill string resonance. In this research the analysis of vibration data from both field and scaled model drill strings is used to develop mathematical models to calculate resonance. These mathematical models are based on wave theory. A case study of axial vibration is discussed and it demonstrates the importance of boundary conditions.

## RESUME

British Gas examine actuellement des méthodes de diminution des coûts de forage par une réduction maximum des temps d'immobilisation des plates-formes dus aux défaillances des trains de forage. Des pannes de trains de forage se sont produites malgré l'observation des méthodes de conception reconnues par l'industrie. Des examens métallurgiques effectués sur des pièces de forage défectueuses ont révélé que ces dernières offrent des signes de fatigue. Une des causes les plus vraisemblables de fatigue est la vibration - en particulier à une vitesse de forage rotary critique ou la résonance se produit et où l'amplitude de la vibration est amplifiée. En outre, il n'y a pas de méthode de calcul des vitesses critiques reconnue par l'industrie. Par conséquent, British Gas a instauré un programme de recherche afin d'examiner des méthodes pratiques de calcul de la résonance des trains de forage. Dans cette recherche, l'analyse des données de vibration provenant à la fois de trains de forage sur le terrain et de modèles réduits de trains de forage est utilisée pour mettre au point des modèles mathématiques destinés au calcul de la résonance. Ces modèles mathématiques sont basés sur la théorie ondulatoire. Une étude de cas sur la vibration axiale est examinée et elle démontre l'importance des conditions aux limites.

## INTRODUCTION

British Gas is examining numerous ways of reducing drilling costs. One area that is currently being investigated, because of its potential for cost saving, is rig down time due to drill string failures. Two common types of failure are twist-off and washout. The total cost of a typical washout is approximately 1 rig day at £40 000 to £50 000 for a North sea operation (this amount represents the total cost of returning the drill bit to the same depth where the failure occurred and it includes: tripping, make-up and breakout times and hole conditioning). A twist-off may cost between 1 to 3 rig days (assuming a successful fishing operation) and the cost of losing a section of hole and side-tracking.

British Gas has experienced some drill string failures. These failures have occurred in:      • new and used drill string components
• different hole sizes
• a variety of operating conditions
and despite:
• following the industry accepted practices for drill string design
• stringent inspection of all components before being sent to the rig

A metallurgical analysis on some of the failed drill string components showed that they fatigued. Vibration - probably a resonance (References 1 to 5) - was thought to be one of the most likely causes of this fatigue. At this moment in time, the Drilling Industry does not have an accepted method of calculating the rotary drilling speed causing resonance - called a "Critical Rotary". This is because the critical speed formulae, detailed in the 12th and earlier editions of API RP7G (References 6 and 7), were withdrawn when field studies showed that these simple equations were not sufficiently accurate. As a consequence of the failures and lack of guidance on the critical rotary, British Gas initiated a research programme to investigate practical methods of calculating drill string resonance.

This paper presents a case study of axial vibration. It describes the analysis of field data from a drilling rig, the results from scaled model testing and the mathematical models. It also demonstrates the importance of boundary conditions at the top and bottom of the drillstring.

## ANALYSIS OF FIELD DATA

A vertical land well was drilled as part of an operation to create a salt cavity storage facility for natural gas. Essentially, the procedure for making this cavity was to drill a vertical well into a thick layer of salt and then leach out the salt to form a cavity. This particular well was drilled to a very high specification - as detailed in Table 1. The rig employed to drill the well used a conventional drawworks, hook (IDECO 360) and swivel (IDECO 400) to suspend the drill string. A standard rotary table provided torque to rotate the drill string at the kelly (5 1/4 inch hexagonal, 41.54 ft in length). The drill string comprised standard drill collar, stabilisers and a 26 inch tricone drill bit.

The field measurement equipment is detailed in the Appendix.

Vibration data was recorded from several drill strings during a variety of operations. This data included:

- Putting the kelly into the "Rat Hole".
- Lowering the drill string down the hole after making a connection.
- Drilling with "Kelly Bounce".

**Putting the Kelly into the "Rat Hole"**

The hook, swivel and kelly remained together as an assembly. This assembly was disconnected from the drill string and moved to the "Rat Hole". The weight on hook (WOH) was $11.3*10^3$ kg (25,000 lb). As the assembly was moved the measurement equipment captured vertical vibration. The acceleration with respect to time, Figure 1, of this vibration showed a smooth waveform with no discontinuities. This suggested that the hook and swivel remained in contact and they vibrated together as a single body. The vibration was transient and the amplitude of vibration decayed as the assembly oscillated. This indicated the presence of damping. A frequency spectrum (this is a plot of amplitude against frequency for all of the vibration components contained within the acceleration time trace data) showed a single vibration frequency at 4.74 Hertz (Hz), Figure 2. This single frequency combined with the fact that the assembly vibrated as one body showed that it behaved dynamically like a single-degree-of-freedom (SDOF) spring/mass system - References 1 and 2. The vibration of the assembly was analysed further using SDOF theory. The damping ratio, effective spring stiffness of the ropes (drawworks) and the mass (hook and swivel) were calculated: 0.0552, 10.1 $*10^6$ N.m$^{-1}$ (57.7$*10^3$ lbf.in$^{-1}$) and 9.94$*10^3$ kg (21.9$*10^3$ lb) respectively.

**Lowering the Drill String Down the Hole After Making a Connection**

The last piece of heavy wall drill pipe (HWDP) was connected to complete the bottom hole assembly (BHA) - as detailed in Table 2. The tool joint connection was made and torqued up, the drill string was raised up by the drawworks and the slips were removed. This drill string was suspended by the swivel with the drill bit several metres above the bottom of the hole. Axial vibration at the swivel was measured and recorded as the drill string was lowered down the hole. The vibration data from this operation produced a spectrum with frequencies at 2.07, 9.40, 16.94, 27.90, 40.90 Hz - as shown in Figure 3 (and also listed in Table 4). It was thought that this transient vibration occurred when either the drill bit or a stabilizer contacted a small discontinuity in the well bore as it was being lowered.

**Drilling with "Kelly Bounce"**

The drill string discussed above, and detailed in Table 2, was used to drill through chalk (The well is defined in Table 3). Axial vibration data from this drill string captured the drilling operation from start-up to severe axial vibration at the surface - called "Kelly Bounce". The duration of    recorded vibration was approximately 7 minutes.

Data from drilling with kelly bounce is shown in Figures 4, 5 and 6. Figure 4, a plot of acceleration against time, showed the vibration at the swivel. This data showed a sudden increase in the amplitude of vibration. This is when kelly bounce was observed. Further analysis of this data, in the form of a "waterfall" spectrum (a 3-dimensional frequency spectrum display with time as the third axis) showed how vibration frequencies in the 0 to 10 Hz bandwidth changed with respect to time - Figure 5. This data showed the run-up to kelly bounce. At 118 rpm (1.96 Hz) there was no significant vibration. The drilling speed was dropped to 96 rpm (1.60 Hz) and vibration frequencies at 4.67 and 9.42 Hz suddenly appeared on the waterfall plot.    Figure 6 showed a frequency spectrum covering the 0 to 50 Hz bandwidth for the complete sample of captured data (i.e. Figure 4). Vibration frequencies were measured at: 1.60, 3.20, 4.67, 6.92, 9.42, 14.50, 19.42, 30.37, and 38.42 Hz (these frequencies are also listed in Table 6).

It was observed that 3.20 Hz was 2 times the rotational drilling speed. 4.67 Hz was very close to 3 times the speed (4.80 Hz). Also, there were multiples of times 3 - for example 9.42 (*6), 14.5 (*9) and 19.42 (*12).

## SCALED MODEL DRILLSTRING RIG

It is impossible to control the boundary conditions and make vibration measurements at any location on an operational drill string in the well. Consequently, it was thought that an accessible, scaled model would be beneficial to a study on the dynamic behaviour of a drill string. A rig to accommodate scaled model drill strings was built.

The rig provides both access to all parts of the scaled drill string and complete control of the boundary conditions. It has a working length of 6m within its total height of 8m (see Figure 7). The variable speed drive sits on top of the rigid vertical support and from here the model drill string is suspended vertically. A series of carriages positioned vertically constrain the transverse displacements of the model drill string under test. An electro-magnetic vibration shaker is positioned at the base of the rig to provide a periodic load at the position of the drill bit.

Scaled drill strings have been tested and the data has been analysed to determine their natural frequencies.

The axial scaled model used to research the vibration of the field measurements detailed previously will be presented. Both the method used to determine the scaling parameters and the results will be discussed.

**Scaling Parameters**

The Buckingham Pi method of dimensional analysis (Reference 8) was used to determine the scaling parameters. The derived Pi groups were:

$$\pi_1 = \frac{a}{l^2} \qquad\qquad (\tfrac{a}{l^2})_{ms} = (\tfrac{a}{l^2})_{ds}$$

$$\pi_2 = \frac{l_s}{l_t} \qquad\qquad (\tfrac{l_s}{l_t})_m = (\tfrac{l_s}{l_t})_d$$

$$\pi_3 = \frac{k}{l \times E} \qquad\qquad (\tfrac{k}{l \times E})_m = (\tfrac{k}{l \times E})_d$$

$$\pi_4 = l \times f \sqrt{\tfrac{\rho}{E}} \qquad\qquad (l_t \times f \times \sqrt{\tfrac{\rho}{E}})_m = (l_t \times f \times \sqrt{\tfrac{\rho}{E}})_d$$

$$\pi_5 = \frac{M}{\rho \times l^3} \qquad\qquad (\tfrac{M}{\rho \times l^3})_m = (\tfrac{M}{\rho \times l^3})_d$$

Where:                                                          and subscripts:

a =   cross sectional area.
l =   length.
k =   spring stiffness of the steel        m =   scaled model.
      ropes and drawworks.                 d =   actual drill string.
M =   total mass of the drill string       t =   total length of drill string.
      plus the hook and swivel.            s =   a section of the drill string (for
$f$ =   frequency.                              example, the length of HWDP).
$\rho$ =   mass density.
E =   Young's Modulus.

A computer program was written to use standard diameters of circular bar (rod) and their material properties in the Pi groups to find a scaled model to fit in test rig. The scaled model of the field study drill string is detailed in Figure 8. This model had a frequency scaling factor of 27.1 to 1.

**Scaled Model Results**

The scaled model was installed in the test rig. It was suspended from the top (hook and swivel) and was free at the bottom (drill bit). The measurement equipment used during the testing of this model is detailed in the Appendix.

This was a difficult structure to test and measure in a purely axial direction because it was very light, and consequently, even small excitation loads caused bending and introduced additional vibration frequencies on the measured data. However, the results showed the 4 most prominent vibration frequencies - i.e. natural frequencies - at 53.0, 267.5, 537.5 and 682.5 Hz respectively. See Figure 9 (and listed in Table 5).

## MATHEMATICAL MODELS

A brief overview of the mathematics is presented. A more detailed description of the derivations and solutions is presented in References 1, 2, 9 and 10.

A suitable mathematical model was developed to provide quick, quantitative information on the resonant frequencies of the drill string. This model was based on elastic displacement as a function of both position within the drillstring and time. To provide the flexibility and allow change to the configuration, the drill string was considered to be a succession of individual items connected end-to-end. This arrangement produced a common boundary at each connection between 2 items. Each item of the drillstring was modelled on either lumped elements (for example the mass of the hook and swivel, the stiffness of the steel ropes and drawworks, etc.) or as a continuous elastic system (all tubulars, for example drill collars, pipe, etc.) and the calculated result was expressed in terms of impedance. The complete drill string was configured form these items and the drill bit was considered to be the source of a periodic driving force generating outgoing displacement waves. These waves travelled up the drill string and down into the rock. The resultant steady state vibration of the complete drill string was the sum of generated and reflected waves. As the drillstring and the rock shared the same force at the point of contact, this complete system was modelled as 2 separate sub-systems. Both sub-systems calculated the impedance at the drill bit and then they were combined for the solution of the complete system.

### Description of Drill String Model (Free at Bit)

The mathematical model for both the full-size field study and the scaled model drill strings (detailed in Table 2 and Figure 8 respectively) was based on lumped elements for the hook, swivel and drawworks and a succession of continuous elements for the collars. The calculation procedure was to treat the surface elements as a load acting on the top of the kelly. This was the top boundary condition. This load was then used to calculate the impedance input at the bottom of the kelly. As the kelly was connected to a piece of HWDP, they both share a common boundary where they join. Consequently, the impedance at the bottom of the kelly is the load acting on the top of this piece of HWDP. This HWDP load was used to calculate the impedance input at the bottom of this element. This procedure was followed down the drillstring until the impedance at the drill bit was calculated. The results were plotted (actually the reciprocal of impedance, i.e. mobility, was plotted because it shows a peak at resonance - see Figures 10, 11 and 12).

**Model for Lumped Elements.** The hook and swivel were modelled by a lump mass. The steel ropes and drawworks were modelled using an effective spring stiffness and damping.

$$\hat{Z} = \frac{F}{\hat{V}}$$

$$\hat{Z}_{HSD} = R_D + j\left[\omega M_{HS} - \frac{K_D}{\omega}\right]$$

Where:

$\hat{Z}$ = impedance (a complex quantity)
$F$ = excitation force
$\hat{V}$ = velocity response (a complex quantity)
$R$ = equivalent viscous damping
$M$ = mass
$K$ = effective spring stiffness
$\omega$ = circular frequency, $= 2\pi f$, where $f$ = frequency
Subscripts "H, S and D" represent hook, swivel and drawworks

**Model for a Continuous System.** The wave equation for longitudinal (axial) displacements in an elastic bar was used to model the drill string tubulars (for example, each piece of collar, pipe, etc.).

The wave equation:     $\dfrac{\partial^2 \xi}{\partial t^2} = c^2 \dfrac{\partial^2 \xi}{\partial x^2}$

Damping was introduced into the equation by the use of complex material properties and wave number:

$$\hat{E} = E(1 + j\eta) \quad \text{and} \quad \hat{k} = k\left(1 - j\tfrac{\eta}{2}\right)$$

Therefore:

$$c = \sqrt{\tfrac{E}{\rho}} \qquad \text{and} \qquad \xi = (\hat{A}e^{-j\hat{k}x} + \hat{B}e^{+j\hat{k}x})e^{j\omega t}$$

Where:

$\xi$ = elastic displacement of the axial vibration
$\hat{A}$ and $\hat{B}$ = complex constants
$x$ = distance
$t$ = time
$\omega$ = circular frequency
$k$ = wave number, $(\hat{k})$ the accent represents a complex quantity
$\eta$ = loss factor (in steel tubulars a value of $1*10^{-4}$ in normally used)
$c$ = speed of sound
$\rho$ = mass density
$E$ = Young's modulus, $(\hat{E})$ the accent represents a complex quantity

The solution for each tubular is expressed in terms of impedance:

$$\hat{Z}_1 = \frac{k S \hat{E}}{\omega} \frac{\left[e^{j\hat{k}l_1} - \hat{\Gamma}e^{-j\hat{k}l_1}\right]}{\left[e^{j\hat{k}l_1} + \hat{\Gamma}e^{-j\hat{k}l_1}\right]}, \qquad \hat{\Gamma} = \frac{E S \hat{k} - \omega \hat{Z}_0}{E S \hat{k} + \omega \hat{Z}_0}$$

Where:

$\hat{Z}_1$ = input impedance                     $\hat{\Gamma}$ = reflection coefficient
$\hat{Z}_0$ = load impedance                      $l_1$ = length of element
$S$ = cross sectional area of the element

**Calculated Resonant Frequencies.** Figures 10 and 11 show the calculated results and Tables 4 and 5 list the natural frequencies at which resonance occurs for the field study (full-size) and scaled model drill string respectively. The Tables also include measured data for comparison.

### Description of "Kelly Bounce" Model

It was assumed that the cutting action from the drill bit generates displacement waves that travel through the rock. There was no mechanism for maintaining plane wave motion in the rock. Consequently, it was thought that the waves will radiate from the source (drill bit) in all directions. The exact wave motion was unknown. However, any waves that diverged must have caused a dilation in the amplitude of the outgoing wave front. To model this phenomenon, it was assumed that it was analogous to the study of plane acoustic sound pressure waves in a duct with damping. The damping attenuated the amplitude of the wave as it travelled along the duct. Therefore the mathematical model for the rock was based on the wave theory described above for tubulars.

Impedance at the drill bit was calculated and summed with the results from the drill string to give the response of the complete system. Figure 12 showed the natural frequencies at which resonance occurred. These frequencies are listed in Table 6.

### THE APPLICATION OF THE MATHEMATICAL MODEL TO PREDICT AXIAL RESONANCE.

A comparison was made between the measured and calculated natural frequencies for the field study drillstring with 2 different boundary conditions at the drill bit. The first boundary condition was the drill bit was free to vibrate axially and the second was the drill bit was in contact with the rock.

### The Drill String Free at Bit

The field study drillstring was assumed to be free at the drill bit as it was several meters above the bottom of the hole when vibration data was captured. Figures 3 and 10 showed the measured and calculated vibration frequencies (respectively) from this drillstring. These frequencies were also listed in Table 4. The comparison of frequencies showed that 4 of the first 5 calculated natural frequencies were within +3.8 and -8.6 % of the measured data. The only exception was the third natural frequency which had an error of -14.4%.

A scaled model of the field study drillstring was tested. Figures 9 and 11 showed the measured and calculated natural frequencies respectively. Table 5 lists the frequencies. Three of the first 4 natural frequencies were calculated to within 6.1% of the measured results. The only exception was the third natural frequency which had an error of +23.8%. The results from this test were scaled to full-size and they agreed with the measured data from the field study drillstring (Tables 4 and 5). This confirmed that the field study drillstring was free at the bit.

**The Drill String in Contact with the Rock**

The additional effects of the rock changed the natural frequencies from the free at bit solution (described above). Figures 4, 5 and 6 showed the measured vibration that occurred during kelly bounce. Note that as the speed decreased from 118 to 96 rpm (1.6 Hz) the drill string resonated and caused large amplitude vibrations at the surface. The most prominent frequency was at 4.67 Hz. This was very close to 3 times the rotational drilling speed (4.80 Hz). Figure 12 showed the calculated natural frequency was at 4.31 Hz - an error of 7.7%.

**CONCLUSIONS**

•   The correct definition of boundary conditions is crucial for the accurate prediction of natural frequencies at which resonance occurs.

•   The mathematical models accurately predicted the axial natural frequencies of a drill string.

•   Drilling chalk with a tricone drill bit produced excitation frequencies at the rotary drilling speed (*1) and multiples of it (*2, *3, etc.). The rotational frequency at 4.80 Hz (*3) was close enough to a natural frequency at 4.67 Hz to cause resonance.

**REFERENCES**

1.   Thomson WT, "Theory of Vibration with Applications", George Allen and Unwin Ltd, ISBN 0-04-620008-8, 1981.
2.   Reynolds DD, "Engineering Principles of Acoustics, Noise and Vibration Control", Allyn and Bacon Inc., ISBN 0-205-07283-6, 1985.
3.   Besaisow AA and Payne ML, "A Study of Excitation Mechanisms and Resonance Inducing BHA Vibrations", SPE 15560, October 1986.
4.   Eronini IE, Somerton WH and Auslander DM, "A Dynamic Model for Rotary Rock Drilling", Journal of Energy Resources Technology, May 1991.
5.   Daring DW, "Drill Collar Length is a Major Factor in Vibration Control", Journal of Petroleum Technology, April 1984.
6.   "API Recommended Practice 7G" (RP 7G), 14th Edition, August 1990.
7.   "API Recommended Practice 7G" (RP 7G), 13th Edition, May 1987.
8.   Massey BS, "Units, Dimensional Analysis and Physical Similarity", Van Nostrand Reinhold, ISBN 0-442-05178-6, 1971.
9.   Kinsler LE and Frey AR, "Fundamentals of Acoustics", John Wiley and Sons Inc, 1950.
10.  Beranek LL, "Acoustics", Electrical and Electronic Engineering Series, McGraw-Hill, 1954.

| DEPTH | | DEVIATION |
|---|---|---|
| Metres | Feet | Degrees |
| 0 - 30.5 | 0 - 100 | 1 |
| 30.5 - 1371.6 | 100 - 4500 | 3 |
| 1371.6 - 1706.9 | 4500 - 5600 | 1 |
| 1706.9 - TD | 5600 - TD | 0.5 |

TABLE 1: HOLE DEVIATION SPECIFICATION

| RUNNING ORDER | ACCUMULATED LENGTH (M) | ACCUMULATED LENGTH (FT) |
|---|---|---|
| 26" Tricone Bit | 0.58 | 1.9 |
| NB Stabilizer | 2.89 | 9.48 |
| NMDC | 5.57 | 18.28 |
| 26" Stabilizer | 7.37 | 24.18 |
| 9.5" NMDC | 16.16 | 53.02 |
| 26" Stabilizer | 18.4 | 60.38 |
| 4*9" DC | 55.33 | 181.53 |
| XO | 56.1 | 184.06 |
| 3*8" DC | 85.52 | 280.57 |
| Jars | 97.95 | 321.37 |
| 8" DC | 104.57 | 343.07 |
| XO | 105.08 | 344.77 |
| 10* 6 3/8" HWDP | 194.72 | 638.85 |

TABLE 2: DESCRIPTION OF BHA

| TRUE VERTICAL DEPTH (TVD) | | GEOLOGICAL | |
|---|---|---|---|
| m | ft | AGE | LITHOLOGY |
| 0 - 30.5 | 0 - 100 | QUAT | BOULDER CLAY |
| 30.5 - 552.6 | 100 - 1813 | CRETACIOUS | CHALK |
| 552.6 - 583.1 | 1813 - 1913 | JURASSIC | CLAYSTONE |
| 583.1 - 1500.5 | 1913 - 4923 | TRIASSIC | SHALE/SANDSTONE /CLAYSTONE |
| 1500.5 - 1914.7 | 4923 - 6282 | PERMIAN | SALTS/POTASSIUM |

TABLE 3: DESCRIPTION OF THE WELL GEOLOGY

| MEASURED | CALCULATED | ERROR |
|---|---|---|
| Hz | Hz | % |
| 2.07 | 2.01 | 2.9 |
| 9.4 | 9.04 | 3.8 |
| 16.94 | 19.38 | -14.4 |
| 27.9 | 30.32 | -8.6 |
| 40.9 | 40 | 2.2 |

TABLE 4: MEASURED AXIAL NATURAL FREQUENCIES AT WHICH
RESONANCE OCCURS IN A FULL-SIZE DRILL STRING (FREE AT DRILL BIT)

| MEASURED ON SCALED MODEL | | CALCULATED USING MATH. MODEL | | |
|---|---|---|---|---|
| ACTUAL MEASUREMENT | SCALED TO FULL-SIZE | ACTUAL SCALE MODEL | SCALED TO FULL-SIZE | ERROR |
| Hz | Hz | Hz | Hz | % |
| 53 | 1.96 | 49.8 | 1.84 | 6.1 |
| 267.5 | 9.87 | 259.2 | 9.56 | 3.1 |
| 537.5 | 19.81 | 408.7 | 15.08 | 23.8 |
| 682.5 | 25.2 | 657.8 | 24.27 | 3.7 |

• The frequency scaling factor is 27.1:1

TABLE 5: MEASURED AXIAL NATURAL FREQUENCIES AT WHICH
RESONANCE OCCURS IN A SCALED MODEL DRILL STRING
(FREE AT DRILL BIT)

| MEASURED | CALULATED | ERROR |
|---|---|---|
| Hz | Hz | % |
| 1.60 (*1) | 1.71 | -6.2 |
| 3.20 (*2) | | |
| 4.67 (CLOSE TO *3) | 4.31 | 7.7 |
| 6.92 | 8.82 | -27.4 |
| 9.42 | 10.71 | -13.7 |
| 14.49 | 13.2 | 8.9 |
| Cluster centred about 19.42 | Cluster centred about 19.41 | 0 |
| Cluster centred about 30.37 | Cluster centred about 29.50 | 0.1 |
| Cluster centred about 38.42 | Cluster centred about 38.42 | -8.9 |

TABLE 6: DRILLING WITH "KELLY BOUNCE"

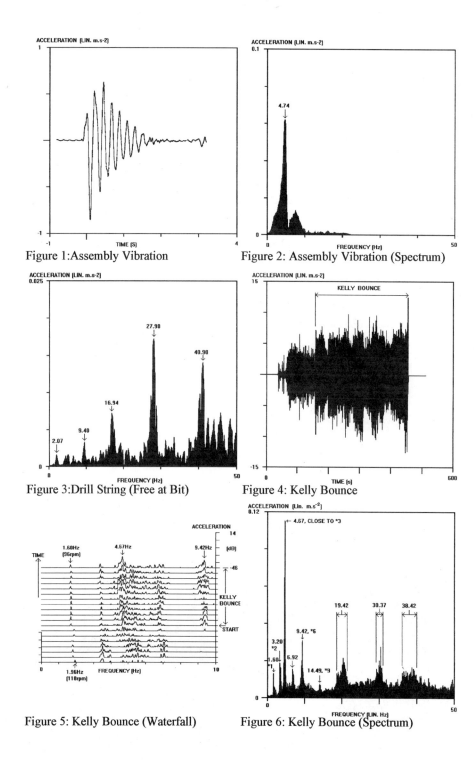

Figure 1:Assembly Vibration

Figure 2: Assembly Vibration (Spectrum)

Figure 3:Drill String (Free at Bit)

Figure 4: Kelly Bounce

Figure 5: Kelly Bounce (Waterfall)

Figure 6: Kelly Bounce (Spectrum)

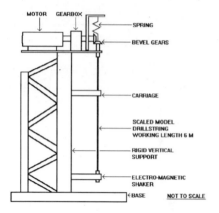

Figure 7:Test Rig For Scaled Drill Strings    Figure:8:Scaled Model Drill String

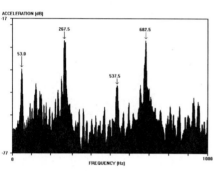

Figure 9:Natural Frequencies Of Scaled
Model Drill String

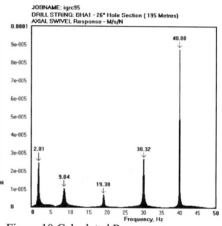

Figure 10:Calculated Resonance

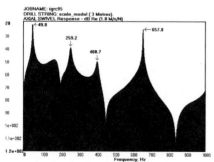

Figure 11:Calculated Resonance, Scaled
Model Drill String (Free at Bit)

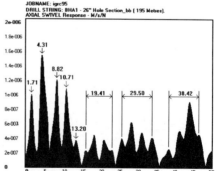

Figure 12:Calculated Resonance, Full-Size
Drill String In Contact With Rock.

## APPENDIX

## DEFINITION OF RESONANCE

Resonance occurs when the frequency of a periodic excitation mechanism is coincident with a natural frequency causing an amplification of the amplitude of vibration - References 1 and 2. The natural frequency is an inherent property of the drill string (geometry, material properties, etc.) and the excitation mechanism is the result of rotation (for example the cutting action of the drill bit, contact between the drill string and the hole, residual imbalance in collars and pipe, etc.) - References 3 to 5.

## FIELD MEASUREMENT EQUIPMENT

The measurement equipment included: transducer, cabling, signal conditioning, tape recorder and a vibration analyser. The transducer was a Bruel and Kjaer (B&K) 4370 accelerometer with an in-house built pre-amplifier. The accelerometer was attached to a stainless steel mounting block (manufactured in-house) by means of a mechanical filter (B&K UA 0553) to protect the accelerometer from excessively high shock vibration. This mounting block was used to fasten the accelerometer on the swivel to measure motion in the vertical, or along the axis, direction of the drill string. The cable from the accelerometer was run along the kelly line, derrick and catenary wires to a safe area. PVC tape was used to secure the cable and prevent it from coming loose. This cable fed the vibration measurement signal into an amplifier (built in-house to match the low energy pre-amplifier on the accelerometer). The output vibration signal from the amplifier was filtered (Barr and Stroud EF4-03 HP/LP) to remove the unwanted high frequency data which may be generated by shock vibration. The conditioned vibration measurement signal was simultaneously recorded on a TEAC XR-510 FM tape recorder and captured on an Ono Sokki CF-910 FFT vibration analyser.

## SCALE MODEL TESTING EQUIPMENT

To simulate the field study results as closely as possible, a miniature accelerometer (DJB A/23/E) was attached to the mass representing the combined hook and swivel acting as a single body. It measured vibration in the vertical (or along the axis of the model). A B&K 2635 charge amplifiers was used to condition the vibration signal from the accelerometer and the Ono Sokki CF 910 vibration analyser was used to capture the vibration data and present the results. A calibrated hammer, PCB K291A, was used to tap the model at the bottom and create a transient vibration in the drill string (Classical vibration theory states that after a structure has been excited to vibrate and left it will oscillate freely at its natural frequencies - References 1 and 2).

## "A NEW QUANTITATIVE TECHNIQUE TO EVALUATE GAS SHOWS DURING MUD LOGGING"

## "NOUVELLE TECHNIQUE POUR L'EVALUATION DES INDICES GAZEUX DETECTEES EN MUD LOGGING"

Patrick L. DeLaune
Texaco Exploration & Production Technology Department

Alan C. Wright
GRI Consultant

Scott Hanson
Texaco Exploration & Production Technology Department

## ABSTRACT

The use of surface gas measurements to identify oil and gas bearing zones has been in use since the 1920s. Early well-site sampling methods were inaccurate and inconsistent, but had little effect on results since measurement and analysis techniques were equally poor. The introduction of gas chromatography in the 1950s created a demand for gas samples more representative of gas in the formation. New techniques were developed, but even these methods of continuous gas extraction at the well-site were recognized to be inconsistent, a fact noted in several publications at the time. However, the basic gas extraction system developed then is still in field use today.

In the late 1980s, Texaco began research to improve the value of mud logging. An early result of this effort was a quantitative fluorescence technique to accurately determine the amount of oil in the drill cuttings. A second more recent result from a joint Texaco/Gas Research Institute (GRI) project is the development of a continuous gas extraction device that enables accurate, consistent gas-in-mud measurements while drilling. This measurement method uses a highly sensitive controlled sample gas trap that provides stable gas extraction over a wide range of operating conditions. Calibration of the trap to actual gas-in-mud values results in accurate gas-in-mud measurements that can be used for meaningful analysis and well-to-well correlations. This new technique not only provides a more accurate measurement of formation gas, but is an actual measurement of formation gas unlike indirect measurements such as wire-line logs or measurement while drilling.

## RÉSUMÉ

Les mesures d'indices gazeux en surface sont utilisées depuis les années 1920 pour identifier les gisements de pétrole et de gaz. Les premières méthodes d'échantillonnage des sites de forage étaient peu précises et peu fiables, mais cela n'avait que peu d'effet sur les résultats, étant donné que les techniques et mesure et d'analyse étaient tout aussi mauvaises. L'introduction de la chromatographie en phase gazeuse au cours des années 1950 créa une demande pour des échantillons gazeux plus représentatifs du gaz dans la formation. De nouvelles techniques furent mises au point, mais même ces méthodes d'extraction continue de gaz au niveau du site de forage furent reconnues comme étant peu fiables, comme cela fut noté dans plusieurs publications à cette époque. Cependant, le système d'extraction de gaz de base fut développé à ce moment-là et il est toujours en usage sur le terrain aujourd'hui.

A la fin des années 1980, Texaco entama des recherches pour améliorer la valeur du mud logging. Un des premiers résultats de ces efforts fut une technique quantitative par fluorescence pour déterminer avec précision la quantité de pétrole dans les carottes de forage. Un deuxième résultat plus récent, provenant d'un projet commun entre Texaco et l'Institut de Recherche sur le Gaz, est le développement d'un dispositif d'extraction continue de gaz qui permet des mesures précises et fiables des idices gazeux pendant le forage. Cette méthode de mesure utilise un piège à gaz d'échantillonnage contrôlé et extrêmement sensible, qui fournit une extraction stable du gaz sur une très large gamme de conditions opérationnelles. L'étalonnage du piège par rapport aux véritables valeurs de l'indice gazeux résulte en des mesures exactes de l'indice gazeux, et celles-ci peuvent être utilisées pour une analyse significative et des corrélations de puits à puits. Cette nouvelle technique fournit non seulement une mesure plus précise du gaz de la formation, mais elle constitue une véritable mesure du gaz de la formation, à l'inverse des mesures indirectes telles que les wire-line logs ou les mesures effectuées pendant le forage.

## BACKGROUND

Mud logging is used during drilling operations as the initial evaluation tool to locate formations which contain gas and oil. Several different analytical techniques are used to obtain this information, and several drilling parameters are monitored to make this determination as accurate as possible. The current perception of mud logging, however, is that it is not adequately reliable or accurate for formation evaluation applications.

The major goal of the Texaco-GRI project was to improve the understanding and reliability of the information obtained from gas detection techniques used in mud logging, and where necessary, to develop new technology. Project efforts focused on improving the accuracy, consistency and interpretation of gas measurements made during mud logging operations at the well-site. Technical tasks were primarily directed toward improvements in gas trap performance, establishing practical means for relating trap gas to actual gas-in-mud, and evaluation of interpretive techniques.

Results reported earlier[1] showed that basic design faults in current traps caused unpredictable gas losses and excessive immersion level sensitivity, both of which contribute to unstable performance. Analytical and empirical methods were used to correct these problems and the new Quantitative Gas Measurement (QGM) trap design (figure 1) was patented [2] and verified in extensive field tests[3, 4]. In common with most traps, the QGM design uses ambient pressure agitation for gas release but incorporates evolutionary improvements for stable performance. To avoid uncontrolled gas loss, the QGM trap includes a mud exit port extended below the mud line, an agitator shaft feed through seal, and a vent line for addition of make-up air. The pyramidal agitator design and internal baffles combine to make the QGM trap insensitive to normal changes in trap immersion caused by variations in the return mud flow rate. A key design goal was to use modifications that would be retrofittable to existing equipment. The enclosed agitator trap design is in common use for a variety of good reasons, not the least of which are simplicity, low cost and low maintenance. Development of a gas trap which sacrificed these qualities would in all probability fail to result in actual improvements in gas logging service. A new technique for direct gas-in-mud measurement (figure 2) was also developed which uses microwave energy to separate gases present in the drilling mud. This new technique is faster, safer and considerably less expensive than other methods.

To accommodate all surface gas measurement requirements, QGM implementation is defined at two service levels. Level 1 service employs the QGM trap and sampling panel to obtain the advantages of more consistent gas extraction. Trap performance based on QGM field tests is used in combination with operational data to estimate in place gas quantities. Level 1 service would normally be used in established fields where requirements dictate a lower level of service and gas data usage is for drilling safety and correlation with known horizons.

Level 2 service adds the microwave gas-in-mud measurement for accurate gas composition determination. A high quality (FID or equivalent) gas chromatograph with peak integration and manual sample injection port is required. Level 2 service is appropriate for exploration wells where accurate gas data can contribute to key decisions. The direct gas-in-mud analysis combined with good chromatograph measurements provides significantly improved quantitative and qualitative formation evaluation capability along with trap performance monitoring. Trap response is tracked for each constituent gas so that actual mud gas compositions can be determined from trap gas measurements.

Field Results using QGM. The performance of the QGM trap and an unimproved trap of similar size and agitator speed are compared in figures 3 and 4 which plot methane read from the gas trap sample against the actual methane in the drilling mud. The data for both figures were obtained over a period of several weeks while drilling with water base muds. The lack of correlation seen in figure 3 for the unimproved trap precludes use of the trap gas for meaningful formation evaluation. In contrast, the tight cross plot of figure 4 demonstrates the long term extraction stability and predictable performance of the QGM trap.

The design modifications preventing gas loss from the QGM trap result in improved detection sensitivity over most traps in common use. Figure 5 shows gas logs from two closely space wells obtained by a commercial logging service using the same gas measurement instruments on both wells. The five to twenty times increase in sensitivity obtained with QGM resulted in significantly improved wire line correlations and delineation of potential pay zones. QGM enables sensitivity control by means of the gas sampling rate. In low gas zones, a low rate can be used to provide a gas measured to gas-in-mud ratio of up to 6:1. For high gas zones, the rate can be increased to avoid trap saturation and still permit accurate gas measurements. Another benefit of higher sample rates is faster response to changes in mud gas levels in high gas zones where fast response is needed most.

Figure 6 compares the QGM gas log from one well with the wire line log for a previously drilled adjacent well. The log provides excellent correlation and shows a constant ten foot formation depth difference between wells. Improved sensitivity and stability provided by QGM gives resolution and accuracy comparable to other formation evaluation tools, thereby enhancing the use and effectiveness of surface gas measurements in formation evaluation applications.

Figure 7 compares raw total gas readings for two closely spaced wells which used similar drilling programs. Peak gas values are similar, enabling unambiguous matching of corresponding sands in the two wells. Over the depths shown, well B displays somewhat thicker bedding with a possible sand pinch-out at the lower depth.

## FORMATION EVALUATION

Because QGM trap performance is tied to the actual gas content of the mud, gas readings can be used for detailed formation evaluation rather than as simple show indicators. Evaluation techniques based on surface gas measurements are divided into two classifications; quantitative and qualitative. In both cases, mud logging has the advantage of providing a near real-time interpretation using direct evidence of formation hydrocarbons. The underlying assumption for formation evaluation applications is that measured surface gas, corrected for trap recovery and recirculated gas, can be taken as representative of the gas in the formation. Equation derivation details are not presented here. The interested reader is directed to reference (4) for additional information.

Quantitative evaluation involves reduction of observed surface gas quantities and operational data to an apparent gas porosity. Means for making this calculation have been well documented, so work in this area contains little original material. The equations presented here, however, are cast in terms familiar to mud logging operations, and problems affecting interpretation are also discussed.

Qualitative evaluation attempts to characterize the total formation fluid from a knowledge of the light gas composition. The effectiveness of published[5] techniques for this application using surface gas measurements was examined using a data base of total reservoir fluid analyses. These techniques included the Pixler ratios, the Exlog ratios, and the triangular plot. The latter two use the uncorrected trap gas composition and thus are subject to considerable error due to recirculated gas and trap recovery variations. In general, it was found that, while all methods indicate generally correct GOR trends, predictive accuracies were far from optimum. In addition, all provide only a qualitative indication of fluid type (such as light gas, condensate, etc.) rather than an actual GOR value. A new method for GOR estimation and a means for detecting unusual gas compositions were developed as part of this project.

## Problems Independent of Trap Operation and Gas Analysis

The accuracy of formation evaluation is limited by several factors outside the direct control of the geologist or logging engineer. These are listed below in the approximate order of their importance.

Formation Flushing. Probably the most serious impediment to the calculation of meaningful gas porosities is the occurrence of flushing ahead of the bit caused by overbalance and bit hydraulics. This effect will be accentuated by slow ROP, low tooth profile bits, and good producibility. Flushing may be difficult to recognize and, in the absence of correlation wells having similar drilling programs, no good means exist for estimating corrections.

Surface Losses (Bell Nipple to Shaker). Limited testing with a water-base mud system indicates that surface losses can become substantial when gas levels exceed about 5% gas-in-mud. The lighter gases tend to be preferentially lost causing apparent compositional changes in the gas sample measured. Corrections may be possible but little reference data is available. An ongoing task of the Texaco-GRI project is to further investigate this issue in field tests comparing gas-in-mud from bell-nipple and shaker tank ("possum belly") samples.

Borehole Influx. Gas influx is caused by underbalanced drilling and hole swabbing, and is accentuated by good producibility. While influx may prevent useful porosity calculations, its occurrence will normally be easy to recognize. If the fluid has retrograde behavior and the formation pressure is below its dew point, lighter gases will be preferentially produced with the heavies remaining in the formation.

Borehole Washout. In poorly consolidated formations the actual volume of cuttings removed may exceed that calculated for the bit size. The effect may be immediate, causing gas shows to be larger than expected, or gradual, in which case the gas background may increase by an undetermined amount due to formation flushing.

Mud Sampling. When acquiring samples for direct gas-in-mud determination, difficulties in obtaining representative samples may occur at higher gas levels due to the presence of gas bubbles in the return mud. The magnitude of this problem and its effect on measured gas compositions may be alleviated by processing duplicate mud samples.

Differential Gas Release. As the cuttings rise to the surface, lighter gases will tend to be expelled first, possibly leading to a component separation effect by the time the gases reach the surface. Differential release will be accentuated when the cuttings are large or oil is present in the pore space.

**Quantitative Formation Evaluation**

The basic model for quantitative evaluation involves the assumption that the gas observed at the surface over a given depth interval may be directly related to the volume of formation drilled. Two steps are involved. First, operational and gas data are reduced to a normalized gas quantity equal to the volume of gas at surface conditions divided by the cuttings volume. The normalized gas is then converted an apparent in-situ gas porosity by dividing by the formation-to-surface expansion factor. This step requires a knowledge of the gas composition so that the appropriate equation of state can be used. Because of various factors previously discussed which can affect the result, the term "apparent porosity" is used.

Normalized Gas. The first step in apparent gas porosity calculation is the conversion of surface gas readings to the volume of gas at surface conditions per volume of cuttings drilled. This ratio is termed "normalized gas" and may be calculated over any desired depth interval. Ideally the interval should match the depth range of the gas show but in practice cut-off points may not be well defined. The interval should be long enough that the effect of gas spreading during the course of circulation from the hole bottom does not have a major effect. This spread can often be estimated quite accurately from the breadth of connection gas or "kelly cut" peaks.

$$\text{Normalized Gas} \;=\; 0.2451 \bullet (\%GAS \bullet V_{mud}) \div ((DIA)^2 \bullet (DIST)) \qquad (1)$$

$$
\begin{aligned}
\text{where } DIA \;&=\; \text{bit diameter in inches,}\\
DIST \;&=\; \text{distance drilled in feet.}\\
\%GAS \;&=\; \text{interval average gas-in-mud (gas/mud basis),}\\
\text{and } V_{mud} \;&=\; \text{total volume of mud pumped in gallons.}
\end{aligned}
$$

When it is clear that a gas peak can be associated with a well defined drilling break over distance DIST, the effects of gas spreading can be accommodated by extending the volume pumped and average gas used in the above equation over the entire peak, since the total volume of gas which came from the interval is what is needed.

When the interval average drill rate and mud flow rate are known, this equation may be recast in the form:

$$\text{Normalized Gas} \;=\; 14.71 \bullet (\%GAS) \bullet (FLOW) \div (\,(DIA)^2 \bullet ROP) \qquad (2)$$

$$
\begin{aligned}
\text{where } FLOW \;&=\; \text{interval average flow in gallons per minute (gpm),}\\
\text{and } ROP \;&=\; \text{interval average drill rate in feet per hour (fph).}
\end{aligned}
$$

For practical reasons, measured gas-in-mud is usually expressed as volume gas per volume gas+mud, whereas the %GAS value needed here is volume gas per volume of gas-free mud. Assuming that the mud cut is due solely to measured gas, the measured gas-in-mud may be corrected by use of the equation:

$$\%GAS \;=\; (\%\text{gas-in-mud}) \div (1 - (\%\text{gas-in-mud} \div 100)) \qquad (3)$$

This correction will be minor except in very high gas situations.

Since the normalized gas by definition measures productivity in terms of surface gas volume, a calculation of total gas per acre from the show interval assuming horizontally uniform formation is straightforward:

$$\text{MMCF/acre} \;=\; 0.4356 \bullet (\text{Normalized Gas}) \bullet (DIST) \qquad (4)$$

Apparent Gas Porosity. Normalized gas is converted to apparent in-situ gas porosity by dividing by the volume expansion experienced by the gas as it is circulated from formation temperature and pressure to surface conditions. Probably the most practical approach is to employ the compressibility factor equation of state often used in reservoir engineering:

$$P\,V \;=\; Z\,R\,T \tag{5}$$

where P　=　absolute gas pressure (psia),

　　　　T　=　absolute gas temperature (deg R = deg F + 460),

　　　　V　=　volume of one mole of gas,

　　　　R　=　gas constant (units dependent),

and　　Z　=　unitless compressibility factor which corrects
　　　　　　　for deviations from ideal gas behavior.

The Z-factor is a complicated function of the total gas composition, temperature and pressure, but the Standing/Katz chart for natural gases (presented in most reservoir engineering books) may be used to estimate Z to adequate accuracy. Use of the Standing/Katz chart requires straightforward but somewhat lengthy calculations of reduced temperature and pressure at reservoir conditions. The apparent gas porosity is calculated by dividing the expansion into the normalized gas:

$$\text{Apparent \% Gas Porosity} = 100 \cdot (\text{Normalized Gas}) \div (\text{Expansion}) \tag{6}$$

## Example from Commercial QGM Service:

### Input Values

| | | Gas Composition (ppm-in-mud) | | | |
|---|---|---|---|---|---|
| Depth Interval: | 25 feet | C1 | C2 | C3 | C4 |
| On-Bottom Time: | 51 min | 54255 | 3078 | 1198 | 550 |
| Hole Diameter: | 7.875 inch | | | | |
| Avg Pump Rate: | 370 gpm | Formation Press: | 5714 psia | | |
| Avg Gas-in-Mud: | 5.91 % | Formation Temp: | 187 deg F | | |

### Calculated Values

$$GAS\% \;=\; 5.91 \div (1 - (5.91 \div 100)) = 6.28 \text{ \% (gas/mud)}$$

$$V_{mud} \;=\; 51 \cdot 370 = 18870 \text{ gal}$$

$$\text{Normalized Gas} \;=\; (0.2451 \cdot 6.28 \cdot 18870) \div (7.875^2 \cdot 25) = 18.7$$

$$\text{Gas/Well (160 acres)} \;=\; (0.04356 \cdot 18.7 \cdot 25 \cdot 160) = 3258 \text{ MMCF}$$

$$\text{Z-factor} \;=\; 1.057 \text{ (from Standing/Katz Nat. Gas Chart)}$$

Expansion assuming 70 deg F, 14.7 psia at surface:

$$((70+460) \cdot 5714) \div [1.057 \cdot (187 + 460) \cdot 14.7] = 301$$

$$\text{Apparent \% Gas Porosity} \;=\; (100 \cdot 18.7) \div 301 = 6.2 \text{ \%}$$

The formation drilled for this example was a tight gas sand having a wire-line porosity of about 10%. When water saturation is allowed for, the calculated gas porosity is quite reasonable.

## Qualitative Formation Evaluation

Qualitative formation evaluation addresses the issue of total fluid typing based on knowledge of the light gas composition measured during mud logging. The equations presented in this section were developed by means of regression techniques applied to a data base of 91 reservoir fluid studies. GOR's ranged from 10 to 200,000 SCF/bbl and oil gravity from 16 to 60 deg API. To avoid production method dependencies, parameters derived strictly from the compositional analyses were used for correlation purposes:

$$\text{Weight Gas (Rel)} = 16 \cdot C1 + 30 \cdot C2 + 44 \cdot C3 + 58 \cdot C4 \tag{7}$$

$$\text{Weight Oil (Rel)} = (\text{moles C5+}) \cdot (\text{mole wt C5+}) \tag{8}$$

$$\text{Compositional GOR} = 100{,}000 \cdot (C1+C2+C3+C4) \div (\text{Weight Oil}) \tag{9}$$

The gas and oil weights are relative to the basis used for the molar composition but the gas/oil weight ratio closely reflects the relative BTU content of two phases. The compositional GOR ignores variations in oil gravity. The factor of 100,000 includes engineering constants and an average oil density term. A plot of actual GOR (corrected for non-hydrocarbon gases) versus compositional GOR is shown in Figure 8. While agreement is good over most of the plot range, some deviation is apparent at the lowest GOR's where lighter components tend to stay in the oil and at the highest GOR's where heavier components tend to be produced as gas. As discussed next, GOR's estimated from mud logging gas compositions are sufficiently imprecise that the use of Figure 8 to correct the estimates is probably superfluous.

Two equations for Weight Oil prediction were developed:

Wt Oil estimated from C2-C4 composition
$$= 1932 \cdot C4^2 \div \sqrt{(C2 \cdot C3)} \qquad (90\% \text{ CF}=4.6) \tag{10}$$

Wt Oil estimated from C2-C5 composition
$$= 3070 \cdot C3 \cdot C5^2 \div [C4 \cdot \sqrt{(C2 \cdot C4)}] \qquad (90\% \text{ CF}=3.0) \tag{11}$$

The compositional basis used for mud logging data is %gas-in-mud. Once the oil weight has been estimated by Equation 10 or 11, the value may be used in Equation 9 to obtain an estimated GOR.

The "90% CF" values are factors to be applied to the calculated results to obtain a 90% confidence range. For example, if a GOR of 5000 is estimated by means of Equation 11 then with 90% certainty the actual value lies in the range 5000/3.0 to 5000x3.0 (or 1667 to 15000). While these accuracies are disappointing from a reservoir engineering standpoint, application of neural network and cluster analysis methods to the data base yielded no improvement. It seems likely that reservoir genesis factors, such as source material, burial history, and the like, also have important influences on GOR which are not directly reflected in gas composition. In contrast to published methods[4], the developed equations provide a realistic basis for GOR estimation since both a value and reliability factor are obtained.

## Field Example of GOR Estimation

| Gas-in-Mud Composition: | C1 | C2 | C3 | C4 | C5 |
|---|---|---|---|---|---|
| | .8633 | 0.0570 | 0.0313 | 0.0194 | 0.0093 % |

Wt Gas = 18.0     (%gas-in-mud basis)

Predicted versus Actual GOR:

| Prediction Composition | Predicted Wt Oil | Predicted SCF/bbl |
|---|---|---|
| C2 to C4 | 17.2 | 5641 |
| C2 to C5 | 12.9 | 7537 |
| Prod. Test | ------ | 9885 |

The main conclusions drawn from this study can be summarizes as follows:

- Accurate knowledge of the relative amounts of methane through pentane allows a prediction of GOR to within a factor of 3.0. When analysis includes methane through butane only, the factor increases to 4.6.

- GOR estimation accuracy suffers by not including pentane but, in actual field practice, the loss is probably minor due to the problems encountered in accurate measurement of the low levels of pentane often present, particularly when background corrections must be applied.

- Published fluid typing methods are far from optimum in predictive accuracy. Use of uncorrected gas trap values instead of background corrected gas-in-mud values can lead to widely divergent GOR estimates.

- Inclusion of additional fluid analyses in study would not significantly improve predictive reliability. Predictions based strictly on the light gas composition have an intrinsic uncertainty due to reservoir genesis factors not considered and usually not known in detail.

- GOR estimation accuracy is not significantly improved by including hexane in the predictive equations.

- Inclusion of iso/normal information for the butanes and pentanes in the predictive equations did not improve accuracy. Iso-fraction monitoring is of value, however, in detection of horizons and classification of fluids.

- Oil gravity is only loosely correlated with gas composition. No useful predictive equations were found.

## Conclusions

QGM has resulted in significant improvements in surface gas measurement and interpretation applicable at all service levels. These results are well documented, and numerous workshops and training programs have been conducted in efforts to transfer this new technology to the industry. QGM is being licensed under terms which encourage use of the new gas trap and related methodology. There are currently over thirty companies licensed to provide QGM service. Increasing Producer usage and direct user feedback indicate that QGM has been accepted as a significant improvement in surface gas measurements, and usage is growing. It is the authors' hope that these developments support application of surface gas measurements as a valid formation evaluation and drilling support tool, and that increased application results in improved methods both for the basic measurements and for better and more consistent interpretation.

## Acknowledgments

Thanks to Texaco and the Gas Research Institute for their support of this project. Special thanks to Howard McKinzie, Texaco EPTD, and Harvey Haines, GRI for their encouragement and support during the development phase of this project, and to Ed Smalley, GRI, for his belief in the product and his substantial support in helping transfer the new technology to the industry. Special thanks also to the EPTD Art Graphics team for their excellent support in preparing this paper for publication.

**References**

(1)    Wright, Hanson and DeLaune; "A New Quantitative Technique for Surface Gas Measurements; SPWLA Annual Conference, June, 1993.

(2)    Gas Trap, U.S. Patent #5,199,509, April 6, 1993.

(3)    Gas Research Institute Contract 5090-212-1945; "A New Quantitative Technique to Evaluate Gas Shows During Mud Logging;" 1991 & 1992 Annual Reports.

(4)    Gas Research Institute Contract 5090-212-1945; "A New Quantitative Technique to Evaluate Gas Shows During Mud Logging;" 1993 Annual Report.

(5)    Whittaker, Alun; "Mud Logging Handbook;" Prentice Hall, Inc., 1991.

Figure 1 - QGM Trap Design

Figure 2 - Microwave Oven for Mud Gas Analysis

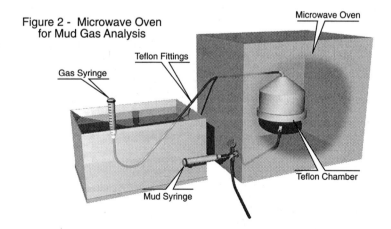

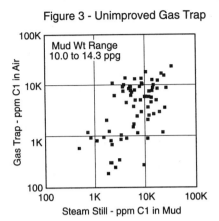

Figure 3 - Unimproved Gas Trap

Mud Wt Range
10.0 to 14.3 ppg

Figure 4 - QGM Gas Trap

Mud Wt Range
9.6 to 16.0 ppg

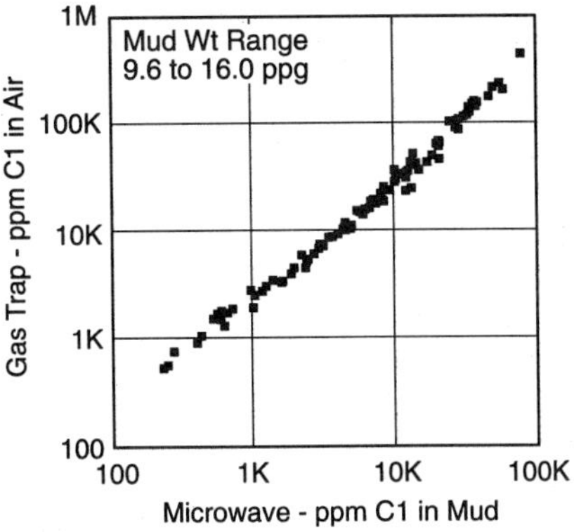

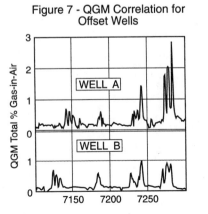

Figure 5 - Comparison of Conventional
and QGM Traps

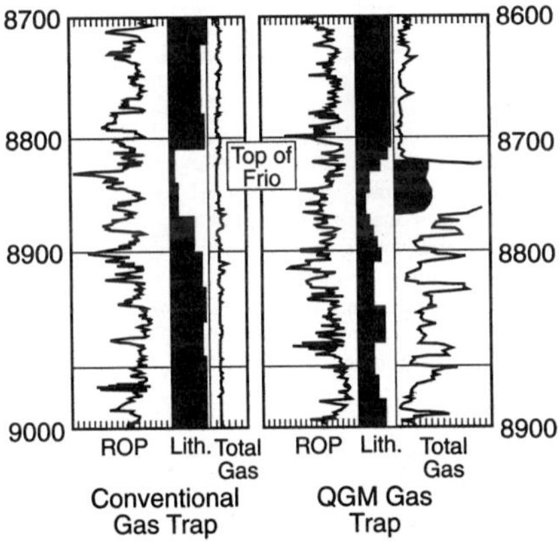

Top of
Frio

ROP  Lith. Total
Gas
Conventional
Gas Trap

ROP  Lith.  Total
Gas
QGM Gas
Trap

Figure 6 - QGM Correlation with
Offset Wireline

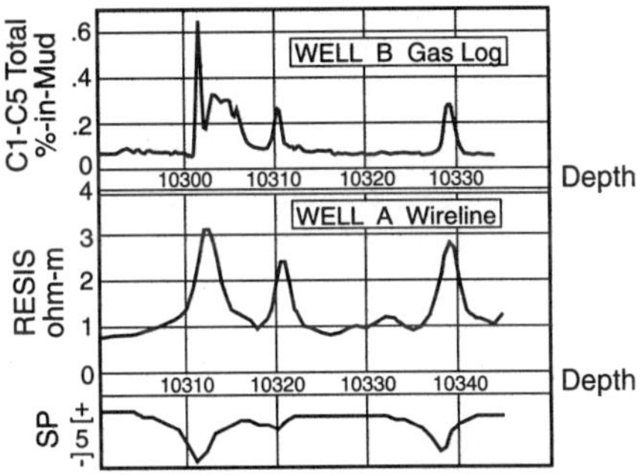

WELL B Gas Log

WELL A Wireline

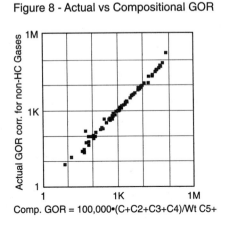

Figure 7 - QGM Correlation for
Offset Wells

WELL A

WELL B

Figure 8 - Actual vs Compositional GOR

Comp. GOR = 100,000•(C+C2+C3+C4)/Wt C5+

NEW INSIGHTS ON HYDRAULIC FRACTURING
FROM THE FRACTURING FLUID CHARACTERIZATION FACILITY

NOUVELLES PERSPECIVES SUR LA FRACTURATION
AU BANC D'ESSAI DE CHARACTERISATION DES FLUIDES

L. R. Brand
Gas Research Institute, USA

S. N. Shah
University of Oklahoma, USA

D. L. Lord
Halliburton Energy Services, USA

ABSTRACT

Accurate design and control of hydraulic fracturing treatments in natural gas wells can only be accomplished if the industry is able to characterize the role of the fracturing fluid in creating the fracture and placing the proppant. At present, assumptions are made on the in-situ performance of fluids based on rheology measurements from laboratory benchtop equipment because fluid performance cannot be measured in the field. The Fracturing Fluid Characterization Facility High Pressure Simulator (HPS), is a new large-scale fracture simulator that enables researchers to measure fluid properties under conditions representative of the downhole environment. Research results discussed in this paper include: significant differences in rheometric data between conventional rheometers and the HPS, differences between expected and measured pressure loss through perforations, dynamic fluid loss measurements, effect of rock texture on filtercake formation, and the importance of measurement technique on crosslinked gel rheology.

RÉSUMÉ

On ne pourra arriver a un controle precis des traitements de fracturation hydraulique dans les puits de gaz naturel que si l'industrie petroliere parvient a caracteriser le role du fluide de fracturation en creant la fracture et en placant le propant. Actuellement des hypothese sont faites quant a la performance in-situ des fluides a partir de measures de rheologie effectuees avec des equipements de laboratoire parce que la performance des fluides ne peut pas etre mesuree sur le terrain. Le Simulateur Haut Pression d'Essaie de Caracterisation du Fluide de Fracturation (HPS) est un nouveau simulateur de fracturation de grande capacite qui permet de mesurer les proprietes du fluide dans des conditions representatives de l'environnement de fond. Les resultats publies dans cette etude comprennent: les differences significatives dans les donnees de rheometrie entre les rheometres conventionnels et le HPS, les differences entre la perte de pression prevue et celle measuree a travers les perforations, les measures de perte de fluide dynamique, l'effet de rugoiste sur la formation du cake de filtration et l'importance de la technique de prise de measures sur la rheologie du gel de liaison.

## INTRODUCTION

Accurate design and control of hydraulic fracturing treatments in natural gas wells can only be accomplished if the industry is able to characterize the role of the fracturing fluid in creating the fracture and placing the proppant. The industry must currently make assumptions on the in-situ performance of fluids based on rheology measurements made with laboratory benchtop equipment because fluid performance cannot be measured in the field. The Gas Research Institute (GRI) conceived of an above-ground fracture simulator that would enable researchers to measure fluid properties in conditions representative of the downhole environment. The Fracturing Fluid Characterization Facility (FFCF) High Pressure Simulator (HPS), which was developed by the University of Oklahoma with support from GRI and the U. S. Department of Energy, is a new state-of-the-art tool now available to industry.

The HPS is a large parallel-plate flow cell, see Figure 1, designed to measure fluid properties under high temperature and pressure conditions. A servo-hydraulic system controls an array of platens that make up both fracture surfaces. The platens are faced with simulated or natural rock to allow the fluid to penetrate the walls of the cell, as it does in the formation, see Figure 2. An optical fiber "vision system" allows the user to see through the simulated rock and steel supports. Laser Doppler anemometers measure fluid velocity profiles, and pressure sensors measure pressure loss within the cell. Several small computers complete the instrumentation package to both provide automatic control of the simulator and collect and analyze the data.

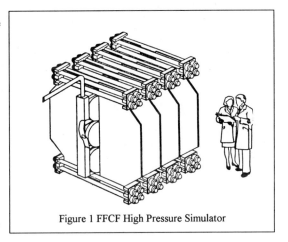

Figure 1 FFCF High Pressure Simulator

There are many other components in the FFCF that enhance the capabilities of the HPS: the shear history simulator, pumps, mixing tanks, a slurry throttling valve, and several types of laboratory viscometric instruments. All of these components, described in further detail in the next section, are designed to study fluid performance and changes in fluid properties. Research at the FFCF centers on five key research needs identified by the gas industry:

1. Identification of fluid properties that predict proppant transport
2. Determining changes in fluid properties along the fracture, including the effects of fluid leakoff
3. Investigating slurry rheology, including characterization of fluid friction and behavior in the fracture and wellbore
4. Finding ways to reduce residual fracture conductivity damage
5. Determining the behavior of nonuniform slurry flow in complex channels, including characterization of nonhomogeneous flow, velocity profiles, and effects of fracture tortuosity and roughness

A research program developed to address these issues has produced results that support some industry assumptions and contradict others. Some assumptions were found to be in excess of 200% in error. Several major results are summarized in this paper.

CAPABILITIES OF THE SIMULATOR

The HPS is a vertical, variable-width parallel plate flow cell capable of operating at elevated temperatures and pressures. The plate surfaces, or facings, can be adjusted for smoothness and permeability. Fluid enters the HPS through manifolds that simulate a wellbore with perforations. The fiber optic vision system and the Laser Doppler Velocimetry (LDV) system of the flow cell facilitate the visualization and accurate measurement of flow behavior of fracturing fluids with or without proppant under certain combinations of simulated reservoir conditions such as formation permeability, temperature, and pressure. The instrumentation system of the HPS is capable of real-time monitoring of temperature, pressure (both system and differential pressure across various positions along the length of the flow cell), gap width at different locations, flow rate and density. The leakoff through the permeable surfaces can also be measured to characterize dynamic fluid loss behavior of the fluids. In addition to the HPS, the FFCF also includes auxiliary equipment for fluid handling and pre-conditioning. This equipment includes mixing and storage tanks, metering pumps, and high pressure and low pressure pumps and 5000 feet of coiled tubing and a fluid heat exchanger.

The HPS has a variable width slot 2.1 m (85 in) high and 2.7 m (119 in) long, formed by two faces, one fixed and the other movable by servo control. The operational limits of the HPS are 8.27 MPa (1200 psi) internal pressure and 120 C (250° F) temperature. Slot width can be adjusted dynamically over the range of 0 to 3.2 cm (0 to 1.25 in) by a system of 12 hydraulically actuated platens. The servo controllers on the individual platens allow the operator to maintain the parallel plate geometry in response to temperature gradients, pressure gradients, and any other factors that would distort the slot geometry. Each platen is 71 cm (28 in) square and the plates are laid out in a 3 high by 4 long matrix to form one face of the simulated fracture.

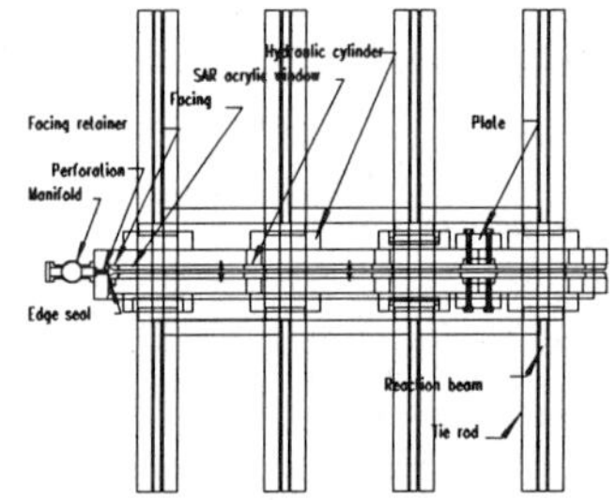

Figure 2 Horizontal Section Through the HPS

Each platen surface is covered with a replaceable simulated rock facing which is instrumented for data acquisition. The movable platen is lined with the desired 2.5 cm (1in) thick facing. The opposite fracture face is a solid fixed slab of steel that is 15 cm (6 in) thick and is covered with a matching 3 by 4 matrix of 2.5 cm (1 in) thick facings having the same permeability as those on the movable side. The facings simulate rock surfaces and can be made with the desired permeabilities. Therefore by changing the facings, different permeabilities and different surface properties such as texture and roughness can be investigated for their effects on the flow behavior and proppant transport. Behind each facing is a network of fluid collection channels which route fluid loss to a point outside the flow cell for measurement.

Inlet and exit manifolds are 7 cm (2.75 in) in diameter, each equipped with 22 perforations that are 13 mm (0.5 in) in diameter and on a 10 cm (4 in) spacing. Inlet manifold perforation configuration and size can be easily changed using a series of blank and sized inserts. The outlet piping exits to a common point located in the midpoint of the height of the HPS to insure uniform flow through the system.

Pre-conditioning and shear history simulation of the test fluid is accomplished by shearing the system through coiled tubing and a tube-in-tube heat exchanger. The coiled tubing system consists of three spools of 3.8 cm (1.5 in) outside diameter coiled tubing in lengths of 305 m, 610 m, and 610 m, (1000 ft, 2000 ft, and 2000 ft), respectively. Each spool can be used or bypassed, so the simulator can shear the fluids from 305 m (1000 ft) to 1524 m (5000 ft) in 1305 m (1000 ft) increments. For example, when the fluid is pumped through the entire length of tubing at 0.227

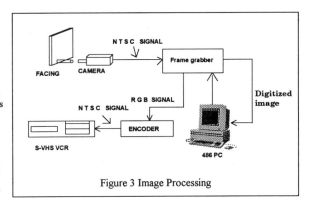

Figure 3 Image Processing

m³/min (60 gpm), it receives a shear rate of 1400 sec⁻¹ for 4.8 min. The heat exchanger consists of 152 m (500 ft) of 5 cm (2 in) tubing inside 7.6 cm (3 in) tubing. The fluid can be heated to the desired temperature, up to 107 C (225 °F) using this apparatus.

The HPS, auxiliary pumping equipment, preconditioning loop, and instrumentation systems can be configured to measure many characteristics of fracturing fluids. Fluid rheology can be measured using 5 differential pressure transducers that are reconfigurable with each experiment. Flow rates and gap width data are also provided for rheological measurements. An LDV system is available to determine the velocity profile of fluids and slurries with concentrations up to 958.4 kg/m³ (8 pounds per gallon). Proppant transport can be seen visually through the vision system fiber optic instrumentation. Through video image processing, see Figure 3, the a map of proppant concentrations within the HPS slot can be computed. Dynamic fluid loss measurements can be made through measuring leakoff rates, pressure drop, and facing permeability. Perforation pressure loss can be measured in a slot geometry with the HPS using two pressure transducers. Fluid displacement fronts are visible from the fiber optic vision system.

FLUID RHEOLOGY

In the HPS, differential pressure versus flow rate data are collected and converted to wall shear stress and nominal shear rate to calculate apparent viscosity. Based on the data collected, test results from the HPS confirm that industry standard Couette viscometers accurately characterize the rheological behavior of linear polymer solutions in fractures. This finding applies to a shear rate range of 12 to 235 sec⁻¹, within the temperature and pressure limits of the simulator. Flow within hydraulic fractures can be approximated as flow between infinite parallel plates because fractures have a large surface area and a narrow width. The HPS has a large surface area and provides a reasonable approximation of flow between infinite parallel plates. Flow data were collected using a Fann 35 Couette viscometer and the HPS on a fluid with 7.2 kg/m³ (60 lb/Mgal) hydroxypropyl guar (HPG). After the data were analyzed with a power-law rheological model and corrected for differences in test geometry, the viscometric data agreed well with data from the HPS. The simple power law model used for this comparison was: $\tau_w = K_a \gamma^n$. Figure 4 shows the HPS data and +/- 10% bars for the rotational viscometer data.

The opposite result was determined for measurement of the properties of crosslinked fluids: in general, industry standard Couette viscometers cannot be used to reliably characterize the rheological behavior of crosslinked polymer gels in fractures. This conclusion was reached after observing the failure of viscometric data to predict crosslinked fluid behavior in the HPS. Fluids evaluated for this purpose were a borate-crosslinked 3.6 kg/m³ guar (30 lb/Mgal) fluid and titanium-crosslinked 4.8 and 7.2 kg/m³ HPG (40 and 60 lb/Mgal) fluids. Figure

5 provides a comparison between the HPS data and +/- 10% of the rotational viscometer data for the titanium crosslinked fluid. Since the introduction of crosslinked fluids for fracture stimulation more than 20 years ago, the industry has been attempting to use viscometric data to describe the rheological behavior of these fluids in a fracture. This testing indicates it is not appropriate to do so.

PERFORATION PRESSURE DROP

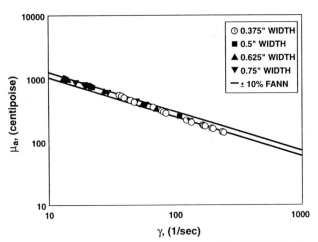

Fig. 4 - Apparent viscosity versus shear rate for a 60 lb HPG/Mgal polymer solution in various HPS gap widths and in a Model 35 Fann Viscometer for comparison.

In the downhole environment, fracturing fluids are exposed to a significant pressure loss through the perforations. Net pressure, used to predict the fracture growth, requires an accurate estimate of the pressure drop through perforations. Measurement of pressure drop through wellbore perforations was found to differ by more than 200% from the predictions made with industry standard correlations. Results of the investigation show that fluid type, perforation size, and fluid viscosity must be considered when selecting a coefficient for use in the standard pressure loss equation. Testing water, a thin fluid, and titanium-crosslinked 7.2 kg/m$^3$ HPG (60 lb/Mgal), a thick fluid, produced perforation coefficients, $C_d$, of 0.879 and 0.589, respectively, in 1.2 cm (0.5 in) perforations. Conventional wisdom is that perforation pressure loss for these two fluids would be the same, but these data,

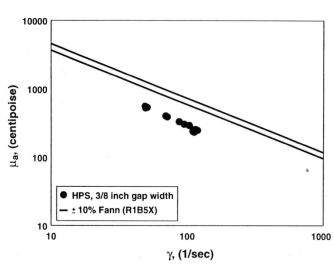

Fig. 5 - Apparent viscosity versus shear rate for a titanium-crosslinked 60 lb HPG/Mgal gel. Comparison of data from the HPS with measurements in an intermediate gap Model 39 Fann Viscometer.

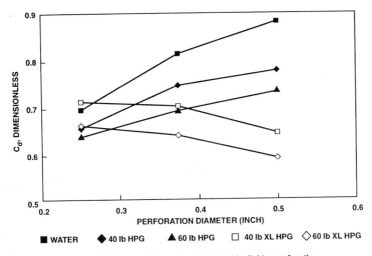

Fig. 6 - **Discharge coefficient of various viscosity fluids as a function of perforation diameter**

shown in Figure 6, indicate the crosslinked fluid pressure loss would be more than twice as much as the thin fluid.

Additional testing was conducted on perforation pressure loss at elevated pressure. Figure 7 shows the pressure drop versus the flow rate squared for a titanium crosslinked 7.2 kg/m³ (60 lb/Mgal) HPG through four 9.5 mm (3/8 in) perforations on 30.5 cm (12 in) spacing. Two sets of data are shown: with and without back pressure. It is evident that elevated pressure did not significantly change the results of the test.

RHEOLOGY AND MIXING

An unusual, and previously undocumented, flow behavior has been observed in the HPS with titanium crosslinked fracturing fluids. Shear stress versus shear rate data collected at various gap widths in the same experiment did not fall on a single line as expected with a well-behaved fluid, see Figure 8. The difference in measured

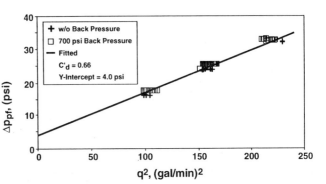

Fig. 7 - **Perforation pressure loss versus flow rate squared for the flow of a titanium-crosslinked 60 lb HPG/Mgal gel through four 3/8 inch perforations on 1ft spacing.**

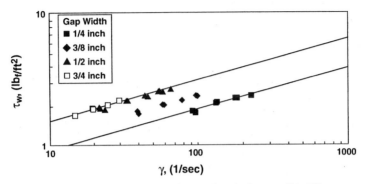

**Fig. 8 - Shear stress versus shear rate for a titanium-crosslinked 60 lb HPG/Mgal gel. Flow rate varied at a fixed gap width to generate the data shown.**

shear stresses among the various gap widths, observed to be as large as 150%, was found to be the result of mixing energy variations present during fluid formulation. A constant flow rate, continuous crosslinking technique with flow diversion was developed in the laboratory to provide a fluid response that can be modeled to predict fracture friction loss. Data from that test, shown in Figure 9, exhibit the expected flow behavior. In the field, the mixing environment present at the point of crosslinker addition and/or reaction must be considered as a factor contributing to the overall performance of these fluids. Similar behavior was observed with borate crosslinked fluids.

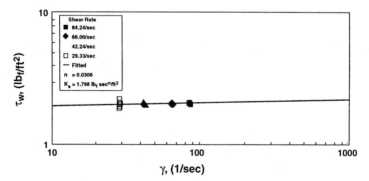

**Fig. 9 - Shear stress versus shear rate for a titanium-crosslinked 60 lb HPG/Mgal gel. Data generated by continuous crosslinking at a fixed flow rate with diversion of portions of the flow into various gap widths to provide the data shown.**

FLUID LOSS ON NATURAL ROCK

A technique was developed to allow natural rock facings to be used with the HPS. First 2.5 cm (1 in) thick slabs are cut from the rock sample and then a step is ground around the edge to allow the facing to be mounted in the HPS. Tests were conducted on a Berea Sandstone natural rock facing with a 3 mD permeability and surface area of 3873 cm². A 4.2 kg/m³ (35 lb/Mgal) crosslinked HPG and 3 kg/m³ (25 lb/Mgal) silica flour (per thousand gallons of solution) for leakoff control were used for this test, see Figure 10. Filtercake was formed on the facing during the experiment and the polymer concentration was 9.68 kg/m³ (80.7 lb/Mgal) caused by the competing forces of slot flow and leakoff. The curve shows a high leakoff rate at the beginning of the test and a lower leakoff rate as the polymer and silica flour is deposited on the surface of the facing.

FLUID LOSS ON
SYNTHETIC ROCK

Synthetic permeable facings were developed to simulate natural rock leakoff characteristics but provide a more durable material for test purposes. These facings are made of plastic resin, plasticiser, and 100 mesh sand, mixed to develop the desired permeability and then baked in an oven. During the initial tests, linear polymer solutions were found to flow unimpeded through these facings under 6.9 Mpa (1000 psi) differential pressure although the facings had a 5 to 16 mD permeability to water. The addition of fluid loss control agents such as a silica flour or a crosslinker were sufficient to reduce fluid loss to an expected level. As fluid loss was reduced by these agents, the cumulative fluid loss was approaching a linear relationship with the square root of time, which is indicative of filtercake buildup on the surfaces. After the tests, however, the HPS was opened and no filtercake was found. It was theorized that the filtercake was being built up beneath the surface of the facing, but the reason for this phenomenon was not determined. Subsequent tests with natural rock facings did produce a filtercake on the surface of the rock.

Upon examination of the facings it was determined that the natural rock surface was more coarse due to the type of saw used to cut the 1 inch slabs. The synthetic rock surfaces came out of the curing process very smooth. Additional tests were then conducted with synthetic rock after they were exposed to a surface sandblasting. The test conditions were 50 sec⁻¹ shear rate and 5.5 MPa (800 psi) back pressure, using a 4.2 kg/m³ (35 lb/Mgal) HPG polymer solution containing 3 kg/m³ (25 lb/Mgal) silica flour. The synthetic rock permeability

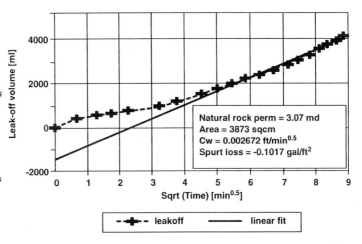

Fig. 10 - Cumulative volume versus square-root-of-time for dynamic fluid loss test with a borate crosslinked 35 lb /Mgal HPG + 25 lb / Mgal Silica Flour

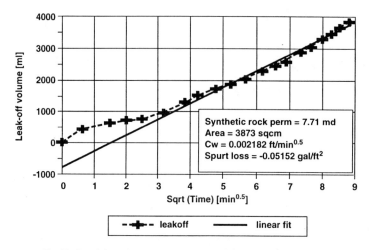

**Fig. 11 - Cumulative volume versus square-root-of-time for dynamic fluid loss test with a borate crosslinked 35 lb /Mgal HPG + 25 lb /Mgal Silica Flour**

was 7.71 mD. The test results are shown in Figure 11. This test shows the expected wall-building characteristics, a linear leakoff volume with the square root of time. When the HPS was opened after the test, a filtercake was found on the surface roughened synthetic rock. The polymer concentration was 8.44 kg/m$^3$ (70.3 lb/Mgal), indicating a slight densification of the polymer. Subsequent testing with other surface-roughened facings confirmed the formation of filtercake on these surfaces.

CONCLUSIONS

The FFCF HPS provides a window into the performance of hydraulic fracturing fluids under conditions representative of the downhole environment. The major findings to date are as follows:

- The use of rotational viscometers is acceptable to measure the rheology of linear gels used in hydraulic fracturing.
- The use of rotational viscometers is not appropriate for measuring the rheology of crosslinked gels.
- Higher than expected perforation friction losses are occurring. Higher losses impact the total pressure drop of the system and reduce the calculated net pressure used in most fracture treatments.
- Fluid mixing or shear history is an important part of borate and titanate-crosslinked gel rheology and must be considered in the field before calculated viscosities are used in a fracture treatment.
- The surface roughness of formations is a significant factor in whether or not a filtercake will build up and affect the leakoff characteristics in the formation.

Several instrumentation upgrades are planned that will further enhance the versatility of the simulator. Future tests of fracturing fluid rheological behavior, the effect of leakoff into the rock matrix, and the migration of proppants within the flow stream will further improve our understanding of the performance of fluids used for hydraulic fracturing of natural gas wells.

REFERENCES

"Functional Capabilities of the High Pressure Simulator for Fracturing Fluid Characterization," December, 1994, Gas Research Institute report number GRI-94/0438

Subhash N. Shah and David L. Lord, "Tests Confirm Operational Status of a Large Slot Flow Apparatus for Characterizing Fracturing Fluids," SPE Production Operations Symposium, April 1995 (SPE 29499).

"Fracturing Fluid Characterization Facility Annual Report," January 1994 -- December, 1994, Gas Research Institute report number GRI-95/0091

"Fracture Fluids, FFCF Simulates Downhole Conditions to Improve Fracture Treatments," Gas Research Institute Digest, Winter 1994/1995.

"Fracturing Fluid Characterization Facility," Gas Research Institute Fact Sheet

"New Facility Aids in Fracture Fluid Study," Gas Research Institute Tech Profile, September, 1994.

WIRELINE OPEN-HOLE STRESS TESTS IN A
TIGHT GAS SANDSTONE

MESURES DE CONTRAINTES EN PUITS OUVERT
DANS DES GRÈS GASÉIFÈRES DE FAIBLE PERMÉABILITÉ

J. Desroches
Schlumberger Cambridge Research, UK

J.R. Marsden
Imperial College London, UK

N.M. Colley
British Gas Exploration and Production, UK

ABSTRACT

This paper presents a series of open-hole stress tests carried out with a wireline tool in a tight gas sandstone reservoir. The measurements were based
on a combination of sleeve fracturing and hydraulic fracturing. Integration of
these measurements with imaging logs and differential strain analysis (DSA)
on cores allowed quality control of the measurements and the determination
of a profile for the complete stress tensor in the reservoir.

RÉSUMÉ

Cet article présente une série de mesures de contraintes effectuées en puits
ouvert à l'aide d'un outil sur cable dans un réservoir de gaz constitué de grès
de faible perméabilité. La technique employée consiste en une combinaison
d'essais de pressiométrie et d'essais de fracturation hydraulique. L'intégration
de ces mesures avec des diagraphies d'imagerie et les résultats d'analyse
différentielle de la courbe de déformation effectuées sur des carottes (DSA),
a permis non seulement un contrôle de la qualité des mesures, mais aussi la
détermination d'un profil complet de l'état de contraintes dans le réservoir.

## INTRODUCTION

The need for stress measurements has been recognised for a long time in the oil and gas industry, with applications to hydraulic fracture containment, wellbore stability and production management of fractured reservoirs. The most reliable way to carry out these measurements at great depth is the micro-hydraulic fracturing technique (for a review, see for example [5]). This is based on an analysis of the pressure response obtained during the initiation, propagation and closure of a hydraulic fracture.

The paper presents a series of open-hole stress measurements carried out on an offshore well in a tight $2.0 \, 10^{10}$ m$^3$ (700 BCF) gas field in the Irish sea. The underlying purpose for these tests was to evaluate the stress tensor with a view to drilling horizontal wells in the appropriate orientation to minimise the likelihood of wellbore instability. These tests were performed with a wireline tool that uses a combination of sleeve fracturing and hydraulic fracturing. As the wellbore was nearly vertical, these measurements allowed the magnitudes of the three principal stresses to be pointwise determined in the reservoir, which consists of tight gas sandstones. These measurements have then been integrated with other measurements, such as calliper logs, resistivity images, sonic logs and laboratory measurements on cores. This allowed not only thorough quality control of the information, but also the estimation of the complete stress field in the reservoir from a small number of direct measurements.

The analysis of the stress tests will first be presented, followed by the information gathered from the other methods. Finally, the stress model in the reservoir and its applications will be described.

## OPEN-HOLE WIRELINE STRESS TESTS

The analysis presented in [11] showed that a stress tool, in order to be reliable in an openhole environment, should have the capabilities of injecting low flow rates, should minimise the effects of wellbore storage on the pressure response, and should allow one to have a good control over the packer behaviour. The MDT* or Modular Formation Dynamics Tester, used with its recently developed packer module, satisfies these requirements [11]. It is a wireline tool which uses motorised valves and is entirely software controlled. The configuration for stress testing is presented in Figure 1 and includes the packer module, the pump-out module and a gamma ray sonde. The packer module allows a 1 metre section of the wellbore to be isolated for testing. Pressure in the packers and in the test interval are recorded simultaneously and can be analysed in real time, which allows real time quality control of the test, especially regarding the packer behaviour. The pump-out module can be used to pump the fluid from the mud column either to the packers or to the interval, and is also used to collapse the packers after a test. Flow rates are of the order of 1 litre/min. Because the pump is downhole, only a small amount of fluid is pressurised and wellbore storage effects are very small. The resulting stiffness of the hydraulic system is almost two orders of magnitude below that of a tool conveyed on pipe. The gamma ray sonde is used for log depth correlation, so that proper tool placement with regard to lithology is ensured.

Such a configuration allows the use of a combination of sleeve fracturing and hydraulic fracturing. During sleeve fracturing, a packer is inflated up to a pressure at which a tensile fracture is created [8]. During hydraulic fracturing, pressurisation of the interval between packers creates a fracture [5]. The combination of these 2 techniques has already been validated to successfully stress test sensitive shales [12]. It is the first time, to the best of our knowledge, that such an approach has been used to stress test sandstones.

---

*Mark of Schlumberger

Three successful tests have been carried out with the following combination of the sleeve fracturing and the hydraulic fracturing technique:
-The sleeve fracturing technique is used to initiate the fracture.
-The hydraulic fracturing technique is then used to propagate the fracture. The drilling mud, which is a high solid content mud, is used as the fracturing fluid. This allows us to create and propagate a micro-hydraulic fracture in a permeable rock while maintaining a low flow rate.
-The sleeve fracturing technique is used again at the end of the test to properly determine the maximum horizontal stress from the reopening pressure.

It is also worth mentioning that the pore pressure at each depth has been interpolated from measurements carried out in the well during the fluid sampling programme, using the same tool.

Interpretation methodology

The interpretation of the tests in term of stresses is based on the analysis of the pressure records obtained during the sleeve fracturing and the hydraulic fracturing tests.

Minimum principal stress. A variety of techniques can be used to estimate the magnitude of the least principal stress. They are all based on the fact that a hydraulic fracture propagates in a plane perpendicular to the minimum principal stress. Note that the direction of fracture initiation can be different. The instantaneous-shut-in-pressure (ISIP) is often taken as a good approximation of the minimum stress (Figure 2). However, errors of the order of several MPa may result when using this approach, especially when there is a large amount of fluid storage. Recently, closure pressure has replaced the ISIP as a measure of the minimum principal stress. The closure pressure is the pressure at which the fracture closes completely. It is currently taken by the industry as the most accurate measure of the minimum stress although modelling shows that stress estimated by this method can be in error by about a quarter of the amount of pore pressure build up due to fluid leak-off [2]. In permeable formations, where the fracturing fluid leaks off from the fracture face, closure pressure is measured at the point at which the pressure decline deviates from a linear dependence on the square root of shut-in time [7]. Alternative methods developed to estimate the minimum principal stress include the reopening test, the step-rate test and the flow-back test [7, 4]. During a reopening test, one reopens a fracture which has already been created, and the point at which the pressure deviates from a linear behaviour is taken as the pressure at which the fracture starts to reopen, or reopening pressure. During a step-rate test, the injection is increased by steps up to the point where the pressure response indicates that a fracture is wide open. An analysis of the propagating pressure vs flow rates leads to an estimation of minimum stress. The flow-back test consists of pumping the fluid out of the fracture once the injection has been stopped. An estimate of the closure stress is provided by an inflexion point in the pressure record during this process.

Maximum horizontal stress. In the case of a vertical wellbore, the maximum horizontal stress can be determined from the fracture initiation pressure, which senses the stress concentration around the wellbore. This stress measurement is less accurate because it depends strongly on the assumed rock behaviour near the wellbore. For example, initiation pressure depends upon whether the formation behaves elastically or inelastically. Initiation pressure depends also on the diffusion of fracturing fluid into the formation, leading to a dependence on the pressurisation rate. The subsequent analysis presented here assumes that the material behaves in a linearly elastic way and the pressurisation rate is low enough to neglect dynamic effects. It is also assumed that the wellbore is perfectly vertical, that the overburden pressure is a principal stress and that the fracture initiates along a vertical line.

If the fluid is a non-penetrating fluid, i.e. if it is not able to penetrate the microcracks intersecting the wellbore, the initiation pressure is given by [6]:

$$P_i = 3\sigma_h - \sigma_H + T_v - P_o \tag{1}$$

where $P_i$ is the initiation pressure, $\sigma_H$ the maximum horizontal stress, $\sigma_h$ the minimum horizontal stress, $P_o$ the pore pressure and $T_v$ the "vertical" tensile strength of the formation. This equation is valid for sleeve fracturing, and for hydraulic fracturing if there is an impermeable mud-cake. It is worth noting that, in these cases, a fracture mechanics approach agrees with equation 1 (see [10]).

Using a packer to pressurise the wellbore ensures that no fluid enters the formation and is the most practical way to satisfy the hypotheses underlying equation 1 [1]. If such a sleeve fracturing test is carried out at the end of a stress test, when a fracture has already been created, the initiation pressure corresponds to the reopening of the fracture, and so $T_v$ is then effectively equal to zero. If $\sigma_h$ and $P_o$ have been determined by other means, equation 1 can be used to estimate the maximum horizontal stress $\sigma_H$. In such a test, the opening of the fracture induces a change in the radial compliance of the wellbore and is signalled by an inflexion point of a plot of packer pressure versus packer volume.

Vertical stress. In the case of a vertical wellbore, the vertical stress $\sigma_v$ can be determined if the fracture created either by hydraulic fracturing or sleeve fracturing initiates horizontally. The initiation pressure is then given by:

$$P_i = \sigma_v + T_h \tag{2}$$

where $T_h$ is the "horizontal" tensile strength of the rock (note that $T_h$ and $T_v$ may be different if the rock is not isotropic).

Field test results

The reservoir consists of mostly tight gas sandstones interbedded with mudstones. As the geological structure of the reservoir does not exhibit any major tectonic feature, it was assumed that the overburden is a principal stress.

The parameters extracted from the analysis of the pressure records are summarised in the Table below.

| location | pore pressure MPa | sleeve breakdown MPa | hydraulic breakdown MPa | reopening pressure MPa | closure pressure MPa | step-rate test MPa | sleeve reopening MPa |
|---|---|---|---|---|---|---|---|
| Station 1 | 14.43 | 40.7 | - | 21.3±0.4 | 18.27 | 17.9 | 20.83 |
| Station 2 | 15.78 | 24.65 | 24.8 | 22.4 | 20.93 | 21.8 | 22.25 |
| Station 3 | 15.95 | 41.45 | >39.0 | >39.0 | | | |

Table 1. Summary of pressure record analysis

An example of sleeve fracturing is presented in Figure 3, and an example of hydraulic fracturing including a breakdown is presented in Figure 4. Figure 5 shows a reopening test, and Figure 6 an example of closure pressure determination.

As described above, the closure pressure is an estimate of the value of the minimum principal stress. This has been successfully determined for the first two stations, and leads to a fracture gradient (minimum principal stress divided by depth) of around 0.0136 MPa/m (0.6 psi/ft). As this gradient is much less than the overburden gradient, it is deduced that the minimum principal stress is horizontal at these depths.

Analysis of the sleeve fracturing tests carried out at the end of the tests (sleeve reopening) allows us to estimate the maximum horizontal stress. Its value is found to be almost equal to the minimum horizontal stress.

During the test carried out at Station 3, it was impossible to reopen the fractures created by sleeve fracturing with the fracturing fluid. The maximum hydraulic pressure achieved during the test $P_{max}$ allows us to determine a lower bound on the closure stress acting on the created fracture. Two cases can be considered. Firstly, if a vertical fracture has been created, a lower estimate for the minimum horizontal stress can be determined by:

$$P_{max} < 3\sigma_h - \sigma_H - P_o \qquad (3)$$

With the assumption that the maximum horizontal stress is not very different from the minimum horizontal stress, it leads to a fracture gradient of over 0.018 MPa/m (0.8 psi/ft). As there is no major structural feature in this area of the reservoir, the large discrepancy between this value and the fracture gradient determined for the two other stations can only be explained if the elastic properties of the rock do influence the state of stress, and if the considered sequence exhibits large variations of elastic properties. Secondly, if a horizontal fracture has been created, $P_{max}$ is simply a lower bound for the overburden $\sigma_v$. It leads to a minimum overburden gradient of 0.026 MPa/m (1.15 psi/ft). This value is close to the weight of the sediments as calculated from the density logs. This hypothesis of a horizontal fracture is therefore preferred. Confirmation will be given by the analysis of the resistivity and sonic logs.

The stress estimates determined by the full analysis of the pressure response of the various tests are summarised in the following Table.

| location | $\sigma_h$ MPa | fracture gradient MPa/m (psi/ft) | $\sigma_H$ MPa | $\sigma_h/\sigma_H$ | overburden gradient MPa/m (psi/ft) |
|---|---|---|---|---|---|
| Station 1 | 18.1±0.1 | 0.0136 (0.60) | 18.55±0.45 | 0.975±0.025 | |
| Station 2 | 20.93 | 0.0141 (0.62) | 24.75 | 0.85 | |
| Station 3 | | | | | >0.026 (1.15) |

Table 2. Estimates of the principal stress values for the 3 stations

## RESISTIVITY IMAGING LOGS

A complete resistivity imaging log was run before the stress tests. Two such logs were run after the tests, between Station 2 and 3 only. The comparison between the pre- and post-frac images allowed us to determine the possible location and orientation of the fractures created during the stress tests for Station 2 and 3.

Station 3

Two sleeve fracturing tests were performed at Station 3. The pressure records indicate in each case that the formation was successfully fractured. The locations of the top and the bottom packers during these two tests are known and do not overlap. This implies that at least two different fractures have been created, one during each sleeve fracturing test.

Figure 7 shows images around the location of Station 3 acquired before and after the stress test. A clear new horizontal feature is observed at a depth of xxx8, at the location of the bottom packer during the second sleeve fracturing test. It is highlighted by a black ellipse. This new feature is present on both images acquired after the MDT stress tests, which happen to have different orientations: it is therefore not an artifact. It appears in white on the image because it is filled with squeezed mud cake, which is much more resistive than the surrounding sandstone. No feature appears at the location of the top packer during that test.

No completely new feature appears at the location of the packers during the first sleeve fracturing test. However, there is at the level of the top packer (xxx6) a pre-existing subhorizontal healed fracture (on the right of the images) whose extension is much larger after the MDT stress test (see Figure 7). It is therefore proposed that the first sleeve fracturing test has indeed reopened and extended these preexisting horizontal features.

The images demonstrate that both the sleeve fracturing tests carried out at station 3 have induced horizontal fractures, which is consistent with the fact that the sleeve fracturing pressure is the same for both stations (within less than 0.1 MPa). These images also confirm that the overburden has been measured.

Station 2

The images acquired around the depth of Station 2 (Figure 8) can be analysed in view of what has been observed on the images presented in the previous subsection. One will look for white vertical features that did not exist on the original image, which would correspond to the intersection between the wellbore and the hydraulic fracture which has been created at this depth.

Such features do appear on the second post fracturing image, although not as clearly as in the previous case, on the right side of the first and the third pad. These features, outlined by black ellipses in Figure 8, are roughly vertical, and correspond to an orientation of around N255E and N65E, which means that they are roughly separated by 180 degrees. This is in accordance with fracture mechanics which predicts that a symmetrical two wing fracture has been created during this stress test. These features are not picked up by the first log run after the stress test, because the tool had a different orientation then: the two new features actually lie in the blind zone between the pads.

If these features correspond to the propagation direction of the created fracture, they can be used to determine the orientation of the minimum principal stress. As the fracture plane is perpendicular to the minimum principal stress, it is proposed that the minimum principal stress is horizontal, with an azimuth of N160E $\pm$ 15°. This orientation is actually consistent with the one determined by other means as discussed later.

A series of four arm calliper logs was also run at the same time. The overgauged sections do not exhibit any ovalisation. If the overgauge sections occur because of mechanical failure of the rock around the wellbore wall, this is an indication that the two horizontal stresses are nearly equal. This is also in accordance with the MDT stress tests.

DUAL SHEAR SONIC LOGS

The dynamic elastic constants of the rock formation can be computed from the speed of compressional and shear waves, and the density of the formation. These dynamic constants are positively correlated to the static ones. Overall, there are strong variations in the computed elastic properties: Poisson's ratio $\nu$ varies between 0.2 and 0.45, Young's modulus $E$ varies between 20 GPa and 65 GPa.

MEASUREMENTS ON CORES

Cores were retrieved from the top part of the reservoir and oriented with the help of the resistivity images.

A series of triaxial tests with varying confining pressure was carried out on 8 plugs taken from these cores, 4 under dry conditions and 4 under brine saturated conditions. The static Young's modulus averaged over each plug showed strong variations (from 24 to 41 GPa) whereas the average Poisson's ratio varied from 0.21 to 0.27. Variations of mechanical properties could be observed within less than a metre variation in depth, which is in agreement with the observation of the sonic logs.

Cubic samples were then cut into these cores and instrumented with strain gauges to carry out Differential Strain Analysis (DSA). DSA is a technique for determination of stress orientation which uses the density and the orientation of micro-cracks which are induced by the relaxation of a sample following the coring process (see for example [9]). It relies on the assumption that the density and the distribution of the microcracks are directly proportional to the stress reduction the core has sustained during its recovery. The outcome consists of the direction (azimuth and dip) of the 3 principal stresses as well as the ratio between the magnitudes of the principal effective stresses. It was checked that the petrofabrics of the sandstones that were tested was suited to this technique following the methodology presented in [3], and the cubes were cut so that the faces make an angle with the laminations of the rock, which allowed testing for any influence of the laminations on the final results.

The results for the orientation of the principal stresses is presented in hemispherical projection in Figure 9, and the results for the principal effective stress ratios are presented in the Table below.

| sample | $\sigma_1^*/\sigma_3^*$ or $(\sigma_1 - P_o)/(\sigma_3 - P_o)$ | $\sigma_2^*/\sigma_3^*$ or $(\sigma_2 - P_o)/(\sigma_3 - P_o)$ |
|--------|--------|--------|
| 1b | 1.327 | 1.080 |
| 2 | 1.428 | 1.158 |
| 5 | 1.473 | 1.041 |
| 6 | 2.462 | 1.469 |
| 7 | 1.396 | 1.182 |
| 8 | 1.251 | 1.046 |
| mean | 1.56 | 1.16 |

Table 3. Estimates of the principal stress ratios from the DSA analysis

These results indicate that the maximum principal stress is nearly vertical, that the intermediate and minimum stress are nearly horizontal and also nearly equal in magnitudes. The consistency between the various samples, with the exception of sample 6, indicates that there is no effect of the laminations (or the elastic properties of the material) on the final results.

Although the analysis can determine the direction of the principal stresses, it cannot fully differentiate between the minimum and the intermediate stress as their values are too close. A consequence is that 2 possible conjugated azimuths can be inferred for either the minimum or the maximum principal stress from Figure 9: N25E and N115E. Results from the image analysis will help us to choose between these 2 possible orientations.

PROPOSED STRESS MODEL

In this section, the information gathered from the various measurements is combined to produce a model of the stress field in the reservoir versus depth.

From the sonic log, we observe large variations in the elastic constants of the rock. In particular, the values at the two depths where the minimum in-situ stress has been measured are:

- $E$=31.9 GPa and $\nu$=0.22 for Station 1, $E$=44.6 GPa and $\nu$=0.3 for Station 2

As the computed fracture gradient (ie minimum stress divided by depth) is very similar for the two stations, it is deduced that the elastic properties do not influence the overall state of stress. This implies that the stress gradients determined for the two first stations should hold for the rest of the wellbore.

This is backed up by the resistivity images which inform us about the structure of the rock. These images clearly indicate that the deposits are lenticular. The rock consists of lenses of variable elastic characteristics, which are by definition not continuous: their characteristic length is small compared to that of the field, ie small compared to the one governing the state of stress of the field. The overall state of stress is governed by far-field boundary conditions acting on some "equivalent" material with averaged elastic properties. Because of this discontinuity of the rock deposit, the local variations, sensed by the sonic log and by the mechanical testing of cores, do not affect the local stresses measured with the MDT.

The resistivity images acquired around Station 2 also allow us to choose between the 2 minimum principal stress directions that come out of the DSA analysis, as the trace of the new feature agrees within less than 25 degrees with one of these directions.

Taking all the information into account, the overall picture of the stress field is therefore as follows:

- the stress field is governed by far field boundary conditions and does not exhibit strong local variations

- the maximum principal stress is vertical, with a vertical gradient greater than 0.026 MPa/m (1.15 psi/ft)

- the minimum principal stress is horizontal, with a vertical gradient between 0.0136 and 0.0141 MPa/m (0.6-0.62 psi/ft), and an orientation roughly NNW-SSE

- the intermediate principal stress is the maximum horizontal stress, with a vertical gradient nearly equal to that of the minimum horizontal stress

Note that this picture is in complete accordance with the regional picture of the stress field as determined from other proprietary data from other wells, as it should be if the stress field is indeed governed by far field conditions.

CONCLUSIONS AND APPLICATIONS

A series of openhole stress tests has been carried out with a wireline tool in tight gas sandstones, with a combination of sleeve fracturing and hydraulic fracturing. The fact that the tool is conveyed on wireline allowed the measurements to be carried out quickly. Its down-hole pump enhances the stiffness of the hydraulic system and hence the overall quality of the measurements. It has been demonstrated that using a drilling fluid with good fluid loss properties to fracture the formation yielded very good measurements with a technique which was formerly limited to very low permeability formations.

Together with information from imaging logs and core measurements, these have enabled us to build a model for the entire stress field in the reservoir. This highlights the importance of combining information from various sources in order to construct such a model. Moreover, the agreement between the stress estimates derived from the micro-hydraulic fracturing technique, the DSA method on cores and prior knowledge of the stresses in the region is a powerful quality control test for both methods.

In the particular case reported in this paper, it is concluded that the basin is in a very relaxed state. One of the consequences is that the variation of stresses between the sandstones and the mudstones is less than expected. Such information is very useful for the planning of any subsequent drilling and completion phase. For example, any stimulation based on hydraulic fracturing must be carried out with great caution to avoid communication between various layers.

## ACKNOWLEDGEMENTS

The authors would like to thank British Gas and Schlumberger for permission to publish this work.

## REFERENCES

1.      Desroches, J., "stress testing with the micro-hydraulic fracturing technique: focus on fracture reopening", 35th U.S. symposium on rock mechanics, 4-7 June 1995, Lake Tahoe, NE, USA, 217-224, 1995.

2.      Detournay E., Cheng A., "plane strain analysis of a stationary hydraulic fracture in a poroelastic medium", Int. J. Solids Structures, vol. 27, 13, 1645-1662, 1991.

3.      Dyke C.G.,"in-situ stress indicators for rock at great depth", Ph.D. thesis, University of London, 1988.

4.      *Reservoir Stimulation*, Economides M. J., K. Nolte (editors), Prentice Hall, 2nd edition, 1989.

5.      Haimson, B., "the hydraulic fracturing method of stress measurement: theory and practice", in J. Hudson (editor), comprehensive rock engineering, chapter 14, Pergamon Press, 1993.

6.      Hubbert M. K., Willis D. G., "mechanics of hydraulic fracturing", transactions of AIME, 210, 153-163, 1957.

7.      Nolte, K.G.: "fracture design considerations based on pressure analysis", paper SPE 10911 presented at the 1982 SPE Cotton Valley symposium of the SPE, Tyler, May 20, 1982.

8.      Stephansson, O., "sleeve fracturing for rock stress measurements in boreholes", international symposium on soil and rock investigations by in-situ stress testing, Paris, France, vol. 2, 571-578, 1983.

9.      Strickland, F., M. Ren, "predicting the in-situ stress for deep wells using differential strain curve analysis", SPE 8954, SPE/DOE symposium on unconventional gas recovery, Pittsburgh, USA, 1980.

10.      Thiercelin, M., "the influence of microstructure on hydraulic fracturing breakdown pressure", symposium on structure and mechanical behaviour of geomaterials, Nancy, France, 419-428, 1992.

11.      Thiercelin, M., J. Desroches, "improving the performance of open hole stress tools", Int. J. of Rock Min. Sci. & Geomech. Abstr., vol. 30, 7, 1249-1252, 1993.

12.      Thiercelin, M., J. Desroches, A. Kurkjian, "open hole stress tests in shales", SPE 28144, SPE/ISRM conference on rock mechanics in petroleum engineering, Eurock'94, Delft, The Netherlands, 29-31 August 1994, pp. 921-928, 1994.

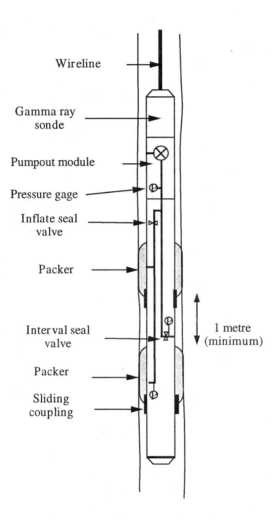

Wireline

Gamma ray
sonde

Pumpout module

Pressure gage

Inflate seal
valve

Packer

Interval seal
valve

Packer

Sliding
coupling

1 metre
(minimum)

Figure 1. Schematic diagram of the tool

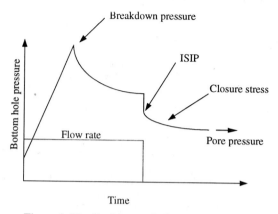

Figure 2. Idealised bottomhole pressure record

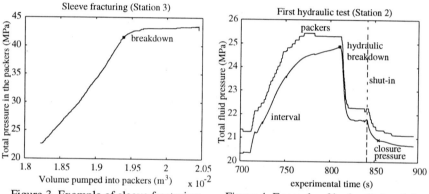

Figure 3. Example of sleeve fracturing

Figure 4. Example of hydraulic breakdown

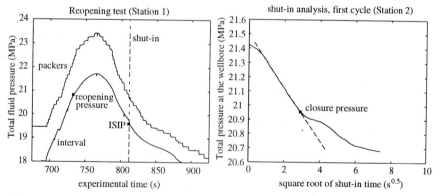

Figure 5. Example of fracture reopening

Figure 6. Example of closure analysis

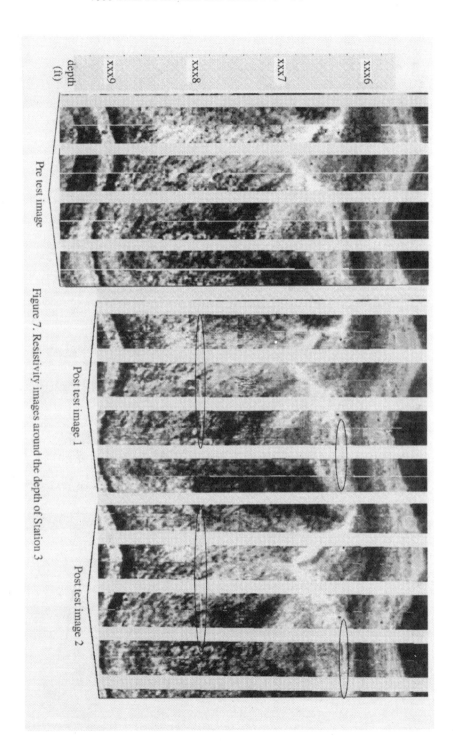

Figure 7. Resistivity images around the depth of Station 3

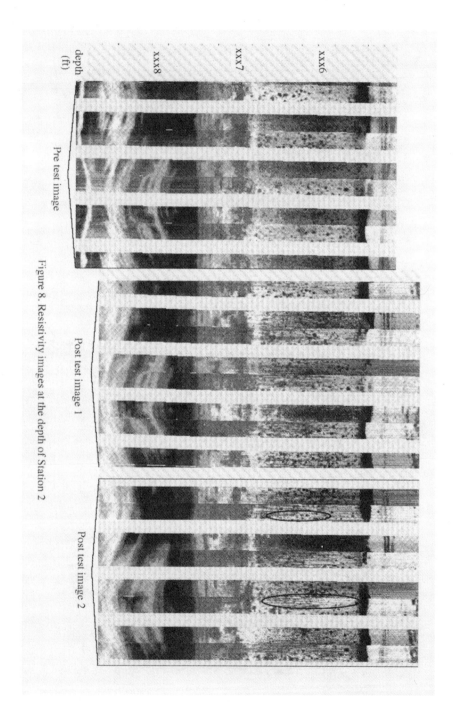

Figure 8. Resistivity images at the depth of Station 2

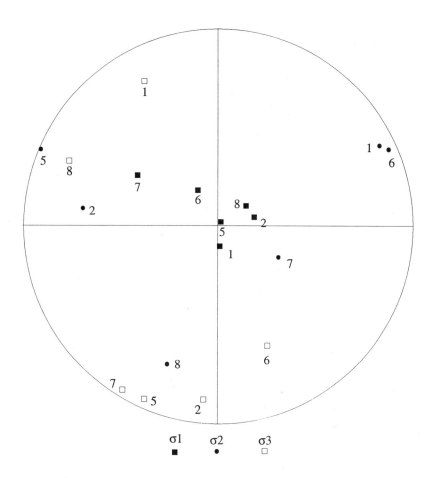

Figure 9. Equal angle hemispherical projection of the principal stresses directions as determined from DSA analysis for cores 1,2,5,6,7 and 8.

PHASE EQUILIBRIA OF GAS-CONDENSATES
IN LOW PERMEABILITY POROUS MEDIA

EQUILIBRE DE PHASE DE GAZ Ä CONDENSAT
DANS UN MILIEU POREU DE FAIBLE PERMÉABILITÉ.

Bedrikovetsky, P.G., Magarshak, T.O. and Shapiro, A.A.
State Gubkin Oil & Gas Academy, Moscow, Russia

ABSTRACT

Study of thermodynamic equilibrium conditions for two-phase multicomponent mixtures in porous media is of critical importance for the description of physical processes in oil-gas-condensate fields in order to estimate the reserves, to perform a recovery methods screening and to predict the recovery factor. We study phase equilibrium of two-phase fluid in porous media under the action of capillary forces and wettability. Equations for phase equilibria in stochastic porous media are derived. An asymptotic method of flash calculations taking into account capillary forces and wettability is developed. This method allows to estimate the reserves of heavy components in a gas-condensate field from a sample of the reservoir gas. Basing on the model above, we have studied the effect of capillary redistribution of the components in multicomponent mixture. The most sufficient effect of capillary forces has been observed in a neighborhood of the dew point (25 - 28 MPa) for high concentrated components and in the region of low pressures (10 - 18 MPa). The capillary effect on the values of condensate saturation is found out to be negligible.

**INTRODUCTION**

Study of thermodynamic equilibrium conditions for two-phase multicomponent mixtures in porous media is of critical importance for the description of physical processes in oil-gas-condensate fields in order to estimate the reserves, to perform a recovery methods screening and to predict the recovery factor. Description of phase equilibrium in porous media requires to take into account capillarity and wettability. Capillary effects lead to the formation of disperse liquid phase (condensate) in thin capillaries. The condensate can contain considerable amount of heavy hydrocarbons which is necessary to take into account in reserves estimates.

During the depletion of a gas condensate field increase of the dew point pressure due to capillary effects leads to earlier separation of liquid condensate which negatively affects the production of heavy hydrocarbon components. Capillary and wettability forces form phase distribution between thin and thick capillaries, which determines shapes and values of relative phase permeabilities. Thus, the action of the capillary forces governs the recovery of condensate.

Experimental observations [1,2] show that dew points of gas-condensate mixtures in porous media can be several percent higher than those measured in a conventional PVT cell test.

It is remarkable that essential condensate saturation can be reached even if the thermodynamic conditions are far away from the dew point experimentally defined in a PVT cell test. However previous theoretical studies of hydrocarbon mixtures equilibria [3,4] contradict these experimental results. The point is that either capillary effects have not been considered in these studies or a porous medium was described as a capillary with effective average radius. Such an approach makes it impossible to estimate saturation of porous medium by liquid phase as a function of pressure. More detailed studies of condensation-evaporation processes of a one-component liquid have been carried out in connection with different processes of chemical technologies [5]. Taking account of scatter in pore sizes has been shown to be significant for correct simulation of these processes. It is pore size distribution that defines the dependence of liquid phase saturation in porous medium on pressure.

One of the features of a reservoir gas-condensate mixture is a variety of low-concentrated components significantly affecting thermodynamic behavior of the mixture. One could expect that the capillary forces lead to redistribution of these components between the phases. However, to the best of our knowledge, this effect has not been studied yet.

The objectives of our study are to obtain general equilibrium conditions for two-phase multicomponent mixtures in porous media and to investigate on this basis the effects mentioned above.

The structure of a porous medium is simulated by a system of independent capillaries with wide pore size distribution (a model of independent domains [5]). The model chosen is proven to be sufficient in order to describe the most important peculiarities of the condensation-evaporation processes in a porous medium including the hysteresis of saturation. This hysteresis is completely determined by the Leverett function which has been defined on the basis of micro-geometrical characteristics of a porous medium. The expression suggested for the Leverett function has turned out to be adequate in all the diapason of saturation values, unlike the usual case when it can be determined only between phase mobility thresholds.

**GENERAL CONDITIONS FOR PHASE EQUILIBRIA**

Consider phase equilibria of two-phase multicomponent fluids in porous media taking into account the wettability and capillary forces. General conditions of equilibrium of connected liquid and gas regions having mutual boundary are defined by the minimum of one of the thermodynamic potentials, for example, Gibbs potential.

In the minimum point intensive thermodynamic variables obey the following system of equations [3-5]

$$\gamma_i^L(p^L, x_j^L) = \gamma_i^g(p^g, x_j^g)$$

$$i = 1,n, \quad j = 1,n-1; \tag{1}$$

$$p^g - p^L = p_c = \sigma C,$$

$$\sigma = \sigma(\gamma_1, ..., \gamma_n) \tag{2}$$

where $\gamma_i^g$, $\gamma_i^L$ = chemical potentials, $x_i^g$, $x_i^L$ = mass fractions of $i^{th}$ component in gas ($g$) and liquid ($L$) phases, $p^g$, $p^L$ = pressures in these phases, $p_c$ = capillary pressure, $\sigma$ = interfacial tension (IFT) coefficient, $C$ = curvature of the interfacial surface. System of Eqs. (1), (2) describes the most general conditions of equilibrium for two phases in contact.

If pressure and composition of gas phase are known then Eqs. (1) may be considered as a system of $n$ independent equations from which $n$ intensive characteristics of liquid phase $p^L$, $x_1^L, \ldots, x_{n-1}^L$ may be uniquely determined. Therefore, if several liquid-filled volumes border a gas-filled volume then all pressures and compositions in liquid are equal. It follows from Eq.(2) that the curvatures of all the surfaces separating liquid-filled and gas-filled volumes are equal too. These arguments are valid in a more general case, when several separated liquid and gas volumes are in contact. The pressures and compositions in all liquid (gas) volumes are equal, as these volumes are connected, and the curvatures of interfacial surfaces are equal too.

Presence of solid phase (porous matrix) shows itself in the wettability conditions at contact lines of three phases. **Fig. 1** presents the picture of forces at the liquid-gas meniscus contact line with the wall of a capillary in a porous medium. Forces of interfacial tension are as follows: $F^{gL}$ (between gas and liquid phases), $F^{gS}$ (gas - solid) and $F^{LS}$ (liquid - solid). Interaction between gas-liquid system and solid is expressed by the reaction force $F^N$ in normal direction to the wall. Vector sum of the above forces is to be equal zero according to the condition of mechanical equilibrium. This equality defines the contact angle $\theta$ between the gas-liquid interfacial surface and the wall of the capillary:

$$\cos(\vartheta) = \frac{|F^{LS}| - |F^{gS}|}{|F^{gL}|} \qquad (3)$$

We shall consider mainly the case of wetting liquid and non-wetting gas, when the angle $\vartheta$ is positive. The case of non-wetting liquid is considered by analogy.

If the absolute value of $F^{gL}$ is less than the difference of values $F^{gS}$ and $F^{LS}$ than the angle $\vartheta$ can not be found from Eq. (3). It is the case of absolute wettability when this angle is supposed to be equal zero.

## GEOMETRIC MODEL OF A POROUS MEDIUM

To choose a model of a porous medium is necessary for evaluation of the saturation of liquid phase. Here we consider the model of the porous medium as a system of cylindrical capillaries of equal lengths $l$ and wide radii distribution which is expressed by the pore size distribution function $\alpha(r)$ (**Fig.2**). Total volume of the capillaries is characterized by the porosity $\phi$.

Conditions of condensation-evaporation processes in different capillaries are considered to be independent. This assumption corresponds to the so-called model of independent domains (the Everett model) [5]. However, the capillaries are supposed to be connected with each other in that component mass exchange between them is possible.

An example of such a system of cylindrical capillaries in contact with a gas volume is presented at **Fig.3**. Connection between separated liquid ganglia is performed by transport in gas phase. More complicated percolation models of phase equilibria in porous media might be considered by analogy. In the framework of these models the effect of capillary interaction on condensation-evaporation processes can be studied more accurately. However the model of independent capillaries suffices to simulate   characteristic features of these processes including the hysteresis of liquid saturation [5].

We will specify general conditions of phase equilibrium (Eqs. (1) - (3)) for the model of independent domains. Recall that these conditions formulated above are that chemical potentials of each component in liquid and gas phases are equal (Eq.1) as well as all the curvatures of interfacial surfaces (Eq.2) and all the contact angles on the separating boundaries (Eq.3).

At given thermodynamic conditions one can define two characteristic radiuses for the processes of condensation and evaporation. The radius characterizing the mechanism of condensation "from walls" is denoted as $r_c$ (**Fig.4**). The radius $R_c$ characterizes the mechanism of evaporation "from meniscus". These radiuses are defined by

$$p_c = \frac{2\sigma \cos(\vartheta)}{R_c} = \frac{\sigma}{r_c}$$

The following three statements describe the thermodynamic equilibrium of two phases in a system of independent capillaries:

1) All the capillaries with radii in excess of $R_c$ are filled by gas;
2) If the contact angle $\theta$ does not exceed 60° (the inequality $R_c > r_c$ takes place; the case of high wettability) then all the capillaries of radii below $r_c$ are filled by liquid;
3) If the contact angle exceeds 60° (the case of low wettability) then all the capillaries of radiuses below $R_c$ are filled by liquid.

In particular, if the condensation has begun with the porous medium initially filled by gas, then all the capillaries of the radii below $r_0 = \min(r_c, R_c)$ are filled by liquid. Inversely, during the evaporation process from the porous medium completely filled by liquid all the capillaries of radii above $R_c$ are filled by gas and the rest of them by liquid. At high vettability, this leads to the hysteresis of saturation in condensation and desorbtion processes.

## DETERMINATION OF THE LEVERETT FUNCTION

The Leverett function is defined as the dimensionless dependence of capillary pressure versus saturation. To determine this dependence consider some thermodynamic process in which liquid saturation changes monotonously. The value of capillary pressure defines curvatures of all the menisci and, therefore, geometry of liquid phase distribution in a porous space. Hence we can define the distribution function $\alpha(r,p_c)$ of pores occupied by liquid. Since the volume of a capillary of radius $r$ equals $\pi l r^2$ then the volume saturation of liquid $S$ can be expressed as

$$S = \int r^2 \alpha(r, p_c)\, dr \quad / \quad \int r^2 \alpha(r)\, dr \tag{4}$$

In particular, it follows from the results of the previous section that saturations $S_C$, $S_E$ for the processes of complete condensation and evaporation are expressed as follows

$$S_C = \int_0^{r_0} r^2 \alpha(r)\, dr \quad / \quad \int_0^{\infty} r^2 \alpha(r)\, dr; \tag{5}$$

$$S_E = \int_0^{R_c} r^2 \alpha(r)\, dr \quad / \quad \int_0^{\infty} r^2 \alpha(r)\, dr \tag{6}$$

The difference between these two equations is in the values of the upper limit ($r_o$ or $R_c$) of the integrals. Since $r_o < R_c$ then the saturation during the process of condensation is less than the saturation during the evaporation.

Reversal of Eq. (5) gives the dependence of capillary pressure $p_c$ versus saturation $S$. The dimensionless capillary pressure (Leverett function) $J(S)$ is defined by the following equality

$$p_c = \sigma \left( \frac{\phi}{k} \right)^{1/2} \cos(\vartheta)\, J(S) \tag{7}$$

where $k$ = permeability; $(k/\phi)^{1/2}$ is the expression for the characteristic capillary radius in a porous medium.

In the case of high wettability Leverett functions for the processes of complete condensation and evaporation are as follows

$$J_C(S) = \frac{(k/\phi)^{1/2}}{\cos(\vartheta)\, r_0(S)}; \qquad J_E(S) = \frac{2(k/\phi)^{1/2}}{R_c(S)} \tag{8}$$

In the case of low wettability the only dependence $R_c(S)$ is used for both condensation and evaporation processes. Note that above formulae for the Leverett function are valid not only within the limits of phase mobility, as usual, but also beyond these limits.

If the contact angle is prescribed then the Leverett function is the only merely geometrical characteristic defining the hysteresis of saturation. This statement appears to be general and to do not depend on the actual micro geometric model of a porous medium. Really, the most general expression for $J$ follows from Eq. (2)

$$J = \frac{(k/\phi)^{1/2}\, C}{\cos(\vartheta)} \tag{9}$$

Thus the Leverett function is determined by the curvature of an interfacial surface. On the other hand, this curvature completely defines possible locations of menisci in a porous medium and, finally, saturation of liquid phase.

It follows from previous discussion that if the contact angle is fixed (for example, in the case of complete wettability) the Leverett function does not depend on the composition of mixture. This can simplify its experimental determination.

**ASYMPTOTIC MODEL FOR PHASE EQUILIBRIUM IN A POROUS MEDIUM**

We suggest here an asymptotic method to calculate capillary corrections to the conditions of phase equilibrium of two-phase multicomponent mixture.

Assume that the pressure $p^g$ and component concentrations $x_i^g$ in gas phase are predetermined. The pressure, saturation and composition of liquid phase is to be evaluated.

In the absence of capillary forces the conditions of phase equilibria may be written as

$$\gamma_i^g(P^0, x_j^g) = \gamma_i^L(P^0, x_j^0) \qquad (10)$$

For given composition of gas phase, initial pressure $P^0$ and initial composition of liquid phase $x^0$ can be defined from these equations. Introduce the following designations:

$$\varepsilon = \frac{\sigma \cos(\vartheta)}{(k/\phi)^{1/2} p^0}; \quad p_D^g = \frac{p^g}{p^0}; \quad p_D^L = \frac{p^L}{p^0}; \quad p_D = \frac{p^0 - p^g}{\varepsilon\, p^0} \qquad (11)$$

In ordinary conditions (pressure of order $10^7 \dots 10^8$ Pa, pore sizes of order $10^{-7} \dots 10^{-5}$ m, IFT of order $10^{-3} \dots 10^{-1}$ N/m) the parameter $\varepsilon$ may be considered as small one (usually of order $10^{-4} \dots 10^{-2}$, no more than $10^{-1}$). Hence the solution $x_i^L$ of Eqs. (1) can be decomposed by this small parameter in the neighborhood of the point $(P^0, x^0)$:

$$x_i^L = x_i^0 + \varepsilon x_i^1 + o(\varepsilon) \qquad (12)$$

Dimensionless pressures are represented as follows

$$p_D^g = 1 - \varepsilon p_D; \qquad (13)$$

$$p_D^L = 1 - \varepsilon(p_D + J(S)) \qquad (14)$$

Substitute Eqs. (12) - (14) into Eqs. (1) of phase equilibrium and decompose these equations by $\varepsilon$. The zeroth approximation coincides with the system of Eqs. (10) of phase equilibrium in absence of capillary forces. It can be determined by usual flash calculations [3,4].

The first approximation is the system of $n$ linear equations in the $n$ values $x_i^1$, $J$ of the form

$$\sum_{j=1}^{n-1} \frac{1}{p^0} \frac{\partial \gamma_i^L}{\partial x_j^L} x_j^L - \frac{\partial \gamma_i^L}{\partial p^L} J = \left( \frac{\partial \gamma_i^L}{\partial p^L} - \frac{\partial \gamma_i^g}{\partial p^g} \right) p_D \quad i = 1,n \qquad (15)$$

After solving this system the saturation can be determined by the value of Leverett function $J(S)$.

The higher order approximations can be determined similarly. However, the estimations show that they are usually negligible.

The system of linear equations (15) solves the problem of determination of the pressure and composition in liquid by those in gas phase. Other similar problems can be also transformed to various systems of linear equations. For example, it is the problem of evaluation of the compositions in both phases by the composition of mixture as a whole and pressure in gas or liquid phase.

**ESTIMATION OF RESERVES**

In practice, testing of composition of a reservoir gas-condensate mixture is as follows. Sampling of gas phase and its chromatography analysis are carried out. A phase state of a reservoir mixture is determined either by PVT cell experiments or by the data of mathematical simulation of phase equilibria.

Suppose that the mixture is considered to be homogeneous gas phase. Reserves of each component are estimated by formula

$$M_i = \phi\, \rho^g(P,T,x_1^g,\dots,x_{n-1}^g)\,x_i^g$$

Describe the above situation in a framework of phase equilibria model taking account of capillary forces. Consider a gas sample under reservoir conditions. The corresponding saturation of liquid phase is found by the method developed in the previous section. The reserve of i-th component is determined as

$$M_i = \phi\left\{\rho^g x_i^g(1-S) + \rho^L x_i^L S\right\}$$

The density of liquid is higher than the density of gas. Additionally, fractions of heavy components in liquid phase exceed ones in gas phase. Therefore, the taking into account of even small saturation of liquid phase can lead to a significant contribution into the values of reserves of heavy hydrocarbon components.

## EFFECT OF CAPILLARY FORCES ON COMPONENT DISTRIBUTION. CASE STUDY.

The works [1,2,4,11-16] discuss theoretical and experimental studies of the capillary effect on a thermodynamical state of a multicomponent mixture in a porous medium. Basically, the capillary effect on a dew point has been studied. Unlike the earlier works [1,2,11-13] where significant effects have been observed the modern estimations [14-16] show that the capillary forces are noticeable only in a very thin capillaries. In natural reservoirs such capillaries are usually occupied by the wetting connate water.

The effect of capillary forces on mixture compositions has been previously studied for binary mixtures [15]. The case of hydrocarbon binary mixtures in an artificial porous medium has been considered. No significant change of mixture composition has been observed. Such a change could show itself only in the area where the concentration of one of the components is small. However this area has not been studied in detail.

In a multicomponent mixture the order of an absolute correction due to capillary forces to the concentration of each component is independent on this concentration. This means that the relative corrections are much higher for the low-concentrated components. Thus one can expect that the action of capillary forces results in redistribution of low-concentrated components in a multi-component mixture. In mixtures present in natural reservoirs there is a number of heavy low-concentrated hydrocarbon components significantly affecting their behavior.

We have studied the effect of capillary redistribution of the components in multicomponent mixture. The composition of mixture considered is presented in the **Table 1**. The dew point of this mixture is 28.5 MPa at the field temperature 78⁰C.

A characteristic feature of this mixture is the presence of enormously high-concentrated $CO_2$ (see Table 1). Another feature of the mixture considered is that it contains a variety of heavy hydrocarbon components which manifests itself in a relatively high concentration of $C_{7+}$. The most low-concentrated components in the mixture are the hydrocarbon components $C_3$ - $C_6$ and nitrogen.

The porous medium is characterized by a uniform set of pore size distributions with variable average radius of pores $r_{av} = (k/m)^{1/2}$. This radius has changed from $0.7*10^{-7}$m to $1.7*10^{-7}$m. The corresponding interval of permeability changes from 0.5 to 3 mD which is of the order of permeabilities of low-permeable carbonaceous rock.

The case of a water-saturated porous medium with initial water saturation 0.1 is also considered. The water is supposed to be the most wettable phase occupying thin capillaries. Thus, the presence of water changes the size distribution of the pores accessible for gas and condensate.

The K-values (the ratios of concentrations in gas and liquid phases) for the components $C_1$, $C_2$, $C_7$, $N_2$, $CO_2$ have been chosen for the mixture characterization. The dependencies of K-values on the pressure for different permeabilities and initial water saturation are presented at **Figs. 4-8**. Additionally, the dependencies of condensate saturations on pressure are calculated (**Fig. 9**). On these Figures, the curve 0 corresponds to the absence of capillary forces, the curves 1, 3, 5 to the permeabilities 0.5, 1, 3 mD and zero initial water saturation, the curves 2, 4, 6 to the permeabilities 0.5, 1, 3 mD and initial water saturation equal 0.1, correspondingly.

The following regularities are observed in these calculations.

Capillary forces change saturation of two-phase mixture only at low pressures (less than 20 MPa for current mixture). The dependence of saturation on the permeability is monotone: the less is the permeability (the more is characteristic capillary pressure) the more is the difference between the saturations in absence and in presence of capillary forces as well as for zero initial water saturation so for initial water saturation equal 0.1.

Basically, similar conclusion is valid for the K-values of the components. For relatively high concentrated components, the deviations in K-values of a given component have the same sign for different pressures. The greatest deviations in K-values have been observed for low concentrated $C_2$ and $N_2$.

The insufficient effect of capillary forces on $C_{7+}$ should be pointed out. If we subdivided these pseudocomponents into a number of low-concentrated fractions their concentrations probably would be changed by capillary forces. This example shows that detailed analysis of a mixture composition is necessary for correct estimation of capillary effects.

The most sufficient effect of capillary forces has been observed in a neighborhood of the dew point (25 - 28 MPa) for high concentrated components and in the region of low pressures (10 - 18 MPa). The capillary effect on the values of condensate saturation is found out to be negligible. It becomes valuable only in the region of low pressures.

Our calculations show that the effect of capillary forces becomes negligible if the permeability exceeds 10 mD.

## CONCLUSIONS

1. The radii of gas-liquid menisci in pores of a different radii under the equilibrium conditions are equal. Compositions of gas and liquid phases are the same in all the pores.

2. Under the action of capillary forces saturation becomes an intensive thermodynamic parameter. It allows to determine the saturation of liquid from the sample of the reservoir gas. As a result, reserves of the reservoir liquid and heavy components can be estimated from the sample of the gas phase.

Neglecting the capillary forces results in significant errors in estimation of reserves of condensate from gas sample when reservoir conditions are near to the dew point.

3. J-function of the capillary pressure for partly miscible phases is determined by the geometry of a porous medium. J-function decreases monotonously from infinity to zero with variation of saturation from zero up to unity. So J-function is also determined for small and large values where only one phase is mobile.

4. Conditions of phase equilibrium in capillary porous media contain small parameter which is a ratio between the average capillary pressure and pressure of a gas phase. It allows a singular asymptotic expansion of equilibrium equations. Zero approximation gives conditions of phase equilibrium under the absence of capillary forces. First order approximation is given by a linear system of equations. It gives capillary corrections to the conditions of phase equilibrium.

5. The most valuable effect of capillary forces on the two-phase multicomponent mixture equilibrium in a porous medium is the redistribution of components between liquid and gas phases.

6. The capillary forces significantly change the distributions of low-concentrated components, both hydrocarbon and non-hydrocarbon, between gas and liquid phases. The less is the concentration of a component the more is the contribution of capillary forces into its K-value.

7. The effect of capillary forces is sufficient only in low permeable porous media, the permeabilities of which do not exceed 10 mD. The less is the permeability the more are the deviations in the K-values of the components.

## NOMENCLATURE

$C$ = curvature of the interfacial surface
$F$ = interfacial tension force, N
$J$ = Leveret function
$k$ = phase permeability, $\mu m^2$
$l$ = length of a capillary, m
$L$ = characteristic length, m
$M$ = reserve of a component, kg
$n$ = number of components
$p$ = pressure, Pa
$r$ = radii of capillaries
$S$ = saturation of liquid phase
$t$ = time, s
$T$ = absolute temperature, K
$V$ = molar volume, $m^3$
$x$ = mass fraction

$\alpha$ = pore size distribution, m$^{-1}$
$\gamma$ = chemical potential J/mole
$\mu$ = viscosity, Pa.s
$\rho$ = density
$\sigma$ = IFT, N/m
$\theta$ = contact angle, degrees
$\phi$ = porosity

## REFERENCES

1. Trebin, F.A. and Zadora, G.I.:"Experimental Study of the Effect of a Porous Medium on Phase Transitions in Gas-Condensate Systems," *Neft i gas* (1968) 8, 41.

2. Tindy, R. and Raynal, M.:"Are Test-Cell Saturation Pressures Accurate Enough?" *Oil and Gas J.* (1966) **64**, 126.

3. Namiot, A.Yu.: *Phase Equilibria in Oil Recovery*, Nedra, Moscow (1983) 183.

4. Brusilovsky, A.I.: "Mathematical Simulation of Phase Behavior of Natural Multicomponent Systems at High Pressures Using Equation of State," paper SPE 20180 presented     at the 1990 SPE/DOE 7th Symposium on Enhanced Oil Recovery, Tulsa, Oklahoma, April 22-25.

5. Kheifets, L.I. and Neimark, A.W.: *Multiphase Processes in Porous Media*, Khimiya, Moscow (1982) 320.

6. Stepanova, G.S.: *Phase Transitions in Oil and Gas Reservoirs*, Nedra, Moscow (1983) 192.

7. Amyx, J.W., Bass, D.M. and Whiting, J.R., Petroleum Reservoir Engineering. Physical Properties, McGraw-Hill, New York, 1960.

8. Fanchi, J.R., Calculations of parachors for compositional simulator , JPT, 1985, p.2049-2050.

9. Fanchi, J.R., Calculations of parachors for compositional simulator: an update, SPE Reservoir Engineering, 1990, p.433-436.

10. Margulov, R.D., Vyakhirev, R.I., Leontiev, I.A. and Gritsenko, A.I., Development of Reservoirs with Complex Composition, Moscow, 1988.

11. Sadykh-Zade, E.S., Mamedov, J.G. and Rafibejli, N.M.: "Determination of the Dynamic Pressure of the Beginning of Condensation in the Presence of a Porous Medium," Neft' i Gaz. (1963) Vol.12, 268-270.

12. Durmishian, A.G., Mamedov, Y. H. and Mirzadzhansade, A. J.: "Experimental investigation of Hydrodynamic and Thermodynamic Properties of Gas Condensate Systems During Flow Through Porous Media", Isvestia Akademii Nauk USSR (1964) No. 1, 133-136.

13. Sadykh-Zade, E.S., Ismailov, D.K., Karakashev, V.K. and Addullaev, A.A.: "A Study of the Process of Equilibrium Rate Attainment During Condensation in Gas Condensate Systems", Neft' i Gaz. (1968) Vol.8, 41.

14. Kent S. Udell: "The Thermodynamics of Evaporation and Condensation in Porous Media", SPE 10779, California Regional Meeting of the SPE, San Francisco, March 24-26, 1982.

15. Sigmung, P.M., Dranchuk, P.M., Morrow, N.R. and Purvis, R.A.: "Retrograde Condensation in Porous Media", SPE 3476, SPE AIME 46th Annual Fall Meeting, New Orleans, Oct. 3-6, 1971.

16. Perepelichenko W.F. "Component recovery of oil-gas-condensate reservoirs", Nedra, Moscow, 1990.
17. Bedrikovetsky P.G. Mathematical Theory of Oil & Gas
Recovery (With applications to ex-USSR oil & gas condensate fields), 1993, Kluwer Academic Publishers, London-Boston-Dordrecht

TABLE 1. COMPOSITION OF THE MIXTURE

| $CO_2$ | $N_2$ | $C_1$ | $C_2$ | $C_3$ | $iC_4$ | $nC_4$ | $C_5$ | $C_6$ | $C_7$ |
|--------|-------|-------|-------|-------|--------|--------|-------|-------|-------|
| 15.37  | 2.3   | 68.3  | 5.35  | 2.68  | 0.70   | 0.95   | 0.73  | 0.58  | 3.04  |

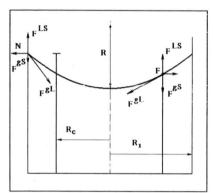

Figure 1. Force balance on interfacial tension on the contact line 'gas-liquid-solid'

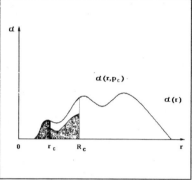

Figure 2. Pore size distribution curve and filling on thin capillaries by wettable liquid

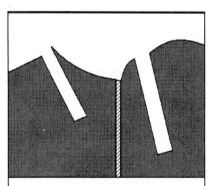

Figure 3. Wettable liquid is located in thin capillaries, gas filles thick ones.

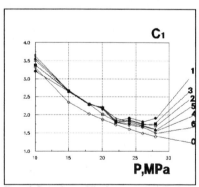

Figure 4. Dependence of K values on pressure for $C_1$.

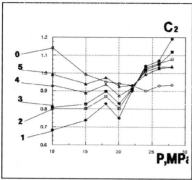

Figure 5. Dependence of K values on pressure for $C_2$.

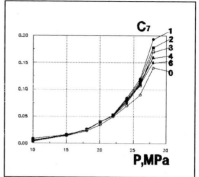

Figure 6. Dependence of K values on pressure for $C_7$.

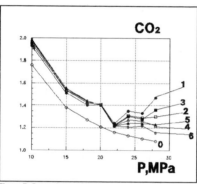

Figure 7. Dependence of K values on pressure for $CO_2$.

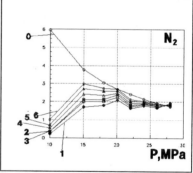

Figure 8. Dependence of K values on pressure for $N_2$.

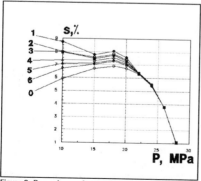

Figure 9. Dependence of saturation on pressure.

BIO-SR™ PROCESS FOR SUBQUALITY NATURAL GAS

PROCEDE BIO-SR POUR GAZ NATUREL DE SOUS-QUALITE

Amir Rehmat
Institute of Gas Technology, USA

Junji Yoshizawa
NKK Corporation, Japan

Dennis Dalrymple
Radian Corporation, USA

Linda Echterhoff and
Michael P. Quinlan
M. W. Kellogg Co., USA

Dennis Leppin
Gas Research Institute, USA

## ABSTRACT

The BIO-SR™ process is an emerging liquid redox technology for the removal of hydrogen sulfide from subquality natural gas. Based on experience in treating sour gases from chemical plants, refineries and sludge digesters, the BIO-SR process has already exhibited good potential for upgrading natural gas to pipeline-quality specification (less than 4 ppm $H_2S$) in a single step. The BIO-SR liquid reagent is maintained at a pH in the range of 1.5 to 2.0 to sustain its selectivity for hydrogen sulfide even in the presence of carbon dioxide. The distinguishing feature of the process is the use of nondegradable ferric sulfate solution which is regenerated by robust and resilient *Thiobacillus ferrooxidans* bacteria, thereby eliminating the costs associated with replenishing degradable liquid redox reagents, such as chelated iron. This is also a primary driving force behind the favorable economics and low operating costs of the BIO-SR process. Sulfur is recovered from the process as elemental sulfur.

## RÉSUMÉ

Le procédé BIO-SR est une technologie d'oxidation-réduction liquide émergente pour le retrait d'acide sulfhydrique de gaz naturel de sous-qualité. Basé sur son expérience de traitement de gaz sulfureux d'usines chimiques, de raffineries et de putréfacteurs de boues, le procédé BIO-SR a déjà démontré un bon potentiel d'amélioration de qualité du gaz naturel aux spécifications de qualité de gazoduc (moins de 4 ppm $H_2S$) en une seule étape. Le réactif liquide BIO-SR est maintenu à un pH situé entre 1,5 et 2,0 pour conserver sa sélectivité d'acide sulfhydrique même en présence de gaz carbonique. La caractéristique bien particulière de ce procédé réside dans l'utilisation d'une solution de sulfate ferrique non-dégradable régénérée par des bactéries *Thiobacillus ferrooxidans* robustes et résilientes. Cela élimine de fait les coûts associés au réapprovisionnement en réactifs d'oxidation-réduction liquides dégradables, tels que le fer chélaté. Ceci représente également une force principale derrière l'aspect économique favorable et les faibles coûts d'exploitation du procédé BIO-SR. Le soufre est récupéré du procédé sous forme de soufre élémentaire.

## INTRODUCTION

A commonly employed method for removing hydrogen sulfide ($H_2S$) from sour natural gas is to treat the gas with a solvent to separate and concentrate the $H_2S$ and then recover elemental sulfur in a Claus plant. For small-capacity sulfur recovery (less than 10 tons per day), Claus plants are difficult to operate and control. This is the impetus for seeking alternate processes, such as liquid redox, to remove the $H_2S$ and recover sulfur from small-scale subquality gas treating applications.

Liquid redox sulfur recovery processes can be employed by a variety of industries where the need exists to remove small quantities of $H_2S$ from gas streams and to produce elemental sulfur for sale or disposal. Liquid redox processes offer high $H_2S$ removal efficiency, conversion of $H_2S$ to elemental sulfur in one processing step, ambient temperature operation, the ability to handle fluctuating inlet gas flows and concentrations, and the ability to treat both low- and high-$H_2S$ content gas streams at pipeline pressures. The overall reaction of liquid redox processes entails reaction of oxygen with $H_2S$ to produce water and elemental sulfur. The key element of the process is a mediating redox couple, which must be reasonably priced and should yield acceptable reaction rates and a high conversion to elemental sulfur.

The most popular liquid redox processes utilize either vanadium or iron as a mediating couple. However, environmental concerns about vanadium have resulted in most new plants being based on iron. In the forefront of these chelated-iron-based processes are LO-CAT®, LO-CAT II™, and SulFerox$^{SM}$ as well as the non-chelated-iron-based BIO-SR. In-depth economic evaluations of these processes have been conducted by the Gas Research Institute (1).

In addition to subquality natural gas, the BIO-SR process is also applicable to gas treatment in chemical plants, sulfur recovery from amine scrubber off gases, oil refinery gases, digester gas from sewage treatment plants, tail gas sweetening in geothermal power generation, and gas sweetening in coal and oil shale gasification and retorting.

The BIO-SR process was originally developed by Dowa Mining Co., Ltd. (2) and is exclusively licensed to NKK. The Institute of Gas Technology is under agreement with NKK to develop the process further and to exploit it for upgrading subquality natural gas. The Gas Research Institute is providing financial support for the process demonstration at an actual field site that is processing subquality natural gas. The Radian Corporation is providing an independent assessment of the process demonstration, whereas Joy Environmental Technologies is providing market support for commercial exploitation.

The process description, inherent advantages of the process, and the current status of the process development are described in this paper.

## PROCESS DESCRIPTION

A schematic flow diagram for the BIO-SR process is shown in Figure 1. Subquality natural gas containing $H_2S$ is contacted with a ferric sulfate [$Fe_2(SO_4)_3$] solution in an absorber such as a jet scrubber, bubble column, or packed column. The $H_2S$ is absorbed into the solution and oxidized to elemental sulfur. At the same time, the ferric sulfate is reduced to ferrous sulfate ($FeSO_4$). The overall reaction is shown below:

$$H_2S + Fe_2(SO_4)_3 \rightarrow S\downarrow + 2FeSO_4 + H_2SO_4$$

The elemental sulfur formed is agglomerated to a larger particle size in the slurry tank. Sulfur is then separated from the solution using settlers and filters.

---

BIO-SR is a registered trademark of the Dowa Mining Company, Ltd.

The ferrous sulfate solution is then introduced into a bio-reactor where *Thiobacillus ferrooxidans* bacteria are employed for the regeneration of the solution. The bacteria oxidize the ferrous sulfate into ferric sulfate through air assist by the following reaction:

$$2FeSO_4 + H_2SO_4 + 1/2O_2 \xrightarrow{\quad bacteria \quad} Fe_2(SO_4)_3 + H_2O$$

The oxidation reaction takes place in the presence of sulfuric acid at a pH value in the range of 1.5 to 2.0. The bacteria accelerate the oxidation rate by a factor of almost 200,000 over a simple chemical reaction at this pH range.

The oxidizer solution is recycled to the absorber to repeat the cycle. In this closed loop system, there is no degradation of the solution, no waste, and neither catalyst nor any chemicals need to be added.

Some of the inherent advantages of the BIO-SR process include:

a)      High $H_2S$ removal efficiency where by the concentration of $H_2S$ in the treated gas is reduced to less than 4 ppm.

b)      Low operating cost because there is no degradation of the liquid redox solution through side reactions. Also, no special catalysts or chemicals are needed for the process. Unlike LO-CAT, LO-CAT II, and SulFerox, the BIO-SR process employs a non-chelated-iron mediating couple in the redox solution. As a result, very little chemical makeup is required by the process. In contrast, the chelated-iron solution is susceptible to degradation. Some of the chelates are lost through the formation of degradation products either by oxidation with $Fe^{3+}$ or through free radical induced oxidation (3).

c)      Ease of operation and maintenance emanating from ease of process control and stable bacterial oxidation.

d)      High $H_2S$ selectivity because of high acidic absorbent solution.

e)      Good flexibility over load fluctuations because the bacterial population in the bio-reactor increases rapidly to adjust to load fluctuations.

PROCESS ECONOMICS

For some years now, GRI has been performing cost evaluations of small-scale $H_2S$ removal processes. Quinlan and Echterhoff (1) compared LO-CAT II costs to Amine/Claus, SulFerox, BIO-SR and other processes. The basis and methodology for the cost comparison is detailed in their paper. In one of their cases, they developed relative total costs based on a gas flow of 56,600 $Nm^3$/day at 7.0 MPa containing 1000 kg/day of sulfur and assuming a payback period of 5 years.

Using this case and incorporating the results of the GRI/Radian testing of SulFerox at high gas pressure (4), Figures 2 and 3 have been developed. These are for a 5-year and a 10-year payback, respectively. For both figures, the baseline process is an Amine/Claus plant. The relative total costs for LO-CAT II, SulFerox, and BIO-SR are compared against the baseline.

In both figures, the relative total costs for LO-CAT II and SulFerox are given for a range of chemical costs. In any redox plant, chemical usage can vary depending on certain factors. Chelant can be lost through degradation, or with solution that remains in the sulfur cake, or through leaks. In addition, the presence of $CO_2$ in the gas impacts the system pH, and buffer chemicals are required to maintain the solution at optimum pH for $H_2S$ removal. The solution is also prone to foaming and plugging, and chemicals are required to suppress these tendencies.

For SulFerox, chemical costs of $400, $600 and $800 per ton of sulfur removed are assumed in both Figures 2 and 3. The SulFerox chemical costs projected by Dow in 1991 were $180 per ton (5). At the 1994 GRI Liquid Redox Sulfur Recovery Conference, the lowest quoted SulFerox chemical costs was just over $400 per ton (6). The SulFerox pilot unit at Kermit had chemical consumptions on the order of 1 kg per kg of sulfur processed. While this was a small pilot unit where high consumptions would be expected, it is doubtful that these consumptions are an order of magnitude above the expected commercial level. Based on these various information sources, it appears that the original $180 per ton estimate may be low. Therefore, we have assumed higher chemicals consumptions for SulFerox for this comparison to BIO-SR to evaluate chemical cost sensitivities between the two processes.

Similarly, the chemical costs assumed for LO-CAT II in Figures 2 and 3 are $150, $225, and $300 per ton of sulfur removed. The chemical costs projected by Wheelabrator Clean Air Systems, Inc. for LO-CAT II in 1991 were $115 per ton of sulfur. This was before any high pressure LO-CAT II units were built and before GRI/Radian testing of the LO-CAT II pilot plant began in April 1995. The latest projections from Wheelabrator Clean Air Systems, Inc. are that an autocirculation unit would have chemical costs of $150 to $200 per ton, and that direct treat units would have a maximum chemical cost of $250 to $300 per ton.

Quinlan and Echterhoff (1) has pointed out that BIO-SR costs are sensitive to the size of the bio-reactor, because size determines whether the reactor can be shop built or must be field fabricated. The differences in construction methods on BIO-SR costs are illustrated in Figures 2 and 3.

For the 1991 cost estimate (1), NKK proposed that the sulfur-laden solution from the absorber be sent to the surge tank then filtered in a filter press. The sulfur cake from the filter then would be fed to an autoclave for melting using a conveyor and hopper. From the autoclave, the sulfur would be settled in a vertical tank or vessel.

A less expensive alternative to remove the sulfur from the solution prior to the bio-reactor may be to direct-melt the sulfur-laden solution from the absorber. Elimination of the surge tank, filter press, conveyor and hopper should result in lower capital investment. This alternative may require more chemical make-up and sulfur quality may be less. However, BIO-SR chemical costs are extremely inexpensive compared to SulFerox or LO-CAT II and, typically, sulfur is not sold at these small volumes so sulfur quality is not a major issue. Some preliminary cost savings for the direct-melt BIO-SR process can be seen in Figures 2 and 3.

The cost graphs show that under most circumstances, BIO-SR costs are less than those for SulFerox. Both LO-CAT II and BIO-SR remain to be proven at high pressures and, while existing BIO-SR costs are higher, replacement of the filter with a direct-melt system, shop built reactors or higher-than-projected LO-CAT II chemical costs could make BIO-SR the process of choice.

OPERATING EXPERIENCE

Thus far, BIO-SR has been successfully deployed on low-pressure gas streams covering a wide range of $H_2S$ concentrations. Table 1 summarizes the operating experiences from four different applications.

The first commercial application of the BIO-SR process was for treating barium chemical processing off gas containing 70% $H_2S$ at the Barium Chemicals Co. of Japan. The capacity of this treatment plant was 150 tons of sulfur per month, which was sold as a by-product for the manufacture of sulfuric acid. Sulfur purity exceeded 99.98% and the concentration of $H_2S$ in the clean gas was consistently maintained below 10 ppm.

The second application was a pilot-scale demonstration at a refinery in Japan to treat amine and Claus feed gases containing up to 1.9 mol % $H_2S$ and up to 93 mol % $H_2S$, respectively. Jet scrubbers were employed for the absorber which yielded $H_2S$ concentrations ranging from 10 to

20 ppm in the treated gases. The pilot plant was operated continuously for two weeks. The activity of the redox solution remained fairly constant throughout the test. The reactivity of the bio-reactor also remained unaffected due to the presence of hydrocarbons in the redox solution.

The third application was a pilot-scale demonstration at a sewage treatment plant in Japan for the treatment of digester off gases. During the sixty-day operating period, the $H_2S$ content of the feed gas fluctuated between 400 and 2000 ppm. However, the $H_2S$ concentration of the treated gas was consistently below 10 ppm. The oxidation rate of the spent solution remained unaffected in spite of fluctuations in the feed gas $H_2S$ concentration or slight variations in the feed gas temperature.

The most recent attribute of the process can be signified by a commercial exploitation at a sewage treatment plant in Sendai, Japan to treat a full stream of 400 $Nm^3/h$ of digester gas containing up to 3000 ppm of $H_2S$. The absorber is a packed tower which reduces the concentration of $H_2S$ in the treated gas to less than 4 ppm (Figure 4). Except for the scrubbing tower, which is made from stainless steel, PVC and FRP (polyvinyl chloride and fiberglass reinforced plastic) material are extensively utilized in the construction of other vessels and tanks including the bio-reactor to contain the cost of the plant.

All of these experiences with the BIO-SR process demonstrate its significant potential for application to upgrading subquality natural gas.

TESTS WITH SUBQUALITY NATURAL GAS

To date, all of the above demonstrations and the commercial applications of the BIO-SR process have taken place at or near atmospheric pressure. These results have been quite encouraging. The process has met pipeline specifications for sulfur, the material of construction for the processing units has been shown to be quite economical, sulfur has been removed from the circulating loop with a simple filter press and there has been very little problem with sulfur plugging or foaming. Despite the success of the process in low-pressure applications, there are several research issues that need to be addressed for application of the process to high-pressure subquality natural gas. These needs are summarized in Table 2.

With its favorable economics and with the resolution of key barrier issues specific to subquality natural gas, the BIO-SR process could become a viable alternative for upgrading subquality natural gas.

Currently, two designs for the demonstration of the BIO-SR process for subquality natural gas are being prepared: one to treat 118 $Nm^3/h$ of subquality natural gas and the other to treat 1180 $Nm^3/h$ of subquality natural gas. Depending upon the cost of these units and the continued support of the host company, Natural Gas Pipeline Company of America (NGPL), one of them may be tested at NGPL's Processing Plant 164 located near Kermit, Texas with cooperation from the Gas Research Institute. The Gas Research Institute and NGPL maintain and provide this facility for specific testing of liquid redox processes (4,7,8).

The NGPL gas processing facility at Kermit uses a diethanolamine (DEA) system and a glycol dehydrating system to remove $H_2S$ and water from a field of five wells located near the plant. NGPL processes from $0.3 \times 10^6$ to $1.3 \times 10^6$ $Nm^3/day$ of sour natural gas at the facility. Table 3 depicts typical characteristics of the sour gas. Presently, the acid gas from the amine unit is flared. The BIO-SR demonstration unit, which is planned to be housed in the GRI pilot unit facility (Figure 5), will receive a slipstream of sour gas and return sweetened gas to the main stream prior to treatment by NGPL's amine unit.

ACKNOWLEDGMENTS

Financial support from the Gas Research Institute under Contract No. 5090-220-3291 is gratefully acknowledged.

REFERENCES

1.    M. Quinlan and L. Echterhoff, "Technical and Economic Comparison of LO-CAT II™ With Other Iron-Based Liquid Redox Processes," paper presented at 1992 GRI Liquid Redox Sulfur Recovery Conference, Oct. 4-6, 1992; Austin, TX, GRI-93/0129.

2.    H. Sonta and T. Shiratori, U.S. Patent 4,931,262 "Method of Treating $H_2S$ Containing Gases," assigned to Dowa Mining Co., Ltd., Tokyo, Japan.

3.    D. DeBerry, D. Seeger, B. Petrinec, and K. Krist, "Mechanisms of Chelant Degradation in Iron Based Liquid Redox Processes," paper presented at 1992 GRI Liquid Redox Sulfur Recovery Conference, Oct. 4-6, 1992, Austin, TX, GRI-93/0129.

4.    K. McIntush, B. Petrinec, and D. Leppin, "GRI Testing of SulFerox® for the Direct Treatment of High-Pressure Natural Gas," paper presented at the Sixth Sulfur Recovery Conference, May 15-17, 1994, Lakeway, TX, GRI-94/0170.

5.    Dow Gas/Spec Technology Group, private communication, July 1990.

6.    D. Mamrosh and M. Allen, "Status of the SulFerox Technology and Recent Developments," paper presented at the Sixth Sulfur Recovery Conference, May 15-17, 1994, Lakeway, TX.

7.    D. Leppin, C. Holloway, and D. Dalrymple, "GRI Testing of LO-CAT II® for the Treatment of High-Pressure Natural Gas," Paper to be presented at the Seventh Sulfur Recovery Conference, September 24-27, 1995, Austin, TX.

8.    D. Leppin and D. Dalrymple, "Test Results for Sulfur Removal From Gas Streams." Paper to be presented at the IGRC 95 Conference, November 1995, Cannes, France.

Table 1. BIO-SR Process Applications

| Gas Source | Pilot Plant | | | Commercial Scale | |
|---|---|---|---|---|---|
| | Refinery Amine Feed Gas | Refinery Claus Feed Gas | Digester Bio-Gas | Barium Chemicals Co. Off-Gas | Digester Off-Gases (Sendai Municipal Plant) |
| Gas Flow Rate, $Nm^3$/h | Up to 0.5 | Up to 0.5 | Up to 20 | 200 | 400 |
| $H_2S$ in Sour Gas | 1.4 - 1.9% | 85 - 93% | 400 - 2000 ppm | 70% | max 3000 ppm |
| $H_2S$ in Sweet Gas, ppm | 10 - 20 | 0 - 10 | 0 - 10 | < 10 | < 4 |
| Sulfur Recovery Rate, kg/day | — | — | — | 5,000 | 36 |
| Absorber Type | Jet Scrubber | Jet Scrubber | Packed Tower | Jet Scrubber | Packed Tower |
| Bio-reactor Type | Fixed Bed | Fixed Bed | Fixed Bed | Fluidized Bed | Fluidized Bed |
| Operation Start | 1986 | 1986 | 1988 | 1984 | 1993 |
| Remarks | | | | Plant stopped in 1992 | On-going |

Table 2. Additional Data Required For High-Pressure Natural Gas Applications

|  | HIGH PRESSURE | LOW PRESSURE |
|---|---|---|
| Absorber materials of construction | Required | Demonstrated |
| Plugging of packed absorber | Required | Demonstrated |
| Liquid-filled absorber |  |  |
| efficiency and ppm $H_2S$ out | Required | Demonstrated |
| circulation rate | Required | Demonstrated |
| Other absorber types |  |  |
| (non-packing or liquid filled | Required | Demonstrated |
| Foaming and plugging |  |  |
| Effect of pH 1-2 vs pH 7 | Required | Demonstrated |
| Effect of no chelant, surfactant, etc. | Required | Demonstrated |
| Effect of less/no sulfur in recycle | Required | Demonstrated |
| Effect of HC in inlet gas | Required | Required |
| Effect of other inlet gas contaminants |  |  |
| (RSH, COS, metals) | Required | Required |
| Actual Costs for range of gas & sulfur rates | Required | Required |
| Filter sparing Requirements | Required | Demonstrated |
| In line sulfur melter | Required | Required |
| Use of PVC & FRP in chemical plants, gas plants, and/or refineries | Required | Demonstrated |

Table 3. Typical Properties of Sour Gas Feed to the NGPL Site

| Temperature, °C | 21 - 49 |
|---|---|
| Pressure, MPa | 6.2 - 6.9 |
| Flow rate, $10^6$ $Nm^3$ /day | 0.3 - 1.3 |
| Gas composition, (dry basis) | Mole % |
| Hydrogen sulfide | 0.30 |
| Nitrogen | 0.51 |
| Methane | 96.15 |
| Carbon dioxide | 1.17 |
| Ethane | 1.59 |
| Propane | 0.22 |
| Isobutane | 0.02 |
| Butane | 0.02 |
| All others | 0.02 |

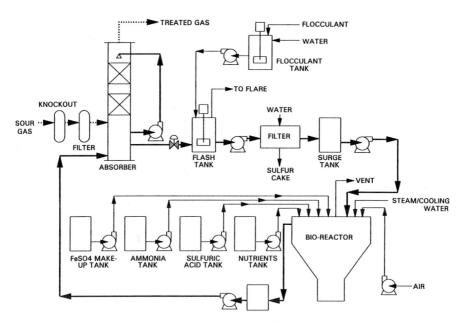

Figure 1. Flow Diagram of the BIO-SR Process

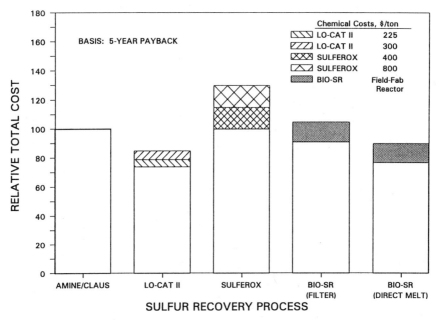

Figure 2. Comparison of Relative Total Costs to Recover
Sulfur by Different Liquid Redox Processes (5-year Payback)

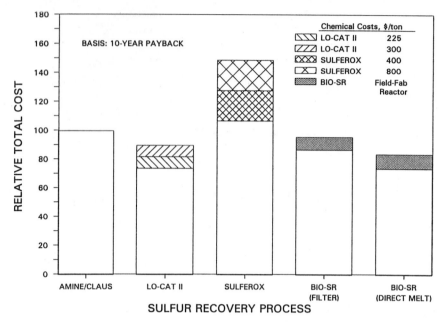

Figure 3.  Comparison of Relative Total Costs to Recover
Sulfur by Different Liquid Redox Processes (10-year Payback)

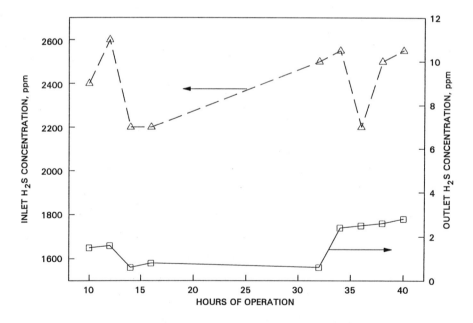

Figure 4. BIO-SR Performance at a Sewage Treatment Plant (Sendai, Japan)

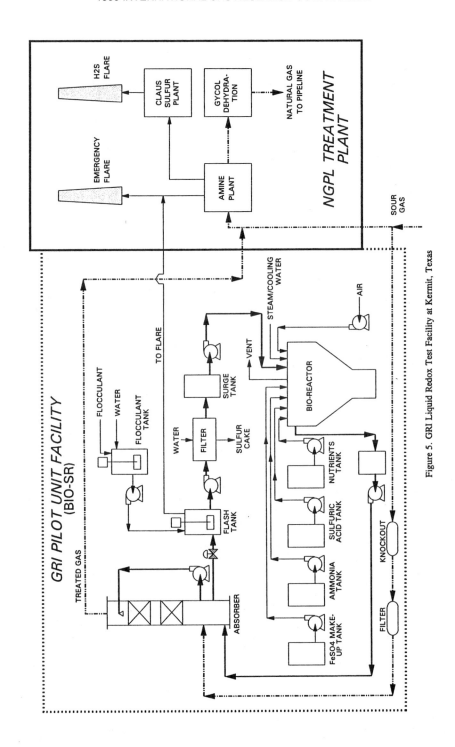

Figure 5. GRI Liquid Redox Test Facility at Kermit, Texas

1995 - International Gas Research Conference

THE ELF ACTIVATED MDEA PROCESS:
NEW DEVELOPMENTS AND INDUSTRIAL RESULTS

LE PROCEDE ELF A LA MDEA ACTIVEE :DEVELOPPEMENTS ET
RESULTATS INDUSTRIELS RECENTS

Jean ELGUE

ELF AQUITAINE PRODUCTION, FRANCE

ABSTRACT

The ELF ACTIVATED MDEA process is the latest development by Elf Aquitaine Production in the field of gas sweetening processes. Compared to the well-known SNPA-DEA process, the new MDEA-based solvents meet the same performance requirements as regards $H_2S$ and $CO_2$ removal, but are far more economic in terms of energy consumption. The adequate activator, chosen among a series of activators, is added to the MDEA solution, at the proper concentration adapted to each specific case. From a practical point of view, most existing MEA or DEA units may easily be retrofitted with the ELF ACTIVATED MDEA process.

The results obtained on industrial units are presented, showing both the high level of performance and the significant reduction in operating costs the ELF ACTIVATED MDEA process procures.

As far as industrial design is concerned, ELF AQUITAINE has made use of its own knowledge in the field of gas-liquid mass transfer with chemical reactions, for computer-aided model calculations extrapolating the laboratory and industrial results.

RESUME

Le procédé à la MDEA ACTIVEE est la plus récente amélioration parmi les procédés d'adoucissement de gaz mise au point par ELF AQUITAINE PRODUCTION. Par rapport au procédé déjà ancien SNPA-DEA, les solvants MDEA ACTIVEE permettent d'atteindre les mêmes degrés d'épuration d'$H_2S$ et de $CO_2$, mais sont beaucoup plus économiques.

Le choix de l'activateur et sa concentration dans la solution de MDEA sont adaptés à chaque cas particulier de traitement.

Dun point de vue pratique, la plupart des installations de lavage à la MEA ou à la DEA peuvent être facilement converties au procédé ELF à la MDEA ACTIVEE.

Cette communication présente les résultats industriels obtenus, en particulier la réduction des coûts de production. Pour la définition des nouvelles installations, ELF AQUITAINE a utilisé ses résultats de recherche en laboratoire, directement extrapolés à l'aide de son simulateur maison.

## PRESENTATION

In the past, Elf Aquitaine has periodically been confronted with the treatment of sour natural gas. The most well-known are:

– the Lacq field (France) in the fifties,
– and the Ram River field (CANADA) in the seventies, with more than 30% $H_2S$.

Similar occurrences may be encountered even now, in prospected zones such as the North Sea or Western Asia (KAZAKHSTAN).

With the general objective of reducing production costs, Elf Aquitaine has been working at improving their amine treatment processes. This particularly involves the $CO_2$ – removal phase. Elimination of $CO_2$ with amines, conventionally using DEA (diethanolamine), is effectively costly in energy because of the high solution enthalpy of $CO_2$ – amine systems.

It is under this context that a new process was industrialised at the Lacq plant, in 1990. The new process is based on the use of an Activated MDEA solvent and rich-amine regeneration system by flash. This significantly reduces the energy consumption in the reboiler.

The final industrial assessment of the 5-year operating period is presented in this paper. It produced several interesting results: a decrease in operating costs, due essentially to reduced energy consumption, for solvent regeneration, but also an increased treatment capacity and enhanced reliability of operation on these old installations, in return of some investments in equipment and control improvements.

## REVAMPING OF LACQ UNITS
## FOR AN ACTIVATED MDEA PROCESS

### The activation principle

One of the problems encountered when basic aqueous solutions are used to absorb gaseous $CO_2$ is the low-rate reaction of $CO_2$ with water, producing carbonic acid. However, this transformation step is inevitable when a carbonate solution (HOT CARBONATE process) or a tertiary amine solution (MDEA process) is used.

With primary or secondary amines, the difficulty lies in the direct reaction between the $CO_2$ and the amine, which produces an amine carbamate. This carbamate reacts with water to form carbonic acid. The reaction mechanisms involved here are complex, and are still within the field of background research.

A basic expression of $CO_2$-amine reactions suffices to understand the activation mechanism, which has been in use for several decades with hot aqueous carbonate solutions [4] and is now used with aqueous MDEA solutions:

reaction with primary or secondary amine:

$$CO_2 + R_2NH \rightleftharpoons R_2NCOO^- + H^+ \qquad (1)$$

carbamate hydrolysis:

$$R_2NCOO^- + H_2O \rightleftharpoons R_2NH + HCO_3^- \qquad (2)$$

Consecutive reactions (1) and (2) can be epitomised as a process which produces carbonic acid, but with much faster reaction rates than direct $CO_2$ - $H_2O$ or $CO_2$ - $OH^-$ reactions.

Nevertheless, since (1) and (2) are balanced reactions, the original quantity of the amine molecule is never totally recovered. This effect is particularly sensitive to high $CO_2$-amine loading.

As the activation process was known, what remained to be done was to find primary or secondary amines with the best kinetic characteristics, physical properties best-adapted to industrial conditions, and the concentrations required to optimise solvent efficiency. The optimisation phase was carried out at the Lacq site, partly under laboratory conditions, and partly on industrial units.

Laboratory tests were used to select amines with carbamate formation rates that could sufficiently activate the $CO_2$ - MDEA reaction. The tests showed, in particular, that several amine families were satisfactory on an industrial scale. The final choice favoured amines with qualities that could help optimise the industrial behaviour of the solvent, rather than the activation performances themselves, which are rather widespread. [2]

**Regeneration by flash**

Regeneration of a rich solvent by pressure draw-down is a common industrial operation, widely used to regenerate physical solvents.

Although the chemical bonds have a negative effect on the flash efficiency, the equilibrium curves of the tertiary amines are favourable enough that degassing by pressure draw-down can yield very good partial regeneration.

This system, already used by BASF for regenerating $CO_2$-rich Activated MDEA in synthesis gas treatment, was applied here for partial regeneration of Activated MDEA containing large amounts of $H_2S$ and $CO_2$, in natural gas treatment.

## Revamping of installations and new performances

The process employed in this system results in the creation of a "precontact" zone in the lower part of the absorber and a second solvent loop, partially regenerated by flash (Figure 1).

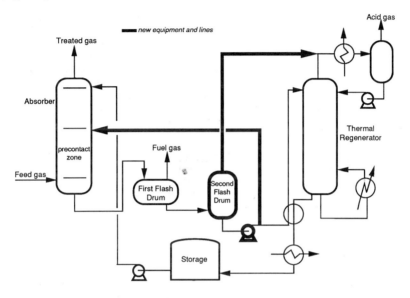

**Figure 1 - Modified process with semi-lean amine regenerated by flash**

The new solvent and regeneration system were tested on a former DEA washing unit. A detailed description of the revamped design of this unit is given in a 19th International Gas Congress publication [1]. Only the essential points are covered in this paper.

A new treatment unit was reconstructed using the old equipment. The new unit comprises two absorption trains and one common thermal regenerator.

Each of the absorbers was equipped with a precontact zone and with a flash-regeneration circuit.

The common regenerator treats the entirety of both amine lean flows injected at the top of each absorber.

This design offers the most efficient use of the thermal regeneration column capacity. The overall result is a 30% increase in total gas-treatment capacity.

A brief list of the recorded performance after revamping (Table 1) illustrates the advantage of using an Activated MDEA solvent and partial regeneration by flash for treating natural gases rich in $H_2S$ or $CO_2$ (Lacq gas: $H_2S$ = 15% vol., $CO_2$ = 10% vol.).

**Table 1**

| Comparative performance | | |
|---|---|---|
| | **Before revamping** | **After revamping** |
| Solvent | DEA | Activated MDEA |
| Absorber pressure ($10^5$ Pa) | 70 | 70 |
| Treated gas:<br>- $H_2S$ ppm vol.<br>- $CO_2$ ppm vol. | < 10<br>< 50 | < 10<br>< 50 |
| Energy consumption per $10^6 Sm^3$ of gas:<br>- reboiling energy (MWh/h)<br>- pump energy (MWh/h) | 10<br>0.46 | 5.40<br>0.83 |

The results procured by revamping reveal an overall 25% decrease in the utilities cost. This result was recorded during a test run at high gas throughput after optimisation of operating conditions.

Nevertheless, the result is closely related to site-specific treatment conditions, notably:

– the raw gas composition,

– treated gas specifications, which are particularly stringent for $CO_2$

Thus, the performance comparison between DEA and Activated MDEA processes cannot be extended to any site. However, with this result as a basis for evaluation, some practical rules can be given, to pinpoint the potential advantage of regeneration by flash:

– the greater the partial pressure of the $H_2S$ and $CO_2$ components in the raw gas, the greater the efficiency of the flash,

In this case, the partial pressure is 18 bar. In comparison with the 2 bar pressure in the flash drum, this gives a ratio of 9. The advantage of regeneration by flash starts at a ratio greater than 3.

– The energy consumption of the activated MDEA process increases as treated gas specifications get more severe, because the portion of rich amine flowrate that is to be thermally regenerated increases very rapidly.

The Activated MDEA process will be effectively energy-efficient when partial $CO_2$ removal only will be required (sale gas specification around 2% $CO_2$). In some cases it might even be possible to completely eliminate thermal regeneration, despite the additional restrictions generated by this option.

## POTENTIALITY FOR OPERATING COST REDUCTION

The industrial development, which began in 1990, rapidly brought to light the potential advantage, in terms of costs, of this process.

Consequently, an in-depth study into production cost reduction was conducted. Three main axes of enhancement were studied:

– improve the control of operations by using a digital control system,

– select the most efficient gas – liquid contactor technology for the activated MDEA

– among families of potential activators, seek out the molecule most adapted to industrial operating conditions at Lacq.

### Optimising Operations

With the addition of a semi-lean amine flow loop, the optimisation and control of operating conditions are theoretically more complex.

Furthermore, to maintain the reliability of the production tool, the design of the new system must reserve the possibility of returning to the initial situation, i.e. a single solvent flow thermally regenerated in the regenerator.

Even more, economic studies show that it is advantageous to make use of the thermal regeneration capacity at its most. In the end, optimisation involved a complex system of two absorber trains, each being able to operate either on the rich amine flash system, or on thermal regeneration only.

The technical solution retained was to equip this installation with a digital control system (DCS). This investment, which was needed because of the complexity of the new system, is now economically advantageous. The most noteworthy points are:

– a decrease in production loss due to delicate operations: the control algorithms are very reliable under complex operations.

– a decrease in the personnel workload.

This work is now followed up by the development of a calculator upstream of the DCS, which would predetermine optimal flowrates for regenerated and semi-regenerated amines, depending on variations in operating parameters. The expected gain is about 10% on the cost of thermal regeneration.

## Structured packing

On the old DEA washing installations, the absorbers were equipped with valve trays or perforated trays. The first results obtained on these columns with the new solvent demonstrated the efficiency of the activator, even for the high objectives that were fixed: less than 100 ppm vol. residual $CO_2$.

A more detailed analysis showed that there was an advantage in increasing the efficiency of the gas-liquid contact so as to be able to tolerate a lower driving force for the mass transfer, and thus to be able to allow higher $CO_2$ loading, all while reducing the solvent flowrate.

This analysis meets with the theoretical considerations: the reactions between $CO_2$ and Activated MDEA are, generally fast, pseudo-first order reactions, represented by simple expressions.

The acceleration of the mass transfer in the liquid film appears to be very close to Hatta's number:

$$H_a = \frac{\sqrt{\mathcal{D}_{co_2} k_1}}{k_L}$$

Using the Lewis film formula, the amount of $CO_2$ transferred is then given as follows:

$$N_{CO_2} = k_L \cdot a \cdot \left( x^{int}_{CO_2} - x^{bulk}_{CO_2} \right) \cdot \frac{\sqrt{\mathcal{D}_{co_2} k_1}}{k_L}$$

hence:

$$N_{CO_2} = \sqrt{\mathcal{D}_{co_2} k_1} \cdot a \cdot \left( x^{int}_{CO_2} - x^{bulk}_{CO_2} \right)$$

This expression demonstrates that, theoretically, the most appropriate type of contactor is the one which has the greatest surface area "a" for given geometric characteristics of the column. The physical mass transfer coefficient, $k_L$, which reflects the molecular diffusion of $CO_2$ in the solvent, and the turbulence of the liquid phase, only has a secondary role in the transfer. Liquid retention has no influence.

Although the trays or packings are known to be well-suited to this kind of mass transfer [3], [5], it has been observed that structured packing, presently used little in absorption under high pressure conditions, simultaneously offers a high surface area and high capacity (Table 2).

The behaviour of the MELLAPAK 250 packing, relative to mass transfer, has been experimentally studied on a pilot installation (column diameter = 30 cm).

The test results were the basis of more in-depth deliberation on how to optimise the process. Use of such packing in replacement of existing perforated trays would effectively reduce the flow of regenerated amine and hence the cost of thermal regeneration.

Once this adaptation was made, the performance tests confirmed that the regenerated amine flowrate was reduced by about 25 - 30 %.

The resulting cost reduction in consumed utilities is about 20 to 25%. In the Lacq context of gas-treatment, this operation turns out to be cost-effective, with the return on investment estimated at about 16 months.

### Table 2

### Geometric area of different types of packing and trays

| Random packing | $m^2 / m^3$ |
|---|---|
| 1" Pall Rings (Metal) | 207 |
| 2" Pall Rings (Metal) | 102 |
| 1" Packing Rings (ceramic) | 190 |
| 2" Packing Rings (ceramic) | 92 |
| **Structured Packing** | $m^2 / m^3$ |
| MELLAPAK 250 | 250 |
| INTALOX 2T | 215 |
| **Trays** | $m^2 / m^3$ * |
| valves (interfacial area) | 50 - 100 |

\* the interfacial area is expressed relative to the full volume of column between 2 successive trays.

### Choice of the best activator

The core of the Activated MDEA process is based on use of MDEA, which allows partial regeneration of the solvent by flash.

As far as the activation is concerned (see § 2.1), its main characteristic is to provide fast absorption of $CO_2$ using the amine carbamate production step.

Several families of molecules are known to have very fast carbamate formation kinetics. For example:

– polyalkylene polyamines and especially polyethylene polyamines (primary amines)

– piperazine and its derivatives (secondary amines and / or primary amines)

– alkyl alcanolamines and, more specifically, alkyl ethanolamines (secondary amines)

However, use of an activator in an industrial context requires a certain number of additional constraints, which are often determining elements in the final choice:

- complete miscibility with water and with MDEA

- lack of sensitivity to thermal deterioration

- no degradation with impurities in the gas (for example, no degradation products with COS).

- low vapour tension

- availability on the market

- low cost

- etc.

The choice of an activator is directed first by the sweetening specifications required and also by the particular operating conditions of the treatment (pressure, temperature, impurities in the raw gas, location of the site, etc.). This has been studied in detail and the advantages and disadvantages of each activator product are now well known. The activator selected for use at Lacq was subject to losses by vapour tension in the gas at the top of the absorber, due to high pressure-temperature conditions (75 bar, 60°C). Among the possible solutions available to reduce these losses, the most economical (and instructive) was to change the activator. But could the activator product be changed on the industrial unit without generating operating problems ? Since the new activator had similar reaction rates to the first, the industrial operation was organised in a very simple manner, by continuous injection of the replacement product in the solvent loops. During the transition period, 2 activator products were present simultaneously. This had no adverse effects on the performance. No production decrease was observed and the behaviour of the new solvent was found to be comparable to the old one.

## CONCLUSIONS

The results related here essentially concern practical problems of the Operator, in using a relatively new type of process and also using an amine mixture, Activated MDEA, as the solvent.

Actually, there is great energy-saving potential in using solvent regeneration by flash.

Modelling of this kind of process is very easy to handle and provides information on rich amine flash efficiency that is accurate enough to estimate its economic interest.

The conclusions gathered from this industrial experiment at the Lacq site are highly instructive in this area: the new Activated MDEA process is well appreciated by the operators who are used to working on DEA washing units. The quality of the amine mixture can be easily followed and controlled. It has also been demonstrated that the strong component in this solvent really is the MDEA and that the activator product can be changed without generating adverse effects in the process.

## REFERENCES

1- PEYTAVY, J. ELGUE, Y. CARTRON, "ELF Activated MDEA: an important improvement in natural gas sweetening process", 19th WORLD GAS CONFERENCE (1994)

2- EUROPEAN PATENT APPLICATION n° 89401397.8 (Pub. n° 0348251)

3- PEYTAVY, M.H. HUOR, R. BUGAREL, A. LAURENT, "Interfacial area and gas side mass transfer coefficient of gas-liquid absorption column", Chem. Eng. Processing, 1990, n°27, pp. 155 - 163

4- MADDOX, "Gas and Liquid Sweetening", Third Edition, 1982, edited by CAMPBELL PETROLEUM SERIES

5- Ch. PONDEBAT, J.L. PEYTAVY, M.H. HUOR, M. PREVOST, A. LAURENT, "Hydrodynamics of a gas-liquid column equipped with structured packing", DISTILLATION AND ABSORPTION, BIRMINGHAM, Sept. 1992

EXPERIENCE OF DEVELOPMENT AND INDUSTRIAL
APPLICATION OF THE ADSORPTION PROCESS AT
GAS FIELD

ELABORATION ET MISE EN EXPLOITATION DU PROCESSUS
D'ADSORPTION DE PRÉPARATION DE GAZ SUR LES CHANTIERS

Lakeev V.P.

Russia

## ABSTRACT

Comprehensive investigations were carried out at the laboratory,
pilot and pilot-industrial units in order to work out adsorption
process of gas site preparation of the Northern fields of Siberia.
Adsorption and desorption of water vapours at zeolites, silicagel and
aluminium oxide were investigated in the widerange of pressure and
temperatures, including also the temperatures lower than 0°C. During
these investigations, humidity desorption mechanism was established
from adsorbents layer in the. regeneration gas hot stream. The results
of investigations were used for designing Messojacha gas preparation
unit. With the help of zeolites and units of silicagel gas drying at
Medveja. Below described are the results of these investigations and
operation experience of industrial units at Messojacha and Medveja.

## RÉSUMÉ

Des études approfondies ont été effectuées dans les laboratoires des
installations pilotes et au niveau des installations experimentales sur les
chantiers afin d'élaborer le processus d'adsorption pour la préparation de
gaz sur les chantiers du Nord de la Sibérie. A cet effet on a étudie
l'adsorption et la désorption des vapeurs d'eau sur les zeolithes, sur le
sélicogèle et sur l'oxyde d'aluminium dans une large gamme de pressions et de
temperatures y compris les temperatures au-dessous de 0°C.Au cours de ces
recherches on a réussi à determiner le mécanisme de la desorption de
l'humidité à partir de la couche d'adsorbants dans le courant de gaz chaud de
la regénération. Les résultats de ces recherches ont été utilisés lors de
l'élaboration du projet d'installation de rechauffement de gaz du gisement de
Messojacha en utilisant les zéolithes et le sechage à l'aide de sélicogeles
sur le gisement de Medveja. Le present rapport donne des précisions sur les
résultats de ces recherches et sur l'expérience d'exploitation des
installations industrielles au niveau de gisements de Messojacha et Medveja.

INTRODUCTION

Extensive research on the laboratory, pilot and semiindustrial units has resulted in the development of a dry-disiccant adsorption process for gas field applications in the northern districts of Siberia. The adsorption and desorption of water was studied in the wide range of pressures and temperatures, including the temperature below 0°C. During this experiments was discovered mechanism desorption of water from layer of desiccant in the hot gas stream. The result of this research has been used to design industrial units and to develop statue to operate it. This units had been built at the Messojacha and Medveja gas fields. The Messojacha's unit was built to dry natural gas and to extract methanol from it and use methanol again. At the Medveja field now operating are five dry bed desiccant units by the capacity 120x10$^6$ cu. m per day. This units were constructed by the french firm "CresoLaure enterprise" and have equipment which was made by the german firm "Bomac". At the same time with the water from the natural gas is extracting heavy hydrocarbons, the temperature evaporation of which is higher than regeneration gas temperature. Silicagel is an adsorbent, which is used here. Service life of it limited by the mechanical stability of the granules, but adsorptive capacity is enough high duration 4-5 years and dew point of dry gas is lower than minus 30° C.

The main criterion while selecting the method of gas site preparation is the gas dew point in terms of water and hydrocarbons. After discovering the first northern fields of Messojacha and Medveja, it was then planned that gas gathering and transportation will be done by pipelines (surface and underground) and, therefore, actual gas temperature will be equal to the ambient temperature, which in winter time drops down to minus 40°-60° C. In this connection the adsorption process of gas site treatment for the above fields was selected. Later on, the decision was made: to dry gas of the northern fields to the dew point not higher than minus 30° C. And, finally, at the present time, after accumulating the northern fields operation experience, it was admitted sufficient to dry gas in winter to the dew point not higher than minus 20° C and in summer not higher than minus 10° C. In this connection at the other fields, put into operation later, glycol gas drying is used, which provides the specified depth of drying.

ADSORBENTS

All the investigations were done on the home-made adsorbent:

- synthetic zeolite NaA$_1$ without binding inert material;

- synthetic zeolite NaA$_2$ with binding inert material;

- small pore silicagel KSM;

- aluminium oxide Sferal IT;

- aluminium oxide A-2.

EQUILIBRIUM AND DYNAMIC ADSORPTION OF WATER VAPOURS

Fig.1 shows isotherms of water vapours adsorption on the adsorbents at 25° C.

While studying the water adsorption in dynamic conditions, the inlet curves of methane drying were taken at various velocities of gas stream, various humidity and heights of adsorbents layer. It was found out, that, the depth of methane drying by zeolites corresponds to the dew point minus 59° C - lower minus 72° C, by silicagel minus 57°-68° C, aluminium  oxide minus 50°-68° C.

As it is seen from Fig.2, the greatest degree of the use of the boundary adsorption capacity at the work in the layer, has silicagel followed by aluminium oxide and zeolite. Therefore, water vapours adsorption velocity at zeolite from methane stream is less than at silicagel and aluminium oxide. Concerning the zeolite working layer height (zone of mass-transfer), than at the temperature lower than 25° C, it drastically increases, and in the range 25°-50° C remain minimum and practically permanent (~1.5 cm).

Thus, natural gas zeolite drying optimum temperature is the temperature not lower than 20°-25° C.

Experiments on methane drying by adsorbents at the temperatures lower than 0° C were done at 0°, -10°, -20° C. It was found out that silicagel grains even at 0° C crack and go to pieces, so silicagel was not tested at -10° and -20° C. All the adsorbents at these temperatures dry methane to the dew point minus 50°-60° C. Here it turned out that the humid capacity of adsorbents at 0° C is 4-5 times less than at -10° and -20° C. Adsorbents humid capacity before the coming through at 0o C showed to be 3-5 times less than the humid capacity at the layer operation till the complete saturation occurs and was, respectively, was zeolite with binding 3.0 and 9.4 % of mass, for aluminium oxide 2.6 and 10.9 % of mass and for silicagel 3.0 and 9.4 % of mass.

HUMIDITY DESORPTION FROM ADSORBENTS

Humidity desorption investigations was done from zeolite layer with binding and aluminium oxide A-2 in the stream of the heated methane. It was stated that heat exchange between gas and adsorbent in the process of humidity desorption is charactesed by 3 successive periods: temperature front formation along the height of sorbent layer, shift of this front along the layer with constant speed and, finally, the period of step by step damping. 3 periods of humidity desorption from adsorbent layer correspond to the 3 periods of heat exchange. During formation and attenuation of temperature front, the humidity volume, desorbed from adsorbents layer is insignificant. The main humidity amount is recovered from adsorbents during the temperature front shift around the layer. Humidity desorption velocity during this time is maximum and constant that latter fact is illustrated by Fig.3.

ADSORPTION INDUSTRIAL IMPLEMENTATION

Fig.4 and 5 show technological scheme of Messojacha unit of drying and methanol recovery from gas and scheme of technological train of gas silicagel drying units at Medveja. The mechanism of coadsorption of water and methanol vapours is quite clear from outlet curves of laboratory experiment (Fig.6) and adsorption cycle in adsorber A-1 (Fig.7), the main parameters of which are shown in Table 1. Messojacha unit has been operated for 5 years, only one loading of zeolite NaA with binding was used.

TABLE **1**. METHANOL AND WATER RECOVERY BY ZEOLITE NAA AT MESSOJACHA
(A-1 - A-4 - ADSORBERS; 1,2 - CYCLES)

| Parameters | A-1 | | A-2 | | A-3 | | A-4 | |
|---|---|---|---|---|---|---|---|---|
| | 1 | 2 | 1 | 2 | 1 | 2 | 1 | 2 |
| Break through, h | 36 | – | 48 | – | – | – | 48 | – |
| Cycle time, h | 58 | 24 | 58 | 20 | 24 | 24 | 70 | 20 |
| Dew point, °C | -49 | -55 | -60 | -60 | -49 | -48 | -48 | -45 |
| Water/methanol in desorption condensate | 84/16 | 59/41 | 78/22 | 53/47 | 88/12 | 50/50 | 96/4 | 45/55 |
| Zeolite capacity for desorption condensate, % of weight | 17.9 | 11.5 | 18.1 | 7.2 | 18.2 | 10.1 | 22 | 9.45 |
| Zeolite for water (before coming through), % of weight | 12.9 | – | 15.3 | – | 12.4 | – | 12.8 | – |

Comparison of adsorption parameters at zeolite from Messojacha units adsorber after 2.5 years of operation and the initial parameters are shown in Table **2**.

TABLE **2**.

| | Zeolite gone through operation | | Initial zeolite | |
|---|---|---|---|---|
| | water/methanol vapours | water vapours | water/methanol vapours | water vapours |
| Dew point, °C | -56 | -57 | -52 | -54 |
| Capacity before breake through weight, %: | | | | |
|   methanol | 11.7 | – | 11.3 | – |
|   water | – | 15.8 | – | 18 |

Thus zeolite NAA with the binding during long operation time high adsorption properties for water and methanol vapours.

Gas silicagel drying units operation at Medveja showed that in the presence of highboiling hydrocarbons vapours, natural gas is dried to the dew point minus (32-52)° C. Simultaneously with water vapours silicagel recovers from gas also those hydrocarbons. Fig. 8 and 9 show the hydrocarbons desorption curves and fractions composition of hydrocarbons samples, selected in the process of regeneration from separator 6 (Fig. 5). Sample 1, selected in the moment II, when the get inlet temperature and outlet temperature from the desorber was amounting to 70° C and 140° C respectively, is boiling away within the limits 160-270° C. Hypothetically this occurrence could be explained by the fact, that obviously high boiling hydrocarbons vapours are in the adsorbent pores not in the form of free liquid but in the state of liquefied vapour. Besides, desorbing matter is methane, i.e. homogenuous substance, from which earlier in the stage of adsorption, moleculas of these hydrocarbons diffused into the silicagel pores. So for hydrocarbon moleculas transit from silicagel pores into regeneration gas stream it was enough to increase, these moleculas activation energy with simultaneous reduction of surface adsorption forces effect by means of silicagel. Increased, compared to adsorption cycle, temperature of regeneration gas provides for the process of all such occurrences. Due to taht, eliminated is the irreversible accumulation of highboiling hydrocarbons moleculas in the silicagel pores and their ckaking with carbon formation.

SOME TECHNICAL-ECONOMIC PARAMETERS OF GAS DRYING AT MEDVEJA

At Medveja, 5 units of silicagel drying and 4 units of 4 gas drying by diethyleneglycol are constructed and operated. Each unit of silicagel drying has 4 technological trains with the capacity of $6.0-6.6 \times 10^6$ m$^3$/day. The units of glycol drying have 10 to 20 trains with productivity $3 \times 10^6$ m$^3$/day. Construction experience and first 10 years of operation of Medveja showed that technological equipment units and its weight in the process of adsorption drying is 2 times less than in the glycol process (35 against 65 and 419576 ton against 815519.1 ton). Later on from the units of silicagel drying excluded were the regeneration gas blower and the amount of the equipment units reduced down to 29; after the glycol drying units modernization, the equipment weight also reduced to 633980.4 ton. These figures refer to the equivalent units productivity equal to $24 \times 10^6$ m$^3$/day. Here not taken into account is the boilers equipment, necessary for glycol regeneration. Specific costs for silicagel turned out to be 8-10 times less, than for glycol, power consumption is also 2 times less than at gas drying by silicagel, after elimination of gas blowers from the scheme it became even less.

If we take into account that at the equivalent amount of dried gas ($24 \times 10^6$ m$^3$/day) at the units of silicagel drying, 4-5 m$^3$ of HC condensate is recovered, and at the glycol - only 0.6-0.8 m$^3$, than adsorption drying parameters look even more attractive.

And finally adsorption drying of gas at the sites is an ecologically pure process. The major drawback of adsorption process is periodical character and presence of a big amount of shut-off valves.

Besides, at the parameters of dried gas close to the equilibrium conditions of hydrate formation, the process parameters for the gas drying depth and drastically aggravated. Application of inhibitors of hydrateformation in this case doesn't solve the problem and the heating of gas will result in capital expenses increase and operation costs. It stimulated the glycol drying process improvement and its application at the other northern fields.

* Domestic adsorbents: zeolites NAA, small-pore silicagel, aluminium oxide provide for quality gas preparation for transport at the site.

* Temperature of dried gas should exceed the hydrateformation equilibrium temperature for 5-10° C. At gas parameters, close to hydrateformation equilibrium conditions, gas drying depth by silicagel is increased to minus 8-12° C. Dynamic humid capacity of zeolite and silicagel also reduced for 3-4 times.

* Zeolite and silicagel service life is about 5 years with drying properties preservation and is limited to going to pieces and mechanical grains wear.

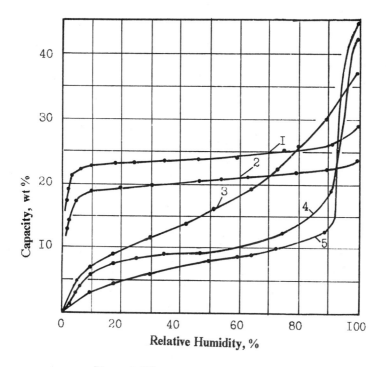

Figure 1. Water capacity of adsorbents:
1. Zeolite $NaA_1$;
2. Zeolite $NaA_2$;
3. Silicagel;
4. Aluminagel Spheral 1T;
5. Aluminagel A-2.

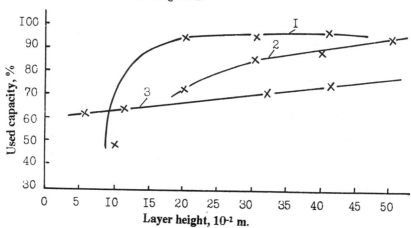

Figure 2. Dependence of used desiccant capacity on layer height.
1. Silicagel; 2. Aluminagel; 3. Zeolite NaA1

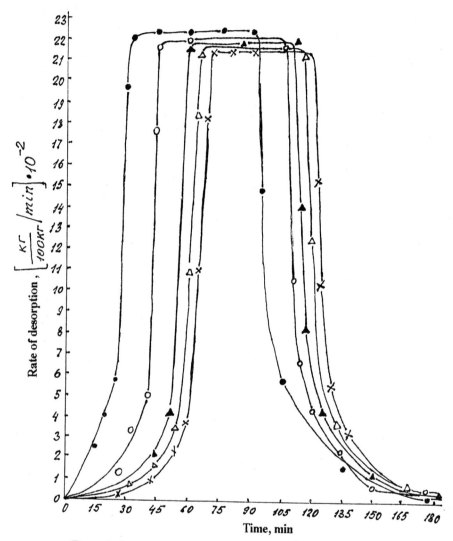

**Figure 3. Rate desorption of water from zeolite NaA₁ under 300⁰C.**
●- 0,1 MPa; O- 1,5 MPa; ▲ - 2,5 MPa;△ - 3,5MPa; ✕ -4,5 MPa.

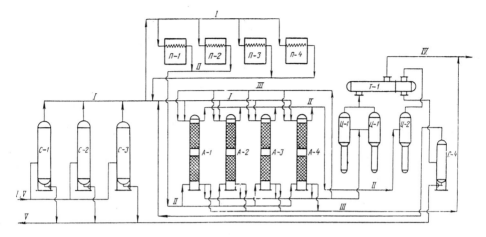

**Figure 4. Flow chart of Messojacha unit.**
C-1,2,3 - feed gas separators; П-1,2 - regeneration gas
heater; П-3,4 - feed gas heater; A-1 - A-4 - adsorbers;
Ц-1,2 - dust catcher; C-4 - regeneration gas separator;
T-1 - heat exchanger; *I* - feed gas; *II* - regeneration gas;
*III* - cooling gas; *IV* - dry gas; *V* - water solution of me-
thanol.

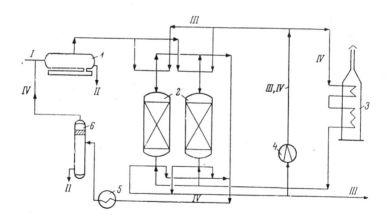

**Figure 5. Flow chart of Medveja dry deciccant unit (technological line).**
1,6 - feed and gas regeneration separators; 2 - adsorbers;
3 - heater; 4 - compression pump; 5 - air cooler; *I* - feed gas;
*II* - water and heavy hydrocarbons; *III,IV* - dry, regenerating,
cooling gas.

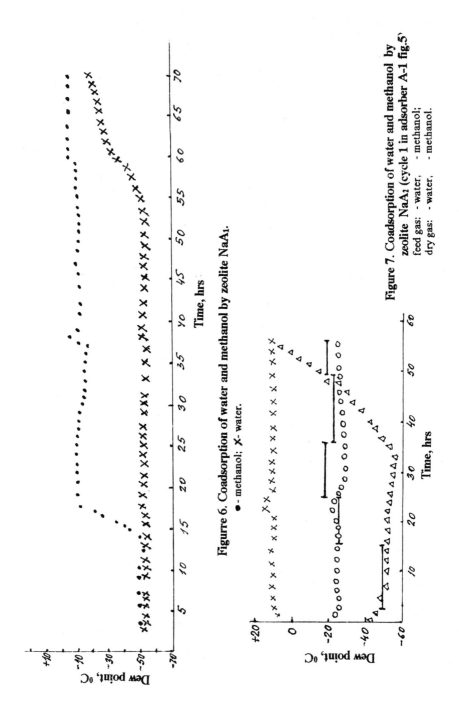

Figurre 6. Coadsorption of water and methanol by zeolite NaA₁.
●- methanol; ✗- water.

Figure 7. Coadsorption of water and methanol by zeolite NaA₂ (cycle 1 in adsorber A-1 fig.5)
feed gas:  ✗- water,   △- methanol;
dry gas:   ✗- water,   ○- methanol.

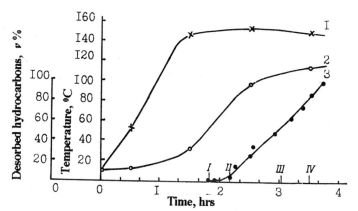

**Figure 8. Desorbtion of hydrocarbons from silicagel .**
1,2 - gas regeneration temperature before and after
adsorber; 3 - volume of desorbed hydrocarbons;
*I* - appearance of hydrocarbons in separator 6,
*II,III,IV* - samples 1,2,3 (fig.9) , *IV* - appearance of
water in separator 6.

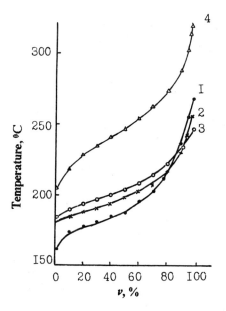

**Figure 9. Curves of boiling hydrocarbons.**
1,2,3 - samples from separator 6
(fig.5); 4 - sample from separator 1.

NATURAL GAS SWEETENING:
THERMODYNAMIC PROPERTIES EVALUATION

DÉACIDIFICATION DU GAZ NATUREL:
ÉVALUATION DES PROPRIÉTÉS THERMODYNAMIQUES

Jeffrey L. Savidge
Gas Research Institute, USA

Lloyd L. Lee, Li-Jun Lee, and Dhananjay Ghonasgi
University of Oklahoma, USA

## ABSTRACT

Gas sweetening represents a 2.2 billion dollar industry in the U.S.A. with annual investments of 40 million dollars. Thermodynamic modeling is needed for process design and operation. An accurate correlation, *ElecGC*, for aqueous amine solutions is developed in this work. It can handle high loading (up to $L = 1.6$) as well as low loading ($L = 0.02$) cases of acid gas. We calculate for the vapor-liquid equilibria of $CO_2$ and $H_2S$ in aqueous MDEA (methyldiethanolamine), DEA (diethanolamine), and MEA (monoethanolamine) at process conditions. *ElecGC* yields speciation of the ionic and molecular species. We show that speciation is at the center of the understanding and control of acid gas treating. Speciation determines the reaction rates. Enthalpy of reaction actually contributes to more than 90% of the total energy requirements. Mass transfer of $CO_2$ and $H_2S$ is increased across the vapor-liquid interface because of the depletion of the molecular species by reactions. As a consequence, this research offers the benefits of process optimization, energy savings, enhancement of absorption, lower corrosion, pinch-point breaking , reduction of VOC emission, formulation of amine blends, and selection of new amines.

## RÉSUMÉ

La déacidification du gaz naturel représente aux USA une industrie remontant à 2.2 billion dollars avec invêtissements annuels au niveau de 40 milliards. Une modélisation thermodynamique *ElecGC* est développée pour les solutions aqueuses des amines qui traite précisément les processus. Des calculs sont effectués pour l'équilibre de phases vapeur-liquide de $CO_2$ et de $H_2S$ dans les amines MDEA, DEA, et MEA de concentrations à partir de L=0.02 jusqu'à L=1.6. Nous montrons que la spéciation est au centre de la compréhension et du contrôle de l'efficace de l'opération. Par conséquent, on profite de l'optimisation du processus, l'épargne d'énergie, l'augmentation d'absorption, corrosion abaissée, emission réduite, et sélection des amines en formule.

## INTRODUCTION

The purpose of this paper is to elucidate the use of accurate thermodynamic modeling for prediction of the vapor-liquid equilibria, enthalpy of absorption, and P-v-T behavior of aqueous amine solutions during acid gas treating. These quantities are responsible for the mechanical and chemical driving forces that enable the removal of the acid gases $CO_2$ and $H_2S$ from the natural gas stream. In addition, we show that speciation is the key to the control of acid gas treating processes.

In 1991 GRI (Gas Research Institute, USA) initiated an integrated research program on the thermodynamic, transport and kinetic properties of acid gases with mixed amine solutions. The objective of the program is to provide a basis for the industry to optimize existing processes and to design for new amine processes. To achieve this goal, GRI sponsored research to obtain specific physical and chemical property data to support development of rigorous thermodynamic and kinetic models for use in process design, analyses, and modeling. The present work is a key element of the program based on new and highly sophisticated thermodynamic models for the studies of vapor-liquid equilibria and thermodynamic properties of amine solutions in gas sweetening operations.

## OVERVIEW

The solubility and amounts of acid gas removed are determined by the vapor pressures upon vapor-liquid equilibrium over the aqueous amine solutions at the top of the absorber tower. Thermodynamic modeling is used to determine the equilibria. At the University of Oklahoma, a fundamental thermodynamic model, *ElecGC*, for electrolyte solutions, is developed. This model combines the mean spherical approach (MSA) in statistical mechanics (1) and the group contribution theory (2-4) to treat the ions, amines, and molecular species in the acid gas solutions. This model has been applied to some 40 acid gas $CO_2$-$H_2S$/amine systems including MDEA (methyldiethanolamine), DEA (diethanolamine), MEA (monoethanolamine) and their blends. The predictive results are highly accurate. The conditions cover

(1) top and bottom of the absorber
  $290 < T$ (K) $< 350$,
  $1 < P$ (bar) $< 70$,
  with acid gas partial pressures for the absorber
  H2S   3E-5 $< P$ (bar) $< 1.4$E-2
  CO2   7E-4 $< P$ (bar) $< 7$;
(2) top and bottom of the regenerator
  $270 < T$(K) $< 390$
  with acid gas partial pressures and loadings for stripper conditions over the ra:._.
    H2S:
  .02 mol H2S/mol amine to 1.6/1,
    CO2:
  .02 mol CO2/mol amine to 1.6/1.

Figure 1 provides a schematic of a general amine treating unit. Absorption of acidic gas in gas treating is achieved by contacting the acidic components in with the basic aqueous amine solution in the absorber. This is followed by an amine regeneration step in the amine stripper. The absorber generally operates at the pressure and temperature of the inlet gas stream. Pressures typically range from 5 bar to over 70 bar. The gas enters the bottom of the absorber and flows upward, contacting the amine solution which flows counter-currently. Contact is achieved either through the use of packing or trays in the absorber.

The rich amine solution leaving the bottom of the absorber flows to a flash tank operated at relatively low pressure, and then to a heat exchanger where its temperature is increased to around 366 K. It is then sent to the stripper or regenerator. The chemical reactions which occurs in the absorber are reversed with increased temperature and reduced pressure in the regenerator. This liberates the acid gases. Lean solvent is then cooled and pumped back to the top of the absorber to 14 bar in the bottom of the absorber. $CO_2$ partial pressures range from 7E-4 to 7 bar in the bottom of the absorber.

Aqueous alkanolamines have been used over fifty years to remove sour gas constituents in industrial gas purification applications. The common amines are MEA, DEA, diglycolamine (DGA), MDEA, and diisopropanolamine (DIPA). Recently amine blends, consisting of MDEA and formulations with DEA and MEA, have received significant attention because they offer important gas treating advantages over single amines. The advantages include:
- low energy requirements for regeneration,
- optimal acid gas solubilities,
- low solvent losses,
- low inert gas solubilities,
- reduced need for reclaimer,
- flexibility for solution swaps and revamping of existing facilities,
- easy biodegradation,
- and lower toxicity.
- reduced capital cost for new treating applications by producing more accurate designs;
- identifications of opportunities for selective treating which minimize operating costs by slipping
      $CO_2$ in the absorber;
- avoiding capital and operating costs in the sulfur recovery and tail gas clean-up facilities,
- improved Claus feed,
- improved process selection for any gas sweetening applications.


## THERMODYNAMIC MODELING

We have developed a state-of-the-art electrolyte model for high ionic strength solutions coupled with a group contribution approach for the amine moieties to accurately predict the thermal, phase, and solubility properties of mixed acid gases in blended amine solutions. The model is referred to as *ElecGC* (the Electrolyte Group Contributions). The purpose of the model is to reliably predict vapor-liquid equilibria (salting-out), heats of absorption, hydrocarbon solubility, chemical speciation as functions of temperature, pressure and loadings of mixed acid gases in aqueous solutions of single and blended amines. Our model provides for the first time a framework for integrating both equilibrium and kinetic properties of a wide variety of reactive and neutral solvents including the amines and alkanolamines used in the natural gas and petroleum industries.

*ElecGC* is based on molecular thermodynamics principles, with wide applicability (high ionic strengths, correct ionic size effects, and modular group contributions without binary interaction parameters). It can be used to accurately predict the activities and speciation of the 12 to 14 species present in the amine solution. A schematic description of the mechanisms by which acid gas is absorbed is provided in Figure 2. The species produced are shown in Figure 3, as a gas bubble rises in the liquid solution. Basically, the reaction of hydrogen sulfide with all aqueous alkanolamines (MEA, DEA, and MDEA) is essentially the same. It proceeds through an almost instantaneous proton transfer reaction with a theoretical maximum molar ratio of one mole $H_2S$ to one mole of amine. The removal of $H_2S$ from the gas is limited by mass transfer from the gas into the liquid. Carbon dioxide reacts at finite rates with alkanolamines. With MEA and DEA, $CO_2$ reacts to form a carbamate. The carbamate reaction is slow. With MDEA, by contrast, $CO_2$ dissociates to from bicarbonate with MDEA serving as a proton acceptor from water. Because tertiary amines do not react directly with $CO_2$ they can be used in combination with more reactive amines to achieve selective removal of $H_2S$ over $CO_2$. If process conditions are not right, the solution chemistry of $CO_2$ absorption may lead to the protonation of all the available amine and a subsequent reversal of the $H_2S$ reactions. This will result in the desorption of $H_2S$ from solution. The variation of $CO_2$ reaction rate and mass transfer with amine type provides the basis for selective removal.

The center piece for the understanding and control of gas treating is *speciation* (distribution of species concentrations in solution at a given temperature and pressure). The limit of speciation is given by solution thermodynamics modeling. Figure 3 shows the species that are produced by chemical reactions during acid gas absorption upon vapor-liquid contact. There are about 11-14 species, ionic and neutral, from dissociation of acid gases ($CO_2$, $H_2S$, $CO_2/H_2S$) in contact with various aqueous solutions of single and mixed amines (MDEA, DEA, and MEA). The mass transfer of $CO_2$ and $H_2S$ through the vapor-liquid interfaces is enhanced due to chemical reactions in the liquid phase that remove rapidly the molecular carbon dioxide/hydrogen sulfide in the bulk. The reaction rates are determined by the activities (or compositions) of the species in the bulk solution. This reactive removal increases the concentration gradient ($|C_{Ai} - C_{A,bulk}|$), thus accelerates the mass transfer (gas absorption). The ratio of the absorption rates before and after the reactions is called the enhancement factor, $E$. Thus speciation information is important in determining enhancement and reaction rates. The total enthalpy consists of three contributions: nonideal mixing, gas-liquid dissolving, and chemical reactions in the liquid phase. The chemical component of enthalpy is huge: amounting to 80-90% of the total enthalpies required. Thus knowing the extent of reaction will yield essentially the enthalpy of absorption. Figure 4 shows the relative importance of the three major contributions to the total enthalpy: mixing, dissolving, and reaction for aqueous MDEA/CO$_2$ solution. Here the reactive part is about 85 - 95 % of the total enthalpy. Since this enthalpy of reaction can be determined from the speciation data, we can estimate with high accuracy the total enthalpy consumption..

Our model can directly predict the vapor-liquid equilibria of aqueous amine solutions. Figure 5 shows the results for aqueous MDEA/CO$_2$ system at 28$^\circ$ C. Side by side is plotted the speciation data of the same system. We note the molecular CO$_2$ concentration (moles/liter) in the liquid solution: at low loading (moles CO$_2$/mole of amine), CO$_2$ concentration is very low (1.0E-5). Thus the CO$_2$ gas is absorbed readily from the vapor phase via steep concentration gradient. As the loading increases, CO$_2$ concentration in liquid also increases. MDEA is protonated to MDEA-H+ in order to neutralize the bicarbonate ions generated. However, as loading reaches 0.6-0.7, the molecular CO$_2$ concentration shows marked increase. This signals the onset of rapid vapor pressure increases of CO$_2$ in the gas phase. It also signifies that additional CO$_2$ is now only weakly absorbed by chemical means. The mechanism starts to shift from chemical absorption (due to exhaustion of basic amine species) to physical absorption (by increased pressure). This is clearly seen in the vapor pressure vs. loading chart of Figure 5. Beyond L=0.7, CO$_2$ partial pressure increases precipitously (with steep slope). Beyond L=1, MDEA is used up (mostly in protonated form). No more protonation is possible. CO$_2$ is absorbed predominantly by the mechanical pressure driving force. Thus the vapor phase pressure of CO$_2$ also increases exponentially.

## CONCLUSIONS

We have shown that our thermodynamic model (in a group contribution MSA framework - namely, *ElecGC*) accurately predicts a wide variety of physical properties of high ionic strength solutions of mixed acid gases and blended amines. The properties predicted include the vapor-liquid equilibria, heats of absorption, P-v-T values, and speciation. We have demonstrated clearly that *ElecGC* reliably predicts chemical speciation, provides accurate evaluation of heats of absorption, and determines the coupling of these quantities to changes in the vapor pressures of soluble gas constituents. In addition, our methodology for the first time delineates the linkage of equilibrium and kinetic properties necessary for enhancement factor prediction. The factors (5-6) which determine capital and operating costs are related to the driving force for mass transfer of acid gas from the vapor to liquid phase and to the energy requirements to strip the acidic constituents. Reactive solvents, such as the amines, increase the solvent capacity and rate of mass transfer by reducing the concentration of free acid gas in the bulk solution. This significantly increases the driving force for mass transfer over physical solubility by providing greater concentration gradients. Because of the high heats of solution, reactive amines also increase the energy required to regenerate the solution relative to physical solvents. Enhancement factors are used to provide a measure of the relative mass transfer due to reaction plus physical solubility over physical solubility alone. An accurate knowledge of the enhancement factor is essential to rate-based modeling and predictions of column performance. These quantities dictate the capital and operating costs in gas sweetening plants, especially relating to the height of the tower, solvent/feed rates, and regeneration costs. Our thermodynamic model directly addresses these issues and contributes to their solution.

## ACKNOWLEDGMENTS

The authors wish to express their appreciation to GRI and GPA for support of this project.

**REFERENCES**

1. K. L. Gering, L. L. Lee, L. H. Landis,  J. L. Savidge,  "a molecular approach to electrolyte solutions: phase behavior and activity coefficients for mixed-salt and multisolvent systems", Fluid Phase Equil. **48**, 111, 1989

2. L. L. Lee and J. M. Haile, "group contribution methods for molecular mixtures. I. interaction site models", Fluid Phase Equil. **43**, 231, 1988

3. C. Massobrio, J. M. Haile, L. L. Lee, "group contribution methods for molecular mixtures. II. computer simulation results", Fluid Phase Equil. **44**, 145, 1988

4. J. M. Haile, L. L. Lee, "group contribution methods for molecular mixtures. III. solution of groups tested via computer simulation", Fluid Phase Equil. **44**, 175, 1988

5. H. Meyer, J. Gomez, "GRI programs in sulfur removal and recovery - 1995 update" proceedings of  74th annual gas processors association, march 13-15, 1995.

6. D. Leppin, et al., "GRI programs in H2S scavenging - 1995 update" proceedings of 74th annual gas processors association, march 13-15, 1995.

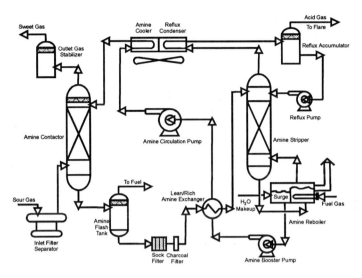

**Figure 1.  Conventional Amine Treating System Schematic.**

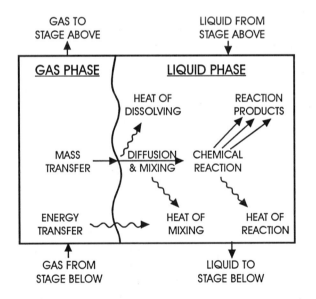

**Figure 2. Interfacial Transport in Acid Gas Absorption.**

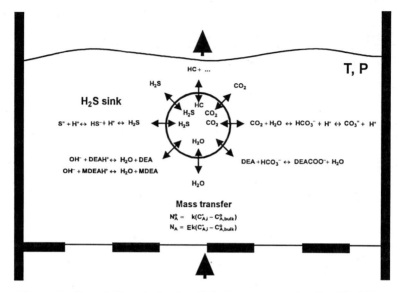

**Figure 3.  Speciation in Amine Solutions around a Gas Bubble.**

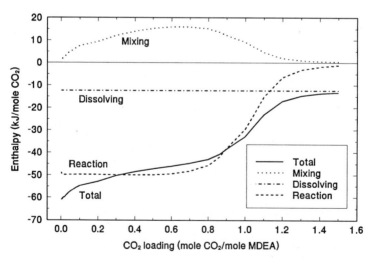

**Figure 4. Heats of Absorption as Composed of Mixing, Dissolving and Reaction. (CO2 in 50wt%MDEA at 77C)**

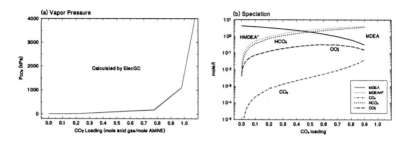

**Figure 5. Effect of Speciation on Vapor Pressure of CO2 in 50wt% MDEA at 28C (Note the CO2 molecular concentration changes in figure b)**

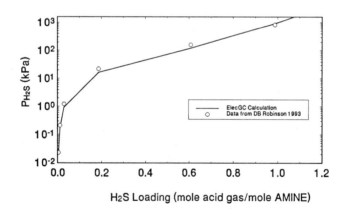

H2S Loading (mole acid gas/mole AMINE)

Figure 6. Vapor Pressure of H₂S in MDEA 50wt% solution at 70°C

A GENERAL PURPOSE COMPUTATIONAL FLUID DYNAMIC CODE
AND ITS APPLICATION TO SAFETY PROBLEMS

PROGICIEL UNIVERSEL DE DYNAMIQUE DES FLUIDES ET SON
APPLICATION AUX PROBLÈMES DE SÉCURITÉ

K.P. Dimitriadis and M. Fairweather
British Gas plc, Gas Research Centre, Loughborough LE11 3QU, U.K.

S.A.E.G. Falle and J.R. Giddings
Mantis Numerics Ltd., 46 The Calls, Leeds LS2 7EY, U.K.

ABSTRACT

A novel computational fluid dynamic code is described
in terms of is general capabilities, and the numerical
and physical sub-models embodied within it.    Its
ability to predict a wide variety of safety related
problems of importance to the gas industry is
demonstrated through its application to gas dispersion,
gas build-up, fire and explosion problems.  Comparison
of model predictions is made with data obtained from
both small and large scale experiments.   Overall, the
paper demonstrates that the code represents a uniquely
powerful fluid flow modelling capability, and
illustrates its ability to predict not only the details
of a given flow but also its usefulness for providing
predictions for use in consequence and risk assessments
of real industrial plant.

RÉSUMÉ

Une description est faite des capacités générales du
nouveau progiciel de dynamique des fluides et des
sous-modèles numériques et physiques réunis dans
celui-ci. Sa capacité de prédire une grande diversité
de problèmes de sécurité importants pour l'industrie du
gaz est démontrée à travers son application à la
dispersion du gaz, l'accumulation du gaz et les
problèmes d'incendie et d'explosion.  Une comparaison
des prévisions sur modèle est faite avec des données
obtenues d'expériences à la fois à petite et grande
échelle.  Dans l'ensemble, la communication démontre
que le progiciel offre une capacité exceptionnelle de
modélisation de l'écoulement des fluides.   En outre,
elle illustre non seulement sa capacité de prédire des
informations sur un écoulement donné mais aussi
l'utilité de ses prédictions utilisées dans
l'estimation du risque et des conséquences d'un
établissement industriel réel.

INTRODUCTION

     The routine operations of any gas industry involve a wide variety
of fluid flow related phenomena.  These range from flows associated
with the exploration and production of gas (reservoir flows, bore
hole flows of non-Newtonian fluids, etc.), with gas transportation,
distribution and storage (flows in pipes and pipe networks, flow
metering, etc.), and finally with its ultimate use in the industrial,
commercial and domestic markets (furnace and boiler flows, gas
powered internal combustion engines, etc.).  Throughout these
activities it is also essential to ensure the safety of all
operations, so that assessments of the consequences of gas release
must be performed.  In particular, the results of operational and
accidental releases of gas must be assessed in terms of gas
dispersion in the atmosphere or build-up in confined spaces, and the
damaging thermal load (from fires) or blast load (from explosions)
that might occur should a release of gas ignite.

     Mathematical models are frequently used in order to provide fluid
flow information of relevance to design and operational activities.
Due to the complexity of many of the fluid flow problems encountered,
however, and the requirement for quick engineering solutions, there
is a long standing tradition of using simple empirical or
phenomenological models in the prediction and analysis of such flows.
The simplicity and economy of this approach is usually achieved at
the expense of physical rigour, with the resulting mathematical
models either providing little detailed information or having ranges
of applicability that are strictly limited by the extent of the
experimental data used in their development or validation.  Such
models are also in general developed to be conservative, resulting in
unnecessary over-engineering and expense.

     In contrast, computational fluid dynamics (CFD) offers a
framework for the detailed and accurate analysis of fluid flow
problems because it is based on solutions of differential equations
which describe the transport of all important flow variables.
Despite their relatively high computational cost, CFD techniques can
today be applied usefully even to the most complex of fluid flows.
The ongoing and dramatic reduction in the cost of computing power,
and the accompanying increases in performance, also seem set to
ensure the extensive future use of such models.

     Despite its potential, however, CFD has not reached the maturity
of, for example, stress analysis packages, largely due to unsolved
problems regarding the nature of complex physical processes.  Many of
these processes are represented within any CFD package by as yet
inexact sub-models, and the development of more accurate and reliable
descriptions remains an ongoing, leading-edge research activity.  In
addition, various flow characteristics such as unsteadiness,
compressibility and geometric complexity often necessitate the use of
specific numerical methods if accurate model solutions are to be
obtained at acceptable computational cost.  These considerations have
driven British Gas R&T away from a "black-box" approach to
computational fluid dynamics.  Instead, a novel CFD code, tailored to
meet the needs of the gas industry, has been developed.  This code
incorporates the most appropriate numerical techniques for any given
problem, and undergoes continual enhancement due to ongoing in-house
and externally sponsored research in the area of physical sub-models.
The development of this code has been carried out jointly by British
Gas plc and Mantis Numerics Ltd, based on the Mantis Numerics Ltd.
code COBRA.

     This paper describes the important features of the code in terms
of its general capabilities and the physical sub-models which have
been implemented within it.  Most importantly, the capabilities of

the code are demonstrated through its application to a wide variety
of safety related problems of importance to the gas industry.

CODE DESCRIPTION

Geometry and Grid

COBRA is particularly well suited to handling complex geometries
involving a variety of objects of different shapes and sizes, e.g.
offshore platform modules. Such geometries can be built within the
code with considerable ease through the use of an extensive library
of generic shapes included in the code. The philosophy behind this
approach is the use of Cartesian finite-volume and collocated
(non-staggered) numerical grids which are constructed automatically
by the code irrespective of the problem. In many cases, like the
offshore module problem mentioned above, a simple Cartesian mesh is
the only practical gridding solution because the construction of a
smooth body-fitted grid would be particularly difficult and
time-consuming, if possible at all. The obvious disadvantage of
Cartesian meshes is the inevitable misalignment of some solid
boundaries with the grid, resulting in a stepped approximation to
some surfaces. This problem is, however, alleviated by local
refining of the grid (1) using the adaptive grid techniques described
below.

The Cartesian mesh approach is time saving and very easy to use,
but it does have its limitations. For example, in certain
three-dimensional confined flows, such as pipe bends or pipe
junctions, it is expensive to achieve the grid resolution necessary
to produce grid-independent solutions. As a consequence, a
curvilinear, adaptive grid capability is also available within the
code.

Numerical Solution Methods

The code incorporates a variety of equation solvers that are
suitable for different flow conditions. For compressible flows, a
second-order accurate variant of Godunov's method is employed in
conjunction with techniques such as adapted linear and non-linear
Riemann solvers, and second-order upwinding with limiting functions.
The method falls into the range of total variation diminishing (TVD)
schemes, and can resolve with great accuracy standing and moving
shock waves and other compressible flow features, as well as shear
layers. A detailed description of the method may be found in (2).
Low Mach number flows are more efficiently predicted using a pressure
correction (SIMPLE) algorithm (3). To avoid the well known
chequerboard oscillations that occur when this method is applied to
collocated grid arrangements, the so called momentum-weighted
interpolation (4) has been adopted within the present code. A
second-order accurate, bounded discretisation scheme, of the TVD
type, is also used in conjunction with this solver in order to
combine accuracy and robustness.

Adaptive Grids

Embedded, dynamically adaptive gridding is a very powerful
feature of the code which enables complex flows to be simulated with
great efficiency. With this method finer numerical resolution is
only provided at points in the flow where it is demanded by the
physical situation being modelled. This means that predictions can
be obtained more cheaply, in terms of computer time, than by other
fixed-grid codes because of the reduced need for computational
points. Alternatively, for given computer resources, this implies
that complex problems, which would otherwise be too demanding of
computer time and memory, can be tackled. Grid adaption within the

code is achieved by bisecting computational cells in each space direction to create a sequence of progressively finer grid levels. A dynamic algorithm removes or generates new computational cells during a calculation, following the evolution of flow features. Grid control is normally based on local truncation errors or property gradients.

The adaptive grid capabilities of the code are demonstrated here by computation of the Riemann problem (5) on a two-dimensional plane with the initial pressure discontinuity placed at an angle to the computational grid. This arrangement results in a flow that is skewed to the numerical grid, thereby ensuring that the effects of any numerical smearing are amplified. Figure 1a) shows the initial grid distribution, with finer grids only existing along the pressure discontinuity. Figure 1b) depicts the grid at a later time when a shock wave, a contact discontinuity and an expansion fan have formed and are moving away from the position of the initial discontinuity. This figure shows clearly how the grid refinement follows faithfully the moving flow features. The accuracy of the solution is demonstrated in Figure 2 which compares the predicted density distribution normal to the shock wave with the exact analytic solution (5). The agreement between model predictions and the analytic solution is seen to be good, and the shock, despite the fact that it is moving and skewed to the mesh, is captured on only four grid points. More details about the adaptive grid method are given in (1).

Sub-Models of Physical Processes

Apart from the conservation laws for mass, momentum and energy which govern any fluid flow, the code also incorporates a large number of additional transport equations which can be optionally invoked if the physics of the problem so demands. In addition, the code also includes a radiation model, a particle-tracking and laminar flame kinetics facility, and various models describing the viscoelastic behaviour of non-Newtonian fluids. Space limitations preclude an exhaustive description of all the physical sub-models embodied in the code, but it is useful here to outline those sub-models which were used in demonstrating the overall capabilities of the code below.

The most commonly used turbulence model within the code is the standard k-epsilon model (6). This model has also been augmented to incorporate additional terms which account for the effects of large density variations, pressure waves and high Mach numbers on turbulent mixing. Another extension of this two-equation turbulence model is a semi-empirical variant which simulates the presence of solid objects too small to be represented on the computational grid. In this approach, the effects of sub-grid obstacles are manifested through drag terms in the momentum equations and extra turbulence energy generation terms. The latter model is mainly used in simulations of explosions in congested areas where it is not possible to represent every small scale object, e.g. pipes. Because of the weakness of the k-epsilon model for predicting flows with significant streamline curvature, recirculation, swirl or buoyancy, various versions of Reynolds stress transport equation models (e.g. (7)) are also available within the code. Lastly, in wall-bounded flows, the damping effect of the wall on the turbulence field is not properly accounted for by the models described above. The code therefore uses wall functions or low Reynolds number modelling approaches close to solid surfaces (e.g. (8)).

Various combustion models were also used in deriving the results discussed below. Turbulent premixed combustion was described using an eigen value method (9) which ensures that a flame propagates at a prescribed turbulent burning velocity, with the latter velocity being determined from local turbulence parameters via empirical correlations. A variant of this model was also used for application to congested environments in conjunction with the sub-grid representation of objects mentioned above. Turbulent non-premixed combustion was described using a conserved scalar/prescribed probability density function approach which used the laminar flamelet concept (10). In addition, a pseudo-kinetic approach (10), based on a modified laminar flamelet method, for predicting soot formation and consumption in flames is also available within the code.

## DEMONSTRATION OF CODE CAPABILITIES

In the remainder of this paper the capabilities of the CFD code are demonstrated through its application to a wide variety of safety related problems. More specifically, predictions of gas dispersion, gas build-up, fires and explosions are given, and compared with available experimental data for model validation purposes. Comparisons with data are made at both a small and a large scale in order to illustrate the ability of the code to predict not only the details of a given flow, but also its usefulness for providing predictions for use in consequence and risk assessments of real industrial plant.

Accidental releases of gas from high pressure pipes and vessels often result in the formation of sonic jets. Such jets are characterised by the existence of shock waves in the near field of the jet which lead to significant compressibility effects on the turbulent mixing process. Depending on the ratio of pressure in the exit plane of the release to the ambient value ($P_o/P_a$), such jets can be classified as either moderately or highly underexpanded. Figure 3 gives Mach number predictions for a highly underexpanded, supersonic release. This release is seen to be characterised by the existence of a normal shock downstream of the release point, known as the Mach disc. Predictions of concentration decay in such jets are used in order to assess those positions where an ignition source could lead to jet light-up and the establishment of a stable flame. Figure 4 compares data (11) on centre-line concentration decay in axisymmetric, highly underexpanded jets of natural gas with model predictions, with good agreement being found.

In reality, the dispersion of gas from such a release is likely to be modified by impact of the jet on nearby process equipment or plant. Because of the high velocities involved, such an impact can also lead to significant loading on the impinged object. Figure 5 compares predictions of density and experimental shadowgraph data (12) in the near field of a supersonic air jet impinging a perpendicular flat plate. Results derived from the model are seen to be in good agreement with observations for both the location and shape of the bow shock which forms in such situations. Predictions of loading on the flat surface, in terms of non-dimensionalised local pressures, are compared with data (12) from another supersonic impinging jet in Figure 6, with good agreement again being found.

Sonic, or even subsonic, releases of gas in confined and congested environments can lead to gas build-up. In order to demonstrate the ability of the CFD code to predict this phenomena, runs were performed for a large, steady release of natural gas on an approximately one-third scale representation of part of an actual offshore platform (13). This rig, which was used in explosion experiments considered further below, contained scaled pipe work and vessels, with confinement being provided by a floor, roof and up to three walls. The rig was 9m square and 2.3m high, and is illustrated in Figure 7. Computations were performed using a cross-wind loading of 5m/s. Figure 8 illustrates that the code predicts gas build-up with time in terms of two monitoring locations, one close to the release in a highly confined part of the rig, and the second in a less confined area where the effects of the cross-wind were felt.

High pressure releases of flammable gas can ignite to give rise to jet fires. For sonic releases, the near-field of the jet will be non-reacting, and identical in form to the dispersing jets considered above. The flame itself will be stabilised some way downstream in the case of a free fire, or closer to the release point should the jet impinge on adjacent pipe work or vessels. Predictions of the model for a sonic free jet fire which has been studied experimentally (14) are given in Figures 9 and 10. The fire considered was approximately 25m in length and was supported by a release rate of 3.7kg/s of natural gas. Figure 9 compares measured and predicted radial temperatures within the fire at three downstream (z) locations, whilst Figure 10 shows radiative heat fluxes external to the fire. In the latter figure, the circles are used to indicate the location of the radiometers, with the arrows showing the orientation of the centre of their field of view. Agreement between model predictions and experimental data is good, both in terms of internal flame structure and external thermal loading. The thermal loads to pipe work and vessels which are impacted by such fires are of course much higher than the external loads illustrated in Figure 10. Total heat fluxes (both radiative and convective) to a 2.2m diameter, 8.8m long cylindrical tank have been studied experimentally (15) using calorimeters maintained at constant temperature. Figure 11 compares measured and predicted total heat fluxes on the stagnation line along the front surface of such a vessel which was impinged by a 32m long fire arising from a 8.2kg/s sonic release of natural gas situated 21.5m away from the target vessel. Agreement between theory and experiment is again good.

Finally, the code was used to simulate explosion experiments carried out at both a laboratory and a field scale. Figures 12 and 13 compare predictions with, respectively, measured flame shapes and overpressures obtained from experiments carried out in a 0.29m diameter, 0.86m long cylindrical Perspex tube which contained three turbulence generating rings. These experiments were performed in order to gain understanding of how turbulent premixed flames propagate in obstacle containing environments, and to permit detailed validation of the eigen value based model of turbulent premixed combustion noted above. Results on the rate of propagation of premixed flames for ignition at the closed end of the vessel, and overpressures generated within the vessel, given in the latter figures show good agreement between model predictions and observations. As noted above, explosion experiments have also been performed (13) in the one-third scale representation of an offshore module illustrated in Figure 7. Predictions of flame propagation in this rig following the ignition of a stoichiometric natural-gas air mixture on the middle of one of three confining walls are given in Figure 14. Figure 15 compares model predictions and experimentally measured overpressures at two locations within the rig, this time for ignition at its centre. The predictions shown in these figures demonstrate the way in which the CFD code can be used not only to calculate the damaging overpressures that might result from the ignition of an accidental release, but also to provide flame propagation information which is of value in allowing design changes in order to mitigate the effects of any explosion. The reduction of explosion overpressures caused by the use of water sprays can also be simulated by the code.

CONCLUSIONS

A novel CFD code has been described in terms of its general capabilities, and the numerical and physical sub-models embodied within it.  Its overall usefulness for predicting a wide variety of safety related problems of importance to the gas industry has been demonstrated through its application to gas dispersion, gas build-up, fire and explosion problems.  Validation of the model has also been performed, in part, by comparison of model predictions with data obtained from both small and large scale experiments.

Overall the paper demonstrates that the CFD code represents a uniquely powerful fluid flow modelling capability, with the code undergoing continual enhancement in all areas due to the results of in-house, externally sponsored and published research findings.  Its application to problems related to the design of domestic burners and appliances is described elsewhere in these proceedings.

ACKNOWLEDGEMENTS

The authors would like to thank colleagues at British Gas for their help in preparing this paper, and in particular P.S. Cumber for his work on the figures.  This paper is published by permission of British Gas plc.

REFERENCES

1.  S.A.E.G. Falle, J.R. Giddings, "Body Capturing Using Adaptive Cartesian Grids", Proc. ICFD Conf. on Numerical Methods for Fluids, 1992.

2.  S.A.E.G. Falle, Mon. Not. of Roy. Astr. Soc., 250, 581, 1991.

3.  S.V. Patankar, "Numerical Heat Transfer and Fluid Flow", McGraw-Hill, 1980.

4.  C.M. Rhie, W.L. Chow, AIAA Jl., 21, 1525, 1983.

5.  C. Hirsch, "Numerical Computation of Internal and External Flows", John Wiley & Sons, 1990.

6.  W.P. Jones, B.E. Launder, Int. J. Heat Mass Transfer, 15, 301, 1972.

7.  M.M. Gibson, B.E. Launder, J. Fluid Mech., 86, 491, 1978.

8.  V.C. Patel, W. Rodi, G. Schreuer, AIAA Jl., 23, 1308, 1985.

9.  C.A. Catlin, M. Fairweather, S.S. Ibrahim, Combust. Flame, to appear, 1995.

10. M. Fairweather, W.P. Jones, R.P. Lindstedt, Combust. Flame, 89, 45, 1992.

11. A.D. Birch, D.R. Brown, M.G. Dodson, F. Swaffield, Combust. Sci. and Tech., 36, 249, 1984.

12. J.C. Carling, B.L. Hunt, J. Fluid Mech., 66, 159, 1974.

13. D.M. Johnson, G. Johnson, "Explosions Research and its Application in Hazard Management", IBC Conference, 1994.

14. J.P. Gore, G.M. Faeth, D. Evans, D.B. Pfenning, Fire and Materials, 10, 161, 1986.

15. J.F. Bennett, L.T. Cowley, J.N. Davenport, J.J. Rowson, "Large-Scale Natural Gas and LPG Jet Fires Final Report to the CEC", TNER.91.022, Shell Research Ltd., 1991.

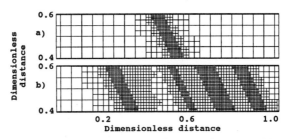

Figure 1. Grids used to solve the Riemann problem.

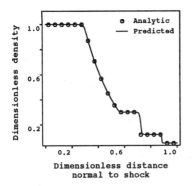

Figure 2. Density distribution normal
to a shock wave.

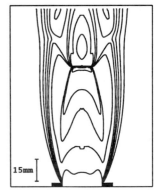

Figure 3. Mach number contours in an
underexpanded jet.

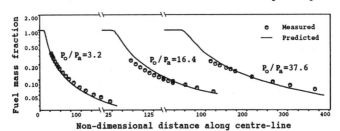

Figure 4. Concentration decay in axisymmetric jets of natural gas.

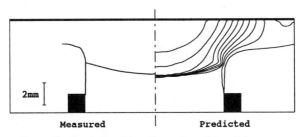

Figure 5. Shock location in an impacting jet.

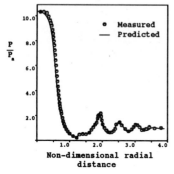

Figure 6. Pressure distribution
on an impacted surface.

Figure 7. One-third scale representation
of an offshore module.

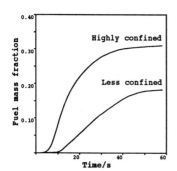

Figure 8. Gas build-up in an
offshore module.

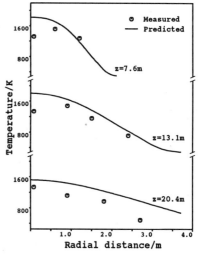

Figure 9. Temperatures within a free
jet fire.

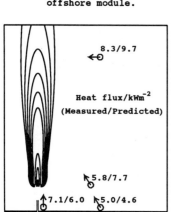

Figure 10. Heat fluxes around a
free jet fire.

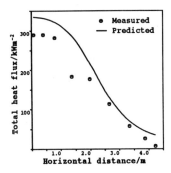

Figure 11. Heat fluxes to the
surface of a tank.

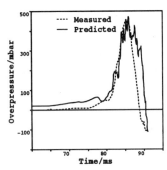

Figure 13. Overpressures generated
in a small scale explosion.

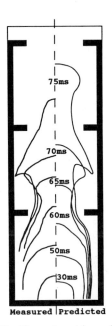

Figure 12. Flame locations in a
small scale explosion.

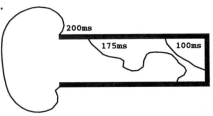

Figure 14. Flame locations in a
large scale explosion.

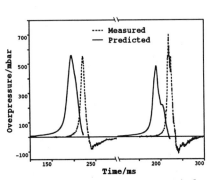

Figure 15. Overpressures generated
in a large scale explosion.

PAPER SUMMARY

## NON-LINEAR BEHAVIOR OF 3D FRAMED STRUCTURES

## COMPORTEMENT NON-LINÉARE DES STRUCTURES EN OSSATURE EN 3 DIMENSIONS

Dr M G Kirkwood and Mr T E Turner

*British Gas plc*
*Engineering Research Station*
*Killingworth*
*Newcastle upon Tyne*
*England*

1. SUMMARY

The design of offshore structures has traditionally been accomplished on a component by component basis using linear elastic frame analysis techniques where joints are represented by rigid connections. However, the ability of the jacket to resist extreme loads, as in the case of a ship collision, fire and blast loading, depends not only on component strength, but also performance at a system level.

This paper is concerned with the static strength and redundancy of jacket and topside structures when subject to extreme events. Frame action and system redundancy are implicit sources of reserve strength that are not accommodated for in the design phase. Emerging design codes have recognised the contribution of these factors (API RP2A - LRFD) and global indicators such as non-linear deformation or resistance to total collapse can be shown to provide a better indication of the structural resistance to extreme loads.

It is recognised that the component level is still important and that there is a reserve of strength beyond the first yield point. However, what is important is how this strength, and accompanying increase in flexibility, affects the overall performance of the jacket or topside structure as a system.

British Gas have investigated the use of a non-linear finite element analysis program (ABAQUS (1)) to the problem of frame collapse and have analysed a series of frame configurations to assess the applicability and accuracy of the approach. The non-linear finite element method has also been applied to four British Gas operated jackets subjected to a boat impact.

Further analyses have been conducted by use of a dedicated frame collapse program (USFOS (2)) and the solutions have been compared.

2. ANALYSIS TECHNIQUES

2.1 Simple Frames

The non-linear analysis of simple two dimensional framed structures has been conducted using both the non-linear finite element technique (ABAQUS) and the phenomenological modelling approach (USFOS) which allows the progressive formation of plastic hinges as the structure deforms plastically. The finite element method requires that each member is modelled by several discrete elements which are able to deform in a non-linear manner and redistribute loading to remaining elements as they begin to fail. The number of elements is critical in assessing the true behaviour of the frame collapse problem. To assess the accuracy of the finite element method a simple K braced frame was analysed. The dimensions of this frame are given in Fig.1 and are those from a full scale push-over test where the frame was subjected to an in line load causing failure(3).

The results from this analysis provided information on the minimum number of elements per member to give the correct load-displacement behaviour. The finite element analysis and test data provided a basis for which to compare the results of the phenomenological USFOS model shown in Fig.2. Both the ABAQUS and USFOS methods are comparable in result but the advantages of the USFOS approach is that only single element members are required for the model and the analysis is very quick to solve whereas the ABAQUS solver requires many time increments to converge on a solution.

The USFOS collapse mechanism for the simple frame is shown in Fig.3(a to d) in which the *plastic utilisation* is plotted on the deformed model with each point identified on the load-deformation plot shown in Fig.4. What is clear from these plots is that there is one critical member which buckles (in the experimental test cracking was also seen at the joint). Once this member fails, the load redistributes to the other members and portal action takes place. After component failure the integrity of the structure is retained, albeit diminished, and there is a fall off in load capacity but portal frame action takes over and a plateau of strength occurs (Fig.4)

2.2 Jacket Analysis

The experience gained in the analysis of the simple, two dimensional frames has provided a basis for the more complex analysis of a complete jacket. Three jackets were selected from the British Gas Rough Field (Fig.5) for an assessment of reserve strength and redundancy. This area of the Southern North Sea has a high density of shipping and the structures are in close proximity to specified shipping lanes. Each jacket chosen was distinct in its design - AP has 8 legs primarily X braced, BP is again 8 legged but primarily K braced and CD is 4 legged with K bracing.

Each of the jackets were subjected to a push-over analysis using both ABAQUS and USFOS. The primary objective of this analysis was to assess the energy absorption levels for each type of jacket when subjected to a ship impact. The energy value were then subsequently used to postulate likely ship tonnage and velocities that would cause ultimate collapse of the structure.

More recent work has concentrated on the behaviour of a British Gas platform in the Morecambe Bay Field (Fig.6). A full push over analysis and a storm wave assessment has been completed to assess the reserve strength and resistance to ship impact (Fig.7). The analysis of this jacket has clearly shown the level of redundancy and reserve strength and has identified the dominant load paths for collapse of the full structure.

## 3. CONCLUDING COMMENTS

Although the results of this assessment are preliminary, the analysis techniques have now been proven and it has been possible to conclude that:

- An improved understanding of the level of reserve strength of existing structures when subjected to extreme loads can be achieved by both non-linear finite element analysis and phenomenological analysis tools.

- Current design codes do not consider system redundancy when assessing the acceptance criteria for components and the total probability of failure is taken as component failure. This is incorrect and requires non-linear frame analyses to provide the overall system reliability.

- Major cost saving through targeted inspection, extended life operation and topside enhancement can be accommodated through an assessment of reserve strength of existing structures. Such techniques can also be utilised for the design of new structures that allow improvements in safety, reduced weight (allowing lift in place jackets) and optimised framing layout to provide acceptable levels of redundancy at minimum cost.

## 3. REFERENCES

(1) Anon, ABAQUS, Hibbit, Karlson and Sorenson.

(2) USFOS - A Computer Program for progressive Collapse Analysis of Steel Offshore Structures - Joint Industry Project, SINTEF, Trondheim, Norway, 1990.

(3) Joint Industry Tubular Frames Project Phase II, Billington Osborne Moss Ltd, Nine Volume Report, BOMEL ref. C556R003.50 to 58, 1992 (Confidential to Contributors until 1995).

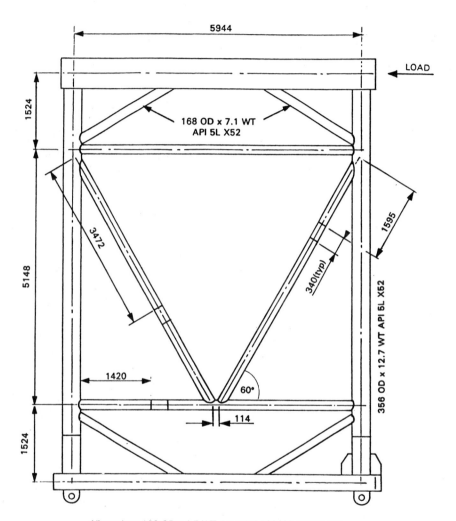

All members 168 OD x 4.5 WT Annealed BS3602 ERW U.N.O

Fig.1 Test Frame Dimensions and Layout

Fig.2 USFOS Model of Test Frame

(a)                                                    (b)

(c)                                                    (d)

Fig.3 Collapse Sequence of Test Frame

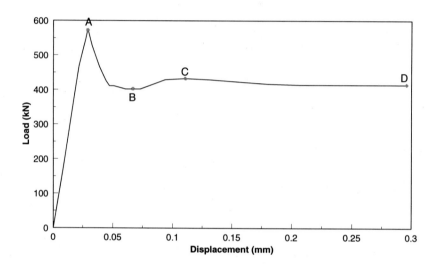

Fig.4 Load-deformation Curve for Test Frame

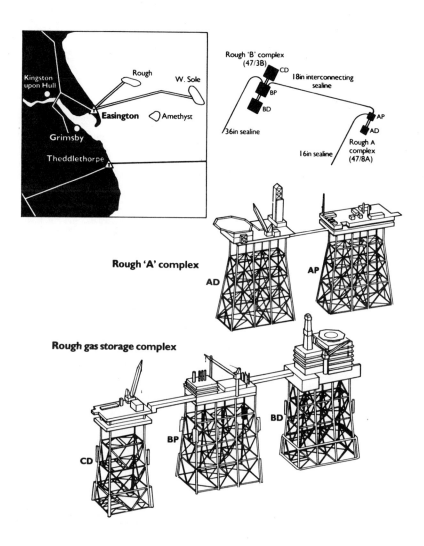

Fig.5 Rough Field Platforms

Fig.6 USFOS Model of Morecambe Bay Jacket

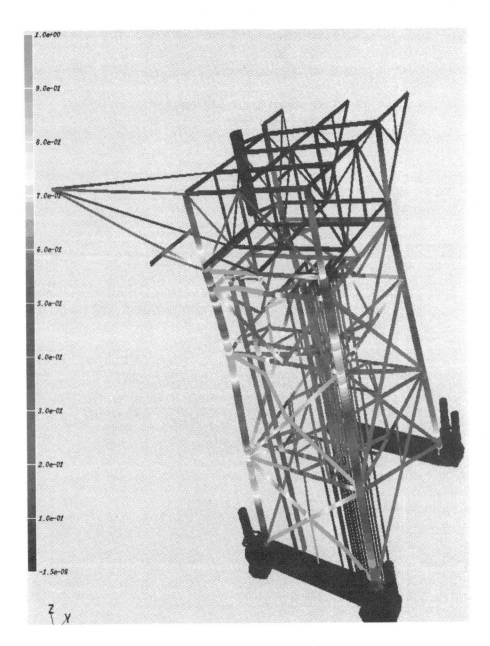

Fig.7 USFOS Impact Analysis - Plastic Interaction

Mechanisms of Natural Gas Hydrate Inhibition

Mechanisms d'inhibitions des hydrate de gaz naturels

J.L. Savidge[1], C.A. Koh[2], R.E. Motie[2], R..I. Nooney[2], X. Wu[2]

[1]Gas Research Institute, Basic Research, Chicago, IL 60631, U.S.A. ;
[2]King's College London, Department Of Chemistry, Strand, London,
WC2R 2LS, U.K.

Abstract

Gas clathrate hydrates have important implications to gas and oil
production and processing, and separation technology.  Growth and
inhibition mechanisms for carbon dioxide and propane gas hydrates at
pressure and temperature conditions close to the gas industry operating
conditions have been determined from in-situ time-resolved spectroscopic measurements.  Kinetic data for carbon dioxide and propane
hydrate formation and decomposition were obtained.  Precursor hydrate
structures were identified during hydrate formation and decomposition.
Our data show several mechanistic options exist for inhibiting hydrate
formation.

**Introduction**:

Energy supply projections for the U.S. indicate that approximately twenty percent of the U.S. gas supply is expected to be obtained by production from the deep-waters of the Gulf of Mexico.  In Europe, operators predict that deep-water resources will contribute nearly 50% of North Sea reserves within the next ten years.  Because of the low seabed temperatures and inaccessibility of the deep subsea pipelines many technical obstacles exist for the production and transport of natural gas and oil from deep-water resources.  Design studies for a variety of production scenarios have been conducted through the Texaco led Deep-Water Stage Recovery consortium.  The studies show that the technical obstacles will have a significant impact on the commercial risks of deepwater projects.

Operating conditions for deep-water fields are considered severe due to the costs associated with applying current production technology.  High economic risks are incurred in these projects due to the likelihood of corrosion, hydrates, waxes, and scale deposition.  Overcoming the technical challenges requires a better understanding of the static and dynamic physico-chemical properties of the produced fluids.

The purpose of this paper is to present some results from GRI's basic research at King's College on the dynamics and inhibition of natural gas hydrates.  Our work has provided the first detailed molecular level data on hydrate formation, decomposition and inhibition[1].  It is being applied, through coordination with other GRI research,  to develop the means to control pipeline blockages caused by gas hydrate formation.  The research program has technical participants from Texaco, Conoco, Amoco, Chevron, and Shell.

## Background

Gas hydrates are solid inclusion compounds. Their existence has been reported in the literature since the early nineteenth century[2-4] The most common types of natural gas hydrates are structure I and structure II which consist of hydrogen-bonded water molecules which form cavities in which a gas molecule is constrained. There are only weak van der Waals forces between the guest and cavity molecules. Structure I consists of pentagonal dodecahedron and tetrakaidecahedron cages, while structure II consists of pentagonal dodecahedron and hexacaidecahedron cavities (see figure I).

Previous hydrate research work has concentrated on macroscopic measurements to establish the equilibrium aspects of hydrate formation[5] . Fundamental research has focused on performing model calculations [7-9] to help determine gas hydrate formation mechanisms and on obtaining spectroscopic information at low temperatures[10-12]. Our early work focused on infrared studies[13] and complementary molecular simulations[14] to begin to understand associating fluid behavior, nucleation, and inhibitor interactions. Our studies suggested the presence of tetrameric hydrogen-bonded water rings. These structures were also suggested by Benson[15]. We have extended single crystal x-ray studies on gas hydrates to dynamic in-situ measurements at solution temperatures and pressures. Dynamic structural data have not been obtained to date by others. Our new results indicate this is important in determining kinetic mechanisms of hydrate formation and decomposition.

## Results

The results presented here are selected examples of the type of data we obtain. In Figure 2 we show results for carbon dioxide and propane which form hydrate structures I and II respectively. Our data have shown that the unit cell parameters of these two hydrates is sensitive to temperature and pressure[16]. We also present a time-resolved profile for carbon dioxide hydrate which illustrates the structural dynamics (see figure 3). Lastly, we illustrate the effect of two additives which may alter both the structure and energetics of the formation process for hydrate crystals (see figure 4).

## Conclusions

GRI's fluid properties research on gas hydrates has produced the first detailed molecular level structural data in order to provide insight into the dynamic process by which natural gas hydrates form. The data demonstrates that the current model for natural gas hydrate formation has some significant limitations since it does not account for the time and structure dependencies occurring during the hydrate formation and decomposition processes. This can produce both modeling and design errors and lead to poor project development decisions.

Our methodology is being extended to many other systems of interest to the gas industry.

## References

1.  Koh C. A., Savidge J. L. and Tang, C.C. 1995, submitted.

2.  Davy, H. Philos. Trans. R. Soc. London 1811, 101, (Part I), 1-35.

3.  Faraday, M. Quant. J. Sci. Lit. Arts 1823, 15, 71-74.

4.  Lowig, C. Ann. Chem. Phys. Sci. 1829, 42, 113-119.

5.  Bishnoi, P.R. and Dholabhai, P.D. Fluid Phase Equilibria, 1993, 83, 455-462.

7.  Van der Waals, J.H. and Platteeuw, J.C. Adv. Chem. Phys. 1959, 83, 455-462.

8.  Tanaka, H. and Kiyohara, K. J. Chem. Phys. 1993, 98, 4098-4109.

9.  Rodger, P.M. Mol. Simulation 1990, 5, 315-328.

10. Jeffrey, G. A. & McMullan, R.K. Prog. Inorg. Chem. 1967, 8, 43-108.

11. McMullan, R.K., and Jeffrey, G.A. J. Chem. Phys. (1965) 42, 2725-2731.

12. von Stackelberg, M and Muller, H.R., J. Chem. Phys. (1951) 19, 1319.

13. Koh, C.A., Muller, E., Zollweg, J.A., Gubbins, K.E. and Savidge, J.L. Annals N.Y. Acad. Sci. 1994, 715, 561-563.

14. Baez, L. and Clancy, P. Annals N.Y. Acad. Sci. (1994).

15. Benson, S.W. and Siebert, E.D. J. Am. Chem. Soc. 1992, 114, 4269-4276.

**Figure Captions**

Figure 1.  Carbon dioxide and propane gas hydrate structures.

Figure 2.   *In-situ* x-ray spectra before (lower trace) and after (upper trace) crystallization for (a) carbon dioxide hydrate, (b) propane hydrate.

Figure 3.  *In-situ* time-resolved x-ray spectra during growth of carbon dioxide hydrate.

Figure 4.  *In-situ* x-ray spectra of carbon dioxide hydrate with (a) polyvinyl pyrrolidone, (b) tyrosine, T= 273.8 K, P = 3.29 MPa.

**Figure 1**

### Structure I

Pm3n

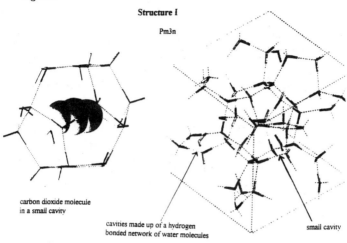

carbon dioxide molecule
in a small cavity

cavities made up of a hydrogen
bonded network of water molecules

small cavity

### Structure II

Fd3m

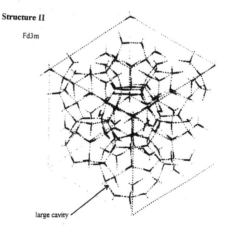

propane molecule
in a large cavity

large cavity

Figure 2(a)

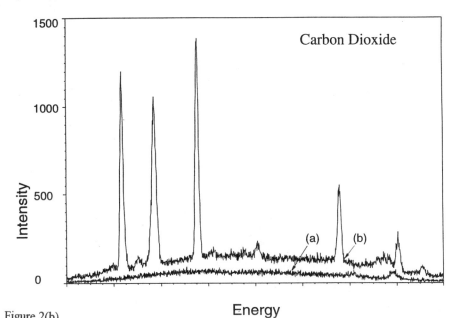

Figure 2(b)

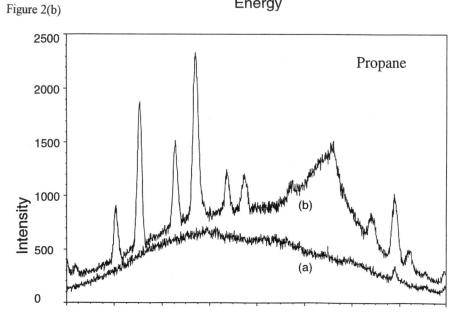

Figure 3

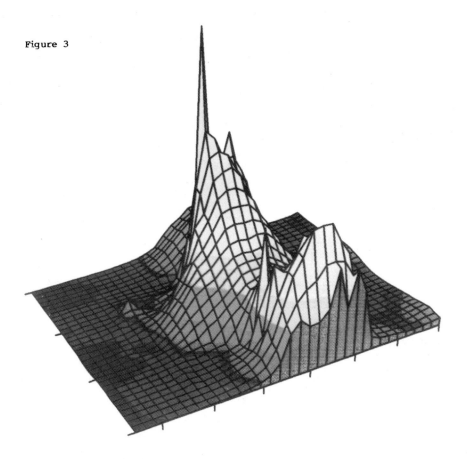

Figure 4

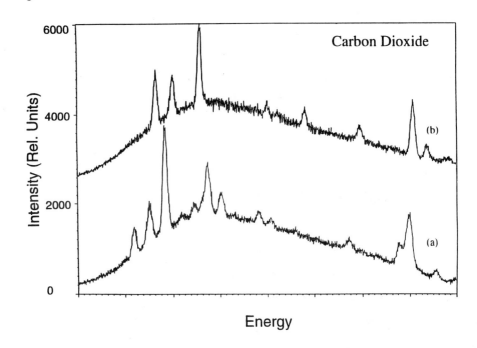

SUBMARINE NATURAL GAS HYDRATES:
RISK TO GAS AND OIL PRODUCTION

LES HYDRATES DE GAZ NATURELS SOUS-
MARINS: LE DANGER POUR LE FORAGE ET
LA PRODUCTION DU GAZ ET PETROLE BRUT

V.S.Yakushev
All-Russian Scientific Research Institute of
Natural Gases and Gas Technologies,
GAZPROM, RUSSIA

D.A.Dubrovski
State Academy of Oil and Gas, RUSSIA

E.M.Chuvilin
Moscow State University, RUSSIA

V.A.Istomin and V.G.Kvon
All-Russian Scientific Research Institute of
Natural Gases and Gas Technologies
GAZPROM, RUSSIA

ABSTRACT

Natural gas hydrates are well-known as element of bottom sediments in seas and oceans.
The sediments are often cemented by hydrates and the hydrates are in equilibrium with
environment. Violation of this equilibrium in the course of drilling through and production
from underlying ordinary oil and gas fields in deep waters (more then approximately 300
m in polar regions and 600 m in tropic altitudes) can result in strong damage of
production facilities. Thawing out of *in-situ* hydrates around production wells can lead to
deformation of the wells, strong uncontrolled gas liberation from sea bottom around
production facility and even submarine landslides. Experimental research and natural
observations of processes caused by gas hydrates presence in sediments confirm
prediction of their strong influence on bottom production facilities


RESUME

Les hydrates de gaz naturels sont bien connus comme l'élément des sédiments de fond des
mers et des océans. Ces sédiments sont souvent cimentés par les hydrates, et les hydrates
se trouvent en équilibre avec l'environnement. Le déséquilibre au cours du forage et de la
production du gaz et de pétrole brut a partir des gisements typiques, se trouvant au
dessous des couches contenant des hydrates, dans les régions profondes (plus de 300
mètres pour les régions polaires et 600 mètres pour les latitudes tropiques) peut amener
aux dommages importants des installations de production. La dégelation des hydrates
naturels autour des puits d'exploitation peut amener à la déformation des puits, aux jets
de gaz non contrôlés à partir du fond sous marin autour des installations de production et
même aux glissements sous-marins. L'étude expérimentale et les observations naturelles
sur les processus dûs à la présence des hydrates de gaz aux sédiments confirment la
prévision de leur influence importante sur les installations au de production fond sous-
marin.

## INTRODUCTION

More than 40 regions of natural gas hydrates occurrences are discovered by the present time with a high trustful rate and this number is continuing to increase. The majority of discovered fields is located in sea and ocean areas. American geologists consider that gas (methane) reserves in discovered hydrate accumulations 10 times exceed explored free gas reserves (Kvenvolden, 1988). During last 20 years the natural gas hydrate problem had been considered from unconventional source of natural hydrocarbons point of view, e.g. investigations were directed for determination of their reserves in deposits and development of the ways of gas recovery from them. However some decreasing of industrial interest to gas hydrate occurrences was marked recently that was related to absence of economically profitable ways of gas recovery. All ways of a gas production from natural hydrate formations offered to the present time are more expensive then a free gas production.

But some new reasons for intensification of natural gas hydrates investigation have appeared recently. One of them is hydrate role in ecological balance of the planet. The global rise in temperature can reach shallow occurrences of hydrate-bearing rocks, especially in arctic regions. Methane and other natural gases liberation from hydrates may result in further increasing of greenhouse effect.

The negative technological and ecological consequences of technical influence on hydrate-containing strata during development of ordinary oil and gas fields on land as well as offshore can represent the most interest for oil and gas industry.

## COMPLICATIONS RELATED TO NATURAL GAS HYDRATES

The first difficulties related to the hydrates decomposition during development of arctic oil and gas fields were registered recently (L.J.Franklin,1983; V.S.Yakushev and T.S.Collett,1992). These difficulties were linked mainly with unexpected gas blowouts in the space beyond casing from shallow permafrost and underpermafrost intervals. Some of them had led even to fires on wellheads. Liquidation of these complications is making in the course of drilling- by pumping in cooled and heavy mud and in the course of operation - by keeping the well in ease until gas educing will over.

Submarine (sea) hydrate formations could be of more danger. They can provoke large breakdowns during the oil and gas fields development in deep submarine areas of seas and oceans. Following two factors determinate this proposal. On the one hand investigations show that gas hydrates mainly are situated in the upper level of a sedimentary cover in areas of seas and often are located above oil and gas fields. On the other hand the solution of construction problems of ice condition platform building should allow soon to pass to a wide development of oil and gas fields concentrated on northern sea shelf, but these regions have a great concentration of gas hydrate accumulations at relatively small water depth (250-300 m for methane hydrate).

The events of complications related to natural hydrates are renowned from the practice which took place during a submarine hydrocarbon fields development. So the data concerning damage of deep-water pipelines foundations because of natural hydrates thawing in Mexican Gulf near the Jolliet TLP platform were represented by E.D.Sloan [ 1 ] .

Detailed prediction of hydrate-containing accumulations behaviour during technical influence on them was not carried out yet. Therefore probable technological and ecological consequences of influences on hydrate rocks during oil and gas fields development can be predicted on a qualitative level only.

## GENERAL INFORMATION ABOUT HYDRATE-CONTAINING SEDIMENTS

Hydrate formation conditions are created in seas and oceans by pressure of water column and ground pressure and by low bottom temperature (fig.1). Depending on thermodynamic conditions gas hydrates can occur at different depths from the bottom level. For northern seas these depths are 250-300 meters, for tropical latitudes- 600-700 m. Gas hydrates can be situated in geologic section in a form of single little inclusions as well as hydrate layers of several meters thickness.

So as a specific content of methane hydrate (the most spread hydrate in nature) reaches 168 m3/m3, it is evidently that violation of gas hydrate thermodynamic balance with environment can lead to stormy liberation of gas and rock structure break-down.

Because of natural properties of hydrates they can execute not only accumulation function but the rock skeleton forming function too. By other words natural hydrates can determine elastic characteristics of saturated intervals. Seismoacoustic exploration of bottom in hydrate accumulated regions confirms it. A lot of wide fields of submarine hydrate-containing rocks were discovered by specific sign - Bottom-Simulating Reflector, BSR, which corresponds to a border between hydrate cemented bottom rocks and underlying gas saturated rocks as sea geophysicists consider. But it is worth to mention that some data on deepwater drilling and coring appeared last time have shown presence of gas hydrates in bottom rocks while the BSR method gave no information about them. It makes hydrate-containing strata exploration more difficult in sea conditions.

Recent natural observations made by seismoacoustic profiling around North America have evidently shown periodical gas hydrate decomposition at low boundary of hydrate stability zone as a reason for large submarine landslides [2]. Observations made from deep-water submarines NR-1 and Johnson Sea Link 1 in Mexican Gulf have shown annual floating up of exposed gas hydrate bottom lobs caused by regular changes in water temperature [3]. These processes could be of large danger for any gas production facility installed on places of gas hydrate spreading.

For the further consideration it will be convenient to split hydrate-containing rocks on the two groups. The first- the rocks there hydrates don't influence on the mechanical characteristics of base rocks ,e.g. those are rocks where hydrate is situated in a form of single disseminations and is accessor mineral.

The second- the rocks where hydrates determine elastic properties of the exploring interval, e.g. hydrate is rock-forming mineral.

## BEHAVIOUR OF HYDRATE-CONTAINING SEDIMENTS IN THE COURSE OF PLATFORM INSTALLATION AND WELL DRILLING.

The Tension-Leg Platforms (TLP) are being planned to use for deepwater ( the depth more than 300 m.) oil and gas fields development. They haven't direct contact with bottom sediments therefore there is no real threat for such platforms from hydrate-containing strata. However some platforms in northern seas at the depths more than 300 m are being planned to put on the hard bases. In this case it is necessary to explore the hydrate deposits near the bottom and to avoid platform setting within such areas if it is possible, since the properties of such deposits as a base for platform foundation are unknown now. Besides in the course of the field development the shift of thermodynamic conditions of deposits near a riser can occur and hydrate rocks can lose their firmness. When TLP platforms are used, wells are drilling at different distances from the platform and have a link with it by flexible risers.

The well drilling and cementing inside hydrate rocks when some light and warm muds are used can be accompanied by a cave formation, by the lacking of adhesion between cement ring and surrounding rocks, by outside columns gas motion between hydrate and underlying gas containing intervals. It should be characteristically for the second group of rocks which represents the main danger during setting and operation of wells.

However in the majority of cases, even strongly hydrate-saturated rocks would not reveal themselves during drilling and cementing since the modern drilling technology supposes rather usage of heavy muds for the gas hydrates decomposition prevention. Muds containing hydrate-formation inhibitors (for example calcium chloride), which provoke hydrate decomposition, are of danger, but in this case it is necessary to calculate conditions of hydrate stability in the presence of the inhibitor for the decomposition prediction.

## HYDRATE-CONTAINING INTERVALS BEHAVIOUR IN THE COURSE OF GAS (OIL) RECOVERY.

It's known that while field exhausting the change of natural Earth temperature distribution around well bore as well as strained parameters of rock massif surrounding the deposit take place. Consideration of the consequences of temperature changing around a well shows that the rocks temperature increasing takes place around casing during oil or gas production. The well bore can be considered as permanently acting heat source in hydrate-saturated intervals. The permanent heat transfer will lead to beginning of hydrate dissociation process in this intervals. Dependence of radius of thawing on time for different hydrate-saturation values is represented on fig.2. Analysis of curves represented on fig.2 shows that the thawing zone diameter can reach 10-20 meters. Taking into account the fact that there can be up to 40 operating wells on the one site and the distance between well bores at depths near 500 m from the bottom is comparable with a size of thawing zone and applying for the each well bore influence the superposition principle, one can affirm that at the definite moment large hydrate-saturated zone should undergo phase change.

We made certain experiments on gas hydrate decomposition in closed cell to determine intensity of gas liberation from the same sand with different initial humidity (5, 10, and 15%) and the same rate of external heating. Description of the experimental equipment is represented in the work [4]. Results have shown that pressure rise is most fast in case of low initial humidity, but total volume of liberated gas in this situation is relatively small. The more is initial humidity, the more is total volume of liberated gas and the less is the rate of the gas edusing. Taking into account this regularity, it could be predicted the character of gas liberation in the course of hydrate-containing sediments heating around well bore. Sediments with low humidity well produce gas in large volumes, but relatevely short time and sediments with high humidity (and hydrate content) will produce gas more weakly, but for a long time.

Hydrate dissociation will lead to qualitative change of strength parameters of rocks directly under recovery equipment. Following consequences are predictable:

1.The influence on platform stability.

2.Possibility of column fracturing and breaking.

3.Gas blowouts appearing ( gas liberation caused by hydrate decomposition).

The platform stability will be directly dependent on the stability of gas hydrates situated near the bottom in the case of platform foundation fixing on bottom deposits. Hydrate decomposition will decrease deposit strength characteristics. Usually the upper part of submarine sediment cover is represented by weakly consolidated clays, silts and sands. Hydrate decomposition in the sediments will lead to sharp slacking of ground cohesion with the well cement ring and columns can be broken by their own weight.

Hydrate cement decomposition in sediments and ground structure breach by the gas educing from hydrate create preconditions for formation of favourable ways for gas filtration to the bottom from hydrates as well as from underlying gas-saturated deposits along channels created by the gas educed as a result of hydrate thawing. This process can result in uncontrolled gas blowouts around well head.

Hydrate-saturated intervals behaviour during changing of rock massif strained condition was simulated by special mathematical model of rock massif above oil pool, which works when the ratio of pool depth to pool diameter is more than 10. Field development leads to ground level subsidence. This subsidense can be of considerable size (first meters) in the case of several hundred meters depth of water above the field or exhausting of shallow productive horizons.

Irregular tension and squeeze strains in hydrate interval will provoke rocks cracking and formation of new filtration ways for under-hydrate gas that should result in further lowering of bottom surface. Besides lowering of hydrate-saturated interval and pressure drop in the under hydrate stratum (because of gas escape) can lead to hydrate decomposition on lower border of hydrate stability zone. This process in the presence of small slope on the bottom will promote submarine landslide along lower border and could result in sea equipment damage.

Bottom subsidence will lead to loading on casing too and can result in column fracturing.

So the hydrate-saturated interval subsidence can have following consequences:

1.Cracking of hydrate-saturated intervals and gas blowouts formation over considerable area of developing field.

2.The shift of lower border of hydrate stability zone to zone of unequilibrium thermodynamic conditions and as a result - submarine landslide possibility.

3.Well bore loading increase.

CONCLUSION

The natural submarine hydrates investigation is in the very initial stage now and a lot of additional information about formation and bedding of hydrate-saturated rocks and their mutual affection are required. However current theoretical and experimental data and the data about complications related to natural gas hydrates in northern oil and gas fields witness about the fact that development of deepwater hydrocarbon fields, located in regions of natural gas hydrate spreading can have heavy ecological and technical consequences.

The base grounds stability loss under deepwater submarine platforms as a result of gas hydrates thawing leads to platform warp and other accompanied breakdowns.

The well breaking results in uncontrolled oil and gas blow-out into seawater and atmosphere. It is very difficult to liquidate such flow in deepwater conditions, that is why an extensive water and air pollution around platform can be predicted. Hydrate-saturated interval cracking will lead to gas escape from underlying gas-saturated deposits and near-bottom water pollution by methane. Deepwater landslides could result in submarine equipment damage or even platform loss.

Oil and gas industry just began deepwater regions development. But it is evidently that at the nearest decade intensity of such regions development will increase. Accordingly probability of possible complications caused by submarine gas hydrates will increase too. It is not proper to speak that their influence on built constructions will lead to disastrous effects from technical as well as ecological point of view. Danger for operating staff health can appear.

It is not obligatory that enumerated above complications will be met on every deepwater platform standing above hydrate contained rocks , but if these damages occur even on one platform, liquidation of them will demand huge expenses.

## REFERENCES

1.    E.D.Sloan. "Natural Gas Hydrates". Jornal of Petroleum Technology. December 1991.

2.    I.R.MacDonald, N.L.Guinasso, R.Sassen, J.M.Brooks, L.Lee and K.T.Scott. "Gas hydrate that breaches the sea floor on the continental slope of the Gulf of Mexico". Geology, August 1994.

3.    Submarine Landslides: Selected Studies in the U.S. Exclusive Economic Zone. (Edited by W.C.Schwab, H.J.Lee and D.C.Twichell). U.S.Geological Survey Bulletin N 2002, 1993.

4.    E.D.Ershov and V.S.Yakushev. "Experimental research on gas hydrate decomposition in frozen rocks". Cold Regions Science and Technology. V.20, 1992.

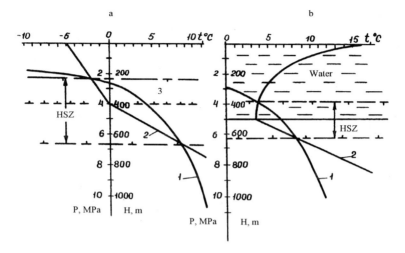

Figure 1.  Definition of Hydrate Stability Zone  (HSZ) on land (a) and offshore (b).
1- Hydrate - formation curve
2- Curve of pressure - temperature distribution in-situ
3- Permafrost boundary

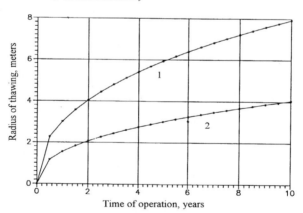

Time of operation, years

Figure 2.  Dynamics of thawing radius  increasing around well
casing (conductor) within time when gas hydrate content
of sediment is 100 kg/cub.m (1) and 500 kg/cub.m (2)
respectively and gas temperature inside well is 25 C .

DIAGENESIS IN OIL AND GAS RESERVOIRS; BARRIERS
TO HYDROCARBON MOVEMENT?

DIAGENÈSE DANS LES RÉSERVES DE PÉTROLE ET DE GAZ: OBSTACLE AU MOUVEMENT DES HYDROCARBURES?

Jon Seedhouse
British Gas Research and Technology
Ashby Road, Loughborough

ABSTRACT

Porosity and permeability in sedimentary rocks both need to be preserved or enhanced at depth in order to produce good hydrocarbon reservoirs. The growth from aqueous solution of diagenetic minerals in pore spaces can greatly decrease porosity and reduce permeability, making extraction of hydrocarbons more difficult. Experiments using salt solutions, and analogues from igneous geology in high viscosity melts, show that fluid convection can be driven by crystallisation which takes heavy elements out of solution and decreases the density of the residual solution. Such convection results in vertical fluid movement which is concentrated in channels and chimneys. The rate of diagenetic mineral growth is higher in these channels and chimneys and so porosity may be dramatically reduced, producing low permeability zones which act as barriers to hydrocarbon migration into reservoirs, and compartmentalize reservoirs – markedly reducing the potential for hydrocarbon recovery.

RESUME

La porsité et la perméabilité des roches sédimentaires doivent être toutes deux conservées en profondeur afin de produire de bonnes réserves d'hydrocarbures. Provenant de la solution aqueuse, la croissance de minéraux diagénétiques dans les volumes des pores peut diminuer considérablement la porosité et la perméabilité, rendant l'extraction des hydrocarbures plus dificile. Des expériences utilisant des solutions de sel et des analogues provenant de la géologie ignée dans des masses en fusion d'une grande viscosité montrent que la convection des fluides peut être soumise à une cristallisation, retirant des éléments lourds de la solution et réduisant la densité de la solution résiduelle. Ceci entraîne un mouvement vertical des fluides concentré dans les cheminées et les canaux. Le taux de la croissance minérale diagénétique est plus élevé dans ces cheminées et canaux et donc la porosité peut être considérablement réduite. Ceci peut engendrer des zones de faible perméabilité qui font office d'obstacles à la migration des hydrocarbures vers les réserves et compartimentent les réserves, réduisant sérieusement le potentiel de régénération des hydrocarbures.

INTRODUCTION

In this paper the results of recent studies in crystal growth in high viscosity silicate melts are presented. It is shown that crystal growth in high viscosity melts causes compositional differences in residual fluids. These compositional differences cause small density variations (in the order of 1 %) in fluids at crystal-liquid interfaces. These density differences are sufficient to drive fluid movement by buoyant "compositional convection".

Over the past 15 years several studies (see Sparks, Huppert and Turner, 1984, for summary) have modelled convection in molten magma chambers by inducing crystallisation in observable analogues. These experimental analogues comprise of perspex tanks of salt solutions. This work has shown that during crystal growth a thin boundary layer is formed at the crystal-liquid interface. This boundary layer is depleted in elements that are incorporated into the crystal lattice and is enriched in solvent (see figure 1). If the growing crystal contains heavy elements (e.g., Mg in crystallizing dolomite or Ba in barite) then the boundary layer will be less dense than the original solution and is likely to convect buoyantly. Conversely, if dissolution takes place, the solvent is enriched in solute, causing a compositionally distinct boundary layer to form. This will convect in a direction governed by its density compared with that of the original solvent.

When such convection takes place in crystallizing igneous bodies (McBirney, 1995) fluid movement is concentrated in vertical chimneys where distinct mineralogies develop. Crystal growth in these zones causes a decrease in porosity and permeability if fluid flow is rapid. If such a process takes place in porous sedimentary rocks, it could result in zones of high degrees of diagenesis which will inhibit hydrocarbon migration through otherwise porous bodies and will make reservoirs more heterogeneous.

Experiments in this study grow olivine ($[CoMg]_2SiO_4$) from a synthetic silicate melt in an attempt to assess compositional-driven convection in a viscous medium.

EXPERIMENTAL DESIGN

Experiments were carried out in cylindrical alumina crucibles (18 mm internal diameter and 24 mm height) in which olivine seeds were cemented to the base with alumina cement, with their long axes approximately vertically aligned. Unlike the boundary layer adjacent to a horizontal crystal face, low density boundary layer melt produced on an inclined surface can never be stable, in fact it is instantaneously unstable (Martin, Griffiths, and Campbell, 1987). The alignment of the olivine seeds in these experiments therefore encourages rapid onset of flow of boundary layer melt and maximises the chances of detecting compositional-driven convection in the viscous melt system (400 poise at 1200°C).

The crystals were covered in a superheated synthetic rock melt (at 1300°C) in which iron had been replaced by cobalt to avoid redox problems in an air atmosphere. The crucibles were loaded into the furnace and held at olivine subsolidus (1230°C) temperatures to promote crystallization on the olivine seed. On run completion the crucibles were quenched, and vertical thin sections were made through the crucibles for optical and electron-probe micro analysis. The run products comprise a pink olivine overgrowth around the olivine seed, and a blue glass which is the result of freezing the silicate melt.

A JEOL JCXA 733 Superprobe microanalyser was used for glass analysis. Back-scattered-electron imagery (BSEI) and wavelength-dispersive spectrometry were used to examine compositional variations in the quenched runs. Operating conditions for analysis were 15kV and 20nA throughout, using pure metals, oxides and minerals as reference standards and a 1 micron diameter electron beam.

The approach adopted for analysing the compositional variation in the glass involved examining closely-spaced points for cobalt x-ray count rates which are indicative of CoO concentrations at the analytical point. Stage movements were set at 1, 2, 5, or 10 microns; by this means the width of boundary layers can be determined to a few microns. X-ray count rate data are converted to CoO wt % equivalents for display purposes, and for comparison with natural Fe-normative quenched magma systems. The data, which are displayed as contoured maps, were produced using a programme called "UNIRAS, UNIMAP 2000". This programme allows data from several analytical tracks to be brought together on a single map, and has been successful in producing contoured maps of Co concentrations around apexes of crystal seeds.

EXPERIMENTAL RESULTS

It had initially been hoped that stripping $Co^{2+}$ from the glass, and incorporating it in the overgrowth, would   produce a fading of the blue colour in the cobalt glass. Paler glass was only visible in sections that were ground to much less than the standard 30 micron thickness. This technique proved unsuccessful as pieces of glass were plucked from the slide during grinding. It was therefore necessary to rely on EPMA for compositional analysis of the glass.

Glass immediately above crystal apexes was the primary target for analysis in order to detect whether or not boundary layer melt was convecting away from its source. For this reason several analytical tracks were made across these areas in thin sections of quenched experimental runs. The results from two such areas are presented in this paper.

Using the contouring software on a workstation it has been possible to combine several tracks of X-ray count-rate data to produce contoured maps of cobalt concentration in the glass analysed. This programme produces contours for several hundred data points over a few mm².

Preliminary traverses for Co X-rays in experiment A (1230°C for 24 hours) identified a 5 x 4 mm area of glass above the seed for compositional mapping. 750 data points were analysed in this area and these data are presented in figure 2. This map reveals a vertically-elongate region of Co-depleted glass above the crystal apex.    This is interpreted as a plume of melt that has flowed from the boundary layer produced at the Co-olivine – melt interface. The plume appears directly above the crystal apex, indicating that boundary layer melt has flowed up the sides of the crystal and has detached from the apex, not from its actual point of origin on the sloping crystal sides. Contours give the plume a boudinaged form which may reflect an irregular three-dimensional structure, ie  the plume may curve in and out of the plane of the section, or it could be caused by pulses of melt rather than a continuous stream leaving the crystal apex.

The presence of Co-depleted glass 4 mm above the seed apex is evidence that chemical diffusion is not fast enough to smooth out compositional gradients in these experiments, and that boundary layer melt has a high enough viscosity and density contrast with the surrounding melt to enable it to remain discrete. This experiment shows that a Co-depleted boundary layer is produced by olivine growth on crystal seeds, and that the melt from such a  layer detaches from the upper reaches of the crystal and convects buoyantly.

Glass in experiment B (1230°C for 72 hours.  See figure 3) was examined to check whether compositional convection was taking place in a longer duration experiment. Figure 3 is a map of CoO concentration in an area 2 mm by 0.7 mm (400 data points) positioned 1 mm above the crystal apex. This map again shows areas of CoO depletion directly above the crystal apex.  As with the previous experiment, the indication is of release of boundary layer melt from the upper parts of the seed in pulses, rather than as a continuous plume of melt.  From a single  section  of  the  glass  it  is impossible to tell whether the blob effect is the result of pulses of boundary layer melt leaving the crystal, or is an artefact of a 3-d plume snaking in and out of the plane of the section.  In order to decide between the two it would be necessary to make multiple sections through the glass to characterize the 3-d nature of the Co-depleted bodies.  This map indicates that olivine growth was still occurring and producing buoyant boundary layer melt after 3 days.

Densities and viscosities were calculated using the methods of Bottinga and Weill (1970) and Shaw (1972) respectively. The calculated density difference in the boundary layer melt is 1 % less than the original melt (Seedhouse, 1994). If this small density difference is responsible for fluid convection in viscous silicate melts (400 poise) then compositional convection in aqueous solutions (<<<10 poise) should also occur readily.

OTHER RELEVANT EXPERIMENTAL WORK

Recent work (e.g., Walker, Jurewicz and Watson, 1988 [see figure 4]; Tait and Jaupart,1992; Bedard, Kerr and   Hallworth, 1992 [see figure 5]) indicates that convection driven by compositional differences is responsible for accelerated crystal growth or dissolution along channels of fluid movement.  These channels were originally zones of high porosity and permeability (see figure 6). However, increased flow and crystal growth may cause the pores to become smaller as crystallisation fills the available space. In igneous rocks this results in chimneys containing distinct mineralogies (McBirney, 1995).

## IMPLICATIONS FOR HYDROCARBON EXPLORATION AND EXTRACTION

Temperature gradients in sedimentary reservoirs are not thought to be high enough to drive convection of reservoir fluids by thermal density differences. Compositional differences caused by crystallisation have been shown in this study to be large enough to drive convection in high viscosity melts. Aqueous solutions have viscosities orders of magnitudes lower than those in silicate melts, as such we can deduce that compositional convection is likely to take place in aqueous solutions.

Recent work on high viscosity melts in porous media shows that convection in porous bodies of rock is partly driven by compositional differences. Again, with the lower viscosities associated with aqueous solutions in reservoir rock, one would expect convection to take place. This may result in heterogeneous diagenesis in reservoirs, with regions of low permeability appearing in high permeability strata.

In sedimentary reservoirs the process described above could be responsible for zones of increased diagenesis, and may produce barriers to hydrocarbon migration in carrier beds from source to reservoir, or barriers to oil and gas extraction from reservoirs.

When wells are drilled in sedimentary reservoirs only tiny portions of individual strata are sampled, while logging tools only analyse the rock immediately adjacent to the well. If low permeabilities and porosities are measured in a reservoir rock that contains heterogeneous diagenesis, possibly caused by compositional-driven convection, then this interval may be written off as a potential hydrocarbon producer when in fact a majority of the interval could have excellent reservoir properties.

Zones of tightly cemented sandstones may act as barriers to hydrocarbon flow if the diagenesis predates hydrocarbon migration. Such a scenario may stop the filling of attractive hydrocarbon traps. It could also prove problematic to hydrocarbon production, as the zones of high cementation will cause less efficient sweeping of sandstone units when such methods as water flooding are used.

## REFERENCES

BEDARD JH, KERR RC and HALLWORTH MA, 1992. Porous sidewall and sloping floor crystallisation experiments using a reactive mush: Implications for the self-channelization of residual melts in cumulates. *Earth and Planetary Science Letters, vol 111, pp 319-329.*

BOTTINGA Y and WEILL DH, 1970. Densities of liquid silicate systems from partial molar volumes of oxide components. *American Journal of Science, vol 269, pp169-182.*

MCBIRNEY AR, 1995. Mechanisms of differentiation in the Skaergaard Intrusion. *Journal of the Geological Society of London, vol 152, pp421-435.*

MARTIN D, GRIFFITHS RW, AND CAMPBELL IH, 1987. Compositional and thermal convection in magma chambers. *Contributions to Mineralogy and Petrology, vol 96, pp465-475.*

SEEDHOUSE JK, 1994. Testing for compositional convection in silicate melts; crystal growth experiments and a petrographic study of a differentiated ring dyke. *PhD thesis, University of St Andrews.*

SHAW HR, 1972. Viscosities of magmatic silicate liquids: an empirical method of prediction. *American Journal of Science, vol 272, 870-893.*

SPARKS RSJ, HUPPERT HE, and TURNER JS, 1984. The fluid dynamics of evolving magma chambers. *Philosophical Transactions of the Royal Society of London, vol A310, pp 511-534.*

TAIT S and JAUPART C, 1992.   Compositional Convection in a Reactive Crystalline Mush and Melt Differentiation.  *Journal of Geophysical Research, vol 97, pp 6735-6756.*

WALKER J *et al* , 1988.  Adcumulus dunite growth in a laboratory thermal gradient.  *Contributions to Mineralogy and Petrology, vol 99, 306-319.*

Figure 1.   Production of a buoyant boundary layer by crystal growth. Heavy elements are incorporated into the crystal lattice and are therefore depleted in the melt at the crystal-liquid interface.  This causes a density decrease in the boundary layer and allows it to convect buoyantly away from its source.

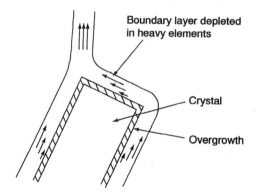

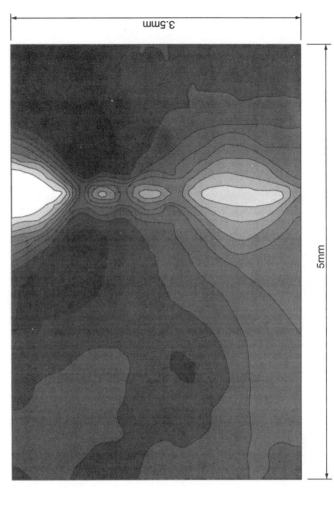

Figure 2.    Map of cobalt concentration in glass above the crystal seed in experiment A.   The database for
this map comprises 750 data points.   Note the boudinaged form of the CoO-depleted glass directly
above the crystal apex.   This may be indicative of pulses of boundary layer convecting buoyantly
from crystal apex.

CoO wt %

>11.94
11.46 - 11.94
10.97 - 11.46
10.49 - 10.97
10.01 - 10.49
9.52 - 10.01
9.04 -  9.52
8.56 -  9.04
8.07 -  8.56
7.59 -  8.07
7.29 -  7.59
<7.29

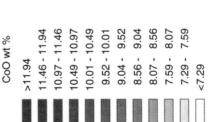

Figure 3.    Map of CoO concentration in glass above the crystal seed in experiment B.   Note the blobs of depleted melt directly above the crystal apex, indicating that boundary layer melt is being produced by olivine growth and is convecting buoyantly.   The map contains data from 400 analytical points.

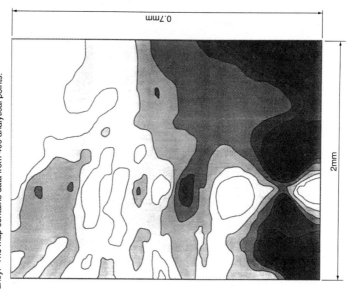

CoO wt %

>11.34
11.28 - 11.34
11.19 - 11.28
11.1  - 11.19
11.03 - 11.1
10.97 - 11.03
10.88 - 10.97
10.79 - 10.88
10.73 - 10.79
10.67 - 10.73
10.58 - 10.67
<10.58

Figure 4.   Textures observed in igneous cumulates (from Walker et al, 1988) . The escape of
            intercumulus fluid from the crystal pile on the floors of magma chambers is thought
            to be driven by compositional density changes. This flow is frequently focussed along
            pathways which, on solidification of the body, have contrasting mineral assemblages.

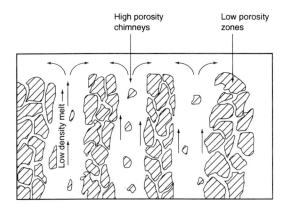

Figure 5.   Channelized fluid flow in a porous medium. Convection is driven by compositional
            density differences in solution (from Bedard, Kerr and Hallworth, 1992). Experiments
            growing a crystal-liquid network in aqueous solutions indicate that buoyant, residual
            liquid flows through the network in channels and is discharged from a focal point as
            a plume. The channel along which the fluid flows has a higher porosity than the rest
            of the network due to crystal dissolution.

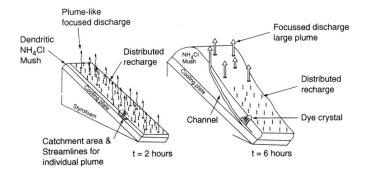

Figure 6.  Self-focusing mechanism of compositional convection in a porous medium (after Tait and Jaupart, 1992). **a)** Initial velocity profiles are similar in upwelling and downwelling regions.  This initial movement may be triggered by temperature or compositional density differences. **b)** Porosity increases in central parts of upwellings, increasing the permeability and therefore the intensity of the flow.  This increased flow could continue to increase porosity if it can dissolve minerals in this region.  On the other hand it may cause precipitation of diagenetic minerals, decreasing permeability, and forcing buoyant fluids to escape via another route. **c)** Porosity fluctuations eventually develop into chimneys.

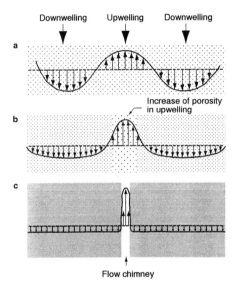

TECHNIQUES FOR DETERMINING
SUBSURFACE STRESS DIRECTION

TECHNIQUES POUR LA DÉTERMINATION
DE LA DIRECTION DE TENSION SOUSTERRAINE

R.E. Hill and R.E. Peterson
CER Corporation

N.R. Warpinski, J.C. Lorenz and L.W. Teufel
Sandia National Laboratories

J.K. Aslakson
Gas Research Institute

ABSTRACT

Knowing the maximum horizontal stress direction ($\sigma_H$) is important for patterning hydraulically-fractured field development wells and waterflood wells. Where natural fractures are a significant component of reservoir permeability, the relationship between natural fractures and $\sigma_H$ can be critical to fracture permeability.

This paper describes 15 techniques for determining hydraulic fracture azimuth. The techniques described are categorized into core-based, borehole-based, near-wellbore, and regional geologic indicators; all can be used to predict or measure hydraulic fracture azimuth. Experience has shown that the more techniques that are used in a single well or field, the more reliable the interpretation of hydraulic fracture azimuth will be.

RESUME

Il importe de connaître la direction horizontale maximale de tension ($\sigma_H$) pour pouvoir établir un modèle de puits de développement de champs fracturés hydrauliquement et de puits d'inondation. Lorsque les fractures naturelles constituent une composante importante de las perméabilité du réservoir, la relation entre les fractures naturelles et $\sigma_H$ peut être cruciale pour la perméabilité des fractures.

Le présent document décrit 15 techniques permettant de déterminer l'azimuth des fractures hydrauliques. Les techniques décrite sont classifiées selon qu'elles se basent sur le noyau, sur le trou de sonde, sur le sondage à proximité d'un puits et les indicateurs régionaux géologiques; chacune d'entre elles peut servir à prédire ou à mesurer l'azimuth des fractures hydrauliques. L'expérience a démontré que l'on obtiendra une interprétation de l'azimuth des fractures hydrauliques d'autant plus correcte que l'on aura eu recours à un plus grand nombre de techniques dans un puits ou un champ donné.

## INTRODUCTION

This paper summarizes the techniques that can be used to determine maximum horizontal stress direction ($\sigma_H$) for oil and gas field development. Maximum horizontal stress direction is important for patterning hydraulically-fractured field development wells to optimally drain a reservoir and patterning waterflood wells to optimize recovery. Where natural fractures are an important part of the reservoir permeability, understanding the in situ stress conditions and their effect on the properties of the fracture system is critical.[1,2] In situ stress affects the measurement and interpretation of geophysical data, petrophysical properties (such as porosity and permeability), rock strength and ductility. In addition, the stress field can change as the reservoir pressure is depleted; this can severely impact reservoir and fracture permeability.[3] The techniques for determining subsurface stress direction described in this report are divided into core-based techniques, borehole-based techniques, near-wellbore techniques, and regional geologic indicators.

## CORE-BASED TECHNIQUES FOR DETERMINING STRESS DIRECTION

Cored-based techniques require oriented core. Therefore, obtaining good quality, oriented core is of primary importance for any of these techniques to work.

### Techniques Based on Core Relaxation Microfracturing

Strain relief of the core after coring is the basis for each of these techniques which include Circumferential Velocity Anisotropy (CVA), Anelastic Strain Recovery (ASR), Differential Strain Curve Analysis (DSCA) and Differential Wave Velocity Analysis (DWVA), axial point load tests, petrographic examination of microcracks, and overcoring of archived core. Relaxation microfractures occur because individual sand grains become stressed during burial and lithification of the sedimentary materials, resulting in compression and distortion of the grains. Fluids permeating through the sediments then precipitate cementing materials which lock in the altered shape of the sand grain. There is considerable stored energy within the grain, and it may vary in different directions depending upon the amount of stress that was applied in each orientation. Obviously, the directions of energy storage, or strain, within a single sand grain are entirely dependent upon the contact points with neighboring particles. However, if a large enough ensemble of grains is chosen, then the domain-averaged principal directions of stored strain will be co-aligned with the principal stress directions. Thus, for relaxation techniques to be valid, there are two primary conditions that must be met. First, the geologic processes are slow and equilibrium conditions are maintained so stored energy within the rock is proportional to the current stress on the sample. Second, the grain size of the sample is small compared to the sample size.

When a rock stratum is cored, the sand grains attempt to expand elastically when the external stresses are relieved, but they are held back by cement materials which form bonds across grains. Many of these cement bonds will eventually be broken, leaving grain-boundary microcracks. The end result of the relief of the in situ stresses by coring is the formation of a population of microcracks that is preferentially aligned with the stress field.[4] A schematic of this population is shown in Figure 1, where it can be seen that there are more (and probably larger) cracks that are opening normal to the maximum in situ stress direction. However, it is important to note that there still are a large number of microcracks with different orientations.

A population of preferentially-oriented microcracks will have observable effects on petrophysical properties in a homogeneous isotropic material, but their effects may not be evident if the rock is highly anisotropic. Examples of core anisotropies, or rock fabric, are bedding planes, bedding structures, large grains, shale clasts, and fractures. Fractures include macroscopic and microscopic natural and induced fractures. The macroscopic fractures can be avoided through careful sampling, but the tectonic microfractures can make all of the strain relaxation techniques unreliable.

### Circumferential Velocity Anisotropy Techniques

Circumferential velocity anisotropy is a technique used to determine the stress azimuth and to deduce information about rock fabric problems. Acoustic velocity through the core is anisotropic because of the population of preferentially oriented microcracks. The velocity around the core will vary because of the effect of crossing a different number of open microcracks in each orientation. Since the averaged direction of maximum crack opening is co-aligned with the maximum in situ stress, the minimum velocity orientation is co-aligned with the maximum stress orientation. Thus, if one can measure the velocity at several orientations around the core, the orientation that has the lowest velocity will be the maximum stress orientation.

In actual practice, there are a number of factors which can cause problems with the CVA technique. In some rocks, there is very little microcrack development, microcracks are overwhelmed by other factors, or the microcracks have little effect on the velocity, so that the anisotropy is small. A good example is a high porosity rock, where additional microcracks have a minimal effect on velocity through the highly voided rock. When velocity variations are on the order of 2 to 3 percent or less, the inferred stress orientation is considered unreliable. A second major problem for the CVA technique is the prior existence of a rock fabric. However, fabrics usually have a completely different velocity character than microcracks, and this becomes very apparent in fitting the theoretical curve to the data. This difference between actual data and the theoretical curve provides a qualitative diagnostic for fabric problems.[5,6]

An advantage to CVA is that it can be performed at any time after oriented core is available, and archived core provides excellent results. It should be considered as a diagnostic anytime that ASR or DSCA/DWVA are used; it can also be used as a primary technique.

## Anelastic Strain Recovery Technique

The Anelastic Strain Recovery (ASR) estimates stress orientation and magnitude from time-dependent strain relaxation measurements of oriented core. Immediately after being cut, the core undergoes differential relaxation in relief of the in situ stresses. The total strain includes both an instantaneous, elastic component and an anelastic component which may relax over tens of hours. Principal in situ stress directions can be determined directly from partial ASR measurements of oriented core by making the assumption that anelastic strains are proportional to the total recoverable strains and that the relaxation process can be described by linear viscoelastic behavior.

The displacements associated with anelastic strain recovery are determined with spring-loaded, clip-on gages, which incorporate precision gage heads.[7] If cores are from vertical wellbores in flat-lying to shallow dipping strata, only three independent displacement measurements are required to determine the directions of the two principal horizontal strains. One procedure is to use three gages that are mounted at 45° to each other in the horizontal plane of each core. Using combinations of any three gages, the principal horizontal strains can be calculated from strain-rosette equations.[8] An alternative analysis technique is to fit the data to a theoretical model.[9,10] This procedure is usually performed when estimating stress magnitudes, but it also provides an orientation that is determined in a least-square procedure, which can be beneficial for data with large scatter.

In addition to core orientation quality, ASR measurements may also be adversely affected by temperature, dehydration, pore-fluid pressure diffusion, homogeneous recovery deformation, anisotropy, drilling mud-rock interaction, residual strains, and core recovery time. Proper understanding of how these parameters influence ASR behavior and the interpretation of ASR results is critical to the successful application of the method.

## Differential Strain Curve Analysis Technique

Differential Stain Curve Analysis (DSCA) is a laboratory technique that estimates stress orientation and magnitudes by comparing the relative strain induced in different directions with the application of confining pressure.[11,12] As discussed earlier, relaxation microcracks have a significant effect on the various rock moduli, and a preferentially oriented set of microcracks will yield different moduli in different orientations, at least for low stress values (until the cracks close).[13] This differential strain behavior is used to extract the stress information.

Figure 2 shows the strain response in one direction due to the application of a hydrostatic confining stress on a core sample with a population of preferentially-oriented microcracks. At low-confining stresses, the rock is highly compliant because of the existence of open or partially-open microcracks. As confining stress is increased, the cracks begin to close (the transition zone), and eventually only the response of the matrix rock remains (low compliance or high modulus). The slope of the initial strain behavior has two components, that of the microcracks and of the matrix. By subtracting out the matrix portion as determined from the high-confining stress conditions from the total, the microcrack contribution can be obtained directly. Of course, if the matrix is homogeneous and isotropic, there is no need to subtract it out for orientation purposes.

These types of measurements are made in multiple orientations, and the differential behavior is used to deduce relative differences in the strain response. Assuming the microcracks are relaxation and not fabric, then two assumptions are needed to use this information for stress purposes. First, the cracks must be proportional volumetrically to the corresponding in situ stress. This assumption was verified by Teufel[14] using acoustic emissions. Second, by reversing the expansion of the sample by subjecting it to hydrostatic pressure, the contraction of the rock in any specific direction will be analogous to the original strain in that direction. This last assumption is not strictly true, as the strain relaxation process is irreversible (as evident from the fact that it always takes more stress to close the microcracks than was originally on the rock at depth), but it appears to be sufficiently applicable that the technique provides good results for many conditions.

Differential Wave Velocity Analysis (DWVA) follows a similar development, except that the acoustic velocity of the material is measured, rather than the strain. Differences are compared in the acoustic travel time between low-stress (cracks plus matrix) and high-stress (matrix alone) conditions for several orientations.

## Axial Point Load Technique

Strength anisotropy tests have been found to be useful for determining the stress azimuth from oriented core.[15] Tests conducted in the Wattenburg Field found that strength anisotropy correlated with hydraulic fracture azimuth. Gregg[16] also used point-load and Brazil tests to determine the rock microstructure. However, in attempting to relate the microstructure to stress azimuth, he failed to account for the differences between relaxation microcracks and other fabric. As a result, his analysis gave inconsistent results. Laubach and others[17] used point-load testing to determine stress orientations in the Frontier Formation and found a bimodal distribution of strength.

Point-load testing, being the easier procedure, is the one recommended for such tests. It is performed by applying a hemispherical indenter to the top and bottom of a core disk and loading the indenter until the rock fails. The pattern of failure is used to deduce the microstructural fabric of the rock. If the microstructure is due entirely to relaxation microcracks, then the induced fractures will align with the microcracks and their orientation will be perpendicular to the maximum stress. If the microstructure is due to tectonic microcracks, then the induced fractures will align with these, and thus, will not be perpendicular to the maximum stress. As with all of the other core-based techniques, it is important to know if fabric is present.

Brazil tests consist of a compression of a core disk across its diameter until failure occurs. This test can be used for strength anisotropy but was generally used by researchers to check the point-load results.

Point load tests are a good technique for determining strength anisotropy in a core sample, and they are fast and easy to conduct. Some machining of the core is required, but the apparatus is simple and so is the analysis. Data analysis consists of measuring the orientations of fractures within the core disks for several samples and obtaining a statistical average and standard deviation of the orientations. Since there is no method to determine if fabric is dominating the response, point-load tests should be performed in tandem with CVA or petrographic examination. The major difficulty with this technique is that there is no way to tell if the strength anisotropy is due to relaxation microcracks or due to other fabric, as all resulting fractures will look similar. Thus, this technique should not be used by itself.

## Petrographic Examination of Microcracks

One of the most valuable techniques for assessing the microstructure of a core is to perform petrographic analyses on thin sections. Such an examination will often provide information on the stress azimuth and rock fabric. Many structural features, including those lumped into the category of "fabric," can be seen under a microscope. Standard blue-dyed thin sections can often be used to detect important features, but techniques using fluorescent-dyed thin sections have made detection even easier.[18,19,20]

Petrographic examination can often be used to distinguish between relaxation microcracks and tectonic microcracks. Relaxation microcracks are primarily intergranular; they typically have uniform widths, or at least monotonically varying widths. Tectonic microcracks can be either intergranular or intragranular; their widths typically are quite variable, presumably because of solution processes that have occurred since the cracks were created. Thus, an experienced examiner can often distinguish between different crack types; petrographic examination becomes a valuable technique for deducing fabric as well as stress orientation.

This technique should be used to diagnose rock fabric whenever there is any doubt about the reliability of other core-based measurements. It is the only technique that can immediately determine if subvisible fabric is affecting the data.

## Overcoring of Archived Core

Overcoring is a technique that can be used to determine the stress azimuth and has potential for use in determining stress magnitudes as well. Apparently, the coring process causes the rock to relieve much of the stored energy through microcracking (as measured with ASR), but not all of the residual stress can be relieved. Successively smaller overcores will continue to relieve additional stored energy, and this energy can be measured in terms of residual strains. The procedure is fairly simple, as it only requires that a strain-gage rosette be epoxied onto the core and a plug be taken. The change in strain (post-coring minus pre-coring) in each direction gives a measure of the differential residual strains/ stresses stored in the rock. Since such strains are likely to be generally aligned with the in situ stresses, the principal strain orientation can be determined using the rosette equations.[5,8]

Overcoring of archived core has the potential to be a valuable technique for estimating stress azimuth because it is simple to use and it can be used on any archived oriented core. Unlike CVA, which requires measurements at a large number of orientations because it is not a tensor, the strain field in one plane can be deduced from only three points.

The principal difficulties with this technique are (1) not all rocks will exhibit much strain recovery upon overcoring and (2) fabric will cause errors in this technique, the same as in any of the other core-based techniques. However, this is an inexpensive technique that can be routinely applied on any oriented core.

## Drilling-Induced Fractures in Core

Drilling-induced fractures can be a reliable indicator of $\sigma_H$.[21] There are two important aspects to the use of induced fractures for stress information. First, the induced fracture must be distinguished from natural fractures, and second, a clear understanding of the fracture, its source, and its relation to drilling parameters must be made. Kulander and others[22,23] and Pendexter and Rohn[24] have described the criteria for differentiating induced fractures and natural fractures in core. Induced fractures can be subdivided into drilling-induced, coring-induced and handling-induced fractures. Of the many types of induced fractures, only petal, petal-centerline and scribeline fractures are appropriate here.

Petal and petal-centerline fractures are drilling-induced fractures created ahead of the bit. They are believed to form in response to the compression of the rock due to the weight of the bit inducing local tensile stress at flaws in the rock. The flaws concentrate the tensile stress and serve as origins for initiating extension fractures that grow parallel to the bit-induced maximum stress. These fractures will open against the minimum in situ stress; therefore, they strike parallel with $\sigma_H$.

In core, petal and petal-centerline fractures are recognized by this distinctive geometric relationship to the core axis. The initial petals curve into the core at angles between 30° to 75° and then curve to become vertical near the central portion of the core (petal-centerline). It is possible to have petals without the centerline portion and many petals may converge to a single centerline as shown in Figure 3.

Scribe-line fractures are coring-induced features created by the orientation scribe knives. Whereas petal fractures form below the bit, scribeline fractures are created above the bit where the core passes the scribe knives as it enters the core barrel. These fractures are more common when the scribe lines are badly-scarred as a result of dull scribe knives. Presumably, dull knives impart more stress than does the clean cut of a sharper scribe knife. The scribe-line fractures originate at grooves created by the scribe knives and are preferentially oriented, approximately parallel with the $\sigma_H$ as shown in Figure 4.

Where present, these induced fractures have been found to be a reliable indicator of $\sigma_H$. If found in conjunction with natural fractures, they can be used to interpret whether present-day stress direction is parallel with natural fractures, even in cores that are not oriented.

## Direct Observation of Overcored Open-Hole Microfractures

A micro-hydraulic fracture initiated in the open-hole environment can provide definitive information on hydraulic fracture azimuth and possibly stress magnitude. A microfracture is induced by conducting an open-hole stress test (OHST), as shown in Figure 5. The fracture induced through this controlled breakdown will propagate laterally and vertically (upward and downward) and align with the prevailing $\sigma_H$. The orientation of the induced fracture can then be determined by coring over the induced fracture which had propagated downward into previously undrilled formation.[25]

The induced fracture can be oriented with a successful overcoring and core orientation operation. The character of the stress-test fracture may be quite variable depending on the rock fabric and includes the following range of possibilities: (1) singular fracture, multiple parallel fractures or fractures which branch and rejoin; (2) smooth fracture faces or rough fracture faces; (3) long (10 to 15 ft) or short (inches) fractures; and (4) fractures which start at the top of the core or fractures which enter from the side of the core at a low angle. The apparent strike and dip of the induced fracture are measured and corrected to true orientation with the core orientation data. The fracture strike will parallel $\sigma_H$.

The accuracy of the azimuth determination based on overcored induced fracture is a function of the reliability of the core orientation data, accuracy of the fracture measurements, and character of the induced fracture. In general, overcoring can result in an accuracy of $\pm 5°$ at best. There are several limitations to successfully determining hydraulic fracture azimuth of overcoring induced fractures. These limitations include: (1) core barrel jamming caused by the induced fracture; (2) poor core orientation of the induced fracture; or (3) the induced fracture does not grow down or is incline and not present in the core.

## BOREHOLE-BASED TECHNIQUES FOR DETERMINING STRESS DIRECTION

### Borehole Imaging of Induced Fractures

Borehole image log data provide a continuous, oriented, 2-dimensional "unwrapped" image of the borehole wall. Image data logs are capable of resolving basic vertical stratigraphy and fractures (natural and induced) as they occur in the borehole. Identification and orientation of induced fractures using borehole image logs can result in an interpretation of hydraulic fracture azimuth.

The relationship of drilling-induced fractures to hydraulic fracture azimuth was previously discussed. Just as drilling-induced fractures measured in core can be used to determine $\sigma_H$, so too can drilling-induced fractures measured on borehole image logs.

First, to provide a meaningful set of data, a statistically significant number of drilling-induced fractures must be detected. Logging an interval of several hundred feet which includes the zone of interest may provide the necessary data for this type of analysis. Once fractures have been imaged, they must be differentiated into drilling-induced, open-hole stress-test-induced and natural fractures. Using only image log data, this task may be difficult or impossible. The best criteria for distinguishing induced from natural fractures is their respective orientations, if known. However, this approach is of little use in an area where induced and natural fractures have the same orientation or where relative orientations are unknown. Image logs can be used to orient conventional cores, and the cores can be used to provide reliable fracture classification. Thus, comparative fracture descriptions acquired from core can greatly enhance image log interpretations, and image log analysis can be used to verify core orientations.

Induced fractures are usually within a few degrees of vertical, and often have vertical lengths which extend several feet or more in the borehole. The drilling-induced fractures often lack the sinusoidal peaks and troughs on the images indicating the fracture origin was within the borehole. Thus, the cause of fracturing may have been a result of the drilling process. Natural fractures can have these characteristics but they are more likely to cross the borehole, giving the familiar sinusoid shape with the peaks and troughs present. Under some circumstances, the natural fractures may have a unique appearance on the log that can allow them to be distinguished from induced fractures.

### Borehole Image Logging of Open-Hole Stress Test Fractures

Using borehole image log data to orient open-hole stress test fractures is similar to orienting drilling-induced fractures, except the approximate depth of the fracture is known in advance. Recognition of breakdown-induced fractures is relatively easy. The open-hole stress test fractures often have very large apertures relative to other fractures in the well. The fractures tend to extend only a few feet below the bottom of the borehole where the open-hole stress test was performed, but the fracture may grow up the borehole for more than 10 ft. In finer-grained (i.e., higher stress) rocks, injecting proppant may hold the fracture open for imaging. This is strongly recommended when using an acoustic image logging tool. Open-hole stress tests described in core often have multiple fracture planes very closely spaced. The image logs will often image multiple stress test fractures as a single, large aperture fracture.

Another potential problem which has not been quantified is the stress field around the borehole may be altered; therefore, the hydraulic fracture azimuth may be altered. Thus, it is possible that a portion of fracture azimuth determined through borehole imaging may not represent the true far-field azimuth. However, the portion of the fracture below the stress-test depth provides a more reliable orientation.

Imaging of fractures induced in the borehole, either as OHST fractures or drilling-induced fractures, can be a simple and effective method for determining hydraulic fracture azimuth. Definitive drilling-induced fractures, however, do not form in all formations. Thus, when attempting to determine fracture azimuth in an area where it is unknown if drilling-induced fractures will form, it is advisable to combine borehole image logging with several other azimuth-predictive techniques to add confidence to the results.

Both electrical and acoustic imaging tools are constantly being improved as are data processing and analysis programs. These improvements include image clarity and data interpretation tools. Computer workstation analysis is highly recommended as it permits the best possible interpretation of the data.

### Borehole Breakouts

Breakouts were first interpreted as a stress-related phenomenon by Bell and Gough.[26] Breakouts are a form of wellbore failure that occur when the stress concentrations at or near the borehole wall exceed the strength of the rock. The resulting microfractures grow and coalesce to form closely-spaced macrofractures. Small pieces of rock between these failure-induced fractures are spalled or eroded and the borehole becomes elongated in the minimum horizontal stress direction.[27,28] Hydraulic fracture azimuth direction can then be determined by adding 90° to get the $\sigma_H$. Borehole breakouts, where the data are unequivocal, are one of the best indicators of $\sigma_H$ because breakouts form in direct response to the in situ stress field. Many of the other stress indicators, such as drilling-induced or hydraulic fractures, are features whose creation is not caused by the stress field. Rather, their orientation aligns with the stress field following crack initiation. However, other factors can influence fracture growth direction. For example, pre-existing natural fractures, faults and bedding can influence fracture propagation.[29]

Most of the problems associated with breakout-derived stress directions are from two causes. First, breakouts must be correctly distinguished from other causes of borehole ellipticity including drill pipe wear and washouts. Second, breakouts may not form parallel with the minimum stress direction when the borehole deviates from vertical or where the vertical stress is not one of the principal stress directions.[30] For instance, topographic relief can cause the vertical stress to be inclined.[31] Current research is presently focusing on qualitative and potentially quantitative stress interpretation using borehole breakouts.[32,33]

Numerous commercially available logging tools can be used to detect and measure breakouts. The best data for measuring breakouts is obtained using one of the sonic pulse-type tools (e.g., Circumferential Borehole Imaging Tool, Borehole Televiewer, Circumferential Acoustic Scanning Tool, and the Ultrasonic Borehole Imager). These tools give a nearly continuous caliper around the well that significantly enhances breakout recognition and measurement when compared with oriented calipers and borehole cameras.

Oriented calipers can also be used for breakout analyses. However, caliper tools do not provide the complete circumferential data that sonic-pulsed tools provide which makes breakout recognition more interpretative. There are several criteria that can be used to distinguish true breakouts from other types of borehole enlargements.[34] Any oriented four- or six-arm caliper tool, if properly analyzed, can be used for breakout detection. Examples of the these types of tools include the Formation MicroScanner and Formation MicroImager. In addition, old wells with dipmeter or other oriented caliper logs can be analyzed for breakouts.

An oriented borehole video imager may be used to analyze breakouts. Poorly-developed breakouts may be difficult to identify, but these tools are capable of detecting well-developed breakouts under proper wellbore conditions. Since breakout interpretations with video data rely on a clear image of the borehole wall, they can only be used in air-filled or optically-clear fluid-filled boreholes. Borehole cameras may provide an acceptable choice for air-filled boreholes since electrical or acoustic tools cannot be used in this medium.

## Borehole Deformation

R&D efforts have been made by Halliburton Services, in conjunction with TOTAL Compagnie Francaise des Petroles, to develop a downhole tool that can measure borehole deformation before, during and after open-hole fracturing. These deformation data acquired during fracture initiation and propagation can be used to calculate fracture orientation and width. The downhole device used for these measurements is termed TOTAL-Halliburton Extensometer or THE Tool.

THE Tool incorporates one or two conventional compression-set testing packers for isolating the zone of interest in the open hole. The device incorporates two sets of six-arm extensometers which utilize linear variable differential transformers (LVDTs) to accurately measure radial borehole displacements as small as 0.001 inches. The two sets of sensors (12 total) are offset from each other to measure displacements at 30° intervals. Orientation, pressure and temperature sensors are also incorporated into the tool assembly. Pressurization of the borehole interval beneath the packers causes radial deformation of the borehole wall. Wellbore pressure reaches the breakdown point of the formation as injection continues and an anisotropic displacement field is produced. The extensometer's displacement pattern determines the fracture direction and directional shear modulus when the formation breaks. Additional information which may be acquired during the injections includes in situ rock modulus; minimum in situ stress magnitude; induced fracture width; and in situ shear modulus.[35,36]

The induced fracture width and direction are calculated from a set of measured wellbore displacements. The orientation of the extensometer pairs is known and therefore can be used to determine fracture azimuth. These results are used to generate an idealized data set of transducer displacements based upon the initial results (e.g., calculated fracture azimuth, width and wellbore expansion) of the original data set. The idealized data are then compared to the actual transducer data which allows for a check to be performed on the transducers. This process may be continued iteratively until the ideal and actual readings are within a prescribed range of agreement. The fracture azimuth is generally interpreted to be perpendicular to the maximum borehole deflection during the tests. The maximum borehole deflection is usually on the axis in which two semi-circular halves, which initiate parallel to the wellbore axis, move during fracturing.[34]

## Directional Gamma Ray Logging

Halliburton Logging Services has developed a wireline gamma ray logging tool designed to statistically determine the azimuthal pattern of gamma ray emissions from completion material (e.g., fluid or proppant) that has been tagged with a radioactive isotope and injected into the formation of interest.[37] These data can then be interpreted to determine fracture propagation azimuth.

The design of the directional gamma ray logging tool (DGRT) incorporates two Halliburton Logging Services measurement instruments, the TracerScan and the RotaScan tools, connected together. The TracerScan tool is a gamma ray spectroscopy device used to determine the vertical and horizontal distributions of radioactive tracers used in hydraulic fracture operations. The RotaScan tool, via a rotating detector, measures gamma ray count rates with respect to rotational position. These data can be oriented using a triaxial accelerometer package incorporated into the RotaScan tool.

Either a fluid-only mini-frac or a propped hydraulic fracture treatment is performed prior to performing the directional gamma ray survey. In each case, the injected materials would be tagged with a radioactive tracer (e.g., liquid gold for a mini-frac or liquid scandium for a propped frac). Data collected after microfrac and mini-frac operations may give better directional results, possibly because the smaller volumes being pumped create a smaller near-wellbore fracture zone than larger propped treatments.

## DETERMINING STRESS DIRECTION BY HYDRAULIC FRACTURE MONITORING

### Microseismic Logging Technique

The Microseismic Logging Technique uses microseismic signals occurring during and after a hydraulic stimulation to estimate fracture azimuth and fracture height. Hydraulic fracturing and fluid injection or fluid withdrawal from a previously-fractured and produced formation alter the in situ stress and pore pressure of a formation in the vicinity of a perforated wellbore. In the process of establishing stress equilibrium, the formation induces localized, abrupt shifts along planes of weakness, including the bedding planes and fractures within the affected region. These small-scale shifts are induced microseismic sources that act as acoustic emitters radiating measurable levels of seismic motion energy into the formation. Microseismic logging detects and locates this cloud of microseismic activity surrounding a hydraulic fracture.[38,39,40,41,42] Tensile failures predominate perpendicular to the direction of the minimum horizontal stress and along zones of weakness in the roughly elliptical central zone of the cloud of microseismic activity.

Surrounding the tensile zone is a zone of shear failure. The shear zone is activated by the fracture fluids leaking off into the formation. The additional pressurized fluid increases the pore pressure and reduces the effective pressure. Both the tensile failures and the shear failures continue for hours after the fracture pumping stops, allowing sufficient time to record the microseismic activity.[43,44] The maximum energy of the largest fracture-induced seismic energy is estimated to be $2 \times 10^{11}$ dyne-centimeters, equivalent to an earthquake Richter magnitude of about negative 2. The typical frequency content of these signals is between about 50 and 450 Hz although recent results indicate that there may be measurable energy up to about 2,000 Hz. These small high-frequency signals can only be detected at ranges up to about 500 ft from the source. Consequently, the receiving geophone must be downhole in the vicinity of the fractured zone, as shown in Figure 6.

Azimuth is determined by plotting either a rose diagram of azimuths or a stereographic projection graph of the unit-normalized direction polarization vectors. The azimuth of the largest number of signals on the rose diagram is interpreted as the fracture direction. The data will show the fracture azimuth plane as a narrow band of data points on a stereographic projection.

### Earth Tilt Technique

Earth tilt mapping is a technique which provides a broad-scale interpretation of hydraulic fracture azimuth. The underlying principle of the tiltmeter technique is to determine the deformation field (gradients of displacement) at the earth's surface that results from growth of a hydraulic fracture in the subsurface. Fracture opening deforms the surrounding rock and, because the earth is elastic, the resulting deformation field extends to the earth's surface. The total surface relief produced by fracture opening is no more than a few thousandths of an inch but the attendant slope changes are measurable with sensitive tiltmeter instrumentation.

This time-evolving deformation field then can be used in conjunction with models derived from elastic continuum theory to resolve geometric features of the hydraulic fracture. The extent to which fracture geometry is recoverable from the data depends principally on completeness of the data in describing the actual surface deformation field and the degree to which the well environs conform to a homogeneous linear-elastic half-space of known Poisson's ratio. A well-chosen array of sample points is often adequate to resolve (in decreasing order of resolvability) fracture orientation, dip, depth-to-center, and height.[45]

In deploying an array of tiltmeters about a treatment well, the intent is to obtain as complete of a description of the fracture-induced surface deformation field as is possible with a finite set of sensors. Tiltmeters, extremely sensitive devices with a resolution 10 nanoradians (0.01 microradians), measure the rotational component of the deformation field induced by the inflation and growth of a hydraulic fracture. This instrument sensitivity corresponds to the angle change caused by a relative vertical uplift of 2mm over a horizontal distance of 400 km.

Ideally, the tiltmeters should be emplaced in 10- to 15-ft deep auger holes several weeks before the fracture treatment to allow for "curing" or settling of the instrument and to acquire periodic (i.e., 10-minute frequency) background earth tilt data. The background tilt noise present in the environment can include solar or lunar tides induced in the Earth's crust; thermoelastic surface strains associated with daily heating of the Earth; local effects, such as the influence of wind on nearby trees, rain and changes in subsurface water; and surface traffic, such as cars, trucks and livestock.[46]

The data acquisition technique during a hydraulic fracture treatment is identical to the background monitoring except that sampling frequency is increased (e.g., 30-second frequency). The earth tilt data acquired in the field during the hydraulic fracture treatment are recorded and may result in a preliminary estimate of hydraulic fracture azimuth in the field. Final confirmation of fracture geometry and azimuth are provided at a later date after more careful examination of the data.

The earth tilt technique is sensitive to broad-scale features of the hydraulic fracture geometry rather than having a field of view restricted to the immediate vicinity of the wellbore. The use of tiltmeter analysis to determine hydraulic fracture azimuth should be considered if borehole or core-based techniques do not yield suitable data. However, fracture detection with tiltmeters is limited, in most cases, to treatment depths shallower than 5,000 ft.[47] This technique also requires a greater degree of logistical coordination to set and cure instrumentation.

## REGIONAL GEOLOGIC INDICATORS OF STRESS DIRECTION

Regional geologic indicators of subsurface stress direction, although locally useful, are not generally part of a data acquisition program for production companies. The various techniques which can be used as regional geologic indicators include fault slip data,[48] earthquake focal mechanisms,[49] trends of joint sets,[50] and volcanic vent alignment.[47]

Fortunately, these data, incorporated with some of the other techniques described previously, have been compiled by scientists from all over the world to produce a world stress map.[47] Consulting this map or some of the previously published maps[51,52] is a good first step for any project where knowledge of $\sigma_H$ is of concern. Experience has shown that the individual techniques described in this report are commonly supported by the stress directions indicated on these maps and, thus, adds a level of confidence to individual well results. Individual well data, however, may vary significantly from those indicated on the stress map, especially near the boundaries between stress provinces.

## ACKNOWLEDGEMENTS

This paper was prepared under GRI Contract No. 5093-211-2602. The original GRI Topical reports, which were the basis of this paper, were prepared under GRI Contract No. 5093-221-2589 (CER Corporation) and Grant No. 5089-211-2059 (Sandia National Laboratories). We also thank James E. Fix for his contribution to the section on microseismic techniques.

## REFERENCES

1.  Laubach, S.E., S.J. Clift, H.S. Hamlin, S.P. Dutton, T.F. Hentz, H. Baek and B.A. Marin, 1994: "Geology of a Stratigraphically Complex Natural Gas Play: Canyon Sandstones, Val Verde Basin, Southwest Texas," Gas Research Institute Topical Report, GRI-94/0167, 135 p.

2.  Lorenz, J.C., N.R. Warpinski and L.W. Teufel, 1993: "Rationale for Finding and Exploiting Fractured Reservoirs, Based on the MWX/SHCT-Piceance Basin Experience," Sandia Report, SAND93-1342, UC-132,150 p.

3.  Teufel, L.W., D.W. Rhett and H.E. Farrell, 1991: "Effect of Reservoir Depletion and Pore Pressure Drawdown on In Situ Stress and Deformation in the Ekofisk Field, North Sea," in Roegiers, J.C. Ed., Rock Mechanics as a Multidisciplinary Science, Proceedings of the 32nd U.S. Symposium, A.A. Balkema, Rotterdam, Netherlands, p. 62-72.

4.  Teufel, L.W., 1982: "Prediction of Hydraulic Fracture Azimuth from Anelastic Strain Recovery Measurements of Oriented Core," 23rd U.S. Symposium on Rock Mechanics, Berkeley, CA, June, pp. 238-246.

5.  Hill, R.E., R.E. Peterson, N.R. Warpinski, J. Lorenz and L.W. Teufel, 1993, "Techniques for Determining Subsurface Stress Direction and Assessing Hydraulic Fracture Azimuth," Gas Research Institute Topical Report GRI-93/0429, prepared by CER Corporation and Sandia National Laboratories, 133 p.

6.  Warpinski, N.R., L.W. Teufel, J.C. Lorenz and D.J. Holcomb, 1993: "Core Based Stress Measurements: A Guide to Their Application," Gas Research Institute Topical Report GRI-93/0270, June, 140 p.

7.  Holcomb, D.J. and M.J. McNamee, 1984: "Displacement Gauge for the Rock Mechanics Laboratory," Sandia National Laboratories Report SAND84-0651.

8.  Jaeger, J.C. and N.G.W. Cook, 1979: *Fundamentals of Rock Mechanics*, 3rd Ed., Chapman and Hall, London, 593 p.

9.  Warpinski, N.R. and L.W. Teufel, L.W., 1989: "A Viscoelastic Constitutive Model for Determining In Situ Stress Magnitudes from Anelastic Strain Recovery of Core," SPE Production Engineering, Vol. 4, August, pp. 272-280.

10. Warpinski, N.R., 1989: "ASR4: A Computer Code for Fitting and Processing 4-Gage Anelastic Strain Recovery Data," Sandia National Laboratories Report SAND89-0484, May.

11. Strickland, F.G. and Ren, N-K., 1980: "Predicting the In situ Stress for Deep Wells Using Differential Strain Curve Analysis," SPE 8954, Proc. 1980 Symposium on Unconventional Reservoirs, Pittsburgh, PA, May 18-21, pp. 251-255.

12. Ren, N-K. and J.-C. Roegiers, 1983: "Differential Strain Curve Analysis - A New Method for Determining the Pre-Existing In Situ Stress State from Rock Core Measurements," 5th Congress of the International Society for Rock Mechanics, Melbourne, Australia, pp. F117-F127.

13. Nur, A. and G. Simmons, 1969: "Stress-Induced Velocity Anisotropy in Rock: An Experimental Study," J. of Geophys. Res., Vol. 74, No. 27, December 15, pp. 6667-6674.

14. Teufel, L.W., 1989: "Acoustic Emissions During Anelastic Strain Recovery of Cores from Deep Boreholes," Proc. 30th U.S. Symposium on Rock Mechanics, Morgantown, WV, June, pp. 269-276.

15. Logan, J.M. and L.W. Teufel, 1978: "The Prediction of Massive Hydraulic Fracturing from Analyses of Oriented Cores," 19th U.S. Symposium on Rock Mechanics, Lake Tahoe, California, May 1-3, pp. 340-347.

16. Gregg, W.J., 1986: "Mechanical Fabric and In Situ Stress Orientations in the Devonian Gas Shales of the Appalachian Basin," 27th U.S. Symposium on Rock Mechanics, Tuscaloosa, Alabama, pp. 709-715.

17. Laubach, S.E., S.J. Clift, R.E. Hill and J. Fix, 1992: "Stress Directions in Cretaceous Frontier Formation, Green River Basin, Wyoming," Wyoming Geol. Assoc. Guidebook.

18. Gies, R.M., 1987: "An Improved Method for Viewing Micropore Systems in Rocks with the Polarizing Microscope," SPE Formation Evaluation, Vol. 2, June, pp. 209-214.

19. Soeder, D.J., 1990: "Applications of Fluorescence Microscopy to the Study of Pores in Tight Rocks," AAPG Bulletin, Vol. 74, January, pp. 30-40.

20. Walls, J.D., J. Packwood, L. Hyman, D. Malek and C. Admire, 1991: "Improvements of Formation Evaluation and Reservoir Engineering in Tight Gas Sands through Selected Core Analysis Procedures," Topical Report GRI-92/0080, December.

21. Lorenz, J.C., N.R. Warpinski, A.R. Sattler and D.A. Northrop, 1990: "Fractures and Stresses in the Bone Spring Sandstones, 1989 Annual Report," Sandia National Laboratories Report SAND90-2068, Sept.

22. Kulander, B.R., C.C. Barton and S.L. Dean, 1979: "The Application of Fractography to Core and Outcrop Fractures Investigations," METC/SP-79/3, U.S. DOE, Morgantown Energy Technology Center, 174 p.

23. Pendexter, C. and R.E. Rohn, 1954: "Fractures Induced During Drilling," J. of Pet. Tech., March, pp. 15 & 49.

24. Kulander, B.R., S.L. Dean and B.J. Ward, Jr., 1990: "Fractured Core Analysis: Interpretation, Logging and Use of Natural and Induced Fractures in Core," AAPG.

25. Daneshy, A.A., G.L. Slusher, P.T. Chisholm and D.A. Magee, 1986: "In situ Stress Measurements During Drilling," Journal of Petroleum Technology, V. 38, No. 9, pp. 891-898.

26. Bell, J.S. and D.I. Gough, 1979: "Northeast-Southwest Compressive Stress in Alberta: Evidence from Oil Wells," Earth and Planetary Science Letters, V. 45, p. 475-482.

27. Gough, D.I. and J.S. Bell, 1982: "Stress Orientation from Borehole Wall Fractures with examples from Colorado, East Texas, and Northern Canada," Canadian Journal of Earth Science, V. 19, p. 1358-1370.

28. Zoback, M.D., D. Moos, L. Mastin and R.N. Anderson, 1985: "Wellbore Breakouts and In situ Stress," Journal of Geophysical Research, V. 90, p. 5523-5530.

29. Warpinski, N.R. and L.W. Teufel, 1987: "Influence of Geologic Discontinuities on Hydraulic Fracture Propagation," Journal of Petroleum Technology, January, p. 209-220.

30. Mastin, L., 1988: "Effect of Borehole Deviation on Breakout Orientations," Journal of Geophysical Research, V. 93, N. B8, pp. 9187-9195.

31. Liu, L. and M. Zoback, 1990: "Effect of Topography on State of Stress at Depth in the Crust: Application to the Site of the Cajon Pass Scientific Drilling Project," Stanford Rock and Borehole Project, V. 40.

32. Barton, C., 1988: "Development of In-Situ Stress Measurement Techniques for Deep Drillholes," PhD Dissertation published by the Stanford Rock and Borehole Project, V. 35, 192 p.

33. Plumb, R.A., 1989: "Fracture Patterns Associated with Incipient Wellbore Breakouts in Rock at Great Depth," Maury & Fourmaintraux (Eds), Proceedings ISRM-SPE International Symposium, p. 761-768.

34. Plumb, R.A. and S.H. Hickman, 1985: "Stress-Induced Borehole Elongation: A Comparison Between the Four-Arm Dipmeter and the Borehole Televiewer in the Auburn Geothermal Well," Journal of Geophysical Research, V. 90, No. B7, pp. 5513-5521.

35. Kuhlman, R.D., T.R. Heemstra, T.G. Ray, P. Lin and P.A. Charlez, 1993: "Field Tests of Downhole Extensometer Used to Obtain Formation In Situ Stress Data," SPE 25905, presented at the 1993 SPE Rocky Mountain Regional/Low Permeability Reservoirs Symposium, Denver, Colorado, April 12-14.

36. McMechan, D.E., J.J. Venditto, T. Heemstra, G. Simpson, L.L. Friend and E. Rothman, 1992: "Microfracturing and New Tools Improve Formation Analysis," Oil & Gas Journal, Dec. 7, pp.75-80.

37. Simpson, G.A. and L.L. Gadeken, 1993: "Interpretation of Directional Gamma Ray Logging Data for Hydraulic Fracture Orientation," SPE 25851. presented at the 1993 SPE Rocky Mountain Regional Meeting/Low Permeability Reservoirs Symposium, Denver, Colorado, April 26-28.

38. Green, A.S.P., R. Baria and R. Jones, 1987: "VSP and Cross-Hole Seismic Surveys Used to Determine Reservoir Characteristics of a Hot Dry Rock Geothermal System," Paper presented at Institut National Des Sciences de L'Univers, 1987 Workshop on Forced Fluid Flow Through Strongly Fractured Rock Masses, Garchy, France, April 12-15.

39. Parker, R., 1989: "The Camborne School of Mines Hot Dry Rock Geothermal Energy Project: Scientific Drilling, 1, 34-41.

40. Hanson, M.E., P.E. Nielsen, G.G. Sorrells, C.M. Boyer II and R.A. Schraufnagel, 1987, "Design, Execution, and Analysis of a Stimulation to Produce Gas from Thin Multiple Coal Seams," SPE 16860, presented at the 1987 SPE Annual Technical Conference and Exhibition, Dallas, Texas, September 27-30.

41. Vinegar, H.J., P.B. Wills, D.C. DeMartini, J. Shlyapobersky, W.F.J. Deeg, R.G. Adair, J.C. Woerpel, J.E. Fix and G.G. Sorrells, G.G., 1992: "Active and Passive Seismic Imaging of a Hydraulic Fracture in Diatomite," J. Petr. Soc., 44, 28-24,88.

42. Wills, P.B., D.C. DeMartini, H.J. Vinegar, J. Shlyapobersky, W.F.J. Deeg, R.G. Adair, J.C. Woerpel, J.E. Fix and G.G. Sorrells, 1992: "Active and Passive Imaging of Hydraulic Fractures," The Leading Edge, 11, 15-22.

43. Fix, J.E., R.G. Adair, K.D. Mahrer, B.C. Myers, J.G. Swanson and J.C. Woerpel, 1990: "Development of Microseismic Methods to Determine Hydraulic Fracture Dimensions," GRI Final Report (December 1987 - November 1989) GRI-90/0220; Teledyne Geotech Report No. 89-6, 110 p.

44. Mahrer, K.D., 1991: "Microseismic Logging: A New Hydraulic Fracture Diagnostic Method," SPE 21834, presented at the 1991 SPE Rocky Mountain Regional Meeting and Low-Permeability Symposium, Denver, Colorado, April 15-17.

45. Evans, K., G. Holzhausen and D.Wood, 1982: "The Geometry of a Large-Scale Nitrogen Gas Hydraulic Fracture Formed in Devonian Shale: An Example of Fracture Mapping with Tiltmeters," Journal of Society of Petroleum Engineers, October, p. 755-763.

46. Lacy, L.L.,1984: "Comparison of Hydraulic Fracture Orientation Techniques," SPE 13225, presented at the 59th Annual Technical Conference of the Society of Petroleum Engineers, Houston, September 16-19.

47. Holzhausen, G.R. and H.N. Egan, 1987: "Detection and Control of Hydraulic Fractures in Water Injection Wells," SPE 16362, presented at the 1987 Society of Petroleum Engineers California Regional Meeting, Ventura, April.

48. Angelier, J., 1979: "Determination of the Mean Principal Stress Directions of Stresses for a Given Fault Population," Tectonophysics, V. 56, p. T17-T26.

49. Zoback, M.L., 1992: "First- and Second-Order Patterns of Stress in the Lithosphere: The World Stress Map Project," Journal of Geophysical Research, V. 97, n. B8, p. 11,703-11,728.

50. Hancock, P.L. and T. Engelder, 1989: "Neotectonic Joints," Geological Society of America Bulletin, V. 101, p. 1197-1208.

51. Zoback, M.L. and Zoback, M.D., 1989: "Tectonic Stress Field of the Continental United States," in Pakiser, L.C. and W.D. Mooney, Geophysical Framework of the Continental United States: Boulder, Colorado, Geological Society of America, Memoir 172, p. 523-539.

52. Zoback, M.D. and M. L. Zoback, 1991: "Tectonic Stress Field of North America and Relative Plate Motions," in The Geology of North America, Decade Map Vol. 1, Neotectonics of North America, edited by B. Slemmons et al, V. 46, p. 339-366.

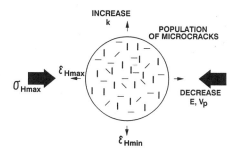

Figure 1  Schematic of Microcrack Effects

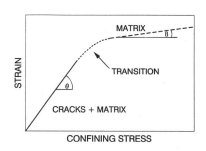

Figure 2  Schematic of Differential Strain Behavior

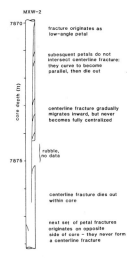

Figure 3  Schematic of Petal-Centerline Fractures and Associated Petal Fractures in Core

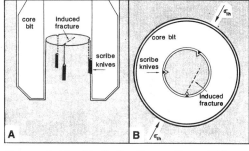

Figure 4  Origin of Scribe-Line Fractures Due to Wedging of Core by Scribe Knives A) Vertical Section and B) Horizontal Section Showing Relationship Between $\sigma_H$ and Strike

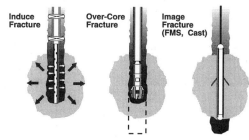

Figure 5  Concept Diagram Illustrating and Induced Open-Hole Fracture to Determine Hydraulic Fracture Azimuth

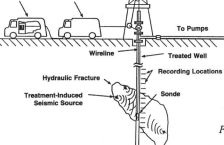

Figure 6  Schematic of Microseismic Logging Data Acquisition

STUDY ON ANOMALIES OCCURRING DURING GAS
FILTRATION IN LOW-PERMEABLE RESERVOIRS

ETUDE DES PHÉNOMÈNES ANORMAUX AU COURS DE
LA FILTRATION DU GAZ DANS DES RÉSERVOIRS
IMPÉRMÉABLES

Rihzov A.E., Savchenko N.V.

Russia

## ABSTRACT

The present paper discloses the results of investigation into low-permeable
rocks with the view to assessing the potentialities of producing gas
therefrom, the result of the laboratory tests on the samples of carbonate and
terrigenous rocks. It has been found that the gas flow in low-permeable
reservoirs have material distinguishing traits, that is, significant
influence of the effective rock pressure on the pore volume and filtration
resistance of reservoirs, the necessity in building up the initial pressure
gradient important for triggering the process of filtration of gas in a
series of rocks containing residuls fluids, plus the pulsating character of
the gas flow. The investigation has revealed the mechanism of the occurrence
of the abnormal phenomena during the filtration process, initial pressure
gradients and pulsation of the gas flow in compact rock reservoirs. With the
above-mentioned phenomena taken into account, the researchers have studied
the dynamics of the exhaustion of gas and the amount od gas recovered from
low-permeable reservoirs.

## RÉSUMÉ

Dans le présent rapport les roches-réservoirs à faible perméabilite sout
étudiées du point de vue d'évaluation des possibilités de production de gaz,
de mise au point des conditions pour introduire les couches compactes dans la
production du gisement, du point de vue de la récupération potentielle de
gaz. Les résultats des travaux complexes de laboratoire sont présentés qui
ont été effectués avec les échantillons des carbonates et des roches
terrigènes provenant de gisements gaziers. Les recherches effectuces ont
demontré que le deplacement du gaz dans des réservoirs à faible perméabilite
a des differences considérables: influence importante sur le volume des pores
et sur la résistance à l'écoulement des réservoirs de la pression efficace
dans la roche; la necessité de créer un gradien initial de pression pour
initier l'écoulement de gaz dans certains roches contenant de fluides
résiduels, le caractère à pulsation du courant de gaz. Le mécanisme
d'apparition des phénomènes anormaux d'écoulement a été étude tels que
gradiens initiaux de pression et pulsations du courant de gaz dans des
réservoirs compacts. Tenant compte de phénomènes examinés des appréciations
ont été faites en ce qui concerne la dynamique du traitement et la
récupération la plus complète possible de gaz à partir les roches-réservoirs
à faibles perméabilite.

INTRODUCTION

At present, low-permeable dense rock are still remaining in the focus of researchers regarding it as a substantial gas reserve. The fraction of oil and gas occuring in low-permeable reservoirs located in the newly discovered fields is constantly growing. This particularly applies to reservoirs associated with carbonate mass. The portion of reserves relating to compact rock in the presently exploited fields where highly productive beds have been to a considerable extent exhansted is also building up.

Dence low-permeable rock has a number of material distinguishing features, that is, complex thin porous and ultrathin porous structure of the pore space, large specific surface area, high content of interstitial water, high gas saturation, nonuniformity of selective texture of gas saturated pores, and substantial pore toruosity. Carbonate low-permeability rock usually form complex reservoirs having several types of voids, namely, thin porous, ultrathin porous, fissured, and those having a certain number of microcaverns.

The present paper is devoted to investigation into dense rock from the viewpoint of assessing the potentialities of producing gas therefrom, revealing the conditions for switching dense rock formations over to gas production and evaluating the contemplated gas recovery potential.

Samples of carbonate and terrigenous rock taken from gas and gas condensate fields have been subjected to a series of special laboratory studies for the above purpose.

Investigation into the process of filtration in low-permeable reservoirs has been made under the conditions simulating stratal ones. Rock pressure was simulated by exerting confining pressure on the sample (up to 80 MPa) and formation pressure was simulated by the intrapore pressure of the gas being filtered (up to 30 MPa). The effective test stress was varied by both stepping down the intrapore gas pressure and increasing the sample confining pressure. The test samples contained residual water in an amount corresponding to that formation interstitial water content. The structure of the rock void space was studied by the methods of mercury porometry and by thin sections.

Experiments have shown that the gas flow in low-permeable reservoirs is substantially different from the filtration gas flow in an ordinary (high-permeable) reservoir. Amongst the differences are the following:

- pronounced effect on the pore volume and filtration properties of low-permeable reservoirs characterized by effective rock pressure;

- marked influence on the gas permeability of liquid fluids (interstitial water, oil and condensate);

- necessity in building up a certain initial pressure gradient for initiating filtration of gas in the rock, and

- pulsating character of the gas flow.

Let us consider in greater detail the results of investigation into the process of variation in the pore volume and gas permeability at a decline in the intrapore pressure and increase of the effective stresses in the samples.

The analysis of the obtained results of the investigation into the various types of rock, both terrigenous and carbonate, has disclosed the following. The structure of the pore space and the specific traits thereof determine the extent and dynamics of the changes occuring in the reservoir parameters. The dynamics of the elastic permeability changes taking place in the low-porous carbonate rock are pictorially illustrated in Figure 1 which disclosed the character of the permeability and pore volume decline caused by the increase in the load imposed on the rock samples of different types of the void space structure which is described by the pore size distribution histograms.

The effective stress to the greatest extent manifests iteself in different ultrathin porous structures where the relative decrease of the pore volume amounts to 80 % and the rock permeability at the effective pressure corresponding to the occurrence depth drops ten to twenty times as compared with the absolute one (Ref. Fig.1).

The presence of thin and particularly medium-size pores (0.5 to 10 mm) in the pore space of larger dimensions. Substantially attenuates the influence of effective stress on permeability. In these conditions, the relative decrease in the pore volume accounts for 7 to 8 % and that of permeability constitutes about 20 to 25 %.

It is apparent that in different kinds of ultrathin porous rock the rising effective stress is relatively uniform and prolonged (up to 60 to 80 MPa) and reduced pore volume and permeability. The presence of pore channels and microcaverns in the rock drastically reduced the influence of the effective stress at 40 to 50 MPa. This is explained by the fact that the intergranular dislocations brought about by the increase in the effective stress have the greatest influence on the thin-pore matrix because of its small pore volume. On the other hand, the same or similar displacements of the rock containing large porous channels produce a significantly lesser effect on the pore volume.

Thus, the experimental studies have outlined the qualitative picture of the influence of the effective stress on the filtration-volume properties of the different terrigenous and carbonate rock, which is actually the same. But, the quantitative evaluation of the changes in the pore volume and permeability of the stressed rocks of various kinds has revealed the fact that the reservoir properties of the terrigenous rock are susceptible to a greater influence of effective stresses.

Investigation into the process of filtration of gas in low-permeable reservoirs containting large amounts of interstitial water has shown that a decrease in the intrapore pressure and increase in the effective pressure are accompanied by a drastic reduction of gas pearmeability down to termonation of the filtration process. Reinitiation of the gas flow proved possible at a certain initial pressure gradient.

Let us now consider in greater detail the phenomenon of origination of the initial pressure gradient in the process of filtration occurring in compack rocks. The manifestation of the

initial pressure gradient mat be caused by a number of diverse
physico-chemical factors associated with the specific qualities of
the filtered fluid and porous medium.

In such cases, the gas filtration process can described by the
following Darcy law formula:

$$V = \frac{K}{\mu} \cdot gradP \cdot \left(1 - \frac{\gamma}{|gradP|}\right), \quad |gradP| > \gamma$$

With $|gradP| < \gamma$, there is no filtration in the rock.

Scrupulous investigation into the initial pressure gradients
characterizing the process of filtration of gas through dense
carbonate rocks under residual water and oil saturation and declining
intrapore pressure conditions has revealed the following mechanism of
initiation thereof.

Gas exhibits mobility in a porous medium when the extent of
saturation thereof by such liquid fluids as water, oil and condensate
is lower then the equilibrium one, but exceeds the residual level.
The reservoir properties deteriorate as the content of thin and
ultrathin pores filled by liquid fluids builds up. The smaller the
size of the pores constituting the rock pore space, the higher the
gas equilibrium saturation, the level of saturation at which the
gaseous phase becomes intermittent and stationary.

The range of gas saturation values at which the gaseous phase
remains stationary naturally constricts as the reservoir parameters
diminish. True, various kinds of rocks possessing characteristic
lithologic traits, particular material constitution, void space
structure, and quantitative relationship between the parameters are
individually colored. Hence, the gas permeability-to-liquid fluid
content curve  becomes increasingly steeper. Even a negligeable
increase in the extent of wetting phase saturation is likely to
result in a drastic decrease of gas permeability to the extent of
complete cessation of the filtration process.

In thin-pore rocks having low permeability, falls in the
reservoir pressure cause migration of liquid fluids into the
gas-saturated pores and fractures to disturb the gaseous phase
continuity and terminate filtration. This mechanism of origination of
the initial pressure gradient is illustrated in Figure 2.

Low-permeable samples containing different amounts of liquid
hydrocarbons have been tested with the object of revealing the effect
of the content of liquid hydrocarbons on the gas filtration process.
The test condensate has been simulated with the use of low-density
oil. The effect of the initial pressure gradient on the "liquid
hydrocarbon-gas" system is substantially lower than that on the
"water-gas" system. The quantity of the initial pressure gradient is
governed by the quantity of the capillary pressure which should be
surmounted for breaking the water and liquid hydrocarbon films
overlapping the gas-saturated pores and fractures. Breakthroughs take
place in the largest pore channels characterized by the smallest
capillary pressure existing at the interface.

In real strata having low permeability and low-porous structure
of reservoirs, the initial pressure gradient disturbs the continuity
of the gaseous phase and brings about the pulsation of the gas flow.

The cyclic recurrence of the filtration process corresponds to the relaxation cycles, that is, the gas flow from the stratum region remote from the near-hole zone of the drastic pressure drop. Such phenomena usually encountered in developing formations exhibiting low filtration-capacity properties significantly complicate production of gas therefrom.

The experimental studies have shown that the initiation of he initial pressure gradient and its magnitude are dependent on the structure of the pore space and degree of saturation with fluids. Variation in the nature of the filtration process, pulsation of the flow, manifestation of the initial pressure gradient and increase in its values under the reservoir pressure drop conditions all together constitute an important factor governing the gas recovery capacity of low-permeable reservoirs.

The field experience and numerous experiments affect that influxes from dense interbeds directly into the well appear considerably suppressed. Low-permeable sections are frequently found either completely or partially blocked. On the one hand, this can be related to a severe contamination of the hear-hole zone by the washing fluid in drilling and on the other hand to substantial deterioration of the filtration characteristics of the near-hole rock space surrounding a well under completion. Hence, with drawal of gas from compact beds is usually associated with the crossflow of gas from these beds over the entire area of contact with the highly permeable reservoirs under development. A great number of researchers believe that such rocks can be fully exhausted due to gas cross-flows between beds.

Let us now consider the dimension of the crossflow in the system consisting of two beds, that is, high-and low-permeable. A low-permeable bed overlays above a drained highly permeable bed. Gas is extracted from solely a highly productive stratum and uniform reduction of pressure is performed in a "sound" drained bed. The lower boundary of a low-permeable bed is considered to be impermeable.

The nonlinear dual-phase filtration equation, supposing the macroimmobility of the liquid phase, is employed as a mathematical model of the process of running a low-permeable startum.

This equation makes allowance for gravity and initial pressure gradient.

$$\begin{cases} V = \frac{K}{\mu} \cdot \left( \frac{\delta P}{\delta z} - \rho \cdot g - \gamma \right), & \text{with } \left| \frac{\delta P}{\delta z} - \rho \cdot g \right| > \gamma \\ V = 0, & \text{with } \left| \frac{\delta P}{\delta z} - \rho \cdot g \right| < \gamma \end{cases}$$

The data on the initial pressure gradient and the porosity-to-pressure and permeability-to-pressure relationships have been obtained on the basis of results of experiments carried out at the Orenburg field. The data on the water saturation fluctuations have been derived from numerically solving the boundary-layer problem by the method of terminal differences. The dynamics of fluctuation of the gas recovery process occuring across the low-permeable stratum are illustrated in Figure 3.

The coefficients of gas recovery in the reservoirs possessing low filtration properties (the results have been obtained from the

calculations made by the above-described method) are excessive
(estimated to a maximum). The calculations performed involved a
uniform average weighted reservoir pressure drop across the entire
bed-to-bed contact area throughout the volume of a sound formation
drained by boreholes. In real strata, the amount of gas recovery due
to crossflows is lower than that indicated in the design pattern
because of the nonuniformity of the pressure field in the stratum
under drainage.

Thus, low-permeable reservoirs can be exhausted owing to the
crossflow of gas into more permeable reservoirs solely at a small
thickness of dense beds (2 to 5 m). The rate of gas recovery
estimated with the use of the data on the specific traits of the
filtration process taking place in compact rocks accounts for 25 %
maximum.


LEGEND:

   V - filtration rate

   K - permeability

   m - porosity, md

   $\mu$ - viscosity, cp

   P - pressure, MPa

   $\gamma$ - initial pressure gradient

   $\rho$ - gas specific gravity, g/cu.cm

   g - gravitational acceleration, m/sq.cm

   z - coordinate

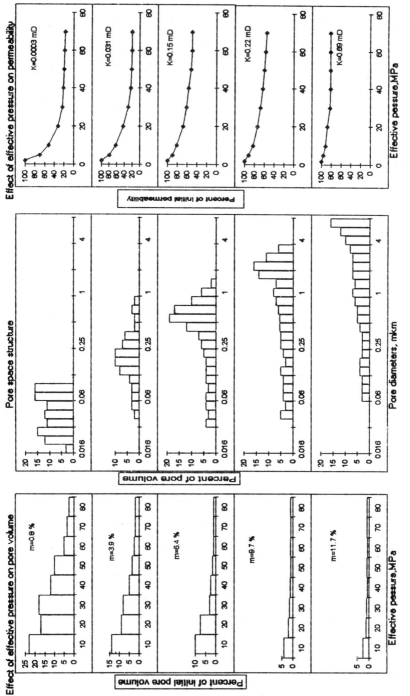

Figure I. Decrease in pore volume and permeability with increasing effective pessure for different pore space carbonate cores

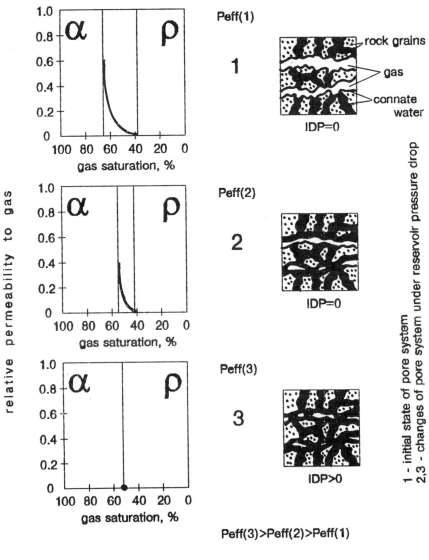

α - connate water saturation

ρ - balance gas saturation

Figure 2. Mechanism of appearance initial differential pressure (IDP) with deformation changes in pore system under reservoir pressure drop.

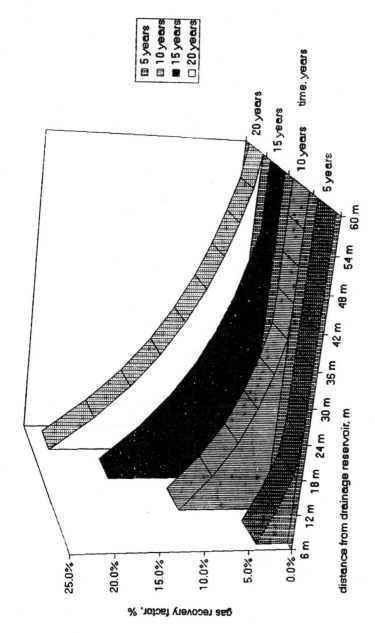

Figure 3 . Changes in gas recovery factor and drainage thickness with time for tight reservoir.

MODELLING NATURAL GAS PROPERTIES
THROUGH MOLECULAR SIMULATION

MODÉLISATION DES PROPRIÉTÉS DU GAZ NATUREL
PAR MODÉLISATION MOLÉCULAIRE

Nick Quirke
University of Wales at Bangor, Gwyned, U.K.

Alexandre Rojey, Bernard Tavitian, Philippe Ungerer
Institut Français du Pétrole, Rueil-Malmaison, France

**ABSTRACT**

The exploitation of natural gas reserves requires a good knowledge of natural gas properties within a wide range of operating conditions, taking into account the possible presence of various contaminants. This paper presents the application of a Gibbs ensemble Monte-Carlo method for the prediction of phase equilibria. Simulation data have been obtained for ethane and the case of more complex molecules is discussed. Some indications are also given concerning the way non-equilibrium molecular dynamics could be used in the future for predicting natural gas transport properties.

**RÉSUMÉ**

L'exploitation des réserves de gaz naturel nécessite une bonne connaissance des propriétés du gaz naturel dans une large gamme de conditions opératoires, en tenant compte de la présence possible de différents contaminants. La publication présente l'application d'une méthode de Monte-Carlo dans l'ensemble de Gibbs pour prédire les diagrammes de phases. Des données de simulation ont été obtenues pour l'éthane et le cas de molécules plus complexes est également discuté. L'utilisation dans le futur de la dynamique moléculaire en non-équilibre pour la prédiction des propriétés de transport du gaz naturel est également abordée.

## BACKGROUND

Reliable predictions of natural gas properties are essential in optimising the exploitation of natural gas reserves. The accuracy of current macroscopic models based on Equations of State used by the gas industry to estimate gas properties depends upon the availability of extensive data bases of experimental results. Such data are required over a wide range of temperature, pressure and composition.

Increasingly, operators are faced with the necessity of producing gas under extreme conditions. In some fields, pressures exceeding 100 MPa and temperatures up to 200°C are found. Phase diagrams under such conditions are not known precisely, while models are inaccurate. This can be a major uncertainty in the development of high pressure and temperature fields.

Better and more extensive data are also required for other aspects of natural gas operations: various contaminants are found in natural gas, examples include water, acid gases such as $H_2S$, $CO_2$, RSH, inert gases such as $N_2$ and He, and small quantities of mercury and arsenic. In order to remove them to meet gas specifications it is necessary to know how they split between different natural gas phases and their solubility in various solvents and adsorbents. An improved knowledge of low temperature and boiling point properties of methane and its mixtures with nitrogen as well as other hydrocarbons would be helpful in optimising the design of natural gas liquefaction plants.

To obtain these data experimentally would be prohibitively expensive. This paper describes an alternative procedure; the use of novel molecular simulation techniques to generate reliable pseudo-experimental data which can be used to systematically improve current macroscopic thermodynamic models. Data are presented for natural gas fluids.

## PHASE EQUILIBRIA

It is the overall aim of molecular simulation to predict thermodynamic (e.g. the relationships between pressure, volume and temperature), interfacial (e.g. surface tension), and transport (e.g. viscosity) properties of gases, liquids, and solids. To this end, one requires (a) the intermolecular forces between the constituent molecules are known to a good approximation, (b) the microscopic time scale over which these properties are determined is less than or in the region of nanoseconds ($10^{-9}$ s) and (c) the molecules are relatively small. These three conditions have been met for the mixtures of interest to the natural gas industry.

Molecular simulation takes as input the intermolecular potential function $U(\underline{R})$ which depends on the coordinates $\underline{R}$ of all the atoms in the system. Given the desired conditions of temperature and pressure it provides as output averages of molecular configurations that correspond to the phase properties of interest. This is shown schematically in figure 1.

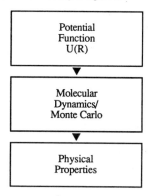

**Figure 1.** The direct route to physical properties of materials. Starting from a potential function $U(\underline{R})$ which describes the interaction energy of the system as a function of the molecular coordinates, molecular simulation methods such as molecular dynamics and Monte Carlo generate configurations from which the physical properties of condensed phases may be predicted.

Once the intermolecular potentials have been determined the temperature, pressure and composition of the liquid may be varied at will. For the case of coexisting phases a new molecular simulation method, Gibbs ensemble Monte Carlo, has been developed. This provides the computational means to reliably predict liquid-liquid and liquid-vapour coexistence. The software is currently being developed for natural gas and related mixtures.

Gases

Preliminary results are displayed in figures 2 and 3 illustrating the accuracy with which the liquid-vapour coexistence and high pressure properties of methane and ethane can be predicted using the simplest possible effective potential functions.

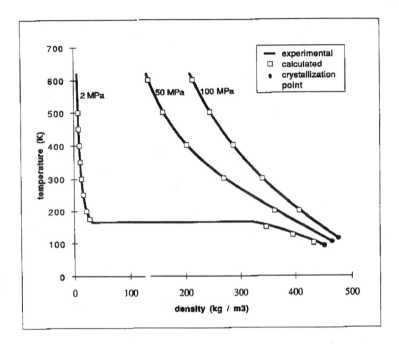

**Figure 2.** Computed density of pure methane at high pressures and temperatures by Monte-Carlo molecular simulation in the NPT ensemble with a Lennard-Jones potential (parameters $\varepsilon/K = 147.9$, $\sigma = 3.73$) compared with experimental densities (Younglove & Ely, 1987).

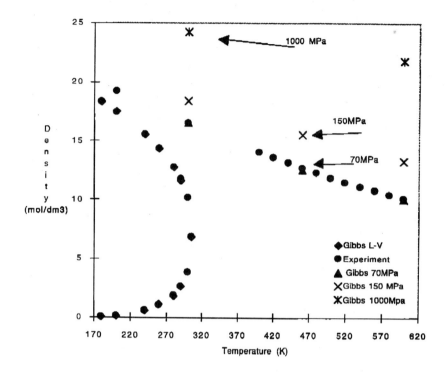

**Figure 3.** High pressure isobars for ethane (1) predicted using Monte carlo (Gibbs ensemble) with a two centre Lennard-Jones effective potential. The solid circles show experimental data (2) and the diamonds, triangles and crosses are the predictions of Gibbs ensemble simulation. In the coexistence region the simulation data are obscured by the experimental data points. The experimental data in reference 2 do not go above 70 MPa, molecular simulation data has been obtained for pressures of 150 MPa and 1000 MPa.

For the coexistence region of ethane (figure 3) the average deviations from experiment were 1% for the liquid density, 3% for the vapour density and 3% for the vapour pressure. The estimated critical temperature for ethane is 305.7K (experiment 305.34K) and the estimated critical density is 6.82 mol/dm$^3$ (experiment 6.88 mol/dm$^3$). Figure 3 shows predicted isobars at 150 MPa and 1000 MPa, obtained by fitting the parameters of the Lennard-Jones potential ($\sigma$, $\varepsilon$) on one single experimental value of ethane density; they can be expected to be accurate to < 2%. Methane density is also well predicted (figure 4) up to 100 MPa and 600 K at least.

More Complex Molecules

Many of the mixtures of interest to the gas industry are associated fluids which form hydrogen bonds and whose thermodynamic properties are dominated by molecular association. van Leeuwen and Smit (3) recently used the Gibbs ensemble to predict the vapour-liquid and critical properties of methanol. Excellent agreement was obtained, for example the critical temperature was determined to be $T_C$ = 512.6 K (exp. Tc = 512.64 K) and the critical density 277.8 kg/m$^3$ (exp. 272 kg/m$^3$). Recent simulation predictions for the associating mixture water-methanol are also in good agreement with experiment (4). Finally, Siepmann et al (5) used similar methods to predict the properties of long chain alkanes of interest to the oil industry. They were able to reproduce the liquid-vapour and critical properties of such fluids where they are known for short chains ($C_n$, n<16) and predict the required properties where they were unknown (n=48). Such data are important for reservoir simulations of gas condensate fields.

## OTHER PROPERTIES

Molecular simulation is not limited to thermodynamic properties, transport properties may also be predicted. Non-equilibrium molecular dynamics (NEMD) has been successful in calculating transport properties of molecular fluids. NEMD simulates a system in a steady state induced by the action of an external field. In order to calculate viscosity, shearing boundary conditions are used to produce an external strain field that results in a steady state Couette flow permitting the calculation of the shear viscosity from the ratio of the off-diagonal element of the pressure tensor to the strain rate. The Newtonian viscosity is obtained as the zero strain rate extrapolation of the strain rate dependent shear viscosity. This method has been used recently to predict the viscosity of carbon dioxide-ethane mixtures (6) using simple effective molecular Lennard-Jones potentials derived from fitting to mixture phase equilibria data.

## CONCLUSION

Modern molecular simulation methods of predicting phase behaviour may provide a promising alternative to experiment under normal and extreme conditions especially for natural gas mixtures. In the future they may be used to enrich data bases from which parameters are obtained for industry equations of state. In this paper new data and new methods for natural gas property prediction have been presented.

## REFERENCES

1. N. Quirke, Molecular Simulation, 1995, in press.

2. B.A. Younglove, J.F. Ely, J. Phys., Ref. Data 16, 642, 1987.

3. M.E. van Leeuwen, B. Smit, J. Phys. Chem., 1994, in press.

4. H.J. Strauch, P.T. Cummings, Fluid Phase Equilibria, 83: 213, 1993.

5. J.I. Siepmann, S. Karaborni, B. Smit, Nature 365: 330, 1993.

6. B.Y. Wang, P.J. Cummings, Molecular Simulation, 10: 1, 1993.

# SOUND VELOCITY MEASUREMENTS

# ON NATURAL GASES

François Montel
Elf Aquitaine, France

Pierre Labes, Jean-Luc Daridon, Bernard Lagourette and Pierre Xans
Université de Pau et des Pays de l'Adour, France

## SUMMARY

Measurements of sound velocity were performed in two natural gases over a large pressure (10 to 100 MPa) and temperature (-10 to 150°C) range.
Sound velocity is related in a simple way to the various coefficients of compressibility, isentropic, isenthalpic and isothermal and its measurements appears to be a severe and relevant test for the selection of the most efficient equation of state for the modelling of the behaviour of natural gases at the various production and transport stages.
Six equations of state have been retained for the restitution tests and six external mixing rules have been studied. The most accurate restitution of the overall data, is supplied by the Lee-Kesler equation of state associated with the Teja mixing rule.

## RESUME

Des mesures de vitesse du son ont été exécutées sur deux gaz naturels entre 10 et 100 MPa pour l'intervalle de pression et entre -10 et 150°C pour l'intervalle de température.
La vitesse du son est reliée, par des formules simples, aux différents coefficients de compressibilité isentropique, isenthalpique et isotherme et sa mesure s'est révélée être un test sévère et pertinent pour la sélection de l'équation d'état la mieux adaptée pour modéliser le comportement des gaz naturels dans les installations de production et de transport.
Six équations d'état ont été retenues pour les tests de restitution en liaison avec six différentes règles de mélange.
La meilleure restitution a été obtenue avec l'équation de Lee et Kesler combinée avec la règle de mélange de Teja.

## INTRODUCTION

Thermodynamic models are widely used in the Oil and Gas industry and the number of new Equations of State (EOS) and new mixing rules increases sharply since several years. Facing a new problem, engineers encounter more and more difficulties to select the best model. This selection is generally made after comparison of the calculated and experimental fluid phase equilibria in the pressure/temperature/composition domain of interest.
We claim that this selection could be greatly improved if we include ultrasonic velocity measurements in the experimental data base.

Ultrasonic velocity "U" is related in a simple way to the various coefficients of compressibility, isentropic, isenthalpic and isothermal.
These coefficients are fundamental for the characterization of the behaviour of natural gases at the various production and transport stages. Hence the importance of measuring the ultrasonic velocities in temperature and pressure conditions encountered by the fluid and to include these measurements into the selection data base.

## MEASUREMENTS

Experimental measurements of sound velocity were made in two natural gases in a large pressure (10 to 70 MPa) and temperature (-10 to 150°C) range. The experimental system and measurement method have been described in detail by Ye et Al[1]. All the measurements were made at Pau University.

Usually the speed of sound within the fluid is obtained by a pulse method called the "echo overlap method" as proposed by Papadakis[2], but, when the attenuation of ultrasonic waves is strong, like for gases, only the first echo can be use and the echo overlap method does not work. Therefore another measurement technique was applied[3].

Two natural gases, supplied by GAZ DE FRANCE, were studied:

- natural gas from North sea (H)
- natural gas from Algeria (A)

The compositions of these two gases are indicated in table 1 and 2 and the sound velocity measurements are given in the tables 3 and 5. Densities were also measured up to 40 MPa using an ANTON PAAR densimeter DMA 45 model equipped with a high pressure cell DMA 512 and results are given in the tables 4 and 6.

## MODELLING

Sound velocity $U$ can be expressed from the system free energy $A$ by the following formula:

$$U = \frac{V}{M^{1/2}} \left( \left( \frac{\partial^2 A}{\partial V^2} \right)_T - \frac{(\partial^2 A/\partial V \partial T)^2}{(\partial^2 A/\partial T^2)_V} \right)^{1/2}$$

$M$     Molecular weight
$V$     Molar volume
$T$     Temperature

But, in the practice, a free energy analytical expression is not always available to perform direct calculation and in the numerical tests, for which results are further reported, the calculation of the velocities lies on the formula:

$$U^2 = \frac{1}{\rho \cdot [\beta_T - (\alpha^2 \cdot V \cdot T)/C_p]}$$

with $\alpha$ thermal expansivity, $\beta_T$ isothermal compressibility, $\rho$ density and $C_p$ specific heat capacity at constant pressure.

The calculation procedure applied consists, for each (P,T) set, in numerically resolving the equation of state with respect to the unknown V. the value of the density is derived from this first operation. Then, the following formulae are applied in order to obtain the other quantities :

$$\alpha = -\frac{1}{V} \frac{(\partial P/\partial T)_V}{(\partial P/\partial V)_T}$$

$$\beta_T = -\frac{1}{V(\partial P/\partial V)_T}$$

and the departure function for the heat capacity at constant pressure :

$$C_p - C_p^* = \int_\infty^v T\left(\frac{\partial^2 P}{\partial T^2}\right)_v dV - T\frac{(\partial P/\partial T)_v^2}{(\partial P/\partial V)_T} - R$$

The various partial derivatives and the integral term appearing as the departure function for the heat capacity are expressed analytically on the basis of the equation of state under consideration, the numerical values are calculated using the value of V given by the previous operation.

In order to determine the specific heat capacity, it is necessary to adopt an expression of the ideal part $C_p^*(T)$, we selected the Aly and Lee[4] representations:

$$C_p^*(T) = C1 + C2\left(\frac{C3/T}{sh(C3/T)}\right)^2 + C4\left(\frac{C5/T}{sh(C5/T)}\right)^2$$

Six equations of state have been retained for the restitution tests :

| | | |
|---|---|---|
| 1 - | SRK | Soave-Redlich-Kwong |
| 2 - | PR | Peng-Ropbinson in its form of origin |
| 3 - | PR-RP | Peng-Robinson as modified by Rauzy-Peneloux method[5] |
| 4 - | SBR | Simonet-Behar-Rauzy[6] |
| 5 - | LK | Lee-Kesler[7] |
| 6 - | COR | Chain of Rotators[8] |

All these equations are currently used for thermodynamic calculations in oil and gas production and processing.

The calculation of parameters from the equation of state for mixtures implies the application of mixing rules to the parameters of pure compounds. Such rules are empirical but of prime importance on the quality of results. Among the equations applied, the Lee-Kesler's model is based on corresponding states. There is a distinct calculation step to get the fluid pseudo-critical coordinates by application of the mixing rules to the critical coordinates of the compounds. It is therefore reasonable to seek for the mixing rule best adapted to the restitution of optimum pseudo-critical properties with respect to the thermodynamic properties to be restituted.

Such approach has been extended to the other equations of state with regard for homogeneity, mixing rules are marked "external rules" in this case.
In practice these equations are not used with other mixing rules than those set by the authors on the parameters involved, marked "internal rules" in this text.

Six external mixing rules have been studied :

1 : Pedersen-Fredenslund-Christensen-Thomassen[9]
2 : Spencer-Danner[10]
3 : Teja[11]
4 : Hankinson[12]
5 : Lee-Kesler
6 : Plocker-Knapp-Prausnitz[13]

Previous comparison between the various mixing rules was made over a data set of $U$ relative to alkane binary mixtures. Results are collated in Ye et Al[14]. For asymmetric mixtures, whose two compounds display very far apart critical properties, we note that the mean deviations vary very significantly following the compositional rule considered and for a same equation of state. Generally Teja external mixing rule leads to good results:

$$Vc_m = \sum_i \sum_j z_i z_j \frac{1}{8} (Vc_i^{1/3} + Vc_j^{1/3})^3$$

$$Tc_m = \frac{1}{Vc_m} \sum_i \sum_j z_i z_j (Vc_i \cdot Vc_j \cdot Tc_i \cdot Tc_j)^{1/2}$$

$$Zc_m = \sum_i z_i \frac{Pc_i Vc_i}{RTc_i}$$

$$Pc_m = \frac{R \cdot Tc_m \cdot Zc_m}{Vc_m}$$

$$\omega_m = \sum_i z_i \omega_i$$

In the case of low asymmetric mixtures the effect of the choice of the external mixing rule makes practically no difference with respect to the deviations observed. As in the case of pure compounds[15], LK equation is that leading to the most accurate restitution.

## APPLICATION TO NATURAL GASES

All the components in natural gases are identified individually and for each of them we know the mole fraction , molecular weight, critical properties and acentric factor. Calculation of pseudo-critical properties and acentric factor of the two fluids were performed by applying the various mixing rules previously cited.

Results of the comparisons performed between the calculated values of $U$ and the experimental values relative to the fluids are summarized in the tables 7 and 8.

The most accurate restitution of the overall data, is supplied by the Lee-Kesler equation of state.

## CONCLUSION

The results we presented show that the ultrasonic velocity measurements are a severe test for the equations of state and associated mixing rules. Its measurement is reliable and accurate, and is more easily accessible in pressure and temperature than the other properties. It can therefore serve as an useful database to discriminate the thermodynamic models.

The characterization of oil fluids by ultrasonic velocity measurements should greatly develop in the coming years. A lot of work has still to be achieved : in the experimental field to complete the databases necessary for testing the models and, in the modelling field, for evidencing defects and qualities in the thermodynamic models.
This work was performed within the framework of a Joule program, contract JOUF-CT91-0066: "Integration of calorimetric and velocimetric measurements in the thermodynamic modelling of synthetic hydrocarbon mixtures representative of natural gases"

Nomenclature

| | |
|---|---|
| $A$ | Helmotz free energy |
| $U$ | Sound velocity |
| $M$ | Molecular weight |
| $V$ | Molar volume |
| $P$ | Pressure |
| $T$ | Temperature |
| $C_p$ | Specific heat at constant pressure |
| $\alpha$ | Thermal expansivity |
| $\rho$ | Density |
| $\beta_T$ | Isothermal compressibility |
| $Pc$ | Critical pressure |
| $Tc$ | Critical temperature |
| $Vc$ | Critical volume |
| $Zc$ | Critical compressibility |
| $\omega$ | Acentric factor |
| $z_i$ | Molar fraction of component i |

TABLES

| Component | mole% | Component | mole% |
|---|---|---|---|
| Nitrogen | 3.187 | Benzene | 0.0272 |
| Carbon dioxide | 1.490 | Cyclohexane | 0.0065 |
| Methane | 88.405 | iso Heptanes | 0.0100 |
| Ethane | 5.166 | nHeptane | 0.0041 |
| Propane | 1.176 | Methyl Cyclohexane | 0.0052 |
| iso Butane | 0.149 | Toluene | 0.0030 |
| nButane | 0.226 | iso Octanes | 0.0029 |
| iso Pentane | 0.056 | nOctane | 0.0008 |
| nPentane | 0.049 | iso Nonanes | 0.0009 |
| iso Hexanes | 0.0216 | nNonane | 0.0002 |
| nHexane | 0.0136 | | |

Table 1. Composition of the natural gas from North Sea (H)

| Component | mole% |
|---|---|
| Nitrogen | 3.187 |
| Methane | 89.569 |
| Ethane | 8.348 |
| Propane | 1.197 |
| iso Butane | 0.149 |
| nButane | 0.226 |
| iso Pentane | 0.015 |

Table 2. Composition of the natural gas from Algeria (A)

| T °K | Sound velocity (m/s) | | | | | | | |
|---|---|---|---|---|---|---|---|---|
| | 262.4 | 273.1 | 283.8 | 294.0 | 303.3 | 313.6 | 334.0 | 354.0 |
| P MPa | | | | | | | | |
| 12 | 393.1 | 397.2 | 405.0 | 413.6 | 421.4 | 430.1 | 446.5 | 461.7 |
| 14 | 428.0 | 422.8 | 424.6 | 429.3 | 434.8 | 441.6 | 455.8 | 469.8 |
| 16 | 469.7 | 455.5 | 450.7 | 450.6 | 452.8 | 457.2 | 468.0 | 480.2 |
| 18 | 511.5 | 490.6 | 479.9 | 475.1 | 474.3 | 475.8 | 482.8 | 492.4 |
| 20 | 553.0 | 527.5 | 511.8 | 502.6 | 498.6 | 497.2 | 499.7 | 506.5 |
| 22 | 591.9 | 563.7 | 544.0 | 531.2 | 524.3 | 519.9 | 518.2 | 521.8 |
| 24 | 628.4 | 598.3 | 575.9 | 560.2 | 550.5 | 543.7 | 537.7 | 538.4 |
| 26 | 664.3 | 632.6 | 607.4 | 589.4 | 577.7 | 568.7 | 558.6 | 556.1 |
| 28 | 696.0 | 663.7 | 637.2 | 617.8 | 604.1 | 593.0 | 579.6 | 574.3 |
| 30 | 727.1 | 694.4 | 666.9 | 645.5 | 630.4 | 617.8 | 600.6 | 593.1 |
| 32 | 756.8 | 723.3 | 694.4 | 672.3 | 656.0 | 641.8 | 622.9 | 611.8 |
| 34 | 784.2 | 750.4 | 721.3 | 698.2 | 680.7 | 665.5 | 643.5 | 630.6 |
| 36 | 810.8 | 776.6 | 747.3 | 724.1 | 705.3 | 689.1 | 665.3 | 650.3 |
| 38 | 835.8 | 801.9 | 772.0 | 748.9 | 728.9 | 711.4 | 686.0 | 669.2 |
| 40 | 860.1 | 826.1 | 795.9 | 772.4 | 751.5 | 734.1 | 706.5 | 687.9 |
| 42 | 883.1 | 849.3 | 818.8 | 794.5 | 774.2 | 756.0 | 726.8 | 706.9 |
| 44 | 904.8 | 871.3 | 840.8 | 815.7 | 794.9 | 776.3 | 746.4 | 725.2 |
| 46 | 926.4 | 893.2 | 862.7 | 837.2 | 816.4 | 797.3 | 766.2 | 743.9 |
| 48 | 947.0 | 913.6 | 883.2 | 857.8 | 836.4 | 816.7 | 785.1 | 761.4 |
| 50 | 967.2 | 933.5 | 903.6 | 878.1 | 856.4 | 836.2 | 803.5 | 779.0 |
| 52 | 986.9 | 953.5 | 923.2 | 897.6 | 876.3 | 855.3 | 822.0 | 796.7 |
| 54 | 1005.3 | 972.5 | 942.3 | 916.2 | 894.8 | 873.6 | 840.0 | 813.3 |
| 56 | 1023.7 | 991.0 | 960.5 | 934.7 | 912.7 | 891.9 | 857.5 | 830.5 |
| 58 | 1041.4 | 1008.7 | 978.7 | 952.3 | 930.9 | 909.7 | 874.8 | 846.9 |
| 60 | 1058.6 | 1026.3 | 996.2 | 969.8 | 948.0 | 926.5 | 891.4 | 863.0 |
| 62 | 1075.8 | 1043.4 | 1013.4 | 987.0 | 965.3 | 944.0 | 908.0 | 879.3 |
| 64 | 1091.4 | 1059.9 | 1030.0 | 1004.0 | 981.8 | 959.6 | 923.7 | 894.5 |
| 66 | 1107.8 | 1076.4 | 1046.7 | 1019.9 | 998.5 | 977.0 | 939.7 | 910.5 |
| 68 | 1123.3 | 1091.8 | 1062.7 | 1035.9 | 1014.3 | 992.3 | 955.0 | 925.4 |
| 70 | 1138.7 | 1107.2 | 1077.8 | 1051.8 | 1029.6 | 1008.1 | 970.5 | 940.1 |

Table 3. Sound velocity in the natural gas from North Sea (H)

| T °K | Density kg/m3 | | | | | | |
|---|---|---|---|---|---|---|---|
| | 293.2 | 303.2 | 313.2 | 323.2 | 333.2 | 343.2 | 353.2 |
| P MPa | | | | | | | |
| 12 | 115.4 | 106.8 | 99.3 | 93.8 | 89.3 | 85.4 | 82.2 |
| 16 | 157.8 | 146.1 | 136.2 | 127.9 | 120.9 | 115.4 | 110.2 |
| 20 | 191.4 | 178.6 | 167.5 | 157.8 | 149.4 | 142.6 | 136.7 |
| 24 | 219.1 | 206.3 | 194.4 | 184.1 | 175.0 | 167.4 | 160.5 |
| 28 | 240.7 | 228.4 | 216.8 | 206.3 | 198.4 | 190.5 | 183.5 |
| 32 | 259.2 | 247.5 | 236.7 | 226.5 | 217.2 | 209.3 | 201.6 |
| 36 | 274.0 | 262.8 | 251.9 | 242.3 | 233.3 | 225.3 | 217.6 |
| 40 | 286.0 | 275.4 | 265.4 | 255.7 | 246.9 | 238.9 | 231.7 |

Table 4. density of the natural gaz from North Sea (H)

| | | | | | Sound velocity (m/s) | | | | | | |
|---|---|---|---|---|---|---|---|---|---|---|---|
| T °K | 272.9 | 293.7 | 303.4 | 313.2 | 323.3 | 333.2 | 343.4 | 353.2 | 373.4 | 393.5 | 413.6 |
| P | | | | | | | | | | | |
| MPa | 549.3 | 514.7 | 508.0 | 505.1 | 504.6 | 505.2 | 507.6 | 510.8 | 519.1 | 528.7 | 538.5 |
| 20 | 587.6 | 545.7 | 535.9 | 529.9 | 526.6 | 525.2 | 525.8 | 527.4 | 533.2 | 541.0 | 549.5 |
| 22 | 624.3 | 577.2 | 564.5 | 555.9 | 550.3 | 546.6 | 545.2 | 545.3 | 548.5 | 554.4 | 561.4 |
| 24 | 659.5 | 608.7 | 593.6 | 582.9 | 574.9 | 569.3 | 566.0 | 564.5 | 565.1 | 568.9 | 574.4 |
| 26 | 692.3 | 638.3 | 621.3 | 608.9 | 599.1 | 591.8 | 587.0 | 584.0 | 581.9 | 583.8 | 587.9 |
| 28 | 723.6 | 667.6 | 649.4 | 635.3 | 623.7 | 615.1 | 608.4 | 604.2 | 599.5 | 599.3 | 601.7 |
| 30 | 753.6 | 696.4 | 676.8 | 661.0 | 647.9 | 638.0 | 629.8 | 624.2 | 617.4 | 615.1 | 616.2 |
| 32 | 780.9 | 723.3 | 702.6 | 686.0 | 671.9 | 660.5 | 651.3 | 644.5 | 635.4 | 631.5 | 630.7 |
| 34 | 808.8 | 749.7 | 728.3 | 710.7 | 695.3 | 683.2 | 672.9 | 665.3 | 654.0 | 648.1 | 646.0 |
| 36 | 834.2 | 774.7 | 753.0 | 734.4 | 718.2 | 705.2 | 693.8 | 685.3 | 672.2 | 664.7 | 661.1 |
| 38 | 858.6 | 799.1 | 776.6 | 757.8 | 740.6 | 726.8 | 714.7 | 705.3 | 690.5 | 681.4 | 676.5 |
| 40 | 882.3 | 822.7 | 800.2 | 780.7 | 762.8 | 748.2 | 735.4 | 725.1 | 708.7 | 698.2 | 692.1 |
| 42 | 905.5 | 845.2 | 822.3 | 802.1 | 783.8 | 769.0 | 755.0 | 744.4 | 726.6 | 714.6 | 707.3 |
| 44 | 927.2 | 867.6 | 844.1 | 823.9 | 804.8 | 789.5 | 775.0 | 763.5 | 744.6 | 731.3 | 722.8 |
| 46 | 948.6 | 888.2 | 864.9 | 844.3 | 825.1 | 809.0 | 794.2 | 782.2 | 762.0 | 747.5 | 738.1 |
| 48 | 969.7 | 909.0 | 885.4 | 864.6 | 845.0 | 828.6 | 813.2 | 800.7 | 779.5 | 764.0 | 753.4 |
| 50 | 989.4 | 929.3 | 905.6 | 884.5 | 864.6 | 847.9 | 832.1 | 819.0 | 796.8 | 780.4 | 768.7 |
| 52 | 1008.3 | 948.5 | 924.8 | 903.5 | 883.5 | 866.2 | 850.5 | 837.0 | 813.6 | 796.2 | 783.6 |
| 54 | 1027.6 | 967.9 | 943.6 | 922.8 | 902.3 | 885.0 | 868.5 | 854.8 | 830.2 | 812.1 | 798.7 |
| 56 | 1045.7 | 986.2 | 962.4 | 940.6 | 920.0 | 902.7 | 885.9 | 871.7 | 846.6 | 827.7 | 813.6 |
| 58 | 1063.4 | 1004.1 | 980.2 | 958.7 | 937.6 | 919.9 | 903.0 | 888.4 | 862.6 | 842.9 | 828.2 |
| 60 | 1080.7 | 1021.7 | 997.8 | 976.1 | 955.0 | 937.0 | 920.0 | 905.1 | 878.7 | 858.6 | 843.0 |
| 62 | 1097.6 | 1038.7 | 1014.7 | 992.9 | 971.6 | 953.5 | 936.3 | 921.1 | 894.5 | 873.4 | 857.2 |
| 64 | 1114.1 | 1055.4 | 1031.7 | 1009.9 | 988.2 | 970.1 | 952.4 | 937.2 | 909.6 | 888.4 | 871.6 |
| 66 | 1130.1 | 1071.9 | 1047.7 | 1025.6 | 1004.1 | 986.0 | 968.5 | 952.9 | 925.2 | 903.0 | 885.7 |
| 68 | 1146.6 | 1088.0 | 1063.7 | 1041.7 | 1020.2 | 1002.0 | 983.9 | 968.2 | 940.5 | 917.8 | 899.8 |
| 70 | | | | | | | | | | | |

Table 5.  Sound velocity in the natural gas from Algeria (A)

| | | | Density kg/m3 | | | | |
|---|---|---|---|---|---|---|---|
| T °K | 293.2 | 303.2 | 313.2 | 323.2 | 333.2 | 343.2 | 353.2 |
| P | | | | | | | |
| MPa | 90.6 | 84.4 | 78.3 | 74.1 | 70.5 | 66.4 | 62.3 |
| 10 | 145.5 | 134.4 | 125.0 | 116.7 | 110.8 | 104.4 | 98.2 |
| 15 | 190.3 | 176.8 | 166.4 | 156.0 | 147.8 | 138.9 | 131.3 |
| 20 | 222.3 | 210.0 | 198.4 | 187.6 | 178.8 | 169.4 | 160.9 |
| 25 | 246.3 | 234.4 | 224.0 | 213.1 | 204.2 | 194.4 | 185.3 |
| 30 | 264.9 | 254.2 | 243.7 | 234.0 | 224.9 | 215.5 | 206.6 |
| 35 | 279.5 | 269.9 | 260.3 | 250.5 | 241.7 | 233.4 | 224.2 |
| 40 | | | | | | | |

Table 6.  density of the natural gaz from Algeria (A)

Average deviation (%) between experimental and calculated sound velocities.

| EOS | MIXING RULES | | | | | | |
|-----|------|------|------|------|------|------|----------|
|     | 1    | 2    | 3    | 4    | 5    | 6    | Internal |
| SRK | 19.4 | 18.9 | 19.5 | 19.7 | 19.5 | 19.5 | 19.3 |
| PR  | 9.3  | 8.2  | 9.5  | 9.7  | 9.4  | 9.5  | 9.4  |
| PR-RP | 4.1 | 2.8 | 4.3 | 4.5 | 4.2 | 4.3 | 4.7 |
| SBR | 2.1  | 2.5  | 2.1  | 2.1  | 2.1  | 2.1  | 2.0  |
| LK  | 1.3  | 3.0  | 1.2  | 1.0  | 1.3  | 1.2  | -    |
| COR | -    | -    | -    | -    | -    | -    | 7.8  |

Table 7. Restitution tests for the natural gas from North Sea (H)

Average deviation (%) between experimental and calculated sound velocities.

| EOS | MIXING RULES | | | | | | |
|-----|------|------|------|------|------|------|----------|
|     | 1    | 2    | 3    | 4    | 5    | 6    | Internal |
| SRK | 17.8 | 17.3 | 17.8 | 18.1 | 17.8 | 17.8 | 17.6 |
| PR  | 9.7  | 8.8  | 9.8  | 10.0 | 9.7  | 9.7  | 9.7  |
| PR-RP | 3.8 | 2.7 | 3.9 | 4.2 | 3.9 | 3.9 | 3.7 |
| SBR | 1.8  | 1.8  | 1.8  | 1.9  | 1.8  | 1.8  | 1.7  |
| LK  | 0.8  | 2.0  | 0.7  | 0.6  | 0.7  | 0.7  | -    |
| COR | -    | -    | -    | -    | -    | -    | 9.2  |

Table 8. Restitution tests for the natural gas from Algeria (A)

REFERENCES

1. YE S., ALLIEZ J., LAGOURETTE B., SAINT-GUIRONS H., ARMAN J. and XANS P., Réalisation d'un système de mesure de la vitesse et de l'atténuation d'onde ultrasonores dans les liquides sous-pression, Revue Phys. Appl. (1990) 25.

2. PAPADAKIS E.P., Ultrasonic attenuatin and velocity in three transformation products in steel, J. Appl. Phys. (1964) 35 p 1474-1482.

3. DARIDON J.L., LAGOURETTE B. and SAINT-GUIRONS H. Ultrasound velocity measurement in fluids under pressure composed of gaseous and liquid component. Acoustica (1993)

4. ALY F.A. and LEE L.L. Self consistent equations for calculating the ideal gas heat capacity enthalpy and entropy, Fluid Phase Equilibria (1981) 6 , pp.169-179

5. PENELOUX A., RAUZY E. and FREZE R. A consistent correction for Redlich-Kwong-Soave Volumes, Fluid Phase Equilibria, (1982) 8, pp.7-23.

6. BEHAR E. SIMONET R. and RAUZY E., A new non-cubic equation of state, Fluid Phase Equilibria (1985) 21, 237-255

7. LEE B.I. and KESLER M.G. A generalized thermodynamic correlation based on three parameters corresponding states, AIChE Journal (1975) Vol.21, N°3 pp.510-527

8. CHIEN C.H., GREENKORN R.A. and CHAO K.C. Chain of Rotators equation of state, AIChE Journal (1983) Vol.29, pp.560-571

9. PEDERSEN K.S., FREDENSLUND A., CHRISTENSEN P.L. and THO-MASSEN P. Viscosity of crude oils, Chem Eng. Sci. (1984) 39 (6) pp.1011-1016.

10. SPENCER C.F. and DANNER R.P. Improve equation for prediction of saturated liquid density, J. Chem. Eng. Data (1972) 17 (2) pp 236-241

11. TEJA A.S., A corresponding states equation for saturated liquid densities, AIChE J., (1980) 3 p 337-345

12. HANKINSON R.W. THOMSON G.M. A new correlation for saturated densities of liquids and their mixtures, AIChE Journal (1979) (25) 4 pp 653-663

13. PLOCKER U. KNAPP and H. PRAUSNITZ, Calculation of high pressure vapour liquid equilibria from a corresponding states correlation with emphasis in asymmetric mixtures, J. Ind. Eng. Chem. Process Dev. (1978) Vol.17 N°3 pp 324-332.

14. YE S., LAGOURETTE B., ALLIEZ J. SAINT-GUIRONS H., XANS P. and MONTEL F., 1992, Speed of sound in binary mixtures as a function of temperature and pressure. Fluid Phase Equilibria 74 pp.177-202.

15. YE S., LAGOURETTE B., ALLIEZ J., SAINT-GUIRONS H., XANS P. and MONTEL F. Comparison with experimental data of ultrasound velocity in pure hydrocarbons calculated from equations of state, Fluid Phase Equilibria 1992, 74, pp157-175.

FOAM MEDIATED REMEDIATION TECHNOLOGY FOR GAS INDUSTRY
APPLICATIONS

TECHNOLOGIE DESTRAITMENTS BASÉS SUR L'EMPLOI DE LA MOUSSE
DANS SES APPLICATIONS À L'INDUSTRIE DU GAZ

Thomas D. Hayes
Gas Research Institute, USA

Vipul Srivastava
Institute of Gas Technology, USA

ABSTRACT

This paper describes an effort to develop foams for *in-situ* soil
remediation. The principal advantage of using a novel foam-based
fluid as an alternative to water as a carrier of chemicals and
pollutants is that it poses a reduced risk to the underlying
groundwater. Aqueous and non-aqueous foams were tested for
their performance in the extraction of polynuclear aromatic (PAHs)
and petroleum hydrocarbons (TPHs) from the soils obtained from
manufactured gas plant sites, and for their flow properties through
sandy soil. Extraction data shows that after two volumes of foams
were passed through a column of contaminated MGP soil, less than
30 percent of total PAHs were removed with the aqueous foams
versus 40-100 percent removal achieved with the ethanol foam
within 30 minutes of contact time. Initial experiments also showed
far less surfactant sorption to soil with ethanol foams (below 1%),
compared to aqueous foams (70-95%). This paper discusses
potential benefits of foam remediation to the gas industry.

RÉSUMÉ

Ce document décrit l'effort consacré au développement de mousses
pour le traitement des sols sur les sites. Le principal avantage
procuré par l'emploi d'un noveau fluide à base de mousse, en
remplacement de l'eau pour le transport des produits chimiques et
des polluants, consiste en la diminuation des risques de
contamination pour les eaux souterraines. Les résultats produits
par des mousses aqueuses et non-aqueses, ainsi que leurs propriétés
d'écoulement dans un sol sableux, ont été testés dans l'extraction
des hydrocarbures aromatiques polunucléaires (PAHs) et
pétrolifères (TPH) de sols provenant de sites de fabrication de gaz.
Les données d'extraction démontrent qu'après le passage de deux
volumes de mousse parune colonne de sol contaminé MGP, moins
de 30 pour cent des PAHs étaient extraits par les mousses aqueuses,
alors que de 40 à 100 pour cent étaient extraits par la mousse
d'éthanol avec un contact d'une durée de 30 minutes. Les premières
expérimentations ont également démontré que l'absorption parle sol
des agents tenso-actifs avec les mousses d'éthanol était inférieure
(mons de 1%), à celle qui a lieu avec les mousses aqueuses (70-
95%). Ce document met en valeur les avantages potentiels du
traitement par la mousse pour l'industrie du gaz.

## INTRODUCTION

Past practices in industrial waste management have led to contamination at numerous sites which involved the release of various types of organic pollutants to significant depths below the subsurface. Although soil venting and bioventing have been shown to be cost-effective in the removal of volatile organics in situ, these techniques have limitations in achieving reductions of concentrated semivolatile hydrocarbon pollutants (such as PAH's, tars, and heavy hydrocarbons). Specific examples of sites that have the potential for deep subsurface contamination include abandoned manufactured gas plants or MGP's (tars and polynuclear aromatic hydrocarbons or PAH's), creosote treatment sites (tars, PAH's, pentachlorophenol), spills at refineries (oils, PAH's), gas dehydration facilities (triethylene glycol and benzene, toluene, ethylbenzene and xylene or BTEX), military bases (fuels, chlorinated hydrocarbon solvents) and oil and gas production pits (heavy alkanes, PAH's and BTEX). Through the research at the Institute of Gas Technology, the reliability and economics of bioremediation has been substantially improved with the use of chemical pretreatment such as Fenton's Reagent and surfactants (1). With the support of GRI and the utilities, this technology has been successfully tested in pilot- and large-scale, ex-situ field experiments at a number of gas industry sites (1). However, because deep subsurface contamination (4 feet or more below the surface) is expensive to remove by excavation, there is a need to develop low-cost, environmentally acceptable approaches for in-place (in-situ) treatment.

If the groundwater protection is a goal in site cleanup, the challenge in dealing with deep semi-volatile contamination is two-fold. First, the most mobile fraction of concentrated non-aqueous phase liquids (NAPL) must be removed from the subsurface. Then chemicals that enhance mass transfer of pollutants from soil/NAPL and nutrients have to be adequately distributed in the subsurface to stimulate biological degradation. The conventional method for chemical enhancement of *in-situ* bioremediation consists of the introduction of chemicals using hundreds or thousands of cubic meters of water into the subsurface through infiltration galleries or pressurized injection systems (2, 3). The main disadvantage of this technique is that the water carrier stream provides poor penetration into clay lenses and non-aqueous phase liquids (NAPL) and moves in a downward direction, due to gravity, into the underlying groundwater. As a part of the GRI Remediation Program, the objective of this work was to evaluate the use of pressure-gradient-guided foams for the transport of pollutants and enhancement chemicals in the contaminated subsurface, while reducing the risk of groundwater contamination.

## BACKGROUND

A survey of the literature indicates that foams have many uses in the U.S. today, from the manufacture of food and beverage to firefighting, from ice cream to shaving cream (4). However, in a search of the open literature since 1975, no references were found that described the use of foams for site remediation. The areas of prior art, however, that have the most relevance to site remediation include the use of foams for enhanced oil recovery and the implementation of foams in separations found in the basic research and mining industry literature.

## Enhanced Oil and Gas Recovery

Foams have been used for many years for the purpose of achieving control of gas and oil flow downhole. The properties of aqueous foams are of great importance in this application. In oil production, for example, it is rare for more than about half of the oil in place in an oilfield to be recovered economically by application of existing technology. The oil which remains is dispersed as small globules throughout the pores of the geological structure. Foams have been investigated for both direct enhancement of oil recovery and as a selective blocking fluid in heterogeneous reservoirs (5). Foam has also been employed in a number of other ways in field operations, particularly in near-well operations such as sand clean-out, stimulation and sealing the formation to control ground water movement or losses of injected fluids such as gas in underground gas storage reservoirs. Literature relevant to art of applying the technology to the recovery of oil from porous media is summarized by Nutt and Burley (6). This body of literature indicates the technical feasibility of utilizing aqueous foams in porous media to mobilize a type of non-aqueous phase liquid for enhanced oil recovery which is performed more than 900 meters (3,000 feet) below the surface.

The successful application of foams to enhanced oil recovery suggests that foams can be effectively injected into the ground and used to influence the mobility and flow of non-aqueous phase liquids in the subsurface. Foams used in the petroleum industry, however, are designed for use at extremely high pressures (thousands of psi). Since high pressures tend to stabilize these foams, their use in shallow formations, where pollutants are located at contaminated sites (less than several hundred feet below the surface), would most likely result in a failure to maintain stable bubble formation. Oil-production foam formulations are also tailored in rheological properties to achieve specific tasks related to petroleum recovery or gas storage and would be inappropriate for site remediation applications. A certain body of know-how on foam formulation and implementation is therefore necessary for applying this principle to enhancing in-situ treatment for pollutant cleanup.

## Foam Separations

The use of foams for achieving separations and transporting chemicals is also described in the literature. Historically, interfacial separation via flotation has been investigated since the turn of the century. Initial studies examined the use of foam fractionation to remove sodium-oleate from aqueous solutions and verify the Gibbs adsorption equation (7). Since then, various studies have been conducted to demonstrate that a wide variety of substances can be removed from solution using flotation methods. Over the years these methods have multiplied and have been classified according to their function and application. These methods have been reviewed by Lemlich and are classified in Figure 1 (7).

As seen in Figure1, interfacial separations using foams is a well developed discipline with more than a dozen categories that have been investigated and employed in industry. Foams have been used for separations of particulate organic materials for sewage treatment (8, 9), dissolved organics (10, 11), soluble inorganic metals and anions (12, 13), particulate heavy metals (14,15), metallo-cyanide complexes (16) and even microbes (17).

The separations literature seems to suggest that foam can serve as a carrier for many different types of pollutants as well as carrier for chemicals that could be used to enhance bioremediation in the subsurface. In particular, it would be useful if foams could be used to scour concentrated NAPL mass from soil surfaces and flush most of the NAPL from the subsurface. It would also be useful if foams could be used to deliver chemicals into the subsurface to enhance bioremediation of NAPL and pollutant residuals that remain in the subsurface after "hot spot" removal. Questions that need to be addressed in the development of foams for these purposes include the following: 1) Can foams be passed through soil columns at reasonable pressure drops? 2) Can surfactant losses be minimized as foams are passed through the subsurface? 3) What is the effect of foam remediation on the abundance of aerobic microbes in the subsurface? The objective of the work described in this paper was to address these and other questions regarding the performance of foams in order to determine the technical feasibility of developing foam treatment systems for in-situ remediation at gas industry sites. Specifically, initial experiments focused on soils from manufactured gas plant sites containing tar NAPL and PAH's and waste pit soils from gas production sites containing weathered petroleum hydrocarbons.

FOAM REMEDIATION CONCEPT

The concept of using foams for NAPL removal and for the delivery of chemicals for enhanced bioremediation is schematically shown in Figure 2. A foam is produced by passing a gas through a finely divided frit submerged in an aqueous solution containing a surfactant and the desired enhancement additives (i.e. nutrients, trace metals, bacteria, oxidants, solvents, etc.). Gas used for the foam may also contain nutrients (e.g. $NH_3$), oxidants (e.g. $O_2$, $O_3$) or solvents (e.g. methanol and ethanol). The foam is produced under pressure (>30 psig) and introduced into vertical or horizontal wells into the treatment zone. Alternatively, liquid surfactant may be introduced into the injection well followed by air to create a foam in-situ. If the foam is injected below the contaminated zone under pressure and a vacuum extraction well is located above the contamination, the foam is expected to flow in the direction of the pressure gradient, upward through the contamination zone. Other modes of foam flow may be induced by similar methods of establishing soil pressure gradients; these modes include radial flow and lateral flow. Since gravitational forces on the foam are relatively low compared to other forces that control flow (i.e. pressure gradients, buoyant forces and capillary forces), the flow of the foam is anticipated to be in the lateral and upward directions in the subsurface, away from groundwater. Even more precise control of foam placement could be achieved through strategic placement of slurry walls in the subsurface.

Basically, two modes of foam remediation are envisioned. One mode would use foams to flush the contaminated zone for NAPL removal. These foams would be formulated to separate masses of NAPL (e.g. tar and oils) and other pollutants from soil particles. It is expected that the removal of NAPL would not be quantitative and that some NAPL and pollutant residuals would remain in the soil requiring added treatment for pollutant stabilization. A second foam application would then be employed to deliver foams for enhancing aerobic bioremediation of the remaining residues. This foam would be used to deliver enhancement chemicals and cultures to stimulate bioremediation. Subsequent introduction of oxygen or air into the injection well would stimulate bacteria feeding off of the nutrients and supplemental carbon (excess solvent and biodegradable surfactant) to degrade pollutant residuals in the treatment zone.

To address development issues and evaluate the feasibility of "foam-mediated site remediation technology", IGT conducted several tests to determine:

- Extractability of PAHs from MGP site soils
- Ability of soil microorganisms to survive foam exposure
- Sorptivity of surfactant in foams (both aqueous and non-aqueous) to soil particles
- Pressure drop during foam flow through the porous media
- Extraction of TPH from E&P site soils

FOAM EXPERIMENTS AND DISCUSSIONS

Desorption of PAHs From MGP Site Soils

Soil column experiments were conducted to determine the capability of aqueous and ethanol-based foams in the extraction of PAHs from MGP soils. The aqueous foam solution contained 1% (w/v) each of NOVEL and Tween-80. These surfactants were chosen because the literature indicates that they are both capable of increasing the solubility of PAHs, and they are both biodegradable. The ethanol foam solution employed 8% (w/v) of a specially synthesized surfactant, IGT FF-1, based on a derivative of polyethylene glycol (PEG). The formation of very stable foams in ethanol was not possible using commercially available surfactants.

The six soils used in these experiments consisted of three clean (no PAHs or other contaminants were present) sands and three MGP soils contaminated with PAHs. The clean sand samples were derived from the same sandy aquifier sample W22C. One W22C sample was exposed to two volumes of concentrated sulfuric acid for 24 hours at room temperature with constant shaking to oxidize all of the organic matter present in this sand. Two other W22C samples were similarly exposed to two volumes of either aqueous surfactant or ethanol surfactant solutions for 24 hours and were then washed free of surfactants. These samples were designated W22C-(aqueous surfactant washed) and W22C-(ethanol surfactant washed), respectively. The three MGP soils were designated 114A, 1145, and TGS22. The 114A and 1145 samples came from the same site as the W22C sample. The 114A sample was lightly contaminated with PAHs (about 25 ppm total PAHs) and other hydrocarbons, whereas the 1145 sample was more heavily contaminated (about 500 ppm total PAHs). Thus, the three W22C-derived samples along with the 114A and 1145 samples comprised a related series of sandy samples that could be used to assess the effect of organic content on the removal of PAHs from soil using foams. To extend this analysis, the TGS22 sample, a silty loam with high organic content collected from a different MGP site, was included in the study.

Soil-column foam experiments (as shown schematically in Figure 3) involved twelve soil columns: six different soil types treated with either organic or ethanol foams. The amount of foam passing through the column was determined by collecting condensed foam solutions. These foam experiments utilized a total of 25 ml of condensed foam solutions. Table 1 and Figure 4 summarize the results in terms of total amount of PAHs extracted during the test period of approximately 30 minutes.

These results clearly indicate that foams can efficiently extract PAHs from soils. It also shows that ethanol foams are far more efficient than aqueous foams in desorbing PAHs from soil particles. It also appears that the sandy soil samples (1 through 5, and 7 through 11) respond much better than the silty soil sample (TGS22 Samples 6 and 12). Visual observation suggests this may be due to channeling of foam through TGS22 soil columns, as compared with the sandy soil samples and may not simply be due to the different compositions of these soils. It also appears that the ethanol surfactant-washed W22C samples show better desorption than the $H_2SO_4$-treated and the aqueous surfactant-washed W22C sample.

Table 1. EXTRACTIONS OF PAHs FROM SOIL COLUMNS BY AQUEOUS AND ETHANOL FOAMS*

| Sample No. | Sample Identification | Foam Type | Foam Volume, ml | % PAH Extracted |
|---|---|---|---|---|
| 1 | W22C ($H_2SO_4$ Treated) | Aqueous | 24 | 18.6 |
| 2 | W22C(Aqueous Surfactant Washed) | Aqueous | 25 | 8.6 |
| 3 | W22C (Ethanol Surfactant Washed) | Aqueous | 26.5 | 26.0 |
| 4 | 1145 | Aqueous | 25.5 | 10.8 |
| 5 | 114A | Aqueous | 25 | 22.0 |
| 6 | TGS22 | Aqueous | 25.5 | 5.3 |
| 7 | W22C ($H_2SO_4$ Treated) | Ethanol | 26 | 51.8 |
| 8 | W22C(Aqueous Surfactant Washed) | Ethanol | 25.3 | 55.3 |
| 9 | W22C (Ehtanol Surfactant Washed) | Ethanol | 28 | 64.0 |
| 10 | 1145 | Ethanol | 22 | 71.8 |
| 11 | 114A | Ethanol | 28 | 102.1 |
| 12 | TGS22 | Ethanol | 25 | 19.3 |

* Each of the above soil sample columns contained 15 g of soil.

Activity of Soil Microorganisms After Foam Flow

An experiment was performed to examine the ability of soil microorganisms to survive exposure to foam solutions. Aqueous foam was formed using distilled water containing 1% each of the nonionic surfactants Tween 80 and Novel, while ethanol foam was formed using 8% of IGT FF-1. Externally generated foam was passed through laboratory-scale soil columns containing 15 grams of the MGP soil 1145. In one sample, a brief pulse of aqueous foam was delivered to the soil column such that as soon as foam was observed emerging from the top of the soil column, the soil was immediately processed to determine the number of heterotrophic bacteria. Another sample received aqueous foam continuously for an hour, after which time the number of heterotrophic microorganisms present in the soil or in the collected foam was determined. Ethanol foam was delivered continuously for an hour to yet another soil sample, and the data is reported in Table 2. It can be seen that while the ethanol foam caused a dramatic decrease in cell viability, aqueous foam shows no significant cell toxicity. Subsequent tests showed that after a short period following the exposure to ethanol foams, soil microorganisms regained activity and number.

Table 2. SURVIVAL OF SOIL MICROORGANISMS EXPOSED TO FOAM

| Sample | Colony Forming Units per Gram of Soil (or per ml of Foam Liquid) |
|---|---|
| Untreated | $4.27 \times 10^6$ |
| Pulse of Aqueous Foam | $8.75 \times 10^6$ |
| Soil After 1 Hour Aqueous Foam | $1.07 \times 10^7$ |
| Foam From 1 Hour Aqueous | $4.19 \times 10^6$ |
| Soil After 1 Hour Ethanol Foam | $9.67 \times 10^2$ |

The data suggest that if aqueous foam is employed to promote in-situ aerobic biormediation of the contaminants, the microbial activity of soil organisms would not be affected adversely. Results also show that ethanol-foam, which could be used for flushing the contaminated zone for NAPL removal, did not completely sterilize the soil, suggesting the feasibility of *in-situ* bioremediation as a final polishing step.

Sorption of Surfactant to Soil Particles

Experiments were conducted to determine the amount of sorption of the surfactant in foam to soil particles during the foam-mediated soil remediation. test columns utilized clean sand (as a control), PAH containing MGP soils, and petroleum hydrocarbons containing E&P soils. Loss of surfactant to soil particles was determined by passing a known amount of surfactant solution of fixed surfactant concentration through the soil column, and then determining the residual concentration of surfactant in the liquid. Other test protocols were similar to those described for soil column experiments. Solution was passed as a liquid as well as a foam fluid. The amount of soil in the column and the flow-rate of the solution were also maintained comparable throughout the test period. Table 3 summarizes the key test results in terms of percentage of the initial amount of surfactant sorbed to the soil particles. The ethanol foam surfactant showed practically no (less than 1%) affinity toward the soil particles, but the aqueous foams lost as much as 99% of the surfactant through the sorption process.

Table 3. SORPTION OF SURFACTANT TO SOIL PARTICLES

| Soil | Aqueous Surfactant (% Sorption) | Ethanol Surfactant (% Sorption) |
|---|---|---|
| TGS21 | 88 | <1 |
| EP-6689 | 90 | <1 |
| EP-W01 | 0 - 35 | <1 |
| Sand | 99 | <1 |

It was also observed that the sorption of surfactant from solution on some soils was up to 50% greater than from foams suggesting yet another benefit of microbubbles of gas in the solution. However, an important issue was identified that a unique foam formulation had to be developed which would result into: a) least sorption of surfactant to soil as in the case of ethanol foam; b) high extraction capability for PAHs from soils; and c)least impact on soil microorganisms. Mixtures of aqueous and ethanol foams are being evaluated for their merits in these contexts.

Desorption of TPH From E&P Soils

Soil column tests were also conducted to determine the extractability of total petroleum hydrocarbons (TPHs) from the exploration and production (E&P) soils. The experimental set up and the type of foams ( both aqueous and non-aqueous/ethanol foams) used in these experiments were very comparable to those in experiments with MGP soils described in a previous section.

Six different E&P soils ranging in TPH concentration from approximately 500 ppm to over 20,000 ppm, were used in these experiments. Results, shown in Figure 5, demonstrate the removal efficiency for foam to be extremely good (60% to 95% of the initial concentration). The ethanol foam generally outperformed the aqueous foam as well as a 40:60 mixed ethanol-aqueous foam that was specially formulated for this project. As mentioned earlier, mixtures of ethanol foam and aqueous foam are being evaluated for their properties related to all the key components of "foam-mediated site remediation". A 40:60 mixture of ethanol-aqueous foam appears to be quite satisfactory.

Pressure Drops Associated With the Movement of Foam Through Soil

Several experiments were conducted to determine the pressure drop as a function of foam type ( aqueous foam, ethanol foam, and ethanol-aqueous mixed foams), foam quality (percentage of air in the foam), and foam flow rate. Test results, shown in Figure 6, indicates that the pressure drop is directly proportional to the foam flow rate and inversely proportional to the foam quality.

These experiments extend previous work that indicated that significant decreases in pressure drop could be achieved with aqueous foams having volumetric gas contents exceeding 90%. As illustrated in Figure 6 and mentioned earlier, increasing foam quality to 99% resulted in a pressure drop of 1.1 to 1.3 bar per meter (5 to 6 psi per foot) of soil at a foam flow rate of 32 ml/min. To eliminate the risk of soil heaving, pressure drops in the range of 0.23 to 0.45 bar per meter (1 to 2 psi/ft) are preferred. A pressure drop of 5 psi/ft may still be somewhat problematic as these tests were performed using sand and soil would likely result in higher pressure drops. Moreover, foam qualities exceeding 99% may be impractical. The data suggest that the minimum pressure drop achievable with aqueous foam formulations is about 1 bar per meter (5 psi/ft). Experiments are being conducted with the ethanol-aqueous mixed foam, which are expected to result in significantly lower pressure drops.

CONCLUSIONS

Foam-mediated site remediation technology for *in-situ* application appears to have all the key attributes required for an efficient process to remediate MGP sites, E&P sites, and other gas industry waste contaminated sites.   Results obtained from actual contaminated sites show that:

- TPH removal efficiencies of 60-95% and PAH removal efficiencies of 60-99% can be achieved with extractions using ethanol foams.  Some E&P soils responded very favorably by aqueous foams.
- Soil microorganisms do not adversely respond to aqueous foams but are affected when exposed to ethanol foams, but the activity appears to be affected only marginally.
- Pressure drop during the foam flow can be minimized by increasing the foam quality, reducing the foam flow, and mixing the ethanol foam with the aqueous foam.

FUTURE DIRECTIONS

Based on the results of this work, the Gas Research Institute has initiated the development of in-situ foam remediation for application to gas industry sites containing subsurface NAPL.  This work is being performed by the Institute of Gas Technology assisted by the Illinois Institute of Technology with modeling support from Argonne National Laboratory.  Commercial partners, including equipment manufacturers, remediation firms and geotechnics companies in partnership with GRI, are combining commercial tools with emerging know-how to accelerate the development of this technology.  Laboratory experiments are under way in 1995 to define the physics of foam flow behavior as a function of foam chemistry, foam stability, lamella characteristics, and introduction modes.  Enhancements to foam flow are currently under investigation.  Development issues include the following:

- How can foams be designed to achieve the desired extraction and flow characteristics for *in-situ* treatment at gas industry sites at depths of 5 to 50 feet?
- How can foams be passed through with tight soils including clay?
- How can foams be controlled and directed in porous media?
- Can foam surfactants be designed to be biodegradable?
- What is the effect of foams on soil structure and microbial ecology?
- Can foam surfactants and solvents be separated from pollutants at a reasonable cost to further reduce the cost of foam flushing?
- Can foam be used to provide NAPL treatment below the water table level?

Good progress has been made to  date in resolving these issues.  Scale-up criteria and remediation system designs are currently being developed.  Field experiments of foam remediation are planned at MGP and gas production sites for 1996 and 1997.  This work will be performed in cooperation with gas companies and commercial partners.

ACKNOWLEDGEMENT

The authors are grateful for the contibutions of Dr. John Kilbane, Dr. Prasan Chowdiah, and Ms. Kathy Jackowski in the conduct of the experimental program. This project was funded by the Gas Research Institute.

REFERENCES

1.  Kelly, R L., V. Srivastava, and S. Nelson. "Field-Scale Evaluation of an Integrated Treatment for Remediation of PAH's in Manufactured Gas Plant Soils," Presented at the 1992 Spring National AIChE Meeting, New Orleans, LA   March 29, 1992. Available from the Institute of Gas Technology, Chicago, IL (1992).

2.  Sims, J. L. *et al.*  In Situ Bioremediation of Contaminated Unsaturated Subsurface Soils, USEPA Engineering Issue No. EPA/540/S-93/501, Robert S. Kerr Environmental Research Laboratory, Ada, OK (1993).

3.  Wunderlich, R. W.  "*In Situ* Remediation of Aquifers Contaminated with Dense Nonaqueous Phase Liquids by Chemically Enhanced Solubilization,"   Journal of Soil Contamination   1(4):361-378 (1992).

4.  Ross, S.  "Foams,"  in Kirk-Othmer Encyclopedia of Chemical Technology, 11:127-145, Wiley and Sons, New York, NY, (1980).

5.  Ettinger, R. A. and C. J. Radke.  "Influence of Texture on Steady Foam Flow in Berea Sandstone,"   SPE Reservoir Engineering, February Issue, pp. 83-90  (1992).

6.  Nutt, C. W. and R. W. Burley.  "The Influence of Foam Rheology in Enhanced Oil Recovery Operations,"  in Foams: Physics, Chemistry and Structure,"   pp. 105-147, Springer-Verlag, New York, NY (1989).

7.  Lemlich, R.  "Adsorptive Bubble Separation Methods," Industrial and Engineering Chemistry 60(10):17-29 (1968).

8.  Komline, T. R.   "Dissolved Air Flotation Tackles Sludge Thickening," Water and Wastes Engineering, February issue, pp 63-69 (1978).                                    .

9.  Zabel, T.  "The Advantages of Dissolved-air Flotation for Water Treatment," Journal of the American Water Works Association - Managment and Operations Section, May issue, pp 42-46 (1985).

10. Brasch, D. J. and K.R. Robilliard.  "Rates of Continuous Foam Fractionation of Dilute Kraft Black Liquor," Separation Science and Technology 14(8):699-709 (1979).

11. Michelsen, D. L., *et al.* "Feasibility Study of Use of Predispersed Solvent Extraction/Flotation Techniques for Removal of Organics from Wastewaters," Chem. Eng. Communications 49:155-163 (1986).

12. Kubota, K. and S. Hayashi. "The Removal of Sodium, Cadmium and Chromium Ions from Dilute Aqueous Solutions Using Foam Fractionation," The Canadian Journal of Chemical Engineering 55:286-292 (1977).

13. McDonald, C. and A. Suleiman. "Ion Flotation of Copper Using Ethylhexadecyldimethyl-Ammonium Bromide," Separation Science and Technology 14(3):219-225 (1979).

14. Huang, S. and D. J. Wilson. "Foam Separation of Mercury(II) and Cadmium(II) from Aqueous Systems," Separation Science 11(3):215-221 (1976).

15. Rubin, A. J. and W. L. Lapp. "Foam Fractionation and Precipitate Flotation of Zinc(II)," Separation Science 6(3):357-363 (1971).

16. Clarke, A. N. *et al.* "The Removal of Metallo-Cyanide Complexes by Foam Flotation," Separation Science and Technology 14(2): 141-153 (1979).

17. Rubin, A. J. and S. C. Lackey. "Effect of Coagulation of the Microflotation of Bacillus Cereus," Journal of the American Water Works Association, 60(10): 1156-1166 (1968).

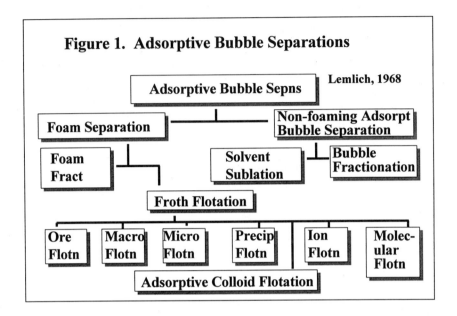

Figure 1. Adsorptive Bubble Separations

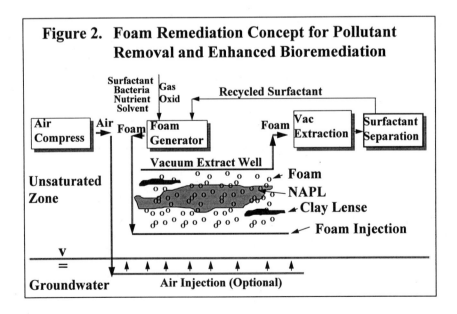

Figure 2. Foam Remediation Concept for Pollutant Removal and Enhanced Bioremediation

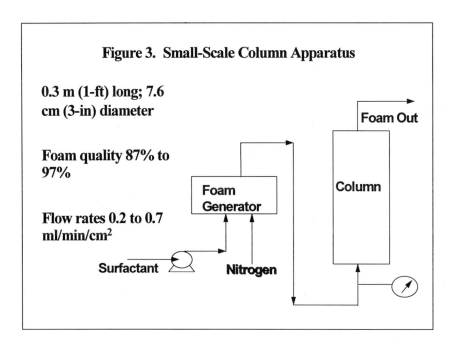

Figure 3.  Small-Scale Column Apparatus

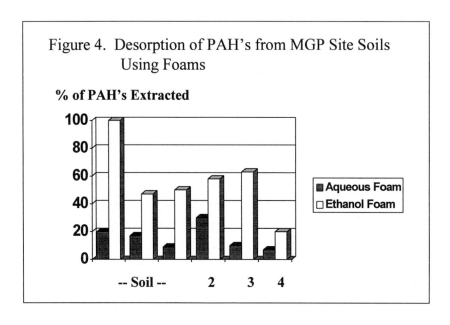

Figure 4.  Desorption of PAH's from MGP Site Soils Using Foams

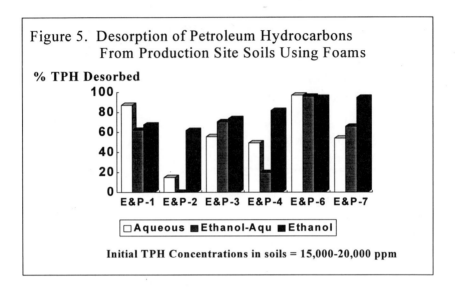

Figure 5. Desorption of Petroleum Hydrocarbons
From Production Site Soils Using Foams

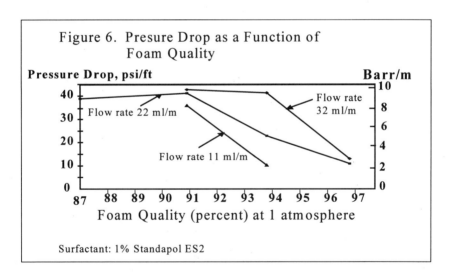

Figure 6. Presure Drop as a Function of
Foam Quality

# REMEDIATION OF AN EX-GASWORKS SITE - A CASE STUDY

PJ Daly, AJ Hart, RS Morris, TPL Smith, PL Walker

## ABSTRACT

Former coal gas manufacturing plants were situated close
to the point of use and to communication links and hence
are now frequently in prime areas for modern inner city
redevelopment.  Unfortunately, the processes associated
with coal gasification may have resulted in areas of
chemical contamination and physical obstructions.
Therefore, prior to redevelopment these sites, like other
contaminated land, require a site surveys to determine the
extent of any contamination and, when necessary, to
specify appropriate remediation measures.  This paper
charts the successful development of such a site located
in the North of England. A full survey was undertaken to
characterise the condition of the site.  This utilised
geophysical methods to augment the more traditional
methodology of trial pits and boreholes.  Following
identification and delineation of the contamination,
potential remediation techniques were identified and
feasibility studies undertaken to establish their
suitability to the site.  Appropriate, cost effective
validation measures were introduced to verify the success
of the selected remediation methods.  The importance of
rigorously defined objectives and an appropriate
validation method (including QA/QC procedures) is clear.

**RESUME**

Les anciennes installations de fabrication de gaz de
houille sont souvent situées dans les endroits qui ont le
plus besoin d'être rénovés.  Toutefois, les procédés qui
entrent dans la gazéification du charbon ont peut-être
entraîné la contamination chimique ou physique de
certaines zones.  Avant les travaux de rénovation, ces
installations doivent être entièrement inspectées afin de
déterminer l'ampleur de toute contamination et, si
nécessaire, les mesures de redressement adéquates.  Cette
communication décrit l'aménagement réussi d'une
installation de ce type située dans le nord de
l'Angleterre.

Une inspection complète a été faite pour déterminer l'état
dans lequel l'installation se trouvait. Celle-ci a fait
appel à des méthodes géophysiques pour ajouter à la
méthodologie traditionnelle des puits de recherche et des
trous de sonde.  Après l'identification et la délimitation
de l'ampleur de la contamination, des techniques de
redressement possibles ont été identifiées et des études
de faisabilité ont été faites pour déterminer si ces
techniques convenaient à ce type d'installation.  Des
mesures de validation adéquates et rentables ont été
adoptées pour vérifier si les méthodes de redressement
sélectionnées avaient réussi.

Cette communication souligne l'importance de la
détermination des objectifs requis et la nécessité
d'adopter une méthode de validation appropriée comprenant
des procédures d'assurance et de contrôle de la qualité
rigoureuses.

## 1.  Introduction

The processes associated with coal gasification generated a
number of by-products which were treated, disposed of, or
stored.  During the working life of these gasworks, typically
150 years, these by-products may have resulted in chemical
contamination of certain areas.  In addition, the owners
frequently updated and/or rebuilt the manufacturing plants and
today physical obstructions are frequently encountered in the
sub-surface soil.  Prior to redevelopment these sites require a
full survey to determine the extent of any contamination and,
when necessary, to specify appropriate remedial measures.

The remediation described in this paper was undertaken on a
disused former gasworks site located in the North of England
which operated from 1835 until 1967, and at its peak
manufactured 118 million cubic feet of gas per day.  The site
was expanded and the technology used to manufacture town gas was
changed several times during the working life of the plant.
With the advent of natural gas from the North Sea in the 1960s,
the need for manufactured gas diminished and this site was
decommissioned in 1967.

## 2.  Site Investigation

Traditionally, site investigations are undertaken using trial
pits and bore holes, however, here these were augmented with
geophysical methods in order to sample a larger percentage of
the site and increase the confidence of identifying sub-surface
structures.

Two geophysical techniques were used: electromagnetic (EM)
conductivity, and magnetometry.  The first of these measures
average electrical conductivity of the sub-surface materials to
depths of up to 6 m, whereas the second measures absolute
geomagnetic field variations caused by large buried metallic
objects.

Measurements were taken on a 5m grid, although in certain areas
this was not possible due to rubble and construction debris
which restricted access.

The EM-conductivity survey was undertaken using a Geonics  EM-31
instrument.  Readings were taken in two orientations, one
parallel to the north-south site grid lines and the other
parallel to the east-west site grid lines.  This was considered
essential due to the strongly directional nature of the EM
measurements.  The geomagnetic survey was undertaken using a
Geometrics  G-856 proton precession magnetometer.

Existing reinforced concrete foundations were detected with both
survey techniques, however the presence of the reinforcing
prevented the instruments from "seeing" below the foundations.
Significant areas of the site demonstrated low to intermediate

conductivity indicating a mixture of brick, rubble, and
demolition debris mixed with gasworks waste such  as clinker and
purifier waste (spent oxide).  The subsequent trial pit and
borehole survey adequately covered these areas of the site.

A number of very distinct anomalies were identified indicating
the presence of sub-surface ferrous objects.  One anomaly
clearly coincided with an old gas holder basin and indicated
that this was still present below ground.  Excavation confirmed
the presence of this structure, which contained water
contaminated with organic substances.  In other locations the
high conductivity resulted from increased proportions of
conductive waste such as clinker and spent oxide.  A significant
linear conductivity anomaly was also identified and correlated
with buried pipes, services or similar linear conductors, as
well as the surrounding pipe fill.  Other  anomalies could be
related to remaining structures and suggested the presence of
metal reinforcing within the concrete.  This was confirmed on
site when the bases were 'broken out'.

### 3.  Laboratory analysis and QA/QC

Throughout the site investigation and remediation works a number
of contract analytical laboratories were used to analyse samples
from the site.  Initially, there was little or no agreement in
data obtained between laboratories.  In desperation, British Gas
R&T instituted a range of QA/QA procedures at these contract
facilities including generation and supply of contaminated
reference materials and carrying out quality audits of
laboratory procedures.  These efforts greatly improved
reliability and reproducibility of data and were vital to
subsequent decision making.  R&T currently organise a "round
robin" assessment of laboratory performance on a six-monthly
basis for those companies wishing to carry out work for British
Gas.

### 4.  Site Remediation

During the initial desk study and site investigation it became
clear that some remediation work on the site would be required,
this provided an opportunity for alternative remediation
techniques to be evaluated alongside the conventional removal of
material to landfill.

Three potential treatment options were considered:
bioremediation, electrokinetics and soil washing.  These
technologies were already under investigation through the
on-going research programmes carried out by British Gas, R&T.
Of these, electrokinetics was shown to be unsuitable for the
site in laboratory tests carried out by R&T.  However,
bioremediation and soil washing were considered possible and a
draft tender document was issued to companies operating in these
areas.  Subsequently, a short list of respondents were invited
to feasibility discussions

On the advice of R&T a number of laboratory based treatability
tests were commissioned to ensure that the techniques were fully
suited to the particular site.  Treatment targets were set in
particular to:

*     reduce the total PAH to below 800 mg kg$^{-1}$ **and**
*     reduce the pyrene concentration by 50%.

These compared favourably with the UK guideline (ICRCL) value of
5,000 mg kg$^{-1}$ .
A full tender document was then issued for the works and bids
were received.

## 4.1  Soil Washing

Laboratory trials to establish the feasibility of utilising soil
washing on this site were undertaken  by MB Geosphere Ltd. on a
3 kg sample of mixed waste.  The approximate physical
composition of the material was:   loam aggregates (<5%), sand
(25%-40%), stones (<5%), slag (<5%), coal/coke (10%-25%) and
Tar-solid agglomerates (<5%).

A series of washing and separation processes were used, these
included:

*     cone mixer with silicon carbide pellets for attrition to
      break up agglomerates.
*     classification by wet screen and laser diffraction to assess
      particle size distribution
*     density separation with material separated at 1.9 kg dm$^{-3}$ and
      2.85 kg dm$^{-3}$
*     floatation for fines removal (<0.5 mm fraction with solids
      concentration of <50 g l-1).

The most important result was that 75% of the total quantity of
contaminants were found in the <0.5 mm fraction.  This is an
effective size fraction to use as a 'cut off' for treatment
because floatation can be used as an additional stage to treat
this particle size range.  Surprisingly, a relatively high
percentage of contamination was also found in the >2 mm fraction
due to the presence of a few highly contaminated agglomerates.

The tests indicated that the most effective soil washing
remediation strategy would therefore employ:

1.    Separation of coarse materials and reduction to <20 mm.
2.    Attrition scrubbing to reduce particle size through
      disaggregation.
3.    Classification by screening to 0.5 mm and 2 mm.
4.    Sorting of < 0.5 mm fraction through flotation.
5.    De-watering.

While the studies demonstrated that soil washing was technically feasibly, an examination of the costs showed that for the particular site circumstances, it was not economically viable. The early tender information reflected this and as a result the technology was not used on this site

## 4.2 Bioremediation

Treatability studies were also carried out to investigate the potential for bioremediation of some of the material on the site. All the specialist bioremediation companies involved were confident that their approaches could provide good results and meet the specification targets. A full tender document was issued for the works and bids were received. One of the tenders was selected and a specialist bioremediation contractor (BioTal Ltd) engaged for the work.

The bioremediation followed a landfarming approach. Excavated soil was laid (on an impermeable liner) to an approximate depth of 80 cm. The soil was rotovated and irrigated daily. Inorganic nutrients were applied weekly along with selected degradative bacteria. Over 8,000 $m^3$ of soil was treated.

Two contract laboratories were appointed to assess the work, one as a validating laboratory and one working on behalf of the main site contractor. However, insufficient data was obtained to fully assess the work and so British Gas, R&T performed the analyses for the data shown below.

Unfortunately, the mean starting value for material laid on the bed was already below the 800 mg/kg total PAH target. It was originally anticipated that starting values would be an order of magnitude higher than this. Furthermore, during the course of the bioremediation contract managers encountered considerable difficulties in interpreting and validating the results from different laboratories. Analysis of subsequent data was also complicated by delays during excavation which resulted in the landfarm area being split up into a number of small plots each with different starting times. The sampling density from each plot was less than would normally be considered acceptable for statistical analysis to demonstrate with any degree of confidence that remediation has occurred. These may have contributed to the disappointing results obtained which are shown in Figures 1 and 2. An additional factor may be extremely optimistic forecasts for treatment performance made by most of the bioremediation contractors in their tenders.

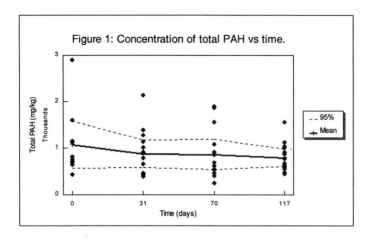

Figure 1: Concentration of total PAH vs time.

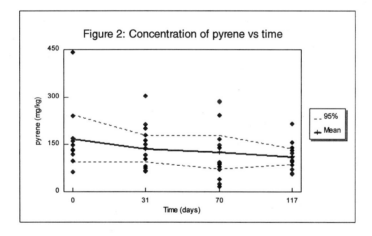

Figure 2: Concentration of pyrene vs time

Fiure 1 shows the change in total PAH
concentration over time, very limited reduction was
achieved and it is by no means clear that this is s
statistically significant change.

Figure 2 shows pyrene concentration as a
function of time.  The concentration does
appear to fall substantially but not by the 50%
specified in the contract.

The problems encountered in the validation of the contract
highlight:

*      the importance of a full site investigation before such
       works commence.

* sampling strategy (including the number of samples taken), is of paramount importance, especially where the inherent variation is high.
* such works must be planned as an integral part of the site development, and key requirements of the remediation works accommodated.
* the statistical method by which such remediation works will be verified must be very clearly defined before work commences.

## 4.3  Removal to landfill

In the UK, removal of contaminated material to landfill remains an option for site developers and often remains the most cost effective procedure.  On this site approximately 12,000 m³ were disposed of in this way.  Landfill costs per unit volume (including transportation) were almost identical to bioremediation, however on-site treatments (including bioremediation) do not incur a cost for importation of clean fill and in this case represented a saving of £60,000 on the 8,000 m³ treated on-site.

## 5.0  Conclusions

* Traditional site investigation of the site was enhanced by the use of remote geophysical techniques.
* The remote sensing data correlated well with later excavation experience and represents an extremely efficient way to increase the information available about a site..
* Soil washing could potentially provide an effective treatment for former gasworks contamination  even though the economics were not suited to its use here
* Bioremediation performance was disappointing due to a combination of factors including unexpected delays on site and over optimistic forecasting.
* The statistical method by which such remediation works will be verified must be very clearly defined before work commences.

ACCELERATED BIOREMEDIATION OF GAS EXPLORATION AND
PRODUCTION SITE SOILS CONTAMINATED WITH ORGANIC AND/OR
INORGANIC POLLUTANTS

TRAITEMENT BIOLOGIQUE ACCÉLÉRÉ DES SOLS DE SITES DE
PRODUCTION ET D'EXPLORATION DE GAZ, CONTAMINÉS PAR DES
POLLUANTS ORGANIQUES ET/OU INORGANIQUES

V.J. Srivastava, J.J. Kilbane II, J.R. Paterek, L.E. Rice
Institute of Gas Technology, USA

and

T. Hayes
Gas Research Institute

ABSTRACT

Bioremediation is an efficient and cost-effective means of treating
soils, sediments, and sludge contaminated with a variety of organic
pollutants. However, soils containing inorganic pollutants, such as
those from exploration and production, are not generally
considered good candidates for bioremediation processes.
Research at the Institute of Gas Technology (IGT) has shown that
leaching solutions can be formulated that are capable of treating
soil that is contaminated with heavy metals such that it can pass
the U.S. Environmental Protection Agency's Toxicity
Characteristic Leaching Procedure (EPA Method 1311). This
leachate can subsequently be treated using microbiological-
physical processes to precipitate heavy metals and salts. IGT's
Chemical/Biological Treatment, the MGP-REM Process, discussed
in another paper, can then be applied to treat the hydrocarbons
either in the leachate or in the soil. Laboratory studies, as well as
related field studies, show that combined chemical, physical, and
microbiological techniques can successfully treat both organic and
inorganic contaminants in gas industry exploration and production
site soils.

RÉSUMÉ

Le traitement Biologique est un moyen efficace et économique pour
remédier à la contamination des sols, sédiments et boues par divers
polluants organiques. Ce procédé de traitement biologique n'est
cependant pas applicable aux matériaux contenant des polluants
inorganiques tels que les sols de sites de production et
d'exploration. Les reserches de l'Institute of Gas Technology (IGT)
ont démontré qu'il est possible de formuler des solutions de
lixiviation capables de traiter des sols fortement contaminés par des
métaux afin d'assurer leur conformité au Procédé de Lixiviation de
la Toxicité de l'Agence pour la Protection de l'Environnement
Américaine (Méthode EPA 1311). Le produit de lixiviation peut
ensuite subir des traitements microbiologiques et physiques qui
résultent en la précipitation de sels et métaux lourds. Le traitement
chimique et biologique de IGT, le procédé MGP-REM, peut alors
être appliqué aux hydrocarbures soit dans le produit de lixiviation
soit directement dans le sol. Des études en laboratoire ont
démontré que les techniques chimiques, physiques et
microbiologiques produisent un traitement efficace des
contaminants organiques et inorganiques dans les sols des sites de
production et d'exploration de l'industrie du gaz.

INTRODUCTION

Exploration and production E&P site soils often contain undesirable high levels of petroleum hydrocarbons, metals, and salts. Generally, petroleum hydrocarbons respond well to biodegradation; however, the presence of metals and salts inhibits most hydrocarbon degrading microorganisms. Fortunately, some microorganisms such as sulfate reducing bacteria (SRB) can not only tolerate high metal and salt environments, but can also aid in purifying their environment through the precipitation of metal sulfides.[1,4,6,11,12] The biodegredation of organic pollutants is generally inhibited by the presence of heavy metals and/or salts; however, sulfate reducing bacteria are not only capable of treating leachates containing metals and salts, but can also degrade some organic contaminants.[8] Organic contaminants that are recalcitrant to biodegredation by SRB can subsequently be effectively biodegraded by aerobic microorganisms after SRB remove/reduce the metal salts.

Chemical oxidation using Fenton's Reagent (hydrogen peroxide plus ferrous sulfate) can be employed in the presence or absence of inorganic contaminants to initiate the oxidative degradation of recalcitrant organic contaminants that can subsequently be completely degraded by microorganisms.[3,7,9,10] This combined chemical and biological treatment for the degradation of organic contaminants is the essence of IGT's CBT process. The application of the CBT process to the remediation of Manufactured Gas Plant (MPG) sites is called the MGP-REM Process. The CBT approach has been demonstrated to increase the rate and extent of the degradation of PAH's, PCB's, and cyanides. A schematic outline of the CBT process is presented in Figure 1.

Therefore, a combined biological, chemical, and physical process may be an effective means of treating exploration and production site soils. In future research, the in-situ treatment of contaminated soils, using these integrated processes may be facilitated through the use of foam-assisted remediation technology. In this instance, foams can be formulated to serve a variety of purposes: leaching/extraction of organic/inorganic contaminants; delivery of chemical oxidants; delivery of nutrients to stimulate in-situ biodegradation; and/or immobilization of inorganic contaminants. This paper describes the current status of laboratory-scale research concerned with the development of integrated biological, chemical, and physical technologies for the remediation of soil contaminated with organic and inorganic pollutants, such as E&P site soils.

RESULTS AND DISCUSSION

Desorption of Organic Contaminants From E&P Soils

Since an organic carbon source is required by SRB in order to precipitate metals in soil leachates, and because ethanol is a good environmentally benign solvent for the extraction of organic contaminants from soil as well as a good carbon source for SRB, experiments were initiated to determine the efficiency of water, ethanol, and water/ethanol mixtures to extract/desorb organic and inorganic contaminants from E&P soils.

Six different E&P soils were collected from different sites so that a range of contaminant types and concentrations, and a range of soil types (sandy, silty, and clay types) were used. Contaminant desorption tests were performed using 130g (dry wt.) samples of E&P soils and 300 ml. of water, ethanol and 40%

ethanol/60% water. Each desorption test was performed in duplicate and consisted of three consecutive changes of the desorption solution every 24 hours, during which time the soil was thoroughly mixed in a tumbling reactor. The soil pellets were recovered by centrifugation and analyzed to determine total petroleum hydrocarbon levels. The results are shown in Figures 2 and 3.

Figure 2 shows the actual levels of petroleum hydrocarbons (ppm/g. soil) present in each soil sample before and after the desorption treatments, while Figure 3 reports the same data as the percent of total petroleum hydrocarbons removed by each treatment. Figure 2 illustrates the variability of contaminants found in different E&P soils, ranging from a few hundred ppm total petroleum hydrocarbons per gram of soil, to more than 2000 ppm. Figure 3 makes it clear that while effective desorption of total petroleum hydrocarbons (TPH's) can be achieved, the results are variable and highly dependent on soil-specific conditions. Generally speaking, ethanol is the most effective solution resulting in from 65% to 95% desorption of TPH from these E&P soils.

## CBT Treatment for the Degradation of Organic Pollutants

In order to optimize the evaluation of a soil and to determine the engineering approach (soil slurry bioreactors, solid treatment, or *in-situ* application) that should be the most successful, a treatability protocol was developed. This protocol development was funded by GRI and the IGT Sustaining Membership Program, and has been used to evaluate the treatability of MGP soils. The second phase of this protocol applies the use of laboratory-scale soil slurry reactors to determine the basic effectiveness of a treatment.

A sample of the E&P site soil, RTS6689, was used to prepare a 10% soil slurry in basal salts medium.[7,9] Replicate reactors were prepared and operated under conditions defined as biological alone (conventional bioremediation), chemical treatment alone (addition of Fenton's reagent with BSM replaced with distilled water), and Chem-Biol.-Treatment (CBT). The reactors were incubated at room temperature (approximately 20°C) for 20 days. The reactors were mixed constantly on a orbital shaker at 150 r.p.m. for aeration.

The hydrocarbon concentration was determined at time zero (labeled as original soil) and at the termination of the experiment. The concentrations were determined using a petroleum hydrocarbon analyzer (General Analysis Corporation, South Norwalk, CT. USA), and report as parts per million (ppm) of total petroleum hydrocarbons (TPH). The results of two separate experiments with this soil are presented in Figure 4.

The CBT treatment was the most effective treatment tested. The TPH concentration was reduced from 90,000 ppm to an average of 20,000 ppm. Conventional bioremediation (biological alone) only removed the hydrocarbons to approximately 40,000 ppm. The rate of removal for the CBT was nearly twice that of the conventional biotreatment (data not shown).

## Soil Slurry Bioreactor: CBT Treatment Plus Surfactant

The soil slurry experiments were repeated with another exploration and production soil (RTS1260) with similar results to those presented above. In addition, a surfactant was added to determine if this would enhance either the biological or chemical-biological treatment. The surfactant added was Novel II 1412-60 (Vista Chemical Company, Austin TX, USA), and the final concentration was 0.01%. Incubation conditions were the same as discussed above.

The results of the experiment are presented in Figure 5, and the CBT (Chem-Bio-Treatment) was again the most effective treatment approach. The addition of the surfactant under chemical alone and biological alone conditions resulted in a decrease in TPH removal. Under chemical conditions, this may have been due to the surfactant acting as reactant with the Fenton's reagent, thus lowering the amount of hydrocarbons that were degraded. The decrease in TPH removal observed in the biological treatment may have been due to the microorganisms using the surfactant as a nutrient in preference to the hydrocarbons and/or the surfactant was directly toxic to the microbial community.

This research indicated that the CBT process is the most successful of the techniques tested both in extent of removal and rate. The addition of other surfactants at varying concentrations is being investigated to verify or refute the results observed with Novel II 1412-60. Novel is being tested at varying concentrations and hydrocarbon-degrading microorganisms to determine toxicity.

Removal of Inorganic Contaminants

Desorption experiments similar to those described above were performed using aqueous or ethanol solutions, containing chelating agents, so that the ability to desorb inorganic contaminants could be evaluated. The metal chelating agents used were the water soluble compound, Ethylene Diamine Tetra Acetic Acid (EDTA), and five ethanol soluble chelating agents: tributyl phosphite (Ech-1), diphenyl thiocarbazone (Ech-2), 2-2'- Iminodibenzoic acid (Ech-3), 2-2'-Thoi-bis (4, 6-dichlorophenol) (Ech-4), and diethylenetriamine (Ech-5). Each chelating agent was used at a concentration of 10 g/L either in distilled water or in ethanol, as appropriate. The desorption experiments were performed using 50 g (dry wt.) of soil and 250 ml of solution in continuously tumbled, zero-head-space reactors for 24 hours at room temperature. The tumbled samples were centrifuged at 10,000 x g for 15 minutes. The supernatant was decanted, then the soil pellet was removed, air dried, and analyzed to determine the concentrations of inorganic contaminants. The results are presented in Figure 6, which shows that the aqueous solution containing EDTA was quite effective in removing inorganic contaminants from this soil: from 75% to 90% of all inorganic contaminants, with the exception of mercury, were removed. However, the ethanol-soluble chelating agents were largely ineffective in desorbing inorganic contaminant from this soil. In no case, was the amount of inorganic contaminants removed by ethanol-soluble chelating agents greater than 34% (Zn) and only the best results are shown in Figure 6. The results of a similar soil leaching experiment, in which an aqueous-EDTA solution was used to desorb inorganic contaminants from soil, are shown in Table 1, which lists the US EPA regulatory limits for toxic metals, the concentration of these metals in a gas industry soil sample before and after leaching, and the results of US EPA Toxicity Characteristics Leaching Procedure (TCLP, EPA Method 1311).[2] As Table 1 shows effective removal of metals from soil, with the exception of mercury, was achieved. Other experiments performed at IGT demonstrate that mercury can be effectively removed from soil using different leaching solutions containing oxidants and pH adjustment.

Once inorganic contaminants are removed from the soil by a leaching procedure, the soil leachate needs to be treated. This can be accomplished by using sulfate-reducing bacteria (SRB). Fixed film bioreactors containing SRB were used in a reactor configuration that allowed continuous feed of metal-laden wastewater/soil leachate at a rate resulting in a hydraulic retention time of 3 days. The soil leachates were supplemented with 3g/L citric acid, 1g/L lactic acid, 0.5g/L $NH_4Cl$, 0.25g/L $K_2HPO_4$, and 0.5g/L yeast extract to stimulate the growth of SRB. The concentration of inorganics in the soil leachate fed to the SRB reactors was 28 ppm Al, 340 ppm Ca, 6.9 ppm Cd, 150 ppm Fe, 77 ppm Mg, 13 ppm Ni, and 14 ppm Zn. The results of treatment of the soil leachate by SRB are shown in Figure 7. Essentially complete removal of Cd, Zn, Al, and Fe was achieved, more than 85% removal of Ca and Ni was achieved, and about 40% removal of Mg was observed. Similar experiments have shown that SRB can remove a wide range of inorganic contaminants and that by manipulating process conditions, essentially complete removal of all inorganics can be achieved. It is particularly relevant that soil leachate solutions containing chelated metals and/or metals associated with colloidal material can be effectively treated using SRB as these solutions are problematic for conventional treatment processes for inorganic waste streams such as ion exchange.

## CONCLUSIONS

Removal of both organic and inorganic contaminants from soil has been demonstrated. Also, the treatment of soil leachates using SRB to precipitate inorganic contaminants from soil leachates, in order to yield clean water, has been demonstrated. In addition, the combined chemical and biological oxidation approach utilized in IGT's CBT process, has been shown to effectively degrade organic pollutants in soil slurries. Therefore, combinations of biological, chemical, and physical processes have been shown in laboratory-scale experiments to effectively treat E&P soils, containing both organic and inorganic contaminants. Future work will focus on the development of an efficient integrated process, particularly a process that is compatible with the *in-situ* remediation of E&P sites.

## ACKNOWLEDGMENTS

The research program presented in this paper was made possible through funding by the Gas Research Institute. GRI's continuing support should allow the successful translation of laboratory techniques and processes into remedial technologies with great potential for the solution of several environmental problems.

We recognize the significant technical contribution of the staff of IGT, including John Conrad, Robert Kelley, Kathy Jackowski, Laura Rice, Salil Pradhan, and, as well as the staff of the Gas Research Institute and the U.S. Environmental Protection Agency.

# REFERENCES

1. W.A Apel, M.R. Wiebe, and P.R. Dugan, "Separation and Concentration of Hazardous Metals From Aqueous Solutions Using Sulfate-Reducing Bacteria," in Bioprocess Engineering Symposium, R.M. Hochmuth, Ed. New York: Amer. Soc. Mechan. Eng., 1990.

2. Appendix II - Method 1311, Toxicity Characteristic Leaching Procedure (TCLP), Federal Register/Rules and Regulations, 55(61), 11863-11877 (1990).

3. N. Barkley and R. Kelley, Chemical and Biological Treatment, EPA Superfund Innovative Technology Evaluation, Emerging Technology Bulletin. EPA/540/F-94/504, May, (1994).

4. D.H. Dvorak, R.S. Hedin, H.M. Edenhorn, and P.E. McIntire, P.E., "Treatment of Metal-Contaminated Water Using Bacterial Sulfate Reduction: Results From Pilot-Scale Reactors," Biotechnology and Bioengineering 40, 609-616 (1992)

5. J.J. Kilbane, J. Xie, and D.K. Cha, "Leaching of Metals From Contaminated Solids," Appl. Microbiol. (Submitted).

6. J.J. Kilbane, B.Y. Liu, J.R. Conrad, and V.J. Srivastava, "Novel Application of Foam for In-Situ Soil Remediation," Project Report, GRI Contract No. 6092-253-2336, April (1995).

7. B.Y. Liu, S. Pradhan, V.J. Srivastava, J.R. Pope, T.D. Hayes, D.G. Linz, C. Proulx, D.E. Jerger, and P.M. Woodhull, "An Evaluation of Slurry-Phase Bioremediation of MGP Soils," Seventh International IGT Symposium on Gas, Oil, and Environmental Biotechnology, Colorado Springs, CO. Institute of Gas Technology, Des Plaines, IL, 1994.

8. R. Rabus, R. Nordhaus, W. Ludwig, and F. Widdel, "Complete Oxidation of Toluene Under Strictly Anoxic Conditions by a New Sulfate-Reducing Bacterium," Appl. Environ. Microbiol. 59, 1444-1451, (1993).

9. J.R. Paterek, B.N. Aronstein, L.E. Rice, V.J. Srivastava, J. Chini,and A. Bohrnerud, "Bioremediation of Soil of a Manufactured Gas Plant Utilizing an In-Situ Treatment Mode," Seventh International IGT Symposium on Gas, Oil, and Environmental Biotechnology, Colorado Springs, CO. Institute of Gas Technology, Des Plaines, IL, 1994.

10. V.J. Srivastava, R.L. Kelley, J.R. Paterek, T.D. Hayes, G.L. Nelson, and J. Golchin, "A Field-Scale Demonstration of a Novel Bioremediation Process for MGP Sites," Appl. Biochem. Biotechnol. 45/46: 741-755, 1994.

11. J. Xie, D.K. Cha, and J.J. Kilbane, "The SRB Biosystem Process for the Treatment of Wastewater and Leachates Containing Heavy Metals," in Eviron. Sci. Technol. (Submitted).

12. J.X.Xie, "Bioremediation of Inorganic Pollutants in Wastewater and Contaminated Solids," Masters Thesis submitted to Illinois Institute of Technology, (1993).

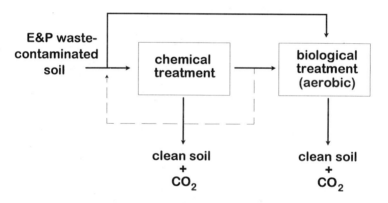

Figure 1. Schematic Diagram of the MGP-REM Process

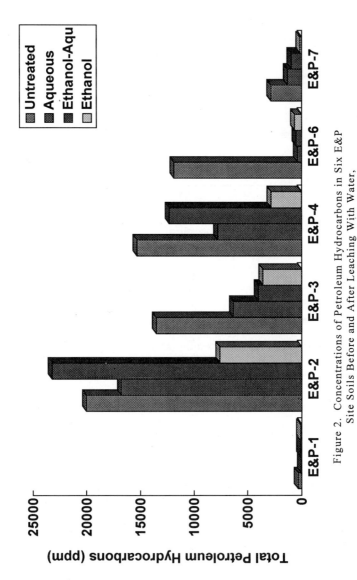

Figure 2. Concentrations of Petroleum Hydrocarbons in Six E&P
Site Soils Before and After Leaching With Water,
Ethanol, or Ethanol-Water Mixtures

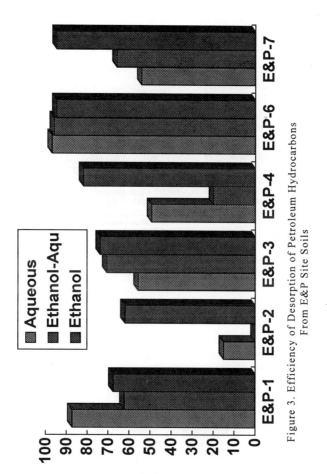

Figure 3. Efficiency of Desorption of Petroleum Hydrocarbons
From E&P Site Soils

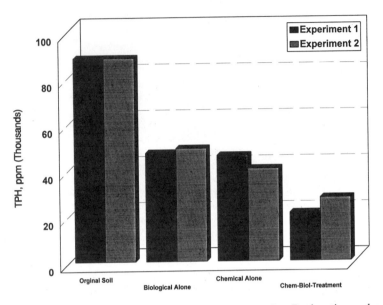

Figure 4.  Application of Various Treatments to Gas Exploration and
Production Soil RTS6689

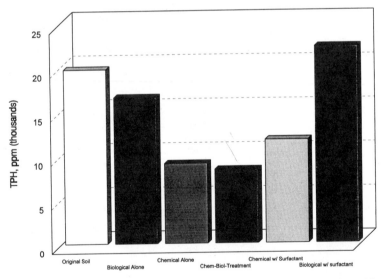

Figure 5.  Application of Various Treatments to Gas Exploration and
Production Soil RTS1260

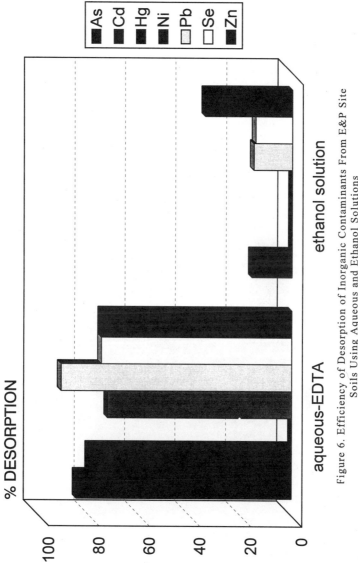

Figure 6. Efficiency of Desorption of Inorganic Contaminants From E&P Site
Soils Using Aqueous and Ethanol Solutions

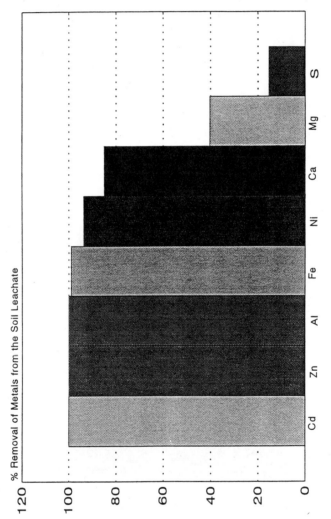

Figure 7.  Sulfate-Reducing Bacteria Can Efficiently Remove Inorganic
Contaminants From Soil Leachates

Table 1.  Controlled Leaching Can Efficiently Remove Inorganic
Contaminants From Soil

**TCLP TEST RESULTS FOR TOXIC METALS OF
LEACHED AND UNLEACHED CONTAMINATED SOIL**

| Toxic Metals | Regulatory Level | Unleached Soil | Leached Soil | Passes ± TCLP Test |
|---|---|---|---|---|
| | | ppm | | |
| Ag | 5.0 | <0.083 | <0.083 | + |
| Ar | 5.0 | 0.035 | 0.0067 | + |
| Ba | 100 | 0.26 | 0.49 | + |
| Cd | 1.0 | 6.75 | 0.28 | + |
| Cr | 5.0 | <0.033 | <0.033 | + |
| Hg | 0.2 | 7.0 | 0.93 | - |
| Pb | 5.0 | 1.26 | <0.33 | + |
| Se | 1.0 | 38 | 0.74 | + |

INTEGRATED NATURAL GAS TREATMENT: GAINED INDUSTRIAL
EXPERIENCE WITH IFPEXOL PROCESS.

TRAITEMENT INTEGRE DU GAZ NATUREL: EXPERIENCE
INDUSTRIELLE ACQUISE AVEC LE PROCEDE IFPEXOL.

Suru PATEL
(Petro-Canada, Calgary, CANADA),
Joseph LARUE, Ari MINKKINEN, Jean-François LEVIER
(Institut Français du Pétrole, Rueil-Malmaison, FRANCE)

RESUME

L'Institut Français du Pétrole a développé et breveté une nouvelle
technique de traitement du gaz naturel, le procédé IFPEXOL, basé sur
une nouvelle mise en oeuvre de méthanol à basse température, qui
intègre dans un procédé unique les 3 fonctions de déshydratation,
extraction des liquides de gaz naturel (LGN) et désacidification. Le
procédé IFPEXOL se compose de deux sections successives: IFPEX-1
effectue la déshydratation et l'extraction des LGN, IFPEX-2 effectue
la désacidification lorsqu'elle est nécessaire. Après un programme de
développement au laboratoire et sur une unité pilote, le procédé
IFPEXOL a été industrialisé. La première unité IFPEX-1 a démarré avec
succès en Juin 92 au Canada sur le champ d'East-Gilby en association
avec Petro-Canada; par la suite, sept autres unités d'IFPEX-1, dont
trois sont en opération, ont été vendues. Les résultats obtenus sur
les unités industrielles confirment les modèles de calcul. La section
IFPEX-2 est en cours de commercialisation.

ABSTRACT

The Institut Francais du Petrole has developed and patented a new
natural gas treatment technique, the IFPEXOL process, based on the use
of methanol at low temperature, and which includes 3 functions in only
one step: dehydration, NGL recovery and acid gases removal. The
IFPEXOL process is split into two successive sections: IFPEX-1 removes
NGL and water, IFPEX-2 removes the acid gases when necessary. After a
development program at laboratory scale and on a pilot plant, the
IFPEXOL process has reached the industrial step. The first IFPEX-1
unit has successfully started up in June 92 in Canada at Petro-
Canada's East-Gilby field. Subsequently, seven other units, of which
three are running, have been licenced. The results obtained from the
industrial plants confirm the simulation models. The IFPEX-2 section
is in its commercialisation phase.

The Institut Français du Pétrole (IFP) has developed and patented[1,2] a new natural gas treatment technique which includes three functions in only one step: dehydration, natural gas liquids (NGL) recovery or dew point control adjustment and acid gases removal.

This process called IFPEXOL is based on the use of a physical solvent, methanol, at low temperature. The principle is to take benefit from the cooling of the gas which is necessary to extract the NGLs to achieve concurrently a solvent enhanced absorption which accomplishes the dehydration and the acid gases removal. IFPEXOL introduces new patented concepts; in particular a novel solvent recovery technique which avoids the classical distillation step.

As all gases are wet but less than half are sour, it is important to be able to comply with only the dehydration aspect of the gas process. Thus, although IFPEXOL was conceived for integration, it is also convenient to be split into two integral sections : IFPEX-1 and IFPEX-2, according to the gas treatment requirements. IFPEX-1 removes condensable hydrocarbons and water from the raw wet gas; IFPEX-2 completes the full gas treatment when acid gases need also to be removed.

IFPEXOL PRINCIPLE

IFPEX-1 section. As shown in Figure 1, inlet gas is split into two streams: one stream is flowed countercurrently through the IFPEX-1 contactor against rich methanol solution, while the other stream bypasses the tower. The bypass stream and the IFPEX-1 contactor outlet are recombined, methanol make-up injected and the stream is then fed to the cold process. During its subsequent cooling, the gas stream is chilled to the required temperature, thereby condensing hydrocarbons, methanol and water. The two liquid phases and the gas phase are separated in a three-phase low temperature separator (LTS); the methanol-water mixture (heavy phase) is recycled to the contactor, whereas the residue gas and NGL phases leave the IFPEX-1 section. In the contactor, the flow of gas is countercurrent to the methanol-water mixture. During its passage upwards through the packed tower, the relatively warm gas is able to strip the methanol from the mixture due to methanol's high volatility. The methanol-water mixture gets progressively leaner with respect to methanol during its downward passage through the packing. As the gas entering the contactor is water saturated, it does not have any additional water carrying capacity and hence the water makes its way down the tower and out. The water leaving the tower contains only traces of methanol. The flow split of inlet gas that is fed to the contactor and the packing height in the contactor are optimized to minimize the total cost of the column, including the packing.

The net results for the gas are that the water and the NGL are removed and the methanol recovered efficiently for recycling without having to use either additional solvent recovery or water stripping facilities or external heat.

IFPEX-2 section. With the water and condensable hydrocarbons removed in the IFPEX-1 section, the already-cold sour gas flows up a second column where it is contacted countercurrently with a chilled methanol solvent stream as shown on figure 1. The IFPEX-2 contactor operates at the same conditions generally as the IFPEX-1 LTS. In the IFPEX-2 contactor, all of the H2S and most of the CO2 and some of the hydrocarbons are absorbed by the methanol solution. Generally the solvent is flashed to some intermediate pressure whereby most of the hydrocarbons some of the CO2 and very little H2S is liberated to the flash gas stream. Sometimes this flash gas can be utilized as such in plant fuel gas systems.
The acid components, notably H2S and CO2, are absorbed in the solvent allowing the exiting gas to meet the sweet gas specifications. A conventional regeneration process desorbs the acid gas from the solvent which is recycled to the IFPEX-2 column. The continuation of the regeneration procedure is a thermal stripper to remove H2S and remaining

$CO_2$ and hydrocarbons as completely as required to meet product gas specifications. The purified solvent is recycled to the IFPEX-2 contactor. A small methanol make-up is needed to compensate for the losses in the treated gas and in the acid gas streams. A slipstream of the regenerated solvent is used as a make-up for the IFPEX-1 section.

The IFPEXOL process development program, achieved by IFP with the EC's financial support, firstly included laboratory experiments to acquire the basic thermodynamic knowledge necessary to design the process. A large number of VLE and VLLE data sets have been determined. In a second step the process was further studied in a pilot plant having a capacity of $5000 Sm^3/d$. The pilot plant was located in Solaize within the Centre de developpement industriel of IFP. Runs of the IFPEX-1 gas-liquid contactor with low L/G ratio have allowed determination of the packing efficiency. At the same time a particular emphasis has been given to the computer simulation of the process. Thermodynamic models based on the EOS approach and including dedicated mixing rules allowed to correlate and predict the phase behaviour of complex mixtures including hydrocarbons, water and polar solvents as methanol at high pressure and low temperature. The importance of the development of appropriate models is illustrated by the plot of the methane molar solubility in a methanol-water mixture (figure 2), which shows the excellent matching quality of the experimental data and the predictions by IFP's model. This is to be compared with the results of a commonly recommended model such as SRK equation of state.

The excellent results of the IFPEXOL process R&D program led to construction of the first industrial application of IFPEX-1, at East-Gilby gas plant in Canada.

IFPEXOL INDUSTRIAL APPLICATIONS

IFPEX-1 application at East-Gilby[3,4,5]

The East-Gilby gas plant located in Alberta (Canada) is wholly owned and operated by Petro-Canada. It was originally built in 1970 and consisted of a gas sweetening unit using MDEA, a refrigeration type NGL extraction unit (hydrocarbon dew point control) processing at -26°C and utilizing MEG injection for hydrate prevention with a design capacity of $700 \ 10^3 Sm^3/d$. In 1990, Petro-Canada decided to revamp the East-Gilby facility to IFPEX-1. The capital investment required for this transformation was relatively small, and there was no process risk associated as the design allowed switching back to original MEG injection mode if required. The specific equipment of IFPEX-1 were added to the plant: IFPEX-1 contactor filled with packing, methanol-water recycle pump, methanol storage tank and methanol make-up pump.

The unit was started up for the first time in September 1991 as a demonstration test to prove the process and also to determine any deficiencies for continuous unmanned operation. As it was the first application, minimum equipment was installed until the IFPEX-1 concept was validated. Once proven, the unit was shut down during the normal plant maintenance program to allow for installation of additional instrumentation and modifications to be carried out.

Following modifications, which consisted essentially of instrumentation, the IFPEX-1 unit was restarted in June 1992 and has been running continously since except for short periods for annual plant maintenance. The unit operation has been very reliable and trouble free and although the MEG system was available as back-up, it was never required or used. As a result, the MEG injection and regeneration equipment was removed when the capacity of the plant was expanded in 1993.

Petro-Canada decided to increase the capacity of the plant to 1475 $10^3 Sm^3/d$. However, as all the installed IFPEX-1 equipment had adequate capacity, no modifications were required for this equipment. The refrigeration system was debottlenecked by addition of one more compressor. The original gas/gas exchangers (3 shells in series) and the gas chiller were removed and replaced by a brazed aluminium heat exchanger (BAHX) designed for a 2°C approach between the hot and cold streams. A new properly sized separator vessel was added upstream of the LTS to act as a gas/liquid separator for it. With a high efficiency demister, in addition to the separator's proper sizing, the amount of liquid droplets entrainment with the vapor is reduced to a minimum. With the original LTS now acting as only a liquid/liquid separator, separation of the two liquid phases has been improved. Both these improvements have resulted in significant reduction in methanol make-up requirements. Figure 3 shows the revamped IFPEX-1 scheme of the East-Gilby plant.

Several performance tests were conducted at East-Gilby after the start-up period and after the plant was stabilized and debugged. The results can be appreciated at two levels: the methanol content of the rejected water at the bottom of the contactor and the methanol make-up rate. Other than physical losses, there are three ways in which methanol is consumed from the IFPEX-1 process: in the water stream from the contactor bottom, in the NGL phase and in the treated gas.

Since the first continuous run in June 1992, the water originating from the IFPEX-1 contactor bottom was sampled and analysed to measure its methanol content. The IFPEX-1 contactor has actually clearly demonstrated its ability to strip the methanol from methanol-water mixture to levels below 100 ppm consistently. An average value of 40 ppm was obtained almost continuously. These results confirm the rightness of the correlations, established to predict the packing's efficiency and based upon the results of the pilot plant tests, and for which the extrapolation to high pressure was not evident. Hence the methanol make-up requirement due to loss through this water stream can be ignored.

During the first tests in June 1992, methanol make-up rate varied about 110% of values predicted in the IFP process book. The performance on a day-to-day basis, after this initial period and prior to 1993 expansion, varied somewhat and over a longer term period, methanol make-up rates averaged 120%. This high methanol make-up rate was probably attributed to poor separation and entrainment as the LTS was handling gas rates considerably in excess of its design, with resultant high gas velocities. In addition, one of the sweet inlet gas streams was prone to periodic liquid slugging. These liquids when dumped into the NGL extraction unit caused a sudden jump in the differential pressure, triggering the high differential pressure switch which in turn started the standby methanol make-up pump. During the 1993 expansion, this liquid dump line was redirected to the deethanizer tower, which has eliminated this problem. So that after the 1993 extension, methanol make-up rate, based on two months of unmanned operation, has dropped to levels very close to IFP process book predictions. These results demontrate the accuracy of the thermodynamic models specifically developped for this system, which calculate reliable values for the amount of methanol in the treated gas phase and in the NGL as well. The average consumption of methanol is 400 $1/10^6$ $Sm^3$. It should be noted that this consumption can be reduced substantially by water washing the NGL product stream and recovering the corresponding methanol. This water-methanol mixture is recycled back to the IFPEX-1 contactor.

With an improved return on investment and the good operating results, Petro-Canada decided to select IFPEX-1 for a new application in Brazeau River plant expansion project.

IFPEX-1 application at Brazeau River

Petro-Canada operates the Brazeau River gas processing complex which processes solution gas from a number of sweet oil pools, slightly sour gas-condensate pools (around 1% $H_2S$) and gas from some very sour reservoirs (25% to 28% $H_2S$). All these are very high pressure (350 Bars) reservoirs and gas cycling has been employed for pressure maintenance (gas reservoirs) and for miscible flooding (oil pools). The scheme has now matured to the point where some of these reservoirs will be commencing blowdown, requiring expansion of the gas processing facilities.

The existing complex consists of the following facilities:
-two high pressure (70 Bars) solution gas processing trains, employing glycol injection and chilling, operating at $-37^{\circ}C$ for propane plus recovery, with a capacity of 200 $10^3 Sm^3/d$ each;
-two low pressure (25 Bars) solution gas processing trains utilizing similar scheme, with a capacity of 85 $10^3 Sm^3/d$ each;
-a sour gas processing train consisting of amine treating and sulphur recovery (MCRC[TM] sub- dewpoint process), gas dehydration (Drizo process) and chilling, operating at $-40^{\circ}C$ for propane plus liquids recovery, with a capacity of 700 $10^3 Sm^3/d$ and 80 te/d Sulphur; and
-a sour gas processing train consisting of amine treating and sulphur recovery (MCRC[TM] sub-dewpoint process), molecular-sieve dehydration and turbo-expander for ethane plus liquids recovery with a capacity of 2,100 $10^3 Sm^3/d$ and 375 te/d Sulphur.

With the oil pools nearing blowdown, expansion of the solution gas handling facility was required as the existing solution gas handling capacity is only 570 $10^3 Sm^3/d$ and the new requirement is 2,000 $10^3 Sm^3/d$. In order to reduce the operating costs and optimize the facilities, it was decided to build a completely new train to handle the full volume of solution gas and salvage the existing high and low pressure trains. The existing utilities (heat-medium and propane refrigeration systems) were to be re-employed, thereby minimizing new capital. The same processing scheme in general was selected for the new train as is utilized in the existing trains. The larger capacity sour train is also being expanded but this required addition of a new contactor only and is not discussed further.

The existing solution gas processing trains utilize ethylene glycol injection for suppressing hydrates. For the new train the following options were considered:

(a) Continue with the existing glycol injection scheme. This option was rejected as the glycol losses tend to be high due to separation difficulties at the $-37^{\circ}C$ operating temperature. Also, the present trains experience ice build-up in the cold exchangers almost weekly, requiring a thaw-out. While gas is being reinjected, this does not cause loss of production as there is no hydrocarbon dewpoint specification to be met. However, when the facility goes on blow-down, residue gas will have to meet water and hydrocarbon dewpoint specifications.

(b) Drizo scheme was considered but rejected as the Drizo unit capital and energy costs were higher than those of an IFPEX-1 unit. In addition, the solution gas feed occasionally carries over large quantity of oil into the processing train (based on present operating experience) and it was considered very likely that the circulating glycol would be contaminated a number of times a year, causing significant production upsets and loss of revenue.

(c) Molecular sieve dehydration was considered but rejected as the capital and operating costs of this scheme were also higher than the Ifpex-1 scheme.

(d) IFPEX-1 methanol injection and recovery unit was evaluated and finally selected, based on its lower capital and operating costs. Petro-Canada's experience at East Gilby, based on over 3 years of operation, has been very favorable. Plant upsets have also been minimal. The only concern with the Ifpex-1 unit is methanol consumption, due to its higher vapor pressure and solubility in liquid hydrocarbons. At East Gilby, methanol recovery from LPG product is not carried out; however, due to its larger size and hence

better economics, a unit for methanol recovery from LPG product is being
installed at Brazeau.

The gas is chilled to -37$^{\circ}$C for propane plus recovery, utilizing a
conventional scheme. To reduce refrigeration requirements to existing
system capacity, brazed aluminum heat exchangers, designed for very close
temperature approach, are employed. In addition, the refrigeration system
was debottlenecked by adding an interstage economizer and subcooler. To
reduce the existing deethanizer overheads compressor load, a high pressure
"Demethanizer" column is installed which strips the light ends  from the
LTS liquids with vapors generated in the demethanizer reboiler. The heat
for the reboiler is provided by the propane refrigerant thereby aiding in
refrigeration load reduction. This is believed to be the first time such a
scheme is used anywhere.
The deethanizer system is standard, except an integral overhead condenser
is employed which eliminates the need for reflux pumps.

The Brazeau River IFPEX-1 unit is shown in figure 4; upgrades have
been incorporated in the Brazeau design based on operating experience
gained at Petro-Canada's East Gilby facility which is the first commercial
application of IFPEX-1 worldwide.

At East Gilby, methanol is not recovered from the liquid hydrocarbon
stream at present. In the design of Brazeau, it was decided to incorporate
this feature in order to reduce methanol consumption.

Methanol is recovered in two steps. First, the  rich methanol
(condensed methanol-water) stream is knocked out in the deethanizer feed
drum, separated from the lighter liquid hydrocarbon phase and recycled back
to the top of the IFPEX-1 column for regeneration. Secondly, the
deethanizer bottoms product, after cooling, is mixed with wash water
(IFPEX-1 column bottoms) in an in-line mixer and then after pre-filtering
(which further aids in mixing LPGs and wash water) sent to a
coalescer/separator for coalescence of the smaller water droplets into
larger ones and subsequent separation from the LPGs. The
coalescer/separator consists of dual elements, the top element acts as a
coalescer for the dilute methanol droplets, whereas the lower
hydrophobically treated Teflon/polymeric fibre separation membrane prevents
water from going through,  allowing only water-free hydrocarbons to flow
through. It is expected that approximately 90% of the methanol in LPGs will
be recovered in this manner. No further product treatment (drying) is being
installed as the LPG stream is expected to contain less than 15ppm of
water. The recovered methanol-water stream is pumped back to the middle of
the IFPEX-1 column for methanol recovery.

The existing gas processing trains are controlled using local
pneumatic controls, whereas the sour gas processing trains (added later on)
are controlled from a central DCS system. To reduce operating costs, the
new train will also be controlled from the central control room utilizing
the spare capacity of the existing DCS system.

Control of the methanol makeup rate is most critical, as smooth plant
operation and methanol losses are directly related to how well this part of
the control system functions. If rich methanol concentration is below the
required value, hydrates will be formed; if it is maintained too high,
methanol makeup will increase. Ideally, methanol makeup rate is set to
achieve just above the required concentration in the rich methanol so as to
prevent hydrates and minimize losses. At Brazeau, this will be achieved by
controlling the ratio of makeup methanol to inlet gas rate as the methanol
requirement is directly proportional to the inlet gas flow rate under
steady state. Finer adjustment, to allow for system variations,  will be
made by a rich methanol density controller, which resets the ratio
controller set point.

Even though adequate control system is provided, possibility of hydrate formation always exists as system upsets or mechanical failures can occasionally occur. To prevent this, high differential pressure indicator and alarm are provided to warn the operator of possible problems.

The gas flow through the IFPEX-1 column is maintained at a fixed rate, regardless of plant throughput, by a flow controller which operates the bypass valve around the column. It is felt that the extra complexity of ratio control, to maintain constant stripping gas ratio, is not warranted. East Gilby experience supports this viewpoint.

The level control in the IFPEX-1 column is maintained by a conventional level controller. The level of the interface in the rich methanol boot is maintained by a level controller which regulates the speed of the rich methanol return pump.

The flowrate of the wash water, used for methanol recovery from LPG product stream, is controlled by a flow controller. The wash water return is controlled by a level controller which regulates the speed of the wash water return pump. A mass flow meter is provided which also indicates the density of the returning water and methanol mixture. If this density drops to a preset value, the operator gets a warning that the coalescer/separator unit needs to be checked  for LPG contamination.

The unit is being installed at Brazeau at press-time and is scheduled to be operational by end of June 1995.

IFPEXOL cryogenic applications

A process can usually be considered to be cryogenic when the lowest operating temperature is below potential propane refrigeration chilling levels; that is to say approximately below -50°C. Glycols cannot be effectively used at such low temperatures to inhibit freezing. However, it is well established that the methanol water hydrocarbon system can effectively operate even down to -100°C levels without freezing. In fact, methanol has long been and still remains the choice antifreeze for most cryogenic processes. It is for these reasons that the application of the IFPEX-1 process to cryogenic temperature levels below -50°C is not only feasible but very attractive. Costly and complex molecular sieve dehydration and/or enhanced glycol extraction schemes can be avoided with significant capital and operating cost savings. One recent example of a cryogenic application of the IFPEX-1 process is illustrated by the Dagang oil field's associated gas LGP recovery project in Dagang (China). This project, which successfully started up in April 1995, processes over 1,125 $10^3 m^3$/d of rich associated gas to recover over 98% of the propane and heavier hydrocarbon components from the feed gas. The cold technology which achieves the desired propane plus recovery was designed by PRO-QUIP. This technology uses a turbo expander coupled with a novel cryogenic distillation system operating in the region of -80°C at the coldest point of the process. Ordinarily conventional molecular sieve dehydration by water extraction would be recognized as the appropriate upstream step to prevent water ice build up in the cryogenic process. Emergency methanol injection would nevertheless be incorporated in case of molecular sieve upsets. PRO-QUIP, as engineering contractor was quick to recognize the advantages that the IFPEX-1 process could bring to their client. Consequently molecular sieve dehydration costing 2 to 3 times more was replaced by continuous methanol inhibited IFPEX-1 dehydration technology.

As depicted in the simplified process flow diagram on figure 5 the essential features of the gas process are: IFPEX-1 methanol stripper, cryogenic turbo expander, low temperature distillation and methanol-water wash system. Upstream associated gas compression and downstream recovered liquids fractionation follow conventional process design and are not described further.

Part of the compressed associated gas feed is sent through the IFPEX-1 contactor to serve as stripping gas and thus recover methanol from both the decanted cold separator concentrated methanol water stream and the dilute methanol wash water return stream. The water leaving the bottom of the contactor is free of methanol. A slip stream of this water is used as a wash water in the methanol water wash system.

The gas leaving the top of the IFPEX-1 contactor containing all the recovered methanol is compressed by the turbo expander driven compressor, is cooled by air and coldstreams in a plate exchanger upstream of which is injected some make-up methanol. The chilled compressed feed is passed to a cold separator drum (LTS) where water/ methanol, hydrocarbon condensate and vapor streams are separated. The vapor stream is expanded to the distillation pressure while attaining -80°C temperature in the mixed phase expander discharge. Additional make-up methanol is injected to the turbo expander suction to assure ice free discharge condition. The hydrocarbon condensate from the LTS is also expanded through a JT valve and after passing through the plate exchanger is taken to the distillation section.

The turbo-expander discharge and flashed condensate are treated in the distillation column consisting of a special cryogenic fractionator combined with a deethanizer to attain over 98% propane recovery with over 99% ethane rejection. The methanol dissolved in the feed finds itself concentrated in the deethanized liquid leaving the section. The overheads contain less than 1 ppm (mol) of methanol at the prevailing operating conditions.

In order to reduce the methanol losses to a strict minimum the recovered liquid containing approximately 5700 ppm (mol) of methanol is washed with methanol free water in the water wash column. Over 99% methanol recovery is attained by using approximately 20 to 1 water methanol ratio in a four theoretical stages countercurrent contact column. The dilute wash water is pumped to the upstream IFPEX-1 contactor to recover the methanol to the cold process. The overall methanol consumption of the complete gas process is less than 6 kg/h.

The Dagang plant was started up in April 95, and operating data will soon be available.

Besides the three applications described above, the IFPEX-1 process has been licenced for five other applications as shown on table 1.

ACID GAS REMOVAL

The IFPEX-2 part of the IFPEXOL technology is destined for efficient acid gas removal from cold to cryogenic temperature gases. For good H2S and selective CO2 solubility the methanol concentration used in the IFPEX-2 process is generally less than 100% but higher than required in the upstream IFPEX-1 step to avoid hydrate formation. The fact that water is present in the refrigerated solvent from 0 to 25% distinguishes the IFPEX-2 methanol absorption process from the well known RECTISOL process. The RECTISOL process was conceived for chemical gases other than hydrocarbons because of the strong co-absorption of hydrocarbons to pure methanol. The presence of water in the methanol solvent was a way to decrease drastically the hydrocarbon co-absorption. This has been amply demonstrated in several years of IFPEXOL pilot plant experiments.

Since methanol is a physical solvent there are no heats of reaction to deal with as there are with amines. Regeneration of the rich solvent is easier to achieve first by flashing and then by mild thermal stripping at relatively low temperatures when compared with amine processes. Moreover the stripper pressure can be kept as high as 10 to 14 bar without exceeding bottoms temperature of 150°C. The latter attribute is especailly important when considering acid gas recovery for reinjection or enhanced oil recovery applications. Moreover the acid gases recovered are virtually dry.

Many new design features have been developed and tested for the IFPEX-2 process to tailor it to most acid gas removal projects. One of the most important of these is the selective regeneration to multi quality acid gas streams. In this design the rich solvent is regenerated to yield a dry hydrocarbon rich fuel gas stream, a dry $CO_2$ rich acid gas stream at higher than 10 bar and a dry $H_2S$ rich acid gas stream of Claus plant quality containing a minimum of hydrocarbons. Hence the IFPEX-2 process can today be considered even for acid gas removal to Claus type sulfur recovery. Limitations in regard to $CO_2$ solubility still restrict the economic application of the IFPEX-2 process to around 1000 ppm (mol) $CO_2$ in the product gas. A finishing step, preferably non-wetting, is needed to attain LNG plant feed quality gas specification in respect to $CO_2$. In all cases the $H_2S$ specification below 3.0 ppm (mol) can be easily achieved.

CONCLUSION

The IFPEXOL process can now be considered as fully industrial. As a matter of fact, the successful three years experience has demonstrated the performance of the IFPEX-1 section. The simulation model resulting from the R&D program is fully validated by the industrial scale operations. The process has shown its reliability and its possibility to merge with different application cases.

Today several proposals have been made for complete IFPEXOL gas treatment, including IFPEX-1 and IFPEX-2 sections; with the gained experience, this process will soon find an industrial application.

REFERENCES

1. US Pat. 4775395, "Integrated Process for the Treatment of a Wet Hydrocarbon Gas", Oct. 86
2. US Pat. 4979966, "Process and Apparatus for Dehydration, Sweetening and Separation of a Condensate from a Natural Gas", Sept. 88
3. J. Larue, A. Minkkinen and S. Patel "IFPEXOL for Environmentally Sound Gas Processing", GPA Convention, Anaheim, California, March 16-18, 1992
4. A.Minkkinen, J.Larue, S.Patel, J.F.Levier "Methanol gas-treating scheme offers economics, versatility", Oil&Gas J., 1 June, 1992
5. S. Patel "IFPEXOL - A Year+ Later" Can Energy '94, Calgary, April 19-20, 1994

| CLIENT | FIELD OR PLANT | LOCATION | CAPACITY Million Sm3/d | COLD PROCESS | START-UP DATE |
|---|---|---|---|---|---|
| PETRO-CANADA | East-Gilby | Canada | 1.47 | C3 refrig. | Jun-92 |
| MARATHON OIL Co. | Markham | U.S.A. | 0.23 | JT valve | Oct-92 |
| JAPEX | Yufutsu | Japan | 2x1.30 | C3 refrig. | May-96 |
| DAGANG PETROLEUM (CNPC) | Dagang | China | 1.21 | Turbo-exp. | Apr-95 |
| MAERSK O&G | West Harald | Denmark (*) | 10.15 | Turbo-exp. | Oct-97 |
| CONWEST EXPLO. | Sexsmith | Canada | 4.08 | C3 refrig. | End-95 |
| PETRO-CANADA | Brazeau | Canada | 2.00 | C3 refrig. | Jun-95 |
| WESTCOAST ENERGY | Aitken Creek | Canada | 2x4.63 | Turbo-exp. | End-95 |

(*) Offshore

**Table 1: IFPEXOL References**

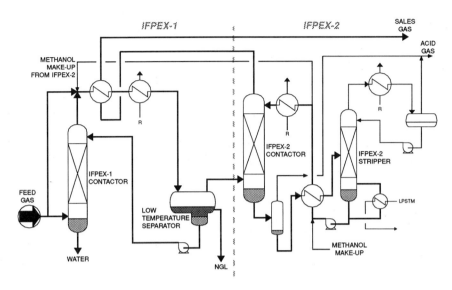

**Figure 1: Principle of the IFPEXOL process**

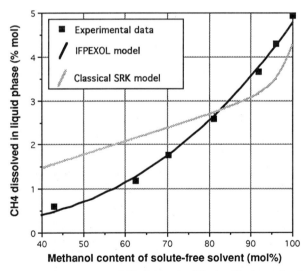

**Figure 2: Solubility of Methane in Water-Methanol mixture
P= 5000 kPa - T= 253 K**

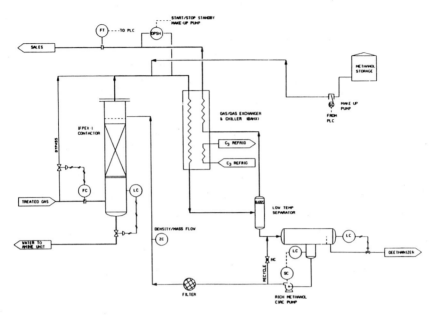

**Figure 3: Revamped IFPEX-1 scheme of the East-Gilby gas plant**

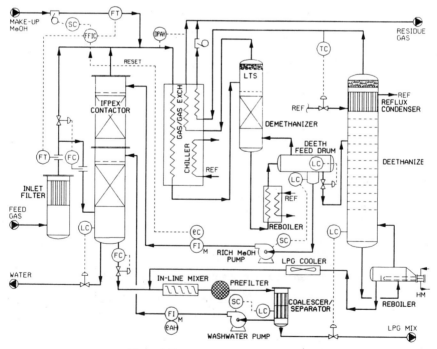

**Figure 4: Brazeau process flow diagram**

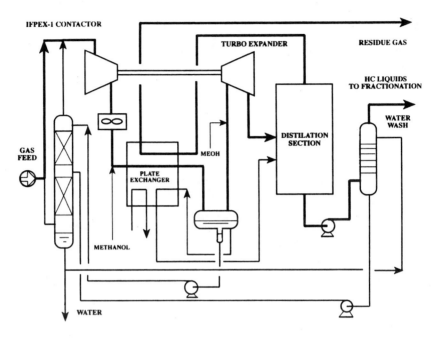

**Figure 5: Dagang simplified flow diagram**

TEST RESULTS FOR SULFUR REMOVAL FROM GAS STREAMS

DESULFURATION DES GAZ NATURELS: RESULTATS D'ESSAIS

Dennis Leppin
Gas Research Institute, USA

Dennis A. Dalrymple
Radian Corporation, USA

## ABSTRACT

Significant amounts of sour gas have been discovered and are being produced in Eastern Europe, the former Soviet Bloc, the Middle East, Canada, United States and elsewhere. Because sulfur-contaminated resources are important to the natural gas supply, the Gas Research Institute (GRI) has funded research into technologies to economically treat sour gas. This is especially important in an environment where increasingly stringent sulfur emissions limits are being adopted globally. Specifically, GRI is generating data to compare and validate the advantages of direct-treat approaches and scavenging processes for sulfur removal/recovery in natural gas processing. This type of comparative data has never been gathered before. This paper presents an overview of the available data which has been generated to date. In addition, information is presented on the beneficial reuse by the utility industry of the by-product sulfur from these direct-treat approaches.

## RÉSUMÉ

Des quantités considérables de gaz naturel sulfureux ont été découvertes et sont actuellement produites en Europe de l'est, dans l'ex-URSS, au Moyen-Orient, au Canada, aux Etats-Unis et dans d'autres parties du monde. Ces ressources sulfureuses constituant un part importante des réserves mondiales, le Gas Research Institute (GRI) subventionne la recherche de technologies économiques pour le traitement des gaz naturels acides. Ceci importe d'autant plus que les émissions de soufre sont globalement de plus en plus strictement limitées. Plus spécifiquement, le GRI a engagé un programme de recherche pour comparer et valider les avantages du traitement direct et des procédés d'épuration pour l'élimination ou la récupération du soufre. C'est la première fois que des données comparatives de ce genre sont recueillies. Cette étude présente un aperçu général des données recueillies jusqu'ici. De plus, nous présentons des informations sur les bénéfices liés à la réutilisation par les entreprises de distribution d'électricité, du soufre récupéré par ces procédés de traitement direct.

## INTRODUCTION

The Gas Research Institute (GRI) has developed a research program in sulfur removal and recovery from natural gas. Hydrogen sulfide ($H_2S$) is a poisonous gas which must be removed from natural gas before the gas can be shipped in the interstate pipeline network. A specification of 4 parts per million volume (ppmv) $H_2S$ is common in gas pipelines. Gas which is prone to containing $H_2S$ comprises some 14% of gas reserves in the lower 48 U.S. states.[1] This resource of $H_2S$-contaminated gas constitutes about $5.4 \times 10^{12}$ $Nm^3$ of the natural gas reserves in these states. If the sulfur in this gas cannot be vented or flared in new plants because of stricter environmental requirements, traditional amine/Claus approaches may be too costly or even impractical. Technology to reduce the cost of sulfur removal/recovery is therefore of considerable interest to the natural gas production industry. Over the past decade, the GRI program has focused on liquid redox technology, and in the last several years has expanded into the area of scavenging-type processes.

Technology transfer of the GRI program results is paramount. This and other papers represent a key avenue of technology transfer.[2] Another very important vehicle has been the GRI-hosted international conferences on liquid redox and scavenging technology and research which convene at 18-month intervals.[3,4,5,6,7,8] The 1995 GRI Sulfur Recovery Conference was held September 24-27 in Austin, Texas.

## SCAVENGING TECHNOLOGY FOR $H_2S$ REMOVAL

For relatively small quantities of $H_2S$ removal, on the order of around 0.1 metric tons per day and less, nonregenerable or "throwaway"-type scavengers are the least expensive options, depending on a number of factors including cost of disposal. Iron sponge is a well-known example of this type of approach, and a number of liquid-based processes using amines, nitrites, caustic or formaldehyde are known. Further, certain scavenging agents can be injected in-line and then removed downstream. Since there is a stoichiometric relationship between the quantity of sulfur removed and the amount of chemical agent needed, the economics of scavenging processing is a strong function of sulfur removal capacity.

GRI has contracted Radian Corporation and The M.W. Kellogg Company to carry out a program to evaluate $H_2S$ scavenging processes.[9] Commercially-available processes are being screened in the laboratory and tested in the field. Evaluation criteria are being developed prior to testing in the areas of performance, economics, and environmental impacts.

A growing segment of the gas producing industry uses $H_2S$ scavenging processes to remove low concentrations of $H_2S$ (usually less than 100 ppm) from subquality natural gas at remote locations. For this gas segment, conventional amine sweetening is not economically feasible, especially when carbon dioxide ($CO_2$) removal is not required. Historically, the gas production industry has used nonregenerable $H_2S$ scavenging processes to treat this gas. The four major categories of $H_2S$ scavengers are listed below:

- Caustic/sodium nitrite solutions (e.g., Nalco/Exxon's SULFA-CHECK® 2420[a]);
- Nonregenerable amines (e.g., Champion Technologies' Gas Treat 114, Petrolite Corporation's HSW-330-L);
- Triazines (e.g., Petrolite Corporation's SULFA-SCRUB® HSW 700[b]); and
- Solid adsorbents (e.g., iron sponge, The SulfaTreat Company's SulfaTreat®[c]).

These processes can produce solutions and solids which are contaminated with elemental sulfur, sulfides, and other constituents such as the chemicals themselves. As regulations have become

---

[a] SULFA-CHECK® is a registered trademark of Nalco/Exxon Energy Chemicals, L.P.

[b] SULFA-SCRUB® is a registered trademark of Petrolite Corporation.

[c] SulfaTreat® is a registered trademark of The SulfaTreat Company.

stricter and heightened awareness related to waste generation and disposal has developed in the gas industry, a keen interest in identifying better and more environmentally-acceptable $H_2S$ scavenging processes for these applications is emerging. This increasing interest in scavenging processes has generated a need by industry for applications and operating guidelines which would allow them to make a more informed selection and use of the various classes of scavengers. GRI's research in this area is aimed at addressing this need for information. The research program includes several components:

- Technical evaluation of information obtained from literature, vendor, and process user sources;
- Laboratory testing; and
- Field testing at commercial facilities.

Each of these areas is discussed in the following sections.

Scavenger Technical Evaluation

The M.W. Kellogg Company is undertaking a task to evaluate and rank various scavenger technologies in a systematic way. The status of the SeleXpert™:$H_2S$ Scavenger Module being developed was reported by Kellogg at the 1995 GPA annual meeting and at the 1995 GRI Sulfur Recovery Conference.[10] A brief overview of the scavenger technical evaluations is given here. Kellogg has evaluated fifteen scavenging technologies based on scavenger material cost and performance information obtained from vendor and literature sources. Based on this public domain information, Kellogg's work established the relative cost and acceptability of the fifteen technologies for removing $H_2S$ from a $2.2 \times 10^3$ Nm³/hr natural gas stream (60, 1100, and 1900 grams of sulfur per hour with 0.13 mol % $CO_2$). The evaluation results were used to screen those technologies with the greatest potential technical and economic merit for further study in GRI's field evaluation program. The SeleXpert: $H_2S$ Scavenger Module prototype was developed using the results from the screening evaluation.[11]

Scavenger Laboratory Evaluation

The objective of the laboratory testing is to evaluate scavengers from each scavenger class to obtain general behavioral characteristics and performance data. The laboratory-scale test apparatus operates at ambient pressure. The test variables include $H_2S$ concentration, $CO_2$ concentration, and the presence of liquid hydrocarbon condensate (to evaluate the potential for hydrocarbon-induced foaming). The data collection includes qualitative data on reaction rates, $H_2S$ capacity, effect of $CO_2$, effect of liquid hydrocarbons, solids formation/characteristics, and tendency to foam. The laboratory data tends to be more qualitative in nature due to the limitations in contact times and heights. Therefore important parameters such as the sulfur capacity of the scavenging agents are best obtained under field conditions.

Table 1 gives the capacity values obtained on the laboratory apparatus for the representative scavenger liquids tested. This table also shows representative data from the field evaluations conducted as part of the GRI program. Representative capacity values for each scavenger class are also given in the table. These values should not be regarded as absolutes, or as necessarily representative of any particular scavenger. They do, however, provide the potential scavenger user with a starting point to evaluate options and costs

Field Evaluations of $H_2S$ Scavengers -- Liquids and Solids in Towers

The primary objective of the field evaluation program is to obtain accurate and reliable performance, cost, and environmental data on each class of scavenging agents to use in developing application and operating guidelines for optimum use of these processes by the gas industry. The project also identifies data gaps and research and process development needs in this increasingly important area of gas processing.

The initial field testing was for liquid scavengers in tower applications at an operating site of a major gas producer in south Texas. Figure 1 is a photograph of the facility. The plant has two parallel towers, each capable of treating up to $17 \times 10^3$ $Nm^3$/hr of sour natural gas containing up to 20 ppm $H_2S$. The measured capacities of the liquid scavengers was shown in Table 1; a complete report of the tests results has been published.[12]

Field testing of a solid-based scavenging agent is currently in progress and nearing completion at a natural gas treating plant near Waco, Texas. The scavenging agent under evaluation is SulfaTreat®, which is an iron-oxide based scavenger. This scavenger is being evaluated at two separate gas treating facilities operated by the host company. Site one treats approximately 2 - 14 $Nm^3$/hr of natural gas with 5 - 10 ppmv $H_2S$ and 2 - 3 % $CO_2$. Natural gas enters the plant at 32 - 46 bar. Site two treats approximately 2 - 18 $Nm^3$/hr of natural gas with 4 - 14 ppmv $H_2S$ and 2 % $CO_2$. The gas is gathered at approximately 15 bar and compressed to 40-70 bar prior to scavenging treatment. Observations have been made and data have been collected in several areas:

- Changeout procedures required;
- Scavenging capacity;
- Bed pressure drop characteristics;
- Water balance analysis;
- Sulfur compound removal;
- Pyrophoric behavior of the spent scavenger;
- Waste characterization and disposal practices;
- Health and safety requirements; and
- Capital and operating costs.

Samples of the spent scavenger are being analyzed to determine their waste disposal characteristics. Initial results indicate the importance of air-drying the spent scavenger. Air-dried samples leached benzene in concentrations less than $0.5 \times 10^3$ g/L, whereas samples of the wet scavenger collected during the tower changeout had levels above $0.5 \times 10^3$ g/L (A concentration of $0.5 \times 10^3$ g/L is the regulatory level established for determining benzene toxicity under 40 CFR Part 261.)

Capital and operating costs for the liquid and solid agents are being developed based on information gathered at the host site facilities. A normalized treatment cost for the agents is being developed which will include costs for tower changeouts, scavenging agent replacement, operating and maintenance labor, and waste disposal. Table 2 gives a comparison of the liquid and solid scavenging costs for tower applications for an example plant treating $17 \times 10^3$ $Nm^3$/hr of sour gas with 19 ppmv $H_2S$. The operating cost parameters and usages are from data and measurements made in this GRI program. The capital costs shown are estimates for new equipment, and do not necessarily reflect the actual costs at the GRI host sites.

Field Evaluation of Liquid-Based $H_2S$ Scavengers In Direct-Injection Applications

Direct injection involves pumping the scavenging agent directly into the sour natural gas pipeline with a positive displacement pump. The scavenging agent may be introduced into the line using 1) a simple pipe connection, 2) an extended "quill" tube to deliver the agent to the center of the pipe, or 3) atomization nozzles. The gas and scavenging agent mix together either under open flow conditions or with static mixing devices. In some cases, the tortuous flow paths through process equipment may be used to enhance the mixing. Following the mixing and reaction, the liquid (and potentially solid) reaction products are removed in a downstream knockout device.

Direct-injection scavenging with liquid absorbents has several potential advantages over the conventional tower applications with liquid or solid scavengers, including:

- No pressurized tower contactor required;

- No costly changeout of towers required;
- Less potential for foaming/carryover problems; and
- Potential for lower chemical usage requirements.

However, direct-injection scavenging has several process characteristics which require careful consideration by the gas producer. The performance of direct-injection scavenging is more difficult to predict than for tower-based processes, in part because of the complexities involved in the two-phase mixing of scavenging agents with natural gas in the pipeline. Direct injection processes must operate over a wide range of gas/liquid ratios, gas velocities, atomizer/spray nozzle types, and injection pump designs (e.g., pulse flow or continuous flow). Trial and error design appears to be typical with these systems. Performance is some cases may be limited by contact time available in the existing piping system. High-pressure injection pumps may also lead to higher maintenance costs and reliability problems. The potential for solids deposits to accumulate in pipelines is also a concern.

Despite these potential concerns, direct-injection remains an attractive alternative to some gas producers because of the potential for reduced chemical costs and that the capital cost of a pressurized tower contactor is avoided. GRI is currently evaluating liquid-based $H_2S$ scavengers in direct-injection applications and will publish the results as they are available.

Advanced Scavenger Process

Current scavenging methods use nonregenerable chemicals which could pose problems for disposal. A GRI exploratory research project conducted by Radian Corporation examined the feasibility of a regenerable process for scavenging $H_2S$ from natural gas. The new scavenging process would remove the $H_2S$ from the gas stream, but maintain it in a soluble form (to prevent maintenance problems in the towers) until the sorbent capacity is reached. At that point, the sorbent could be regenerated for reuse while simultaneously generating solid sulfur for sale or disposal. Feasibility was demonstrated at the laboratory scale, and a patent application has been filed on the process. Additional development of the regeneration options for this process concept is planned.

LIQUID REDOX TECHNOLOGY FOR $H_2S$ REMOVAL/SULFUR RECOVERY

For large-scale treatment, amine treating followed by modified-Claus and various tail gas treating (TGT) options, depending on the ultimate recovery required, is the least expensive recovery route. For sulfur recovery on the order of 20 metric tons per day down to around 0.1 metric ton per day, liquid redox processes appear advantageous over other options. To provide the most economical treatment using this approach, the amine plant is replaced by a high-pressure liquid redox contactor. Liquid redox units can also be used following an amine plant at low pressure, such as when $CO_2$ needs to be removed in any event, but in this application the liquid redox units are operating as TGT units. This application is generally accepted as commercially available and is not addressed in GRI's program. The direct-treat application, which offers the greatest benefits if it can be realized, was chosen by GRI for field validation efforts. Technical evaluation process comparison studies confirmed the potential of this approach.

GRI's liquid redox research consists of fundamental studies of liquid redox kinetics and mechanisms, early-stage development of advanced processes (e.g., Hysulf[SM][a]) and pilot-scale testing of commercially-available direct-treatment processes such as SulFerox®[b] and ARI-LO-CAT II®[c]. A report giving chemistry and operating guidelines for Stretford-type redox processes has been issued,

---

[a] Hysulf[SM] is a service mark of Marathon Oil Company.
[b] SulFerox® is a registered trademark of Shell Oil Company.
[c] ARI-LO-CAT® and ARI-LO-CAT II® are registered trademarks of Wheelabrator Clean Air Systems, Inc.

as well as a report describing the results of tests on the SulFerox process in high-pressure natural gas treatment.[13,14]

Liquid redox processes occur through an oxidation reduction cycle. For the iron-based processes, the iron (Fe) is alternately oxidized and reduced to the ferrous and ferric oxidation states as follows:

$$H_2S + Fe^{+3} \rightleftharpoons S^- + 2H^+ + Fe^{+2} \quad (1)$$

$$\tfrac{1}{2}O_2 + Fe^{+2} \rightleftharpoons Fe^{+3} + H_2O \quad (2)$$

The overall reaction is then:

$$\tfrac{1}{2}O_2 + H_2S \rightleftharpoons S + H_2O$$

The sour gas enters an absorber (Figure 2) where it contacts fresh solution (ferric chelate) and reaction (1) takes place, oxidizing the sulfide ion in $H_2S$ to sulfur and reducing the ferric chelate to ferrous chelate. The solution containing the sulfur and ferrous chelate is sent to a retention or settling vessel where the sulfur is removed. The ferrous solution is then sent to an oxidizer vessel where it contacts air for regeneration back to the ferric form. The sulfur slurry is generally sent to filtration for removal as a wet (~50% moisture) cake.

The iron in these processes is typically in the form of chelated iron which is much more soluble in the aqueous solution at the pH of operation (generally above 7). The complex chemistry associated with the chelates, especially with regard to degradation reactions and stability, is the source of much of the proprietary know-how held by the vendors. Fundamental studies to elucidate the actual mechanisms, which are much more detailed than indicated in the simple description above, are being carried out under GRI funding at Caltech and Radian Corporation.[15,16]

Drawbacks of liquid redox processes are the losses of rather expensive chelant due to degradation and purge (removed with the sulfur cake). The requirement for stainless steel in any pressure vessels coming into contact with the solution contributes to high capital cost.

Liquid Redox Technical Evaluation

Kellogg has completed a technical and economic evaluation of the iron-based liquid redox processes for small-scale (~2 metric tons per day of sulfur) $H_2S$ removal from natural gas based on inputs from the process licensors.[17,18] Information was obtained from Wheelabrator Clean Air Systems, Inc., for the ARI-LO-CAT and ARI-LO-CAT II processes, from Dow Chemical USA for the Shell SulFerox process, and from NKK Japan for the Bio-SR process. The economic evaluations encompassed two different cases as shown in Table 3.

The study found that the liquid redox sulfur recovery (LRSR) processes have a number of advantages over amine/Claus/SCOT. The LRSR processes can remove $H_2S$ to pipeline quality while recovering over 99.8% of the sulfur in a single unit. The LRSR processes easily handle sulfur capacities of less than 5 metric tons/day, have very large turndowns, can process lean $H_2S/CO_2$ gases, do not require fired equipment, and adapt easily to variations in gas flow and $H_2S$ concentrations, all of which cause problems in Claus units. The investment costs for the LRSR processes are of the same order of magnitude as amine/Claus, but the addition of the SCOT unit to obtain equivalent sulfur recoveries makes amine/Claus/SCOT more expensive. The sulfur produced by the LRSR processes is not Claus grade; but it can be disposed of easily as a slurry or cake or sold either as a cake or in the molten state.

The ARI-LO-CAT process uses a chelated iron solution with a low iron concentration. (Chelating agents are necessary to keep the iron from precipitating at neutral pH.) The process has a relatively high pumping cost due to this low concentration of scrubbing solution. Similar to ARI-LO-CAT and ARI-LO-CAT II, the SulFerox process uses a chelated iron solution, but at a much higher iron concentration.[19] This reduces equipment sizes and pumping costs, but makes management of the solution more expensive and difficult. The cost of SulFerox for the rich gas case is comparable to direct-treat ARI-LO-CAT II.

The Bio-SR process does not use chelates, operates at low pH, and uses bacteria to enhance the kinetics for the regeneration (by air oxidation) of the reduced iron solution. While the chemical make-up costs for Bio-SR are less than for the chelated LRSR processes, the size of the bioreactor is very large. The field construction of the bioreactor results in a high capital cost for the Bio-SR process.

Kellogg's studies indicate that LRSR processes have the potential to be more economical than amine/Claus/SCOT for small-scale applications. When the operating benefits are also considered, the studies indicate strong advantages for LRSR for small-scale $H_2S$ removal. For direct applications, however, the lack of operational data from full-scale plants should be considered. The GRI pilot plant program should help to reduce the uncertainty of using this potentially lower-cost approach.

Liquid Redox Process Testing

In the field experiment program, which is being administered by the Radian Corporation, data is being gathered on such important parameters as salts buildup, energy and utility requirements, degree of sulfur removal, solution loss, and sulfur quality. In addition, process operability, reliability, and flexibility are being evaluated. The field experiment program is being conducted at the Natural Gas Pipeline Company's (NGPL) sour gas facility near Kermit, Texas. The SulFerox pilot plant which was tested at the Kermit site is shown (photograph) in Figure 3. This plant has since been removed, and the ARI-LO-CAT II pilot plant installed at the same location (shown in Figure 4). The pilot plant design basis feed gas composition at this facility is shown in Table 4.

During most of 1993 and the first few months of 1994, the SulFerox process was tested at this facility. The process was consistently able to meet pipeline specification for $H_2S$, but foaming and plugging in the high-pressure section of the plant prevented stable, reliable operation. A complete report of the GRI testing is available.[5]

Following the SulFerox program, a pilot unit based on the ARI-LO-CAT II process was installed at the site for testing under substantially the same conditions. Initial startup occurred in November of 1994. A test program funded by the licensor, Wheelabrator Clean Air Systems (formerly ARI Technologies), for developmental purposes and to establish baseline conditions was conducted from November 1994 through mid-May of 1995. As of the submission date for this paper, GRI's evaluation testing had just been completed and analysis of the data was beginning. The preliminary observation is that direct desulfurization of natural gas with ARI-LO-CAT II is technically feasible, but there are some operational areas where revisions in a commercial unit design will be needed. The pilot unit operation confirms that static mixer absorbers in this service have an inherent tendency to plug. Provisions for cleaning the static mixers in place will be required for this service. Also, the high-pressure solution recirculation pump seals and packing fail quickly; improvements in this area are also needed. Table 5 provides a comparison of the design conditions versus observed process values.

BASIC SULFUR RECOVERY RESEARCH

The goal of GRI basic research is to provide much improved methods for treating subquality natural gas reserves containing $H_2S$, including compact methods for offshore use. Problems with the current systems include chemical degradation of the sorbent, operational difficulties associated with separating and purifying the sulfur product, and high liquid flow rates and inventories. Since the chemistry of liquid redox sulfur recovery processes is complex, an understanding of the basic chemistry may be key to ensuring reliable and economical operation. In the absorber section of these processes, the rates of reaction of the oxidized redox agent with $H_2S$ determine the effectiveness of scrubbing. Yet excessive rates of sulfur formation in the scrubber can lead to plugging. Detailed mechanistic understanding could lead to sufficient control of the kinetics to satisfy these conflicting requirements. In the air-driven regeneration step of liquid redox processes, the reoxidation rate of the reduced form of the redox couple is relatively slow and requires fairly large equipment. Most of the reagent degradation and loss occurs in the regeneration step. Fundamental understanding is needed to improve the long-term stability and rate of regeneration of the redox catalyst.

GRI 's basic research program in sulfur recovery is examining these fundamental issues with the goal of improving the technologies (especially with respect to reducing costs) and developing new technologies where needed. Laboratory and field experiments are measuring reaction rates and products; complex kinetic models are being developed; reaction pathways are being postulated and tested; and concepts for process improvements are being developed and tested. One promising development has been the invention of a concept for a novel liquid redox process which provides inherently better control over sulfur formation in the scrubber and which produces high quality, easy-to-separate sulfur without use of surfactants. Radian and GRI have submitted a patent application on this process. Development is continuing.

Researchers at the California Institute of Technology have developed electrochemical sensors for monitoring the ratio and individual concentrations of oxidized and reduced forms of iron chelate redox agents. The initial form of the sensor used a polymer-coated, carbon-fiber electrode. The sensor responded well in the presence of sulfur over a wide redox agent concentration range, but proved to be less durable than expected. The sensor design was modified and has recently been tested by Radian at on the ARI-LO-CAT II pilot plant at Kermit. This new design proved to be very robust. Even after repeated use, the new sensors were more active than freshly polished platinum electrodes. One sensor retained practically all of its activity after overnight exposure in the oxidizer box. Figure 5 illustrates that the new sensors gave generally good agreement with the phenanthroline spectrophotometric method.

OTHER GRI SULFUR RECOVERY ACTIVITIES

GRI is interested in evaluating other processes if they offer significant advantages through novel approaches. One candidate is the Bio-SR process, which has been developed by NKK Industries of Japan.[20] If initial lab and engineering studies are favorable, then the next step would likely be to conduct very small scale tests in the field to gather intial data on the performance of the high-pressure section of the design. This testing would occur sometime in 1996. Following a go/no go decision, then this process could be evaluated at the NGPL Kermit site

Other processes of potential interest to GRI include Marathon Oil Company's HYSULF[SM] process[*], the Idemitsu Kosan sulfur recovery process, and the Paques process. The HYSULF process uses redox chemistry under mild operating conditions to convert $H_2S$ into sulfur and hydrogen.[21] GRI is co-funding development of this process. The Idemitsu process involves redox reactions at elevated temperatures and features an electrolytic regeneration approach. Initial technical data gathering by GRI and Radian has occurred. Following additional development by Idemitsu (Japan), small-scale tests in the United States may be conducted in the mid- to late-96 time frame. The Paques process uses microbes to treat the gas. GRI is in the information gathering stage regarding this process' potential for treating sour natural gas.

USE OF LIQUID REDOX SULFUR IN WET FGD SYSTEMS

In a related development, GRI, the Electric Power Research Institute, and several U.S. utilities are funding a joint effort to evaluate the beneficial reuse of byproduct liquid redox sulfur from the

---

[*] HYSULF[SM] is a service mark of the Marathon Oil Co.

gas industry.[22] This program has included lab-, pilot-, and commercial-scale testing. A key result of the work has been the development of methods to convert solid sulfur cake from liquid redox plants into a water-based suspension commonly called "emulsified" sulfur. This emulsion can be used by the utilities in their wet flue gas desulfurization (FGD) systems to inhibit oxidation and improve process operations. The utilities have been purchasing a high cost sulfur material. This joint research has shown that this gas industry byproduct, which is often disposed of in a landfill, can be used instead -- thus producing cost savings for both industries.

## CONCLUSIONS

GRI has an active effort in sulfur removal and recovery for natural gas processing. GRI's information products in this area should provide the industry with much needed data and tools for lowering their costs of treating gas. Additional developments, expected to be available over a longer time frame but before 2000, include new processes for liquid redox and scavenging and tools for measuring and controlling liquid redox processes.

## REFERENCES

1.  Hugman, R.H., P.S. Springer, and E.H. Vidas (Energy and Environmental Analysis, Inc.), "Chemical Composition of Discovered and Undiscovered Natural Gas in the United States - 1993 Update (3 volumes)" report to Gas Research Institute, Report No. GRI-93/0456.1, .2, .3, December 1993.

2.  Leppin, D. (Gas Research Institute), and D.A. Dalrymple (Radian Corporation), "GRI Program in Sulfur Recovery from Natural Gas -- 1995 Update," paper presented at the GPA 74th Annual Convention, March 13-15, 1995, San Antonio, Texas.

3.  Dalrymple, D.A. and J.K. Wessels (Radian Corporation), "Proceedings of the 1994 GRI Sulfur Recovery Conference," topical report to the Gas Research Institute, Report No. GRI-94/0170, July 1994.

4.  Dalrymple, D.A. and N.L. Gerard (Radian Corporation), "Proceedings of the 1992 GRI Liquid Redox Sulfur Recovery Conference," topical report to the Gas Research Institute, Report No. GRI-93/0129, April 1993.

5.  Dalrymple, D.A. and J.K. Wessels (Radian Corporation), "Proceedings of the 1991 GRI Liquid Redox Sulfur Recovery Conference," topical report to the Gas Research Institute, Report No. GRI-91/0188, June 1991.

6.  Dalrymple, D.A. and J.K. Wessels (Radian Corporation), "Proceedings of the 1989 GRI Liquid Redox Sulfur Recovery Conference," topical report to the Gas Research Institute, Report No. GRI-89/0206, August 1989.

7.  Dalrymple, D.A. and T.W. Trofe (Radian Corporation), "Proceedings of the 1987 GRI Liquid Redox Sulfur Recovery Conference," topical report to the Gas Research Institute, Report No. GRI-88/0078, April 1988.

8.  Scheffel, F.A. and V.D. Edge (Radian Corporation), "Proceedings of the 1986 GRI Stretford Users' Conference," topical report to the Gas Research Institute, Report No. GRI-86/0256, November 1986.

9.  Dalrymple, D.A., K.S. Fisher (Radian Corporation), and D. Leppin (Gas Research Institute), "GRI Research Program in $H_2S$ Scavenging -- 1995 Update," paper presented at the GPA 74th Annual Convention, March 13-15, 1995, San Antonio, Texas.

10. Echterhoff, L.W., A.J. Foral, R.L. McKee, S.T. Schamp (M.W. Kellogg Company), and D. Leppin (Gas Research Institute), "SeleXpert™: $H_2S$ Scavenging Module PC-Based Computer Program Simplifies Screening of $H_2S$ Technologies," paper presented at the GPA 74th Annual Convention, March 13-15, 1995, San Antonio, Texas.

11. Foral, A.J. and B.H. Al-Ubaidi (M.W. Kellogg), "Evaluation of $H_2S$ Scavenger Technologies," topical report to the Gas Research Institute, Report No. GRI-94/0197, May 1995.

12. Fisher, K.S. and D.A. Dalrymple (Radian Corporation), "GRI Field Evaluation of Liquid-based $H_2S$ Scavengers in Tower Applications at a Natural Gas Production Plant in South Texas," topical report to the Gas Research Institute, Report No. GRI-94/0437, February 1995.

13. Trofe, T.W., K.E. McIntush, and M.C Murff (Radian Corporation), "Stretford Process Operations and Chemistry Report," final report to the Gas Research Institute, Report No. GRI-93/0121, November 1993.

14. K.E. McIntush and B.J. Petrinec (Radian Corporation), "GRI Testing of SulFerox® for the Direct Treatment of High-Pressure Natural Gas at NGPL's Kermit, Texas Site, " topical report to the Gas Research Institute, Report No. GRI-94/0432, January 1995.

15. DeBerry, D.W. (Radian Corporation), "Rates and Mechanisms of Reactions of Hydrogen Sulfide with Iron Chelates," topical report to the Gas Research Institute, Report No. GRI-93/0019, April 1993.

16. DeBerry, D.W. (Radian Corporation), Regeneration of Chelated Iron Liquid Redox Sulfur Recovery Sorbent," draft topical report to the Gas Research Institute, December 1993.

17. Quinlan, M.P., and L.W. Echterhoff (M.W. Kellogg Company), "Technical and Economic Comparison of LO-CAT II with Other Iron-based Liquid Redox Processes," paper presented at the 1992 GRI Liquid Redox Sulfur Recovery Conference, October 4-6, 1992, Austin, Texas.

18. Quinlan, M.P. (M.W. Kellogg Company), "Technical and Economic Analysis of the Iron-based Liquid Redox Processes," paper presented at the GPA 71st Annual Convention, March 16-18, 1992, Anaheim, California.

19. Hardison, L.C. (ARI Systems, Inc.), "Early Experience with ARI-LO-CAT II for Natural Gas Treatment," paper presented at AIChE Spring National Meeting, March 29 - April 2, 1992, New Orleans, Louisiana.

20. Rehmat, A., (Institute of Gas Technology), et. al., "Bio-SR Process for Subquality Natural Gas," paper presented at the 1995 International Gas Research Conference, November 6-9, 1995, Cannes, France.

21. Plummer, M.A. (Marathon Oil Company, "The HYSULF$^{SM}$ Process: A Valuable Hydrogen Resource from Hydrogen Sulfide," paper presented at the GPA 74th Annual Convention, March 13-15, 1995, San Antonio, Texas.

22. McIntush, K.E. (Radian Corporation), et. al., "Use of Sulphur from Liquid Redox Processes as an Oxidition Inhibitor in Wet Flue Gas Desulphurization Systems," paper presented at the Sulphur 94 conference, November 6-9, 1994, Tampa, Florida.

Table 1
Comparison of $H_2S$ Scavenger Capacity Data

|  | Field Test Results | | Radian | Host | Representative |
|  | Tower 1 | Tower 2 | Lab Test | Database | Values |
|---|---|---|---|---|---|
| Nitrite | | | | | |
| g sulfur/L | 40 | 106 | 600[a] | 35-90 | 90 |
| lb sulfur/gal | 0.33 | 0.88 | 5.03[a] | 0.29-0.75 | 0.75 |
| Nonregenerable Amine | 66,49 | NA | 103 | 47-107 | 72 |
| g sulfur/L | 0.55, 0.41 | NA | 0.86 | 0.39-0.89 | 0.60 |
| lb sulfur/gal | | | | | |
| Triazine | | | | | |
| g sulfur/L | 61 | 89 | 97 | 56-102 | 72 |
| lb sulfur/gal | 0.51 | 0.74 | 0.81 | 0.47-0.85 | 0.60 |

[a] High capacity resulted from absence of $CO_2$.

Figure 1  Photograph of scavenging towers at the South Texas site

Table 2
Scavenger Cost Comparison for a $17 \times 10^3$ Nm³/hr,
19 ppmv $H_2S$, 70 Bar, Batch Tower Operation

|  | Nitrite Liquid | Nonregenerable Amine Liquid | Triazine Liquid | Solid Based |
|---|---|---|---|---|
| Capital cost, $ | 464,000 | 464,000 | 464,000 | 316,000 |
| Operating costs, $/yr | | | | |
| Scavenger material | 64,600 | 147,600 | 153,300 | 22,800 |
| Operating labor | 7,200 | 7,200 | 7,200 | 7,200 |
| Maintenance | 17,300 | 1,300 | 1,300 | 0 |
| Tower chg out | 12,600 | 18,400 | 18,400 | 11,000 |
| Annual operating cost, $/yr | 101,700 | 174,500 | 180,200 | 41,000 |
| Amortization, $/yr | 100,400 | 100,400 | 100,400 | 66,800 |
| Annual treatment cost, $/yr | 202,100 | 274,900 | 280,600 | 107,800 |
| Total treatment cost | | | | |
| $/Nm³ | 1.38 | 1.90 | 1.94 | 0.75 |
| $/10³ g sulfur | 51 | 70 | 71 | 27 |

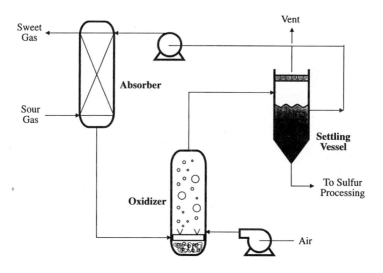

Figure 2  Liquid redox process schematic

Table 3
Design Basis

|                        | Rich Case | Lean Case |
|------------------------|-----------|-----------|
| H$_2$S, mol%           | 2.7       | 0.5       |
| CO$_2$, mol%           | 1.2       | 2.0       |
| Sulfur, metric tons/day | 2.1      | 1.9       |
| Pressure, bar          | 69        | 69        |

Figure 3  Photograph of SulFerox pilot plant at the NGPL Kermit site

Figure 4  Photograph of LO-CAT II  pilot plant at the NGPL Kermit site

Table 4
Typical Properties of NGPL Site Feed

| | |
|---|---|
| Temperature, C | 45-50 |
| Pressure, bar | 66 |
| Flow rate, Nm³/hr | 1520 |
| Molar gas composition, (dry | Mole % |
| basis) | 0.30 |
|   Hydrogen sulfide | 0.51 |
|   Nitrogen | 96.15 |
|   Methane | 1.17 |
|   Carbon dioxide | 1.59 |
|   Ethane | 0.22 |
|   Propane | 0.02 |
|   Isobutane | 0.02 |
|   Butane | 0.02 |
|   All others | |

Table 5
Preliminary ARI-LO-CAT II Pilot Plant Performance Summary

| Parameter | Design | Actual |
|---|---|---|
| Flow, Nm³/hr | 1230 | 780 |
| Inlet $H_2S$, ppmv | 3000 | 4550 |
| Outlet $H_2S$, ppmv | <4 | 1.9 |
| Solution Circulation, L/min | 120 | 64 |
| Desulfurization rate, metric tons per day | 0.13 | 0.13 |

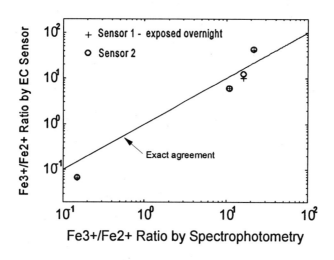

Figure 5 CalTech sensors performance versus spectrophotometric method

THE MEMBRANE-RECTIFICATION METHOD OF $H_2S$
PURIFYING GAS

LA MÉTHODE PAR MEMBRANES DE LA RÉCUPÉRATION $H_2S$ DU
GAZ

A.Gritsenko,B.Bergo,B.Hamaker,

J.Thurley, Yu.Yampolsky

Russia, USA, UK

ABSTRACT

At the processing of natural gas containing condensate, the big amount of $H_2S$
and $CO_2$; the hybrid technology is applied, in compliance with which the greater
part of $H_2S$ is removed from gas by means of fractionating condensation; and at
final purification, the selective absorbent of physical effect is used. For gas
purification from $CO_2$, membrane is used.
From gas saturated condensate in the fractionating evaporator, firstly $CO_2$ and
the lighter are removed. Then, in the rectification column $H_2S$ is removed, here
the components $C_3$ and $C_4$ are concentrated in the bottom product. The top product
of this column, fraction $H_2S$-$C_3$ is separated at membrane with production of $H_2S$
with high concentration; the enriched $C_3$ unpermeat is returned to the column.
Methods of physical and mathematical simulation showed the possibility of the
significant expenses reduction (20-40 % reduction), energy consumption
reduction at gas fractionating and in the absorption processes by means of
column-heat-exchanging devices use. Worked out is the compact design of the
devices of such type with the use of screw packing, for which velocity factor
in ratio to the free section of the apparatus reaches 10, and the number of
separation stages is 6-8 for 1 m of the apparatus height.

RÉSUMÉ

Lors du traitement du gaz naturel qui contient du condensat et des quantités
considérables de $H_2S$ et de $CO_2$ on applique la technologie hybride selon
laquelle la plus grande partie de $H_2S$ est eliminée par la condensation
fractionnée tandis que pour la rectification finale on utilise un absorbent
sélectif de l'action physique. Pour purifier le gaz de $CO_2$ on utilise une
membrane. Au niveau du vaporisateur fractionnaire on élimine du condensat
saturé en gaz d'abord $CO_2$ et les fractions plus légères et ensuite au niveau
de la colonne de rectification on élimine $H_2S$, les composants $C_3$ et $C_4$ étant
concentrés dans le produit de cube. Le produit supérieur de cette colonne, la
fraction $H_2S$-$C_3$ est divisé en membrane pour obtenir $H_2S$ de haute concentration
tendis que $C_3$ enrichi est renvoyé en colonne.
Le possibilité de diminuer considérablement les dépenses d'énergie (de l'ordre
de 20-40 %) est présentée par les methodes comportant des modeles physiques et
mathématiques lors de fractionnement de gaz et dans les processus d'absorption
avec l'utilisation des appareils de type colonne-échangeur. Une construction
compacte des appareils de ce type est elaborcé avec l'utilisation d'une
rallonge à vis pour laquelle le facteur de vitesse rapporté a la section libre
de l'appareil atteint 10 et le nombre de degrés de séparation est de 6-8 sur
1 m de la hauteur de l'appareil.

INTRODUCTION

While processing the natural gas, containing condensate, the increases quantities of $H_2S$ and $CO_2$, sulfur-organic components use, as a rule, the process of $H_2S$ and $CO_2$ absorption by amine solutions with further low temperature condensation of sulfur-organic components and hydrocarbons $C_{3+}$. Acc. to this technology, energy consumption, capital and operational expenses turn out to be overstated. Lately the membrane technology has been developing successfully; rectification and absorption fractionation and also to produce cool. Use of new technical solutions opens the possibility of technologies elaboration, satisfying the highest economical and ecological requirements. Fulfilled based upon the example of Astrakhan field gases processing, this investigation has the purpose of working out the economical, ecologically pure gas treatment process with separate extraction of $H_2S$ and $CO_2$. While solving the set task, the most prospective directions of gas treatment processes and equipment improvements were taken into account. General direction of gas fractionation and absorption technology improvement is connected with the use of the differential heat supply. The process with the differential heat supply and carry-away is done in the device of the type column-heat-exchanger. The most simple and reliable device design is vertical straight pipe apparatus with the packing, located in the pipes, annulus space; or in both of them. The tubular column can function in the mode of highly-volatile components concentration (fractionating condensor), obtaining low-volatile components (fractionating evaporator) or in the mode of complete coulmn with obtaining both products. In tubular columns it is possible to use the low-potential heat or cold and thus significantly reduce energy consumption. While simulating it was found out that the value of energy saving in tubular columns at separation of such mixtures $C_3-C_4$, $iC_4-NC_4$, $C_1-C_2$, $N_2-O_2$ amounts to 20-40 %. During the last years the $CO_2$ and $H_2S$ extraction technology by membrans method has been developing successfully. The problems of selectivity, permeability, and membrane properties stability increase in the medium with agressive components, are solved. Energy use while expanding the gas and liquid streams, is a very significant stand-by in energy supply thus, for example, at entries of gas saturated liquid into the vessel and exit of it, it is possible to compress (in the range of high pressures) practically all the gas dissolved in the liquid.

THE CONCEPT OF ENERGY SAVING TECHNOLOGY ELABORATION FOR PROCESSING OF THE GAS WITH HIGH SULFUR CONTENT

Below, based upon the example of the Astrakhan gas condensate field gases processing, the conceptual solutions are considered; such solutions, which to the greatest extent take the advantage of the separate processes and their new modifications. The reservoir mixture has the following breakdown (hereby and further on in the text in % mol):

| He | $N_2$ | $C_1$ | $C_2$ | $C_3$ | $C_4$ | $C_{5+}$ | $H_2S$ | $CO_2$ | RHS | COS |
|------|------|------|------|------|------|------|------|------|------|------|
| 0,02 | 0,34 | 53,3 | 2,43 | 1,1 | 0,88 | 3,82 | 25,09 | 12,95 | 0,05 | 0,05 |

The mixture pressure at the entry to the gas pumping units is 80 bar, temperature 35° C. In the process of possible technologies analysis, purely rectifying process has been considered with separation acc. to key components $H_2S-C_2H_6$. The area of phase conditions of the deethanisation top product is shown at Fig. 1.

During the simulation it is prisumed that the process pressure is 30
bar, i.e. is signuficantly lower than the critical and far from the
solid phase area.

Simulation results are as follows:

| Number of stages | Reflux ratio | $H_2S$ impurity in the product, PPM |
|---|---|---|
| 50 | 3 | 126 |
| 57 | 3.5 | 34 |
| 62 | 3.5 | 19 |
| 62 | 5 | 12 |

Based upon these data, the following conclusions are made. In
principle it is possible to remove by rectification $H_2S$ from gas,
having in gas $CO_2$ and $C_2$, however in this case greater amount of trays
and reflux are needed. If the presume, that in the top product there
can remain part of $H_2S$, than the amount of reflux will be reduced
significantly. At deep rectificating gas purification from $H_2S$, the
energy consumption can be reduced, if the inter-column heat-exchange
between the top zone of the apparatus and adjacent zone (where $H_2S$
concentration is 2-3 %) will be done. Average difference of the
temperatures in these zones will be several degrees, so the pressure
differential in the compressor, acting as the heat pump, will be not
big.

The mentioned method of rectification $H_2S$-purification
development demands additional investigations, and before their
completion we should adopt the concept of partial $H_2S$ removal. For HS
removal from gases of condensate stabilization and liquid obtained at
low-temperature gas treatment, it was suggested to use membrane. At
the pilot unit, they was studied the process of $H_2S$ membrane
separation from gases of condensate stabilization with the
composition

| $C_1$ | $CO_2$ | $C_2$ | $H_2S$ | $C_3$ | $C_4$ | $C_{5+}$ |
|---|---|---|---|---|---|---|
| 2,5 | 5,3 | 2,4 | 79,6 | 4,6 | 4,4 | 1,2 |

The feed gas pressure is 16 bars, temperature $30^0$ C. The
material of membrane is acetate cellulose. The type of membrane is
fibre. The pilot sample had the dimensions diameter of fibre plait
10 mm, length 900 mm. Membrane selectivity in the experiments was
about 10, which is considered to be not sufficiently high. The
negative factor, explaining the obtained result, is high partial
pressure of $H_2S$, enhancing HC dissolving in membrane. Based upon the
carried out experiments, the conclusion is made on the feasibility of
gas pressure reduction before membrane down to 4-6 bar and $H_2S$
concentartion increase in this gas up to 85-90 % by means of
preliminary removal of $CO_2$ components and lighter components from
condensate.

TECHNOLOGICAL PROCESSES OF HIBRID TECHNOLOGY

Taken separately typical processes and devices can not meet the
set perposes, so it's necessary to update and functionally unite
them. Low under consideration are the main components of such hybrid
technology. The main mass of $H_2S$ and sulfur-organic components are
separated from gas in fractionating condenser, including 2 sections
acc. to the layout, presented at Fig. 2. In section A as cool-carries
perform propane or liquid fraction $H_2S$-$C_3$, obtained at condensate

stabilization (see Fig. 4). In section B cooling agent is the reverse stream of dry gas. To prevent hydrates depositions the method is used, described in the work (1).

Recompression of gases dissolved in condensate is done by the method of volumetric compressor in the switching capacity by means of entry there of liquid under high pressure and its exit at reduced pressure in turns. Parameters of fractionating condensation, obtained by simulation are shown in Table 1.

TABLE 1.

| Process pressure, bar | Number of stages | Temperature | | $C_{4+}$ content in dry gas, % | Cool consumption kj/nm³ of raw gas |
|---|---|---|---|---|---|
| | | top | bottom | | |
| 70 | 5 | - 6.5°C | 25°C | 0.2 | 59.2 |

At the final $H_2S$ purification (see Fig. 3) gas is being washed by N-methylpyrrolydone (MPD) or other selective solvent. Gases dissolved in absorbent return to absorber with the help of volumetric compressor. Degassed absorbent is distributed in agent in fractionating condenser, the second is heated by the heat of regenerated absorbent and introduced into the desorber as feed. $H_2S$-purified gas is let through membrane to eliminate $CO_2$ from gas. At simulation of the process, the following results were as follows (see Table 2).

TABLE 2.

| Absorbent consumption (2.1 l/nm³ of raw gas), % | | Number of stages | Temperature | | $H_2S$ impurity in puri- fied     gas, ppm | $H_2S$ content in sour gas, % |
|---|---|---|---|---|---|---|
| NMP | $H_2O$ | | top | bottom | | |
| 70 | 30 | 20 | 40°C | 55°C | 0.3 | 97.5 |

The process of condensate processing is shown at Fig. 4. In deethanizer, designed as fractionating evaporator, $CO_2$ and lighter are separated from condensate. In stabilizer provided with fractionating condensor, from the top they obtain $H_2S$ with some $C_3$, from the bottom $C_3$ fraction purified from $H_2S$. Top product of the column is condensed and choked to 6 bar, obtaining the cool at the level of -20° C. Fraction $H_2S$-$C_3$ at 6 bar and 20° C is let through the membrane, getting 98 % $H_2S$. In apermeata $C_3$ concentration amounts to 60 %. This stream is compressed and delivered to the lower part of the stabilizer into the zones of low concentrations of $H_2S$. While simulating the process, the following results were obtained (see Table 3).

TABLE 3.

| | Deethanizer | Stabilizer |
|---|---|---|
| Pressure, bar | 40 | 25 |
| Number of stages | 30 | 20 |
| Temperature, °C top bottom | 33.5 95.5 | 46 275 |

SCIENTIFIC AND TECHNICAL PROBLEMS

Non-adiabatic rectification and absorption, being the new
processes, have not yet been sufficiently studied and need
elaboration of mathematical models and R&D and design works. 2 models
of the process have been developed. One - on the basis of matrix
method, the other - relaxation method. The additional change in the
system of equations, describing the process, is the amount of heat
delivered to the arbitrary tray, as function of the temperatures
differential, surface of heat-transfer and thermal properties of
heat-carrier. The simulation experience showed, that relaxation
method is more reliable, however demands more time for calculations.

Energy gain of non-adiabatic rectification processes application
is indused by concentration pressures reduction during masstransfer;
so it is necessary to increase the number of separation stages. At
dislocation of column, the working section of the apparatus is
rediced. Thus, the main tasks of the columns-heat-exchangers design
is streams high speeds obtaining and securing increased amount (2-3
times more) of separation stages compared to typical apparatus.

As basic design, the straight pipe heat-exchanger design was
adopted. Some possible variants were studied to equip the tubular
columns with packings. For the conditions of fractionating
condensation and absorption the most suitable is the screw packing,
for which the velocity factor in ratio to the column free section
reached 10. In the experiments, carried out with the laboratory
mixture, it was found out that the separation effect of 1 m of screw
packing is equal to 4-8 stages.

For the apparatus of the type of fractionating evaporator, the
preferance was given to the flooded mode, when the interpipe space,
where approximately 2/3 of the height is filled with the liquid
phase. In the flooded mode at the appropriate gas velocity in 1 m of
apparatus, the quantity of separation stages reached 8. Due to the
tendency of the formation of the azeotrope$H_2S$-$C_3H_8$ in processing of
acid gases or gases of stabilization of condensates, the question is
arisen of the separation of these mixtures by nontraditional, in
particular, membrane methods.

Two different strategy of the separation of hydrogen
sulfide-propane mixtures can be imagined. In one case, permeate
stream is enriched with hydrogen sulfide, in other with propane. As
the feed mixture contains more $H_2S$ than $C_3H_8$ (70:30), the first
strategy seems to be more attractive, because it makes possible to
save the surface area of the membrane and, therefore, the cost of
membrane unit. However, a feasibility of a separation strategy
strongly depends on:

- properties of gases;

- properties of membrane materials;

- "coupling effects", i.e. the interactions between the
penetrants with each other during the separation, or between
separated mixture and membrane material.

GASES

The analysis of how gas and polymer properties affect the
efficiency of membrane separation is based on several simple

relationships, which are necessary, but not sufficient conditions of successful membrane separation. Permeability coefficients P which determine the unit fluxes through a film can be given by

$$P = D \ S$$

where D is the diffusion coefficient and S is the solubility coefficients. Separation factors which determine the selectivity of membrane material

$$\alpha_{ij} = P_i/P_j = (D_i/D_j) \ (S_i/S_j)$$

Both D and S values are strongly related to gas properties. Solubility coefficients are functions of thermodynamic properties of gases:

$$\log S = a_k Z + b_k$$

where Z can be boiling point $T_b$, critical temperature $T_c$, or Lennard-Jones parameter $\varepsilon/k$ and $a_k > 0$. On the other hand, diffusion coefficients depend on molecular sizes of penetrant molecules

$$\log D = - c_1 Y + d_1$$

where Y is a function of penetrant's cross section: $Y = d^n$, where $1 < n < 3$, and $c_1 > 0$. Hence, solubility increases with $T_b$, $T_c$ or $\varepsilon/k$, whereas diffusivity decreases with the accompanied increase in the size of penetrant molecules.

Table 4 shows that thermodynamic properties of $H_2S$ and $C_3H_8$ are relatively similar.

TABLE 4. PROPERTIES OF HYDROGEN SULFIDE AND PROPANE

| Characteristics | $H_2S$ | $C_3H_8$ |
|---|---|---|
| Boiling point $T_b$, K | 212.9 | 231.1 |
| Critical point $T_c$, K | 373 | 370 |
| Lennard-Jones parameter $\varepsilon/k$, K | 190 | 242 - 254 |
| Molecular size, A | 3.2 | 5.1 - 5.6 |

Although the boiling points and Lennard-Jones parameters of propane are somewhar higher, the critical temperatures of two gases nearly coinside. Therefore, it is difficult to perform the solubility controled strategy of separation of this mixture with propane as a fast component, which is often performed in membrane made of rubbery polymers, e.g. for separation of hydrocarbons of natural and petroleum gases. On the other hand, propane molecule is much bulkier, and this is reflected in larger kinetic diameter of this molecule (see Table 4). Hence, one can expect much higher diffusion and permeability coefficients for hydrogen sulfide. Because of it, mobility or diffusivity controlled membrane separation can be anticipated for this mixture. Normally, this type of membrane separation is realized with glassy polymers.

POLYMERS

A paucity of the data in the literature can be noted for $P(H_2S)$, $P(C_3H_8)$ and ideal separation factors for this gas pair (2). Because of it, a search was performed in a Data Base on gas permeation

properties of polymers that has been developed and exists in
A.V.Topchiev Institute of Petrochemical Synthesis (TIPS). This search
included:

- search for original data on $P_i$ and $\alpha_{ij}$ for different glassy,
rubbery and semicrystalline polymers;

- use of correlations to find the $P(C_3H_8)$ values for those
polymers, for which the $P(H_2S)$ but not the $P(C_3H_8)$ values have been
reported; for this purpose a correlation of $P(C_nH_{2n+2})$ versus n in
different polymers were used.

Additionally, some of the polymers deliberately synthesized in
TIPS were tested, and the found values of $P_i$ and $\alpha_{ij}$ were included
into consideration. Some of the results obtained are shown in Fig.5.
It can be seen that there is a number of polymers which are
characterized by the combination of relatively high $P(H_2S)$ values in
the range 10-100 Barrers and separation factors $\alpha(H_2S/C_3H_8)$ in the
range 10-100. Rubbers, e.g. polydimethylsiloxane, are usually more
permeable but less permeselective ($\alpha<10$). On the other hand, many
glassy polymers are distinctive by high permeselectivity ($\alpha>20$) and
permeability coefficients in excess of 10 Barrers. It means that high
performance gas separation membranes can be manufactured from such
polymers as polyphenyleneoxide or Ge-containing derivative of
polynorbornene. A combination of high permeability in respect to $H_2S$
and high permselectivity can be anticipated for some
fluorine-containing polymers.

Penetrant-penetrant and penetrant-polymer interactions are the
least investigated aspect of the problem.Both components of this
mixture can be considered as active vapours. Therefore, the fluxes
and composition of permeate streams during coupled transport can
differ significantly from the values, that can be calculated for
individual gas transport. Literature gives examples of both increased
and decreased performance of membranes in coupled transport. Propane
at higher pressure can exert a plasticizing action on many polymeric
materials. Hydrogen sulfide can form hydrogen bonds with many oxygen-
and nitrogen-containing polymers increasing its permeation rates and
separation factors. Many other components, primarily hydrocarbon
impurities in technical propane streams can affect the performance of
membrane. Usually such information can be obtained only during bench
tests. Another aspect of the problem is the long term stability of
the membrane material in contact with the mixture to be separated or
with permeate and retentate streams. Some of the results illustrating
the compatability of different polymers in contact with hydrogen
sulfide and propane are given in Table 5.

TABLE 5.

| Material | $H_2S$ | $C_3H_8$ |
|---|---|---|
| Natural Rubber | P | P |
| Neoprene | G | F |
| Buna N | F | G |
| Cellulose Acetate | F | G |
| Polyamides | P | G |
| Polytetrafluoroethylene | G | G |
| Polystyrene | F | P |

P - poor, F - fair, G - good

It is seen that an additional difficulty may stem from the fact that sometimes a conflicting behaviour is observed for the stability of a certain polymer in contact with $H_2S$ and $C_3H_8$. For example, polyamides exhibit poor stability in $H_2S$ but good stability in $C_3H_8$. Once again, very good stability and extended range of working temperatures can be noted for fluorine-containing polymers (e.g. polytetrafluoroethylene). These properties should be also taken into account in developing the membrane polymeric materials suitable for the separation of propane/hydrogen sulfide mixtures.

In conclusion, the analysis of the available in the literature data and some domestic transport parameters indicated that some of the polymers studied, mainly glassy polymers, can be good candidates for the material of membranes to separate $H_2S/C_3H_8$ mixtures. The membranes prepared from these polymers would allow to obtain, in one stage, the permeate from these polymers would allow to obtain, in one stage, the permeate with hydrogen sulfide content of 98 $\pm0.5\%$ at low stage cuts, the recycling or multiple stage separation must be organized. All these polymers are soluble, so the preparation of phase inversion or composite membranes is possible. As for stability of membrane materials, only assumptions can be made at the moment. However, the most stable polymers are those containing fluorocarbon groups in main chain and side chains.

CONCLUSION

The use of hybrid technology solves the following tasks.

Klaus unit processes highly concentrated $H_2S$, that allows to reduce the expenses for the purification of off-gases, reduce the volume of harmful emissions into the atmosphere, and when substituting the air by oxygene, practically totally eliminate such emissions.

The obtained highly concentrated $CO_2$ stream is stream is injected into the well, that enhances the condensate recovery and prevents the emission into the atmosphere of $CO_2$ big volumes.

Energy consumption for the own purposes are reduced in such a way, that instead of power consumption from outside in the volume 25 $MWatt/10^9$ $m^3$ acc. to the existing current technology with the use of DEA the plant can produce for outer needs about 8.5 $MWatt/10^9 m^3$ of power.

REFERENCES

1. Patent US N 4775395

2. Gas Encyclopedia

   Elsevier (Air Liquid, 1976)

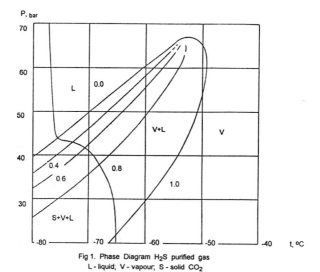

Fig 1. Phase Diagram H₂S purified gas
L - liquid; V - vapour; S - solid CO₂

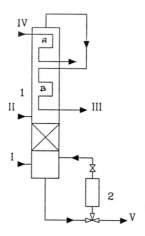

Fig 2 Scheme of H₂S preliminary removal

1. fractionating condensor;     I Feed
2. volumetric compressor        II Methanol
                                III Dry gas
                                IV Cooling agent
                                V Degassed condensate

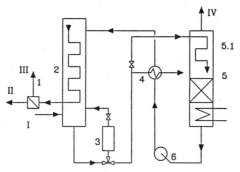

Fig 3 Scheme of final H₂S purification of gas

1 membrane
2 absorber–heat–exchanger
3 volumetric compressor
4 heat–exchanger
5 desorber
   5.1 fractionating condensor
6 pump

I Feed
II CO₂
III purified gas
IV H₂S

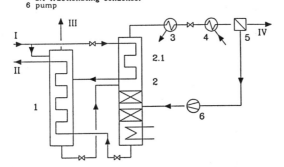

Fig 4 Scheme of condensate H₂S purification process

1. fractionaling evaporator–deethaniser
2. column of H₂S extraction
   2.1 fractionaling condencator
3 condensor
4 evaporator
5 membrane
6 compressor

I Feed
II H₂S purified condensate(C₃+)
III gas of deethanisation
IV H₂S

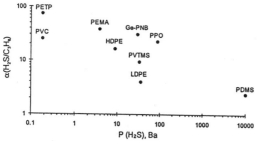

Fig 5. Characteristics of some polymers

PDMS  - polydimethylsiloxane
LDPE  - low density polyethylene
HDPE  - high density polyethylene
PVTMS - poly (vinyltrimethyl silane)
PPO    - poly (phenylene oxide)

Ge-PNB - Ge-containing polynorbornene
PEMA  - poly (ethyl methacrylate)
PVC   - poly (vinyl chloride)
PETP  - poly (ethylene terephtalate)

## GAS AND OIL INDUSTRY EFFLUENT AND CONTAMINATED GROUNDWATER TREATMENT USING THE BIOLOGICAL GAC-FBR PROCESS

## TRAITEMENT DE L'EFFLUENT DE L'INDUSTRIE PETROLIERE ET DES EAUX SOUS TERRAINES CONTAMINEES UTILISANT LE PROCEDE BIOLOGIQUE GAC-FBR

Robert Hickey, Dan Wagner, April Sunday, Veronica Groshko, Bob Heine and Raj Rajan
EFX Systems, Inc., USA

Tom Hayes
Gas Research Institute, USA

## ABSTRACT

Although physicochemical approaches are effective in removal of the BTEX and other petroleum hydrocarbons from water, they suffer several drawbacks. These are costly processing options, and the BTEX is simply transferred from the water to GAC or the atmosphere. An alternative to physicochemical remedial techniques is biological treatment. Biological treatment processes result in the complete oxidation of the contaminants requiring treatment. The perceived problem associated with this treatment alternative, however, is the greater amount of uncertainty that regulatory personnel and design engineers have with biological treatment being able to reliably meet stringent performance requirements.

During the past five years, an extensive effort developing the know-how required to successfully apply the Granular Activated Carbon-Fluidized Bed Reactor (GAC-FBR) for treating a variety of gas and oil industry effluent streams has been performed. Presented is a compendium of results that includes work conducted at the laboratory-pilot (1500 liters/day) and field-pilot (100 liters/minute) scale on produced water brines, and groundwater contaminated with BTEX, aliphatic hydrocarbons and PAHs due to gas and oil production activities.

## ABREGE

Bien que ces approches physico-chemiques s'avèrent être un moyes efficace pour retirer des eaux le BTEX et d'autres hydrocarbures provenants du pétrole, ils presentent plusieurs inconvenients. Ce sont des méthodes côuteuses de traitement des eaux, et le BTEX est simplement transformé en GAC (Carbone Grenu Radioactif) ou relaché dans l'atmosphère. Une alternative à ces téchniques physico-chemiques est le traitement biologique. Le procédé biologique résulte en l'oxidation complète des agents contaminateurs nécessitants le traitement. le problème associé à cette méthode vient du doute qu'ont les ingenieurs de conception et le personnel réglementaire envers les capacités qu'a le procédé biologique à repondre regoureusement aux severes exigences de performance.

Durant les cinq dernières années, un effort considerable a été effectué, afin de developper le savoire-faire requis pour l'application avec succés du GAC-FBR (Carbone Grenu Radiactif-Reacteur a Banc Fluide) au traitement d'une diversité de courant d'effluent de l'industrie pétrolière. Un manuel de résultats comprenant des travaux effectués à l'échelle du laboratoire-pilote (1500 litres/jour) et du terrain-pilote (100 litres/minute) est presenté. Ces travaux ont été effectués sur des eaux salees créés et des eaux sousterraines, contaminées par le BTEX, par des hydrocarbures aliphatiques et par les PAH résultants des activités de la production pétrolière.

## INTRODUCTION

The clean-up of contaminated soils and groundwater may represent the largest public works program ever attempted. Conventional pump and treat type systems, such as carbon adsorption or air stripping with vapor phase control are often quite expensive from an operating expense perspective. These high costs are associated with replacement or regeneration of the activated carbon or the power required for catalytic oxidation of the off-gases from air stripping systems.

Biological processes can oxidize or degrade contaminants at significantly reduced overall costs, particularly long-term operational costs. One process configuration offers the advantages of cost effective biological treatment with the positive removal mechanism of carbon adsorption without the need for frequent replacement of the carbon, the Granular Activated Carbon - Fluidized Bed Reactor (GAC-FBR) process.[1-5]

Presented in this paper are some results of using the GAC-FBR for treating groundwater contaminated with benzene, toluene, ethylbenzene and xylenes (BTEX), aliphatic hydrocarbons and polynuclear aromatic hydrocarbons (PAHs) associated with past and current gas and oil industry operations.

## BACKGROUND

The biological fluidized bed is a high rate, biological fixed-film treatment process in which the water to be treated is passed upwards through a bed of fine-grained media, such as granular activated carbon (GAC), at a velocity sufficient to impart motion to or fluidization the media. This occurs when the drag forces caused by the liquid moving past the individual media particles are equal to the net downward force exerted by gravity (buoyant weight of the media). As the water passes by the media, a thin, highly active biological film (biofilm) grows on the surface of each grain. This biofilm oxidizes the organic pollutants in the water as it passes by.

Fluidization of fine grained media allows the entire surface of each individual particle to be colonized resulting in surface areas on the order of 300 $m^2/m^3$ of bed. This results in accumulation of biomass concentrations of up to 50,000 mg VSS/L of fluidized bed, which is an order of magnitude greater than the cell mass concentrations obtained in most other biological processes.[1] By manipulating the volume of media added to a system, the fluidization velocity and the height the bed is allowed to expand to, a great deal of control can be extended on manipulating the average biofilm thickness and mean cell retention time to optimize overall process performance. In most cases, the influent is pre-oxygenated using high purity oxygen in a sealed vessel. Virtually all the oxygen added is dissolved. As a result, no off-gases containing volatile or semi-volatile contaminants are produced. The conceptual advantages of biological fluidized bed reactor systems over conventional biological processes include:

- Large surface area for biomass attachment;
- High biomass concentrations;
- Ability to control and optimize biofilm thickness;
- Minimal plugging or channeling;
- High mass transfer properties;
- No off-gas produced, therefore, no air quality concerns; and
- The biomass carrier can be tailored to optimize system performance.

The use of an adsorbent carrier, such as GAC, allows two removal mechanisms to operate. During steady-state, the GAC-FBR system performs essentially as a regular biological FBR system with the microbial biofilms degrading the target compounds. During start-up, shock loads or other perturbations, however, the adsorptive capacity of the GAC augments the biological removal capacity resulting in enhanced removal and more stable, robust performance. The advantages of using GAC in FBR systems are:

- During start-up GAC adsorbs contaminants; high removal efficiency from time zero;
- Once a biofilm is established, the system performs with the cost effectiveness of a biological system;
- Contaminants such as BTEX adsorbed onto the GAC during start-up are to a large extent desorbed and degraded (bioregeneration);
- Dual biological and adsorptive removal mechanisms ensure robust performance during perturbations;
- Slow-to-degrade contaminants are held in the system for a longer time resulting in more complete degradation; and
- Non-degradable compounds are removed via adsorption.

The GAC-FBR process is one of the most technically advanced and cost-effective biological treatment process configurations available for treating dilute waste streams such as contaminated groundwater. This process "platform" has a well-established track record for treating petroleum hydrocarbons aerobically.[2-5] Treatment times of minutes rather than hours or days are generally possible while maintaining the ability to provide removal efficiencies of 99+%. More than 30 full-scale GAC-FBR systems have been installed and are successfully treating groundwater and process effluents ranging in size from several gallons per minute to greater than 5 million gallons per day.[3] A simplified representation of the GAC-FBR is shown in Figure 1.

## RESULTS

Treatment of Groundwater at a Gas Dehydration Site

An Envirex 100-liter per minute GAC-FBR system was inoculated with a BTEX-degrading consortia and set at an initial applied organic loading rate (OLR) of 4.0 kg $COD/m^3$-d. System performance during the initial 40 days is presented in Figures 2a and 2b.

Total BTEX removals were >99% from start-up through the entire first week. This was due to a combination of adsorption and some biological removal. Effluent benzene concentration was consistently <1.0 µg/L. After the first week, a peak concentration of benzene 15 µg/L and total BTEX concentration of 83 µg/L were observed in the effluent. By day 10, effluent benzene concentration was again below detection limits (<1.0 µg/L). By day 14, benzene and total BTEX removal efficiency exceeded 99% as biodegradation became the predominant removal mechanism.

After a one-month start-up period, performance was judged to have equilibrated and a steady-state data set (n=10) was collected. During this period, benzene was always below detection limits and total BTEX removals averaged 99.8% (Table 1). System performance remained stable at this level during the remainder of the project.

Approximately five months later, a second steady-state data set was collected. Results are presented in Table 2. As observed previously, benzene concentration was consistently below detection limits (<1.0 µg/L) and, total BTEX removal averaged 99.4%. This is despite the fact that the influent concentration had decreased to less than 20% of the previous steady-state sampling period and the groundwater temperature decreased to 9°C.

Response During Perturbations. The GAC-FBR system was subjected to several planned and unplanned perturbations. These included a prolonged starvation period (no feed to reactor), total system shutdown and free product spike loading to the system. Performance was robust during all of these events. During a one week starvation trial, dissolved oxygen (DO) consumption through the reactor remained at the same level as before the cessation for one day and then gradually decreased over the next six days. Analysis of biomass levels and DO profiles indicated that two thirds of the DO consumption was utilized for bioregeneration of the adsorptive capacity of the GAC carrier. The consumption of DO increased immediately upon restoration of forward feed to the system.

Free product was inadvertently forwarded to the GAC-FBR system on several occasions. These shock loadings, due to excessive drawdown in the production well, resulted in an immediate decrease in effluent DO and a concurrent rapid increase in inlet oxygen concentration. In one case, oxygen consumption through the reactor increased from ca. 2.5 mg/L to over 40 mg/L in less than ten minutes in response to the shock loading (Figure 3). Benzene levels in the effluent remained below detection limits and BTEX removal efficiencies remained above 96% throughout this incident. TVH removal efficiencies remained above 75%. Following the spike of free product, the oxygen consumption through the reactor decreased to ca. 20 mg/L for a 3-hour period and then asymptotically decreased to the pre-spike load level over the ensuing 10 hours. During this period, BTEX and aliphatic hydrocarbons adsorbed onto the GAC during the spike load diffused back off of the GAC and were degraded, resulting in bioregeneration of the adsorptive capacity.

Treatment of PAHs at MGP Site

At a Manufactured Gas Plant (MGP) site in Pennsylvania, a hot water treatment to remove DNAPL from the subsurface, is being used. This process generates a liquid effluent stream that, based on pilot testing, contains BTEX, PAHs and some nitrophenols. A synthetic waste stream was prepared and tested to determine the efficacy of GAC-FBR for treatment.

The laboratory-pilot system (1500 liters/day) was originally inoculated with a mixed culture able to degrade 2- to 4-ring PAHs developed from MGP-site soil samples. The system was initially fed a mixture of 8 PAHs (2- to 5-ring) that represented those most prevalent in the process effluent. Microtox assays were performed on influent and effluent samples.

Complete removal of naphthalene (and other PAHs) occurred as soon as forward flow was started to the reactor, as shown in Figure 4. Oxygen consumption did not reach levels commensurate with oxidation of the amount of naphthalene and other PAHs in the influent until several weeks after start-up. During this initial period, adsorption was the primary removal mechanism operative. After this point in time, increased oxygen consumption showed that removal was primarily due to biological oxidation. This was verified by conducting batch activity tests with the 2- to 4-ring PAHs and biomass removed from the reactor.

Results of system performance at an applied organic loading rate of 4.6 Kg COD/m$^3$-d is presented in Table 3. Naphthalene, the PAH of the highest concentration, was removed by greater than 99.9%. The 3- and 4-ring PAHs were removed by 97.2 to 98.7% and the 5-ring PAHs by ca. 85%. Overall, total PAH removal averaged 99.7% at a hydraulic retention time of 5.8 minutes.

Microtox™ assays were performed on influent and effluent samples to get some idea of toxicity reduction levels. This also served as a check that breakdown products of PAHs were not accumulating and causing an actual increase in toxicity. Complete reduction in toxicity from an $EC_{50}$ of 12-16%, as measured by Microtox, was achieved by treatment with the GAC-FBR process.

Based on these results, a full-scale system was installed at the site. The process, schematically presented in Figure 5, includes acid addition for emulsion breaking, caustic and oxidant addition for ion oxidation followed by gravity separation of precipitated iron and free oils and coal tars.

Preliminary data from the full-scale system are provided in Figure 6. Results to date are similar to those observed in the laboratory-pilot system despite intermittent operation due to fouling problems encountered with the reinjection wells.

Treatment of Produced Water Brines

A gas and oil research consortia was performing work on deoiling produced waters using a 40 liter per minute closed loop system where oil was added to artificial seawater.

This synthetic produced water was treated through a hydrocyclone to remove the larger droplets. After treatment in the hydrocyclone, the water was passed through an induced gas floatation cell.

Summary of Preliminary Pilot-Scale Treatability Test. As a preliminary test, four 55 gallon barrels of synthetic produced water, pretreated with a hydrocyclone for free oil removal, were sent from the site to EFX Systems, Inc. for treatment using the GAC-FBR process. The GAC-FBR process performed well for the removal of BTEX and other volatile hydrocarbons. The total volatile hydrocarbon was removed by 90-99% at organic loading rates of up to 6.3 Kg volatile COD/$m^3$-d. Results for the highest applied OLR are presented in Table 4.

Complete removal of toxicity, as measure by the Microtox™ assay was achieved at all applied OLRs, even at hydraulic retention times of less than 10 minutes. Influent samples had an average $EC_{50}$ of 26.6%. Preliminary results indicate that complete removal of benzene, BTEX, total volatile hydrocarbons and toxicity was achieved in as few as 6 minutes treatment time for the produced water treated herein.

Results of Field Test. Following the positive results of the laboratory pilot test, an Envirex Model 30 GAC-FBR was installed at the site to determine how well the system could treat BTEX and naphthenic acids in the artificial produced water.

The "mock" produced water was stored in two, 2000 gallon tanks. This water was continuously recycled through the treatment train. The water was changed once over the three month period of operation. Filters (5 μm) were placed in line during a portion of the experiment, to remove oil solids and oxidized iron that had built up in the large storage tanks. The system is schematically shown in Figure 7.

Initially, to verify the preliminary results, BTEX was mixed with crude oil (20% by volume) and fed to the recycle line of the GAC-FBR system. BTEX was added to the reactor for 45 days. During this period, greater than 99.5% of the BTEX added was degraded by the GAC-FBR process. Total petroleum hydrocarbon (TPH) removal was not measured. Influent soluble TPH was less than 5 mg/L.

Analysis of BTEX adsorbed to the GAC (based on samples taken at the end of this period) from the GAC-FBR (analyzed using thermal desorption) indicated less than 0.1% of the BTEX fed during this period was adsorbed onto the GAC.

Naphthenic acids, a group of partially unsaturated cyclic hydrocarbons with carboxylic substitutions can be a significant portion of the soluble TPH in produced waters. The potential of the GAC-FBR system to remove these acids was tested subsequent to the work listed above. The naphthenic acid used in this study was supplied by JT Baker. The JT Baker naphthenic acid was a darkish straw color liquid, with an average molecular weight of approximately 211.

The naphthenic acid was mixed with crude oil (80% naphthenic; 20% crude) and dispersed into the produced water being fed to the GAC-FBR. The resulting produced water was sent through the hydrocyclone, then on to the GAC-FBR at 2.5 to 5 gpm.

Results at three different OLRs are presented in Table 5. Significant removal rates of naphthenic acid were observed. Only soluble TPH was removed during treatment on the GAC-FBR. The dispersed oils were not removed to any significant degree.

## SUMMARY

Three applications of the GAC-FBR for use in meeting oil and gas industry needs for treatment of contaminated groundwater and process effluent problems are presented in this paper. Treatment of BTEX, aliphatic hydrocarbons, and PAHs was successfully accomplished at relatively high organic loading rates (on the order of 4-5 Kg COD/$m^3$-d) and short hydraulic retention times, 6 to 13 minutes. The use of an adsorptive biomass carrier, GAC, permitted essentially complete removal of contaminants to be realized from the instant forward flow was introduced to the reactors. Once a mature biofilm was established, removal was due to biological oxidation during normal operation.

Treatment of contaminated groundwater at a natural gas dehydration site was demonstrated using a commercial-scale reactor. Removal of BTEX as well as the aliphatic hydrocarbons present consistently exceeded 99%. The system performance during several perturbations, including starvation for one week, and a shock loading, was robust with little to no loss of removal efficiency occurring. This was the result of the high capacity for biological oxidation coupled with temporary adsorption of the inlet petroleum hydrocarbons that were not biologically degraded.

The ability of the GAC-FBR to treat PAHs typically found at MGP was proven at the laboratory-pilot scale (ca. 1500 l/d). The removal of 2- to 4-ring PAHs at an OLR of 4.6 Kg COD/m$^3$-d was primarily due to biological oxidation once a mature biofilm developed (ca. 2-3 weeks). The removal of 5-ring PAHs was likely due to a combination of biological oxidation and adsorption onto the GAC. Preliminary results at full-scale indicate similar performance can be attained as observed for the pilot-scale system.

Treatment of BTEX and naphthenic acids, soluble hydrocarbons of concern in produced waters, was effectively accomplished. High removal rates were observed for soluble TPH in a "mock" produced water generated from trials conducted for testing deoiling equipment. Free oil droplets that were not captured in the up-front hydrocyclone and/or induced gas flotation system were not removed.

Complete removal of toxicity from this synthetic produced water was observed during pilot testing.

The GAC-FBR process is certainly no "magic bullet" for providing remediation of contaminated groundwaters. The process does appear, however, to have a wide range of applications where it can be effectively used. Three such applications are presented here. Other applications, such as the treatment of chlorinated solvents and mixtures of chlorinated solvents and petroleum hydrocarbons, are also currently being tested at the laboratory-pilot and field demonstration scale.

## REFERENCES

1.  Hickey, R. F., Wagner, D. J. and Mazewski, G. (1991). Treating Contaminated Groundwater using a Fluidized Bed Reactor. *Remediation*, 1(2):447-460.

2.  Hickey, R. F., et. al. (1993). Application of the GAC-FBR for Treatment of Gas Industry Wastewaters. *Proceedings, Institute of Gas Technologies 6th International Symposium on Gas, Oil and Environmental Biotechnology*, Colorado Springs, CO.

3.  Hickey, R. F., et. al. (1994). Treatment of Oil and Gas Industry Effluents and Contaminated Groundwater using the Biological GAC-FBR Process. *Proceedings, International Petroleum Environmental Conference*, Houston, TX (in press).

4.  Voice, T. C., Zhao, X., Shi, J. and Hickey, R. F. (1992). Biological Activated Carbon in Fluidized Bed Reactors for the Treatment of Groundwater Contaminated with Volatile Aromatic Hydrocarbons. *Water Res.*, 26:1384-1401.

5.  Xing, J. and Hickey, R. F. (1994). Response in Performance of the GAC-Fluidized Bed Reactor Process for BTX Removal to Perturbations in Oxygen and Nutrient Supply. *J. of Biodegradation and Biodeterioration*, 33:23-39.

**Table 1**
**Summary of Steady-State Monitoring (n=10) of GAC-FBR Treating Groundwater at a Gas Dehydration Site in Michigan - one month after start-up**

| Constituent | Influent (µg/L) | Effluent (µg/L) | % Removal |
|---|---|---|---|
| Benzene | 120 (26)* | <1.0 | >99.2 |
| Toluene | 1590 (450) | 3.8 (9.3)* | 99.8 |
| Xylenes | 860 (270) | 2.2 (4.7) | 99.7 |
| BTEX | 2570 (660) | 6.0 (13) | 99.8 |
| TVH** | 9420 (2290) | 54 (37) | 99.4 |

HRT = 12.5 minutes; OLR = 3.4 Kg COD/m³-d;   * ( ) = standard deviations
Temp = 11°C; pH = 7.0                          ** TVH = total volatile hydrocarbons

**Table 2**
**Summary of Performance Data for a GAC-FBR Treating Groundwater at a Gas Dehydration Site in Michigan - six months after start-up**

| Constituent | Influent (µg/L) | Effluent (µg/L) | % Removal |
|---|---|---|---|
| Benzene | 20 (±3)* | <1 | >95.0 |
| Toluene | 234 (±34) | 2 (±2) | 99.2 |
| Xylenes | 122 (±17) | <1 | 99.0 |
| BTEX | 375 (±53) | 2 (±2) | 99.4 |
| TVH** | 1673 (±244) | 170 (±90) | 89.9 |

HRT = 13 minutes; OLR = 0.6 Kg COD/m³-d;   *( ) = standard deviation;
Temp = 9°C; pH = 6.9 to 7.0                   **TVH = total volatile hydrocarbons

**Table 3**
**Steady-State Performance Data for a Laboratory-Pilot GAC-FBR Treating PAHs**

|  |  |  |  |
|---|---|---|---|
| Naphthalene | 5600 (±672) | <3.0 | >99.9 |
| Acenaphthene | 413 (±169) | <10.0 | >97.2 |
| Phenanthrene | 103 (±26.8) | 1.4 (±1.3) | 98.7 |
| Fluoranthene | 41.6 (±9.2) | 1.1 (±0.8) | 97.8 |
| Pyrene | 30.3 (±7.6) | 0.98 (±0.73) | 97.2 |
| Benzo(b)fluoranthene | 0.55 (±0.20) | 0.11 (±0.13) | 85.2 |
| Benzo(a)pyrene | 0.62 (±0.22) | 0.12 (±0.11) | 83.6 |
| Total 3 + 4 ring PAHs | 588 | 13.5 | 97.7 |
| Total PAHs | 6189 | 16.7 | 99.7 |

OLR = 4.6 Kg COD/m³-d; Ratio DO/COD = 0.73;     DO consumption = 13.6 (±2.9); HRT = 5.8 minutes
Temp = 23°C

**Table 4**
**Performance of Laboratory-Pilot GAC-FBR Treating Produced Water (TDS = 3%)**

| Compound | Influent (μg/L) | Effluent (μg/L) | % Removal |
|---|---|---|---|
| Benzene | 82 | <1 | >98.8 |
| Toluene | 269 | 3 | 98.9 |
| Xylenes[1] | 639 | 8 | 98.7 |
| TVH | 3935 | 379 | 90.4 |

[1]Includes ethylbenzene          OLR = 6.3 Kg COD/m³-d
[2]Total Volatile Hydrocarbons     TDS = 3%

**Table 5**
**Performance of GAC-FBR Treating a Mixture of Naphthenic Acids and Crude Oil**

| OLR (Kg COD/m³-d) | % Removal Soluble TPH | Removal Rate TPH (mg/L-min) |
|---|---|---|
| 5.9 | 69.0 | 0.74 |
| 8.1 | 50.0 | 1.21 |
| 10.6 | 51.4 | 0.96 |

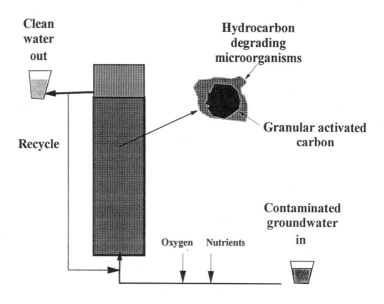

**Figure 1.  Schematic of GAC-FBR Process**

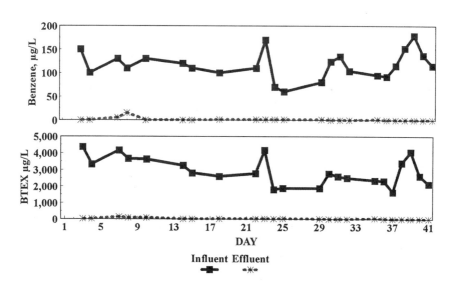

**Figures 2a & 2b.  BTEX Performance Data from a GAC-FBR Treating Groundwater at a Gas Dehydration Site in Michigan**

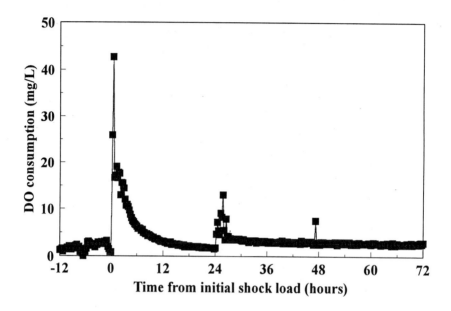

**Figure 3.  DO Consumption Versus Time during Shock Loading**

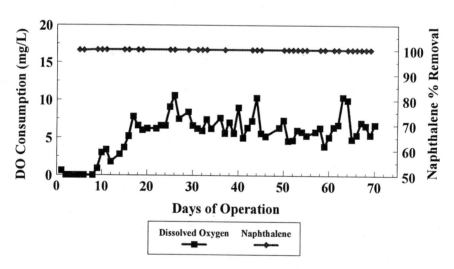

**Figure 4.  Dissolved Oxygen Consumption and Naphthalene
Removal for a GAC-FBR Treating PAHs**

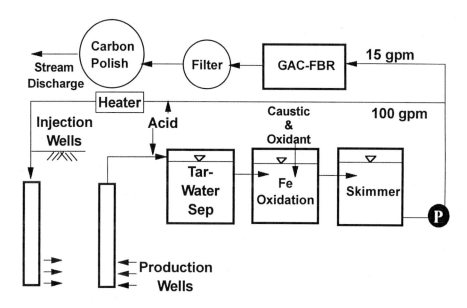

**Figure 5.  Process Schematic - Groundwater Extraction and DNAPL
Removal from Subsurface**

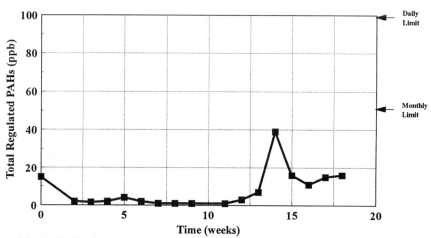

Max. Daily Discharge Limit: 100 ppb;
Max. Monthly Discharge Limit: 50 ppb

**Figure 6.  Preliminary Data from a Pennsylvania MGP Site**

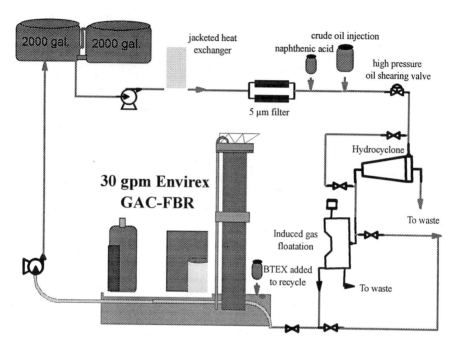

**Figure 7.  Schematic Depiction of the Synthetic Produced Water Deoiling System for Field Test of the GAC-FBR for Soluble Oil Removal**

A COMPREHENSIVE AND ROBUST OXIDATIVE METHOD FOR THE
TREATMENT OF PRODUCED WATER FROM GAS AND OIL PRODUCTION


UNE MÉTHODE OXYDANTE COMPLÈTE ET ROBUSTE POUR ÉPURER
L'EAU POLLUÉE PAR LA PRODUCTION DE GAZ ET DE PÉTROLE

C.W. Sweeney *, A.M.I. Younes and C. Taylor
British Gas plc., Gas Research Centre, Loughborough
LE11 3QU, United Kingdom.

ABSTRACT

The catalytic wet air oxidation (CWAO) process has been investigated for the treatment of toxic production chemicals and naturally-occurring contaminants in saline produced water. Test-rig experiments have been conducted over the temperature range 423K to 543K, and at pressures between 5 and 10 MPa. Removal efficiencies up to 100% have been achieved for hydrate and corrosion inhibitors and for hydrocarbons. Reductions in chemical oxygen demand (COD) of between 80% and 100% were obtained, depending on the conditions and the nature of the COD. It is concluded that the whole range of organic components that may be present in produced water may be effectively removed by the CWAO process to meet environmental discharge standards. The process offers a comparable removal efficiency to that of wet air oxidation (WAO) but at much milder process conditions; which ameliorates the operating problems encountered at the high temperatures and pressures required for conventional WAO.

RÉSUMÉ

Le procédé catalytique d'oxydation à l'air humide (CWAO) à été examiné pour le traitment des produits chimiques, provenant de productions toxiques, et des polluents qui apparaissent naturellement dans l'eau saline produite. Des expériences ont été effectuées dans un intervalle de températures de 423 à 543K et à des pressions entre 5 et 10 MPa. Des rendements de suppression atteignant 100% ont été réalisés pour l'hydrate, les inhibiteurs de corrosion et les hydrocarbones. Des réductions de la demande chimique en oxygène (DCO) allant de 80% à 100% ont été réalisées en fonction des conditions et de la nature de la DCO. On en conclue que tous les éléments organiques qui sont peut-être présents dans les eaux produites peuvent être retirés efficacement grâce au procédé CWAO afin de répondre aux normes environnementales d'évacuation. Le procédé offre un rendement de suppression conparable à celui des procédés d'oxydation à l'air humide mais dans des conditions de traitement beaucoup plus douces.

* Author to whom correspondence should be addressed.

## INTRODUCTION

Water produced during the exploitation of gas and oil reserves requires treatment before discharge to the environment. The degree of treatment is generally set by legislation or voluntary agreement, and in the UK continental shelf region depends upon whether the discharge is directly from an offshore platform or from an onshore gas treatment facility. As a consequence of the move towards simplified platforms with minimum offshore processing, increasing quantities of produced water will be brought onshore in the future. Much more rigorous treatment is required onshore: whereas treatment for offshore discharge is generally confined to dispersed oils, onshore discharge consents and pricing formulae may cover a wide range of dispersed and dissolved components as well as the total organic load.

For both the existing onshore water treatment needs and any future offshore treatment of dissolved components (1), there are some common requirements of the technology employed: the process should comprehensively and thoroughly treat the range of organic components present in produced water; it should require minimum pre- and post-treatment facilities, and it should be sufficiently robust to withstand some of the characteristic problems associated with produced water; primarily the high salinity, the toxicity of some components, and variable compositions arising from process upsets. None of the currently popular water treatment technologies is entirely satisfactory in these respects, in particular biological and chemical oxidation and membrane processes (reverse osmosis and nanofiltration).

Wet air oxidation (WAO) and supercritical water oxidation (SCWO) are two processes that have the potential to meet the requirements of produced water treatment (2,3). The processes have a much better oxidation efficiency for organic compounds compared with biological and other chemical oxidation processes, but they have the disadvantages of high capital costs and process complexity owing to the very high process temperatures and pressures (typically 550K and 10 MPa for WAO and higher for SCWO). A related process is catalytic wet air oxidation (CWAO), which is based upon the WAO process but makes use of a heterogeneous catalyst to assist the oxidation processes.

This paper reports an experimental investigation at test-rig scale to investigate the CWAO process for produced water treatment, particularly with regard to its efficiency at milder process conditions than those used in WAO, and its ability to deal with the wide range of disparate contaminants at varying concentrations. The following were the major objectives of this work:

1. To investigate the efficiency of the CWAO process at typical WAO conditions (543K and 10 MPa) in removing COD and produced water components that are representative of three major categories of contaminants present. These were: methanol (a refractory production chemical which is poorly oxidized by hydrogen peroxide, ozone, and ultra-violet processes); a long-chain amine corrosion inhibitor which is poorly treated by biological oxidation, and pentane, which is representative of the less refractory naturally-occurring components.
2. To investigate the performance of the CWAO process over a range of lower temperatures and pressures in order to identify the lowest temperature at which adequate treatment may be achieved.
3. To obtain information on the effect of changing the composition at constant operating conditions in order to assess the influence of upstream process upsets on CWAO performance.

4. To estimate the importance of the air/liquid ratio (i.e. the stoichiometric excess of oxygen) on the oxidation efficiency.
5. To investigate the corrosion rate and identify suitable materials of construction or CWAO plant treating saline produced water.

PRODUCED WATER TREATMENT

Produced water from gas reservoirs typically contains a higher level of dispersed hydrocarbons, with smaller droplets, than that from oil production; the salinity varies from relatively low levels, when the major constituent is condensation water, up to around 135 kg m$^{-3}$ when formation water is present. A wide range of naturally-occurring organic and inorganic components and production chemicals is present, and also high levels of iron and heavy metals. This presents a formidable water treatment task, despite the common imputation that the organic constituents of produced water are readily degradable (this is more applicable to water discharged offshore than to that brought onshore).

The naturally-occurring dissolved organics include aliphatic hydrocarbons, monocylic aromatic hydrocarbons (BTEX), polyaromatic hydrocarbons, aldehydes, ketones, phenols and carboxylic acids. The major production chemicals are corrosion inhibitors, which are frequently long-chain amines and amides in a hydrocarbon matrix, and hydrate inhibitors (usually methanol and glycols at present, but newer surfactant additives are under development). This mixture of environmentally harmful substances finds its way onshore in wet sealines, much of it contained in the water fraction of the three-phase fluid. The production chemicals, carboxylic acids and phenols make up the bulk of the chemical oxygen demand in produced water that is brought onshore, with the production chemicals each having levels around 100 - 1000 ppm before treatment. The same type of mixture can also arise from inland natural gas and coal-bed methane production.

The nature of the water to be discharged depends on the processing scheme. For example when methanol is used as the hydrate inhibitor, it is regenerated by distillation, which leads to a contaminated produced water effluent. When glycols are used as hydrate inhibitors, it is sometimes more economic not to recover them from the water if they are present at low levels; this leads to an effluent stream which may require treatment. However, it is more usual to regenerate glycols, in which case a produced water effluent does not result, but any condensate from the regenerator will contain contaminants such as BTEX components.

Strict discharge levels are often set for the contaminants. For example, Her Majesty's Inspector of Pollution has set maximum levels of 0.25 ppm for the corrosion inhibitor amines and 1 ppm for methanol for discharges into waters controlled by the UK National Rivers Authority. In some sensitive coastal waters, the local environmental quality standards require zero discharge levels for these components. Levels for discharge into sewers are generally much higher, but here the chemical oxygen demand is an important factor since this may be subject to discharge limits and also determines the discharge fee.

A review of produced water treatment options has recently been published by Hansen and Davies (2) which demonstrates that, with the exception of processes for removing dispersed components, little progress has been made in addressing the particular difficulties of treating produced water: it cannot be said that there is one obvious process to meet the need. Membrane processes such as nanofiltration do not as yet show the required rejection for organic components, and reverse osmosis is limited by the osmotic pressure at higher salinities. The salinity also places restrictions on the use of biological processes, and some of the components are poorly bio-degradable or toxic to the biomass. Membrane and biological processes also give rise to a residual waste disposal problem, which can be expensive and would be particularly inconvenient for any future offshore applications.

One of the most promising of the chemical oxidation methods is the UV/ozone process, and a plant has been successfully commissioned at a British Gas onshore facility to treat produced water from a North Sea field. This process is particularly useful for cracking refractory and non-biodegradable compounds, but it does not meet all the requirements: some pre-treatment is required; the process is too expensive to operate for the removal of high levels of organics, and some components are only poorly treated. Wet air oxidation can be used to treat components that are resistant to other forms of chemical or biological oxidation.

## CATALYTIC WET AIR-OXIDATION

The CWAO process is a development of WAO processes such as the Zimpro process (4), in which organic and some inorganic contaminants are oxidized in the liquid phase by contacting the liquid with high-pressure air at temperatures which are typically between 500 and 580K. The operating pressure is maintained well above the saturation pressure of water at the reaction temperatures (usually about 10 MPa) so that the reaction takes place in the liquid phase. This enables the oxidation processes to proceed at lower temperatures than those required for incineration. Residence times are from 15 minutes to 120 minutes, and the chemical oxygen demand removal may typically be about 75% to 90%. Organic compounds may be converted to carbon dioxide and water at the higher temperatures; nitrogen and sulphur heteroatoms are converted to molecular nitrogen and sulphates. A problem with the WAO process is that incomplete oxidation can sometimes result in the formation of carbon monoxide. The high temperatures can lead to corrosion which often necessitates the use of expensive materials such as titanium.

In the CWAO process the liquid phase and high-pressure air are passed co-currently over a stationary bed of catalyst. The effect of the catalyst is to provide a higher degree of COD removal than is obtained by WAO at comparable conditions, or to reduce the residence time. Carbon monoxide formation can also be eliminated. The process becomes autogenic at COD levels of about 5-10 g/l, at which the system will require external energy only at start-up.

The catalyst is a transition metal on supports such as alumina, zeolites and zirconia. Few studies have been carried out on the relative activities of transition metals catalysts in wet air oxidation. It is known that homogeneous copper is more active than heterogeneous catalysts, but the toxic copper ion must be removed after use. In this study a ruthenium catalyst has been used which has a comparable or superior activity to platinum, rhodium, iridium, palladium, and manganese. It has been demonstrated that the support is not inert and can appreciably affect the activity of the catalyst by the formation of mixed oxides (5).

## EXPERIMENTAL

Experiments were carried out on samples of synthetic produced water and actual produced water with salts levels up to 20 kg m$^{-3}$. The synthetic samples were dosed with methanol, pentane, and one of four different amine/amide based proprietary corrosion inhibitors which are currently in use at natural gas production installations. These are designated CI(I) to CI(IV). The samples of actual produced water were taken after methanol recovery from the methanol still sumps, and were supplemented where necessary with methanol and the appropriate corrosion inhibitor. A series of 27 test-rig runs were carried out; the conditions for each run, compositions of the feed and treated water and process conditions are given in Tables 1 and 2.

Test Rig Experiments

Operating Procedure

A schematic diagram of the CWAO test rig is given in Figure 1. Untreated effluent is stored under nitrogen to prevent oxidation taking place. Effluent is withdrawn from the storage tank, pressurized using an air-driven reciprocating metering pump and passed into the bottom of the electrical (4kW) pre-heater. Air is pressurized using an air-driven reciprocating gas booster and passed to a buffer tank before being metered into the pre-heater. The two phases then flow from the pre-heater to the reactor. This is a hastelloy C-276 vessel 3.6 cm in diameter and 2.88 m long. The reactor is packed with 3.4 kg of the catalyst. The heated effluent and air flow co-currently upwards through the reactor. The reaction is exothermic and a discernible temperature profile builds up as the reaction proceeds. Although the reactor is lagged, it is electrically heated along its length, at a rate just sufficient to balance the heat losses, in order to simulate adiabatic conditions. The reaction products pass from the reactor to a heat exchanger, where the effluent is cooled and filtered before passing into a two-phase separator via a back-pressure regulator. The process conditions for the series of 27 runs are given in Table 3.

Sampling And Analysis

Although the reactor is fitted with seven sampling points along its length, for the series of experiments described here it was necessary to sample the feed and treated effluent only. The effluent vapour was analysed for carbon dioxide using an infra-red detector, and for oxygen with a solid-state detector. The following chemical analyses were carried out on the liquid samples:

1. COD by the photometric Hach method which was suitably modified for saline solutions,
2. methanol by gas chromatography,
3. chloride and nitrate by ion chromatography,
4. the corrosion inhibitors were determined by the manufacturers' recommended methods which included solvent extraction followed by titrimetric or spectrophotometric analysis.

The analytical results for the feed and treated samples from runs 1 to 27 are given in Tables 1 to 3.

Corrosion Studies

During the course of this work, sections of the stainless steel pipework in contact with the hot fluid were found to be severely corroded, so all parts of the test-rig that came into contact with the hot fluid were replaced with hastelloy pipework. A study was also carried out on a range of materials to determine which would withstand the most extreme CWAO conditions. Static autoclave tests at 573K and 10 MPa oxygen pressure were conducted for a period of 60 days on pre-stressed pipe samples of hastelloy C22, incalloy 625, zirconium, titanium, and titanium/palladium alloy. The results showed that only titanium/palladium would give a satisfactory equipment lifetime at these conditions. This result formed part of the impetus to reduce the reaction temperature and pressure. The hastelloy reactor and pipework in the CWAO test-rig were inspected by ultrasonic, X-ray and dye-penetration tests before and after the series of runs on the real produced water samples. No corrosion was observed from these tests.

DISCUSSION

The CWAO test-rig results for the produced water samples at typical WAO conditions (runs 1 to 6 and run 20) show that all four corrosion inhibitors are eliminated to below detectable levels, and that (as indicated by the COD results) methanol and pentane are also reduced to below detectable levels. Virtually complete COD removal is obtained for the synthetic samples, which is better than is reported for WAO at these conditions.

Runs 7 to 19 on synthetic produced water samples show that the very good corrosion inhibitor treatment is maintained as the temperature and pressure are reduced, and there is an insignificant decline in methanol and COD removal down to 480K and 7 MPa. At the lowest temperatures, the corrosion inhibitor is still effectively removed, but the COD reduction drops from over 99% to 95%, which is still a very good result for a temperature reduction of 110K. The removal efficiencies towards methanol and corrosion inhibitor in the real produced water samples are also unaffected by a reduction in temperature by up to 120K. Methanol and corrosion inhibitor are components that are not treated well by chemical (e.g. uv/ozone) and biological processes, respectively. CWAO effectively removes these components at considerably milder conditions than those for WAO. In common with biological and chemical processes, CWAO effectively removes pentane.

The total COD for the synthetic samples is made up of the components listed in Table 1. Clearly the COD is easily removed by CWAO even at the lowest temperatures. Less complete COD removal is obtained for the actual produced water samples (runs 21 to 27). However, the 92.6% removal at 543K is still superior to that which would be expected by WAO, and the residual COD is made up of non-toxic components which may be safely discharged. The COD removal declines from 93% to 65% for a 120K reduction in temperature (at corresponding air/liquid ratios).

The corrosion inhibitor and methanol comprise about half of the COD in the untreated real produced water samples; gas chromatography-mass spectrometry (gc-ms) analyses show that the balance of the COD in  is made up a variety of phenols, carboxylic acids and ketones, and also a small amount of a silicone anti-foaming agent (added to the water before the methanol stills). Phenols have been shown to be very effectively removed by CWAO, therefore the bulk of the residual COD in the treated samples must consist of the carboxylic acids and carbonyl compounds. This has been demonstrated by gc-ms analyses, but the levels of these components in the feed accounts for less than 20% of the residual COD in the treated samples. It has been proposed (6,7) that carboxylic acids and ketones are intermediates in the oxidation of organic compounds; but the results for the synthetic samples show that methanol, corrosion inhibitors and pentane do not give rise to stable intermediates and are completely oxidized to carbon dioxide, water and nitrogen (or nitrate). It may be reasonably inferred therefore that these compounds have been completely oxidized in the real samples, and that the residual COD in the treated samples arises from the incomplete oxidation of natural components originally present in the untreated water.

Foussard and co-workers (8) have calculated standardized oxidation fractions for acids and ketones (1 hour residence, 533K and 10MPa). Most carboxylic acids are resistant to WAO, but ketones and methanoic acid are almost completely oxidized. Ethanoic acid is reported to be exceptionally resistant, which is readily explained in terms of the resistance of the methyl hydrogens to abstraction by free radicals that is brought about by hyperconjugation between the $\pi^{*}_{CH3}$ antibonding and $\pi_{CO}$ bonding molecular orbitals. Bi and Han (7) have studied the formation of acids during the degradation of hydrocarbons by CWAO, and conclude that carboxylic acids are relatively stable intermediates. This is not consistent with the results for pentane, which implies that this is oxidized via ketones or methanoic acid, and might reflect the effect of different catalysts in modifying the mechanism for hydrocarbons.

Temperature is clearly the most important parameter determining the performance of the CWAO process; and runs 26 and 27 show that pressure also has a significant effect on COD removal. At constant pressure the stoichiometric excess of oxygen, as determined by the air/volume ratio, is evidently important in COD reduction. Runs 21 to 24 show this effect: when the temperature is reduced from 543K to 473K, at constant pressure and a constant air/volume ratio, there is 12% reduction in COD removal; but at constant temperature and pressure, variations in the relative air rate lead to a 33% reduction in COD removal.

Runs 15 to 19 indicate the effect of substantially increasing the feed composition at constant conditions in order to simulate the effect of upstream process upsets. It can be seen that there is a decline in removal performance but this is small compared with the magnitude of the variation. This is in marked contrast to biological processes, which may be seriously affected by such a change, unless they were over-designed for such contingencies.

CONCLUSIONS

(1)  CWAO can effectively remove representative components of three major categories of organic contaminants in produced water at very much milder conditions than those used for WAO. Unlike biological and most chemical oxidation processes, CWAO performs comparably well for each category.
(2)  The process may be operated for produced water applications at conditions which obviate the need for very expensive construction materials such as Ti and Pd. The results to date indicate that hastelloy is suitable.
(3)  Further process optimization (for example air/liquid ratios and catalyst screening) may enable the temperature to be reduced further, and improve COD removal at the lower temperatures.
(4)  The process is robust, being largely unaffected by salinity and changes in composition.

Table 1.  Summary of CWAO test-rig results: synthetic produced water samples

| No. | Temp. (K) | Pressure (MPa) | Feed Concentrations ($g\,m^{-3}$) | | | | Oxidized Fraction | |
|-----|-----------|----------------|------|----------|---------|------|---------|---------|
| | | | CI | Methanol | Pentane | COD | CI | COD |
| 1 | 543 | 10 | 1500 | 25000 | 400 | 42000 | >0.9999[a] | >0.9998 |
| 2 | 543 | 10 | 1500 | 25000 | 400 | 46500 | >0.9999 | >0.9998 |
| 3 | 543 | 10 | 1500 | 25000 | 400 | 24000 | >0.9999 | >0.9997 |
| 4 | 543 | 10 | 1500 | 25000 | 400 | 27500 | >0.9999 | >0.9998 |
| 5 | 543 | 10 | 1500 | 25000 | 400 | 38000 | >0.9999 | >0.9998 |
| 6 | 543 | 10 | 1500 | 25000 | 400 | 33500 | >0.9999 | >0.9998 |
| 7 | 483 | 9.7 | 750 | 0 | 0 | 660 | >0.9933 | 1 |
| 8 | 483 | 9.7 | 1500 | 0 | 0 | 2500 | >0.9967 | 1 |
| 9 | 483 | 9.7 | 1500 | 1000 | 0 | 3000 | >0.9967 | 1 |
| 10 | 483 | 9.7 | 1500 | 10000 | 0 | 10200 | >0.9967 | 1 |
| 11 | 483 | 9.7 | 1500 | 25000 | 0 | 28500 | >0.9967 | 1 |
| 12 | 483 | 9.7 | 1500 | 25000 | 200 | 25500 | >0.9967 | 1 |
| 13 | 483 | 9.7 | 1500 | 25000 | 400 | 29500 | >0.9967 | >0.9993 |
| 14 | 480 | 7 | 1600 | 25000 | 0 | 32000 | >0.9900 | 0.9958 |
| 15 | 475 | 7.1 | 1000 | 0 | 0 | - | >0.9990 | - |
| 16 | 473 | 3.6 | 1600 | 25000 | 0 | 32000 | 0.9625 | 0.9534 |
| 17 | 443 | 5.5 | 1000 | 0 | 0 | - | 0.994 | - |
| 18 | 433 | 4.8 | 1600 | 25000 | 0 | 32000 | 0.9688 | 0.9556 |
| 19 | 427 | 4.6 | 1600 | 0 | 0 | 0 | 0.996 | - |

(a) ">" indicates that the treated component was below the limit of detection

Table 2. Summary of CWAO results: actual produced water samples

| No. | Temp. | Pressure | Air/liquid | Oxidized Fraction | | |
|---|---|---|---|---|---|---|
| | (K) | (MPa) | | CI | Methanol | COD |
| 20 | 543 | 10 | 116 | >0.9995 | 0.9919 | 0.9265 |
| 21 | 473 | 10 | 116 | >0.9995 | >0.9995 | (0.65)[a] |
| 22 | 473 | 10 | 151 | >0.9995 | 0.9991 | 0.8088 |
| 23 | 473 | 10 | 33 | >0.9995 | 0.9991 | 0.6471 |
| 24 | 473 | 10 | 8.3 | >0.9995 | >0.9995 | 0.4705 |
| 25 | 453 | 10 | 49.5 | >0.9995 | >0.9995 | 0.0441 |
| 26 | 423 | 10 | 116 | >0.9995 | >0.9995 | 0.6471 |
| 27 | 423 | 5 | 116 | >0.9995 | 0.9919 | 0.4853 |

(a) The COD result for this run is approximate owing to a suspected error in the Hach test

Table 3. Experimental details

| | Conditions for Table 1 | Conditions for Table 2 |
|---|---|---|
| Reactor residence time: | 1 hour | |
| Liquid flowrate: | 3.3 l/hour | |
| Air flowrate: | 50% $O_2$ excess | 27-378 l/hour |
| Treated liquid pH: | 3.6-7.1 | 3.2-4.8 |
| Outlet $CO_2$: | 2.4%-10.6% | 0.3%-24.4% |
| Outlet $O_2$: | 5.8%-17% | |

Runs 1,2 CI(I); Runs 3,4 CI(II); Runs 5,6 CI(III); Runs 7-27 CI(IV)

REFERENCES

1. D.A.Hadfield, I.Chem.E., Oil and Gas subject group meeting (London), 1993
2. B.R.Hansen, and S.R.Davies, Trans I.Chem.E., 176,72(A), 1994
3. C.Caruana, Chem.Eng.Prog., 10,91(4), 1995
4. E.J.Zimmerman, Chem.Eng.,117, 1958
5. S.Imamura, I.Fakuda, and S.Ishida, Ind.Eng.Chem.Res.,718,27, 1988
6. L.Li, P.Chen and E.F.Gloyna, AIChE Journal, 1687,37(11), 1991
7. D.Bi and J.Han, Proc.23rd. Oil Shale Symp., Golden (USA), 1990
8. J-N Foussard, H.Debellefontaine, J. Besombes-Vailhe, J.Env.Eng., 367, 115, 1989

# Figure 1. Schematic diagram of the Catalytic Wet Air Oxidation (CWAO) test rig

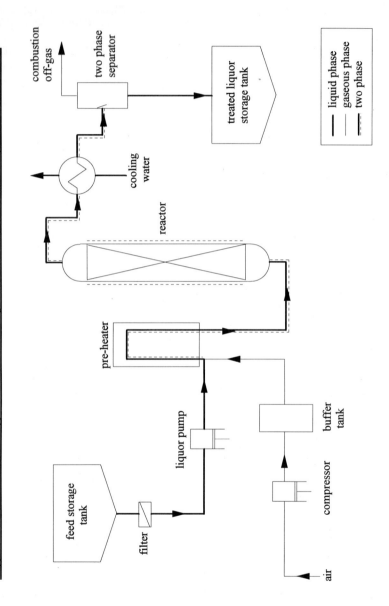

# A HYBRID ED/RO PROCESS FOR TDS REDUCTION OF PRODUCED WATERS

by

Shih-Perng Tsai, Rathin Datta, and James R. Frank
Argonne National Laboratory, Argonne, IL, USA

Lonny Lawrence
Remediation Technologies, Inc., Pittsburgh, PA, USA

Thomas D. Hayes
Gas Research Institute, Chicago, IL, USA

submitted to

1995 International Gas Research Conference

November 6-9, 1995

Conference and Exhibition Centre
Cannes, France

Sponsored by

Gas Research Institute
International Gas Union
American Gas Association
U.S. Department of Energy

The submitted manuscript has been authored by a contractor of the U. S. Government under contract No. W-31-109-ENG-38. Accordingly, the U. S. Government retains a nonexclusive, royalty-free license to publish or reproduce the published form of this contribution, or allow others to do so, for U. S. Government purposes.

A HYBRID ED/RO PROCESS FOR TDS
REDUCTION OF PRODUCED WATERS


UN PROCÈS ÉLECTRODIALYSE/OSMOSE
INVERSE HYBRIDE POUR REDUCTION
DES SELS DISSOUS EN L'EAU "PRODUITE"

Shih-Perng Tsai, Rathin Datta, and James R. Frank
Argonne National Laboratory, Argonne, IL, USA

Lonny Lawrence
Remediation Technologies, Inc., Pittsburgh, PA, USA

Thomas D. Hayes
Gas Research Institute, Chicago, IL, USA

## ABSTRACT

Large volumes of produced waters are generated from natural gas production. In the United States the prevailing management practice for produced waters is deep well injection, but this practice is costly. Therefore minimizing the need for deep well injection is desirable. A major treatment issue for produced waters is the reduction of total dissolved solids (TDS), which consist mostly of inorganic salts. A hybrid electrodialysis/reverse-osmosis (ED/RO) treatment process is being developed to concentrate the salts in produced waters and thereby reduce the volume of brine that needs to be managed for disposal. The desalted water can be used beneficially or discharged. In this study, laboratory feasibility experiments were conducted by using produced waters from multiple sites. A novel-membrane configuration approach to prevent fouling and scale formation was developed and demonstrated. Results of laboratory experiments and plans for field demonstration are discussed.

## RÉSUMÉ

L'extraction de gas naturel est accompagnée d'une grande quantité d'eau (nommeé l'eau "produite"). Les régulations ne permettent pas la décharge d'eau produite dans l'environment. Aux Étas-Unis, l'eau produite est reinjecter sous terre, un procès qui est très cher. Il est possible de décharger l'eau produite dans l'environment si les sels inorganiques dissolues sont réduits. Un procès électrodialyse/osmose inverse hybride est étudié qui a comme but de concentrés les sels inorganiques. Ce procès produit une petite quantité de liqueur-mère qui contient la majeur partie des sels. Ensuite, la masse d'eau produite peut être déchargé à l'environment ou être beneficielment utilise. L'encrassment de la membrane est diminuée par une nouvelle configuaration de la membrane utilisée. Ce procès a ete' étudié en laboratoire avec l'eau produite venant de plusieurs emplacements, et des plans de demonstration sous lieu seront présentés.

## BACKGROUND

Large volumes of produced waters are generated from natural gas production. An estimated $5.4 \times 10^{10}$ L of produced water were generated in the United States in 1990 from non-associated gas (NAG) and coal bed methane (CBM) production. Because of the large volume of produced water, the cost of its management could impact the profitability of the natural gas industry. Produced water is not a hazardous waste as defined by the Resource Conservation and Recovery Act (RCRA). Its disposal, nevertheless, is subject to various other regulations, such as those associated with the Clean Water Act (CWA) and the Safe Drinking Water Act (SDWA), depending on the method of disposal. Of the $5.4 \times 10^{10}$ L of produced water generated in 1990, it was reported that $3.4 \times 10^{10}$ L (63%) were managed by injection (Daly et al. 1992). The prevailing management practice for produced water is class II injection through enhanced oil recovery (EOR) and salt water disposal (SWD) wells. Other management options, including surface discharge, surface evaporation, land application, and off-site commercial disposal, are also practiced, but to a lesser extent. Whereas produced water from oil and associated-gas (AG) production are typically injected to SWD or EOR wells, NAG- and CBM-related produced water are more often injected into SWD wells.

The cost of injecting produced water through SWD wells is high, ranging from U.S. \$3.15 to U.S. \$11.02 per 1,000 L. Installing new SWD wells costs from U.S. \$400,000 to over U.S. \$3,000,000 per well and can be time-consuming for technical and regulatory reasons. With more stringent environmental regulations, this management option can be expected to become more difficult and expensive. Therefore, minimizing the need for deep well injection is desirable. Treatment of produced water followed by surface discharge or beneficial reuse of the treated water can be an attractive management approach. The major issue associated with the surface discharge or beneficial reuse of produced water is the reduction of total dissolved solids (TDS), which consist mostly of inorganic salts. The most abundant salt is sodium chloride, but other cations (such as potassium, calcium, magnesium, barium, etc.) and anions (such as sulfate, bicarbonate, etc.) can also be present at considerable concentrations. In addition, produced waters contain volatile and semivolatile organic compounds, including aromatic hydrocarbons and aliphatic petroleum hydrocarbons. These organic compounds may or may not be subject to environmental regulations. However, their presence can affect the feasibility of the technologies selected for TDS reduction, a consideration that needs to be addressed for the development of treatment technologies. The quantities and characteristics of produced waters vary widely. Compared with the NAG-produced water, the CBM-produced water is typically generated at a larger volume per well per day but contains lower concentrations of TDS. Even among the CBM- or NAG-produced waters, wide variations exist. Therefore, the feasibility of any treatment technology is expected to be highly case-specific.

Argonne's proposed treatment process for produced water is an integrated ED/RO process for TDS. A biological fluidized-bed reactor (FBR) that removes organics precedes the ED/RO process. The applications of these two membrane technologies, RO and ED, for produced water treatment, have been investigated by some researchers (Nakles et al. 1992; Simmons 1992; Kok 1993), but only to a limited extent and not as an integrated ED/RO process. RO is a pressure-driven membrane process that can concentrate the TDS from produced water into a retentate stream while producing a permeate stream that is sufficiently clean for discharge or reuse. The performance of RO is affected by the osmotic pressure of the process stream, which is proportional to the total concentration of the ionic and non-ionic solutes. In general, RO can concentrate a salt-laden water to one molar (e.g., 58.45 g NaCl/L) before cost of the treatment becomes prohibitive. ED is an electrical field-driven process that uses ion-exchange membranes for salt removal or concentration. ED is able to produce a highly concentrated salt solution by transporting dissolved salts from a solution on one side of the membranes to a concentrated salt solution on the other side of the membranes. For the production of table salt from sea water, a 20% (3.4 M) sodium chloride solution is generated from the sea water, which contains 3% (0.5 M) sodium chloride. Successful applications of ED are widespread in Japan. The scale of Japanese plants ranges from very large (over $2 \times 10^8$ kg/yr) for table-salt plants to small-scale flavor extraction plants. Long membrane life (4 yr) has been established for several operations. Automated cleaning-in-place (CIP) techniques have been developed for specific applications to extend membrane life and to improve process consistency. Several ED membrane manufacturers have developed desalting ED membranes that are highly efficient and stable, moderately priced, and energy efficient (e.g., Japanese plants for desalting sea water consume 130—150 kWh/ton of NaCl). These new membranes are now available for process development and commercial applications. The biological FBR process developed by EFX uses acclimated microbial culture immobilized on granular activated-carbon support. The system has been demonstrated to be very efficient (capable of removing a high percentage of salt at a hydraulic retention time of several minutes) for treating waters containing aromatic and aliphatic organic compounds commonly associated with gas production operations. The system has also been shown to be effective even at the salt concentrations found in produced waters.

A schematic of the proposed process is shown in Figure 1. The produced water is first pretreated in the biological FBR to remove organics, then fed to the ED system. In the ED step, salt ions are removed from the produced-water feed and are transported through ion-exchange membranes into a concentrated salt stream. This concentrated salt stream is of a much smaller volume than that of the original produced water and, therefore, can be more easily and economically managed by deep well injection, surface evaporation, or off-site commercial disposal. The desalted produced water from ED is fed to the RO unit to generate a permeate that will be suitable for surface discharge or beneficial uses and a retentate that contains a re-concentrated salt stream that is recycled to ED for further concentration. This process combines ED and RO in a synergistic manner.

In field applications of the ED/RO treatment of produced water, it would be desirable to pump the produced water from several production wells to a central treatment site where the treatment system could be operated for long periods with minimal human intervention. Fouling is a potential problem for the long-term operation of all membrane separation processes. Proper integration of ED and RO can reduce the tendency of fouling, and CIP techniques can be practiced, as needed, to restore membrane performance. Long-term, unattended operation of the process can be accomplished by computer-based, on-line monitoring of process parameters, in conjunction with protocols for automated process operation and CIP procedures. Automated processing is common in several small- and large-scale ED plants in Japan and has been widely practiced for RO.

## R&D PROGRESSES AND RESULTS

### Scope and Objectives

This ED/RO process development work is being performed at Argonne National Laboratory (ANL) in collaboration with Gas Research Institute (GRI), Remediation Technologies, Inc. (ReTec), and EFX Systems, Inc. (EFX). GRI and ReTec manage the overall project, identify the treatment needs of produced water and potential technological solutions, and develop a knowledge base for the selection of the most promising treatment approaches for the specific situations of each produced water generator (i.e., gas producer). EFX applies its FBR technology for the removal of organics from produced waters. The principal objectives of the ED/RO work at ANL are as follows:

- Evaluate the applicability of the proposed ED/RO process with respect to the varying characteristics of produced waters generated at different gas production sites,

- Determine the technical and economical feasibility of the process with laboratory data,

- Develop and optimize the integrated ED/RO produced water treatment process at the laboratory scale, and

- Demonstrate the long-term process feasibility at selected gas production sites.

### Major Technical Parameters

The major technical parameters that can critically affect the technical and economic feasibility of the ED/RO process are as follows.

- Brine volume reduction factor: The objective of the treatment is to reduce the volume of brine. The volume reduction factor is determined by the ratio of achievable TDS level in the concentrated brine to the TDS level of the produced water feed. For sodium chloride solution, the ED process has been shown to be able to generate a 20% brine. For produced waters that contain high levels of multivalent cations and anions, however, the maximum achievable brine concentration is also limited by potential membrane fouling or scale formation, as discussed below.

- Membrane fouling and scale formation: Salts of multivalent cations and anions (e.g., $CaSO_4$ and $CaCO_3$) often have very limited solubility in water. When produced waters are being concentrated, the sparingly soluble salts can precipitate in the brine solution or in the concentration boundary layer near the membrane at a high TDS level and cause scale formation or membrane fouling. In fact, precipitation of inorganic salts has been known to be a major problem for RO applications in produced water treatment. ED is inherently more resistant to salt precipitation. However, care must be taken in selecting the process conditions and cleaning-in-place protocols to prevent membrane fouling and extend membrane life. In addition, intelligent integration of ED and RO can reduce the overall problems of membrane fouling and scale formation.

- ED energy requirement: Besides the cost of replacing the membrane, the electricity cost of the ED step is a major operating cost. At a given current density, the ED energy requirement is proportional to the electrical resistance of the ED membranes and process solutions. The use of low-resistance membranes can significantly reduce the energy requirement.

- ED flux: The flux is proportional to current density and current efficiency. For a given salt removal rate, the size of the ED system required is inversely proportional to the flux. Because the capital cost of the ED system is a significant factor of process economics, it is important that the ED process can be operated at a reasonably high current density and current efficiency.

Laboratory Feasibility Experiments

Produced water samples generated at several sites were tested at ANL. Table 1 shows the characteristics of these samples. They varied widely not only in the TDS concentration, but also with respect to cation and anion profiles. For example, sodium chloride was the predominant salt in Sample C, whereas the sulfate concentration in Sample D was higher than the chloride concentration. Laboratory screening tests were conducted with these samples. Initially, only simple ED feasibility experiments were performed by using the produced water samples as received without biological FBR pretreatment or integration with RO. The experiments were carried out by using a laboratory ED system equipped with a Tokuyama TS-2 stack, which contained several pairs of anion- and cation-exchange membranes (usually 10 pairs) with an effective membrane area of 200 cm$^2$/sheet. The laboratory system used is a true process development unit (i.e., process data collected with this unit are directly scaleable to full-sized commercial systems). Membranes for each test were selected for their electrical resistance properties, compatibility with the solution to be desalted, and for their capability to separate the ions of interest.

In the batch-desalting mode, the ED process was started with a constant DC current applied to the stack. As dissolved salts were transferred from the produced water feed (diluting stream) to the brine (concentrating stream), the conductivity of the diluting stream decreased and the voltage drop of the stack increased until a preset upper limit was reached. The system was then switched into a constant voltage operation with decreasing current, until a low conductivity of the diluting stream was reached and the run was then stopped. The batch desalting experiments generated such feasibility data as the ED energy requirement, salt removal flux, and the compositions of the desalted water and concentrated brine. In addition to the batch experiments, membrane stability was tested in separate experiments with the recycle of the brine stream to the diluting stream for continuous operation up to 24 h, which is the expected interval for cleaning-in-place techniques.

The technical feasibility of ED desalting was demonstrated for all the produced waters tested. The significant findings are as follows:

- The ED process was shown to concentrate sodium chloride, the predominant salt in most produced waters, to about 18%, suggesting the potential of a significant volume reduction of the brine.

- There was no evidence of rapid fouling of the ED membranes, even without pretreatment for organic removal.

- Some migration of organics into the brine stream was observed. This observation suggests that some organics were able to enter the matrix of the ED membranes. Although this did not cause membrane fouling, the use of a biological FBR as a pretreatment to remove organics from the produced water before it enters the ED/RO system will prevent potential fouling of ED and RO membranes. The presence of organics in the concentrate should not be a problem, however, if brine disposal is managed by reinjection.

- The ED energy requirement was strongly affected by the selection of membranes. A membrane configuration using low-resistance membrane was found to reduce the energy consumption of ED by 20%.

- A novel approach to preventing membrane fouling of the ED/RO process was developed and demonstrated.

Process Simulation

A spreadsheet computer program is being developed to simulate the material balance of this ED/RO process and to predict the potential of membrane fouling and scale formation. For a given composition of the produced water feed, the program calculates the composition of each process stream on the basis of the TDS concentration factor and the membrane selectivity and compares these valves with the solubility of sparingly soluble salts to predict the potential of scale formation. Taking into account concentration polarization near the membrane surface, the program also predicts the potential for membrane fouling.

Process Economics and Sensitivity Analysis

In addition, a process costing model is being developed. The ED module of the model has been completed and used to calculate the ED processing costs, including the costs of the system depreciation, electricity consumption (for stack and pumping), and membrane replacement. Sensitivity analyses were performed to predict the effects of technical parameters and process conditions (e.g., current efficiency, plant size, and salinity of the produced water feed and the desalted water) on the process economics. For a model system that has 5% TDS in the produced water feed, the ED processing cost was estimated to be about U.S. $2.33/1,000 L. This cost compares favorably with the costs of alternative methods of produced-water management. The model is being expanded to perform cost estimation of the integrated ED/RO process. The total costs of the ED/RO-based management method, including the costs of

ED/RO, pre-treatment, and final disposal costs, should still be lower than or comparable with the cost of SWD well injection. However, the flexibility and reliability of this aboveground treatment process should it more attractive than injection, considering the intensive capital investment and uncertainties related to establishing new injection wells.

## CONCLUSIONS

The laboratory experiments and economic analyses to date have demonstrated the technical and economic feasibility of ED desalting of produced waters. The characteristics of produced waters varies widely, and the optimal process conditions and membrane configuration will need to be selected accordingly. The laboratory work is being continued to integrate the ED process with the biological FBR and RO and to determine the long-term performance of the integrated ED/RO process. Cleaning-in-place techniques and automation protocols will be developed. A field demonstration is being planned to perform a slip-stream operation of the integrated FBR-ED/RO process at a gas production site, starting fall 1995 or spring 1996.

## ACKNOWLEDGMENT

This work has been supported by the Gas Research Institute and Remediation Technologies, Inc.

## REFERENCES

Daly, D.J., R.S. Stoa, J.A. Sorensen, and S.A. Bassingthwaite, 1992, "Gas Industry Related Produced Water Management Demographics," Gas Research Institute report, Chicago, Ill.

Kok, S., 1993, personal communication.

Nakles, D.V., I. Oritz, and J.R. Frank, 1992, "An Analysis of Management Strategies for Produced Waters from Natural Gas Production," presented at the 1992 International Produced Waters Symposium, February 4-7, 1992, San Diego, Calif.

Simmons, B. F., 1992, "Treatment and Disposal of Wastewaters Produced with Coalbed Methane by Reverse Osmosis," in J.P. Ray and F.R. Engelhardt (eds.), Produced Water Technological/Environmental Issues and Solutions, Plenum Press, N.Y.

Table 1.  Characteristics of Various Produced-Water Samples

| Analyses | Site A | Site B | Site C | Site D | Site E |
|---|---|---|---|---|---|
| pH, SU | 6.4 | 7.6 | 7.2 | 7.2 | 7.4 |
| Conductivity, mS/cm | 67.0 | 12.6 | 18.6 | 33.7 | 75.4 |
| Total Suspended Solids, mg/L | 195 | 18.0 | 14 | 24 | 318 |
| Fixed Suspended Solids, mg/L | – | 12.0 | 8 | 15 | 110 |
| Volatile Suspended Solids, mg/L | – | 6.0 | 6 | 9 | 208 |
| Total Dissolved Solids, mg/L | – | 8,000 | 14,700 | 28,900 | 83,400 |
| Oil & Grease, mg/L | – | 98.4 | < 5 | < 5 | < 5 |
| Total Recoverable Petroleum Hydrocarbons, mg/L | – | 243.0 | 1.1 | 73.5 | 695 |
| TOC, mg/L | – | 143.0 | 22.2 | 383 | 40.7 |
| Chloride, mg/L | 29,930 | 3,630 | 1,920 | 8,400 | 61,600 |
| Sulfate, mg/L | 1,500 | 6.9 | 10.6 | 9,290 | 6 |
| Sulfide, mg/L | 900 | 3.5 | 1.8 | 6.1 | 2.2 |
| Fluoride, mg/L | – | 2.4 | 0.92 | 0.77 | 0.88 |
| Sodium, mg/L | 15,400 | 2,640 | 6,200 | 8,600 | 23,600 |
| Potassium, mg/L | 306 | 48.2 | 24.0 | 66.0 | 146 |
| Calcium, mg/L | 2,010 | 18.9 | 22.10 | 284.0 | 1,900 |
| Magnesium, mg/L | 575 | < 5 | 17.4 | 52.9 | 264 |
| Barium, mg/L | – | 10.1 | 27.2 | < 0.2 | 21.5 |
| Iron, mg/L | 0.1 | 3.87 | 3.16 | 5.34 | 4.76 |
| Total Alkalinity, mg/L | – | 1,620 | 9,590 | 1,000 | 128 |
| Carbonate Alkalinity, mg/L | – | 0 | 0 | 0 | 0 |
| Bicarbonate Alkalinity, mg/L | – | 1,620 | 9,590 | 1,000 | 128 |
| Total BTEX, mg/L | 4.6 | 9.5 | 0.0326 | 41.4 | 161.5 |
| Total TPH, mg/L | 12.2 | 215.2 | < 0.8 | 29.33 | 123.5 |

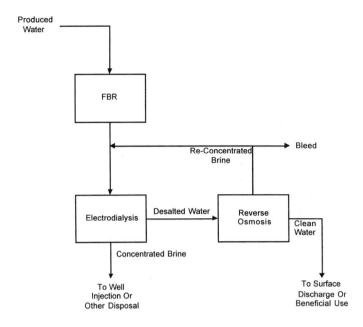

Figure 1.  Schematic of the Integrated ED/RO Process for Produced-Water Treatment

RECUPERATION DU SOUFRE AVEC UN RENDEMENT SUPERIEUR A 99,9 %

GRACE A UNE NOUVELLE VERSION DU PROCEDE SULFREEN

99.9 % SULPHUR RECOVERY WITH A NEW VERSION

OF SULFREEN PROCESS

Sabine SAVIN, Jean NOUGAYREDE

ELF AQUITAINE PRODUCTION

**RESUME**

Les besoins croissants d'une meilleure protection de l'environnement incitent au développement de nouveaux procédés capables de réaliser l'objectif d'une conversion globale de l'$H_2S$ en soufre supérieure à 99,9 % à moindres coûts d'investissement et de fonctionnement.

ELF AQUITAINE PRODUCTION étudie actuellement une nouvelle voie entièrement catalytique pour le traitement des gaz résiduaires d'usines à soufre. Ce traitement consiste dans l'oxydation directe et sélective de l'$H_2S$ en soufre à l'aide d'un catalyseur adéquat. Les schémas de procédé en cours d'évaluation opèrent à une température inférieure au point de rosée du soufre, selon le concept de la technologie Sulfreen

**ABSTRACT**

Increasing environmental concern leads to the development of new process concepts to achieve the objective of a 99.9 % mini. overall sulphur recovery from H2S gas streams, at better investment and operating costs.

ELF AQUITAINE PRODUCTION is currently elaborating a new totally catalytic route for treating tail gases of sulphur recovery units. It consists in the selective direct oxidation of H2S into sulphur through the use of a new appropriate catalyst.Process schemes under consideration are given, which operate below sulfur dew-point, according to the Sulfreen technology concept.

BACKGROUND

Reducing atmospheric pollution by SO2 has become a major environmental concern for natural gas industries.

ELF AQUITAINE PRODUCTION has contributed for many years to the development of new technologies aimed at increasing sulphur recovery from sulphur recovery units, by first introducing the concept of implementing the catalytic Claus reaction below sulphur dew point which resulted in improved Claus yields.

The so -called Sulfreen process jointly developed with LURGI in the 70's and its further extensions with Hydrosulfreen and Oxysulfreen in the 80's thus brought a significant breakthrough in the art. Nevertheless, as they are based on the Claus reaction, their performance is limited to overall recovery yields not exceeding 99.7 % on a regular basis.

The further 99.9 % challenge supposed to basically reconsider both process and reaction philosophies.

Taking advantage of the expertise acquired with the Sulfreen technology, ELF AQUITAINE PRODUCTION decided to explore the potentiality of a totally catalytic route that would proceed according to the 2 following stages :

1. Catalytic conversion into H2S of all the sulphur species which are contained in the tail gases of sulphur recovery units, including SO2, COS and CS2, through hydrogenation-hydrolysis over a Co/Mo type catalyst ;

2. Direct oxidation of the resulting H2S into sulphur over a new appropriate catalyst

Compared with the existing best available technology, which is based on tail gas reduction followed by H2S recycling through liquid solvent absorption, this new approach should present the following advantages :

* lower operating costs, in particular as far as energy consumption is concerned

* absence of liquid effluent streams to be further treated before disposal.

The first hydrogenation-hydrolysis step is well known in the art and commercially proven. The second step is the innovative sequence under current investigation.

As the fruit of a preliminary research study, conducted in collaboration with RHONE-POULENC, a new catalytic material came up, which is now being experimented successfully on the laboratory scale, the main quality of which being its ability to directly oxidize H2S into sulphur in the presence of air, with a selectivity only slightly affected by the ratio of oxygen to H2S at low temperature.

Because the reaction of H2S with oxygen on the new catalyst should take place at a temperature below 150°C, the technology which will be developed will benefit a lot from the industrial experience acquired through the development of the Sulfreen concept, i.e. the cyclic succession of an adsorption-reaction phase, where the sulphur formed from H2S remains adsorbed within the catalyst, and of a regeneration phase, where the sulphur is expelled from the catalyst by heating to 300°C.

THE DIRECT OXIDATION OF H2S INTO SULPHUR

A laboratory pilot was designed so as to best simulate all the sequences of the process, and follow the mid-term evolution of the catalysts performances over periods as long as 6 months.

Tests have been carried out with tail gas compositions ranging from 0.25 to 1.5 % H2S in order to evaluate the performances to be expected according to the various process options which will be further developed within this presentation.

The main parameters governing the H2S conversion and selectivity rates, could be experimentally identified both in terms of operating procedures and catalyst formulation.

For example, the results obtained brought to light the positive influence of the presence of water towards the kinetics of the H2S conversion, levelling to its maximum at water contents above 20 %, i.e. concentrations fortunately corresponding to the usual composition of the industrial streams to be treated.

However, the main operating parameters controlling the overall selectivity towards sulphur against SO2 clearly appeared to be the oxygen to H2S ratio, correlated to the temperature of the reaction.

Figure 1 illustrates the significant influence of temperature towards the selectivity of the reaction expressed as the percentage of SO2 that is formed from the H2S content of the feed. The experimental data shown in this figure were collected with an equimolar O2/H2S ratio, i.e. twice the theoretical amount necessary to produce sulphur.

The results also give evidence of the influence of the quantity of active material deposited on the support, the chemical nature of which, silica or alumina, being of little significance. With the least selective formulation, which contains 4 % of active material, the oxygen to H2S ratio can be increased to values exceeding four times the stoichiometry of the reaction with a rate of SO2 formation remaining below 5 % of the total H2S of the feed at temperatures up to 110°C (figure 2). With only 1 % of active material, no SO2 could be traced at the outlet of the reactor (<30 ppm) with O2/H2S ratios as high as 6 times the stoichiometry under the same temperature conditions.

The kinetics of H2S conversion also appears to be somewhat affected by the amount of active material deposited on the support, as can be seen from Figure 3.

Another interesting feature is the dependence of the maximum H2S conversion rate with the H2S content of the feed, at least in the case of alumina supported samples ; experimental data including catalysts analysis and tests with silica supported samples suggest that this phenomenon should be related to the intrinsic texture of the porous network resulting from the stabilization of the formulation during the first cycles (figure 4).

PROCESS EXTRAPOLATIONS FROM EXPERIMENTAL RESULTS

The above experimental results led to the conception of two process schemes which could be implemented respectively :

* downstream of the sulphur recovery unit

* downstream of a Hydrosulfreen tail gas treatment unit

Both schemes are based on the operation of a minimum of 2 reactors, one working according to the adsorption-reaction phase, while the other one is being regenerated. The automatic switch from one reactor to the other through programmed sequences make it possible to ensure an overall continuous tail gas treating.

## 1. Direct treatment of SRU tail gas

This is the most demanding case due to the high level of H2S content in the gas to be treated : 1.5 % H2S corresponds to a SRU recovery yield of 95 %.

Figure 5 illustrates the successive steps which have to be considered :

* hydrogenation-hydrolysis of the sulphur containing tail gas components over a Co/Mo type catalyst at 300°C in the reactor R1.

* cooling of the resulting gases down to 90°C (i.e. above water dew point) through the heat exchanger E2.

* smooth oxidation of H2S in the Sulfreen reactors, alternatively R2 and R3 ; each reactor is designed with 3 catalytic stages separated by intermediate coolers E3/E4 and E5/E6 to ensure an interstage cooling down to 90°C.

Thermodynamics data indicate that the oxidation of around 5000 ppm H2S, i.e. 1/3 of the H2S to be expected from the SRU tail gas, generates a temperature increase of 30°C under adiabatic conditions.

Above experimental results give evidence that a correct catalyst formulation make it possible to ensure the required selectivity versus SO2, while maintaining the H2S conversion at each catalytic level, up to 120°C.

Thus, in the first two catalytic stages, the reaction is allowed to proceed under adiabatic conditions, with the temperature not exceeding 120°C through the controlled addition of air ; it is considered that a 1 % concentration of H2S can thus be treated.

In the last (third) catalytic stage, the reaction is pushed forward by introducing air in excess ; under these conditions, the selectivity control requires the design of a cooled reactor to keep the temperature below 120°C. The preliminary feasibility study of the total process design led to the conclusion that this third cooled stage is the sizing element of the unit.

The above described process is illustrated in figure 5, and constitutes the basic process scheme.

## 2. Tail gas treatment downstream of a Hydrosulfreen unit

In this case, the option which is considered and is illustrated in figure 6, consists in the following :

* SRU tail gas is pretreated according to the Hydrosulfreen process, within a unit composed of a reactor R1 dedicated to the hydrolysis of COS/CS2 at 300°C, followed by a cooler E2 which brings back temperature down to 135°C and by a first catalytic stage being located in the 2 Sulfreen reactors R2 and R3.

Tail gas at the outlet of this pretreatment contains 2500 ppm of residual H2S, free from COS/CS2 thanks to the hydrolysis stage and free from SO2 thanks to the controlled shift of the H2S/SO2 ratio towards H2S in excess, downstream of the sulphur plant (H2S - 2 SO2 = 0.25 %).

* The gas coming out of the first catalytic stage (Sulfreen) are cooled down to 90°C through a system of 2 exchangers E3 and E4 ("switch condensers").

* The final purification of the tail gas through the selective oxidation of H2S into sulphur is performed in a second catalytic stage, which is integrated within the Sulfreen reactors, in the presence of air in excess. As in the former case, the control of the H2S oxidation selectivity towards sulphur requires to keep the temperature below 120°C, which entails the implementation of cooled reactors as above described.

CONCLUSION

Although still in the development phase, the process route under investigation by ELF AQUITAINE PRODUCTION shows promising and the results obtained to date confirm the accessibility of the ambitious 99.9 % objective through totally catalytic pathways.

**SO2 formation rate (%)**
**(integrated over 24h)**

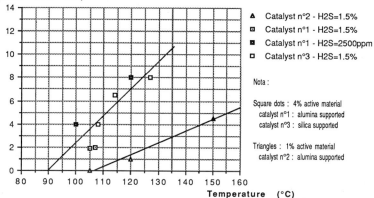

*Figure 1 :*
*Comparison of the selectivity performances of 3 catalyst formulations, based on the same active material, according to temperature*

Conditions of the reaction (adsorption phase) :
Contact time = 4s at the reaction temperature (i.e. : 5.5 sNTP at 100°C and 6.2 sNTP at 150°C)
Feed composition : H2S=see diagram key ; O2/H2S=1mole/mole ; H2O=30% ; N2=complement to 100%

**SO2 formation rate (%)**
**(integrated over 24h)**

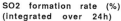
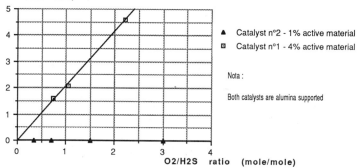

*Figure 2 :*
*Influence of the catalyst composition over the selectivity of the oxidation reaction, evaluated from the oxygen to H2S ratio in the feed*

Conditions of the reaction (adsorption phase) :
Temperature = 105-110°C
Contact time = 5,5 sNTP
Feed composition : H2S=1.5% ; O2/H2S=see diagram ; H2O=30% ; N2=complement to 100%
Duration = 24h

**H2S conversion (%)**
**(Integrated over 24h)**

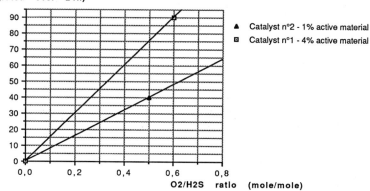

**Figure 3 :**
*Influence of the catalyst composition over the kinetics of the H2S conversion, evaluated from the oxygen to H2S ratio in the feed*

Conditions of the reaction (adsorption phase) :
Temperature = 105-110°C
Contact time = 5.5 sNTP
Feed composition : H2S=1.5% ; O2/H2S=see diagram ; H2O=30% ; N2=complement to 100%
Duration = 24h

**H2S conversion rate (%)**
**(Integrated over 24h)**

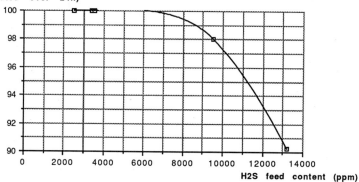

**Figure 4 :**
*Evolution of the maximal H2S conversion rate as a function of the H2S content of the feed over alumina supported formulations, as examplified from the results obtained with the 1% active material sample.*
Conditions of the reaction (adsorption phase) :
Temperature = 100-105°C
Contact time = 5.5 sNTP
Feed composition : H2S=see diagram ; O2/H2S>1.45 mole/mole ; H2O=30% ; N2=complement to 100%

**Objective 99.9 : Claus unit tail gas treating process by selective oxidation of H2S into sulfur**

*Fig.5*

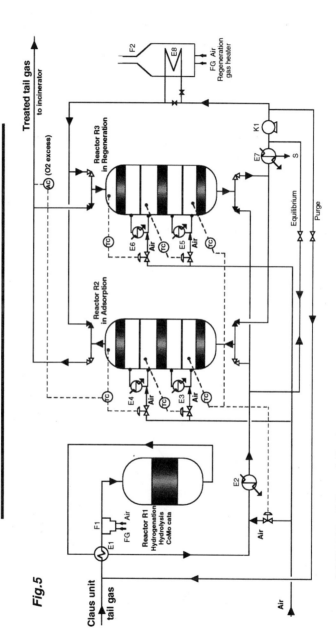

A.P./J.N. / EPS 179AB - Dialogues - 1515

Switching valves : Open — Closed

## Objective 99.9 : Claus unit tail gas treating based on hydrosulfreen process and selective oxidation of H2S into sulfur

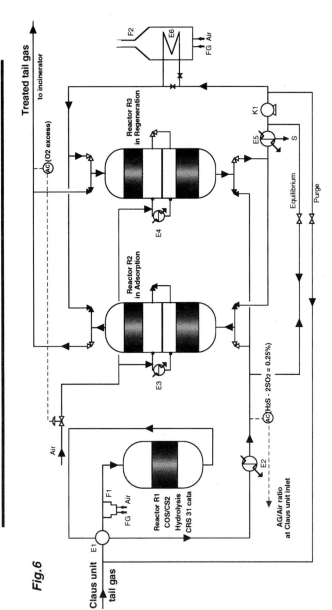

*Fig.6*

A.P./J.N. / EPS 179AC - Dialogues - 1515

Switching valves : Open    Closed

NEW TYPE OF FRONT-END REACTION FURNACE FOR CLAUS PROCESS

NOUVEAU RÉACTEUR-FOUR POUR LE PROCÉDÉ CLAUS SOMMAIRE

P.A.TESNER, M.S.NEMIROVSKY

VNIIGAS, Russia.


V.I.NASTEKA
Orenburg Gas Processing Plant, Russia

ABSTRACT

This work presents the results of kinetic and aerodynamic investigations laid in the foundation of the new reactor design. The new reactor provide a minimum time for reaching the thermodynamic equilibrium. Three years of industrial operation of the reactor with capacity 1200 t of elementary sulphur per day have proved a possibility to reach the thermodynamic equilibrium for Claus reaction and COS formation within 0.7 sec. The combustion products was shown not to contain oxygen. The new reactor produce elementary sulphur by 30% more as compared with tangential flame burner reactor. This results in decrease of temperature difference at the catalytic convertors by 30-40°C as well as in increase of Claus unit conversion degree by 1-2%. Rebuilding the existing flame burner thermal reactors by the new burner is not very complicated and expensive procedure but ecologically and economically advantageous one.

RÉSUMÉ

Le présent rapport contient l'exposé des études cinétiques et aérodynamiques qui ont servi de base pour l'élabaration de la nouvelle construction du réacteur. Ce réacteur-là assure le temps minimum de la réalisation de l'équilibre thérmodynamique. Trois années d'exploitation industrielle du nouveau réacteur à la capacite de production egale à 1200 tonnes de soufre par jour ont montré qu'il assure la realisation de l'equilibre thérmodynamique de la réaction Claus et celle de la formation de COS dans 0.7 sec. Il est aussi démontré les produits de la combustion pratiquement ne contiennent pas d'oxygène. Le nouveau réacteur produit a 30% plus de soufre par rapport au réacteur au brûluer torche tangentiel. Il en résulte la diminution de 30 a 40% du gradient de température des réacteurs catalytiques et l'augmantation du 1 a 2% du degré de conversion dans l'unité Claus. La réconstruction des brûleurs torche en brûleurs a tourbinnement contraire n'est pas compliquée et n'est pas chère; elle donne des éffets économiques et écologiques considérables.

INTRODUCTION

Nowadays a great amount of hydrogen sulfide is produced during natural gas and crude oil treatments as well as during hydrofinig of petroleum fractions at refineries. Claus process is the main one in elementary sulphur manufacturing from hydrogen sulphide.

The first stage of the Claus process is a thermal one wherein an incomplete combustion of hydrogen sulphide in the air or oxygen occurs. This process takes place in the apparatus called a Reactor-Furnace and represented the combination of a burner unit and a chemical reactor. Thermodynamic calculations performed [1-3] demonstrate that 60-70% conversion of hydrogen sulfide entering the reactor to elementary sulphur can be reached at the thermal stage. Therefore, a proper reactor design is of great importance to the Claus unit operation. There are many designs available of such reactors [4]. However, in the most of them the thermodynamic yield of sulphur cannot be reached. Evidentely, these apparatus were not designed as the chemical reactors but the burner units.

To design the reactor properly one has to know the Claus process kinetics. This paper deals with the results obtained during kinetic investigation of the reaction:

$$2H_2S + SO_2 = 1.5S_2 + 2H_2O \qquad (1)$$

as well as with a new design of the reactor.

KINETIC INVESTIGATION

Kinetics of the reaction (1) were studied experimentally in the laboratory conditions. Kinetic studies have shown that the reaction order for hydrogen sulphide is 1.0 and for sulphur dioxide it is 0.5. The activation energy is 14.3 kcal/mole [5]. Integration of the differential kinetic equation with the account of the reverse reaction permitted us to find a relation between the degree of hydrogen sulfide conversion and the gas residence time. On the basis of kinetic studies, temperature variations and conversion degrees of the hydrogen sulfide reaction (1) were calculated [6,7]. The calculations were performed for two cases: an ideal plug flow reactor (PFR) and ideal back-mixed reactor (BMR). In both cases it was assumed that reaction (1) begins at the temperature reached by the mixture of gases when the combustion reaction (2) goes to completion.

$$H_2S + 3/2O_2 = SO_2 + H_2O \qquad (2)$$

This tempetature was calculated by the thermal balance.
The systems of equations of PFR and BMR material and thermal balances were numerically solved by a computer. The results of calculations for various acid gas composition are plotted in Figs. 1 and 2. Curves 1 and 4 relate to the PFR, curves 2 and 3 to the BMR. In Fig.1 the reactors are operated on acid gas containing 46% $H_2S$, 13.4% $H_2O$, 40.6% $CO_2$. In Fig. 2 acid gas composition is 71% $H_2S$, 7% $H_2O$, 22% $CO_2$. In both cases the stoichiometric amount of air was taken according to reaction (3).

$$H_2S + 1/2O_2 = 1/2S_2 + H_2O \qquad (3)$$

As one would expect, comparison of the results for PFR and BMR shows a considerable advantage for an ideal PFR. For example, when acid gas containing 71% $H_2S$ is processed, the reaction in the PFR is practically completed (95% of a thermodynamic limit) within 0.05 sec, whereas in the BMR the conversion within this time reaches only 30%.

A kinetic model of an adiabatic PFR was used to calculate the required residence time for various concentrations of hydrogen sulfide in acid gas. Doing these calculations it was assumed that: 1) acid gas contained hydrogen sulfide and carbon dioxide, 2) combustion took place in the stoichiometric amount of air according to equation (2), 3) temperature of initial gases was 300K. The time required to reach conversion of 95% of that thermodynamically possible was calculated.

The results of calculation are given in Fig. 3. They demonstrate that as hydrogen sulfide content in acid gas increases from 30 to 90%, the required residence time decreases from 0.41 to 0.02 sec. This is mainly due to the growth of the combustion temperature with increasing concentration of hydrogen sulfide in acid gas. The relation between residence time and hydrogen sulphide concentration in acid gas is approximated by the equation (4), which can be used in engineering calculations for the front-end furnace of the Claus process:

$$t = 3800 \cdot C^{-2.7} \qquad (4)$$

where, t — the required residence time, sec
      C — $H_2S$ concentration in acid gas, % mol.

REACTOR DESIGN

The results obtained during the kinetic calculations of the Claus reactors demonstrated the following. To reach the thermo-dynamic equilibrium of the reaction (1) in a mimimum possible time it is necessary to provide in the reactor a plug flow regime i.e. the flow rates vectors of the combustion products at any section points of the reactor to be parallel to its axis. The time (t) required to obtain 95% of the thermodynamic equilibrium can be calculated according to equation (4).

The residence time in the reactor includes (t) + the time required to complete the combustion reactions. Acid gas and air are introduced in the reactor separately. So, the time required to hudrogen sulfide combustion is mainly limited by the mixing time. Hence, the reactor design has to provide first and the foremost an ideal mixing regime followed by an ideal plug flow regime. It goes without saying that diffusion flame cannot be applicable for obtaining this goal. Therefore, a new approach was applied here, i.e. a creation of two opposingly rotated flames, their interaction resulting in the flames rotation decaying as well as in the ideal plug flow regime generation in the main part of the reactor. Feasibility of the method proposed was confirmed at aerodynamic pilot testings. There was proved that two on-coming wirls rotated opposingly really suppress each other resulting in the creation of the unrotary streams simmilar to those observed in plug flow regime. A length of the zone where the on-coming wirls are suppressed can be taken as equaled to diameter of the reactor. The results obtained during the aerodynamic pilot testings will be published elsewhere. At the new reactor designing the results of kinetic and airodynamic investigations were used.

A scheme of the industrial scale reactor is given in Fig.4 [8,9]. The reactor dimentions were as follows: diameter — 4m, length 10m.  The Claus unit had two catalytic convertors and was constructed to produce 1200 t of elementary sulphur per day. The Claus unit was designed to process acid gas with hydrogen sulfide content from 45 up to 65%.  It was the reason to install the forechambers there to ensure a stable combustion of the rotary flames.  These forechambers provide also the reactor heating during the Claus unit start-up as well as at catalysts regeneration stage.  Heating of the forechambers proceeds by fuel gas combustion.

The two external burners installed opposingly constitute a common burner, acid gas and air being fed there by a single pipe. To provide the equal acid gas and air consumption by both burners the feeding pipes were constructed symmetrically.  The new reactor was created as a result of rebuilding of the existing reactor with tangential burners.  The rebuilding was performed by the Orenburgh GPP personnel.

RESULTS OBTAINED DURING OPERATION OF THE NEW REACTOR

The new reactor was put into operation in September, 1992. The results obtained have validated the design calculations. Reaching the equilibrium of reaction (1) was proved by a direct mesuarement of the liquid sulphur production at acid gas consumption 40000 $m^3$/h and hydrogen sulfide concentration in acid gas 51–52%. At these conditions the liquid sulphur production was 157 liters per minute.  The calculation showed that $H_2S$ conversion degree in the reactor was 61%, which compared favourably with the thermodynamic equilibrium conversion 64% calculated for this acid gas. Since at least 2–3% of the sulphur comes out with the combustion products as vapour and mist, we concluded that thermodynamic equilibrium is reached in the reactor. The residence time in the reactor is 1.1 sec.

In the reactor with a tangential burner the conversion degree was about 48%. Consequently, in the operation of the new reactor the conversion degree is 30% higher. This increase led to an appreciable decrease in the temperature gradient in the catalytic reactors. The total temperature gradient in the two convertors has been lowered from 110–120°C to 80–85°C. When the reactor was operating at the largest capacity 60000 $m^3$/h there was not any change in the temperature difference in the catalytic convertors. Therefore, the thermodynamic equilibrium was also reached at the residence time 0.7 sec.

Analysis of the combustion products sampled after the new reactor showed a decrease in COS concentration compared with other reactors.

| Reactor design | COS concentration, vol.% |
|---|---|
| With an axis flame | 0.9–1.0 |
| With a tangential flame | 0.4 |
| The new reactor | 0.2 |

The measurements performed by the Central Laboratory of Astrakhan GPP [10] demonstrated that COS concentration in the processing gas leaving the thermal reactors accounts for 0.65% when H2S concentration in acid gas is 66–67%. This matter will be examined in Discussion.

It could be mentioned that when the new reactor operates there are no flame visible on the tube grid of the boiler as it occurs during operation of the reactor with a tangential burner. One cannot register the flame presense in the watching ports of the forechambers. The flame is completely transparent and it is the evenly red hot refractory that can only be seen. Hydrogen sulfide conversion degree in the Claus unit does not practically change during approximately three years operation period and makes up 95.5-96.0%.

DISCUSSION

The reactor described is evidently the first one designed on the basis of the results obtained during both kinetic and aerodynamic investigations. The reactor ensures a reaction of acid gas and air to proceed in two stages. The first stage is an intensive mixing of acid gas and air when the exothermic reactions with oxygen occur. This stage is considered to terminate in exterior lateral burners. The second stage is the endothermic reaction of hydrogen sulfide and sulphur dioxide. This stage proceeds in the reactor-furnace. In the beginning zone of the reactor a decaying of the rotary streams coming from the lateral burners occurs, whereas in the second part of the reactor the plug flow regime is available. It makes possible to use effectively the reactor volume and decreases the time necessary to reach the thermodynamic equilibrium.

The necessary time to reach the thermodynamic equilibrium when processing acid gas containing 51% of hydrogen sulfide is 0.7 sec. It goes without saying that the time will be less at higher concentrations of hydrogen sulfide. A lower concentration of COS observed in the combustion products permits us to conclude that the reaction of COS formation also reaches the equilibrium.

$$H_2S + CO_2 = COS + H_2O \qquad (5)$$

Really, the results of thermodynamic calculations performed in VNIIGAS [3] and presented in Table 1 prove it.

Table 1.

Thermodinamic concentrations of COS for different

acid gas ($H_2O$ - 5.6%, $CH_4$ - 2.0)

| Temperature, K | Concentration, vol.% | | |
| --- | --- | --- | --- |
| | in acid gas $H_2S$ | $CO_2$ | in combustion products COS |
| 1220 | 42.4 | 50.0 | 0.322 |
| 1342 | 62.4 | 30.0 | 0.197 |
| 1516 | 92.4 | — | 0.0102 |

The results given in Table 1 show that at processing the acid gas containing $H_2S$ - 62.4%, the concentration of COS formed makes up 0.197% that coincides with experimentally obtained value (0.2%).

Reaching the equilibrium for reactions (1) and (5) permit us to conclude that the combustion reactions which proceed some oders of magnitude faster than endothermic reactions [11] also reach the equilibrium. It means the oxygen concentratiion in the combustion products are less than $10^{-10}$ mol.fractions or $10^{-4}$ ppm. So, oxygen is practically absent in the combustion products.

Let's consider the advantages that gives the reaching thermodynamic equilibrium. An increase of sulphur yield by 30% at the thermal stage results in the decrease of temperature difference at the first catalytic convertor by 30-40°C. Besides, the less concentration of sulphur compounds entering the first catalytic convertor makes it possible to decrease temperature of the processing gas at the convertor inlet. These factors result in increase of the Claus unit conversion degree by 1-2%. (The catalyst ageing degree is higher, conversion increase is greater). A decrease in sulphur dioxide release into atmosphere as compared with that obtained at the reactors with flame burners depends on the presence as well as the type of tail gas cleaning units. For Claus units with small capacity at refineries and without the cleaning units a real decrease in tail gas release may achieve 20-40%. For the large-sized GPP Claus units with Sulfreen tail gas cleaning facilities and taking into account the lower concentration of COS, the decrease in $SO_2$ release into atmosphere may be 30-50%. For each Claus unit there exist obvious advantages in no using the special oxygen protective catalysts as well as in prolongation of the catalyst service life.


CONCLUSIONS

The new reactor ensures a reaching the thermodynamic equilibrium for the Claus reaction as well as for COS formation during a residence time 0.7 sec. The combustion products was shown not to contain oxygen. Rebuilding the existing flame burner thermal reactors by the on-coming wirls burner is not very complicated and expensive procedure but ecologically and economically advantageous one.

REFERENCES

1. H.Fischer, "sulfur costs vary with process selection", Hydrocarbon Processing, 1979, N3, p.125.

2. R.M.Schurin, V.M.Pliner. M.S.Nemirovsky, "thermodynamic investigations of the thermal stage of the sulfur recovery process", Gasovaya Promishlennost, 1983, N6, p.38.

3. A.M.Tsybulebsky, L.V.Morgun, "the Claus process thermodynamic studies", Moscow, VNIIEGASPROM, 1991.

4. J.B.Hyne, "optimum furnace configuration for sulphur recovery units", Sulphur (198), 1988, p.24.

5. P.A.Tesner, M.S.Nemirovsky, D.N.Motyl, "kinetics of the Claus reaction at 800-1200°C", Kinetika i Kataliz, 1989, 30(5), p.1232.

6. P.A.Tesner, M.S.Nemirovsky, "calculation of the Claus unit thermal stage reactor", Fizika Goreniaya i Vzryva, 1990, 26(5), p.85.

7. P.A.Tesner, M.S.Nemirovsky, D.M.Motyl and R.Kh.Rubinov, "the Claus SRU Front-End Reaction Furnace", Sulphur-91, British Sulphur, London, 1991.

8. P.A.Tesner, N.Y.Zaitzev, M.S.Nemirovsky and I.S.Slavkin. Patent of Russian Federation N 1600074, "thermal stage reactor of the Claus process", october 1993.

9. P.A.Tesner, V.I.Nasteka, M.S.Nemirovsky and D.V.Motyl, "new Front End Reaction Furnace", Sulphur-93, British Sulphur, London, 1993, p.53.

10.I.F.Belova, G.I.Litvinova, "Report of the Central Laboratory of Astrakhan GPP", 1994.

11.B.V.Potapkin, V.D.Rusanov et al, "Influence of oxygene addition on $H_2S$ dissociation kinetics at thermal plasm" Khimiaya Vysokich Energiy, 1990, 24(2), p.156.

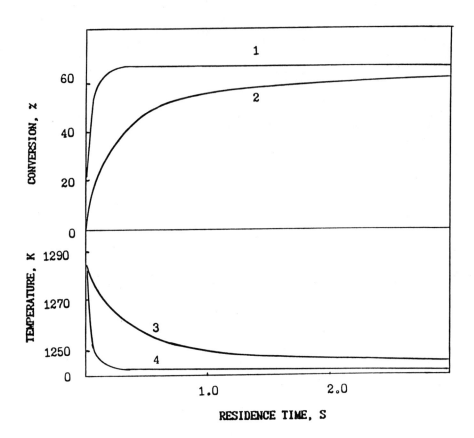

Fig. 1. Conversion (1,2) and temperature of combustion
products (3,4) vs. residence time

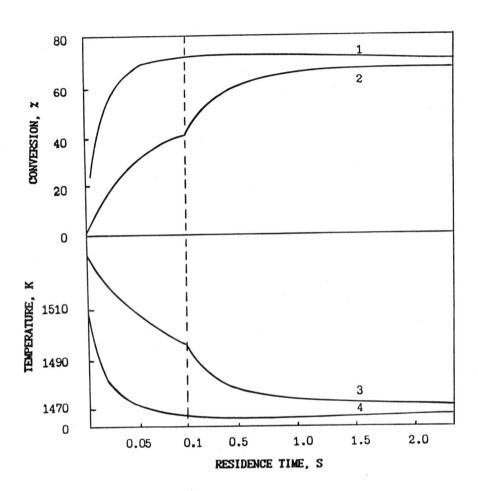

Fig. 2. Conversion (1,2) and temperature of combustion
products (3,4) vs. residence time

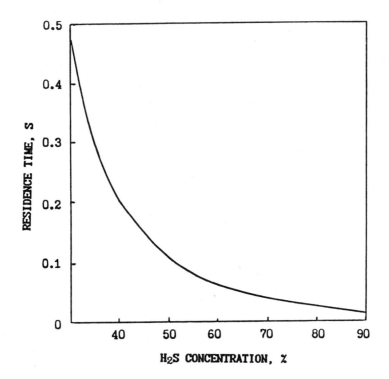

Fig. 3. Residence time vs. hydrogen sulfide concentration in acid gas

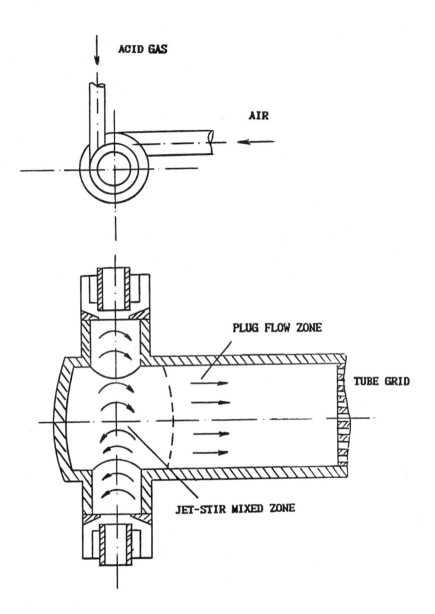

Fig. 4. Scheme of the new front-end reaction furnace
for Claus process

ESTIMATION OF FUGITIVE GASEOUS EMISSIONS

ESTIMATION DES DEGAGEMENTS GAZEUX FUGITIFS

David I. Bradshaw, David C. Carslaw and Gerard Hall
Gas Research Centre, Research and Technology, British Gas plc
Ashby Road, Loughborough, Leicestershire, LE11 3QU, UK.

## ABSTRACT

Fugitive emissions from gas treatment, storage and
transmission can be difficult to estimate accurately.  These
emissions are environmentally undesirable, and a loss of
valuable product.  British Gas has developed a methodology for
the estimation of fugitive emissions based upon a combination
of a fully mobile laboratory and Gaussian dispersion
modelling.  Validation exercises using controlled releases of
methane and comparison with results obtained simultaneously by
DIfferential Absorption Lidar (DIAL) provide confidence in
this technique as a means of estimating losses from medium to
large scale plant and a way of locating emission sources.

## RÉSUMÉ

Les dégagements fugitifs provenant du traitement, du stockage
et de la transmission du gaz peuvent être difficiles à estimer
avec précision.  Ces dégagements sont non seulement
indésirables pour l'environnement mais ils entraînent la perte
d'un produit précieux.  British Gas a mis au point une
méthodologie pour l'estimation des dégagements fugitifs basée
sur l'association d'un laboratoire entièrement mobile et d'une
modélisation de la dispersion de Gauss.  Des exercices de
validation utilisant des dégagements de méthane contrôlés et
une comparison avec des résultats obtenus simultanément par un
lidar différentiel d'absorption (DIAL) démontrent la fiabilité
de cette technique et offrent un moyen d'estimer les pertes
provenant des installations à moyenne et grande échelle et une
méthode de localisation de la source des émissions.

INTRODUCTION

Airborne emissions from large-scale plant can be a cause of concern
to local communities, environmental pressure groups, politicians
and regulatory authorities. Likewise, they are of concern to the
operators because they may be indicative of equipment performing
inefficiently. Emissions from plant fall into three main
categories. The first is from planned, continuous operations such
as flue gases from combustion plant. The second is from discrete
operations such as venting for maintenance. The third is fugitive
emissions. In the first two cases gaseous emissions can readily be
estimated from plant design, operating conditions and continuous
monitoring of vent stacks. Fugitive emissions are, however,
unplanned and are a function of a plant's propensity to leak.

Fugitive emissions of methane and of odoriferous materials are two
issues of particular concern to British Gas. Odoriferous materials
are a potential source of public nuisance and consequently their
emissions must be minimised. Methane is also an important
greenhouse gas and therefore its releases to atmosphere need to be
minimised: British Gas has already supplied estimates of emissions
of methane from its operations to the Watt Committee (1). Fugitive
emissions from plant can pose potential safety hazards and their
early identification reduces risk. Methane emissions are also a
source of lost revenue and consequently quantification of losses
allows appropriate loss reduction strategies to be adopted.

British Gas has developed and tested a methodology for measuring
total airborne emissions which means that the impact of fugitive
emissions, such loss of methane from valves and from incomplete
combustion, can now be accounted for with greater accuracy. This
methodology consists of combining results from a fully mobile
laboratory, which is known as the Area Survey Vehicle (ASV), with a
Gaussian dispersion model.

THE AREA SURVEY VEHICLE

The Area Survey Vehicle has been designed to allow it to collect
the three sets of data required to determine emission rates, namely
gas concentration, position and meteorology.

Instrumentation

The Area Survey Vehicle (ASV) is a fully mobile laboratory designed
to sample and analyse a range of airborne pollutants at one second
intervals whilst on the move. Typically it is configured to
monitor for methane and for total hydrocarbons using flame
ionisation detectors. These analysers are sensitive enough to
measure concentrations to within ± 10ppb and are manufactured by
Rotork.

Concentrations of reduced sulfur compounds are measured by using a
sulfur converter with a sulfur dioxide fluorescence analyser. The
converter removes sulfur dioxide from the sample and then oxidises
any reduced sulfur compounds into sulfur dioxide which is then
detected by the sulfur dioxide fluorescence analyser. Additional
concentrations of oxides of nitrogen are detected by means of a
chemiluminescence analyser and sulfur dioxide by means of a
fluorescence analyser. The analysers used for these species were
obtained from Monitor Labs.

Determination of the profile of a pollution plume requires
knowledge of the position of the ASV at the time of measuring the
concentrations of the pollutants. Three methods of achieving this

have been used.  The first is known as Datatrak and is a location
system developed by Securicor.  This system determines its position
by monitoring signals from land based radio beacons and is limited
to use in the UK.  The second system is a Navstar global
positioning system (GPS) which determines position from US Defense
Department satellites and thus permits operation outside the UK.
The third method is by use of a distance counter and site plans or
maps.  In this case a file is opened at a known location and closed
at another known location.  From this it is possible to relate data
from the analysers to position by linear interpolation of results
from the distance counter.

The portable meteorological station transported by the ASV consists
of a 10m mast and tripod base, which can be located on site, and a
Gill sonic anemometer.  From this wind-speed, wind-direction and
atmospheric turbulence can be calculated for the period of the
survey.

DETERMINATION OF EMISSION RATES

Concentrations measured by the ASV are a function of the dispersion
process.  As a gaseous release disperses it spreads in both the
vertical and horizontal planes.  If concentrations in the vertical
and horizontal planes are known then the total flux can be
estimated readily.  However, the ASV can only provide data from the
horizontal plane and therefore it is necessary to use a suitable
model to relate the concentrations measured to the emission rate of
the site.  A variety of models can be used and in our case we have
incorporated the NRPB-R91 Gaussian dispersion model (2) into the
software used to analyse data collected by the ASV.

The first stage of calculating the emission rate consists of
identifying the location of the principal emission sources by
driving the ASV around the site.  Figure 1 shows a typical map of
fugitive emissions of methane around a compressor site and a
superposition of the modelled plume.  The ASV is driven downwind of
the site along roads that are close to right angles to the wind
direction.  The resultant pollution plume is projected onto a line
at right angles to the plume centre and the emission source, and
the area under the plume is then calculated.  The next stage is to
perform dispersion modelling using the measured windspeed,
atmospheric turbulence, atmospheric mixing height and the roughness
of the terrain for an assumed emission rate of one gram per second.
The emission rate can now be determined by ratioing the measured
plume area against the predicted area.

Because emission rates are calculated by comparing plume areas, the
extent of horizontal plume spread is unimportant and hence a
potential source of uncertainty is avoided.  The use of plume areas
as a means of estimating emission rates is also important because
on many sites fugitive emissions arise from a number of sources.
Therefore, the measured peak is broader and less intense than would
be observed for a single source emitting the same amount of gas.
However, providing the distance between sources is small compared
with the distance to the ASV, the area under the plume will yield
the correct total emission rate for the site.

Variabilty of a plume's concentration profile in the vertical plane
is a potential source of inaccuracy.  This is most pronounced under
conditions giving rise to unstable atmospheres such as strong
sunlight, and takes the form of plume looping.  Therefore, the
emission rate calculated from a single traverse may not be
representative of the emission rate of the site.  This source of

inaccuracy is addressed by performing multiple traverses so that a
representative rate can be calculated.

Improved confidence in calculated emission rates can be gained by
consideration of plume width and the downwind distances at which
measurements are performed.  Comparison of observed and predicted
plume widths provides a valuable check on modelling assumptions.
This is useful because there is a strong correlation between
horizontal and vertical dispersion rates.

Performance of multiple traverses at a range of downwind distances
establishes whether the calculated emission rate varies with
distance.  If the assumptions made about vertical dispersion,
source location and source height in the dispersion model are
correct then the emission rate should be independent of distance.
Traverses performed at various distances can enable multiple
sources of differing heights to be distinguished and quantified
because high level sources will not produce measurable plumes in
the near-field.  Therefore, for the case shown in Figure 1
traverses across the plume at several distances downwind should be
compatible with the modelled concentrations if the modelling
assumptions are correct.

PERFORMANCE IN THE FIELD

The current methodology has undergone a number of validation trials
and has been used extensively to measure fugitive methane emissions
from British Gas operations.  Operations monitored vary in size and
complexity from terminals and offshore rigs down to pressure
reduction stations and district governors.

Validation of the ASV method has been achieved by measuring
controlled releases of methane and by comparison with alternative
methods such as Differential Absorption Lidar (DIAL).  Unlike the
ASV, DIAL can provide a concentration profile across the entire
plume.  This is achieved by firing a pulsed infra-red laser beam
through the plume. Light is scattered back from dust in the air and
returns to the detector.  By comparing the returning signal from
frequencies at which methane is absorbing and non-absorbing the
amount of methane in the beam path can be measured.  The range of
points in the gas plume is measured by the time taken for the pulse
of light to return as in radar.  It is then possible to determine
the emission rate from the plume flux and windspeed.

Controlled releases of methane have been studied using a
combination of various emission heights, rates and distances.  A
typical traverse of a plume is shown in Figure 2.  Multiple
traverses of plumes demonstrated good repeatability, and emission
rates of about 70% of the actual were calculated using NRPB-R91.
Emission rates were subsequently re-calculated using the United
Kingdom Atmospheric Dispersion Modelling System (UKADMS).  UKADMS
provides a more rigorous approach to the mechanics of dispersion
than simple Gaussian models and hence a better estimate would be
expected.  This indeed proved to be the case and an emission rate
of better than 90% of the actual rate was found.  Apart from
measuring absolute emission rates it is important to be able to
compare sources of different strengths.  Doubling the emission rate
resulted in the ratio of the calculated rates from NRPB-R91 to be
within 5% of the actual value thus demonstrating that excellent
comparison can be achieved between emission sources.

Comparison of results from a joint survey with the National
Physical Laboratory (NPL) operating their DIAL facility provides
further confidence in the ASV method.  Fugitive emissions of

methane from a liquefied natural gas (LNG) storage site have been
monitored using the ASV and NPL DIAL.  The rate calculated by the
ASV is dependent upon a range of modelling assumptions, but DIAL
provides an estimate of the emission rate directly from the flux of
the pollutant and the windspeed without recourse to dispersion
modelling.  Figure 3 shows a typical concentration map of methane
measured by the ASV downwind of the site, and Figure 4 shows the
same data plotted as concentration versus distance.  These results
clearly indicate the presence of multiple sources and thus the
contribution of each can be estimated.  Results from the DIAL also
confirmed the presence of multiple sources.  Emission rates
calculated from the two methods were within 15% of each other.

Surveys performed offshore are not constrained by the location of
roads and hence traverses over a wider range of distances can be
collected readily.  A map of methane concentrations found downwind
of two offshore platforms is shown in Figure 5.  Emission rates
were calculated for each plume and a high degree of consistency was
found over the range of distances studied which in turn improves
confidence in the modelling assumptions made in the methodology.
From the results the relative emission rates of the two rigs were
shown to be 3 to 1.  This data, used in conjunction with knowledge
of each rig's complexity, can be used to allow resources to be
allocated to plant improvements in a more efficient manner.

Measurement of emission rates requires that the location of sources
and conflicting sources from other sites are determined.
Collection of data immediately upwind of the area of interest
ensures that the presence of sources other than those of immediate
interest can be identified.  Identification of sources on site can
be provided by driving the ASV along site roads and producing a
concentration map.  From this map, and knowledge of the plant and
its operations at the time, it is possible to deduce the likely
major sources of gaseous emissions.  Although site roads are useful
for source identification, they are usually too close for modelling
to give accurate release rates.  A typical map of concentrations on
site is shown in Figure 6.  Thus from determination of the
locations of the emission sources, using a mobile laboratory to
measure the ground level concentration profile of the plume at
various downwind distances, and measurements of the local
meteorology, it is possible to provide a good estimate of the rate
of fugitive emissions from a site.

This work is now being complemented by use of a DIAL facility that
has been purchased jointly by British Gas, Shell Research and
Siemens Environmental Systems Ltd.  This system is particularly
powerful for providing detailed profiles of methane plumes and will
make a major contribution to our environmental programme.  Initial
trials have been successful in monitoring unburnt methane exiting
from a compressor stack and emissions from flare stacks.  In these
cases where the emission source is at a significant height there
are distinct advantages to be gained by using DIAL.  The choice of
whether to use the ASV method or DIAL will be a function of site
complexity, terrain and required speed of response;  however, cost,
availability and speed of deployment of the ASV will still make it
the favoured method for many sites for the foreseeable future.

CONCLUSIONS

The ASV allows rates of fugitive emissions to be determined readily
and with a good accuracy.  Various monitoring exercises have
demonstrated the modelling assumptions to be sound and the method
can resolve between separate sources that are on the same or
adjacent sites.

ACKNOWLEDGEMENTS

The authors wish to thank British Gas for permission to publish this paper.

REFERENCES

1.   Watt Committee Report Number 28, 1994

2.   R. H. Clark, Report NRPB-R91, HMSO, 1979

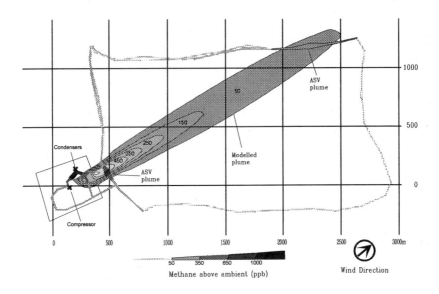

Figure 1.  Map of Measured and Modelled Methane Emissions from a Compressor

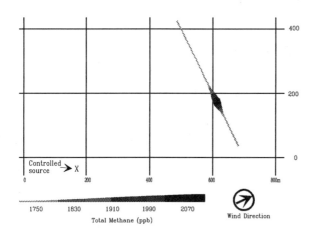

Figure 2.  Methane Plume from a Controlled Release

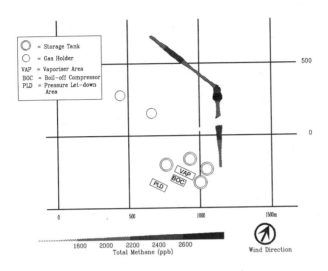

Figure 3. Methane Emissions from a Storage site

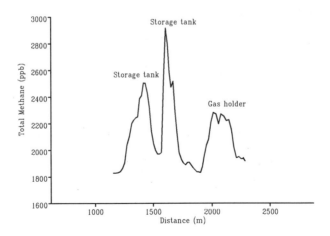

Figure 4. Cross-section of Methane Plume from a Storage Site

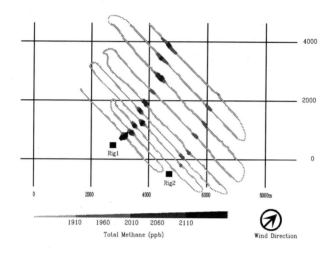

Figure 5.  Methane Emissions from Offshore Rigs

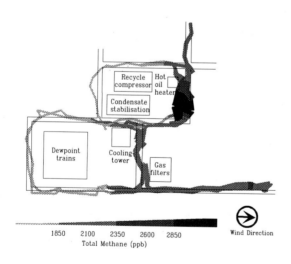

Figure 6.  Map of On-site Methane Emissions

PRESSURE ANALYSIS OF FRACTURED GAS WELLS
IN PRESSURE SENSITIVE FORMATIONS

ANALYZE DE PRESSIONS DANS LES PUITS DE GAZ FRACTURES
DANS LES MILIEUX POREUX SENSIBLES A LA PRESSION

Sergio Berumen
University of Oklahoma & PEMEX (MEX)

Djebbar Tiab
University of Oklahoma (USA)

## ABSTRACT

The forecasting of fractured gas well production is based on the assumption of constant fracture conductivity. However, when the pore pressure is reduced the porous network is deformed and tends to close, causing the fracture conductivity and formation permeability to be sensitive to pressure.

In this study, a pressure analysis method to evaluate this non-linear problem in fractured gas wells is discussed. The method of analysis is based on the direct synthesis approach which allows to analyze log-log plots of pressure and pressure derivatives without using type curve matching. Specific type curves were developed for pressure-sensitive formations by solving numerically the non-linear model. The proposed method allows to evaluate a fracture conductivity modulus, and then, the fracture conductivity as a function of pressure.

Results indicate that the pressure dependency of the conductivity effect can invalidate some of the classical results used to evaluate fractured wells.

## RESUME

Les prévisions sur la production des puits de gaz fracturés sont basées sur l'hypothese d'une conductivité constante de la fracture. La conductivité de la fracture et la perméabilité de la formation sont fonction de la pression, parce que une fois la pression de réservoir reduite, le milieux poreux se deforme et tend a se fermer.

Dans cette étude une methode d'analyse de la pression est développée pour evaluer ce problème non-lineaire dans les puits de gaz fracturés. La methode d'analyse est basée sur l'approche "Direct Synthesis" qui permet d'analyser en coordonneès log-log la pression et sa derivée sans utiliser une approximation par un type de courbe. Des types de courbes ont été developpés pour des formations sensibles à la pression, par résolution numérique d'un modèle non-lineaire. La methode proposée permet d'evaluer le module de conductivité de la fracture, et donc la conductivité en fonction de la pression.

Les resultats indiquent que la dependance de la pression sur l'effet de conductivité peut rendre invalides certains des resultats classiques utilisés pour évaluer les puits fracturés.

INTRODUCTION

Conventional well test analysis correlates field information with theoretical models on pressure responses behavior. Those models are derived from analytical solutions which use several assumptions. Even though this approach has undergone some evolution, such as the pressure derivative function[14], it has been used systematically along the well test analysis history. This approach is limited for multiphase flow, and particularly for non-linear problems.

Amongst the most important non-linear problems remaining unsolved yet, is the evaluation of fractured wells in permeable systems sensitive to pressure. The non-linearity of this problem results from the fact that as pore pressure declines the porous system tends to deform causing the formation permeability and fracture conductivity to be a function of pressure[1,3], i.e., $k(p) = f(p)$ and $C_{f_D}(p) = f(p)$. Experimental evidences demonstrate that this phenomenon is even stronger in gas tight formations than in liquid saturated formations[3,6,16,17,19,20]. Ultimately this phenomenon partially dominates the flow rate performance of fractured wells.

The introduction of the pressure derivative function by Tiab[14] in 1980 constitutes the landmark of the modern methods in well test analysis. Likewise, the first comprehensive study on pressure analysis of fractured wells considering the finite nature of the fracture conductivity was that of Cinco et al[2]. in 1981. They discovered the theory of bilinear flow, which allows to characterize finite conductivity fractures. In 1986, Wong et al[18] extended the Cinco's et al. work, and introduced new type curves to analyze fractured wells considering finite conductivity and damage conditions along the fracture. That is probably the most widely used technique to analyze artificially fractured wells. Recently in 1993, Tiab[15] introduced the direct synthesis approach, which is a method to analyze well pressure tests without using type curves matching. Based on specific characteristics of the type curves, he was able to construct simplified equations that allow to interpret the pressure behavior at different flow situations. The method overcomes the uniqueness error and/or the imaginary type curve selection error commonly introduced in the type curve matching procedure. The method has been developed for homogeneous reservoirs and also for fractured wells with infinite conductivity fractures.

The available technology previously described is based on the assumption of rigid fractures, that is, fractures whose conductivity $C_{f_D}$ is constant. However, the physics of this problem should strictly be related to a deformable fracture whose conductivity is a function of pressure, $C_{f_D} = f(p)$. Thus, the pressure dependence of the fracture conductivity leads to a non-linear problem[1].

This paper describes a method to detect and quantify the intensity of the pressure sensitive effect in artificially fractured wells, by using well test analysis. The approach used in the investigation presented in this study is based on numerical simulation of gas flow through finite-conductivity fractures sensitive to pressure, i.e. $C_{f_D}(p) = f(p)$.

PRESSURE DEPENDENCE OF PERMEABILITY AND FRACTURE CONDUCTIVITY.

Experimental results demonstrate that the permeability and conductivity of several permeable formations show an exponential behavior with pore pressure[10,13,16,17,20]. Even though the pressure sensitivity on the fracture conductivity plays a dominant role in the well pressure response, the formation permeability is also subject to deformation, and sensitive to pressure. The first formal application of this phenomenon in reservoir engineering was discussed by Vairogs et. al.[16] in 1971. They concluded that for gas tight formations the results of test analysis are not accurate unless the pressure dependence is taken into account.

Formation permeability modulus and fracture conductivity modulus are used in this work to investigate the effect of pore pressure on, respectively, formation permeability and fracture conductivity. These moduli are related to pore pressure as follows[1]:

(1)
$$\gamma = \frac{1}{k}\frac{\partial k}{\partial p} \qquad ; \quad k(p) = k(p_i)e^{-\gamma \Delta p}$$

(2)
$$\gamma_f = \frac{1}{C_{f_D}}\frac{\partial C_{f_D}}{\partial p} \qquad ; \quad C_{f_D}(p) = C_{f_D}(p_i)e^{-\gamma_f \Delta p}$$

where $k(p_i)$ and $C_{f_D}(p_i)$ are the formation permeability and fracture conductivity at initial pressure conditions, respectively.

Based on Coyner's[3] experimental results of $k$ vs $p$, Berumen[1] observed that the behavior of the formation permeability modulus $\gamma$ follows a smooth variation with pore pressure, and eventually takes a constant value. A relationship between the modulus $\gamma$ and elastic rock properties was derived coupling the Kozeny's equation and the Mackenzie's model[7,4] for spherical pore geometry with Equation 1,

(3)
$$\gamma = \frac{6a(1+\nu)}{4E}\left(\frac{p_c}{p} - b\right)$$

where $p$ is the pore pressure, $b$ is the Biot coefficient, $p_c$ is the confining pressure, $a$ is the power law in Kozeny's equation, $E$ is the Young's modulus, and $\nu$ is the Poisson's ratio. The $\gamma$ modulus can also be obtained by pre-fracturing pressure well tests analysis according to the method developed by Pedroza[11]. The fracture conductivity modulus $\gamma_f$ can be obtained by using the proposed well test method described in the following sections of this paper.

THE MATHEMATICAL MODEL.

The mathematical model developed in this study treats flow in the formation and flow in the fracture, separately. Then, some convenient boundary conditions were implemented at the interphase fracture-formation and at the wellbore. The reservoir is considered to be an infinite, horizontal slab of a deformable porous media with isotropic properties, uniform thickness saturated with a single, compressible gas fluid. Constant-rate production through a well intersected by a symmetric or asymmetric finite-conductivity vertical deformable fracture is considered. Figure 1 depicts graphically the modeling of this system.

Introducing the gas potential flow function $m(p)$, the reservoir gas flow model is given by

(4)
$$\left(\frac{\partial^2 m_D}{\partial x_D^2}\right) + \gamma_D\left(\frac{\partial m_D}{\partial x_D}\right)^2 + \left(\frac{\partial^2 m_D}{\partial y_D^2}\right) + \gamma_D\left(\frac{\partial m_D}{\partial y_D}\right)^2$$
$$+ 2\pi\left(e^{\gamma_D m_D}\right)q_{f_D}(x_{D_i}, t_D) = \alpha_D\left(e^{\gamma_D m_D}\right)\left(\frac{\partial m_D}{\partial t_D}\right)$$

where $\alpha_D$ is a dimensionless term that accounts for the changes in the viscosity-compressibility product, and $m_D$ is the dimensionless function of gas. The new parameter $\gamma_D$ is the dimensionless formation permeability modulus[1]. No-flow boundary conditions are imposed at the external boundaries of the reservoir both in $x$ and $y$ direction.

The gas flow equation for the fracture flow model is defined as

$$(5) \qquad \left(\frac{\partial^2 m_{f_D}}{\partial x_D^2}\right) + \gamma_{f_D}\left(\frac{\partial m_{f_D}}{\partial x_D}\right)^2 - \frac{\pi}{C'_{f_D}}q_{f_D}(x_D,t_D) + \frac{2\pi}{C'_{f_D}}q_{w_D}(t_D) = \pi\frac{C^{\bullet}_{f_D}}{C'_{f_D}}\left(\frac{\partial m_{f_D}}{\partial t_D}\right)$$

where the parameter $\gamma_{f_D}$ is the dimensionless fracture conductivity modulus. The wellbore condition for the gas flow model is obtained by integrating Equation 5 over the domain of the fracture. This condition is mathematically expressed as

$$(6) \qquad q_{w_D}(t_D) = \frac{1}{2}\int_{-1}^{1}q_{f_D}(x_D,t_D)dx_D + \frac{C^{\bullet}_{f_D}}{2}\int_{-1}^{1}\frac{\partial m_{f_D}}{\partial t_D}dx_D$$

where $C^{\bullet}_{f_D}$ is the dimensionless fracture storage. Other dimensionless parameters follow the standard definitions. Continuity conditions, flux density and pressure, along the interphase fracture-formation were also implemented.

It should be noted that Equations 4 and 5 are partial differential equations that exhibit a highly non-linear structure. The non-linearity of the model is due to the presence of the quadratic pressure gradient terms. These terms are introduced in the model since the formation permeability and fracture conductivity are functions of pore pressure. Likewise, the non-linearity is caused by the fracture storage and by the viscosity-compressibility terms on the right hand side of the model equations.

By introducing the transformations $p_D = \frac{1}{\gamma_D}\ln(1-\gamma_D u)$ and $p_{f_D} = \frac{1}{\gamma_{f_D}}\ln(1-\gamma_{f_D}u_f)$ the partial differential equations take a somewhat simpler form, and the non-linearity due to the squared terms are considerably weakened.[1]

SOLUTION OF THE FORMATION-FRACTURE MODEL EQUATIONS.

A numerical method based on the standard finite differences approach was used to solve the non-linear model problem. The numerical model was formulated in terms of the fully implicit procedure of Newtonian iteration. The spatial discretization of the system was designed by using a non-uniform grid whose nodes distribution was carefully selected[1]. The criterion used in selecting the nodes position was based on the fact that more nodes are needed close to the well and fracture, as well as close to the fracture's tip. Figure 2 shows the schematic grid and its nodes distribution in describing the spatial domain of the reservoir fracture model.

The fully implicit time implemented in a block centered irregular spatial grid was found to be consistent and accurate. The pentadiagonal matrix system was solved by using standard Gaussian elimination for sparse matrices[5].

DISCUSSION OF SIMULATION RESULTS.

The validation of the model was carried out by comparing the numerical solutions with those semi-analytical of Cinco et al[2] for finite conductivity fractures. The consistency of the numerical solutions were successfully tested, and it was found that the relative error was less than 1%.

Several wellbore pressure drawdown tests for different levels of pressure sensitivity in both the fracture( $\gamma_{f_D}$ ) and the formation ( $\gamma_D$ ) were simulated. As a result, several type curves were generated for different combinations of $\gamma_{f_D}$, $C_{f_D}$ and $\gamma_D$. For illustrative purposes, Figures 3 and 4 show only two of all type curves generated. The variables of interest are $C_{f_D}$, $\gamma_{f_D}$, $\gamma_D$. The results of the analysis of the new type curves showed that under pressure-sensitive conditions, the pseudo-bilinear slope takes values from 0.25 up to 0.35 depending on the $\gamma_{f_D}$ and $C_{f_D}$ combination.

Figure 5 depicts the effect of varying the formation permeability modulus on the well pressure response in a low fracture conductivity under high pressure-sensitive conditions, $\gamma_{f_D}$. It is concluded that only the pressure sensitive effect in the fracture governs the magnitude of the slope $\kappa$ on this period, so that this flow period may be characterized by $m_{w_D} = f(t_{D_{xf}}, C_{f_D}, \gamma_{f_D})$. The trend of the pressure response on this flow regime can be captured by the following general equation

$$(7) \qquad\qquad m_{w_D} \cong \frac{\alpha}{C_{f_D}^b}\, t_{D_{xf}}^{\kappa}$$

A multivariate non-linear least square fitting[8,9] was carried out to obtain the relationship between the pseudo-bilinear slope $\kappa$ and $C_{f_D}$ and $\gamma_{f_D}$,

$$(8) \qquad\qquad \gamma_{f_D} = \frac{1}{\beta} ln\left\{ \frac{\kappa - 0.25}{\zeta C_{f_D}^{\nu}} + 1 \right\} \qquad \left\{ \begin{array}{l} 0.1 \leq C_{f_D} \leq 500 \\ 0 \leq \gamma_{f_D} \leq 3 \end{array} \right.$$

where $\beta = 0.09384$, $\nu = -0.391469$ and $\zeta = 0.12104$ are constants. The initial fracture conductivity $C_{f_D}$ can be approximated by using the method of Wong et al[18].

An additional phenomenon detected in the new type curves was the pressure closure effect. The maximum points observed in the derivative function curve represents the pressure at which the fracture conductivity has lost at least 50% of its initial value. It was observed that as the pressure sensitivity along the fracture becomes stronger, the fracture closure effect causes a gradual increase in the wellbore pressure drop. This effect is also non-linearly related to the degree of fracture conductivity, $(t_D m'_D)_{max} = f(C_{f_D}, \gamma_{f_D})$. Again, the multivariate non-linear least square fitting was applied yielding the following equations to predict the pressure of occurrence of the closure fracture effect

$$(9) \qquad\qquad \Delta m(p) = \frac{1424 q_w T}{k(p_i) h_f} 10^D$$

where      $D = 0.69043 exp(-0.9532\gamma_{f_D}) - 0.40276 C_{f_D}^{-0.13585} + 0.93925$

Solving Equation 7 for the half-fracture length and the initial fracture conductivity in real dimensions gives, respectively:

$$
(10) \qquad x_f = \left\{ \frac{3488.8(0.0002637)^\kappa q_w T \, \kappa}{h_f(t*\Delta m'_w)_{b1} C_{fD}^{0.5} \{k(p_i)\}^{(1-2\kappa)} \{\phi(p_i)\mu c_t k(p_i)\}^\kappa} \right\}^{1/2\kappa}
$$

$$
(11) \qquad (k_f(p_i)w)^{0.5} = \left\{ \frac{3488.8(0.0002637)^\kappa q_w T}{h_f m_{bf} \{x_f k(p_i)\}^{(1-2\kappa)} \{\phi(p_i)\mu c_t k(p_i)\}^\kappa} \right\}
$$

where $m_{bf}$ is the slope of a graph of $\Delta m(p)$ vs $t^\kappa$, and $(t*\Delta m'_w)_{b1}$ is the value of the product $t*\Delta m'_w$ at time $t = 1hr$ on the pseudo-bilinear flow straight line ( extrapolated if necessary) of the log-log plot.

This methodology used to analyze the new type curves is known as direct synthesis[15], and is based on the proper recognition of the specific characteristics of the type curves. The procedure for interpreting fractured gas wells tests under pressure sensitive conditions is:

1. A diagnostic log-log plot of gas flow function ($\Delta m_w$) and pressure derivative ($t*\Delta m'_w$) versus time is made.

2. Apply a regression analysis to the data that define the approximate straight line with a slope close to 0.25, and calculate the exact slope $\kappa$.

3. Obtain the value of $(t*\Delta m'_w)$ at $t = 1hr$ from the pseudo-linear flow line ( extrapolated if necessary ), $(t*\Delta m'_w)_{b1}$

4. A plot of ($\Delta m_w$) versus $t^\kappa$ gives a straight line of $m_{bf}$.

5. Calculate the half fracture length $x_f$ from Equation 10. Calculate the fracture conductivity modulus by using Equation 8.

7. Calculate the pressure at which the fracture closure occurs by using Equation 9.

CONCLUSIONS

- Type curves were generated for a fractured well intercepting a pressure-sensitive fracture of finite conductivity.

- The evaluation of the pressure dependence on fracture conductivity $\gamma_{f_D}$ requires a precise slope of the data lying on the pseudo-bilinear flow period.

- The pseudo-bilinear slope takes values from 0.25 up to 0.35 depending on the conductivity and fracture conductivity modulus combination.

- The occurrence of the partial closure fracture effect can be anticipated by using the equation provided in this work.

## REFERENCES

1. Berumen, S.: "Evaluation of Fractured Wells in Pressure Sensitive Formations", *Ph.D. dissertation, University of Oklahoma, Norman, OK 1995.*

2. Cinco-Ley, H. and Samaniego, V.F.: "Transient Pressure Analysis for Fractured Wells", *J. Pet. Tech., 1749-1766, Sept. 1981.*

3. Coyner, K.B.: "Effects of Stress, Pore Pressure, and Pore Fluids on Bulk Strain, Velocity, and Permeability of Rocks", *Ph.D. dissertation, Mass. Inst. of Technol., Cambridge, Ma. 1984.*

4. Detournay, E. and Cheng, A., H-D.: "Fundamentals of Poroelasticity", *Chapter 5 in Rock Mechanics Continum Modeling, 113-171, 1991.*

5. Duff, I.S., Erisman, A.M. and Reid, J.K.: <u>Direct Methods for Sparse Matrices</u>, *Oxford University Press, Monographs on Numerical Analysis, New York, 1990.*

6. Jones, F.O. and Owens, W.W.: "A Laboratory Study of Low-Permeability Gas Sands", *J. Pet. Tech., 1631-1640, September. 1980.*

7. Mackenzie, J.K.: "The Elastic Constants of a Solid Containing Spherical Holes", *Proceedings of the Physical Society of London, 63(B1), 2-11, 1950.*

8. "Macsyma: A Symbolic Mathematics and Numerical Computation Software", *PC Macsyma 2.0, August 1994*

9. Marquardt, D.W.: "An Algorithm for Least-Squares Estimation of Nonlinear Parameters", *J. Soc. Indust. Appl. Math., Vol. 11, 431-441, Jun., 1963.*

10. Ostensen, R.W.,: "The Effect of Stress-Dependent Permeability on Gas Production and Well Testing", *SPE Formation Evaluation, v.1,n. 3, 227-235, June 1986.*

11. Pedrosa, O.A., Jr.: "Pressure Transient Response in Stress-Sensitive Formations", *paper SPE 15115 presented at the 56th California Regional Meeting of SPE, Oakland, Ca., April 2-4, 1986.*

12. Poe, B.D., Shah, P.C. and Elbel, J.L..: "Pressure Transient Behavior of a Finite-Conductivity Fractured Well With Spatially Varying Fracture Properties", *paper SPE 24707 presented at the 67th Annual Technical Conference and Exhibition of SPE, Washington, DC, Oct. 4-7, 1992.*

13. Snow, D.T.: "Fracture Deformation and Changes of Permeability and Storage Upon Changes of Fluid Pressure", *Colo. Sch. Mines Q., 63, 201-244, 1968.*

14. Tiab, D. and Kumar, A..: "Application of $P_D'$-Function to Interference Analysis", *J. Pet. Tech., 1465-1470, Aug. 1980.*

15. Tiab, D.: "Analysis of Pressure and Pressure Derivative without Type- Curve Matching - Vertically Fractured Wells in Closed Systems", *paper SPE 26138 presented at the western Regional Meeting, Anchorage, Alaska, May 26-28, 1993, J. of Petr. Science, p323-333, 11(1994)*

16. Vairogs, J., Hearn, C.L., Dareing, D.W. and Rhoades, V.W.: "Effect of Rock Stress on Gas Production from Low-Permeability Reservoirs", *J. Pet. Tech., Sept. 1971.*

17. Walls, J. and Nur, A.: "Pore Pressure and Confining Pressure Dependence of Permeability in Sandstone", *7th Formation Evaluation Symposium of the Canadian Well Logging Society, 7pp., Calgary, Alberta Canada, Oct. 21-24, 1979.*

18. Wong, D.W., Harrington, A.G. and Cinco-Ley, H.: "Application of the Pressure-Derivative Function in the Pressure-Transient Testing of Fractured Wells", *SPE Formation Evaluation, 470-480, Oct. 1986.*

19. Yves, P. and Robin, F.: "Note on Effective Pressure", *J. Geophysical Res., v.78, No.14, 2434-2437, May 10, 1973.*

20. Zoback, M.D. and Byerlee, J.D.: "Permeability and Effective Stress", *Bull. Am. Assoc. Pet. Geol., 59, 154-158, 1975.*

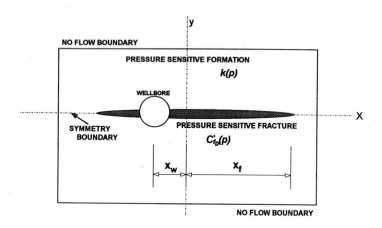

*FIG. 1 - Modeling of the pressure-sensitive fracture formation system.*

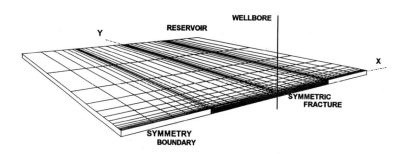

*FIG. 2 - Spatial discretization of the symmetric fracture-reservoir model by using an irregular grid system.*

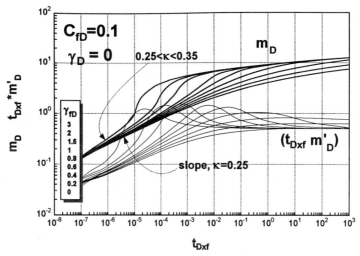

FIG. 3 Type curve showing the effect of varying the fracture permeability modulus, initial fracture conductivity, $C_{fD}$=0.1. No pressure-sensitive effect in the formation, $\gamma_D$=0.

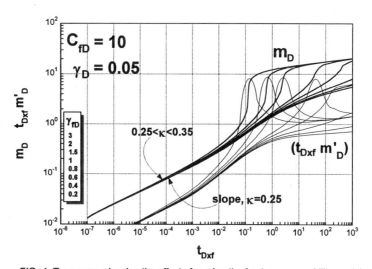

FIG. 4 Type curve showing the effect of varying the fracture permeability modulus, initial fracture conductivity $C_{fD}$=10. Pressure-sensitive effect in the formation, $\gamma_D$=0.05

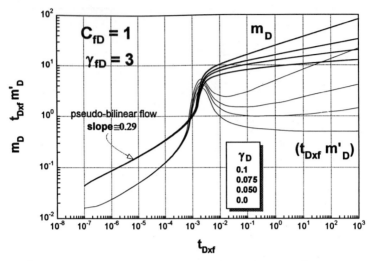

FIG. 5 *Effect of varying the formation permeability modulus on well pressure response in a fracture of low conductivity and high pressure-sensitive conditions.*

SEISMIC MONITORING SYSTEM PROJECT
FOR ARCTIC SHELF HYDROCARBONS FIELDS

PROJECT DU MONITORINGU SISMIQUE
DES GISEMENTS DES HYDROCARBURES DANS
LES REGIONS DE CHELF ARCTIGUE

M.B.Rapoport and S.Yu.Pigusov
Gubkin Oil and Gas Academy, Russia

M.M.Tikhomirov
Oil and Gas Research Inst., Russia

## ABSTRACT

While developing oil and gas fields it is necessary to monitor the exploited deposit outline. Onshore this is done through observation of operating and monitor holes which are quite sufficient in number whereas similar monitoring offshore fields is hindered due to scarcity of the holes which are extremely expensive. Seismic monitoring is possible because of the presence of hydrocarbons in rock pores influences on the seismic waves parameters - amplitude and its change with offset , time and difference of times of reflections, velocity and its dependence on frequency, wave impedance and attenuation of oscillations. This paper includes the analysis of physical effects, which was possible to be used for monitoring, and description of one of the possible design of monitoring systems using stationary sea-bottom receiving hardware and real time data processing. The drawings adduced in texts illustrate the use of some indicators.

## RESUME

Lors de l'exploitation des gisements du petrole et du gaz on a besoin du contole de demlacement du contour des hydrocarbures (le monitoring). En exploitation terrestre on ce base sur l'information deduit dans les puits, le nombre lequels est considerable. En offshore le controle est complique lorsque le nombre des puits est limite. Le monitoring par le procede sismique est possible grasse a liaison entre la presance des hydrocarbures dans les roches magasins et les pharametres du champ des ondes sismiques - amplitude, temps et la differance de temps des reflexion, impedance d'onde et attenuation des ebranlements. Dans cet article il s'agit d'analyse des effets physiques, dont on utilise dans le monitoring, on donne aussi une de construction du systeme de controle avec un dispositif d'acquisition des donnes sismiques situes sur le fond de la mer et un systeme de tretement de l'information sismique en temps reel (real time).

INTRODUCTION

The task of the seismic monitoring of the field contour
is close to the task of investigation of deposit by seismic
data ( 2,3 ), but considerable differences are present. For
monitoring, as well as for investigation, it is necessary to
use the parameters of seismic wave field, significance of which
depends on the hydrocarbons saturation. At monitoring, the high
accuracy of contour definition is more necessary. The
availability of repeated observations at study of pool changes
permits to exclude the distortions, caused by factors, not
dependent from fluid type and remaining constant during deposit
exploitation.

Important seismic effect of the field is its influence on
seismic waves velocity and on parameters determined by
velocity, for example, amplitude of reflections. At monitoring
the role of this effect grows due to elimination of influence
of other factors marked above. The other effect is the
increasing of the seismic energy dissipation, which also can be
found out by seismic data. The parameters determined by this
effect - decrement of absorption or seismic quality factor and
phase velocity dispersion - are measured independently of
measurement of velocity parameters and their joint
interpretation increases the reliability of results.

Seismic prospecting is rather expensive kind of
researches. Seismic monitoring using periodically repeated
observations is especially expensive. Such observations are
especially difficult to conduct on Arctic shelǐ with difficult
ice conditions. The opportunity of successful development of
the seismic monitoring method and its economic efficiency
depends from decision of this task.

We consider both mentioned problems.

THE INFLUENCE OF HYDROCARBONS FIELD ON SEISMIC WAVES

The effects displayed the influence of hydrocarbons field
are good investigated at oil and gas prospecting. The
parameters - indicators of hydrocarbons are subjected to
difficult, multifactorial influence of various physical
processes, but at monitoring, in difference from prospecting,
many from acting factors remain constant ones. It facilitates
the revealing variations of wave field parameters, caused by
field variations.

The parameters of all volume waves (P-waves and S-waves)
are subjected to variations, but the study of S-waves is
complicated, especially offshore. Therefore we below consider
only the P-waves.

The real geological media in field area is nonlinear and
nonelastic, while seismic prospecting is usual based on ideal
and elastic model. In frameworks of such model it is possible
to investigate the velocity of waves propagation and its
variations, amplitude of reflections, wave impedance and some
other parameters.

We use the parameters of seismic inelasticity, connected
with seismic energy dissipation - absorption and velocity
dispersion as hydrocarbons indicators. Study of these
parameters requires of nonelastic model assumption. These
indicators are investigated in frameworks of linear model of

the media. The application of nonlinear model the media can give the new opportunities, over than we now work.

The seismic waves velocity

The seismic waves velocity is one of the important parameters of the media, determined by seismic data. The velocity is considerable increased when fluid replacement in layer ( from hydrocarbons to water ) takes place (Figure 1). Velocity depends and from other factors - lithology, porosity, depth, fluid pressure. Only last factor - fluid pressure - changes during field exploration. This change can mask the change, caused by hydrocarbons replacement, and to distort results of monitoring.

The difference of times of reflections

It is possible to use the difference of times of reflections from two boundaries upper (A) and below (C) productive layer (B) (Figure 2,3).This parameter is sensitive to velocity variations and can be measured independently.

Thus velocity variations in layer are averaged on all thickness between reflectors, that reduces the effect. Velocity definition in seismic data processing also requires the use of interval of depth, which usually considerably surpasses the capacity of productive layer. This is results in velocity averaging and its variation in interval of analysis and in reduction of field effect.

The amplitude of reflection

The amplitude of reflection is determined by contrast of the seismic border, i.e. velocity relation in contacting layers. In comparison with parameters of velocity and differences of times amplitude values can be in addition distorted by influence of second from contacting layers, but this influence remains constant and at monitoring does not distort the result.

The amplitude of reflections as the indicator of hydrocarbons presence is the most easily determined in case of sand-clay section ( Figure 3 ). If the 3-D seismic data are present, it is possible to make up a map of normalized amplitudes and the of abnormal amplitudes will image productive zone and its change during exploration.

Instead of direct measurements of amplitudes of seismic oscillations it is possible to use parameters, determined on the basis of Hilbert transformation. The amplitude of reflections as the indicator of hydrocarbons is found out in papers on seismic monitoring often than other parameters (1).

The new method AVO ( Amplitude Variation with Offset ) is more closely than amplitude connected with fluid type. The application of AVO is possible when large angles of fall of seismic wave on the boundary take place. This fact practically limits depth of analysis at monitoring and the AVO advantages in comparison with method of amplitudes are less, than at prospecting. But data AVO should be used.

The wave impedance

Seismic section of wave impedance, obtained as the

reversive decision of one-dimensional dynamic task ( method
VELOG ), permits to find favorable for field allocation the
sites of layer, describing by lowered significances. Except
reduction of velocity, reduction of density has an effect.
Usually the lowered wave impedance can be interpretated as the
result of porosity increasing, but fluid influence takes place
undoubtedly. Therefore wave impedance variation analysis is one
of means for field contouring at monitoring.

The seismic waves absorption

        The nonelastic absorption of seismic oscillations is
displayed in additional ( to divergence and scattering )
attenuation of amplitudes and in gradual downturn of
frequencies of oscillations. The absorption can be determined
as the vertical gradient of module of frequent spectrum. As
well as other parameters - indicators, its measurement is
accompanied by distortions, mainly - owing to interferension.
For noise weakening it is necessary to low vertical resolution,
which is less, than at velocity measurements. The absorption
value is usually described by quality factor Q. But it is
inconvenient to operate with it , because at Q grows infinitely
absence of absorption. More suitable value is the decrement of
absorption, which is reverse value of Q.

        In modern seismic data processing the absorption is used
as the auxiliary parameter for improvement of deconvolution and
migration. However, absorption is a parameter, the most closely
connected with HC availability (2,3) (Figure 4). If field has
single or considerably distinguished in depth productive
layers, the absorption is the main indicator for monitoring.
But if distance between productive layers is measured by tens
of meters, the use of absorption at monitoring is complicated
due to low resolution of the method.

The phase velocity dispersion

        In ideal-elastic media the velocity does not depend on
the frequency. In seismic prospecting velocity dispersion is
usually less than error of measurements and does not play a
practical role. It is experimentally found out that in  pools
velocity dispersion can be very strong ( 2-5 % ) at frequency
band 10-50Hz. This fact permits to consider this parameter as
the HC indicator ( 4,5 ). Velocity dispersion existence is
closely connected with absorption and was predicted by theory
for linear model, but because of nonlinearity of the media the
quantitative ratio can be different from theoretical ones.

        Velocity dispersion can be determined by vertical
gradient's of phase spectrum. Therefore its vertical resolution
is the same as for absorption measurements. At present velocity
dispersion is basically used together with analysis of
absorption, as correlation of both parameters permits to
exclude the false anomaly, caused by distortions.


        All these parameters are complicated by measurements
errors and distortions. But use their sets in complex
interpretation allows us to increase the accuracy of study of
field contour. Interpretation includes the editing of separate
parameters, their weighing in accordance with their
informativity and calculation of average weighted summary
parameter, the most precisely describing change of field
contour.

THE OBSERVATION SYSTEM

3-D Seismic observations are necessary for detailed study of changes of field contour. The total system of 3D observations, which was necessary to be repeated each some months, is too expensive. But at monitoring the repeated observations are necessary only in areas of contours and its probable changes. Besides in difference from seismic prospecting, the monitoring is carried out on known structure with known contour and field depth, and it is enough to study the narrow area along the contour and to calculate the necessary aquisition system using wave field modelling.

One of possible systems of observation is shown in Figure 5. The line of geophones is placed along the line of contour at its internal part, as the contour displaces in this part. The lines of explosions are orthogonal to line of geophones and in common form the system of 3D observation, elucidating the area of contour.

Usual floating streamer can be used for seismic data aquisition. But if the work is conducted in the ice presence or, if the streamer passing is interfered of building, it is preferable to use sea-bottom aquisition telemetering system. The absence of low-velocity noise permits to lower its cost, after reducing or after removing the grouping of geophones. The output of telemetering system is connected to computer, installed on the sea-coast on one of buildings.

The small vessel lay the line of explosion . In ice conditions it can be the ice breaker or vessel, following ice breaker. The navigating information also arrives on computer.

The total scanning of investigated contour or its) important site is proceeded with periodicity, determined by simulation of layer exploitation. This period can be the few months. At this time it is necessary to conduct all observations and to process data on computer.

THE PROCESSING SYSTEM

The investigated area at monitoring is limited by area of contour and by interval of depth (time), containing the field. Therefore for processing it is possible to use the usual computing platform of average productivity. The regime of processing follows to relate to real-time regime, as it should be executed at time, not exceeding period of monitoring.

The software package of processing system executes the following functions:

1. Reception of oscillations and geometry assignment in formats SEG-Y in view of navigating information.

2. Restoration of amplitudes, editing, statics and record in data base.

3. Velocity analysis and interval velocity calculation.

4. Hilbert transformation, calculation of instant amplitudes.

5. Prestack 3D migration.

6. Semiautomatic interactive phase tracing.

7. Definition of difference of times.

8. Spectral analysis of oscillations.

9. Estimation of parameters of seismic inelasticity.

10. Processing of fields of separate indicators ( elimination of background, definition of variations, weighing etc. ).

11. Calculation of field of summary parameter - indicator of field changes.

12. Visualization of the map of summary parameter and conclusion about change of contour.

CONCLUSIONS

* For seismic monitoring of exploited hydrocarbons fields it is possible to use variations of parameters of wave field, which are described as by elastic model of geological media (velocity, difference of times, amplitude of reflections etc.), as model with dissipation ( decrement of absorption or quality factor, dispersion of phase velocity ).

* The economic system of monitoring, consisting from receiving system located along line of contour and orthogonal lines of sources, which provides 3D seismic prospecting in area of contour of deposit is offered. The system of observations is calculated by modeling of wave field on deposit.

* Receiving system can be realized as a stationary sea-bottom telemetering system, which can work in heavy ice conditions and on site with numerous buildings. The real-time data processing at the time, not exceeding period of observations, permits operatively to receive the information about field change at its exploitation.

REFERENCES

1.   Anderson A.N., Boulanger A, Wei He et al., 1995, Method described for using 4D seismic to track reservoir fliud movement: Oil and Gas Journal, vol.93, N14, p. 70-74

2.   Rapoport, M.B., Rapoport L.I., Ryjkov, V.I., 1992, Usage of seismic waves absorption method in exploration of hydrocarbons: Abstract of papers,54 EAEG Meeting,Paris

3.   Rapoport, M.B., Rapoport L.I., Ryjkov, V.I., Parnikel V.E., Kately V.A., 1994, Method AVD (Absorption and Velocity Dispersion): Testing and Using on the oil deposit in Western Siberia,Abstract of papers,56 EAEG Meeting,Vena

4.   Rapoport, M.B., Ryjkov, V.I., 1994, Seismic velocity dispersion: An indicator of hydrocarbons: Abstract of papers,64 SEG Meeting,Los Angeles

5.   Ryjkov, V.I., Rapoport, M.B., 1994, Study of a seismic inelasticity from VSP: Abstract of papers,56 EAEG Meeting,Vena

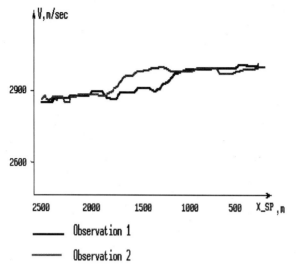

Figure 1. Interval velocity changes during field exploitation.

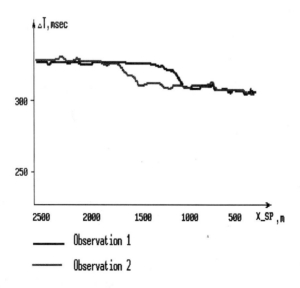

Figure 2. Difference of times of reflections changes during
field exploitation.

A.

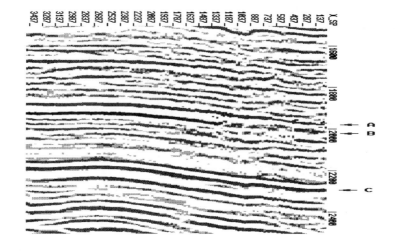

B.

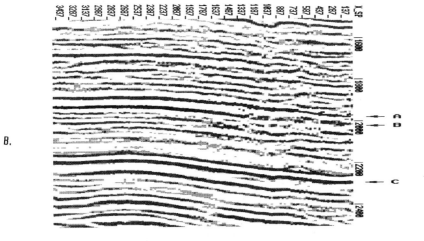

Figure 3. Amplitude of reflection changes during field
         exploitation.
         ( A- Observation 1, B- Observation 2 )

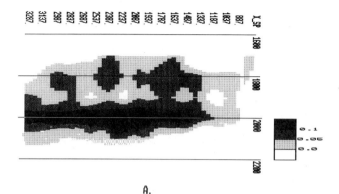

A.

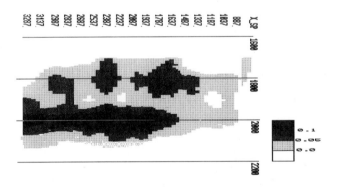

B.

Figure 4. Changes of seismic waves attenuation during
          field exploitation.
          ( A- Observation 1, B- Observation 2 )

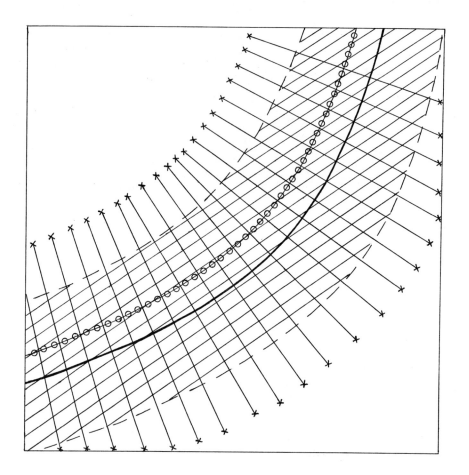

Figure 5. The observation system for monitoring.

×——×  Sources line

••••••  Receivers Line

⁄⁄⁄⁄  Investigated area

——  Contour line

RELATIVE PERMEABILITY AND THE MICROSCOPIC
DISTRIBUTION OF WETTING AND NONWETTING
PHASES IN THE PORE SPACE OF BEREA SANDSTONE

PERMÉABILITÉ RELATIVE ET DISTRIBUTION MICROSCOPIQUE
DES PHASES MOUILLANTE ET NON MOUILLANTE
DANS LES ESPACES POREUX DES GRÈS DE BÉRÉA

E.M. Schlueter and P.A. Witherspoon
Lawrence Berkeley Laboratory, University of California, USA

## ABSTRACT

Experiments to study relative permeabilities of a partially saturated rock have been carried out in Berea sandstone using fluids that can be solidified in place. 2-D SEM photomicrographs of rock cross-sections are employed to examine the occupied pore space after the experiment. The effective permeability of the pore spaces not occupied by the wetting fluid (paraffin wax) or the nonwetting fluid (Wood's metal), have been measured at various saturations after solidifying each of the phases. The tests were conducted on Berea sandstone samples that had an absolute permeability of about 600 mD ($600 \times 10^{-15}$ m$^2$). The shape of the laboratory-derived relative permeability vs. saturation curves measured with the other phase solidified conforms well with typical curves obtained using conventional experimental methods. The corresponding wetting and nonwetting fluid distributions at different saturations are presented and analyzed in light of the role of the pore structure in the invasion process, and their impact on relative permeability and capillary pressure. Irreducible wetting and nonwetting phase fluid distributions are studied. The effect of clay minerals on permeability is also assessed.

## RÉSUMÉ

Des études experimentales relatives à la perméabilité de roches partiellemment saturées ont été effectuées sur du grès de Béréa et cela en en utilisant des fluides pouvant être solidifiés sur place. La photomicrographie 2-D SEM des sections de roches a été employée pour examiner l'espace occupé après experience. La perméabilité effective des espèces des pores non occupés par le fluide mouillant (Paraffine solide) ou par le fluide non mouillant (Métal Wood's) a été mesurée à différents degrés de saturations après solidification de chaque phase. Les tests ont été conduits sur des échantillons de grès de Béréa qui ont une perméabilité absolue de 600 mD ($600.10^{-15}$ m$^2$). L'allure des courbes obtenues par la méthode choisie et relatives aux tracés de la perméabilité en fonction de la saturation est semblable à celle obtenue par d'autres méthodes classiques. La correspondance de distribution entre fluide 'mouillant' et fluide 'non mouillant' à différents degrés de saturation est présentée et analysée en mettant en jeu le rôle de la structure des pores dans les processus d'invasion et leur impact sur la perméabilité relative et la pression capillaire. La distribution entre phases mouillante et non mouillante est aussi étudiée. L'effet des argiles minérales sur la perméabilité a été aussi examiné.

## INTRODUCTION

Relative permeability and its associated capillary pressure effects are relevant to problems such as enhanced oil recovery and waste remediation and/or isolation. About 50% or more of the original oil-in place is left in a typical U.S. oil reservoir by traditional primary and secondary (i.e., water-flooding) techniques (1). This unrecovered oil is a large target for enhanced or tertiary oil recovery methods that are being developed. The concept of relative permeability is introduced when extending Darcy's law for single phase flow to the multiphase realm (2). It is generally assumed that relative permeabilities to immiscible fluids are only functions of saturation. A great number of experimental investigations (3,4) substantiate this assumption, within limits. For example, Calhoun (5) found that the chemical composition of the fluids do not matter much, and that the relative permeability functions are approximately the same for any 'wetting-nonwetting' fluid system. This is a direct consequence of the fact that the microstructure of reservoir rocks strongly influences the mobilization and distribution of fluids in the pore space. Moreover, such factors as (1) fluid/fluid properties-interfacial tension (IFT), viscosity ratio, density difference, phase behavior, and interfacial mass transfer; (2) fluid/solid properties-wettability, ion exchange, adsorption, and interaction; and (3) magnitude of applied pressure gradient, gravity, and aging have been found to play roles in interpreting the motion and distribution of oil in petroleum reservoirs (6,7).

The relative permeabilities are empirical coefficients which appear in the continuum form of Darcy's law for two-phase flow through porous media:

$$\frac{q_w}{A} = \frac{-k_{rw}k}{\mu_w}\frac{dp_w}{dx} \tag{1}$$

$$\frac{q_{nw}}{A} = \frac{-k_{rnw}k}{\mu_{nw}}\frac{dp_{nw}}{dx} \tag{2}$$

where $q_w$ and $q_{nw}$ are the volumetric flowrates of the wetting and nonwetting phases, $\mu_w$ and $\mu_{nw}$ are the viscosities of those phases, $dp_w/dx$ and $dp_{nw}/dx$ are the macroscale pressure gradients in those phases, and $A$ is the cross-sectional area, perpendicular to the flow, of the porous medium. $k_{rw}k$ and $k_{rnw}k$ are the permeabilities to the wetting and nonwetting phases. $k$ is the permeability of the porous medium when only one phase is present, and $k_{rw}$ and $k_{rnw}$ are the wetting and nonwetting phase relative permeabilities. The relative permeabilities depend upon wetting-phase saturation, $S_w$ - the fraction of pore volume occupied by the wetting phase. $S_{nw}$, the nonwetting phase saturation, is always given by $S_{nw} = 1 - S_w$.

As Eqs. (1) and (2) show, the relative permeability factor is an empirical representation of a well-defined transport process in a highly complex pore space geometry and topology. In spite of this complexity, symplified models of the pore structure have been proposed (8,9,10). However, such parameters as pore body and pore throat distributions, pore coordination numbers and individual fluid-phase coordination numbers as a function of saturation which are implemented in the mathematical models have not been determined experimentally. This is due in part to the lack of good experimental techniques required for visualizing three-dimensional (3-D) microstructures in natural porous media while maintaining the original pore and phase geometry. Therefore, we decided to work on this problem with several main objectives in mind: (1) to further develop an experimental technique initiated by Yadav et al. (11) that would allow measurement of relative permeability for the full range of saturation, (2) to visualize directly 2-D pore structure and wettabilities for the full range of saturation, (3) to interpret experimental data and fluid distributions qualitatively and quantitatively with respect to pore geometry and topology, (4) to evaluate relative permeability data in terms of microphysics and microchemistry of the processes involved (i.e., effect of clay minerals coating pores), and (5) to compare relative permeability and associated capillary pressure experimental data obtained using conventional methods.

## APPARATUS AND PROCEDURE

The apparatus that was used in this study was designed to measure simultaneously both hydraulic and electrical conductivity (12). The rock core (5 cm in diameter and 5 cm in length) is encased in its rubber jacket and placed in the test cell. The test cell base is connected directly to the bottom of the sample, and a centrally-located orifice is attached to allow fluids to flow through the mounted core. A confining pressure of 50 psi (3.4 atm) is applied using nitrogen gas. Fluid flow through the core is controlled by a syringe pump that provides constant flow rates. The basic procedure used for measuring permeability is first to vacuum saturate each core completely with triple-distilled water. Distilled water is then pumped through the core, and flow is continued for a sufficient time to establish constant pressure readings. It was found that about four pore volumes of water are required to achieve steady state. In our experiments, we used samples of Berea sandstone, which is a homogeneous sedimentary rock used as a reference rock in the petroleum industry. The intrinsic permeability and porosity of a Berea sandstone core are about 600 mD (600 $\times$ 10$^{-15}$ m$^2$) and 22%, respectively.

## EFFECT OF WETTING PHASE SATURATION

To determine the effect of partial fluid saturation on permeability, we utilized Berea sandstone samples that had been permeated with triple-distilled water to measure the single phase hydraulic conductivity. This procedure was applied to every sample to find the permeability before paraffin application. The samples were then oven dried. After measuring the permeability, the samples were partially filled with paraffin wax at controlled saturations of 20%, 30%, 40%, 50%, 60%, and 70%. Paraffin wax is a wetting phase composed of a mixture of solid hydrocarbons of high molecular weight with a density of 0.76 g/cm$^3$, a dynamic viscosity of about 3 $\times$ 10$^{-3}$ Pa·s at 150°C, and a melting point of 56°C. The paraffin is applied at temperatures higher than its melting point in the core axial direction, and until uniform saturation is observed throughout the sample. The paraffin is then solidified in place at ambient temperature conditions. After paraffin application, the rock grain surfaces became hydrophobic. To measure the effective permeability, the rock samples that were partially saturated with paraffin were permeated with distilled water. The effective permeability of the pore spaces not occupied by the wetting fluid was measured in core samples in which electrical conductivity had been measured previous to paraffin impregnation (Case A). Experiments in which electrical conductivity had not been measured previous to paraffin impregnation were repeated on a new and clean set of samples. Good agreement, within experimental error, was found between the two sets of experiments A and B. The extrapolated value of permeability at zero paraffin saturation obtained from experimental set B ($\sim$ 600 mD) is higher than the measured value of permeability obtained at the same saturation when using triple-distilled water ($\sim$ 300 - 400 mD). A possible explanation of this phenomenon is given in a later section. The relative permeability to the nonwetting phase obtained as a ratio of effective permeability data of the pore spaces not occupied by the wetting fluid to absolute permeability is shown in Fig. 1a.

### Effect of Pore Structure and Topology

To understand how pore structure and topology control permeability, the relative permeability to the nonwetting phase (Figure 1a) has been studied in light of the wetting-fluid distributions at each saturation regime (Figures 2 to 4) with the aid of a complete rock pore cast. The rock pore cast was obtained from a rock specimen that had been fully impregnated with Wood's metal alloy and the quartz grains removed by hydrofluoric acid. The rock pore cast clearly reveals that the pore space is composed of grain-contact porosity and intergranular porosity. Paraffin imbibition occurs because surface tension effects encourage the displacing fluid to advance. The overall dynamics of the wetting phase imbibition process is as follows: In the grain-contact pore space, in the smaller throats, and in the surface capillary grooves, capillary pressure is high, and the paraffin will advance quickly to the next pore. The pores exert much less capillary pressure, and for a given pressure difference between the phases only the smaller pores will fill. Once a pore is filled, the paraffin will next fill all throats leading from it, again rapidly. A new set of pores will be reached and the process continues. Therefore, during paraffin imbibition the flow dynamics are pore-dominated.

Figure 2 shows a scanning electron microscope (SEM) photomicrograph collage of a Berea sandstone specimen that has been partially saturated with approximately 20-30% paraffin. The gray phase corresponds to quartz grains, the white phase corresponds to pores that have been impregnated with paraffin, and the black phase corresponds to the remaining pore space, which was filled with blue epoxy for imaging purposes. Paraffin has invaded grain-contact pore space (i.e., thin sheets and micropores) and intergranular pore space connected by smaller throats, but has only coated the available intergranular channels connected by larger throats. A minor effect on effective permeability is observed (Figure 2). Therefore, the fraction of the pore structure connected by smaller constrictions (e.g., grain-contact pore space) do not contribute much to effective permeability. Figure 3 shows an SEM photomicrograph collage of a rock specimen partially saturated with approximately 40-50% paraffin. At this stage, we are filling main intergranular conduits connected by the larger throats. A substantial effect on effective permeability is observed. Figure 4 shows an SEM photomicrograph collage of a rock specimen partially saturated with approximately 60-70% paraffin. We have filled almost all intergranular conduits connected by larger throats. A few intergranular pores not well connected still remain unfilled. When paraffin saturation is $\sim$ 70%, the whole pore structure behaves as though hydraulically disconnected.

Irreducible Wetting Phase Saturation

Overall, it is observed that that the wetting phase is confined to a continuous network of conduits throughout the porous medium (Figure 2). It is composed of clusters of intergranular pores, edges, corners and wedges of intergranular pores, capillary channels present on rough surfaces of pores, and single grain-contact pores. Since the wetting fluid at the 'irreducible saturation' limit forms a hydraulically connected continuum, it is possible to reduce the 'irreducible wetting phase saturation' progressively, at least in principle. Therefore, the 'irreducible wetting phase saturation' is not constant and becomes a function of the externally applied pressure.

Thus, the existence of the 'irreducible wetting phase saturation' in a consolidated rock such as Berea sandstone is due to the fact that (1) grain-contact pores have narrow throats and large surface area, (2) pores have corners (angular cross sections), and (3) the pore surface is rough at the microscopic scale.

## EFFECT OF CLAY MINERALS

X-ray diffraction studies by Khilar and Fogler (13), in conjunction with scanning electron microscopy and energy-dispersive x-ray analysis (12) indicate that Berea sandstone contains about 8% by weight of dispersable and swelling clays (mainly kaolinite with some illite and smectite). The injection of a fluid such as triple-distilled water whose solution chemistry is not compatible with the porous rock in its natural state can bring significant reductions in the permeability. This is just the manifestation of peptization and flocculation of clay particles in Berea sandstone. Khilar and Fogler (13) found that when flow is switched from salt water to fresh water, clay particles are released from the pore wall. The particles then migrate in the direction of the flow and are trapped at throats which results in blockage of the pores of the sandstone, decreasing the permeability. For electrolyte solutions with cations of valence 1, at pH = 7, a critical salt concentration (0.07 M for sodium chloride solution at 30°C) has been found below which clay particles are released from Berea sandstone pore walls (13). Particle migration is thought to be the most important mechanism in water-sensitive Berea sandstone due to the fact that the amount of swelling clays is minimal. The peptization and flocculation of clay particles in Berea sandstone may be explained in terms of double-layer theory. The major forces that hold the clay particles to the pore walls are the London-van der Waals forces of attraction. The forces causing the detachment of the clay particles are the double-layer forces of repulsion and possibly, under conditions of high flow rate, the hydrodynamic shear. Calculations show these two forces of double-layer repulsion and hydrodynamic shear to be the most probable cause for particle release (14). Experimental observations (13) strongly suggest that the double-layer force of repulsion may be the dominant cause of particle release. These observations include the two most important parameters that govern the stability of the colloidal suspension of clay particles: temperature and type of cation. More importantly, the phenomenon occurs only at relatively low salt concentration, where the double-layer repulsive forces are large.

It is important to recognize that the clay minerals present in the rock have been immobilized by coating pores with hydrocarbon paraffin. Therefore, the permeability extrapolated to paraffin saturation of zero (i.e., no hydrocarbon paraffin) corresponds to either the permeability of the clean rock without clays or the permeability of the rock with clay, but with brine as flowing fluid (with concentration above critical salt concentration if monovalent cations are employed). This hypothesis was verified by partially removing clays in a Berea sandstone core by acid treatment with a mixture of 6% hydrochloric and 1.5% hydrofluoric acids (Suarez-Rivera, personal communication, 1991). After the core was treated and clays flushed out, the permeability was found to be 574 mD, higher than the measured value obtained using triple-distilled water ($\sim$ 300 - 400 mD).

## EFFECT OF NONWETTING PHASE SATURATION

In this experimental investigation, we have sought to examine the relationship between the microscopic pore occupancy by the nonwetting fluid and its effect on effective permeability and capillary pressure.

We have used three-dimensional imbibition of a nonwetting Wood's metal alloy instead of the conventional mercury porosimetry. This technique offers the advantage of allowing analysis of the occupied pore space after the experiment. Wood's metal is an alloy of about 43% Bi, 38% Pb, 11% Sn, and 9% Cd, with a specific gravity of 9.6, a viscosity of about $1.3 \times 10^{-3}$ Pa·s at 75°C, and a surface tension of about 400 mN/m (11). The apparatus for the three-dimensional imbibition experiments consists of a metallic container of Wood's metal placed in a metal vacuum chamber provided with a lucite window and surrounded by a heating element to keep the metal molten (melting point varies from about 50°C to 70°C, depending on its composition). A micrometer is attached to the metallic container to determine the pressure at which the Wood's metal first enters the specimen. The 5 cm-long and 5 cm-diameter sandstone sample is first oven-dried, and then immersed in the molten Wood's metal in the metallic container and placed in the metal vacuum chamber. Then the sample is de-aired by applying a full vacuum for about 60 minutes, until no air bubbles are observed through the lucite window. A sub-atmospheric pressure is applied by drawing a partial vacuum, which is maintained at the desired value by a regulating valve until capillary equilibrium is achieved. Each sample was allowed to imbibe at a fixed equilibrium pressure for approximately 90 minutes, at a fixed pressure, until no movement of Wood's metal was noticed through the lucite window. At a pressure of about 5 to 6 psia, the micrometer signaled the first indication of Wood's metal entering the pore space (probably an edge effect on the sample sides). The Wood's metal imbibition experiment was repeated on several samples by applying pressure externally under quasistatic conditions in the range of approximately 6 to 14 psia. The imbibed samples were cut into four axial quarters, each of which had a different saturation. To minimize the effect of gravity (hydrostatic) gradient, we took the top quarter of each imbibed specimen at a particular equilibrium pressure and measured its saturation. Figure 1b shows the Wood's metal imbibition curve, in which the volume of Wood's metal intruded (normalized by the total pore volume) is plotted vs. the applied pressure. Fluid saturation increases rather sharply with a corresponding small increase in capillary pressure in the saturation range from about 10 to 50% (Fig. 1b). After Wood's metal application, the rock samples were vacuum-saturated and permeated with triple-distilled water to measure the effective permeability. Figure 1a shows the relative permeability curve to the wetting phase, measured at various saturations (in a Berea sandstone of absolute permeability of $\sim$ 600 mD).

Effect of Pore Structure and Topology

To understand how pore structure and topology control the physical property under consideration, we have studied the effective permeability and capillary pressure data in light of the nonwetting fluid distributions observed at each equilibrium pressure. For this purpose, optical and scanning electron microscopic examinations of the tops of samples (after cutting off 3 mm) have provided valuable insights into the pore-level complexity of the natural porous media. In the Wood's metal imbibition process, some external pressure is needed to overcome surface tension and push the Wood's metal through the pores and throats. Large throats, with their comparatively weak capillary pressures, will fill more readily than small throats. Once the fluid reaches a pore, capillary pressure is reduced, and the pore will fill rapidly. In this process, the flow dynamics are mainly controlled by the throats. Isolated regions will occur because a region of large throats surround a region of constricted throats.

Figure 5 shows an optical photograph of the nonwetting fluid distributions obtained in axial quarters in the pressure range 6.8 to 7.7 psia. It is observed that the nonwetting fluid flow network is composed of a set of imbibing clusters correlated in space. At every pressure step, the nonwetting fluid resides in the pores accessible through throats with a radius larger than that corresponding to the current equilibrium capillary pressure. As the pressure increases, the nonwetting phase saturation increases, and the nonwetting fluid invades successively smaller pores and becomes connected to regions which were separated from this phase by small throats. At 6.8 psia (Fig. 5), the fluid has preferentially penetrated the sample sides. The saturation is greatest near the perimeter of the sample, and least at the center. This observation suggests that pores near the cylindrical surface of the sample are better connected than those towards the center. This interconnection could arise from exposure of pores where they intersect the surface, or from damage adjacent to this surface. At 6.9 psia (Fig. 5), a saturation gradation is observed in the direction of flow at this pressure (preferentially horizontal). The longer flow paths are connected by smaller constrictions, so fewer flow channels are going to the sample center starting from all available channels at the sample surface. At pressures of 7.2 psia (Fig. 5) and greater, the nonwetting fluid invades more and more smaller pores, becoming connected to regions that were separated to this phase by smaller pores, and the clusters of nonwetting phase become larger and larger.

Figure 6 shows an SEM photomicrograph collage of a rock specimen saturated with about 30% Wood's metal at 7.2 psia equilibrium pressure. Large percolating clusters have been formed. There are relatively few intergranular conduits connected by larger throats filled with the nonwetting phase. At this stage, a substantial effect on effective permeability is observed. Thus, we have found that a large percentage of the permeability of the medium is contributed by a relatively small number of intergranular conduits connected by larger throats of narrow size distribution and of high hydraulic conductance.

Irreducible Nonwetting Phase Saturation

In contrast to the previously discussed 'irreducible wetting phase saturation', it is observed that the trapped clusters of a nonwetting fluid are separate entities that are not hydraulically interconnected with each other (Figure 3). We have found that when the wetting phase saturation is about 70%, the effective permeability is zero. Thus the nonwetting fluid simply ceases to flow when its saturation falls below the irreducible nonwetting phase saturation limit ($\sim$ 30%) because its continuity breaks down, leaving isolated stranded clusters of disconnected fluid.

RESULTS AND DISCUSSION

Experimental studies have been conducted aimed at studying permeability of a partially saturated rock. For this purpose, the effective permeabilities of the spaces not occupied by the wetting fluid (paraffin wax) or the nonwetting fluid (Wood's metal), respectively, have been measured at various saturations, while solidifying the other phase. The experiments were conducted on Berea sandstone samples of $\sim$ 600 mD absolute permeability. The absolute permeability was extrapolated from the effective permeability curve after partially filling the rock pore space with paraffin. The extrapolated value of permeability at zero paraffin saturation ($\sim$ 600 mD) is higher than the measured value of permeability obtained at the same saturation when using triple-distilled water ($\sim$ 300 to 400 mD). A possible explanation is that the paraffin immobilizes the effect of clay present in the rock pore space (e.g., prevents clay migration, swelling, etc.).

The relative permeabilities, $k_r$, obtained as a ratio of effective permeability to absolute permeability of the rock, are shown in Figure 1a. The wetting phase relative permeability is concave upward while the nonwetting phase relative permeability has an $S$ shape. The shape of the nonwetting phase relative permeability in the steep-sloped zone indicates that for a small reduction in nonwetting phase (increase in wetting phase) there is a relatively large decrease in relative permeability. This rapid decrease is due to the occupation of larger pores or flow paths by the wetting phase. The nonwetting relative permeability curve reaches nearly 100% at a nonwetting phase saturation less than a 100% which means that part of the interconnected space composed by smaller pores (e.g., grain-contact) does not contribute to the nonwetting phase relative permeability of the porous medium, but does contribute to electrical conductivity (12). The sum of the relative permeabilities is less than unity. One of the reasons is that part of the pore channels available for flow of a fluid may be reduced in size by the other fluid present in the rock. Another reason is that immobilized droplets of one fluid may completely plug some constrictions in a pore channel through which the other fluid would otherwise flow. The laboratory-derived relative permeability data conforms with typical relative permeability curves using oil and gas as the wetting and nonwetting phase, respectively, in Berea sandstone using conventional methods (15). It is observed that the two curves have similar trends. The relative permeabilities are nearly symmetric within the same range of saturation at which intergranular channels connected by larger throats control effective permeability. This observation then is consistent with fluid flow studies that show that when immiscible fluids flow simultaneously through a porous medium, each fluid follows its own flow path (16). When Darcy's law is applied to the measurement of relative permeabilities of immiscible fluids, it is assumed that the interfaces are steady, the phases flow through their respective channels as if the other phase were absent, and each fluid phase obeys Darcy's law (11). These conditions are met in the application of this technique. Thus, it is possible to measure the macroscopic properties using only single-phase experiments, while the other phase is frozen in place. It is worth noting that strong phase interference has been found experimentally for the relative permeability function (e.g., $k_{rw} + k_{rnw} << 1$) of a 3-D porous media. Moreover, the fluid phases are allowed to flow together in a rather narrow range of saturation.

The effective permeability data have been studied in light of the fluid distributions observed at different saturations with the aid of a complete pore cast and its associated rock section. Our analysis shows that (1) $\sim$ 30% of the pore space consists of grain-contact pores (i.e., thin sheets and micropores) and intergranular pores connected by smaller throats, (2) $\sim$ 40% of the pore space comprises intergranular conduits composed of pores connected by larger throats, and (3) $\sim$ 30% of the intergranular pore space remains hydraulically disconnected. The grain-contact pore space of large surface areas (thin sheets), micropores, and intergranular pores connected by smaller throats provide only minor alternate paths for the fluid to flow to the intergranular conduits connected by larger throats.

Finally, the irreducible nonwetting phase saturation, $S_{rnw}$, is found to have a value of about 30% (percolation threshold). In contrast, since the wetting phase constitutes a continuous network even at low wetting phase saturations, the irreducible wetting phase saturation becomes a function of applied external pressure (e.g., $S_{rw} < 30\%$).

REFERENCES

1. "Reserves of crude oil, natural gas liquids, and natural gas in the U.S. and Canada as of December 31, 1977" American Petroleum Institute, 32, 1978

2. A.E. Scheidegger "The Physics of Flow through Porous Media" University of Toronto Press, 1974

3. G.L. Hassler, R.R. Rice, E.H. Leeman "investigations of recovery on the oil from sandstones by gas-drive" Transactions AIME, 118, page 116, 1936

4. H.G. Botset "flow of gas liquid mixtures through consolidated sands" Transactions AIME, 136, page 91, 1940

5. J.C. Calhoun "Fundamentals of Reservoir Engineering" University of Oklahoma Press, Norman Oklahoma, 1953

6. F.A.L. Dullien "Porous Media Fluid Transport and Pore Structure" Academic Press, 1979

7. G.L. Stegemeir "mechanism of entrapment and mobilization of oil in porous media" Improved Oil Recovery by Surfactant and Polymer Flooding, D.O. Shah and R.S. Schechter (eds.), Academic Press, 1977

8. I. Fatt, H. Dykstra "relative permeability studies" Transactions AIME, 192, page 249, 1951

9. W. Rose, P.A. Witherspoon "studies of waterflood performance: II. trapping oil in a pore doublet" Producers Monthly 21(2), page 32, 1956

10. I. Chatzis, F.A.L. Dullien "modelling pore structure by 2-D and 3-D networks with application to sandstones" Journal of Canadian Petroleum Technology, 16, page 97, 1977

11. G.D. Yadav, F.A.L. Dullien, I. Chatzis, I.F. Macdonald "microscopic distribution of wetting and nonwetting phases in sandstones during immiscible displacements" SPE Reservoir Engineering, May, page 137, 1987

12. E.M. Schlueter "Predicting the Transport Properties of Sedimentary Rocks from Microstructure" Ph.D. Thesis, University of California at Berkeley, Lawrence Berkeley Laboratory Report LBL-36900, Berkeley, California, U.S. Department of Energy Report DOE/BC/95000129 Distribution Category UC-122, 1995

13. K.C. Khilar, H.S. Fogler "the existence of a critical salt concentration for particle release" Journal of Colloid Interface Science, 101, page 214, 1984

14. N. Mungan "permeability reduction due to salinity changes" Journal of Canadian Petroleum Technology, 7(8), page 113, 1968

15. A.T. Corey, C.H. Rathjens "effect of stratification on relative permeability" Transactions AIME, 207, page 358, 1956

16. M. Honarpour, L. Koederitz, A.H. Harvey "Relative Permeability of Petroleum Reservoirs" CRC Press, Inc., Boca Raton Florida, 1986

ACKNOWLEDGEMENTS

This work was supported by the Assistant Secretary for Fossil Energy, Bartlesville Project Office, Advanced Extraction Process Technology (AEPT), under U.S. Department of Energy Contract No. DE-AC22-89BC14475. Thanks are due to L.R. Myer and N.G.W. Cook for providing technical expertise with the experimental apparatus. Thanks are also due to R. Wilson for assistance with the SEM and to R. Curtis for support with the experimental apparatus. We thank R.W. Zimmerman and C. Doughty of Lawrence Berkeley Laboratory for carefully reviewing this paper.

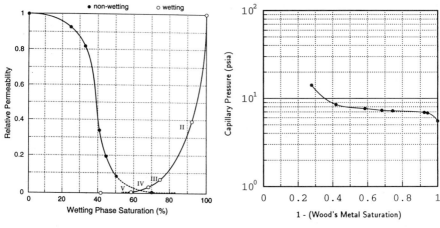

Figure 1a. Relative permeability vs. saturation curve for Berea sandstone using two fluids, serving as the wetting and nonwetting phases, that can be frozen in situ, one at a time. The effective permeability of the spaces not occupied by the wetting fluid (paraffin wax) and the nonwetting fluid (Wood's metal), respectively, have been measured at various saturations in Berea sandstone samples of absolute permeability of 600 mD. The applied pressures (in psia) for the points on the plot are II = 6.9, III = 7.2, IV = 7.3, and V = 7.7 psia.

Figure 1b. Experimental Wood's metal imbibition curve of Berea sandstone. The rock has been impregnated with a nonwetting fluid (Wood's metal) at different equilibrium pressures and solidified in place. The procedure allows for direct observation and analysis of the fluid distribution at a fixed pore pressure and saturation level.

Figure 2. Scanning electron micrograph collage of a Berea sandstone specimen impregnated with approximately 20% - 30% paraffin. The actual width of field is about 6 mm. The gray phase is quartz grains, the white phase consists of pores saturated with paraffin, and the black phase comprises remaining pores filled with blue epoxy for imaging purposes.

Figure 3. Scanning electron micrograph collage of a Berea sandstone specimen impregnated with approximately 40% - 50% paraffin. The actual width of field is about 6 mm. The gray phase is quartz grains, the white phase consists of pores saturated with paraffin, and the black phase comprises remaining pores filled with blue epoxy for imaging purposes.

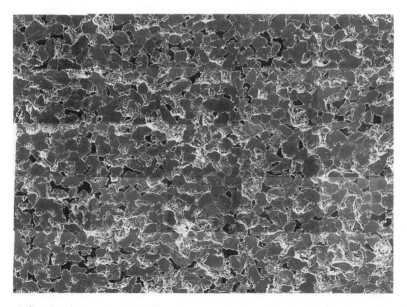

Figure 4. Scanning electron micrograph collage of a Berea sandstone specimen impregnated with approximately 60% - 70% paraffin. The actual width of field is about 6 mm. The gray phase is quartz grains, the white phase consists of pores saturated with paraffin, and the black phase comprises remaining pores filled with blue epoxy for imaging purposes.

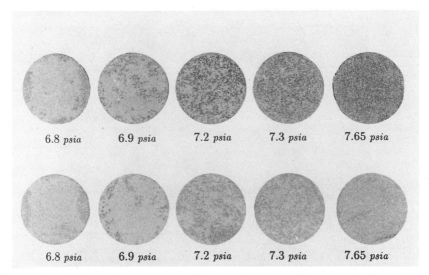

Figure 5. Top and bottom axial quarter sections of Berea sandstone cores partially saturated with a nonwetting fluid (Wood's metal alloy) at different equilibrium pressures, and solidified in place. The light phase is quartz grains and the dark phase is pores saturated with the alloy. The procedure allows for direct observation and analysis of the fluid distribution at a fixed pore pressure and saturation level. The sections reveal that the fluid distributions are composed of a set of imbibing clusters correlated in space.

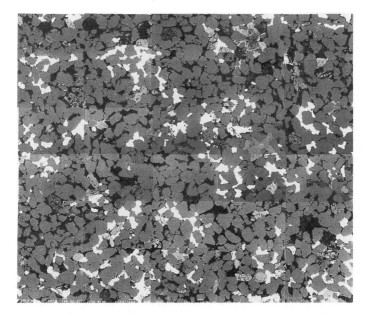

Figure 6. SEM photomicrograph collage of an enlarged partial section obtained from a Berea sandstone sample partially saturated with approximately 30% Wood's metal (white phase) at 7.3 psia pressure. Actual width of field is about 5 mm.

EVALUATION OF GAS CONTENT IN COALS OF THE UPPER SILESIAN
COAL BASIN BY USING WELL LOGGING

APPLICATION DES DIAGRAPHIES A L'EVALUATION TENEUR EN GAZ DES
CHARBONS SILESIENS

Kazimierz Twardowski, Stanisław Rychlicki
University of Mining and Metallurgy in Cracow, Poland

ABSTRACT

In order to investigate the possibility of assessing the methane content of coals in Upper Silesian
Coal Basin on the basis of well logging data, a regression analysis was employed for the gas
parameters of coal seams in USCB, as well logging results recorded in the borehole conditions.
The analysis was based on a set of empirical data, imparted by the Upper Silesian Section of the
Polish Institute of Geology in Sosnowiec, which related to the 12 selected, deep (to over 2000 m of
depth) parametric boreholes in the USCB area. The results of the investigations show to the
possibility of methane content evaluation in coal of USCB, using the complex well logging
interpretation.

RÉSUMÉ

Pour évaluer la teneur en méthane des charbons á Bassin Houiller d'Haute Silésia on a étudié des
relations statistiques entre des diagraphies et des résultats des essais de laboratoire unié avec la
teneur en méthane des charbons. On a obtenu des données á l'analyse de Filiale Silesien d'Institut
Géologique National de Sosnowiec. Elles a été unié avec 12 profond sondages paramétriques
(au - dessus 2000 m) de la région Silesien. Les résultats des études montrent qu'il y a la
possibilité d'évaluation de la teneur en méthane des charbons á l'aide des diagraphies.

INTRODUCTION

Apart from the Rhura and Donieck Basins, Upper Silesian Coal Basin (USCB) is
one of the biggest ones all over Europe. It covers the area of over 5000 km$^2$ , about
4500 km$^2$ in Poland, and the remaining part in the Czech Republic. As far as geological
build is concerned the basin represents an orogenic type with coal-bearing layers of the
Upper Carboniferous (the so-called Silesian).

Estimations of the size of the USCB coalbed methane resources, recently carried out by the Polish and American experts, vary to a great extent. The presented values amount to $100 \times 10^9$ mld $m^3$ in some of the Polish sources, to reach the value of $1300 \times 10^9$ $m^3$ in the Raven Ridge Resources assessment. The Polish Bureau for Geological Concessions states that the resources should be estimated for $500 \times 10^9$ $m^3$ (1).

CHARACTERISTIC OF METHANE CONTENT IN COAL OF THE USCB

The USCB hard coals methane content varies considerably both in the surfacial and in the depth scale (2, 3). The presently observed variability of coalbed methane content to over 20 $m^3$ CH /t is determined by the whole range of primary and secondary factors, connected with the origin, accumulation and migration of gases in the coal-bearing series of the productive Carboniferous. In the light of literature data, the most important ones are as follows: advancement of the process of organic matter coalification (degree of coal metamorphism), bed conditions (temperature and pressure), physicochemical properties and petrographic composition of coals (especially their sorptive properties), chemical composition of gases, reservoir-filtration properties of the carbonaceous series (especially their fracturing), presence of a sealing overburden. These factors are, as a rule, interrelated and interdependent, which shows to the necessity of applying a complex approach to the quantitative description of coalbed methane content.

For obvious reasons the USCB coalbed methane content is considerably well recognized in the depth areas and zones subjected to the mining activity. Quantitative estimations of methane content, especially beyond the areas covered by coal mining, and at greater depths, are based on laboratory analyses of coal samples taken from cores (2). Such analyses are by their nature difficult to carry out, both technically and methodically; previously they were conducted with the help of various laboratories and various methods. The comparative analysis of the results of at least two independent laboratory determinations for the USCB coalbed methane content, obtained with different methods and referring to the same coal beds, proved (4) that the results obtained with the use of the total vacuum degassing method (called "container method") should be treated as reliable and fully comparable. This method is an adaptation of a traditional sidewall method applied by the Central Mining Institute in Katowice for determining methane content from chase samples.

The analysis of chemical composition of coalbed gas constitutes an integral part of the "container method". It shows that this gas generally consists of saturated hydrocarbons (alkanes), among which methane and nitrogen dominate significantly. The sum of these components usually makes over 97% vol. of the whole gas; among the remaining components carbon dioxide (average content ca. 2.5%) and hydrogen ca. (0.3%) prevail. Carbon oxide and helium are in trace quantities.

The ultimate result of the laboratory determination of coalbed methane content gives the summaric content of hydrocarbons of alkanes series in m per 1 t of pure coal substance (pcs). Calculations are made with the use of the correction coefficient, taking into account the loss of methane in the process of sampling and testing. The total vacuum degassing method, used in the USCB by the end of the 1960s, gives comparable results to those obtained through the US Bureau of Mines method (2).

The results of multiple (at least twice) independent laboratory determinations of coalbed methane content in relation to the same coalbeds in practice often exhibit very significant differences. They are often very distinct. Differentiation of the results was subjected to detailed studies carried out by the Authors with the use of the variance analysis, presented in (5). It was indicated in the mentioned paper that the general, observed variability of laboratory determinations of methane-content the USCB coals is conditioned by, among others, intralayer variability (random), resulting from the nonhomogeneity of physicochemical properties and methane-content of individual coalbeds as well as inaccuracy of the laboratory experiments. It explains about 9% of the general, observed variability of results of laboratory analyses of coalbed methane-content, and is described by standard deviation $S_r \approx 1.43$ m$^3$ CH$_4$/t pcs. In practice this value can be interpreted physically as the upper limit of standard random error of laboratory determinations of coalbed methane-content, resulting from physical nonhomogeneity of coal beds and random errors of the applied laboratory method.

Practically most interesting expected values of 95% single confidence intervals of the individual laboratory determinations of coalbed methane content DM$_{95\%}$ grow with the increasing methane content M, following the formula:

$$DM_{95\%} = 0.19 + 0.244 \, M \qquad\qquad /1/$$

The above values simultaneously determine the theoretically obtainable in practice accuracy of indirect methods of quantitative evaluation of methane-content in the USCB coals, e.g. based on well logging.

RESULTS OF EXPERIMENTS ON QUANTITATIVE PROGNOSIS OF METHANE-CONTENT IN HARD COALS OF THE USCB USING WELL LOGGING

The possibility of a quantitative estimation of methane-content in the USCB hard coals based on well logging follows from physical premises and practical experience of the Authors (6, 7).

Recognition of the USCB coalbed gas-bearingness (beyond the area of mining activity and at greater depths) is for apparent reasons weaker and more fragmentary. This situation can be changed through the elaboration of methodics for coalbed gas content estimation based on well logging. Coalbed gas parameters depend on a number of the same geological factors, concurrently determining the variability of other physicochemical parameters, well logged physical parameters in particular. This can be unambiguously confirmed by publications which present the results of experiments in a general form (8, 9, 10). General methodic solutions have a regional or local character, and base on the correct utilization of correlations existing between the results of laboratory experiments and well logging. The Authors know the COALAN interpretation system elaborated for the coal basins San Juan and Black Warrior.

In order to find the correlations between the gas parameters of the USCB coalbeds determined in laboratory conditions and by well logging in borehole conditions, preliminary experimints were carried out. They were based on empirical data imparted by the Upper Silesian Polish Mining Institute in Sosnowiec, relating to 12 selected deep parametric coal boreholes, especially in the central and SW part of the USCB.

A typical complex of geophysical measurements was carried out in the analysed boreholes: gamma ray log (GR), formation density log (FDL), neutron log (NL), caliper, lateral device log L=2.63 m, mud resistivity log (ML), sonic log (SL) and temperature log (TL).

Laboratory experiments were conducted in relation to 320 coal seams, out of which N=152 were qualified for further analysis as fulfilling the following selection criteria:

– geologically homogeneous bed (no interbeddings),

– full gain of the core (100%),

– bed thickness h ≥ 0.3 m.

They were ascribed a set of data, embracing characteristic indications obtained by the well logging and laboratory methods of coalbed methane-content. Observation vector describing individual coalbeds encompassed the following parameters:

• H - depth,

• h - bed thickness,

• $T_w$ - natural temperature of layer,

• $\rho_{pl}$ - electric resistivity of drilling mud,

• $t_{pom}$ - time between the moment of drilling through the bed and well logging,

• d - actual borehole diameter,

• $d/d_n$ - relative actual borehole diameter to nominal diameter ratio,

• $\Delta I_g$, $\Delta I_{gg}$, $\Delta I_{PN}$ - characteristic relative double difference parameters in reference to the gamma ray log, formation density log and neutron log,

• $\Delta t$ - characteristic value of interval time (sonic log),

• $\rho_{g2,63}$ - characteristic value of apparent electric resistivity (lateral device 2,63m)

• M - coalbed methane content obtained from the laboratory tests and expressed in $m^3$ $CH_4$/tpsc.

In order to analyse the interrelations between the methane-content M and the geological-geophysical parameters of coal beds (x) (taken into account in the studies), the empirical material was subjected to the correlation-regression analysis. There were determined empirical estimations of coupled linear correlation coefficients r(M,x) between coalbed methane-content M and the analysed geological-geophysical characteristics x, treated separatelly, and the coefficient of nonlinear multiple correlation R(M,X) between coalbed methane-content M and their characteristics(X), treated jointly.

Table 1. Results of correlation analysis for relations between methan content M and geological-geophysical characteristics x of the USCB coalbeds

| Parameter x | H | h | $T_w$ | $t_{pom}$ | $\rho_{pl}$ | d | $d/d_n$ | $\Delta I_g$ | $\Delta I_{gg}$ | $\Delta I_{PN}$ | $\Delta t$ | $\rho_{g2.63}$ | X |
|---|---|---|---|---|---|---|---|---|---|---|---|---|---|
| r (M,x) | +.61 | +.06 | +.72 | -.05* | -.09* | -.13* | +.30 | -.34 | +.33 | -.33 | +.26 | +.42 | .87 |
| N | 152 | 152 | 143 | 146 | 146 | 151 | 151 | 151 | 151 | 151 | 145 | 151 | 123 |

"*" - no significant coupled correlation at significance level q=0.05

From Table 1 follows, among others, the possibility of constructing a polydimensional regression model for the prognosis of coalbed methane-contents M based on their geological-geophysical characteristics . Such a model was constructed with the use of an algorithm for the nonlinear multiple regression analysis, including the interrelations between the analysed parameters (elements of the mixed type regression). Almost all geological-geophysical parameters used in the analysis (except for $t_{pom}$ and $\rho_{pl}$) were included as variables. This explains over 75% of the observed variability of the USCB coal methane-content with the characteristic error of prognosis equal to about 1.8 $m^3$ $CH_4$/t pcs, comparable with the upper limit of the standard random error of laboratory determinations of methane-content.

CONCLUSIONS

- The vacuum degassing method, practically used for the estimation of the USCB coal methane-content based on individual laboratory determinations is very inaccurate. The upper limit of the standard random error of these determinations significantly grows with the increment of coalbed gas-content. The expected values of 95% single-sided confidence intervals of individual laboratory determinations of methane-content can be assessed from relation /1/.

- Methane-content of the USCB coalbeds typically has significant coupled correlations (at significance level q = 0.05) with the predominant domination of geological-geophysical characteristics encompassed in the analysis. The methane-content most strongly depends on natural deep temperature $T_w$ (r =+ 0.72) and depth of beds deposition H (r=+0.61). Coupled correlation coefficients between the methane-content and individual geophysical parameters of beds sensu stricto have definitely lower estimations.

- The obtained equation of multiple nonlinear regression for the estimation of the USCB coalbed methane-content contains in the character of the depend variables almost all geological-geophysical characteristics taken into consideration in the analysis, especially indications of individual well loggings (except for mud log $PO_{pl}$). It explains over 75% of the observed variability of coalbed methane-content.

- Results of the conducted analyses show to the possibility of efficient prognosis of the USCB coalbed methane-content, based on a complex interpretation of well log data without the necessity to conduct noxious and costly laboratory experiments.

REFERENCES

1.  „Rozmowa z Markiem Hoffmannem, Dyrektorem Biura Koncesji Geologicznych w Ministerstwie Ochrony Środowiska, Zasobów Naturalnych i Leśnictwa". Metan Pokładów Węgla. Biuletyn Centrum Informacji - Katowice, nr 4, czerwiec 1993.

2.  M. Karwasiecka, J. Kwarciński „Zestawienie wyników badań laboratoryjnych dotyczących gazonośności węgli kamiennych GZW wraz z ich weryfikacją i wstępną analizą przestrzennej zmienności". Oddział Górnośląski Państwowego Instytutu Geologicznego, Sosnowiec 1994.

3.  S. Rychlicki, K. Twardowski, J. Kwarciński, M. Karwasiecka „Jakościowo-ilościowa charakterystyka gazonośności węgli kamiennych Górnośląskiego Zagłębia Węglowego". Spr. z pos. Komisji Naukowych PAN, Oddz. w Krakowie, tom za styczeń-grudzień 1995 (w druku).

4.  S. Rychlicki, K. Twardowski „Analiza porównawcza wyników badań laboratoryjnych metanonośności węgli kamiennych Górnośląskiego Zagębia Węglowego". Mat. XIX Sympozjum Naukowego "Zastosowanie metod matematycznych i informatyki w geologii", Kraków 1995.

5.  K. Twardowski, S. Rychlicki „Ocena niedokładności laboratoryjnych oznaczeń metanonośności węgli kamiennych Górnośląskiego Zagłębia Węglowego". Mat. XIX Sympozjum Naukowego „Zastosowanie metod matematycznych i informatyki w geologii", Kraków 1995.

6.  K. Twardowski, S. Rychlicki, K. Krochmal „Badanie zmienności własności fizycznych węgli kamiennych w aspekcie ich gazonośności i zagrożeń wyrzutowych w górnictwie". Spr. z bad. własnych, Wydział Wiertniczo-Naftowy AGH, Krakow 1994.

7.  K. Twardowski „Wstępne wyniki badań dotyczących oceny gazonośności węgli kamiennych GZW w oparciu o dane geofizyki wiertniczej". Mat. Konf. Nauk.-Techn. „Wydział Wiertniczo-Naftowy AGH dla Kraju", Kraków 1994.

8.  P. Howard „Log Analysis of Coalbed Methane in San Juan Basin". Schlumberger GFE paper, 1985.

9.  U. Ahmed, D. Johnston, J. L. Colson „An Advanced and Integrated Approach to Coal Formation Evaluation". Paper SPE 22736. 66-th Annual Technical Conference and Exhibition of the SPE, Dallas 1991.

10. J. L. Colson „Evaluating Gas Content of Black Warrior Basin Coalbeds from Wireline Log Data". SPE Gas Technology Symposium, Houston 1991.

THERMODYNAMIC OF HYDROCARBONS
EVAPORATION BY NON-EQUILIBRIUM GAS

THERMODYNAMIQUE DE  LA VAPORISATION
DES HYDROCARBURES PARLE GAZ NON
EQUILIBRE

A.I.Gritsenko, R.M.Ter-Sarkisov, N.A.Guzhov,
V.A.Nikolaev, M.I.Fadeev, A.N.Shandrygin
All-Russian Scientific-Research Institute of Natural
Gas and Gases Technology (VNIIGAS), Moscow,
Russia

ABSTRACT

High losses of hydrocarbons when developing gas condensate fields under
reservoir energy depletion call for developing new methods of enhancing
hydrocarbon recovery (EHCR).The paper describes EHCR methods based on
the evaporation mechanism. The results of thermodynamics of hydrocarbons
evaporation by nonequilibrium gas presented.

RESUME

Les pertes importantes des hidrocarbures en cours de l'exploitation des giments
de gaz à condensat en régime d'épuisement de l'énergue de la couche ditriment
l'actualité du développement des méthodes de l'influence sur la couche pour
l'augmentation de sa récupération des hydrocarbures. A l'article présent il s'agit
des méthodes de l'influence, qui sont baseés sur l'utilisation du mécanisme de la
vaporisation. Les méthodes et les résultats des études thermodynamiques de la
vaporisation des hydrocarbures par le gaz non équilibré y sont présentés.

## INTRODUCTION

The all gas condensate fields  (GCF) in Russia and many GCFs in gas-producing countries are being developed only on the basis of reservoir natural energy (depletion condition).The efficiency of such development as object of gas production is  sufficiently  high, gas recovery factors  for pay beds reaching 60-80 per cent and in some case 90 per cent and higher. However, at a high content of condensate this method is not enough effective for recovery gas condensate of gas condensate ($C_{2+}$), condensate recovery factor generally reaching 30-40 per cent. Solution to this problem is very important for the gas industry since the residual reserves of condensate having been a valuable feed stock for the gas chemical sector account for thousands million tonnes only in Russia.

VNIIGAS has developed and tested under field conditions several EHCR methods (1). One of these methods is being  used in Vuctyl GCF for commercial recovering retrograde condensate.The efficiency of a stimulation method is defined, to a great extent,  by the current thermobarical  conditions and hydrocarbon system composition of a pool. A  choice of a stimulation method depends on comparative data on   economical   efficiency   and   the   efficiency   of   hydrocarbons additional   recovery.  A   final   choice   is   made   based   on   the peculiarities of transportation system and structure of  a regional field demand.

By  the  mechanism  of  retrograde  condensate  stimulation  the methods can be divided into two groups. The first group is directed to  involve  retrograde  condensate  into  the  filtration  process   as  a fraction of liquid phase. The second group is directed to recover hydrocarbons of retrograde condensate in composition of easily-flowed gaseous phase. The  paper presents the results of thermodynamic tests on   interaction   between   hydrocarbon   systems   and   injected   non-equilibrium gas as applied to the second group.

## INVESTIGATION METHODS

Study   of   thermodynamic   features   of   phase   behaviour    of hydrocarbon system during its interaction with a gaseous agent injected into reservoir has been carried out along with the use of experimental and theoretical methods.

In experimental study of gas-condensate system conducted on PVT unit a choice of a particular hydrocarbons mixture simulating most efficiently    natural    mixture    in    the    process    of    differential condensation has been made.Simulation of agent injection process was performed on a 5 m thermostated linear model filled with porous media with porosity and permeability 24 % and $10^{-14}$ $m^2$  respectively. The mixture composition at the model's outlet and inlet was changed by chromatography method.

Theoretical  investigations  were  based  on  the  use  of  estimation method for parameters of phase equilibrium  of hydrocarbons mixtures based  on  Peng-Robinson  equations.  The  analysis  of  distribution  of

.   rvoir system compo '  on and parameters during the process of gas
injection has been co...ucted with the help of mathematical two-phase
multicomponent filtration model developed by VNIIGAS (2).   The
mathematical model was constructed on the basis of finite-
differential method being explicit by concentrations and implicit by
pressure. A  heavy residue  of natural condensate was simulated,
during  thermodynamic calculation, by a set  of fractions totalled
from 15 to 25. To cut computation  time and requirements to computer
memory during computation of multi-component filtration only 4-8
fractions were used.

     A preliminary analysis of main trends in interaction between
injected gas and reservoir system was carried out on the basis of
ternary diagrams. A multicomponent gas condensate system was taken
arbitrarily as a set of three pseudocomponents and the results of
thermodynamic calculations of its phase state were given in the form
of ternary diagrams.

PRELIMINARY  ANALYSIS

     A main possibility of influence on gas evaporation capability
under field conditions is a change  in intermediate components
content, such as ethane, propane, butane and carbon dioxide. A
typical ternary diagram of hydrocarbon system is illustrated in
Fig.1.The first pseudocomponent ($C_1$) combines methane and nitrogen,
the second - intermediate components and the third - highly-boiling
hydrocarbons ($C_{5+}$ ).  Such phase diagram is typical for range  of
pressures which is lower than a dew point pressure and higher than
that  of  unlimited  miscibility  of  the  first  and  second
pseudocomponents.Point S corresponds to a current composition of
depleted system, while points G and L correspond a composition of
gaseous and liquid phases respectively. A section GL  is tie line. It
is know that a state of mixture is formed immediately behind
replacement front. This state corresponds a point located on the tie
line the extension of which crosses a  point corresponding the
injected gas. For example, during the injection of gas B or D the
state E or F are realised respectively. A line tangent to the
boundary of two-phase area in a critical point (K-C) limits the area
above which a complete miscible displacement takes place.

     When using the agent described by a point which lies on the tie
line extension, GL, a shift of the point S along its tie line to
gaseous phase will take place during evaporation process. A change in
phase composition does not occur. It may be considered that in this
case we have the realisation of nonequilibrium of the injected agent
and initial mixture only by a heavy pseudocomponent. The use of the
agent with a light (point D) or low (point B) intermediate components
content results not only in a change of phase relationship but in
change of phase composition due to the transition to the other tie
line. Compared to the above case, such gases are more nonequilibrium
relative to the reservoir system.A nature of influence of an
intermediate component content in the injected gas on the evaporation
of fraction $C_{5+}$  is defined by the dew point line slope to the
horizontal axis $C_1$ - $C_{5+}$ . At a slope of 60 $^0$ ,  the content of the

third pseudocomponent in gaseous phase is constant and does not depend on the content of the second pseudocomponent in the injected gas. At a slope of less 60⁰ , the enrichment of injected gas by pseudocomponent $C_{2-4}$ increases  the evaporation capability of fraction $C_{5+}$  . At a slope of higher than 60 ⁰ , it is advisable to use gas with less content of intermediate components in order to increase evaporation efficiency.

Fig.2 illustrates phase diagram of Vuctyl gas condensate system at two pressures plotted by the thermodynamic calculation results on the basis of 32 components. As the reservoir pressure decreases, two-phase area extends and reaches the $C_1$- $C_{2-4}$ axis at a pressure lower than that for an unlimited miscibility of the first and second pseudocomponents. At the same time, a slope of dew point line of the two-phase area boundary is observed. Hence  at high pressures the enrichment of gas with an intermediate component results in increasing evaporation capability of gas relative to fraction $C_{5+}$ , whereas at the low pressures we have inverse dependence. Similar tendencies have been observed for other gas condensate systems.

The study of retrograde condensate evaporation intensity does not require a complete construction of phase diagram of a system. It will suffice to restore only its lower part in order to find a  $C_{5+}$ content in gaseous phase and the influence of intermediate components on this value. A design dependence  of mean value of the derivative ($\Delta C_{5+}$ / $\Delta C_{2-4}$) of the lower part of the dew point line on pressure is given in Fig.3 for Urengoy gas condensate system.The sign change at P=21 MPa separates the areas of preferable use of dry and enriched gas.

It  should  be  noted  that  the  analysis  based  on  the pseudocomponent approximation is conventional since the composition of  the  same  pseudocomponent  in  different  phase  is  different. Conclusions on general tendencies and a state of system immediately after injected agent front are the most reliable when performing such analysis. That is why, after choosing  a range of simulation conditions, the estimation of efficiency and the main indicators of process is performed on the basis of mathematical and physical simulation  of the multicomponent flow.

HIGH PRESSURE

At high pressure the increase in exploration capability of gas taken place due to increasing intermediate components. Compared to a typical cycling-process the injection of intermediate component-rich gas would allow to reduce a volume of the injected gas and a required level of  injection  pressure  both  due  to  increasing  evaporation capability of gas and due to increasing a gas column weight in a hole.A problem of the intermediate component resources which are needed for providing this process should be solved with regard to the gas production, transportation and the other  economical sectors of a region.

The peculiarities of reservoir mixture phase behaviour during the injection of gases of different composition at a relatively early stage of field development have been studied both theoretically and experimentally on a gas condensate system of Urengoy field of West Siberia. The dew point pressure was 28 MPa, the content of intermediate hydrocarbons $C_{2-4}$ was 11 %, and the content of high-boiling hydrocarbons $C_{5+}$ was 220 $g/m^3$. Averaged values of saturation of an undisturbed zone and of a zone subjected to injection are presented in Fig.4. The same dependences under a partial dry gas repressuring are given in Fig.5. Within a sufficient range of pressure, the enriched gas evaporates condensate completely. However, as the pressure declines lower than 16 MPa, the evaporated condensate begins precipitate intensively from the enriched gas. Thus on performing the process under high pressure condensate as a fraction of gaseous phase can be recovered completely.

The mechanism of condensate transfer is of special interest. The first portion of enriched gas are completely saturated with heavy hydrocarbons through evaporating condensate. Since under partial maintenance of reservoir pressure the latter decreases as the displacement front advances, condensate precipitation from the enriched gas is observed. The precipitated condensate evaporates by the next portion of displacing agent. Thus, the condensate advance through a reservoir is accompanied by the processes of condensation and evaporation. The effect of hydrocarbons output increase is defined both by a partial maintenance of reservoir pressure and evaporation of retrograde condensate. The process regularities as deduced from mathematical simulation have been supported by experiments conducted on a linear reservoir model.

LOW PRESSURE

At present there are several gas condensate fields entering a final phase of development. For different reasons these fields has been developed without using enhanced hydrocarbons recovery methods. However, problem of residual condensate recovery and the maintenance of the production potentialities of gas processing plants is of great importance. As stated above , the enrichment of gas with intermediate components has an adverse effect on its evaporation capability under moderate and low reservoir pressures. Besides, dry gaseous mixtures enable a more complete recovery both heavy and intermediate components dissolved in condensate.

The simulation of retrograde condensate evaporation process into the injected gas under pressure of 10-30 % of initial pressure was conducted for gas condensate systems of the Urengoy and Vuctyl gas condensate fields. Methane and reservoir gas without heavy hydrocarbons (separator gas) were used as an injection agent.

The computation results from the mathematical model of two-phase multicomponent filtration and the experiments made on the linear reservoir model are in good agreement. When using dry gas (methane), hydrocarbons evaporation is more active compared to separator gas. The study shows a selectivity of evaporation process. First of all,

light hydrocarbons with a molecular mass less than 100 g/mol are
primarily evaporated. On further pumping, a share of these
hydrocarbons in the recovered gas declines. A small increase in the
evaporation of condensate heavier components, which takes place at a
next stage due to their larger molecular mass, leads to the
maintenance and even to a temporal growth of condensate weight
content in the recovered gas.

Fig.6 illustrates content change in recovered gas observed in
the linear reservoir model during methane injection. The results
show that ethane and propane are recovered more rapidly. Content of
evaporated butanes is maintained at an initial level under injection
volume up to three pore volumes. A content of high-boiling
hydrocarbons is hold close to initial level for a long time.

CONCLUSIONS

•     The regularities of evaporation of retrograde condensate
      hydrocarbons in injected gas were studied on mathematical and
      physical models. The results obtained from the mathematical
      model are in good agreement to those for the linear reservoir
      model.

•     The analysis of gas condensate system behaviour based on
      ternary diagrams enable to estimate the main features of
      stimulation. In order to obtain more reliable indicators of
      stimulation one should use methods of direct mathematical and
      physical simulation of the multicomponent flow process.

•     The results show that enriched gas has a positive effect on the
      evaporation efficiency under high reservoir pressure. At an
      initial stage the enrichment of injected gas with intermediate
      components makes it possible to recover the bulk of heavy
      components being in one-phase state.

•     Under moderate and low pressure a content of intermediate
      components increases the heavy component evaporation. Low
      pressure dry gas stimulation enables to enhance intermediate
      component recovery. High-molecular hydrocarbons can be produced
      for a long time.

REFERENCES

1.    R.Ter-Sarkisov, A.Gritsenko "hydrocarbon injection improves
      condensate recovery in U.S.S.R", Oil&Gas Journal, June 24, 1991
2.    N.Gujov, V.Mitlin "effect of interphase surface in studies of
      miscible displacement of multi-component systems", Izwestija AN
      USSR, Mehanika zhidkosty i gaza, No.4, 1986

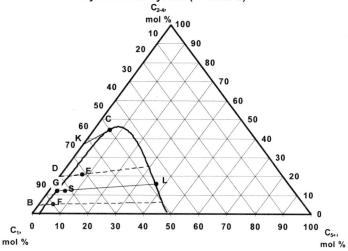

Fig. 1 Ternary phase diagram for simulatial hydrocarbon system (P=18 MPa)

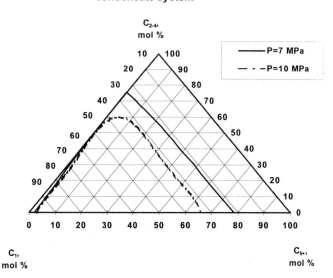

Fig. 2 Ternary phase diagram for the Vuktyl gas condensate system

**Fig. 3    Tangent dew point line slope vs. pressure (Vuctyl GCF)**

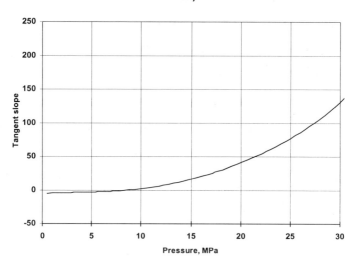

**Fig. 4    Condensate gas ratio (CGR) and liquid saturation (SL) vs. pressure under partial rich gas repressuring**

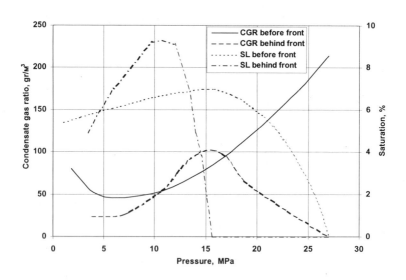

**Fig. 5      Condensate gas ratio (CGR) and liquid saturation
(SL) vs. pressure under partial dry gas repressuring**

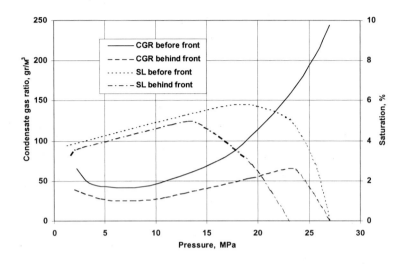

**Fig.6    Hydrocarbon component content (C₂, C₃, C₄, C₅₊) in
the recovered produce gas vs. injected dry gas volume
(P=5.0 MPa, T=62⁰C)**

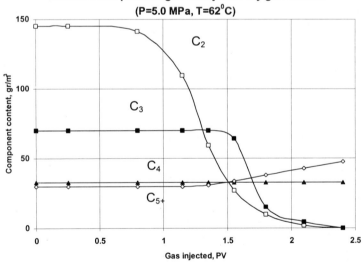

THE MEASUREMENT AND MODELLING OF HYDROCARBON PHASE BEHAVIOUR AT RETROGRADE
AND NEAR CRITICAL CONDITIONS

LA MESURE ET LA MODELISATION DU COMPORTEMENT DES PHASES D'HYDROCARBURES DANS
DES CONDITIONS RETROGRADES ET QUASI CRITIQUES

P.J. McGauley
British Gas plc, Research and Technology, UK.

ABSTRACT

Cubic equations of state are used throughout the oil and gas industry to model the phase behaviour
of hydrocarbon streams. From original applications for processing conditions, such modelling is
often performed at the high temperatures and pressures encountered in oil and gas reservoirs where
near critical behaviour may be encountered.

This paper describes the experimental apparatus and procedures used to generate a database of
high pressure and temperature phase equilibria and volumetric data using model gas condensate
mixtures. The experimental data were used to evaluate the predictive capabilities of three leading
cubic equations of state at retrograde and near critical conditions. A new set of binary interaction
parameters was generated for each equation of state which significantly improved fluid property
prediction. Poor liquid density predictions at near critical conditions were overcome by
introducing a second binary interaction parameter ($l_{ij}$) for the equation of state $b$ parameter.

RÉSUMÉ

Les équations d'état du troisième degré sont utilisées dans toute l'industrie du pétrole et du gaz
pour simuler sur modèle le comportement des phases des flots d'hydrocarbures. A partir des
application initiales pour des conditions de traitement, cette modélisation est souvent réalisée aux
températures et pressions élevées rencontrées dans les réserves de pétrole et de gaz, dans
lesquelles un comportement quasi critique peut être constaté.

La communication décrit l'équipment expérimental et les méthodes d'expérimentation utilisés
pour produire une base de données des équilibres des phases à des tempértures et des pressions
élevées et des données volumétriques en utilisiant des simulations sur modèle de mélanges de
condensats de gaz. Les données expérimentales ont été utilisées pour évaluer les possibilités de
prévision des trois équations d'état du troisième degré principales dans des conditions rétrogrades
et quasi critques. Une nouvelle série de paramètres d'interaction binaires a été produite pour
chaque équation d'état, ce qui a considérablement amélioré la prévision de la propriété des fluides.
Le problème des mauvaises prévisions de densité des liquides dans des conditions quasi critiques a
été résolu insérant un second paramètre d'interaction binaire ($l_{ij}$) pour le paramètre b de l'équation
d'état.

## INTRODUCTION

The cubic equation of state is widely used throughout the petroleum industry to provide estimates of hydrocarbon fluid properties at reservoir conditions. Accurate estimates of these properties are required when determining hydrocarbon reserves and selecting the most efficient recovery schemes. Since many gas condensate reservoir fluids are found at high pressures (above 24 MPa) and temperatures, it is important that the reliability of the cubic equation of state at these conditions can be validated.

A search of the British Gas database revealed that less than forty of the twenty thousand experimental vapour-liquid equilibria (VLE) data points were measured at pressures typical of gas condensate reservoir conditions. Most of these data were generated from experiments performed by Yarborough (1972), Vairogs et al. (1970) and Li et al. (1981), using multicomponent systems and a range of hydrocarbons from methane to decane. The number of high pressure VLE points and the range of hydrocarbons reported do not provide a sufficient data base to comprehensively evaluate the cubic equation's predictive capabilities at high pressure conditions.

Experimental PVT studies using real gas condensate fluids have been performed by the Gas Processors Association (Ng et al., 1987) and Winfrith (Bennison and Element,1991), from which a large database of high pressure and temperature VLE data were generated. These data are subject to compositional uncertainty arising from the procedures used to characterise the fluid's heaviest fraction. Compositional uncertainty introduces an unknown into the equation of state calculations, which obscures the true predictive capabilities of the equation of state.

To avoid the problem of compositional uncertainty and provide a sufficient database of VLE properties, experimental measurements were made on five model gas condensates consisting of four and six component mixtures. These measurements were made at retrograde and near critical conditions from which over 150 K-values, 30 VLE densities and compressibility factors, and series of liquid saturations were measured.

These data represent a significant contribution to the current high pressure and temperature VLE data base and provide sufficient information to evaluate and improve the cubic equation property predictions at reservoir conditions.

## EXPERIMENTAL MIXTURES

The following four and six component model gas condensates were studied:-

1: $C_1 / C_2 / C_{10} / C_{16}$

2: $C_1 / C_2 / C_{12} / C_{14}$

3: $C_1 / C_2 / C_3 / C_5 / C_8 / C_{16}$

4: $C_1 / C_2 / C_6 / C_{12} / C_{16} / N_2$

5: $C_1 / C_2 / C_6 / C_{10} / C_{16} / CO_2$

These mixtures were chosen to provide experimental data for a comprehensive range of n-alkanes, $C_1$-$C_{16}$, as well as the two important non-hydrocarbon components nitrogen and carbon dioxide. The latter components are found naturally in many hydrocarbon reservoirs but they may also be introduced during enhanced oil recovery processes. These range of components will allow the cubic equation to be evaluated for molecules of varying molecular size and nature.

EXPERIMENTAL

Apparatus

The principal parts of the PVT apparatus and some of the ancillary equipment used to perform the experimental measurements are shown in Figure 1.

Volumetric changes within the PVT cell were controlled using a 100 cm$^3$ mercury displacement pump accurate to within ± 0.01 cm$^3$. Cell pressures were measured with a 0-10,000 psia Heise gauge, which had been calibrated to within 2-3 psi over the experimental pressure range. The PVT cell temperature was maintained to within ± 0.1°C inside an oven using a air bath to control the temperature. Cell temperature readings were taken by a thermocouple placed inside the wall of the cell.

To ensure proper mixing of the cell contents, the cell was seated on a mechanical arm which was rocked with the aid of a motor. Fluid samples were flowed into and out of the cell through a valve at the top of the cell. This valve was operated from outside the oven using a detachable long stem valve handle.

The pipe work leading from the top of the PVT cell to the outlet valves was wrapped in heating tape to maintain a constant temperature during transfer of fluid from the cell. Narrow bore 1/16" piping was used to avoid excessive dead volumes within the system and so minimise the pressure drop when the cell was initially opened to the pipe work. The laboratory temperature was maintained at 20 ± 1°C to ensure the PVT apparatus remained inside its calibration limits.

Liquid Saturation Measurements

Liquid volumes were measured by isothermally expanding the mixtures from single to two phase conditions over the experimental pressure range 55.1 to 3.5 MPa. The volumes of liquid formed during this expansion process were measured using a camera and linear transducer mounted outside the oven window. The isothermal experiments were repeated at several temperatures ranging from conditions close to the mixture's cricondentherm and down to the critical temperature. A partial phase envelope was constructed by plotting the liquid volume fractions across the experimental temperature and pressure range. Quality lines of constant liquid volume fraction were drawn and these lines were extrapolated to a point of convergence where the mixture's critical point was determined.

Vapour Liquid Equilibria Measurements

Vapour liquid equilibria measurements were performed by isobarically displacing the equilibrium phase from the cell to the shut-off micrometering valve, Figure 1. Initially, part of the equilibrium fluid was purged through the micrometering valve to flush out any heavy components which had precipitated into the pipe work. The sample was then flashed into a catchpot under controlled conditions. The heavier liquid components condensed out at room temperature and the produced gas was piped into a gasometer via the gas chromatograph. The composition of the gas and liquid produced by flashing were determined by gas chromatographic analysis. These compositions were mathematically recombined to determine the high pressure phase equilibrium compositions.

The phase equilibrium measurements were made at a series of pressures along a selected isotherm both at retrograde and non-retrograde conditions. Using the experimental compositions and volume of displaced fluid, the phase equilibrium ratios (K-values) and VLE densities and compressibility factors at each of the experimental pressure points were determined. The quality and integrity of the experimental VLE data were evaluated using molar balances and Hoffmann-Crump-Hocott plots (1953) plots as consistency checks.

EQUATION OF STATE MODELLING

Three cubic equations of state were selected for evaluation, which included the extensively used Peng-Robinson (PR, 1976) equation, the British Gas (Gibbons and Laughton, 1984) and the three parameter Schmidt-Wenzel (SW, 1980) equations. The accuracy of the cubic equation's phase volumetric and compositional predictions were evaluated separately using experimental VLE densities and equilibrium ratios respectively.

Phase Volumetrics

Poor predictions of liquid volumes have been identified as one of the main limitations of the cubic equation of state, Abbot (1979) and Firoozabadi (1988). Accurate estimates of liquid volumes are required for reservoir simulation purposes, where the values are used to calculate fluid flow parameters and determine the deliverability of the reservoir. In order to assess the true liquid volumetric accuracy of the cubic equation and avoid phase equilibria uncertainties, the VLE liquid densities have been calculated using the experimental liquid phase compositions.

A total of 30 experimental liquid densities were evaluated and the average absolute deviations between the calculated and experimental liquid densities for each of the cubic equations are presented in Figure 2. The two parameter BG and PR equations do not provide accurate estimates of the liquid phase volume as shown by the 13 % and 6% overprediction of liquid densities respectively. The introduction of a third parameter into the cubic equation state by Schmidt and Wenzel (SW) is shown to markedly improve the equation's liquid volumetric predictive capabilities, enabling liquid densities to be estimated to within 2.5% of the experimental values. The volume translated (VT) versions of the PR (Jhaveri and Youngren, 1988) and BG (Peneloux et al., 1982) equations were also investigated. Figure 2 shows that the volume translated form of the PR and BG equations provide highly accurate liquid density predictions. The improvement in predicted liquid densities is most marked for the BG equation where liquid density errors are reduced by almost an order of magnitude.

These results show that both the volume corrected and the three parameter Schmidt-Wenzel cubic equations can provide good estimates of liquid phase volumes for model gas condensates mixtures at high pressures and temperatures. The calculations were repeated using a range of binary interaction parameters but the predicted liquid volumes are insensitive to the value of the interaction parameter. Further testing is required to assess the validity of the volumetric results at near critical conditions.

Phase Equilibria

The equation of state phase equilibria predictions were evaluated using the experimental equilibrium ratios (K-values) and dewpoint pressure data. The calculation of these properties are particularly sensitive to the choice of binary interaction parameters ($k_{ij}$), which are used to correct the combining rules for molecular pairs, Prausnitz et al. (1987). Currently, the binary interaction parameters proposed by Katz and Firoozabadi (1978) are used with the PR equation to predict gas condensate phase behaviour but no similar sets of interactions for the BG and SW equations could be found in the literature.

In this study three sets of binary interaction parameters were developed for PR, BG and SW equations based on the generalised correlation proposal by Trebble and Sigmund (1990). These interaction parameters were derived by varying the correlation variable until the deviations between the predicted and experimental dewpoints of the model gas condensates were minimised. The interaction parameters from this work were further evaluated using pressure composition (P-X) data from a range of binary methane-$n$-alkane data, (ethane to hexadecane). It was shown from these P-X plots that the new interaction parameters accurately predicted the binary VLE behaviour over most of the two phase region; the calculations were least satisfactory in the near critical region where the saturation pressures were over-predicted.

Previous studies by Yarborough (1979) and Danesh (1991) have shown that the equilibrium ratios of the $C_{7+}$ components are not predicted accurately by the cubic equation. In order to assess the effect of the new set of binary interaction parameters on the PR phase equilibria predictions, the $C_{7+}$ equilibrium ratios were calculated using the new (BG) interaction parameters and the current default Katz-Firoozabadi set. The results from these calculations in Figure 3 show that the new set of interaction parameters enable the PR equation to predict the $C_{7+}$

K-values with an accuracy of twice that of the current Katz-Firoozabadi $k_{ij}$ set. Similar calculations were performed using the experimental saturation pressure data, and the results are presented in Figure 4. The new set of $k_{ij}$ values are also shown to halve the deviations between the experimental and predicted dewpoint pressures

The new set of interactions parameters, derived from the Trebble and Sigmund correlation, clearly improve the PR EoS phase equilibria predictions however, further work is still needed to provide satisfactory estimates for the $C_{7+}$ equilibrium ratios.

Liquid Volume Fractions

The calculated liquid volume fractions are derived from a combination of the liquid molar phase fraction and liquid molar volume. It is therefore essential that the cubic equation predicts both these phase equilibria and volumetric properties accurately.

The experimental and calculated liquid volume fractions are presented graphically in Figures 5 and 6, both at temperatures away from (375.75K) and close to the critical point (324.45K). These calculations were performed using the volume translated PR and BG equations, and as shown in the figures the PR equation provides the most accurate results. The SW equation has been omitted for clarity but this equation has an accuracy similar to the BG equation. Although the PR equation is shown to provide satisfactory predictions at higher temperatures away from the critical point, the predicted liquid volumetric behaviour remains unsatisfactory at lower temperatures or near critical conditions, Figure 6.

Near Critical Calculations

The poor prediction of a mixture's critical point by the cubic equation will have a significant effect on the calculated VLE properties in the near critical region. Recently, Chou and Prausnitz (1989), Mathias et al. (1989) and Danesh et al. (1990) have attempted to improve the EoS predictions in this region through the use of near critical volume correction terms. These volumetric corrections were evaluated by Danesh et al. using near critical PVT data but only limited improvements in predicted properties were achieved.

Firoozabadi et al. (1994) showed that the near critical phase behaviour of binary mixtures could be accurately predicted by the PR equation by relating the interaction parameter to the bulk modulus of the fluid. However, when these interactions were applied to ternary mixtures only limited improvements were achieved compared with using a constant $k_{ij}$ value. Chou and Prausnitz (1989) showed that improved near critical phase predictions could be made if a second binary interaction coefficient ($l_{ij}$) were used with the combining rule for the repulsion term, **b**.

In this study a second binary interaction parameter was introduced for the $C_1$-$C_{16}$ pair only. The effect of this parameter on the predicted liquid volume fractions for the mixture $C_1/C_2/C_3/C_5/C_8/C_{16}$ at near critical conditions is shown in Figure 7. The results show that the introduction of the $l_{ij}$ term significantly improves the predicted liquid volume fractions, reproducing the experimental results very accurately. The generality of this result requires further investigation to determine whether the $l_{ij}$ parameter is sufficient to correct for poor liquid volume predictions in the critical region.

CONCLUSIONS

.   The volume corrected and 3 parameter cubic equations have been shown to provide accurate estimates of liquid volumes at retrograde conditions.

.   A new set of binary interaction parameters have been developed for the PR equation which enable improved predictions of saturation pressures and $C_{7+}$ equilibrium ratios to be achieved. However, the prediction of the $C_{7+}$ equilibrium ratios still remains unsatisfactory. Further improvements to the equations of state are necessary.

.   The prediction of critical points by the cubic equation remains inaccurate. Partial success has been achieved in improving near critical property predictions through the use of a second binary interaction parameter ( $l_{ij}$ ). The use of a second binary interaction to correct liquid volume predictions in the near critical region requires further investigation.

Acknowledgement

The author would like to thank Andrew Laughton (British Gas) for testing the new binary interaction parameter sets and for his helpful suggestions and corrections to this paper.

Internet address: patrick.mcgauley@bggrc.co.uk

REFERENCES

1.  Abbott, M.M.
    Cubic Equations of State: An Interpretive Review.
    Advances in Chemistry Series 182, American Chemical Society, pp. 47-70, (1979).

2.  Bennison, T.G., and Element, D.J.
    A Study of The Thermodynamic And Transport Properties of Gas Condensates and Volatile Oils.
    Winfrith AEA Petroleum Services, (October, 1991).

3.  Chou. G.F., and Prausnitz, J.M.
    A Phenomenological Correction to an Equation of State for The Near Critical Region.
    AIChE Journal, Vol.35, No.9, pp. 1487-1496, (September 1989).

4.  Danesh, A., Xu, D-H., and Todd, A.C.
    An Evaluation of Cubic Equations of State for Phase Behaviour Calculations Near Miscibility Conditions.
    SPE/DOE 20267, pp. 915- 924, (1990).

5.  Danesh, A., Xu, D-H., and Todd, A.C.
    Comparative Study of Cubic Equations of State For Predicting Phase Behaviour and Volumetric Properties of Injection Gas-Reservoir Oil Systems.
    Fluid Phase Equilibria, Vol. 63, pp. 259-278, (1991).

6.  Firoozabadi, A.
    Reservoir-Fluid Phase Behavior and Volumetric Prediction With Equations of state.
    J.Pet. Tech., pp. 397-406, (April 1988).

7.  Firoozabadi, A., Arbabi., S., and Dindoruk, B.
    Near-Critical Phase Behaviour of Mixtures Using Equations of State.
    Canad.J.Chem.Eng., Vol.72, pp.134-141, (February 1994).

8.  Gibbons, R.M., and Laughton, A.P.
    An Equation of State for Polar and Non-polar Substances and Mixtures.
    J.Chem.Soc., Faraday Trans. 2, Vol. 80, pp. 1019-1038, (1984).

9.  Hoffmann, A.E., Crump, J.S. and Hocott, C.R.
    Equilibrium Constants for a Gas Condensate System.
    Trans. AIME, Vol. 198, pp. 1-10, (1953).

10. Jhaveri, B.S., and Youngren, G.K.
    Three Parameter Modification of The Peng-Robinson Equation of State to Improve Volumetric Predictions.
    SPE Res. Eng, pp 1033-1040, (August,1988).

11. Katz, D.L., and Firoozabadi, A.
    Predicting Phase Behaviour of Condensate/Crude-Oil Systems using Methane Interaction
    Coefficients.
    J. Pet.Tech., pp.1649-1655, (November, 1978).

12. Li, Y.H., Dillard, K.H., and Robinson, R.L Jr.
    Vapour-Liquid Phase Equilibria in The Methane-Ethane-Propane-Toluene-1-Methylnaphthalene
    system at 220-400 °F
    J.Chem.Eng.Data, Vol.26, pp. 200-204, (1981).

13. Mathias, P. M., Tarik, N., and Edwin, M.
    A Density Correction for The Peng-Robinson Equation of State.
    Fluid Phase Equilibria, Vol.47, pp. 77-87, (1989).

14. Ng, H.J., Schroeder, H., and Robinson, D.B.
    Vapour-Liquid Equilibrium and Condensing Curves For A Gas Condensate Containing Nitrogen.
    Gas Processors Association, Research Report RR-105, (1987).

15. Peneloux, A., Rauzy, E., and Freze, R.
    A consistent Correction for the Redlich-Kwong-Soave Volumes
    Fluid Phase Equilibria, Vol. 8, pp. 7-23, (1982).

16. Peng, D.Y. and Robinson, D.B.
    A New Two-Constant Equation of State
    Ind.Eng.Chem.Fundam., Vol.15, pp. 59-64, (1976).

17. Prausnitz, J. M.,  Reid, R.C., and Poling, B.E.
    The Properties of  Gases and Liquids, Chap.4, 4th ed., McGraw-Hill, (1987).

18. Schmidt, G., and Wenzel, H.
    A modified Van der Waals Type Equation of State
    Chem.Eng.Sci, Vol.35, pp. 1503-1512, (1980).

19. Trebble, M.A., and Sigmund, P.M..
    A Generalised Correlation for the Prediction of Phase Behaviour in Supercritical Systems.
    Canad.J.Chem.Eng., Vol. 68, pp. 1033-1039, (December, 1990).

20. Vairogs J., Klekers, A.J., and Edmister W.C.
    Phase Equilibria in The Methane-Ethane-Propane-n-Pentane-n-Hexane-n-Decane System.
    AIChE Journal, Vol.17, pp. 308-312, (1970).

21. Yarborough, L.
    Vapour-Liquid Equilibrium Data for Multicomponent Mixtures Containing Hydrocarbon and
    Non-hydrocarbon Components.
    J.Chem.Eng.Data, Vol.17, pp. 129-133, (1972).

22. Yarborough, L.
    Application of a Generalised Equation of State to Petroleum Reservoir Mixtures.
    Advances in Chemistry Series 182,  American Chemical Society, pp. 385-439, (1979)

Figure 1
PVT Experimental Apparatus.

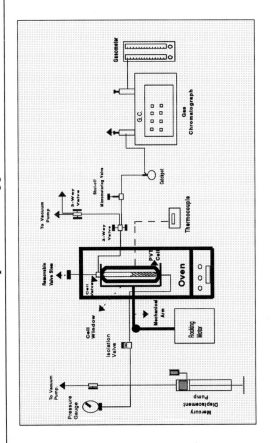

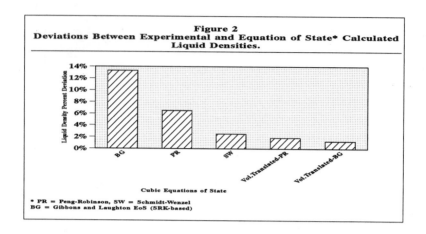

**Figure 2**
**Deviations Between Experimental and Equation of State\* Calculated Liquid Densities.**

\* PR = Peng-Robinson, SW = Schmidt-Wenzel
BG = Gibbons and Laughton EoS (SRK-based)

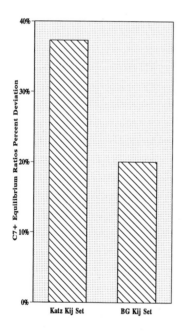

Figure 3
Deviations Between Experimental and PR EoS Calculated C7+
Equilibrium Ratios for Two Sets of Binary Interaction Parameters

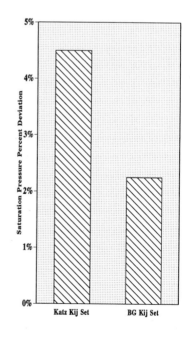

Figure 4
Deviations Between Experimental and PR EoS Calculated
Saturation Pressures For Two Sets of Binary Interaction Parameters.

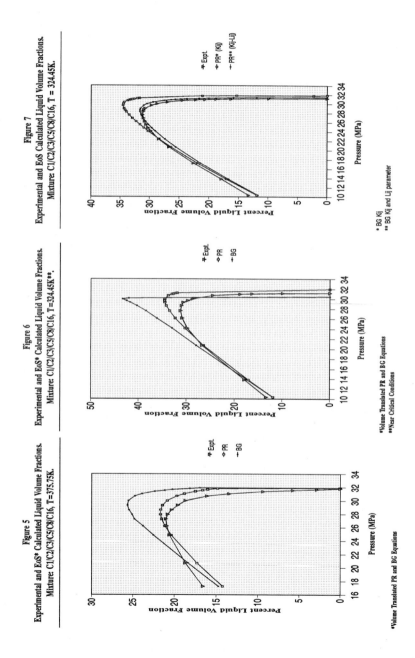

Figure 5
Experimental and EoS* Calculated Liquid Volume Fractions.
Mixture: C1/C2/C3/C5/C8/C16, T=375.75K.

*Volume Translated PR and BG Equations

Figure 6
Experimental and EoS* Calculated Liquid Volume Fractions.
Mixture: C1/C2/C3/C5/C8/C16, T=324.45K**.

*Volume Translated PR and BG Equations
**Near Critical Conditions

Figure 7
Experimental and EoS Calculated Liquid Volume Fractions.
Mixture: C1/C2/C3/C5/C8/C16, T = 324.45K.

* BG Kij
** BG Kij and Lij parameter

GAS RECYCLING IN GAS-CONDENSATE RESERVOIRS
USING HORIZONTAL WELLS
(3-D ANALYTICAL MODEL)


GAZ RECYCLING DANS LES GISEMENTS DE GAS
À CONDENSAT UTILIZANT DES PUITS HORIZONTALS
(3D MODEL ANALYTIQUE)


Bedrikovetsky, P.G., Evtjuchin A.V.,
Magarshak, T.O. and Shapiro, A.A.
Gubkin Oil & Gas Academy, Moscow, Russia.


## ABSTRACT

The development of horizontal well technology requires new methods to predict the recovery parameters for different well systems. Our way around this problem is to develop an fast three-dimensional analytical-numerical simulator. The simulator is used to predict gas recovery during the lean gas injection in regular systems of vertical, horizontal and slanted wells. It allows to run multivariant comparative studies of displacement processes in different systems of wells and to find the parameters of well locations and lengths providing optimal recovery. We have applied our model to optimisation of geomrtrical parameters of a regulary five-spot system of wells with vertical injectors and horizontal multihole producers and to determine an optimal well location for cycling of small marginal field using horizontal injector and horizontal producer.

## INTRODUCTION

Presently a number of horizontal wells are put into operation in several oil-gas-condensate fields. They are proven to be more effective than vertical ones in thin or layer-cake reservoirs. Horizontal wells are also used in submarine and other reservoirs where one faces with the difficulties in the organization of multi-well systems. An advantage of horizontal wells over vertical ones is in more intensive and uniform inflow providing better recovery. The development of horizontal well technology requires new methods to predict the recovery parameters for different well systems.

Exact analytical simulation of the reservoir development with a well system containing horizontal wells is possible only in some simplest cases, in view of the complex, sufficiently three-dimensional structure of flows. In previous studies only the formulae for the one-phase inflow to a single horizontal well were obtained, and these solutions were compared with the productivity of a vertical well in similar conditions.

The numerical simulation of lean gas recycling in a system of horizontal wells is also rather difficult since the singularities of flows take place at the displacement fronts and in the neighborhoods of wells. Numerical calculation of the recovery in a system of horizontal wells desires a powerful computer and is a time-consuming problem.

Our way around this problem was to develop an approximate analytical-numerical simulator [1,2]. It allows to run multivariant comparative studies of displacement processes in different regular systems of horizontal, vertical and slanted wells and to find the parameters of well locations and lengths providing optimal recovery.

The simulator is based on the advanced streamline concept [7,8]. A curvilinear coordinate system connected with the streamlines of an incompressible liquid flow is introduced. The incompressible flow field is calculated by the method of reflections. We accept the only assumption that the pressure change normal to a stream line is negligible as compared with the pressure change along the line. Application of this assumption together with curvilinear coordinates allows to bring the problem to a set of 1D problems which are solved analytically. The total recovery of each component is obtained as a sum of the recoveries along each stream line.

Analytical solutions of 3D displacement problems and their fast realization on PC enable us to compare different periodical well systems (parallel lines of wells, 5 or 7 spot patterns) and to choose a system providing maximal sweep efficiency. In particular, we applied the solutions obtained for the calculation of condensate recovery factors for for five-spot horizontal well systems. We study also effect of well locations in case of development of small marginal field using horizontal wells.

Dependence of heavy hydrocarbons recovery on different dimensionless geometrical parameters was studied. Dependence of the recovery efficiency on different length relations of injection and production wells as well as dependence of the recovery on different intervals between the wells were also studied. An optimal length of a horizontal well relative to the thickness of the reservoir was determined.

The analytical method developed is especially efficient for the preliminary feasibility study and design of performance of a gas-condensate reservoir with application of horizontal wells. After choice of optimal parameters of a well system numerical calculations on the basis of exact models must be run to predict the recovery more precisely.

## EFFICIENCY OF HORIZONTAL WELLS WITH THE LEAN GAS RECYCLING

There is a number of advantages of application of horizontal wells for the gas recycling in gas-condensate fields. The viscosity ratio under the lean gas injection into a condensate bearing formation is the unfair one. This results in the instability of the frontal displacement, viscous fingering and fast breakthrough of the gas injected. Production of condensate after the breakthrough declines fastly because of the fall of hydraulic conductivity in the lean gas occupied channels. The sweep under the unstable displacement is particularly low when the density of stream lines is non-uniform, which is the case in a system of vertical wells.

Lengths of horizontal wells are usually higher than of the vertical ones, and the stream lines in horizontal well systems are more uniform. Thus the sweep efficiency can be also higher.

Another advantage of the application pf horizontal wells is in lower pressure drops around injectors and producers. The reason for this is as follows: the longer is a source (sink) the lower is a pressure drop providing the same flow rate.

Low pressure drops on the production wells provide low precipitation of the liquid condensate under the depletion of a field. It also reduces the danger of the aquifer water breakthrough into production wells.

## MODELS OF DISPLACEMENT AND METHODS OF SOLUTION

We consider miscible displacement of a reservoir gas-condensate mixture by gas (at the pressure higher than the minimum miscibility one). The cases of displacement from a homogeneous reservoir and from a fractured-porous one are discussed.

The model of displacement from a homogeneous porous medium is of a one-phase two-component type. It includes the continuity equations for one component (the gas injected) and for the mixture as a whole, as well as the Darcy's Low for the flow rate. The corresponding equations are shown in Appendix B.

The 3-D model of miscible displacement in fractured-porous media contains velocities in blocks and fractures, concentrations of solvent gas in fractures and blocks. System of equations consists of equation of mass balance for the total flux, for gas component both in fractures and blocks and in the system of blocks only [4-6].

The model takes into consideration both convective and diffusive mechanisms of the block-fracture mass transfer. The fractional flow function $F(c_1,c_2)$ distributes the total flux between fractures and blocks.

The boundary conditions for both models correspond to the displacement in a system of injection and production wells in a bounded reservoir. We set the conditions of impermeability of the reservoir boundaries, values of the pressure drops between injectors and producers and values of the concentrations at the injection wells.

An analytical stream line method for 3D displacement using horizontal wells was developed in [1-3] for the case of two-phase immiscible flows (waterflooding). Mathematical backgrounds of this method for miscible displacement are discussed in Appendix B. A procedure for calculation of the stream lines is based on the methods of reflection and superposition. It is presented in Appendix A.

## CYCLING WITH DIFFERENT LOCATIONS OF INJECTOR AND PRODUCER

Horizontal wells are put into operation in large reservoirs as well as in small marginal fields. Determination of an optimal well location in such a fields allows to increase sweep efficiency varying not only well length, but also well locations relatively to reservoir boundaries.

Let us consider a small marginal reservoir of the square horizontal cross-section 300m*300m and the thickness 50m. The reservoir is being developed by one injection and one production well. Well locations are symmetrical (Fig.1). The lengths of injector and producer are equal. We characterize the well locations by the dimensionless distance 'reservoir side - well axes' b and by the dimensionless well length a. These parameters are the ratios between the corresponding linear sizes and the reservoir size. The value of b equals zero if the wells are located on the side of the formation. The unity value of a means that the well length coincides with the reservoir size.

The dependence of oil recovery (in reserves) on the value of injection volume (in porous volumes of the element) has been calculated as the most significant characteristic of the sweep efficiency. Table 1 shows the recovery factor for 2 pore volumes injected and different values of a and b.

A more influential parameter is b. The reason is that decrease of b results in straightening of stream lines. Correspondingly, the breakthrough times for different stream lines equalize. If b is equal to zero then the flow is close to linear-parallel one. Decrease of b under constant well length increases the recovery. For example, for a equal to 0.5 decrease of b from 0.15 to 0.05 results in two times increase of the recovery.

**Table 1.**
**Dependence of the recovery on dimensionless parameters a and b**

| a<br>b | 1.00 | 0.90 | 0.70 | 0.50 | 0.30 | 0.10 |
|---|---|---|---|---|---|---|
| 0.05 | 0.58 | 0.58 | 0.57 | 0.55 | 0.51 | 0.44 |
| 0.15 | 0.33 | 0.32 | 0.30 | 0.28 | 0.25 | 0.24 |
| 0.25 | 0.25 | 0.25 | 0.23 | 0.22 | 0.20 | 0.19 |
| 0.35 | 0.21 | 0.20 | 0.19 | 0.18 | 0.17 | 0.16 |
| 0.45 | 0.16 | 0.15 | 0.15 | 0.13 | 0.12 | 0.11 |

Our calculations show that the value of **a** is not influential on the recovery for the well geometry being studied. For example, the time of breakthrough is independent on this parameter, in view of the symmetric location of wells. Of course, the most effective sweep efficiency corresponds to **a**=1. However increase of the well length from **a**=0.1 to **a**=0.9 results in increase of the recovery only by 4-14% for different values of **b**.

In order to evaluate the efficiency of application of horizontal wells for small marginal fields, let us compare above values of recovery with the recovery when the two vertical wells are applied to the same field. Our calculations show, that for every horizontal well length, even if the length of a vertical well is larger than of the horizontal one (50 m vertical well and 30 m horizontal well), the recovery is 3-10 times higher for cycling with horizontal wells. This is explained by a more advantageous geometry of flow in the horizontal well system.

## APPLICATION OF MULTIHOLE WELLS

Let us consider now a regulary five-spot system of wells with vertical injectors and horizontal multihole producers. A horizontal cross-section of this system is shown on Fig.2.

The dimensionless geometrical parameters for this system are the ratios of the well length and of the element size to the thickness of the reservoir.

Fig.3 presents dependence of recovery (in initial reserves) on the volume injected (in pore volumes) for different well lengths (the size of the element is equal to 20). The dependence of recovery on the well length in such a case is not monotonous. It allows to determine an optimal length. In our case this length equals to 12.

Results of recovery calculations for different sizes of the element are shown on Fig.4. In these calculations the length of a well is equal to a half of the reservoir size. The less is the size of an element the more is the efficiency of the displacement process. However, a small size of the element means a large number of elements on the area. It results in a large number of wells and is not economically efficient. Our observations show that for the sizes of elements larger than 20 the recovery changes insignificantly.

## GAS RECYCLING IN A FRACTURED-POROUS RESERVOIR

Discuss now lean gas recycling in a fractured-porous reservoir. As above, we consider a rectangular reservoir with one horizontal injector and one horizontal producer. A characteristic dependence of recovery on geometrical parameters is similar to one in the case of gas recycling in a homogeneous reservoir.

Fig. 5 shows the effect of the flow rate on the recovery. The flow rate affects on the block-fissure mass transfer. The faster is the displacement the less time is left for the diffusive and convective mass exchange between blocks and cracks. The reservoirs fluid remains in blocks and the recovery decreases. At the increasing of the displacement rate from $10^{-6}$ m/s to the $10^{-4}$ m/s the recovery factor at two pore volume injection decreases from 0.51 to 0.47.

Fig. 6 presents the effect of cracks opening on the recovery factor under a constant block size. The higher is the opening of the cracks the higher is the fractional flow in fractures. Thus the recovery factor decreases with the opening. In our case 100 times increase of the crack opening changes the recovery factor from 0.83 to 0.03.

Fig. 7 shows the effect of the permeability ratio on the recovery factor. The higher is the permeability of the block system the higher is the fractional flow via blocks and the more intensive is the convective displacement of the condensate from blocks. On the contrary, the higher is the permeability of fractures the higher is the fractional flow in them and the lower is the convective mass transfer between blocks and fractures. With increasing of the block permeability under a constant permeability of fractures the recovery increases monotonously. 100 times increase in block permeability changes the recovery factor from 0.02 to 0.82. Dependence of the recovery on the fracture permeability under the constant block permeability is not monotonic.

Fig. 8 shows the viscosity ratio effect (viscosity of the condensate to the viscosity of the gas injected) on the recovery factor. The higher is the viscosity of the condensate the lower is the condensate mobility in blocks. So with the raise of the viscosity ratio the fractional flow in fractures increases and the convective block-fracture mass transfer decreases, which negatively affects the recovery. Five times condensate viscosity increase results in decrease of the recovery factor from 0.51 to 0.25.

## CONCLUSIONS

1. An analytical model has been developed for the simulation of gas recycling in a system of horizontal, vertical and slanted wells. The model is based on an advanced stream line concept. The 3D miscible displacement from homogeneous and fractured-porous reservoirs is described analytically.

2. Geometry of well locations can significally change the recovery in small marginal fields. In the case of two wells (injector and producer) an optimal well location is near the boundaries of a reservoir. The well length is not highly influential parameter on the recovery.

3. There is no optimal size of an element for the five-spot system including horizontal multihole producers. However, increase of the element size more than 20 times of reservoir thickness does not significantly affect the recovery. For every size of the element there does exist an optimal well length.

4. For the displacement in a fractured-porous reservoir, the effects of structural parameters (permeability ratio, opening of the fractures) have been studied, as well as the effects of the viscosity ratio and of the displacement flow rate. It is shown that the effect of microgeometry on the recovery is more significant than the effect of displacement flow rate and than the ratio of viscosities of the injected and produced fluids.

## REFERENCES

1. Bedrikovetsky P.G., Magarshak T.O. and Shapiro A.A. 3D Analytical Model for Displacement of Oil Using Horizontal Wells. SPE 26996, III Latin American/Carribean Petroleum Engineering Conference, 22-24 March 1994
2. Bedrikovetsky P.G., Magarshak T.O. and Shapiro A.A. Waterflooding in a System of Horizontal Wells (Analytical Reservoir Model. Offshore Case). SPE 29876, Bachrein, 11-14 March 1995
3. Basniev, K.S., Bedrikovetsky, P.G., and Shapiro, A.A. (1991), "Analytical Method of Simulation of 2D Flows under the Displacement of Oil in a System of Wells" Engineering Physical Journal (Injenerno-fizicheskii jurnal), V.58., No.4., p.103-111.
4. Bedrikovetsky P.G. Mathematical Theory of Oil & Gas Recovery (With applications to ex-USSR oil & gas condensate fields), 1993, Kluwer Academic Publishers, London-Boston-Dordrecht
5. Basniev K.S., Bedrikovetsky P.G. Miscible displacement in fractured-porous media (Theory and Experiments). Proc of VI European Symposium on Improved Oil Recovery. Norway, Stavanger, 1991, vol 1, p 803-812.
6. Bedrikovetsky P.G. Horizontal miscible displacement in fractured-porous media. Fluid Dynamics. USSR Academy of Sciences. (Izvestija AN SSSR. MJG) 1992, No. 3, p 87-95.
7. Martin, J.C. and Wegner, R.E. (1979),"Numerical solution of multiphase two-dimensional incompressible flow using stream-tube relationships", Trans. AIME,267 : 313-323.
8. Muscat, M. "Flows of heterogenous liquids in porous medium" -Moscow, "Gostoptechizdat", 1949.

## APPENDIX A  CALCULATION OF STREAM LINES

Let us consider an auxiliary problem on a 3D 1-phase flow of an incompressible liquid. Such a flow is described by the Darcy's law and the mass conservation law:

$$\operatorname{div} u = 0, \quad u = \nabla \phi \quad (\phi = \frac{k}{\mu} P)$$

In this section the wells are supposed to be linear, with infinitely small radii. As boundary conditions, the flow rate distributions along well lengths are given. For the sake of simplicity these distributions are chosen constant. We accept also the conditions of impermeability on the top and on the bottom of a reservoir which are assumed to be two horizontal planes.

To solve this problem the following algorithm based on the reflection and superposition methods is proposed:

    1. The solution for one isolated point source in a bounded layer is derived by the use of the reflection method;

    2. This solution is integrated along a well to obtain its flow rate;

    3. The impact of each well is summed over all the system of wells.

Let us obtain the flow rate field for a point source in a bounded layer with impermeable boundaries. To do so, we reflect the layer, with the source inside it, about its boundaries. Then we reflect the layers reflected and continue this process to infinity. The solution is the superposition of the flow rates of the initial point source and all the sources obtained by reflections

$$u = \sum_{k=-\infty}^{\infty} \frac{q}{4\pi} \frac{r_k}{r_k^3} \tag{A1}$$

where $r_k$ is the position vector to the $k^{th}$ source obtained by reflection.

The flow rate field for a linear source of the flow rate $Q$ and the length $L$ is obtained by integration of each term of the series (A1) along the well

$$u = \frac{Q}{4\pi} * \sum_{k=-\infty}^{\infty} \frac{R_k^1/R_k^1 + R_k^2/R_k^2}{(R_k^1 + R_k^2 + L)(R_k^1 + R_k^2 - L)} \tag{A2}$$

Here $R_k^1$ and $R_k^2$ are position vectors to the ends of the $k^{th}$ well.

Eq.(A2) describes the flow rate of an 1-phase incompressible liquid in a bounded layer for the only injection or production well. To solve the problem for a system of wells we sum the solutions for all the wells in the system according to the principle of superposition.

$$u = \sum_{i=1}^{N} \sum_{k=-\infty}^{\infty} \frac{Q_i}{4\pi} * \frac{R_{k_i}^1/R_{k_i}^1 + R_{k_i}^2/R_{k_i}^2}{(R_{k_i}^1 + R_{k_i}^2 + L_i)(R_{k_i}^1 + R_{k_i}^2 - L_i)} \tag{A3}$$

Thus the solution of the auxiliary problem is represented by the series (A3). The convergence of this series is accelerated by the condition of flow rate balance. For further improvement of the convergence we couple symmetrical terms.

$$u = \sum_{i=1}^{N} \left( u_{0_i} + \sum_{k=1}^{\infty} (u_{k_i} + u_{-k_i}) \right) \tag{A4}$$

We retain only a finite number of terms in the series (A4) which satisfy the inequality

$$|u_k| \geq |u_0|\varepsilon$$

## APPENDIX B. THE STREAM LINE METHOD

We will demonstrate the modified stream-line method on the example of miscible displacement from a homogeneous reservoir. The governing system of equations for such a displacement has the form of

$$m\frac{\partial c}{\partial t} + U\nabla c = 0$$

$$div\ U = 0$$

$$U = -\Pi(c)\nabla P, \quad \Pi(c) = \frac{k}{\mu(c)}$$

The wells are disposed in a reservoir, represented by a homogenous porous layer bounded by the two parallel planes. The boundaries of the reservoir are impermeable:

$$\frac{\partial P}{\partial n} = 0, \qquad z = z_0, \quad z = z^0$$

The displacement takes place due to the pressure drop between the injection and production wells. This drop is defined by the pressure values at wells

$$P|_{L_i} = P_i \qquad i = 1,N$$

To complete the couple of initial and boundary conditions the value of concentration at the injection wells and initial concentration must be preassigned.

$$c|_{l_i} = c^0 \ (i=1,M); \qquad t=0: \ c=0$$

Consider now a curvilinear orthogonal system of coordinates $(\varphi, \ \psi, \ \eta)$ . Dependence $\varphi = \varphi(x,y,z)$ is determined by integration of the flow rate field which was calculated in Appendix A. Coordinates $\psi, \eta$ do not vary along each stream line.

The condition for this system to be orthogonal is given by

$$A*A^T = E \ \{u(\varphi,\psi,\eta)\}^2,$$

where $E$ is the 3*3 unit matrix, $A$ is the transformation matrix of the grid system of $(x,y,z)$ into the system $(\varphi, \ \psi, \ \eta)$ .

Transforming the flow equation to the system of curvilinear coordinates $(\varphi,\psi,\eta)$ we obtain

$$m\frac{\partial c}{\partial t} + (w_x\frac{\partial \varphi}{\partial x} + w_y\frac{\partial \varphi}{\partial y} + w_z\frac{\partial \varphi}{\partial z})\frac{\partial c}{\partial \varphi} +$$
$$(w_x\frac{\partial \psi}{\partial x} + w_y\frac{\partial \psi}{\partial y} + w_z\frac{\partial \psi}{\partial z})\frac{\partial c}{\partial \psi} + (w_x\frac{\partial \eta}{\partial x} + w_y\frac{\partial \eta}{\partial y} + w_z\frac{\partial \eta}{\partial z})\frac{\partial c}{\partial \eta} = 0 \tag{B1}$$

It can be shown [1,2] that under the assumption that the stream lines are constant the equation for pressure is transformed to

$$\Pi(c)\frac{\partial P}{\partial \varphi} = H(\psi,\eta,t) \tag{B2}$$

and the equation for the flow rate to

$$w = H\frac{\partial \varphi}{\partial n} = Hu_n \tag{B3}$$

Thus, Eq.(B1) accepts the form of

$$m\frac{\partial c}{\partial t} - H \ |u|^2\frac{\partial c}{\partial \varphi} - H(\frac{\partial \varphi}{\partial x}\frac{\partial \psi}{\partial x} + \frac{\partial \varphi}{\partial y}\frac{\partial \psi}{\partial y} + \frac{\partial \varphi}{\partial z}\frac{\partial \psi}{\partial z})\frac{\partial c}{\partial \psi} -$$
$$H(\frac{\partial \varphi}{\partial x}\frac{\partial \eta}{\partial x} + \frac{\partial \varphi}{\partial y}\frac{\partial \eta}{\partial y} + \frac{\partial \varphi}{\partial z}\frac{\partial \eta}{\partial z})\frac{\partial c}{\partial \eta} = 0 \tag{B4}$$

Rewriting Eq.(B5) in account of orthogonality of the system of curvilinear coordinates $(\varphi, \ \psi, \ \eta)$ we obtain the following equation

$$m\frac{\partial c}{\partial t} - H \ |u|^2 \frac{\partial c}{\partial \varphi} = 0 \tag{B5}$$

Eqs.(B2), (B3) and (B5) describe the 3D displacement process in terms of curvilinear coordinates $(\varphi,\psi,\eta)$ . Note that Eq.(B5) has become 1D hyperbolic displacement equation in a stream tube of variable cross-section. The stream functions $\psi,\eta$ are the parameters identifying the stream tubes.

Introduce the following new variables instead of $\varphi$ and $t$

$$\xi = \int_{\varphi}^{\varphi_0} \frac{\partial\varphi}{|u|^2(\varphi,\psi,\eta)} \qquad \text{(B6)}$$

$$\tau = \int_0^t \frac{H(\psi,\eta,t')dt'}{m} \qquad \text{(B7)}$$

After substitution of $\xi$ and $\tau$ into (B5) for $\varphi$ and $t$ we obtain the piston-like displacement equation for each stream line

$$\frac{\partial c}{\partial\tau} + \frac{\partial c}{\partial\xi} = 0 \qquad \text{(B8)}$$

with the following initial and boundary conditions

$$\begin{aligned} \xi = 0 &: c = c^* \\ \tau = 0 &: c = c_0 \end{aligned} \qquad \text{(B9)}$$

The dependence $H(\psi,\eta,t)$ is determined from the boundary conditions. Integrating Eq.(B2) by $\varphi$ we find that

$$P = P_0 - \int_{\varphi}^{\varphi_0} \frac{d\varphi}{\Pi(c)} \qquad \text{(B10)}$$

In view of Eqs.(B6), (B7) concentration of gas depends on $\xi$ and $\tau$. For stream line $(\psi,\eta)$ from well $i$ to well $j$ we have

$$\Delta P_{ij} = H(\psi,\eta,t)*\Gamma$$

$$\Gamma = \int_{\varphi}^{\varphi_0} \frac{d\varphi}{\Pi(\xi(\varphi,\psi,\eta),\tau)} \qquad \text{(B11)}$$

By definition (B7),

$$H = m\frac{\partial\tau}{\partial t} \qquad \text{(B12)}$$

Substituting this equality into Eq.(B11) we obtain the differential equation

$$\frac{\partial\tau}{\partial t} = \frac{\Delta P}{m\int_{\varphi}^{\varphi_0} \Pi(\xi,\tau)d\varphi} \qquad \text{(B13)}$$

The initial condition for this differential equation for $\tau$ is $\tau(0,\psi,\eta) = 0$. The equation obtained can be solved by the separation of variables.

Some integral characteristics of the solution (flow rate of each phase and total flow rate for any moment, recovery and phase saturations at production wells) are of the most importance. We will show how to calculate these characteristics without calculation of all the pressure and saturation fields in a reservoir.

First we will clarify the physical meaning of the function $H(\varphi, \psi, \eta)$. Consider an arbitrary bounded part $\omega$ of an equipotential $\varphi = const$. The total flow rate through $\omega$ is expressed as

$$Q = \int_\omega w_n ds = \int_\omega H u_n ds = \int_\omega H |u| ds$$

Due to the orthogonality conditions of transformation $(x, y, z) \rightarrow (\varphi, \psi, \eta)$ one can prove that the product $|u| ds$ equals $d\psi d\eta$. Thus we have

$$Q = \int_\omega H(\psi, \eta, t) d\psi d\eta$$

and the value of H expresses the flow rate per one stream line at the time moment t. Therefore, according to Eq.(B12), $m\tau$ is the volume of liquid which has been flown to the moment t along the stream line $(\psi, \eta)$. Hence the total quantity of liquid T(t) having been flown to the moment t through an injection (production) well, in porous volumes, is expressed by

$$T(t) = \iint \frac{m\tau(\psi, \eta, t)}{\Omega} d\psi d\eta \tag{B14}$$

Since the physical meaning of the function F is share of the water a in flow then the recovery to the moment t (in reserves) is expressed by

$$B(t) = \frac{1}{\Omega} * \int_0^t \iint (1 - c(\psi, \eta)) \Big|_{\substack{prod. \\ well}} H(\psi, \eta, t) d\psi d\eta dt \tag{B15}$$

Eqs.(B14), (B15) have been used in our program for the calculation of recovery.

NOMENCLATURE.

$k$　- permeability;

$L$　- length of a well;

$r_c$　- radius of a well;

$m$　- porosity;

$R_1, R_2$　- distance to the first and second ends of a well;

$u = (u_x, u_y, u_z)$　- the velocity of an incompressible liquid;

$w = (w_x, w_y, w_z)$　- the rate of two-phase flow;

$z_0, z^0$　- the bottom and top boundaries of a layer.

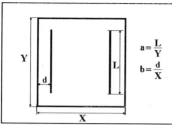

Figure 1. The horizontal cross-section of the small field. Locations of the injection and production wells.

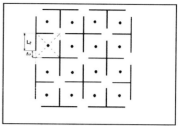

Figure 2. Location of wells in the five-spot periodical system.

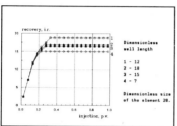

Figure 3. Recovery for different lengths of the branches of multihole wells.

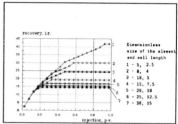

Figure 4. Recovery for different sizes of an element.

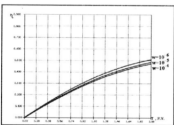

Figure 5. Recovery from a fractured-porous reservoir under different displacement velocities.

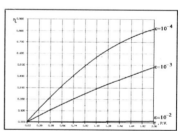

Figure 6. Recovery for different crack openings under a constant block size.

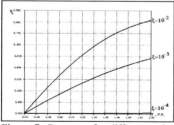

Figure 7. Recovery for different ratios of block and crack permeabilities.

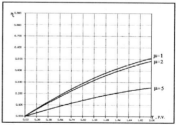

Figure 8. Recovery for different viscosity ratios.

STUDY OF NOVEL TECHNOLOGY TO DEVELOP
GAS CONDENSATE FIELD WITH OIL RIM


ETUDE D'UNE TECHNOLOGIE NOUVELLE DE LA PRODUCTION
D'UN GISEMENT DE GAZ À CONDENSAT AVEC UNE BANDE D'HUILE

S.N. Zakirov
Oil and Gas Research Institute, Russia

ABSTRACT

Oil production from oil rims of gas condensate fields is characterized by low efficiency, namely, by low ultimate oil recovery factors. One of the main cause is connected with gas and water cones for mation. There are different ways of struggle with them which are not very successful. Therefore, inves tigation results of new approach to oil rims development are given in this paper. It is based on gel screen creation and the use of liquid barrier, i.e. advantages of screens and barrier flooding are realized simultaneously. The study was fulfilled with application of three- or fourphase, 2D or 3D mathematical models. It appears that gel screen creation at the level of GOC with given extent and configuration is real but not simple problem. The technology effectiveness was evaluated as applied to oil rims similar to TWOP and TWGP of Troll field (Norway) and Lantorskoe field (Russia). Alternative variants were made in supposition that producer was operated under depletion regime with critical gas free oil (liquid) rate. Simulation results show that development efficiency according to the considered technology depends on formation anisotropy.

RÉSUMÉ

La production d'huile des anneaux d'huile des gisements de gaz à condensat se distingue par l'efficacité reduite, notamment par par petite récupération d'huile. Une des raisons principales est lieé avec la formation des cônes d'eau et de gaz. Il existe des approches differentes de lutte contre ces phénomènes. Cet exposé démontre les résultats des rechrches d'une nouvelle approche dans la production d'huile des anneaux d'huile. Cette approche se base sur la création d'un écran de gel et d'une barriere liquide, c'est à dire utilise des avantages des écrans et de l'injection barrière d'eau. Les recherches ont été executeés sur la base des modèles 2D soit 3D pour les écoulements triphasiqus ou quatrephasiques. Il a été établi, que la création d'un écran de gel au niveau du contact gas-huile avec une longueur donnée peut être réalisée, mais présente un problème difficile. L'efficacité de la technologie a été prouvée sur l'exemple des anneaux d'huile du gisement Troll (Norvège) et du gisement Lentorskoé (Russie). Comme les variantes de base ont été retenues les variantes de production des puits en régime d'épuisement avec les débits critiques sans gaz de l'huile (du liquide). Les résultats de la simulation démontrent, que l'efficacité de la production suivant l'approche proposée se trouve en dépendance de l'hétérogénéité de la couche productive.

INTRODUCTION

It's well known that a lot of oil reserves all over the world are confined to oil rims of gas-oil-condensate fields and rather frequently - to thin oil rims (the thickness of oil column is about 10 m). At the same time the efficiency of oil recovery from them is very low. It differs from several percents to approximately 20%, being equal in average to about 10%. Obviously, it is difficult to put up with such situation.

The main reason for low oil recovery from oil rims is connected with the phenomenon of the coning, i.e. with breakthrough of gas and water to the bottom hole of the operating wells. Therefore, M.Muskat and R.Wyckoff suggested the theory of stationary coning [1].

M.Muskat's and R.Wyckoff's theory was developed concerning the oil well with partial penetration into formation. Such well drains oil field with bottom water. According to this theory anybody can find so called critical oil rate (oil rate without water in the output). They say, that the use of such rate leads to stationary water cone below well and absence of water breakthrough to the bottom hole of operating wells.

Later on a lot of theoretical and experimental results were published on the problem of stationary coning [2-13]. Some investigations were devoted to the critical water free oil rate [2-5,7,10-12], some of them consider the critical water free gas rate [9,12]. And other papers deal with estimation of the critical oil rate without water and gas in case of gas-and-oil fields and indicate the ways of defining the best drain interval in oil rim [6,11-13].

Recently horizontal wells have been widely used in the practice of oil and gas production. So the theory of stationary coning was developed for such wells [12,14-18].

There are some papers proposing creation of different screens in gas bearing part of reservoir in order to prevent gas breakthrough to bottom hole [12,19-21]. Sometimes barrier flooding allows to separate gas cap and oil rim and to increase gas free oil rates [22-24].

Nevertheless further investigations are necessary to the problem of effective oil recovery from oil rims, as, on the one hand, each new gas-and-oil field is characterized by its own features and, on the other hand, everywhere they have very low oil recovery factors of oil rims. The results given below were undertaken in order to further advance the most difficult problem of the oil rims development.

ESSENCE OF THE CONSIDERED TECHNOLOGY

Practice shows that gas cone is the most undesirable one from above two cones. Mathematical simulation permits to understand why screen creation or barrier flooding application do not give good results. It turned out to be that screens can not prevent gas breakthrough through screen or below one. For barrier flooding injected water falls down into oil rim and water cuts well production. Therefore, it is worth to combine its advantages in order to remove their shortcomings.

Proposed novel technology consists in two stages:
1. immovable gel screen creation at the level of gas-oil contact;
2. mobile liquid barrier creation by means of working agent injection over the screen into gas cap.

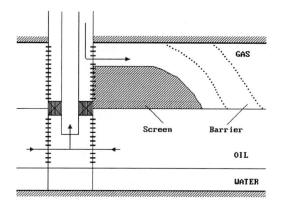

**Fig. 1. Scheme of considered technology in case of vertical wells usage.**

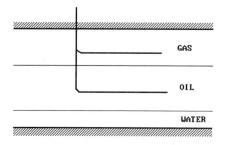

**Fig. 2. Location of operating and injecting holes in case of horizontal wells usage.**

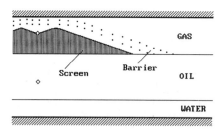

**Fig. 3. Scheme of considered technology in case of horizontal wells usage.**

The goal of the local screen development (operation number 1) does not consist in struggling against gas breakthrough. The main purpose of this stage is to prevent the injected fluid (water) downfall into the well during realization of operation 2.

The aim of operation 2 are the following:
• creation of increasing in size and volume barrier between gas and oil to avert gas cone breakthrough;
• formation pressure maintenance to escape uncontrolled oil rim shift beyond the initial boundaries.

The considered technology foresees application for both vertical and horizontal operating and injecting wells systems (see Fig. 1-3). Stated below results were received for horizontal wells system (see Fig. 2,3).

GEL SCREEN CREATION

Simulation of gel screen creation process is an important constituent of the proposed technology. Obviously all technical and economical figures depend on success of that technological stage.

Simulation of gel screen creation consists in the following. Gel solution is pumped through injection horizontal hole located in gas cap in order to receive after gelling immobile screen at the level of GOC.

First results of simulation showed that gel screen creation process is quite complicated problem. Uncontrolled "freeze" gel screen near injection hole has taken place under gel injection with definite gelling time. Gel screen expanded eventually with very whimsical configuration without any aspiration to dispose at the level of GOC.

Further investigations showed that it was necessary to control gel screen formation at the expense of different technological parameters. It appears that it is expediently
• gel solution injection process has to be divided for sepa rate stages,
• gelling time for each injection portion (for corresponding stage) should be completely definite,
• gel solution injection rate has to submit to optimal dy namics.

Immovable gel screen with given configuration and location, for instance, as applied to TWOP manage to be created under condition that the duration of separate injection stages changed from 2.1 to 3.5 days, gelling time of individual portion of gel solution was from 4.3 to 107 days and gel solution injection rate grew in time from 300 to 3010 $m^3$/day. The corresponding gel screens as applied to fields similar to TWOP and Lantorskoe field had length about 150 m and 250 m accordingly (see Fig. 4). These screens were used in further research.

INVESTIGATION RESULTS FOR TROLL FIELD

First of all the applicability of immovable gel screens against gas breakthrough was evaluated with using data reported in paper [25]. Therefore the calculations were made as applied to variants with and without gel screen under different distance between horizontal wells holes. In both cases the wells operation was simulated under regime of critical gas free oil rates at each current moment. The results comparison showed that the production indices with immovable screen got worst than in case without screen. Time of first

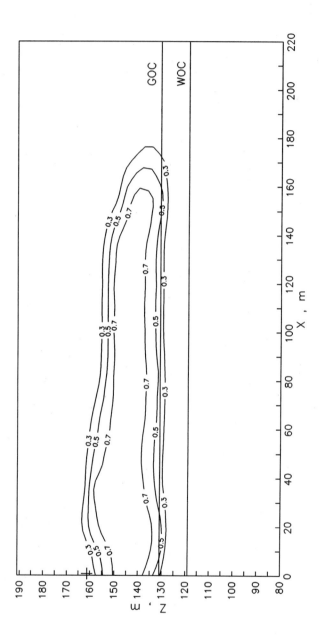

**Fig. 4. Isolines of immovable gel saturation in case of screen as applied to TWGP.**

gas breakthrough to well is reduced, ultimate oil recovery happens less in case of the screen creation and use. It is explained by gas breakthrough below gel screen towards to the operating horizontal hole. Considerable gas inflow takes place at the expense of vertical flow if body of gel screen has even negligible permeability.

Simulation of considered technology was fulfilled for different variants. It turned out to be that time of putting into operation of the lowest horizontal hole is significant. Here time is accounted from beginning of liquid barrier development. Therefore some variants were studied when, for example, oil was produced for a long time under absence of screen and barrier and then lowest horizontal hole was putted into operation.

All examined variants gave the negative results. It is connected with very large reservoir qualitaties of TWOP and TWGP deposits and also with low anisotropy grade. Here permeability along lateral is in average equal to 6D and horizontal to vertical permeability ratio is equal to only 2. As a result injected water beyond screen downfalls in oil rim and cuts off considerable oil reserves. Therefore ultimate oil recovery factor is less than in case of depletion regime realization and the use of critical gas free rates.

Thus in cases of large permeability and low anisotropy it is impossible to enhance oil recovery of thin oil rims by means of immovable screen usage, liquid barrier or their different combination.

INVESTIGATION RESULTS FOR LANTORSKOE FIELD

Lantorskoe field is one of the largest in West Siberia. The basic oil reserves are sandwiched between gas cap and bottom water. The thickness of gas-bearing formation changes from several meters to 20-25 m, the oil column thickness makes up 8-10 m. In our simulation initial data for one of zones were following: initial reservoir pressure is equal to 21 MPa, porosity m=0.24, horizontal permeability $k_h$=285 mD, vertical permeability $k_v$=2,85 mD, oil density amounts to 914 kg/m$^3$, oil viscosity $\mu_o$=3.57 mPa·s, initial gas-oil ratio R=73 m$^3$/m$^3$, gas column thickness $h_g$=12 m, oil column thickness $h_o$=8 m, water column thickness $h_w$=10 m. Grid block dimensions changed from 1 m to 90 m along axe OX and from 1 m to 5.25 m along axe OZ. Length of horizontal holes were equal to 500 m. The distance between wells was 1000 m. Considered well is put into production at the initial oil rate equal to 50 m$^3$/day. Under depletion regime and maintenance of current critical gas free rate ultimate oil recovery is equal to 8.6 %.

Then the efficiency of so called barrier flooding was studied for Lantorskoe field. For this purpose different working agent injection variants in gas bearing zone were examined to make barrier between gas cap and oil rim. Liquids with various viscosity were considered, their viscosity was less or equal or more than oil viscosity at formation conditions. Viscosity of working agents changed from 0.5 mPa·s to 20 mPa·s. Liquid screen with viscosity equal to 10 mPa·s provides the largest oil recovery factor. Unfortunately, it is only equal to 8.2 %, i.e. less than under depletion regime.

Investigated technology foreseeing gel screen creation and water barrier formation turned out to be effective as applied to Lantorskoe field development (see Table). In considered variants wells were exploited under constant mass fluid rates which corresponded to the initial mass rates. It was possible because of strong restriction absence on gas-oil ratio. In some variants outward formation element boundaries were taken as permeable on gas and impermeable on another one.

**Table. Immovable gel screen. Formation element of the Lantorskoe field. Duration time 30 years.**

| I t e m | Variant number | | | | | | | | | |
|---|---|---|---|---|---|---|---|---|---|---|
| | L007a | L007b | L071 | L071a | L072 | L072a | L073 | L074 | L074a | L075 |
| Barrier creation before bringing well into production | − | + | + | + | + | + | + | + | + | + |
| Screen agent viscosity , cp | 8 | 8 | 8 | 8 | 8 | 8 | 8 | 8 | 8 | 8 |
| Completion above WOC , m | 3 | 3 | 3 | 3 | 6 | 6 | 5 | 4 | 4 | 5 |
| Barrier creation rate , Sm³/day | 50 | 50 | 50 | 100 | 50 | 100 | 50 | 50 | 100 | 100 |
| Initial oil production rate , Sm³/day | 50 | 50 | 100 | 100 | 50 | 100 | 50 | 100 | 100 | 100 |
| Cumulative oil production , $10^3$ Sm³ | 121 | 175 | 180 | 217 | 198 | 228 | 189 | 191 | 223 | 226 |
| Ultimate oil recovery factor , % | 16,8 | 24,3 | 25,0 | 30,2 | 27,5 | 31,7 | 26,3 | 26,5 | 31,0 | 31,7 |
| Cumulative water production , $10^3$ Sm³ | 204 | 322 | 440 | 803 | 313 | 844 | 299 | 422 | 797 | 794 |
| Cumulative water injection , $10^3$ Sm³ | 548 | 602 | 602 | 1150 | 602 | 1150 | 602 | 602 | 1150 | 1150 |
| Difference between cumulative water injection and production , $10^3$ Sm³ | 344,0 | 280,0 | 162,0 | 347,0 | 289,0 | 306,0 | 303,0 | 180,0 | 353,0 | 356,0 |
| Gas recovery factor , % | 122,7 | 32,5 | 258,0 | 43,2 | 38,5 | 47,2 | 36,3 | 260,04 | 44,4 | 45,2 |

Analysis of results given in Table shows that proposed technology is quite promising when anisotropy is large. For example, the best variant **L075** allows to attain oil recovery factor equal to 31.3 % instead of 8.6 % under depletion regime and 8.2 % when we use liquid barrier. There are technological parameters which help to enhance oil recovery factors, namely, horizontal well standoff relatively WOC, rate of liquid injection under creation of liquid barrier, initial oil rate and so on.

CONCLUSIONS

Horizontal wells usage under oil rims development allows in some cases to produce oil effectively with critical gas free oil rates.

Immovable screens creation at GOC level with goal to avert the gas breakthrough is probably unperspective direction of enhanced oil recovery from oil rims.

Sometimes movable liquid barrier with optimal viscosity of working agent may permit increasing of oil recovery factor.

Considered in this paper technology deserves attention as applied to gas-and-oil deposits with anisotropic reservoir.

ACKNOWLEDGMENTS

Author would like to thank very much Statoil for this research support and permission to publish corresponding results, A.Henriques and O.Scontorp for their kind support and help under our investigations fulfillment, V.Gordon and V.Levochkin for calculations, B.Palatnik and I.Zakirov for their help to create 3D fourphase simulator.

REFERENCES

1. Muskat M., Wyckoff R. An approximate theory of water-coning in oil production. Trans. AIME, Petr. Dev. Techn., vol. 114, 1935.
2. Charnyi I. A. On the critical rates and differential pressures in the oil fields with bottom water or gas cap. Trans. of the conference on the development of scientific research in the region of the secondary oil production methods, Baku, 1953 (in Russian).
3. Meyer H. J., Garder A. O. Mechanics of two immiscible fluids in porous media. J. Applied Physics, vol. 25, № 11, 1954.
4. Chaney P. G., Noble M. W., Henson W. L. and Rice J. D. How to perforate your well to prevent water and gas coning. The Oil and Gas J., May 7, 1956.
5. Efros D. A. , Allahverdieva R. A. Calculation of the water-free critical rates of the partially penetrated wells by using the modelling data. Trans. VNII, vol. X, 1957 (in Russian).
6. Kurbanov A. K. On operating of the oil fields with gas cap. Izvestia vuzov, series "Oil and Gas", № 6, 1958 (in Russian).
7. Perez Rosales C., Hefferan J. V., Loreto Mendoza E. G. Graphical solution of fluid-coning problems. The Oil and Gas J., vol. 57, № 33, 1959.
8. Piskunov N. S. The estimation method of the water-free critical rates in the field with bottom water under different types of penetration. Trans. VNII, vol. 19, Gostoptechizdat, 1959 (in Russian).
9. Lapuk B. B., Brudno A. G., Somov B. E. On cones of the bottom water in gas fields. Gazovaia promishlennost, № 2, 1961 (in Russian).
10. Stklanin Y. I., Telkov A. P. The calculation of the water-free critical rates in the homo-anisotropic formations with the axe symmetry. J. Appl. Mathem. and Techn. Phis. Acad. Scien. USSR, № 5,

1961 (in Russian).
11. Telkov A. P., Stklanin Y. I. The calculation of water-free and gas- free critical rates in the oilgas fields. Trans. MING and GP named after Gubkin, vol. 42, Gostoptechizdat, 1963 (in Russian).
12. Telkov A. P., Stklanin Y. I. The formation of the water cones in the oil and gas production. Publ. House "Nedra", 1965 (in Russian).
13. Kurbanov A. K. The design and calculation of the technological figures of the oilgas fields development. Manual on the design of the oil fields development and production (edited by Gimatudinov S. K.) Publ. House "Nedra", 1983 (in Russian).
14. Chaperon I. Theoretical study of coning toward horizontal and vertical wells in anisotropic formations: subcritical and critical rates. Paper SPE 15430 presented at the SPE Annual technical conference and exhibition, New Orleans, Oct. 5-8, 1986.
15. Kararas M., Ayan C., Productivity and coning behavior of phased horizontal completions. Paper SPE 22928 presented at the 66 SPE Annual technical conference and exhibition. Dallas, Oct. 6-9, 1991.
16. Boyun Guo, Molinard J.- E., Lee R. L. A general solution of gas/water coning problem for horizontal wells. Paper SPE 25050 presented at the Europec, Cannes, Nov. 16-18, 1992.
17. Weiping Yang, Wattenbarger R. A. Water coning calculations for vertical and horizontal wells. Paper SPE 22931 presented at the 66 SPE Annual technical conference and exhibition. Dallas, Oct. 6-9, 1991.
18. Ekrann S. On the protection against coning provided by horizontal barriers of limited lateral extent. The paper presented at the 6th European IOR- Symposium in Stavanger, Norway, May 21-23, 1991.
19. Zakirov S. N., Korotaev I. P., Perepelichenko V. F. Novel in the technology of oil production from the oil rims of gas fields. Publ. House VNIEGasprom, vol. 2, 1982 (in Russian).
20. Medvedsky R. I., Krakin A. B., Balin V. P. Modern and perspective ways of the West Siberia gas- condensate fields exploitation. Publ. House VNIEGasprom, 1980 (in Russian).
21. Hanssen J. E., Dalland M. Foam barriers for thin oil rims: gas blockage at reservoir conditions. Paper presented at the 6 th European IOR- Symposium in Stavanger, Norway, May 21- 23, 1991.
22. Amelin I.D. Peculiarities of gas-and-oil fields development. Publ. House Nedra, 1978 (in Russian).
23. Afanasieva A.V., Zinovieva L.A. Analysis of gas-and-oil fields development. Publ. House Nedra, 1980 (in Russian).
24. Durmishian A.G. Gas condensate fields. Publ. House Nedra, 1979 (in Russian).
25. Hang B.T., Ferguson W.I., Kydland T. Horizontal wells in the water zone: the most effective way of tapping oil from thin oil zones? Paper SPE 22929 presented at the 66th Annual technical conference and exhibition. Dallas, Oct. 6-9, 1991.

## IN SITU BIOVENTING/BIOSPARGING FOR REMEDIATING SOIL AND GROUNDWATER AT A NATURAL GAS DEHYDRATOR SITE

## BIOASPERSION/BIOPERÇAGE IN SITU POUR L'AMÉLIORATION DU TERRAIN ET DE LA NAPPE PHRÉATIQUE D'UN SITE DE DÉSHYDRATATION DE GAZ NATUREL

A. W. Lawrence, D. L. Miller, J. A. Miller, R. L. Weightman
Remediation Technologies, Inc., USA

T. D. Hayes
Gas Research Institute, USA

## ABSTRACT

This paper describes a GRI sponsored bioventing/biosparging field demonstration which was conducted over a thirteen month period at a former glycol dehydrator site located near Traverse City, Michigan, USA. The goal of the project was to determine the feasibility of this technology for site remediation and to develop engineering design concepts for application at similar sites. The chemicals-of-interest are BTEX and alkanes ($C_4$ through $C_{10}$). A pump and treat system has operated since 1991 to treat the groundwater BTEX plume. Bioventing/biosparging was installed in September 1993 to treat the contaminant source area.

Three different operating modes were tested and compared by performing in situ respirometry studies to establish biodegradation rates. A hydrocarbon mass balance based on soil and groundwater sampling was compared to the estimate of hydrocarbons biologically degraded based on the respiration studies. Gaseous phase nutrients were added to stimulate the rates of biodegradation.

The results of the study suggest that bioventing/biosparging is a feasible technology for in situ remediation of soil and groundwater at gas industry glycol dehydrator sites.

## RÉSUMÉ

Cette étude traite d'une démonstration sur le terrain relatif au bioperçage et à la bioaspersion, qui a été soutenue par GRI et conduite au cours d'une période de plus de treize mois à un ancien site de déshydratation de glycol situé près de Traverse City (Michigan, États-Unis). L'objectif de ce projet était de déterminer la faisabilité de cette technologie de traitement de site et de développer des concepts de design technique applicables à d'autres sites similaires. Les produits chimiques d'intérêts sont les BTEX (Benzène - Toluène - Éthène - Xylène) et les alcanes (de $C_4$ à $C_{10}$). Une pompe et un système de traitement ont été opérationnels depuis 1991 pour traiter la partie de la nappe phréatique polluée par le BTEX. Le bioperçage et la bioaspersion ont été installés en Septembre 1993 pour traiter la partie où se situe la source de contamination.

Trois modes d'opérations différents ont été essayés et comparés en accomplissant des études de respirométrie in situ afin d'établir les taux de biodégradation. Une mesure de la masse d'hydrocarbures fondée sur des échantillons de sol et de la nappe phréatique a été comparée aux estimations d'hydrocarbures dégradés biologiquement issues des études respiratoires. Des nutrients en phase gazeuse ont été ajoutés afin de stimuler le taux de biodégradation.

Les résultats de l'étude laissent à penser que le bioperçage et la bioaspersion sont des technologies faisables pour le traitement in situ du sol et de la nappe phréatique de sites de déshydratation de glycol de l'industrie du gaz.

## INTRODUCTION

This GRI field experiment at a member company's site was performed to investigate the feasibility of using bioventing\biosparging for cost effective remediation of natural gas glycol dehydrator site contamination. Daily field activities began on September 1, 1993, and ended July 4, 1994. Post-demonstration groundwater and soil sampling was conducted in October 1994, and a post-demonstration respirometry study was conducted in November 1994. A final sampling event is scheduled for the end of the 3rd quarter 1995 to document long term performance of bioventing/biosparging.

A series of air sparge wells and multilevel monitor points were installed in the location of the former glycol dehydrator, which was the source of a 580 m (1900 ft) BTEX groundwater plume. Figure 1 is a site plan for this field experiment.

A number of process equipment configurations and process operational programs were field tested to determine which approach resulted in maximum biodegradation rates. Groundwater, soil, and soil gas samples were collected and analyzed to determine the effectiveness of the system. Realtime soil gas and groundwater field measurements were taken to monitor performance. Gaseous phase nutrients were added when biokinetic rates determined from the respiration studies declined sufficiently to suggest that nutrients had become rate limiting. When nutrients were added, the field measured biokinetic rates increased.

## EXPERIMENTAL DESIGN

### Experimental Plan

The bioventing/biosparging system consists of two linked process operations; i.e., a biosparging process and a bioventing process. The biosparging process was designed to inject air into the saturated zone while the bioventing process was designed to collect soil gas to control and monitor subsurface air flow.

The experimental plan consisted of a mechanical system design, an analytical sampling plan, a field monitoring plan, and an operating plan. The following equation was used to estimate the mass biodegraded as determined by soil, groundwater, and vapor analytical sampling:

$$IMASS - TMASS - PTMASS - SVEMASS = BDMASS_{ANALYTICAL} \tag{1}$$

where:   $IMASS$ = hydrocarbon mass initially in treatment zone
$TMASS$ = hydrocarbon mass at time (t) in treatment zone
$PTMASS$ = hydrocarbon mass leaving treatment zone from pump
             and treat system
$SVEMASS$ = hydrocarbon mass extracted with soil vapor
             extraction system
$BDMASS_{ANALYTICAL}$ = hydrocarbon mass biologically degraded

Zero-order biodegradation rates for the unsaturated zone were estimated by measuring oxygen depletion in monitor points screened in the unsaturated zone following periodic cessation of the air sparging. The saturated zone biodegradation rates were estimated by measuring dissolved oxygen utilization in the groundwater in the monitor points screened in the saturated zone. The average biodegradation rates for both the saturated and unsaturated zones were then used to estimate the mass biologically degraded based on the following equation:

$$UMASS + SMASS = BDMASS_{RESPIROMETRY} \tag{2}$$

where:   $UMASS$ = hydrocarbon mass removed from the unsaturated zone
$SMASS$ = hydrocarbon mass removed from the saturated zone
$BDMASS_{RESPIROMETRY}$ = hydrocarbon mass biologically degraded

Finally, the two calculated biologically degraded masses were compared for agreement,

$$\frac{BDMASS_{ANALYTICAL}}{BDMASS_{RESPIROMETRY}} = 1 \tag{3}$$

### Facility Design

An air sparging blower, six air sparge wells, and soil gas monitor points had been installed prior to initiation of the field experiment. Figure 1 is a site plan and Figure 2 is a process and instrument diagram for the biosparging system. Mathematical modeling confirmed the need for a soil vapor collection blower (bioventing) to control subsurface air flow. Flow meters, nutrients, nutrient delivery equipment, and a soil vapor collection blower (bioventing) were added to the existing biosparging system. The bioventing blower was added to the treatment system to control subsurface air flows so that soil gases sparged into the unsaturated zone by biosparging were collected and the hydrocarbon concentration was measured prior to release to the atmosphere. Vapor phase nutrients, nitrous oxide and triethyl phosphate, at approximately 100:10:2 C:N:P ratios were selected for this demonstration based on reported experience at the Savannah River Site (1). Nitrous oxide is a vapor at ambient conditions and was easily introduced into the biosparge flow. Triethyl phosphate is a liquid at ambient conditions but has a high vapor pressure. Thus, processing equipment was required to volatilize the triethyl phosphate in the biosparge flow. A chemical feed pump and injection nozzle were used to accurately measure the triethyl phosphate feed and improve volatilization. A trap was also added to the biosparge piping to collect and measure the triethyl phosphate that did not volatilize.

## FIELD OPERATIONS AND RESULTS

### Operations Monitoring

Phase I operations, a pulsed biosparging mode, began on September 29, 1993. Table 1 summarizes the operation dates for the four phases of the field experiment. Phase II, a stepped continuous air flow mode, began on October 25, 1993, and continued through February 4, 1994. Gaseous nutrient addition began November 18, 1993. Nutrients were added to both the saturated and unsaturated zones. However, mechanical problems developed with the triethyl phosphate nutrient feed pump and injection system, and material compatibility problems were also experienced. The mechanical problems and material incompatibilities were resolved and Phase II was restarted January 11, 1994. The second Phase II respirometry study (fourth respiration) was performed beginning January 29, 1994, and suggested that the addition of nutrients had improved the biodegradation rates. A controlled laboratory study showed that dissolved triethyl phosphate was not air stripped from water. This confirmed that triethyl phosphate could not easily enter the unsaturated zone through biosparging from the saturated zone and, thus, nutrients were added to the unsaturated and saturated zones.

In Phase III, a soil gas recycle mode, a continuous reading lower explosive limit meter (LEL) was installed to monitor and shut down the system if the measured hydrocarbon vapor concentration was above 25% of the LEL. The respirometry study conducted during this phase indicated no significant improvement in biodegradation rates compared to those observed in Phases I and II. Additionally, the hydrocarbon concentrations of the offgas were higher than for the other two operating modes.

The GRI sponsored field experiment ended July 4, 1994 (279 cumulative days). Site remediation is continuing under the direction of the site owner's consultant. While several modifications have been made to the equipment configuration and operations since July 1994, one respirometry study was performed in November, 1994 to document the ongoing remediation progress (2).

### Mass Balances of Source Area Hydrocarbons

Table 2 summarizes the hydrocarbon mass balance for the source area soil and groundwater samples. Soil BTEX concentrations ranged from Non Detect to 3,923 mg/kg and total alkanes ($C_4$ - $C_{10}$) ranged from Non Detect to 16,496 mg/kg. Groundwater BTEX ranged from Non Detect to 85.9 mg/L and total alkanes ranged from Non Detect to 1757.2 mg/L. As shown in Table 2, the estimated initial mass of hydrocarbons was less than the mass estimated from event two. This can be explained because the sampling intervals were changed as a result of the first event samples. The average of events one and two is assumed to be the best estimate of the initial hydrocarbon mass. An average of the hydrocarbon mass from events three and four was 574 kg (1,262 lbs.), which was the remaining mass. Using equation (1), the hydrocarbon mass biologically degraded was estimated to be 2266 kg (4,985 lbs.) (see Table 2).

### Biokinetic Rates of Hydrocarbon Degradation Determined by Field Respirometry Measurements

Seven respirometry studies were performed. Oxygen depletion as percent oxygen in the soil gas and dissolved oxygen in the groundwater were measured over time during periods when the bioventing blower and the biosparging blower were turned off.

Table 1 shows calculated zero order biodegradation rates for each of the seven respirometry studies. Based on these respirometry determined biodegradation rates, the estimated contaminant mass biologically degraded during the study period is 895 kg (1,970 lbs). Four of the seven respiration measured biodegradation rates from this field experiment compare well with published biodegradation rates from other projects (1-21 mg/kg day) (3). It should be noted that the high rate measured in the seventh respiration is most probably a result of the injection of bacterial seed into the capillary fringe and groundwater approximately one month prior to the seventh respiration event. Thus, it is probably not representative of the preceding bioactivity at the site.

**ENGINEERING EVALUATION**

According to the National Research Council (4) recommended criteria for evaluating the efficiency of in situ bioremediation, this study showed that:

- Hydrocarbon contaminant concentrations declined in the groundwater and soils;

- Indigenous microorganisms in site soil and groundwater samples were shown to have the potential to transform the contaminants as shown by the microbial counts (see Figure 3), and;

- Biodegradation was realized as shown by the increase in carbon dioxide in the soil gas and the soil gas oxygen utilization observed in the respirometry studies (see Figure 4).

According to equation 3, the ratio of the biodegraded hydrocarbon mass balance based on analytical sampling to the respirometry-based biodegraded hydrocarbon mass should equal unity. The calculated ratio for this study was 2.5. Variability was observed in the soil hydrocarbon concentrations between sampling events most probably due to the difficulty of obtaining truly representative samples of the contaminant distribution in the subsurface and the use of relatively few samples to characterize relatively large soil masses. The mass balance technique appears to be highly sample specific and thus is a relatively insensitive tool for evaluating the effectiveness of the bioventing process. The only way to overcome this difficulty would be to significantly increase the number of soil and groundwater samples used to compute the mass balances, which would entail considerably greater expense both in terms of field sample collection and analytical expense.

Conversely, the in situ respirometry technique of evaluating the rate of oxygen depletion both in the soil vapor and groundwater following periodic cessation of biosparging appears to be a more useful tool both for monitoring the progress of in situ bioremediation and estimating the total mass of hydrocarbons which are biologically degraded and physically removed from the subsurface.

Respiratory studies performed at the site suggested that biological oxidation of the hydrocarbon contaminants became nutrient (nitrogen and/or phosphorus) limited. Introduction of nutrients into the saturated and unsaturated subsurface zones appeared to be a critical element in increasing the effectiveness of the bioventing/biosparging and achieving remediation at this site. The site soils were predominantly sand and gravel with background total organic carbon concentrations consistently below laboratory detection limits. The nutrient limitation hypothesis is supported by the measured nutrient concentrations in both soil and groundwater that were consistently below laboratory detection limits and the increase in the biodegradation rates following successful injection of nutrients into the subsurface. It does not appear that oxygen concentration was a limiting factor in the rate of biodegradation. A dissolved oxygen (D.O.) level of 1 mg/L would be sufficient to support aerobic biological activity and was supported by field measurement of D.O. concentrations above 1.0 mg/L at the groundwater wells. Figure 3 is a graph showing the change in microbial populations measured as colony forming units/gram of soil from the baseline soil sampling event and for the three additional soil sampling events. This graph shows an increase in biological activity. Figure 4 is a trend plot for hydrocarbons, oxygen and carbon dioxide concentrations for the monitor well location screened in the capillary fringe which is located in the center of the treatment zone. The hydrocarbon and oxygen concentrations declined, while carbon dioxide concentrations increased during the respiration studies.

**Biosparging System Operational Analysis**

The four bioventing/biosparging operating modes evaluated in this study appear to successfully achieve contaminant source removal. Controlled laboratory studies have indicated that pulsed air flow operations may produce higher biodegradation rates while minimizing volatilization. (5) Based on stoichiometry, atmospheric air containing approximately 21 percent oxygen by volume can supply sufficient oxygen to biodegrade a maximum of 20 mg of hexane equivalents/kg of soil utilizing all available oxygen. Thus, during continuous operations, any hydrocarbons volatilized above this concentration would be vented. Stated another way, the maximum vapor phase concentration that can be biologically degraded is 2.5 percent hexane by volume; any concentration above 2.5 percent would be vented to the atmosphere. Pulsed operations would minimize volatilization. This hypothesis was not positively confirmed in this field experiment. Based on the field results, recycling the hydrocarbons (Phase III) does not appear to improve remediation. The offgas hydrocarbon concentrations during the Phase III recycle mode were higher than those observed during the other operating modes. Also, the recycle system is more capital expensive than the non-recycle system. A generalized engineering evaluation, in terms of implementability, performance, and cost, indicates that biosparging using continuous flow through operations or pulsed air flow mode of operations may be more cost effective than recycling the soil gases.

## CONCLUSIONS AND RECOMMENDATIONS

This project has demonstrated that bioventing/biosparging at natural gas dehydration sites is a feasible remediation alternative. The objective of identifying and quantifying engineering design parameters has been partially achieved. However, to fully understand and apply the technology at a wide spectrum of natural gas dehydrator sites, it will be necessary to evaluate the technology at additional dehydrator sites with different soil and groundwater characteristics.

Soils from this site have been archived and may be used in controlled laboratory studies to more fully evaluate the kinetics of the bioventing/biosparging process. These laboratory results could be used in conjunction with the field results obtained in this field experiment to develop a design hypothesis for remediation of natural gas industry glycol dehydrator sites by bioventing/biosparging. The design hypothesis will be refined in the projected additional field experiments of in situ bioremediation of natural gas industry glycol dehydrator sites.

## ACKNOWLEDGMENTS

This field demonstration was performed for GRI by Remediation Technologies, Inc., under GRI Contract No. 5091-253-2215 entitled "Technical Assessments of Environmental Control Strategies in the Natural Gas Production Industry," and by Global Remediation Technologies, Inc., of Traverse City, Michigan, under subcontract to Remediation Technologies, Inc. The ongoing support and encouragement of the GRI staff are greatly appreciated.

Global Remediation Technologies, Inc., of Traverse City, Michigan, performed the majority of the field work and assisted with data collection and reduction. The field activities could not have been performed without their assistance.

## REFERENCES

1.    Hazen, T. C., C. B. Fliermans, M. Enzien, J. M. Dougherty, and K. Lombar. In Situ Methanotrophic Bioremediation Using Horizontal Well Technology. Savannah River Project-U.S. Department of Energy, Westinghouse Environmental Corporation. 1993.

2.    Lawrence, A. Wm., D. L. Miller, J.A. Miller, R. M. Raetz, and T. D. Hayes. "In Situ Bioventing for Environmental Remediation of a Natural Gas Dehydrator Site: A Field Demonstration." SPE Paper 28351 presented at the 1994 SPE Annual Technical Conference and Exhibition, New Orleans, LA. September 25 - 28, 1994.

3.    Hinchee, R. E., S. K. Ong, R. N. Miller, D. C. Downey, and R. Frandt. Test Plan And Technical Protocol For A Field Treatability Test For Bioventing, for U.S. Air Force Center for Environmental Excellence, Brooks Air Force Base, TX. 1992.

4.    Committee on In Situ Bioremediation Water Science and Technology Board, Commission on Engineering and Technical Systems, and National Research Council. In Situ Bioremediation When Does It Work?, National Academy Press, Washington, DC. 1993.

5.    Dupont, R. R. and T. Lakshmiprasad. "Assessment of Operating Mode and Nutrient Amendment on Performance of a Pilot Scale Bioventing System." IGT Biotechnology Symposium, Colorado Springs, CO. 1993.

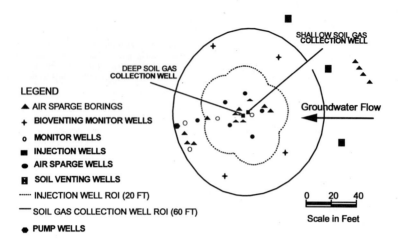

**Figure 1. Site Plan**

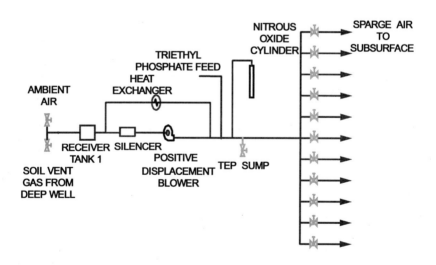

**Figure 2. Biosparging Process Flow and Instrument Diagram**

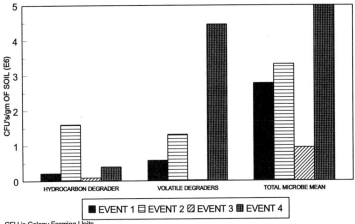

EVENT 1  EVENT 2  EVENT 3  EVENT 4

CFU is Colony Forming Units
Total Microbes for Event 4 had one sample with
5 E7 CFUs/gm of soil

**Figure 3. Soil Microbial Counts**

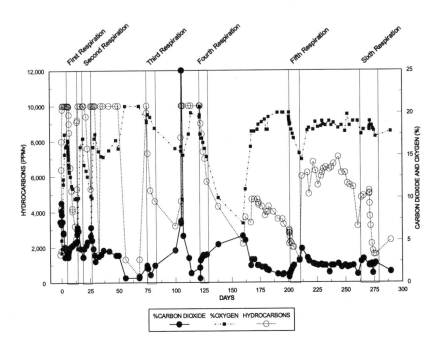

**Figure 4. Trend Plot of Soil Gas Concentration at the Centrally Located Subsurface
Soil Gas Monitoring Location for the Duration of the Field Demonstration**

**Table 1.  List of System Operational Dates and Respiration Rates**

| System Operational Dates | | | Respiration Rates | |
|---|---|---|---|---|
| Dates | | Number of Days | Cumulative Number of Days | Unsaturated Zone Soil mg/kg-day | Saturated Zone Soil mg/kg-day |
| Background | 09/27/93 to 09/28/93 | (2) | | | |
| Phase I Cycle I | | | | | |
| Operation | 09/29/93 to 10/04/93 | 6 | 6 | | |
| Respirometry | 10/05/93 to 10/12/93 | 8 | 14 | 3.65 | 0.0695 |
| Phase I Cycle II | | | | | |
| Operation | 10/13/93 to 10/17/93 | 5 | 19 | | |
| Respirometry | 10/18/93 to 10/24/93 | 7 | 26 | 0.65 | 0.071 |
| Phase II Cycle I | | | | | |
| Operation | 10/25/93 to 12/12/93 | 49 | 75 | | |
| Respirometry | 12/13/93 to 12/19/93 | 7 | 82 | 0.21 | 0.0319 |
| No Operation | 12/20/93 to 01/10/94 | 22 | 104 | | |
| Phase II Cycle II | | | | | |
| Operation | 01/11/94 to 01/28/94 | 18 | 122 | | |
| Respirometry | 01/29/94 to 02/4/94 | 7 | 129 | 5.92 | 0.4327 |
| No Operation.  System Modified for Mode III Soil Gas Recycle | 02/5/94 to 03/7/94 | 31 | 160 | | |
| Phase III Cycle I | | | | | |
| Mechanical Shake Down | 03/08/94 to 03/17/94 | 10 | 170 | | |
| Operation | 03/18/94 to 03/28/94 | 11 | 181 | | |
| Operation w/increase in flow | 03/29/94 to 04/17/94 | 20 | 201 | | |
| Respirometry | 04/18/94 to 4/26/94 | 9 | 210 | 1.22 | 0.0915 |
| Phase IV Cycle I | | | | | |
| Operation | 4/27/94 to 6/19/94 | 54 | 264 | | |
| Respirometry | 6/27/94 to 7/4/94 | 15 | 279 | 0.28 | 0.0118 |
| Continued Operations | 7/5/94-Present | | | | |
| Bacterial Seed Added | August-September 1994 | | | | |
| Respiration | November 1994 | | | 4.28 | 0.42 |

**Table 2. Hydrocarbon Mass Balance**

| Media | Pounds of Hydrocarbon Event One September 1993 kg (lbs) | Pounds of Hydrocarbons Event Two December 1993 kg (lbs) | Pounds of Hydrocarbons Event Three June 1994 kg (lbs) | Pounds of Hydrocarbons Event Four October 1994 kg (lbs) |
|---|---|---|---|---|
| Groundwater | 11 (24) | 155 (340) | 11 (24) | 11 (24) |
| Unsaturated Soil | 1,074 ( 2,362) | 1,796 (3,952) | 281 (619) | 301 (662) |
| Saturated Soil | 1,302 (2,864) | 2,143 (4,715) | 258 (567) | 285 (628) |
| Total | 2,387 (5,521) | 4,094 (9,007) | 550 (1,210) | 597 (1,314) |

| Biodegraded Mass Balance | kg (lbs) |
|---|---|
| Average Hydrocarbon Mass Events One and Two | 3,240 (7,129) |
| Average Hydrocarbon Mass Events Three and Four | 574 (1,262) |
| Mass Removed from Pump and Treat | 155 (342) |
| Mass Volatized | 245 (540) |
| Biodegraded Mass | 2,266 (4,985) |

INTEGRATED CHEMICAL AND BIOLOGICAL TREATMENT OF
POLYNUCLEAR AROMATIC HYDROCARBON CONTAMINATED SOILS AT
MANUFACTURED GAS PLANT SITES

TRAITEMENT CHIMIQUE ET BIOLOGIQUE INTÉGRÉDES SOLS CONTAMINÉS
PAR LES HYDROCARBURES AROMATIQUES POLYNUCLÉAIRES DANS LES
USINES DE FABRICATION DE GAZ

V.J. Srivastava, J.R. Paterek, B Y. Liu
Institute of Gas Technology, U.S.A.

and

T.D. Hayes
Gas Research Institute, U.S.A.

ABSTRACT

The Institute of Gas Technology has developed, field demonstrated, and deployed an integrated biological-chemical treatment to efficiently remediate soil contaminated with hazardous organic compounds. The process is called MGP-REM when applied to polynuclear aromatic hydrocarbons (PAHs) contaminated soils at manufactured gas plant sites. Bench-scale and/or field-scale experiments show that MGP-REM is far superior to conventional biotreatment in the common treatment modes - slurry-phase, solid-phase, and *in-situ* phase treatments. The MGP-REM process allows the activity of the native microbial population to degrade PAHs to necessary levels. The soil investigated for *in-situ* MGP-REM was tested in laboratory bioreactors in which the removal rate was 3 times greater than conventional biotreatment. Field-scale evaluation of MGP-REM in soil slurry bioreactors showed a 4-fold improvement over conventional bioremediation at a small fraction of the cost of incineration. Field evaluations in solid-phase treatment show up to 100% improvement over conventional bioremediation.

RÉSUMÉ

L'Institute of Gas Technology a développé, démontré sur le terrain et déployé un traitement biologique et chimique intégré pour remédier efficacement à l'état des sols contaminés par des composés organiques dangereux. Le processus est désigné sous l'appellation MGP-REM lorsqu'il s'aapplique aux sols contaminés par des hydrocarbures aromatiques polnucléaires (PAHs) sur les sites des usines de fabrication de gaz. Des expériences en laboratoire et sur les chantiers ont démontré que le traitement au MGP-REM est de loin supérieur au traitement biologique conventionnel utilisé dans les modes de traitement habituels - phase boue, phase solide - et pour les traitements sur le site. Le sol traité au MGP-REM permet l'action d'une population microbienne indigéne qui assure la dégradation des PAHs aux niveaux requis. Le sol traité au MGP-REM sur le site a été examiné sur des bioréacteurs en laboratoire où le taux d'élimination était trois fois plus élevé que celui dérivé d'un traitement biologique conventionnele. L'évaluation au niveau chantier de boues traitées au MGP-REM a démontré une amélioration quatre fois plus élevée que celle produite par la solution biologique conventionnelle et cela, à une fraction minme du prix du coùt de l'incinération. Les études au niveau chantier dans la phase solide montrent jusqu' à 100% d'amélioration sur la solution biologique conventionnelle.

## INTRODUCTION

The Institute of Gas Technology (IGT) has been developing engineering processes to treat soils, sediments, and water at former manufactured gas plant (MGP) sites contaminated with polynuclear aromatic hydrocarbons (PAHs), cyanides, and metals (2,3,4,5,6,7,8,9,10). The ultimate goal of this development is to provide a cost-effective waste treatment technology that furnishes an efficient alternative to land filling, thermal treatment (incineration), and other technologies.

IGT has identified the rate-limiting steps of conventional biological treatment systems, and then developed approaches to overcome these limitations. As a result of extensive bench-scale studies carried out since 1987, IGT has developed and demonstrated a process for PAH-contaminated soils that is a combination of biological and physical /chemical treatment -- the MGP-REM process.

The MGP-REM process combines two complementary remedial techniques -- chemical oxidation and biological treatment. A schematic diagram of the process is presented in Figure 1. The chemical treatment can be performed as a pre-treatment before the biological degradation, or can be integrated as a step between biological treatments. The MGP-REM process uses a mild chemical treatment with Fenton's reagent ($H_2O_2$ plus $Fe^{2+}$) that produces hydroxyl radicals that start a chain reaction with the organic contaminants. The contaminants, specifically PAHs, are modified or degraded to forms that are more readily degraded by native or supplemented microorganisms. The ultimate products of this process are carbon dioxide, water, and biomass. Results, including the ones presented in this paper, with approximately 25 MGP soils, show that the MGP-REM process is capable of enhancing the rate as well as the extent of PAH degradation.

The sequence of each treatment step, as well as its extent or concentration, is controlled by the conditions of the site and soil under investigation. For example, a soil that is dominated by 4-6 ring PAHs may require a Fenton's reagent addition as a pre-treatment. If the soil contamination is primarily 2-3 ring compounds, or if a high total organic carbon content is present, then an initial biological treatment improves the performance of the process. To optimize the evaluation of a soil, and to determine the engineering approach (soil slurry bioreactors, solid treatment, or *in-situ* application) that should be the most successful, a treatability protocol was developed. This protocol development was funded by GRI, and the IGT Sustaining Membership and has been used to evaluate the treatability of MGP soils. Figure 2 is a schematic diagram of this protocol.

This paper presents data generated in two of the phases of this protocol. Application of MGP-REM using an *in-situ* treatment method, is in the laboratory evaluation phase, and the soil slurry bioreactor approach is in the field experimentation or demonstration phase. MGP-REM solid-phase treatment has progressed through all the protocol phases and has enter the full-remediation stage. Data on this approach are not presented in this report.

## SLURRY-PHASE BIOREMEDIATION

In slurry-phase bioremediation, excavated contaminated soil is screened to remove debris and large objects before being placed in a on-site stirred tank reactor where the soil is combined with water to form a slurry. Typical solids contents range from 10% to 40% by weight. If required, nutrients, microorganisms, or surfactants are added to the slurry to enhance the biodegradation process. Once biodegradation of the contaminants is completed, the treated slurry is typically dewatered and the cleaned soil can be reused depending on the regulatory constraints.

To effectively remediate soil in a bio-slurry reactor, all oversize material must be removed. The excavated contaminated soil is first sieved through a 2-inch screen to remove large objects, such as rocks or bricks. The screened soil is then slurried up in an attrition scrubber to wash contaminants from the larger soil particles. After this, it passes through a shaker screen to remove any gravel, debris, and other oversize material. Most of the sand and gravel will be clean after the washing step and can be discharged. The finer materials and the excess wash water that cannot be recycled are then passed into slurry reactors for treatment. The soil passing through the shaker screen is then fed into the slurry reactor. The schematic diagram of the slurry-phase bioremediation is shown in Figure 3.

### Field Conditions

As shown in Figure 3, excavated soil was screened to remove objects greater than 2 inches. The screened soil was then transported to an attrition scrubber where soil was mixed with water to make a 50% soil slurry. Slurry from the attrition scrubber was sent to the 20-mesh vibrating screen to remove particles greater than 1 mm, which were sent to the reject stockpile. The slurry reactor, chemical reactor, and biological reactor have the identical capacity of 2100 gallons. Slurry passing through the screen was diluted to 10%-35% solids in the slurry reactor in preparation of the following chemical/biological treatment. In the chemical treatment, 50% hydrogen peroxide ($H_2O_2$) was added to the chemical reactor to achieve the designed volume $H_2O_2$ / volume slurry ratio. Commercial-grade $FeSO_4 \cdot 7H_2O$ was added prior to the addition of $H_2O_2$ to achieve a predetermined $Fe^{+2}$ concentration during the chemical treatment.

The slurry-reactor system was operated in a batch mode. The 1994 tests started with soil of low PAH concentration and approximately 10% solids concentration. The tests generally started with a biological treatment, followed by a chemical treatment and a biological polishing treatment.

During the biological treatment, oxygen was provided through aeration and nutrients (nitrogen and phosphorus) were added to ensure optimal conditions for microbial growth. Only solids were treated with Fenton's reagent during the chemical treatment because PAHs are insoluble and should remain in the solid matrix. Prior to chemical treatment, slurry was allowed to settle for 4 hours, and the supernatant (about an half of the total volume) was aerated in the slurry tank for later addition in the biological reactor. This procedure served as a way to oxidize only the PAHs in soil and keep the microbial population in the supernatant unaffected. After the chemical oxidation was completed, which was indicated by the complete utilization of added hydrogen peroxide, the supernatant with active microbial population was added back to the soil slurry.

## PAHs Results After Field-Scale Soil Slurry Bioreactor Treatment

The complete test results of one example test run 1 are plotted in Figure 4, showing the overall decreasing trend of the treatment. Samples taken at days 0, 20, and 40 were compared in Table 1 and Figure 4, in which the day 40 sample was taken from the sludge thickener 20 days after the biological treatment was completed. Table 1 shows that a 95% removal efficiency was achieved for total PAHs. Table 1 also displays a better removal efficiency of non-carcinogenic than carcinogenic PAHs. These results agree that the PAHs with fewer (2 and 3) aromatic rings were degraded more effectively than those with more (4, 5, and 6) aromatic rings. Table 2 further reports individual PAHs ring numbered compounds and these data demonstrate the same trend presented in Table 1. In addition, Figure 5 compares the PAH concentrations, before and after MGP-REM treatment, for the carcinogenic PAH compounds.

Table 1. PAHs Degradation over time in Soil slurry bioreactor Field-scale Experiment: Test 1

| PAHs, (mg/kg) | Day 1 | Day 20 | Day 40* | % Degraded |
|---|---|---|---|---|
| Total | 1164 | 157 | 53 | 95 |
| Non-Carcinogenic | 974 | 86 | 33 | 97 |
| Carcinogenic | 191 | 71 | 20 | 90 |

* Samples taken from the thickener.

Test 1 results demonstrated the effectiveness of MGP-REM process, especially the 90% removal of the carcinogenic PAHs and the 95% and above removal for the lower-ring PAHs. Test 2, summarized in Table 3, shows the similar trend as Test 1. Since Test 2 was conducted for a shorter duration, only 11 days versus 20 days for Test 1, its treatment efficiency was slightly lower that of Test 1.

Table 2. PAH Degradation by Individual Ring PAHs - Test 1

| PAHs, (mg/kg) | Day 1 | Day 20 | Day 40* | % Degraded |
|---|---|---|---|---|
| 2-ring | 202 | 21 | 7.6 | 96 |
| 3-ring | 516 | 29 | 13.2 | 97 |
| 4-ring | 337 | 41 | 18.2 | 95 |
| 5-ring | 85 | 46 | 11.3 | 87 |
| 6-ring | 24 | 21 | 2.8 | 88 |

* Samples taken from the thickener.

Table 3.  PAH Degradation Data for Test 2

| PAHs, mg/kg | Day 1 | Day 11 | Day 27* | % Degraded |
|---|---|---|---|---|
| Total | 722 | 97 | 72 | 90 |
| Non - Carcinogenic | 565 | 61 | 48 | 92 |
| Carcinogenic | 157 | 36 | 24 | 85 |
| | | | | |
| Group Ring PAHs | | | | |
| 2, 3 -Rings | 359 | 36 | 33 | 91 |
| 4, 5, and 6 -Rings | 363 | 61 | 39 | 89 |
| | | | | |
| Individual Ring PAHs | | | | |
| 2-Rings | 59 | 14 | 13 | 78 |
| 3-Rings | 301 | 21 | 20 | 93 |
| 4-Rings | 266 | 26 | 20 | 92 |
| 5-Rings | 74 | 22 | 14 | 81 |
| 6-Rings | 23 | 13 | 5 | 80 |

\* Samples taken from the thickener.
\*\* Appears low due to initial concentration


Toxicity Test Results

    Soil samples for Tests 1 and 2 were tested for toxicity to determine the
effect of MGP-REM process on reducing its level in MGP soils.  The samples
tested were soils before treatment, soils after treatment, and treated soils after
grass was planted and allowed to grow for 2 weeks.  The toxicity results,
reported on a dry soil basis, are presented in Table 4.  The measure of toxicity
used here is EC50, meaning the percentage of soil slurry that will inhibit 50 % of
a known bacterial activity.  Therefore, the lower the EC50 reading, the higher is
the toxicity in the soil.

    As seen from Table 4, the soil prior to testing for Test 1 was very toxic and
the MGP-REM process decreased the toxicity by more than 50 times.  For Test 2,
the original soil was not as toxic as Test 1, but still the MGP-REM process
managed to reduce the toxicity by a factor of 5.  In addition, the grass further
reduced the toxicity of the treated Test 3 soil, as indicated in Table 4.
In order to identify the benefits of MGP-REM process, the system was also
operated in the conventional bioremediation mode.  Since PAHs degradation
follows a first-order kinetics, the PAH degradation rates are directly proportional
to PAH concentration in the slurry bioreactor.

    However, this study found that the conventional first-order degradation
kinetics do not describe PAH degradation very well.  Instead, the first-order
kinetics fits better if the degradation is divided into two distinct portions: the

first 5 to 10 days of treatment and the remaining time of the process. In the first part of treatment, the biodegradable compounds were rapidly removed and PAH

Table 4.  Toxicity Test Results

| Test | Soil Sample Description | EC50 @ 5 minutes | Interpretation |
|------|------------------------|------------------|----------------|
| 1 | Before Treatment | 0.212 | Very toxic |
| 1 | After Treatment (day 20) | >10 | Non toxic |
| 1 | After Treatment with Grass* | 8.84 | Non toxic |
| 2 | Before Treatment | 0.803 | Toxic |
| 2 | After Treatment (day 11) | 3.35 | Non toxic |
| 2 | After Treatment with Grass* | 5.44 | Non toxic |

*Tested after grass was planted on the soil.

concentrations drop drastically. After the first part of treatment the rate decreased drastically where only the recalcitrant PAHs remained in the reactor.

Table 5 summarizes the first-order kinetics for the MGP-REM test and the conventional bioremediation test, dividing them into the overall kinetics (for conventional bioremediation only), and two parts of the treatment (for MGP-REM bioremediation). As shown in Table 5, MGP-REM increase the first-order kinetics between 3 to 4 times, from 0.12 to 0.36 (Test 1), and 0.53 (Test 2) day$^{-1}$ confirming the effects of the chemically enhanced bioremediation.

Table 5.  First-Order Kinetics (day$^{-1}$)

| Test | First Part Constant | Second-Part Constant | Overall Constant |
|------|--------------------|--------------------|-----------------|
| MGP-REM - Test 1 | 0.36 | 0.04 | NA |
| MGP-REM - Test 2 | 0.53 | 0.12 | NA |
| Conventional | NA | NA | 0.12 |

NA: not applicable

The 1994 field test results indicated that the MGP-REM Process can effectively remediate MGP soils to satisfactory levels. As a result, two more pilot-scale tests are scheduled for 1995. In addition, based on the 1994 field test, a full-scale slurry-phase remediation employing MGP-REM is in the planning stage.

In summary, the MGP-REM process successfully reduced the PAHs concentration of and toxicity in the MGP soils tested in this study. Over 90% of the PAHs were removed in the two tests presented. As a result, the full-scale remediation is the next reasonable step for this site, as long as the regulatory agency approves this action.

The pilot-scale study demonstrated that the integrated chemical/biological treatment can effectively treat MGP soil in slurry-phase bioremediation. Results of the pilot-scale study showed that total carcinogenic PAHs can be removed to below 25 mg/kg.

## SOLID-PHASE TREATMENT (LANDFARMING)

The solid-phase treatment utilizing MGP-REM was the first to be successful tested following the GRI/IGT Treatability Protocol. This included laboratory-scale and three years of field-scale experimentation. Because of the success of the field-scale trials, the solid-phase application of MGP-REM is scheduled in 1995-96 for use in a full-scale site remediation. No additional data on this treatment type are included in this paper.

## IN-SITU BIOREMEDIATION

The approach of this phase of the study was to evaluate and enhance the abilities of the native microbial community, enriched directly from the contaminated site soil, to degrade PAHs in an *in-situ* treatment mode. The enhancement tested was the application of Fenton's reagent, with and without the addition of a non-ionic surfactant. The phase of the treatment protocol (Figure 2) examined in this study was Phase 1 where the soil slurry reactors were monitored using computer-controlled respirometry. The measurement of oxygen utilized by the biological community generated data on the rates of PAH degradation under various conditions and treatment regimes. IGT is currently performing tests for three field demonstrations of the MGP-REM Process during 1995-96.

### Site Evaluation

Three sites in Southern California, USA, were investigated for future field application of MGP-REM in an *in-situ* treatment mode. A number of chemical, physical, and biological factors are considered. This represents the first phase in the GRI/IGT treatability protocol (Figure 2). A summary of the results of this investigation is presented in Table 6.
Because of the acceptable levels of microorganisms ($6.0 \times 10^7$ organisms/gram soil), physiological pH (7.7), and the concentration of PAHs, the Olympic Base #2 site was chosen for further study. The remaining data on the *in-situ* remediation part of this paper were generated with this soil.

### Soil Slurry Reactors

Soil slurry reactors were prepared in flasks designed for use with the respirometer system. The working volume of the systems was 200 ml and contained 10% soil by weight. A water bath was used to maintained the temperature at 30°C, and the soil slurries were constantly stirred.

Computer controlled and monitored respirometry was carried out using a *Comput-Ox* WB512 Series Respirometer (N-Con Systems Company, Inc., Larchmont, NY).

Table 6.  Critical Characteristics in Application of MGP-REM in the *In-Situ* Treatment Mode: California USA Sites

| Characteristic | Hanford Site | Santa Barbara Site | Olympic Base Site #1 | Olympic Base Site #2 |
|---|---|---|---|---|
| pH | 4.5 | 6.5 | Not Determined | 7.7 |
| Total PAHs, ppm | 293 | 592 | 85 | 350 |
| Carcinogenic PAHs, ppm | 115 | 192 | 23 | 125 |
| Bacterial Population, per gram of soil | less than $10^5$ | Not Determined | $2.0 \times 10^6$ | $6.0 \times 10^7$ |

All experiments were executed in the BOD flask systems using procedures furnished with the apparatus.  The initial gas phase and all gas additions were 100% oxygen.

The chemical treatment of the MGP-REM process consists of the addition of iron and hydrogen peroxide.  The compounds are added sequentially, with the iron added first.  The iron is added as a volume of 0.1 $M$ $FeSO_4$ in distilled water.  The final concentration in each treatment is 1 $mM$ of iron. The hydrogen peroxide is added as varying amounts of a 30% solution of hydrogen peroxide in water.  The volume added is determined by the total volume of the experimental systems.  The final concentration of hydrogen peroxide for each treatment is 1.0% of the total volume.  Treatments may be cycled with reagents being added again.  The final treatment concentration of each reagent is the cumulative.

This method has been found to be effective in our laboratory and others for the determination of biodegradability of slightly soluble organic compounds, such as PAHs (1,9).  The results of an experiment comparing the MGP-REM process to conventional biotreatment is present in Figure 6. The results of the soil slurry reactor studies as shown in Figure 6 present clear evidence that MGP-REM activity is greater in both extent and rate when compared with conventional bioremediation systems.  This should allow the development of an *in-situ* process that is more rapid than conventional biotreatment, thus saving capital and operating expenses.  The MGP-REM has the potential to be an efficient and cost-effective alternative for conventional bioremediation.

Microbiological Studies

In support of this *in-situ* evaluation, microbial cultures were isolated, characterized, and cultivated from the town gas waste sites' soils.  This is necessary to understand the complex ecological processes involved and to determined what "engineered" additions or conditions might enhance the rate, extent, or dependability of the *in-situ* application of enhanced biodegradation. In addition, the enhancements and production of competent (able to degrade the targeted compounds) microorganisms were executed. This production of microbial inoculum would be necessary if augmentation of soils lacking in a suitable competent microbial community is required.

The tentative identification of the key microorganisms is the examined soils is presented in Table 7. The microorganisms were characterized based on their metabolic activities, cellular appearance (morphology), and the chemical composition of the cell wall surround each bacterial type. The cell wall data are the basis for Table 7. The large number of different types of microorganisms (diversity) degrading the PAHs indicates a system with the stability and predictability characterized of this degree of redundancy.

Table 7.  Microorganisms Isolated from *In-Situ* Sites (Southern California USA) and Identified by Fatty Acid Methyl Esters Analysis

| IGT Isolate Number | Specific Epithet | Similarity Index |
|---|---|---|
| BAP-1 | *Phyllobacterium rubiacearum* | 0.441* |
| BAP-2 | *Sphingobacterium multivorum* | 0.374 |
| BAP-3 | *Xanthomonas maltophilia* | 0.613 |
| BAP-4 | *Pseudomonas aeruginosa* | 0.825 |
| BAP-5 | *Alcaligenes faecalis* | 0.901 |
| BAP-6 | *Rhodotorula rubra* (yeast) | 0.676 |
| BAP-7B | *Flavobacterium thalpophilum* | 0.384 |
| BAP-7S-1 | *Xanthomonas maltophilia* | 0.552 |
| BAP-7S-2 | *Bacillus subtilis* | 0.015 |

* Closer the number to 1.0, higher the FAME similarity to type strain profile

Ongoing research includes the enumeration of these PAH-degrading microbial populations under various treatment conditions. The methods being developed in the laboratory will have direct application when the MGP-REM process is being tested under field-scale *in-situ* conditions.

SUMMARY

The application of IGT's MGP-REM technology for the remediation of MGP sites in the USA and elsewhere is a cost-effective and efficient option. Our laboratory and field-scale experiments and trials prove that the process is far superior to conventional bioremediation in both the rate of degradation and the extent of PAH removal. The cost estimates give below indicate that, based on capital and operating expenses, the MGP-REM is extremely cost-effective when compared to thermal treatment, such as incineration.

## Estimated Soil Cleanup Cost

The estimated costs for soil treatment using the MGP-REM process in the soil slurry bioreactors and solid-phase mode were estimated. These evaluations were generated by an independent contractor of GRI (published by GRI) and do not include permitting costs. Soil slurry bioreactors treatment is estimated to cost $100-$150 per cubic yard of soil and solid phase treatment (landfarming) at $60-$80 per cubic yard. These estimates do not include permitting or evaluation support. The preliminary estimates for *in-situ* application of bioremediation and enhanced bioremediation, such as MGP-REM range from $25-$75 per cubic yard. The estimate of the *in-situ* application of MGP-REM was generated by us and is based on laboratory-scale experiments only. As a means for comparison, we estimate incineration costs to range from $400 to $2000 per cubic yard, depending on the waste type and amount. All estimates are based on non-site specific characteristics and may vary based on the geological, hydrogeological, biological, and engineering factors.

## ACKNOWLEDGMENTS

The research program presented was this paper was possible through funding from the Gas Research Institute, IGT's Sustaining Membership Program, U.S. Environmental Protection Agency, and several gas industry members. Their continuing support should allow the successful translation of laboratory techniques and processes into remedial technologies with great potential for the solution of several environmental problems.

We recognize the significant technical contribution of the staff of IGT, including John Conrad, Robert Kelley, John Kilbane, Laura Rice, Salil Pradhan, and Kathy Jackowski, as well as the staff of Gas Research Institute and the U.S. Environmental Protection Agency.

## REFERENCES

1.   Aichinger, G., C.P.L. Grady Jr., and H.H. Tabak. 1992. "Application of Respirometric Biodegradability Testing Protocol to Slightly Soluble Organic Compounds." Water Environ. Res. 64(7): 890-900.

2.   Gauger, W.K., J.J. Kilbane, R.L. Kelley, and V.J. Srivastava. "Enhancement of Microbial Degradation of Hydrocarbons in Soil and Water." *In* IGT's Second International Symposium on Gas, Oil, Coal, and Environmental Biotechnology, New Orleans, LA, December 1989.

3.    Kelley, R.L. and V.J. Srivastava. "Field-Scale Evaluation of an Integrated
      Treatment for Remediation of PAHs in Manufactured Gas Plant Soils." *In*
      Spring National A.I.Ch.E. Meeting, New Orleans, LA, March 1992.

4.    Kelley, R.L. W.K. Gauger, and V.J. Srivastava. "Application of Fenton's
      Reagent as a Pretreatment Step in Biological Degradation of Aromatic
      Compounds." *In* IGT's Third International Symposium on Gas, Oil, Coal,
      and Environmental Biotechnology, New Orleans, LA, December 1990.

5.    Kelley, R.L., V.J. Srivastava, J.R. Conrad, J.R. Paterek, and B.Y. Liu.
      1993. "Application of IGT's MGP-REM Process in Landfarming Mode."
      Sixth International IGT Symposium on Gas, Oil, and Environmental
      Biotechnology, Colorado Springs, CO. Institute of Gas Technology, Des
      Plaines, IL.

6.    Liu, B.Y., S. Pradhan, V.J. Srivastava, J.R. Pope, T.D. Hayes, D.G. Linz,
      C. Proulx D.E. Jerger, and P.M. Woodhull. 1994. "An Envaluation of
      Slurry-Phase Bioremediation of MGP Soils," Seventh International IGT
      Symposium on Gas, Oil, and Environmental Biotechnology, Colorado
      Springs, CO. Institute of Gas Technology, Des Plaines, IL.

7.    Liu, B.Y., V.J. Srivastava, J. R. Paterek, S.P. Pradhan, J.R. Pope, T.D.
      Hayes, D.G. Linz, and D.E. Jerger. 1993. "MGP Soil Remediation in a
      Slurry-Phase System: A Pilot-Scale Test." Sixth International IGT
      Symposium on Gas, Oil, and Environmental Biotechnology, Colorado
      Springs, CO. Institute of Gas Technology, Des Plaines, IL.

8.    Paterek, J.R. 1993. "The Role of Bioremediation in the Treatment of Gas
      Industry Wastes." Hazardous and Environmental Sensitive Waste
      Management in the Gas Industry.Symposiuim, Albuquerque, N.M. Institute
      of Gas Technology, Des Plaines, IL.

9.    Paterek, J.R., B.N. Aronstein, L.E. Rice, V.J. Srivastava, J. Chini, and A.
      Bohrnerud. 1994. "Bioremediation of Soil of a Manufactured Gas Plant
      Utilizing an *In-Situ* Treatment Mode," Seventh International IGT
      Symposium on Gas, Oil, and Environmental Biotechnology, Colorado
      Springs, CO. Institute of Gas Technology, Des Plaines, IL.

10.   Srivastava, V.J., R.L. Kelley, J.R. Paterek, T.D. Hayes, G.L. Nelson, and
      J. Golchin. 1994. "A Field-Scale Demonstration of a Novel Bioremediation
      Process for MGP Sites." Appl. Biochem. Biotechnol. 45/46: 741-755.

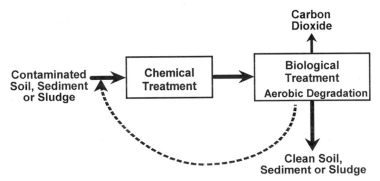

Figure 1.  Schematic Diagram of the MGP-REM Process

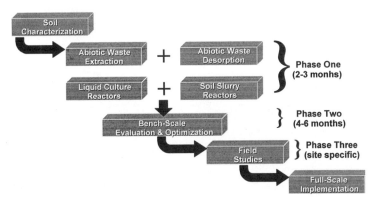

Figure 2.  GRI/IGT MGP-REM Treatability Protocol

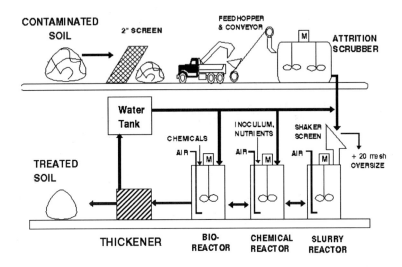

Figure 3.  Slurry Phase Bioremediation Diagram

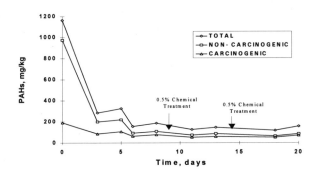

Figure 4.  PAHs Degradation Over Time in Soil Slurry Bioreactor Field-Scale
Experiment: Test 1

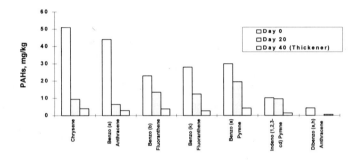

Figure 5. Carcinogenic PAH Reduction in Test 1

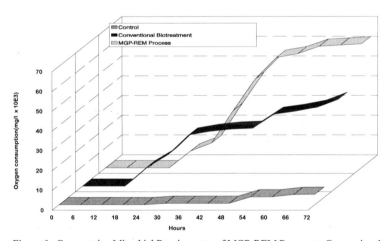

Figure 6. Comparative Microbial Respirometry of MGP-REM Process to Conventional
Bioremediation Using Olympic Base #2 Soil

# METHANE PRODUCTION SYSTEM FROM HOUSEHOLD
# WASTES BY CATALYTIC AND BIOLOGICAL TREATMENT

## SYSTÉME DE PRODUCTION DU MÉTHANE PAR TRAITMENT
## CATALYTIQUE ET BIOLOGIQUE DES ORDURES MÉNAGÉRES

Shin-ichi Ueda, Michio Futakawa, Nobuyuki Matsumoto
Osaka Gas Co., Ltd., JAPAN


Gen-nosuke Inoue, Tetsuo Fujioka
Water Re-Use Promotion Center, JAPAN

ABSTRACT

This report details the innovative system in which household wastes and wastewater are treated and simultaneously converted to energy and re-usable water. In this system, organic contaminants contained in household wastes and wastewater are converted to organic acid catalytically and finally gasified in a methane fermentation process. Establishment of this system enables us to expel wastes and bad smell from the kitchen and the street and create valuable energy. Besides, the clean reclaimed water is re-used efficiently. A study of energy balance shows that total energy efficiency of the system is better than that of conventional one due to improvement in carbon conversion ratio during the solubilization process. A feasibility study of the total system indicates that the cost of the system is competitive with that of conventional one.

RÉSUMÉ

Le présent rapport rend compte de la mise au point d'un système révolutionnaire qui, tout en permettant de résoudre les problèmes de traitement des ordures ménagères et des eaux usées, permet de récupérer l'énergie et de recycler l'eau régénérée. Selon ce système, les polluants organiques contenus dans les ordures et les eaux ménagères sont convertis en acides organiques par traitement catalytique et finalement en méthane en phase gazeuse en séjournant dans un bac de fermentation. La mise au point définitive de ce système permettra de nous libérer des opérations fastidieuses de traitement des ordures ménagères et de produire une précieuse énergie. De plus, l'eau récupérée peut être réutilisée. Les études sur le rendement énergétique global démontrent la supériorité de ce système sur les systèmes conventionnels, supériorité qui provient de l'amélioration du taux de conversion du carbone organique total à l'étape du traitement de solubilisation. Quant aux études de faisabilité de l'unité de traitement complète, elles indiquent que le coût de ce système est compétitif avec celui des systèmes conventionnels.

## INTRODUCTION

Most existing landfills are approaching their capacities.  Immediate solutions are required throughout the world to manage the problems of disposal regarding municipal solid waste (MSW).  Nowadays in Japan, MSW has immense energy potential comparable to the total amount of natural gas consumed in the country.  Therefore many attempts have been made to recover energy by combustion of MSW to convert waste into heat and electricity in recent years.  But construction of new incineration plants have become increasingly difficult due to the problem of public acceptance.  On the other hand, wastewater from houses is normally treated at sewage plants.  From these treatment plants, secondary pollutants such as nitrogen oxide, dioxins, sludge and ash are discharged.

Under existing conditions, since 1991 the Ministry of International Trade and Industry (MITI) has been developing a new system in which household wastes and wastewater are treated and, simultaneously methane gas and heat energy are produced (Figure 1).  Ten private companies have been cooperating with New Energy and Industrial Technology Development Organization (NEDO) to develop the entire system.  The project began research and development on the elementary technologies in 1991 and have been conducting an operation study at Chigasaki plant in Kanagawa Prefecture.  The research conducted by Osaka Gas, with its proprietary OG Catalytic Wet Oxidation (OG-CWO) process, has focused on developing a physico-chemical solubilization process in order to produce a raw material for methane  fermentation.  A feasibility study regarding the entire system has been conducted since 1993[1].

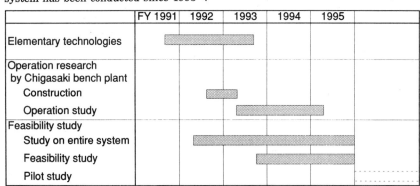

Figure 1.  Schedule

## DESCRIPTION OF THE MHW SYSTEM

### System Configuration

Figure 2 shows a schematic configuration of the METHANE FROM HOUSEHOLD WASTE (MHW) system.  The crushed garbage, suspended in water, is carried into the biological solubilization process to convert it into organic acid biologically.  Other waste such as plastics and papers, introduced into the OG-CWO process after crushing, are solubilized into the water without catalyst.  Then, the physico-chemically solubilized organic matters are also catalytically oxidized and converted into organic acids like acetic acid.  In the following methane fermentation process, the organic acids from both solubilization processes are converted into methane, which is supposed to be utilized as a fuel for co-generation units or refrigerators.  After further treatment, treated water is utilized as a substitute for low grade tap water. The thermal energy produced in the CWO process is recovered and utilized as well.

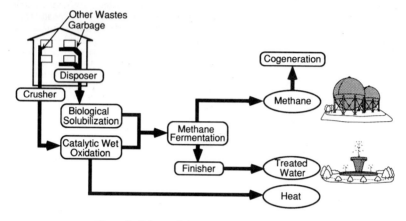

Figure 2. Schematic Configuration of MHW System[2)]

## Features

From the environmental point of view, NOx or the ash, both of which are discharged from conventional incinerators are not emitted from the MHW system. Moreover, organic sludge is not left in the system. Discharged materials from conventional treating processes cause secondary pollution in the atmosphere. Collecting the garbage by a garbage truck is another annoyance to traffic. From the viewpoint of resources, this system enables us to produce methane gas and thermal energy from wastes and to reclaim reusable water from wastewater. Living conditions will be improved by treating waste out of sight. Accordingly, it is certain that this new system is a globally friendly system from the view points of environment and resources.

## RESULTS AND DISCUSSIONS

### Operation Study

In this project, two major technologies: solubilization by the CWO process and high-temperature methane fermentation, have been developed successfully. Figure 3 shows the schematic flow diagram of Bench Plant constructed at Chigasaki in Kanagawa Prefecture. Using this plant, experiments on standard wastes or actual wastes was conducted. To achieve optimal energy utilization it is necessary to maximize the methane yield. This can be achieved by optimizing conditions of the CWO process and the methane fermentation process. The liquor obtained from the CWO process contains solubilized materials from the wastes, suitable for fermentation. It was found that mainly aldehides obstruct fermentation reaction. Furthermore, the CWO process is able to reduce aldehides in the effluent without significantly decreasing the organic acids necessary for methane production. High-temperature methane fermentation technology has proved to be able to increase the rate and efficiency of methane reaction. Twenty-three percent of the carbon in the waste is converted to the raw material of methane fermentation as DOC (dissolved organic carbon), from which about 0.6 liters of methane gas is recovered from each gram of DOC.

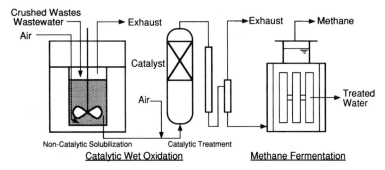

Figure 3. Schematic Flow Diagram of Bench Plant

**Feasibility Study**

**Study on Energy Balance.** Assuming a large condominium style residential area with a population of 28,000, a feasibility study has been conducted using the experimental data obtained. As a result, 0.4 Mm³ of methane gas can be recovered from the fermentation process per year. Figure 4 and 5 show comparison between the energy balance of the MHW system and that of the conventional one.

In the conventional system, 12.6 tera joule per year [TJ/y] of electric power is consumed, and 45.2 TJ/y of thermal energy and 5.4 TJ/y of electric power is produced. The resulting energy utilization efficiency is 42 percent.

In the MHW system, 14.2 TJ/y of electric power is consumed. 40.5 TJ/y of thermal energy is produced in the catalytic wet oxidation reaction of the organic material in the waste. The energy of the methane is converted to 7.9 TJ/y of electric power and 7.9 TJ/y of thermal energy. The total thermal energy produced from the two processes is 48.5 TJ/y. The resulting energy utilization efficiency is 47 percent. These figures of efficiency surpass those of the conventional system.

**Feasibility Study.** Assuming the same condominium residential area, the energy balance economic study of the entire system has been conducted using the results of energy balance. Figure 6 shows detailed system formation of the MHW system. This system consists of pre-treatment, crushing and separation, catalytic wet oxidation, biological solubilization, methane fermentation, advanced water treatment, methane utilization and so on.

Using the cost data of each components, the total cost of the MHW system is calculated. Figure 7 and 8 show the investment and operating cost of the MHW system compared with those of the conventional one.

The investment costs of incineration and advanced water treatment in the conventional system are $6.7 \times 10^9$ and $0.80 \times 10^9$ yen. The total investment cost of the conventional system is about $7.5 \times 10^9$ yen. On the other hand, the investment costs of each process in the MHW system are $3.5 \times 10^9$ yen for CWO, $1.9 \times 10^9$ yen for biological solubilization and methane fermentation, $1.5 \times 10^9$ yen for crushing and separation, $0.97 \times 10^9$ yen for advanced water treatment and $0.63 \times 10^9$ yen for pre-treatment. Eventually the total investment cost of the MHW system is about $9.8 \times 10^9$ yen.

The operating costs of incineration and advanced water treatment in the conventional system are $1.4 \times 10^6$ and $0.11 \times 10^6$ yen per day respectively. The total operating cost of the conventional system is about $1.5 \times 10^6$ yen per day. On the other hand, the investment costs of each process in the MHW system are 0.45 million yen per day for CWO, $0.40 \times 10^6$ yen per day for biological solubilization

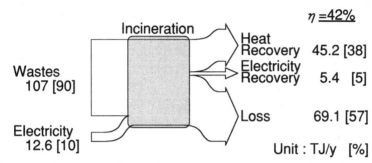

Figure 4.  Energy Balance in Conventional System (28,000 residents)

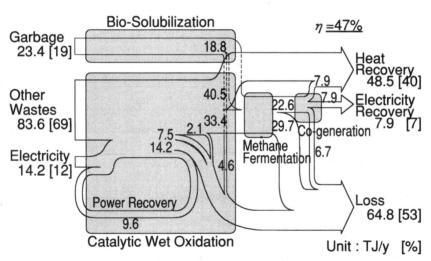

Figure 5.  Energy Balance in MHW System (28,000 residents)

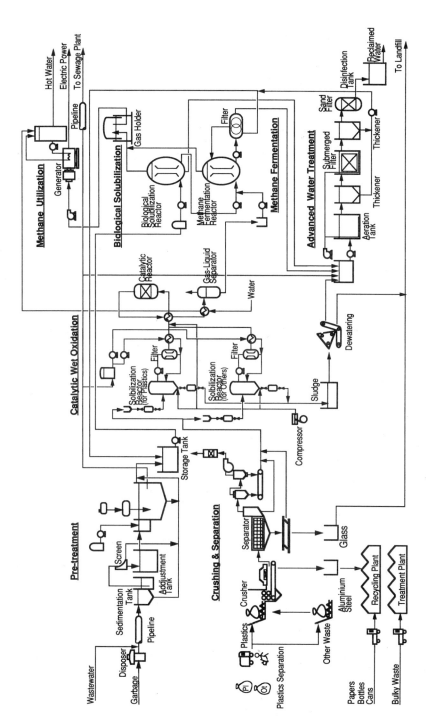

Figure 6. Flow Diagram of MHW System

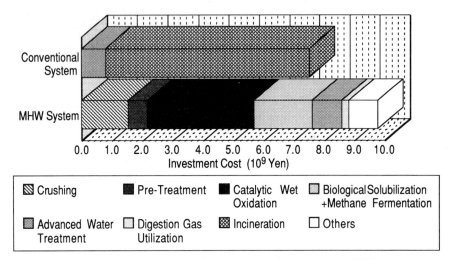

Figure 7.  Investment Costs of Conventional System and MHW System

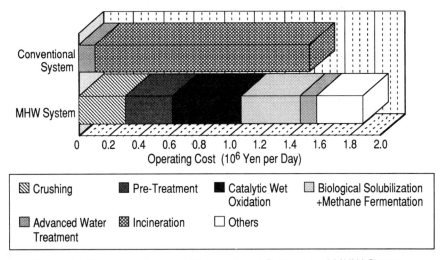

Figure 8.  Operating Costs of Conventional System and MHW System

and methane fermentation, $0.31 \times 10^6$ yen per day for crushing and separation, $0.32 \times 10^6$ yen per day for advanced water treatment and $0.11 \times 10^6$ yen per day for pre-treatment. Eventually the total operating cost of the MHW system is about $1.9 \times 10^6$ yen per day.

In consequence, the MHW system is more expensive than the conventional one by 30 percent in investment cost and 25 percent in operating cost.

## CONCLUSIONS

The conventional system which consists of MSW incinerator and sewage treatment has a number of problems from environmental point of view. Elementary technologies were developed and evaluated at the first stage of the project. Then the economic feasibility of the entire system was examined if the MHW system could be accepted in society. The most important target of this project is, maintaining a system with the least impact to global environment, to maximize energy utilization from waste. Although the target was achieved, the cost of the MHW system proved to be a little higher than that of the conventional one. But considering that the MHW system has several advantages that cannot be described quantitatively, it is sufficiently competitive with the conventional one. Moreover, in order to judge the feasibility of implementing the MHW system, economic studies have been continued covering concrete scenarios. It is believed that the MHW system and the conventional one have the potential to supplement each other.

## REFERENCE

1)M. Futakawa, G. Inoue, H. Ogasawara, Y. Murakami " Methane from Household Wastes by Catalytic and Biological Treatment", International Gas Union /19th World Gas Conference, Milan, June, 1994.
2)MITI brochure, "Development of Methane Recovery System from Wastes." 1991.

# A PROBABILISTIC APPROACH TO INSPECTION SCHEDULING

Mike Brown
British Gas, Research and Technology

## ABSTRACT

British Gas initially used probabilistic techniques to develop optimised schedules for the sub-sea inspections of the tubular joints of offshore structures. Inspections were scheduled when the calculated probability of failure of a tubular joint, rose above a target level. Current work is integrating all aspects of this methodology into a one-stop software package for sub-sea offshore structure inspection scheduling. Probabilistic techniques have now been applied to the assessment of future operational and inspection requirements of pipelines subject to corrosion and fatigue. Similar methods have been developed for the assessment of defects in pressure vessels. Probabilistic analysis allows the use of quantified 'risk-based' criteria in the determination of optimum inspection intervals. This paper discusses: the development and application of a number of probabilistic models; structural degradation models; and risk based optimisation approaches.

INTRODUCTION

Probabilistic Analysis

A number of differing industries are now adopting probabilistic and risk based methodologies. For example, on the financial side of project planning, a number of specialised PC software packages are available to help in the assessment of the relative merits of alternative investment strategies (e.g. 1).

Probabilistic analysis involves the use of structural mechanics failure equations, but with the input variables represented as statistical distributions, rather than as single, fixed values. The equations are usually re-arranged such that 'load' and 'resistance to load' terms are created. Calculating the probability that the 'load' is greater than the 'resistance to load' determines the probability of failure of the structure or component. Alternatively 'load' is replaced by 'stress' and 'resistance to load' by 'strength' and the terminology 'stress~strength interference model' is adopted, see Figure 1.

Why Use Probabilistic Analysis ?

Probabilistic analysis can be very complex; the quality of input data needs to be much higher than for a conventional analysis, to get the best from the technique.

There are a number of advantages.


i) Bringing the conceptual model closer to the physical reality

In any engineering system, the parameters considered are known only within a tolerance. Examples are:
The properties of engineering materials. Nominally identical material always shows some variability when the results of material tests are considered.
Manufactured components. Nominally identical, practically show variability in their dimensions (e.g. wall thickness of pipe spools), within the tolerance band of the manufacturing process.

Perhaps less obviously, corrosion rate and the wave loading of an offshore structure are both best suited to statistical representation.

ii) Avoiding excessive conservatism

For example, a conventional assessment of a pipeline, might use: the specified minimum yield strength (SMYS) of the pipeline material; a pipeline wall thickness at the lower end of the manufacturing tolerance; upper bound prediction of corrosion rates; pressure loading with a safety factor applied; upper bound assumptions, due to measuring tolerances, on the size of reported defects.

The result could well be a combination of conservatism's which are mutually incompatible.

The probabilistic assessment allows the Engineer to realistically take account of the probability that a combination of unfavourable events / parameters will be such as to result in a failure.

iii) Making sense of safety factors / quantified risk assessment

A number of standards (e.g. 2), have used probabilistic methods to provide guidance on the level of partial safety factors. However the magnitude of safety factors is often a question of engineering judgement and the setting of an appropriate safety factor may be problematical.

In simple terms, is it worth spending an extra £100,000 to increase a safety factor from 1.5 to 2.0 ? Or acceptable to reduce the safety factor from 2.0 to 1.5, saving £100,000 ? By introducing risk based arguments, which consider the probability and the consequence of a failure, and the cost of reducing the risk, it is possible to rationalise this decision making process.

It should be noted that in this context, risk of failure could refer to a risk of financial loss or make reference to a permissible level of risk to life. Reference (3) reviews and discusses some recent thinking on risk issues.

PROBABILISTIC TECHNIQUES

General

In broad terms, the assessment of probability of failure can be carried out in one of two ways, by using a sampling method, or an analytical approach. It should be noted that when dealing with very small probabilities of failure, it is common, especially in the offshore sector, to refer to reliability index, $\beta$, rather than probability of failure. The reliability index is a conveniently sized measure defined as the argument of the standard normal distribution which yields (1-the event probability), see Figure 3.

Assuming then, that the structural mechanics problem has been formulated in terms of a stress strength interference model and that the input variables are represented by statistical distributions:

Sampling Methods

The most primitive and robust sampling approach is the 'Monte-Carlo' method. Monte-Carlo simulation consists of repeatedly taking a 'sample' from each of the statistical distributions of the input parameters. For each sample set , an assessment of whether this set of values would lead to a failure made. The parameters are sampled according to their input distributions, that is, for a normal distribution for example, there would be more simulations with values near to the mean of the distribution, than there would be simulations with values in the tails of the distribution.

When sufficient samples have been taken, an assessment can be made of the probability of failure, based on the proportion of samples which gave failure. The major advantage of the Monte-Carlo method is that it will always produce an unbiased result. The major disadvantage is that, for small probabilities, a very large number of samples is required. As a indication, if the true probability is 1 in a million, many more than one million samples should be taken to produce an accurate result. Obviously this can result in cumbersome and timetaking analysis.

There are other simulation methods (e.g. Directional Simulation, Latin Hypercube) which are more efficient than Monte-Carlo. However Monte-Carlo simulation is the simplest and probably still the widest used simulation method.

Analytical Methods

The probability of an event can be determined by solution of the appropriate multidimensional integral;

$$P_{failure} = \int_{failure} f_x(x)dx$$

Where the variables 'x' are the input variables to the failure equation.

However where there are many input variables, the integral becomes very complex and difficult to evaluate.  The FORM and SORM (First and Second Order Reliability Methods) are approaches which can, usually very accurately, approximate the solution of the failure equation integral.

To simply  visualise the FORM approach, consider Figure 2 which shows the failure area for a problem with two input variables, both normally distributed. Each unit of the graph axes, represents one standard deviation of the distribution of that variable. The failure line, that is the line describing where the values of the two input variables combine so as to just cause failure, is as shown. The FORM solution is an estimate of the failure area as defined by the linear approximation shown. The SORM solution would approximate the failure line as a second order line. For more input variables the principles are similar but the problem becomes multi-dimensional.

With some research, the mathematics of the FORM approach will be found to be relatively straightforward, simple PC packages being sufficient to produce specific useful working models (4). However sophisticated software is available (e.g. 5) which aids the user in the development of probabilistic failure models and makes use of a wide range of solution methods, via easy to use graphical user interfaces.

BRITISH GAS EXPERIENCE

Offshore Structure Tubular Joints

Offshore structures on the United Kingdom Continental Shelf (UKCS) must satisfy National requirements which specify that sufficient underwater surveys be undertaken to ensure the continued integrity of the structure. For platforms operated by British Gas Exploration and Production (BGE&P) on the UKCS, the intersection welds (tubular joint welds) of the tubular members of the frame structures (the Jacket) are most sensitive to deterioration due to fatigue crack growth. Previously, BGE&P had used partly subjective appraisal of: the deterministic fatigue life; service history and consequence of failure of individual joints, to determine inspection requirements. However recognising the need to rationalise inspection costs, while maintaining structural integrity, BGE&P initiated a project to determine the optimum location and frequency of inspections, using probabilistic techniques.

The platforms considered were all shallow water structures (26m to 37m water depth), the structure age being between 1 and 19 years. Prior to this project BGE&P carried out a rationalisation exercise, essentially to standardise the structural models see Figure 4. These beam type models were used to determine the nominal stress in the tubular members of the jackets. More detailed finite element models, see Figure 5, being developed to determine accurately the stress state at the intersection welds of the tubular members.
To determine the fatigue loading on the joint, the maximum stress at the intersection welds is combined with statistical data on the wave frequency and height.

Using methods developed from in-house research into fatigue crack growth in tubular joints (6), British Gas Research and Technology (BGR&T), developed a probabilistic fracture mechanics fatigue crack growth model. Together with the results of other work (7), this probabilistic method was applied to the consideration of all critical tubular joints on the BGE&P UKCS platforms, and improved sub-sea inspection schedules developed for these platforms.

Fracture mechanics fatigue analysis relates growth of a crack to the range of stress intensity to which the crack tip is subjected. It is common to represent fatigue crack growth data in the form of a log(da/dN) versus log $\Delta K$ curve. The Paris Law being widely used to represent the crack growth relevant to the central portion of the curve.

The Paris Law is given by

$$\frac{da}{dN} = C\Delta K^m$$

Where

a = crack depth
N= number of stress cycles
C=crack growth constant (material property)
m=crack growth exponent (material property)
$\Delta K$=range of stress intensity

also

$$\Delta K = Y(a)\Delta\sigma\sqrt{(\pi a)}$$

where:

Y(a)=a structural compliance factor (often referred to as the 'Y-calibration')
$\Delta\sigma$=stress range

The value of Y(a) changes as the crack depth increases.

The analysis procedure to determine the Y-calibration, used for this project was based on the research referred to above (6), which included parametric finite element studies of a number of cracked tubular joint geometries.

The probabilistic analysis was implemented via the general purpose probabilistic analysis program, PROBAN (5). That is, FORTRAN77 code of the failure model was produced and this code linked to PROBAN to gain access to the PROBAN statistical and probabilistic functions. This is very similar to the way in which any suite of software may be built up from a library of subroutines.

Due to the degradation process of fatigue, the probability of failure of each tubular joint increases with time (the reliability falls). Inspections are scheduled when the reliability has fallen below an allowable target value, see Figure 6. This value may be defined by reference to recommended values (e.g. 9) or by a more complex consideration of the contribution of the individual joint to the overall integrity of the structure, (e.g.7).

Following the inspection, the reliability will be restored for one of two reasons. Either the inspection has found that no fatigue crack exists, or else a crack has been found and repaired.
Due to the high man-power requirements of the initial project, an integrated software package was later produced by BGR&T, to enable BGE&P to cost-effectively run analyses and carry out sensitivity studies, to further optimise the inspection schedules (8).

Pipelines

Corrosion can be a major problem for the operator of on and offshore pipelines. The periodic use of on-line inspection vehicles (magnetic and ultrasonic 'intelligent pigs') allows the operator to gain accurate information on the depth, length and frequency of corrosion within a pipeline.

Methods for determining the acceptability of corrosion defects have been widely published (e.g. 10, 11, 12). The combination of these methods, high accuracy on-line inspection vehicles (e.g. the British Gas "smart pig"), and sophisticated probabilistic analysis techniques, has meant that predictions for the probability of failure of corroding pipelines can be obtained.

Failure Equation for the Assessment of part-through pipe wall defects

A semi-empirical criteria, derived from the results of burst tests of pipes containing axially oriented defects (10), is as shown:

$$\sigma_{fail} = \sigma_{flow}\left[\frac{1-\frac{A}{A_o}}{1-\left(\frac{A}{A_o}\right)M^{-1}}\right] = \frac{P_{fail}R}{t}$$

Where M, accounts for the stress concentration at the defect due to radial bulging, is referred to as the Folias factor and has been defined as:

$$M = \left[1 + 0.4\left(\frac{2c}{\sqrt{Rt}}\right)^2\right]^{\frac{1}{2}}$$

$\sigma_{fail}$ = pipeline hoop stress at failure
$P_{fail}$ = failure pressure
$\sigma_{flow}$ = 'flow' stress ( a function of the pipeline yield strength)
d = defect depth
t = pipewall thickness
2c = defect axial length
R = pipe radius
A = defect cross-sectional area
$A_o$ = 2c . t

By rearranging the failure equation an expression may be formed for the maximum tolerable corrosion area in the pipeline, $A_f$

$$A_f = A_o\left[\frac{\sigma_{flow} - \sigma_{fail}}{\sigma_{flow} - \sigma_{fail}M^{-1}}\right]$$

Failure is predicted to occur when the actual corrosion (as measured), $A_m$, exceeds the tolerable corrosion area, $A_f$, that is

$A_m > A_f.$

Hence the "limit-state function", which describes the failure set is:

$A_f - A_m < 0$

Considering a pipeline with active corrosion, Figure 7 shows diagrammatically the basis for a changing probabilistic assessment as defects worsen.

Problems exist when attempting to establish the variability's of the input parameters (see 13 for more detail).

Generally, SMYS represents a lower bound to the yield strength of the pipe material. It is possible (perhaps the probability can be quantified) that the pipe material will be of lower strength than the SMYS. It is more likely that the material will be of higher yield strength. If the pipe mill certificates are available (or a sample large enough to be statistically significant), then a statistical distribution may be developed for the material yield strength.

Tolerances on the pipeline geometry, that is the diameter and the wall thickness, may be found in the relevant National or International Standard, (e.g.14).

Recommendations on the future operating strategies of a pipeline (e.g. de-rating of a deteriorating pipeline to ensure a constant level of reliability, repair and/or replacement decisions) can thus be made on a quantified basis. This method has been successfully applied to the assessment of a number of pipelines and is available as a commercial service.

Pressure Vessels

The assessment of the significance of flaws in pressure vessels, has generally been carried out within British Gas by the use of procedures which assume that a structure may fail due to either fracture or plastic collapse (e.g. 2, 15).

By applying probabilistic techniques, it is possible to redefine the assessment criteria such as to determine the theoretical 'probability of failure' of a detected defect and the relative likelihood of each failure mode.

Combination of 'probability of failure' with the possible consequences of the failure of the pressure vessel, allows the determination of the total risk associated with the presence of a flaw in a vessel. An inspection schedule or repair/replacement strategy may thus be developed, based on a combination of risk to life and risk of financial loss.

This area of work is the subject of continuing research within British Gas.

CONCLUDING COMMENTS

Probabilistic methods provide quantified information on integrity which allow more cost effective operation of structures and plant.

The effectiveness of probabilistic methods depends on the development of appropriate deterministic deterioration and failure models and the availability of data on input parameter variability.

British Gas have demonstrated the usefulness of these methods in a number of areas, and are continuing to extend the use of probabilistic techniques into new areas of structural integrity.

REFERENCES

1. @RISK - Risk Analysis for Spreadsheets, Palisade Corporation.

2. British Standards Institute, Published Document, PD 6493:1991, "Guidance on methods for assessing the acceptability of flaws in fusion welded structures".

3. I.Corder, G.Fearnehough and R.N.Knott,"Pipeline design using risk based criteria", IGE 129th Annual General Meeting and Spring Conference, May 1992.

4. M.G.Kirkwood, I.Keilty, H.Rabbia,"Structural Reliability of Drill String Casing Threaded Connectors", To be published SPE, 1996.

5. Veritas Sesam Systems, "PROBAN General purpose probabilistic analysis program", developed by Det norske Veritas.

6. J.V.Haswell, "Predicting the Fatigue Life of Offshore Tubular Joints", International Gas Research Conference, Orlando, Florida, 1992.

7. A.Oakley, M.Brown, P.A.Warren, N.D.P.Barltrop, "Optimised Inspection Scheduling for Offshore Structures: A Probabilistic Approach", BOSS '94, U.S.A.

8. Inspection Maintenance Planning System, IMPS, British Gas internal report and software.

9. Anon, "Structural Reliability Analysis of Marine Structures", Classification Notes No. 306, Det Norse Veritas, July 1992.

10. J.F. Kiefner, et al, "Failure Stress Levels of Flaws in Pressurised Cylinders", ASTM STP 536, 1973.

11. P.Hopkins, D.G.Jones, "A Study of Long and Complex-Shaped Corrosion in Transmission Pipelines", 11th International Conference on Offshore Mechanics and ArcticEngineering, Calgary, 1992.

12. R.W.E.Shannon, "The Failure Behaviour of Linepipe Defects", Int J Press Vess and Piping, Vol 1., 1974.

13. D.G.Jones, S.J.Dawson, M.Brown, "Reliability of Corroded Pipelines", 13th International Conference on Offshore Mechanics and Arctic Engineering, 1994.

14. Anon., API Specification for Linepipe (5L, 5LS, 5LX).

15. I.Milne et al, R/H/R6, "Assessment of the Integrity of Structures Containing Defects", Central Electricity Generating Board.

## Figure 1

### Stress~Strength Interference Model

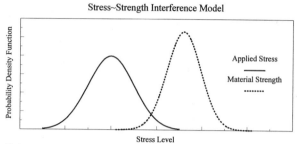

Note:

Failure occurs when the Applied Stress > Material Strength

## Figure 2

### Visual Representation of FORM solution

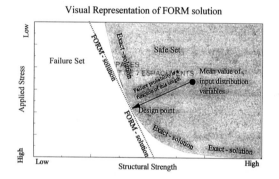

## Figure 3

### The Reliability Index

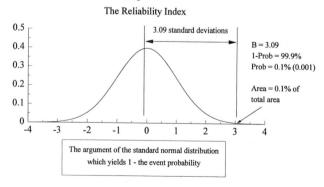

Figure 4

Structural Model of Offshore Jacket

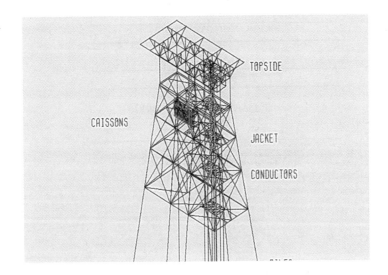

Figure 5

Detailed Shell Finite Element Model of Tubular Joint

Figure 6

Significance of Inspection to Reliability

# Reliability versus Time Plots

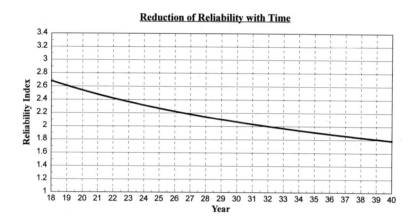

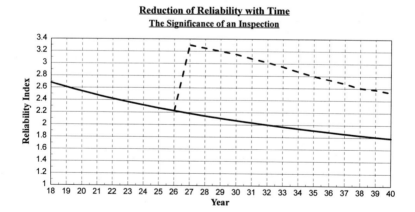

## Figure 7

## The significance of active corrosion

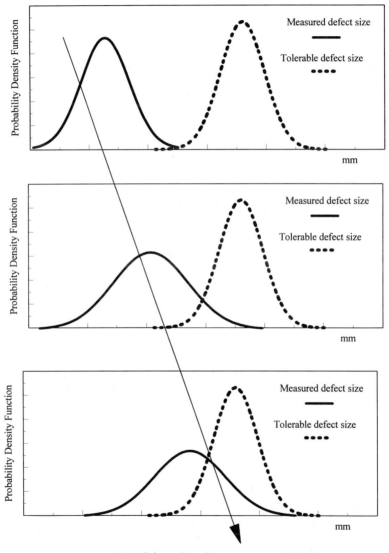

Defect size increases with time,
increasing probability of failure

LARGE SCALE JET FIRE IMPACTION
ONTO A FLAT SURFACE

IMPACT DE FLAMME JAILLISSANTE À GRANDE ÉCHELLE
SUR UNE SURFACE PLANE

A.J. Gosse and M.J. Pritchard
British Gas Research and Technology, UK

ABSTRACT

During the storage or processing of pressurised flammable liquid or gas an accidental release may lead to a jet fire. To assess the thermal impact of jet fires on the surroundings and structures an investigation has been undertaken to study heat transfer from vertical natural gas jet fires impacting onto the underside of a flat 20m by 20m deck at flowrates of up to 3kgs⁻¹. The effect of a wide range of parameters on the fire characteristics were assessed, including varying the distance between the release point and the deck, the height of the deck above the ground, the exit diameter and the release pressure. Measurements were made of the total and radiative heat flux distribution over the deck and of the velocity and temperature distribution in the flames. The paper discusses the test facility, the experimental programme, the data obtained and its use for the development and validation of predictive models.

RÉSUMÉ

Pendant le stockage ou le traitement de gaz ou liquide inflammable sous pression, un dégagement accidentel peut provoquer l'apparition d'une flamme faillissante. Afin d'évaluer l'impact thermique des flammes jaillissantes sur l'environnement et les structures, un examen a été entrepris pour étudier la transmission de la chaleur d'un impact vertical de flammes jaillissantes de gaz naturel sur une plate-forme de 20m sur 20m à des débits allant jusqu'à 3kgs⁻¹. Les effets d'une grande variété de paramètres sur les caractéristiques du feu ont été évalués. Ces paramètres comprenaient la variation de la distance entre le point de dégagement et la plate-forme, la hauteur de la plate-forme au-dessus du sol, le diamètre de sortie et la pression du dégagement. Des mesures ont été faites de la distribution du flux de3 chaleur radiative et globale sur la plate-forme et de la distribution de la vitesse et de la température dans les flammes. La communication examine le matériel d'essai, le programme expérimental, les données obtenues et leur utilisation pour la mise au point et la validation de modèles prédictifs.

## INTRODUCTION

During the storage or processing of pressurised flammable liquids or gases, a particular hazard which may arise following an accidental release, is that of a jet fire. For onshore and offshore installations where limitations of space lead to areas of high congestion, a jet fire may impact on adjacent structures such as pipework or process plant. If the rate of heat transfer is sufficiently high, further damage could ensue and lead to additional releases, thereby escalating the event. Although the probability of an accidental release remains low the consequences of such events need to be taken into account in undertaking risk assessments and designing appropriate fire protection systems. For this reason a significant proportion of the work undertaken within the British Gas R&T programme contributes to the prevention of such accidents by helping to establish correct engineering design, construction, operation and maintenance procedures.

In order to be able to develop methodologies for calculating as accurately as possible the consequences of an accidental release, it is necessary to conduct some experiments at as near as practical to full scale because many of the physical processes involved in the release and combustion of flammable materials are scale dependent. To date, a large number of jet fire experiments with a variety of fuels have been conducted to study the thermal loading on cylindrical obstacles such as storage vessels or pipe-work[1,2]. To extend this work to study jet fire interaction with more complex geometries a purpose built rig has been constructed, enabling a wide range of experimental investigations to be undertaken, providing high quality data for the development and validation of prediction models used in hazard assessment. This paper describes the initial experimental programme of work to study jet fires in which natural gas was released vertically upwards on to the underside of a large flat surface and includes the range of experimental techniques employed and the results obtained.

## TEST FACILITY

The tests were carried out within a test facility located at the British Gas test site at Spadeadam in northern England. The facility (Figure 1) consists of a 20m x 20m flat surface (deck) suspended on steel ropes from legs located near to the four corners of the rig. The ropes are connected to a winch allowing the deck height to be varied between 2 and 8m above a similar sized flat base. The under-side of the deck is covered in a 25mm thick layer of a Mandolite fire protective coating enabling the deck to withstand the rigorous nature of an impacting jet fire and protect the steel construction of the rig from excessive temperature rises during the tests. The deck incorporates a range of fixed instrument positions on radial lines allowing a wide range of instruments to be either mounted through the surface or suspended underneath on supports. These include heat flux calorimeters, radiometers, pitot probes and thermocouples.

Natural gas is supplied to the facility from a high pressure reservoir system with a sophisticated flow control system enabling the gas to be released at a constant flow rate. For the tests described in this paper a 50mm diameter supply pipework was configured to allow gas to be released vertically upwards from heights of 2 to 7m above the ground and at pressures of up to 130 bar through an interchangeable orifice.

## SCIENTIFIC MEASUREMENTS

Instrumentation was installed in the rig to obtain detailed measurements on the release conditions of the natural gas, the convective and radiative heat loading to the deck, the temperature and dynamic pressure of the gases within the flame, the thermal emission characteristics of the flame and the flame geometry. A brief description of the instrumentation used is given below.

## Release Conditions

Measurements of stagnation and static pressure and stagnation temperature were made within the gas supply pipeline at three locations. The mass flow rate was also determined using an orifice plate.

## Ambient Weather Conditions

The wind speed and direction can affect the geometry of the flame and these parameters were monitored using a number of anemometers and wind vanes at locations nominally upwind and downwind of the rig. Relative humidity and temperature were also measured in order to calculate atmospheric transmissivity.

## Flame Emission Characteristics

Incident thermal radiation levels were measured at various locations around the fires to provide data for model validation. These data were obtained using up to 6 wide angle radiometers. Information on the thermal radiation emitted at the surface of the flame is also required. This is not a straightforward measurement as it is dependent upon fuel type and the size of the fire. For a given fuel, it also varies with local flame temperature and gas composition. Thermal radiation from hydrocarbon fires normally has two components; the continuous black body radiation from soot particles (responsible for the luminous nature of the flame) and discrete radiation bands of hot gases, predominantly $H_2O$ and $CO_2$. To simplify analysis, the effect of the temperature and composition of the flame gases is usually characterised by defining a flame surface emissive power (SEP), with the flame considered to be a solid body with the radiation originating at its surface. During some of the tests an infrared thermal imaging camera was used, allowing both the flame geometry and a distribution of the SEP over the flame to be obtained, greatly enhancing the understanding of the flame emission characteristics. In addition to the thermal imaging camera, video cameras were installed at various locations around the rig to obtain data on the flame geometry.

## Internal Flame Characteristics

Gas temperatures within the flame were made using up to 24 100μm exposed bead, nickel chromel/alumel (type K) thermocouples. The thermocouples were mounted on four supports suspended from the flat surface at different radial distances from the centre and at different distances below the surface. Measurements of the dynamic pressure within the flame ($\frac{1}{2}\rho V^2$) were made using up to 20 simple pitot probes mounted on the same supports as the thermocouples. This measurement can be used directly for model validation, and additionally, if an estimation of the density is made, to obtain gas velocities.

## Heat Loading to the Flat Surface

In an accidental release scenario in which a jet fire impinges upon a flat surface, a knowledge of the rate of heat transfer to the surface is required in order to ascertain its thermal response to the fire. The total heat transfer (radiative and convective) was measured using up to 33 heat flux calorimeters, with the radiative component measured separately using up to 7 ellipsoidal radiometers. These calorimeters measure the total heat loading flux to a surface (the sensing element of the calorimeter) whose temperature is maintained at 60°C. The convective component of heat loading was obtained by subtracting the radiative load measured by the radiometers. By using data on the temperature of the gases within the flame, convective heat transfer coefficients can be calculated and used as input to mathematical models to define the convective heat load to a structure when predicting thermal response.

EXPERIMENTAL PROGRAMME

A series of commissioning tests were undertaken to investigate the range of flow conditions, rig configuration and wind conditions which could be studied. Based on these tests an experimental programme was devised and test conditions were varied to look at the effect of certain parameters on the fire characteristics. A release and rig configuration with a nominal mass flow rate of 2.1kgs$^{-1}$ through a 30mm diameter exit orifice, a deck height of 7.96m and a release point height of 6.04m was chosen as a "base case" release. The effect of varying the following parameters on this release was investigated:

- Combination of exit pressure and exit orifice diameter:
    - Exit pressures in the range 1.36 to 113 barg (All sonic releases)
    - Exit diameters of 10.0, 20.0, 30.0 and 50.8mm

- Mass flow rate:
    - Mass flow rates in the range 0.42 to 3.13kgs$^{-1}$

- Stand-off distance (the distance between the flat surface and the gas release point):
    - Stand-off distances in the range 0.42 to 5.91m

- Partial confinement (reducing the flat surface to floor spacing):
    - Flat surface height in the range 2.56 to 7.96m

- Wind speed:
    - Wind speeds in the range 0.1 to 7.8ms$^{-1}$

Table 1 contains a list of the 32 tests conducted in the main test programme. Also included in this table are the rig configuration and time averaged values of exit pressure, mass flow rate and wind speed.

RESULTS AND DISCUSSION

A detailed study of the time averaged data from individual tests has been undertaken enabling the effect of the test parameters on heat loading to the flat surface and the internal flame characteristics to be investigated. The findings of this study are discussed in the following sections.

In general, the impacting flames investigated were thin and of low luminosity (Figure 2). The "base case" release stabilised on the impacted surface and had a diameter of about 12m and a depth of less than 0.4m. A plot of the total heat flux to the flat surface during Test 20 is shown in Figure 3. In this plot, the measured total heat flux distribution along the three instrument lines, nominally upwind, downwind and crosswind from the centre of the flat surface, is presented. It is seen that there was excellent agreement between values from each line, and that for this release, which was conducted in negligible wind speed, the flame impingement was approximately axisymmetric. The shape of the radial distribution of total heat flux seen in Figure 3 was typical of tests where the flame stabilised on the flat surface rather than in the free jet below the flat surface. For tests where the stand-off distance was greater than 3m, the flame was seen to stabilise in the free jet. This is important in relation to the maximum flux levels measured and the shape of the distribution and this will be discussed later.

Effect of Exit Pressure/Exit Orifice Diameter

The effect of varying the exit pressure and exit orifice diameter to achieve the same nominal mass flow rate (2.1kgs$^{-1}$) and similar stand-off distance was investigated by comparing the results from Test 29 (39.8barg exit pressure through a 20.0mm exit diameter), Test 20 (17.6barg exit pressure through a 30.0mm exit diameter) and Test 6 (6.1barg exit pressure through a 50.8mm exit diameter). The data from these tests showed, for these sonic releases, that varying the exit pressure and exit orifice diameter to achieve the same nominal mass flow rate (2.1kgs$^{-1}$) had no significant effect on the flame characteristics.

Effect of Mass Flow Rate

The total heat flux distributions from Tests 8, 10, 7 and 6 are presented in Figure 4. The mass flow rates for these releases were 0.69, 1.12, 1.73 and 2.10kgs$^{-1}$ respectively and the stand-off distance was approximately 2m so that the flame stabilised on the impacted flat surface during each release. It can be seen that up to 1.5m from the centre of the deck there was little dependence on the total heat flux with increasing mass flow rate over the measured range. The maximum total heat flux was seen to increase and the location of the maximum seen to shift outwards from the centre of the flat surface with increasing flow rate. As expected, the radial decay of total heat flux was affected by the increased mass flow rate due to the radial spread of the flame being largest for the highest mass flow rate.

The gas temperature distributions measured within the flame for these tests are presented in Figure 5. It can be seen that for Support 1 at 2.02m from the centre of the flat surface, the gas temperature distribution was similar for all of these mass flow rates. However, for the other support positions, higher temperatures were measured at all measurement locations with a higher mass flow rate. This indicates that, as observed, the thickness and radial spread of the flame increased with increased mass flow rate.

Effect of Stand-off Distance

The effect of stand-off distance, which has been defined as the distance between the release point and the flat surface, has been investigated by comparing results from Tests 11, 20, 25 and 16, which had stand-off distances of 0.42, 2.01, 3.81 and 5.91m. The nominal mass flow rate for each of these four tests was 2.1kgs$^{-1}$. For logistical reasons, the different stand-off distances listed above were achieved with a variety of deck heights. However, it was established that the minimum deck height investigated (4.06m) was sufficiently high that it would not effect the characteristics of the flame, enabling the affect of stand-off distance to be investigated in isolation. The peak measured total heat flux increased with increasing stand off distance, from approximately 200kWm$^{-2}$ at a 0.42m stand off distance to 300kWm$^{-2}$ at a 5.91m stand off distance. This can be seen in Figure 6 which shows the variation of total heat flux with radial distance from the centre of the flat surface for each test. For Tests 11 and 20, the flame was observed to stabilise on the flat surface and it can be seen that these tests have similar total heat flux distributions. For Test 25, the flame was seen to stabilise in the free jet just below the flat surface resulting in higher measured heat fluxes in the central region of the flat surface. For Test 16, where the stand-off distance was 5.91m the flame stabilised in the free jet approximately 3m below the flat surface and it can be seen that much higher heat fluxes were measured in the central region of the deck. The reason for the higher peak fluxes could therefore be attributed to the observation that the flame stabilised in the jet resulting in high velocity hot gases impacting normal to the flat surface. At the 5.91m stand-off distance the peak values were also to be found closer to the impaction point. However, as expected, the radial spread of the flame observed during Test 16 was less than for Test 11 and this was reflected in the measured total heat flux which showed a faster rate of decay radially from the centre of the rig.

The gas temperatures measured close to the centre of the flat surface were higher for the largest stand-off. However, since, for a given flow rate, the radial spread of the fire decreases with increasing stand-off distance the gas temperatures at measurement points furthest from the deck centre were lower for the highest stand-off distance.

Effect of Partial Confinement

Partial confinement of the flame was achieved by lowering the height of the flat surface to reduce the distance between it and the rig floor. The lowest flat surface height investigated was 2.56m with a 2.05m release height (Test 22) producing a stand-off distance of 0.51m. The effect of partial confinement was investigated by comparing this test with Test 11 which had a similar stand-off distance and a flat surface height of 6.46m. This flat surface height can be considered to be sufficiently high that the floor has no influence on the flame characteristics. Examination of all the data suggests that for these tests conducted in low wind speeds, which had similar mass flow rates and stand-off distances, this degree of partial confinement had no significant effect on the measured total heat flux distribution.

Effect of Wind Speed

Whilst undertaking the commissioning tests it was observed that the flame was not significantly affected by the wind in speeds of up to 5ms$^{-1}$. However, some releases were conducted in high gusting wind conditions and it was seen that large variations in the flame geometry occurred. To enable more reliable comparisons of the measurement parameters it was decided that the main test programme should be conducted, where possible, in wind speeds of below 5ms$^{-1}$.

The effect of wind speed on the flame characteristics can be determined by comparing Test 20, conducted in negligible wind, with Test 5 which was undertaken in a moderate wind (5.5ms$^{-1}$). For Test 20 there was close agreement between the total heat flux values obtained from each radial line, indicating the flame impingement was approximately axisymmetric. However, during Test 5, the total heat flux distributions showed a departure from the symmetry seen in Test 20.

The effect of wind speed was further exaggerated in the partial confined configurations. Test 32 was conducted in high gusting wind conditions where, for a short period, a time averaged wind speed of 7.8ms$^{-1}$ was measured. During this period, the appearance of the flame was seen to be significantly altered, with the flame filling the space between the deck and the rig floor over a significant area of the deck. The flame became more luminous and soot was seen to emanate from the flame. After the test it was observed that soot had been deposited on areas of the deck and some of the instrumentation. This period of high wind speed was chosen to produce time averaged results and the total heat flux distributions from instrument lines upwind, downwind and crosswind during this period are presented in Figure 7. It is clear that the flame characteristics were significantly affected by the combination of the partial confinement and high wind speed. The upwind portion of the flame appeared to be stalled by the wind and to recirculate back towards the release point. Also, the radial spread of the flame downwind and crosswind was greater than for a low wind speed test. During the high wind speed period, a maximum total heat flux of approximately $350kWm^{-2}$ was recorded.

CONCLUSIONS

- Changing the release pressure and exit diameter whilst maintaining the same flow rate was seen, for these sonic release, to have no significant effect on the heat loading to the flat surface or the internal flame characteristics.

- The maximum total heat flux was seen to increase and the location of the maximum seen to shift outwards from the centre of the deck with increasing flow rate. As expected, the radial decay of total heat flux was affected by an increase in mass flow rate with the radial spread of the flame being largest for the highest mass flow rate.

- Changing the stand-off distance between the deck and the release point significantly affected the heat loading to the surface. It was seen that the position of the stabilisation of the flame greatly affects the localised maximum flux level, with the highest local flux levels occurring when the flame stabilised in the free jet rather than on the impacted surface.

- Partial confinement of the fires by reducing the separation distance between the deck and the rig floor to 2.56m had no noticeable effect on the heat loading to the surface in low wind speed conditions.

- Flame impaction on the deck, and hence the heat loading to it, was symmetrical at low wind speeds. The flame was also seen to be little affected by wind speeds of below $5ms^{-1}$. High wind conditions were seen to significantly affect fire characteristics, particularly the partial confined configuration. Under such conditions, large variations in the flame geometry and in the heat loading to the deck where seen, with heat fluxes of up to $350kWm^{-2}$ being measured.

REFERENCES

1.    Bennet, J.F, Cowley, L.T., Davenport, J.N., Rowson, J.J., 'Large Scale Natural Gas and LPG Jet Fires', Shell External Report TNER.91.022, 1991.

2.    Acton, M.R. and Sekulin, A.J. 'Large Scale Tests to Study Horizontal Jet Fires of Mixtures of Natural Gas and Butane', Final Report, CEC Contract No. STEP-CT90-0098 (DTEE), 1995.

Table 1 - Experimental Programme

| Test No. | Deck Height (m) | Release Height (m) | Exit Orifice Diameter (mm) | Average Exit Stagnation Pressure (barg) | Average Mass Flow Rate (kgs$^{-1}$) | Average Wind Speed (ms$^{-1}$) |
|---|---|---|---|---|---|---|
| 1 | 7.96 | 6.04 | 10.0 | 113.0 | 1.60 | 5.7 |
| 2 | 7.96 | 6.04 | 10.0 | 85.4 | 1.22 | 6.0 |
| 3 | 7.96 | 6.04 | 30.0 | 15.8 | 1.90 | 6.3 |
| 4 | 7.96 | 6.04 | 30.0 | 9.2 | 1.14 | 7.3 |
| 5 | 7.96 | 6.04 | 30.0 | 17.4 | 2.10 | 5.5 |
| 6 | 7.96 | 6.04 | 50.8 | 6.1 | 2.10 | 2.5 |
| 7 | 7.96 | 6.04 | 50.8 | 4.8 | 1.73 | 2.2 |
| 8 | 7.96 | 6.04 | 50.8 | 1.4 | 0.69 | 1.3 |
| 9 | 7.96 | 6.04 | 50.8 | 1.7 | 0.78 | 1.3 |
| 10 | 7.96 | 6.04 | 50.8 | 2.8 | 1.12 | 1.5 |
| 11 | 6.46 | 6.04 | 30.0 | 17.2 | 2.08 | 0.3 |
| 12 | 6.46 | 6.04 | 30.0 | 9.4 | 1.18 | 0.6 |
| 13 | 6.46 | 6.04 | 30.0 | 12.0 | 1.49 | 0.3 |
| 14 | 7.96 | 2.05 | 30.0 | 9.8 | 1.20 | 3.8 |
| 15 | 7.96 | 2.05 | 30.0 | 17.1 | 2.02 | 3.2 |
| 16 | 7.96 | 2.05 | 30.0 | 17.6 | 2.09 | 2.2 |
| 17 | 7.96 | 2.05 | 30.0 | 20.9 | 2.48 | 3.3 |
| 18 | 7.96 | 2.05 | 30.0 | 24.9 | 2.93 | 4.6 |
| 19 | 4.06 | 2.05 | 30.0 | 9.7 | 1.19 | 0.7 |
| 20 | 4.06 | 2.05 | 30.0 | 17.6 | 2.09 | 0.1 |
| 21 | 2.56 | 2.05 | 30.0 | 9.9 | 1.21 | 0.7 |
| 22 | 2.56 | 2.05 | 30.0 | 17.8 | 2.10 | 0.6 |
| 23 | 2.56 | 2.05 | 30.0 | 17.5 | 2.07 | 2.8 |
| 24 | 5.86 | 2.05 | 30.0 | 9.7 | 1.18 | 2.9 |
| 25 | 5.86 | 2.05 | 30.0 | 17.6 | 2.07 | 1.7 |
| 26 | 7.96 | 2.05 | 20.0 | 45.7 | 2.34 | 3.8 |
| 27 | 7.96 | 2.05 | 20.0 | 24.3 | 1.25 | 2.7 |
| 28 | 7.96 | 2.05 | 20.0 | 38.1 | 1.98 | 2.6 |
| 29 | 4.06 | 2.05 | 20.0 | 39.8 | 2.07 | 1.8 |
| 30 | 4.06 | 2.05 | 20.0 | 23.9 | 1.24 | 1.8 |
| 31 | 2.56 | 2.05 | 30.0 | 2.7 | 0.42 | 4.9 |
| 32 | 2.56 | 2.05 | 30.0 | 17.6 | 2.09 | 7.8 |

Figure 1. Experimental Rig

Figure 2. Typical Impacting Fire Test

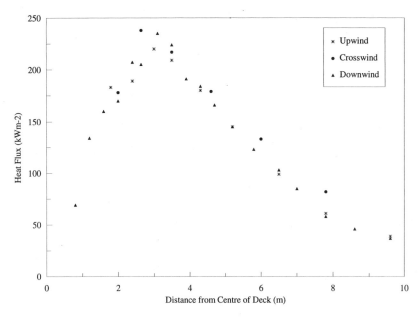

Figure 3. Total Heat Flux Distribution (Test 20)

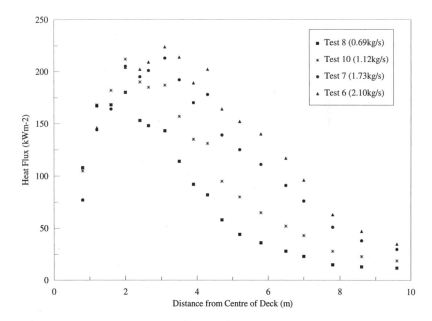

Figure 4. Effect of Mass Flow Rate on Total Heat Flux Distribution

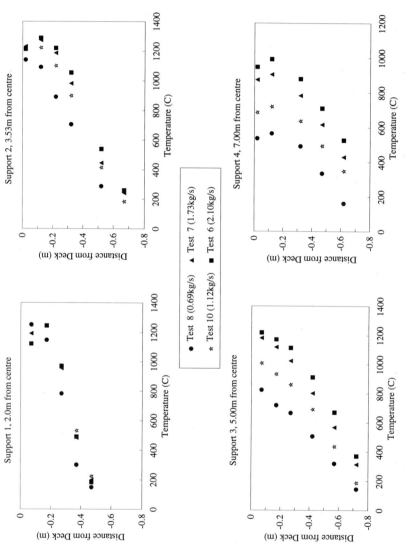

Figure 5. Effect of Mass Flow Rate on Gas Temperature

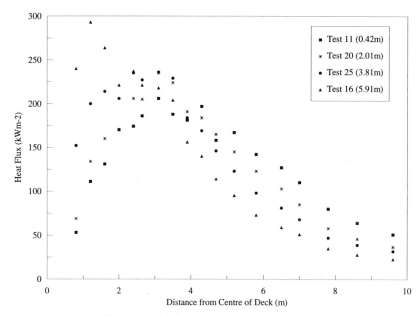

Figure 6. Effect of Stand Off distance on Total Heat Flux Distribution

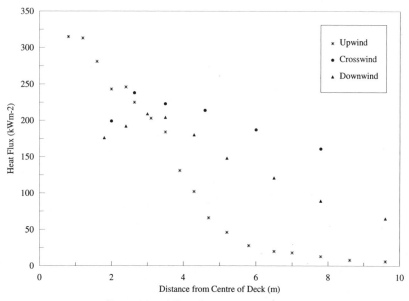

Figure 7. Total Heat Flux Distribution (Test 32)

A LABORATORY AND FIELD STUDY OF THE MITIGATION OF NORM SCALE
IN THE GULF COAST REGIONS OF TEXAS AND LOUISIANA

UNE ÈTUDE LABORATOIRE ET SUR LE TERRAIN DE RÈDUCTION DE
DEPÔT CALCAIRES NORM DANS LES RÉGIONS DU GOLF DU
MEXIQUE DU TEXAS A LA LOUISIANE

John E. Oddo, Xinliang Zhou
Water Research Institute, Inc., USA

Jorge Gamez
Gas Research Institute, USA

Shiliang He and Mason B. Tomson
Rice University, USA

## ABSTRACT

Some oil field scales have the potential to contain regulated levels of naturally occurring radioactive materials (NORM), generally in the form of radium-226. It is estimated that between 300,000 and 1,000,000 tons of NORM scale are produced in the United States each year, if all NORM scales are included. However, these estimates drop dramatically to 15,000 to 50,000 tons/year if included scales are limited to >2,000 pCi/gram. Due to the uncertainties in the amount of material produced and the low average radionuclide content, it is difficult to assess the risk. However, government agencies have defined and are further defining regulations to monitor and dispose of NORM scale materials and scaled equipment. In addition, scale deposition in producing wells and associated facilities negatively impacts rates of production and is expensive to treat and remediate, regardless of the environmental regulations involved. The most common NORM containing scale is $BaSO_4$, or barite. This paper presents the results of a Gas Research Institute (GRI) study that investigates the causes of NORM scale formation and mitigation techniques employed in the field.

Chemical threshold scale inhibitors are generally employed to inhibit scale formation in production systems. However, there is little agreement on which scale inhibitor is most effective with respect to differing water chemistries, temperatures and conditions encountered in the field. Laboratory work using a GRI patented inhibitor evaluation apparatus has produced results that can be used to determine the most effective inhibitor for a specific field application. GRI sponsored work in the Michigan Basin (United States) presented in the last IGRC Conference indicated that a phosphinopolycarboxylate was most effective against NORM barium sulfate scale formation at low temperatures in relatively fresh water. Further work in this study identifies phosphonates as being more effective in the higher ionic strength (TDS) waters and higher temperature regimes that can be expected in the Gulf Coast Region of the United States. The matrix of ionic strength and temperatures and the most effective inhibitors are outlined in the paper.

A new method to evaluate inhibitors has been determined which is based on the delayed nucleation times of scale crystals in the presence of scale inhibitors. This method is faster than flow through (tube blocking) inhibitor evaluations and has been found to correlate well with flow through results. Although flow through testing is still recommended for definitive evaluations, the new method is recommended as a screening procedure.

Three NORM fields have been studied in the Gulf Coast Region. In these fields, three causes of NORM scale have been identified. 1) Incipient scale in a well caused by the temperature/pressure changes that occur during production. 2) Barium sulfate scale formation due to previous seawater floods that introduce high sulfate levels to reservoirs containing barium. 3) The commingling of waters from different zones within a well or from different wells that are not compatible with respect to barium and sulfate. Treatment procedures can vary depending on the type of NORM scale encountered to realize optimum results. Field treatment techniques employed in the three fields studied are summarized in the paper.

The process of fixing a scale inhibitor chemical in a reservoir is called a scale inhibitor squeeze. When the well is produced, the produced water has scale inhibitor dissolved in it and scale may be inhibited if certain criteria have been met. Inhibitor squeeze procedures have been studied in the laboratory and in the field. A squeeze simulation apparatus was constructed to research inhibitor squeeze practices in the laboratory. Results from this work resulted in successful inhibitor squeeze applications in the field. The inhibitor squeeze apparatus and the field results are discussed in the paper. Squeeze life has been extended from an average of two to six months to two to three years or more as a result of this work.

## ABSTRAIT

Certains dépôts de champ pétrolifères ont le potentiel de contenir des "niveaux stabilisés de materiaux radioactifs naturellement produits" (NORM), généralement sous la forme de raduim-226. Il est estimé qu'une quantité mesurant entre 300.000 et 1.000.000 de tonnes de dépôts calcaires NORM sont produits aux Etats-Unis chaque année, si l'on inclut tous les dépôts NORM. Cependant, ces estimations déclinent de 15.000 à 50.000 tonnes par an si les dépôts que l'on inclut sont limités à >2.000 pCi/gramme. Dû à l'imprévisibilité du montant de matériaux produits et à la basse moyenne du contenu radionuclide, il est difficile d'évaluer le risque. Cependant, des agences gouvernementales ont défini et continuent à définir des réglementations pour contrôler et se débarrasser de matériaux NORM et de l'équipement contaminé. De plus, une accumulation de ces dépôts lorsqu'on creuse des puits et autres installations qui y sont associèes, a un effet négatif sur les taux de production et est coûteuse à traiter et à remédier, quelque soient les règles environnementales qui s'y rapportent. Le dèpôt calcaire qui contient le plus fréquemment du NORM est le BaSO$_4$ ou baryte. Cet article présente les résultats d'une étude de L'Institut de Recherche du Gaz (GRI) qui recherche les causes de la formation de dépôts calcaires NORM et les techniques de réduction employées sur la terrain.

Des inhibiteurs de dèpôts calcaires à effet chimique sont généralement employés pour réduire la formation de dépôts calcaires dans les systèmes de production. Cependant, on n'est par toujours d'accord pour définir lequel des inhibiteurs est le plus efficace afin de différencier les propriétés chimiques, températures et conditions de l'eau qu'on rencontre sur le terrain. Des travaux de laboratoire utilisant un appareillage pour évaluer l'inhibition brevetée GRI ont produit des résultats qui peuvent être utilisés pour déterminer l'inhibiteur le plus efficace pour une application pratique spécifique. Des travaux financés par GRI dans le Bassin du Michigan (Etats-Unis) et présentés lors de la dernière Conférence IGRC indiquent qu'un phosphinopolycarboylate est le plus efficace contre la formation de dépôts de sulfate de baryum à températures basses dans de l'eau relativement douce. Un travail plus pousse dans cette étude identifie les composés du phosphore comme étude les plus efficaces dans les eaux à plus grande force ionique (TDS) et dans les conditions de plus haute température qu'on peut attendre de la région du Golfe du Mexique aux Etats-Unis. Cet environnement de force ionique et de températures ainsi que les inhibiteurs les plus efficaces sont brièvement présentés dans cet article.

Une nouvelle méthode pour évaluer les inhibiteurs a été déterminée: elle est basée sur le temps ralenti de nucléation de cristaux de dépôts calcaire en la présence d'inhibiteurs de dépôts. Cette méthode est plus rapide que les évaluations d'inhibiteurs par écoulement (en bloquant le tube) et s'est trouvée être en bonne corrélation avec les résultats basés sur l'ecoulement. Bien que des analyses basées sur l'écoulement soient toujours recommandées pour achever des évaluations définitives, cette nouvelle méthode est recommandée en tant que procédure de filtrage.

Trois catétories de NORM ont été étudiés dans la région de la Côte du Golfe. Parmi ces catégories, trois causes de dépôts NORM ont été identifiées. 1) Un début de dépôts calcaires dans un puits causés par les changements de tempérture et de pression qui se passent pendant la production. 2) La formation de dépôts de sulfate de baryum due à des inondations précédentes d'eau de mer ce qui introduit de hauts niveaux de sulfate dans les réservoirs contenant du baryum. 3) Le mélange d'eaux venant de différentes zones dans un puits ou de différents puits qui ne sont pas compatibles en raisin du baryum et du sulfate. Les procédures de traitement peuvent varier selon le type de dépôt calcaire NORM que l'on recontré de façon à réaliser les meilleurs résultats. Les techniques de traitement sur le terrain qui sont employées dans les trois catégories étudiées sont résumées dans l'article présent.

La procédure qui consiste à utiliser un produit chimique inhibiteur de dépôts calcaires dans un réservoir s'appelle une compression d'inhibiteurs de formation. Lorsque le puits est créé, on dissout un inhibiteur de dépôt calcaire dans l'eau produite et ces dépôts peuvent être empêchés si l'on adhère à certains critères. Les procédures de compression d'inhibiteur ont été étudiées en laboratoire et sur le terrain. Un appareillage de simulation de commpression fut constuit pour pouvoir pratiquer la compression d'inhibiteur en laboratoire. Les conséquences de ces travaux curent pour résultat les applications pratiques de compression d'inhibiteur sur la terrain. L'appareillage de compression d'inhibiteur et les résultats pratiques sont discutés au cours de cet article. Le temps de compression a été prolongé d'une moyenne de deux à six mois à deux à trois ans ou plus conséquemment à ces travaux.

**INTRODUCTION**

As part of the introduction, it is appropriate to briefly describe the NORM problem and some of the vocabulary involved. Radioactive materials are categorized by the United States Nuclear Regulatory Commission (NRC) by the amount of radiation they are likely to produce, and hence, the potential hazard:

**Special Nuclear Material** - Uranium-233, Uranium enriched in Uranium-233, Uranium-235, Plutonium and any other materials designated by the NRC except source materials.
**By-Product Materials** - Radioactive materials (except Special Nuclear Materials) that are yielded radioactive by exposure to radiation incident to the process of producing Special Nuclear Materials.
**Source Material** - Materials that contain uranium, thorium or any combination thereof in excess of 0.05% by weight except Special Nuclear Material.
**NORM** - Naturally Occurring Radioactive Materials
**NARM** - Naturally or Accelerator Produced Radioactive Material

Not all NORM materials occur in the gas and oil fields. Other NORM materials are produced from uranium mining, fly ash, mineral and phosphate rock processing, etc. Due to the high volumes, but low average activity of scale materials from the production of hydrocarbons, it may not be prudent to include these wastes in the same category as other NORM's. The State of Texas has recently differentiated gas and oil field NORM wastes from NORM materials produced from other sources.

The activity of NORM materials in soils, scales, etc., is commonly expressed in picocuries of radiation per gram of soil, scale or other material. A Curie (Ci) is defined as $3.700 \times 10^{10}$ disintegrations per second (dps) which is the number of dps from one gram radium-226. A picocurie, then, is one trillionth of the radioactivity of one gram of radium-226. Since most gas and oil field NORM is composed of radium co-precipitated in scale, 2,000 picocuries/gram of soil or scale material has approximately two-billionths of a gram of radium included. The US EPA drinking water standard is 5 picocuries/l or $5 \times 10^{-12}$ grams of radium-226/liter of drinking water. Radiation due to scale material on equipment or in pipes, separators, etc., is commonly expressed in terms of the human body dose related unit, microrems/hour ($\mu$rems/hr.).

Chemically, radium is a metal cation with a charge of plus two (2+) and is slightly mobile in the produced water. Worldwide produced waters have from nil to a few thousand picocuries/l of radioactivity due to radium-226 and radium-228. Some oil field scales have the potential to contain regulated levels of NORM, generally in the form of radium-226 and radium-228. It is estimated that between 300,000 and 1,000,000 tons of NORM scale are produced in the United States each year, if all NORM scales are included. However, these estimates drop dramatically to 15,000 to 50,000 tons/year if included scales are limited to >2,000 pCi/gram.[11] Due to the uncertainties in the amount of material produced and the low average radionuclide content, it is difficult to assess the risk. However, state agencies have defined and are further defining regulations to monitor and dispose of NORM scale materials and scaled equipment.       Mineral scales are deposits produced in field production facilities due to temperature and pressure changes during the gas and oil recovery processes. Scale deposition in producing wells and associated facilities negatively impacts rates of production and is expensive to treat and remediate, regardless of the environmental regulations involved. The most common NORM containing scale is barium sulfate, or barite.[6, 10, 11] Although the radionuclides responsible for NORM in barium sulfate scales are radium-226 and radium-228, these radionuclides do not precipitate directly, but are co-precipitated in the barium sulfate scale causing the scale to be radioactive as in the following equation:

$$Ba^{2+} + Ra^{2+} + SO_4^{2-} \Rightarrow Ba(Ra)SO_4 \text{ (barite solid)}$$

The concentration of radium in the barite solid is always far less than the concentration of barium.

The concentration of radium in the flowing brine is generally not high enough to be regulated, but when concentrated in scale deposits radiation levels can be in excess of regulated limits. Unlike most other common scales, no economic method exists to chemically remove barium sulfate from field equipment. Furthermore, the scale often forms near or at the bottom of a well. The scale is usually removed by mechanical means. This results in lost production, damaged or ruined equipment and downtime. In addition, the recovery of solid NORM scale materials leads to storage problems of the regulated material. Barium sulfate scale occurs during gas and oil production in many places throughout the world and in the United States including the Michigan Basin, the Gulf Coast, Oklahoma and Alaska to name a few.

Though radium in scale decays to radon gas, there is no build-up of radon in conjunction with NORM scales due to the 1620 year half-life of radium-228 combined with the relatively short time since the scale formation.

**LABORATORY RESULTS**

Chemical scale inhibitors are commonly used to prevent or inhibit scale formation in production systems.[1, 13] These chemicals inhibit crystal growth and are generally effective at less than 10 - 20 mg/l in the produced water. It is extremely important to evaluate scale inhibitors for field use under conditions similar to those that will be encountered in the field. Inhibitor performance is dependent on temperature, overall water chemistry and the ratio of barium to sulfate in the case of barium sulfate scale. An inhibitor that performs well under a certain set of circumstances may not perform as expected under a different set of conditions. It is important to find the most effective inhibitors to use before weighing secondary issues such as cost per pound.

An inhibitor squeeze is performed by pushing scale inhibitor into a producing formation and fixing the inhibitor in the formation. When the well is flowing, inhibitor is produced along with the formation water. Evaluating inhibitors is even more important with respect to a squeeze since the life of the squeeze may be determined by the effectiveness of the inhibitor. That is, if two inhibitors return at the same concentration with one being effective and the other not, the well with the less effective scale inhibitor will need to be treated much more often. This difference can be weeks or months instead of years of successful inhibitor performance from one squeeze.

Inhibitors were evaluated in the laboratory using a dynamic flow-through simulation system. A GRI patent is pending on the inhibitor evaluation apparatus.[7] Scale inhibitors should not be evaluated using so-called open beaker tests. These tests yield inaccurate and often costly results due to inherent problems associated with the technique.[12]

Previous work suggested that the phosphinopolycarboxylate-29 scale inhibitor was most effective for barium scale inhibition.[4, 5] However, this inhibitor is known to be incompatible with many medium - high calcium brines. Further tests have been performed using simulated brines of varying water chemistries at different temperatures to identify scale inhibitors that will perform well under these varying conditions. Although this work is in progress, available results suggest other inhibitors are more effective under different conditions. Inhibitors have been evaluated using the water chemistries outlined in Table 1. Results of the evaluations are shown in Table 2. The results of the inhibitor evaluations are presented as the minimum effective dose (MED) to inhibit scale under the conditions of the evaluations. During the dynamic tests, scale must be 100% inhibited, therefore, percent inhibition is not applicable. Concentrations are "as product" of the concentrated material that is normally obtained from the manufacturer. None of the products were neutralized or diluted before the evaluations.

Although much more testing remains to be done for the inhibitors and for other inhibitors not shown, some conclusions can be drawn from the data. BHMDTMP (bishexamethylenediaminetetra(methylene phosphonic) acid and BHMTPMP (bishexamethylenetriaminepenta(methylene phosphonic) acid may have applications over a wide range of conditions.

The phosphonate evaluated at $75^0$ F does not perform well. This is consistent with the observations of others, and with results from our own laboratory that phosphonates are not as effective at temperatures below approximately $120^0$ F. Note the effectiveness of the PPPC-29 material in the 0.5 M ionic strength water consistent with previously reported results.[4] The overall results of these evaluations are also consistent with the results of He.[2, 3] At lower temperatures, phosphate esters[5] and tripolyphosphate (He, Personal Communication) are also effective and may have cost advantages.

## FIELD RESULTS

Over one hundred and eighty water samples have been obtained from wells and facilities in the Gulf Coast region. These waters have been analyzed for scale forming components including barium and sulfate. The scale forming tendencies of the produced waters were determined using saturation index equations developed by the authors.[8] NORM scale in the Gulf Coast region has three primary mechanisms of formation:

1) A high saturation index and resultant scale formation can also be generated simply by the temperature and pressure changes exerted on a reservoir water that is at equilibrium with barium sulfate at reservoir conditions.

2) Scale can form due to the introduction of sulfate into a reservoir containing barium by seawater flooding and;

3) NORM scale can also form by the commingling of waters from different zones or wells where one zone is relatively high in barium and the other relatively high in sulfate.

All three of these causative factors have been observed in the field and are discussed below.

### Field A - Offshore Gulf of Mexico

Field A is an offshore gas and oil field in the Gulf of Mexico. The field has been seawater flooded to maintain production levels. Produced water and hydrocarbons are piped onshore for processing. Data, radiation readings and water samples were collected in the filed in multiple occasions.[9] Sixty-seven water samples from wells and surface facilities were obtained from this field. Only one wellhead was identified as concentrating NORM in scale. In addition, only one of the surface facilities was found to be contaminated with NORM. Produced water and hydrocarbons are piped onshore for processing. Water transfer pipes and vessels beyond the individual platform sites are contaminated with NORM scale. The scale has been identified as barium sulfate by x-ray spectroscopy.

The produced waters from the wells are typically characterized by being either relatively high in barium or sulfate, although some wells are relatively equal in their barium and sulfate concentrations. Barium sulfate scale is predicted[8] in the well where NORM readings above background were detected and in two surface facilities. However, barium sulfate scale was not predicted nor found in any of the other wells. Figure 1 shows the sulfate vs. chloride concentrations of the produced waters. The dramatic increase in the sulfate concentrations near 20,000 mg/l chloride demonstrates the seawater breakthrough in these wells. (Seawater sulfate and chloride concentrations are about 2700 mg/l and 19,375 mg/l, respectively.) The higher sulfate concentrations noted at about 95,000 mg/l chloride are due to production from a high sulfate low barium zone. Figure 2 is a plot of the barium vs. sulfate concentrations of the waters of Field A showing that an increase in one variable essentially drives the other variable to a very low or non-detectable level due to the low solubility of barium sulfate. Unlike other barium sulfate scaling locations, such as the North Sea, barium sulfate scale in this field does not form in the production wells as a result of past seawater flooding. This may be a result of the much smaller flow rates encountered in the field ($\cong$ 500 - 1000 BFPD).

The primary causative factor for the formation of NORM scale in Field A is the commingling of waters at the surface from the different wells and platforms in the field. The produced water is transported on-shore in pipelines and these pipelines are the most contaminated with NORM scale. The pipeline begins at the furthest point from shore and continues toward shore with the highest NORM scale readings being in the pipeline just after the facility closest to shore. Scale does not form in the wells from the past seawater flooding nor as a result of changes in temperature and pressures associated with production (except for one well).

Current plans for this field involve surface treatment with a phosphate ester scale inhibitor. This is reasonable based on the lower cost of phosphate esters, as opposed to phosphonates, and the relatively low temperatures encountered in the subsea flowlines. Phosphate esters have been found to be effective barium sulfate scale inhibitors in previous studies[5], as well as by others.

Based on the study of this field and others, the commingling of waters from different wells or zones, with or without seawater flooding is the prevalent cause of NORM scale deposition in the Gulf Coast. Incipient scale in a well as a result of production changes in temperature and pressure may be less prevalent, but does occur as in Field B below.

**Field B - Atchafalaya River Marsh Area**

Field B is an example of wells that produce scale in the well tubulars and in the surface facilities due only to the temperature and pressure changes associated with production. The field has been visited several times to collect water samples and radiation data.[9] NORM scale has been found in the wellheads, the production tubulars and in the surface facilities. The NORM scale has been identified as barium sulfate. All of the wells will scale NORM materials if the temperature is cool enough. (The solubility of barium sulfate decreases as the temperature decreases, unlike calcium carbonate.[8])

The wells produce into flowlines that carry fluids to central facilities where the hydrocarbons are separated from the water. The waters are then commingled and injected into a disposal well. No NORM materials have been identified in the disposal well system.

Several wells are predicted to form calcium carbonate scale. These wells which scale calcium carbonate generally do not scale extensively with barium sulfate at wellhead. However, these wells will scale barium sulfate and will precipitate specifically at chokes and bends or any points of turbulence. In addition, these wells may scale barium sulfate downhole at points of turbulence, such as, gas lift valves. Although some wells may be supersaturated with calcium carbonate at the wellhead, it should be noted that calcium carbonate may be undersaturated or only slightly scaling in some wells downhole due to the increased downhole pressure and may therefore scale barium sulfate. The tubing was pulled in a treated well for replacement due to corrosion failure. Figure 3 is a plot of the radiation counts of the pulled tubing vs. depth in the well. The dark diamonds on the figure are the locations of the gas lift valves in the well. The gas lift valves were notably scaled upon inspection. It can be observed from Figure 3 that the turbulence caused by the gas lift valves was the cause of the barium sulfate NORM scale deposition.

All of the wells in this field with the except for the pulled well are being treated with a combination scale inhibitor to prevent the deposition of calcium carbonate scale at high temperature and barium sulfate scales at relatively lower temperatures. The scale inhibitor is being injected into the gas lift systems of the wells until a decision is made to squeeze the wells with scale inhibitor. The two inhibitors being used are ATMP (aminotrimethylene phosphonic acid) and BHMDTMP (bishexamethylene-triaminetetra(methylene phosphonic) acid). This procedure has inhibited scale above the lowest gas lift valve, although there is still some scale deposition below the gas lift valves in two of the wells. The pulled well was squeezed in late 1994 to prevent future scale deposition. The tubing was pulled again on March 20, 1995 and was found to be scale free. However, due to unrelated production problems, the well was completed in a different zone. This new zone may be squeezed depending on the water analyses and the scaling tendency of the new zone. Water samples have been collected from this zone.

**The squeeze parameters used for were:**

**Pre-flush -** 15 barrels of produced water with surfactant and sodium bisulfite.

**Inhibitor Pill -** 80 barrels of 1.6% ATMP for calcium carbonate inhibition and 1.6% BHMDTMP for barium sulfate inhibition in produced water with sodium bisulfite.

**Overflush -** 147 barrels of produced water with sodium bisulfite.

This squeeze is expected to last two - three years, but the influence of the turbulence caused by the gas lift valves makes this somewhat uncertain.

**CONCLUSIONS**

1. Barium sulfate scale inhibitors vary dramatically in performance depending on temperature, water chemistry and barium:sulfate ratios.
2. Preliminary work indicates that at lower temperatures (below about $120^0$ F), phosphate esters and polycarboxylates may be more effective than phosphonate scale inhibitors for barium sulfate.
3. At higher temperatures, BHMDTMP and BHMTPMP appear to have a wide range of application and are more effective than other scale inhibitor, both in terms of cost and performance.
4. Three causes of NORM scale deposition have been identified in the Gulf Coast Region:
    1) A high saturation index and resultant scale formation can also be generated simply by the temperature and pressure changes exerted on a reservoir water that is at equilibrium with barium sulfate at reservoir conditions.
    2) Scale can form due to the introduction of sulfate into a reservoir containing barium by seawater flooding and;
    3) NORM scale can also form by the commingling of waters from different zones or wells where one zone is relatively high in barium and the other relatively high in sulfate.
5. The most prevalent cause of NORM scale formation is the commingling of produced waters from different wells or production zones, with or without seawater flooding.
6. Based on the work, scale in the production tubing due to past seawater flooding may not be as severe a problem in the Gulf Coast as in other areas, e.g., the North Sea.
7. Incipient scale occurring in a well due to the temperature/pressure changes exerted on the reservoir brine during produced water may not be as prevalent, but does occur.
8. NORM scale deposition can be inhibited in the field with scale inhibitors currently available. However, it is essential to perform scale inhibitor evaluations to find the most effective scale inhibitor at conditions similar to those encountered in the field.

## ACKNOWLEDGEMENTS

This work was supported by GRI but in no way does this constitute an endorsement by GRI of any products or views contained herein. In addition, the cooperation of Chevron Producing Co., Texaco, Inc. and Hilcorp Energy is acknowledged.

## REFERENCES

1. J. C. Cowan , D. J. Weintritt "Water Formed Scale Deposits" Gulf Publishing Co., Houston, Tx, 1976, 586 p.
2. S. He, J. E. Oddo , M. B. Tomson "The Inhibition of Gypsum and Barite Nucleation in NaCl Brines at Temperatures from 25 to 90 C" App. Geochem., 1993.
3. S. He, J. E. Oddo , M. B. Tomson "The Inhibition of Calcium and Barium Sulfate Nucleation and the Relationships to Scale Control", Baltimore, Md., NACE, CORROSION 94, 1994
4. J. E. Oddo "Evaluating Economic Gas Well Scale Control in the Traverse City Area of the Michigan Basin with Special Attention to Naturally Occurring Radioactive Materials (NORM)" Gas Research Institute Final Report, (in press)
5. J. E. Oddo, A. Y. Al-Borno, I. Ortiz, R. Anthony, D. Pope, D. Hill, D. Linz, J. Frank, D. Becker , M. B. Tomson "The Chemistry, Prediction and Treatment of Scale Containing NORM's in Antrim Gas Fields" SPE Production Operations Symposium, Oklamhoma City, 1993
6. J. E. Oddo , S. C. "Naturally Occurring Radioactive Materials (NORM) in Scales: Inhibition, Remediation and Disposal" Hazardous and Environmentally Sensitive Waste Management in the Gas Industry, Albuquerque, NM, Institute of Gas Technology, 1993
7. J. E. Oddo , M. B. Tomson "Elevated Temperature-Pressure Flow Simulator" United States Patent Office, Patent Number 5,370,799, 1994
8. J. E. Oddo , M. B. Tomson "Why Scale Forms and How to Predict It." SPE Prod. and Fac. Journ. (Feb.), 1994.
9. J. E. Oddo, X. Zhou, D. G. Linz, S. He , M. B. Tomson "The Mitigation of NORM Scale in the Gulf Coast Regions of Texas and Louisiana: A Laboratory and Field Study" SPE/EPA Expl. and Prod. Conf., Houston, TX, SPE 29710, 1995
10. G. H. Otto "A National Survey on NORM in Petroleum Producing and Gas Processing Facilities" The American Petroleum Institute, 1989
11. P. W. Spaite , G. R. Smithson "Technical and Regulatory Issues Associated with Naturally Occurring Radioactive Material (NORM) in the Gas and Oil Industry" Gas Research Institute, GRI-92/0178, 1992
12. M. B. Tomson , J. E. Oddo "Handbook of Calcite Scale Prediction and Control" Pennwell Press, Houston, TX, 1995, (in press)
13. M. B. Tomson, L. A. Rogers, K. Varughese, S. M. Prestwich, G. G. Waggett , M. H. Salimi "Use of Inhibitors for Scale Control in Brine-Producing Gas and Oil Wells" 61st Ann. Conf., New Orleans, La, SPE, SPE 15457, 1986

**Table 1. The chemistries of the four waters used in the chemical inhibitor evaluations. This work is in progress, and more inhibitors are being evaluated. This work should not be interpreted as presenting the most effective known inhibitors at the indicated conditions.**

| Water Component | A | Concentration (mg/l where applicable) B | C | D |
|---|---|---|---|---|
| Ba | 200 | 135,175,220,260* | 225,320,420,500 | 275,385,500,615 |
| Ca | 7000 | 518 | 1500 | 3000 |
| Mg | 1000 | 400 | 500 | 500 |
| $HCO_3$ | 25 | 88 | 88 | 100 |
| Cl | 135000 | 15880 | 51000 | 85000 |
| $SO_4$ | 250 | 135,175,220,260 | 225,320,420,500 | 275,385,500,615 |
| Ionic Strength (M) | 4.03 | 0.5 | 1.5 | 2 |
| TDS | 221000 | 27000 | 84000 | 140000 |

* Inhibitors are being evaluated at four different temperatures with a constant saturation index of 2.3. Therefore, the concentrations of barium and sulfate had to be increased at each temperature to maintain a constant supersaturation due to the increased solubility. The pressure is 150 psi.

**Table 2. The minimum effective dose (MED) of scale inhibitor required to inhibit scale under the designated conditions. This work is in progress, and more inhibitors are being evaluated. This work should not be interpreted as presenting the most effective known inhibitors at the indicated conditions. All MED concentrations are as product.**

| Water Inhibitor | A | Concentration (mg/l) B | C | D |
|---|---|---|---|---|
| **Temperature 75 F** | | | | |
| BHMDTMP | | 0.8 | 0.5 | 1.5 |
| PPPC-29 | | 1.0 | 0.5 | 0.5 |
| PPPC-30 | | 1.0 | 0.8 | 0.5 |
| Phosphate Ester | | 0.5 | 0.5 | 2.3 |
| DTPMP | | 1.0 | 1.0 | 2.0 |
| BHMTPMP | | 0.5 | 0.5 | 0.8 |
| DETHMP | | 0.5 | 0.5 | 2.3 |
| **Temperature 125 F** | | | | |
| BHMDTMP | | 0.5 | 0.5 | 0.5 |
| PPPC-29 | | 0.5 | 1.3 | 2.5 |
| PPPC-30 | | 1.0 | 1.8 | 4.0 |
| Phosphate Ester | | 1.5 | 0.5 | 2.5 |
| DTPMP | | 0.5 | 1.3 | 5.5 |
| BHMTPMP | | 0.5 | 0.5 | 0.7 |
| DETHMP | | 0.5 | 0.5 | 3.5 |
| **Temperature 175 F** | | | | |
| BHMDTMP | | 0.8 | 1.0 | 5.5 |
| PPPC-29 | | 1.8 | 1.5 | >25 |
| PPPC-30 | | 2.3 | 2.5 | 22.5 |
| Phosphate Ester | | 1.0 | 1.3 | 10.5 |
| DTPMP | | 3.5 | 1.5 | >25 |
| BHMTPMP | | 0.8 | 0.8 | 2.5 |
| DETHMP | | 1.0 | 2 | 12 |
| **Temperature 225 F** | | | | |
| BHMDTMP | 3.2 | 0.5 | 5 | 20 |
| ATMP | 8.8 | | | |
| PPPC-29 | >20* | 18 | >25 | >25 |
| PPPC-30 | | 3.5 | 24.5 | >25 |
| Phosphate Ester | | 1.5 | 15 | 19 |
| DTPMP | | 10 | >25 | >25 |
| BHMTPMP | | 0.5 | 4 | 15 |
| DETHMP | | 15 | >25 | >25 |

* Incompatible with the brine before inhibition.
BHMDTMP - bishexamethylenediaminetetra(methylene phosphonic) acid; PPPC-29 - phosphino-polycarboxylate-29; PPPC-30 - phosphinopolycarboxylate-30; DTPMP - diethylenetriaminepenta-(methylene phosphonic) acid; BHMTPMP - bishexamethylenetriaminepenta(methylene phosphonic) acid; DETHMP - diproplethylenetetraaminehexa(methylene phosphonic) acid; ATMP - aminotrimethylene phosphonic acid.

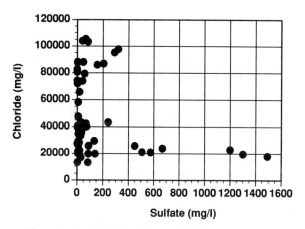

Figure 1. A plot of the sulfate vs. chloride concentrations showing the increase in sulfate at chloride concentrations near that of seawater (19,375 mg/l). This is probably due to water breakthrough from past seawater flooding in Field A.

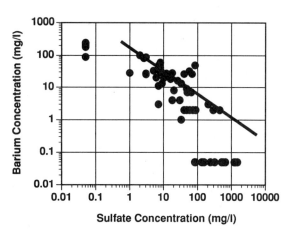

Figure 2. The concentrations of barium and sulfate in the produced waters from Field A illustrating when one variable is high, the other is low.

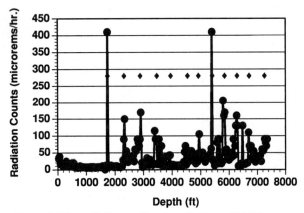

**Figure 3. The radiation readings in well 5 from Field B vs.
depth. The dark diamonds are the locations of the gas lift
valves in the well.**

II. TRANSMISSION AND STORAGE

MODEL PREDICTIONS AND FIELD MEASUREMENTS ON THE
CONDENSATION BEHAVIOR OF LEAN NATURAL GAS

PREDICTIONS DU MODELE ET MESURES SUR LE TERRAIN CONCERNANT
LE COMPORTEMENT DE CONDENSATION DU GAZ NATUREL

M.E. Voulgaris, C.J. Peters and J. de Swaan Arons
Delft University of Technology, The Netherlands.

P.A.H. Derks and R. Janssen-van Rosmalen
N.V. Nederlandse Gasunie, The Netherlands

ABSTRACT

The occurrence of liquid dropout in natural gas pipelines may cause operational problems during storage, transport and processing. Therefore, the availability of a model that accurately predicts the amount of liquid formed is of great importance for the natural gas industry. The objective of this study is to develop a thermodynamic model for the accurate prediction of small amounts of liquid formed in natural gas pipelines at transportation conditions. As input, the model requires an accurate gas analysis. A modified Peng-Robinson equation of state was selected for the phase equilibrium calculations. The equation of state contains adjustable binary interaction parameters, which must be evaluated from experimental vapor-liquid equilibrium data. Since there is little published data available for that purpose, an extensive experimental program was carried out to obtain this information for a number of well-chosen systems. Binary interaction parameters were optimized from the experimental data obtained at conditions of practical interest ($10 < p < 70$ bar and $250 < T < 290$ K). Since the heavy-end fractions of natural gas contain a large variety of compounds substantiality different in their behavior from n-alkanes (iso-paraffins, aromatics and naphthenes), a characterization procedure has been developed to represent the heavy-end fractions by a limited number of pseudo-components. From a sensitivity analysis, it could be concluded that the liquid dropout is mainly influenced by the concentration and characterization of $C_7$ - $C_{13}$ fractions. In this work, two different characterization procedures to represent these fractions are compared. For three different types of treated natural gas, the model predictions are compared with field measurements.

RESUME

Les pertes liquides dans les canalisations de gaz naturel peuvent causer des problèmes opérationnels pendant le stockage, le transport et le traitement. Voilà pourquoi il est très important pour l'industrie gazière de disposer d'un modèle prédisant avec précision les quantités de liquide formées. L'objectif de la présente étude est de développer un modèle thermodynamique en vue de prédire avec précision les petite quantités de liquide formées dans les canalisations de gaz naturel dans des conditions de transport. Comme entrée, le modèle demande une analyse exacte du gaz concerné. Une équation d'état Peng-Robinson modifiée a été sélectionnée pour les calculs de l'équilibre des phases. Cette équation d'état contient des paramètres variables d'interaction

binaire, devant être évalués sur base des données résultant des essais
d'équilibre vapeur-liquide. Etant donné qu'il existe très peu de données
publiées à ce sujet, un large programme d'essai a été mis au point afin
d'obtenir ces informations pour un certain nombre de systèmes bien choisis.
Ensuite, les paramètres d'interaction binaire ont été optimisés à partir des
données expérimentales obtenues dans des conditions d'intérêt pratique (10 < p
< 70 bars et 250 < T < 290 K). Vu que les fractions lourdes du gaz naturel
comportent une grande variété de substances dont le comportement diffère
beaucoup de celui des n-alcanes (iso-paraffines, hydrocarbures aromatique et
naphtènes), une procédure de vérification des caractères a été élaborée afin
de représenter les fractions lourdes par un nombres restreint de
pseudocomposantes. Il ressort d'une analyse de sensibilité que les pertes
liquides sont principalement influencées par la concentration et la
caractérisation des fractions $C_7$ - $C_{13}$. Cette étude établit une comparaison
entre deux procédures de caractérisation différentes pour représenter ces
fractions. Pour trois différentes types de gaz naturel traité, les prédictions
du modèle sont comparées aux mesures effectuées sur le terrain.

## INTRODUCTION

During storage, transportation and processing, natural gas may form small
amounts of liquid at pressure decrease. This phenomenon is called retrograde
condensation, and sometimes may lead to problems in the operating facilities.
Obviously, the availability of an adequate computational tool to predict the
condensation behavior of natural gas is of interest to prevent liquid formation and
its accumulation in the operating facilities.

For that purpose The Technical University of Delft and N.V. Nederlandse
Gasunie decided to define and to carry out a research project to develop a
thermodynamic model for the accurate prediction of the amount of liquid formed in
natural gas pipelines, based on a gas analysis. Figure 1 shows schematically the
various aspects of the project that have to be considered to develop the
thermodynamic model (item 5 in Figure 1).

In literature it has been pointed out (1 - 3), that the variable most commonly
used for expressing the condensation behavior of a multicomponent mixture is the dew
point, because it is very sensitive to the presence of heavy compounds in
natural gas (4). However, there may be a large difference between the dew point
temperature and the temperature where the amount of liquid formed may cause
operational problems. In practice, this makes the dew point inappropriate for
estimating the amount of condensate to be formed at a specified pressure,
temperature and composition of the natural gas. A more appropriate property is the
Potential Hydrocarbon Liquid Content (PHLC) of natural gas. It is defined as the
mass of condensable liquid (in milligrams) at the pressure and temperature of the
measurement, per unit volume of gas at normal conditions, that is at T = 273.15 K
and p = 1.01325 bar. The pressure and temperature range in which the model has to be
accurate, is: 10 < p < 70 bar and of 250 < T < 290 K respectively, which may
correspond to PHLC-values typically from 5 up to 200 mg/Nm$^3$.

As the only input information for the model a natural gas analysis was used,
which was specially developed by N.V. Nederlandse Gasunie for the accurate
determination of the heavier hydrocarbons. This novel method has a detection limit
of 0.05 ppm instead of 1 ppm which is the detection limit of the extended version of
ISO-6974 (5).

The Technical University of Delft carried out an experimental program to
determine the vapor-liquid (VLE) equilibrium of a number of "key-binary" mixtures.
For that purpose a saturation apparatus was developed to determine the extremely low
solubilities of some selected low-volatile hydrocarbons in methane. This
experimental information was used to calculate binary interaction parameters
occurring in the mixing rules of the equation of state applied.

It was also studied experimentally how minute amounts of nitrogen, ethane and
carbon dioxide in methane may influence the solubility of decane in these gas
mixtures. The latter information was used to investigate the capability of the

equation of state to represent the small changes in the extremely low solubilities of decane in the synthetic gas mixtures studied. Decane was not an arbitrary choice: from a thorough sensitivity analysis it could be concluded that the liquid dropout of lean natural gas is mainly governed by hydrocarbons ranging in carbon number from 7 up to 13. Based on the experimental results and the sensitivity analysis, a modified Peng-Robinson equation of state (6) was selected for the model.

In the carbon number range crucial for the liquid dropout (i.e., from 7 until 13), the gaschromatographic analysis of natural gas only gives the concentration of the n-alkanes and that of each discrete compound up to a carbon number as high as 6. For higher carbon numbers, the gaschromatographic analysis gives a sum of the concentration of a large number of compounds of different chemical nature (iso-paraffins, naphthenes and aromatics), the so-called heavy-end fraction. Therefore, for the heavy-end fraction a suitable characterization technique is necessary for its proper representation. Essentially, a characterization technique transforms the heavy-end tail into a limited number of pseudo-components. It turned out that the nature of the characterization procedure has an essential influence on the accuracy of the model predictions. Consequently, in this study much attention was given to this aspect. In this work two different characterization procedures to represent the heavy-end fractions have been compared.

In order to validate the model predictions, N.V. Nederlandse Gasunie carried out field measurements on the liquid dropout of three different types of lean natural gases referred to as Gas A, B and C. A comparison of the field measurements with the model predictions showed that the model is capable to predict the amount of condensate within the requirements of the project. In terms of the dew point temperature, this means that the model predictions and the field measurements are not allowed to differ more than approximately 1 K. Note that a change of 1 ppm in, for instance, the hexadecane concentration in natural gas may cause a shift in the dew point temperature of about 10 K.

VAPOR-LIQUID EQUILIBRIUM MEASUREMENTS

In order to develop the predictive thermodynamic model, two different types of vapor-liquid (VLE) experiments were performed (item 1 in Figure 1):
a. determination of the phase behavior of a selected number of binary mixtures (bubble and dew points);
b. solubility measurements of heavy hydrocarbons in mixtures of gaseous components representative for natural gas.

Experimental

Windowed autoclave. Under vacuum conditions samples of known composition were introduced into a glass vessel, which was subsequently mounted into a stainless steel autoclave. To observe the sample visually, the autoclave was equipped with two sapphire windows. Pressure and temperature can be independently controlled and measured within the ranges 0.2 to 100 MPa and 250 to 350 K respectively. Phase boundaries between a homogeneous fluid phase (either liquid or gas) and two fluid phases can be located by varying the pressure at constant temperature. Details about the instrumentation involving both the windowed autoclave and the sample preparation system are described elsewhere (10,11).

Saturation apparatus. Phase boundaries between a homogeneous vapor phase and two fluid phases, removed from the critical region, can be located with a for this purpose developed dynamic apparatus operating according to the saturation technique. In Figure 2 the principle of operation is shown schematically. A supercritical gas is supplied at constant temperature, pressure and constant flow rate to a saturation system in which the gas stream is intensively contacted with the solute. After achieving saturation, the gas is withdrawn from the thermostated saturators and heated in order to prevent premature condensation. Subsequently the gas stream is allowed to expand to atmospheric pressure. Downstream the gas can either be directed to a solute recovery system or to an absolute flow measuring device. A gas washing unit filled with a suitable solvent appeared to fully recover the solute from the gas stream. The concentration of the solute can readily be monitored by gaschomatography. For further details of this apparatus, one is referred to elsewhere (12,13).

## Vapor-Liquid Equilibria of Selected Binary Mixtures

It is assumed that for the accurate prediction of the condensation behavior of natural gas, the thermodynamic model requires VLE information for only a limited number of carefully selected binary mixtures. This assumption is based on the possibility to generalize experimental data obtained for the "key" binary mixtures to related binary mixtures. The main purpose of the experimental work on the "key" binary mixtures can be summarized as follows:
a. to select an appropriate equation of state;
b. to test mixing rules to be used in the equation of state;
c. to calculate binary interaction parameters.

Since in literature the availability of accurate experimental data of binary mixtures of interest for this study is scarce, it was decided (13) to carry out an extensive experimental program to measure the vapor-liquid equilibria of a number of selected binary mixtures. Because of the strong influence on the PHLC prediction, emphasis has been given to a better representation of the VLE behavior of asymmetrical binary mixtures, i.e., mixtures containing a supercritical gas and a heavy hydrocarbon. Dew points were determined indirectly with a specially developed gas saturation apparatus allowing the measurement of very small amounts (ppm) of heavy hydrocarbons in a supercritical gas (12,13). Bubble point measurements were carried out in a windowed autoclave equipment (10). Four binary systems were studied (12,13), each containing the main constituent of natural gas, methane, and one of the condensable hydrocarbons decane, dodecane, hexadecane and benzene. Figure 3 shows some experimental results for the binary mixture methane + dodecane (14).

As pointed out by Boyle (18), these systems are very important for the understanding of natural gas condensation behavior. For details one is referred to elsewhere (12-19).

## Solubility of Decane in Gas Mixtures Representative for Natural Gas

For the following reasons, the solubility of heavy hydrocarbons in gaseous mixtures representative for natural gas were experimentally determined:
a. to obtain insight into the sensitivity of the selected equation of state used in the model to describe minute fluctuations in the concentration of heavy hydrocarbons;
b. to obtain quantitative information about the increasing solubility effect of heavy hydrocarbons caused by ethane and carbon dioxide, and the decreasing solubility effect of heavy hydrocarbons caused by nitrogen.

Therefore, it was decided to carry out an experimental program to obtain solubility data of a representative hydrocarbon in mixtures of methane, nitrogen, carbon dioxide, and ethane, with methane as the main constituent. The composition of the gas mixtures was chosen in such a way that, with respect to the main volatile consituents, representative mixtures for the extremes in composition of the used validation gases were obtained. The selection of the representative hydrocarbon (decane) was not arbitrary, but based on a sensitivity analysis (20,21). On a molar basis, these mixtures were composed as follows:

1. methane (85%) + nitrogen (15%)
2. methane (80%) + carbon dioxide (20%)
3. methane (80%) + carbon dioxide (5%) + nitrogen (15%)
4. methane (80%) + carbon dioxide (2%) + nitrogen (15%) + ethane (3%)

As an illustration of the experimental work, isothermal data for the solubility of decane in mixture 3 are shown in Figure 4. For further details on this part of the experimental program, one is referred to elsewhere (22,23).

## EQUATION OF STATE

The accurate calculation of the PHLC of natural gas necessitates the use of an equation of state (EOS) to predict the correct fluid phase behavior. In this work, for binary mixtures of natural gas components the predictive capabilities of two different EOS - the simplified-perturbed-hard-chain theory (SPHCT) (24) and the Peng-Robinson equation (PR) (25) - were compared in the temperature and pressure range of interest (item 2 in Figure 1). Compared with the original PR equation, the modified version introduced by Magoulas and Tassios (6) predicts better pure component vapor pressures. Therefore, the latter version was used in this work. For mixture calculations, the conventional Van der Waals one-fluid mixing rules have been used. The PR equation of state and the mixing rules used in this study read as follows:

$$p = \frac{RT}{V - b} - \frac{a(T)}{V(V + b) + b(V - b)},$$  (1)

with mixing rules:

$$a = \sum_i \sum_j x_i x_j a_{ij}, \text{ with } a_{ij} = (a_{ii}a_{jj})^{1/2} (1 - k_{ij})$$  (2)

$$b = \sum_i \sum_j x_i x_j b_{ij}, \text{ with } b_{ij} = \frac{1}{2} (b_{ii} + b_{jj}) (1 - l_{ij})$$  (3)

The temperature dependence of the parameter $a_{ii}$ is defined by:

$$a_{ii}(T) = a_{ii}(T_{c,i}) \cdot \alpha_{ii}(T_{r,i}), \text{ with } a_{ii}(T_{c,i}) = 0.45724 \frac{R^2 T_{c,i}^2}{P_{c,i}},$$  (4)

$$\alpha_{ii}(T_{r,i}) = [1 + m_i(1 - T_{r,i}^{1/2})]^2$$  (5)

$$m_i = 0.384401 + 1.522760 \, \omega_i - 0.213808 \, \omega_i^2 + 0.034616 \, \omega_i^3 - 0.001976 \, \omega_i^4$$  (6)

The relationship between the parameter $b_{ii}$ and the critical temperature and pressure is given by the equation:

$$b_{ii}(T_{c,i}) = 0.07780 \frac{RT_{c,i}}{P_{c,i}}$$  (7)

From the Eqs. (1-7), it can be concluded that each component in the mixture is represented by three characteristic parameters: the critical pressure $p_c$, the critical temperature $T_c$ and the acentric factor $\omega$. In Eqs. (2 and 3), $k_{ii}$ and $l_{ii}$ are adjustable binary interaction parameters to be evaluated from the VLE measurements. The other symbols in the equations have their usual meaning.

The calculation of the PHLC of natural gas requires an accurate prediction of the vapor and liquid phase composition from the flash calculation of the natural gas under study. Therefore, the equation of state to be used must be as accurate as possible in predicting these properties. Both candidate equations of state have been tested accordingly. For a number of binary mixtures of methane and n-alkanes the average absolute error (AAD) has been calculated and compared with experimental data. The results are summarized graphically for the liquid and vapor phase in Figures 5 and 6 respectively.

## LEAN NATURAL GAS

As input information, the model requires an accurate natural gas analysis (item 3 in Figure 1). This section deals with the composition of natural gas, its gaschromatographic analysis and sampling technique. The large differences in composition may result in substantial differences in the condensation behavior of the various types of natural gas. This work focuses on lean natural gas for which the amount of heavy compounds ($C_7^+$ fractions) is less than 0.03% of the total number of moles.

## Composition

The three validation gases used in this study, show large differences in concentration levels of the various components. For example, methane is typically present in amounts 16,000,000 times larger than tetradecane. Moreover, on a molar basis the amount of carbon dioxide varied from 1% up to 20%, nitrogen varied from 3% up to 14% and heavy hydrocarbons are present in very small amounts. For further details on the composition of two of the three gases considered in this study, one is referred to IGRC-1992 (7).

With an exception of the n-alkanes, for components with carbon numbers beyond 6, the gaschromatographic analysis is not capable to identify all the components individually, because of the large number of isomers. Therefore, the sum of the concentrations of all unidentified compounds with a boiling point ($T_b$) between those of the n-alkanes with a carbon number k-1 and k, is indicated by y-$C_k$ fraction (k = 7, 8) or x-$C_k$ fraction (k > 8). The y-$C_7$ fraction does not contain benzene and cyclohexane and in the y-$C_8$ fraction toluene and methylcyclohexane are not included since these four components are detected as individual components in the gaschromatographic analysis (7,8).

## Gaschromatographic Analysis

From a sensitivity analysis, it became apparent that the condensation behavior of natural gas close to its dew point is mainly governed by the concentration of the heavy hydrocarbons. In order to determine these concentrations, a gaschromatographic analysis was used. The complexity of performing such an analysis is mainly related to the large concentration range in which the components in natural gas may occur. Standard gaschromatographic analysis are not sufficiently detailed and accurate for the objectives to be attained in this work. Therefore, N.V. Nederlandse Gasunie developed a proprietary analysis technique (8). The detection limit of this new method is approximately 1 ppm of dodecane. In summary, the method consists of three steps:
a. An extended gaschromatographic analysis of natural gas, using a packed column for the separation of inert gases and methane, and an open tubular capillary column for the separation of carbon dioxide and hydrocarbons from ethane and higher. This analysis is similar to the improved ISO-6975 (9) with a 1 ppm detection limit;
b. A gaschromatographic analysis of higher hydrocarbons, using an open tubular capillary column and on-column injection. This is performed after pre-concentration on octadecyl silica gel of the heavier hydrocarbons present in natural gas and followed by liquid desorption;
c. A combination of the first two steps into one analysis, called detailed analysis, using heptane as the bridge component.

The concentrations of helium, nitrogen, carbon dioxide, hydrocarbons up to $C_7$ and heptane are taken from the extended analysis (step a.), whereas concentrations of hydrocarbons from heptane and higher are obtained from the analysis after pre-concentration (step b.). The detection limit of the detailed analysis is 0.05 ppm of hexadecane.

## Sampling Technique

Apart from the gaschromatographic technique, the sampling procedure is also a key issue for a representative natural gas analysis. N.V. Nederlandse Gasunie has tested several sampling methods. Indirect sampling by means of storage in gas bottles is not recommended. In all cases, the samples of the three natural gases (Gas A, B and C) were taken directly from the pipeline by a special technigue.

## SENSITIVITY ANALYSIS

In order to design a characterization procedure to represent the unidentified heavy-end fractions by a limited number of pseudo-components, it is important to get insight in the factors that dominate the PHLC predictions. For that purpose a sensitivity analysis has been performed for the two natural gases A and B (20,21). The sensitivity analysis has been performed with the aid of a preliminary characterization procedure. This procedure takes into account all individual

compounds up to $C_8$ with their related physical properties ($p_c$, $T_c$ and $\omega$). In this approach, a x-$C_k$ or y-$C_k$ fraction, is reduced to a single n-$C_k$ component, i.e., for that particular fraction the physical properties of the corresponding n-alkane have been used. The following aspects were considered in the sensitivity analysis:
a. concentration of the natural gas constituents;
b. pure component parameters;
c. undetectable components;
d. fluctuations in temperature and pressure;
e. effect of the binary interaction parameters.

An important conclusion obtained from the sensitivity analysis was that the constituents of natural gas belonging to the $C_7$-$C_{13}$ fractions are the most important ones for the PHLC prediction (see Figure 7). Among them, $C_9$ and $C_{10}$ are the most crucial ones. Therefore, a suitable characterization technique for these fractions will be essential for an accurate PHLC prediction. Details on the sensitivity analysis have been published previously (20,21).

## CHARACTERIZATION OF THE HEAVY-END FRACTION

In one of the previous sections it was discussed that components with carbon number heavier than 6, in general, could not be identified individually from the gaschromatographic analysis. This was due to the large number of components and the very small concentration of various compounds present in the boiling point range of two subsequent n-alkanes. For this reason, a procedure is necessary that converts the unidentified fractions of natural gas into a limited number of pseudo-components with known properties, i.e., with known equation of state parameters ($p_c$, $T_c$ and $\omega$). The conversion of the gaschromatographic analysis into a number of well-defined pseudo-components is called characterization (item 4 in Figure 1).

### Characterizing Parameters

The proposed characterization procedure for the description of natural gas, based on the detailed gaschromatographic analysis only (8), can be separated into the following steps:
a. All discrete components up to $C_6$ are taken into account with their pure component parameters ($p_c$, $T_c$ and $\omega$) and optimized binary interaction parameters ($k_{ij}$ and $l_{ij}$) with respect to the main volatile constituents (methane, nitrogen, carbon dioxide and ethane) present in natural gas.
b. The y-$C_7$ and y-$C_8$ fractions include nearly all components with a boiling point $T_b$ between that of the n-alkanes n-$C_6$- n-$C_7$ and n-$C_7$- n-$C_8$ respectively. In these two fractions the aromatics, benzene and toluene, and the naphthenes, cyclohexane and methylcyclohexane, are not included because they are detected separately. Consequently, these y-fractions do not show any aromaticity. There is only a small probability that a considerable amount of naphthenes will be present, since the most important ones have already been detected. Therefore, these y-fractions are considered as iso-paraffins.
c. For the $C_8^+$ fraction, only the mole fractions of the n-alkanes and the sum of the mole fractions of all the other compounds (iso-paraffins, naphthenes and aromatics), which have a $T_b$ between that of two corresponding n-alkanes, are included. Consequently, for these fractions, a representative property must be introduced that relates the concentrations of the unidentified fractions to the a and b parameters in the equation of state.

For that purpose, two properties have been tested:
1. The boiling point ($T_b$);
2. The logarithm of the ratio of the saturation pressure ($p^{sat}$) over the critical pressure $p_c$. In the property $\ln(p^{sat}/p_c)$, the saturation pressure $p^{sat}(T)$ was taken at the temperature of the flash calculation.

The choice of both properties as candidate characterizing parameters was not arbitrary. Model calculations with the selected equation of state on the solubility of hydrocarbons with carbon numbers larger than 4 in a mixture of the major volatile natural gas constituents (81 % methane, 3% ethane, 2% carbon dioxide and 14 %

nitrogen), at the pressure and temperature conditions of interest, have revealed that the logarithm of the solubility y of each individual hydrocarbon can be correlated to $T_b$ by a second-order polynomial with a correlation coefficient equal to 0.995 (see Figure 8). Only heavy polynuclear aromatics are not satisfactorily represented by this correlation. If only the $C_8^+$ n-alkanes are taken into account, the second-order polynomial reduces to a straight line.

In addition, it was also found that the logarithm of the solubility is a linear function of the parameter $\ln(p^{sat}/p_c)$. In this case the correlation coefficient is equal to 0.998 (see Figure 9). It is striking that all hydrocarbons (paraffinic, naphthenic and aromatic) satisfy this linear relationship. For further details on this solubility behavior, one is referred to elsewhere (26).

## Representation of the Heavy-End Fractions by Pseudo-Components

For a real natural-gas mixture, it was found that the concentration of the $C_8^+$ n-alkanes follow qualitatively the same exponential decrease either as a function of $T_b$ (Figure 10) or as a function of $\ln(p^{sat}/p_c)$ (Figure 11). Based on this behavior, it is assumed that the concentrations of all compounds present in the natural gas under study, follow the same exponential trend as a function of $T_b$ or $\ln(p^{sat}/p_c)$. Both characterization procedures were tested.

In the section on the sensitivity analysis, it has been established that the most important fractions in natural gas are x-$C_9$ and x-$C_{10}$ (see Figure 7 and the related table), especially at lower temperatures (high PHLC yield). On the other hand, at higher temperatures (low PHLC yield), the $C_{11}$ fraction is the most important one. Therefore, it was decided to split the unidentified heavy-end fraction into two major fractions. The first major fraction covers the region between n-$C_8$ and n-$C_{10}$, whereas the second major fraction starts at n-$C_{10}$ and ends with the last detected fraction.

The next step is to decide how these two major fractions can be represented most effectively by a limited number of pseudo-components. Based on the truncated exponential distribution function, which exists for the concentration of n-alkanes with carbon number ($N_c$) $8 \le N_c \le 16$ as a function of their $T_b$ or $\ln(p^{sat}/p_c)$, the Gaussian quadrature method can be applied. This technique allows to find the molar composition and the value of the characteristic property $T_b$ or $\ln(p^{sat}/p_c)$ of the subfractions which represent in an optimum way each major cut. For further details on this method, one is referred to literature (27,28).

For the prediction of the PHLC, three pseudo-components for each major cut is sufficient. It was established that a four point integration does not influence significantly the PHLC yield. On the other hand, decreasing the number of pseudo-components to two for each major fraction, on the average, results into a difference in the VLE equilibrium temperature of 0.3 K.

The a and b parameters (Eq. 1) and the molecular weight of each pseudo-component must be known in terms of its $T_b$ or $\ln(p^{sat}/p_c)$, as derived from the Gaussian quadrature method. As PNA (paraffinic, naphthenic and aromatic) information is lacking, the pseudo-components were considered as n-alkanes, which properties can be represented as a function of one variable only.

It has already been noticed that the concentration of n-alkanes heavier than n-$C_8$ in natural gas decreases exponentially as a function of both characteristic properties. The same holds for the x-$C_k$ fractions, assuming that the value of their $T_b$ is the average of the $T_b$'s which correspond to the n-$C_{k-1}$ and n-$C_k$. Therefore, the amount of the non-detected fractions can be predicted by extrapolating these curves to higher carbon number, assuming that the same exponential trend holds. All the non-detected components are considered as one pseudo-component with properties corresponding to a n-alkane with a $T_b$ equal to the average of the $T_b$'s of all the non-detected fractions.

**FIELD MEASUREMENTS**

In order to validate the model predictions, field measurements of the condensate formed along the pipelines of the network are a prerequisite. For that purpose N.V. Nederlandse Gasunie performed these measurements (item 7 in Figure 1).

**Experimental Techniques**

A manual method (29) for the determination of the potential condensate content according to ISO-6570/2 (1984) was used to measure the PHLC of a natural gas of interest. Its principle is to measure the quantity of liquid accumulated during a certain period by comparing the mass of the condensate separator at the beginning and at the end of this period. The following experimental steps have to be taken:
a. A representative sample of the gas is led through the measuring device and allowed to reach a specified pressure and temperature. The hydrocarbon condensate formed in the natural gas is separated from the gas flow and collected in a small separator;
b. The volume of the gas passing through the system is measured with a gasmeter after pressure has released to atmospheric;
c. The amount of liquid in the separator is determined by weighing the separator before and after the measurement.

Each measurement takes approximately 24 hours; four to five measurements could be carried out simultaneously.

Because the manual method is time consuming and expensive, the development of its automatic counterpart was justified. In this apparatus (named Gacom) condensate formed is measured continuously with the aid of a sensitive pressure difference gauge, that monitors the hydrostatic pressure caused by the condensate formed in the cell. The gas flow has to be maintained between 0.5 and 1.5 $Nm^3/h$ and was accurately measured with a calibrated gasmeter. During the measurement, the temperature and pressure of the gas are continuously monitored and recorded. Before entering the measuring device, the gas is brought to the temperature of the measurement in a heat exchanger coil that is submerged in an iso-thermal cooling bath. The desired pressure is obtained by means of a calibrated pressure control valve.
With Gacom, the PHLC can be measured semi-continuously, yielding one measurement within one hour. Because the gas source is monitored during the measurements, the accuray of this method will be an improvement compared to the manual method.
The field measurement data were obtained either by the manual or by the semi-automatic method.

**VALIDATION OF THE MODEL**

In the previous sections an equation of state and a characterization procedure with two optional characterizing parameters have been proposed for the modelling of the condensation behavior of lean natural gas. Obviously, the evaluation of the proposed model and the selection of the appropriate characterizing parameter can only be performed after comparing the model predictions with field measurements of lean natural gas (item 6 in Figure 1). Some of the PHLC measurements perfomed by N.V. Nederlandse Gasunie were published already (7). In this section model predictions are compared with some of the field measurements (Figures 12 - 14).

**Natural Gas A**

Figure 12 shows the results at 26, 41 and 61 bar. From this figure it becomes apparent that $T_b$ has to be preferred as characterizing parameter over $\ln(p^{sat}/p_c)$.

**Natural Gas B**

From Figure 13 it can be seen that the model with $T_b$ and $\ln(p^{sat}/p_c)$ as characterizing parameters shows a systematic overprediction of approximately 1 and 2.5 K respectively. Because in this natural gas the concentration of carbon dioxide is as high as 20%, it is obvious that this error must be attributed to the interactions between carbon dioxide and the other constituents, and not to the characterization procedure used.

This conclusion is based on the observation that, even if the more accurate characterizing parameter $T_b$ is used, such a systematic overprediction is not observed in the other investigated gases with lower concentrations of carbon dioxide. For Gas B, it can be concluded that the model predictions with $T_b$ as characterizing parameter are on the average, within the prescribed accuracy.

**Natural Gas C**

For Gas C, all measurements have been performed with the automatic version of ISO-6570/2 (29), Gacom. Figure 14 compares the predicted PHLC with the corresponding measurements at 16.1, 26 and 41.1 bar. Also for Gas C it can be concluded that the model with $T_b$ as characterizing parameter is the most accurate. The model predictions have a comparable accuracy as those for Gas A.

TUNING OF THE MODEL

The general conclusion from the results obtained is that for all the gases, the model with $T_b$ as characterizing parameter is the most accurate. An accuracy within the specifications of the project can be achieved, i.e., within approximately 1 K. Therefore, adjusting one or more suitable model parameters, using the field measurement data to match the experimental results (tuning), is not needed (item 8 in Figure 1).

Only for Gas B, it can be argued that the model predictions need further improvement, which can be achieved by, for instance, simply tuning one interaction parameter for carbon dioxide and an unidentified component. However, for two reasons this is not recommended:

a. The model predictions also for Gas B are still within the prescribed accuracy;
b. Tuning limits the capability of the model to extrapolate to other types of gases, i.e., the predictive capability of the model will decrease.

DISCUSSION AND CONCLUSIONS

In one of the previous sections, the validation of the model with two different characterizing parameters has been performed using field measurements for three different types of gases. The maximum error in the equilibrium temperature does not exceed 1.2 K, i.e., the predictions are close to the accuracy required for the project. Although the performance of the characteristic parameter $\ln(p^{sat}/p_c)$ seems to be more accurate for the PNA description, $T_b$ is found to be more accurate for the PHLC prediction.

Tuning of the model, which will limit its predictive capability, is not needed. In addition, tuning is not justified if one takes into account the magnitude of the total uncertainty in both the measurements and the model predictions.

REFERENCES

1.   L. Oranje. Description of natural gas quality in relation to condensate formation in pipelines. Paper presented at the 14th World Gas Conference of the IGU, Toronto, Canada (1979).

2.   J.L.K. Banell, A.G. Dixon, and T.P. Davies, T.P. in Gas Quality: Proceedings of the Congress of "Gas Quality - specification and measurement of physical and chemical properties of natural gas", Groningen, The Netherlands, April 1986. Ed: G.J. van Rossum (Elsevier, Amsterdam, 1986) pp. 263-271.

3.   K.S. Pedersen, Aa. Fredenslund, and P. Thomassen, in: "Properties of Oils and Natural Gases", (Gulf Publishing Company, Houston, Texas, 1989).

4.  J. Lammers, and J. de Swaan Arons. Etudes Thermodynamiques sur le phénomène de condensation rétrograde des gaz naturels. Chimie et Industrie-Genie Chimique, 106 (1973) 615-621.

5.  International Organisation for Standardisation, ISO 6974: Natural Gas - Determination of hydrogen, inert gases and hydrocarbons up to $C_8$- Gas chromatographic method, Geneva (1984).

6.  C. Magoulas, and D. Tassios. Thermophysical properties of n-alkanes from $C_1$ to $C_{20}$ and their prediction for higher ones Fluid Phase Equilibria 56 (1990) 119.

7.  P.A.H. Derks, L. van der Meulen-Kuijk, and A.L.C. Smit. Detailed analysis of natural gas for an improved prediction of condensation behaviour. International Gas Research Conference, Orlando, U.S.A. (1992) 378-389.

8.  L. Kuijk, R.J. Beks, M. Struis, and A.L.C. Smit. IGT Gas Quality Measurement Symposium, Chicago, U.S.A. (1991).

9.  International Organisation for Standardisation, Revision of ISO 6975: Extended Analysis for natural gas - gaschromatographic method, Geneva (in preparation).

10. M. Glaser, C.J. Peters, H.J. van der Kooi, and R.N. Lichtenthaler. Phase equilibria of (methane + n-hexadecane) and (p, $V_m$, T) of n-hexadecane. J.Chem. Thermodynamics, 17 (1985) 803-815.

11. H.J. van der Kooi. Ph.D. Thesis. Metingen en berekeningen aan het systeem methaan-n-eicosaan. Delft University of Technology, Delft, The Netherlands (1981).

12. M.P.W.M. Rijkers, M. Malais, C.J. Peters, and J. de Swaan Arons. Measurements on the phase behavior of binary hydrocarbon mixtures for modelling the condensation behavior of natural gas. I. The system methane + decane. Fluid Phase Equilibria, 71 (1992) 143-168.

13. M.P.W.M. Rijkers. Retrograde Condensation of Lean natural Gas, Ph.D. Thesis, Delft University of Technology, Delft, The Netherlands, (1991).

14. M.P.W.M. Rijkers, V.B. Maduro, C.J. Peters, and J. de Swaan Arons. Measurements on the phase behavior of binary hydrocarbon mixtures for modelling the condensation behavior of natural gas. II. The system methane + dodecane. Fluid Phase Equilibria, 72 (1992) 309-324.

15. M.P.W.M. Rijkers, M. Malais, C.J. Peters, and J. de Swaan Arons. Experimental determination of the phase behavior of binary mixtures of methane + benzene. Part I. Vapor + liquid, solid benzene + liquid, solid benzene + vapor and solid benzene + liquid + vapor equilibria. Fluid Phase Equilibria, 77 (1992) 327-342.

16. M.P.W.M. Rijkers, M. Hathie, C.J. Peters, and J. de Swaan Arons. Experimental determination of the phase behavior of binary mixtures of methane + benzene. Part II. The solubility of liquid benzene in supercritical methane. Fluid Phase Equilibria, 77 (1992) 343-353.

17. M.P.W.M. Rijkers, C.J. Peters, and J. de Swaan Arons. Measurements on the phase behavior of binary hydrocarbon mixtures for modelling the condensation behavior of natural gas. III. The system methane + hexadecane. Fluid Phase Equilibria, 85 (1993) 335-345.

18. G.J. Boyle. Retrograde condensation from lean natural gas. Paper presented at the 2nd conference on natural gas research and technology, Atlanta, Georgia, U.S.A. (1972).

19.  D.L. Pearce, C.J. Peters, and J. de Swaan Arons. Measurement of the gas phase solubilty of decane in nitrogen. Fluid Phase Equilibria, 89 (1993) 335-343.

20.  M.E. Voulgaris, C.J. Peters, and J. de Swaan Arons, P.A.H. Derks, R. Janssen-van Rosmalen, and A.L.C. Smit. Prediction of the potential hydrocarbon liquid content of lean natural gas. Comparison with field tests. Proceedings of the Seventy-Third GPA Annual Convention, New Orleans, Louisiana, U.S.A., March 7 - 9, 1994, U.S.A., pp. 40 - 48.

21.  M.E. Voulgaris, C.J. Peters, and J. Swaan Arons. On the retrograde condensation behavior of lean natural gas. International Journal of Thermophysics, (1995), in press.

22.  E.J.M. Straver, M.E. Voulgaris, C.J. Peters, and J. de Swaan Arons. On the solubility of decane in supercritical mixtures of methane, nitrogen, carbon dioxide and ethane. Fluid Phase Equilibria, in preparation.

23.  D.L. Pearce, C.J. Peters, and J. de Swaan Arons. The solubility of decane in a mixture of methane and nitrogen. Fluid Phase Equilibria, 97 (1994) 61-66.

24.  C.H. Kim, P. Vimalchand, M.D. Donohue, and S.I. Sandler. Local composition model for chainlike molecules : A new simplified version of the perturbed hard chain theory. AIChE J., 32 (1986) 1726-1736.

25.  D.-Y. Peng, D.B. Robinson. A new two constant equation of state. Ind. Eng. Chem. Fundam., 15 (1976) 59-64.

26.  C.J. Peters, M.E. Voulgaris, and J. de Swaan Arons. On the solubility of hydrocarbons in supercritical gases. J. of Supercritical Fluids, in preparation.

27.  S.K. Shibata, S.I. Sandler, and R.A. Behrens. Phase equilibrium calculations for continuous and semicontinuous mixtures. Chem. Eng. Science, 42 (1987) 1977-1988.

28.  P.J. Davis, and P. Rabinowitz. Methods of numerical integration, 2nd Edition, Academic Press, Inc. (1984).

29.  International Organisation for Standardisation, ISO 6570/2: Natural Gas - Determination of potential hydrocarbon liquid content - Part 2: Weighing method, Geneva (1984).

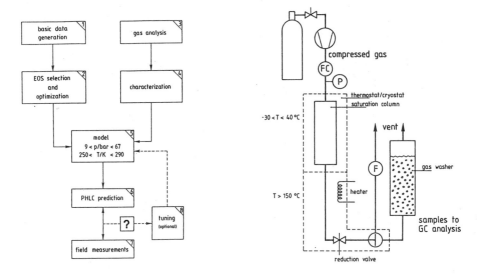

**Figure 1.** Schematical overview of the procedure followed for the prediction of Potential Hydrocarbon Liquid Content (PHLC).

**Figure 2.** Schematical overview of the gas saturation apparatus.

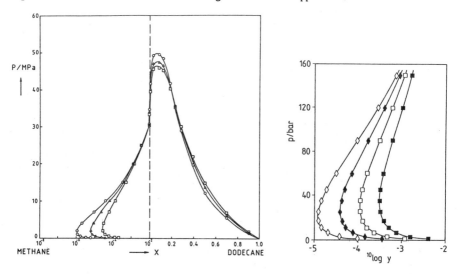

**Figure 3.** Experimental p,x,y-sections of the system methane + dodecane at constant temperature. o, T = 263.15 K; Δ, T = 283.15 K; □, T = 303.15 K.

**Figure 4.** Solubility of decane in a gas mixture of methane (80 mole%), carbon dioxide (5 mole%) and nitrogen (15 mole%). Open diamonds 263.15 K; filled diamonds 278.15 K; open squares 293.15 K; filled squares 310.85 K. Solid lines represent best fits to the experimental data.

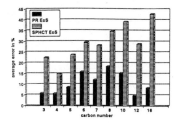 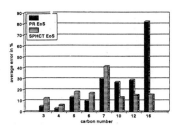

**Figure 5.** Average errors (% AAD) in the prediction of the liquid phase composition in binary systems of methane and n-alkanes. Comparison between the PR and the SPHCT equations of state (binary interaction parameters are taken zero).

**Figure 6.** Average errors (% AAD) in the prediction of the vapor phase composition in binary systems of methane and n-alkanes. Comparison between the PR and the SPHCT equations of state (binary interaction parameters are taken zero).

| Code | Component |
|------|-----------|
| 1  | helium |
| 2  | nitrogen |
| 3  | methane |
| 4  | carbon dioxide |
| 5  | ethane |
| 6  | propane |
| 7  | isobutane |
| 8  | n-butane |
| 9  | 2,2-dimethylpropane |
| 10 | isopentane |
| 11 | n-pentane |
| 12 | cyclopentane |
| 13 | 2,2-dimethylbutane |
| 14 | 2,3-dimethylbutane |
| 15 | 3-methylpentane |
| 16 | n-hexane |
| 17 | benzene |
| 18 | cyclohexane |
| 19 | heptanes |
| 20 | methylcyclohexane |
| 21 | toluene |
| 22 | octanes |
| 23 | nonanes |
| 24 | decanes |
| 25 | undecanes |
| 26 | dodecanes |
| 27 | tridecanes |
| 28 | tetradecanes |
| 29 | pentadecanes |
| 30 | hexadecanes |

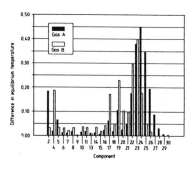

**Figure 7.** Absolute change of the equilibrium temperature at a PHLC level of 50 mg.N.m$^{-3}$ and a pressure of 40 bar, when the concentration of each constituent in the natural gases A and B increases 10%. For reasons of clarity, the influence of methane is not included. The numbers on the horizontal axis are explained in the table.

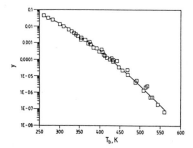 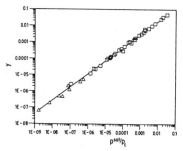

**Figure 8.** Solubility of hydrocarbons as a function of their $T_b$ (correlation coefficient r = 0.995) in a mixture of methane (81%), nitrogen (14%), carbon dioxide (2%) and ethane (3%), calculated by the PR EOS at T = 263.15 K and p = 60 bar. Open squares, calculated by the PR EOS; solid curve, best fit to the black squares.

**Figure 9.** Solubility of hydrocarbons as a function of their $p^{sat}/p_c$ (correlation coefficient r = 0.998). For additional specifications see legend of figure 8.

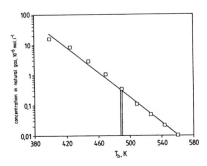 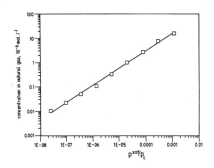

**Figure 10**. Concentration of n-alkanes with carbon number $N_c \geq 8$ in one of the validation natural gases as a function of $T_b$.

**Figure 11**. Concentration of n-alkanes with carbon number $N_c \geq 8$ in one of the validation natural gases as a function of $\ln(p^{sat}/p_c)$.

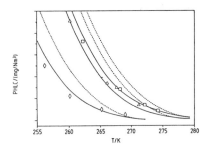

**Figure 12**. Comparison of the calculated amount of PHLC with measurements as a function of the equilibrium temperature for Gas A (first set of field measurements). Experimental data: □, 26 bar; Δ, 41 bar; ◇, 60.7 bar. Calculations: ........, $\ln(P^{sat}/P_c)$ as characterizing parameter; ———, $T_b$ as characterizing parameter.

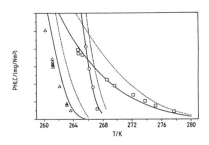

**Figure 13**. Comparison of the calculated amount of PHLC with measurements as a function of the equilibrium temperature at P=41 bar. Experimental data: □, Gas A; Δ, Gas B; ○, Gas C. Calculations: ........., $\ln(P^{sat}/P_c)$ as characterizing parameter; ———, $T_b$ as characterizing parameter.

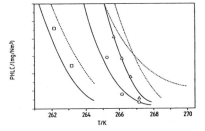

**Figure 14**. Comparison of the calculated amount of PHLC with measurements as a function of the equilibrium temperature for Gas C. Experimental data: □, 16.1 bar; o, 25.8 bar; Δ, 41.2 bar. Calculations: .........; $\ln(P^{sat}/P_c)$ as characterizing parameter, ———, $T_b$ as characterizing parameter.

TESTING OF EQUATIONS OF STATE USING SPEED OF SOUND DATA
OF THE GERG ROUND ROBIN TEST

VERIFICATION D'EQUATIONS D'ETAT
EN UTILISANT DES DONNEES DE VITESSE DU SON
OPERATION DES MESURES COMPARATIVES DU GERG

Dr. M. Jaeschke
Ruhrgas AG, Germany

Dr. J. de Boer
Gasunie, The Netherlands

Dr. P. Zambarbieri
SNAM, Italy

Dr. H. Knappstein
Thyssengas, Germany

Dr. S. Kimpton
British Gas, United Kingdom

Dr. J.J. Pinvidic
Gaz de France, France

ABSTRACT

The GERG round robin test to measure speeds of sound in methane, a binary mixture and a multi-component test gas is part of a project to examine existing equations of state for their suitability for calculating calorific data for pressures up to 30 MPa and in the 250 K to 350 K temperature range. This test is supplemented by measurements of isobaric enthalpy changes. As this experimental work programme has not been finished, a preliminary check on the selected equations of state has been carried out with published speed of sound and density data for methane and speed of sound data for a binary methane and ethane mixture. So far, of the equations tested, only the AGA8-D92 equation can meet the target uncertainty of 0.1 % for calculated speeds of sound over a restricted range. A more substantiated statement will be possible after completion of the GERG round robin test and the current enthalpy change measurements.

RESUME

L'opération des mesures comparatives effectuée par le GERG pour mesurer la vitesse du son dans le méthane; dans un mélange binaire et dans un mélange à plusieurs composants fait partie d'un projet pour examiner différentes équations d'état en vue de leur aptitude à calculer des données calorifiques pour des pressions allant jusqu'à 30 MPa et pour des températures entre 250 K et 350 K.. Le programme d'essai qui n'est pas encore terminé inclue également des mesures de changements d'enthalpie isobare. Une première vérification a été faite pour des équations d'état sélectionnées dont les valeurs de la vitesse du son et de la densité pour le méthane et les valeurs de la vitesse du son pour le mélange binaire de méthane et d'éthane avaient été publiées. Il s'est avéré que seul l'équation AGA8-D92 est à même de fournir une précision de 0,1% pour des vitesses du son calculées à l'intérieur d'une marge restreinte. L'accomplissement de l'opération des mesures comparatives et des mesures de changements d'enthalpie fournira des conclusions encore plus pertinentes.

INTRODUCTION

High accuracy thermodynamic property calculation methods are needed for a wide variety of applications in the gas industry. Areas of application are

• flow metering using critical nozzles, orifice meters or ultrasonic flowmeters,

• process simulation such as gas storage simulation, the evaluation of compressor performance tests or the design of interstage coolers,

• energy flow measurements which might be simplified by measuring speed of sound instead of gross calorific value.

For such an approach, an improved fundamental equation of state is needed. Therefore, a GERG working group (Groupe Européen de Recherches Gazières) focusing on this problem has been set up.

The objective of the GERG project is to recommend a fundamental equation using a molar composition analysis which can accurately and reliably calculate speed of sound data and isobaric enthalpy changes of natural gas. The expected uncertainty is less than 0.1 % (speed of sound) and 1 to 2 % for isobaric enthalpy changes. The maximum pressure is 30 MPa and the temperature range is 250 K to 350 K.

WORK PROGRAMME

The work programme consists of an experimental part and a theoretical part and is contracted out to several groups. Speed of sound measurements are part of the experimental work and are being performed on three gases in four laboratories. The test gases used are methane, a binary mixture of methane (0.85) and ethane (0.15) and a multi-component test gas similar to a high-calorific value natural gas. The contractors for the experimental work are

• Gaz de France, Paris, France,

• Imperial College of Science, Technology and Medicine, London, United Kingdom,

• Murdoch University, Murdoch, Australia, and

• University College, London, United Kingdom

The GERG round robin test on speed of sound data is supplemented by measurements of isobaric enthalpy changes for the three test gases at

• Karlsruhe University, Germany, and

• SINTEF, Trondheim, Norway.

The theoretical work is conducted by Ruhr University, Bochum, Germany. The theoretical work of the project involves searching literature, collecting existing experimental data on speed of sound or isobaric enthalpy changes and setting up a databank.

The selected data has been examined

• on the basis of the information given by the authors,

• by using the best available equation of state for pure gases and

• by cross-correlating the different data sets.

The data selected and the round robin data collected during the experimental work programme are being used to assess existing equations of state, such as

• the Benedict-Webb-Rubin equation [1]

• the Peng-Robinson equation [2]

• the AGA8-DC92 equation [3]

- the VNIT equation [4] and

- the NGAS equation [5].

Before testing some of the equations in question, ideal heat capacity values need to be selected. During the next but one sections, the selected heat capacity values will be used in an assessment of equations of state using data on speed of sound and enthalpy changes.

SELECTION OF IDEAL HEAT CAPACITY VALUES

For the selection of isobaric heat capacity values of ideal gases, the summarising works of Laughton and Humphreys [6] and Savidge and Shen [7] were critically examined and compared with the original data published. To describe isobaric heat capacities, the expanded approach of Aly and Lee [8] as proposed by Savidge and Shen, was adopted.

$$Cp^{\circ}(T) = B + C\left[\frac{D/T}{\sinh(D/T)}\right]^2 + E\left[\frac{F/T}{\cosh(F/T)}\right]^2 + G\left[\frac{H/T}{\sinh(H/T)}\right]^2 + I\left[\frac{J/T}{\cosh(J/T)}\right]^2 \quad (1)$$

The parameters of the expanded equation (1) were reconciled with original experimental data for all pure gases needed for the AGA8-DC92 equation [3]. The parameters were adjusted over a maximum temperature range of 10 K to 1,000 K. In most cases, it was sufficient to determine the first seven parameters. For noble gases, it is sufficient to use the first term only since translation and rotation energies are already fully excited over the relevant temperature range. However, for improving data adjustment for methane, carbon dioxide, ethane and propane, it was essential to determine all nine parameters. Reports on the results are published separately [9, 10]. The maximum deviation of the data so determined with the isobaric heat capacities used in the correlation work is less than 0.05 % (except for n-pentane) and in many cases is even less than 0.01 % (e.g. methane, nitrogen, carbon dioxide).

TESTING OF EQUATIONS OF STATE WITH METHANE

Initial testing of the selected equations of state was carried out using published experimental speed of sound and density data for methane.

Comparison with Speed of Sound Data

A first test of the selected equations has been made using speed of sound data for pure methane. Fig. 1 shows the percentage deviations of data calculated with the selected equations from the new speed sound data measured by Pinvidic and Desenfant [11] as a function of pressure.

Benedict-Webb-Rubin and Peng-Robinson Equation. Results are plotted for the 225 K to 350 K isotherms. For the Benedict-Webb-Rubin equation in the modification of Wolowski [1] and the Peng-Robinson equation [2] the deviations are often about 1 %. For lower temperatures (T < 275 K) the Benedict-Webb-Rubin equation and for higher pressures (p > 15 MPa) the Peng-Robinson equation exceed the 2 % limit. Both equations of state have been improved by about 0.1 % by using the new selected heat capacities [10].

The AGA8-DC92 equation [3] and the NGAS equation [5] agree with the experimental data [11] to within 0.1 %, except for the 225 K isotherm. The VNIT equation [4] predicts to within 0.3 % the experimental speed of sound data, except for pressures above 17.5 MPa.

AGA8-DC92 Equation. In Figure 2, the latter three equations [3 - 5] are compared in more detail with other published methane data and the Setzmann-Wagner equation for methane [12].

Five temperature regimes are selected between 250 K and 350 K. The percentage deviation between experimental and calculated (AGA8-DC92 equation) values are plotted for pressures of up to 25 MPa. In addition, the results for the other equations are given. The agreement of the AGA8-DC92 equation with the experimental speed of sound data is generally within 0.1 %. The data by Sivaraman [13], used in setting up the AGA8-DC92 equation for curve fitting deviate on the 250 K and 275 K isotherms for a pressure of 12 MPa by a maximum of + 0.33 % and + 0.19 %, respectively, while the Pinvidic [11] data deviate for a pressure of 20 MPa by 0.23 % at 250 K and by 0.14 % at 275 K. At low temperatures (250 K) the Pinvidic data seem to be systematically too high and the Beckermann data [14] too low. At 10 MPa the difference between the results of Sivaraman [13] or Pinvidic [11] and Beckermann [14] significantly exceeds the specified uncertainties of the authors (see Table 1).

The very precise data of Ewing [15] and Trusler [16] (measuring uncertainty better than 0.02 %) and the results of the equation of Setzmann et al. (12) (with the exception at 250 K and pressures above 15 MPa) agree with the AGA8-DC92 equation to within 0.05 %.

VNIT and NGAS Equation. The NGAS equation [5] which is valid for pressures up to 10 MPa agrees with most experimental data to within 0.1 %. The Beckermann data [14] differ by up to 0.2 % for the 250 K isotherm. Even for the highly accurate Ewing [15] and Trusler [16] data, the agreement between the calculated values for the 250 K and 275 K isotherms and the experimental data is no better than 0.1 %.

The VNIT equation is capable of calculating speed of sound values at high pressures, yet the results deteriorate for pressures above 17.5 MPa to differences of more than 0.3 % from the experimental results.

Testing of the various equations of states with data from published literature for the speed of sound in methane can be summarised as follows:

- The AGA8-DC92 and the NGAS equations meet the target uncertainty of 0.1 % for predicting speed of sound values.

- The NGAS equation is only valid for pressures up to 10 MPa.

- The uncertainty of the AGA8-DC92 equation in this restricted pressure range is often better than 0.05 %.

Comparison with Density Data

A second test of the selected equations of state was carried out using published density data for methane. For the Benedict-Webb-Rubin and the Peng-Robinson equation the calculated values often differ by more than 1 %. In Figure 3, results are shown for the three other equations (AGA8-DC92, VNIT and NGAS), compared with experimental data (see Table 2) [18 - 24] and the Setzmann-Wagner equation [12]. For the three selected isotherms, 273 K, 323 K and 348 K, the AGA8-DC92 equation agrees with the experimental data to within 0.05 % for pressures up to 30 MPa. For pressures up to 22 MPa the VNIT equation often also shows differences of less than 0.05 %. The NGAS equation however, often shows differences of more than 0.1 % even in the restricted pressure ranges to 10 MPa, which is not acceptable. Together with the results from the speed of sound comparison, which already excludes the VNIT equation from further investigations, only the AGA8-DC92 equation remains for further evaluations.

TEST WITH A METHANE AND AN ETHANE MIXTURE

Following the previous assessment, a further preliminary test with a binary mixture was only carried out for the AGA8 DC92 equation. For the binary methane and ethane (0.15) mixture Boyes [25], Younglove [5], and Beckermann [14] have published speed of sound data for temperatures from 250 K to 350 K and pressures up to 11 MPa (see Table 3). A similar binary mixture will also be examined in the GERG round robin analysis.

For temperatures from 275 K to 350 K, the measured values of Younglove [5] deviate from the calculated values (see Figure 4) by no more than 0.1 %. At a temperature of 250 K, however, the deviations reach as much as - 0.5 % (for 10 MPa). For temperatures of 300 K and 350 K, the measured values of Boyes [25] match those of Younglove [5] well. At 250 K and 270 K, however, there are major discrepancies. In his work Boyes describes problems for these temperatures caused by precondensation and condensation of the ethane component in the mixture at high pressures. At 250 K the ethane vapour pressure is only approx. 1.3 MPa and, therefore, lower than the partial pressure of ethane at a pressure of 10 MPa of the gas mixture.

Part of the ethane precondensated at high pressure re-vaporises at lower pressures. Therefore, e.g. at 250 K and 275 K, the molar fractions of ethane have increased by approx. 0.004 or about 2.5 % causing a shift in the speed of sound data of about - 0.15 %.

At 250 K the values of Beckermann [14] match those of Younglove [5] quite well, while at 300 K and 350 K the Beckermann values are systematically higher (by 0.05 - 0.15 %) than the values of Younglove and Boyes. The discrepancies between the various sets of data are to be resolved in the round robin test planned by GERG.

CONCLUSION

A GERG round robin test on speed of sound measurements in methane, a binary mixture and a multi-component test gas has been started and supplemented by enthalpy change measurements. A preliminary test on selected equations of state indicates that only the AGA8-DC92 equation is likely to meet the target uncertainty of 0.1 % for calculated speeds of sound.

REFERENCES

[1]   E. Wolowski, Über das Kompressibilitätsverhalten von wasserstoffhaltigen Gasgemischen bei Drücken bis zu 150 Atm, Dissertation, Rheinisch-Westfälische Technische Hochschule Aachen (1971).

[2]   O. LeNoë, Gaz de France, CERSTA, La Plaine St. Denis, France, Private Communication (1995).

[3]   K.E. Starling and J.L. Savidge, AGA Transmission Measurement Committee Report No. 8, 2nd edition, November 1992.

[4]   V.I. Otrokhov, Gosstan of Russia, Moscow, Private Communication (1993).

[5]   B.A. Younglove, N.V. Frederick and R.D. McCarty, Speed of Sound Data and Related Models for Mixtures of Natural Gas Constitutents. NIST Monograph 178, January 1993.

[6]   A.P. Laughton and A.E. Humphreys, Proceedings of the 1989 International Gas Research Conference, Tokyo, pp. 1769 - 1778, Government Institutes Inc., Rockville (1990).

[7]   J.L. Savidge and J.J.S. Shen, Proceedings of the 1989 International Gas Research Conference, Tokyo, pp. 511 - 525, Government Institutes Inc., Rockville (1990).

[8]   F.A. Aly and L.L. Lee, Fluid Phase Equilibria, 6, 169 - 179 (1981).

[9]   P. Schley, Entwicklung von Korrelationsgleichungen für isobare Wärmekapazitäten im Zustand des idealen Gases, Diplomarbeit, Ruhr-Universität, Bochum (1994).

[10]  M. Jaeschke and P. Schley, Ideal Gas Thermodynamic Properties for Natural Gas Applications, 12th Symposium on Thermophysical Properties, Boulder, 19 - 24 June 1994, and Int. J. Thermophysics, accepted for publication (1995).

[11]  J.J. Pinvidic and P. Desenfant, Experimental Determination of Sound Velocity in Methane, Gaz de France, private communication (1995).

[12]  U. Setzmann and W. Wagner, J. Phys. Chem. Ref. Data, 20 (6) 1061 - 1116 (1991).

[13]  A. Sivaraman and B.E. Gammon, Speed of Sound Measurement in Natural Gas Fluids, Gas Research Institute, Report 86/0043 (1986).

[14]  W. Beckermann, Messung der Schallgeschwindigkeit an Arbeitsstoffen der Energietechnik, VDI-Fortschritt-Berichte, Reihe 19, Heft 67, VDI-Verlag, Düsseldorf (1993).

[15]  M.B. Ewing and A.R.H. Goodwin, J. Chem. Thermodyn., 24, 1257 - 1274 (1992).

[16]  J.P.M. Trusler and M. Zarari, J. Chem. Thermodyn., 24, 973 - 991 (1992).

[17]  B.E. Gammon and D.R. Douslin, J. Chem. Phys., 64, (1) 203 - 218 (1976)

[18]  H.W. Schamp, E.A. Mason, A.C.B. Richardson, and A. Altman, Phys. Fluids, 1, 329 - 337 (1958)

[19]  D.R. Douslin, R.H. Harrison, R.T. Moore and J.P. McCullough, J. Chem. Eng. Data, 9, 358 - 363 (1964)

[20]  N.J. Trappeniers, T. Wassenaar, and J.C. Abels, Physica, 98A, 289 - 297 (1979). Erratum: Physica, 100A, 660 (1980)

[21]  R. Kleinrahm,. W. Duschek, W. Wagner, and M. Jaeschke, J. Chem. Thermodyn., 20, 621 - 631 (1988)

[22]  N. Pieperbeck, R. Kleinrahm, W. Wagner and M. Jaeschke, J. Chem. Thermodyn., 23, 175 - 194 (1991)

[23]  M. Jaeschke and M. Hinze, Ermittlung des Realgasverhaltens von Methan und Stickstoff und deren Gemische im Temperaturbereich von 270 K bis 353 K und Drücken bis 30 MPa, Fort.-Ber. VDI-Z., Reihe 3, Heft 262, (VDI-Verlag, Düsseldorf, 1991)

[24]  H.J. Achtermann, J. Hong, W. Wagner, and A. Pruss, J. Chem. Eng. Data, 37, 414 - 418 (1992)

[25]  S.J. Boyes: PhD Thesis. Univ. of London (1992)

| Source | | No. of data | temperature range [K] | pressure range [MPa] | uncertainty [%] |
|---|---|---|---|---|---|
| Gammon [17] | (1976) | 197 | 113 - 323 | 0.1 - 24 | 0.01 |
| Sivaraman [13] | (1986) | 95 | 193 - 423 | 1.4 - 27.5 | 0.01 |
| Ewing [15] | (1992) | 35 | 255 - 300 | 0.17 - 7 | 0.001 |
| Trusler [16] | (1992) | 80 | 275 - 375 | 0.38 - 10 | 0.002 |
| Beckermann [14] | (1993) | 92 | 250 - 350 | 0.5 - 10 | 0.025 - 0.06 |
| Pinvidic [11] | (1995) | 46 | 225 - 350 | 2.5 - 20 | - |

Table 1. Experimental speed of sound data of methane.

| Source | | No. of data | temperature range [K] | pressure range [MPa] | uncertainty [%] |
|---|---|---|---|---|---|
| Schamp [18] | (1958) | 118 | 273 - 423 | 1.8 - 26 | 0.02 |
| Douslin [19] | (1964) | 374 | 273 - 623 | 1.6 - 38 | 0.03 - 0.2 |
| Trappeniers [20] | (1979) | 472 | 273 - 423 | 2 - 260 | 0.05 |
| Kleinrahm [21] | (1991) | 169 | 273 - 323 | 0.1 - 8 | 0.02 |
| Pieperbeck [22] | (1991) | 164 | 263 - 323 | 0.1 - 12 | 0.02 |
| Jaeschke (BUR) [23] | (1991) | 169 | 273 - 353 | 0.2 - 30.3 | 0.05 |
| Jaeschke (OPT) [23] | (1991) | 436 | 269 - 353 | 0.3 - 28.7 | 0.05 |
| Achtermann [24] | (1992) | 654 | 273 - 373 | 1 - 34 | 0.05 |

Table 2. Experimental density data of methane.

| Source | | No. of data | temperature range [K] | pressure range [MPa] | uncertainty [%] |
|---|---|---|---|---|---|
| Boyes [27] | (1992) | 73 | 250 - 350 | 0.1 - 10 | - |
| Younglove [5] | (1993) | 67 | 250 - 350 | 0.5 - 11 | 0.05 |
| Beckermann [14] | (1993) | 103 | 250 - 350 | 0.1 - 10 | 0.025 - 0.06 |

Table 3. Experimental speed of sound data of the binary $CH_4 + C_2H_6$ mixture.
The ethane molar fraction for the data of Boyes is 0.1500, for Younglove 0.1501
and for Beckermann 0.1353.

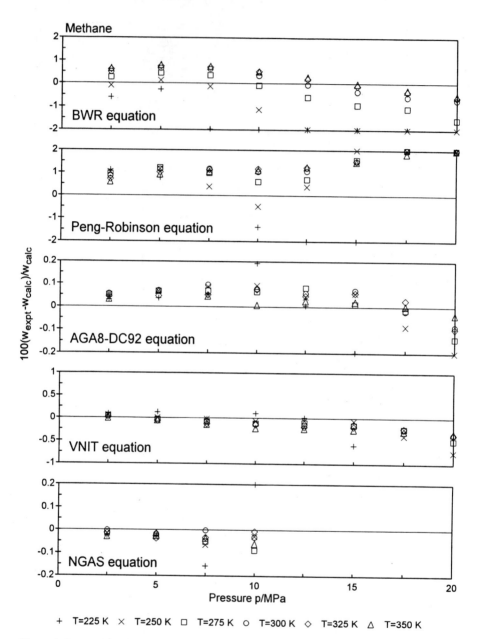

Figure 1: Comparison of calculated speed of sound data of methane for various
equations with experimental data from Pinvidic [11].

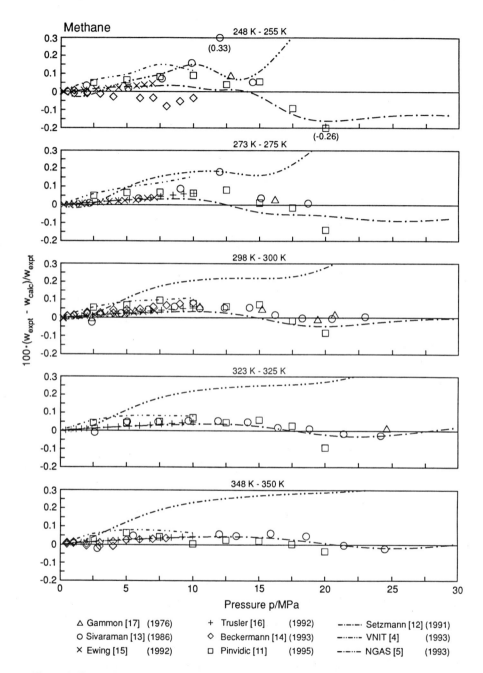

Figure 2: Percentage deviations of experimental speed of sound values of methane from values calculated (AGA8-DC92 equation as baseline).

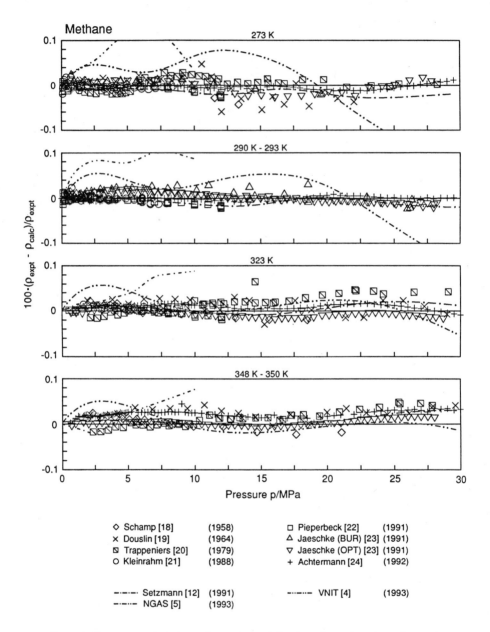

Figure 3: Percentage deviations of experimental density values of methane from values calculated (AGA8-DC92 equation as baseline).
BUR: Burnett measurements, OPT: refractive index measurements.

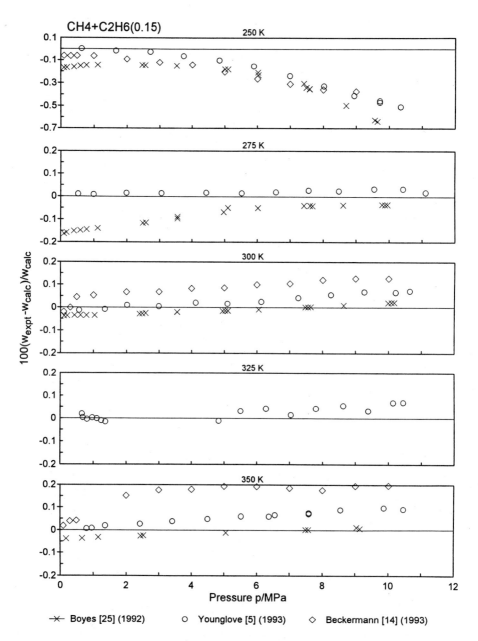

Figure 4: Percentage deviations of experimental speed of sound values of the binary CH4+C2H6(0.15) mixture from values calculated (AGA8-DC92 equation as baseline).

DEVELOPMENT OF A MATHEMATICAL CORRELATION
BETWEEN WATER CONTENT AND WATER DEWPOINT

DEVELOPPEMENT D'UNE CORRELATION MATHEMATIQUE
ENTRE TENEUR EN EAU ET POINT DE ROSEE EAU

O. Le Noë
Gaz de France

L. Schieppati, B. Viglietti
SNAM, Italy

L. Oellrich, K. Althaus
Karlsruhe University, Germany

F. Pot, L. van der Meulen
Gasunie, Netherlands

H. Kaesler
Ruhrgas, Germany

G. Moncó
Enagas, Spain

G. Wismann
Thyssengas, Germany

ABSTRACT

This paper presents the experimental phase of a project set for the development of a new mathematical correlation between water content and water dewpoint in natural gas. Current models were derived from experimental data obtained at temperatures higher than 300 K. It is shown that they are inadequate for pressure and temperature conditions of natural gas in transmission pipelines. Gases from the european network were used for the achievement of a practical data base. The experimental techniques are presented ; they are based on the principle of a temperature controlled water condensation. Significant results are reported.

RESUME

Cet article présente la phase expérimentale d'un projet ayant pour but le développement d'une nouvelle corrélation mathématique entre la teneur en eau et le point de rosée eau du gaz naturel. Les modèles actuels furent déduits de données expérimentales obtenues à des températures supérieures à 300 K. Nous démontrons qu'ils sont inadaptés aux conditions de pression et de température rencontrées dans les réseaux de transport. Des gaz du réseau européen ont été utilisés pour l'élaboration d'une base de données exploitable. Les techniques expérimentales sont présentées ; elles sont basées sur le principe d'une condensation d'eau à température contrôlée. Des résultats significatifs sont exposés.

## INTRODUCTION

Water vapour has always been considered as an impurity in natural gas because of the damages caused by water condensation : corrosion, mostly in presence of $H_2S$ or $CO_2$, hydrates or ice formation. Water vapour condenses if the gas is cooled down, which can occur during pipeline transmission in cold areas or during expansion from transmission to supply pressures. Considering the importance of water vapour for safety of natural gas transmission equipment, gas companies tend to implement dehydration units and on-line water content control.

The measurement of water vapour concentration is nowadays very accurate, in laboratory conditions as well as on-line conditions. Most of the instruments are based on Karl Fischer titration, according to the standard method ISO 10101, electrolytic cells, or hygroscopic vibrating quartz. It is more accurate and reliable than the measurement of water dewpoint, and can be achieved at low pressure. However, from the physical point of view, the water dewpoint of natural gas makes more sense than the water concentration. It gives knowledge about the phase equilibrium conditions, ie the temperatures at which water condenses at production and transmission conditions of pressure. Furthermore gas sales contracts often specify the limit of water content in natural gas in terms of water dewpoint at a specified pressure. The natural gas industry thus needs an accurate correlation between water vapour concentration and water dewpoint, at temperatures from 258.15 K to 278.15 K, and pressures from 0.5 MPa to 10 MPa.

The existing correlations, among which the widest used are Bukacek's and Campbell's, have proven to be impractical when applied to a wide temperature range, though they give very similar results. Moreover their accuracies are not known at water concentrations lower than 100 ppm, ie in the concentration range gas companies are interested in. Most of these correlations are based on experimental works of IGT from the 50's [1,2], achieved at high temperature up to 470 K. A lack of experimental data is obvious in a range more practical for the gas industry. Consequently, GERG (European Gas Research Group) set up a research program to develop a new mathematical correlation between water dewpoint and water content in natural gas. The metrological objective is a maximum error of ± 2 K on the dew temperature calculated from the real water content and the real pressure values. The scope of work consists of three phases : reliability tests on experimental methods, experimental data collecting and mathematical development. The project is developed by GERG Working Group 1.6, under supervision of GERG Program Committee 1. It is supposed to be completed by mid-1997. The present phase in development is the experimental data collecting ; it is supposed to be completed by mid-1996. In order to study the influence of gas composition on the water vapour saturation, pure methane and six most representative gases from the European network have been selected for this work.

## EXPERIMENTAL

### Principle

The experimental method selected for this work is based on the generation of wet calibrated natural gases by water condensation in a temperature controlled condenser, with continuous gas flow at specified pressures. The water concentration of the gas is measured at the outlet of the moisture generation bench, using a Karl Fischer titration, according to the standard method ISO 10101/3. Doing so, a water content reference value of the gaseous phase is obtained, and will be used for the development of a new correlation. The water dewpoint reference value is obtained by setting the thermodynamic parameters of the bench, ie the pressure and the water condensation temperature. Their values are measured and regulated. Moreover, a dew temperature measurement is achieved at line pressure, in parallel with the Karl Fischer titration at atmospheric pressure.

The pressure values range from 0.5 MPa to 10 MPa and the temperature values range from 258.15 K to 278.15 K. It appears that most of the generated water dewpoints lie within P-T domain of hydrate stability. This domain, whose limits depend slightly upon the composition of the gas, can be calculated by market available programs, based on statistic thermodynamics of hydrates stability. We used for our work Sloan [3] and Gaz de France models to calculate these stability limits. However the purpose of this work is to examine the metastable water dewpoint, ie the water condensation point before hydrates formation. It is admitted that natural gas hydrates cannot form in a water liquid free fluid ; water dewpoint measurement, for instance on-line at pipeline pressure, thus leads to a metastable dewpoint value when achieved in the P-T hydrate stability domain. As revealed by recent works [3,4] in natural gas hydrate kinetics, the hydrate ignition needs a particular interface between gas and liquid (or ice) : usually in absence of gas turbulences, the liquid has to be stirred or the ice has to be ground in order to increase the contact surface. Karlsruhe University implemented an endoscopic video system in order to trace the possible occurence of hydrates into the condensers. This equipment is presented in the following section.

We thus assume to generate metastable water dewpoints. In all the present work, no distinction is made between water vapour condensation as liquid and water vapour solidification as ice. Both are called "dewpoint". Seven gases are being used for this work : pure methane and the 6 most typical natural gases on the European transmission network. The natural gases and their sampling places are the following :

- Russian gas, sampled in Waidhause (Germany) by Ruhrgas,
- Ekofisk gas, sampled in Emden (Germany) by Ruhrgas,
- Groningen gas, sampled in Aalten (Germany) by Thyssengas,
- revaporized LNG, sampled in Montoir-de-Bretagne (France) by Gaz de France,
- Netherlands gas, sampled in Masera (Italy) by SNAM,
- Algerian gas, sampled in Terranuovo-Bracciolini (Italy) by SNAM.

Karlsruhe University achieves the dewpoint generations along isobars (0.5 MPa, 1.5 MPa, 4 MPa, 6 MPa, 8 MPa, 10 MPa). Each dewpoint is generated twice. The first series of dewpoint generation for each isobar is performed with increasing values of temperature : 258.15 K, 263.15 K, 268.15 K, 273.15 K, 278.15 K. Whereas the second series is performed with the same temperature values randomly selected. In order to avoid any bias or systematic error in the measurements, Gaz de France performs checking measurements on the same gas samples : for each isobar, one dewpoint was generated with a temperature randomly selected in the above mentioned list. Each water content or dewpoint result, presented in §Results, is an average value of 10 successive measurements performed after stabilization of all the parameters of the system.

Gas sampling procedure and gas analysis

All the natural gases studied were sampled in same quantity, ie 12 cylinders of 50 litres at 20 MPa, and according to the same method : the 12 cylinders were parallely connected to a heated standard sampling line from a pipeline. A compressor was placed in between  in order to fill the cylinders up to 20 MPa. A vent outlet vacuum pump was connected in parallel with the cylinders for purging the line.

The cylinders were supplied by Messer Griesheim Company, with a slight overpressure of dry nitrogen (grade 4.6). The purge consisted first in evacuating the nitrogen and the oxygen from the cylinders and the connecting lines. Second it consisted in filling the cylinders at a few bars with the pipeline gas and evacuating them at least five times.

A 2 litre cylinder was also filled in parallel up to 4 MPa ; it was used for a preliminary specific chromatographic analysis of the gas. Gasunie was in charge of this analysis, achieved according to ISO 6975. A hydrocarbon phase envelope was calculated from the detailed composition, in order to predict the interferences between water and hydrocarbon dewpoints during the experimental work. The sulphur components of the sampled gases were carefully analysed because it was previously shown [1] that they heavily modify gas-liquid water equilibria. In order to check the stability of the gas composition, another specific analysis was achieved by Gasunie after complete experimental work on each gas, using residual gas from a 50 litre cylinder. Table 1 contains the approximative compositions of the natural gases on which results are presented in §Results. The purity of the methane used for our work was 99.995%.

| component | Russian | Ekofisk | Groningen |
|-----------|---------|---------|-----------|
| $CO_2$    | 0.11    | 1.73    | 1.25      |
| $N_2$     | 0.85    | 0.88    | 13.08     |
| $CH_4$    | 98.17   | 84.25   | 82.15     |
| $C_2H_6$  | 0.57    | 8.72    | 2.78      |
| $C_3$     | 0.22    | 3.30    | 0.47      |
| $C_4$     | 0.05    | 0.90    | 0.17      |
| $C_5$     | 0.01    | 0.18    | 0.05      |
| $C_6+$    | 0.01    | 0.03    | 0.05      |
| He        | 0.01    | 0.01    | 0.00      |

Table 1. gas compositions (mole percent)

Karlsruhe University equipment

The water dewpoint generation bench used for our experimental data collecting is presented in figure 1. It was set up and it is operated by Institute of Technical Thermodynamics and Cryogenics (ITTK). After controlled expansion (PI1) the gas is saturated with water vapour by flowing through liquid water in a saturator held at a temperature well above hydrate formation. The temperature controlled water condensation is then achieved into two successive stainless steel condensers. The first condenser temperature (TIR3) is set to a value lying between  ambient and temperature of the second condenser (TIR4). Doing so the quantity of ice or liquid collected into the second condenser is minimized. The water dewpoint being finally set into the second condenser, a special attention is paid to TIR4 and PIR4 measurements :

- temperature is measured using a Pt100 sensor, Sensycon Type 28635. It is traceable to a Pt25 Rosemount sensor and its accuracy is better than ± 0.02 K. The sensor is immersed into the condenser.

- pressure is measured using a Wika sensor, Class 0.05, Type 891.10.500. The sensor was calibrated against a Desgranges-Huot precision dead weight gauge. Its accuracy is better than 0.05% of actual value.

In order to avoid any recondensation , the line is heated in the vicinity of RV2, RV3 and RV4 valves. The instrumentation implemented for water content and water dewpoint measurements are the following :

- Mitsubishi CA02 and CA06 Karl Fischer Titrators, coupled with an Elster wet gasmeter, Type Gr.00, E51, 0.2% accuracy. Before each water content measurement, the KF system was checked with a Hydranal-water-methanol standard solution (1 mg/ml) supplied by Riedel de Haen company.
- Marquis Dewpoint Mirror Type 1300 chilled mirror instrument, operating according to standard method DIN 51871-A (ISO 6327). The cooling of the mirror is achieved by a refrigerant fluid, and the detection of the water condensation on the mirror is visual. The uncertainty on the dew temperature is better than ± 2 K.

The endoscopic system consists of two endoscopes guides, connected to cameras, a video switchbox controlled by a 286 computer and connected to a 486 computer for data storing. Data are visualized on a video monitor. The system, called "Eagle" (Opticon) is presented in figure 2. The visualization is made from outside the condensers because of the severe conditions of pressure and temperature inside. The endoscopes endings are coupled to saphir windows on the top of the condensers. An optical fiber cold light source  is placed with the endoscope on the window. A flow of dry nitogren is maintaining the endoscope-window interface dry. Photographs obtained with the Eagle system are presented in §Results.

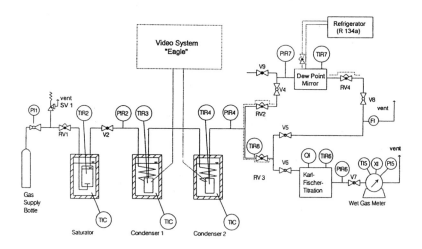

figure 1. moisture generation bench
RV : control valve   SV : safety valve      V : ball valve
TI.. : temperature measurement    PI.. : pressure measurement
QI : coulometric measurement      XI : volume measurement

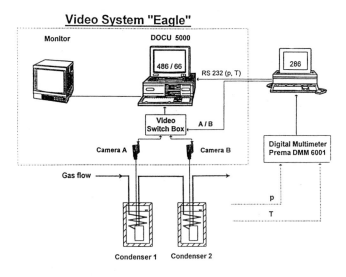

figure 2. endoscopic and video system

Reliability tests

The first phase of the project, completed in 1993, determined the performance of the methods used for the present work. Repeatability and reproducibility of the Karl Fischer titration and the dewpoint generation were calculated, according to ISO 5725, after inter-laboratory tests and repeatitive measurements. The results are presented in Table 2. Reference conditions for volume are 273.15 K and 0.101325 MPa. Test A was achieved by 5 laboratories on one standard gas prepared by BOC. Test B was achieved by 3 laboratories, on a water dewpoint of 263.15 K and 6 MPa in pure methane and in pure nitrogen. The reliability tests results are taken as consistency criteria for the present experimental phase : the maximum acceptable standard deviation of ITTK measurements is derived from the repeatability value, and the maximum acceptable discrepancy between ITTK and Gaz de France measurements is derived from the reproducibility value.

| | TEST A Karl Fischer | TEST B Dewpoint generation 263.15 K , 6 MPa | |
|---|---|---|---|
| | $H_2O$ in $N_2$ BOC mixture | $H_2O$ in $N_2$ | $H_2O$ in $CH_4$ |
| mean value (mg/m3) | 61.5 | 42.6 | 36.0 |
| repeatability (mg/m3) | 5.1 | 2.2 | 1.6 |
| reproducibility (mg/m3) | 9.1 | 10.4 | 4.2 |

Table 2. performance evaluation of water content measurements

RESULTS

Physical phenomena visualization

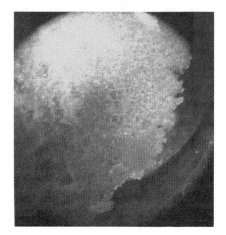          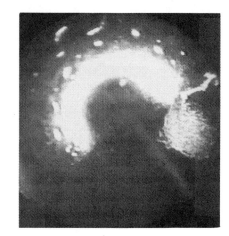

figure 3. hydrates in 1st condenser                    figure 4. ice in 2nd condenser

Some hydrocarbon condensates can interfere with water dewpoint at the highest pressures and the lowest temperatures. But the visual detection of condensation on the mirror allows to distinguish between hydrocarbon and ice owing to the differences of viscosity and light reflection. It is also possible to distinguish hydrates from ice, as shown in figures 3 and 4, photographs of respectively hydrates in the first condenser and ice in the second condenser. Hydrates have snow-like aspect, while ice forms a translucent layer (right side of figure 4). For kinetics reasons hydrates are only observed in the first condenser.

Moisture measurements

Complete results on pure methane and partial results on Russian gas, Ekofisk gas and Groningen gas are presented. Reference conditions for volumes are 273.15 K and 0.101325 MPa.

Dewpoint verification with chilled mirror instruments. Figure 5 represents the differences between generated dew temperatures, by setting the temperature of the second condenser (see §Experimental), and measured dew temperatures, according to ISO 6327, for all pressure values on pure methane.

One can see that, almost all the measurements lie within the expected uncertainty on dewpoints, ie ± 2 K. The dew temperature of the (10 MPa, 258.15 K) generated point could not be achieved because of a failure of the mirror cooling system. The differences increase with pressure, but this observation is related to the operation of a chilled mirror instrument at high pressure : the thermal equilibrium between the mirror surface and the surrounding gas is difficult to reach when the gas density is high. The agreement between generated and measured dew temperatures was confirmed on natural gases.

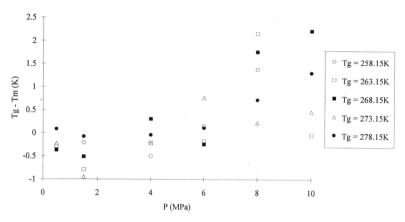

figure 5. differences between generated ($T_g$) and measured ($T_m$) dew temperatures

Water content measurements. Figure 6 represents the complete isotherms set of water content measurements in pure methane. One can see the consistency of the data, expressed as the regular distance between isotherms. Moreover, the shape of the curves may be compared, as a gross approximation, to a hyperbola which is consistent with the ideal gas behaviour assumption of Dalton and Raoult laws leading to $[H_2O] = \dfrac{P_s(T)}{P}$ . Where $P_s(T)$ is the vapor pressure of water, P is the absolute total pressure and $[H_2O]$ the molar fraction of water in the gaseous phase.

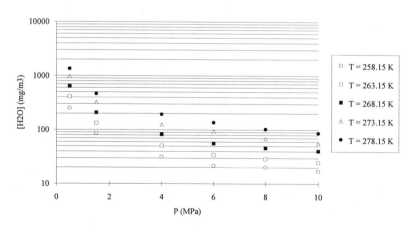

Figure 6. water content measurements for water dewpoint generation in pure methane

Figure 7 represents water content measurements on 3 natural gases. One temperature, indicated on the graph, was chosen for each pressure. The correlated values, obtained from [1], are included. They are composition independent. One can see that the relative differences between measured and correlated values increase with pressure. They reach 80 % at 8 MPa and

10 MPa. Figure 7 also shows that the effect on the water content of the composition of the gas is negligible, as far as we have investigated, compared to the discrepancies between measured and calculated values.

The differences observed between the correlation and our experimental results confirm the importance of our present work. The results on revaporized LNG, algerian gas and gas from Bocholtz should confirm the inadequacy of the current models. The existing correlations being the extrapolations of high temperature liquid-gas data, one reason for their inadequacy at temperatures lower than 273.15 K might be the presence of ice as the stable phase for water. This point will be examined during the correlation development phase.

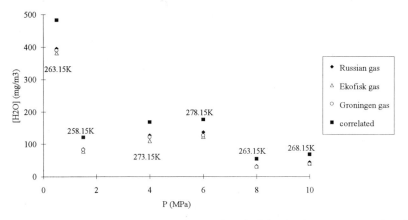

figure 7. water content measurements on Russia, Ekofisk, Groningen gases, and Bukacek correlated values.

CONCLUSION

The experimental work in progress will provide an exhaustive reference moisture database to the members of the project. It was shown that we generate metastable water dewpoints because of the absence of hydrates in the dewpoint setting condenser and because of the agreement between generated and measured dew temperatures. Indeed metastable dewpoint is the physical property measured by a chilled mirror instrument, in laboratory as well as in field conditions. Considering the discrepancies between measured and correlated dewpoints, reaching 80 % at the highest pressures, a new correlation is obviously needed.

The last phase of our project will consist in the development of a new correlation using the new database. Depending on the discrepancies in water contents between all the different gases of this work, we will decide to take into account the gas composition or not (main components, sulfur components...) in the new correlation. A special attention should be paid to the differences in physical behaviour between liquid water and ice.

REFERENCES

[1]    R.F. Bukacek, "Equilibrium moisture content of natural gases", IGT Research Bulletin 8, Nov. 1955.

[2]   S. Sharma, J.M. Campbell, "Water content of natural gas", 48th NGPA annual convention, 1969, pp 70-71.

[3]   E.D. Sloan, "Clathrate Hydrates of Natural Gases", Marcel Dekker Inc, NY,1990.

[4]   P.R. Bishnoï, A. Vysniauskas, GRI report, Contract no 5080-363-0312, 1980.

THE DEVELOPMENT OF RISK ASSESSMENT METHODOLOGIES FOR ONSHORE AND
OFFSHORE PLANT


LA MISE AU POINT DE METHODOLOGIES D'ESTIMATION DU RISQUE POUR LES
INSTALLATIONS ONSHORE ET OFFSHORE.

H.F.Hopkins and S.J.Potts
British Gas plc, Research and Technology

## ABSTRACT

The paper describes the way in which the methodology for carrying out hazard and risk
assessment for plant and pipelines operated by British Gas is being developed. A
collaborative knowledge based approach is being followed in order to achieve an agreed
consistent means of accessing and managing the information, data and calculation methods
required. As a consequence of this approach the release and its effects are more realistically
modelled, the derivation of the output is more accessible, and the results can be used with
greater confidence to support design and operational decisions. The development is
illustrated with examples for gas transmission pipelines and gas releases on offshore
platforms.

## RESUME

La communication décrit la mise au point de la méthodologie d'estimation du risque pour les
installations et les pipelines utilisés par British Gas. Une approche d'expert faite en commun
est utilisée afin de convenir d'une procédure logique d'accès et de gestion des informations,
des données et des méthodes de calcul nécessaires. En conséquence de cette approche,
le dégagement et ses effets sont simulés sur modèle d'une facon plus réaliste, la dérivation
des données de sortie est plus accessible et les résultats peuvent être utilisés avec plus de
confiance pour aider à la prise de décisions concernant la conception et l'exploitation. La
mise au point est illustrée par des examples de gazoducs et de dégagement de gaz sur des
derricks en mer.

## INTRODUCTION

Risk assessment forms part of a procedure to ensure the achievement of safe, reliable, efficient plant, which can clearly be shown to meet statutory requirements. A representation of such a procedure is shown in Figure 1. The basic elements, which are well known (1), are: hazard identification; hazard reduction; quantification of frequency; and consequences, the combination of which is the risk; and risk reduction. The process is iterative at all stages, and as the procedure progresses, for example through the design stages of a project, the scope of the assessment becomes more focused and the level of detail increases. The procedure is followed in a progressive manner until it can be demonstrated that a criterion of acceptability has been satisfied. In the United Kingdom the criterion is that the risk has been reduced to a level which is 'as low as reasonably practicable', commonly referred to as ALARP. The process described is consistent with the 'identify, assess, control' philosophy of UK legislation.

Each element involves a range of techniques and sources of data and information. Hazard identification generally involves well established techniques such as Failure Mode and Effects Analysis (FMEA) and Hazard and Operability Studies (HAZOP), approaches are now being followed however to develop this along a more knowledge based, automated route (2). The hazard reduction phase takes account of principles such as inherent safety, i.e. sources of hazard will not be quantified at a later stage where they could more easily have been designed out.

The quantification of frequency will rely on historical failure data, failure models or structured techniques such as fault tree analysis. The quantification of consequences will access a range of data and models appropriate to the failure being considered, the validation of which is an important element in supporting the overall assessment (3). This paper is concerned with the assessment of these two elements, to enable the calculation of risk in a way which takes account of the behaviour and response of plant in a realistic manner. The use of the results to demonstrate that the risk has been reduced to an acceptable level is also an important aspect of this development.

## RISK ASSESSMENT METHODOLOGY

The failure frequency, consequences, and their effects are assessed using a structured approach as shown in Figure 2. This consists of three basic elements:

* the logic chart; or problem definition,
* the data, rules and procedures; the knowledge base, and
* the calculation procedures; the model library (or toolkit).

The logic chart can in turn be considered to consist of five sub-elements:

* the input data- on the plant or pipeline being assessed, the system of which it forms a part, the fuel, the environment (or surroundings), and the weather;
* the failure parameters- the causes of failure, with the associated frequencies of each possible failure mode;
* the calculation of the consequences for each of the failure modes;
* the effect of the consequences on the surrounding plant and population; and
* the combination of these effects with the failure frequency to calculate the output risks required.

This generic description of the logic diagram can be extended further. The failure parameters relate the failure mode and frequency to each of the possible causes. The consequences typically follow the pattern of gas release, dispersion (and accumulation), and ignition- leading to fire and/or explosion. The magnitude of each of these will be influenced by the behaviour of the system following failure, and by the response of operators and safety critical protective systems such as gas detection and emergency shutdown. The effects of the consequences are typically those of thermal radiation, overpressure or toxic dose. Many of the models and sources of data used in these calculations will be common to a range of release situations.

What we have done thus far is to set out the way in which the hazard and risk from flammable gas and liquid releases is calculated in a generic manner which is applicable to the range of plant types to be considered. The challenge is to use this generic approach and the data, models, and techniques available in a way which takes more account of the nature and behaviour of realistic plant. This requires the assessment to manage, in a consistent way, the many variables involved in plant failures and their effect on the surrounding population. The way in which this is addressed, for pipelines and for offshore platforms, is described below.

## KNOWLEDGE BASED APPROACH

A consequence of adopting a more realistically modelled approach is the increased amount of data and knowledge required to carry out the assessment, and to access the calculation models in the required way. Safety assessments have depended on engineers using software models according to a set of rules, and applying their knowledge about the models and the way in which the data is processed. The assessment relied on the skill of the engineer in applying the knowledge to the particular situation. The more complex and detailed the methodology becomes the more difficult it is for the process to continue in this way.

The development described here is aimed at moving the methodology a stage further, embodying not only the rules but also the associated knowledge, while still requiring the assessor to use their skill and experience to apply it correctly. This might appear to be reducing the input from the assessor however this is not the case. By incorporating more knowledge in the assessment methodology, the assessor has more freedom to consider the detailed nature of the plant and process being assessed, thus improving the level of detail, confidence and applicability of the results. It follows that when additional detailed knowledge has been defined this too can be incorporated. Thus the process can become a continual one of adding to the methodology that knowledge which can be specified and agreed. An additional benefit of this approach is that the knowledge base for the assessment becomes more accessible to safety engineers, operational managers, or regulatory bodies.

Two examples of the way in which this knowledge based approach is being developed are described below: for high pressure gas transmission pipelines; and for gas releases on offshore platforms. The same approach is being followed for other plant and pipelines where hazard and risk assessments are required, or where operations can be improved by the application of hazard and risk assessment in this way.

### Gas Transmission Pipelines

Knowledge based software for the risk assessment of gas transmission pipelines has been in use within British Gas for a number of years (4). This provides a means of making available in the form of an accessible agreed methodology the results obtained from an extensive research programme into pipeline failure and its consequences. This software continues to be extended as a result of the continual development of the knowledge base in these areas and from experience in its use.

Failure of the pipeline to give a leak (puncture) or break (rupture) could result from a range of possible causes. For a modern pipeline system such as that operated by British Gas the design, testing, inspection and maintenance of the pipeline should virtually eliminate many of these causes, and the development of sophisticated inspection vehicles is aimed at assuring this. These vehicles provide data on the condition of the system, and together with reports of damage and other events, produce an extensive database which can be used to direct research activities and to validate predictive techniques for causes such as corrosion and cracking which are not at present routinely addressed in risk assessments.

Third party damage, and ground movement in specific areas, are the dominant failure causes and hence are addressed quantitatively in assessments. Historical data on pipeline failure for modern high toughness systems is sparse and can be of relatively limited value. British Gas has therefore developed a predictive approach for third party damage failures (5) based on determining the critical length and depth of damage defects required to cause failure as a puncture or rupture, as a function of diameter, wall thickness, and hoop stress, and assigning the frequency of this damage occurring from a statistical analysis of data on damage events on the British Gas system, whether or not any failure occurred.

Figure 3 illustrates the variables to be managed in the assessment of the consequences and in the risk calculations for a natural gas pipeline failure, where the hazard is that of thermal radiation resulting from an ignited release. For a major failure the gas outflow varies significantly with time over the period for which the effect on people and property, and the response of the operator and emergency services, are critical to the resulting consequences. The outflow model is run for the appropriate boundary conditions, which relate to the operation of the system, taking account of any response, such as the operation of isolation valves, which can affect the consequences, in order to obtain a realistic outflow time profile to form the basis of the assessment.

Gas dispersion modelling can be used to give an indication of the extent of any unignited plume to assist with determining the possibility of ignition of the release, however because ignition can occur from a variety of sources both close to and remote from the failure historical data is more typically used.

Ignition of the release results in a short duration transient fireball or flash fire depending on how soon ignition occurs after the failure, followed by a quasi steady state impacted jet (crater) fire fuelled by the steadily decaying gas outflow. The variation of thermal radiation with distance from the fire can be calculated using a crater fire model. Such models are typically steady state, because of the complexity of modelling the combustion process, however for the long duration transient decay referred to here successive runs of a steady state model with interpolation between them is a satisfactory approach. The transient nature of the event means that the effects cannot be based simply on a thermal radiation level, particularly if the opportunity for people to escape to safe shelter or a safe radiation level is taken into account. The radiation is summed as a dose, typically in the form of probit dose units (6), and compared with a definition (or criterion) of casualty. The dose to property is summed to a criterion for the ignition of wood, and allowance can be made for the possibility of people evacuating unsafe shelter, and escaping to safe shelter or a safe radiation level further away. The variation of wind speed and direction may also need to be taken into account. This procedure results in the calculation of the probability of people reaching safe shelter (and hence the casualty probability) at a range of distances from the failure.

For any plant or pipeline being assessed the point of failure may be specified. In the general case however it could be anywhere on the system, the risk at any given location has therefore to take into account the likelihood of the failure being at a specific point. For a pipeline there is an interaction length within which a failure can affect a location, with the extent of the hazard being dependent on the exact failure position. The shelter probability will be obtained by `averaging' the hazard along this length.

In this way a realistically modelled casualty probability and hence individual risk level, is obtained. For so-called major hazard plant the societal risk, the frequency at which numbers of casualties could occur, is likely to be a more important parameter (7) and would need to be taken into account in determining pipeline routes or operating conditions. In order to calculate the societal risk data on the number of people present at a location at different times (of the day or week for example) will also need to be accessed. This complete process results in very detailed output data which can be used more effectively in considering measures to reduce risk using for example cost benefit studies or acceptability criteria. This detailed approach can also be used to assist with the definition of criteria, for example by quantifying the risks inherent in operation to accepted design codes and standards.

## Gas Releases - Offshore Platforms

While the assessment of a release on an offshore platform follows the same generic approach to that for a transmission pipeline, there are a number of important differences:

\*the consequence calculations are required for near field effects necessitating the calculations to take account of the detailed nature of the release surroundings;
\*the consequences can vary significantly for different release positions and orientations;
\*the release may give rise either to a fire hazard or an explosion hazard depending on the time of ignition and whether a flammable mixture can be produced in a confined or partially confined space;
\*the operation of safety critical systems such as gas detection is central to the rate and quantity of gas released.

To consider the detailed calculation of the consequences of releases in process areas of offshore platforms and the response of process and structural components, a software package CHAOS has been produced by British Gas (8) for use in safety cases required by UK legislation arising from the Cullen Report into the Piper Alpha disaster. However in order for a quantitative risk assessment to be carried out, this package must be used in conjunction with information relating to the relevant frequencies involved. These include the failure frequency for different failure modes (release sizes), failure location and orientation, ignition, safety critical systems availability, wind speed and direction. The way in which these have been used to calculate the frequency of explosion and fire loading on the structure is detailed below.

The gas release rate, in the form of the outflow-time profile, which determines the later consequences, is derived using a reliability study to determine the availability of the safety critical systems installed. This is indicated in Figure 4 in the form of a section of the event tree for the operation of the gas detection, Emergency Shut Down (ESD) and blowdown systems. These active protection systems can limit the consequences of any release by confining each isolatable section (sections of pipework and associated components between ESD valves) limiting the inventory which can be released, and by venting a proportion of the trapped inventory. The transient decay of the gas released from the isolatable section is calculated, using a transient gas and two phase release model, as a function of release size, initial pressure, initial temperature, blowdown orifice size, and blowdown delay time. Three different outflow-time profiles are shown and each will have an associated probability. The availability of the water deluge system will also be included in the reliability study since deluge can affect the magnitude of any predicted explosion overpressure. A similar approach to the frequency calculation is being followed by at least one other operator (9).

Whether the consequences predicted are those of fire or explosion depends initially on whether an ignition source is assumed to be encountered immediately, when a fire is assumed to occur. Otherwise if there is a degree of confinement in the area of the release a build up of gas concentration could take place, which may lead to an explosion if the gas concentration becomes flammable and an ignition source is subsequently encountered. The immediate ignition probability is based upon the flammable volume of a free jet from the release and the ignition source density (based upon historical data). Delayed ignition probability is based upon the volume of flammable mixture, the length of time that it is present, and the ignition source density.

Calculations are carried out for each isolatable section within each module. The frequency of releases from an isolatable section is determined by multiplying the amount of equipment (pipework in selected size ranges, and components such as valves and pumps) by historical failure rate data for each component class (10).

The consequence calculations are progressed separately for the branches of the event tree leading to fires and to gas-build up giving rise to the possibility of an explosion overpressure. Both will however consider the same range of release conditions; release position, orientation and diameter.

Fires. For each release combination the failure frequency and immediate ignition probability are calculated. The availability of the protective systems; fire detection, ESD and blowdown are used to determine the probability for each of the outflow-time profile options. These frequencies are combined with the release conditions to give a range of scenarios of known frequency. The thermal radiation is calculated using the models within the CHAOS package. The interaction of these models with the geometry database for the module being assessed will automatically take account of whether the fire behaves as a free jet or is impacted on a part of the structure. For transient decaying releases the models are run for a succession of points along the outflow decay curve, taking into account the times for safety critical systems to operate (which determine the length of time for which the release is steady state). The output of the fire models is used to calculate:

*the area of modules where the thermal flux is above a threshold which could result in immediate casualties.
*the thermal flux along user defined escape routes and at life saving equipment to determine whether they become impaired (unavailable, either temporarily or permanently) due to the fire; and as input to thermal response models to consider:
*the response of user defined targets: pipes, vessels, structural elements, which on failure could cause the event to escalate significantly (and the time which they fail).

The output data for the impairment of escape routes and life saving equipment, and for escalation, is input to an Escape Evacuation and Rescue (EER) model to enable the calculation of the casualty probability and the number of casualties for persons escaping to the Temporary Refuge (TR) and evacuating the platform. These are combined with the frequency data to give the individual and societal risk.

Gas-Build Up. A range of release conditions are considered in the same manner as that described for fires, except that variations in the external wind conditions are also taken into account, and gas detection will be considered instead of fire detection. The time above a range of gas concentrations between the Lower (LFL) and Upper (UFL) Flammability Limits is calculated using the jet dispersion and gas-build up models from the CHAOS package, thus taking account of any confining structure, taking as input the appropriate pressure-time profile for the release scenario. These times are used to determine the probability of ignition occurring while the mixture is above each specified gas concentration, as a function of the volume of the module and the time spent above each gas concentration. This in turn can be combined with the overpressures resulting from ignition at the relevant gas concentration, for a range of ignition positions, in order to calculate the frequency of specified overpressures being exceeded.

Each overpressure calculated (for each gas concentration and ignition position) can be used to calculate the casualty probability and number of casualties in a similar manner to that for fires. The immediate casualties within and adjacent to the module involved are assessed. The immediate escalation due to failure of walls, floors, structural elements, pipes and vessels, and the unavailability of escape routes and life saving equipment can be obtained by calculating the blast loading and response from the predicted pressure-time profile and velocity data.

## CONCLUSIONS

The development described in this paper and illustrated with the pipeline and offshore platform applications, is aimed at progressing the methodology for hazard and risk assessment along a continually developing knowledge based approach, where the skill of the safety assessment engineer can be developed into agreed procedures and rules to be incorporated into the methodology. In this way expert judgement, when applied to standard situations, can be eliminated, and simplifying assumptions can be replaced with a more realistic treatment of the variables involved. This process is aided by the availability of ever more powerful computers, and to developments in computer software to act as an interface with the user. A further objective of the approach is to preserve, as far as possible, the detail of the calculated risks i.e. the combinations of frequency and number of predicted casualties associated with each release, by minimising the averaging of data at intermediate stages of the assessment. The provision of more detailed frequency and consequence data facilitates the use of the output in a range of forms such as FN curves, potential casualties per year, or in cost benefit studies.

While the treatment of the societal risk is the main issue with major hazard plant there is no simple way of presenting it. This is a consequence of the range of events, with their associated frequencies and consequences, on the one hand, and the public perception and political judgements which are applied to them on the other. The UK legislative approach using the concept of `reasonable practicability' involves a comparison of any reduction in risk with the `cost' of achieving it. Such decisions are not made solely on the basis of quantifying risks however they will in general make use of data on the overall level of harm such as the `potential casualties' per year and the distribution of risk in the form of for example an FN curve; the ability to retain these data in sufficient detail is therefore important.

The quantification of risk does not in itself determine the acceptability of the operation of plant or pipelines since in addition to the judgmental factors involved, there remain uncertainties and simplifications in the models and methods used in the assessment. The acceptability of a risk will also depend on other factors such as how often the risk is repeated, either locally or nationally, and who is imposing the risk and on whom. Nevertheless, it should be the case that where decisions are made on the basis of information on the hazards and risks imposed by an operation, the more realistic and detailed the information, the better the decision is likely to be.

## ACKNOWLEDGEMENTS

This paper is published by permission of British Gas plc. The contribution of many of our colleagues whose work is interfaced into the risk assessment methodologies described is acknowledged.

## REFERENCES

1.      Health and Safety Commission- Advisory Committee on Major Hazards: Second Report, 'The Assessment of Major Hazards', London, HMSO, 1979.

2.      P.W.H.Chung, 'Qualitative Analysis of Process Plant Behaviour', Proc. 6th Int. Conf. IEA/AIE, Edinburgh, June 1993, Gordon and Breach Science Publishers.

3.      B.J.Flood and R.J.Harris, 'Hazard Assessment at Full Scale, the Spadeadam Story', IGE Communication 1381, 1988.

4.      H.F.Hopkins and S.E.Lewis, 'TRANSPIRE: an Expert System  Package for the Assessment of the Risks and Hazards of Gas  Transmission Pipelines', Gas Eng. and Mgt, Vol.34, Jan/Feb  1994.

5.      I.Corder and G.D.Fearnehough, 'Prediction of Pipeline Failure  Frequencies', 2nd International Conference on Pipes, Pipelines  and Pipeline Systems, Utrecht, 1987.

6.      N.A.Eisenberg et al. 'Vulnerability Model. A Simulation System  for Assessing Damage Resulting from Marine Spills'. Final  Report June 1975, AD/A015/245.

7.      J.D.Rimington 'Overview of Risk Assessment', in Proceedings of  HSE Conference on Risk Assessment, HSE 1992.

8.      K.Greening, M.J.A.Mihsein, D.Piper and M.W.Vasey, 'The  Development and Application of CHAOS: a Computer Package for  the Consequence and Hazard Assessment of Offshore Structures',  IGE Communication 1493, 1993.

9.      J.Andrews, R.Smith and J.Gregory, 'Procedure to Calculate the  Explosion Frequency for a Module on an Offshore Platform',  Trans.I.Chem.E., Vol.72, Part B, May 1994.

10.     Oil Industry International Exploration and Production Forum,  'Hydrocarbon Leak and Ignition Database', Report No. 11.4/180.

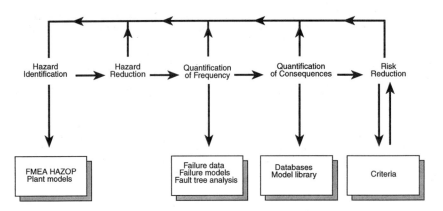

Figure 1. Safety Assessment Procedure

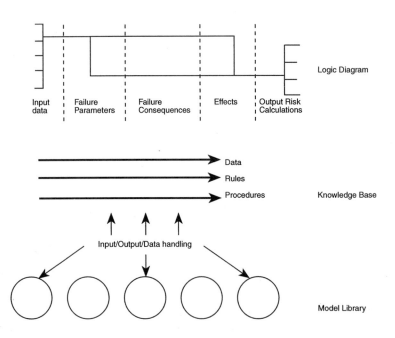

Figure 2. Elements of Knowledge Based Package

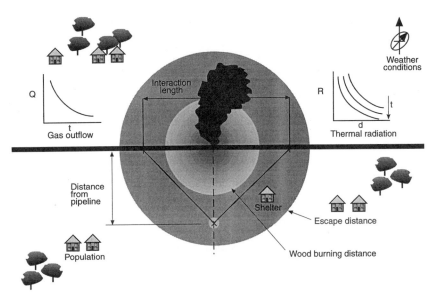

Figure 3. Variables Involved in Pipeline Risk Assessment

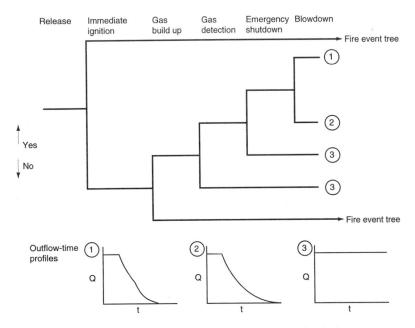

Figure 4. Section of Release Event Tree and Resulting Gas Outflows

RISK METHODOLOGY IN SAFETY ANALYSIS
OF TYPICAL GAS INDUSTRY FACILITIES

LA ME'THODOLOGIQIE DU RISQUE DANS LE PROBLE'ME DE L'ANALYSE DE LA
SURETE' DES INSTALLATIONS TYPIQUES DE L'INDUSTRIE DU GAZ

G.E.Odisharia, V.S.Safonov, A.S.Yedigarov
Research Institute of Natural Gases & Gas Technology, Russia
A.A.Shvyryaev
Lomonosov Moscow State University, Russia

ABSTRACT

The paper presents an analysis of methodological aspects of hazard sources identification and explosive and toxic hazards maps creation for risk assessment of hydrocarbons production, transport, storage and refinery facilities. Risk assessment procedure was performed in view of facility technological peculiarities and climatic-geographical characteristics of a region where a facility is sited. Special attention was paid to a time-space distribution of potential hazard sources and affected individuals and also to factors of direct influence on accident development, type and scale of a damage, such as vapor cloud ignition sources distribution, phisical-chemical transformation of substances, presence and efficiency of alarm-safety systems, "domino" effects etc. Consequences prediction of toxic and explosive chemicals accidental emissions was performed on the base of a complex of original mathematical models (including three-dimensional hydrodynamic numerical models) and computer codes which enable to reproduce probable accidents scenarios and obtain time-space distribution of probable damage with an adequate accuracy. The proposed methodology and computer software were used in practice for a risk assessment of a number of gas industry facilities.

RESUME

Un expose considere des aspects methodiques de l'identification et de l'edification des champs d'un danger potentiel de l'explosion de l'incendie et de l'infection toxique lors de prevois des risques de l'exploitation des entreprises de prodaction de transport, de stockage et de tractement de la matiere premiere hydrocarbonee et aussi des method de calcul et de disposition d'apres le rang des entreprises influencees selon des degres des risques compte tenu des specifications techniques de l'entreprise consideree des conditions climatique set geographique d'une region.
La prevision des cosequences des emissions incidentes des products toxiques et inflammables est realisee a l'aide de l'ensemble des model mathematique d'ocigine (y compris des models tridimentionnels hydrodynamiques numerique) et des programmes d'ordinateur, susceptibles de reconstituer des images probables des incedents et obtenir des distributions spaccales et temporeles du dommage avec precasion suffisante.

## INTRODUCTION

In spite of the significant efforts taken in some countries lately to elaborate the technical safety systems, the industrial emergency parameters have been growing much faster than the production scale. This circumstance confirms that the problem of industry safety increase cannot be solved only by means of technical protection components and demands detailed study of "inner mechanisms" of emergency and accidents as the inherent feature of complicated technological system, possessing potential energy reserve.

In this connection VNIIGAS in co-operation with Moscow State University and some academic and industrial branch scientific-research institutes fulfilled the complex of investigations to work out the methodological foundation and practical analysis of safety and risk parameters of operating the hydrocarbon production, transport, storage and feed processing facilities.

In gas industry there could be observed all the typical emergency processes of chemical technology, including explosions of hydrocarbons clouds, fires of spilled matters and toxic impact upon people and environment. In their essence all those emergencies and accidents can be conventionally subdivided into 2 typical subgroups: Firstly, emergencies, when the potential energy is realized at the very place of occurrence (gas or vapours explosions in the closed rooms and spaces, flying fragments of ruptured vessels, "BLEVE" effect, jet flames, liquid hydrocarbons burning at the limited areas, etc.). This emergency group is defined mainly by technological peculiarities of a facility and physical-chemical characteristics of hazardous materials and depends little or not at all upon the environmental parameters. The damage degree here is determined by the initial energy potential of the facility, however, as a rule, the damage has the limited character and localizes in the zone directly adjoining the emergency area.

The second subgroup includes the emergencies, potential of which is not realized at the initial point; and the emergency development scenario and the degree of impact upon the environment and human beings are significantly determined by the environmental parameters (toxic gases spreading distantly with the wind as well as hydrocarbons cloud, potential sources of burning of various types distribution on the territory and their influence upon the respective exploding transformations and harm induced, etc.).

From the practical viewpoint, the second emergency group represents the greatest complication in the quantitative assessment of the damage and requires elaboration of the special methodical tool.

## LOGICAL DESIGN OF POTENTIAL HAZARD DISTRIBUTION

As it is well-knowing in the world practice the risk is being implied as the mathematical expectation of the certain type of damage for the selected influenced object. The procedure of risk analysis comprises:

-Analysis of the specific features of the facility, dangers identification
and analysis of undesirable occurenses, drawing to the destruction of
equipment or pipelines and into unpredicted releases of hazardous materials into the environment.

-Determination of the probability of the undesirable occurrences ( $\varpi$ ).

-Distinguishing the peculiarities and intensities assessment (W), total
amounts and time of emission of hazardous materials into the
environment for the whole spectrum of the undesired occurrences.

-Determination of specific features and criteria of negative influence of
the "source" upon the environment.

-Substantiation of physical-mathematical models of the initial danger
distribution in the environment.

-Defining the direct and indirect consequences of the emergency
influence upon various objects (i.e. damage), taking into consideration their

space and time distribution around the potential danger source.
-Assessment and analysis of risk parameters for the affected objects.

The distinguishing feature of the proposed method is calculation of potential danger distribution for each facility, based upon the adopted criteria of negative influence upon the various groups of risk, taking into account the technological specifics of the facility and reason-consequence logic of typical accidents occurrences and their development, as well as the probable impact of environmental parameters upon the scale of transfer and the specifics of transformation of the initial danger within space and time framework. Transition to the quantitative estimation of the particular types of damage from the potential emergencies at the facility requires additional consideration of distribution over the territory (in the zone of negative influence) of both: the risk (affected) objects and factors (sources) resulting in the realization of the initial danger, for example, ignition sources for hydrocarbons vapour clouds.

As characteristic examples we can consider the succession of damage analysis in emergency cases with toxic gases emissions and explosion-fire inducing vapours.

The succession of calculations of the territorial distribution of potential danger for people from toxic gas emission is shown on fig.1. At the first stage, concentrations distribution is calculated based upon the scenario of the accident development (fig.1a). Further on, taking into account the specifics of toxic matter physiological influence and the time of the cloud existence, the integral absorbed dose is calculated (fig.1b). The degree of damage is estimated with the use of "probit-function" characterizing the probability of damage depending upon the dose (fig.1c). For the considered case the damage zone (fig.1d,e,f) is characterized by the width of area, where 100% damage is possible. At constructing the territorial distribution of potential danger (fig.1g), meteorological information is observed according to L grades of the wind velocity and 6 classes of atmosphere stability condition. And the probability of damage in some definite point $(r,\theta)$ is determined by summarizing the damage zones according to M - compass points grid of the winds directions repeatability (fig.1g).

$$R_M(r,\theta) = \sum_{v=1}^{M} \left\{ \sum_{l=1}^{L} P_{vl} \sum_{k=1}^{6} (P_k(u_l)) * R(W, u_l, k)/(2\pi r/M) \right\} \qquad (1)$$

where $P_{vl}$  - wind repeatability with velocity $u_l$ in sector $v$
$P_k(u_l)$  - the probability of atmosphere stability class realization
      "k" at the wind velocity $u_l$

$R(W, u_l, k)$  - width of damage zone (100% damage) in section $v$ for the
      distance "r" from the source, depending upon the emission
      rate, wind velocity and class of atmosphere stability.

Due to the fact that in practice we deal with range of various emergency cases (j=1,J), then integral evaluation of potential danger distribution R(x,y) within the territory is obtained by means of summarizing the separate fields for each scenario, taking into account its frequency $\varpi_j$

$$R(x, y) = R(r, \theta) = \sum_{j=1}^{J} \varpi_j * R_{M_j}(r, \theta) \qquad (2)$$

Obtained field of potential danger characterizes the individual damage probability in the concrete point in case of this individual presence in that very point during the selected time interval (field of individual risk).

Further on, taking into account real layout of individuals around the danger source, N-R diagram is calculated (fig.1h), which characterizes integral distribution of the individuals according to the degree of risk in the zone of negative influence of the facility.

The methodological approach under consideration allows also to select concrete factors and directions with maximum impact into the integral risk parameters. While evaluating risk, connected to the expended distribution in the atmosphere of vapour clouds, it was taken into account that damage realization occurs as a rule only at exploding burning of the cloud (fig.2).

Due to the fact that construction of the potential risk fields is carried out in the uniform scale on the real map-graphical basis the account of the actual layout of ignition sources and their type (capacity) becomes of great importance. The field $R_m$ $(r,\theta)$ characterizes the probability of the explosion-dangerous cloud reaching of the particular point of the territory. The worked out algorithms take into account both real layout and specifics of the sources of the clouds ignition at the emergencies of such type.

The closer source to the emission place has influence on "snaping into action" of the next one in succession if their angular sectors $2*L/r_{source}$, (where L- the cloud width and $r_{source}$ - distance to the source of ignition) cross. Then the probability of "n" ignition source snaping into action is defined as

$$P_n^*(r_{source}, \theta_{source}) = P_n * \prod_{i=1}^{n-1} (1 - P_i) \qquad (3)$$

where $P_i$ - the relative probability of the cloud ignition by the sources of various types (the probability of the cloud ignition by the open flame is qualified as equal to "1").

For the ignition sources, acting permanently or coming effective at the moment when the cloud rim reaches them, the second member (S) in the equation (4) is equal to 0. In cases when the ignition source comes effective (inside the cloud) with delay after the cloud reaches the maximum size , at calculating the potential danger the second member is added for $r > r_{source}$ ,which takes into account the possible cloud location at the distances further than $r_{source}$ :

$$P_{MY}(r, \theta) = \sum_{i=1}^{N} P_D(r_{source}, \theta_{source}) * P_i^*(r_{source}, \theta_{source}) + S \qquad (4)$$

where the second member is equal to $S = \sum_{i=1}^{N} P_D(r > r_{source}, \theta_{source}) * P_i^*(r_{source}, \theta_{source})$ , $r_{source}$ , $\theta_{source}$ - coordinates of ignition source, $P_D$ $(r_{source}, \theta_{source})$ - the probability of explosive cloud reaching of various ignition sources.

Due to the mentioned peculiarities, the obtained field of potential hazard has radial form with rays directed to ignition sources.

Succession of carring out the analysis at emergencies with explosive clouds formation is shown in fig.2. And the ignition sources, "snaping into action" when the cloud reaches them, characterize the lower border of the damage scale (fig.2d,f); and the sources "snaping into action" with delay represent the upper limit (fig.2e,g).

For other types of accidents (the accidents of the 1 subgroup) the methodology of the risk level assessment is similar to the one described above.

It's important to emphasize that if in its essence the hazard is potential, then risk can be only of concrete contents. The assessment and analysis of the risk parameters should be done only based upon the real map-graphical foundation, taking into account the concrete space-time distribution around the territory both of the factors of hazard and the effected individuals. Due to the mentioned circumstances, the typical accidents at the similar technological facilities can have significantly different risk levels and damage degree for the technical personnel, regional population and environment.

## MATHEMATICAL MODELLING

Risk assessment of industrial facilities involves consequences prediction of accidental releases of hazardous materials. Practically the only tool available for making such prediction is the mathematical modeling of associated physical processes. It is well known, that such important features of an accident as probable hazardous zone, number of fatalities, etc., can be found if a toxic or explosive gas cloud propagation is determined with an adequate accuracy.

The complex of original mathematical models was developed for consequences predicions, which enable to reproduce probable accidental releases of liquefied or compressed chemical substances from industrial facilities by means of numerical experiments. The complex of developed numerical algorithms and computer codes is based on numerical solution of sets of differential equations which describe thermo-gas dynamics and heat-mass transfer processes running while an accident takes place. Up-to-date concepts of phenomenology of physical effects in question and experimental data in conjunction with original computational methods were use in working out physical and mathematical models and numerical algorithms. In particular, simulation of non-isothermal dense vapour cloud evolution was based on numerical integration of a complete set of Reynolds three-dimensional unsteady nonlinear equations for viscous compressible heat conductive gas in the field of gravity within the scope of algebraic eddy viscosity submodel. The problem of compressed gas blowout dispersion was solved using quasi three-dimensional hydrodynamic jet-diffusion model, which enables to take into account such peculiarities as time varying mass flow rate, presence of ground surface, wind velocity and atmospheric turbulence intensity distribution, etc.. The main advantage of suggested approach for safety analysis is the possibility to reproduce accidental releases of hazardous materials close to reality , and obtain time-space distribution of flow parameters.

The represented methodological approaches and the respective complex of mathematical models and software were approbated while carrying out the risk analysis of some gas industry typical facilities. The results for some of them are reported in short terms below.

## CASE STUDIES

Bovanenkovo gas/condensate field facilities at the Yamal peninsula

Within the frames of the unite dynamic model of geotechnical system functioning and development, the complex investigation of reason-consequence logic of occurrence and development scale of potential accidents and fires including cascade effects at the drilling sites (wells clusters), at gathering pipelines grids and units of complex gas preparation was done. The specific features were also investigated for the negative influence of industrial emissions on the environment: first of all on the flora, the vegetation covering, the area (mainly moss and lichen), having the function of heat protection for the permafrost. Based upon the results of investigations, the economical and ecological harm level prediction was compiled, related to the emergencies at technological facilities of the industrial zone, and the complex of preventive measures is substantiated for the equipment reliability increase. The predicted dynamics of falling out and restoration (on basis of new plant types) of the flora on the territory of the industrial zone (35 km*45 km), related to the operation of booster compressor stations, has been calculated. Fig.3 shows the dynamics of the areal surface coverage change with the main types of vegetation at different stages of the field development.

It is found out that for the extreme conditions of the Far North there is obvious relationship between the vegetation falling out, frost soil melting and increase of emergency level at the facilities of the industrial complex.

Main Gas and Condensate Pipelines

As a typical example we took the Yamal Centre main gas pipeline which has a diameter of 1420 mm at an operating pressure 75 atm., a total length 2300 km, and spans different climatic zones, including the zone of permafrost. The whole length of gas pipeline was subdivided according to the arrangement based upon the influence of natural-climatic and engineering-geological factors on the distribution of expected emergency faults along the route. Here, first of all taken into the consideration was presence of frosted soils, marshlands, rivers, valleys along the route , types of soil and their bearing ability. Taken into account was also the impact of the human industrial activity, location of compressor stations and technological blocks of gas pipelines and degree of transport infrastructure development.

Taking into account the influence factors, the anticipated frequency of emergency failures was determined, development scenarios and the possible consequences of accidents for the population, inhabiting the area adjoinig to the Yamal-Centre gas pipeline route , and environment (forest, crops). It was found out that the value of individual risk for the population is below the level $10^{-6}$ /yer, adopted in the world practice as the conventional limit of the acceptable risk. Stated also is that the expected material damage for the forest and agricultural crops from the potential fires in case of accidents at the gas pipelines is significantly lower than the actual values of these types of damage, related to the ignitions from the lightning , fires induced by human activity, etc.

The methodical peculiarities of risk evaluation for the pipelines pumping thermodynamically non-stable hydrocarbons and liquefied gases, breaking the sealing integrity of which can induce the formation and distribution in the space of explosion-hazardous clouds, are shown at the example of safe parameters analysis for the Minnibaevo-Kazan butane pipeline with diameter of 300 mm and length of 300 km . The product pipeline goes close to the big amount of inhabited settlements and crosses multiple other pipelines and transport communications. Fig.4 illustrates the distribution along the route of individual risk. Analysis has shown relatively high level of risk at the product line operation and also high level of possible economic expenses , related to the compensation for the potential damage to the population and personal property.

Processing facilities

Hydrocarbons feed processing facilities operation risk analysis have been perfomed on the examples of Orenburg Gas Processing Plant and Astrakhan Gas Complex (AGC), the specifics of which is processing of significant gas and condencate volumes with great $H_2S$ content. Within the framework of the investigation the surface and subsurface pipelines of sour gas and non-stable condensate, technological units and vessels, field facilities of AGC were under consideration; as well as reservoir facilities (tank farm) for condensate processing stable products storage and some other. As risky groups the facilities personnel and the population of the nearly settlements were considered . Fig.5 shows the hazards distribution around the territory of AGC, connected to the potential emission of sour gas. It's shown (fig.6) that for the regional population the risk level from accidents at AGC facilities is close to acceptable. Should be noted that for the various settlements the impact of different AGC facilities into the integral risk is inhomogeneous that explains the differentiated approach for the working out of organizational measures in conditions of emergency situation.

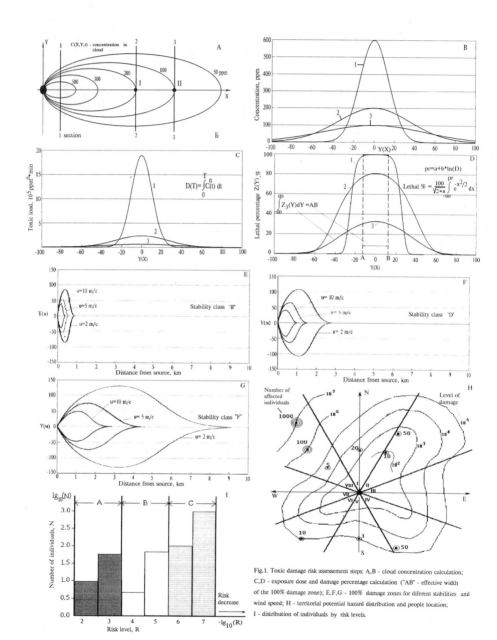

Fig.1. Toxic damage risk assessement steps: A,B - cloud concentration calculation; C,D - exposure dose and damage percentage calculation ("AB" - effective width of the 100% damage zone); E,F,G - 100% damage zones for diferent stabilities and wind speed; H - territorial potential hazard distribution and people location; I - distribution of individuals by risk levels.

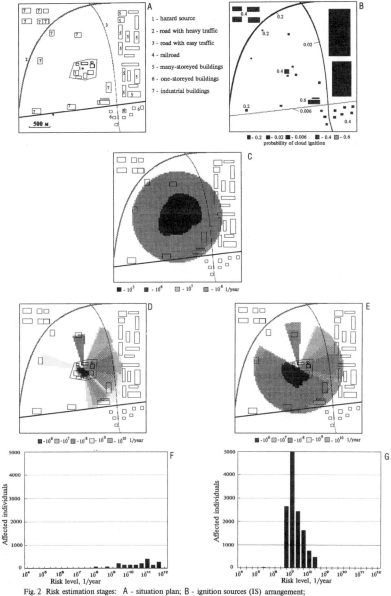

Fig. 2 Risk estimation stages:  A - situation plan; B - ignition sources (IS) arrangement;
C - covering zone probability map; D - risk map for constant IS; E - risk map for occasional IS;
F,G  - affected persons distribution by risk level for the cases "D" and "E"  accordingly

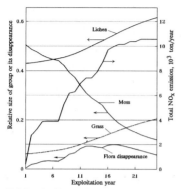

Fig.3. Dynamics of flora changing on Bovanenkovo gas field
as a result of $NO_x$ pollution.

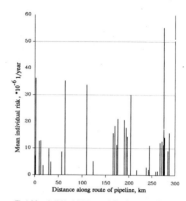

Fig.4. Mean individual risk for population alone route of pipeline
Minnibaevo - Kazan (butan, D=300 mm).

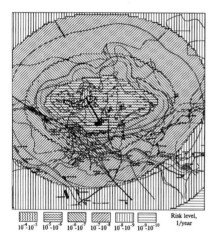

Fig.5. Integral potential toxic hazard distribution from accidents with $H_2S$
emmision at the Astrakhan gas condensate complex.

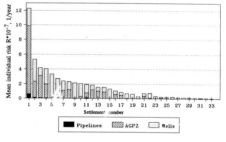

Fig.6. Influence of AGCC technical systems on the individual risk for

various populated areas

**Study of a Methodology of Safety Assessment
for High-Pressure Natural Gas Pipelines**

**Méthodologie d'étude de sécurité
des canalisations de gaz naturel à haute pression**

by G. Hamaïde\*, M. Cazade\*, K. Schwier\*\*, G. Vareschi\*\*\*

( \* ) Gaz de France - R&D Division, Saint Denis, France
Production and Transmission Division, Paris, France
( \*\* ) Ruhrgas AG, Technical Controlling Division, Essen, Germany
( \*\*\* ) SNAM - R&D Division, Safety Section, Milan, Italy

ABSTRACT

Gas installations are designed to ensure a maximum level of safety, but as in any industry, there is still a possibility of an incident occurring even if the probability of having an incident is constantly decreasing.

A methodology has been developed to assess the safety of high pressure natural gas pipelines.

A deterministic analysis gives the failure modes and their consequences.

Potential damage to people and structures are quantified requiring a survey of the urbanisation around the pipeline. These methods indicate the population distribution around the pipeline and the definition of special buildings.

The failure frequency is determined from a historical database on incidents and with an analytical mechanical model which takes into account urbanisation and land use. The present methodology allows both a deterministic safety assessment study to be performed and leads to determine: individual risk, inhabitant risk, societal risk, threshold values and cost/benefit ratios for safety measures.

RESUME

Les installations gazières sont construites pour assurer un niveau de sécurité maximal, mais comme dans toute industrie, la possibilité d'avoir un incident subsiste même si cette probabilité est en régression.

A partir des données sur la canalisation et d'une base de données d'accidents, les modes d'accidents sont déterminés. Le type d'accident ainsi que sa probabilité d'occurrence sont analysés.

Une analyse déterministe permet d'obtenir les conséquences physiques de chaque type d'incident. Les effets sur les personnes et les structures sont définis par différentes méthodes qui requièrent un relevé d'urbanisation, la distribution de population ainsi que l'utilisation des bâtiments.

La fréquence d'accident est déterminée à partir d'une base de données d'accidents et d'un modèle analytique tenant compte de l'urbanisation et l'utilisation du sol. La méthodologie permet d'obtenir une analyse déterministe des conséquences, le risque individuel, le risque pour un habitant, le risque sociétal, les valeurs "seuil" et le rapport coûts/réduction du risque.

## INTRODUCTION

Gas installations are designed to ensure a maximum level of safety. Through a good engineering experience, gas industry can claim a remarkable and very low number of incidents. Nevertheless, there is still a possibility of an incident occurring.

Prompted by a growing market, gas companies are constantly concerned with improving the safety of their high pressure natural gas pipelines.

To improve the gas installations safety, a methodology has been developed in a collaborative project. the objectives were to define the risks associated with pipeline operations and also to identify the key factors that influence the safety. This analysis will allow to optimise the allocation of resources to increase the level of safety in an efficient process and to avoid gross disproportion between the cost of the countermeasures and the risk reduction they would achieve.

## THE METHODOLOGY

### Description

According to the principle "many roads lead to Rome" this methodology was developed to allow both a deterministic safety assessment as well as a probabilistic analysis, i.e. quantitative risk calculations by determining the possible types of failure, their probabilities and damage to people or property for each type of failure.

The methodology follows a logic chart (figure 1) to estimate different results.

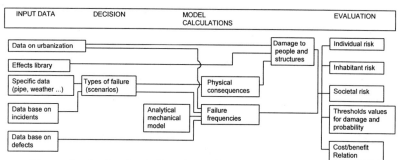

**Figure 1. Logic chart for the safety assessment methodology**

From the specific data on the pipeline (diameter, pressure, thickness ...) and from a historical data base on incidents, a number of failure modes are determined. Both the type of failure and the probability of occurrence are considered.

The physical consequences (flowrate, heat radiation, over-pressure, missiles ...) for each failure mode are calculated.

Damage to people and structures is quantified by different methods which are applied to the real surroundings of the pipeline, thus requiring a survey of the urbanisation around the pipeline. This survey is made by remote data acquisition techniques or by using numerical topographic databases. The present methodology incorporates the possibility of escaping when considering the hazard to people. These methods indicate the population distribution around the pipeline and the definition of special buildings (distance from the pipeline, number of people, fraction of time of person being present).

The failure frequency is determined from a historical database on incidents and with an analytical mechanical model which takes into account urbanisation and land use in the area around the pipeline.

The present methodology allows performing both a deterministic and a probabilistic safety assessment study depending on the needs of the operator, and leads to the following results :

Individual risk. Risk associated with the pipeline for a man standing permanently at a given distance from the pipeline.

Inhabitant risk. Risk associated with a pipeline for an inhabitant living at a given distance from the pipeline. That risk is weighed by probabilities of presence.

Societal risk. Societal risk is defined as the probability to have a certain number of casualties due to a pipeline incident for a given pipeline. Societal risk is calculated by considering the population in the area around pipelines. Societal risk can be expressed with different forms : number of fatalities and probability as a function of the position of the incident along the pipeline ; for the whole pipeline, frequency (F) of an incident leading to more than N fatalities as a function of N (F/N curves) ; for the whole pipeline, a single figure giving the statistical expectation value of fatalities per unit time (year) anywhere due to a pipeline incident.

Threshold values. Assessment criteria may be also threshold values for the maximum credible damage or probability of occurrence.

Cost/benefit analysis. Analysis that links for example the benefit of some additional solutions in terms of societal risk and the cost of this solution, allowing an optimisation of the resources available for further improving the level of safety of the pipeline.

Types of Failure and Incident Frequencies

A historical database for incidents on transmission networks in Europe shows that the probability of an incident occurring is very low and this probability is constantly decreasing (1).

From this data base and from the knowledge acquired by gas companies on safety matters, it can be shown that primarily two types of failure must be considered for high pressure natural gas pipelines : a full rupture and a puncture.

The most likely event that is able to cause these types of failure on a gas pipeline is external interference that accounts for up to 50% of pipeline incidents (1). The other causes have a lower influence:

- external interference:    52%
- corrosion:    14%
- construction defect:    17%
- ground movement:    7%
- others:    10%

At first stage, the project was concentrated on the influence of external interference because of its major weight. For the others cause, the incident frequencies are directly deducted from the figures given above.

When looking for more detailed data that would take in account the type of pipeline (diameter, thickness, grade, depth of cover ...) and the environment (rural or urban area, land use ...), the small number of incidents having occurred in high pressure natural gas pipelines makes a statistical evaluation difficult.

Thus a model has been developed to predict for a specific pipeline the incident frequency due to external interference depending on the pipeline characteristics and environment.

From the environment data (urban or rural area, land use ...) the types of machines that are likely to work in the surroundings, are defined. Then the probability to meet a specific type of machine is deducted from a data base on the number of existing machines.

Whether or not the machine is able to create a puncture or a rupture, is determined by the pipe characteristics (diameter; thickness, grade ...).

The incident frequency is then calculated in combining the probability to have the machine working close to the pipeline and its ability to damage the pipeline.

Deterministic Analysis of the Physical Consequences of a Gas Release

When a loss of containment for a high pressure natural gas pipeline occurs the most severe consequences are due to the thermal heat radiation if the gas is ignited.

Different models have been developed to estimate these physical consequences of a gas release.

Flowrate. The flowrate is calculated using a model which solves the basic Navier-Stokes equations of fluid mechanics. The system is completed with an equation of state.

The model gives the evolution in time of the flowrate in case of a rupture as well as in case of a puncture.

Thermal heat radiation. The thermal heat radiation is predicted with an integral steady state model. The received heat flux is obtained as a function of the distance between the flame and the target.

The computer program developed is flexible enough to enable easy replacement of individual models and to add models for additional failure types and additional categories of consequences if need be.

Damage on People and Property

Little is known on the effects of thermal heat radiation on structures such as individual houses, offices buildings...

So it was assumed that the resistance threshold of structures is equivalent to the mean value for wood spontaneous ignition. If the received thermal heat radiation is less than this threshold value (25 kW/m$^2$) the structure can be considered as a safe place. Above this value, the structure is no more a shelter.

This approach is a very simple one but is conservative because in fact a building cannot be completely burnt out in a second.

To study the effect of thermal heat radiation on people, experiments have been undertaken in laboratories. It is clear that during these experiments only part of the body was exposed to the heat flux and only the pain threshold was determined. So, it was decided to use a method based on statistical observation of incidents. The method is the method of probit with Eisenberg formulation (2).

To estimate the effect on people, it is not a threshold approach that is used but a dosage approach.

For people outdoors at the time of ignition, the only possibility is to escape in the best direction, radially away from the centre of the fire, to get a safe place : a shelter or at a distance where the thermal radiation is less than 1.5 kW/m$^2$. It is also assumed that they need a reaction delay before taking a decision for escaping.

For people indoors, the building is a shelter as long as the received thermal radiation is less than 25 kW/m$^2$. If the heat flux is higher, the dosage is calculated in the same way as for people outdoors.

Thus the relations used to estimate the dosage are:

$$dosage = \int_{escape} I^{4/3}(D(t), t)dt$$

$$D(t) = D_0 + v_{escape} \cdot (t - t_{reaction})$$

| | |
|---|---|
| I | received heat flux (W/m$^2$) |
| D(t) | distance (m) to the rupture at time t (s) |
| D$_o$ | initial distance to the rupture (m) |
| v$_{escape}$ | escape velocity (m/s) |
| t$_{reaction}$ | reaction delay (s) |

From the dosage, a probit value is obtained by Eisenberg relation :

$$probit = -14.9 + 2.56 \cdot \ln(\frac{dosage}{10^4})$$

Finally, the probit value gives the percentage of lethality (see figure 2).

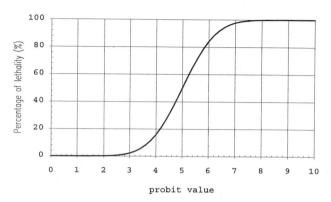

**Figure 2. Relation between probit and percentage of lethality**

Risk Assessments and priorities on Safety Measures

The deterministic analysis of the consequences of a failure combined with the analysis of potential damages provides the percentage of lethality as a function of the distance to the pipe. To determine the number of casualties that would happen in case of a incident, precise data are required on the urbanisation around the pipe and on the number of people actually present.

<u>Urbanisation data collecting.</u> To know the number of people in the surroundings of the pipeline, it is necessary to determine the type of land use or building use close to the pipe. Two methods have been identified which give these data : a satellite survey or a plane survey. In fact the photographs obtained by satellite or plane are then processed to give the position of buildings, the people distribution and the land use.

Then for each type of building (individual house, school , hospital, public building) or land use (cultivation, forest ..), there is a number of people associated with a probability to be present. for example, in a building where there is only offices, it is possible to know the number of people and to assume that there is nobody during the night time.

<u>Individual risk.</u> Individual risk is the probability per unit time (year) of a person being permanently present at a specified location, to become a casualty due to a pipeline incident.

$$IR = \int_{pipeline} (F_{incident} \cdot P)$$

$F_{incident}$          incident frequency as a function of the position of the incident along the pipeline.

P                  percentage of lethality (for people outside or inside) as function of the initial position of a person and the position of the incident along the pipeline.

Inhabitant risk. Inhabitant risk is the probability per unit time (year) of a person living at a specified location, to become a casualty due to a pipeline incident.

The inhabitant risk differs from the individual risk only by a factor taking into account a possible absence of the person some time.

$$IHR = f_{inside} \cdot IR_{inside} + f_{outside} \cdot IR_{outside}$$

$IR_{outside}$    Individual risk for people outside
$IR_{inside}$    Individual risk for people inside
$f_{outside}$    fraction of time of person being outside
$f_{inside}$    fraction of time of person being inside

Societal risk. Societal risk is the statistical expectation value of fatalities per unit time (year) anywhere due to a pipeline incident, for a specific pipeline section.

$$SR = \int_{pipeline} \int_{A} (d \cdot F_{incident} \cdot P)$$

A      total area surrounding the pipeline
d      population density.

Threshold values. Incidents occurring at a probability exceeding a certain value are not tolerable, even if the damage caused by them is quite small.

On the other hand, incidents occurring at probabilities below a certain other value are normally regarded as not being relevant for planning counter measures. What has just been stated for probabilities also hold true for damage. Minor damage is usually accepted even at high probabilities, whereas catastrophic damage is usually not accepted even at very low probabilities.

The model identifies for a given pipeline in a given environment the sections along the pipeline, where the damage or probabilities exceed certain threshold values, and the sections, where damage and probability undershoot, certain threshold values.

Cost/Benefit analysis. The model gives a comparison between the risk reduction due to different counter measures and their cost to help the operator to make a decision among the different possibilities (3). For a section of pipeline defined as a part of the pipeline having constant parameters, the reduction of the risk associated to each countermeasure or a combination of countermeasures is determined. The costs for these countermeasures are calculated.

APPLICATION

Safety Assessment Tool

A computer program has been developed for conducting the assessment of the safety of high pressure natural gas pipeline. This computer program is based on the logic chart of the methodology. It can be described as a shell inside which modules or computing programs have been incorporated. The shell defines the user surface, the relations between the working or computing programs and the storing of the data.

The modules are the computing programs that calculate the consequences
(flowrate, heat radiation,...), the failure frequencies, the effects,
the risks, ...

Some examples

   Calculation have been undertaken on a real pipeline.

   Urbanisation survey. Figure 3 gives an example of the data obtained
on the urbanisation (different types of building, land use ...)

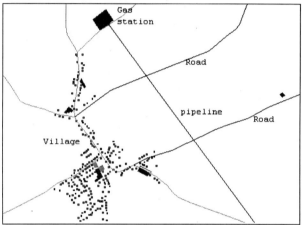

**Figure 3. Data on urbanisation**

   Individual risk. Individual risk is represented on figure 4 as a
function of the distance to the pipeline for a 800 mm diameter pipeline
at 67 bar in case of a rupture.

   Inhabitant risk. Inhabitant risk has been calculated in function of
the distance to the pipeline (Figure 4).

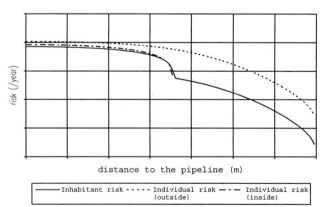

**Figure 4. Individual and inhabitant risk**

Societal risk. The urbanisation data have been collected along a certain 40 km long pipeline. The number of potential casualties along this pipeline is presented in figure 5.

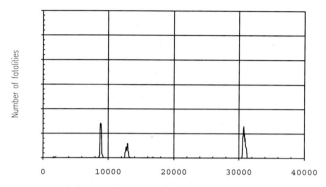

Position of the incident along the pipeline (m)

**Figure 5. Number of potential casualties**

CONCLUSION

Applying the present methodology indicates to the operator possible differences in the safety level of different pipe sections, shows where first to allocate the available resources for further improvements in safety and allows a sound judgement of the effectiveness of additional safety measures. The nowadays widely discussed safety distances for high pressure natural gas pipelines, for example, can be shown to have very limited effectiveness and are inferior to alternatives from both a technical and an economic viewpoint.

This methodology allows the level of safety achieved with natural gas transmission networks to be defined and the relevant parameters for the safety of a pipeline evaluated. It helps management to improve the level of safety of such a network.

REFERENCES

(1)    European Gas Pipeline Incident Data Group IGU Milan, June 1994.

(2)    Eisenberg N.A. and al, Final report AD/A015/245, National Technical Information Service, June 1975

(3)    Merz H.A. and Bohnenblust H., Second World Congress on Safety Science, Budapest.

FATIGUE CRACKING FROM A NOTCH:   EFFECTS OF RESIDUAL STRESSES

FISSURATION EN FATIGUE A PARTIR D'UNE ENTAILLE:   EFFETS DES CONTRAINTES RESIDUELLES

R. BATISSE [*], Y. MEZIERE[*], C. MOKHDANI[**], A. PINEAU[**]
*Gaz de France, France
**Ecole des Mines de Paris, URA CNRS 866, France

ABSTRACT

The Gaz de France transmission network is subject to mechanical damage of the gouge type due to the interference by excavators.
A new criterion of fatigue crack initiation was established to estimate the residual life of damaged pipelines subjected to varying gas pressures. The validation of the criterion gave satisfactory results, although without taking into account the possible existence of residual stresses in applying the crack initiation criterion and the propagation laws.
After a short presentation of the crack initiation criterion and its validation, this article will examine, in quantitative terms, the role played by residual stresses on fatigue cracking. The study utilized laboratory specimens which had known residual stresses and were loaded in fatigue.

RESUME

Le réseau de transport du Gaz de France peut être sujet à des agressions mécaniques de type "griffures" dues à des impacts de pelles mécaniques.
Un nouveau critère d'amorçage de fissuration par fatigue a été établi pour estimer la durée de vie résiduelle des canalisations endommagées soumises à des pressions variables de gaz. La validation du critère a donné des résultats satisfaisants sans pour autant prendre en compte l'existence éventuelle de contraintes résiduelles dans l'application du critère d'amorçage et des lois de propagation.
Après une brève présentation du critère d'amorçage et de sa validation, cet article s'intéresse de manière quantitative au rôle joué par les contraintes résiduelles sur la fissuration par fatigue. L'étude met en oeuvre des éprouvettes de laboratoire comportant des contraintes résiduelles bien contrôlées et sollicitées en fatigue.

## INTRODUCTION

Machinery on work sites may cause "gouge only" or "gouge in dent" type damage on pipelines in service. To lower maintenance costs without impairing pipeline safety, the nocivity of gouge must be quantified, particularly as regards fatigue loading, because the transmission network is subjected to gas pressures varying between 40 bar and 67.7 bar.

One approach to fatigue cracking was chosen in order to obtain a crack initiation criterion meeting the following conditions:

      - ease of use
      - applicability over the entire range of pipeline operation, from low cycle fatigue up to $10^5$ cycles.

The criterion was successfully validated through comparison with the results of tests subjecting damaged pipes to fluctuating internal pressure. However, the possible existence of residual stresses in the damaged zones had thus far been ignored. The residual stresses may have originated with the creation of the defect or as a result of the shaping of the pipe. Thus, it is important to measure their effects not only on crack initiation but also on its propagation.

After a brief review of the crack initiation criterion and its validation, we will deal with the impact of residual stresses on that criterion and on the laws of propagation, according to an experimental methodology using laboratory specimens.

## 1. THE CRACK INITIATION CRITERION AND ITS VALIDATION

The crack initiation criterion chosen was deduced from a local elastic analysis of crack initiation proposed by DEVAUX and al [1] for grade 316 L stainless steel. Supported by the work of ERDOGAN and SIH [2], these authors linked the number of crack-initiation cycles Na to the stress variation $\Delta\sigma_{\theta\theta}$ computed in elasticity at a characteristic distance d from the defect. The notion of characteristic distance had already been utilized by WILLIAMS and EWING [3] in studying PMMA rupture. This method linking Na to $\Delta\sigma_{\theta\theta}(d)$ was used in the nuclear industry by MASSON [4] to predict crack initiation in sleeves subjected to repeated thermal shock.

More recently, MOKHDANI [5] applied this local approach to an API X65 grade ferrito-pearlitic steel used in gas transmission pipelines. The criterion $\Delta\sigma_{\theta\theta}(d)$ as a function of Na was established using stress-relieved CHARPY type specimens loaded in 4-point bending (Figure 1).

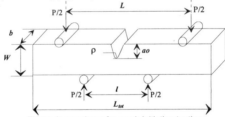

Figure 1:  specimen for crack-initiation testing

A potential drop technique detected the presence of a crack 0.1 mm long, which was the length selected conventionally to obtain the number of crack-initiation cycles Na. The stress variation $\Delta\sigma_{\theta\theta}$ at distance d was computed in elasticity, either numerically by bidimensional finite elements meshing of the specimen, or by the CREAGER formula [6] for notch radii under 0.5 mm. The characteristic distance d is the distance at which, for a given number of crack-initiation cycles Na, the stress variation $\Delta\sigma_{\theta\theta}$ is the same whatever the notch geometry, was determined to be 44 µm. The resulting master line for X65 steel is represented in Figure 2.

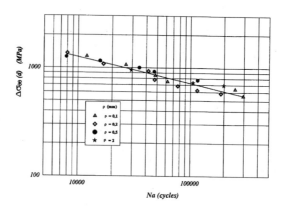

<u>Figure 2</u>: crack-initiation criterion for grade X65

Damaged pipes with idealized "notch only" or "notch-in-dent" type defects were subjected to fluctuating internal pressure of between 40 bar and 70 bar to validate the criterion. The testing was conducted up to a maximum of 30,000 cycles. When the pipes did not break before 30,000 cycles, a metallurgical inspection was performed to measure the depth of the crack from the notch root.

Alongside the testing on pipes, the measured transverse geometries of the defects were taken into account in a bidimensional numerical computation in elasticity to determine the stress variation $\Delta\sigma_{\theta\theta}$ at distance d=44 μm from the notch root. The number of crack-initiation cycles Na corresponding to a 0.1 mm-long crack was then deduced directly from the criterion in Figure 2. To obtain the total number of cycles, we added the number of propagation cycles to Na and computed it by integrating the PARIS law, established on a stress-relieved metal for a load ratio R=0.10 (see below), on the basis of a crack between 0.1 mm long and the actual measured length or a critical length $a_c$ for pipes having burst before 30,000 cycles. Figure 3 compares the results for the number of observed cycles and for the total computed number of cycles.

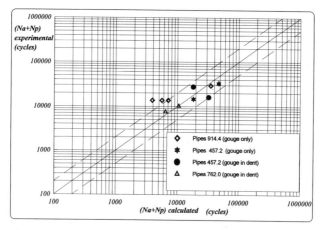

<u>Figure 3</u>: validation of the crack-initiation criterion on the pipes

These results show a good agreement between the observed and the calculated number of cycles to failure. However some scatter is observed. The following assumptions were made to explain this scatter:

- The actual transverse geometry of the defect is not known with sufficient accuracy, in particular the radius of curvature at the tip of the notch. The assumption is very realistic because it is true for the points furthest from the bisector. Moreover, the crack-initiation criterion has been shown to be highly sensitive when applied to the defect's actual geometry.

- Some of the pipes chosen for the validation were grade X42 and X60, unlike the grade X65 which was chosen for the crack-initiation criterion. In reality, there is little likelihood of the steel grade causing the differences observed, because recent work has shown no sensitivity of the criterion to a low-resistance grade such as A42 and grade X65 [7].
   - The effects, not taken into account, of the possible presence of residual stresses in the damaged zones. This assumption is tested in more detail in this article.

## 2. EFFECT OF RESIDUAL STRESSES ON CRACK-INITIATION CRITERION

### 2.1. Experimental procedure and results

Residual stresses were created in CHARPY type notched specimens, which were first stress-relieved after machining of the notches and then mechanically pre-loaded under 4-point bending. The stress-relieving was achieved by holding the specimens at 600°C for 8 hours, in accordance with CANONICO's recommendations [8]. Depending on whether the notched portion was pre-stressed in tension or compression, the residual stresses were either compressive or tensile at the notch root (Figure 4).

(a): residual compressive stresses

(b): residual tensile stresses

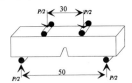 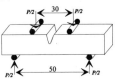

Figure 4: introduction of residual stresses

The specimens with residual compressive stresses in the notched portion were labelled PC, while those with residual tensile stresses were labelled PT. Table 1 lists the preloading and fatigue test conditions.

| Specimen | Radius at notch root ρ (mm) | Preloading (kN) | Pmax/Pmin (kN) | Frequency f (Hz) |
|---|---|---|---|---|
| PT1 |  | 8,5 | -0,5/-5 | 10 |
| PT2 |  | 11,9 | -0,35/-3,5 | 10 |
| PT3 |  | 7,5 | -0,35/-3,5 | 10 |
| PT4 | 0,2 | 7,5 | -0,28/-2,8 | 10 |
| PT5 |  | 7,5 | -0,26/-2,6 | 10 |
| PT6 |  | 7,5 | -0,25/-2,5 | 10 |
| PC1 |  | 8 | -0,5/-5 | 10 |
| PC2 |  | 7,5 | -0,45/-4,5 | 10 |
| PC3 | 0,2 | 7,5 | -0,4/-4 | 10 |
| PC4 |  | 7,5 | --0,35/-3,75 | 10 |
| PC5 |  | 7,5 | -0,35/-3,5 | 10 |

Table 1: loading conditions of specimens PC and PT for crack-initiation testing

The specimens with residual compressive stresses at the notch root were generally loaded more heavily. The results of the crack-initiation tests are given in Table 2.

| Specimen | Number of cycles for $\Delta a=100\mu m (V/Vo=1.01)$ | $\Delta\sigma_{99}(d = 44\mu m)$ (MPa) |
|---|---|---|
| PT1 | 27000 | 972 |
| PT2 | 119000 | 680 |
| PT3 | 119970 | 680 |
| PT4 | 295000 | 544 |
| PT5 | 724936 | 484 |
| PT6 | 3470400 | 515 |
| PC1 | 35200 | 930 |
| PC2 | 52000 | 875 |
| PC3 | 117000 | 778 |
| PC4 | 184718 | 729 |
| PC5 | 1955005 | 680 |

Table 2: results of the crack-initiation tests

Figure 5 gives the master curves of the criterion corresponding to the stress-relieved state and to the states containing residual compressive and tensile stresses at notch root. For the stress-relieved state, the curve is like that of the criterion in figure 2, but extends to the higher fatigue strength ranges.

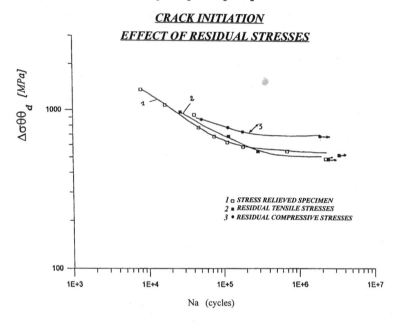

### CRACK INITIATION
### EFFECT OF RESIDUAL STRESSES

*1 □ STRESS RELIEVED SPECIMEN*
*2 ■ RESIDUAL TENSILE STRESSES*
*3 ● RESIDUAL COMPRESSIVE STRESSES*

Figure 5: effect of residual stresses on fatigue crack initiation

These curves show that introducing residual compressive stresses leads to a significant increase in the number of crack initiation cycles beyond $10^5$ cycles. Residual tensile stresses, on the other hand, do not modify the fatigue strength curve. The latter result is less obvious and must be interpreted.

2.2. Interpretation of the effect of residual stresses

Using numerical simulation, we were able to compute the residual stresses at the notch root and estimate the relaxation of the initial stresses during fatigue loading. A model of kinematic and non-linear isotropic work hardening with superposition succeeded in satisfactorily reproducing all the low cycle fatigue tests performed on a grade X60 similar to grade X65. The details of the approach are described in [5].

Case of initial residual compressive stresses (figure 6):

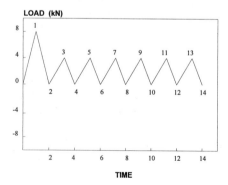

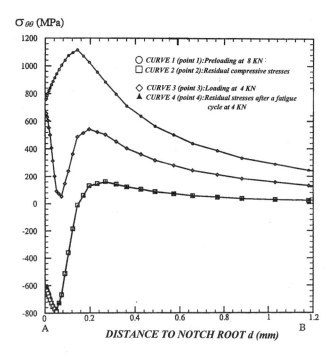

Figure 6: Results of numerical computation of residual compressive stresses

After tensile preloading at 8 kN (curve 1, point 1), the residual stresses were compressive (curve 2, point 2). Then a subsequent loading at 4kN caused limited plastic deformation at the notch root (curve 3, point 3). Hence curve 4 shows that unloading at 0 kN (curve 4, point 4) did not change the range of initial residual stresses represented by curve 2. This means that, after a fatigue cycle, the specimen conserved the initial residual compressive stresses at the notch root.

Case of initial residual tensile stresses (figure 7):

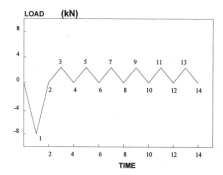

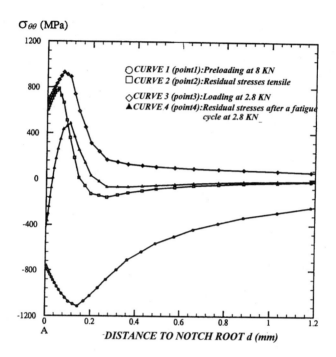

Figure 7:  Results of the numerical computations of residual tensile stresses

Compressive preloading at - 8 kN (curve 1, point 1) introduced residual tensile stresses after unloading (curve 2, point 2). Curve 3 shows that subsequent fatigue loading at 2.8 kN in this case caused significant plastic deformation at the notch root (curve 3, point 3). After unloading, the yield point was substantially lower (curve 4, point 4) and the initial residual tensile stresses were thus considerably relaxed after a fatigue cycle (comparison of curves 4 and 2). At the characteristic distance of 44 μm, the residual stresses were close to zero after a fatigue cycle. As was demonstrated, this result did not change even after a number of subsequent fatigue cycles [5]. Hence initial residual tensile stresses have no effect on the crack initiation criterion.

To summarize, the initial residual stresses at notch root are not changed unless subsequent loadings cause significant plastic deformation. This condition is achieved only when the residual stresses are compressive and the subsequent fatigue loadings are minor. This is why the master curve in figure 2 was modified only slightly by the initial residual compressive or tensile stresses within the pipeline operating range (< $10^5$ cycles). At this point, we need to examine whether the initial residual stresses have a significant effect on the laws of propagation.

## 3. EFFECT OF THE RESIDUAL STRESSES ON THE LAWS OF PROPAGATION

### 3.1. Experimental procedures and results

The residual stresses were introduced by subjecting unnotched stress-relieved bars to 4-point bending. After this pre-bending, the relatively shallow notches (length 0.6 mm) were machined, first to keep relaxation to a minimum and redistribute the residual stresses and second to avoid problems of plasticity due to the thinness of the specimens. Specimens on which the notches were machined on the side with residual compressive stresses were labelled PC and those on which the notches were machined on the side with residual tensile stresses were labelled PT. Figure 8 gives the bar geometries and the preloading conditions.

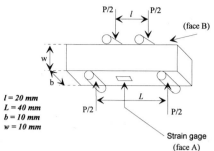

Figure 8:  Conditions of bar preloading in bending

Two bars were preloaded at 27 kN (PT1 and PC1) and two at 29 kN (PT2 and PC2). Table 3 gives the conditions for the fatigue testing. It should be noted that the tests were conducted at a load ratio of R=Pmin/Pmax=0.10.

| Specimen | Pmax(kN)/Pmin(kN) | f (Hz) |
|----------|-------------------|--------|
| PT1 | -0,8/-8 | 10 |
| PT2 | -0,7/-7 | 10 |
| PC1 | -1/-10 | 10 |
| PC2 | -1,2/-12 | 10 |

Table 3:  Conditions of fatigue loading of specimens PT and PC

Figure 9 shows the propagation curves corresponding to the stress-relieved state (results corresponding to the indicated scatter and again obtained with R=0.10), the compressive state and the tensile state.

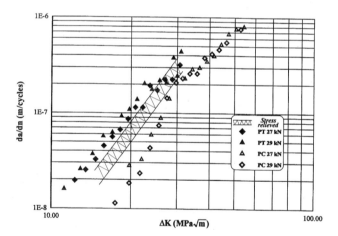

Figure 9:  Effect of residual stresses on crack propagation rates

Figure 9 shows that introducing residual compressive or tensile stresses in the specimens had respectively a retarding and an accelerating effect on propagation rate. This effect was only pronounced at low propagation rates (around $10^{-7}$ m/cycles). The explanation for this phenomenon may lie in the introduction of an effective stress intensity factor $\Delta$Keff.

3.2. Interpretation of the effect of residual stresses

The factor $\Delta$Keff is taken as the stress intensity factor that actually helps propagate the crack. For that reason, $\Delta$Keff takes into account the stress intensity factor Kr related to the residual stresses as well as Kouv related to the closure of the crack. Figure 10 illustrates the three configurations studied.

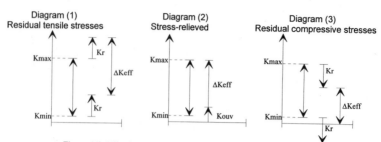

Figure 10: Effective stress intensity factor in the three configurations

- Case of stress-relieved specimens: When the loading tends toward zero, the crack closes and no longer propagates when K falls below Kouv. Thus:

$$\Delta Keff = Kmax - Kouv$$

- Case of specimens with residual tensile stresses: Due to the residual tensile stresses, the crack is open enough for Kouv to be zero. $\Delta Keff$ is then equal to $\Delta K$:

$$\Delta Keff = Kmax - Kmin$$

- Case of specimens with residual compressive stresses: When Kr is large, the material may undergo some rubbing effect due to the interference of the crack lips, in which case Kouv is zero:

$$\Delta Keff = Kmax - Kr$$

These three cases show that the values of $\Delta Keff$ for specimens PT are higher that the $\Delta Keff$ values for specimens PC. This explains the differences in propagation rate observed in figure 9: for the same $\Delta K$, the crack propagation rates are higher for specimens PT than for specimens PC.

Kouv may be estimated experimentally by plotting the applied load curve as a function of the crack mouth displacement δ [9]. MOKHDANI [5] estimated Kouv indirectly by comparing the curves in figure 9 corresponding to the PT specimens to the specimens stress-relieved to the lower $\Delta K$. The Kouv found accordingly has a value of 4.2 MPa√m, close to the results obtained on steels of a similar strength [10].

Kr was deduced either through numerical bidimensional finite element computation or through the integration of the residual stress range using a weight function given by TADA and al [11].

This time, we plot the values of the measured propagation velocity as a function of $\Delta Keff$, which gives us a single curve representing the material's intrinsic PARIS law (figure 11).

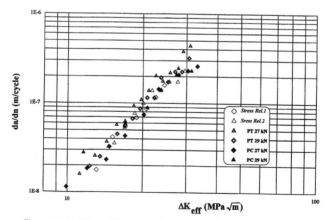

Figure 11: Matching of the curves for the specimens with residual stresses

It should be noted that in the computing on the pipes (§ 1), when we needed to compute the number of propagation cycles, we used the PARIS curve for stress-relieved materials with a load ratio of R=0.10, as indicated earlier. Strictly speaking, it would have been preferable to use a curve established at a higher load ratio, the same as that of the pressures applied (≅ 40bar/70bar). This would have resulted in a slightly lower number of propagation cycles than that we computed. Nevertheless, any corrections this might entail are very slight, because of the high propagation rates computed. Moreover, the resulting difference between the computed and the observed values (Na + Np) would have in fact been somewhat greater.

## CONCLUSION

The influence of residual compressive and tensile stresses on fatigue cracking was quantified by handling the crack initiation phase and the propagation phase separately.

As regards the crack initiation phase, the residual stresses, whether compressive or tensile, have little effect on the number of crack initiation cycles predicted by the criterion within the pipeline operating range, for fewer than $10^5$ cycles. The residual compressive stresses only slow down crack initiation perceptibly near the endurance limit.

The study on crack propagation, on the other hand, showed that residual tensile stresses accelerate the propagation rate by eliminating the crack closure effect, while residual compressive stresses slow propagation due to a stress intensity factor Kr related to those residual stresses.

Hence, taking residual stresses into account in predicting numbers of cycles to fatigue crack failure on the basis of gouge type defects in pipe walls is justified only in computing the number of propagation cycles, but not in using the criterion to determine the number of crack initiation cycles.However, the corrections to be made are always minor, insofar as the crack propagation rates computed very rapidly attain values for which the effects of the residual stresses are low.

## REFERENCES

[1] DEVAUX J.C., D'ESCATHA Y., RABBE P. and PELLISSIER-TANON A. " A criterion for analysing fatigue crack-initiation in geometrical singularities", Transaction of the 5th International Conference on Structural Mechanics in Reactor Technology (SMIRT), Berlin 1979.

[2] ERDOGAN F. and SIH G.C. "On the crack extension in plate under plane loading and transverse shear" Trans ASME, J. Basic Eng, December 1963, p 519.

[3] WILLIAMS J.G. and EWING P.D. "Fracture under complex stress. The angled crack problem" International Journal of Fracture Mechanics, Vol 8, N°4, December 1972, p 441-446.

[4] MASSON J.C. "Utilisation de l'approche locale pour la prévision de la fissuration par fatigue de manchettes soumises à des chocs thermiques". Séminaire international sur l'approche locale de la rupture, Moret Sur Loing, France 1986, p 347-358.

[5] MOKHDANI C. "Amorçage et propagation de fissures de fatigue dans un acier pour tubes de transport de gaz" Thèse de docteur de l'Ecole Nationale des Mines de Paris, 6 avril 1995.

[6] CREAGER M. and PARIS P.C. " The elastic field near the tip for a blunt crack", Thesis, Lehigh University, 1966.

[7] BATISSE R., MEZIERE Y., MOKHDANI C. and PINEAU A. "A fatigue crack-initiation criterion for the assessment of the residual life on gas transmission pipelines with gouge only or gouge in dent", EPRG-PRC 10th biennal joint technical meeting on line pipe research, 18-21 april 1995.

[8] CANONICO D.A. "Stress-relief heat treating of steels" American Society for Metals, Metal Handbook, 9th ed, Vol 4, p 3-5.

[9] ELBER W, "The significance of fatigue crack closer" ASTM STP 486, 1971, p 230-242.

[10] BREAT J.L., MUDRY F. and PINEAU A. "Amorçage et propagation des fissures de fatigue dans les zones de concentration de contraintes" Société Française de Métallurgie, Commission de fatigue des métaux, Journées Internationales de Printemps, Paris 1984, p143-158

[11] TADA H., PARIS P. and IRWING G. "The stress analysis of cracks handbook" Del Research Corporation Hellertown, Pennsylvanie 1973.

DAMAGE MONITORING SYSTEM FOR PIPELINE

SYSTÈME DE DIAGNOSTICET ET DE SUIVI
DES DÉFAUTS POUR LES CANALISATIONS

Satoru Miura
Trunkline Depertment, Osaka Gas Co., , Japan

Takeshi Mishima
Engineering Department, Osaka Gas Co., , ,Japan

## ABSTRACT

In a pipeline that consists of steel pipes coated with high-insulation coating material such as polyethylene-coated steel pipes and is provided with a cathodic protection system powered by a single external power sypply, damage to the coating caused by a construction vehicle or the like operated for earthworks of other purposes can be detected by monitoring a change in the cathodic protection current.

Osaka Gas Co., Ltd. hav been monitoring intergerence to some of its gas pipelines incurred in earthworks of other purposes by applying this principle. In areas crowded with much stray currents such as current leakage from railway tracks and cathodic protection current of other underground structures, however, monitoring for the gas pipeline has been disturbed by the ever-changing stray currents, resulting in great difficulty of discriminating damage to the pipeline coating from electric noise.

To solve this problem, we have been making research on the use of alternate current applied exclusively as the signal current for damage detection, instead of direct current (cathodic protection current) which can be greatly affected by electric noise originating in stray currents from railway tracks and other sources. This research resulted in the developement of a damage monitoring system featuring high immunity to noise and greatly improved accuracy of detection, which proved its practical applicability. This system was not put into practical use in a section between Himeji and Sanda of Kinki Western Trunkline II in 1991.

In order to further improve the detection accuracy and enable to locate the point of damage, we started in 1994 to develop a new system, We plan to deploy the new system in our high-pressure gas pipelines coated with polyethylene lining.

## RÉSUMÉ

Dans une conduite qui se compose de tuyaux en acier doubles d'un materiau avec un revetement a haute isolation, tels que des tuyaux en acier revetus de polyethylene et munis d'un systeme de protection cathodique alimente par une alimentation en courant exterieure unique, l'endommagement du revetement, provoque, par des vehicules de chantiers ou du meme genre fonctionnant pour des travaux de terrassement realises dans d'autres buts, peut etre detecte an surveillant le changement survenant dans le courant de protection cathodique.

La S.A. Osaka Gas a surveille les interferences qui etaient survenues a certaines de ses canalisations de gaz a grande distance, eprouvees lors de tavaux de terrassement effectues dans d'autres buts, en appliquant ce principe. Cependant, dans zones encombrees de courants de fuite, telle qu'une perte de courant provenant de voies ferrees et d'un courant de protection cathodique d'autres structures souterraines, la surveillance pour les canalisations de gaz a grande distance est perturbee par des courants de fuite se produisant sans cesse, provoquant de ce fait de grandes difficultes pour distinguer l'endommagement du revetement de la conduite provenant de bruits parasites electriques.

Pour resoudre ce probleme, nous avons effectue des recherches sur l'utilisation d'un courant alternatif applique exclusivement en that que courant de signal d'appel pour la detection d'un endommagement, a la place d'un courant direct (courant de protection cathodique) qui peut etre grandement affecte par un bruit parasite electrique ayant pour origine des courants de fuite provenant de voies ferrees et d'autres sources. Ces recherches ont permis d'aboutir a la mise au point d'un systeme de surveillance sur l'endommagement se caracterisant par une immunite elevee aux bruits perturbateurs et une precision amelioree plus grande de la detection, ce qui est prouve par sa possibilite d'application pratique. Ce systeme a commence a etre utilise dans une section de la ligne principale Kinki II de l'ouest, entre Himeji et Sanda et 1991.
De maniere a pouvoir ameliorer ulterieurement la precision de la detection et de permettre de localiser l'endroit de l'endommagement, nous avons commence en 1994 a mettre au point un nouveau systeme. Nous prevoyons de deployer ce nouveau systeme dans nos canalisations de gaz sous haute pression a grande distance revetues d'une doublure en polyethylene.

## INTRODUCTION

In Japan, gas pipelines , even if high pressure lines are embedded under roads which are public space in town area. So, we must not have an accident with high pressure gas pipelines even by third party's works. Therefore, we have been installing steel protection plates and marking sheets over the gas pipelines, while making patrol along the pipeline routes two rounds or more a day to check for other earthworks conducted without notice.

Further, to make assurance double sure, we have been developing a damage monitoring system for pipeline that enables it to detect damages instantaneously and to take quick remedial action. Most of other earthworks conducted without notice are geological surveys by means of boring machines. Therefore object of the system development was set to the detection of damage to the coating, particularly to the detection of metal contact by boring machine.

## HIGH-PRESSURE GAS PIPELINE OPERATED BY OSAKA GAS CO., LTD.

Since 1972, we have been using polyethylene-coated steel pipes in the construction of high-pressure gas pipelines. In pipelines laid in and after 1975 including Kinki Western Trunkline II, high insulation of coating has been achieved with $10^6$ $\Omega$ -m$^2$ or higher insulation resistance measured in the embedded pipeline thanks to the improved construction technology. Also taking advantage of the improved cathodic protection technology, we provide cathodic protection of a pipeline extending over a total length of several tens to about one hundred kilometers by means of a single external power supply unit. The high-pressure pipelines are sufficiently insulated from medium-pressure lines, instrumentation, building and other facilities and structures at every station. System diagram of our high-pressure gas pipelines is shown in Fig.1.

## BACKGROUND OF THE DEVELOPMENT

In pipeline provided with cathodic protection as described above, damage to the coating of the line caused by other earthwork, namely a metal contact by a construction vehicle, results in decreased equivalent resistance of the pipeline observed from the external power supply unit thereby causing an instantaneous increase in the cathodic protection current. By applying this principle, we developed a damage detection system based on continuous monitor of cathodic protection current (DC current). With this detection system, however, it has been very difficult to distinguish damage to the coating from electric noise due to the influence of stray current which constantly change, in such an area as is crowded with much stray current including current leakage from railway tracks and cathodic protection current of other underground structures. To solve this problem, we have been making research on the use of AC current applied exclusively as the signal current for damage detection, instead of DC current (cathodic protection current) which can be greatly affected by electric noise originating in stray currents from railway tracks and other sources.

OPERATING PRINCIPLE OF THE DAMAGE DETECTION SYSTEM

Fig.2 is a diagram illustrating the operating principle of the damage detection system.

Application Of Alternate Voltage. An AC voltage for damage detection is superposed on the cathodic protection voltage (DC) provided by an external power supply, with the resultant voltage being applied across the pipeline and the groaned, Magnitude of the alternate voltage is set within such a range that does not cause alternate current corrosion. Frequency of the AC voltage is set to one that is not included in the electric noise and has greater response to a damage.

Measurement Of AC Current. From the current flowing in the pipeline at various points, only the AC current component having the frequency of the applied voltage is detected by means of a band-pass filter. The current component can be detected either by connecting a pair of wires at two points of the pipe separated several tens of meters along the pipeline and measuring the voltage difference across these points, or by winding a coil around the pipe and measuring the voltage induced in the coil. The former method is employed in the existing system and the latter method is employed in the new system currently under development.

Damage Detection Logic. Distribution of electric noise at the frequency of the applied voltage is determined in advance by continuous measurement of the voltage under normal condition (defect-free condition) over an extended period. This measurement is used to set the criterion to determine whether a monitored voltage level is due to a damage caused by other earthwork or not. Because the electric noise distribution is different in daytime when railways are in operation and in midnight when they are not in operation, and also varies by the day of the week, as a matter of course, different criteria are set for different hours of the day and for different days of the week. Further, since the maintenance personnel must be dispatched to patrol the suspected section of the line even in midnight when a damage caused by other earthwork is detected, we set the rate of detection of spurious damage signals within one per year.

METHOD OF SYSTEM EVALUATION

To make it easier to estimate the seriousness of a damage to the coating, we employed the current (DC) flowing through the point of damage from the pipeline to the ground (hereafter called damage current) as the evaluation parameter. It was presumed that the ratio of damage current (DC) to AC current component of the applied frequency is approximately constant in the pipeline to be monitored independent of the distance from the point of voltage input and the soil conditions. Under this assumption, we conducted the following experiment.

Measurement Of Damage Current Caused By Construction Vehicle. A short pipe of the same specifications as the main pipe of the pipeline was embedded near the main pipe by the same pipe laying procedure as

that of the main pipe.   The main pipe and the short pipe were
electrically connected with a wire.   A construction vehicle such as
boring machine, earth auger or back hoe was operated to touch the
short pipe, while measuring the magnitude and waveform of the damage
current.   Photo 1 shows the short pipe being embedded, and photo 2
shows an earth auger being operated to damage the short pipe.   Fig.3
shows the waveform of damage current, flowing from the pipe through
the earth auger to the ground, measured at this time.

   Measurement Of Damage Current By Means Of Test Piece.   Test
pieces were made by coating pieces of the same steel as that of the
main pipe with epoxy resin and processing them to have the same steel
surfaces.   Test pieces having four different surface areas were
prepared : 100, 200, 500 and 1000cm$^2$.   The test pieces were embedded
near the main pipe by the same pipe laying procedure as the main pipe,
and electrically connected to the main pipe with wires to provide
dummy defects.   Then damage current was measured at different points
of the pipeline.   The measurements show that the damage current is in
approximately constant relationship with the damaged surface area
independent of the distance from the point of voltage input and the
soil conditions such as specific resistance of the ground.   Photo 3
shows the test pieces and Fig.4 shows the values of damage current
measured at different stations.

   Dummy Defect Represented By Variable Resistor.   The two
experiments described above showed that the intensity of the damage
current could be translated to the damaged surface area of the coating
and the type of construction vehicle that caused the damage.   So we
decided to estimate the extent of damage by making such an arrangement
as a constant damage current flows between the pipe and the ground at
any point of the line by using variable resistor.   Object of the
damage detection system is set at detecting metal contact by boring
machine used in other earthwork.   And the goal for the suction between
Himeji and Sanda of Kinki Western Trunkline II, where the new system
under development is to be introduced, is set at detecting equivalent
damage current of 30mA.

EXISTING DAMAGE MONITORING SYSTEM

   Decision On The Pipeline To Introduce The New Damage Monitoring
System.   We made prototypes of the damage monitoring system as shown
in photo 4, which were installed in three sections of Kinki Western
Trunkline II ; Himeji to Sanda, Sanda to Nishibetsuin, and
Nishibetsuin to Fushimi in 1989.   Monitoring test was conducted with
these prototype systems for about half a year. (Insulation joints are
installed in the pipeline at Sanda and Nishibetsuin, so that these
three sections regarded as electrically separate lines.)   In the test,
the system installed in the section between Himeji and Sanda showed
the most remarkable effect, and we decided to introduce the system in
this section.   The section between Himeji and Sanda has a total line
length of 86km and comes close to railway tracks at many locations,
and therefore monitoring by the conventional method (DC method) is
disturbed by much electric noise and it has been difficult to detect
even heavy construction vehicles.   On the other hand, sections between
Sanda and Nishibetsuin and the section between Nishibetsuin and
Fushimi are about 30 to 40km in total length and hardly come near to
railway tracks, and therefore interferences to these sections by
construction vehicles of such a size as of earth auger can be detected
satisfactorily by the conventional method (DC method).   For this
reason, the section between Himeji and Sanda was selected to introduce
the new system.

   System Configuration.   We made a practical version of the new
damage monitoring system as shown in photo 5, and installed it in
Seishin governor station located at near the center of the line, and
put it in operation in 1991.   Fig.5 shows its system configuration.

Since damage detection by the system is made only one point, location of the point of damage was made only to determine whether it was in the section between Himeji and Seishin or the section between the Seishin and Sanda. Accuracy of detection was as described below.

Accuracy Of Detection. Dummy defect having an area of $100cm^2$ was connected to the line at Kakogawa station for 30-sec. period at intervals of 30 minutes, to obtain the result shown in Fig.5. Assuming the rate of detecting spurious damages to be one per year, the result indicates that boring machines can be detected in midnight when railways are not in operation and earth augers and back hoes can be detected in daytime.

GOAL OF DEVELOPING THE NEW SYSTEM

Based on the technology of the existing damage monitoring system, we have been engaged in the development of the new system since 1994. Objects of the development are as follows.

Improvement In The Detecting Accuracy. As described in the introduction, object of the system development is to detect metal contact by boring machine. Therefore accuracy of detection must be improved so that metal contact of a boring machine can be detected even in daytime when there is much electric noise.

Location Of The Point Of Damage. The existing system, as it measures the damage current at only point, can only determine whether the point of damage is on the upstream or downstream of the measuring point. In fact, it is difficult to find other earthwork by patrolling along the line extending over a total length of about 40km. In practice, it is necessary to locate the point of damage within a range of several kilometers.

BREAKTHROUGH OF THE NEW SYSTEM

Breakthroughs of the new system are as follows.

Current Sensor. The existing system has been using a current measuring wire installed in the pipeline for the purpose of corrosion protection. The current measuring wire is an unshielded wire bonded to the pipeline by thermit welding and runs from the pipeline to the monitoring system over a distance of 30 to 40km. Such a long unshielded wire can easily be affected by electric noise propagating on and under ground. The new system employs the coil sensor as shown in photo 6 which is connected to the monitoring system with a shielded wire about several kilometers in total length.

Cost Reduction. The existing damage monitoring system required an initial cost of not less than 10 million yen for each unit, because it was built by using off-the-shelf precision instruments. We succeeded in reducing the cost of the new system down to one million yen per unit through in-house manufacture including circuit boards. This made it economically feasible to install the damage monitoring system of all stations of the line and, as a result, to locate the point of damage within a range of 4 to 8km.

Combined Use Of Two Detecting Methods. In addition to the measurement of current flowing in the pipeline based on the conventional method, we measured the pipeline potential to the ground at the same time, and reduced the detection of spurious damage signals by comparing the two measurements.

PROGRESS OF DEVELOPMENT OF THE NEW SYSTEM

We tested the first prototype monitoring system on the section between Himeji and Sanda of Kinki Western Trunkline II in August 1994.

The test showed that the system can detect a metal contact by a boring machine even in daytime. Fig.7 shows the configuration of the new system, Fig.8 shows the locations of the new system, and Fig.9 shows the results of measurements. While this test used the conventional current measuring wire installed in the pipeline, we expect that a higher detecting accuracy could be achieved with a production type prototype system.

As of April 1995, the production type prototype system is under test in the section between Himeji and Sanda of Kinki Western Trunkline II.

OUTLINE OF THE MONITORING TEST

Transmitter. A transmitter that applies AC voltage is installed at Senshin governor station located at middle of the line. Photo 7 shows the transmitter and a personal computer used in the system control and measurement.

Receiver. Receivers that measure the current flowing in the pipeline and the pipeline potential to the ground are installed at five stations in the line. Four receivers are installed in a section between Seishin station where the transmitter is installed and Himeji, because measurements in the past show that the section of the pipeline on Himeji side has lower insulation resistance of coating and more frequently come near to railway tracks, making it more difficult to detect damages in this section than in the section on Sanda side. Photo 8 shows the production type prototype monitoring system and a personal computer used in measurement.

Dummy Defect. The dummy defect is a device to short-circuit the pipeline to the ground via a variable resistor for the purpose of damage detection and location, as described in the section of system evaluation. Dummy defects are installed at two stations in the line. Duration, current and interval of short-circuiting can be freely set by remote control. In the monitoring test, damage current corresponding to a boring machine and a heavy construction machine was set to flow for 10 to 30 seconds at intervals of 30 minutes. Photo 9 shows a circuit board consisting of resistor and relay, a shunt box for measuring the damage current and a personal computer used in the control and measurement.

CONCLUSION

Results of the test obtained so far indicate that the goals of the development with regard to the detection performance and cost reduction have already been achieved. It was verified that one unit of the new monitoring system capable of detecting metal contact by a boring machine even in daytime can be manufactured at a cost of about one million yen. Evaluation of the damage location performance will be completed in August 1995.

Based on the results of testing the production type system currently under way, we plan to introduce the new damage monitoring system at all stations (25 locations) of Kinki Western Trunkline II in 1996 and at all stations (9 locations) of Kinki Western Trunkline III in 1997.

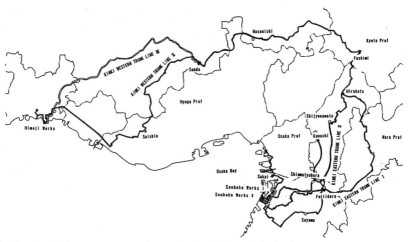

Fig. 1 : High pressure gas transmission line at Osaka Gas

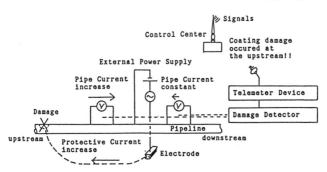

Fig. 2 : operating principle

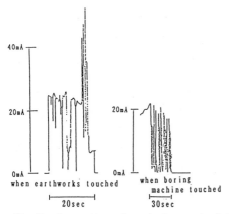

Fig. 3 : Current waveform during contact by a construction vehicle

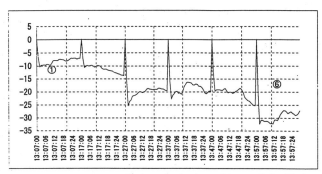

Fig. 4 : Damage current when test piece (dummy defect) is connected

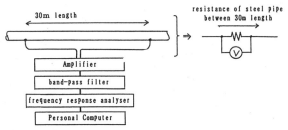

Fig. 5 : Configuration of practical sysytem installed at Seishin station

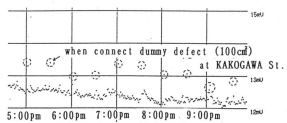

measure at SEISHIN St.when dummy defect connect
between 30sec every 30 minutes at KAKOGAWA St.

Fig. 6 : Waveform measured with dummy defect connected at Kakogawa (protoype)

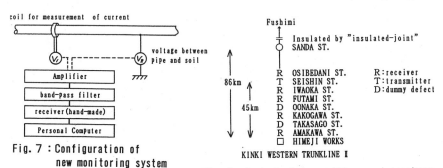

Fig. 7 : Configuration of
new monitoring system

Fig. 8 : Layout of transmitters and receivers
for the test of new system

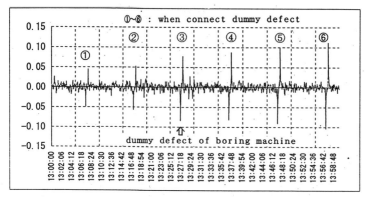

Fig. 9 : Waveform measured with dummy defect sonnected
to first prototype of the new system

Photo. 1 : Experimet with construction
vehicle: short pipe being embedded

Photo. 2 : Earth auger making
metal contact with the pipeline

Photo. 3 : Test piece

Photo. 4 : Prototype

Photo. 5 : Practical system

Photo. 6 : Ring coil (Current sensor)

Photo. 7 : Second prototype: transmitter

Photo. 8 : Receiver

Photo. 9 : Dummy defect

ASSESSING PIPELINE STEELS FOR SOUR SERVICE

EVALUATION DE LA RESISTANCE DES ACIERS DES GAZODUCS
POUR L'UTILISATION DE GAZ CORROSIFS

C L Jones and P R Kirkwood
British Gas plc
Research and Technology

R F Dewsnap and W J Rudd
British Steel plc
Swinden Technology Centre

ABSTRACT

This paper describes a programme of work carried out to
establish the optimum laboratory scale test for predicting the
service performance of linepipe steels under sour gas
conditions. Four full-scale tests were carried out in a sour
gas facility (designed to provide a realistic simulation of
typical sour gas pipelines in service) and the results
compared with a comprehensive series of standard and
specialised laboratory hydrogen induced cracking (HIC) and
sulphide stress corrosion cracking (SSCC) tests. The results
of the tests are described and the implications for sour gas
testing are assessed.

RÉSUMÉ

Cette communication décrit un programme de travail réalisé
afin de déterminer les essais en laboratoire optimaux pour la
prévision de la performance de service des aciers des gazoducs
dans des conditions d'utilisation de gaz corrosifs. Quatre
essais dans les conditions d'utilisation ont été réalisés dans
une installation de gaz corrosifs (destinée à fournir une
simulation réaliste des gazoducs de gaz corrosifs type en
service) et les résultats ont été comparés à une série
complète d'essais en laboratoire normalisés et spécialisés de
fissuation provoquée par l'hydrogène (HIC) et de fissuration
par corrosion sous tension au sulfure (SSCC). Les résultats
de ces essais sont décrits et les implications des essais sur
les gaz corrosifs sont évaluées.

INTRODUCTION

Pipeline steels transporting wet sour gas (or oil) can suffer from two types of cracking.  One is hydrogen induced cracking (HIC), also termed stepwise cracking or blistering, which can occur in steels of any strength level and does not require the action of an applied stress (1).  The other is sulphide stress corrosion cracking (SSCC) which normally only occurs in high strength steels and requires the action of an externally applied or residual stress (2).

Both types of cracking have been well documented for many years and have caused many service failures.  As a result laboratory tests have been developed to predict service performance.  Thus, since the majority of service failures due to SSCC were confined to steels with hardness values in excess of HRC 22, the NACE recommendations (3) to prevent SSCC have been based on limiting hardness levels to less than this value (approximately equivalent to HV 248).  Tensile and bend tests have also been employed.  The most common HIC test is the "BP test" which was adopted as a procedure in a NACE specification (4).  A later variation of the test used the solution employed in the NACE SSCC tests (3) which employs an acetic acid addition to give a pH in the range 3.5 - 3.8 for the majority of the test.

However, doubts have been raised (3) about the validity of using these tests for predicting service performance.  This led to the establishment of a major joint industry project to study sour gas cracking.  The project was funded jointly by the HSE and Shell, Statoil, Britoil, British Steel and British Gas who were all represented on the steering groups which advised on the development and progress of the project.  The overall programme was managed by British Gas Research and Technology.

The main objective of the programme was to establish the optimum laboratory scale tests for predicting sour gas cracking.  In order to achieve this it was necessary to establish the relationship between the full-scale performance of pipeline steels (in a facility designed to provide a realistic simulation of typical sour gas pipelines) and a comprehensive series of standard and specialised laboratory HIC and SSCC tests.

A previous paper (5) described the full-scale sour gas test facility, its operation and the results generated.  This paper concentrates on a comparison of the results of the full-scale and laboratory tests.

EXPERIMENTAL

Materials

Nine pipeline steels were included in the programme.  The pipes were all 910mm (36 inch) diameter, with a range of wall thicknesses, and had specified minimum yield strengths (SMYS) in the range 414-482MPa (60-70Ksi).  Their chemical analyses are summarised in Table 1.  The table uses identification codes for each steel and they are used hereafter for simplicity.

Full-Scale Test Rig

The full-scale test facility was designed to provide as realistic a simulation as possible of typical sour gas pipelines in service.  The test rig (shown schematically in Figure 1) consisted of a series of eight or nine sections welded together to form a

continuous 12m length of 910mm OD pipe.  The test loop was designed
to operate under flowing gas conditions at a maximum pressure of
100bar using various combinations of hydrogen sulphide ($H_2S$) carbon
dioxide ($CO_2$) and natural gas.  A detailed description of the rig
and its operation is given in an earlier paper (5).

Four full-scale tests were carried out (designated 1,2,3A and
3B).  The specified conditions of each test are summarised in
Table 2.  During each test HIC initiation and development in a
pre-selected section of the test line was monitored by an automatic
ultrasonic P-scan system (Corroscan).  Following each test the
Corroscan was used to survey the full test section for HIC.

Laboratory Testing

## Standard HIC Tests

From each of the original 11m long pipes, three 1m long
equidistantly spaced full pipe rings were supplied for the
laboratory testing programme.  HIC testpieces were prepared from the
180° body position on all three rings and from the seam weld (0°),
90° and 270° body positions on the middle ring, giving a total of
six sampling positions from each pipe.  In addition girth welds were
also tested.

Duplicate testpieces were taken from each test location and HIC
tests were conducted according to NACE specification TM0284 (now
TM0284-87)(4) in $H_2S$ saturated pH5 artificial seawater formulated to
ASTM D1141-52 (BP solution) and also in $H_2S$ saturated pH3 solution
formulated to TM01777(6) (NACE solution).  All the exposure periods
in the test solutions were 96 hours.

For the crack assessment, standard sectioning of testpieces was
used throughout and crack length ratio (CLR%), crack thickness ratio
(CTR%) and crack sensitivity ratio (CSR%) were calculated.

## Single Sided HIC Tests

Single sided exposure HIC tests were carried out to provide a
more reasonable comparison with service conditions.  They were
conducted in a multi-testpiece cell, illustrated in Figure 2.  An
area of the pipe inner wall approximately 95 cm$^2$ and having a
surface finish comparable with that required for standard HIC
testing was exposed to the BP and NACE test solutions for 1,000 hrs.
HIC development was monitored each day during the early stages of
test using ultrasonic inspection with the testpieces in situ on the
test cell.  Crack area ratio (CAR%) was expressed as a percentage of
the total exposed area of the testpiece.

## Sulphide Stress Corrosion Cracking (SSCC) Tests

The SSCC resistance of the parent pipe steels was assessed using
NACE tensile and fracture mechanics tests to give the threshold
stress, $\sigma_{Th}$, and threshold stress intensity, $K_{ISCC}$, respectively.
The tensile testpieces were transverse to the pipe axis.  The
fracture mechanics samples were small three point bend testpieces
transverse to the pipe axis with a through-thickness crack (YZ
orientation).  In both cases testing was carried out under constant
load for up to 720 h in NACE solution.  $\sigma_{Th}$ was determined to an
accuracy of 5% SMYS, and $K_{ISCC}$ to an accuracy of ± 1 MPam$^{\frac{1}{2}}$.

The SSCC performance of seam welds was assessed using a
transverse four point bend testpiece measuring 115 x 15 x 5mm.

Testpieces were machined from flattened pipe with the inner surface and weld bead intact.  Stressing was conducted in a four point bend jig under constant deflection using a simple elastic beam formula, i.e. no account was taken of stress concentration at the weld toe. Tests were conducted for 96 h in NACE and BP solutions.  Threshold stress values were obtained to an accuracy of 10% SMYS, except where values were above SMYS.

RESULTS

Full-scale Tests

The test conditions for the four full-scale tests were always maintained within the levels specified in Table 2, except for a short period in tests 2 and 3B when the rig had to be depressurised to correct faults on the Corroscan.

Two full-scale test failures occurred.  One was due to a through-wall SSCC defect in the seam weld of pipe GBV in test 3A (Figure 3) which caused leakage less than twenty hours after the start of the test.  The other failure (in test 3B) occurred after 77 days due to gross, mid-wall HIC in the body of pipe GBQ which initiated a through-wall SSCC defect (Figure 4).

Most pipes exhibited HIC in at least one of the full-scale tests and the cracking was predominantly associated with segregated bands at the mid-wall position.  The only pipes which did not exhibit any HIC were GCT and GBV.  A summary of levels of HIC in the full scale tests (expressed as % crack area) is given in Table 3.

Full details of the results have been given earlier (5).

Laboratory Results

HIC Results

Standard HIC (Pipe Body).  The laboratory HIC and single sided test results are summarised in Table 4 and indicate a wide range of susceptibility dependent on steel quality and test conditions.  In the tests in NACE solution the bulk of the materials sustained major hydrogen damage and a laboratory ranking based on CLR and CSR values showed pipes EUZ, GAN, FZS and GBQ to be substantially the most susceptible with average CLR values for two of the  pipes exceeding 100%.  This group had the highest sulphur content ranging from about 50 ppm to 110 ppm and (except for pipe FZS) also had the highest alloy content expressed as carbon equivalent value (CEV), Table 1. Of the remaining steels (three of which were manufactured to a sour quality with low sulphur and calcium treatment), only the spiral weld pipe GCT could be considered as fully HIC resistant in NACE solution.  No consistent effect of sampling position on HIC susceptibility could be established, variability being found both along the pipe axis and round the circumference.

In BP solution GCT and GBV exhibited zero cracking, together with the four copper bearing steels which showed high to moderate susceptibility in NACE solution, thereby demonstrating the  powerful beneficial effect of copper in a relatively mild (pH5) test environment.

Weld Metal HIC Tests.  All seam welds were free from cracks under pH5 test conditions.  However, in the pH3 test, four pipes EUZ, FZS, GBE and GBW developed weld metal HIC.  All except GBE were copper containing steels.

Cracking was also detected in a number of girth weld specimens which were different from the cracked seam weld pipes.  In NACE solution, GCT, GBV and GBE exhibited cracking wholly within girth weld metal, while cracks were found between the HAZ and weld metal in pipes EUZ and GBB.  Only one girth weld developed HIC in BP solution and this was again pipe GCT while a single crack was found between HAZ and weld metal of pipe EUZ.

Single Sided HIC Tests.  As in the standard HIC test, none of the copper containing steels developed HIC in BP solution.  Cracking was confined to pipes GAN, GBQ and GBB which had exhibited the highest levels of HIC in the standard test in BP solution.  In NACE solution all the pipes except GCT and GBV exhibited cracking.

Microstructure and HIC.  All the steels had basically ferrite-pearlite microstructures although the morphology and distribution of the phases and consequently the cracking modes differed depending on composition, processing route and HIC testing procedure.  Except for the fully HIC resistant pipe GCT and to some degree GBV, all the steels exhibited HIC associated with segregation bands, particularly at or near the mid-wall position (Figure 5).  This was frequently accompanied with severe blister cracking at the pipe outer surface in the higher sulphur content controlled rolled steels.  It is also significant that the two most susceptible pipes GBQ and GAN developed substantial stepwise cracking in the standard HIC test.  In the case of the high sulphur content, normalised steel EUZ all cracking modes were present with cracks uniformly distributed across the testpiece sections.

SSCC Results

All the laboratory SSCC are summarised in Table 4.  They indicate a very wide range of SSCC resistance in NACE tensile tests with threshold stress values ranging from 40% SMYS (GBQ) to 95% SMYS (GBV and GBW)  In contrast $K_{ISCC}$ in these steels is relatively insensitive to composition, microstructure, inclusion type etc.

NACE Tensile Tests.  Metallographic examination of NACE tensile testpieces showed that the steels GAN, GBE, FZS, EUZ and GBQ which had poor HIC performance, suffered SSCC by a mechanism of HIC linkage.  These steels also had the lowest values of threshold stress.  The other steels, with CLR values <60 in HIC tests, appeared to crack by classical SSCC, i.e. a single crack initiating at the surface rather than internal cracking linking back to the surface.

It can be expected that steels which have a poor HIC resistance might also have poor SSCC resistance in NACE tensile tests due to SSCC by HIC linkage.  However, the antithesis of this is not true, and steels with the best HIC resistance are not the best performers in SSCC tests (Table 4).  This is because once a certain degree of HIC resistance is achieved, the steels fail by classical SSCC which is clearly not controlled by the same internal features which control HIC.

$K_{ISCC}$ Tests.  $K_{ISCC}$ can be used to calculate the critical defect size for stress corrosion in a pipe using the analysis of Newman and Raju (7).  For a semi-elliptical surface crack with a 4:1 length to depth ratio, a critical defect of 4 mm is required to exceed $K_{ISCC}$ for pipe EUZ, the pipe under highest hoop stress in the full scale tests.  Such large defects should not be present in pipes which are all ultrasonically examined and proof tested by the manufacturers.  Hence threshold stress would appear to be the most important measure of SSCC in these linepipe steels.

Four Point Bend Tests. The results summary of threshold
stresses is shown in Table 4 for NACE solution. In BP solution no
stress corrosion cracks were observed at stress values up to 100%
SMYS. The steels tested in NACE solution showed a wide range of
threshold stress from 40% SMYS for GBB to >100% SMYS for FZS, GBQ,
GBW and GCT. Many of the steels which performed well in NACE
tensile tests had a poor performance in these bend tests where
cracking always occurred in the coarse grain HAZ at the weld toe.
Only steels GCT and GBW met a 72% SMYS design criterion for both
NACE tensiles and 4 point bend tests.

DISCUSSION

   Correlation of Laboratory HIC Tests and Full Scale Performance

   A comparison of the laboratory and full scale test results
allows some important observations to be made on the optimum
laboratory tests for predicting service performance. In particular,
it is apparent from an examination of Tables 3 and 4, and Figure 6
which plots CLR in the laboratory tests as a function of % crack
area in the full scale tests, that the laboratory HIC tests in BP
solution (either standard or single sided) can not be used to give a
reliable prediction of full scale performance. This is most clearly
demonstrated by the results of the second full scale test when three
copper containing steels (EUZ, FZS and GBW) exhibited extensive HIC
under conditions similar to the laboratory HIC test in BP solution
(in terms of the levels of $H_2S$ in solution). In the laboratory test
no cracking was observed in these steels. This is significant
because the HIC test in BP solution has been widely used in
specifications for pipelines for sour gas service over the last 20
years and has been incorporated in the NACE standard on HIC testing
(4).

   The beneficial effect of a 0.3% copper addition in completely
suppressing HIC during the laboratory BP test has been attributed to
the formation of a surface protective film which reduces corrosion
and minimises the ingress of hydrogen. It is possible that in the
full-scale tests, disruption of the protective film occurred due to
mini-stress cycling brought about by small temperature changes
leading to variations in gas pressure. A further possible
explanation arising from recent work (8) is that a galvanic effect
was induced in the full scale tests, with the more noble Cu, Cr, Mo
and Ni containing steels becoming cathodic and evolving hydrogen in
the corrosion process.

   A substantially better correlation was obtained between the
laboratory standard HIC test in NACE solution and full scale test
performance (Figure 6). There is still considerable scatter in the
data but the test appears to be capable of indicating which steels
would be resistant to cracking in the full scale tests, i.e. those
steels which exhibited zero cracking in the standard HIC test in
NACE solution did not crack in the full scale tests. In fact, tests
in NACE solution appear to be conservative with steels exhibiting
12% CLR in the laboratory NACE test, showing zero cracking in the
full scale tests (Figure 6). Thus, it appears that small amounts of
cracking could be tolerated in the laboratory specimens exposed to
NACE solution without risking HIC in the full scale tests (and hence
in service).

   Also, despite the scatter in the data, it appears that
categories of susceptibility to HIC can be established from the
results of the laboratory NACE tests (Table 4). Pipes GBQ, GAN, EUZ
and FZS were by far the most susceptible and therefore would be

predicted to be most likely to develop HIC under full scale exposure
conditions.  Of these, GAN and GBQ which had the highest CSR values
also showed the highest crack area in the full scale tests, with EUZ
and FZS exhibiting lower, but substantial crack areas.  Some overlap
inevitably occurred between the high susceptibility and the medium
susceptibility group comprising GBE, GBB and GBW, with GBW tending
to fall towards the lower susceptibility end of the higher group
based on a maximum crack area criterion in the full scale test.
Pipe GBV had low susceptibility in both laboratory and full scale
tests while the fully resistant, spirally welded pipe GCT
manufactured from coil mill accelerated cooled plate showed
excellent agreement in both the laboratory and full scale tests.

The single sided test appears to be less discriminating than the
standard HIC test in NACE solution but it did identify the very poor
steels and the good steels, although the full scale performance of
the intermediate susceptibility steel GBB was grossly overestimated
whilst that of GBV was underestimated, probably due to sampling
variability.

Correlation of SSCC Tests and Full Scale Performance

Although the seam weld SSCC failure in test 3A was not predicted
by any test, the failure of GBQ in test 3B was indicated by the
laboratory results.  This steel displayed the worst NACE tensile
result in the laboratory tests.  The severity of the full scale test
to SSCC is also determined by the stress in the pipe.  GBQ had a
high hoop stress in the full scale test (Table 3) combined with a
low threshold stress (Table 4).  Indeed Figure 7 shows that this was
the only steel in which the hoop stress divided by the lowest
failure stress in the NACE tensile test, had a value significantly
above 1.  It is impossible to assess the severity of the full scale
tests compared to the small scale NACE tensile test.  The threshold
stress for the full scale could be higher or lower than those
determined in the laboratory.  Nevertheless it is possible from
Figure 7 to assess that GBQ was the most likely pipe body to suffer
SSCC.  The laboratory tests also suggested that the mechanism would
be HIC linkage.  As indicated earlier the $K_{ISCC}$ results did not
distinguish between the steels and the test appears totally
irrelevant to the full scale test performance.

CONCLUSIONS

1.  Both the standard and single sided laboratory HIC test in BP
    solution may not be a reliable indicator of full scale
    performance, particularly when copper is present in the steel.

2.  Of the laboratory HIC tests examined to date, the standard HIC
    test in NACE solution appears to be the most capable of
    indicating the general susceptibility of pipe body materials in
    a full scale test and thus in service.

3.  The standard HIC test in NACE solution has a high degree of
    in-built conservatism and it appears that, for the steels
    studied to date, small amounts of cracking could be tolerated in
    the laboratory specimens without risking HIC in the full scale
    tests and thus in service.

4.  The single sided HIC test in NACE solution may have some
    potential for predicting full scale behaviour, provided a
    realistic number of coupons is tested from each steel.

5.  The NACE tensile SSCC test was able to distinguish which pipe
    body was likely to fail, and those least likely to fail.

ACKNOWLEDGEMENTS

The authors wish to acknowledge the permission of British Gas plc, Dr R Baker, Director of Research and Development, British Steel plc and the members of the steering group for permission to publish this paper. They also wish to acknowledge the technical contributions made by their colleagues and by members of the steering committee of the sponsor group.

REFERENCES

1. Moore, E M and Warga, J J, Materials Performance, Vol 15, 1976.

2. Biefer, G J, Materials Performance, Vol 21, No 6, p19, 1982.

3. Dewsnap, R F et al, A Review of Information on Hydrogen Induced Cracking and Sulphide Stress Corrosion Cracking in Linepipe Steels, Offshire Technical Report, OTH-86-256, Publ HMSO, 1987.

4. NACE Standard TM-02-84(87) Standard Test Method - Evaluation of Pipeline Steels for Resistance of Stepwise Cracking, 1987.

5. Jones, C L. The Performance of Carbon Manganese Pipeline Steels in Sour Gas Environment, International Gas Research Conference, Orlando, November 1992.

6. NACE Standard TM-01-77 (1986 Revision) Test Method 'Testing of Metals for Resistance to Sulphide Stress Corrosion Cracking at Ambient Temperatures'.

7. Newman, J C Jr. and Raju, I S Trans ASME Ser. J Vol 102, pp342-346, 1980.

8. Kushida, T et al, Full Testing of Linepipe for Sour Service, International Offshore and Polar-Engineering Conference, Edinburgh, August 1991.

**TABLE 1**

**PIPE DETAILS**

| PIPE CODE | PROCESS ROUTE | GRADE | CHEMICAL COMPOSITION, WT % | | | | | | | | | | | | | | | CEV |
|---|---|---|---|---|---|---|---|---|---|---|---|---|---|---|---|---|---|---|---|
| | | | C | Si | Mn | S | P | Al | V | Nb | Ti | Ni | Cr | Mo | Cu | REM | Ca | |
| EUZ | Normalised | X60 | 0.19 | 0.37 | 1.57 | 0.0100 | 0.013 | 0.022 | 0.12 | 0.002 | 0.002 | 0.02 | 0.16 | 0.005 | 0.32 | - | - | 0.48 |
| GAN | Controlled Rolled | X60 | 0.12 | 0.30 | 1.42 | 0.0090 | 0.015 | 0.040 | 0.04 | 0.031 | 0.002 | 0.04 | 0.05 | 0.01 | 0.07 | - | - | 0.37 |
| FZS | Controlled Rolled | X65 | 0.05 | 0.28 | 1.33 | 0.0050 | 0.015 | 0.041 | 0.06 | 0.038 | 0.002 | 0.22 | 0.02 | 0.005 | 0.31 | - | - | 0.29 |
| GBQ | Controlled Rolled | X65 | 0.10 | 0.28 | 1.49 | 0.0110 | 0.020 | 0.016 | 0.05 | 0.037 | <0.002 | 0.02 | 0.03 | <0.005 | 0.03 | - | - | 0.35 |
| GBE | Controlled Rolled | X65 | 0.07 | 0.32 | 1.48 | 0.0020 | 0.017 | 0.040 | 0.08 | 0.036 | 0.002 | 0.03 | 0.17 | 0.005 | 0.07 | - | - | 0.34 |
| GBB | Controlled Rolled | X70 | 0.08 | 0.31 | 1.46 | 0.0020 | 0.012 | 0.040 | 0.07 | 0.035 | 0.002 | 0.03 | 0.04 | 0.005 | 0.06 | - | 0.0012 | 0.33 |
| GCT | Accelerated Cooled Spiral Weld | X60 | 0.05 | 0.26 | 1.41 | 0.0014 | 0.009 | 0.059 | 0.002 | 0.043 | 0.002 | 0.02 | 0.02 | 0.005 | 0.02 | - | 0.0018 | 0.29 |
| GBV | Controlled Rolled | X70 | 0.02 | 0.24 | 1.75 | 0.0005 | 0.007 | 0.022 | <0.002 | 0.110 | 0.011 | 0.016 | 0.27 | <0.005 | 0.3 | - | 0.002 | 0.34 |
| GBW | Controlled Rolled | X65 | 0.05 | 0.31 | 1.29 | 0.0020 | 0.010 | 0.04 | 0.06 | 0.042 | <0.002 | 0.21 | 0.01 | 0.005 | 0.3 | - | 0.0029 | 0.28 |

**TABLE 2**

**SPECIFIED CONDITIONS FOR THE FULL-SCALE TESTS**

| TEST VARIABLE | TEST 1 | TEST 2 | TEST 3A | TEST 3B |
|---|---|---|---|---|
| $H_2S$ Partial Pressure (Bar) | 1.0 ± 0.5 | ~3 | ~3 | ~3 |
| $H_2S$ Levels in Solution (ppm) | - | 2300-3500 | 2300-3500 | 2300-3500 |
| $CO_2$ Partial Pressure (Bar) | - | - | ~5.5 | ~5.5 |
| Total Pressure (Bar) | 100 ± 5 | 100 ± 5 | 100 ± 5 | 100 ± 5 |
| Temperature °C | 25 ± 3 | 25 ± 3 | 25 ± 3 | 25 ± 3 |
| Gas Velocity (m/s) | 1.2 | 1.2 | 1.2 | 1.2 |
| Depth of Artificial Seawater (mm) | ~150 | ~150 | ~150 | ~150 |
| Test Duration (Days) | 42 | 90 | 90 days | 90 |

**TABLE 3**

**HIC/SSCC RESULTS FOR FULL-SCALE TESTS**

| Pipe Code | Hoop Stress % SMYS | FULL SCALE TESTS % Crack Area | | | |
|---|---|---|---|---|---|
| | | Test 1 | Test 2 | Test 3A | Test 3B |
| EUZ | 69.6 | 1.5 | 11.8 | 0 | 1 |
| GAN | 50.2 | 8.8 | NT | 0.05 | 33 |
| FZS | 45.8 | 0 | 2.1 | 0 | 0 |
| GBQ | 64.2 | 0 | 0.5 | 0.15 | 80/2* |
| GBE | 37.8 | 0 | 1.1 | 0 | 0.1 |
| GBB | 42.6 | 0 | 0.4 | 0 | 1.1 |
| GCT | 63.2 | 0 | 0 | 0 | 0 |
| GBV | 52.5 | NT | 0 | 0+ | NT |
| GBW | 37.8 | 0 | 3.6 | 0 | 1.2 |

+ SSCC of Seam Weld
* SSCC by HIC Linkage

**TABLE 4**

**LABORATORY HIC AND SSCC RESULTS**

| Pipe Code | Body HIC+ | | | | Seam Weld HIC* | | Girth Weld HIC* | | Single Sided HIC, % Crack Area | | SSCC Tests | | |
|---|---|---|---|---|---|---|---|---|---|---|---|---|---|
| | BP | | NACE | | BP | NACE | BP | NACE | BP | NACE | NACE % SMYS | KISC MPa√m | Four Point Bend % SMYS |
| | CLR | CSR | CLR | CSR | | | | | | | | | |
| EUZ | 0 | 0 | 114.1 | 1.3 | NC | C | NC | NC | 0 | 25 | 65 | 25.3 | 80 |
| GAN | 53.9 | 1.2 | 102.2 | 3 | NC | NC | NC | NC | 16 | 20 | 45 | 23.8 | 90 |
| FZS | 0 | 0 | 67.4 | 1.5 | NC | C | NC | NC | 0 | 22 | 50 | 28.9 | >100 |
| GBQ | 65.0 | 2.5 | 86.5 | 4 | NC | NC | NC | NC | 64 | 70/100 | 40 | 22.7 | >100 |
| GBE | 37.2 | 0.3 | 59.0 | 0.5 | NC | C | NC | C | 0 | 22 | 75 | 25.1 | 50 |
| GBB | 43.3 | 0.2 | 52.1 | 0.3 | NC | NC | NC | NC | 48 | 120 | 85 | 25.0 | 40 |
| GCT | 0 | 0 | 0.1 | 0 | NC | NC | C | C | 0 | 0 | 75 | 25.7 | >100 |
| GBV | 0 | 0 | 12.4 | 0.7 | NC | NC | NC | C | 0 | 0 | 95 | 24.6 | 60 |
| GBW | 0 | 0 | 58.1 | 0.7 | NC | C | NC | NC | 0 | 2.5 | 95 | 25.2 | >100 |

\*   C   = Cracked
    NC = No Cracks
+   Typical acceptance criteria:   BP Solution   - in principle no stepwise cracking allowed
                                     NACE Solution - 15% CLR max, 2% CRS max

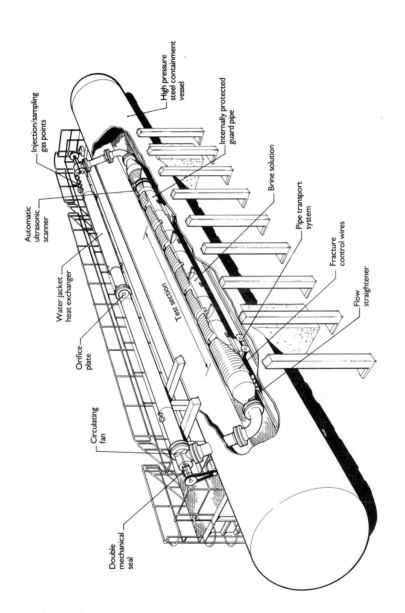

**Fig.1** Large scale sour gas test rig

Injection/sampling gas points

High pressure steel containment vessel

Internally protected guard pipe

Automatic ultrasonic scanner

Brine solution

Water jacket heat exchanger

Orifice plate

Test section

Pipe transport system

Fracture control wires

Circulating fan

Flow straightener

Double mechanical seal

1   Temperature controlled water bath
2   Heater - Stirrer
3   20L Vessel containing NACE solution
4   $H_2S$ to neutralising solution
5   10L Aspirator containing 20% NaOH
    solution
6   Test solution from reservoir
7   Circulation pump
8   HIC Testpieces
9   Single sided test cell
10  Test solution return to reservoir

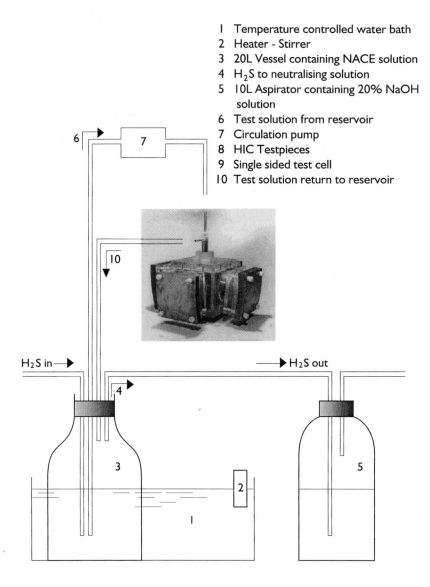

**Fig.2**  Single sided HIC test rig

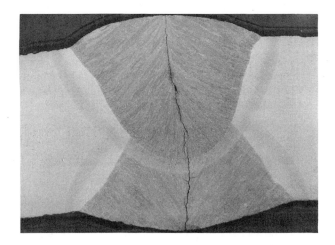

Figure 3    SSCC in the seam weld of pipe GBV

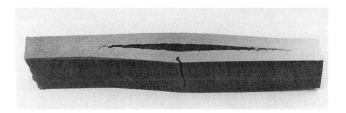

Figure 4    Mid-wall HIC and SSCC in pipe GBQ

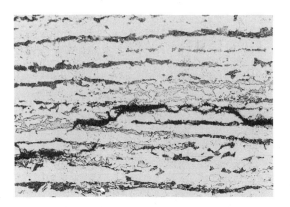

Figure 5    HIC in a mid-wall segregated band

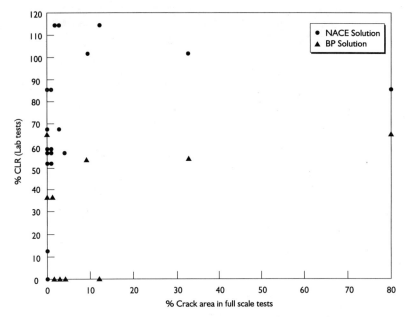

**Figure 6**   % Crack area in full scale tests as a function of
CLR in laboratory tests

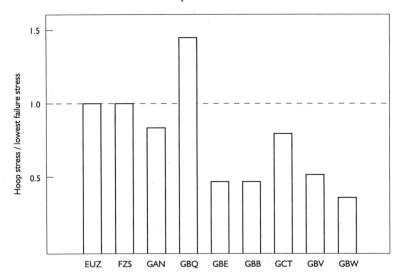

**Figure 7**   Ratio of hoop stress in full scale test divided by lowest
failure stress in NACE tensile test for each steel

ON-LINE MONITORING SYSTEM
FOR DETECTING COATING DEFECT ON PIPELINE


LE SYSTÈME ON-LINE DE CONTRÔLE
POUR DÉTECTION DE DEFAUT D'ENROBAGE EN GAZODUC

Mutsumi SHIBATA and Fumio KAJIYAMA
Tokyo Gas Co., Ltd., Japan

ABSTRACT

The occurrence of a coating defect causes not only an
increase in the current required to maintain cathodic
protection, that is, a reduction in the effectiveness
of cathodic protection, but also a rise in the
possibility of failures affecting pipeline integrity.
Therefore development of techniques for early
detection of coating defect has been required to
ensure pipeline safety.
This paper describes an advanced on-line monitoring
system for detecting coating defect on pipeline. Using
this system to monitor "damage resistance" as
determined by the analysis of pipe-to-soil resistance
can furnish the information indicating not only the
occurrence of coating defect but also the location.
Verification of the system was obtained in the field
using simulated coating defect. This innovative,
continuous 24-hour monitoring system provides early
detection capabilities.


RESUME

L'occurrence de défaut d'enrobage provoque non
seulement l'augmentation du courant requis pour
maintenir la protection cathodique, autrement dit, la
réduction de l'efficacité de la protection
cathodique, mais aussi la possibilité de défaillances
affectant l'intégrité de gazoduc. C'est pourquoi des
techniques permettant la détection précore des dé
fauts de revêtement ont été requises pour maintenir la
sécurité de gazoduc.
Cette thèse décrit un système on-line de côntrole pour
détection de défaut d'enrobage en gazoduc. Le côntrole
de la "résistance aux dommages" réalisée par analyse
de la résistance tuyau/sol du système peut nous donner
des informations sur l'occurrence de défaut
d'enrobage et sur leur emplacement. Le système a été v
érifié avec de défaut d'enrobage simulés sur le
terrain. Ce nouveau système de côntrole permet la dé
tection précore 24 heures sur 24.

INTRODUCTION

Pipelines can be effectively protected from soil corrosion by combination of high-resistivity coating materials and cathodic protection. In cases where coating defects occur, sufficient current must be increased to suppress corrosion at the site of the coating defect where bare steel is in direct contact with the soil. Therefore, in order to achieve the secure, cost-effective maintenance of pipelines, a good coating-to-metal bond is essential.

Various survey techniques for detecting coating defects such as the needle electrode method, the Pearson method, and others [1][2], have been developed, however, these techniques are not practical for everyday use. Therefore, a remote automatic system for the early detection of coating defects is required.

Although coating defects can be attributed to a number of causes, in all cases, the occurrence of such defects always leads to a reduction in pipe-to-soil resistance. Utilizing this phenomenon, the authors have developed an on-line monitoring system for detecting coating defect on pipeline by monitoring "damage resistance" as determined by analysis of variations in pipe-to-soil resistance along the pipeline route. This paper describes the system and its methodology, and presents some examples of its application.

SYSTEM

The system consists of several units. These units monitor the occurrence of coating defect on their respective sections continuously for 24 hours. The length of their sections are determined by coating specifications. The computer used to analyze the data collected by each unit are connected to a computer at the main station, thus an operator at the main station can easily access the data pertaining to the condition of entire pipeline.

An example of how the system may be set up is given schematically in Figure 1, UNIT 1 and UNIT 2 are positioned to monitor the occurrence of coating defect between point 1 and point 3. Each unit has a discrete power supply that enables it to impress an AC signal on a particular frequency (f1 for UNIT 1 and f2 for UNIT 2) from the pipeline to earth. Equipments for monitoring line current and pipe-to-soil potential at one frequency (f1 for UNIT 1 and f2 for UNIT 2) are set at the point nearest the power supply (point 1 for UNIT 1 and point 3 for UNIT 2) and a an intermediate point (point 2 for both UNIT 1 and UNIT 2). In cases where these two points are a great distance apart, the use of additional monitoring equipment is recommended to improve accuracy.

In the case shown in Figure 1, the monitoring section for UNIT 1 is between point 1 and point 2, and that for UNIT 2 is between point 2 and point 3. However, when several additional monitoring points are employed, the section of covered by each unit is divided into several shorter and more detailed sections. The occurrence of coating defect is detected by determining the "damage resistance" of each section between neighboring monitoring points. Thus, the system can detect not only the occurrence of a coating defect but also its location.

In this system, AC signals are impressed continuously between the pipeline and earth by AC power supplies. The use of AC signals is preferable to DC signals, because AC signals are less vulnerable to error caused by interference, especially in environments where electric interference exists.

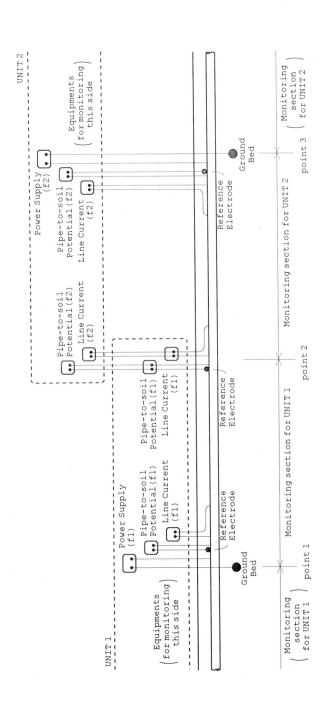

Figure 1.   The arrangement of the system.

ANALYZING PROCEDURE

Pipe-to-soil resistance of the section is calculated by average potential divided by current collected in the section. Thus pipe-to-soil resistance of the section between the neighboring monitoring point x and point x+1, Rp, will be given by equation (1), in which i(x) and i(x+1) stand for line currents, and E(x) and E(x+1) stand for pipe-to-soil potentials at two monitoring points, respectively[3].

$$Rp = \frac{1}{2} \cdot \frac{E(x)+E(x+1)}{i(x)-i(x+1)} \qquad (1)$$

As previously mentioned, monitored pipe-to-soil resistance of each section offers a significant information on the occurrence of coating defect. However, pipe-to-soil resistance varies with its condition at the interface between the pipeline and soil especially influenced by water contents.

To overcome the difficulty caused by interference, special attention was focused on the variation of pipe-to-soil resistance. Studies revealed that variations caused by coating damage, which leads to the occurrence of coating defect, are of short duration (a few seconds), while the variations due to other causes are of long duration (a few hours). Thus, an analysis of shorter variations in pipe-to-soil resistance, reveals damage resistance, that is defect-to-soil resistance. Thus this system detects the occurrence of coating defect by determining damage resistance.

Figure 2 shows electrical equivalent circuits of pipeline in one section (a)undamaged and (b)damaged. As pipe resistance is relatively low compared with coating resistance, an equivalent circuit undamaged is expressed using only the combined pipe-to-soil resistances, Rc(k). However an equivalent circuit with damage at "point d", damage resistance, Rd, will be added in parallel with the pipe-to-soil resistances.

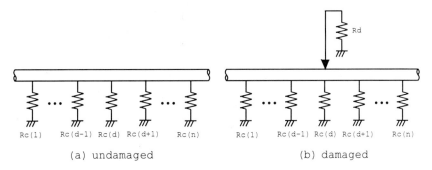

(a) undamaged                    (b) damaged

Figure 2. Electrical equivalent circuits of one monitoring section undamaged and damaged.

The mathematical relationships of these equivalent circuits have been studied. The inverse of the pipe-to-soil resistance of the section undamaged, 1/Rpa, can be expressed as sum of the inverse of pipe-to-soil resistances in an equation(2).

$$\frac{1}{Rpa} = \sum_{k=1}^{n} \frac{1}{Rc(k)} \qquad (2)$$

The inverse of pipe-to-soil resistance of this section damaged, 1/Rp, can also be expressed as a sum of the inverses of pipe-to-soil resistances, except at the location where the coating is damaged, as shown in equation(3). At the location where coating is damaged, the inverse of damage resistance, 1/Rd, is added to the inverses of the pipe-to-soil resistances, 1/Rc(d). And, finally, the simple relationship between the pipe-to-soil resistances undamaged and damaged, and damage resistance can be determined.

$$\frac{1}{Rp} = \sum_{k=1}^{d-1} \frac{1}{Rc(k)} + \left( \frac{1}{Rc(d)} + \frac{1}{Rd} \right) + \sum_{k=d+1}^{n} \frac{1}{Rc(k)} = \frac{1}{Rpa} + \frac{1}{Rd} \qquad (3)$$

The equation for determining damage resistance, as expressed by pipe-to-soil resistance undamaged and damaged, is derived from equation(3) as follows:

$$Rd = \left( \frac{1}{Rp} - \frac{1}{Rpa} \right)^{-1} \qquad (4)$$

Without the damage, damage resistance, Rd, is infinite as Rp is equal to Rpa. However, when coating is damaged, damage resistance decreases due to the reduction in defect-to-soil resistance. Therefore, it is possible to detect coating defect by finding the decreases in damage resistance. The shorter the intervals at which monitoring points are set, the higher accuracy for identifying the location of damage is obtained.

FIELD SURVEY

An evaluation of the system was performed on gas pipeline that runs for 49 km through Tokyo district. The pipeline is cathodically protected by impressed current systems. It crosses under many electric railway systems and so the protection current is frequently modulated to maintain adequate potential to suppress the influence of stray currents. The pipeline studied is 660 mm in diameter with a polyethylene coating.

The conditions set for the system in the field survey are shown in Table 1. The total length of monitoring sections was 4.7 km from point 1 and point 3. The total length was divided into two shorter sections at point 2; the section between point 1 and point 2 was monitored by UNIT 1 and that between point 2 and point 3 was monitored by UNIT 2. AC signals were impressed between pipeline and magnesium electrode using power supplies of UNIT 1 and UNIT 2, bipolar power supply / amps (Takasago, Ltd., BPS40-15) incorporating internal oscillators of lock-in voltmeters (NF Electronic Instruments, 5560). To prevent interference between two units' AC signals, the signals were impressed in the current constant mode. Line currents were measured using the resistance drop method [4]. Pipe-to-soil potentials were measured using buried zinc electrode (at point 2) or copper sulfate electrodes (at point 1 and point 3). Lock-in voltmeters were used to measure these values of the one frequencies.

The appropriate adequate frequencies for AC signals impressed by power supply of UNIT 1 (f1=225Hz) and UNIT 2 (f2=420Hz) were decided on with consideration with responses in damage resistance observed during coating damage, analyses on noise on pipeline and the possibility of interference between the AC signals of UNIT 1 and UNIT 2 (f1 and f2).

Buried sacrificial magnesium anodes of several points along the monitoring sections, usually not in direct contact with the pipeline during the survey, were used to simulate coating damage by making electrical contact with the pipeline. The magnesium-to-soil resistances were controlled to be 10 ohm with variable resistance. The electrical contacts simulating coating damage were applied for 5-second, for a total of 30 to 35 seconds of each 1-minute monitoring interval, so that variations due to damage could be clearly evaluated. The pipe-to-soil resistance without the damage, Rpa, was determined based on pipe-to-soil resistance 1-minute prior to the monitoring interval. All data was recorded at 0.2-second intervals using digital data recorder.

Table 1. Conditions set for the system in the field survey.

|  | UNIT 1 | | UNIT 2 |
|---|---|---|---|
|  | point 1 | point 2 | point 3 |
| Frequency (Hz) | 225 | – | 420 |
| Current (A(rms)) | 0.8 | – | 0.8 |
| Interval of terminals for line current monitoring (m) | 21 | 202 | 51 |
| Monitoring section (km) | 2.2 | | 2.5 |
| Sampling interval (sec) | 0.2 | | |

Results

Damage at 0.1 km away from point 1 (in the section monitored by UNIT 1).

In Figure 3, the variations in line currents and pipe-to-soil potentials for the section monitored by UNIT 1 when damage is present is shown. When damage is present, an increase and an slight decrease in line currents at point 1 and point 2, respectively, were found, and decreases in pipe-to-soil potential at both point 1 and point 2 were found. However, even if these variations were caused by a decrease in pipe-to-soil resistance due to damage in the section studied, these variations themselves are so small that determining whether or not damage is present is quite difficult.

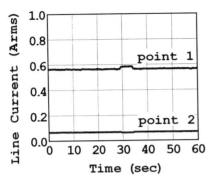 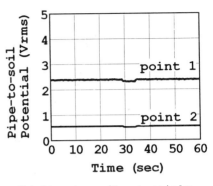

(a) Line currents   (b) Pipe-to-soil potentials

Figure 3. Line currents and pipe-to-soil potentials with damage at 0.1 km away from point 1 (in the section monitored by UNIT 1).

In Figure 4(a), the pipe-to-soil resistance, $R_p$, of the section monitored by UNIT 1 when damage is present is shown. Pipe-to-soil resistance was determined from line currents and pipe-to-soil potentials at point 1 and point 2, shown in Figure 3, according to equation(1). With the presence of damage, pipe-to-soil resistance decreased obviously, unlike the variations in line currents and pipe-to-soil potentials illustrated in Figure 3.

In Figure 4(b), the damage resistance of the section monitored by UNIT 1 when damage is present is shown. Damage resistance was determined by analyzing pipe-to-soil resistance according to equation(4). When damage is not present, damage resistance stays greater than 266 ohm. However, when damage is present, it decreases to 30 ohm, a value similar to that for controlled damage resistance. Even if variations in damage resistance can be seen clearly when damage is present, there still remains the problem that damage resistance can be low even when no damage is present, despite the fact that damage resistance is in theory infinite when damage is not present.

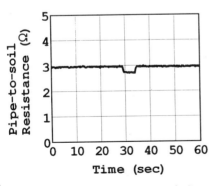 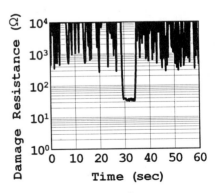

(a) Pipe-to-soil potential   (b) Damage resistance

Figure 4. Pipe-to-soil resistance and damage resistance for the section monitored by UNIT 1, with damage at 0.1 km away from point 1 (in the section monitored by UNIT 1).

To reduce the possibility of misinterpretation, a simple mathematical analysis was performed against damage resistance. Presented in Figure 5 is the result of analysis of damage resistance that plots the maximum of continuous five damage resistances (maximum damage resistances for one second). Application of this analysis effectively decreases the possibility of misinterpretation.

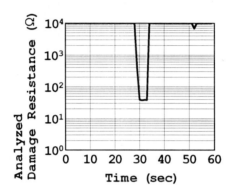

Figure 5. Analyzed damage resistance of the section monitored by UNIT 1 with damage at 0.1 km away from point 1 (in the section monitored by UNIT 1).

In Figure 6, analyzed damage resistance of the section monitored by UNIT 2 is given. As the damage is not present in this section, analyzed damage resistance remained greater than 1936 ohm.

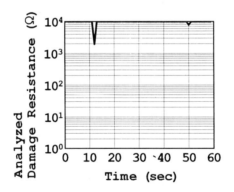

Figure 6. Analyzed damage resistance of the section monitored by UNIT 2 with damage at 0.1 km away from point 1 (in the section monitored by UNIT 1).

Damage at 2.0 km away from point 1 (in the section monitored by UNIT 1, not in the section monitored by UNIT 2).

The effectiveness of the system in detecting damage at a distant point was evaluated. In Figure 7, variations in analyzed damage resistance of UNIT 1 and UNIT 2, respectively, are given. Damage resistance of UNIT 1 decreased immediately with the presence of damage, while that of UNIT 2 remained greater than 1114 ohm. These variations indicate that damage is present in the section monitored by UNIT 1, not in the section monitored by UNIT 2.

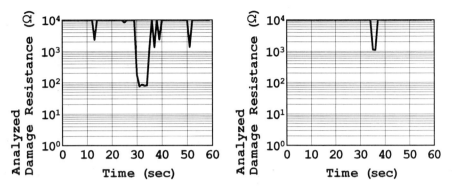

(a) section monitored by UNIT 1     (b) section monitored by UNIT 2

Figure 7. Analyzed damage resistances with damage at 2.0 km away from point 1 (in the section monitored by UNIT 1, not in the section monitored by UNIT 2).

### Damage at 1.9 km and 0.1 km away from point 3 (not in the section monitored by UNIT 1, in the section monitored by UNIT 2).

Further evaluation was performed with the damage at a site not in the section monitored by UNIT 1 but in the section monitored by UNIT 2. Presented in Figure 8 and Figure 9 , are variations in analyzed damage resistances of UNIT 1 and UNIT 2 when the site of damage are located at 1.9 km and 0.1 km away from point 3. In both cases, the level of analyzed damage resistance of UNIT 1 remained high despite the presence of damage, while that of UNIT 2 decreased obviously. These results prove the ability of the system to identify the section where the coating is damaged.

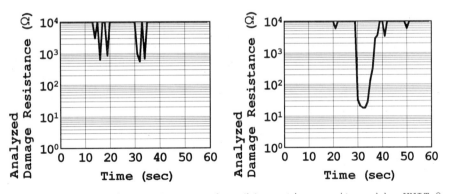

(a) section monitored by UNIT 1     (b) section monitored by UNIT 2

Figure 8. Analyzed damage resistances with damage at 1.9 km away from point 3 (not in the section monitored by UNIT 1, in the section monitored by UNIT 2)

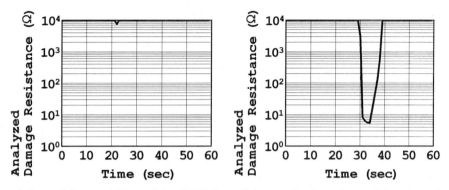

(a) section monitored by UNIT 1    (b) section monitored by UNIT 2

Figure 9. Analyzed damage resistances with damage at 0.1 km away from point 3 (not in the section monitored by UNIT 1, in the section monitored by UNIT 2)

CONCLUSION and FUTURE PLAN

Data obtained in the field survey proved the effectiveness of this system and suggest its high utility as part of pipeline maintenance programs. To improve the system's accuracy, however more-effective analysis is required. Adequate and appropriate conditions for AC signal supply must be determined with particular attention given to analyzing the influence of AC induced corrosion through both laboratory study and field surveys.

By incorporating monitoring system of pipe-to-soil potential of DC, it is possible to construct a total monitoring system for the maintenance on both coating and cathodic protection.

REFERENCES

[1] T.Sato, M.Kawakami, "Development of Underground Pipeline Coating Defect Inspection Systems", Internal & External Protection of Pipes - Proceedings of the 8th International Conference, 1990, p.329-338.

[2] L.Di Biase, H.G.Schöneich, D.Koster, P.Labat, et.al., "G.E.R.G-PC2 Fault Location on Pipeline Coatings", Proceedings of the 19th World Gas Conference, 1994, RC5.

[3] A.W.Peabody, "Control of Pipeline Corrosion", NACE Publication, 1976, p.45-47.

[4] ibid, p.41.

SURVEILLANCE DES MOUVEMENTS DE GAZ DANS UN STOCKAGE SOUTERRAIN EN
AQUIFERE PAR SISMIQUE DE PUITS


MONITORING GAS MOVEMENTS IN AN UNDERGROUND STORAGE FACILITY BY
SEISMIC PROFILING

J-L. MARI*, F. HUGUET**, S.SERBUTOVIEZ*, F. VERDIER**

* Institut Français du Pétrole

** Gaz de France

**RESUME**

Une nouvelle méthode de surveilllance de l'évolution de la bulle de gaz au voisinage d'un puits a été développée par le Gaz de France et l'Institut Français du Pétrole et expérimenté sur un stockage en nappe aquifère en développement.

La méthode de sismique utilisée correspond à une mise en oeuvre de type "walk away" autour d'un puits équipé de capteurs sismiques permanents.

La surveillance des mouvements de gaz est réalisée par la mesure de l'évolution des retards temporels associés aux horizons situés sous le réservoir.

Elle est confirmée par les modifications d'amplitude des marqueurs sismiques associés au réservoir.

Les résultats obtenus montrent qu'il est possible de suivre les différentes phases du remplissage en gaz du réservoir et de mettre en évidence les directions de remplissage préférentielles.

**ABSTRACT**

A new method for monitoring fluid movements in a reservoir in the vicinity of a well has been developped by Gaz de France and Institut Français du Pétrole. This method was tested on a underground gas storage facility where gas was injected into an aquifer.

The method is a borehole seismic technic of a walk away type.
The seismic data are recorded using a array of permanent vertical sensors.

The bubble movement versus time can be checked by comparing seismic data recorded at different times. The movements of gas are monitored by measuring time-delay variations associated with the horizons below the reservoir as well as amplitude anomalies associated with the seismic marker of the reservoir.

The experiment shows that the proposed method can be used both for monitoring fluid movement and for indicating the main axes of gas filling.

## INTRODUCTION

Les méthodes conventionnelles de surveillance des stockages de gaz en nappe aquifère sont basées sur des mesures ponctuelles dans les puits (neutron, plan d'eau, pressions) et ne permettent pas de suivre les mouvements du gaz en dehors d'une zone proche du puits.

De façon à augmenter la distance d'investigation des puits, Gaz de France (G.D.F.) et l'Institut Français du Pétrole (I.F.P.) ont développé une méthode de monitoring basée sur la sismique de puits pour suivre l'évolution de la saturation en gaz à une distance de plusieurs centaines de mètres du puits.

La méthode consiste à effectuer des profils sismiques répétitifs dans le temps en utilisant un dispositif de capteurs sismiques permanents installés dans un puits sans gêne pour l'exploitation du puits.

La structure anticlinale de Céré-la-Ronde est utilisée par G.D.F. comme stockage souterrain de gaz en nappe aquifère. L'objet de la présente communication est de montrer l'aptitude de la sismique de puits à la surveillance des mouvements de fluide dans un réservoir en fonction du temps.

Deux profils de sismique de puits de type balade sismique ou walk away ont été enregistrés sur la structure à quatre époques différentes. La première campagne de mesure, enregistrée en juin 1993 avant la mise en gaz, sert de référence. Les trois autres campagnes ont été acquises au cours de trois périodes de remplissage, en février, avril et novembre 1994.

Le présent article est composé de trois parties : la première partie est une description géologique de la structure, la deuxième partie décrit la mise en oeuvre et le traitement des données sismiques et la troisième partie présente une étude comparative des données de puits aux différentes époques.

## DESCRIPTION GEOLOGIQUE

Le stockage de Céré-la-Ronde est constitué par une structure anticlinale faillée complexe. Deux tops ont été identifiés. Sur le top central, ont été forés les puits CE 12 et CE 112 au voisinage desquels ont été réalisées les premières injections de gaz.

Cette structure centrale, allongée Nord-Sud est bordée par deux failles dont la plus importante assure la fermeture vers l'Ouest.

Le réservoir principal R1 situé à une profondeur moyenne de 900 m est constitué par un amalgame de chenaux gréseux d'excellente qualité réservoir sur une épaisseur moyenne de 20 m. Ce réservoir est couvert soit par une couverture argileuse ou directement par la formation argilo-dolomitique de l'Hettangien.

Le réservoir R2 se situe sous le R1 et est constitué par des chenaux à communication complexe.

## MISE EN OEUVRE ET TRAITEMENT DES DONNEES SISMIQUES
## INTRODUCTION

• Dispositif de mise en oeuvre

Les données de puits ont été acquises sur une antenne réceptrice composée de capteurs permanents disposée dans le puits CE 112 foré pour contrôler l'aquifère Bathonien. Le puits CE 112, situé à proximité du puits CE 12, a une profondeur limitée à 700 m et n'atteint pas l'objectif réservoir (environ 950 m). Le puits CE 12 est un puits profond qui atteint le réservoir. Un profil sismique vertical classique a été enregistré dans le puits CE 12 dans l'intervalle de profondeur 150 - 1 050 m. L'antenne réceptrice (figure 1) est composée de 15 capteurs permanents répartis en quatre groupes sur l'intervalle de profondeur 520 - 680 m. La distance entre deux capteurs est de 10 m. Les capteurs permanents, descendus avec le tubing sont ancrés au cuvelage du puits par l'intermédiaire d'un système composé de ressorts à lames. Les capteurs permanents sont des géophones verticaux dont la fréquence de coupure est de 28 Hz. Aux cotes 640 et 680 m, les géophones verticaux ont été remplacés par des géophones à trois composantes.

Le dispositif émetteur est composé de deux vibrateurs distants de 10 m émettant un signal vibrosismique dans la bande de fréquences 16 - 120 Hz.

La mise en oeuvre de la sismique de puits est de type balade sismique ou walk away. Deux profils appelés M 01 et M 02 ont été enregistrés sur la structure. La figure 2 donne le plan d'implantation des profils M 01 et M 02. Les lignes composées de points donnent la localisation des points de tirs (SP). Les lignes continues donnent la localisation des points miroirs. Le profil M 01, orienté Nord-Sud, est composé de 103 points de vibration (SP). Le déport maximal longitudinal de la source est de 800 m. Le profil M 02, orienté Est-Ouest, est composé de 60 points de vibration avec un déport maximal de 500 m. La zone miroir éclairée (CDP) de part et d'autre du puits CE 112 est de 300 m pour le profil Nord-Sud et de 150 m pour le profil Est-Ouest.

• Traitement des données de puits

Les données de puits ont fait l'objet d'un traitement spécifique en vue d'obtenir des sections de sismique de puits avec un fort rapport signal à bruit. Le traitement est décrit en détail par J-L. MARI, F. HUGUET et J. LAURENT (1994).

Le traitement des données de puits est réalisé en deux phases : la première phase concerne le traitement de chaque PSV déporté composé de 15 cotes, la deuxième phase concerne la mise en collection en point miroir des différents PSV pour obtenir les deux profils sismiques M 01 et M 02.

- Première phase de traitement

Pour chaque PSV déporté, les ondes descendantes P ont été extraites par filtrage matriciel. Ces ondes sont projetées sur la première section propre, les données brutes ayant été horizontalisées pour permettre l'usage d'un opérateur de moyenne en distance et fréquence (F. GLANGEAUD et J-L. MARI, 1994). Après extraction, les ondes descendantes ainsi estimées sont soustraites aux données initiales pour obtenir une section résiduelle. Cette dernière contient les ondes montantes, les ondes converties et le bruit. Les ondes descendantes sont remises à leur position originelle en temps et pointées. Les temps pointés de première arrivée sont utilisés pour déterminer la loi vitesse. Après remise en temps à sa position initiale, la section résiduelle est corrigée dynamiquement puis horizontalisée de façon à mettre à plat en temps double les ondes P montantes. Ces dernières sont ensuite extraites par filtrage matriciel avec une forte moyenne en fréquence.

- Deuxième phase de traitement

La section en ondes montantes associée à chaque PSV déporté est projetée sur la ligne des points-miroir de façon à obtenir une section de sismique de puits de type "VSP-CDP stack" par profil. Chaque trace miroir est identifiée par son numéro de point de tir. Les traces miroir sont corrigées statique de façon à horizontaliser l'horizon sismique associé au Dogger. Sur chaque profil de sismique de puits, le rapport signal sur bruit est amélioré par un filtrace matriciel glissant appliqué sur sept traces adjacentes. La section associée à l'espace signal est la première section propre. La section associée à l'espace bruit est la différence entre la section brute et la section associée à l'espace signal.

- Présentation des résultats

Pour chaque campagne sismique, nous présentons par profil (M 01 et M 02), la section sismique associée à l'espace signal (figures 3 et 4). La figure 5 montre la corrélation obtenue en juin 1993 entre les sections de puits (trace somme et section du PSV classique acquis dans le puits CE 12 avec le profil sismique de puits M 02) et les informations lithologiques (identification des horizons sismiques en profondeur). Les capteurs permanents étant situés dans l'intervalle de profondeur 520 - 680 m, les sections de profil de puits M 01 et M 02 montrent des horizons sismiques cohérents dans l'intervalle temps 400 - 900 ms avec un bon rapport signal sur bruit au niveau du réservoir. La prédiction sous le puits est estimée à 360 m.

Les sections sismiques n'ont pas le même nombre de traces à toutes les époques. Ceci est la conséquence des conditions météorologiques, rendant certains points de tir inaccessibles.

ETUDE COMPARATIVE DES PROFILS DE SISMIQUE DE PUITS

L'évolution de la bulle de gaz au cours du temps peut être mise en évidence en comparant des données sismiques enregistrées à des époques différentes (par exemple, des sections de sismique de surface : E.. BLONDIN et J-L. MARI, 1986). En effet, dans un réservoir gréseux, la vitesse des ondes de compression diminue lorsque du gaz remplace de l'eau. La diminution de vitesse introduit un retard temporel des réflexions situées sous le réservoir. Les profils sismiques ont été suréchantillonnés au pas de 0,5 ms (1 ms étant le pas d'échantillonnage temps à l'acquisition). La mesure des retards temporels a été obtenue par corrélation en utilisant la méthodologie décrite par E. BLONDIN et J-L. MARI (1986).

Les résultats de comparaison sont présentés en figures 6 et 7. Le puits CE 12 est noté A. Les puits injecteurs CE 17, CE 5 et CE 16 sont notés respectivement, b, c et d.

Les figures 6 et 7 montrent les profils de sismique de puits avant mise en gaz du réservoir (juin 1993) ainsi que les retards temporels observés en février 1994 (trait continu) et avril 1994 (pointillé). La comparaison a été réalisée sur 68 points miroir pour le profil M 01 et 51 points miroir pour le profil M 02, correspondant aux points miroir communs aux différentes périodes d'acquisition.

Le profil M 02 montre un retard temporel globalement constant sur l'ensemble du profil. Le retard temporel passe de 0,5 ms en février 1994 à 1 ms en avril 1994. Le profil M 01 montre une courbe de retard temporel plus chahutée. La courbe de retard présente des bosses au niveau des puits injecteurs c et b. Entre février 1994 et avril 1994, l'évolution de la courbe des retards temporels montre une mise en gaz préférentielle dans la partie Nord du profil M 01. Les anomalies de retard temporel ont été reportées sur le plan de position (figure 2). Leur répartition géographique montre une mise en gaz suivant l'axe principal de la structure.

L'analyse des cartes des variations des retards résiduels montre une mise en gaz progressive sur le profil M 02 avec un remplissage plus important vers l'Ouest, en novembre 1994.

La qualité du profil M 01 orienté Nord-Sud est moins bonne dans sa partie la plus au Nord. En prenant comme référence le profil acquis en février 1994, on constate un développement de la bulle de gaz vers le Nord, entre février et novembre 1994.

L'évolution du mouvement de la bulle de gaz a été également suivi en étudiant les amplitudes sismiques et en transformant les sections PSV à déport nul en sections impédance à l'aide du logiciel d'inversion stratigraphique développé par la Compagnie Générale de Géophysique (C.G.G.). Le logiciel utilisé est un logiciel d'inversion non linéaire qui transforme des données sismiques en impédance acoustique. Les données entrées comprennent les données sismiques avec l'ondelette ayant servi au traitement et un macro-modèle initial d'impédance acoustique.

Le macro-modèle d'impédance initial est décrit par couches pour lesquelles on définit une valeur initiale et une plage de variations possibles. Chaque couche est subdivisée en sous-couches dont on donne la résolution en temps double. Le processus d'inversion est itératif et minimise une fonctionnelle sur une fenêtre temporelle par une technique de relaxation.

Le programme fournit en résultat une section synthétique et une section résidu correspondant à la différence entre les données entrées au programme et les données après inversion. Un coefficient de corrélation permet d'apprécier la qualité de l'inversion à chaque itération.

Le macro-modèle d'impédance a été construit dans un premier temps à partir des vitesses de tranche de la courbe temps-profondeur du PSV sur le puits CE 12, la courbe étant extrapolée en profondeur sous le puits. Il a été raffiné en partant du log d'impédance en temps calculé à partir des logs sonique et densité. Le modèle est défini par 8 couches, les sous-couches élémentaires font 3 ms temps double (figure 8-1).

L'ondelette de référence est extraite des traitements PSV au niveau de la déconvolution de l'arrivée directe. L'ondelette brute s'étalant sur plus de 50 ms a été compressée par un filtre triangulaire pour réduire l'extension des lobes latéraux.

Trois variantes d'inversion ont été réalisées. Une inversion 1D de chaque log PSV avec et sans mute et une inversion 2D avant stack de l'ensemble des PSV à la manière d'une section sismique. Les coefficients de corrélation obtenus sur la fenêtre 500 à 900 ms sont de l'ordre de 98 %. L'inversion est très peu contrainte, la plage d'impédance possible va de 3 000 à 15 000.

La figure 8 correspondant à l'inversion 1D des logs sismiques obtenus sans mute met en évidence des variations d'impédance au niveau du réservoir. De février à avril 1994, la chute d'impédance par rapport à juin 1993 est de 8 % et va jusqu'à 18 % au mois de novembre 1994.

Les anomalies d'amplitude observées sur les PSV à déport nul sont également observables sur les profils sismiques de puits. Elles sont mises en évidence sur les profils par pointé (figures 3 et 4) et identifiées par le caractère AA. Les fortes anomalies d'amplitudes corrèlent avec les anomalies de retard temporel. Elles permettent également de suivre la mise en gaz du réservoir.

## CONCLUSION

Une nouvelle technologie de capteurs sismiques permanents et amovibles développée par G.D.F et I.F.P grâce à un couplage optimal des géophones avec le puits assure une qualité d'enregistrement sismique supérieure à une sonde descendue au cable avec un côut d'exploitation très faible.

Une antenne réceptrice composée de capteurs permanents est donc parfaitement adaptée aux enregistrements de sismique répétitive pour surveiller des mouvements de fluide au voisinage des puits dans un stockage souterrain en aquifère, la différence de qualité sismique d'une période à une autre étant uniquement liée aux effets de source et aux conditions de surface. Le traitement des données de puits est réalisé pour obtenir des sections de type VSP-CDP stack avec un rapport signal sur bruit élevé et une haute résolution.

La surveillance des mouvements de gaz peut être réalisée par mesure de l'évolution des retards temporels associés aux horizons situés sous le réservoir, la répartition géographique des anomalies de retard temporel montrant un développement de la bulle de gaz vers le Nord et un remplissage plus important vers l'Ouest. La migration du gaz dans le réservoir est également confirmée par les anomalies d'amplitude observables sur les profils sismiques au niveau de la zone réservoir.

Les résultats obtenus sont conformes aux mesures ponctuelles réalisées dans le puits (hauteur en gaz, satutation). La méthode développée doit permettre à court terme de réaliser un suivi quantitatif de l'évolution de la saturation du réservoir à une distance de quelques centaines de mètres du puits.

## REFERENCES

MARI J-L., HUGUET F. et LAURENT J., 1994. An example of walk away processing based on spectral matrix filtering , paper G029, expanded abstracts of the 56 th meeting of the European Association of Exploration Geophysicsts, Vienna.

BLONDIN E. et MARI J-L., 1986. Detection of gas bubble boundary movement, Geophysical Prospecting, vol 34, n° 1, pp. 73-93.

GLANGEAUD F. et MARI J-L., 1994. Wave separation. Editions Technip, Paris.

## Permanent sensor Walkaway WSP
### SP and CDP locations

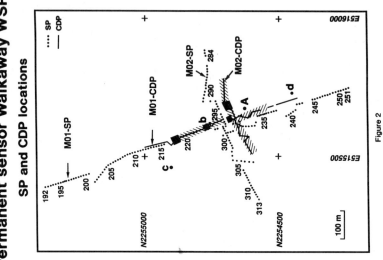

Figure 2

## Geophone array

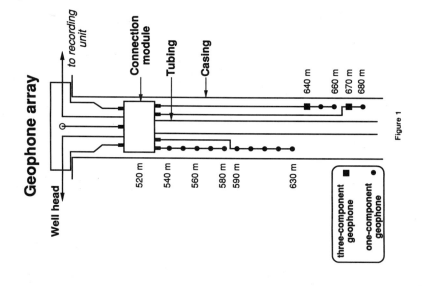

Figure 1

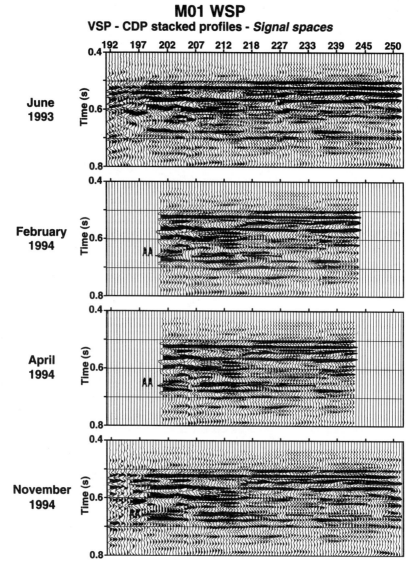

**M01 WSP**

VSP - CDP stacked profiles - *Signal spaces*

Figure 3

# M02 WSP

## VSP - CDP stacked profiles - *Signal spaces*

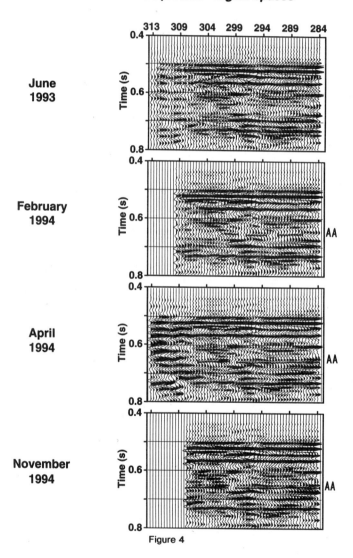

Figure 4

**Correlation of well seismic sections with lithology**

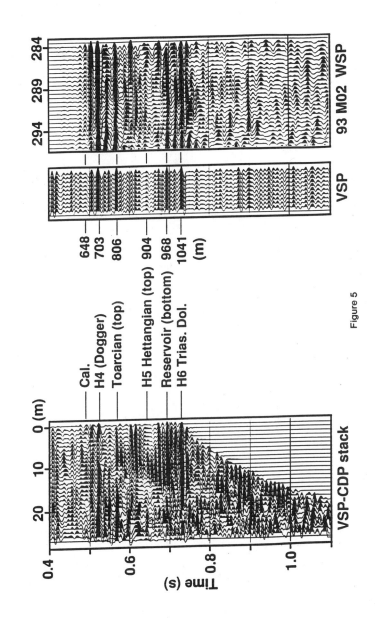

Figure 5

## MO1 WSP : VSP – CDP stacked profile – *Signal space*

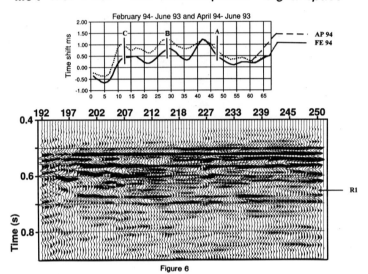

Figure 6

## MO2 WSP : VSP – CDP stacked profile – *Signal space*

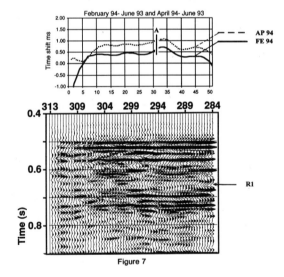

Figure 7

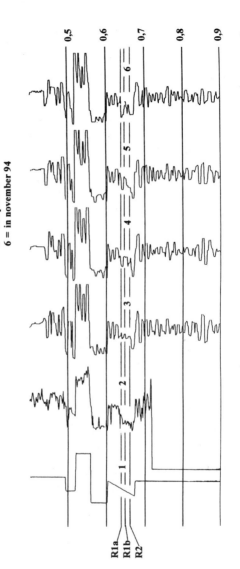

**1 D Stratigraphic Inversion
From VSP data**

**Impedance logs after inversion**

1 = impedance model
2 = impedance log

3 = in june 93
4 = in february 94
5 = in april 94
6 = in november 94

Figure 8

DEVELOPMENT OF LONG DISTANCE DIRECT JACKING METHODS
FOR LARGE DIAMETER STEEL PIPES

DEVELOPPEMENT DE METHODES DE RACCORDEMENT DIRECT SUR
LONGUE DISTANCE POUR TUYAUX EN ACIER DE GRAND DIAMETRE

Katsumi FUCHIMOTO
Distribution Engineering Center, Osaka Gas Co. Ltd., JAPAN

## ABSTRACT

In order to meet projected natural gas demand into the 21th century, a new LNG terminal
and trunklines, whose length is over 150 km, will have to be construct. In the urban area
of Japan, it is difficult to adopt the open cut method. Therefore, we have developed two
types of direct pipe jacking methods for our new trunklies, 750mm diameter steel pipes.
Our two types of pipe jacking method are named "Solid lubricant injectionmethod" and
"Membrane wrapping method".

## RESUME

Afin de répondre à la demande en gaz natural prévue au XXXI ˚ siècle, un nouveau terminal
GNL et de nouvelles conduites interurbaines, dont la longueur est de plus de 150km, devront
être construits. Dans les zones urbaines du Japon, il est difficile d'adopter la methodes
à ciel ouvert. Nous avons donc mis au point deux types de méthodes de raccordement direct
de tuyaux de distribution pour nos nouvelles conduites interurbaines,tuyaux en acier de 750mm
de diamètre. Nos deux types de méthodes de raccordement de tuyaux sont appelés "Méthode
d'injection de librifiant solide" et "Méthode de revêtement à membrane".

## 1. INTRODUCTION

Osaka Gas operates two LNG terminals. In order to meet projected natural gas demand into the 21th century, a new LNG terminal and trunklines, whose length is over 150 km, will have to be construct. Usually the pipes are installed by an open cut method. However, in the urban area of Japan, it is difficult to adopt the open cut method. Therefore, we srarted to research pipe jacking methods for our new trunklies, 750mm diameter steel pipes, and we concluded that two problems have to be solved as below.

(1)How to reduce jack thrust

In our case, 500m long pipe jacking work are required. However, the jack thrust will increase in proportion to thrusting distance(See Fig.1.) and allowable jacking force is 600 ton, which depends on ground reaction behind the jack, or 800 ton, which depends on compressive strength of jacking pipes.

(2)How to inject lubricant and cement mortar

The lubricant have to be injected during jacking operation while the cement mortar have to be injected after completion of jacking operation for the purpose of backfilling. In case of hume pipe, they can be injected from holes, whereas holes cannot be made on high pressure steel gas pipes.

First, we developed pipe jacking method using casing pipes. However, in order to make pipe jacking work effficient, we has been developed two pipe jacking methods without using casing pipes.

Our two types of pipe jacking method are named "Solid lubricant injectionmethod" and "Membrane wrapping method".(See Fig.2 and 3.)

## 2. SPLID LUBRICANT INJECTION METHOD

2.1 Principle

With a view to reduce the jack thrust, lubricant is often injected. In addtion, the lubricant is liquid because it is injected from the starting pit through the tube. Therefore, it often dilute into the ground and so jackthrust cannot be reduced.

We have developed a new lubricant named "ALL MIGHTY", which consists of two kinds of liquid. They are injected at the end of the shiled machine and changed to solid state when they are mixed in the soil. Therefore, the solidlubricant does not dilute into the ground, and the injection holes are not needed in the jacking pipes.

2.2 Properties of "ALL MIGTHTY"

ALL MIGTHTY is consists of Liquid-A and -B. The chemical components of them are shown in Table 1. They do not contain pollutant.

Furthermore, Liquid-A and -B are shot into the ground and mixed. Changingthe ratio of A and B, viscocity of the mixture can be controlled as shown in Table 2 in order to fit various types of soil.

Friction reduction ratio(FRR),which is defined by Eq.1, is measured experimentally.

$$FRR = \frac{\text{coefficient of friction with lubricant}}{\text{coefficient of friction without lubricant}} \quad \text{(Eq. 1)}$$

Fig. 4 shows   normalized FRR of ALL MIGHTY(where A:B=5:5) by the standardlubricant of Japan society of sewage lines. The FRR of ALL MIGHTY is almost 30% of that of the standard lubricant.

## 3. MEMBRANE WRAPPING METHOD

### 3.1 Principle

The Membrane wrapping method is performed in such a way that, at first,the lubricant is injected into between jacking pipes and a membrane, which is wrapping up jacking pipes, then jacking pipes are shoved forward in a tube of the lubricant. Consequently, the friction is greatly reduced, which enable the very long distance pipe jacking works easily. (See Fig.5.)

### 3.2 Membrane

The mambrane must have the following features to be used :

(1)Impermeablity to prevent the lubricant from escaping

(2)Can be neatly folded easily

(3)Tensile strength strong enough to bear the tension force caused by being pulled out from the
  container of the membrane

We checked various types of membranes and have found that polyester(PETP),whose best thickness is 0.26mm. Table 3 shows the properties of the PETP.

This membrane has air permeability, and so we developed the lubricant forthis method. The lubricant is a mixture of bentnite and CMC(Carbonilic Methul Cellulouse). Then, we confirmed experimentally that does not permeate through this membrene when the inject pressure is $2.0kgf/cm^2$. (See Fig.6)

### 3.3 Injection

After completion of jacking, the lubricant between the pipes and the membrane should be displaced with cement mortar for backfilling. The cement mortar can be injected only from the starting pit. Therefore, its viscocity should be low. On the other hand, its compressive strength after solidification should be similar to the natural ground.

Considering the above condition, we developed new cement mortar, whose properties are shown in Table 4.

In order to check the effectiveness of the lubricant to the cement mortar,we performed the experiments shown in Fig.7. First, we wrapped up the steel pipe, whose diamter was 762 mm and length was 50m, and filled the gap between the pipe and the membrane with the lubricant. Next we injected the cement mortar into the gap filled with the lubricant. We stopped the injection after 280 minutes, when the accumulate volume reached 126% of the volume of the lubricant. 7 days later, we took 10 samples of the cement mortar and measured their compressive strengths. Those were 5 or 8 $kgf/cm^2$ , which were satisfactory results.

Fig.8 shows the relationship between injection pressure and accumulate injection volume when the injection flow rate is 30 l/min. The equation of the fitted line as follows.

$$P = 0.048861 + 0.028688 \cdot Q \qquad ( Eq.2 )$$

where  P :Injection pressure($kgf/cm^2$ )
     Q :Accumulate injection volume($m^3$ )

Using this equation, we can obtain the adequate injection pressre of the cement mortar from the injection volume which can be calculated the volume of injected lubricant.

### 3.4 Model test

In order to confirm that the lubricant is displaced with the cement mortar at an actual condition, we carried out the model test.(See Fig.9.)

Fig.10 shows a view of the cement mortar. We concluded that there were no significant problems for practical use.

### 3.5 Records of pipe jacking works on site

Fig.11 shows the change of jack thrust force with jacking length, when jacking pipes are hume pipes of 1500mm in diameter. It was found that the maximum thrust force was 350 ton.

### 4. FUTURE WORK

First, we will test Solid lubricant injectionmethod and Membrane wrappingmethod on actual sites by using hume pipes in 1994. Also we are now developing steel pipes with resin mortar coating. Then, using those pipes, we will adopt both methods for our new trunklines.

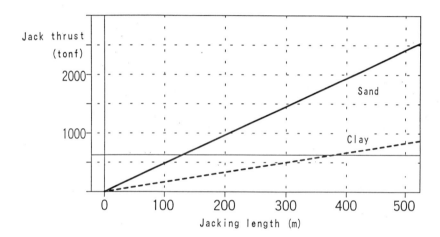

Fig. 1 Required jack thrust
(O.D. of jacking pipe :762mm, Depth of cover : 3m)

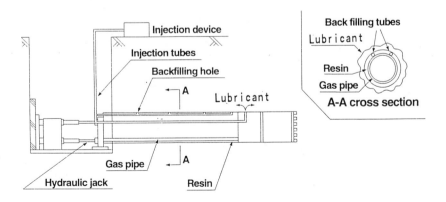

Fig. 2 Solid lubricant injection method

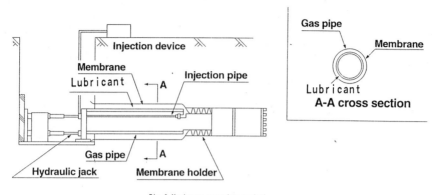

Fig. 3 Membrane wrapping method

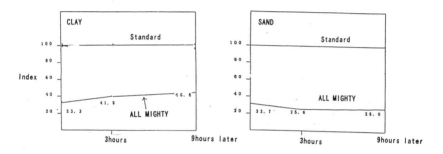

Fig. 4  Friction reduction ratio (Standard lubricant=100)

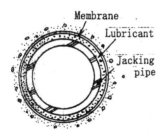

Fig. 5 Typicall cross section of Membrane wrapping method

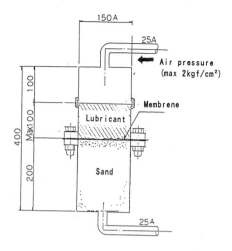

Fig. 6 Membrene permeate test by lubricant

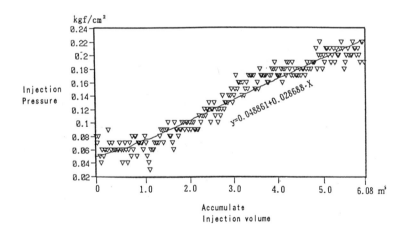

Fig. 8 Relationship between injection pressure and accumulate
injection volume(Cement mortar flow rate is 30 l/min.)

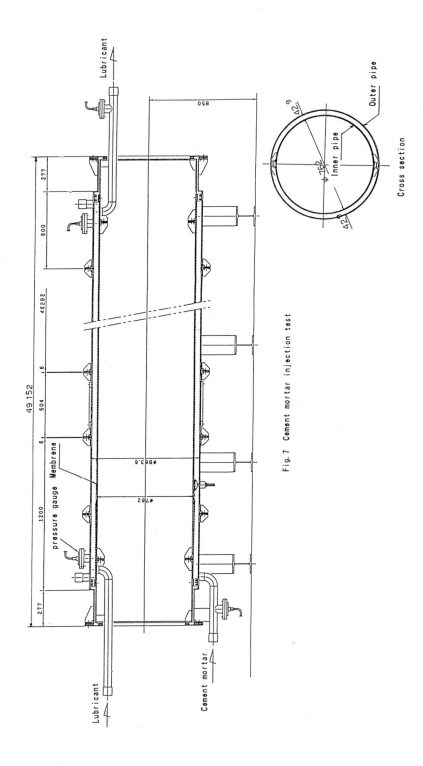

Fig. 7  Cement mortar injection test

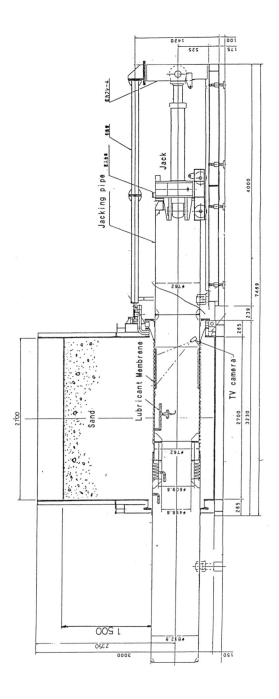

Fig. 9 Model jacking test

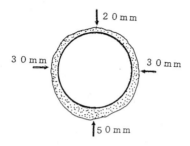

Fig. 10 Results of model jacking test
(View of backfiiling cement mortar)

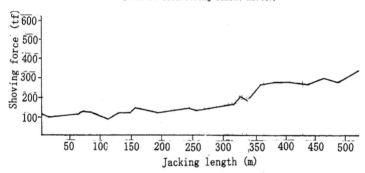

Fig. 11 Record of jack thrust force
(Jacking pipe :Hume pipe, Diameter :1500mm)

Table 1 Components of ALL MIGHTY

| Liquid A | Liquid B |
|---|---|
| Bentnite<br>Sodium nitrate<br>Glucono-δ-lactone<br>Water | Polyacrylate<br>$(RCOONa)_n$<br>CMC<br>Water |

Table 2 Viscosity of ALL MIGHTY

| mixture ratio | | Viscosity (CP) | Type of soil | | | |
|---|---|---|---|---|---|---|
| A | B | | Clay | Sandy Clay | Sand | Rocky sand |
| 10 | 0 | 2,000 | | | | |
| 6 | 4 | 30,000 | | | | ◎ |
| 5 | 5 | 27,000 | | | ○ | ○ |
| 4 | 6 | 26,000 | | | ○ | |
| 2 | 8 | 13,000 | | ○ | | |
| 0 | 10 | 7,000 | ○ | | | |

◎ Very good  ○ Good

Table 3 Membrane properties

| Tensile Strength | (machine direction)<br>(cross diretion) | 160 kgf/cm²<br>160 kgf/cm² | JIS L 1096 |
|---|---|---|---|
| Tear Strength | (machine direction)<br>(cross diretion) | 42 kgf<br>38 kgf | JIS L 1096 |

Table 4 Properties of cement of backfilling

| Composition | Cement bentnite<br>Flyash<br>Fluidify material<br>Hardening delay material<br>Water | |
|---|---|---|
| Viscosity(CP) | 0 hours later<br>6 hours later<br>12 hours later | 1,400<br>2,000<br>2,250 |
| Compressive strength | 7 days later<br>28 days later | 8.0 kgf/cm²<br>15.2 kgf/cm² |

OPTIMAL TEMPERATURE CONDITIONS OF GAS PIPELINES

UNDER THEIR TRANSITION TO COOLING REGIME


REGIME OPTIMUMS DE TEMPÉRATURE DES CONDUITES À GAZ

AU COURS LEUR PASSAGE AU RÉGIME DE REFROIDISSEMENT

Z.T.Galiullin, I.A.Ismailov, P.A.Dubin, V.P.Khankin

Russia

ABSTRACT

The paper deals with the study of permafrost condition around
buried gas pipelines of large diameter transmitting gas with a
temperature of about +20°C. The results are given for two gas
pipelines being under operation during 4 and 15 years. The
recomendations on optimal temperature operating conditions of
these gas pipelines under their transition to a cooling regime
to enhance their reliability are presented along with the
results of a predicted period for recovering permafrost
disturbed.

RÉSUMÉ

Les résultats de l'étude de l'état des permafrosts autour des
conduites à gaz enterrées à gros diamètre, transportant le gaz
à température environ +20°C sout présentés. L'une a été
exploité à ce régime pendant 15 ans et l'autre conduite -
pendant 4 ans. Les recommandations sur les régimes optimums de
température de ces conduites à gaz au cours leur passage au
régime de refroidissement pour l'assurance de la fiabilité de
leur fonctionnement sont données. Les résultats des délais de
prévision de la restitution du permafrost sont représentés.

INTRODUCTION

Large-diameter gas mains crossing lengthy permafrost are generally designed based on through-year transmission of gas cooled to negative temperatures close to soil temperatures. Such technology makes it possible to close soil temperature conditions around a gas pipeline to natural conditions and thus to ensures high soil stability pipeline sticking and environmental equilibrium.

Actually many large-diameter gas mains laid in permafrost have been operated for several years without gas cooling stations. Positive temperatures of the gas flowing along such pipelines have changed considerably a natural temperature pattern around a pipe, resulting in permafrost destruction. The change in the geocryological conditions has led, in its turn, to the destruction of fill-up soil, activization of soil erosion, solifluction and, as sequence, to a loss of pipeline stability (pipeline exposure, arch formation, etc.).

A decrease in temperature of transported gas in a way enchencing gas pipeline reliability.

OPTIMAL GAS TEMPERATURES OF GAS PIPELINES UNDER THEIR TRANSMISSION TO COOLING REGIME

Different initial geocryological conditions, operating life and operating conditions of the gas pipelines transmitting gas at positive temperatures require a separate study of each pipeline in order to predict optimal conditions for their further operation.

For this purpose, a compture programme for studing heat fields around the pipelines during their transition to a through year operation at negative temperatures has been developed based on thermo-moisture conditions of the ground, natural heat field, atmospheric conditions, and a change in pipeline operating conditions.

The correctness of the programme was reached by modelling operation of the pipelines which had passed "a high-temperature period". A good convergence between the predicted and actual heat fields has proved the programme validity.

In order to restive permafrost along the pipeline having been operated during 15 years at a temperature of + 20° C resulting in soil thawing to a depth of 10 meters, temperature conditions were simulated. A soil temperature field around the pipeline after 15 years operation is shown in Fig. 1. A soil temperature field 7 years after putting a gas cooling station into operation and cooling gas in summer to - 2° C is shown in Fig. 2. According to Fig. 2, the soil under a pipe was frozen to a depth of 6,5 metres. The feeezing zone thickness was reached 4 metres. However, in spite of this the permafrost has not been restored completely. A complete restoration will take place in 11 years.

A soil temperature field around the gas pipeline after the permafrost restoration at ~ temperature of transmithed gas of - 2° C is shown in Fig. 3. Under lower temperatures, the permafrost restoration process will be but slightly accelerated. According to Fig. 4, a complete restoration of permafrost will take place in 9 years at a gas temperature of - 5° C, while at a gas temperature of - 10° C this process will be completed in 8 years. Such long period of permafrost restoration around the gas pipeline makes this process unreasonable. Therefore, this gas pipeline is presently considered as a pipeline's temperatures operating between + 5° C and 10° C are enough to stop a further destruction of permafrost.

Parallel with it, the calculation of permafrost restoration around a pipeline, the ground be which had been thawed of a depth of 3 meters, has been made.

The calculations show that the use of a cooling station (gas temperature in summer is - 2° C, in winter $t_g = t_{air} + 10°$ C) will enable cooling the soil under the pipeline to 0° C during one-year cycle. At the same time, at depth from 2 to 4 meters a zone of freezing soil (with a temperature range from 0° C to - 0,6° C) will remain in which a high content of water will shill exist and fine-dispersixe soil will not practically pass into frozen state.

After two years the ground beneath the pipeline will be completely frozen; however, at depths between 4 and 6 meters the ground temperature will be higher compared to that for natural conditions. A complete permafrost restoration will take place at a third year of the pipeline operation.

A relatively small depth of thawing under this gas pipeline makes it possible to operate it under a through-year cooling regime. Two or three years which are necessary to restore permafrost is a relatively short period. This cooling cycle allows to enchance the pipeline reliability considerably.

The transition of gas pipelines to cooled gas should be accomplished together with other works including soil back-filling, drainage, etc. These complex measures will enable both to enchance pipeline reliability and to protect environment.

CONCLUSIONS

*   Transmission of gas having positive temperature through pipelines laid in permafrostresults in considerable change in thermal-moisture conditions of soil. A depth of thawing reaches 10 meters.
*   Thawing leads to soil settlement and pipeline exposure and finally to a loss of pipeline reliability.
*   To solve the problem both of pipeline reliability and environment protection cooling of gas is required.
*   A level of optimal depends upon heat and engineering computations.
*   A level of cooling must ensure a stable zone in the vicinity of the pipeline during a whole period of its operation.

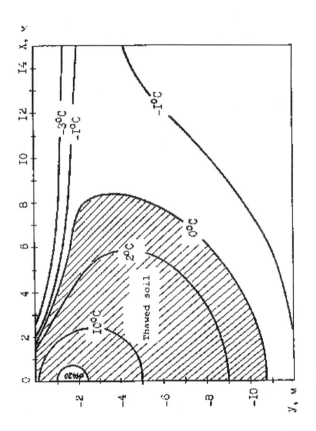

Figure 1. Soil temperature field around the pipeline after 15 years of its operation at a through-year positive temperature of gas (March).

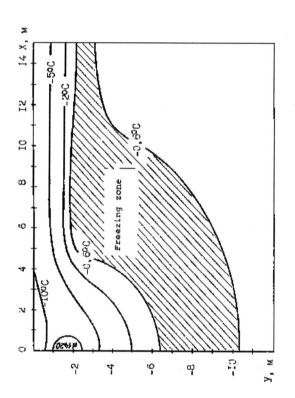

Figure 2. Soil temperature field around the pipeline 7 years after
putting a cooling station into operation ($t_{year} = -2°$ C;

$t_{winter} = -8,3°$ C, March).

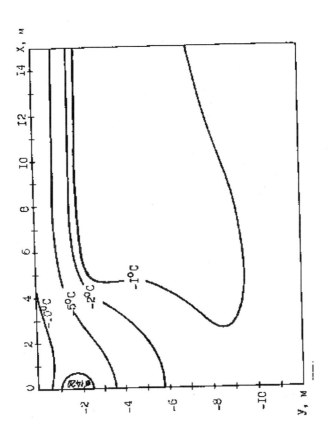

Figure 3. A complete restoration of permafrost around the pipeline after 11 years.

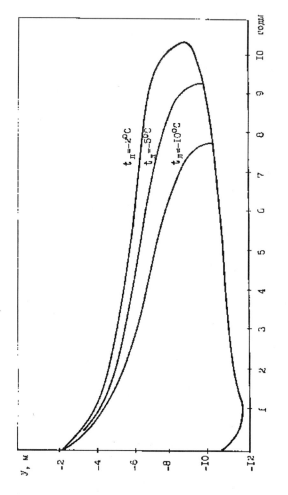

Figure 4. A permafrost period at different temperature conditions of gas cooling station operation.

DEVELOPMENT, DEMONSTRATION, AND DEPLOYMENT FOR TECHNOLOGY TO
ENHANCE RECIPROCATING COMPRESSOR OPERATION

LE DÉVELOPMENT, DÉMONSTRATION, ET DÉPLOYMENT DE LA TECHNOLOGIE POUR
AMÉLIORER LE FONCTIONNEMENT DES COMPRESSEURS ALTERNATIFS

K. M. Kothari
Gas Research Institute, USA

A. J. Smalley
Southwest Research Institute, USA

## ABSTRACT

This paper presents the development and demonstration of software to help control maintenance and fuel costs for reciprocating compressors in gas transmission and storage. It describes the central model which predicts pressure and temperature in a cylinder; the software uses this model to identify and quantify malfunctions by comparing predicted and measured pressures and by adjusting the severity of faults in the model until predicted and measured pressures agree. The paper shows how the software uses this model to aid engineering and problem solving. It summarizes the field test program by the software developer, and by operating company representatives, together with specific test examples documenting the repeatability of diagnosis, and the accuracy of inferred flow. The paper illustrates parametric investigations to improve efficiency of a single stage transmission compressor, and performance prediction for a three stage process compressor.

## RÉSUMÉ

Ce papier présente le développement et la démonstration de software qui peut reduire le coût de la maintenance et du combustible pour les compresseurs alternatifs qui fonctionnent en transport du gaz, et en stockage. Il décrit la modèle au centre qui prévoit la pression et la température dans le cylindre; cette modèle fournit les moyens d'identifier et de quantifier les défauts de fonctionnement; la software compare la pression mesurée et la pression prévue, et il ajuste les grandeurs des défauts dans la modèle jusqu'a la différence entre la pression prévue et mesurée est petite. Le papier montre que l'ingenieur peut utiliser cette modèle pour rèsoudre des problèmes. Le papier résume les épreuves entrepris par les auteurs du software et par des compagnies qui fonctionnent des compresseurs, avec des exemples qui documentent la uniformité des diagnoses et la précision du débit déduit par le software. Le papier montre les ajustements des parametres pour améliorer le rendement prevu d'un compresseur avec un étage, et le prévision de la puissance et du débit pour un compresseur avec trois étages.

INTRODUCTION

Compressor operation contributes substantially to gas pipeline overall operating cost. Nineteen Ninety-Two Federal Energy Regulatory Commission data show fuel and compressor maintenance each totaled $250-300 million for the major U.S. gas transmission companies combined (1). While fuel gas costs fell, maintenance costs rose steadily over the 1980's. This paper describes development, test, and refinement of software to help control fuel and maintenance costs for reciprocating compressors and to assist performance measurement and applications engineering. The Gas Research Institute (GRI) and the Pipeline and Compressor Research Council (PCRC) funded development of the Compressor Diagnostic Software (CDS); a group of industry advisers and evaluators guided its development (2,3). Both the developer (Southwest Research Institute) and various company evaluators performed experiments in the laboratory (4) and tested the software in the field (5). Critical user evaluation stimulated addition and refinement of capabilities. This paper summarizes the field testing program, illustrates the software refinement process, and presents test and application examples. The paper describes the CDS concept and its application, for diagnostic analysis, for performance analysis, and for use as an engineering tool.

CDS CONCEPT

The CDS concept is to combine predicted and measured cylinder pressure for problem diagnosis, performance analysis, and application engineering. It adapts an advanced, generic, model to the compressor of interest, using a data base of design and operating parameters, and pressure measured in each compressor cylinder. It predicts performance of single and multiple stage compressors, forecasts the effect of changes in design or operation, and maps power and throughput as a function of operating parameters. It compares measured pressure when available against predicted cylinder pressure to identify any significant malfunctions, to distinguish the cause, and to guide maintenance action by quantitatively assessing the cost and severity of the malfunction.

Figure 1 illustrates the domain of CDS: the double acting cylinder of a reciprocating compressor; in which piston motion changes volume, pressure and temperature of trapped gas; and passive, spring loaded, check valves control flow into and out of the trapped volume. CDS depends on a model which includes piston motion (driven by a rotating crankshaft); gas properties, based on the Benedict-Webb-Rubin (BWR) equation of state; heat transfer between gas and cylinder walls; valve dynamic response to pressure, spring, and inertia forces; valve flow resistance corresponding to instantaneous flow area; and flow through valve leaks (when included). The model includes an orifice type resistance in series with the valves to account for "close in" piping resistance, which directly affects piston work and temperature rise. The model solves the first law of thermodynamics with mass transfer for the time varying cylinder volume.

The cylinder model supports several CDS functions. It provides the basis for predicting performance of single ends and complete compressors, including for multi-stage compressors, an iteration on interstage pressures, in order to match flows from stage to stage. The model also supports CDS diagnostics, which compare measured and predicted pressure. If it detects significant discrepancy, the software adjusts model clearance and leaks in suction valve, discharge valve, or rings, and seeks to minimize these discrepancies. Iterative adjustment continues until area deviation between predicted and measured pressure volume cards for the extent of the compression and re-expansion-lines fall below 1/2% of total area or the iteration count reaches a specified limit (typically 16).

Once converged, the diagnostic software makes one more prediction with no leaks and, by comparison, establishes flow and horsepower penalties associated with the leak. It presents various graphic and tabular reports, based on diagnosed leak severity information.

The block diagram of Figure 2 illustrates data flow between compressor, data base, model, quantitative diagnosis, graphics, penalty information, performance predictions, load mapping, and on-line monitoring (this last capability is currently under development and test).

SOFTWARE VALIDATION

Table 1 summarizes compressor model, compression ratio, type of valve, speed, gas, type of service, and nature of the test at sixteen field test sites. The test program included four or five repeatability tests of various types; some performed by the software developer and some by software users. Figure 3 presents power penalty and estimated daily cost from a repeatability test, performed by a user on a transmission compressor with poppet valves; the three data sets characterize the compressor "as found", with one poppet out, and with two poppets out. Power penalty increases almost linearly with the number of missing poppets, and the variability within each data set is small (all standard deviations in power penalty are less than one percent).

## COMPANY EVALUATION AND SOFTWARE REFINEMENT PROCESS

Users from operating companies critically evaluated CDS and provided many recommendations. Table 2 summaries a number of these recommendations and shows that, of 21 recommended refinements, the current CDS software release contains 18. A near-future release should complete the remaining 3 items from this list. Some items, now considered standard, required significant modifications when first implemented. The enhanced user interface and graphics have been major ongoing programs, resulting in a transition from DOS to WINDOWS with convenient dialog boxes for the user. A "network ready" version of CDS, planned for near term release, provides a common data base, accessible by multiple users and allows concurrent execution of various CDS modules. Early CDS versions provided a purely diagnostic system, which simply compared measured and predicted pressures for a single end. The "what if" capability required substantial modifications to provide convenient user access to the predictive model. Further substantial modifications built the single end capabilities into multi-cylinder diagnostic analysis and multi-cylinder, multi-stage prediction capabilities. Critical evaluation of then current software, by users involved in compressor engineering and performance analysis, most effectively identified needed refinements, changes, or additions.

## LEAK REPEATABILITY

Figure 4 presents a recent test on a transmission compressor of discharge valve leaks with increasing severity ("as found", "nicked", 1/3 third cut, 2/3 cut). This figure also presents RMS deviations of each penalty value about the mean for that condition. The largest variance occurs for the nicked condition, with a penalty range of 2 to 3%. The overall RMS deviations so obtained are 0.75% and 0.83% for power and flow penalty, respectively.

Table 3 summarizes leak repeatability results covering "as is" conditions, several suction poppet leak tests, and one discharge poppet leak test. The standard deviation from these tests always falls below 1.5, with a low of 0.08, and most frequently falls below 1.0, indicating that the CDS diagnosis repeats satisfactorily from data set to data set.

## FLOW CONSISTENCY TESTS

This section summarizes all available data, comparing CDS inferred flow against electronic flow measurement (EFM). Independent company evaluators provided all the cylinder pressure and EFM data, covering four different stages on three different compressor models, one in gas gathering (a GMV), and two in transmission (an RA and a W62). Figure 5 summarizes the flow comparisons in a bar graph with CDS inferred flow adjacent to the measured flow for each compressor model, stage, or test. CDS and EFM agree closely. A regression analysis of these nine data points shows:

$$\text{CDS Flow} = (0.9924 \pm 0.0064) * \text{EFM Flow}.$$

The mean discrepancy between CDS and EFM flows for these 9 cases is less than 2%.

## MULTI-CYLINDER MULTI-STAGE PERFORMANCE PREDICTIONS

As previously discussed, CDS uses the single end model in multi-cylinder, multi-stage performance prediction. The CDS data base structure and internal logic associate individual cylinders with a particular stage and, for multiple stages, find a self-consistent combination of interstage pressures and flow for the specified first suction and final discharge pressure. Figure 6 presents flow, power per unit flow, temperature rise, valve flutter index (ratio of average to maximum valve motion), and rod load for an eight cylinder, natural gas compressor--with a four cylinder first stage, and two cylinders each for second and third stages, compressing from 1.2 Bara suction to 31.7 Bara discharge. Figure 6 shows three precisely equal stage flows. It indicates well-balanced stages, with almost identical power per unit flow (about 45) for each stage, and similar temperature rise through each stage (about 100°C). The flutter shows some variability, with the most severe index on the first stage (just over 50%) and least severe (80%) on the third stage. Maximum rod load varies stage to stage, with the highest (318,000 N) occurring in the third stage. The rod load limit of 510,000 N still provides significant margins for this highest load. In summary, the multi-stage capability enables design studies, sizing, and stage matching.

PARAMETER STUDIES USING CDS

The CDS user can change data base parameters to study how they influence selected performance characteristics. Figure 7, for a particular combination of cylinder, valves and operating conditions, presents valve motion predicted as a function of crank angle, with substantial flutter matching the frequency of cylinder pressure modulations. Table 4 shows how valve preload influences flutter, closing angle, and power per unit flow (Watt.Hr/m$^3$). The three data sets in this table correspond to preloads of 0, 6 and 12 Newtons. The highest preload data (nominal condition of Figure 7) produces a flutter index of 54.8 and a suction valve closing angle of -13.4° (significant early closing). A well-behaved valve would have a high flutter index (70 percent or above) and a closing angle close to zero. Cutting preload in half increases the flutter index to 65.3% and reduces the severity of early closing to -9.8°. Further reduction in preload to zero increases valve flutter index to 82.6% and the closing angle to 1.8°. Reducing preload to zero also reduces power per unit flow by 5%, because it increases average effective lift and flow area and reduces the average valve pressure drop. Zero preload is difficult to achieve precisely; however, this analysis shows benefit in reducing preload from its nominal value, at least in half, perhaps to some value close to zero.

ON-LINE MONITORING USING CDS

Figure 2 indicated the potential for CDS as a component of an on-line condition monitoring system. Other essential components, including rugged, reliable, affordable, high speed transmitters, and data acquisition hardware, appear to be reaching the status of viable commercial products. An experimental system, installed with the cooperative assistance of Bristol-Babcock and a leading gas transmission company on a TLAD8 compressor, has recently demonstrated initial functionality and is undergoing critical tests and refinement. Based on measured cylinder pressure, this experimental system can display various quantities, including power, flow, effective clearance, temperature rise, and leak severities, on an hourly basis. The user can display supportive details, on demand, including Pressure-Volume (PV) cards, unit summaries and detailed end performance tables. Planned refinements include trend identifying logic and exception reporting. Potential benefits include:

- Consistency of analysis
- More frequent analysis than manual monitoring allows
- User guidance to the most critical problems by means of exception reporting
- Directly measured torque for use in control or in parametric emissions monitoring

SUMMARY

This paper has provided a technical description of the Compressor Diagnostic Software, an illustration of how it works, and various leak detection and flow tests, together with statistics on variability of diagnosis and flow accuracy. The paper has illustrated multi-stage multi-cylinder performance prediction, stage matching, and the application of CDS in parameter studies to help optimize performance. The paper has further discussed on-line performance monitoring, using CDS, from an ongoing field experiment. The following observations summarize the results presented in the paper.

- Model based software, as exemplified by CDS, can, with benefit, assist performance analysis, diagnostics, and applications engineering for reciprocating compressors, with direct benefits to efficiency, and operating cost.

- Improved cost effectiveness of compressor operation will directly benefit a major cost component of pipeline operations.

- CDS has demonstrated self-consistent ability to diagnose implanted leaks.

- Flow inferred by CDS closely reproduces EFM data -- on average within two percent for the combination of cases tested.

- The prediction capabilities provide important performance characteristics of single and multi-stage reciprocating compressors, to assist sizing, stage matching, and applications engineering.

- Use of channel and valve models can help distinguish modulations in the cylinder pressure, including channel resonance, valve flutter and pulsations.

- The prediction capabilities can guide the solution of operating problems, such as valve flutter, with benefit to operating efficiency.

- CDS has potential as a component of an on-line condition monitoring system.

- The close, critical, involvement by representatives of companies, which operate compressors as a business, in the software test, evaluation, and refinement process helps ensure a versatile, user friendly, tool, with a range of beneficial, needed capabilities.

The software is now commercially available from the Pipeline and Compressor Research Council (PCRC) or from its sub-licensee, Beta Monitors. So far five companies have bought a total of 16 copies of CDS.

## REFERENCES

1.   Pipeline Economics - "Natural - Gas Pipeline Transmission Expenses", Oil & Gas Journal, November 22, 1993

2.   A.R. Berry, S.P. Mohan, L.G. Shabi, J.J. Wang, and K.J. Warren, "Compressor Diagnostics Software (CDS) Results of Industry Trials", Seventh Annual Reciprocating Machinery Conference, September 22-25, 1992, Denver, Colorado

3.   D. Harris, D. Cantrell, J. Wells, P.A. Rullman, and K.M. Kothari, "User Experience with Compressor Diagnostics Software", 8th International Reciprocating Machinery Conference, September 20-23, 1993, Denver, Colorado

4.   C.R. Gerlach and A.J. Smalley, "Fault Implantation: A Technique for Reciprocating Compressor Diagnostics", Pipelines October, 1989, Vol. 61, pp. 2-9

5.   R.E. Harris, C.E. Edlund, J.W. Hotzel, K.M. Kothari, and A.J. Smalley, "Compressor Cylinder Performance Analysis: The Next Generation of Software Capabilities", Sixth Annual Reciprocating Machinery Conference, Salt Lake City, Utah, September 23-26, 1991

6.   C.M. Beeson and R.E. Harris, "Channel Resonance Correction for Improved Cylinder Performance and Diagnostic Analysis", 5th Annual Reciprocating Machinery Conference, September 25-27, 1990, Nashville, Tennessee

7.   R.E. Harris and A.J. Smalley, "Computer Based Diagnostic Tools for Compressor Performance Evaluation", ASME #90ICE-28, Energy-Sources Technology Conference and Exhibition, New Orleans, LA, January 14-18, 1990

8.   Leopold Boswirth, "Theoretical and Experimental Study on Valve Flutter"

9.   Southwest Research Institute, "Controlling the Effects of Pulsations and Fluid Transients in Piping Systems", PCRC Pulsation & Vibration Short Course, February 1991

10.  A.J. Smalley, C.E. Edlund, A.R. Berry, L.G. Shabi, and J.W. Fulton, "On-Line Monitoring of Compressor Cylinder Performance - Technology Needs and Experience", 9th Annual International Gas Machinery Conference (GMC), September 26,29, 1994 Kansas City, Missouri

**FIGURE 1.  DOUBLE-ACTING CYLINDER WITH VALVES,
PISTON AND NOZZLE ORIFICES**

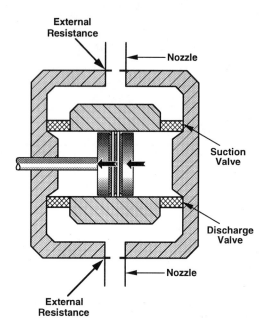

**FIGURE 2.  SCHEMATIC OF DATA FLOW AND
ANALYSIS PROCESS**

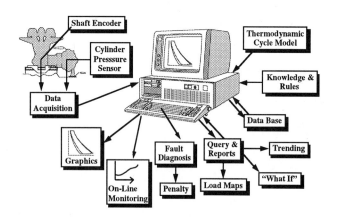

## FIGURE 3.   LEAK REPEATABILITY WITH ESTIMATED COST PER DAY

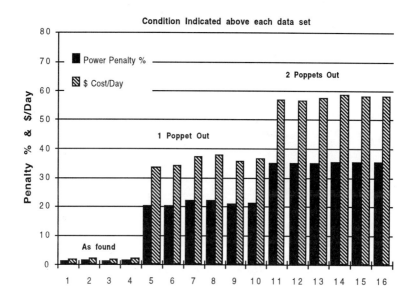

## FIGURE 4.   REPEATABILITY OF DISCHARGE PENALTY DATA FOR PARTIAL DAMAGE TO DISCHARGE POPPETS

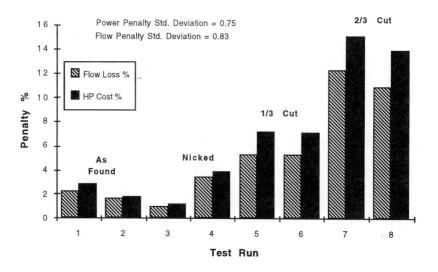

**FIGURE 5.   COMPARISON OF CDS INFERRED FLOW AGAINST ELECTRONIC
FLOW MEASUREMENT**

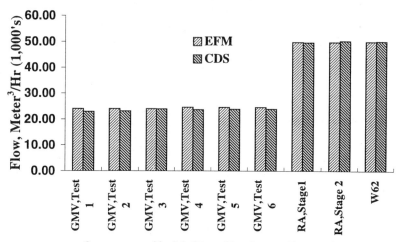

**FIGURE 6. PERFORMANCE PREDICTION FOR 3 STAGE, 8 CYLINDER
COMPRESSOR ON NATURAL GAS**

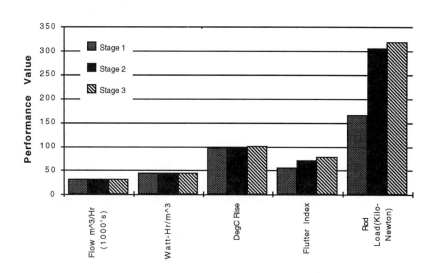

**FIGURE 7.  MEASURED PRESSURE MODULATION (AFTER CHANNEL CORRECTION) SHOWING CORRELATION WITH PREDICTED VALVE MOTION AS AN AID TO DIAGNOSIS AND PROBLEM SOLVING**

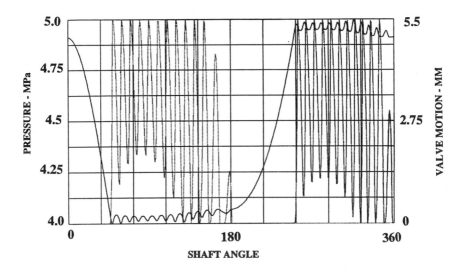

## TABLE 1. CDS FIELD VALIDATION TEST SUMMARY

| Service/ Gas | Model | Speed RPM | Ratio | Stages | Valve | Tests Performed |
|---|---|---|---|---|---|---|
| Transmission/NG* | GMV10 | 300 | 2.25 | 1 | Plate | S-Valve Leak, Severity Range |
| Transmission/NG | GMV10 | 300 | 2.25 | 1 | Plate | Precision & Repeatability |
| Transmission/NG | GMWC | 250 | 1.35 | 1 | Poppet | D-Valve Leak Detection |
| Transmission/NG | GMWA | 300 | 1.4 | 1 | Poppet | Flow Test vs. Installed Instruments |
| Transmission/NG | GMWC | 275 | 1.2 to 1.5 | 1 | Poppet | S-Valve Leak Repeatability |
| Transmission/NG | HHE | 327 | 2.1 | 2 | Channel | Repeatability, "as is" |
| Transmission/NG | KVS | 300 | 1.3 | 1 | Poppet | S-Valve Leak Repeatability |
| Processing/NG | HHE | 327 | 2.5/3.0 | 3 | Channel | Temperature, Clearance, Twall |
| Transmission/NG | KVS | 300 | 1.2 | 1 | Poppet | Flow vs. Tracer Gas |
| Transmission/NG | W62 | 900 | 1.2 | 1 | Plate | Flow vs. EFM |
| Transmission/NG | RA | 300 | 1.3/1.4 | 2 | Poppet | Flow vs. EFM |
| Processing/NG | HHE | 327 | 3.0 | 2 | Channel | Confirm Naturally Occuring Leaks |
| Gathering/NG | GMV | 300 | 3.0 | 1 | Plate | Flow Test vs. EFM |
| Processing/NG, N₂ | HHE | 327 | 2.5/ 3.0 | 2 & 1 | Channel | Clearance Test |
| Processing/N₂ | HHE | 327 | 3.0 | 1 | Channel | On-Line Monitoring |
| Transmission/NG | | 300 | 1.4 | 1 | Poppet | D-Valve Leak Severity, Range, Repeatability |

* NG = Natural Gas

## TABLE 2. SUMMARY OF USER RECOMMENDED ENHANCEMENTS FOR CDS

| RECOMMENDATION | STATUS* |
|---|---|
| Extend Test Program | √ |
| Distinguish Tensile & Compressive Rod Load | √ |
| Add External Resistance to Prediction | √ |
| Add Option to Fix Clearnace in Iteration | √ |
| Add a Clearance Discrepancy Diagnostic | √ |
| Add Input of Suction & Discharge Pressure History | |
| Add Gases to Thermophysical Data Base ($H_2$, $H_2S$, $H_2O$) | √ |
| Allow User Access to Existing Cylinder Prediction Capability ("what if") | √ |
| Add Capability to Handle Inactive Ends | √ |
| Add Front End for More Analyzers | √ |
| Support Different Output Devices | √ |
| Enhance User Interface & Graphics | √ |
| Provide Trending Capability | |
| Add Warning Message if Convergence < 99% | √ |
| Enhance Data Base Management | √ |
| Refine Valve Motion on PV Card | √ |
| Provide a Separate Valve Data Base | |
| Add Load Map Generation | √ |
| Add Cursor Readout | √ |
| Speed-up Software | √ |

* √ = Complete

## TABLE 3.  LEAK REPEATABILITY DATA

| Condition | No. In Sample | Mean Power Penalty % | Standard Deviation |
|---|---|---|---|
| As Is | 4 | 1.36 | 0.08 |
| 1 S-Poppet Out | 6 | 21.01 | 0.79 |
| 2 S-Poppets Out | 6 | 35.15 | 0.25 |
| As Is | 5 | 0.50 | 0.47 |
| As Is | 7 | 0.69 | 1.4 |
| As Is | 29 | 2.41 | 1.15 |
| 1 S-Poppet Out | 27 | 23.05 | 1.49 |
| As Is | 15 | 4.74 | 1.17 |
| Cut D-Poppets | 8 | Varying | 0.75 |

## TABLE 4.  VALVE PERFORMANCE PARAMETERS AS A FUNCTION OF VALVE PRELOAD

| Preload Newton | Flutter Index, % | Closing Angle, Deg | Watt-Hour/$m^3$ | HP/MMSCFD |
|---|---|---|---|---|
| 0 | 82.6 | 1.8 | 5.25 | 8.3 |
| 6 | 65.3 | -9.8 | 5.31 | 8.4 |
| 12 | 54.8 | -13.4 | 5.50 | 8.7 |

# DETECTION OF PHASE BOUNDARIES
# FOR NATURAL GAS MIXTURES

A. R. H. Goodwin and J. A. Hill,
Center for Applied Thermodynamic Studies
University of Idaho, Moscow, ID 83844

and J. L. Savidge,
Gas Research Institute, Chicago, IL 60631

## ABSTRACT

The gas industry encounters phase boundaries in many operating environments. The presence of liquids during natural gas production, gathering, processing, transmission, distribution and end use leads to many costly operational and quality control problems including: large gas measurement errors, liquid drop out, unmarketable aromatics, deterioration of storage facilities, and pipeline corrosion. Phase boundaries determination has traditionally relied on sampling pipeline fluid which is later subjected to laboratory compositional analysis and visual observation of phase behavior. The objective of the basic research presented here is to develop reliable methods to detect the onset of gas-liquid phase transitions.

## 1. INTRODUCTION

Industrial experimental investigations of dew and bubble curves usually rely on visual observation of the first onset of liquid or vapor. Such experiments often suffer significant uncertainties arising from blind regions, dead volumes and surface wetting. There are numerous variants on this method as well as other experimental techniques that can be used to study phase behavior. GRI's research monitors the electromagnetic properties of the fluid. Measurements of change in complex impedance of fluid-filled capacitors (which arise from variations in the fluid relative permittivity) have been used to study phase equilibrium of simple molecules, for example, helium. To detect phase transitions for many different fluids, it is only a matter of determining the relative permittivity.

Capacitors can easily be filled with various test fluids and have a capacitance on the order of a few pF. Thus at audio frequencies, they are very high impedance sources. It follows that the measurements of the dielectric constant at audio frequencies puts great demands on the insulators that are used to maintain stable mechanical spacing between the conducting plates. Furthermore, even the slight conductivity that results from polar impurities in normally insulating fluids may interfere with the measurements. As the temperature is raised, the conductivity of most fluids increases, and the difficulties in measuring the dielectric constant at audio frequencies, with an ac bridge, increase. For example, at radio frequencies the source impedance of capacitors is much lower and, therefore, a greater parallel conductivity can be tolerated. This reduces the dependency on metal-insulator seals that are often trouble some when they are subjected to stresses from differential thermal expansion or applied pressure. One higher frequency method has been discussed in the literature [1,2]. In this experiment a resonant chamber, filled with air, at atmospheric pressure, is mounted at a fluid container with a sapphire window separating the two cavities. Reflections at the sapphire-fluid-interface perturbs the resonance frequency of the air filled cavity. It is the measurement of this frequency shift or variation in resonance quality factor that is observed. This method has degenerate modes. The option which was chosen by us is an extreme reentrant cavity, which is an $LC$ oscillator where $L$ is inductance and $C$ capacitance. It has several advantages over other devices: (1), it completely avoids the use of insulators except for the cable connections; (2), it is self supporting without capacitors spacers; (3), the $LC$ device has a non-degenerate mode; and (4), the style of resonator has great mechanical rigidity, and can be made from the same material and is free from the effects of differential thermal expansion. The cavity has been modeled as a coaxial wave guide coupled to a toroidal inductor [3]. This model includes the effects of the finite conductivity of all cavity walls. The effects of probe coupling and of contact losses within the cavity have been considered also. Thus the problem of measuring changes in permittivity is reduced to an easier one of measuring changes in resonance frequency.

## 2. APPARATUS AND EXPERIMENTAL

Each component of our apparatus is state-of-the-art and has been developed separately, working equations derived and tested. The phase-detection techniques rely on the measurements of frequency. The apparatus, including a spherical resonator to determine sound speed, is shown in Figure 1. The inclusion of all devices in a modular thermostat allows us to determine a number of the thermophysical properties of the fluid. The modular construction lends itself to rapid variations in the devices under test. We required the devices constructed for the apparatus should operate at temperature ranges up to 500 K and pressure up to 42 MPa. All components are manufactured from 316 stainless steel and have either mechanical or electro-polished internal surfaces. The fluid seals are effected with silver o-rings and stainless steel disks; no elastomers are used. The techniques we have used are described below.

Phase boundaries were detected from variations in the relative permittivity using a $LC$ reentrant cavity shown in Figure 2. The reentrant cavity, which served as both the fluid containment vessel and resonator was comprised of two metal parts. The lower was a hollow cylinder closed at the bottom and fitted with a fluid outlet. It had an internal radius of 25 mm. The upper part of the device served as a lid to the cylinder and had a bulbous coaxial extension into the cavity. Near its top the reentrant portion had a radius of 10 mm and an length of 20 mm. The bulbous intrusion had a diameter and length of 24 mm. When the resonator was assembled, an annular gap about 1 mm wide separated the bulbous intrusion of the lid from the inner surface of the cylinder; perturbations arising from imperfect alignment of the concentric cylinder are of second order and insignificant when the device is machined to usual machine shop tolerances. Since this device is also used as a pressure vessel, where the capacitance gap increase so the capacitance decreases and the frequency increases, as the vessel dilates. Values of the permittivity are obtained from a ratio of the experimental quantities. Fortunately, this approach ensures that many systematic errors cancel to high order.

**FIGURE 1.** Left: View of the apparatus showing the concentric cylinder capacitor, isolation valve, reentrant cavity, and spherical resonator with transducer port. Right: View of the apparatus showing the differential pressure transducer, electromagnetic mixing pump and spherical resonator.

All components in the apparatus were connected in series through a magnetically activated piston-cylinder circulating pump, shown in Figure 3, that was used to move the fluid through these devices. All cavities have a fluid inlet and outlet, the latter positioned to eliminate fluid stagnation and collection; dead volumes have been reduced to a minimum.

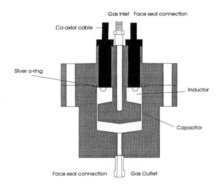

**FIGURE 2.** Cross-section through the reentrant cavity.

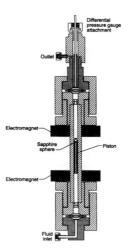

**FIGURE 3**. Cross-section through the magnetically activated circulating pump

The mixtures used in this work were prepared, and composition determined, gravimetrically in the gas phase. Each pure component used in this preparation was research grade with a minimum stated purity of better than 99.995 mole percent for propane and 99.9995 mole percent for methane. Prior to commencing measurements the apparatus was first evacuated at a temperature of 500 K until the pressure in the pumping line was below 1 Pa. The apparatus and filling line temperatures were maintained at about 400 K while the cavities were filled with fluid. The fluid was then circulated for about 30 minutes, the resonance frequency pressure and temperature were measured. The circulating was continued until equilibrium was established. This was taken as indication the fluid was homogeneous.

The temperature was then reduced and the temperature, pressure and frequency $(T, p, f)$ remeasured. This process was repeated until phase separation occurred as indicated by a rapid variation in resonance frequency. The sample was then heated to the mixing temperature and the fluid remixed with the same procedure as outlined above. The sample density was then reduced and another isochore begun. These procedures were repeated until all desired isochores were determined.

The fluid collected from each expansion, and that remaining at the conclusion of the experiments was analyzed to ensure compositional integrity. For the binary mixture, gaseous compositions have also been determined *in situ*, without recourse to sampling and gas-liquid chromatography, with sound speed measurements.

## 4. MEASUREMENTS

Here we will describe the results obtained for the phase boundary in $\{0.62CH_4 + 0.38C_3H_8\}$ and a multi-component gas mixture representative of a natural gas. Both mixtures were prepared, and composition determined, gravimetrically in the gas phase.

In a phase transition experiment, the formation of the second phase is accompanied by the flow of some parent phase into or out of the capacitor, so that there are two distinct mechanisms by which phase transition are observed with relative permittivity experiments that arise from density changes associated with the onset of a phase separation. First, liquid formation in the capacitor and second, by depletion of one or more components from the gaseous phase in the capacitor to form liquid elsewhere.

For the components in this mixture, the ratio of the relative permittivity of the gaseous state, $\varepsilon(CH_4, g)/\varepsilon(C_3H_8, g)<1$, while for liquids the ratio $\varepsilon(CH_4, l)/\varepsilon(C_3H_8, l) >1$. The results are consistent with depletion of gaseous propane from the capacitor. This mechanism is also the least sensitive since $\varepsilon$ for liquid is greater than $\varepsilon$ for a gas. Assuming perfect gas behavior, we can estimate a worst case bound for the gaseous mole fraction change in propane that would be detected in the binary mixture $\{0.62CH_4 + 0.38C_3H_8\}$. At $T=300$ K and $p=7$ MPa, where $\rho\approx3000$ m$^3 \cdot$mol$^{-1}$ and $1/\varepsilon(\partial\varepsilon/\partial x)\approx0.5$, with $\delta\varepsilon/\varepsilon =1\cdot10^{-6}$, as is appropriate for a reentrant cavity, this implies a sensitivity of $2\cdot10^{-6}$.

The reentrant cavity has been used to determine phase transition [4] for $0.5$ CO$_2$ + $0.5$ C$_2$H$_6$. In Reference 4, it was shown that the (p,T) sections obtained were in excellent agreement with literature data, which supports the conclusion that this detection system is accurate. For the system we have studied, $\{0.62CH_4 + 0.38C_3H_8\}$, the (p,T) section differs from those reported by Reamer *et al.* [5] by about 2 per cent. In the absence of other data sources, and in view of the accuracy of measurements reported elsewhere, we conclude that the data of Reamer *et al.* [5] are in error.

## 5. REFERENCES

1.    Rogers, W. J.; Holste, J.C.; Eubank, P.T.; Hall, K.R. *Rev. Sci. Instrum.* **1985**, 56, 1907.
2.    Frørup, M.D.; Jepsen, J.T.; Frederslund, A. *Fluid Phase Equilibria* **1989**, 52, 229.
3.    Mehl, J.B. Private communication, **1995**.
4.    Goodwin, A.R.H.; Moldover, M.R. to be published.
5.    Reamer, H.H.; Sage, B.H.; Lacey, W.N. *Ind. Eng. Chem.* **1950**, 42, 534.

SENSING THERMOPHYSICAL AND TRANSPORT PROPERTIES
OF NATURAL GAS WITH THERMAL MICROSENSORS

CHARACTERISTIQUES THERMOPHYSIQUES ET DE TRANSPORT
DE GAZ NATUREL DETERMINÉES PAR MICROJAUGES THERMALES

U. Bonne
Honeywell Technology Center, Plymouth, MN 55441, USA

V. Vesovic
Dep. of Mineral Resources Eng., Imperial College, London, SW7 2BY, UK

and W.A. Wakeham
IUPAC Transport Properties Project Center,
Dep. of Chem.Eng. and Chem.Tech., Imperial College, London, SW7 2BY, UK

**ABSTRACT**

Deregulation of natural gas distribution in the U.S. and privatization
in Europe have increased the demand for precision metering with greater
emphasis on energy than on mass or volume flow. To meet this demand by
using straight volumetric metering via positive displacement or
ultrasonic approaches would require additional means to compensate for
pressure and temperature, and to sense heating value. A fully
compensated metering solution based on a thermal microanemometric
approach was presented at the 1992 IGRC, but its performance was
limited by the uncertainty in the consistency of thermophysical
property data available for calibration. In addition, the universality
and transferability of the flow compensation coefficients from one
sensor to another was predicted but needed to be proven.
As discussed in the paper, progress towards resolving these issues is
based on (1) computational generation of isobaric specific heat,
thermal conductivity and viscosity of pure and mixed gases, and (2)
experimental verification, respectively.

**RESUME**

La déréglementation de la distribution de gaz naturel aux États Unis et
à l'Europe a élevé la demande pour la mésure précise du gaz, et
notamment pour les mésures basées sur l'énergie du gaz, au lieu de son
volume ou son poids. Afin de réaliser ce but en utilisant les compteurs
à gaz volumétriques déjà existants (de displacement positive ou de
mésures ultrasoniques), il faudrait trouver des moyens supplémentaires
qui pourraient compenser pour les variations de température et de
pression, et pour les différences de potentiel calorifique du gaz. Une
Si-microjauge donc compensée pour l'usage dans les compteurs à gaz
électroniques avait été présenté au 1992 IGRC, mais sa pérformance
était limitée par la consistence des données accessibles pour sa
calibration, et il n'était pas certain si ses coefficients de
corréction d'écoulement du gaz étaient transférables d'une jauge à
autres.
Ce rapport décrit le progrès qu'on a fait vers les solutions aux effets
ci-dessus, à partir de: (1) la génération des données plus consistents
de chaleur specifique, de conductivité thérmique, et de viscosité,
ainsi que (2) la vérification expérimentale de l'universalité des
coefficients ci-dessus, respectivement.

## INTRODUCTION

The purpose of this paper is to present the results of (1) analyzing and proving the transferability of derived compensation coefficients, provided the metering occurred within a reasonable operating envelope of gas composition, pressure (0 to 70 bar), temperature (-40 to 150°C), and mass flux or flow regime (microturbulence), and (2) deriving and implementing a methodology for the generation of internally consistent data of temperature- and pressure-dependent thermal conductivity, viscosity and isobaric specific heat, which are needed here for sensor calibration.

Although consistent and accurate thermophysical property data of natural gases and its constituents are needed for many types of operations involving natural gas, the application singled out here focuses on point flow and property measurement of natural gas, as presented at an earlier IGRC[1]. To avoid repeating the presented microstructure sensor-based measurement approach here, only a brief summary is given below in the first section.

The second section expands on the methodology indicated recently[5] and chosen for the derivation of physical properties of dense and mixed gases of natural gas composition.

## POINT FLOW AND PROPERTY SENSING

The type of silicon-chip-based, thermal microsensors used for point flow measurement here are shown in Figs.1a (cross section, simplified) and 1b (top view, to scale). Fig.1b shows the various elements of the chip involved in measuring temperature, pressure and flow or fluid properties. Two such sensors are positioned as indicated in Fig.1c, whereby one is exposed to flow and senses mass flux, while the second one, protected in its cavity, measures the fluid properties (in a zero-flow environment) needed to correct for errors caused by uncontrolled changes in the fluid composition and physical properties.

Fig.1d illustrates how the property sensor is intermittently energized while recording the sensor element responses to (1) about zero heater energy to sense ambient temperature, $y_1 = T$, (2) temperature rise rate, $y_2 = dT/dz$, and (3) steady-state temperature rise, $y_3 = \Delta T$. These $y_i$ are converted to voltages via the front-end electronics, digitized and converted to thermal conductivity, k, and specific heat, cp, via the converter#1 equations of the microcomputer, and correlated to other fuel properties of interest, $Y_m(y_i)$, such as the listed density, heating value, compressibility factor, viscosity, etc., via the converter#2 equations. Typical sensor data outputs are shown in Fig.1e for flow and Fig.1f for the property sensor[1-4]. The first is shown to cover over 3 orders of magnitude of flow, with signal shifts caused by gas composition changes; the second illustrates the short response time of less than 10 ms.

For the above #1 and #2 equations to be successful and reliable, it is necessary to have:

- A consistent set of $k_j(T,p)$ and $c_{pj}(T,p)$ for the chosen set of preferably **pure calibration gases**, which are needed mostly to determine the #1 equations;

- An accurate procedure to compute the k and cp values of the above set of **gas mixtures**, which are needed mostly to determine the generic #2 equations[3,4], which will then be valid for all sensors; and

- Accurate values of $Y_m$ to generate accurate (or at least consistent) correlations for the #2 equations, $Y_m = f_m(k,c_p)$.

The flow sensor, after its flow calibration[2] (or output verification), also makes use of consistent property data in its flow signal fuel property correction, according to[1]:

$$C_F = (k/k_o)^{n1}(c_p/c_{po})^{n2}(T/T_o)^{n3}(Pr/Pr_o)^{n4} \qquad (1)$$

where the corrected flow signal, $G = G_u/C_F$, and the zero subscripts refer to any arbitrary but constant reference or calibration conditions. The fourth term, with $n_4 \cong 0.33$, can often be ignored, especially when the Prandtl number, $Pr = \eta c_p/(kM)$, is reasonably constant, as would be the case with natural gases. The universality of the other $n_i$ was checked as follows.

**Universality of the $n_i$.** Flow data were analyzed from fifteen off-the-shelf sensors, packaged with their own flow channels for nominal flow rates of up to 100 $cm^3/min$, but tested up to 500 $cm^3/min$ with air, $N_2$, He, Ar-$CH_4$ and $H_2$. We derived the $n_i$ for one sensor according to eq.(1), neglecting the Pr term. The flow signal data had an uncertainty of $\pm0.5$ - 1.1% ($1\sigma$) and covered a flow range from 25 to 500 $cm^3/min$. The maximum composition correction errors were determined for each of the 15 sensors, both for using their own flow curves, $F_u(G)$, as well as for using the one derived for one randomly chosen reference sensor. These data indicate that the $n_i$ exponents can be used for any of the sensors in the group if their individual flow curves are used. This resulted in maximum errors for individual sensors in the above flow range from $\pm1.6$ to $\pm3.5$ (standard errors are about 3x lower), see Fig.3, in spite of the substantial range in gas properties covered by the shown set of test gases. This provides the sought experimental verification of the universality of the $n_i$, with values for $n_1 \cong$ -0.8827 and $n_2 \cong 1.110$. Regarding sensor interchangeability, using the flow curve of one reference sensor for any other increased the obtained maximum errors about threefold.

An additional insight gained from this analysis was that the correction accuracy became visibly better for lower flows with lower Reynolds numbers (closer to laminar flow), as observed for He and $H_2$, which exhibit kinematic viscosities about 6x larger (and Re numbers 6x lower) than air and $N_2$.

One might ask about the existence and extent of the errors, in Fig.3. Part of the answer may lie in the less than perfect upstream flow conditioning of the 0.5 x 2.5 mm flow channel cross section; the transition from laminar to turbulent flow does not appear to cause much of a disturbance. Even in a larger but smoother flow channel as in Fig.1c, flow velocity variabilities in the 14-mm ID Venturi throat of about $\pm10\%$ were found (with higher values at both very high and very low flows), as determined via flow sensor traverses, see Figs.2a and b. The upstream flow conditioning consisted of a 25-mm honeycomb (3-mm cells) and a 16-mesh screen upstream from it. The corresponding Re numbers were Re[ID] = 2000 at about v = 2.2 m/s but did not reach Re[chip] = 2000 until about v = 39 m/s. It would appear that improving conditioning may be worth some effort.

## THERMOPHYSICAL DATA GENERATION

To achieve reliable operation of the sensors described above, accurate, or at least internally consistent, data on isobaric specific heat, $c_p$, thermal conductivity, $k$, and viscosity, $\eta$, are needed. The methodology chosen to determine these data, in view of the extensive body of literature that exists on this subject, is based on the application of statistical-mechanical calculations for the first property and on the Thorne-Enskog equations for rigid sphere systems[5] to real gases for the last two properties.

The gas conditions covered in this effort range up to $30\cdot10^6$ Pa or 300 bar (4500 psi) and from $-40 \le T \le 250^\circ C$. Regarding natural gas constituents, the ones included to date are, for pure $CH_4$, $C_2H_6$, $C_3H_8$, i- and n-$C_4H_{10}$, $N_2$, $CO_2$, CO and $H_2$ for low densities, and for their mixtures (with small concentrations of $C_5H_{12}$, $C_6H_{14}$, $C_7H_{16}$, $C_8H_{18}$ and He); and for mixtures of $CH_4$, $C_2H_6$, $C_3H_8$, i-/n-$C_4H_{10}$, $N_2$ and $CO_2$ for high densities.

## Methodology

For the isobaric heat capacity of the most important components of natural gas, the preferred way of evaluation is through a complete equation of state, which represents all of the thermodynamic properties of the fluid in terms of the Helmholtz free energy as a function of volume and temperature. Such equations exist for many pure fluids and the best available have been use here in each case.

The available kinetic theory of fluids enables one to separate each of the desired transport properties, for pure or mixed gases, into three component parts, as described by eq.(2)[6,7]:

$$X = X^{\circ}(T) + \Delta X(\rho, T) + \Delta_c X(\rho, T) \qquad (2)$$

in which X represents the property of interest. Here $X^{\circ}(T)$ is the dilute gas contribution that represents the property in the limit $\rho \rightarrow 0$[7], $\Delta X(\rho, T)$ is the excess contribution from the effect of elevated density and $\Delta_c X(\rho, T)$ is the critical enhancement contribution arising from the particular behavior of properties in the neighborhood of the critical point. To date, this work has included all three terms for $c_p$ and the first two for k and $\eta$. For the $X^{\circ}(T)$ terms of every gas, the most accurate available representations have been employed that have a pedigree traceable to IUPAC or a similar organization.

This methodology is being incorporated into a FORTRAN computer program, which will then serve as a tool to predict these property data within the given operating gas conditions and constituents. Presently, the user is required to enter gas density, temperature and constituent concentration to obtain $c_p$, k and/or $\eta$.

**Properties of Dense, Pure Gases.** According to the available kinetic theory[7], the excess transport properties of a dense gas, $\Delta X(\rho, T)$, can be represented by a power series in density of the form

$$\Delta X(\rho, T) = X_1(T)\rho + X_2(T)\rho^2 + \ldots \qquad (3)$$

Although the theory is able to give no more than an estimate of $X_1$, and no information at all about higher order coefficients ($X_2$, $X_3$, ...), eq.(3) does form a sensible basis for the representation of experimental data.

Analysis of the experimental data for viscosity and thermal conductivity of methane and ethane have been carried out by Younglove and Ely[8] and for nitrogen by Stephan et al.[9] under the auspices of the IUPAC Subcommittee on Transport Properties. Their results were therefore adopted for excess viscosity and thermal conductivity. When used in conjunction with the sources employed earlier for the zero-density properties, these representations are sufficient to represent the requisite properties of the pure fluids over the entire range of conditions of interest. Their representative equations were used to evaluate the excess viscosity and the excess thermal conductivity of methane, ethane, and nitrogen.

**Transport Properties of Dense, Mixed Gases.** The theory upon which the prediction of the transport properties of the dense gas mixtures is founded has been described in detail before[10,11]. Therefore, only a summary is provided here to illustrate the information employed in the prediction scheme.

The procedure is essentially the same for both viscosity and thermal conductivity and it is based upon the Thorne-Enskog equations[7] for the transport properties of a rigid-sphere gas mixture. These equations are a useful starting point for the prediction scheme because they provide a means of interpolating between the properties of the pure, dense gases in the mixture in a manner based on an approximate theory.

Implementation of the procedure requires that for each pure component in the mixture, the transport property of interest be available as a function of temperature and density. Then, for a prescribed molar density of the mixture of interest, $\rho_{mix}$, and at a particular temperature, T, the first step is to evaluate for each pure component of interest the pseudo-radial distribution function, $\chi_i(\rho_{mix}, T)$. This is achieved by using the viscosity and thermal conductivity data in the Enskog formulation of the density dependence of the transport property for a hard-sphere system. In this process, physically reasonable constraints are applied to the derived values of the pseudo-radial distribution function so that it is monotonic and well behaved at all densities. These constraints serve to determine a single value of $\chi_i(\rho_{mix}, T)$ for each pure component and also a size parameter for the pure hard-sphere fluid, $\gamma_{ii}$, at each temperature and for each pure component. In addition to the density dependence of the pure component property, this procedure also requires the same property in the limit of zero density.

Further information is required on the behavior of mixtures in the limit of zero density. In particular, the interaction viscosity, $\eta_{ij}$, is required for each unlike binary interaction in the mixture. This is the same information as was required to evaluate the mixture transport properties in the limit of zero density[6].

Once all this information is available, two mixing rules based upon hard-sphere theory are employed to construct all the possible pseudo-radial distribution functions, $\chi_{ij}$, for the mixture of interest, as well as the size parameters, $\gamma_{ij}$, that characterize unlike interactions. Then a straightforward calculation yields the transport property of the mixture at the density, $\rho_{mix}$, and temperature, T, of interest. The procedure automatically reproduces the transport property of all pure components exactly, in addition of placing the least possible demands upon the theory, two considerable advantages indeed.

An additional aspect of the procedure needs to be explained that relates to the circumstances when the molar density of the mixture, $\rho_{mix}$, at a particular temperature, T, is such that one or more of the pure components in the system is in its two-phase region. In such a case, it is not possible to evaluate the pure component transport property at the conditions ($\rho_{mix}$, T) because the fluid does not exist in this state. In such circumstances, the density corresponds to a hypothetical fluid density inside the two-phase region. An interpolation between the values of the vapor and liquid at saturation for the same temperature has been shown to yield a density that provides acceptable values of transport properties[10,11]. If the correlation of the transport property is well-behaved as a function of density for both saturation densities (as in the case here) then it is automatically used for this purpose.

**Specific Heat of Dense, Mixed Gases.** The method chosen to predict the isobaric heat capacity or specific heat, $c_p$, of mixtures involves a two-step process, whereby in (1) the residual $c_p$ is obtained via a modified Lee-Kesler method, which in (2) is then added to the result of applying the rigorous statistical mechanical mixing rule for low-density fluids, i.e.:

$$c_p = c_p^0 + c_p^{res}. \qquad (4)$$

The ideal gas (low density) limit of the isobaric heat capacity, $c_p^0$, is obtained simply as the mole fraction average of the values of the pure components. For gas mixtures for which no one constituent exceeds a mole fraction of 0.99, the residual $c_p^{res}$ is evaluated by the conventional Lee-Kesler method.

This procedure as it stands does not ensure consistency between the isobaric heat capacity of the pure fluids and that obtained by the mixture formulation in the limit of vanishingly small impurities in a mixture at elevated pressures. To guarantee that consistency, we have added an interpolation step: For quasi-pure gases in which the mole fraction of one component, $x_j > 0.99$, so that $\Sigma x_i < 0.01$ (i=1 to n, i≠j), the residual $c_p^{res}$ is evaluated by a smooth (linear in mole fraction) interpolation between the best available data for the pure, dominant component, j, and the calculated Lee-Kesler result for the prescribed composition. Because the contribution of the impurities to the overall $c_p$ is small and the Lee-Kesler procedure is quite accurate, this method secures the objective of consistency with the highest quality pure component properties at the small penalty of a mild inconsistency at a level beyond observable limits.

**The Critical Region.** Near the critical point, the thermal conductivity and viscosity of a pure fluid diverge, becoming infinite at the critical point itself[13]. For the viscosity, the region of (p,T) space over which the property diverges is very small. For the thermal conductivity, on the other hand, the extent of the divergence is quite large[13]. For the natural-gas-like mixtures of interest here, the critical points of pure ethane[15] and those of higher hydrocarbons fall within the specified (p,T) space of intended applications, so that for some fluids the term $\Delta_c X(\rho, T)$ in eq.(2) will need to be considered. Todate we have confined our efforts to the so-called background properties, which do not treat the critical region.

The critical enhancement term of transport properties for binary or multicomponent fluids has only recently been studied[13,14]. As the theory of the critical behaviour in mixtures is getting better understood, an evaluation of the $\Delta_c X(\rho, T)$ term will undoubtedly be facilitated, and should then be added to our computations. Note that the critical enhancement effects are already included in the chosen approach to determine specific heat.

## Accuracy, Consistency and Comparisons

**Comparisons with Experimental Data.** Comparisons of the predictive scheme for thermal conductivity and viscosity for some of the mixtures of interest here, as well as for other, similar systems, have been carried out using the limited experimental data available and presented[10,11]. Generally, for the range of conditions listed in the Introduction, the accuracy of the predictions is within about ±3%, which is comparable to the accuracy of the experimental data.

**Accuracy of the Predictions.** Based on these comparisons, it seems safe to assert that, except for the region in the vicinity of the critical region, the procedure set out will not have an uncertainty greater than ±5% and will generally be closer to ±3%. For specific heat, the prediction uncertainty would be less than approximately ±0.5, ±1 and 1.5%, for $N_2$, $CH_4$ and $C_2H_6$, respectively, also based on comparisons with experimental data, without excluding the critical region.

**Consistency of the Predictions.** By virtue of the methodology now applied in the calculation, the portion of data uncertainty contributed by internal data inconsistencies of heat capacity, viscosity and thermal conductivity is estimated to be 3 to 6 times lower, i.e. the data are estimated to be approximately that much more consistent than previously published data.

In an attempt to validate that estimate, we can report that in a comparison between our new data and those from a commercial source, the use of the former data to calibrate a thermal conductivity sensor led to a 2- to 30-fold reduction in error when that thermal conductivity sensor, after being calibrated with methane, ethane and nitrogen data, was used with methane (different $(\rho, T)$ conditions) and argon, respectively. While this is the result of comparing only one set of experiments with the above data, each set consisted of more than 30 measurements, and may thus be viewed as a very satisfactory validation of the consistency improvements being achieved with the data generated by Imperial College in this program.

## CONCLUSIONS

**Natural Gas Properties.** Data of isobaric specific heat, thermal conductivity and viscosity were derived for pressures up to 300 bar (4500 psi) and for $233 \leq T$ in $K \leq 523$ ($-40 \leq T$ in $°C \leq 250$), for pure and mixed gases as follows: For <u>pure</u> $CH_4$, $C_2H_6$, $C_3H_8$, i- and n-$C_4H_{10}$, $N_2$, $CO_2$, CO and $H_2$ for low densities, and for their mixtures (with small concentrations of $C_5H_{12}$, $C_6H_{14}$, $C_7H_{16}$, $C_8H_{18}$ and He); and for <u>mixtures</u> of $CH_4$, $C_2H_6$, $C_3H_8$, i- and n-$C_4H_{10}$, $N_2$ and $CO_2$ for high densities. Judging from the experimental errors in the data upon which the $c_p$ representation is based, and excluding the critical regions, it was estimated that the $c_p$ data uncertainty is less than ±0.5, ±1 and 1.5% for $N_2$, $CH_4$ and $C_2H_6$, respectively. The methodology employed here for the calculation of heat capacity, viscosity and thermal conductivity is estimated to have led to a 3- to 6-fold improvement in data consistency, i.e. the data are estimated to be approximately that much more consistent than previously published data.

While absolute accuracy and internal consistency are very hard to measure, an independent comparison between data resulting from this study and other commercial data found that use of the former led to a 2- to 30-fold reduction in error.

**Fluid Flow:** The hypothesis of the universality of the composition correction factors for thermal anemometers[1] was validated. Experiments with thermal microanemometers in the throat of a 14-mm ID Venturi showed that flow and sensor output variabilities were within about ±10%, despite upstream conditioning over less than 1.5 in. upstream of the point flow sensor.

The results of this effort will enable the development of affordable, on-line and in situ natural gas flow and property sensors, which in turn will enhance the accuracy, efficiency and performance of natural gas operations (processing, transportation/compressing) and user equipment (manufacturing, combustion, metering). One illustration of this emerging capability is provided in Fig.4 by an interim comparison of predicted and measured data of motor octane number, $N_{mon}$, heating value, $\Delta H_c$, and Wobbe number, Wb, as the methane test gas was purposely spiked with various amounts of $N_2$ and $C_2H_6$, at different pressures as indicated by the different size points.

Planned activities for this technology development include assessment and incorporation of means to reduce the effects of

(1) disturbances occurring under conditions near and not so near the critical or pseudocritical conditions of natural gas mixtures, and

(2) flow velocity profile non-uniformities by improving the effectiveness of upstream flow conditioning.

## ACKNOWLEDGMENT

The authors are pleased to acknowledge the support of GRI/Basic Research (Contract No. 5093-260-2556) for parts of this work.

## REFERENCES

1. U. Bonne, "Fully Compensated Flow Microsensor for Electronic Gas Metering," Int'l. Gas Research Conference, Orlando, FL, 16-19 Nov.1992, Proceedings, Vol.III, p.859

2. D. Kubisiak et al., "Microanemometer-Based Flow Sensing," 5th IGT Symposium on Natural gas Quality Measurement, Chicago, IL, 16-18 July 1990, Proceedings

3. U. Bonne and D. Kubisiak, "Determination of Compressibility Factor and Critical Compression Ratio with Si-Based Microstructure Sensors," 7th IGT Symp. on Natural Gas Quality, Chicago, IL, 12-14 July 1993, Proceedings

4. U. Bonne, "New Developments in Natural Gas Transducer Technology," 8th IGT Symposium on Gas Quality and Energy Measurement, Orlando, FL, 20-22 Feb. 1995

5. U. Bonne, V. Vesovic and W.A. Wakeham, "Thermophysical Properties of Natural Gases for On-Line Metering," 12th Symposium on Thermo-physical Properties, Boulder, CO, 19-24 June 1994

6. W.A. Wakeham, A. Nagashima and J.V. Sengers (Eds.), "Measurement of the Properties of Fluids," Exp. Thermodynamics, Vol.III, IUPAC Chemical Data Series No.37

7. J. Kestin and W.A. Wakeham, "Transport Properties, CINDAS Data Series on Material Properties, Vol.I-1 (CINDAS) (1991)

8. B.A. Younglove and J.F. Ely, "Thermophysical Properties of Fluids. II Methane, Ethane, Propane, i-Butane and n-Butane," J.Phys.Chem. Ref.Data 16, 577 (1987)

9. K. Stephan, R. Krauss and A. Laeseke, "Viscosity and Thermal Conductivity of of Nitrogen for a Wide Range of Fluid States," J.Phys.Chem.Ref.Data 16, 993 (1987)

10. V. Vesovic and W.A. Wakeham, "Prediction of the Viscosity of Fluid Mixtures over Wide Ranges of Temperature and Pressure," Chem. Eng.Sc. 44, 2181 (1989)

11. V. Vesovic and W.A. Wakeham, "Prediction of the Thermal Conductivity of Fluid Mixtures Over Wide Ranges of Temperature and Pressure," High Temp.-High Pressures, 23, 179 (1991)

12. T.M. Reed and K.E. Gubbins, "Applied Statistical Mechanics," Chapter 9, McGraw-Hill, N.Y., N.Y. (1973)

13. J.V. Sengers, "Transport of Fluids Near Critical Points," Int'l. J. Thermophys. 6, 203 (1985)

14. J. Luettmer-Strathmann, "Transport Properties of Fluids and Fluid Mixtures," PhD Thesis, University of Maryland (1994)

15. For example, our present computations underestimate the thermal conductivity of ethane by a maximum of about 17, 13 and 9% at (T,p) conditions of (350 K, 100 bar), (400,140) and (500,300), respectively, as obtained via comparisons with tabulated data of ref.(8). For methane those errors would be negligible for $T \geq 250$ K and $p \leq 20$ bar; e.g. 6% at T=250 K and p = 100 bar.
PBIGRC95.W01'19MayCannes

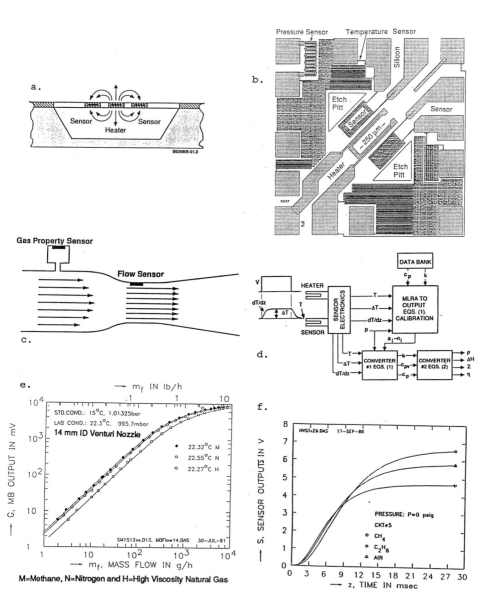

FIG. 1. FLOW AND PROPERTY SENSOR OVERVIEW: a. SCHEMATIC CROSS SECTION,
b. TOP VIEW, c. PLACEM, d. PROPERTY SENSOR ELECTRONICS, e. FLOW
SENSOR DATA, and f. PROPERTY SENSOR DATA

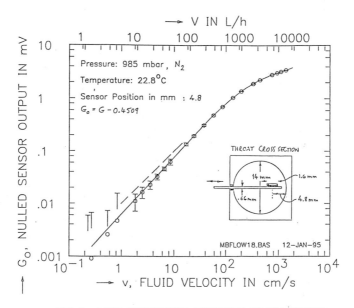

FIG.2a. FLOW MICROSENSOR TRAVERSES IN THE THROAT
OF A 14 mm ID VENTURI. OUTPUT VS. FLOW.
POSITION: 4.8 mm OFF THE FAR SIDE

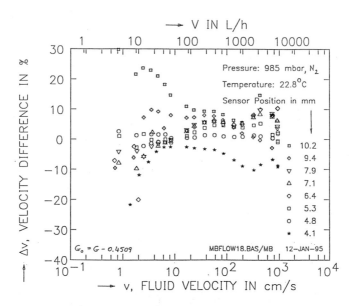

FIG.2b. FLOW MICROSENSOR TRAVERSES IN THE THROAT
OF A 14 mm ID VENTURI. VELOCITY
DIFFERENCE VS. FLOW AND POSITION;
CORRECTED FOR SENSOR BLOCKAGE.

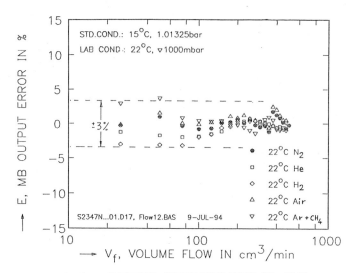

**FIG. 3. MICROSENSOR OUTPUT FLOW ERROR VS. FLOW, AFTER GAS COMPOSITION CORRECTIONS WERE MADE BY USING THE COEFFICIENTS DERIVED FOR ANOTHER SENSOR.**

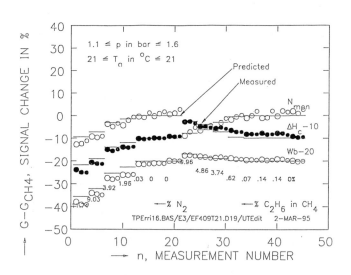

**FIG. 4. INTERIM FUEL PROPERTY SENSOR VALIDATIONS BASED ON METHANE SAMPLES SPIKED WITH THE INDICATED AMOUNTS OF VOL.% $N_2$ AND $C_2H_6$.**

# ACOUSTIC MEASUREMENTS IN
# NATURAL GAS MIXTURES

A. R. H. Goodwin and J. A. Hill,
Center for Applied Thermodynamic Studies
University of Idaho, Moscow, ID 83844

and J. L. Savidge,
Gas Research Institute, Chicago, IL 60631

## ABSTRACT

Acoustic measurements are important to the gas industry for flow metering. In particular, the speed of sound is of interest for obtaining information about the thermodynamic properties of the fluid, as well as an important quantity in the mechanics of fluid flow metering. The method chosen for the determination of speed of sound and data analysis will be described with results for binary and multi-component mixtures representative of those found in natural gas.

## 1. INTRODUCTION

The spherical geometry acoustic resonator has proven to be ideally suited to highly precise measurements of the speed of sound in gases under conditions of relatively small sound absorption and low densities [1] ($< 200$ kg·m$^{-3}$). The principal advantages of the sphere lie in the existence of radially symmetric modes which are characterized by both the absence of viscous damping at the surface and by the resonance frequencies that are insensitive to geometric imperfections. Consequently, resonators can be constructed easily without recourse to special machining techniques. The absence of viscous damping and the most favorable volume-to-surface ratio in the sphere leads to higher quality factors in gases than any other geometry of similar volume and operating frequency, and it in turn contributes to the highest possible precision in the determination of resonance frequencies. A further advantage of the spherical geometry lies in the availability of closed form solution to the problem of coupling between fluid and shell motion; such coupling is important as the gas density is increased.

Our apparatus can be used to simultaneously determine the following thermophysical properties of the fluid: a) location of phase boundary ($p, \rho, T, x$); b) relative permittivity $\varepsilon$; c) speed of sound, $u(T, p)$; d) compression factor $Z(T, p)$; e) heat capacity at constant pressure $C_{p,m}(T, p)$; f) viscosity $\eta$; and, g) thermal conductivity, $\kappa$.

The speed of sound has been determined from measurements of the frequencies of the lowest five radial modes within a spherical resonator. The frequencies $f$ of the radial modes are, at least to first order, related to the sound speed $u$ through the relationship $f = (u/2\pi a)/\nu$, where $a$ is the internal radius of the resonator and $\nu$ is an eigenvalue that can be calculated exactly. A more detailed treatment included the effects of both heat flow between the gas and wall and the finite elasticity of the wall material [1]. These effects account for the boundary, so the experimental speed of sound is identical to the thermodynamic value. To analyze the acoustic measurements with this model, we require estimates of the gaseous thermal conductivity and viscosity with an accuracy of about 5 percent. The resonator radius was determined from measurement with argon for which $u^2 = RT\gamma^{pg}/M$ is known. For any other fluid, the speed of sound is determined from the ratio of two experimental quantities. This approach ensures that many systematic errors cancel to high order.

## 2. APPARATUS AND EXPERIMENTAL

The apparatus, including a radio frequency reentrant cavity and an audio frequency concentric cylinder capacitor, is shown in Figure 1. The inclusion of all devices in a modular thermostat allows us to simultaneously determine various thermophysical properties of a fluid. All components are manufactured from 316 stainless steel and have either mechanical or electro-polished internal surfaces. The fluid seals are effected with silver o-rings and stainless steel disks; no elastomers are used.

We have two spherical resonators, one with an internal radius $a=25.4$ mm, at $T=298$ K, the other, shown in Figure 2, with $a=44.45$ mm $T=298$ K. Each sphere, which served both as a pressure vessel and the resonator, was constructed as two hemispheres from a single cylindrical bar of material. The gas-entry and exit ports were 1 mm diameter with a length $L \approx a$ were machined into the boss in each hemisphere. The tube opened up into a chamber fitted with a face-seal fitting. The internal radius and sphericity, as defined by $\delta a/a$, were determined, from microwave measurements, and found to be better than $3 \cdot 10^{-4}$.

**FIGURE 1.** Left: View of the apparatus showing the concentric cylinder capacitor, isolation valve, reentrant cavity, and spherical resonator with transducer port. Right: View of the apparatus showing differential pressure transducer, electromagnetic mixing pump and spherical resonator.

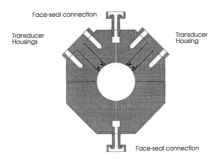

**FIGURE 2.** Cross-section through the spherical acoustic resonator.

The transducers used for the generation and detection of sound and illustrated in Figure 3 were fabricated as removable units. Our choice of materials were determined by the operating conditions and gas-purity requirements. Each was a solid-dielectric capacitance transducer with a 45 mm active area arranged to be nearly flush with the interior surface. Each device had a capacitance of about 22 pF and a fundamental resonance frequency of about 100 kHz at 0.1 MPa.

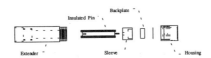

**FIGURE 3.** Electro-acoustic capacitance transducers.

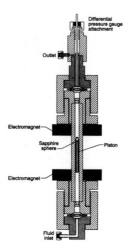

**FIGURE 4.** Cross-section through the magnetically activated circulating pump

All components in the apparatus were connected in series through a magnetically activated piston-cylinder circulating pump, shown in Figure 4, that was used to move the fluid through these devices. All cavities have a fluid inlet and outlet, the latter positioned to eliminate fluid stagnation and collection; dead volumes have been reduced to a minimum.

## 3. RESULTS

Here we will describe isochoric acoustic measurements in the gaseous mixture $\{0.62CH_4 + 0.38C_3H_8\}$ and a multi-component mixture representative of a natural gas in the temperature range 200 K to 450 K at pressures up to 42 MPa. Both mixtures were prepared, and compositions determined, gravimetrically. For the binary mixture, compositions have also been determined *in situ*, with sound speed measurements. The speed of sound has been determined with an uncertainty of about 0.002 %. The compression factor and isobaric heat capacity have been determined from the results of the isochoric sound speed measurements [2]. We estimate, based on extensive analysis with methane and other gas mixtures representative of natural gases, that the derived compression factor has an uncertainty of about 0.05 % and the isobaric heat capacity an uncertainty of 0.2 % [2].

## 4. REFERENCES

1.      Moldover, M.R.; Mehl, J.B.; Greenspan, M. *J. Acoust. Soc. Am.* **1986**, 79, 253.
2.      Trusler, J.P.M.; Zarari, M. *J. Chem. Thermodyn.* **1992**, 24, 973.

# CALORIC PROPERTIES OF GASEOUS MIXTURES OF METHANE-WATER AND METHANE-ETHANE-WATER

## PROPRIETES CALORIQUES DES MELANGES GAZEUX EAU-METHANE ET EAU-METHANE-ETHANE

C. Day and L.R. Oellrich
Institut für Technische Thermodynamik und Kältetechnik,
Universität Karlsruhe (TH)

## ABSTRACT

Water-Hydrocarbon mixtures are dealt with in numerous processing plants.Yet a general procedure to predict or just to represent the thermodynamic properties of these mixtures from experiments within experimental error remains unsolved. A calorimeter has been constructed to measure the isobaric enthalpy change and the integral Joule-Thomson effect for water-hydrocarbon mixtures in the gaseous phase. The apparatus is designed for pressures to 15 MPa and temperatures in the range from ambient to 600 K. Data are reported for pure methane and compared to results reported in the literature and obtained from the fundamental equation of Setzmann and Wagner. Very good agreement has been reached. In addition data for the binary sytem water-methane with 10, 20 and 40 mole% water and for a water-methane-ethane system with 60/20/20 mole % are presented. For the binary and the ternary the experimental results are compared to those calculated from different equations of state.

## RESUME

Les mélanges eau-hydrocarbures sont présents dans de nombreux procédés industriels. Une méthode générale pour prévoir ou juste pour représenter les propriétés thermodynamiques de ces mélanges à partir de données expérimentales dans le domaine de précision des mesures n'a pu encore être développée. Un calorimètre a été construit pour mesurer la variation isobare d'enthalpie et l'effet Joule-Thomson intégral pour les mélanges eau-hydrocarbures en phase gazeuse. L'appareil est conçu pour des pressions allant jusqu'à 15 MPa et des températures de la température ambiante à 600 K. Les résultats sont donnés pour le méthane pur et comparés à ceux de la littérature et ceux obtenus avec l'équation fondamentale de Setzmann et Wagner. Un très bon accord est obtenu. Les résultats pour le système binaire eau-méthane avec 10, 20, et 40 mole% d'eau et le système eau-méthane-éthane à une composition de 60/20/20 mole% sont également présentés. Les résultats expérimentaux obtenus pour ces deux systèmes sont comparés à ceux calculés avec différentes équations d'état.

INTRODUCTION

The knowledge of caloric properties of pure substances and, moreover, of mixtures, play a dominant role in the design of processing plants such as for natural gas processing and transportation. From an economical point of view it is essential to know these properties as accurate as possible. In general they are calculated by means of thermal equations of state (eos) that are able to represent the pVT-behaviour of the system under investigation and from informations on the ideal gas heat capacities. In practice the eos parameters for pure substances are in most cases tuned to give a good representation of the vapor pressures. For mixtures the required binary parameters for the mixing rules are fit by least square methods to binary vapour liquid equilibrium data. However, for highly nonideal systems accurate and reliable data are often lacking, especially in the field of caloric properties.

Due to the fact that the calculation of caloric data from an eos necessarily involves differentiation and subsequent integration the obtainable accuracy is sometimes of a magnitude lower than that of the pVT-properties the eos is based upon [1,2]. Thus the eos methods sometimes can lead to larger uncertainties in the estimated caloric properties. To improve this situation directly measured caloric data of good precision are needed to be incorporated for the determination of the eos parameters. This is especially required for mixtures showing a strong deviation from ideality.

Hydrocarbon-water systems are representatives of this class of mixtures. Eos often fail to accurately represent the caloric properties of these mixtures. As except of the work of Wormald and coworkers [e.g.3] reliable data of the caloric properties of hydrocarbon-water mixtures are lacking a thorough experimental study for various compositions of the methane-water and the methane-ethane-water system has been carried out in the gaseous region at pressures up to 7 MPa and temperatures to 600 K. The data are compared to those that have been obtained from eos methods especially developed for representing the thermodynamic properties of hydrocarbon-water systems.

EXPERIMENTAL SET UP

An adiabatic flow calorimeter has been set up on the basis of Rittmann [5] to determine caloric properties of mixtures with fixed composition : the isobaric enthalpy change $(\Delta h)_p$ and the integral isenthalpic Joule-Thomson effect $(\Delta T)_h$. It has been designed for measurements in the gaseous region for pressures up to 15 MPa and temperatures from ambient to 600 K.

Fig. 1 gives the simplified flow diagram of the calorimeter. The apparatus consists of two cyles, one for the hydrocarbon components that remain in the gaseous state and one for water that undergoes phase transition during the experiment. The hydrocarbon fluid stream (pure methane in the case of the binary and a pre-mixed methane-ethane mixture for the ternary system) is pressurized to appr. 12 MPa and circulated by means of a two stage diaphragm compressor. The pressure then is reduced to the inlet pressure of the calorimeter. In the pre-heater the gas stream is mixed isobarically with the water vapour and the inlet temperature to the calorimeter is adjusted. The mixture first passes the isobaric enthalpy change cell where a defined amount of energy by means of electrical heating is added and then the throttling valve where the pressure is reduced to 0.17 MPa, a value that has always been kept constant during the measurements. Temperatures are continously taken by calibrated Pt 100 sensors, pressures recorded by calibrated piezo-resistive sensors.

After passing the calorimeter the mixture is cooled to ambient temperature against cooling water and passed to a phase separator where the condensed water is separated from the gaseous stream. The gas is returning to the compressor, the liquid water is pressurized by a piston pump to supercritical pressure (appr. 25 MPa) and subsequently heated to supercritical temperature (appr. 680 K). The pressure then is reduced to the desired inlet pressure of the calorimeter. By this procedure it could be ensured that the water always remains in the superheated state so that a continous operation is guaranteed.

The flow rates of both streams were determined separately. Water flow was checked gravimetrically, the gaseous flow was estimated volumetrically with a calibrated dry gas meter. By also taking into consideration the phase equilibrium properties finally the actual composition of the overall mixtures could be determined. For the ternary system the methane-ethane composition was checked during the experiments by gas chromatography.

The gases investigated were of a purity of 4.5, water had been de-ionized (el. conductivity < 0.8 S/cm).

Design of the Calorimeter

Both measuring devices, for isobaric enthalpy change and for throttling have to ensure adiabatic operation. The power $Q_{el}$ added to the stream ṅ must be transferred to the fluid without loss. As no mechanical work is done in the system and the change in kinetic and potential energy of the stream along the calorimeter is of negligible magnitude the first law of thermodynamics reduces to

$$(\Delta h)_p = \frac{\dot{Q}_{el}}{\dot{n}} \tag{1}$$

for the isobaric enthalpy change and to

$$\Delta h = 0 \tag{2}$$

for the throttling device.

The required suppression of heat losses has been realized by three means. Convective heat losses have been eliminated by placing the calorimeter in an evacuated chamber (pressure < $10^{-4}$ Pa), radiative heat losses have been minimized by super insulation and conductive losses have kept to a minimum by using stainless steel piping with a minimum wall thickness according to design. However, the heat losses along the pipes and the temperature sensors are the largest contribution to the experimental error.

An error propagation calculation resulted in the following values:
- For water free mixtures 0.9% for the isobaric enthalpy change and 180 mK for the integral Joule-Thomson effect
- For water containing mixtures a maximum error of 4% in the isobaric enthalpy change and 210 mK for the integral Joule-Thomson effect resulted.

The errors are mainly of dynamic nature and could not be reduced by applying more precise measuring devices.

Possible Gas-Hydrate Formation after the Compressor

The hydrocarbon stream enters the compressor saturated with water at low pressure. The gas stream is cooled after the first and second stage of the compressor. Therefore, depending on pressure and temperature, hydrate formation is possible (and has been experienced) especially in the case of the methane-ethane system. For the highest ethane content used in this study (25 mole%) according to a calculation procedure of Sloan [4] a minimum temperature of abt. 293 K can be tolerated at 12 MPa (the pressure at compressor outlet). Therefore cooling after the second stage had to be performed by means of a thermostat that kept the temperature at about 305 K. In addition a molecular sieve adsorption column has been installed to avoid possible hydrate formation further downstream.

Heating of Water

The supercritical heating of water was chosen to ensure a smooth operation without disturbances due to the evaporation process which could influence composition. The error of scattering in water composition could thus be reduced by one magnitude to 0.2% from about 2% when direct evaporation is applied [5].

Measuring Principle and Evaluation

The basic procedure of the measurements is demonstrated in a schematic h-T-diagram in Fig. 2. The isobaric enthalpy changes were taken in subsequent series of experiments. Keeping the inlet temperature of the calorimeter constant the heating was increased stepwise to a corresponding change in outlet temperature of abt. 12 K each before throttling to the constant pressure of 0.17 MPa (measurements 1a to 1n). When a maximum difference between inlet and outlet temperature of abt. 80 K along the isobaric enthalpy change cell was reached a second set of experiments was performed starting with a constant inlet temperature slightly below the highest outlet temperature of the preceeding set (2a, 2b,...). By doing so an overlap of the series was guaranteed.

In the subsequent evaluation procedure the experimental raw data were corrected to compensate for small fluctuations in pressure and mixture composition during the measurements. In the last step the series of measurements were combined resulting in smooth curves for the isobaric enthalpy as a function of temperature. No heat leak corrections had to be applied.

Finally the total isobaric enthalpy has been fit to cubic polynomials in temperature from which also the specific heat, $c_p$, can be obtained by the definition

$$c_p = \left(\frac{\partial h}{\partial T}\right)_{p,xi} \qquad (3)$$

It could be shown that the residual enthalpy ($\delta h$) can be obtained directly from the measurements without loss of accuracy by extrapolating the throttling experiments (polynomials) to zero pressure. In this case no additional information input for the ideal gas enthalpy is required. The residual enthalpy has been correlated as exponential term in temperature following a proposal of DIPPR [6].

The evaluation procedure results thus in expressions for isobaric $(\Delta h)_{p,xi}$, isothermal $(\Delta h)_{T,xi}$ and isenthalpic $(\Delta T)_{h,xi}$ expressions that are thermodynamically consistent.

RESULTS FOR PURE METHANE

To prove the operability of the calorimeter first measurements were performed with pure methane for which highly accurate fundamental equations have been proposed. Here the comparisons are based on the equation proposed by Setzmann and Wagner [7]. Only a few reliable caloric measurements of methane above ambient temperature are known. So the own data extending to 600 K are an extension of the existing caloric data pool and can be used to check the fundamental equations in this region.

Fig. 3 shows the values obtained for the integral Joule-Thomson effects $(\Delta T)_h$ when throttling from 3 and 7 MPa to 0.17 MPa as function of the throttling valve inlet temperature. The size of the symbols was chosen to also indicate information about the a.m. experimental accuracy. The own data are compared with all data retrievable from the open literature and those calculated from the Wagner-Setzmann equation represented by the solid lines. Agreement between the latter and the own data is very good over the whole range of investigated temperatures as well as with the literature values of Dawe and Snowdon [8], Ayber [9], Eakin et al. [10] and , for 70 bar, of Zemlin [11]. However, some of the older data (Tsaturiants and Mamedov [12], Budenholzer et al. [13] and, for 30 bar, Zemlin [11]) show appreciable deviations from our data. The inconsistency of the data of Budenholzer et al. has already been discussed elsewhere [7,14]. It is believed that they are due to heat losses [15].

Fig. 4 compares the own evaluated data for the residual enthalpy ($\delta h$) with results of the Wagner-Setzmann equation and literature data. The own results are represented as dotted lines. Again the data of Dawe and Snowdon [8] and Eakin et al. [10] as well as those of Dillard et al. [16] show good agreement with the own data. The data of Sage and Lacey [17] give too low residuals. Over the whole temperature range the predicted values from Wagner-Setzmann's equation and the own values stay within the accuracy limit of about 10 J/mol stated for this equation [7].

RESULTS FOR THE METHANE-WATER SYSTEM

Corresponding measurements were performed at 3 and 7 MPa for the methane-water system up to 40 mole% water from slightly above the dew point temperatures to abt. 600 K. To our knowledge no data in the open literature exist to compare with in the composition range examined here.

The upper part of fig. 5 gives the values of integral Joule-Thomson effects (3 MPa to 0.17 MPa) for mixtures with 10, 20 and 40 mole% water and, for comparison, also the own data for pure methane. The solid lines represent the correlation of the data. The lower part of fig. 5 gives the results for the residual enthalpies ($\delta h$) at 3 MPa. In addition values for a 50 mole% mixture as interpolated from isothermal data of Lancaster and Wormald [3] are shown (circles).

The obtained values show a change with composition overproportional to the water content. This is most pronounced in the case of the mixture with 40 mole% water as compared to the 10 and 20 mole% lines. Partly this can be attributed to the fact that our measurements started at temperature values near the respective dew points (for the 40 mole% water, 3 MPa a dew point temperature of abt. 465 K).

In fig. 6 the respective results for the 7 MPa measurements are shown for the mixture containing 20 mole% water. Again the own correlated values for pure methane are included for comparison. In this figure we have also included results obtained from the Soave eos [22] with a binary parameter $k_{ij}$=0.52 [23-25] and equation of state methods that have been developed especially for representing the properties of water-methane mixtures. These are the cubic eos of deSantis et al. [18] and of Wormald [19], a virial type eos proposed by Pitzer et al [20] and a fundamental equation proposed by Larsen and Prausnitz [21]. All these equations use temperature dependent parameters individually fit to the properties of water (and generalized for alkanes for methane) as well as binary interaction parameters obtained from vapor liquid equilibrium data for the methane-water system. It can be seen that the equation of Wormald gives the best results. The Soave eos with the constant kij applied does not perform worse then the other especially proposed equations. One of the reasons of the too flat slope for the residual enthalpy for the Soave eos may be attributed to the fact that the Soave eos also gives too low residuals for water.

## RESULTS FOR THE METHANE-ETHANE-WATER SYSTEM

Measurements were performed with two ternary mixtures, one with 78 mole% methane, 7 mole% ethane and 15 mole% water, the other with 60 mole% methane, 20 mole% ethane and 20 mole% water. Except of a few water dew point data for an equimolar methane-ethane mixture [26] and solubility data [27] no other experimental data exist in the open literature for this ternary mixture.

Fig. 7 shows the results for the mixture containing 20 mole% water. The own results are presented by the bold solid lines. They are compared with results obtained from the Soave [22], deSantis and Wormald eos. For the Soave eos binary parameters from [28-31,24 and 23] have been used in the conventional van der Waals mixing rules. The Soave equation slightly underpredicts the slope of the $(\Delta T)_{h,xi}$ data results, the other two eos overpredict the temperature dependence at both investigated pressures. For the $(\delta h)$ values the temperature dependence (except for the 7 MPa values for the eos of Wormald) is underpredicted by all three eos.

## OUTLOOK

It has been shown that experimental caloric data are indispensable for an eos to give reasonable representation of caloric mixture behavior also for mixtures showing stronger deviation from ideality. Even methods developed especially for the systems under investigation do not represent the measured caloric properties satisfactorily. Therefore it is recommended to take the caloric information into account already during the development of an eos. One of these possibilities to adequately describe both thermal and caloric properties with the same eos is currently under way [15].

Acknowledgement

The authors appreciate the financial support donated by the Deutsche Forschungsgemeinschaft (DFG). LRO would like to thank Prof. H. Knapp for supplying the basic start up equipment.

## REFERENCES

1. Schulz, S.: Archiv Technisches Messen (Germany), Blatt V 2-1 (1973) 181 - 184
2. Miyazaki, T. et al. : Proc. 1st Intern. Conf. Calor. and Therm. Aug. 1969, 617-623
3. Lancaster, N.M.; C.J. Wormald: J. Chem. Eng. Data 35 (1990) 11 - 16
4. Sloan, E.D. Jr. : Clathrate Hydrates of Natural Gases,Marcel Dekker,N.Y. 1990
5. Rittmann, B., Dissertation, Technical University Berlin 1983
6. Daubert, T.E. et al. AICHE Symp. Ser. 86, no. 279 (1992) 62 - 92
7. Setzmann, U.; W. Wagner Phys. Chem. Ref. Data 20 (1991) 6, 1061 -1155
8. Dawe, R.A.; P.N. Snowdon: J. Chem. Eng. Data 19 (1974) 3, 220 - 223
9. Ayber, R. : VDI-Forschungsheft 511, Düsseldorf/Germany 1965
10. Eakin, B.E. et al. : Gas Processors Association, Ann. Conv. 54 (1975) 52 - 58
11. Zemlin, H. : Dissertation, Universität Karlsruhe (TH) 1970
12. Tsaturiants, A.BI.; A.R. Mamedov: Izv. Akad.Nauk. Azerb. SSR Ser. Fiz. Mat., Techn. Nauk.3 (1962) 137 - 144
13. Budenholzer,R.A. et al. : Ind. Eng. Chem. 31 (1939) 3, 369-374

14. Francis, P.G; G.R. Lockhurst: Proc. Roy. Soc. A 271 (1963) 667 - 672
15. Day, Chr. : Dissertation, Universität Karlsruhe (TH) 1995, submitted for
    "VDI-Fortschrittbericht", Düsseldorf/Germany 1995
16. Dillard, D.D. et al. : AICHE-J. 14 (1968) 6, 923 - 928
17. Sage, B.H.; W.N. Lacey: Ind. Eng. Chem. 31 (1939) 12,1497-1509
18. deSantis, R. et al. : Ind. Eng. Chem. Proc. Des. Dev. 13 (1974) 4, 3 74 - 3 77
19. Wormald, C.J. : J. Chem. Soc. Faraday Trans. I 85 (1989) 6, 1315 - 1326
20. Pitzer, K.S. et al. : Fluid Phase Equilibria 79 (1992) 125-137
21. Larsen, E.R., J.M. Prausnitz: AICHE J. 30 (1984) 5, 732 -738
22. Soave, G.: Chem. Eng. Science 27(1972), 1197-1203
23. Erbar et al.: GPA Project 752, Research Report RR-42, 1980
24. Trebble, M.A., Bishnoi, P.R., Fluid Phase Equilibria 40(1988),1-21
25. Tonopoulos, C. et al., Fliud Phase Equilibria 57(1990), 261-276
26. Villareal, J.F. et al.: Producer's Monthly 18(1954)7, 15-17
27. Amirijafari, B. et al.: Soc. Petr. Engineers J. 12(1972)2, 21-27
28. Knapp, H. et al.: DECHEMA Chemistry Data Series, Vol. VI, 1982
29. Knapp, H.: Proc. XV Intern. Congress of Refr., Vol. II (1979), 229-232
30. Gupta, M.K. et al: J. Chem. Eng. Data 25(1980), 313-318
31. Gmehling, J., Kolbe, B.: Thermodynamik, Thieme Verlag Stuttgart 1988

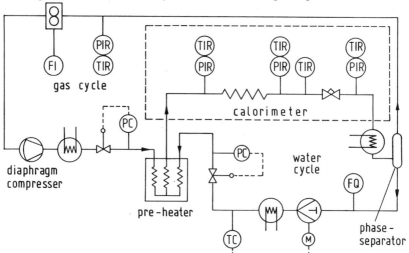

**Figure 1**: Simplified Flow Diagram of the Calorimeter

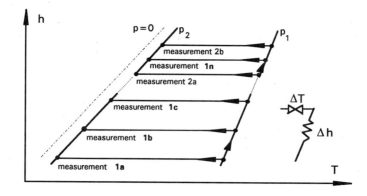

**Figure 2:** Measuring Principle

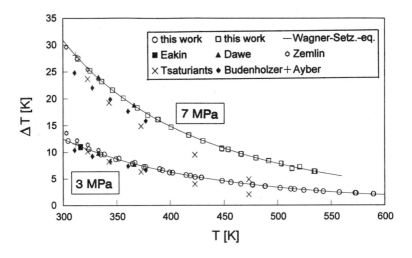

**Figure 3:** Integral Joule-Thomson Effect by Throttling from High Pressure to 0.17 MPa
for Pure Methane as Function of the Throttling Valve Inlet Temperature.
Comparison of Own Results with Literature Data and
Calculated Data (Solid Lines).

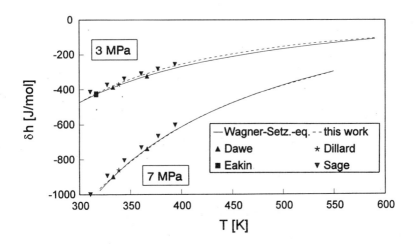

**Figure 4:** Residual Enthalpy for Pure Methane. Comparison of Own Results (Dotted
Lines) with Literature Data and Calculated Data (Solid Lines).

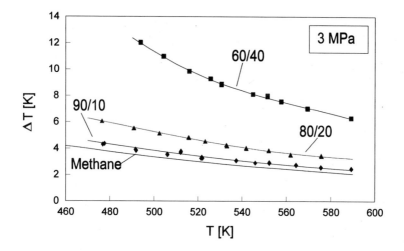

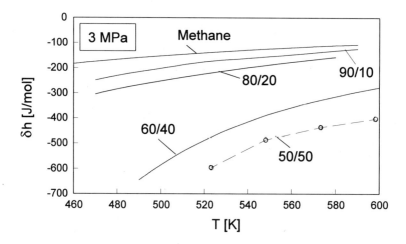

**Figure 5:** Illustration of the Measurement Results for the Joule-Thomson Effect
by Throttling to 0.17 MPa and the Residual Enthalpy for Various
Compositions of the Methane-Water System (Given in
Mole % Methane/Mole % Water). The Points for the Equimolar Mixture
are interpolated values, taken from Wormald [3].

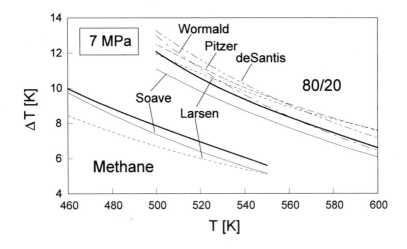

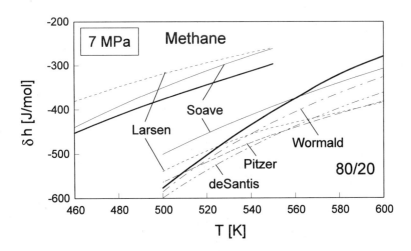

**Figure 6:** Comparison of Measurements for the Methane-Water System
(Bold Lines) with Results Calculated from Various Equations of State.

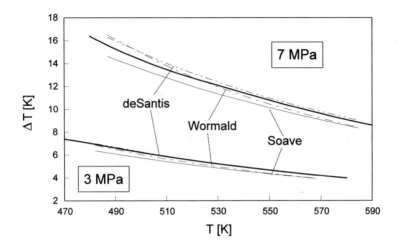

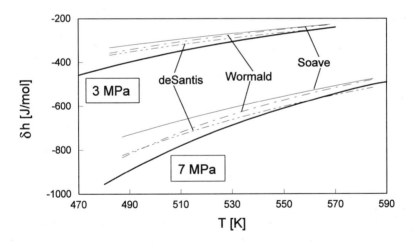

**Figure 7:** Comparison of the Measurements for the Ternary System (60 Mole % Methane, 20 Mole % Ethane and 20 Mole % Water) (Bold Lines) with Results Calculated from Various Equations of State.

## SIMULATION OF VAPOUR CLOUD EXPLOSION AND SUBSEQUENT BLAST PROPAGATION IN BUILD-UP AREAS

## SIMULATION DES EXPLOSIONS DE GAZ ET DE LA PROPAGATION DES ONDES DE SOUFFLE QUI EN RESULTENT EN PRÉSENCE DE BATIMENTS

W.P.M. Mercx , A.C van den Berg and L.H.J. Absil
TNO Prins Maurits Laboratory, The Netherlands

Y. Mouilleau
INERIS, France

C.J. Hayhurst
Century Dynamics Ltd., UK

## ABSTRACT

The processing and storage of large quantities of flammables at chemical plants and refineries constitute a potential explosin hazard for the environment. In particular, in densely populated areas where the mutual distance between plant and residential areas is restricted, the danger of blast damage can be significant.

AutoReaGas is a CFD-tool capable of detailed numerical simulation of any aspect in this problem. AutoReaGas contains both a gas explosion simulator and a blast simulator, each tailored to the specific features of the problem.

In this paper, the AutoReaGas tool is demonstrated in a practical case study.

## RÉSUMÉ

L'utilisation et le stockage de grandes quantitiés de gaz inflammables dans l'industrie chimique et dans ler raffineries constituent pour l'environnement un risque potentiel d'explosion. En particulier, dans les régions où la densité de population est élevée et où les installations industrielles sont proches des zones urbaines, les riques de dommages importants en cas d'explosion accidentelle sont significatifs.

AutoReaGas est un code C.F.D (pour 'Computational Fluid Dynamics') qui permet de simuler l'ensemble des phénoménes mis en jeu lors d'une explosion de gaz. Ce code comprend en particulier deux modèles conçus spécifiquement pour simuler la combustion des gaz d'une part et la propagation des ondes de souffle d'autre part.

Dans cet article, l'emploi d'AutoReaGas est illustré dans un cas pratique.

## INTRODUCTION

Vapour cloud explosions constitute a major hazard for the process industries. An accidental release of a flammable substance in the open, the mixing with air and a subsequent ignition result in a flame propagation process which, under the appropriate boundary conditions, may develop explosive combustion and damaging blast. Petro-chemical plants, where large quantities of highly flammable substances are stored and processed under high temperatures and pressures, often constitute outstanding boundary conditions for a vapour cloud explosion to develop. A list of major vapour cloud explosion incidents in the past is given by the references [1-3].

A characteristic feature of an explosion is a blast wave. An object struck by a blast wave experiences a loading. This loading is a complex function of blast wave properties and the object size and shape. The blast resulting from a vapour cloud explosion may do damage to structures up to a considerable distance from the explosion.

Up to this moment, highly simplified methods [4], such as TNT-equivalency or Multi-Energy methods, are mainly used to assess vapour cloud explosion blast effects. Such methods model vapour cloud explosion blast by means of the blast resulting from an idealised explosive charge whose size and strength can be determined by simple rules of thumb. The blast characteristics can be simply read from blast charts. An implicit assumption using such methods is that the blast effects are fully point symmetric. The consequence of using such methods may often result in blast loading predictions which are not more than an order in magnitude accurate. Such inaccuracies are particularly severe for results calculated for locations close to the blast source.

Today, there is a growing need for more accuracy; this can only be attained through the application of more sophisticated methods. In order to meet this requirement TNO have for several years developed, together with partner companies, computational tools for analysing gas explosion and blast effects. In addition, TNO have carried out extensive experimental research programs widely sponsored by CEC, national authorities and industry.

AutoReaGas is a software package incorporating this expertise and technology and capable of detailed 3-D numerical simulation of any aspect of the vapour cloud explosion problem. AutoReaGas contains both a gas explosion simulator and a blast simulator, each tailored to specific problem features.

After a general description of the phenomena and how they are modelled, this paper demonstrates the software in a practical case study.

## PHENOMENA

### Gas explosion

In a gas explosion a flammable gas mixture is consumed by a combustion process which propagates through the mixture in the form of a flame front. The flame front is the interface between cold reactants and hot combustion products. Because combustion products are of high temperature, the cold flammable medium expands strongly on combustion. The expansion induces a flow field whose structure is fully determined by the nature of its rigid boundaries, i.e. the boundary conditions. In this self-induced flow field the combustion process is carried along. The rate of the combustion process is strongly affected by the flow structure (velocity gradients and turbulence) met. Flow velocity gradients stretch the flame front to enlarge its interface and increase the effective combustion rate. Low intensity turbulence wrinkles the flame front with a similar effect on the combustion rate. Higher combustion rates intensify the expansion. Higher flow velocities go hand in hand with more intense turbulence levels. Higher turbulence levels speed up the combustion, etc. etc....... In other words: under the appropriate (turbulence generative) boundary conditions, a positive feedback mechanism is triggered by which a gas explosion develops exponentially both in speed and overpressure.

## Blast

During the explosion process, the rapidly expanding combustion products do work on the surrounding medium. In this way, the chemical energy (heat of combustion) of the flammable mixture is partly converted into mechanical energy (expansion). Such a process is characterised by a thermodynamic efficiency with a maximum of approximately 40%. The mechanical energy is transmitted from the explosion into the surrounding atmosphere in the form of a blast wave. Such a blast wave may do damage on structures a large distance from the explosion.

An object struck by a blast wave experiences a blast loading which is a combination of two effects. On the one hand, a blast wave is a experienced as a transient change in the static overpressure (pressure wave) and on the other hand as a transient change in the medium velocity (a gust of wind). The pressure wave character induces a static pressure distribution while the medium velocity wave induces a fluid dynamic drag force on an object struck.

## MODELLING

### Gas explosion

As described in Section 2, the basic mechanism of a gas explosion consists of the interaction of a premixed combustion process with its self-induced expansion flow field. The development of this process is predominantly controlled by the turbulent structure of the flow field which is induced by the boundary conditions. Modelling of a gas explosion requires careful modelling of all aspects of this complicated process. The model underlying the AutoReaGas gas explosion simulator can be characterised as follows:

- The gas dynamics is modelled as a perfect gas which expands as a consequence of energy addition. This is mathematically formulated in conservation equations for mass, momentum and energy.
- The energy addition is supplied by combustion which is modelled as a one step conversion process of flammable mixture into combustion products. This is formulated in conservation equations for the fuel mass fraction and the composition. The combustion rate is a source term in the fuel mass fraction conservation equation.
- Turbulence is modelled by a two parameter model (k-$\varepsilon$) which consists of conservation equations for the turbulence kinetic energy k and its dissipation rate $\varepsilon$ [5].
- Turbulent combustion is modelled by an expression which relates the combustion rate to turbulence. Several options are available varying from theoretical relations such as the Eddy Break Up model [6] and the Eddy Dissipation model [7, 8]up to experimental correlations between turbulence and combustion [9,10]. Because the cell size in many applications is often far too large to fully resolve a turbulent combustion zone, the combustion rate is corrected.
- The initial stage of combustion upon ignition is modelled by a process of laminar flame propagation whose speed is controlled on the basis of experimental data.
- Objects too small to be represented by solid boundaries in the computational mesh, are modelled by a subgrid formulation. The presence of a subgrid object is modelled by the specification of appropriate flow conditions, i.e.: a fluid dynamic drag and a source of turbulence.
- Numerical solution of the set of equations is accomplished by means of the "power law" scheme applied within a finite volume approach [11].

**Blast**

As long as objects with large cross-flow dimensions are considered, the interaction of gas explosion blast is predominantly governed by the pressure wave character of a blast wave and the drag component can be neglected. The pressure wave character of blast flow fields is accurately represented by inviscid flow. Often, blast flow fields are characterised by the presence of gas dynamic discontinuities such as shocks. Modelling of blast-object interaction requires careful description of such phenomena. Therefore, the blast simulator models blast-object interaction as follows:

- The gas dynamics is modelled as inviscid compressible flow of a perfect gaseous fluid which can be formulated as the conservation equations for mass, momentum and energy for inviscid flow, i.e. the Euler-equations.
- Description of shock phenomena requires a sophisticated numerical technique tailored to proper representation of steep gradients. To this end, the blast simulator utilises Flux-Corrected Transport (FCT) [12, 13]. FCT makes an optimised use of numerical diffusion so that steep gradients present in shocks are retained. Numerical diffusion is added only where it is required for numerical stability.

## ANALYSIS OF A VAPOUR CLOUD EXPLOSION

### Problem

A small town is situated at some distance from a petro-chemical plant. Beside a storage site of large capacity, the plant consists of a process area of 80x80 m. This area contains two identical units of 20x60 m and 20 m high, which are separated by a 12 m wide lane. The process equipment consists of a large number of vessels, pumps and pieces of apparatus, interconnected by a maze of piping and appendages. The equipment is built in two concrete structures consisting of parallel floors supported by pylons.

In this environment, the possibility of an incident, consisting of a big release of propane is considered. The dense propane disperses in a flat layer above the ground and drifts into the process area where it is ignited. In this paper, the ensuing gas explosion and the resulting blast loading on buildings in the nearby town is analysed by numerical simulation.

### Vapour Cloud Explosion Analysis

The storage site is a relatively open area where the propane cloud can disperse in a flat layer above the ground. Drifting into the process installation, the flammable cloud is ignited at a short distance from the process equipment. The cloud is consumed by a flame front which propagates into the process area. The equipment provides the turbulence generative conditions which speed up the combustion process up to explosive intensity. The strength of the explosion is predominantly dependent on the detailed layout of the equipment present in the process area. Therefore, the development of the flame propagation in the process area is analysed in detail.

A computational domain of 80x80x20 m, covering the process area, is specified. The domain is subdivided into 40x40x20 cells of 2x2x1 $m^3$. Within this domain, the software allows the specification of the physical layout of any configuration of boxes, beams, vessels and tubes by means of a CAD-like user interface. Figure 1 is an AutoReaGas representation of only the larger vessels and piping of the process units specified.

The configuration of objects specified in the domain is automatically converted by the software into the proper input for the explosion simulator. Large objects are represented by solid boundaries while the presence of small objects - the piping and the appendages - is taken into account by the subgrid formulation. The vapour cloud is specified as a layer of stoichiometric propane-air located directly above the ground to a height of 3 m. The flammable mixture is ignited in a location, approximately 5 m outside the equipment at ground level.

The software allows fully interactive simulation of the phenomena showing the distributions of any specified process parameter on the screen during the computation. Figure 3 is a compilation of such a set of pictures showing the temperature field in both a horizontal and vertical cross-section through the ignition point at a few consecutive points of time. The temperature field, which is a good indicator for the flame propagation process, is visualised by means of a suggestive colour gradation. The timing in the pictures indicates that the flame propagation process had a slow initial stage in the cloud outside the process equipment, followed by a gradual speed-up when the flame enters the space underneath the first concrete floor. The presence of a 12 m wide lane between the two units seems to hardly interrupt the flame acceleration process.

During the full time of the simulation, any desired process parameter can be monitored at gauge locations throughout the computational domain. The Figure 2 represents, for instance, the overpressure-time traces recorded for the gauges 1 - 5. The traces demonstrate a characteristic behaviour. A long phase of slow laminar flame propagation producing hardly any overpressure during the first 1.9 s which progresses into an exponential development in speed and overpressure under the influence of the turbulence inducing conditions in the process equipment.

The results show that the turbulence generative conditions in the process area are sufficient to develop damaging blast overpressures. On the other hand, the results also indicate that the high overpressures are generated by the explosive combustion of only a portion of the initially available combustion energy. A substantial part of the available energy is consumed during the initial phase of relatively slow flame propagation. In addition, the timing in the pressure pulses P3 and P4 on the one hand and P5 on the other, seems to indicate a more or less separate development of explosive combustion at different locations within the process area.

The overpressure-time traces demonstrate clearly that the blast effects produced by such a violent vapour cloud explosion have a high degree of directionality. The overpressures observed in the gauges 1, 2 and 3, for instance, show that an order of magnitude higher blast overpressures are produced in the direction of flame propagation than in the opposite direction. This strong directionality in the blast effects is fully in line with experimental observations [14].

The software allows a straightforward computation of blast loading on any object present within the process area. This can be accomplished by recording pressures differentials acting on large objects represented by solid boundaries or by recording drag forces acting on small objects represented by the subgrid formulation.
In this analysis, however, only the interaction of the blast wave with buildings at some distance from the explosion are considered.

**Blast Interaction Analysis**

The strong directionality in the blast near the source disappears with propagation distance. The higher the strength of the blast source, the stronger the tendency to full symmetry. Therefore, the use of data on spherical fuel-air charge blast wave propagation [15] is justified for extrapolation of the blast wave parameters into the far field.
According to these data, the blast wave overpressure has decayed down to 10 kPa and the wave duration has grown up to 0.1 s at the distance the blast wave interaction with buildings is considered. Therefore, a blast wave of 10 kPa overpressure and 0.1 s duration serves as blast simulator input.

Blast loading of an object is a complicated function of blast wave properties and object size and shape. Full simulation of the interaction of the blast flow field with an object enables one to study the phenomena in detail and to compute the blast loading. To this end, the software allows the specification of a computational domain and the specification of any configuration of rigid boundaries within this domain. A blast wave of any desired strength, duration or shape can be specified, coming in from the left boundary of the computational mesh.

The compilation of AutoReaGas pictures in Figure 4 shows the development of the wave phenomena which is characteristic for blast wave interaction with two buildings of 10m width and 15m height. The wave phenomena are visualised in the pressure field by an isobar pattern. Shock phenomena are present where the isobars accumulate.

A 10 kPa overpressure and 0.1 s duration blast wave is initialised, coming in from the left boundary of the mesh. The blast wave reflects at the frontal area of the building. The reflected frontal overpressure is relieved by lateral rarefaction. The blast wave passes the top side of the building nearly unaffected and diffracts down the back side and subsequently reflects at the earth's surface. During the simulation, for three gauge locations at each building (P1, P2 and P3 for the first and P4, P5 and P6 for the second building) the overpressure was monitored. The pressure-time signals are represented in Figure 5. The wave phenomena can be clearly traced back in the overpressures-time signals. They show how the blast wave overpressure approximately doubles on reflection at the front (P1).

The overpressure build-up at the back wall (P3) is clearly the result of the passage of two waves, the diffracted and the ground-reflected wave. The third peak is due to the reflection of the primary wave at the front of the second building. The front of the second building experiences a substantial reduction in blast loading because of the sheltering presence of the first.

The overpressure build-up in between the buildings as well as the sheltering effects, however, appear to be highly dependent on the blast wave duration and the spacing between the two buildings.

**CONCLUSION**

AutoReaGas is a software package for analysis of gas explosion problems. It consists of a gas explosion simulator and a blast simulator, placed in a user-friendly environment. Problems can be defined using CAD-like interface. During simulation, the development of the phenomena can be continuously monitored. Any desired process variable can be recorded in any desired location. Several possibilities of the software were demonstrated in a practical case study.

The case study showed that the process equipment of chemical plants often constitute outstanding conditions for gas explosions to develop damaging overpressures and blast. High blast overpressures were generated locally at different locations in the plant. Only a limited part of the totally available combustion energy actually contributes to the blast. Near-field blast effects from violent vapour cloud explosions were shown have a high degree of directionality.

Simulation of the interaction of the blast with buildings enables one to compute detailed blast loading. The blast loading on a building was shown to be greatly influenced by the presence of other structures in its vicinity.

**REFERENCES**

1.      J.A. Davenport "a study of vapor cloud incidents"
        A.I.Ch.E. Loss Prevention Symposium, Houston (TX), USA, 1977

2.      J.A. Davenport "a study of vapor cloud incidents - an update"
        4th Int. Symp. Loss Prevention and Safety Promotion in the Process Industries, Harrogate
        (UK), IChemE Symp. Series, No.80, 1983

3.      F.P. Lees "loss prevention in the process industries"
        Butterworths, London, 1980

4.      IChE "explosions in the process industries, 2nd edition, a report of the major hazards
        assessment panel, overpressure working party"
        Institution of Chemical Engineers, 1994

5.      B.E. Launder and D.B. Spalding "mathematical models of turbulence"
        Academic Press, London, 1972

6.      D.B. Spalding "development of the eddy break up model of turbulent combustion"
        16th Symp. (Int.) on Combustion, pp. 1657-1663, The Combustion Institute, Pittsburgh
        (PA), 1977

7.      B.F. Magnussen and B.H. Hjertager "on the mathematical modelling of turbulent
        combustion with special emphasis on soot formation and combustion"
        16th Symp. (Int.) on Combustion, pp. 719-729, The Combustion Institute, Pittsburgh
        (PA), 1977

8.      B.H. Hjertager et al. "computer modelling of gas explosion propagation in offshore
        modules"
        J. Loss Prev. Process Ind.,Vol. 5, No. 3, (1992), pp. 165-174

9.      R.G. Abdel-Gayed, D. Bradley and M. Lawes
        "turbulent burning velocities: a general correlation in terms of straining rates"
        Proc. Roy. Soc. London, A414, pp. 389

10.     K.N.C. Bray "studies of turbulent burning velocity" Proc. Roy. Soc. London,
        Vol. A431, (1990), pp. 315-325

11.     S.V. Patankar "numerical heat transfer and fluid flow "
        Hemisphere Publishing Corporation, Washington, 1980

12.     J.P. Boris J.P. and D.L. Book "solution of continuity equations by the method of flux-
        corrected transport"
        Methods in Computational Physics, Vol.16, Academic Press, New York, 1976

13.     J.P. Boris "flux-corrected transport modules for solving generalized continuity equations"
        NRL Memorandum report 3237, Naval Research Laboratory, Washington, D.C.

14.     C.J.M. van Wingerden "experimental investigation into the strength of blast waves
        generated by vapour cloud explosions in congested areas"
        6th Int. Symp. "Loss Prevention and Safety Promotion in the Process Industries", Oslo,
        Norway, 1989, proceedings, pp. 26-1, 26-16

15.     A.C. van den Berg and A. Lannoy
        "methods for vapour cloud explosion blast modelling"
        J. of Haz. Mat., 34, (1993), pp. 151-171

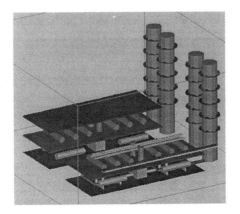

**Figure 1. AutoReaGas Representation of Equipment in the Process Area**

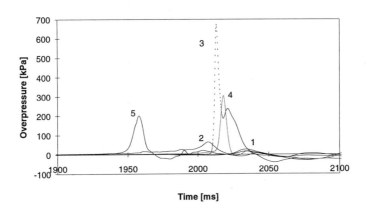

**Figure 3. Overpressure-time Traces Recorded at Gauges 1, 2, 3, 4, and 5**

# HORIZONTAL CROSS SECTION

900 Time 1.192 sec. after ignition                1550 Time 1.866 sec. after ignition

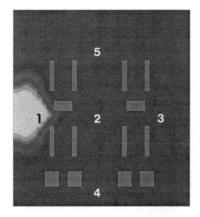 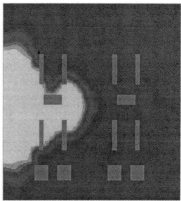

1750 Time 1.961 sec. after ignition                1950 Time 2.016 sec. after ignition

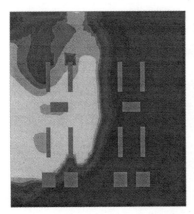 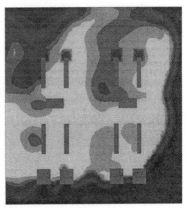

**Temperature [K]**

| 300 | 500 | 700 | 900 | 1100 | 1300 | 1500 | 1700 | 1900 | 2100 |

**Figure 2. Visualisation of the Flame Propagation Process in a Horizontal and a Vertical Cross-section at Consecutive Points in Time**

## VERTICAL CROSS SECTION

0900 Time 1.192 sec. after ignition

1550 Time 1.866 sec. after ignition

1750 Time 1.961 sec. after ignition

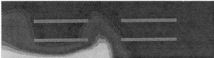

1950 Time 2.016 sec. after ignition

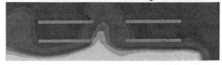

### Temperature [K]

300    500    700    900    1100    1300    1500    1700    1900    2100

**Figure 2. Continued**

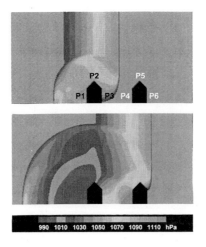

**Figure 4. Visualisation of Blast Wave Interaction with Two Buildings**

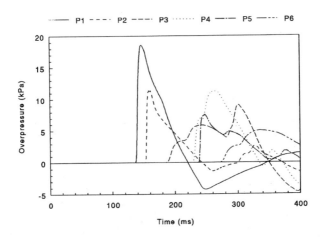

**Figure 5. Overpressure-time Traces Recorded at the Gauges P1, P2, P3, P4, P5 and P6**

STUDY OF HYDROCARBON FLAME PROPAGATION

IN THE PRESENCE OF REPEATED OBSTACLES.

ETUDE DE LA PROPAGATION DE FLAMMES D'HYDROCARBURES

EN PRESENCE D'OBSTACLES REPETES.

V. Vaslier, J.P. Pyrot

Gaz de France - Research and Development Division - Saint-Denis, France

N. Lamoureux, C.E. Paillard

CNRS, LCSR, ORLEANS, France

ABSTRACT

As part of safety studies on the gas chain, and especially in an effort to describe phenomena that appear during a gas explosion in a building, it is important to understand properly the effects of increasing pressure and acceleration of flames due to the presence of repeated obstacles. An experimental device was made to follow flame propagation throughout the entire length. Three removable configurations of obstacles ( half-moon shape plates ) are positioned at 1.4 m from the ignition point. An intensified high-speed video provides frames. Different hydrocarbon-air mixtures ( methane, ethane, natural gas ) were studied at sub-atmospheric pressures in the different obstacle configurations. In each configuration, the ethane-air flame speed is slightly greater than that of methane-air. The trends of the natural gas-air flame ranged between that of methane and ethane. These results will probably be used to validate 3D model calculations of explosions.

RÉSUMÉ

Dans le cadre des études de sécurité de la chaîne gazière, et en particulier pour estimer les effets d'une explosion sur les constructions, il est important de comprendre les phénomènes d'augmentation de la pression et de la vitesse de flamme en présence d'obstacles répétés. Un dispositif expérimental a été construit pour suivre la propagation de la flamme. Trois configurations d'obstacles amovibles ( plaques en demi lune ) sont placées à 1,4 m du point d'inflammation. Une caméra intensifiée rapide permet de suivre la progression de la flamme. Différents mélanges hydrocarbure-air ( méthane, éthane, gaz naturel ) ont été étudiés à des pressions subatmosphériques dans différentes configurations d'obstacles. Pour chaque configuration, la vitesse de la flamme éthane-air est plus importante que celle de la flamme méthane-air. L'évolution de la flamme gaz naturel-air est intermédiaire entre celles de méthane et d'éthane. Ces résultats pourront servir à valider des codes 3D de modélisation des explosions.

INTRODUCTION

When an explosion is initiated in a fuel-air mixture inside partially or confined enclosure, the effects upon the structures depend mainly on the changes in flame speed during its propagation from ignition point. These changes are linked to confinement and obstacles inside the enclosure. Analyses of damage caused by confined vapour cloud explosions having occurred in the last 30 years show that strong blast waves may be generated. A dramatic influence of the turbulence generated by obstacles has been observed in both small-scale and large-scale field experiments (1,2). The maximum flow velocity reached depends largely on the number, the size, the distance between the obstacles, the degree of confinement and the reactivity of gas. While most of these parameters have been studied, little work has been reported on the influence of the reactivity of gas on the flame acceleration phenomena. This paper reports on the results of an experimental investigation of flame propagation in a duct partially filled with obstacles. For different fuel-air mixtures, the effect of various obstacle configurations on flame propagation and acceleration was studied.

EXPERIMENTAL APPARATUS AND PROCEDURE

The experiments were performed in a cylindrical Pyrex tube 150 mm in internal diameter and 2.95 m long. Inflammation was produced at the closed end. The other tube end was separated from a tank by a thin plastic sheet. If the over-pressure during the explosion was too great, the sheet burst. The mixture was ignited by a spark at 8 cm from the end. Fourteen pressure gauges were placed along the top of the tube and separated from each other by 150 mm (Figure 1). The first gauge was located 80 cm from the ignition point. The visualisation was made with a high-speed intensified video ( EKTAPRO EM 1012/2 KODAK ). The camera shot at a rate of up to 2000 images per second. The observations were carried out over a length of 70 cm. Several shots were taken to follow the flame propagation over the entire tube length. A removable obstacles field was placed 140 cm from the ignition point. The obstacles were steel half-moon plates. The blockage ratio was of 0.5 and their thickness was 0.7 mm. The blockage ratio is defined by the obstructed area - tube section ratio. The mixture was prepared by the partial pressure method in two 75 l tanks. Three fuel-air mixtures ( methane, ethane, natural gas ) were studied. The methane-air mixtures were prepared with different equivalence ratios ( 0.7, 1, 1.3 ). The natural gas composition was : 89.533% $CH_4$, 8.367% $C_2H_6$, 1.197% $C_3H_8$, 0.166% i-$C_4H_{10}$, 0.226% n-$C_4H_{10}$, 0.016% $C_5H_{12}$, 0.495% $N_2$. Before each shot, the tube was evacuted.

RESULTS

Flame propagation in smooth tube

First, flame propagation in a smooth tube of stoechiometric methane-air mixture was compared to that obtained with ethane-air. The initial pressure in the tube was about 16 kPa. For both methane-air and ethane-air, the maximum flame front velocity ( 60 m.s$^{-1}$ ) was reached at 70 cm from the ignition point. In the first stage of propagation, the flame propagated in laminar stream. Its shape was quasi hemispherical (Figure 2, frame 1). The higher velocity was due largely to the expansion of the burned gas. After that, the flame velocity decreased. The direction of front propagation and its convexity changed (frame 2). The flame front took on a "tulip" shape. This behaviour has been well described by various authors (3, 4). Next, the flame front became wrinkled (frame 6). Its velocity successively increased and decreased. In this configuration, it was not possible to differentiate between the two mixture behaviours (Figure 3). The characteristic change of front shape was also observed when the obstacles were placed in the flame path.

Flame propagation in the presence of obstacles

    Three obstacle configurations were studied. For all configurations, the first obstacle was placed 140 cm from the ignition point. The distance between the obstacles was fixed at 150 mm in configuration 1, whereas it was fixed respectively at 187.5 and 75 mm for configurations 2 and 3.

    Configuration 1. A field composed of six obstacles spaced at one diameter was placed in the tube. In the first 100 cm from the ignition point, flame propagation was not altered by the obstacles situated in second part of the tube. After that, the flame was slowed because of obstacles which generated a change in the unburned gas flow field. When the flame front reached the obstacles, its propagation velocity increased up to 90 m.s$^{-1}$ with the methane-air mixture (Figure 4). The maximum velocities of the flames of ethane-air and natural gas-air mixtures were respectively 120 and 100 m.s$^{-1}$. An example of flame front frames is shown for methane-air and ethane-air mixtures (Figure 5). The difference between the changes in the flame fronts for the three fuel-air mixtures was very slight.

    Configuration 2. For the stoechiometric methane-air and ethane-air mixtures, the gap between the obstacles was modified. Five obstacles spaced 1.25 diameters apart were positioned. For both mixtures, acceleration was more intense after the third obstacle. However, the velocity decreased just before the flame reached the fourth obstacle (Figure 6). Then, the flame front accelerated again up the last plate. While the ethane-air flame speed was about 140 m.s$^{-1}$, the methane-air speed was about 80 m.s$^{-1}$. All along the obstacle field, the ethane-air flame speed was greater than that of methane-air.

    Configuration 3. By placing 11 obstacles spaced at one-half diameter, both flames had differing behaviours. In the ethane-air mixture, the flame speed increased all over the obstacles field from 20 to 150 m.s$^{-1}$ (Figure 7). In the methane-air mixture, however, the flame speed was almost constant between the first and the fourth obstacle. It then increased up to the last obstacle from 20 to 140 m.s$^{-1}$. Both flame speeds were almost equal.

    Natural gas-air flame propagation was not studied in the latter two configurations. For each three configurations of obstacles studied, the ethane-air flame speed was slightly greater than the methane-air flame speed. With configuration 1, the changes in the natural gas-air flame ranged between that of methane and ethane.

Change in equivalence ratio

    For methane-air mixtures, flame front propagation was observed with different equivalence ratios ($\phi$ = 0.7, 1 ,1.3). As shown by the fundamental combustion velocity measured (5), the faster flame is observed with a composition mixture near stoechiometry. The faster flame propagation was observed in our apparatus with the stoechiometric mixture. The lean mixture flame velocity was very slow. When the flame reached the obstacles field (configuration 1), it accelerated slowly from 5 to 40 m.s$^{-l}$. With the rich mixture, the flame speed was higher. It increased from 10 to 60 m.s$^{-l}$.

Change in initial pressure

    We want to show the influence of the initial pressure in the tube on
the flame speed. Flame propagation for a stoechiometric methane-air mixture
was studied at different pressures with configuration 1. The initial
pressure was varied from 13 to 34 kPa at intervals of 3.5 kPa. The
dependence flame velocity - distance is given in figure 8. From 13 to 31.5
kPa, the flame velocity increased regularly with pressure. However, from
31.5 to 34 kPa, the flame velocity at the end of the obstacles field
increased by a factor greater than 2. The maximum flame speed was up to 350
m.s$^{-1}$. It seems that in this particular configuration, when the pressure was
greater than a definite value, the flame velocity might be dramatically
increased.

DISCUSSION

    The fundamental combustion velocity of both stoechiometric methane-air
and ethane-air mixtures is almost equal (5) (respectively 43.4 and 44.5
cm.s$^{-1}$). When the flame was slightly disturbed in a smooth tube, the flame
front in both mixtures propagated at the same velocity. However, in the
obstacles field, the flame front was strongly disturbed. When the flame
front reached the first obstacle, it was stretched. The amount of gas
consumed increases, causing a more significant flow field in the unburned
gas. The disturbance generates eddies which modify the flame surface and
accelerate its propagation. The flow field velocity increases again and
produces more intense vortices ahead, in the obstacles field. The flame
curls up between the obstacles, trapping unburned gas pockets. They burn
out, further accelerating flame propagation. Within the separated plate, 1)
a standing eddy is formed behind the obstacle, 2) between the separated
flow and the out flow there is a mixing shear layer, 3) and for a large
distance downstream, the flow becomes undisturbed again. The acceleration
process due to a feed-back mechanism has been described in detail by Moen
et al. (1). The distances separating the obstacles ( BR = 0.5 ) were varied
( P = 75, 150, 187.5 mm ). With P = 75 mm, the flame could not fit into a
vortex. The distance between the plates was too small, causing a strong
acceleration of the flame propagation. When P = 150 mm, the distance
between the plates was large enough to allow the flame front to curl up. If
P = 187.5 mm, the distance between the plates was too large to cause
continuous acceleration of the flame front. In this case, the flow field
just ahead of the obstacle was less disturbed and the flame speed
decreased.

    Hjertager et al. (6) have written that the influence of turbulence on
heat release is governed by turbulence parameters, gas dynamics effects and
chemical reaction kinetics. The turbulence may be characterised by the
lifetime of the turbulent eddies. The chemical time may be defined by the
induction time of autoignition. A characteristic gas dynamic time may be
defined as a function of the sound speed in the explosive mixture. This
parameter is almost identical for the various compositions of the mixtures
studied. The interaction between those parameters is very complicated. When
the distance between the plates was decreased, the methane-air and ethane-
air flames propagated at the same velocity. The lifetime of the turbulent
eddies becomes very short. The chemical parameter is less important than
the turbulent parameter. Where the distance between the plates was larger
(187.5 mm), the two mixtures presented very different flame propagation
velocities. The characteristic chemical time becomes more important than
the eddies lifetime.

According to Van Wingerden et al. (7), gas reactivity has no effect on the flame propagation velocity. Without obstacles, the two mixtures presented the same evolution. However, by placing obstacles field in the path of the flame front, differences between methane-air and ethane-air flame velocity were noted. These differences were more evident with 187.5 mm spacing obstacles than with the 75 mm. The degree of turbulence generated by obstacles has not the same influence on flame evolution. This influence was dependent on the nature of the fuel.

CONCLUSION

. This study shows that flame propagation depends not only on the obstacles configuration ( blockage ratio, distance between the obstacles and their shape ) but on the nature of the reactive mixture.

. Flame velocity accelerates considerably in the presence of obstacles. Yet the maximum flame speed reached is less than the sound speed in the unburned gas.

. Now, a few numerical 3D model calculations have been developed and largely validated. However, some questions must be clarified, particularly as regards a good description of the flame folding around different obstacles. This study may be used to improve the numerical simulation of flame folding.

REFERENCES

1.  I. O. Moen, M. Donato, R. Knystautas, J. H. Lee " Flame acceleration due to turbulence produced by obstacles " Comb. and Flame, 39, p 21-32, 1980

2.  I. O. Moen, J. H. S. Lee, B. H. Hjertager, K. Fuhre, R. K. Eckhoff "Pressure development due to turbulent flame propagation in large-scale methane-air explosions" Comb. Flame, 47, p 31-52, 1982

3.  O. C. Ellis " Flame movement in gaseous explosive mixtures " Fuel, Vol VII, N° 11, p 502-526, 1928

4.  D. Dunn-Rankine, P. K. Barr, R. F. Sawyer " Numerical and experimental study of "tulip" formation in a closed vessel " 21st Symp. (Int) on Comb., p 1291-1301, 1986

5.  A. Van Tiggelen Oxydations et combustions, Vol. I, chap. V, Institut Français du Pétrole, 1968

6.  B. H. Hjertager, K. Fuhre, R. K. Eckhoff " Large-scale experiments on turbulent flame and pressure development " Fuel-air explosions, p 585-599, 1982

7.  C.J.M. Van Wingerden, J.P. Zeeuwen " Flame propagation in the presence of repeated obstacles : Influence of gas reactivity and degree of confinement " Journal of hazardous materials, 8, p 139-156, 1983

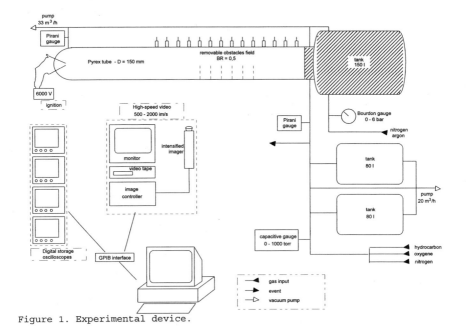

Figure 1. Experimental device.

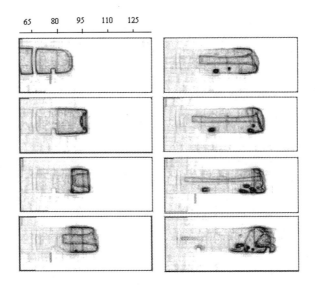

Figure 2. Formation of tulip shape in flame front in stoechiometric methane-air mixture. The initial pressure is equal to 16 kPa. Each frame is taken every 6 ms.

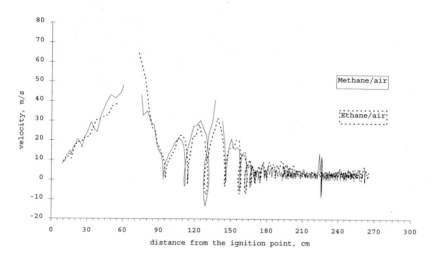

Figure 3. Flame front velocity versus distance from the ignition point for both stoechiometric methane-air and ethane-air mixtures. The initial pressure in the tube is equal to 16 kPa in the smooth tube.

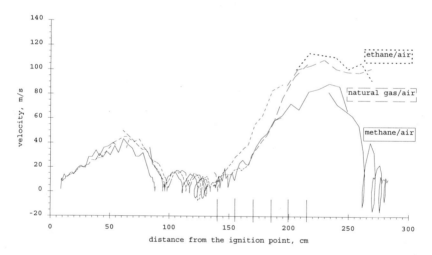

Figure 4. Flame front velocity versus distance from the ignition point for the stoechiometric methane-air, ethane-air and natural gas-air mixtures in the presence of repeated obstacles (space of 150 mm). The blockage ratio is equal to 0.5 and the initial pressure is 16 kPa.

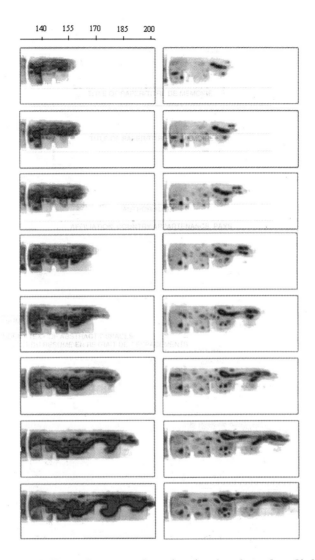

Figure 5. Frames of flame front acceleration in the obstacles field (BR=0.5 - P=150 mm) for both the stoechiometric ethane-air (on the left) and the methane-air (on the right) mixtures. The initial pressure is 16 kPa. Each frame is taken every 1 ms.

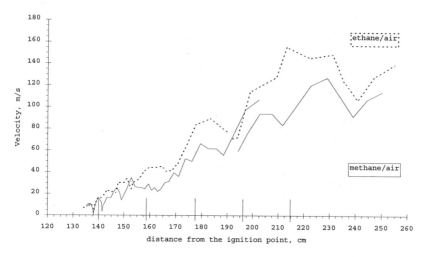

Figure 6. Flame front velocity versus distance from the ignition point in the presence of repeated obstacles (space equal to 187.5 mm) for both the stoechiometric methane-air and the ethane-air mixture. The blockage ratio is equal to 0.5 and the initial pressure is 16 kPa.

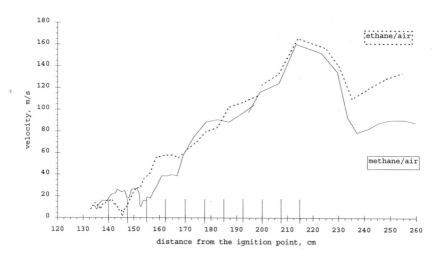

Figure 7. Flame front velocity versus distance from the ignition point in the presence of repeated obstacles (space equal to 75 mm) for both the stoechiometric methane-air and the ethane-air mixture. The blockage ratio is equal to 0.5 and the initial pressure is of 16 kPa.

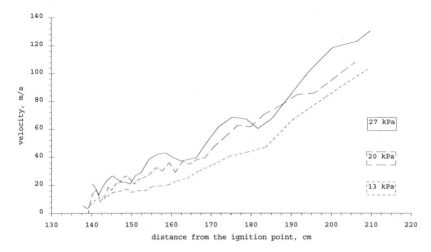

Figure 8. Influence of the initial pressure on the stoechiometric methane-air flame front velocity versus distance from the initial ignition point. The blockage ratio is equal to 0.5 and the plates are spaced 150 mm from each other.

**1995 INTERNATIONAL GAS RESEARCH CONFERENCE**

FINE CALIBRATION OF THE NEW RUHRGAS AG HIGH-PRESSURE GAS METER PROVING FACILITY AT
DORSTEN USING A PISTON PROVER

ETALONNAGE DE PRECISION DU NOUVEAU BANC D'ESSAI POUR COMPTEURS A GAZ HAUTE PRESSION DE
RUHRGAS AG A DORSTEN A L'AIDE D'UN ETALON PRIMAIRE

R. Erbeck, R. Boden, O. Brandt
Ruhrgas AG, Essen, Germany

ABSTRACT

High-pressure gas flow meters should preferably be calibrated using gas at normal working pressure. In November 1993, Ruhrgas AG commissioned a new high-pressure gas meter proving facility in Dorsten to provide a service for customers and reduce the uncertainty of flow measurements for commercial applications. Unlike the previous practice of calibrating working standards on the high-pressure meter proving facility of (NMi) the Dutch weights and measures authority, the new facility is now calibrated using a piston prover, an instrument based on a fundamental measurement technique, also completed in 1993.

The piston prover allows the working standards of the Dorsten proving facility to be calibrated directly at normal working pressure without long calibration chains. The facility was calibrated under the supervision of PTB (the federal institute for physics and technology) and the weights and measures authorities. They have certified that the measurement uncertainties of the facility are very low.

The deviations between results obtained using this procedure and the calibration of working standards by the NMi facilities are about 0.1 % or less, well within the overlapping uncertainties of the two procedures.

RESUME

Les compteurs à gaz utilisés dans de réseaux d'approvisionnement en gaz devraient être étalonnés le plus souvent possible au gaz à la pression de service. Dans le but d'offrir à ses clients un service supplémentaire et pour améliorer encore la précision de mesure dans les applications commerciales, la Ruhrgas AG a mis en service en novembre 1993, dans ses ateliers à Dorsten, un nouveau banc d'essai pour compteurs à gaz haute pression. L'étalonnage du banc n'a pas été réalisé comme dans le passé par l'étalonnage de l'étalon de travail sur les bancs d'essai pour compteurs à gaz haute pression des services d'étalonnage néerlandais (NMi), mais à l'aide d'un étalon primaire qui avait également été réalisé en 1993, appelé piston d'étalonnage.

A l'aide de cet étalon primaire, les étalons de travail du banc d'essai à Dorsten ont pu être étalonnés directement à haute pression sans avoir recours à de longues chaînes d'étalonnage. L'étalonnage a été réalisé sous la surveillance de la Physikalisch-Technische Bundesanstalt (bureau fédéral allemand de physique et de métrologie) et des services officiels de métrologie. Les autorités ont attesté au banc d'essai de très petites incertitudes de mesure. Par rapport à l'étalonnage des étalons de travail sur les bancs d'essai du NMi, on constate des différences allant jusqu'à 0,1% environ, c'est-à-dire elles se situent largement à l'intérieur des bandes d'incertitudes.

## INTRODUCTION

The law in force in the Federal Republic of Germany concerning measurements and calibration requires the calibration of instruments used to determine gas quantities in business and trade use. Such instruments are calibrated by comparison with an instrument referred to as a working standard. The meter to be tested and the working standard are connected by a pipe which must be as short as possible and the same gas is allowed to flow through them (at the same mass flow rate.

Flow meters are normally calibrated using air at atmospheric pressure. When flow meters are used in high-pressure service in gas supply systems, there may be more or less severe deviations from the error curves obtained during low-pressure air calibration. This effect may already be apparent from pressures as low as 2 bar. Where possible, high-pressure gas flow meters should therefore be calibrated using gas at a pressure corresponding to their later working pressure.

Previously, calibration work at pressures in excess of 10 bar or at high flow rates was mainly performed on the high-pressure calibration facilities of the Dutch weights and measures authorities (NMi), because the facilities required were not available in Germany.

In order to cover the increasing demand for high-pressure meter proving services and to reduce the uncertainty of measurements in commercial applications, Ruhrgas commissioned its new high-pressure meter proving facility *pigsar* (an abbreviation of the German expression for gas meter proving facility - a service offered by Ruhrgas) in November 1993. The facility is located at Dorsten, about 25 km to the north of Essen. The design of the facility was already prepared for the implementation of a new procedure for working standard calibration. Appropriately stepped sizes for the working standards were selected and the space required for the installation of a new flow prover was included in the plans. This appeared to be a reasonable approach as DVGW - the German gas and water industry association - would be able to make available a piston prover, a high-pressure flow prover using a fundamental measurement procedure, following the completion of an extensive research programme at the beginning of 1993.

A piston prover is based on the principle of measuring the time taken for a piston to pass between two sensors in a pipe, displacing a defined volume of fluid. For some time, piston provers were only used as flow provers for liquid flow meters. It seemed to be impossible to ensure that the piston was sufficiently gas-tight. In addition, it was feared that the pressure surge resulting from piston start-up would compress the gas, leading to measurement results which would not be reproducible.

Laak et al /1/ describe the implementation of a piston prover for ethylene meters. Since 1984, the turbine meters of Aethylen-Rohrleitungs-Gesellschaft (ARG) of Antwerp have been calibrated using a stationary piston prover. The piston prover used in *pigsar* was built by Budé using design documents similar to those on which the ARG instrument is based.

In order to make the initial measurements needed for the commissioning of *pigsar*, all the working standards were first calibrated at NMi. Following commissioning measurements, the working standards were then proved using the meter prover in order to provide an independent basis for meter proving operations. Two sets of calibration results, both obtained using high-pressure proving facilities with wide pressure and flow ranges, were therefore available for comparison.

## DESIGN AND MODE OF OPERATION OF PISTON PROVER

The schematic in Fig. 1 shows the mode of operation of the piston prover. Before the beginning of a measurement, with start valve 1 closed, gas flows through start valve 2, via openings in the wall of the prover run, through the prover run and to the meter to be tested, installed downstream of the piston prover. The piston is in position 1 and does not move at this stage. If conditions (temperatures, pressures and flow rate) are stable, the measurement may be started by simultaneously closing start valve 1 and opening start valve 2, allowing gas to flow behind the piston. The piston then starts to move.

The time tpp taken by the piston to displace test volume V'pp is measured by inductive sensors. The volume flow rate at flowing conditions is then given by V'pp/tpp.

The test section itself, with a length of 3 m, is located in a decentralized position in the prover tube in order to allow a start-up length of 2 m. This is sufficient to allow the pressure wave built up by piston start-up to subside before measurement starts. The straight length of the prover tube downstream of the test section is 1 m.

The flow measured is only corrected for material temperature and gas pressure in the prover tube.

As the volume of the test section is very small in relation to the flow rate measured, measuring times are also very short, for example only 1.11 sec. at maximum flow of 480 m$^3$/h. Even with a high-frequency pulse transmitter, the turbine flow meter to be tested, installed downstream of the piston prover, only generates about 1000 pulses during the measurement. The rounding error of +/- 1 pulse would result in excessive uncertainty. For this reason, the time between the corresponding pulse flanks is measured using separate timers for the piston prover and the meter to be tested and this value is used to calculate the flow rate. The measurement time for the meter to be tested always starts with the first flank of the pulse following the piston prover pulse. The number of blades on the turbine meter rotor is entered in the computer in order to ensure that the time measurement on the meter tested is continued for a whole number of rotations (avoiding any periodic error which may be in evidence).

The technical data of the piston prover are summarized in Table 1 below:

The output signals of the pressure sensors and the four-wire resistance thermometers are digitized by a data logging unit and transmitted to a computer which also receives signals from the control system, pulse counter and timer. The entire piston prover system can therefore be operated from the computer, which also evaluates the measured data.

A fundamental problem which affects measurements made using systems with small test volumes is the line pack effect. This is the change in gas volume in the connecting pipe between two gas meters during a measurement as a result of pressure and temperature fluctuations in the gas. The error produced by this effect is proportional to the volume of the connecting piping and inversely proportional to test volume. In order to minimize the effective volume of connecting piping and the error, the piston prover is always used in combination with a reference meter installed just downstream of the test section.

The first step is to calibrate the reference meter using the piston prover. The reference standards of the facility are then calibrated in the second stage (indirect method).

In this second stage, gas continues to flow through the piston prover, but the piston remains in its final position. This ensures that gas flows to the piston prover and reference meter at unchanged conditions and that gas flow conditions for the working standards to be tested are the same as in later operation.

RESULTS OF MEASUREMENTS MADE AT THE RUHRGAS AG HIGH-PRESSURE GAS METER PROVING FACILITY IN DORSTEN

For test measurements in the commissioning phase and subsequent test operation of the Ruhrgas AG high-pressure gas meter proving facility /6/, the calibration data for the working standards obtained at the Bergum and Groningen calibration facilities were used.

The completion of the commissioning phase and subsequent test operation coincided with the end of development work on the piston prover (/2/, /3/ and /4/). As a result, it was possible to effect the calibration of *pigsar* already planned in the design phase before starting meter proving work for third parties. In addition, there was a unique opportunity to compare the data obtained during the comprehensive start-up programme of *pigsar* with those obtained following recalibration by the piston prover.

As the piston prover had not yet been used for calibrating a meter proving facility prior to the basic calibration of *pigsar*, a comprehensive programme of tests to validate the functioning and to verify the figures for measurement uncertainties determined by theoretical studies was conducted at the same time as the measurements. Among other things, the test programme, with a duration of several months, verified the reproducibility and repeatability of reference meter calibration and of working standard calibration using the reference meter.

Calibration of Working Standards

When selecting the sizes of working standards ( 1 x G100, 4 x G250 and 4 x G1000) and sizing the building in the design phase, the intention had been to ensure that the proving facility would be ideally suited for the measuring range of the piston prover and that the piston prover could be installed in a position which would allow operation unaffected by ambient conditions.

Figs. 2 and 3 show the configuration used for connecting the piston prover into the proving facility. The piston prover was installed downstream from the nine working standards in an easily accessible position designed specifically for the piston prover and its reference meter (G250). It was decided to install the prover downstream of the working standards in order to avoid interference on the working standards caused by the piston prover and to ensure that flow conditions at the working standards during calibration would be comparable to conditions during later meter proving operation.

The sizes of the working standards installed allow direct calibration of the smaller standards up to their maximum flow rates (190 m³/h for G100 and 480 m³/h for G250 meters). The G1000 standards are calibrated in two stages. Up to the maximum flow rate of the piston prover, the standards are calibrated directly using the piston prover and its reference meter. For flow rates above 480 m³/h, four G250 working standards which have already been calibrated are connected in parallel and used to calibrate a G1000 transfer standard installed in the test position up to its maximum flow of 1920 m³/h. The G1000 working standards are then calibrated from 480 m³/h up to their maximum flows using the G1000 transfer standard (see Fig. 4).

In each calibration stage, calibration was effected at three pressures (18, 35 and 50 bar) and at 10 different flow rates, providing 30 sets of values for the correction curve to be calculated. The results of calibration are presented in detail in /7/.

SIGNIFICANCE OF TEST RESULTS FOR PIGSAR

Comparison Between NMI (Bergum) and *pigsar*

The piston prover, which allows calibration without any dependence on a long calibration chain represents a major improvement in international standards for high-pressure meter proving.

As the *pigsar* standards were calibrated in The Netherlands (at Groningen and Bergum) for the tests to be made in the commissioning phase and fine calibration using the piston prover was then effected within a year, it is possible to compare the results of two entirely independent calibrations. All nine *pigsar* standards were calibrated at three pressures (8 bar, 20 bar and 50 bar) in Bergum and in some cases also in Groningen. In order to allow direct comparison of the error curves determined by the piston prover with the results obtained in The Netherlands, the effects of the higher temperature on the Bergum facility (27°C, compared to 15°C for all the piston prover measurements) have already been taken into account in the following /8/.

Fig. 5 (G250) and Fig. 6 (G1000) show direct comparisons between the Bergum and *pigsar* error curves for two working standards selected as representative of the others. Generally, these curves are representative of those obtained for the other working standards.

The calibration facility computers determine error curves as a function of the Reynolds number. These curves are calculated by forming a correction function (fifth-order polynomial) for all values of the correction curves of the working standards recorded at individual pressures.

On this basis, the difference between the correction curves derived from the Bergum and *pigsar* measurements can be determined. As three or four working standards are always operated in parallel at *pigsar*, the best way of comparing the facilities is to take the average of all working standards of the same size for *pigsar* (Fig. 7). The variation of the individual curves around the mean curve is less than 0.1 %.

In order to plot the results over flow rate, it is necessary to select a fixed reference pressure. Fig. 8 and Fig. 9 show the offset between the two facilities for pressures of 20 bar and 50 bar respectively.

The overlap between the averaged error curves (Figs 5 to 9) is significantly better than the measurement uncertainty specified for Bergum and *pigsar* and these results can therefore be seen to show very good agreement.

Calibration by means of a piston prover is currently one of the most accurate ways of calibrating a high-pressure meter proving facility. As there are only slight differences between this method and results obtained using conventional proving facilities, conventional facilities can also be seen to meet very high quality requirements.

Measurement Uncertainty of Proving Facility

Considering all possible sources of error, including random uncertainty of sensors, line pack effects and errors due to the presentation of all measured values in one correction curve, the measurement uncertainties reached if all the metrological advantages of *pigsar* are utilized are as follows (Table 2):

| | |
|---|---|
| 16 m³/h to 160 m³/h | measurement uncertainty 0.23 % |
| 160 m³/h to 1600 m³/h | measurement uncertainty 0.20 % |
| 1600 m³/h to 6500 m³/h | measurement uncertainty 0.25 % |

Even with such an advanced facility as *pigsar*, with features such as extremely modern instrumentation and the use of several working standards in parallel to minimize random errors, such low uncertainty values can currently only be reached if a piston prover is used.

Further Action

However small the differences which persist between the measurements of the proving facilities may be, further reductions are still desirable. With this aim in view, it will be necessary to harmonize conditions at the facilities, including gas temperature, as closely as possible. In future, the calibration of *pigsar* working standards in the same position as in later meter proving operation, an advantage which it is currently not possible to quantify, will need to be taken into consideration when analysing a proving facility.

The experience obtained with the initial calibration of *pigsar* will permit a reduction in scatter when calibrating working standards in the minimum flow range with the piston prover and reference meter. This will lead to a further improvement in the measurement uncertainty of the entire system.

Although the level of quality reached in high-pressure gas metering is already high, international comparison tests will b e essential if this high level is to be maintained and even exceeded.

REFERENCES

/1/     Bellinga, H., Hoeks, St., Kooi, A., van Laak, F.A.L. and Orbons, P.J.:
        Anwendung einer Rohrprüfstrecke als Eichnormal für Hochdruckgasmessung.
        gwf-gas/erdgas 127 (1986), No. 3

/2/     Brandt, O., Schmitz, G. and Kämper, J.:
        Erfahrungen mit der Rohrprüfstrecke als neues Urnormal für die Bundesrepublik Deutschland zur Überprüfung cvon
        Gaszählern unter Hochdruck.
        gwf-gas/erdgas 133 (1992), No. 3

/3/     Schmitz, G.:
        Erstellung, Erprobung und Einsatz einer Hochdruck-Fundamentalapparatur zur Kalibrierung von Gebrauchsnormalen
        auf Hochdruckgaszählerprüfständen;
        Teil 1: Abnahmemessungen und erste Erprobung.
        Gaswärme-institut e.V. Essen, Report No. 7977 (1989)

/4/     Kämper, J. and Kronenberger, M.:
        Erstellung, Erprobung und Einsatz einer Hochdruck-Fundamentalapparatur zur Kalibrierung von Gebrauchsnormalen
        auf Hochdruckgaszählerprüfständen;
        Teil 2: Einsatz der RPS auf zwei Hochdruckzählerprüfständen.
        Gaswärme-institut e.V. Essen, Report No. 8921 (1992)

/5/     Aschenbrenner, A.:
        Berechnung der Unsicherheit von Messungen mit der Rohrprüfstrecke.
        Physikalish Technische Bundesanstalt, Memorandum (October 1990)

/6/     Brandt, O. and Erbeck, R.:
        Planung, Errichtung und Inbetriebnahme eines HD-Gaszählerprüfstandes.
        gwf-gas/erdgas 133 (1992), No. 10/11, pp. 535-540

/7/     Kronenberger, M. and Erbeck, R.:
        Einsatz der Fundamentalapparatur Rohrprüfstrecke.
        gwf-gas/erdgas 133 (1992), No. 10/11, pp. 535-540

/8/     Aschenbrenner, A.:
        Der Einfluß der Gastemperatur auf das Meßverhalten von Turbinenradgaszählern.
        PTB-Mitteilungen 88 5/78, pp. 319-322

| | |
|---|---|
| Prover tube length: | 6 m |
| Length of test volume: | 3 m |
| Length of half test volume: | 1.5 m |
| Upstream length of straight pipe: | 2 m |
| Prover tube diameter: | 250 mm |
| Wall thickness: | 12 mm |
| Prover tube material: | stainless steel (ASTM 316) |
| Piston material: | aluminium |
| Test volume: | approx. 150 dm³ |
| Flow metering range: | 30 to 480 m³/h natural gas |
| Max. allowable pressure: | 90 bar |
| Temperature: | 0-50°C |
| Differential pressure at piston: | approx. 0.1 bar |
| Connecting flanges: | 4", ANSI 6 lbs RF |

Table 1. Technical data of piston prover for natural gas

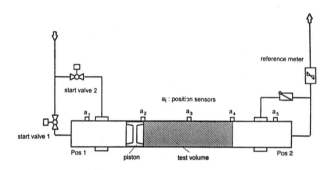

Fig. 1. Piston prover schematic

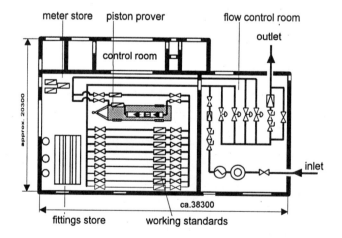

Fig. 2. Connection of piston prover downstream of working standards of *pisgar*, Dorsten

Fig. 3. View of test hall and piston prover during calibration in 1993

# From Paris to *pigsar*

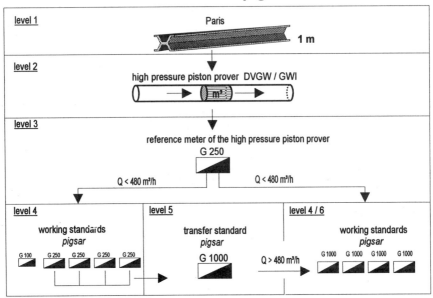

Fig. 4. Calibration schematic for *pigsar* working standards

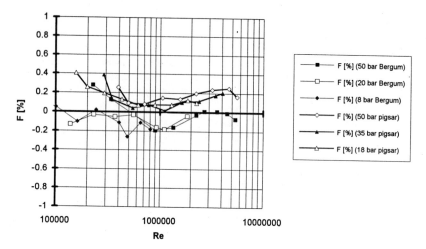

Fig. 5. Comparison of *pisgar* and Bergum error curves for a G250 working standard

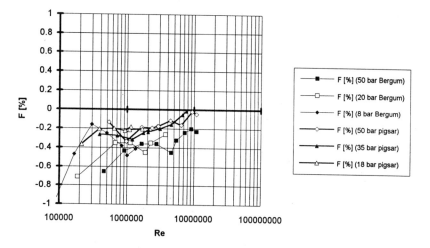

Fig. 6. Comparison of *pisgar* and Bergum error curves for a G1000 working standard

| 16 m³/h to 160 m³/h | measurement uncertainty 0.23 % |
| 160 m³/h to 1600 m³/h | measurement uncertainty 0.20 % |
| 1600 m³/h to 6500 m³/h | measurement uncertainty 0.25 % |

Table 2. Measurement uncertainties reached by *pigsar*

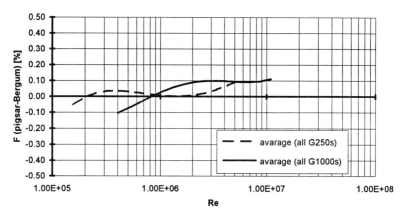

Fig. 7. Average Difference between Bergum and *pisgar* correction curves over all pressures
for standards of the same size

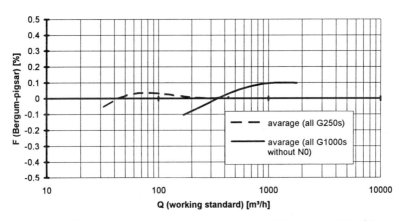

Fig. 8. Average difference between Bergum and *pisgar* correction curves at 20 bar for all standards of the same Size

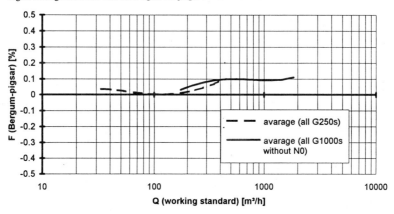

Fig. 9. Average difference between Bergum and *pisgar* correction curves at 50 bar for all standards of the same Size

EFFECT OF LIQUID ENTRAINMENT ON THE ACCURACY OF
ORIFICE METERS FOR GAS FLOW MEASUREMENT

EFFET DE L'ENTRAÎNEMENT DE LIQUIDE SUR LA PRÉCISION DES
DÉBITMÈTRES À DIAPHRAGME EN MESURES DES DEBITS DE GAZ

V. C. Ting
Chevron Petroleum Technology Company
La Habra, CA, USA

G. P. Corpron
Colorado Engineering Experiment Station, Inc.
Nunn, CO, USA

ABSTRACT

This paper presents the results of a study to show that a small amount of liquid entrainment in
an orifice meter can affect the accuracy of gas flow measurement. A series of tests, sponsored
by Chevron Petroleum Technology Company, was conducted under controlled conditions at
the Colorado Engineering Experiment Station, Inc. (CEESI) air flow calibration facility to
study this effect. Eight-inch orifice meters were selected for the experiments. The tests were
conducted at 4.13 MPa (600 psia) over the orifice Reynolds number range from 4 to 9 million using two horizontally mounted orifice meters. Water was injected at a controlled rate
upstream of the orifice meter to simulate field conditions. It was found that the presence of a
small amount of liquid in the gas stream caused the orifice meters to read a lower gas flow
measurement by as much as 1.7% depending on the beta ratio and the liquid rate.

RÉSUMÉ

Cette contribution présente les résultats d'une étude visant à démontrer qu'une petite quantité
d'entraînement liquide dans un débitmètre à diaphragme peut influer sur la précision des
mesures des débits de gaz. Une série de tests commanditée par la Chevron Petroleum Technology Company, a été réalisée sous conditions contrôlées au centre de calibration
d'écoulement d'air à la Colorado Engineering Experiment Station, Inc. (CEESI) afin d'étudier
ce phénomène. Pour les tests on a choisi des débitmètres à diaphragme de huit pouces. Les
tests ont été réalisés à une pression de 4.13 MPa (600 psia) dans la gamme de nombres de
Reynolds de 4 à 9 millions avec l'utilisation de deux débitmètres montés de façon horizontale.
L'injection d'eau à un taux contrôlé en amont du compteur servait à simuler les conditions de
champ. On a trouvé que la présence d'une petite quantité de liquide dans le courant de gaz a
amené les débitmètres à sous-évaluer les mesures, les erreurs pouvant atteindre jusqu'à 1.7%,
selon le rapport beta et le taux liquide.

## INTRODUCTION

Orifice meters are commonly used for processed and unprocessed custody flow measurement of natural gas. The orifice meter is accepted by the industry because of its simplicity in design and reliability. The orifice metering standards such as International ISO 5167,[1] American API 2530 (A.G.A.3)[2] and American ASME MFC-3M[3] offer detailed specifications, and installation and calculation requirements. These standards apply to steady-state, single-phase, homogeneous, and Newtonian fluid flow. When installed, orifice meters require minimum maintenance. The meter can provide 2% accuracy even without field calibration. The accuracy of orifice meters is of great importance because of the monetary value of the large volume of processed and unprocessed natural gas being transferred every day.

In production pipelines between wellheads and a process plant, natural gas generally carries some amount of water and condensate droplets besides the gas being metered. The entrained liquid comes from liquid carry-over in an inefficient production separation process and/or heavy hydrocarbon components condensing from the saturated gaseous phase. When applying measurement standards developed for single-phase fluid to unprocessed fluid with a small amount of liquid entrained in the gaseous stream, measurement uncertainty is expected to increase. However, studies of the measurement accuracy for unprocessed natural gas flow by orifice meters is limited. Most recent works in orifice flow measurement are concentrated on the orifice meter discharge coefficient data base and meter installation effects. Those studies are all conducted using well-defined dry gases such as air, nitrogen and dry processed natural gas.

There are several published correlations of two-phase flow measurements with orifices. The commonly mentioned works are Murdock, James, and Lin.[4-6] For gas-liquid flow measurement in orifice meters, the total flow rate and quality are the parameters to be determined. Most of these correlations were derived from homogeneous and separated flow models with known liquid to gas ratios. The basic assumptions of these models were developed for higher liquid flow rates than are normally present in unprocessed gas flows. It is not certain whether these models are valid for low liquid flow conditions.

In the studies by Ting and Shen[7,8] on field calibration of 15.24, 10.16, and 5.08-cm (6, 4, 2-inch) orifice meters by sonic nozzles for processed and unprocessed natural gas, it was concluded that flow measurement of unprocessed natural gas resulted in an additional uncertainty not found in processed pipeline-quality natural gas. It was shown that the magnitude of the increase in the uncertainty of orifice meters measuring unprocessed gas was from -0.5% to -2.5%. The authors also observed small amounts of liquid hydrocarbon condensate and water entrainment in the gas stream and suggested that without further research, sonic nozzles may not be effective as proving devices for unprocessed gas.

Schuster[9] and Nangea[10] also studied the effects of liquid entrainment on orifice meters. However, data points were collected at much higher liquid rates. McConaghy et al.[11] presented limited results to study the effects of liquid entrainment for 10.16- and 20.32-cm (4- and 8-inch) meters with a 0.6 beta ratio (ratio of orifice plate bore diameter to meter tube internal diameter, d/D) at lower liquid loading conditions. Their results, using the gas equation without a two-phase correction, indicated a relatively large under-measurement error of up to 1.0% for Reynolds number ranging from 3-8 million. Less measurement errors were detected at a lower 0.2 beta ratio.

A paper by Hussein[12] provided a detailed study on flow meter accuracy when measuring high-quality steam. The authors compared test data using several methods for correcting the mass flow rate when water was present and suggested that a high-efficiency separator be installed upstream of the meter to assure measurement accuracy.

Ting[13] investigated this further in the laboratory to determine the effect of liquid entrainment on a 5.08-cm (2-inch) orifice meter at 41.37 kPa (6 psig) at various beta ratios and metering positions. He found that a small amount of liquid entrainment always contributes to under-measurement of gas flow by up to -1.5% in a horizontal flowing position. He also suggested that an orifice meter should be installed in a horizontal position with a beta in the range from 0.5–0.6 to achieve the best unprocessed gas measurement results.

This paper extends the earlier low pressure laboratory work by Ting to a horizontally mounted 20.32 cm (8-inch) orifice meter at 4.13 MPa (600 psia) to simulate field operating conditions. A series of tests was conducted under controlled conditions at the Colorado Engineering Experiment Station, Inc. (CEESI) air flow calibration facility to study this effect for orifice Reynolds numbers from 4 to 9 million and beta ratios of 0.5 and 0.7.

EXPERIMENTAL SYSTEM AND PROCEDURES

The calibrations were performed using a blow down system to supply air to the test section. Systems of this type are typically used to calibrate flowmeters using either a primary calibration method or by using a secondary standard such as a critical flow venturi.[14-20] When secondary calibrations are done with a critical flow venturi, the calibration uncertainty is usually quoted as ±0.5%. In the case of the tests reported here, two orifices were first calibrated with a critical flow venturi using dry air. A turbine meter was also calibrated using dry air. In subsequent tests when water was injected into the line, the turbine meter was used to determine the volumetric flow rate of the dry air component. Temperature and pressure measurements in the vicinity of the turbine meter were used with a state equation for air to calculate density. This was then multiplied by the volumetric flow rate to determine the mass flow rate of the dry air component.

Wet air tests were performed by injecting water directly into the line upstream of the orifices (see Figure 1). The flow rate of water was determined with needle valves that had previously been calibrated in a high pressure water facility.[21] That calibration process consisted of measuring the flow rate through a valve when applying a 344.7 kPa (50 psi) differential pressure across the valve at several different valve stem positions as determined with a micrometer adjusting screw on the valve. The data was fit, and the fit was used to calculate the mass flow rate of water in the wet air tests.

Water was injected into the test section through a horizontal 9.525 mm (3/8") tube having seven sets of radial holes drilled into the tube (see Figure 2). Each set consisted of eight holes spaced at 45°. The spacing between hole sets along the length of the tube was one inch. Two hole sizes were used depending on the desired mass fraction or ratio of the mass flow rate of water to the mass flow rate of dry air. For mass fractions from 0.0012 to 0.021, a 1.27 mm (0.05") hole size was used, and for mass fractions from 0.0002 to 0.0011, a 0.508 mm (0.02") hole size was used. No attempt was made to spray the water into the flow field. Rather, any dispersion of the water was caused by the flow of air past the tube. Although the water injection was not visually observed, it was felt that water which did not evaporate probably accumulated along the bottom half of the pipe or on the orifice. The dew point of the air downstream of the water injection point was also not measured.

In a typical calibration, flow was established at steady conditions and when thermal equilibrium was achieved, the flow rates of both the dry air and water were measured. The discharge coefficient of the orifice was initially established with no water flow by

$$C_{dry} = \frac{4q_{mdry}\varepsilon_2 d^2}{\pi}\sqrt{\frac{1-\beta^4}{2\Delta p \rho_{f2}}} \tag{1}$$

where,  $C_{dry}$ = the discharge coefficient when the flowing fluid is dry air

$q_{mdry}$ = the mass flow rate of dry air as determined with a critical flow venturi

$e_2$ = the expansion factor based on the downstream pressure given by

$$\varepsilon_2 = \sqrt{1+\frac{\Delta p}{p_2}} - (0.41+0.35\beta^4)\frac{\Delta p}{\kappa p_2 \sqrt{1+\frac{\Delta p}{p_2}}}$$

$\pi$ = 3.141592654

d = the throat diameter of the orifice

$\beta$ = beta ratio, d/D

D = the interior diameter of the pipe

$\Delta p$ = the differential pressure across the orifice = $p_1 - p_2$

$\rho_{f2}$ = the density of the dry air based on the pressure, $p_2$, and temperature, $T_2$, downstream of the orifice

$\kappa$ = the isentropic exponent for dry air

When water was injected into the line, the discharge coefficient was calculated using the following equation:

$$C_{wet} = \frac{4q_{mdry}\varepsilon_2 d^2}{\pi} \sqrt{\frac{1-\beta^4}{2\Delta p \rho_{f2}}} \qquad (2)$$

A major difference in this case is that the flow rate of the dry air component ($q_{mdry}$) is determined with the turbine meter using the pressure and temperature measurements at the turbine. The density of wet air at the orifice was calculated using the equation of state for dry air. Because free water was present, the downstream pressure, differential pressure, fluid density and viscosity at the orifice differed from what would have been observed had the air been truly dry. Consequently, by using dry air state equations, an apparent shift was introduced in the discharge coefficient.

The discharge coefficient was determined in both the dry air and wet air cases as a function of the orifice throat Reynolds number, Rd, given by

$$Rd = \frac{\rho v d}{\mu} = \frac{4q_{mdry}}{\pi d \mu} \qquad (3)$$

where $\mu$ = the dynamic viscosity of dry air based on $p_2$ and $T_2$.

When the mass flow rate was calculated from orifice measurements, the calculation process involved first calculating the dry air density, viscosity and k using $p_2$ and $T_2$. A first estimate of the flow rate was then made by setting $C_{dry} = 0.6$ and calculating $q_{mwet}$ using the equation

$$q_{mwet} = \frac{\pi}{4} C_{dry} \varepsilon_2 d^2 \sqrt{\frac{2\Delta p \rho_{f2}}{1-\beta^4}} \qquad (4)$$

The throat Reynolds number was calculated using equation (3), and a second estimate of the discharge coefficient was obtained from the functional relationship between $C_{dry}$ and Rd which was determined under reference conditions with dry air. A second estimate of the mass flow rate was then calculated with equation (4). This process of calculating the flow rate, calculating a throat Reynolds number, calculating a new estimate of the discharge coefficient and then calculating a new flow rate was repeated until the flow rate calculations converged (usually by the third iteration). It is consistent with current practice.[1-3]

The above procedures resulted in values for predicted discharge coefficients and flow rates that could be compared to the reference dry air discharge coefficients and true dry air mass flow rates. These comparisons were carried out for two orifices, one having $\beta = 0.5$ and the other having $\beta = 0.7$ at a variety of water to dry air mass fractions.

## RESULTS AND DISCUSSION

The purpose of these tests was to observe the relative shifts of orifice discharge coefficients and flow rate caused by water injection when using dry air fluid properties. Air flow rate data for Reynolds numbers from 4 to 9 million were collected for 20.32 cm (8-inch) orifice meters with 0.5 and 0.7 beta ratios at a nominal 4.13 MPa and 15.6°C (600 psia and 60°F). A controlled amount of water was injected upstream of the orifice meter during the experiments. The water injection rate with respect to the air injection rate is expressed in terms of mass ratio:

$$\text{Mass Ratio} = \frac{(\text{Water mass flow rate})}{(\text{Air mass flow rate})} \qquad (5)$$

For each sequence of tests, a fixed mass ratio was set over the entire air flow rate range. Seven mass ratios were selected for the tests. Table 1 summarizes the test parameters used in the experiments.

### Table 1. 20.32 cm (8-inch) Orifice Meter Liquid Entrainment Experiment — Test Parameters

| Gas | Liquid | Pressure MPa (psia) | Temperature °C (°F) | Beta Ratio | Gas Flow Range (Orifice Reynolds Numbers) | Mass Ratio |
|-----|--------|---------------------|---------------------|------------|-------------------------------------------|------------|
| Air | Water | 4.13 (600) | 15.6 (60) | 0.5 and 0.7 | 4,000,000– 9,000,000 | 0.0002, 0.0005, 0.0008, 0.001, 0.005, 0.01, and 0.02 |

For each beta ratio, the orifice meter was calibrated with dry air at the beginning of the tests. Orifice meter discharge coefficients at dry air conditions ($C_{dry}$) were developed over the orifice Reynolds number range. For example, Figure 3 shows the $C_{dry}$ calibration curve for a 0.5 beta ratio over a Reynolds number range from 4–9 millions. The $C_{dry}$ data were fit with a second degree equation in terms of the Reynolds number (Rd) and in the case of $\beta = 0.5$, the following equation was obtained.

$$C_{dry} = 0.603483 + 7.7 \times 10^{-11} Rd + 1.28 \times 10^{-14} Rd^2 \qquad (6)$$

The meters were then calibrated at wet conditions with a constant water injection rate. However, the fluid density of the wet stream was assumed dry without the water additions. This was done to simulate actual field computation methods where the amount of liquid entrainment in the orifice meters was generally ignored. A set of orifice meter discharge coefficients ($C_{wet}$) were thus obtained.

To characterize orifice meter performance, the orifice meter discharge coefficients obtained by the experiments at wet conditions ($C_{wet}$) were compared with the dry discharge coefficients ($C_{dry}$). The wet air discharge coefficient deviation from the dry air discharge coefficient for the orifice meter was calculated with Equation (7).

$$\%C \text{ Deviation} = \frac{(C_{wet} - C_{dry})}{C_{dry}} \times 100 \qquad (7)$$

In addition, the wet air mass flow rate ($q_{mwet}$) measured by the orifice meter was compared with the dry air mass flow rate ($q_{mdry}$) measured by the turbine meter. Equation (8) defines the % deviation of the indicated wet flow rate from the reference dry flow rate. Again, the equation of state for dry air was used to calculate the density of the wet air.

$$\% \text{ Deviation} = \frac{\left(q_{mwet} - q_{mdry}\right)}{q_{mdry}} \times 100 \tag{8}$$

Figures 4–8 show the results of the water entrainment experiments for the 20.32 cm (8-inch) orifice meters with 0.5 and 0.7 beta ratios. The deviations of the discharge coefficient (Equation 7) and mass flow rate (Equation 8) are plotted as a function of the orifice Reynolds number for different water injection rates. The water injection rates are expressed in terms of mass flow rate ratios and are therefore dimensionless (see Equation 5).

Orifice Meter at 0.7 Beta Ratio

Figure 4 shows the discharge coefficient deviation (Equation 7) caused by liquid entrainment in the orifice meter at a beta ratio of 0.7. The water injection rate varied from a mass ratio of 0.000196 to 0.0208 over the orifice Reynolds number range form 4 to 9 million. A flow deviation plot is also presented in Figure 5 to show the effect of liquid entrainment on flow rate measurement. Test results at 0.7 beta ratio show that the flow rate deviation becomes increasingly negative with increasing mass ratio and Reynolds number, reaching an extreme of -1.7%.

When measuring wet natural gas in the field, the amount of liquid entrainment in the orifice meters is generally not known and the dry gas properties are used in the calculations even though the fluid was wet. It is also interesting to note that if density and viscosity corrections are made for the small amount of water added in the air in the flow calculations, the deviation do not change significantly. It was observed that the low flow readings were due in part to the lower differential pressure measurement when water was added to the flow.

In order to estimate the measurement uncertainty of entrained liquid in orifice meter measurements, data points are plotted in three mass ratio ranges, <0.0006, 0>, <0.02, 0.0006> and <0.02, 0.002>, as shown in Figure 6. A linear equation was fitted over the mass ratio range to illustrate how measurement bias in wet gas flow measurement can be estimated. It is not, however, the intention of this study to develop a model or best correlations to predict small amounts of liquid entrainment effects on orifice flow measurement. The results show that when the mass ratio was less than 0.006, flow rate measurement deviation was within -0.5%. However, when the mass ratio was greater than 0.002, the flow rate measurement deviation changed from -0.5% to -1.7% with increasing Reynolds numbers. Higher pressure tests conducted at CEESI also confirm earlier low-pressure test results published by the author.[13]

Orifice Meter at 0.5 Beta Ratio

Seven series of tests from mass ratio of 0.0005 to 0.0187 over the orifice Reynolds number range from 4 to 9 million were conducted. Figure 7 shows the discharge coefficient deviation (Equation 7) and Figure 8 presents the flow rate deviation caused by liquid entrainment in the orifice meter at 0.5 beta ratio. Unlike the orifice meter at 0.7 beta ratio, liquid entrainment tests at 0.5 beta ratio show less shift for the discharge coefficient and flow rate. Test results indicated the deviations are within ±0.5%, as shown in Figures 7 and 8.

CONCLUSION

The effect of liquid entrainment on the accuracy of orifice meters was systematically studied under controlled conditions at a flow calibration facility. The following conclusions were drawn:

1.    The flow measurement uncertainty was higher at wet conditions when a small amount of liquid was entrained. Orifice meters undermeasured wet gas flow rate with increasing beta ratio and Reynolds number. Up to a 1.7% lower flow rate measurement was detected at 0.7 beta ratio.

2.   Orifice meters performed better at 0.5 beta ratio when a small amount of liquid entrainment was presented. However, for best performance, entrained liquid should be removed upstream of the orifice meter.

3.   High-pressure air/water tests confirmed natural gas orifice meter performance data collected from the field and low-pressure air/water tests.

ACKNOWLEDGMENT

The authors thank the management of Chevron Petroleum Technology Company and Colorado Engineering Experiment Station, Inc., for permission to publish this work.

REFERENCES

1.   American Petroleum Institute (API), "Manual of Petroleum Measurement Standards" Chapter 14, Natural Gas Fluids Measurement, Section 3, Concentric Squared-Edged Orifice Meters, Parts I–IV, (American Gas Association Report No. 3), 1990–1992.

2.   International Standard Organization, "Measurement of Fluid Flow by means of Pressure Differential Devices — Part 1: Orifice Plates, Nozzles and Venturi Tubes Inserted in Circular Cross-section Conduits Running Full," ISO 5167-1, 1991.

3.   The American Society of Mechanical Engineers, Measurement of Fluid Flow in Pipes Using Orifice, Nozzle, and Venturi," ASME MFC-3M, 1984.

4.   Murdock, J. W., "Two-Phase Flow Measurement with Sharp-Edged Orifices," J. Basic Engineering, Vol. 84, No. 4, pp. 419–433, 1962.

5.   James, R., "Metering of Steam-Water Two-Phase Flow by Sharp-Edged Orifices," Proc. Inst. Mech. Engrs., Vol. 180, No. 23, pp. 549–566, 1965.

6.   Lin, Z. H., "Two-Phase Flow Measurements with Sharp-Edged Orifices," Int. J. Multiphase Flow, Vol. 8, No. 6, pp. 683–693, 1982.

7.   Ting, V. C. and J. J. S. Shen, "Field Flow Calibration of Natural Gas Orifice Meters," ASME Journal of Energy Resources Technology, Vol. 111, No 1, pp. 22–33, 1989.

8.   Shen, J. J. S. and V. C. Ting, "Accuracy in Field Flow Measurement of Unprocessed Natural Gas," presented at the 1992 International Gas Research Conference, Orlando, FL, U.S.A., November 16–19, 1992.

9.   Schuster, R. A., "Effect of Entrained Liquids on Gas Measurement," Pipe Line Industry, February 1959.

10.  Nangea, A. G., L. S. Reid, and R. L. Huntington, "The Effect of Entrained Liquid on the Measurement of Gas by a Orifice Meter," J. of Petroleum Technology, pp. 657–660, June 1965.

11.  McConaghy, B. J., D. G. Bell, and W. Studzinski, "How Orifice-Plate Conditions Affects Measurement Accuracy," Pipe Line Industry, December 1989.

12.  Hussein, I. B. and I. Owen, "Calibration of Flowmeters in Superheated and Wet Steam," Flow Measurement Instrument, Vol. 2, pp. 209–215, October 1991.

13.  Ting, V. C., "Effect of Orifice Meter Orientation on Wet Gas Flow Measurement Accuracy," presented at the SPE Gas Technology Symposium, Calgary, Alberta, Canada, June 28–30, 1993.

14.  Arnberg, B. T. and C. L. Britton, "Two Primary Methods of Proving Gas Flow Meters," Symposium on Flow: Its Measurement and Control in Science and Industry, Pittsburgh, Pennsylvania, U.S.A., May 9–14, 1971.

15.  Arnberg, B. T., C. L. Britton, and W. F. Seidl, "Discharge Coefficient Correlations for Circular-Arc Venturi Flowmeters at Critical (Sonic) Flow," *Journal of Fluids Engineering*, June 1974.

16.  Corpron, G. P., "Correlation of Hydrogen and Air Flow in Critical Flow Nozzles, Part 2: Calibration Results Obtained with Air and Hydrogen," 1994 Conference on Advanced Earth-to-Orbit Propulsion Technology, Huntsville, Alabama, U.S.A., May 17–19, 1994.

17.  Corpron, G. P., "Correlation of $H_2$, $N_2$, Ar, He and Air Flow in Critical Plow Nozzles, 3rd International Symposium on Fluid Flow Measurement", San Antonio, TX, March 1 9–22, 1995.

18.  Kegel, T. M., "Laboratory Calibration of Flow Measurement Systems," American Gas Association Distribution/Transmission Conference & Exhibit, May 16–19, 1993.

19.  Kegel, T. M., "Uncertainty Analysis of a Sonic Nozzle Based Flowmeter Calibration," National Conference of Standards Laboratories 1994 Workshop & Symposium, Chicago, Illinois, July 31–August 4, 1994.

20.  Kegel, T. M., "Uncertainty Analysis of a Compressible Flowmeter Calibration Process," International Mechanical Engineering Congress and Exposition, Chicago, Illinois, U.S.A., November 6–11, 1994.

21.  Corpron, G. P., "High Pressure, Liquid Flow Calibration," ISA/94 Anaheim Technical Conference, Anaheim, CA, U.S.A., October 24–27, 1994.

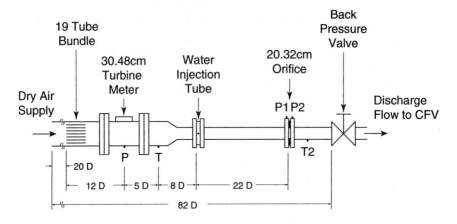

Figure 1. Flow Test Schematic

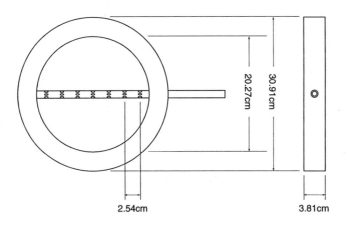

Figure 2. Water Injection Tube and Holder

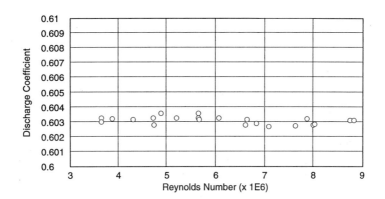

Figure 3

20.32 cm Orifice Meter Calibration Curve at 0.5 Beta Ratio

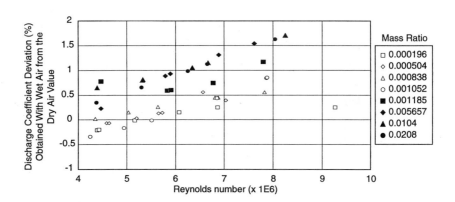

Figure 4

Effect of Liquid Entrainment on a 20.32 cm, 0.7 Beta, Orifice
Meter--Discharge Coefficient Deviation

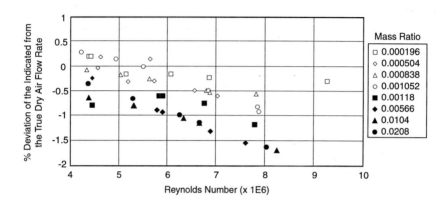

Figure 5

Effect of Liquid Entrainment on a 20.32 cm, 0.7 Beta,
Orifice Meter--Flow Rate Deviation

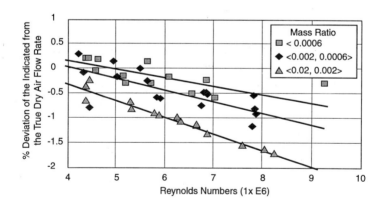

Figure 6

Effect of Liquid Entrainment on a 20.32 cm, Beta=0.7,
Orifice Meter--Flow Rate Deviation

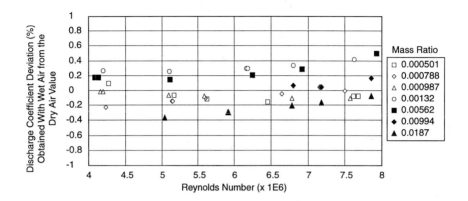

Figure 7

Effect of Liquid Entrainment on a 20.32 cm, Beta=0.5,
Orifice Meter--Discharge Coefficient Deviation

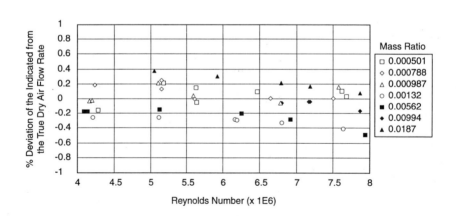

Figure 8

Effect of Liquid Entrainment on a 20.32 cm, Beta=0.5,
Orifice Meter--Flow Rate Deviation

# Pyroelectric Anemometer Calibration for Accurate Flow Measurements

H.-Y. Hsieh, C. Rothey. J. N. Zemel
Department of Electrical Engineering
and
Center for Sensor Technologies
University of Pennsylvania
Philadelphia PA 19104-6314
Tel: (215) 898-8545
Fax: (215) 573-2608
zemel@pender.ee.upenn.edu

**ABSTRACT:** In this paper, we report on several different types of gas flow measurements conducted with the pyroelectric anemometers (PA). These devices have been under investigation at the University of Pennsylvania for several years. They offer an attractive approach to flow measurements that includes, among other things, the following possibilities: spatial metering of gas flow profiles in real time; a signal that is a function only of the pipe Reynolds number; excellent long term stability while delivering 0.5% precision for a wide range of flows. Physically, the pyroelectric anemometer is a small ( 3.8 mm x 3.8 mm x 0.2 mm), rugged and relatively inexpensive device which can be combined in a wide range of measurement configurations. It operates at low power (20 mW or less) and its temperature rise is $\leq$ 3°C above ambient temperature. Studies were conducted at the Southwest Research Institute's (SwRI) Initial Low Pressure Flow Loop with 50 mm and 100 mm inner diameter spools. The goal of these tests was to calibrate 24 PA elements at this well established and controlled flow facility. Two different PA designs were employed: a bayonet sensor inserted into the gas stream to provide local data on the mass flow at the PA position and a wall mounted sensor designed to measure swirl in the gas flow. These measurements covered flows at Reynolds numbers (Re) in the range $16,000 \leq$ Re $\leq 1,200,000$ at pressures of 0.2 MPa and 0.8 MPa. Excellent agreement was obtained in the measurements conducted with the PAs in the two spools at the same pipe Reynolds numbers. A 2", multi-segmented suction wind tunnel was constructed recently at the University of Pennsylvania to measure swirl produced by closely coupled double 90° elbows at various angles using wall-mounted PAs. Decay length of 33 pipe diameters were found at Reynolds numbers of 64,000 at atmospheric pressure. Some measurements of the angular dependence of the PA elements is presented as part of a broader study of swirl phenomena. We also report on calibrations of the PA against absolute piston provers in the range 10 sccm to 5,000 sccm. We find excellent reproducibility ($\leq 0.5\%$ over this entire range) between measurements conducted at NIST two and a half years ago and recent measurements with a Sierra prover.

**INTRODUCTION:** Pyroelectric anemometers are thermal flow meters that use pyroelectricity as the means to measure fluid flow. Earlier studies had demonstrated that pyroelectric anemometer (PAs) based on single crystal LiTaO3 have a very wide range and the promise of interesting response characteristics.(1, 2, 3, 4, 5, 6, 7) The PA is a small (e.g. 3.8 mm x 3.8 mm 0.2 mm), rugged and inexpensive device which can be combined in spatial configurations that yield flow profiles in real time. For industrial flow measurements, the PA must have short and long term reproducibility for a wide flow range with precisions that are at least 1% of measured value. Of particular interest is the possibility that the PA could provide a stable, long term electronic method for gas metering in gas transmission systems. Various aspects of the earlier work on these devices have been reported earlier this year at two flow metering conferences.(8, 9). To put the results of this investigation into perspective, we briefly review the characteristics of a more common thermal flow meter, the hot wire/film anemometer. In recent years, micromachined silicon flow meters have become available but these are variants of the hot /wire film devices. The characteristics of these devices are compared with those of the PA.

**Background Information:** All thermal mass flow-meters employ convective heat transfer between a heated element and the flowing gas as the means to measure the mass flow rate. Almost all of these devices employ the temperature coefficient of resistance of an appropriate conductor as the means to measure the heat transfer. The thermal flow meters can be classified according to the thermal transfer mechanism, i.e. calorimetric or boundary-layer type flow meters.(10) The most common boundary-layer type thermal flow meters are the hot wire and hot film anemometers (HW/FA).(11) A wire or film, in contact with the fluid, is electrically heated above the ambient temperature. The electrical resistance of the heated material itself is used as the temperature transducer in a fashion similar to that used for the capillary meter. The heat transfer process involves a narrow region adjacent to the wire: the thermal boundary layer. The heat loss from the HW/FA follows a semi-empirical law referred to as King's law:(12)

$$\frac{P}{\Delta \theta} = A + B \, u_\infty^{1/2} , \quad 1)$$

where $\Delta \theta$ is the temperature of the heated sensor element relative to the gas temperature, $u_\infty$ is the flow velocity; and A and B are two constants. The flow rate can be measured by keeping either P or $\Delta \theta$ constant. The latter method is used widely because of its better response time. Hot film anemometry is substantially the same as hot wire anemometry except that the metal wire is replaced by a metal film deposited on a suitable insulating substrate. The hot wire anemometer has the advantages of small cross-sectional area in the flow, rapid response, and good sensitivity. However, these device are subject to problems with their stability and gas temperature dependence.(13) Temperature compensation techniques are used but they require the exact matching of the reference resistor's and hot wire's temperature coefficients of resistance (TCR). Unfortunately, there are problems. The TCR is not a simple function of the temperature, $\theta$, and the diameter of each hot wire anemometer is non-uniform along it's length. As a result, each anemometer has to be calibrated at multiple points by a standard flow measurement device prior to use to achieve reasonable accuracy. High temperature operation (above 300°C) is needed for good sensitivity, but the elevated temperature can interfere with the measurements due to self-heating of the gas. High temperatures can induce a variety of physio-chemical reactions within the metal wire or film ranging from crystal grain growth to erosion of the wire or film, especially if corrosive gases are used. These effects lead to the gradual degradation of performance and can cause long term instability. Last but not least, these accurate devices of this class are not rugged and rugged elements have limited accuracy.

Instead of using the temperature dependent resistance, the PAs use the pyroelectric effect to detect the heat transfer process. Pyroelectricity is an intrinsic property of ferroelectric materials. These materials have a spontaneous electric polarization along a particular direction, i.e. the polarization exists even in the absence of an external electric field. The spontaneous polarization creates surface charges. These charges may be neutralized by free electric charges attracted from the surrounding media and conduction currents arising from the surface charge induced internal field in the pyroelectric crystal. Because the spontaneous polarization depends on temperature, new surface charges will be induced if the temperature of the pyroelectric crystal is changed.

One of the most important parameters characterizing the pyroelectric materials is the polar pyroelectric vector, $\tilde{p}$ . The coefficients of the pyroelectric vector are defined as the temperature derivatives of spontaneous polarization $P_s$:

$$\tilde{p} = \frac{\partial P_s}{\partial \theta}. \qquad (2)$$

The dimension of the pyroelectric coefficient is charge per unit area per unit temperature change.

Pyroelectric anemometers are constructed from z-cut wafers of appropriate ferroelectric crystals (the wafer orientation is along the direction yielding the largest pyroelectric coefficient vector) with heaters and electrodes deposited on the front wafer surface and a ground electrode on back wafer surface. The electrodes, with the pyroelectric crystal sandwiched between them and the ground, are in fact capacitors. For each electrode, an equivalent circuit can be described:

$$i = \frac{d\tilde{Q}}{dt} = C_{py}\frac{dV}{dt} + \bar{p}A_e\frac{d<\theta>}{dt} + \frac{V}{R_{py}}$$  (3)

where $\tilde{Q}$ is the total free charge on the electrodes and $A_e$ is the area of the electrodes; $\bar{p}$ is the pyroelectric coefficient in the z-cut direction, $<\theta>$ is the temperature of pyroelectric crystal averaged under the electrode; $R_{py}$ and $C_{py}$ are the internal resistance and capacitance of the electrode. Schematics of the electrode configurations for the PAs used in this study are shown in Figure 1. The PA in Figure 1a) has two electrodes symmetrically disposed about a central heater element. A sinusoidal heating current is supplied to the heater. The dissipation of the ac power creates an oscillating temperature field that propagates into the PA. The oscillating temperature under the electrode induces oscillating charges and a corresponding oscillating current due to the pyroelectric effect. The difference between the pyroelectric current induced on the two electrodes, $\Delta i$, is used to measure the flow rate.

$$\Delta i = \bar{p}A_e\frac{d}{dt}[<\theta>_D - <\theta>_U]$$  (4)

where U and D denote the upstream and downstream electrodes, respectively. Under zero flow, both electrodes will have the same oscillating current because of symmetry and $\Delta i = 0$. As gas flows, the convective heat loss at the upstream electrode is different from the downstream electrode. This effect induces a different pyroelectric current on the two electrodes and $\Delta i \neq 0$.

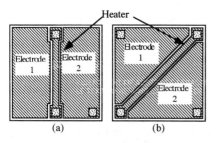

(a)                    (b)

Figure 1. a) Linear electrode used with the bayonet mounting.  b) Diagonal configuration used with the wall mounted structure for measuring the swirl.

**Measurement System:** The pyroelectric anemometer has many attractive features in comparison to other thermal anemometers. Though larger than a HWA, it can be made quite small (~1x1 mm), requires very little power (less than 10 mW in the 3.8x3.8 mm devices discussed here), are just nominally above ambient temperature as a result of their low power operation (the temperature rise of the devices here is much less than 5 degrees for the device used here) and the signal is quite stable. The LiTaO3 pyroelectric material employed in this study is inert to corrosive gases which makes it very attractive in some hazardous environments. The device response does not depend on the temperature and pressure of the gas beyond the ideal gas effects. However, pyroelectric materials like LiTaO3 are fragile. New polycrystalline ceramics offer some promise of more rugged material for this application. Furthermore, they operate as high impedance current sources, requiring considerable care in the design of the electronic measuring system.

Figure 2: (A) Bayonet used in the 1/4" Union T; (B) Bayonet used in the SwRI measurements; (C) Wall mounted PAs for swirl measurements.

Two different PA designs were employed. The type shown in Figure 1a) was designed for use as a bayonet sensor. The bayonet sensor consists of a single PA vertically mounted on a ceramic carrier. One type, shown in Figure 2A), was mounted in the center of 1/4" Union T. This design has been used for over two and a half years for precision measurements as described below. The type in Figure 2B) was used for the SwRI measurements. These elements had three insertion lengths which makes it possible to measure distortion in the flow profile. The type shown in Figure 1b) was designed for use as a wall mounted sensor. The configuration for this is shown in Figure 2C). Two sensors are mounted with their heaters positioned orthogonal to each other. This permits measurements of the corresponding orthogonal components of the flow at the wall and, as a result, the swirl in the gas flow at the wall.

The basic configuration of the measuring system is depicted in Figure 3. In almost all the measurements here, a constant pressure of dry $N_2$ was employed. An HP 3312A function generator was used to supply a 3 Hz electric current to the heater of the PA. Most data were taken with 20 mW power dissipation in the heater. The output of the device is linearly proportional to the power as shown by J. R. Frederick et al.(3). The power dissipation level is so small that the average PA temperature was only 3-5°C above the ambient temperature. The resulting signals from two electrodes of the PA are buffered. They are then sent to a signal conditioner where the amplitudes and phases of two electrode signals are adjusted to achieve a minimum offset differential signal in the absence of flow. From there, the differential signal is sent to the SR530 lock-in amplifier which measures its amplitude.

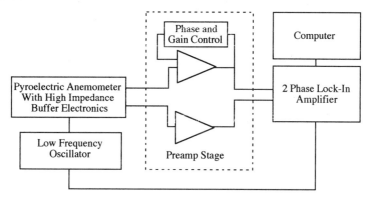

Figure 3. Schematic depiction of the PA measuring system. The oscillator provides a 3 Hz signal to both the PA heater and the lock-in-amplifier. The 6 Hz thermal signal is used to measure the flow.

The method of measurement in all cases were substantially the same. Each measurement consisted of a two minute run during which time the data was read by the lock-in amplifier (LIA) every second. Some of the more recent measurements are being conducted for 128 seconds to simplify the Fourier analysis of the fluctuations. The integration time of the LIA was approximately three seconds. Both the in- and out-of-phase signals were measured and recorded. These data were subsequently processed in a Macintosh computer to obtain the mean amplitude of the signal over a 120 second span, the standard deviation over that self-same two minute period, and the frequency spectrum of the fluctuations.

2" and 4" stainless steel spools were designed and constructed at the University of Pennsylvania for the ILPL measurements at SwRI. Each spool has nine posts: six posts for bayonet mounted PAs and three posts for the wall-mounted PAs. The entire system was designed to conform to the Class 40 required by SwRI. The goal was to calibrate twenty four (24) PA elements. Eight series of measurements were conducted and data were obtained from five bayonet mounted and two wall mounted PAs in the 4" spool and from six bayonet mounted and as many as four wall mounted PAs in the 2" spools. All told, over three hundred and twenty five (325) measurements were conducted on the various devices, aside from standardization runs. Some of the characteristics of the device were reported elsewhere (9,10). Most of these runs were conducted at pressures of ~0.2 MPa. The response of the devices in the two spools were quite similar but because high pressure measurements (~0.8 MPa) were carried out only in the 2" spool, we will give some additional data on this system only. Additional measurements on the PA elements calibrated at the ILPL were conducted in an uncalibrated 2" suction wind tunnel in our laboratory. Striking differences were observed in the data from the run-to-run reproducibility and the magnitude of the signal fluctuations in these two systems.

**Experimental Results-SwRI Studies:** The PA measurements against the piston provers were conducted with a bayonet mounted device Similar measurements were conducted in the suction wind tunnel and in comparative studies with the piston provers. As we are still in the process of analyzing the data, only preliminary results are shown here. Illustrative data for Re ≈ 64,000 is presented in Figures 4 for devices 6 in the 5 cm spool. The fluctuation in the amplitude and the phase are caused by flow fluctuations associated with the closed loop operations as well as turbulence. Because of its small size, the PA can measure the details of turbulent cells in real time. The amplitude data in Figure 4 was analyzed to obtain the spectral density of the fluctuations. As may be seen, the spectral density does not follow a power law $1/(frequency)^n$ type dependence. Instead, it appears to obey a exponential dependence of the form

$$\text{Spectral Density} = 0.0020048*\exp\{\frac{-0.061287}{\text{frequency}}\}$$

with a quality of fit of R = 0.78582. This is not a particularly good fit but the analysis makes it clear that there are no resonances or harmonics in the measurement.

The data from the 2" system is generally more reproducible except at low flow rates and positions close to the wall of the spool. The reproducibility of the 2" system, which is represented by the standard deviation for the three measurements, are well below 10% for almost all runs and for the middle range, the agreement is in the 1% range. The scattering observed results from local variation in flow on a scale smaller than the turbulent structure. The reproducibility of 4" spool is worse and the reason is under investigation.

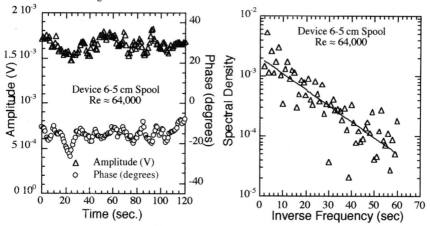

Figure 4: Amplitude and phase for device 6 measured at SwRI at Re ≈ 64,000 in a 5 cm spool

Figure 5: Spectral density of data in Figure 4.

In Figure 5, the averaged signal of devices 4, 5, and 6 over three runs is shown as a function of the Reynolds number for two different pressures, P = 0.2 and 0.8 MPa. The signal amplitude follows closely the square root of the nominal flow rate. This behavior was observed on every PA including the bayonet and wall-mounted PAs. It is also consistent with the laminar, moderate flow behavior of the PA in the Union T discussed below.

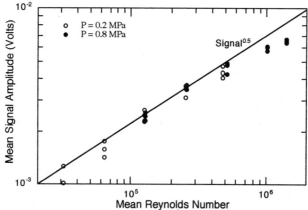

Figure 5: Compilation of data on devices 4,5 and 6 taken at SwRI for two different pressures. Note the excellent agreement between the signal [0.5] line and the experimental data. The fall-off at high Re is due to loss of choking in the SwRI venturis.

A 2", multi-segmented suction wind tunnel was constructed at the University of Pennsylvania for conducting a variety of tests on the PA elements described above. A schematic drawing of the overall system is depicted in Figure 6. The tubing elements were constructed from standard 2" class 40 PVC pipe with a relatively smooth inner surface. The length of the elements was 0.5 m. One of the first

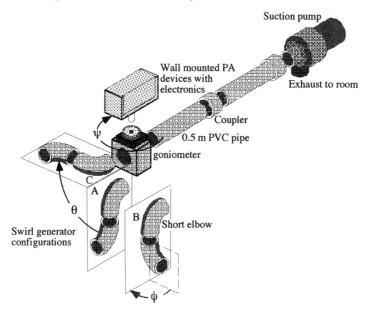

Figure 6: Schematic of the University of Pennsylvania Suction Wind Tunnel showing the elements for straight and swirl flow.

experiments conducted was to measure the signal from several devices located at the same positions as in the SwRI tests. Not having an independent means to measure the Reynolds number, we assumed that the calibrations at SwRI were sufficiently accurate to provide a reasonable indication of the flow. We found that the agreement was excellent for all of the devices at a flow corresponding to approximately Re = 64,000. This is depicted in Figure 7. What may also be observed is the rather good agreement between each class of measurements (at SwRI and at the UP-SWT). In the former case, the agreement is of the order of 6% and in the latter case, 1.5%. As expected, the profile of the turbulent flow was quite flat.

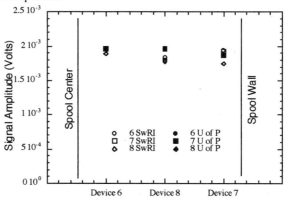

Figure 7: Signal amplitude for three PA devices tested at SwRI and UP. Re ≈ 64,000. The three devices were at different radial positions in the test spool.

As a precursor to studies of swirl in this system, we determined the degree to which the PA elements could be used to measure the angle η of the flow relative to the perpendicular to the heater filament axis in the plane of the chip. The goniometer shown in Figure 6 was employed for these measurements. The experimental results normalized to the maximum signal shown in Figure 8 are reasonable. Also plotted for comparison are the absolute sine and cosine functions corresponding to the ideal response of the device. Further improvements will be needed to obtain better quality angular data.

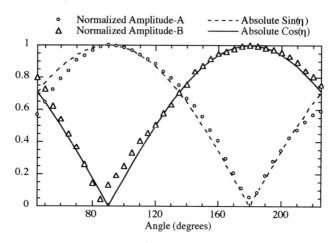

Figure 8: Data from two nominally orthogonal PA chips of the type shown in Figure 1b compared to absolute values of the sine and cosine functions.

A question of considerable importance to us has been the absolute precision of the PA chips. Some years ago, a PA element was bayonet mounted in a 4.76 mm ID 1/4" Union T. The schematic of the arrangement is shown in Figure 9. As can be seen, a 1 m long tube is attached to the T to provide sufficient length so that the flow is completely developed. The preamplifier section consists of a buffer stage for transforming the high impedance signal to a low impedance signal. The output from

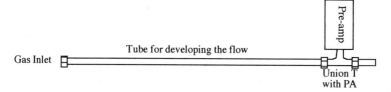

Figure 9. Schematic depiction of the PA transfer standard layout. The ID of the system is 4.76 mm.

the buffer stage then goes to the nulling circuit depicted in Figure 3 where the amplitude and phase are adjusted at zero flow so that there is a minimal signal . This is rarely more than 1 μV. The single electrode signal of the PA is used as a measure of the dissipated power. This signal has been set at 20 mV in the latest set of measurement made with the Sierra prover. In earlier measurements at NIST, the single electrode signal was 19 mV. Because of the linearity of the differential response of the PA to power input, this meant that the NIST values would be approximately 5% lower than those obtained with the Sierra prover. The results of the experiments are shown in Figure 10 with the NIST PA measurements corrected upward by 5%. The Sierra prover measurements were conducted over an eight hour period with the measurements initially made with increasing flow velocities in the morning and decreasing velocities in the afternoon. The agreement between the measurements over the course of the day were within the uncertainty of the repeatability of the Sierra prover. This data is in excellent general agreement with the recent observations of Hsieh et al. (6,7,8,9). In those measurements, we were able to observe the termination of the piston motion when the bypass valve cut in. A careful fitting of this data to an analytic form has not been completed as yet. Until this is

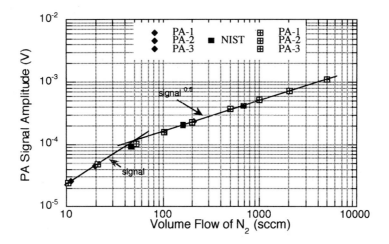

Figure 10: Signal amplitude as a function of volumetric flow of $N_2$ in a 4.76 mm diameter pipe at room temperature.

done. it will be difficult to give a more precise estimate of the agreement between the recent Sierra prover data and the NIST data taken over two and a half years ago.

Based on these measurements, we find that even at flow rates as low as 10 sccm, the reproducibility of the measurements is in the 0.5% range. At this volumetric flow rate, the average linear velocity of the gas is of the order of 100 mm/min with an uncertainty of 500 $\mu$m/min in a 4.76 mm diameter pipe. Whether it will be possible to press this precision to flows of the order of 1 sccm in such a large pipe remains an unanswered question.

**Conclusions:** These measurement provide additional substantial evidence of the broad applicability of the PA to a wide range of flow measurement applications. The SwRI measurements conclusively demonstrate that the device can withstand extremely high velocity flows (Re $\approx$ 1.4e06) and provides interesting information on the spatial and temporal distribution of the flows. The piston prover measurements are particularly informative with respect to the long term stability of these devices. There is no indication of any observable change in the device characteristics during a two and a half year period.

**Acknowledgments:** The authors wish to acknowledge the financial support of the Gas Research Institute for part of this research. They also wish to express their appreciation to Dr. T. K. Wang for making it possible to conduct the Sierra prover measurements and Dr. Max Klein for many useful discussions.

**References:**

1  Rahnamai, H., and Zemel, J.N.,  "Pyroelectric anemometers: preparation and flow velocity measurements", *Sensors and Actuators*, **2**, p 3, 1981/82.
2  Rahnamai H. and Zemel, J.N., "Directional gas-flow measurement with pyroelectric anemometers (PA)", *Sensors and Actuators*, **2**, p 203, 1982/83.
3  Rahnamai H., "Pyroelectric anemometer probe with improved sensitivity", *Sensors and Actuators*, **3**, p 17, 1982/83.
4  Frederick, J.R., Zemel, J.N., and Goldfine, N., "Pyroelectric Anemometers: Experimental Geometric Considerations" *J. Appl. Phys.*, **57**, p 4936, 1985.
5  Hesketh, P., Gebhart, B., and Zemel, J. N., "Heat Transfer Model for the Pyroelectric Anemometer," *J. Appl. Phys.*, **57**, p 4944, 1985.
6  Hsieh, H.Y., and Zemel, J.N., "Pyroelectric Anemometry: Frequency, Geometry and Gas Dependence," in press *Sensors and Actuators*.
7  Hsieh, H.Y., Bau, H.H., and Zemel, J.N., "Pyroelectric Anemometry: Theory of Operation," in press *Sensors and Actuators*.

8    Hsieh, H. Y. and Zemel, J. N., "Recent Advances In Pyroelectric Anemometry", *Third Int. Symp. on Flow Measurements*, San Antonio TX, March 1995

9    Hsieh, H.Y., Dempsey, M., Rothey, C., Thompson M. and Zemel, J.N., "Principles Of Pyroelectric Anemometry: A New Mass Flow Sensor", *Proc. Second Brazilian Symposium on Flow Measurements*, São Paulo, Brazil, March 1995, p.209

10    Hohenstatt, M., in: *Sensors, A comprehensive Survey*, Göpel, W., Hesse, J., and Zemel, J.N. (ed.); VCH, New York, vol. 4, p 323-343, 1992.

11    Perry, A. E., *Hot-wire Anemometry*, Oxford, New York, 1982.

12    King, L.V., *Philos. Trans. R. Soc. London, Ser. A*, **214**, p 373-433, 1914.

13    Lomas, C. G., *Fundamentals of Hot Wire Anemometry*, Cambridge, New York, 1986.

# USING INERT GAS: AN APPRAISAL OF FIFTEEN YEARS' EXPERIENCE

# UTILISATION DU GAZ INERTE: BILAN DE 15 ANS D'EXPERIENCE

Anne DONG, Pierre LEHUEN, Gilbert MEUNIER
Gaz de France, FRANCE

## ABSTRACT

When natural gas is stored in aquifers, cushion gas accounts for the largest part of the investment. In order to reduce costs, Gaz de France started inert gas injection in three storage facilities (Saint-Clair in 1979, Saint-Illiers in 1989 and Germigny in 1982 and 1993). These operations took place under very different practical conditions (inert injection prior to natural gas injection or already in-place cushion gas substitution...). They were designed so that the withdrawn gas could be sent out without any specific operating constraints over several decades. The monitoring of such operations was done using a thorough measuring network or/and modelling tools that correctly handle gas mixing phenomena. The Saint-Clair and Saint-Illiers cases will be detailed in this paper. For the latter, a comparison between the reservoir performance forecasts issued from a model and real measurements is presented.

## RESUME

Pour le stockage en nappe aquifère, l'investissement lié au gaz coussin représente la plus grosse part. Afin de réduire les coûts, Gaz de France a commencé à injecter du gaz inerte dans trois stockages (Saint-Clair en 1979, Saint-Illiers en 1989 et Germigny en 1982 et 1993). Ces opérations ont été effectuées dans différentes conditions pratiques (injection d'inerte avant l'injection du gaz naturel ou substitution d'un gaz coussin déjà en place...). Elles ont été menées de manière à ce que le gaz soutiré puisse être livré sans aucune contrainte d'exploitation supplémentaire et ceci pour plusieurs décennies. Le pilotage de telles opérations a été fait grâce à l'utilisation d'un réseau complet de mesures ou/et de modèles réservoirs qui représentent correctement les phénomènes de mélanges de gaz. Cet article présentera une description détaillée des cas de Saint-Clair et de Saint-Illiers. Dans le second cas, une comparaison entre les prévisions de performance du réservoir fournies par le modèle et les mesures réelles sera présentée.

## I - INTRODUCTION

When natural gas is stored in aquifers, cushion gas accounts for the largest part of the investment (40% of the total investment at the present time despite the low price of natural gas). This shows the interest of replacing the cushion gas by inert gas in UGS.

Nevertheless, this substitution operation is profitable only if it is closely monitored and sized. The quantity of inert gas to be injected and the location of the injections must be optimized so that the withdrawn gas can be sent out with no specific operating constraints (for instance on the higher heating value even for long term behavior).

Therefore inert/natural gas mixing must be intensively screened in:

- evaluating the formation dispersion coefficients (tracer tests, etc.)
- developing tools to model the behavior of reservoirs containing several gases
- setting up a measure network over the storage facility in order to follow inert gas movement, validate the previously built models and improve predictions

First, this paper gives a description of three GDF storage facilities where inert gas has been injected. The second part details, for two cases, how the operational constraints and the use of models interact in the monitoring of inert gas injection and the operating strategy. In the last paragraph, a comparison between the forecasts from a model and real measurements is presented.


## II - INJECTION OF INERT GAS OPERATED IN THREE GDF UGS

GDF started injecting inert gas in a UGS in 1979. The three facilities involved are located in the Paris Basin (Saint-Clair-sur-Epte in 1979, Saint-Illiers in 1989 and Germigny-sous-Coulombs in 1982 and 1993). The reservoirs isobaths are shown in figures 1 (Saint-Clair) and 8 (Saint-Illiers). As shown in Tables 1,2 and 3, the inert injection phases took place under very different practical conditions:

- before the establishment of the natural gas bubble, in two phases: during development and at the end of the development period
- in dispersive carbonate, fairly homogeneous sandstone or multi-layered reservoirs
- with an annual withdrawal of the working volume (Saint-Clair) or limited withdrawal (Germigny)

| | Saint-Clair | Germigny | Saint-Illiers |
|---|---|---|---|
| Formation | limestones | shaly sandstones | sandstones |
| Depth (m/sea level) | 705 | 900 | 340 |
| Closure (m) | 35 | 35 | 120 |
| Thickness (m) | 30 | 80 | 30(R1) , 40(R2) |
| Closed area (km$^2$) | 15 | 100 | 20 |
| Particularities | | heterogeneous reservoir characteristics | multi-layered (R1 and R2) |
| Porosity (%) | 20 | max $\cong$ 30 | 25 |
| Permeability (mD) | 700 | max $\cong$ several Darcy | 1000 (R1) |

Table 1: Geological characteristics of three GDF UGS

| | Saint-Clair | Germigny | Saint-Illiers |
|---|---|---|---|
| Replacement strategy | inert injection before methane injections | a two-phase injection of inert gas: ‹before methane injection ‹during development | replacement of base gas |
| Operating constraints | high heating value zone for deliverability | high heating value zone for deliverability | high heating value zone for deliverability |
| Particularities | | 3 gases in presence (inert, low and high heating value) | |
| Date of inert gas injection | 1979 | 1982 then 1993 | 1989 |
| Total inventory when the inert injection started $(10^6 \ m^3(n))$ | 0 | 2200 (in 1993) | 1260 |
| "Non natural" gas $(10^6 \ m^3(n))$ | 60 of nitrogen/ carbon dioxide mixture (burned natural gas) | ‹ 76 of nitrogen/ carbon dioxide mixture (1982) ‹ nitrogen injection planned to reach 180. $10^6 \ m^3(n)$ by 1995 | 140 of nitrogen |
| Cushion substitution ratio | 20% | | 20% |

Table 2: Gas mixing in three GDF UGS

| | Saint-Clair | Germigny | Saint-Illiers |
|---|---|---|---|
| Total inventory in 1995 $(10^6 \ m^3(n))$ | 670 | 2400 | 1340 |
| Working capacity $(10^6 \ m^3(n))$ | 275 | 670 | 560 |
| Maximum pressure (bar) | 105 | 123 | 70 |
| Number of production wells | 11 | 26 | 31 |

Table 3: Operating characteristics of three GDF UGS

Since operations started, gas quality has been measured regularly:

• a daily analysis of the different components is performed on gas entering or leaving the storage facility

• monthly or even weekly measurements are performed on a number of representative wells during the withdrawal period

With this unique test base and fifteen years' experience, Gaz de France has been able to validate inert gas injection techniques in different practical conditions. A precise methodology has progressively come into use through the continuous interaction between the forecasts for this type of operation and the feedback. This methodology is based on three main points:

- a detailed description of reservoir geology taking into account the vertical contrasts in permeability and lateral continuity of sedimentary bodies
- interpretation of all the mixing data available (tracer tests, injection of gases of different qualities)
- the development and intensive use of compositional gas/water models. Severe operating constraints imply that the behavior of different gases in the reservoir should be correctly forecasted. As the problem of composition in the gas phase is not satisfactorily addressed by most of the tools available on the market, new methods for reducing numerical dispersion have been developed in our simulation model.

In order to illustrate the interaction between operational constraints and the use of numerical models, the cases of Saint-Clair and Saint-Illiers will be detailed in the next paragraph. No appraisal of inert gas injection is available yet for the Germigny case since it started only two years ago.

## III - DETAILED DESCRIPTION OF TWO CASES

The Saint-Clair and Saint-Illiers facilities differ in at least two points :

- the timing of inert gas injection (before natural gas injection for Saint-Clair, replacement of an already in-place cushion gas for Saint-Illiers).
- the state of the art of available numerical models as far as the mixing problem is concerned (1979 for Saint-Clair and 1989 for Saint-Illiers).

In the Saint-Clair case, as there was no gas in place when the inert gas was injected, the development of the inert bubble could be monitored by a measuring network ; the mixing aspect only came into view some years later when natural gas injection started (1981) and its importance increased while gas was cycled during normal operation. For these reasons an empirical approach was applied to the Saint-Clair case and numerical models were used only to predict the performance of the storage facility.

The cushion gas replacement in Saint-Illiers took place in 1989 (10 years after the Saint-Clair case). In the meantime considerable improvements enabled simulation models to handle mixing problems. This was fortunate because the mixture of "in-place" natural cushion gas was inevitable and needed to be carefully studied before the operation began. So, in this second case, the use of numerical models occurred at the assessment phase in order to optimize the volume of natural gas to be replaced and the location of the injection wells. Naturally, as for the Saint-Clair case, simulations were also run for performance predictions. This can be considered as a "forecasted" approach.

### III - 1 - Saint-Clair-sur-Epte : an empirical approach

#### a/ Inert Gas injection and monitoring

Inert gas injection covered the period from August 1979 to August 1981 and began on well Vn7 (figure 1) located 2km south of the structural top. The injection rates increased progressively from 100 000 to 240000 $m^3(n)/d$. The development of the inert zone was carefully monitored :

- on well Vn7, gas analyses by chromatography were carried out to obtain the composition of the inert gas actually injected.
- on the same well, neutron logs were recorded, showing that the injection involved the entire reservoir thickness.

- the gas zone extension was monitored by pressure measurements and neutron logs on the other available wells located near well Vn7. They were still in the water zone. Well Vn 18, located on the top of the structure, was the first to be reached by inert gas in August 1981, just before the first naturel gas injection (corresponding total inventory = 50,4 x $10^6$ $m^3$ (n)).

### b/ Natural gas injection

It began on well Vn19 (located 1.4 km north of Vn7 in the central zone) which was still in water at the beginning of the injection. The consequence of this was that the inert gas in the top zone of the structure was actually swept away during the injection of 57.6 x 106 $m^3$ (n) of natural gas on well Vn19 between August and decembrer 1981.

Frequent gas analyses by chromatography were made to monitor the variation of inert gas concentration on well Vn18, from 100% inert gas in october 1981 to 100 % natural gas in December 1981. The phase during which inert gas was swept by natural gas from the central zone was successful. Well Vn18 has been used for natural gas withdrawal since 1982 without any operating problems. Inert gas injection ceased after March 1982, (total inventory of inert gas $\approx$ 60 x $10^6$ $m^3$ (n)).

### c/ Monitoring both inert and natural gas zones (1981-1983)

A large number of gas component analyses by chromatography were made with the aim of monitoring the inert and natural gas zones (for the period preceding the first major natural gas withdrawal: 1981-1983). Figure 2 represents the extension of inert gas zone at the end of 1983. The measurements were performed on :

- wells located in the top zone (Vn18,Vn21,Vn23 and Vn8) in order to monitor the quality of the injected natural gas.
- on well Vn7 in order to screen the mixing phenomena.
- on edge wells (Vn34, Cv1) as soon as gas reached those zones. One can notice that mixing phenomena sometimes reveal reservoir heterogeneities that would otherwise be unnoticeable with one gas : for instance the appearance of early inert gas in Vn34 and Cv1.

### d/ Storage behavior during cyclic operation

The cyclic operation of the storage began in the winter of 83-84. That year, 52x$10^6$ $m^3$(n) of natural gas were produced by wells Vn19, Vn21 and Vn23 without any trace of inert gas. The following Injection/Withdrawal cycles were quite limited due to a rather low demand and the gas analyses showed effects of reservoir heterogeneities : Vn7 remained in pure inert gas even though it was near the top zone, whereas Cv1 (located further south) showed a methane concentration ranging from 12 to 16 %.

In summer 1986, a significant increase in inventory took place. In order to push the inert gas southward of the structure and to avoid overly rapid gas encroachment in the northern zone (Vn34), a second sweeping phase of inert gas by natural gas injection was performed using wells located in the southern part of the top zone (Vn18,Vn19,Vn23,Vn21). Gas quality was screened in well Vn7 (methane concentration increased from 0% in June 86 to 80% in September 86). From that date on, Vn7 was used as a natural gas injection well.

From 1986 to 1994, inert gas concentration was punctually measured in some producing and monitoring wells (figures 4 and 5). Figure 4 shows that at the majority of the producing wells, the nitrogen ratio stays under 5% except for well Vn29 which is near well Vn7. Figure 5 shows that the nitrogen ratio at monitoring wells Cv1, Vn7 and Vn34 is decreasing every year. The two sweeping phases managed to push the inert gas back to the south east zone (Cv1).

During the winter of 86-87, more than 90% of the working volume was withdrawn. This was performed without any mixing problems. (For each UGS of GDF, the working volume is defined as the maximal volume of gas that can be withdrawn during autumn-winter and entirely reinjected during the rest of the year. According to demands and climate events, this working volume can be partially or entirely operated).

And eversince, no deliverability nor mixing problems have arisen during cyclic operation of this storage facility in which 20% of the cushion is inert.

### e/ Use of numerical models

Using conclusions drawn from geological studies and hydraulic tests, a numerical model was built and validated by the numerous measurements made since the first gas injection. This model may be used to either:

- predict the performance of the reservoir
- test whether an increase of the inventory or the working gas would be profitable under specific operating constraints, or
- predict inert production (rate and cumulative) according to different cycling scenarios.

As far as the last point is concerned, on the basis of data acquired daily, nitrogen injection and withdrawal measurements can be drawn up to determine the volume and rate of inert gas production. The difference in the average nitrogen ratio between the withdrawn and the injected gases is computed : it stabilizes at a value of 0.4% corresponding to an annual inert gas production of roughly $10^6$ m$^3$(n).

Our simulations agree with the values observed during the storage period. Over the coming years, the trend will be toward a balance between the two gases. A small quantity of inert gas is drawn toward the I/W wells by the natural gas during withdrawal and then replaced by the newly injected gas during the following cycle. As a consequence, the inert inventory is expected to drop slowly but steadily over the years (figure 6). (Then a new inert gas injection might even be proposed in a fifty years' time in order to "strengthen" the cushion). Figure 3 shows how relatively well confined the distribution of inert gas is in 1994.

### III - 2 - Saint-Illiers : a forecasted case

In 1989, when cushion gas replacement was envisionned for Saint-Illiers, this storage facility had already been operating for 24 years (created in 1965). It had (and still has) a major role in the overall working capacity of GDF. That is why, in order to deal with mixing problems between inert and natural gases, an intensive preliminary study of the substitution operation was carried out (an empirical approach such as the one used for the Saint-Clair case was considered too risky).

In order to optimize the cushion substitution with regard to the quality of the withdrawn gas and various possible demands in natural gas (low for warm winter or peak demand for a few freezy days) , a two-phase, three-dimensional and compositional numerical model was used taking into account all physical phenomena and including a precise description of the heterogeneities. This study focused on the long-term behavior of the inert gas.

### a/ Description of the model and history matching

The Saint-Illiers reservoir was divided into three layers from top to bottom. Two grid-refinement levels were used, one for the aquifer, the other for the storage reservoir. A history matching was made for the first period (1965 to 1989) during which the storage was operated without inert gas. The matching concerns water saturation and pressure evolution in monitoring and producing wells.

A major preliminary task before gas mixing simulation is to determine the dispersion coefficient. The greater this variable is, the higher the maximum inert gas production at the end of the withdrawal period. The same remark stands for the cumulative annual inert gas production. In the case of Saint-Illiers, the dispersion coefficient was estimated by interpreting changes in the heating values of gas injected during the 1984 injection period. The maximum contrast in heating values was 11.1 to 12.3 $kWh/m^3(n)$, i.e. 1072-1188 $Btu/ft^3$. These contrasted injections were used as a large scale tracer test. The interpretation of these tests was done using a one-dimensional and radial model specifically developped to solve the dispersion equation without numerical dispersion. The dispersion value found here was between 15 and 20 m.

### b/ Simulations of the substitution operation

For the predictions, the inert gas is injected in the upper reservoir layer from June 89 to June 92 at a constant flow rate. Different operating scenarios were tested for the 26-year period lasting until 2014-2015 and particular attention was devoted to studying the influence of the following factors :

- the quantity of cushion substituted (10, 15, 20, 25% or more)
- the distribution of inert gas injections among the selected wells
- the starting moment of the inert gas injection (at the end of a natural gas withdrawal or injection period ?)
- the operating strategy (which production wells should be closed by the end of the withdrawal period in order to limit inert gas production ...)
- the dispersion coefficient and gravity

Three criteria are used to evaluate the tested scenarios:

- the maximum percentage of inert gas mixed with the natural gas produced
- the volume of inert gas withdrawn during a winter
- the ratio of this volume to the withdrawn volume

The first one characterizes the emissibility of withdrawn gas, the two other ones give information about the transit duration of inert gas in the reservoir. So the energy loss due to parasite inert gas production can be estimated.

### c/ Results of simulations

- Substituted volumes: a set of five simulations was run to investigate this parameter (10, 15, 20, 25 and 30% of the cushion gas volume).The results regarding inert gas rate production on the last day of winter are presented in fig. 7; those concerning the annual rate of inert gas withdrawn are similar. According to the criterion of required gas quality, a decision was made about the part of the cushion to be replaced: for instance, since inert gas rate production on the last day of winter was not to exceed 1% then the optimal substituted volume ratio would be 20% (fig. 7). Nevertheless, it must be noted that the economic profit of the operation still increased for a 30% replacement and probably higher volumes.

- Distribution of the inert gas injection: two monitoring wells (SI13, SI4) were meant to be used as inert gas injectors. But was an extra well, located at midway between the two previous ones, necessary? What would be the optimal rate injection distribution? Simulations have shown that if the extra well (SI50) was not used, the inert gas would be split into two regions respectively around SI4 and SI13 and more inert gas would be withdrawn during the first 10 years. On the contrary, the differences in inert gas extension, due to various distribution of injection rates among the wells, were shown to gradually disappear with time; moreover, this phenomenon can be neutralized by an adequate use of the producing wells.

- Withdrawn gas quality: during the withdrawal period, the amount of inert gas mixed with the natural gas produced is very low for most of the time and increases rapidly at the end of the winter. Over the 26 years simulated, this parameter reaches a maximum at around 2005-2010 (for substituted volumes equal to 30 or 20%) and then decreases slowly. When all the producing wells are used, half the volume of the produced inert gas comes from wells located in the north of the top (close to the inert injection zone). This means that an adequate strategy in the use of producing wells at the end of winter can limit inert gas production.

### d/ economic evaluation and the adopted substitution strategy

The injected inert gas is produced by a Pressure Swing Adsorption unit: it is mainly composed of nitrogen and the oxygen concentration is adjustable up to a maximum of 8%.

The evaluation of the financial benefits of a cushion substitution operation takes into account the cost of natural and inert gases (PSA unit, electricity consumption), the drilling and equipment of extra wells if necessary, the connexion operations between injection wells and the PSA unit, the gradual long-term re-substitution of inert cushion gas by natural gas (a small volume of inert gas is withdrawn at each cycle).

According to these calculations, the benefits increase with the rate of cushion substitution (even up to 30%). Nevertheless, because of severe gas quality constraints, a cushion substitution ratio of 20% was decided (according to preliminary studies, this substitution ratio would provide a maximum extra nitrogen concentration in the gas produced of roughly 1%, which is far below the acceptable threshold). Finally, the inert gas was injected in three wells ($50.10^6 m^3(n)$ in each well SI4 and SI13 and $40.10^6 m^3(n)$ in well SI50) and lasted from June 89 to June 92.

### e/ accurate forecast of inert gas production and behavior (1990-1994)

Fig. 9a and 9b represent inert gas concentration in 1992 at the end of the natural gas withdrawal and injection periods (the darker an area the higher inert gas concentration: wells SI13, SI4 and SI50 which were used for inert gas injection are represented by large white dots). Fig. 9a and 9b are obtained using a numerical model that matches the reservoir behavior from 1965 to 1994 (water saturation, pressure changes in monitoring wells and inert gas concentration in producing wells). The dispersion coefficient used is 17m. Due to gravity and reservoir heterogeneities, the inert gas zone has a crescent form and gets round the top zone.

Fig. 10a, 10b and 10c show nitrogen ratio measured in "sentinel" wells SI7, SI28 and S39 located north of the top zone. Because of heterogeneities, the three wells are polluted by inert gas: the nitrogen ratio at the end of the withdrawal period ranges from 5% in well SI39 to 14% in well SI7. One can see that these measurements are correctly estimated by simulation.

Nevertheless, the most important point is the quality of the gas produced by the storage wells as a whole. From 1990 to 1994, the annual ratio of produced nitrogen to the withdrawn gas never exceeded 0.5% (fig. 11) and so far the maximum daily nitrogen ratio produced never exceeded 2%, which is quite acceptable compared to the threshold for the storage gas emissions. Simulations implying higher gas demands have been performed and the results show that we can be very confident about the future.

## IV - CONCLUSION

GDF has perfomed inert gas injection in three of its storage facilities: in the case of Saint-Clair-sur-Epte, the inert gas injection was operated in 1979 before natural gas was injected: it was an empirical approach monitored by a measuring network throughout the reservoir. For the Saint-Illiers facility which has been in operation since 1965, the existing natural cushion gas was partly replaced by inert gas in 1989: this storage is a major gas movements adjustment tool, representing at that time 21% of the working volume available in the Paris area (the largest energy consuming area in France). Moreover, severe gas quality constraints were applied : for instance, it would not be acceptable to have a single day of non deliverability of the withdrawn gas. Therefore, an intensive preliminary study was carried out in order to optimize the substitution strategy (volume of gas substituted, inert gas rate injection...) and to predict the long-term behavior of the reservoir (evolution of the quality of withdrawn gas over time...).

So far, in 1995, in the two previously cited facilities, the working gas is normally cycled without any specific operating constraint. In 1993, one year after the end of the completion of the substitution operation, the working volume of Saint-Illiers increased by 9% and still represented 19% of the working volume available near Paris. The cushion substitution is considered so successful (confirmed financial benefits and no problem of gas emissibility) that a third GDF UGS (Germigny-sous-Coulombs) is being converted since 1993.

Since inert injection operations started, gas quality has been measured regularly. With this unique test base and fifteen years' experience, GDF has been able to validate gas injection techniques in different practical conditions. The PSA unit used for the inert gas production is reliable and easy to handle. Thanks to the continuous interaction between forecasts and real observations, reliable modelling tools are developed in order to fit the real measurements made in the past and to predict the behavior of reservoirs containing a mixture of natural and inert gases.

## REFERENCES

1.  Carrière J.F., Fasanino G., Tek M.R., "Mixing in underground storage reservoirs", 1985, SPE 14202.

2.  Laille J.P., Molinard J.E., Wents A., "Inert gas injection as a part of the cushion of the underground storage of Saint-Clair-sur-Epte, France", 1988, SPE 17740.

3.  Wents A., Rouge J., "Utilisation du gaz inerte dans les réservoirs souterrains en nappe aquifère", Colloque sur l'évolution et les tendances du stockage souterrain du gaz naturel et des GPL, Paris (France), May 29- June 2, 1989.

4.  de Moegen H., Giouse H., "Long-term study of cushion gas replacement by inert gas", 1989, SPE 19754.

5.  Giouse H., de Moegen H., "Replacement of existing cushion gas by inert gas in the Saint-Illiers storage reservoir, France", UIIG, Berlin 1991.

## SAINT-CLAIR

**Fig 1: Reservoir isobaths**

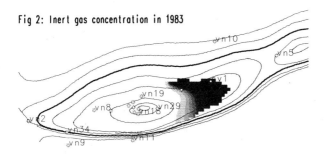

**Fig 2: Inert gas concentration in 1983**

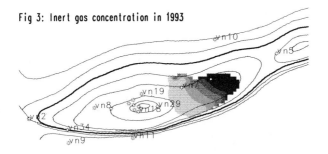

**Fig 3: Inert gas concentration in 1993**

0,950
0,800
0,650
0,500
0,350
0,200
0,050

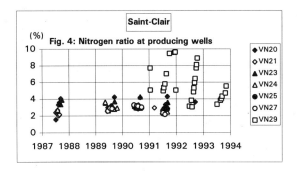

Saint-Clair

Fig. 4: Nitrogen ratio at producing wells

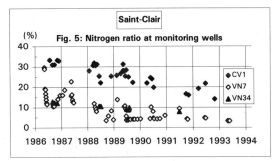

Saint-Clair

Fig. 5: Nitrogen ratio at monitoring wells

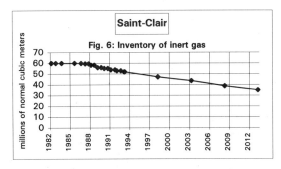

Saint-Clair

Fig. 6: Inventory of inert gas

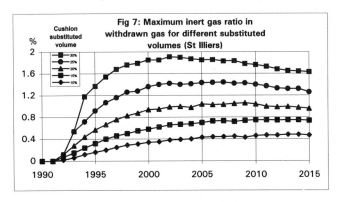

Fig 7: Maximum inert gas ratio in withdrawn gas for different substituted volumes (St Illiers)

SAINT-ILLIERS

Fig. 8: RESERVOIR ISOBATHS

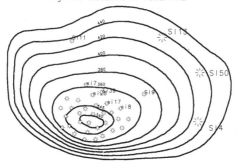

Fig. 9a AND 9b: INERT GAS CONCENTRATION

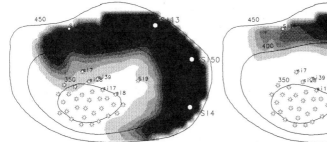
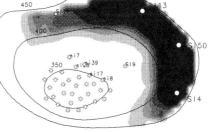

END OF THE WITHDRAWAL PERIOD (91-92)          END OF THE INJECTION PERIOD (92)

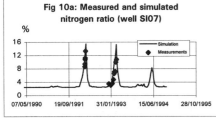

Fig 10a: Measured and simulated nitrogen ratio (well SI07)

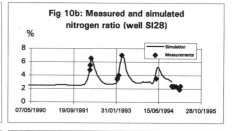

Fig 10b: Measured and simulated nitrogen ratio (well SI28)

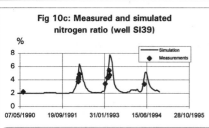

Fig 10c: Measured and simulated nitrogen ratio (well SI39)

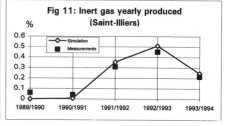

Fig 11: Inert gas yearly produced (Saint-Illiers)

COMPORTEMENT DU SEL IN SITU
SOUS DES PRESSIONS TRES ELEVEES

BEHAVIOUR OF IN SITU SALT
AT EXTREMELY HIGH PRESSURE LEVELS

Patrick DESGREE, Jean-Gérard DURUP
GAZ DE FRANCE, FRANCE

RESUME

Le Département Réservoirs Souterrains de la Direction de la
Recherche du GAZ DE FRANCE a réalisé un programme
d'études sur le thème de la pression maximale tolérable par
des cavités de stockages creusées dans le sel in situ.

Ces études, menées entre 1988 et 1994 ont nécessité un
important volet expérimental sur du sel en place vers 900 m
de profondeur. Les essais ont été réalisés sur le site de
stockage de gaz naturel en cavités salines d'ETREZ (Ain,
France). Divers scénarios de pressurisation ont été étudiés
utilisant comme fluide d'essai d'abord un liquide puis un
gaz.

Les objectifs fixés étaient : (1) de comparer les gradients de
fracturation obtenus avec les deux fluides, (2) d'apprécier
l'influence de la vitesse de pressurisation sur ces gradients
limites, (3) d'étudier la cicatrisation des fractures hydrauliques par la recristallisation du sel, et (4) d'observer les
indices de percolation des deux types de fluides dans le
massif salifère.

Les résultats de ces études permettent de revoir à la hausse
les pressions maximales admissibles dans les cavités
d'ETREZ. Ainsi une augmentation de près de 10 % de
celles-ci est désormais possible.

ABSTRACT

The GAZ DE FRANCE, Research Division, Underground
Storage Department undertook a study programme on the
maximum pressure tolerated by salt in situ.

The studies, which were performed between 1988 and 1994,
required extensive tests on in situ salt at a depth of
approximately 900 metres.

Tests were performed at the Etrez facility in France (Ain department), where natural gas is stored in salt cavities. Various pressurization scenarios. Were studied using two different test fluids : first, a liquid (1988-1990 "brine" campaign) and then a gas (1992-1994 "nitrogen" campaign).

The objectives set were (1) to compare the fracturing gradients obtained with the two fluids, (2) to assess the influence of the pressurization speed on these maximum gradients, (3) to study the cicatrization of the hydraulic fractures by the recrystallizing salt and (4) to observe the percolation indices of both types of fluid in the saliferous massif.

As one of the main consequences of the study programme, the maximum pressure applicable in cavities created in the salt can be upgraded. These cavities are used for storing natural gas at high pressures and the possibility to increase operating pressures safely in them leads to an improvement of performance by approximately 10 %.

## INTRODUCTION

Dans l'optique d'optimiser l'exploitation de ses cavités salines de stockage de gaz, GAZ DE FRANCE a depuis 1988 engagé un programme d'essais in situ visant à mieux caractériser le comportement du sel in situ vis-à-vis de différents fluides à de très fortes pressions. Pendant la première phase (1988-1990), les expériences ont toutes été réalisées avec de la saumure comme fluide d'essai.

Après une année entière de préparation (1991), la deuxième phase d'expériences (1992-1994) a été menée avec de l'azote comme fluide d'essai. Les coûts des deux phases ont été cofinancés par un contrat de recherche soutenu par le Solution Mining Research Institute.

Les deux essais ont été réalisés sur le site d'ETREZ qui se caractérise par deux couches de halite. Seule la couche inférieure, à 1 300 m de profondeur, est équipée de cavités de stockage de gaz naturel. La couche supérieure, à une profondeur de 900 m, a été équipée d'une cavité ainsi que d'un puits expérimental. Les essais dont il est question ici ont été réalisés dans ce puits (EZ 58).

Les principaux objectifs étaient de déterminer les gradients d'hydrofracturation à différentes vitesses de pressurisation, de comparer les valeurs d'hydrofracturation obtenues avec le liquide et le gaz et d'étudier, dans de telles conditions in situ, les effets d'autocicatrisation et l'infiltration des fluides dans le massif salifère. Ces paramètres servent de base pour définir les pressions d'exploitation maximales dans des formations salines et apportent également des données fondamentales pour la définition des scénarios d'abandon des cavités.

Nous verrons donc ici pour chacun des deux essais, le montage expérimental mis en place, les résultats expérimentaux et l'interprétation que l'on peut en donner, et enfin la comparaison des deux essais.

## ESSAI SAUMURE

### Montage expérimental

Le découvert, objet de l'essai (figure 1), a une hauteur d'environ 200 m et se situe entièrement dans le sel gemme. Un tubage central 5" fixé au moyen d'une garniture étanche située juste au-dessus du sabot du tubage a été utilisé pour les injections d'eau glycolée à la tête de puits. L'espace annulaire 5"-9" 5/8 isolé par la garniture étanche agissait comme une enceinte de contrôle évitant d'éventuelles fuites parasites de fluide d'essai à travers le tubage ou les joints de raccordement du tubage central.

Au cours de cet essai d'étanchéité/fracturation en saumure, le découvert a été pressurisé par des incréments de 0,5 MPa. Chaque nouveau palier était maintenu à pression constante pendant un mois par des injections de fluide très précisément contrôlées. Les essais ont duré un an.

Les pressions et les températures à la tête et au fond du puits ont été contrôlées, à la fois dans l'espace annulaire et dans le tubage central. Pour chaque palier de pression, la pression mesurée au fond du trou a toujours été maintenue dans la limite de ± 0,2 MPa par rapport à la pression de référence du fond de trou pendant un mois.

A la partie supérieure du découvert, du fioul a été mis en place afin de confirmer et de faire la distinction entre deux types de pertes de fluide : par infiltration avant la rupture et par fracturation après la rupture. Les mesures de l'interface fioul/saumure avant et après l'expérience ont montré une corrélation précise entre la rupture et la perte de fioul à la partie supérieure du découvert comme prévu, car il s'agit du point où la contre-pression lithostatique est la plus faible. En conséquence, la totalité du fluide injectée à la tête du puits a été attribuée essentiellement à l'effet de compressibilité du système pendant l'application progressive de la pression et à l'infiltration hydraulique entre le découvert et le massif de sel.

**Résultats**

Les principaux résultats sont rassemblés dans le tableau suivant :

| Gradient de pression du fluide d'essai (MPa/m) | Débit injecté stabilisé (litres/heure) |
|---|---|
| 0,0146 | 0,18 |
| 0,0160 | 0,19 |
| 0,0180 | 0,23 |
| 0,0205 | 0,29 |
| 0,0210 | 0,30 |
| 0,0215 | 0,32 |
| 0,0220 | 0,35 |
| 0,0225 | 0,37 |
| 0,0230 | 0,38 |
| 0,0235 | 0,42 |
| 0,0240 * | 0,72 |

* rupture.

Un essai de fracturation de courte durée, réalisé après l'essai de longue durée a donné un gradient de fracturation de 0,0256 MPa/m.

**Interprétation**

Les principes de Darcy ont été appliqués ; ils expriment une proportionnalité linéaire entre le débit Q et la pression différentielle dP. Pour un cas circulaire radial tel que celui d'un découvert d'un puits de forage, il peut s'exprimer comme suit :

$$Q = K2rH.dp/\mu/Ln(R/r)$$

La valeur de perméabilité correspondante K peut être estimée pour n'importe laquelle des paires de valeurs ci-dessus. Par exemple, lorsque le gradient de pression du fluide est de 0,023 MPa/m, le débit stabilisé est de $1,1 \cdot 10^{-7}$ m$^3$/s (0,38 l/heure). Il s'est avéré relativement délicat de choisir la valeur du gradient de pression hydrostatique de la saumure saturée vierge in situ ; elle a finalement été évaluée à environ 0,012 MPa/m car, avec 0,145 MPa/m, on constatait déjà certains écoulements vers le massif. Dans ce cas, la pression différentielle au milieu de la cavité libre (950 m) est de 10,4 MPa. Les paramètres suivants sont la viscosité dynamique de la saumure saturée $\mu = 1,2 \cdot 10^{-3}$ Pa, la hauteur du puits H = 200 m et son rayon r = 0,1 m. Un rayon d'influence maximum du fluide d'essai dans un massif vierge de 1 m a été estimé (5 diamètres). Le facteur K calculé avec ces paramètres a une valeur de $3 \cdot 10^{-20}$ m$^2$.

L'évolution de la valeur de K dans le temps pendant toute la période a été étudiée. Ceci a été obtenu par simulation de l'ensemble du processus d'injection au moyen d'une maquette radiale à différence finie (la maquette utilisée est une version simplifiée d'un simulateur de réservoir à deux phases et en 3D appelé MULTI). La perméabilité et la porosité ont été définies par corrélation entre les valeurs des volumes cumulés injectés au cours de chaque phase (figure 2) et des débits stabilisés à la fin de chaque phase (figure 3) et les valeurs mesurées.

Les autres paramètres pris en considération étaient une compressibilité de la saumure de $2,7 \ 10^{-10}$ Pa$^{-1}$, une compressibilité du sel gemme de $7 \ 10^{-11}$ Pa$^{-1}$ et une densité de saumure de 1,2. L'influence des paramètres a été examinée : si la compressibilité du sel gemme ou du fluide augmentaient, la variation du volume injecté d'un palier de pression à un autre restait inchangée ; toutefois, pour obtenir les mêmes valeurs de volume, le facteur K devait être réduit. Comme la correspondance s'avérait moins sensible à la porosité, elle a été réalisée essentiellement en faisant varier ce facteur K. La meilleure corrélation a finalement été obtenue avec une porosité de 1 % et une perméabilité de $6 \ 10^{-20}$ m$^2$.

## ESSAI GAZ

### Montage expérimental

L'essai gaz a été effectué sur le même puits. Cependant, un certain effritement ayant été constaté à la suite de l'essai saumure sur la partie inférieure, celle-ci a été isolée (figure 4).

Le résultat de ce choix est que la longueur du puits, et donc la surface de sel gemme essayée avec le gaz, peut être considérée comme la moitié de la longueur essayée avec la saumure. Le découvert était tout à fait régulier avec un diamètre de 11 1/4" sur toute la hauteur de 105 m de sel.

Sur la sortie de l'annulaire extérieur, on a enregistré la pression de l'espace annulaire afin de vérifier l'absence de gaz dans cet espace de contrôle.

Des unités de détection P et T (pression et température) plus sensibles ont été installées sur la sortie 5"-2 7/8" pour surveiller les caractéristiques physiques de l'azote pendant les injections et au repos. P et T en fond de cavité ont été mesurées aussi près que possible techniquement du sabot du cuvelage 9 5/8" dont la cote est choisie comme référence. Les relevés ont été envoyés à la surface à des intervalles de 15 minutes environ avec un câble conducteur se trouvant dans l'espace annulaire 9 5/8"-5".

On a eu recours à deux solutions pour l'alimentation en azote. Le premier type d'alimentation en azote a été l'utilisation directe de conteneurs de gaz fournis par un fournisseur de gaz industriel, AIR LIQUIDE dans ce cas. Le deuxième type d'alimentation en azote a été un générateur d'azote. Comme indiqué précédemment, on a surveillé les conditions de pression et de température en fond de cavité. On a donc à nouveau appliqué l'équation d'état du gaz à chaque volume d'azote entrant dans le puits pour déterminer son volume correspondant dans des conditions de fond.

Le processus de remplissage en azote du trou foré a consisté à injecter de l'azote au niveau de la tête de puits dans l'espace annulaire compris entre les tubes de production de 5" et 2 7/8". Pendant le processus de mise en gaz pour la deuxième phase des essais, toute la saumure provenant du trou foré a été soigneusement surveillée de manière à vérifier la géométrie du puits obtenue par des mesures de diamètre.

**Résultats**

Les principaux résultats sont rassemblés dans le tableau suivant :

| PRESSION<br>gradient au sabot du cuvelage<br>en MPa/m | TAUX<br>d'infiltration<br>en litres/jour |
|---|---|
| 0,0160 | 4,08 |
| 0,0180 | 6,26 |
| 0,0200 | 3,96 |
| 0,0205 | 5,30 |
| 0,0210 | 6,16 |
| 0,0215 | 6,28 |
| 0,0217 | 4,74 |
| 0,0222 | 6,63 |
| 0,0227 | 7,61 |
| 0,0232 | 6,33 |

**Nota** : Les volumes de gaz et les vitesses d'écoulement sont indiqués dans les conditions de fond. Ils ne comprennent pas l'azote injecté pour les changements de palier.

La perte d'étanchéité est intervenue à 0,0237 MPa/m pour l'essai de longue durée. L'essai de courte durée, effectué environ 2 mois après l'essai de longue durée à donné une valeur de 0,0236 MPa/m.

Ces résultats sont illustrés par la courbe de pression de la figure 5 avec le premier frac en A et le second en B. Les grands pics vers le bas correspondent à des remontées de capteur.

**Interprétation**

Les fortes diminutions de pression ont été interprétées comme des pertes d'étanchéité au niveau de la cimentation du sabot du cuvelage et/ou du massif de sel gemme.

En se basant sur cette expérience, le gradient de pression ultime le plus conservatif pour l'étanchéité au gaz est par conséquence la valeur obtenue par l'essai de courte durée, c'est-à-dire 0,0236 MPa/m.

Dans l'interprétation des courbes de pression de post-fracturation, la pression stabilisée après confinement est généralement considérée comme représentative de la composante minimale du champ de contrainte in situ. Les valeurs de la pression stabilisée en fond de cavité pour les deux courbes de diminution de la pression étaient équivalentes et correspondaient à un gradient lithostatique de 0,0227 MPa/m.

D'anciennes interprétations de diagraphies de densité provenant de l'ensemble des puits de ce site particulier on établi que la densité moyenne de référence de toute la masse rocheuse de recouvrement était de 2,3, soit un gradient de 0,023 MPa/m. Ceci représente l'état de contrainte primaire au niveau du sabot du cuvelage.

Une comparaison du gradient de pression ultime de l'essai avec les deux valeurs mentionnées ci-dessus tendraient à indiquer que le gradient de pression ultime avant la défaillance mécanique, dans des conditions in situ, se situe à un niveau légèrement supérieur au gradient lithostatique.

L'augmentation de la vitesse de pressurisation de presque deux ordres de grandeur n'a pas conduit à des effets perceptibles sur les valeurs de rupture de la pression avec du gaz :

| Vitesse de pressurisation<br>(MPa/j) | Gradient de pression ultime au<br>sabot du cuvelage (MPa/m) |
|---|---|
| 0,02 | 0,0237 |
| 1,3 | 0,0236 |

Une explication possible est que la pénétration du gaz dans le sel est si rapidement freinée par des forces capillaires que le comportement est en fait très proche de celui pour une pressurisation rapide, sur une très large plage de vitesses de montée en pression.

La capacité du sel gemme de se recristalliser et de confiner une fracture d'origine hydraulique est un phénomène connu souvent mentionné dans la littérature. Dans des conditions in situ, en particulier à de grandes profondeurs, on ne dispose pratiquement d'aucune donnée sur les questions suivantes :

- la résistance mécanique du sel gemme après la cicatrisation,
- le laps de temps nécessaire au processus de cicatrisation.

Ces essais ont apporté des informations concernant ces deux sujets. Premièrement, une simple comparaison des deux valeurs de rupture consécutives montre que la résistance des milieux essayés est demeurée intacte après le processus de cicatrisation.

Le processus de recristallisation concerne seulement le massif de sel gemme et non la cimentation. De ce fait, la fracture cicatrisée a été nécessairement créée dans le sel gemme. La limite de résistance atteinte était donc celle du sel et non celle du ciment.

Le laps de temps entre les deux ruptures de pression a été de 48 jours. Cette durée a cependant été fixée pour des raisons pratiques de manière à observer la diminution naturelle de la pression et à préparer l'essai de courte durée. Il n'est donc pas représentatif du laps de temps réel nécessaire au processus de cicatrisation, mais il établit une limite supérieure vérifiée sur le sel en place de la capacité d'autocicatrisation du sel gemme de moins de 48 jours.

On a repris l'approche à l'aide du code MULTI comme pour l'essai en saumure. Pour ce faire, le code calcule les scénarios d'injection de gaz correspondants dans une cellule centrale représentant le découvert, pour un système biphasique composé d'un fluide compressible, l'azote, et d'un liquide représentant la saumure dans les interstices cristallins du sel.

En plus des caractéristiques physiques de l'azote en fond de cavité, d'autres paramètres ont été pris en compte, à savoir :

- le massif de sel gemme interprété comme un milieu microporeux (avec une compressibilité de $0,7 \times 10^{-10}$ $Pa^{-1}$, une microporosité de 1 % et une microperméabilité de $6.10^{-20}$ $m^2$),

- la saumure interprétée comme le fluide interstitiel original (avec une compressibilité de $2,7 \times 10^{-10}$ $Pa^{-1}$, une viscosité de $1,2.10^{-3}$ $Pa.s$ et une densité de $1,2$),

- une pression de saumure interstielle "vierge" initiale (pour initialiser les calculs).

On a pu évaluer l'étendue de la zone infiltrée de gaz dans le milieu rocheux à 1,8 m.

L'explication pour la zone d'infiltration pourrait être l'existence d'une zone à perméabilité secondaire accrue causée par des microfissures. Celles-ci pourraient avoir été provoquées par des contraintes importantes essentiellement localisées à proximité de la paroi.

Cette zone ne devrait pas s'étendre très loin dans le massif rocheux mais plutôt diminuer rapidement. Or l'infiltration du fluide d'essai n'a pas semblé s'atténuer avec le temps : donc ou bien la limite de la zone microfissurée n'a pas été atteinte ou bien le rôle des espaces intercristallins doit également être pris en compte.

## Comparaison des essais gaz et saumure

Pendant l'essai de longue durée, qui a consisté en 12 plages de pression (10 plages pour l'essai en gaz), la plage de pression totale a été de 8 MPa à comparer à la plage de pression de 9,5 MPa pour l'essai en gaz. Dans les deux cas, la durée totale de l'essai a été d'approximativement 450 jours. Ceci montre que des scénarios de pression raisonnablement similaires ont été appliqués dans ces deux cas.

Il faut tenir compte d'une différence importante : pour l'essai en gaz la hauteur (100 m), et donc l'aire du découvert, était moitié moindre que celle utilisée pour l'essai en saumure (200 m).

Le tableau suivant donne la comparaison des taux d'infiltration avec de la saumure et avec du gaz.

| Gradient de pression au sabot du cuvelage en MPa/m | Saumure débits en l/jour pour un découvert de 200 m | Gaz débits en l/jour pour un découvert de 200 m (pour un découvert de 100 m) |
|---|---|---|
| 0,0160 | 4,46 | 8,16 |
| 0,0180 | 5,52 | 12,52 |
| 0,0200 | 7,08 | 7,92 |
| 0,0205 | 6,96 | 10,60 |
| 0,0210 | 7,20 | 12,30 |
| 0,0215 | 7,68 | 12,56 |
| 0,0217 | 8,04 | 9,48 |
| 0,0222 | 8,64 | 13,26 |
| 0,0227 | 9,00 | 15,22 |
| 0,0232 | 9,60 | 12,66 |

**Nota** : Pour le gaz, les vitesses d'écoulement sont indiquées dans des conditions de fond.

Ce tableau compare les taux d'infiltration obtenus avec la saumure et avec l'azote pour des conditions P et T au fond équivalentes. Pour être comparables aux valeurs de la saumure, les valeurs du gaz ont été doublées de manière à tenir compte du fait que l'aire testée avec le gaz était la moitié de celle essayée avec la saumure. Sur la base de cette approximation, trois remarques principales sont formulées puis discutées :

**Remarque n°1** : Pour des conditions P et T et une surface de paroi de sel gemme équivalentes, les vitesses d'écoulement du gaz sont supérieures aux vitesses d'écoulement de la saumure .

Les dimensions des interstices (espaces intercristallins) dans lesquels l'écoulement est supposé se faire sont cependant extrêmement petites, environ $10^{-8}$ m. Dans de telles conditions, l'écoulement du fluide est entravé par des forces capillaires ($P_C$) fonction de la tension superficielle (T), de l'angle de ménisque ($\theta$) et des dimensions des "pores" (r) :

$$P_C = T \times \cos\theta / r$$

Nous avons estimé raisonnable de supposer que le fluide présent à l'origine dans ces interstices était de la saumure. Il résulte que la pression de seuil ($P_T$) nécessaire pour initialiser l'écoulement doit dépasser la pression hydrostatique "vierge" de la saumure ($P_H$) et la pression capillaire mentionnée ci-dessus ($P_C$) :

$$P_T = P_H + P_C$$

En fait, dans le cas particulier où la pression est appliquée par la saumure il n'y a qu'une seule phase et il n'y a donc pas de pression capillaire. $P_T$ est dans ce cas à sa valeur la plus faible et elle est égale à $P_H$.

Dans l'industrie des cavités salines, de tels systèmes monophasiques représenteraient des puits en saumure et à des cavités remplies de saumure et obturées en permanence. Pour ces dernières, on sait qu'une augmentation de pression est vraisemblable du fait de divers facteurs bien connus tels que le fluage, l'augmentation de température, etc. L'augmentation de la pression dans la cavité réduit la convergence mais graduellement la pression devrait s'approcher de la résistance du sel gemme et tendre à la dépasser. Nous pensons que dans cette situation l'augmentation des vitesses d'écoulement de la saumure devrait durablement empêcher l'hydrofracturation du massif salifère, et en tant que tel, agir comme un mécanisme régulateur de la pression.

Les systèmes biphasiques représenteraient des cavités sous pression contenant du gaz naturel, de l'air comprimé, des hydrocarbures liquides, etc. ; dans de tel cas, $P_C$ n'est pas nulle. Les pressions de seuil correspondantes ont donc des valeurs plus élevées que dans le cas monophasique précédent. Pour cette raison, nous avions fait le pari, avant de commencer les expériences, qu'il n'y aurait pas d'infiltration de gaz avant que la pression de seuil (pression de déplacement) ne soit atteinte ; ceci offrant là un moyen d'évaluation de valeur. Il est clair que les résultats de ces expériences n'ont pas confirmé cette hypothèse étant donné que l'on a observé des vitesses d'infiltration de gaz même pour des niveaux de pression tout à fait bas.

**Remarque n°2 :** Par voie de conséquence, à conditions P et T et à l'aire de sel gemme équivalentes, il pénètre plus de gaz dans le massif que de saumure.

Les gaz sont des fluides moins visqueux que les liquides. Dans des conditions équivalentes (pression, température, dimensions des pores, etc.), les gaz sont donc supposés s'écouler plus librement (avec des vitesses d'écoulement plus élevées) que les liquides. Avec la saumure, les calculs ont montré que 3 $m^3$ de saumure se sont infiltrés sur environ 0,6 m dans le massif. Les conditions P et T étaient équivalentes pour l'essai en gaz. Nous avons calculé que, dans des conditions en fond de cavité, 2,7 $m^3$ de gaz avait pénétré sur environ 1,8 m dans le massif. Le gaz a donc pénétré plus profondément dans le massif ce qui est cohérent (le gaz est un fluide moins visqueux que la saumure).

**Remarque n°3 :** Avec la saumure, les vitesses d'écoulement sont nettement proportionnelles aux niveaux de pression alors que cette proportionnalité n'a pas été démontrée avec le gaz.

Il y a donc une apparente absence de proportionnalité entre les taux d'infiltration et les niveaux de pression lorsque le fluide d'essai est du gaz. Même lorsque l'on prend en compte des imprécisions expérimentales, estimées à Q ± 0,5 litres/jour, la tendance générale des valeurs demeure incertaine avec le gaz. Les vitesses d'écoulement semblent demeurer à un niveau moyen approximatif de 12 l/jour pour 200 m de découvert (sur la base d'une moyenne de 6 l/jour par jour pour 100 m de découvert).

Ceci contraste avec les valeurs de la vitesse d'écoulement de la saumure. Dans ce cas, pendant les plages successives de l'essai de longue durée, les vitesses d'écoulement apparentes en fond de cavité (dues à des réajustements) pour maintenir la pression constante ont augmenté proportionnellement aux niveaux de pression successifs, de 4 l/jour pour la douzième plage. En se basant sur cette proportionnalité, on a démontré que l'infiltration de la saumure dans le massif salifère pouvait être interprétée en termes d'un écoulement de Darcy.

Le processus d'adaptation des courbes entre les vitesses d'écoulement calculées et les vitesses d'écoulement mesurées a été satisfaisant pour les valeurs de microperméabilité et de microporosité du sel gemme et de viscosité de la saumure.

Enfin, on procède à une comparaison pour les deux fluides des gradients de pression lors de la perte d'étanchéité observée. La remarque essentielle à propos de ces valeurs (voir tableau ci-dessous) est qu'elles sont toutes plus élevées que le gradient de pression lithostatique estimé de 0,023 MPa/m.

| | Saumure | Azote |
|---|---|---|
| Essai de longue durée (1 an) | 0,240 MPa/m | 0,237 MPa/m |
| Diminution naturelle de la pression | 38 jours | 48 jours |
| Essai de courte durée (1 jour) | 0,256 MPa/m | 0,236 MPa/m |

La différence maximale de gradient observée a donc été 0,0256 MPa/m - 0,023 MPa/m = 0,0026 MPa/m. A la profondeur du sabot du cuvelage (870,8 m), ce "gradient excédentaire" par rapport au gradient lithostatique correspond à 0,0026 x 870.8 = 2,26 MPa ce que nous avons jugé relativement proche de la résistance apparente à la traction de ce sel gemme particulier (2,5 MPa). Une possible interprétation est que pour fracturer la masse rocheuse, les contraintes appliquées doivent d'abord compenser le poids des terrains sus-jacents et ensuite surmonter la résistance du sel gemme.

CONCLUSION

Le comportement du sel gemme à des essais hydrauliques (destructifs) de fracturation a été étudié in situ par GAZ DE FRANCE de 1989 à 1994.

Les résultats obtenus sont spécifiques au site d'ETREZ dans une certaine mesure. Certaines conclusions sont cependant considérées comme étant raisonnablement représentatives pour toute formation saline en dôme ou en couche.

Les gradients de pression nécessaires au niveau du sabot du cuvelage pour obtenir une défaillance mécanique évidente (perte d'étanchéité) ont été systématiquement plus élevés que le gradient de pression lithostatique du site. Ceci a été vérifié in situ pour le gaz et pour la saumure dans le même sel gemme.

On peut donc penser que, dans des conditions in situ équivalentes, il est possible de procéder à des essais de pression jusqu'à la pression lithostatique sans mettre en danger l'intégrité du sel gemme.

L'augmentation du taux de pressurisation de deux ordres de grandeur n'a pas affecté notablement les valeurs de rupture. Il est donc suggéré que, pour des opérations de stockage, il peut être appliqué in situ des augmentations de pression équivalentes sans courir de risques de défaillance mécanique.

L'essai a apporté la preuve que, in situ, le sel gemme peut récupérer sa résistance initiale, pas seulement lorsque le fluide de fracturation est de la saumure (première phase des expérience) mais aussi lorsqu'il s'agit de gaz. Le temps de récupération a été d'approximativement un mois. Ceci est considéré comme un résultat positif étant donné que, en supposant une cimentation appropriée au sabot du cuvelage, une fracturation hydraulique non intentionnelle peut être réparée naturellement par ce processus d'auto-cicatrisation.

Les vitesses d'écoulement du gaz estimées dans le massif, dans des conditions de fond de cavité, ont été du même ordre de grandeur que celles enregistrées avec la saumure.

Dans ces expériences, les infiltrations de gaz et de saumure dans le massif salifère sont apparues similaires : environ un mètre sur un an pour des pressions quasi-lithostatiques. Ceci est un indicateur intéressant sur la migration à long terme des produits conservés dans des cavités de stockage.

Ce programme d'essai présente un argument déterminant en faveur d'une augmentation du gradient de la PMS à 0,02 MPa/m (gradient 2) sur le site d'ETREZ.

Les essais en place montrent qu'aux pressions d'épreuve prévues (10 % supérieures aux PMS), la résistance mécanique du sel n'était pas atteinte (gradient de
fracturation de l'ordre de 0,0236 MPa/an), aussi bien avec la saumure qu'avec le
gaz. Même à ces fortes pressions, les expériences confirment l'excellent confinement
du gaz par le sel et une infiltration très limitée de gaz dans le massif salifère (de
l'ordre du mètre).

Outre l'amélioration de 10 % des performances des stockages, le passage au
gradient 2 irait dans le sens de la réduction du fluage. Les études menées par
GAZ DE FRANCE ont démontré que cette augmentation de pression ne
compromettait ni l'intégrité mécanique de l'ouvrage, ni le confinement du gaz.

## REFERENCES

1.  Jean-Gérard DURUP
    "Long term test for tightness evaluation with brine and gas in salt".
    Solution Mining Research Institute.
    Research Projet Report n° 90.0002-S et 94.0002-S.

2.  Patrick DESGREE
    "Etude du passage au gradient 2 pour l'exploitation des cavités du site
    d'ETREZ".
    Rapport interne GDF : M.DRS - DGP/MMA - T.3097 - 1994.

3.  Bruno HUGOUT
    "Essais d'étanchéité des puits des cavités salines avant lessivage".
    Rapport interne GDF/DETN - 1984.

4.  Jean-Gérard DURUP
    "Long term permeability field test in rock salt".
    Meeting paper - Congrès international de Mécanique des Roches.
    Aix-La-Chapelle - 1991.

FIGURE 1 : MONTAGE
EXPERIMENTAL DE L'ESSAI
SAUMURE

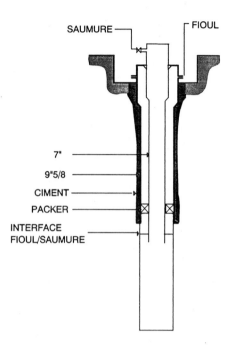

FIGURE 2 :

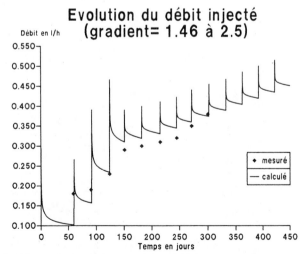

FIGURE 3 :

# Evolution du volume cumulé injecté

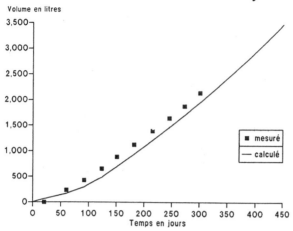

FIGURE 4 : MONTAGE EXPERIMENTAL POUR L'ESSAI GAZ

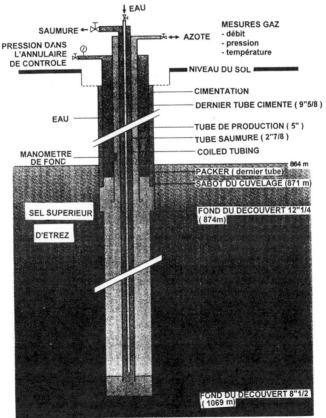

**FIGURE 5 :**

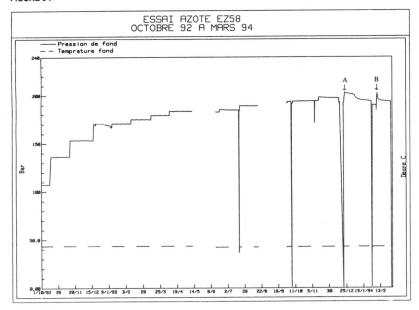

# SYSTEM FOR DETECTION AND COLLECTION OF POTENTIAL GAS LEAKAGES FROM A LRC GAS STORAGE

## SYSTEME DE DETECTION ET DE CAPTAGE DES FUITES DE GAZ EVENTUELLES DANS UN STOCKAGE DE GAZ LRC

J. Johansson
Sydkraft AB, Sweden

U. E. Lindblom
Chalmers University of Technology, Sweden

## ABSTRACT

During the past 10 years the LRC (Lined Rock Cavern) concept for high pressure storage of natural gas has been developed in Sweden. An important part of the concept is the gas drainage system. The aim of the system is to give an early warning in case of a gas leak, to limit the physical damage to the storage plant and to prevent, as far as possible, uncontrolled intrusion of gas into the surrounding rock mass. This paper describes the design principles of such a gas leak control and drainage system and presents some of the gas leak tests performed in the Swedish LRC Pilot Plant.

## RESUME

Le LRC (Lined Rock Cavern), procédé de stockage de gaz naturel à haute pression dans des cavernes revêtues a été développé en Suéde au cours des dix dernières années. Un point essentiel du procédé de stockage est le système de drainage du gaz. Le but du système est de signaler rapidement une fuite de gaz afin de limiter les dégâts matériels dans le stockage et de prévenir, dans la mesure du possible, l'intrusion incontrôlée du gaz dans la masse rocheuse environnante. Cet exposé décrit les principes de conception du contrôle des fuites du gaz et du système de drainage. Il présente aussi certains essais de fuite de gaz effectués sur l'installation suédoise prototype.

## INTRODUCTION

The LRC (Lined Rock Cavern) concept for storage of natural gas is based on constructing a rock cavern in the form of a vertical cylinder. The cavern is lined with a sandwich wall, consisting of a layer of concrete to transfer the gas pressure to the rock and a gas-tight steel lining to safeguard containment (The LRC concept has previously been described by e.g. Rosendal, 1992).

Although every effort will be made to create a high-quality steel lining that can sustain its important service during the lifetime of the storage, the possibility of a failure cannot be ignored. It is therefore important to provide a reliable gas drainage system. The aim of the system is to give an early warning in case of gas leakage, to limit the physical damage to the storage plant and to prevent, as far as possible, uncontrolled intrusion of gas into the surrounding rock mass. Needless to say, a failure in the steel lining would be a serious incident that could lead to economical losses for the storage company and/or consequences for the environment.

This paper describes the design principles of a gas leak control and drainage system for a LRC and presents some of the pilot tests in this field performed in Sweden. It also describes the intended design principles of a gas drainage system for a proposed LRC Demonstration Plant. A brief description of the ongoing comprehensive risk and safety analysis is also included in the paper.

## THE LRC STORAGE CONCEPT

The main components of a LRC storage facility are outlined in Figure 1. The plant consists of one or several storage caverns, a vertical shaft and a system of tunnels connecting the caverns with the ground surface. The storage caverns are excavated as vertical cylinders.

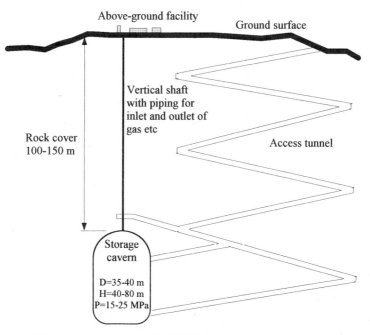

Figure 1     Schematic cross-section of a LRC storage plant

The cavern is planned to be located at a depth of about 150 m below ground. The maximum storage pressure will be in the range of 15-25 MPa. With typical cavern dimensions of 35-40 m diameter and 40-80 m height, a total storage capacity of 8-25 $MNm^3$ of natural gas is achieved. The above-ground facilities include a compressor station, a boiler house, piping and valves.

When the storage pressure is lower than the pipeline pressure, the cavern is filled by means of pressure reduction equipment. In the opposite case, the pressure is increased by a compressor. After compression, the gas is cooled by an air cooler.

Withdrawal is generally done by free-flow from the cavern to the transmission line. Only when the storage pressure falls below the pipeline pressure, is it necessary to use the compressor at withdrawal. To avoid problems with temperature decreases in the cavern during peak withdrawal, the gas can be heated in a heat exchanger and recirculated into the cavern. The gas also needs to be heated before passing the pressure reduction valves.

All rock surfaces inside the storage cavern are covered with a sandwich wall structure composed of a layer of concrete and a gas-tight steel lining. Figure 2 is a detail of the wall structure. Cast into the concrete, next to the rock surface, there is a grid-shaped system of drainage pipes to serve as gas drainage. On the rare occasions when there is very low or zero pressure in the cavern, the system is also used for ground water drainage to avoid damage to the lining.

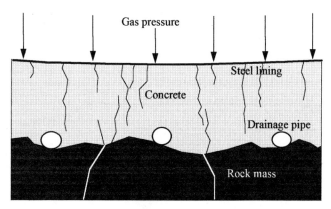

Figure 2     Detail of the cavern wall construction

## GAS DRAINAGE SYSTEM

As mentioned above, the gas drainage system is of central importance for the safe operation and control of the storage. The main components of this system are (see also Figure 3):

- Two systems of parallel subvertical drainage pipes connected to form a grid with a rhombic pattern (1). The grid covers the entire cavern surface. The pipes are spaced 1-2 m apart and are perforated.
- At the intersection between the dome and the top of the wall and at the bottom of the wall, two large-diameter ring-shaped gas collector pipes are installed (2).
- Several large-diameter gas evacuation pipes (3) are connected to the upper collector pipe, leading to the tunnel above and further to the ground surface.

- A large diameter evacuation pipe (4) from the lower collector pipe, leading to the access tunnel. This connection is normally closed and used only for water drainage. However, in case of emergency it can also be used for gas evacuation.
- A curtain of subhorizontal boreholes (5), drilled from the tunnel above to form an "umbrella" over the cavern.

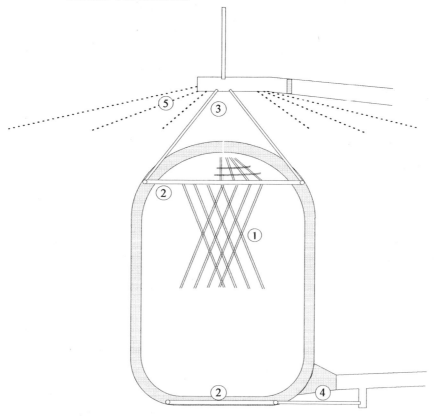

Figure 3     Design principles of the gas drainage system

The gas collector and evacuation pipes must not be perforated. The entire drainage system will be kept waterfilled at all times during operation of the storage, with negligible water circulation rates in the pipes.

Should any gas leakage occur, it will inevitably reach the drainage system after a certain time lapse. A pressure increase will follow in the drainage system as a signal of warning. By monitoring the upper evacuation pipes, the presence of methane in the water may also be detected. In the case of a continuous pressure increase, the pipe system should be drained of water through the lower evacuation pipe and the system be operated solely as a gas collection and drainage system.

At low to medium gas leakage rates, the drainage system should be capable of evacuating all leaking gas safely to the ground surface. The flow capacity of the system must be such that the pressure rise in the drainage pipes is controlled and insignificant. Thereby the risk of gas intrusion into the surrounding rock mass is eliminated.

Drilled from the tunnel above the cavern, a system of inclined boreholes are installed in the rock mass surrounding the cavern. This curtain will serve as an extra safeguard, primarily in the case of a large gas leak and secondly in the case of cavern depletion. In the first case, the curtain is used to monitor gas migration and to drain gas seeping upwards in the rock mass. In the second case, pumping will be done from the curtain to help reduce the external ground-water pressure acting on the outside of the concrete and steel liner.

## THE OCCURRENCE OF GAS LEAKAGE

A LRC storage is designed to be completely gas-tight when taken into operation and to remain so during its lifetime. As the steel lining is a man-made barrier, the success of the storage expressed as mechanical toughness and gas-tightness is very much dependent on the quality of the welds. Primarily, this is ensured by an extremely high level of quality control during construction. All welds are to be tested for internal defects (with radiography and/or ultrasonic methods) and for gas-tightness (with trace-gas methods). This implies that the steel lining is gas-tight when first pressurised after construction. However, despite the fact that highly developed materials and methods and very qualified personnel are used, there will always be some small internal defects remaining in the welds.

The next step in the verification is to pressurise the cavern to a level above the intended maximum storage pressure (e.g. 30% overpressure). This pressure loading is done to test the mechanical stability of the cavern and is most likely performed with water due to practical reasons. The final step is to submit the cavern to a high-accuracy gas-tightness test, performed at a low pressure with gas. If any defect (e.g. small crack) should have occurred during the high pressure loading with water, it is expected to be detectable by pressure monitoring and/or gas detectors in the drainage system also at this low pressure gas test.

### The cause of gas leakage

The steel material of the liner is ductile with a yield stress of 200-300 MPa and possesses a pronounced strain capacity. In principle, there are two mechanisms that can lead to a leakage through such a material. The first one is corrosion. With the assumption that the storage is localised in an area with favourable geochemical conditions, the probability of a leakage induced by corrosion is considered to be low. This is mainly due to the advantageous chemical environment near the steel surface. The thick concrete lining (minimum 0.5 m) creates a strong alkaline environment that protects the steel, the temperature is low and stable and the transportation of substances with the groundwater is negligible (assuming that the system normally is waterfilled).

The second mechanism is high intrinsic strains in the liner, combined with fatigue load. The most sensitive part of the structure is the welds, where the material is affected due to heating and where small internal defects are expected to be present even after a thorough control programme. Around such weaknesses, three-dimensional stress fields may develop. In combination with the general high stress level and cyclic loads, this may give rise to fatigue phenomena. One positive factor is the limited number of cyclic loads; a number of 100-1000 full cycles is expected during the lifetime, depending on the storage operation. Assuming that the welding operation and the weld control are of the highest possible quality, the probability of failure due to high strains is also considered to be low.

### Fault sizes

In order to design a drainage system for detection and collection of a potential gas leakage, three different fault sizes have been studied. These are listed in Table 1 along with the assumed origin of the fault and the calculated maximum gas leakage rate at 20 MPa. The estimation of gas leakage rates is made using a simple approximative method to give an idea of the magnitude. The calculation does not include any retardation of the gas flow caused by the concrete lining. A small pore or a 0.050 m long crack are assumed to be realistic sizes of a failure in the steel liner. As a worst case scenario, a 1.0 m long crack has been studied.

Table 1     Assumed fault magnitude and maximum leakage rates at 20 MPa used for the design of the gas drainage system.

| Leakage size | Assumed fault size | Probable origin of fault | Fault area (x $10^{-6}$ m$^2$) | Estimated maximum leakage rate (Nm$^3$/h) |
|---|---|---|---|---|
| A. Small | Pore | Corrosion | 1 | 150 |
| B. Medium | 0.05 m long crack | Fatigue | 6 | 800 |
| C. Large | 1.0 m long crack | Fatigue | 2 300 | 300 000 |

## CONSEQUENCES OF A GAS LEAKAGE

In the phenomenological description of leakage scenarios, the three leakage levels listed in Table 1 will be used. Figure 5 is an overview graph illustrating the barriers, failure and flow mechanisms the gas will encounter on its way from the cavern to the ground surface. Accompanying this graph is a rough pressure diagram. It is evident from the figure that the pressure draw-down capacity of the drainage system is of central importance.

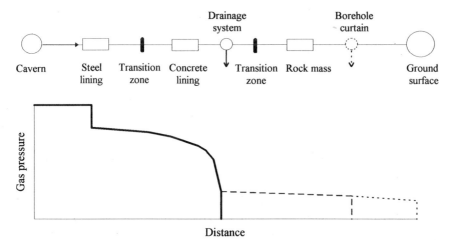

Figure 5     Overview graph illustrating the flow path of leaking gas and the corresponding pressure diagram.

### Scenario A, small size leakage

In the instance of a small pore (fault size $1 \times 10^{-6}$ m$^2$) through the steel liner, the high internal pressure will at some time start to affect the very minimal area of the concrete surface behind the pore. The concrete wall is criss-crossed by numerous tensional cracks. Should the pore develop directly above such a crack in the concrete, the gas will be transferred through the network of concrete cracks. When approaching the rock wall, the gas will be detected as a pressure increase in the drainage system. Should the pressure rise permanently to a level near the surrounding groundwater pressure, then the drainage system should be emptied and switched over to gas collection operation.

However, it must be noted that the occurrence of small pores ($1-2 \times 10^{-6}$ m$^2$ size) in the steel lining may not be detected until after a considerable time since solid concrete has quite a low gas permeability.

## Scenario B, medium size leakage

Case B is a crack of about 0.05 m length (fault size $6 \times 10^{-6}$ m$^2$). In this case, the possibility that the concrete layer retards the gas migration is lower than in Case A. With time one has to assume that a leakage path is established through the interconnected concrete crack network. Upon reaching the rock wall, the migrating gas is detected and then collected in the drainage system. The drainage system should be given a discharge capacity large enough to handle gas flow rates of this magnitude throughout the lifetime of the project. The drainage system must be controlled to operate well below the pressure of the surrounding groundwater. If this is not possible, gas will displace water in the cavern vicinity and start to escape from the cavern. Should such a situation occur, the borehole curtain above the cavern may be used, at least temporarily, to increase the groundwater pressure and prevent gas escape.

Consequently, Case B may or may not lead to operational problems for the storage, depending on the development of the gas flow and the discharge capacity of the drainage system.

## Scenario C, large size leakage

In Case C, the fracture in the steel lining has grown to unacceptable dimensions, length 1.0 m (fault size $2\ 300 \times 10^{-6}$ m$^2$ ). The gas flow is extremely high, in the order of 50 000 Nm$^3$/h or more. A well preserved drainage system may initially be capable of controlling even such a considerable gas flow for a limited time (number of days or weeks). The flow velocity is, however, extremely high in this case, which leads to serious erosion effects in the individual concrete fractures which have to handle the gas flow. The support of the steel plate behind the fracture will sooner or later be jeopardised by this and a much greater hole in the steel will be created.

However, one interesting aspect of the drainage system in a catastrophic event like Case C, is that it might allow sufficient time for depressurisation of the cavern and other extraordinary measures. Should it not be possible to control the gas pressure against the rock walls, a plume of gas will migrate into the tunnel and shaft system above the cavern and move upwards to the ground surface. Arrangements may be made on the ground surface to control this gas flow, for example through a gas blow-off chimney or a flare system.

## PROBABILISTIC RISK ANALYSIS CONCERNING CONCEPT SAFETY

A probabilistic risk analysis concerning the safety of the LRC concept is presently under completion. Within this analysis hazards connected to the different construction elements have been identified. The correlation between different hazards and events has been studied using fault tree analysis. Some examples of important identified hazards are:

- Frequent high stress and strain levels in the steel liner
- Reduced capacity in the drainage system due to clogging or physical damage
- Inadequate quality control during construction

The consequences of a leakage have been studied by performing event tree analyses. The event trees include events starting with the occurrence of a gas leak and eventually ending with the event that the gas reaches the ground surface. The preliminary results indicate that severe consequences even of a fairly large leakage are unlikely and well within the normal acceptance level of facilities of similar type.

## FIELD TESTS

The Pilot Plant for LRC, located in central Sweden 250 km west of Stockholm, comprises three test rooms and was built during 1988 as a joint project by a number of Scandinavian companies interested in developing new techniques for storing natural gas in lined rock caverns. Tests have been carried out in four phases during 1989-93. The test programme includes pressure tests with water to 52 MPa and with air to 15 MPa. The Pilot Tests in general and a comprehensive analysis of the test results have previously been presented by Stille et al., 1994 and Johansson et al., 1994 and 1995.

Figure 6 illustrates the layout of the test rooms. The rooms were excavated as vertical cylinders and are small-scale copies of the proposed design of a full-scale storage.

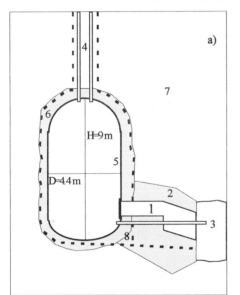

1. Access tube     2. Concrete plug
3. Water fill       4. Gas fill
5. Steel lining     6. Concrete lining
7. Rock mass      8. Drainage system

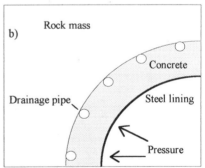

Figure 6     a) General layout of a Pilot Plant test room. b) Horizontal section

The drainage system consists of standard drainage pipes (0,07 m diameter) which were mounted subvertically on the rock surface prior to casting the concrete lining. In all 15 pipes were installed, distributed along the circumference with an average distance of 1.2 m. At the top and bottom of the cavern the pipes are gathered in 7 groups (6x2 and 1x3 pipes).

Air leakage tests with artificially created faults in the steel plate were done on two occasions for the purpose of studying the ability of the drainage system to perform its two main tasks, i.e. to detect and to collect leaking gas. In Grängesberg, gas leakages could be detected both from the drainage system surrounding the cavern and by registration of the cavern pressure. The drainage system is the most sensitive system with an accuracy of $10^{-3}$ $Nm^3/h$.

**Leakage tests at 1.5 MPa**

The first leakage tests were performed at an air pressure of 1.5 MPa in a test room lined with 0.006 m thick steel plates. The leakage was created by placing nozzles in holes drilled through the steel lining before the room was pressurised, see Figure 7. The nozzle size used was 1.05 mm diameter. Laboratory tests to calibrate the nozzles indicated a maximum leakage of 8.6 $Nm^3$/h at 1.5 MPa (the laboratory test was done with free flow behind the nozzle). In all, three holes at different locations on the steel liner were tested. In addition, two of the holes were also tested without the nozzle, leaving a 10 mm diameter hole in the steel.

The test results showed that the leakage was clearly detectable and could be localised by flow measurements in the drainage system. As regards collection, the gas volume collected in the drainage system was compared to the estimated leakage through the steel liner (evaluated from measurements of pressure and temperature inside the cavern). The collecting capacity achieved was in the range 75-100% of the leaked air. The results also gave an indication of the retarding effect of the concrete lining. The highest leakage rate in the field tests only reached 45 % of the rate obtained in the laboratory (the other two holes had rates of 4 % or lower).

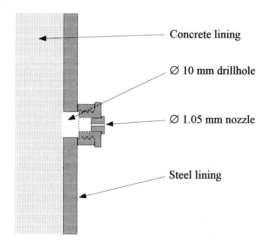

Concrete lining

Ø 10 mm drillhole

Ø 1.05 mm nozzle

Steel lining

Figure 7       Nozzle used for leakage tests at 1.5 MPa.

**Leakage tests at 13 and 11 MPa**

On the second occasion, two air leakage tests were performed at high pressures (13 and 11 MPa) in a test room lined with 0.0005 m thick stainless steel sheets. The leaks were created by two cutting edges triggered by remote control to fall and make holes through the liner at the same time as the room was pressurised. Figure 8 shows the pressure fall during the first leakage test when two cuts were made.

During this test (at a pressure of 13 MPa), no increase in the existing initial leakage (due to minor defects in the welds) was detectable despite two new large defects ($100 \times 10^{-6}$ $m^2$ each) created by the cutting edges. The rate of air leakage and the pressure inside the room were monitored during a holding time of 18 days. During the first half of this period, the leakage rate was 11 $Nm^3$/h. Then a slow increase was noticed and the rate of leakage rose to 15 $Nm^3$/h during the second half. The efficiency of the drainage system in collecting gas was evaluated at about 80%. An inspection of the concrete surface behind the cuts in the liner did not reveal any cracks or other effects. During a second leakage test only one of the two cutting edges was successfully triggered. The collection efficiency of the drainage system was estimated at about 94-100%.

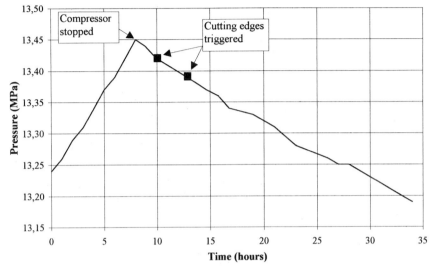

Figure 8          Pressure fall during air leakage test in Test Room 3, Grängesberg. The black squares indicates the times when the cuts were made.

As was the case with the leakage tests at 1.5 MPa, the tests at 13 and 11 MPa also indicate the retarding effect of the concrete lining. The maximum leakage rate through a $100 \times 10^{-6}$ $m^2$ cut at 13 MPa can be estimated at 9 000 $Nm^3/h$ with free flow behind the leak (the same approximative methode as used for Table 1). This can be compared to a maximum measured leakage rate from the test room of 15 $Nm^3/h$, a leakage rate including the original weld defects as well as the two new cuts. The test room had previously been pressurised to 28 MPa and the concrete lining was consequently criss-crossed with numerous tension cracks. The retarding effect of the concrete is thus considerable, despite the presence of cracks and even after several weeks.

**CONCLUDING REMARKS**

The general conclusions regarding the gas drainage system for a LRC storage, based on the field tests and the design work performed in Sweden, can be summarised as follows:

- It is essential to use high-quality materials and methods and to implement a very high level of control during the construction of the steel lining. If this is done, it is possible to construct a lining that is initially gas-tight and to ensure that the risk of any remaining defects in the welds will lead to a failure during operation is minimized.
- To study the complicated questions concerning the probability of a gas leak and the consequences of a gas leak, the use of probabilistic risk analysis methods is recommended, e.g  fault-tree and event-tree analysis.
- The suggested design of the gas drainage system is expected to control and collect small and medium gas leaks and to prevent gas intrusion in the surrounding rock mass.

- Even a large gas leak can initially be controlled. The gas drainage system will in this case allow enough time to reduce the storage pressure. The gas intrusion in the rock mass is therefore expected to be small even in a worst case scenario.
- The retarding effect of the concrete lining is considerable, even if criss-crossed by numerous tensile cracks. However, after long time (weeks) and with high leakage rates the concrete will probably be damaged by erosion effects, leading to an increasing leakage rate.

## REFERENCES

1. Johansson, J., Stille, H., Sturk, R., 1995: " Pilotanläggning för inklädda gaslager i Grängesberg - Fördjupad analys av försöksresultaten". Dept. of Soil & Rock Mechanics, Royal Institute of Technology, Stockholm.

2. Johansson, J., Stille, H., Sturk, R., 1994: "Storage of gas in lined shallow rock caverns - conclusions based on results from the Grängesberg test plant". Presented at the workshop "Natural Gas Rock Cavern Storage", Czech Gas & Oil Association, Prague.

3. Rosendal, T., Tengborg, P., Särkkä, P., 1992: "Scandinavian Concept For Storing of Gas in Lined Rock Caverns," Proc. of 1992 Int. Gas Research Conference, V. III, pp. 1-8, Gas Research Institute, Chicago.

4. Stille, H., Johansson, J., Sturk, R., 1994: "High pressure storage of gas in lined rock caverns - Results from field tests". Proc. of EUROCK'94, pp. 689-696, Balkema, Rotterdam.

## CHARACTERIZATION OF GAS STORAGE FIELDS USING
## NEURAL NETWORK MODELING OF WELL TRANSIENTS

I. Ershaghi and X. Li

University of Southern California, USA

S. Foh

The Gas Research Institute, USA

ABSTRACT

Pressure transient tests are regularly conducted in gas storage reservoirs for inventory verification. Quantitative interpretation of pressure transient test data requires information about reservoir structure, compartmentalization and interface movement. On the other hand, qualitative interpretation of pressure transient test data may contain this required information. As such, pressure transient test data not only can be used for parameter estimation and average reservoir pressure determination, they can also be used for reservoir characterization.

A method using neural network technique was developed which uses the qualitative signals imbedded in pressure transient test data for reservoir model selection. Pressure derivative diagnostic plots are used as the basis for neural network pattern recognition. Neural networks are trained with pressure transient responses generated representing various theoretical models. The real field test data are then measured up against the neural network models to identify the potential conceptual reservoir models. The most plausible model is then selected by using other available information.

A "desktop" computer program has been developed to assist gas storage operators to make full use of the pressure transient test data. The program incorporates modules for pressure transient test design, reservoir model selection, test data analysis and inventory verification. Pressure transient results are also easily correlated to inventory verification.

RESUME

Des tests de pression sont effectues regulierement dans des reservoirs naturels de gaz pour en verifier le contenu. L'evaluation des proprietes du gaz present dans le reservoir, a partir des resultats de ces tests, necessite des informations sur la structure du reservoir et sur la couche d'eau parfois presente sous le gaz. Ces donnees elles memes peuvent etre deduites des mesures obtenues lors des tests. Ainsi ces tests ont un double role : trouver les caracteristiques du reservoir et estimer la pression moyenne du gaz.

Une methode utilisant la technique des reseaux neureaux a ete mise au point pour definir un modele particulier de reservoir. Le reseau neural est entraine a reconnaitre plusieurs modeles theoriques ; a partir des courbes experimentales de la derivee de la pression du gaz par rapport au temps, il choisit alors l' un d' entre eux.

Un programme sur ordinateur portable a ete developpe pour permettre l' interpretation des mesures effectuees sur le terrain. Ce programme comporte plusieurs modules : preparation des tests, choix d' un modele, interpretation quantitative des resultats, estimation du contenu du reservoir.

## INTRODUCTION

Inventory verification in gas storage fields requires information about reservoir structure and interface movements. This information is often obtained in a lumped parameter approach by monitoring static pressures and applying the material balances related to injection and withdrawal. Delineation of the specific aspects of reservoir configuration requires extensive reservoir characterization studies and history matching using reservoir models.

A very powerful characterization approach is the use of qualitative signals imbedded in pressure transient test diagnostic plots. Plausible conceptual models representing the reservoir can be identified prior to any parameter estimation efforts. This ability of well test data has become of significant interest in recent years because of pressure derivative based diagnostic technique and new analytical solutions available for a host of reservoir conditions.

For gas storage operations, where well test data can be obtained on a routine basis, evaluation engineers need a convenient way to conduct both qualitative and quantitative evaluation of pressure transient test data. Existence of numerous classes of well transient responses requires extensive expertise for pattern recognition and model selection. As a substitute for the expertise, the potentials of artificial intelligence approach and the methods of fuzzy sets have been investigated.

This paper presents the fundamental components of a neural network based modeling approach to delineate gas storage architecture from well transients. The neural network models included are pre-trained for several classes of well transients. These include reservoirs of uniform properties as well as those with layering structure, reservoir transmissibility architecture of the composite types and reservoirs with natural fractures. The training process also includes conceptual reservoir models with numerous combination of no flow boundaries such as a single sealing fault as well as multiple boundaries. Theoretical prediction of expected transient responses for numerous conceptual models are generated using the numerical inversion of analytical solutions in the Laplace space. Diagnostic patterns associated with real field data are then measured up against the neural network models to select the most plausible model or models. The computer aided technique presented in this paper includes a non-linear regression method as well as conventional analysis methods for quantitative parameter estimations. These estimation procedures cover essential transmissivity characteristics, proximity to boundaries and parameters depicting interporosity flow plus near wellbore effects.

The combination of neural network modeling and non-linear regression and conventional parameter estimation technique is developed in the form of a "desktop" software for application by gas storage operators. A number of modules are incorporated in this computer aided analysis technique. Well test data can be analyzed individually or in conjunction with other wells in a given field. Under the combined data set, an algorithm is included to estimate the weighted average static reservoir pressure. The estimated value is then automatically incorporated into the inventory verification module to analyze the hysterisis associated with gas leakage and losses. The software is further equipped with design capabilities for selecting test duration which can characterize the important elements of the storage compartments.

The essential purpose of the study was to familiarize the gas storage operators with the merits of conducting pressure transient tests instead of static tests, to develop a software with the necessary know-how to design and analyze tests with on-line training capabilities for users with limited knowledge in well testing.

## IMPORTANCE OF GAS STORAGE FIELD CHARACTERIZATION

Inventory verification is routinely required in gas storage field operation. Because of leakage and influx, a simple pressure-volume material balance study using injection and withdrawal data alone may not correctly estimate the gas inventory with insufficient static pressure data. Estimation of static average reservoir pressure is, therefore, needed to verify the actual gas inventory. While a true static average reservoir pressure requires shutting down all the wells in the field, the generally long shut-in time required for this purpose can not be realized because of operational difficulties and the economics. An alternative approach commonly taken is then to conduct pressure transient tests in some of the wells in the field and to estimate field average pressure by analyzing the limited well transients. Pressure transients are affected by the characteristics of a field. The controlling parameters include formation thickness, formation continuity, structure and rock and fluid properties (e.g. permeability, porosity, viscosity, compressibility). Characterization of the field is thus essential for correct analysis of pressure transient test data.

Heterogeneity of the gas storage rocks often causes differential depletion of different layers or different regions of a field. Gas remaining in the low permeability layers or regions may be mistakenly counted as gas leaked or lost.

An inappropriately designed test may result in insufficient data for estimating interference among different wells. At times, it is not feasible to simultaneously shut in all the wells for estimation of static pressure. To ultimately solve these problems, a reservoir simulator should be constructed for each gas storage field so that the gas inventory can be dynamically simulated on a computer. In such a case, only a few observation pressure points may be needed at different times to verify storage simulation. Pressure transient tests can be run on selected wells for model calibration. Again, the characterization of the field is critical for constructing a good reservoir simulator.

While the nature of a gas storage field is important in analyzing pressure transient test data, such tests can provide both quantitative and qualitative information about the reservoir geometry, storativity and transmissivity characteristics. Pressure transient test data have traditionally been used for quantitative estimation of reservoir parameters. Qualitative reservoir geometry verification has been complex because of non-unique answers to diagnostic plots.

Unlike conventional gas and oil fields, which are abandoned after reaching to their economic limits, gas storage fields are subjected to repeatedly cycling of the injection and withdrawal of gas. These cycles provide opportunities for pressure transient tests which are usually conducted for inventory verification. Repeated cycles of pressurization and de-pressurization may cause fluid-fluid interface movement, potential gas leakage and water influx, which may result in non-linear behavior of the storage pressure responses to gas injection and withdrawal.

GRI - USC Project

The GRI - USC project was aimed to address problems related to the analysis of pressure transient test data in gas storage fields. Advanced mathematical models needed to describe different reservoir types and reservoir configurations and non-uniqueness of the mathematical solutions makes the problem complicated for routine studies by operators. Inadequate test design also results in the test data containing limited useful information. Furthermore, poor data recording makes data unusable. Finally, expertise required to analyze pressure transient test data for field characterization is generally lacking within the staff of most small operating companies.

To overcome the difficulties mentioned above, GRI sponsored a project at the University of Southern California to provide the gas operators with a convenient tool to make full use of pressure transient test data. The objective of the project was to develop a computer software which will incorporate multitude of expected conceptual reservoir models to describe different reservoir types and reservoir configurations. Advanced technology was to be used to take into account of the non-uniqueness of mathematical solutions. Additional features were also incorporated in the software to simplify training and to assist in test design and data analysis.

OVERVIEW OF THE "DESKTOP" COMPUTER PROGRAM

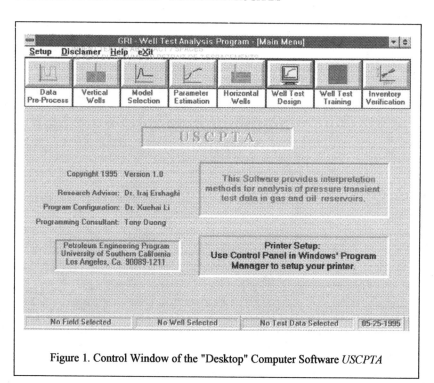

Figure 1. Control Window of the "Desktop" Computer Software *USCPTA*

Figure 1 shows the control window of the computer software *USCPTA*. The main features of this software are briefly described below:

(1) Pre-Processing of Raw Test Data: Raw test data can be viewed on the screen and a portion of the test data (e.g. drawdown part or buildup part) can be selected from the data set, and the selected data can then be filtered from noise when needed. Wellhead pressure data can be converted to bottom hole pressure.

(2) Data Storage: The software organizes and stores pressure transient test data on the given field bases. The field map, well locations, fault locations and test data for each well can be input to the computer. The test data can then be browsed by well name or calendar year and individual test can be retrieved for analysis. The test data for each field can also be backed up or restored.

(3) Model Selection: Neural network method was used to assist in the selection of conceptual reservoir models from pressure derivative plots of actual test data. Different reservoir models are included.

(4) Parameter Estimation: The program uses conventional straight line and type curve match techniques, as well as the method of non-linear regression, to estimate reservoir parameters. Interference test and variable rate test data can also be analyzed. When both pressure and rate changes are monitored in a buildup or falloff test, the early time data can also be analyzed by using pressure and rate convolution method, which usually produces an earlier time data set of significant value in short duration tests. A module is also included to match the test history by using the parameters estimated from all above mentioned methods.

(5) Pressure Transient Test Design: The software generates pressure responses with the user specifying reservoir parameters for a given reservoir model and test type.

(6) Pressure Transient Test Training: Some of the basic concepts related to pressure transient test are included in this program. A module for type curve review is created to help users study the shapes of the pressure derivative diagnostic type curves for different conceptual reservoir models. A module for type curve quiz is also included to test users' knowledge about the expected responses of the pressure derivative diagnostic plots. A module for model comparison is created for users to compare the pressure responses from different reservoir models.

(7) Inventory Verification: For gas storage operations, users can estimate an average reservoir pressure from the analysis results of a group of tested wells. When the user enters the injection and production history of the field, the program will plot the inventory history and generates the diagnostic incremental inventory changes.

## APPLICATION OF NEURAL NETWORKS FOR PATTERN RECOGNITION

Pressure transient test data provide not only the information on the dynamic behavior of a gas storage field, they also contains information related to the characteristics of the reservoir type and reservoir configuration. Since its introduction by Bourdet[1] et al, the loglog pressure derivative technique, which uses the different patterns shown on the pressure derivative plots to identify reservoir models, has become a very powerful tool in the interpretation of pressure transient test data. With the introduction of high resolution and high accuracy pressure gauges, distinguishable features can be easily obtained from pressure derivative plots. With the development of computer technology, automated pattern recognition by using pressure derivative plots have become the subject of studies for qualitatively identifying conceptual reservoir models.

Two basic approaches are used in automated pattern recognition for pressure transient data interpretation. The first approach is the use of knowledge-based expert systems, which establishes if-then rules based on feature extraction or symbolic representation of the type curves. Because this approach is adversely affected by data noise, its application is hindered in practice. The second approach is the use of neural network technique. There has been limited application of neural network in petroleum engineering. Al-Kaabi and Lee[2] first suggested this approach for limited cases of well test data. The method requires the training of the neural network with theoretically generated patterns. The trained neural network is then used for pattern recognition from actual test data.

Detailed discussion on the use of neural networks for pattern recognition in pressure transient test data interpretation can be found in Al-Kaabi and Lee[2], Juniardi and Ershaghi[3] and Ershaghi[4] et al. Briefly speaking, back-propagation neural networks are used for pattern recognition in pressure test analysis. A back-propagation neural network consists of nodes arranged in three layers: an input layer, a middle hidden layer and an output layer. These nodes are then connected by links, with the input layer nodes to be connected to the middle hidden layer nodes and the latter to be connected to the output layer nodes. By training the neural network with a set of known patterns and a set of specified output value for each output node, a weight factor is generated for each link. Pattern recognition is then carried out by inputting an unknown pattern through input layer and comparing the activation number generated from the output layer.

Juniardi and Ershaghi[3] discussed the difficulties encountered in the use of neural networks in well test analysis. Generally speaking, two main problems exist in pattern recognition by the use of pressure derivative plots. The first problem is the non-uniqueness of the shapes of the pressure derivative plots for a specific reservoir model, caused by different combinations of the model parameters. This implies that infinite number of pressure derivative curves can be generated for a specific reservoir model. The second problem is the similarities of the shapes of the pressure derivative plots between different reservoir models, which implies that one shape of the pressure derivative plots may represent more than one reservoir models. Therefore, a definite reservoir model may not be determined from pressure derivative plot alone, and more information are needed for a definite model identification.

Because of the difficulties caused by the above mentioned non-uniqueness and similarity problems, training a comprehensive neural network to include all possible patterns commonly encountered in well test analysis is impractical. Ershaghi[4] et al proposed a method which uses multiple neural networks, with each neural network trained for a specific reservoir model. Each of these individual neural networks is trained to recognize most of the patterns which may be generated from the specific model it represents. By going through all the neural networks trained, one pattern is picked from each neural network for an unknown pattern. These selected patterns can be ranked and all possible models resembling the unknown pattern may then be identified. The objective of this approach is then to provide all possible models that a set of pressure transient test data may represent. As such, a more appropriate reservoir model may be identified and can be substantiated with other information, such as geological, geophysical and performance data. Another advantage of this approach is that new models can be easily added by training new neural networks, with the existing neural networks undisturbed.

APPLICATION OF THE "DESKTOP" COMPUTER PROGRAM

Neural Network Pattern Recognition

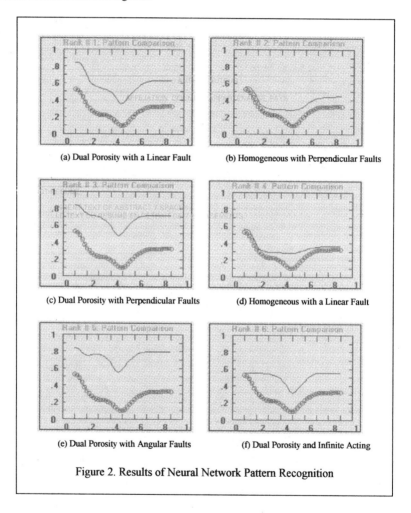

(a) Dual Porosity with a Linear Fault

(b) Homogeneous with Perpendicular Faults

(c) Dual Porosity with Perpendicular Faults

(d) Homogeneous with a Linear Fault

(e) Dual Porosity with Angular Faults

(f) Dual Porosity and Infinite Acting

Figure 2. Results of Neural Network Pattern Recognition

To demonstrate the application of neural network method for pattern recognition, a synthetical pressure derivative curve was generated by using a dual porosity reservoir model with a linear fault. After activating the module for model selection, the patterns ranked from one to six are shown in Figure 2, where the circles are the test pattern and lines are theoretically generated patterns. It can be seen that the pattern ranked number one is from dual porosity model with a linear fault. For insufficient pattern data, additional information is needed for identifying an appropriate reservoir model.

Composite Analysis for Estimating Average Reservoir Pressure

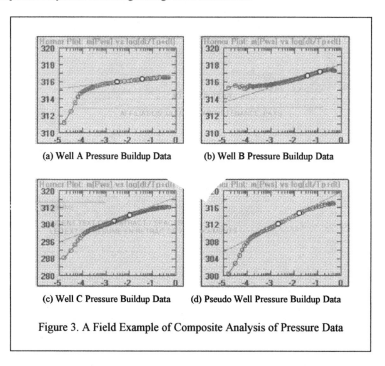

(a) Well A Pressure Buildup Data          (b) Well B Pressure Buildup Data

(c) Well C Pressure Buildup Data          (d) Pseudo Well Pressure Buildup Data

Figure 3. A Field Example of Composite Analysis of Pressure Data

In common practice, pressure transient tests are usually conducted in multiple wells throughout a gas storage field to estimate an average reservoir pressure. In doing so, an average pressure in the drainage area of every individual participating well needs to be determined first. These drainage area average pressures are then averaged, either volumetrically or arithmetically, to obtain a field average pressure. To determine the average pressure in the drainage area of an active well, conventional straight line analysis methods, such as Horner and MDH methods, can be used, which requires the knowledge of the size and the shape of the drainage area. Even though the drainage area and shape can be estimated from pressure drawdown information, rate fluctuations commonly encountered in the pressure drawdown period often makes this task difficult. To avoid determining the sizes and shapes of the drainage area for all active wells, Ershaghi[5] et al devised a composite analysis technique which uses a pseudo well to represent all the active wells in a gas storage field, with the pseudo well data being rate averaged from all active wells. The method assumes all active wells should have a homogeneous reservoir responses and the tests at each active well need to commence at the same time. By using a rectangular to approximate the field shape, a shape factor can be estimated according to the location of the pseudo well. With the use of the total field area and the shape factor estimated, an average reservoir pressure can be directly determined from the analysis of the pseudo well pressure buildup data.

Figure 3 shows an actual field example of this composite analysis method. Three wells were tested on this gas storage field with each well being put on gas flow for three days and subsequently shut-in for three days. The pressure buildup data of these three wells are shown in Figure 3 (a), (b) and (c), respectively. Figure 3 (d) shows the pseudo well pressure buildup data, which is generated by rate averaging the pressure buildup data from all three actual wells.

The average pressure estimated from buildup and drawdown data for the drainage areas of Well A and Well B are 1973.9 psia and 1973.1 psia, respectively. An average pressure can not be estimated for Well C, because of the poor quality of drawdown data caused by rate fluctuations. Fortunately, the pressure in this well leveled off after about 48 hours of shut-in, reaching a value of around 1977.8 psia. An arithmetical average of the three active wells gives an average reservoir pressure of 1975.3 psia, and a volumetric average of these wells gives an average reservoir pressure of 1976.4 psia.

The analysis results of the composite data estimated an average reservoir pressure of 1976.2 psia, which is very close to the volumetrically averaged reservoir pressure from the three active wells.

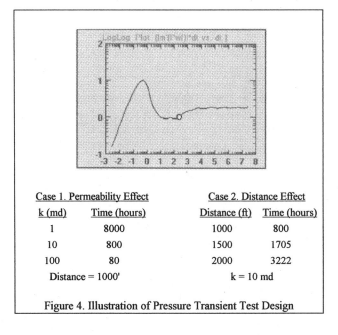

| Case 1. Permeability Effect | | Case 2. Distance Effect | |
|---|---|---|---|
| k (md) | Time (hours) | Distance (ft) | Time (hours) |
| 1 | 8000 | 1000 | 800 |
| 10 | 800 | 1500 | 1705 |
| 100 | 80 | 2000 | 3222 |
| Distance = 1000' | | k = 10 md | |

Figure 4. Illustration of Pressure Transient Test Design

Pressure Transient Test Design

To help gas storage operators in designing their pressure transient tests, a module is included in the computer program which uses theoretical models to predict pressure responses. When a reservoir model and a test type are selected, the program will calculate the pressure response for the reservoir and fluid parameters specified by a user. The program can be used in different ways. For example, a user can vary a specific parameter and study its effect on pressure response. If a specific feature of the reservoir needs to be tested, such as the location of a fault, the program can help to estimate the time necessary for detecting this feature. Illustrated in Figure 4 is an example of determining the minimum testing time for detecting a fault in a homogeneous reservoir. Case 1 shows the effect of formation permeability when the fault distance is specified. Case 2 shows the effect of fault distance when permeability is specified. Other parameters are the same for both cases.

CONCLUSIONS

Pressure transient tests are regularly conducted on gas storage fields for inventory verification purpose. Pressure transient data can be used not only for parameter estimation and average storage pressure determination, but also for the characterization of gas storage fields.

The computer software USCPTA developed at the university of Southern California under the sponsorship of the Gas Research Institute provides the advance tool needed for test design and test data interpretation by gas storage operators. In this software, a method was developed which uses a structured neural network technique to assist in the selection of conceptual reservoir models from pressure derivative data. A composite analysis technique was also incorporated which uses rate averaged pressure buildup data for estimating average reservoir pressures. The software in the current design can also handle pressure test data analysis for gas reservoirs.

REFERENCES

1. D. Bourdet, J.A. Ayoub and Y.M. Pirard: "Use of the Pressure Derivative in Well Test Interpretation," SPE Formation Evaluation (June 1989) 293-302.
2. A.U. Al-Kaabi and W.J. Lee: "Using Artificial Neural Networks to Identify the Well-Test Interpretation Model," paper SPE 20332 presented at the 1990 Petroleum Computer Conference, Denver, June 25-28.
3. I.R. Juniardi and I. Ershaghi: "Complexities of Using Neural Network in Well Test Analysis of Faulted Reservoirs," paper SPE 26106 presented at the Western Regional Technical Conference and Exhibition, Ankhorage, Alaska, May 26-28, 1993.
4. I. Ershaghi, X. Li, M. Hassibi and Y. Shikari: "A Robust Neural Network Model for Pattern Recognition of Pressure Transient Test Data," paper SPE 26427 presented at the Annual Technical Conference and Exhibition, Houston, Texas, October 3-6, 1993.
5. I. Ershaghi, H. Calisgan, J. Chang and Y. Shikari: "A Critical Look at Methods Used for Estimation of Average Shut-in Pressure in Gas Storage Reservoirs,"

INTERPRETATION STRATIGRAPHIQUE DE LA SISMIQUE 3 D :
APPLICATION PRATIQUE A UN RESERVOIR DE GAZ NATUREL EN NAPPE
AQUIFERE

STRATIGRAPHIC INTERPRETATION OF 3 D SHOOTING :
PRATICAL APPLICATION TO A NATURAL GAS STORAGE RESERVOIR IN THE
AQUIFER

Frédéric HUGUET*, Denis MOUGENOT**

*Gaz de France
** Compagnie Générale de Géophysique

RESUME

L'interprétation stratigraphique de la sismique 3 D de SOINGS en SOLOGNE a permis de localiser les limites de la bulle de gaz et les zones à forte saturation du voisinage des puits d'exploitation.

Deux méthodes d'interprétation ont été expérimentées pour évaluer les caractéristiques du réservoir et de son contenu en fluide.

La méthode la plus simple a consisté à cartographier les amplitudes sismiques au toit du réservoir, L'extrapolation des caractéristiques réservoirs à partir des puits en suivant la carte des amplitudes et la forme   structurale a permis d'estimer l'extension de la bulle de gaz.

Une méthode plus détaillée a été expérimentée dans la zone centrale: elle consiste à étudier la répartition spatiale des impédances acoustiques dans la couche réservoir, à en déduire une pseudo-épaisseur saturée et une pseudo-saturation et ainsi à localiser géographiquement les meilleurs réservoirs.

ABSTRACT

The stratigraphic interpretation of a 3 D seismic carried out at SOINGS en SOLOGNE allowed us to delineate the limits of the gas bubble and also the areas with high gas saturation near the production wells.

We tested two methodologies to evaluate the characteristics of the reservoir and its fluid content.

The simplest method is to map the seismic amplitude at the top of the reservoir.
The extrapolation of reservoir characteristics starting from the wells and following  the amplitude map and the structural shape allowed  to estimate the gaz bubble extension.

A more detailed method was tested in the central area of the structure where we studied the distribution of the reservoir acoustic impedance. We obtained a pseudo–saturation map and a pseudo–gas  thickness map. This interpretation characterizes the production area with high gas saturations.

## INTRODUCTION

La réalisation d'un stockage souterrain de gaz naturel en nappe aquifère nécessite des études poussées tant sur la forme structurale que sur la caractérisation du réservoir dont dépend la performance de l'ouvrage.

Les méthodes traditionnelles d'étude des réservoirs sont basées sur les informations de puits acquises en cours de forage et de production. Bien que ces informations soient précises et fiables, elles sont ponctuelles et dépendent de la répartition des puits.
L'interpolation de ces informations entre les puits fournit une image lissée et interprétative du réservoir. Cette image peut être améliorée, de manière significative, en utilisant la sismique 3 D, qui réalise un échantillonnage spatial continu de la réflectivité du sous–sol.

L'interprétation stratigraphique de la sismique 3 D enregistrée sur le stockage de SOINGS en SOLOGNE a permis de mieux caractériser le réservoir et la répartition du gaz (Pinson et Huguet 1994).
Cet article présente deux méthodes d'interprétation utilisant cette sismique et les résultats obtenus.


## PRESENTATION DU SITE ET DES DONNEES

Le stockage de SOINGS en SOLOGNE est situé dans le Loir & Cher au Sud de BLOIS.
Le réservoir situé à une profondeur moyenne de 1050 m par rapport au niveau de la mer est constitué par un ensemble de grès fluviatiles et d'argiles à géométrie complexe sur une épaisseur de 40 m.

Dans cette formation on peut distinguer deux ensembles réservoir. Le réservoir supérieur est formé par une nappe gréseuse continue sur toute la structure. Il est couvert par une formation argilo-gréseuse. Le réservoir principal est isolé du réservoir supérieur par une couche argileuse. Il est formé par un ensemble de chenaux fluviatiles devenant plus argileux à la base avant de passer à des niveaux gréso-conglomératiques et dolomitiques.

La campagne sismique 3D tirée en avril 1991 couvre toute la fermeture structurale et elle est calibrée par 12 puits.

## EXPLOITATION DES DONNEES SISMIQUES

L'acquisition et le traitement des données ont été réalisées par Gaz de France (G.D.F.) par la Compagnie Générale de Géophysique (C.G.G.) de façon à préserver au mieux les amplitudes avec l'obtention d'un bon rapport signal sur bruit.

L'interprétation structurale a permis de mieux préciser la structure et la géométrie des failles, qui n'avaient auparavant été reconnus que par de la sismique 2 D. L'interprétation sismique stratigraphique a été réalisée dans le cadre d'un projet de recherche commun entre le G.D.F et la C.G.G. visant à tester de nouvelles méthodes de traitement et d'interprétation stratigraphiques.

Deux approches différentes, l'une simple,l'autre plus complexe à mettre en oeuvre, ont été expérimentées sur ces données. La première méthode est basée sur l'étude des amplitudes sismiques, la seconde sur l'analyse quantitative des impédances acoustiques.

### *Méthode d'analyse des amplitudes sismiques:*

Le traitement conventionnel des données sismiques a pour objectif l'obtention d'une image sismique 2D - 3D dont les variations d'amplitudes reflètent au mieux les coefficients de réflexion à l'interface des couches géologiques.
Ces coefficients de réflexion de l'onde sismique sont proportionnels aux contrastes d'impédance acoustique, c'est à dire à la variation de la densité et de la vitesse sismique de part et d'autre de l'interface considérée.

Si la réflexion au toit du réservoir est représentée par une amplitude positive, elle correspond à un accroissement d'impédance. A l'inverse le passage d'un grès à une argile de plus faible impédance sera représenté par une amplitude négative.

L'amplitude au toit d'un réservoir augmente quand sa porosité diminue. Par contre, le remplacement de l'eau par du gaz dans les pores de la roche réservoir se traduit par une réduction de son impédance et donc par une diminution de l'amplitude à son toit. Un effet analogue se produit lorsque l'argilosité du réservoir augmente.
Par conséquent, il ne sera pas possible par l'étude des variations d'amplitude de la réflexion au toit d'un réservoir de distinguer un grès propre à gaz d'un grès argileux à eau.
On ne peut lever cet indétermination sans prendre en compte les informations géologiques aux puits et analyser les correspondances entre la forme structurale et les variations d'amplitude (la bulle de gaz se situant à l'intérieur de la fermeture structurale).

La figure 1 représente l'amplitude au toit du réservoir principal et la figure 2 son interprétation . Le puits F se situe dans une zone à forte amplitude, s'expliquant par la présence de grès propre à eau alors que le puits G traverse un réservoir médiocre composé de grès argileux. Aussi l'amplitude de la réflexion est faible de même qu'au niveau du puits A qui est situé dans une zone à gaz.
En extrapolant les informations aux puits par l'intermédiaire des amplitudes sismiques, on montre la présence d'une zone à faible amplitude située à l'emplacement de la culmination structurale et pouvant être interprétée comme zone en gaz, la limite de la bulle dans la direction du puits F qui se matérialise par un accroissement important de l'amplitude est franche.

On notera toutefois que cette interprétation n'est représentative que de l'état des saturations en fluide de la partie supérieure du réservoir principal. Elle suppose également que toutes les variations d'amplitudes sont liées à des changements dans le réservoir principal, sa couverture étant considérée comme ne présentant pas de variations latérale

### *Méthode d'interprétation basée sur l'étude des impédances acoustiques:*

La conversion du volume des amplitudes sismiques en impédance acoustiques nécessite un traitement particulier appelé "inversion stratigraphique". Les impédances, représentées en couches, peuvent ensuite être calées sur les impédances mesurées aux puits, ce qui facilite l'interprétation de la sismique.

Le programme expérimental d'inversion 3D ROV développé par la CGG calcule ensuite un modèle d'impédance optimal constitué de couches, pour expliquer au mieux les réflexions et leurs variations d'amplitudes dans le volume sismique (Gluck et al, 1994).
Un petit bloc de 1 km² a été inversé dans la partie centrale de la structure. Ce mini-bloc est recoupé par cinq puits. Les couches en impédance ont été chargées dans le modeleur surfacique 3D GOCAD pour décrire leurs variations.

La figure 3 présente une section impédance passant par les puits C,A,B. On peut remarquer une diminution importante de l'impédance moyenne du réservoir vers les puits A et C et un épaississement de la couche de faible impédance dans la même direction.
La diminution de l'impédance moyenne est à relier avec la présence du gaz et la limite inférieure de la tranche de faible impédance peut être interprétée comme une pseudo-interface eau gaz. Vers le puits B, cette interface remonte vers le toit du réservoir, dont seule la partie supérieure semble imprégnée par le gaz.

La figure 4 présente la carte iso-impédance de la tranche réservoir et confirme la réduction des impédances moyennes vers le nord par suite de la diminution de la hauteur imprégnée par le gaz . La figure 5 présente l'épaississement de la tranche réservoir imprégnée par le gaz vers le nord.

Afin d'évaluer les quantités de gaz et lever l'indétermination gaz-argile, une démarche originale a été expérimentée . Des "cross plots" impédance porosité ont été représentés au niveau des puits (voir les figures 7 et 8).
Trois pôles essentiels (porosité-impédance) ont été identifiés.
*   le pôle argileux se traduit par de fortes porosités apparentes  et de faibles impédances,
*   le pôle grès propre est caractérisé par de fortes impédances et des porosités apparentes faibles,
*   le pôle grès à gaz présente de faibles impédances et de faibles porosités apparentes.

Sur les puits forés avant la mise en gaz une relation linéaire a été déduite pour calculer la porosité apparente à partir de l'impédance acoustique. Cette porosité intègre l'effet de l'argile. En suivant cette relation, la diminution de l'impédance due au gaz se traduira par une augmentation de la porosité sismique apparente.
A partir des puits de la structure une carte des porosités apparentes réelles a été calculée en prenant en compte l'argile. Alors la comparaison des porosités sismiques avec les porosités réelles traduit l'état de saturation en gaz du réservoir.

La figure 6 présente la carte de pseudo-saturation en gaz du réservoir; on remarque sa cohérence avec les cartes précédentes (fig 4 et 5). Le puits A qui est le plus performant de la structure tombe dans la zone à plus forte saturation.
En combinant l'ensemble des cartes précédentes et en recherchant les zones ayant simultanément des faibles impédances moyennes, des fortes pseudo–épaisseurs de gaz et de fortes pseudo–saturations, il est possible de localiser les zones à plus fort potentiel réservoir.
La figure 9 présente l'intégration des trois cartes en terme de qualité réservoir. Cette démarche séduisante a été expérimentée sur une zone très limitée, elle demande à être étendue à l'intégralité du volume 3D pour être validée par l'ensemble des puits.

CONCLUSIONS

Les progrès récents des méthodes sismiques, tant sur l'acquisition que sur le traitement des données, permettent d'obtenir une bonne image du sous sol avec une résolution verticale suffisante pour étudier les réservoirs utilisés pour le stockage du gaz.

Contrairement aux informations de puits fiables mais ponctuelles, la sismique 3D fournit une image de moins bonne résolution mais qui a l'avantage d'être continue sur l'ensemble de la structure.
Le calage des informations sismiques aux puits est indispensable tant que pour le traitement que pour l'interprétation afin d'obtenir une image cohérente avec les puits.

La méthode d'interprétation la plus simple qui consiste à étudier la répartition spatiale des amplitudes au toit du réservoir fournit un résultat rapide mais qui demande une bonne connaissance de la structure et de la répartition des argiles pour localiser la bulle de gaz dans la partie superficielle du réservoir.

La méthode plus complexe, basée sur l'étude de la répartition spatiale des faibles impédances, nécessite d'associer plusieurs critères liés à la présence de gaz pour réaliser une cartographie des réservoirs de meilleure qualité.
Pour être validée cette démarche demande à être étendue à l'ensemble du bloc sismique 3D de manière à bien identifier les limites de la bulle de gaz et à vérifier les prévisions aux puits.

REFERENCES BIBLIOGRAPHIQUES

–Ch. Pinson et F. Huguet, 1994. –Apport de la sismique 3D pour la caractérisation d'un réservoir de stockage de gaz. Pétrole et Technique,391,pp.6.11
–S. Gluck, Y. Lafet et D. Mougenot, 1994. –3D.ROV: acoustic impedance(pv) in three dimensions. CGG Technical Series, 4p

**FIG. 1**

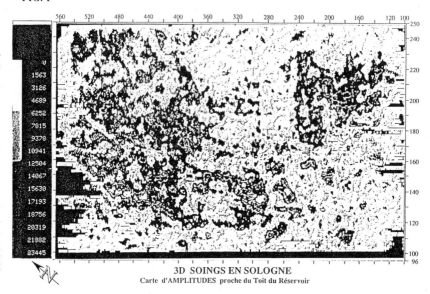

**3D  SOINGS EN SOLOGNE**
Carte  d'AMPLITUDES  proche du Toit du Réservoir

**FIG. 2**

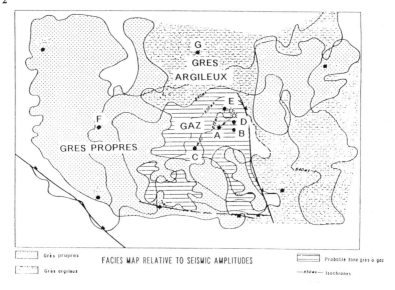

FACIES MAP RELATIVE TO SEISMIC AMPLITUDES

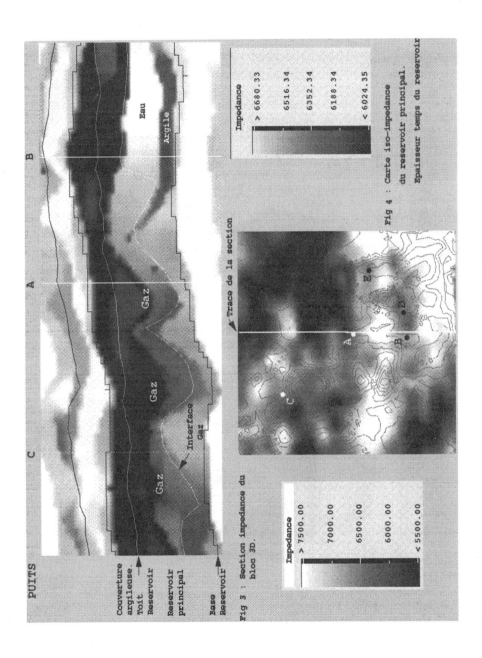

PUITS

A    B    C

Eau

Argile

Gaz

Gaz

Gaz

Gaz

Interface
Gaz

Couverture
argileuse.
Toit
Reservoir

Reservoir
principal

Base
Reservoir

Trace de la section

Impedance
> 6680.33
6516.34
6352.34
6188.34
< 6024.35

Fig 4 : Carte iso-impedance
du reservoir principal.
Epaisseur temps du reservoir

Fig 3 : Section impedance du
bloc 3D.

Impedance
> 7500.00
7000.00
6500.00
6000.00
< 5500.00

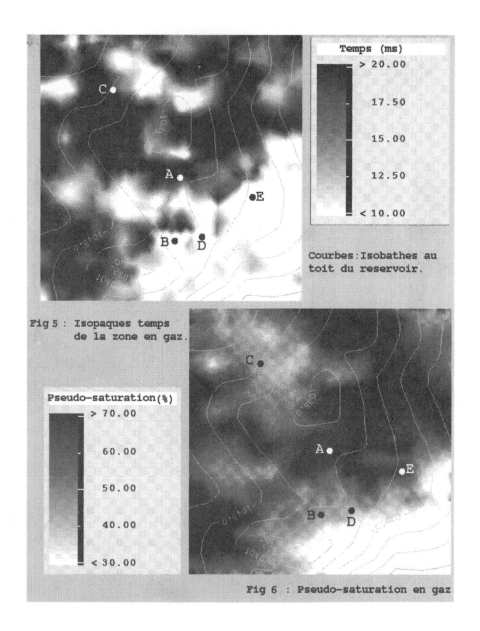

Courbes:Isobathes au toit du reservoir.

Fig 5 : Isopaques temps de la zone en gaz.

Fig 6 : Pseudo-saturation en gaz

FIG. 8 CROSS - PLOT IMPEDANCE- NEUTRON

PUITS C

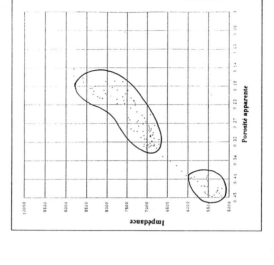

Ce puits foré avant la mise en gaz de la structure montre:
 – Le pôle argileux de la couverture
 – Le pôle grès à eau du réservoir
Contraste d'impédance couverture –réservoir fort
La sismique montre une amplitude faible
 --> réservoir en gaz

FIG. 7 CROSS - PLOT IMPEDANCE- NEUTRON

PUITS A

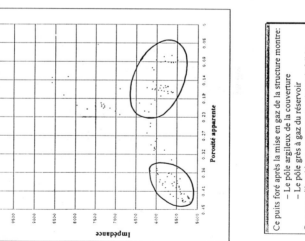

Ce puits foré après la mise en gaz de la structure montre:
 – Le pôle argileux de la couverture
 – Le pôle grès à gaz du réservoir
Contraste d'impédance couverture –réservoir faible
La sismique montre une amplitude faible

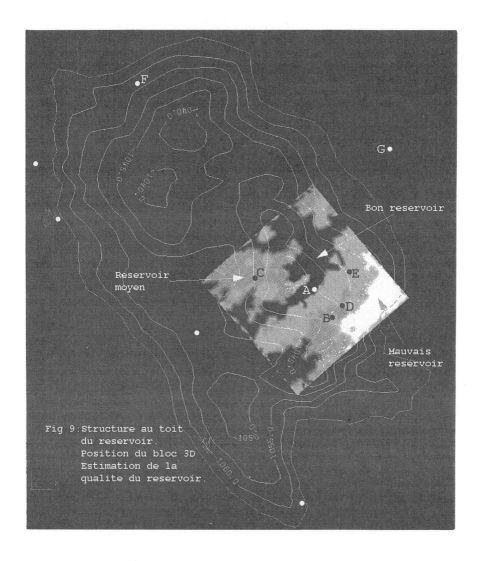

Fig 9:Structure au toit
      du reservoir.
      Position du bloc 3D
      Estimation de la
      qualite du reservoir.

PERFORMANCE TESTING OF A HORIZONTAL GAS STORAGE WELL UNDER VARIOUS
COMPLETION TECHNIQUES

TEST DE CAPACITE D'UN SONDAGE HORIZONTAL DU STOCK DE GAZ SOUS DIVERS
PROCEDURES COMPLEMENTAIRES

PETER R. ZEILINGER
OMV AG

ABSTRACT

Intensive investigations commenced in 1991 to determine the feasibility of converting the
depleted Zwerndorf-Vysoka gas field into gas storage in order to account for the rising
demand in gas supply and gas storage capacity.
The horizontal pilot well ZW 101 was drilled into the Zwerndorf Hauptsand reservoir in
October 1993 to test the performance and suitability of horizontal wells for this project.
The horizontal section of the well was designed and completed with an open-hole and a
cased hole section in order to evaluate and optimize the cost effectiveness and
performance of subsequent wells.
This paper describes the design and testing of the horizontal pilot well ZW 101. Results
from various tests performed in the horizontal section are presented, including
deliverability and production data, hole stability and reservoir parameters.


RESUME

Etant donné la demande croissante d'approvisionnement en gaz de stockage de celui-ci, des
études de faisabilité ont été entreprises en 1991 pour déterminer la possibilité de
transformation des gisements de gaz épuiseés de Zwerndorf-Vysoka en réservoir.
Le sondage-pilote horizontal ZW 101 a été foré dans le réservoir de Zwerndorf Hauptsand
en octobre 1993 afin de vérifier si un sondage horizontal est souhaitable pour ce type de
projet et, si oui, de tester les performances de celui-ci.
La section horizontale du sondage a été réalisée selon les plans avec une section non-tubée
et une section tubée en vue d'évaluer et d'optimiser les coûts et les performances des
sondages subséquents.
Ce document décrit les plans du sondage-pilote horizontal ZW 101 et les tests qui y ont
été effectués. Les résultats des tests différents de la section horizontale sont présenté ainsi
que la stabilité du trou de sonde, les caractéristiques du réservoir, les données de
production, et les possibilités de livraison.

## INTRODUCTION

As in many other industrialized countries gas demand in Austria showed a significant upswing in the last six years and grew more than 5% p.a. Steady improvement of the distribution network, advantages in environmental measures and low prices encouraged this development.
The rising demand in Austria necessitates its import, as domestic production only covers 22% of the total consumption at present.
Austria, which in 1968 was the first West European Country to import gas from the former USSR, is now playing an important role in the transportation of natural gas from the CIS to West European countries.
At the intake point at Baumgarten on the boarder of Slovakia, gas has been delivered since 1974 for transport via the Trans-Austria-Gasleitung (TAG) to Italy, and to former Yugoslavia via the Süd-Ost-Leitung (SOL).
Natural gas for France has been transported since 1980 via the West-Austrian-Gasleitung (WAG).
All three of these pipelines also transport gas for Austria's own needs.
To provide security and flexibility to compensate for the seasonal fluctuations large underground storage facilities have been built in the depleted sandstone reservoirs of the Vienna basin as well as in depleted gas reservoirs in the western part of Austria. They are used to supply the Austrian gas market with an entire working gas volume of more than $2.5*10^9$ m³ and a total capacity of more than $1*10^6$ m³/h.
Figure 1 presents the major gas pipelines and gas storage facilities in Austria.

OMV's forecast indicates that the remaining Eocene reservoirs will not fulfill working gas volume requirements over the next 20 years.
One main criteria of gas storage is the short distance to distributing pipelines. Therefore OMV conducted a study to determine the technical and economic feasibility of converting a large depleted gas field, which is in the immediate vicinity of an important Russian gas export pipeline, into storage.

One major aspect of this study was to investigate the advantages of using horizontal wells in gas storage projects to reduce investments and operating costs and enhance production and injection capacities.

This paper presents the extensive testing of a horizontal pilot well for a gas storage project in the depleted Zwerndorf gas reservoir.
It helps to provide a sound basis for completion evaluation and well performance analysis which can be used in the design and development of a gas storage project.

## THE ZWERNDORF - VYSOKA GAS RESERVOIR

The gas reservoir, located in the eastern part of Austria crossing the border to Slovakia, was discovered in 1952. It produced a total gas volume of $19.9*10^9$ m³ from a maximum of 52 wells during the years 1952 to 1992. Approximately 75% of the IGIP ($27*10^9$m³) has been produced.

The reservoir has an areal extent of 25 km² and is separated by the border into an Austrian and a Slovakian part. The structure of the reservoir is a flat anticline in the upper part of the Zwerndorf Sand which has a total thickness of 500 m. The maximum pay thickness of the gas zone is 80m and occurs at an average depth of 1300m subsea.
The Zwerndorf Sand is a fine to medium grained Sandstone, vertically divided into a series of lithological layers.
The Aquifer acted principally from the north of the reservoir which resulted in a continuous movement of the gas water contact from north to south. The Slovakian wells which were located in the north of the reservoir had to be abandoned by 1975.
In 1991 the top of the reservoir was flooded and only a small gas zone with 6 gas producing wells remained in the far south of the field.
Table 1 shows the initial reservoir data.

| IGIP | $27*10^9$ m³ | (990 BCF) |
|---|---|---|
| Ratio Austria/Slovakia | 1.654 : 1 | |
| Initial Pressure | 146.2 bar | (2119 psi) |
| Formation Temperature | 65 °C | (149 °F) |
| Average Water Saturation | 22% | |
| Average Porosity | 24% | |
| Average Permeability from Cores | 50 mD | |
| Maximum Pay Zone Thickness | 80 m | (262 ft) |
| Initial Gas Water Contact | -1350m (Subsea) | (4429 ft) |

Table 1 Zwerndorf Reservoir Data

## THE ZWERNDORF GAS STORAGE PROJECT

The Zwerndorf gas storage project is designed to handle a working gas volume of $1*10^9$ m³ to $3*10^9$ m³ with a capacity of $10*10^6$ m³/d to $30*10^6$m³/d in the final development stage. The maximum allowable storage pressure was set at 170 bar.
Simulation results in 1991 proved the technical feasibility of converting the subject gas pool into an underground gas storage reservoir.
The drilling of a vertical test well confirmed the model assumptions such as vertical and areal transmissibility reductions within the reservoir.
Additional investigations in the laboratory on reservoir cores as well as field and well tests were carried out, which clarified the technical and physical conditions to convert the reservoir into a gas storage.
An economic study based on these results showed that the high number (180) of vertical storage wells is a critical factor to the economic efficiency of the project.
Therefore, the possibility of using horizontal drilling to reduce the number of wells, by increasing productivity and injectivity was evaluated by drilling and testing the horizontal pilot well ZW 101 in October 1993.

## HORIZONTAL PILOT WELL ZW 101

The main objectives of this test well were to obtain :

- Information about reservoir parameters and maximum production and injection rates due to the technical and geometrical parameters of the well.

- Optimisation of gas flowing capacity and reduction of drilling, workover and completion costs of future wells by use of suitable completion concepts

- Information about the influence of injection and production cycles on borehole stability and performance of the horizontal well section.

The well was drilled from the kick off point at 1148m using a geosteering MWD/LDW tool to achieve a horizontal section of 500m in the top of the uppermost Zwerndorf sand layer.
Lithological information was transmitted with a time lag due to higher priority on directional data. As a result the top of the sand was recognised too late.
Therefore the well penetrated the Zwerndorf A1 to A3 sand layers before returning to the planned well path.

The first 250m of the 8.5" horizontal section were completed based on the monobore concept using a 7" liner. The 6" open hole section was completed with a 4.5" predrilled liner equipped with linerhanger, packer and landing nipple.
Figure 2 presents the completion design of the ZW 101 well.

Test design

One main objective was to test both horizontal sections selectively in order to be able to make a decision towards an optimum future completion procedure.
To achieve the required data mentioned above the following schedule was chosen :

| | |
|---|---|
| 1 | Pre test and Stimulation<br>to plan and optimize logistics and manpower and derive data about<br>borehole damage |
| 2 | Open hole section testing<br>to analyse well and reservoir parameters, flowing capacities, stimulation<br>results and borehole stability |
| 2a | Isolation of the open hole section with a bridge plug and perforating the cased hole<br>section |
| 3 | Cased hole section testing<br>well capacities, confirmation of reservoir parameters |
| 3a | Removal of the bridge plug |
| 4 | Capacity test of the total horizontal section |

Modified isochronal testing was chosen for the open hole capacity tests to minimize inaccuracies in analysis caused by operational constraints and depletion effects. Pressure analysis was carried out using EPS PAN System 2.1c software.
Every test sequence was simulated before testing using the latest well and reservoir results to optimize flowing periods, gauge programming and rate schedules.

Open hole testing

Three different tests were performed in the open hole section which consisted of production, injection and cyclic load testing.
Downhole pressures and temperatures were recorded by two memory gauges set at 1448m (MD).
Surface pressures and flow rates were measured at the wellhead and at the Baumgarten gas processing station, one km apart from the well site.
Figures 3 and 4 present pressures and flowrates documented in the multi-rate capacity tests.

Production test. To account for the depletion of 1.36 bar observed during the test, the recorded pressures had to be corrected according to the actual flowrate.
The different flow regimes occurring during the production test, such as wellbore storage, early vertical radial flow, hemi radial flow and late horizontal flow could be observed from the test analysis diagnostic plots. Figure 5 presents the Log Log Plot of the final build-up.

Conventional Horner analysis, type curve matching and derivative simulation led to the same results; 20 mD effective gas permeability, kh/kv of 10 and an effective well length of 175m.
This effective well length correlates with the above mentioned interbeddings, that have crossed the well path.
A comparison of well log data to the results obtained from the characteristic derivative helped to identify the vertical components of the reservoir taking part in the fluid flow.

The sandface deliverability was calculated to be 350,000 $m^3$/d with a 10 bar draw down and a reservoir pressure of 81.3 bar.
The performance of the well indicated an increased production capacity due to acid stimulation. This was confirmed by a skin analysis which showed a Darcy skin reduction from 1.7 in the pre-test to -1.5 in the production test.
A comparison of surface and downhole pressures showed a maximum $\Delta p$ of 11 bar indicating very small friction losses due to the chosen monobore completion concept.

Injection Test. The test confirmed the reservoir parameters obtained from the production test, however a small reduction in the Darcy skin was observed.
Maximum injection pressures and flowrates were limited by surface flowlines and facilities.

Although both gauges fell back into the hole while beeing removed, they did continue to record downhole pressures and temperatures.

After fishing with coiled tubing, the data was recovered intact as shown in figure 4.
Due to operational constraints in gas supply the last flowrate was limited to 24 hours and no stabilized flow was achieved during the injection stages.
Therefore the first results from the deliverability analysis based on the C&n method were considered as not representative.

A simulation of the injection test was carried out, based on the obtained reservoir parameters, allowing the last injection period to reach stabilized conditions. The results of the analysis of the simulated test are shown in figure 6.

Cyclic Load Test. The test simulated the cyclic load of a gas storage well under conditions of storage and production. Four cycles of injection ($1200*10^3$ m³/d) and production ($720*10^3$ m³/d to $960*10^3$ m³/d) were conducted. Each cycle consisted of 96 hours of injection and 96 hours of production.
A pressure build-up was performed following the last cycle to compare reservoir parameters to the production/injection test results. Sand production was checked at the wellhead and at the Baumgarten station. No substantial mobilisation of formation fines was observed.
Flowing pressure and skin analysis showed further improvement in flowing conditions due to the continuous clean up of the borehole.

Cased Hole Testing

After separation of the open hole section with a bridge plug the 7" liner was balanced perforated on drill pipe using a tubing gun with 6 SPF (0.51" holes, 28" perforation depth).
A flow after flow test was performed in the cased hole section to evaluate the applicability of different capacity tests on data quality and analysis.
Four step-wise flowrates (increasing from $303*10^3$ to $730*10^3$ m³/day) were followed by a final buildup. The total duration of the test was 600 hours, 400 hours flowing time and 200 hours shut in.
As observed in the open hole testing a depletion of approximately 1.4 bar occurred , which was corrected according to the actual rate schedule. The decrease was caused by pseudo steady flow due to reduction of the gas cap.

The quality of the data measured during the flow periods was influenced by variations in flow rates and downhole pressures. The unstable conditions caused great problems in analysing the step rate test for Darcy and variable skin.
A comparison of the total skin (Darcy + variable skin) showed a decreasing trend from the lowest to the maximum flowrate which was due to a continuous clean up of the perforated section.
The total skin from the last flowing period was comparable to the value obtained from the open hole testing.

Deliverability calculations were carried out using measured and simulated data.
Both analyses resulted in an approximate capacity of $400*10^3$ m³/d with 10 bar depletion at a reservoir pressure of 93 bar.
The effective well length contributing to the fluid flow was calculated at 190 m; this corresponds to the penetrated layers and their different reservoir qualities.
Due to the results of the open hole testing and the good matches of simulated and measured test data it was not necessary to perform an injection or cyclic load test in the perforated section.

Following the removal of the bridge plug an isochronal production test was carried out over the total horizontal section to compare the performance of the selectively tested sections to the total horizontal well capacity.
The well was produced at rates increasing from $283*10^3$ to $812*10^3$ m³/d followed by a final buildup.
Analysis of the final buildup revealed an effective horizontal well length of approximately 300 m and no further reduction in total skin. Deliverability results based on measured and simulated data yielded similar capacities of $500*10^3$ m³/d.

Figure 7 presents capacities of the ZW 101 well at different reservoir pressures based on the simulated and analysed results. Vertical well capacities are obtained from an isochronal test of the Zw30 well.

## CONCLUSIONS

The tests showed a positive performance of the open hole section on borehole stability and production/injection capacities.

For the homogeneous Zwerndorf standstone the option of selectively stimulating or production logging the cased hole section does not justify an increase in well costs of 25% for completion and perforation.

The applied test schedule was suitable for analysing the well and reservoir conditions of a horizontal gas storage well in a gas reservoir with an active water drive.
Proper simulation of the subsequent tests, based on previous analysis results helped to optimize the program .

Isochronal testing provided better quality data than flow after flow testing and, therefore allowed a more accurate analysis of turbulent skin and well capacities.

As presented in figure 8 the horizontal well Zwerndorf 101 showed a production capacity of 2.5 times the deliverability of a vertical well.

Effective well lengths obtained from individually tested horizontal sections cannot be added to predict performance over the total intervall. The effective well length represents those parts of the horizontal section contributing to fluid flow according to the predominant pressure distribution and geological properties.

Considering the penetrated interbeddings of lower reservoir quality, 50% of the total horizontal section contributing to the fluid flow is a high number. Despite this fact the well performance was below expectations.
Nevertheless, the required number of horizontal wells for the gas storage project is one quarter of the number of vertical wells. The higher costs of 40% for horizontal wells is outweighed by this fact.

## REFERENCES

(1)   ONDRACEK W., PASCHON F.X., SEITINGER P., "Feasibility Study of Zwerndorf-Vysoka" presented at the EAPG meeting Stavanger 1993.

(2)   FOITL E., WENNINGER G., HEINEMANN H.,"Completion Alternatives for Horizontal wells in Sour Gas",presented at the DGMK meeting Celle 1994.

(3)   JOSHI S., "Horizontal Well Technology" Penn Well Publishing Company 1991

(4)   PITTARD F., MADIGAN J., "Horizontal Gas Storage Wells Can Increase Deliverability presented at the American Gas Distribution Conference in Orlando, 1993

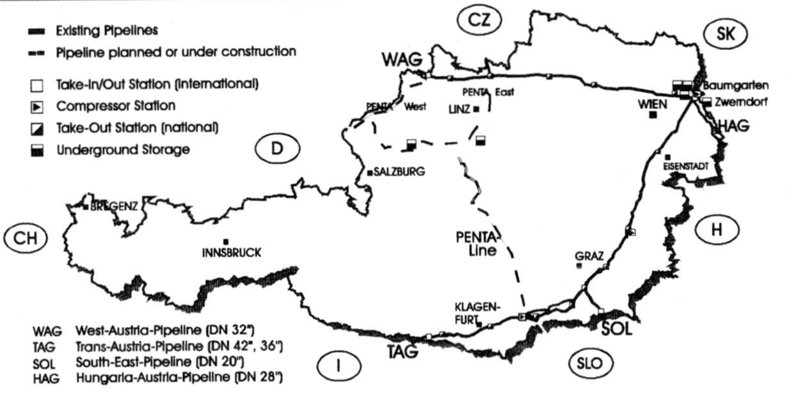
Existing Pipelines
Pipeline planned or under construction
Take-In/Out Station (International)
Compressor Station
Take-Out Station (national)
Underground Storage
CZ
SK
D
CH
H
I
SLO
WAG
PENTA West
PENTA East
LINZ
WIEN
Baumgarten
Zwerndorf
HAG
EISENSTADT
SALZBURG
BREGENZ
INNSBRUCK
PENTA Line
GRAZ
KLAGEN-FURT
SOL
TAG
WAG West-Austria-Pipeline (DN 32")
TAG Trans-Austria-Pipeline (DN 42", 36")
SOL South-East-Pipeline (DN 20")
HAG Hungaria-Austria-Pipeline (DN 28")

Figure 1 Major Gas Pipelines and Gas Storage Facilities in Austria

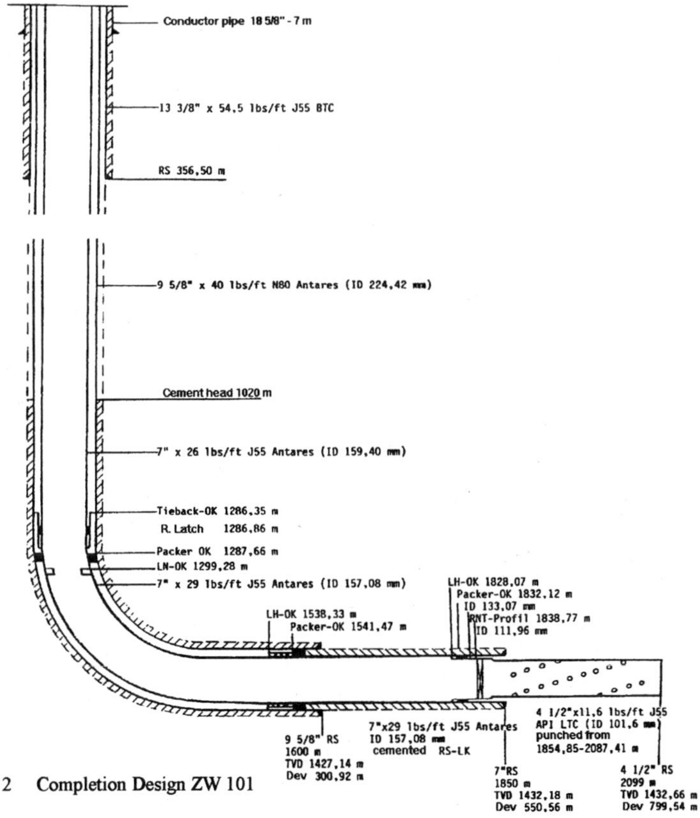
Conductor pipe 18 5/8" - 7 m
13 3/8" x 54,5 lbs/ft J55 BTC
RS 356,50 m
9 5/8" x 40 lbs/ft N80 Antares (ID 224,42 mm)
Cement head 1020 m
7" x 26 lbs/ft J55 Antares (ID 159,40 mm)
Tieback-OK 1286,35 m
R. Latch 1286,86 m
Packer OK 1287,66 m
LN-OK 1299,28 m
7" x 29 lbs/ft J55 Antares (ID 157,08 mm)
LH-OK 1538,33 m
Packer-OK 1541,47 m
LH-OK 1828,07 m
Packer-OK 1832,12 m
ID 133,07 mm
RNT-Profil 1838,77 m
ID 111,96 mm
9 5/8" RS
1600 m
TVD 1427,14 m
Dev 300,92 m
7"x29 lbs/ft J55 Antares
ID 157,08 mm
cemented RS-LK
7"RS
1850 m
TVD 1432,18 m
Dev 550,56 m
4 1/2"x11,6 lbs/ft J55
API LTC (ID 101,6 mm)
punched from
1854,85-2087,41 m
4 1/2" RS
2099 m
TVD 1432,66 m
Dev 799,54 m

Figure 2 Completion Design ZW 101

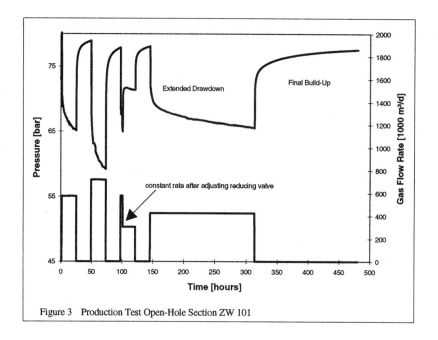

Figure 3    Production Test Open-Hole Section ZW 101

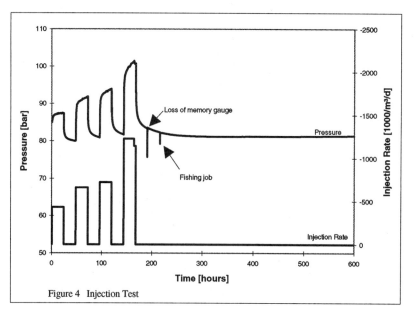

Figure 4    Injection Test

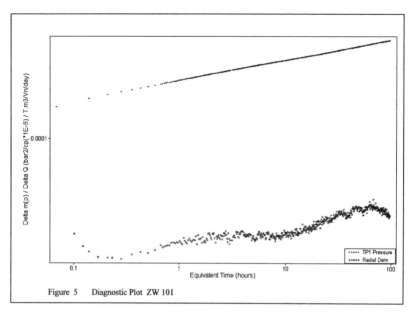

Figure 5    Diagnostic Plot  ZW 101

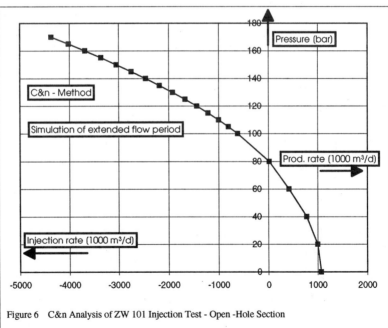

Figure 6    C&n Analysis of ZW 101 Injection Test - Open -Hole Section

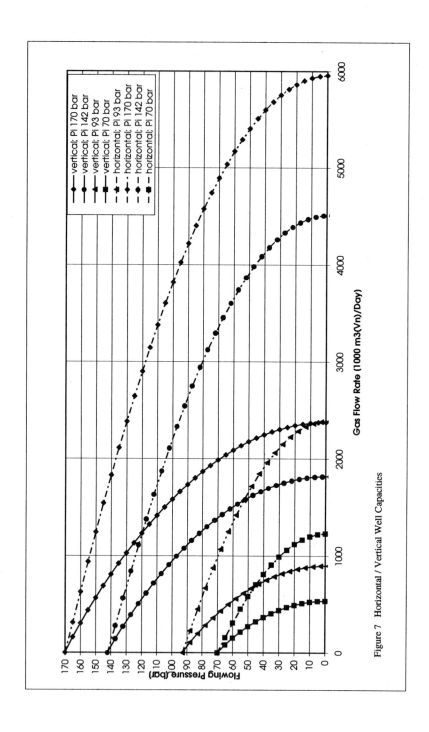

Figure 7   Horizontal / Vertical Well Capacities

**SATELLITE DATA IN DESIGN, MAINTENANCE,
SURVEY PHASES FOR THE GAS TRANSPORT INDUSTRY**

**DONNEES DE SATELLITE DANS LE PROJET, LA
MAINTENANCE, LA SURVEILLANCE POUR L'INDUSTRIE DU GAZ**

**B. Andreetto, A. Cappanera and F. Santangelo
SNAM SpA, ITALY**

## ABSTRACT

The availability of a tool, as a procedure based on the remote sensing, for automatic acquisition of a large number of data on the territory, land use, and population density represents a valid support to collect up-dated information that can be utilized in the definition of design choices, energy policies and in territorial planning from a maintenance point of view. In effect an infrastructure such as a gas transmission pipeline with a linear lay-out extended for hundreds of kilometres and involving a large number of different site typologies, needs a lot of information. To collect this information in a quick and reliable way SNAM is evaluating the remote sensing techniques as a valid support and tool for its activity. In this paper are presented some automatic procedures that have been performed utilizing remote sensing techniques and that have been utilized to build up data banks and different thematic maps.

## RÉSUMÉ

La possibilité d'avoir à disposition une procedure developpée avec l'utilisation des informations de satellites pour l'acquisition automatique d'une grande quantité de données sur le territoire, sur l'utilisation du terrain et sur la densité de la population, représents un bon support pour réunir des information mises a jour. Ces informations peuvent être utilisées pour la definition des choix de projet, des strategies énergétiques, de la planification du territoire pour la maintenance. En effet une infrastructure comme un gazoduc, qui se développe linéairement pour beaucoup de kilomètres et concerne differents typologies d'endroits, a besoin de beaucoup d'informations. Pour réunir ces informations rapidement et dans un moyen adapté à ses besoins, SNAM est en train de considerer les satellites comme une source pour supporter ses activités. Dans cet exposé sont presentées quelques procedures automatiques que ont été réalisées en utilisant les tecniques de satellite et que ont été utilisées pour construire data banks et des differentes cartes thématiques.

## INTRODUCTION

SNAM can satisfy the greater and greater Italian gas demand via a gas pipeline network of some 25,000 km which covers most of the country and which is continuously developed.

This network has to assure an uninterrupted gas supply in highly safe conditions for people, dwellings and environment, complying with environmental and safety regulations that are getting stricter and stricter in Italy and throughout Europe.

This progress needs an effort more and more qualified and onerous in design, construction and management of the gas lines.

Fast and economical management of all the complex data required for these activities is not easy.

To improve the phase of data collection, SNAM has decided to approach the remote sensing techniques by means of satellites.

For the last twenty years, a small revolution has happened in this field because of the large number of information, the rapidity of acquisition, extension, precision and resolution of images, the frequency of the surveys have assured a new knowledge of land geography and more frequent up-dating possibilities for the compilation of territorial thematic maps.

Each image from satellite is composed of millions of square elements that define the structure and the resolution: the pixels (picture elements).

The satellite cannot tell details smaller than a pixel. Each of them carries information of a part of territory recorded from satellites during their flights.

After many years of experiments and development, the use of remote sensing has found many different applications: agriculture, classification of forests, hydrology and oceanography, geology and geophysics, town-planning, meteorology.Moreover, satellite data can be integrated with other sources of information to get a particular precision.

The main difficulties consist in the integration of different data typologies and the research nowadays is fine tuning the existing techniques.

Because of the good results obtained and of the availability of satellites, costs for the compilation of thematic maps are competitive with the traditional techniques on the ground.

On the basis of these considerations, SNAM R&D Division has decided to develop some procedures utilizing remote sensing techniques to collect data and manage a data bank concerning territory and human activities.This information can be utilized in different life phases of lines, from route selection to management.

SNAM procedures have been carried out by AQUATER, a company of ENI Group, with experiences in the treatment of satellite images and in expert software packages on environmental issues.

The current application fields of the procedures are:
- design of pipelines, particularly in the route selection phase;
- acquisition of data on the population distribution (integrated with census data) and land use patterns along the routes of the pipelines;
- individuation of infrastructures potentially utilizing fuel on the territory;
- survey of the network.

The procedures use images obtained from civil satellites with medium resolution. These images on sample areas, treated and corrected, have been utilized in expert systems (i.e. automatic recognition of towns and single buildings) that can build up data banks and different thematic maps: land use, slope state, urban and industrial areas.

Other thematic maps on hydrography and roads are being carried out.

## LAND USE MAP

A land use map can be utilized both in locating a gas line route and in maintenance of an operational gas pipeline.

In this study, territorial data have been automatically generated by means of "passive" sensors able to point out and measure the reflected sun energy from different soil coverings such as woods, meadows, etc.

The percentage of reflected energy depends on wave length and chemical-physical properties of land surface, so that it is possible to define and classify territory shares by similar spectral characteristics.

In this research, a procedure for unsupervised automatic classification - which allows to subdivide the territory in homogeneous classes depending on radiance - has been carried out (see Figure 1).

The procedure is developed in six different phases:

- requirements definition
- image selection
- image correction
- automatic unsupervised classification of images
- interpretation of covering classes
- integration with processing of multitemporal images.

Requirements of a land use map are its geographic precision, the legend definition and its thematic accuracy. Particularly, the procedure does not depend on the chosen legend while geographic precision and thematic accuracy depend on pixel size and field investigations.

The image selection is one of the most important requirements for the realization of a map.

In fact, kinds of data used as primary source and the period to acquire them, affect on characteristics of thematic maps. In this study, images from the Thematic Mapper (TM) sensor of the Landsat 5 satellite (resolution 30x30 m and spectral resolution of seven bands) have been selected.

Further, a multitemporal analysis has been performed and two images have been acquired at different times to obtain an improved discrimination of different coverings. Moreover, the procedure does not depend on the sensor.

Because of the noise effects due to the atmosphere (scattering, absorption, light refraction), images have been corrected by means of techniques that do not depend on the acquisition of atmospheric parameters and on the sensor calibration.

Besides, a geometric correction of the image system has been carried out to avoid possible distortions and to geocode every pixel on plane coordinates.

During the classification phase of a map, the procedure allows to choose different legend on condition that they are legible in the spectrum.

In this case the following operations are performed step by step:

- stratification of the region in homogeneous areas utilizing other sources of information: DTM, agronomic data, statistic data;
- an unsupervised classification for every homogeneous area obtained by the stratification is completed. This activity is splitted in two steps: clustering, that puts pixels in similar spectral groups (clusters) and the cluster interpretation by the operator, to classify them in one of the selected thematic classes;
- the homogeneous areas are automatically assembled to rebuild the whole region.

The possibility to have more than one image of the same region, but recorded at different period, has allowed to perform a reiteration of the process (multitemporal analysis) identifying a very high percentage of classified (see Figure 2).

In effect the clouds affect the performance of the system, and the multitemporal analysis allows to reduce the hidden areas.

These operations produce thematic maps on the scale of 1:25,000.

In this study a map on 1:25,000 has been carried out with the following legend:

- no vegetation areas
- conifer woods
- broadleaf woods

- mixcd woods
- permanent crops
- arable lands
- pastures and productive uncultivated
- urban areas
- surface waters.

By this classification, the map can be a valid support for both design and maintenance phases of a gas line to help technicians in their choices.

## SLOPE STATE MAP

The slope state map is used during localisation phase of a gas line route.
For its definition, it has been necessary to carry out the algorithm for the production of DTM (Digital Terrain Model) by means of the following operations:
- triangulation
- matching
- intersection and interpolation

Two panchromatic images have been used (10 m resolution and different angles of incidence). These pictures have been chosen taking into account the following requirements:
- no cloud covering
- time interval among acquisitions of images as little as possible
- acquisition time in the summer.

During the triangulation phase, cinematic and geometric parameters of the satellite are estimated. Typically, this operation takes 9 seconds for the acquisition of one picture.

The matching phase is a fully automatic process to find homologous points on the two images previously taken. This is obtained by means of a radiometric correlation algorithm and is a critical phase for the DTM procedure, because long processing times are necessary (typically, 1 day for an area of 3.000 km$^2$).

The following intersection phase of homologous points produces a set of points in the space, representing the land surface. The interpolation of these points allows to obtain the DTM in raster format. In this study, a DTM has been provided with cells 50x50 m rectified by hand by means of a map on 1:25.000 for those areas where interpretation was misleaded due mainly to shadow phenomena.

From this DTM, a slope state map has been performed with the following legend:
areas with slope between 0 and 25%
areas with slope between 25 and 50%
areas with slope between 50 and 75%
areas with slope between 75 and 100%.

The slope calculation has been carried out for any pixel by means of a window of 3x3 pixels centered on the considered point. Inside this window, the average slope has been calculated both in direction East-West (Sew) and in direction North-South (Sns).

The average slope of the point has been calculated with the following expression:
$$S = \text{sqrt } (Sew^2 + Sns^2)/2$$

## EVALUATION OF POPULATION DISTRIBUTION DENSITY IN AREAS ALONG GAS LINES.

A panchromatic sensor on the SPOT satellite has been used to identify buildings and population distribution in a geographic area crossed by a gas line. The sensor geometric resolution is 10x10 m, so that data can be collected as far as a single building.

First, the images utilized have been pretreated to eliminate systematic (speed satellite variations, Earth rotation, etc.) and not systematic errors (altitude, trim variations of the satellite).
Then two algorithms have been developed, utilizing the rectified images, to identify the urban surface and to estimate the population distribution density.

Algorithm to identify the urban surface.

The identification of buildings from satellite images has been one of the more difficult research items. To get this result, a quantitative procedure has been produced, overcoming the limits of a qualitative procedure based on interpretation.
This choice has been followed to set objective and, consequently, replicable techniques, to generate procedures that can be implemented on a computer to use a system which is managed by a GIS (Geographic Information System).
From the beginning, the execution of this activity has showed a remarkable complexity due to the large spectral variability (for instance, roof coverings are built by various materials that differ considerably among them), the variable size of the buildings, the different structural frameworks that can be met. The "Mathematical Morphology" technique has been adopted to identify a building. This technique is based on the combination of the geometric characteristics of the object and its own radiometric signal.Considerations about the shape of the objects taken have allowed to distinguish buildings from other kinds of objects that had the same signal spectrum but a different structure like, for instance, roads with their linear shape. The estimation about the different levels of radiometric signal, like "the discountinuity" of the signal passing from an object to another, has allowed to identify buildings located in rural and in urban areas.An application near Pordenone (North-Eastern Italy) has been carried out to verify the methodology and the obtained results have been satisfactory;about 90% of the information were correct. The discordances between indications deriving from the automatic system and from the survey are due to:
- low resolution (pixel 10x10 m)
- impossibility for the system used to distinguish actual buildings from other kinds of construction (for instance, ruins or water conditioners)
- vegetation shield.

Statistical algorithm to define the population distribution

The algorithm, extremely simple, is based on the knowledge of the people number living or working in the interested area and on the building surface of the same area.
The source of data have been the ISTAT (Italian Statistical Institute), from which the people number living in each census area is obtained, and the information getting by the above algorithm from which the position and the surface of each building is obtained. By means of these input data, a number of people has been related to each urbanised surface:

$$np_{kj} = \sum_{j=1}^{ns} \frac{NPj}{SUj} \cdot su_{kj}$$

where:
$np_{kj}$ = number of people evaluated in the building k belonging to census area j
$NP_j$ = total number of people in the whole census area j (ISTAT)
$SU_j$ = urban surface identified by satellite in census area j
$su_{kj}$ = surface of the building k, identified by satellite, belonging to census area j·
$ns$ = number of census areas intersecting building surface

In this way the population has been geocoded with a good precision, to allow users, who can have a GIS software, "to query" the situation of the studied area.

## PIPELINE ROUTING

To be able to plan maintenance and survey interventions on existing gas lines, it has been necessary to connect all the information on territory, that has been obtained from the automatic procedure (for instance the urbanisation of the area), with the gas line routing and more in detail with the positioning of the single pipe.

For this reason it is necessary to locate the line and its components in a computer map, like the other territorial data.

To get it, a digital mapping phase of the pipeline route has been carried out.

Two steps have been followed: first, using a map on 1:25,000 with the pipeline route and a digitizer, the line has been digitized and overlapped on the computer map by the UTM coordinates (Universal Transverse Mercator) of its vertex (points where there is a change of direction); then a digital pipeline tally (obtained, for instance, after pigging) has been used to locate each single pipe ("tube") in the computer map by its UTM coordinates. In fact, these coordinates are achieved considering a pipeline vertex as starting point (with well-known coordinates) and projecting the length and the orientation of the single pipe reported on the pipeline tally on the line path previously digitized. The achievable accuracy depends on the number of check points of pipeline tally of which the correct UTM coordinates are known (these check points can be located in road crossings, river crossings and so on and are reported on pipeline tally). So each single pipe composing the pipeline has been positioned by its geographic coordinates and can now be managed by a GIS system.

The structure of the methodology for the evaluation of population distribution density and for land use soil is showed in Figure 3.

## STRUCTURES POTENTIALLY UTILIZING FUEL

To get information on structures potentially utilizing fuel on the territory, a calculation procedure has been set to estimate dwellings, industrial volumetry and the main road network in any studied area.

The obtained data will be input in an already available SNAM code evaluating the air pollutant sources. Then it will be possible to simulate different scenarios and plan gas market strategies in sectors and territories particularly interesting.

To calculate dwellings and industrial volumetry, ISTAT data about population and industry have been integrated with processed stereoscoping satellite images to estimate the average height of urban areas and with pictures taken by plane to distinguish industrial sites from inhabited areas.

To define the road network, an algorithm has been developed that utilizes SPOT images (10x10 m) able to identify linear elements and to eliminate elements that are not roads.

## CONCLUSIONS - FUTURE DEVELOPMENT

The main purpose of setting procedures, based on the remote sensing for the automatic acquisition of data on territory, land use and population density, is to provide SNAM with an alternative way to get further information relating to its operating reality. This goal has been partially achieved.In fact, knowledge of the land use type, the characteristics of ground morphology, the possibility to evaluate the population distribution in an area can supply more and more useful indications to the user in the design and maintenance of gas pipelines. The completed procedures, even if they offer satisfactory results, can be still improved. First of all, sensors can be chosen overcoming the limitations of resolution. At present, for this research, commercial sensors for civil satellites have been used, but more sophisticated sensors will be available in a short while; in particular, both air-borne and next satellite generation sensors could considerably improve the resolution level. This will overcome inaccuracies and errors now present, but will not invalidate the generated procedure that does not depend on the kind of sensor. This research has to be considered a first step in the use of more sophisticated technologies for achieving and managing computerized knowledge that can come out very useful to run complex plants like SNAM gas pipelines.

## REFERENCES

1.  D. G. Koger "A close look at photogeology, remote sensing, and image analysis", Oil & Gas Journal, December 5th, 1988, p. 54

2.  G. Inghilleri "Topografia Generale", UTET (italian version)

3.  I. Serra "Image analysis and mathematical morphology", Academic Press Inc.

4.  P. F. Fisher, R. E. Linderberg "On distinction among Cartography, Remote Sensing and Geographic Information System", P.E.&R.S., Vol. 52. pp. 1507–1511

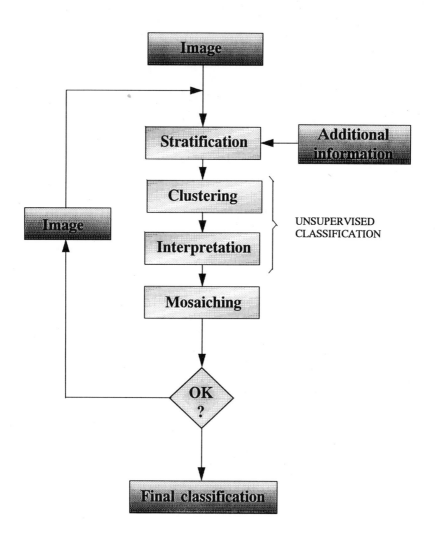

figure 1

IMAGE TM 24/05/94

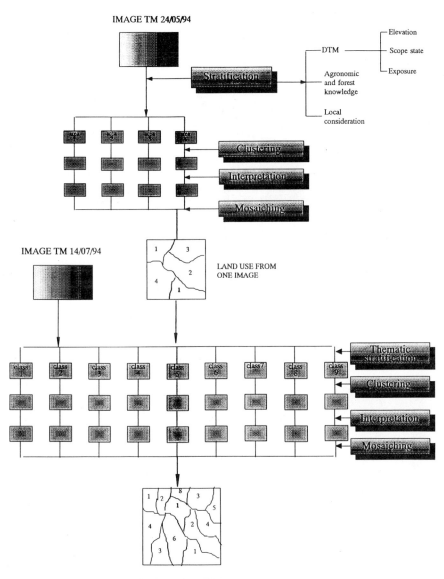

FINAL LAND USE CLASSIFICATION

figure 2

*Methodology for the evaluation of population
distribution density and for
land use soil in areas along gas line*

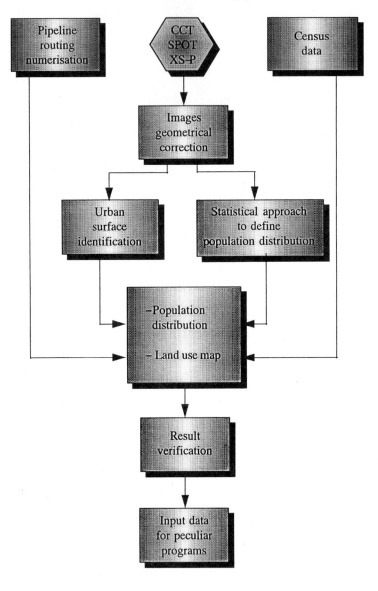

figure 3

ACOUSTIC GAS LEAK MONITORING

AVERTISSEMENT ACOUSIQUE POUR LE COULAGE DE GASE

*Michael Savic*
savic@ecse.rpi.edu
Electrical Computer and System Engineering Department
Signal and Speech Research Laboratory
Rensselaer Polytechnic Institute
Troy, NY 12180
USA
Tel. 518-276-6388

ABSTRACT

Presented are several new approaches to the continuous leak monitoring problem in above ground and underground gas pipelines. The permanently placed monitoring units along the pipeline detect acoustic signals in the pipeline and discriminate leak sounds from other man made or natural non--leak sounds that can occur. The units communicate with a central station to alert the monitoring personnel in case of a leak

RESUME

Nous presentons plusieurs maniere pour decovrir le coulage continuel de gase par des pipe qui sont enterrer ou non. Les transduceurs son placer tout le long de la pipe et donne un signal "son" qui est uniques pour le coulage de gase continuel. En tous de cas de coulage de gase, un signal est presenter a une station centrale pour avertir les personne en charge d'operation.

## 1.    INTRODUCTION

Fast, reliable detection of leaks of hazardous materials from storage and pipeline facilities is an important problem. This paper presents new continuous acoustic leak detection systems for above ground and underground high pressure gas pipelines.

Systems developed in this work can detect leaks as small as 1/32" in diameter in pipelines carrying gas under high pressure. The systems consists of remote signal collection and analysis units placed at a predetermined distance from each other along the pipeline. The units communicate with a central station to alert the monitoring personnel in case of a leak Fig. (1.1). The remote units monitor the acoustic signals in the pipeline. Without a leak present, units $T_1$–$T_N$, will pick up sounds of the substance flowing through the pipeline, compressor and pump noises, and external sound noises such as trains and cars. If a leak is present, the sound that the leak generates will travel through the pipeline and will be picked up by at least one of the remote units. Each unit is able to discriminate the leak sound from all other sounds and to communicate the result to the central station, which in turn will alert the users.

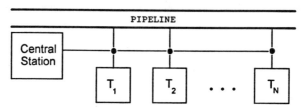

Figure 1.1: Pipeline Monitoring System

Our experiments were conducted on underground and above ground pipelines. The underground pipeline was a Texaco ethylene pipeline running from the storage facility in Sour Lake, Texas, to the chemical plant in Port Arthur, Texas. This approximately 40 mile long pipeline has an internal diameter of 7 inches and 0.5 inch thick walls. The internal pressure of that pipeline is 1,500 PSI and the pipeline is buried in soil that is usually damp. The above ground pipeline is a low pressure Texaco pipeline at the Humble cite in Texas with an external diameter of $D = 6.625$ in. .

## 2.    LEAK DETECTION

In order to find useful features to discriminate leaks from other sounds, the leak signals had to be generated and sampled. Because it was dangerous to generate leaks in the real pipeline, a leak simulator was built from a section of the pipe similar to the buried one. The simulator had a port into which different leak modules with varying hole shapes and sizes could be plugged. The simulator was filled with nitrogen gas to the pressure in the live pipeline, a valve was opened letting the gas escape through the hole in the leak module, and the sound that was generated was recorded.

The next step was to determine the dominant features that represent the leak signals. A leak sound is generated by turbulence due to the difference in pressure between the gas in the pipe and the environment. This turbulence can be modeled by a white noise process. The sound of the leak is generated when this white noise signal passes through a spectral shaping filter. The parameters of this filter predominately depend on the shape and size of the leak , and on pipeline dimensions. Thus a leak signal can be modeled as an output of a rational pole–zero filter driven by a white noise process.

$$H(z) = G\frac{1+\sum_{k=1}^{q}b[k]z^{-k}}{1+\sum_{k=1}^{p}a[k]z^{-k}} \tag{2.1}$$

where $G$ is the gain of the filter, $q$ and $p$ are the number of zeros and poles respectively, and $b[k]$ and $a[k]$ are the moving average and autoregressive coefficients respectively. When the input to this filter is a unit variance white noise process, $w[n]$, the output, $x[n]$, is determined by the difference equation:

$$x[n] = -\sum_{k=1}^{p}a[k]x[n-k]+G\sum_{k=0}^{q}b[k]w[n-k] \tag{2.2}$$

Inversely, the ARMA parameters $p$, $q$, $a[k]$, $b[k]$, and $G$ can be determined from the sampled signal, $x[n]$, using one of the available algorithms [6]. We used for the detection of leaks two different methods, the first is based on LPC cepstrum coefficients, and the other on frequency spectrum of the leak signal.

### 2.1   The LPC cepstrum method

Using the LPC cepstrums as features [7] we have:

$$h[n] = a[n]+\sum_{k=1}^{n-1}\frac{k}{n}h[k]a[n-k] \tag{2.3}$$

The training set was derived from the leak sounds collected using a leak simulator and various non–leak sounds collected in the field and the lab. In order to maximize the detection distance, effects due to propagation must be considered. Using equation (2.3), the pipeline can be modeled as a distance dependent filter of the form:

$$H_P(\omega,x) = e^{-m_o \tau |\omega|/(2\pi T)} e^{j\phi(\omega)x} \qquad (2.4)$$

with $T$, the sampling period, set to 24.4 μs. $m_0$ was experimentally found to be $2.45\times10^{-6}$ sec$^2$/meter, with $x$ in meters. This form assumes that the attenuation constant, $\alpha$, can be approximated by a linear relation with frequency:

$$\alpha = m_0 f \qquad (2.5)$$

the experimental results shown later in this paper proved this assumption to be true. Equation (2.8) represents a lowpass filter with the pass band narrowing with distance $x$. When pipeline effects are ignored, the maximum detection distance does not exceed 50 meters. To solve these problems the propagation effects were taken into account during classifier training. The leak sounds collected using the leak simulator were the signals at $x=0$. Eight distance checkpoints were set-up every 50 meters, $x=0$, 50, ..., 350, and both leak and non–leak signals from the training set were estimated at these checkpoints using equation (2.8). The resulting estimates were added to the training set.

## 2.2 The Frequency Spectrum Method

The sound of the leak signal received at the remote unit is picked up by a piezoelectric transducer attached to the wall of the pipeline and converted into an electric signal. This signal has a complex frequency spectrum that is produced by poles and zeros of the source of the sound, as well as by the poles and zeros of the section of the pipeline between the source of the sound and the location of the transducer. First let us discuss the source of the sound. Gaseous or liquid media under pressure leaking through a small hole undergo turbulent motions. This turbulence produces a Gaussian excitation that tends to cause the pipeline section close to the leak to oscillate at its resonant frequencies. A pipeline has many resonant frequencies that can be found by equations utilizing Bessel Functions, however we will focus only on dominant resonant frequencies which give the largest amplitudes. One of these dominant resonant frequencies is

$f_d = 2/C$ where $C$ is the internal circumference of the pipeline. Consequently $C = \lambda_d/2$; $\lambda_d$ is the wavelength

of the dominant harmonic. The pipeline behaves as a lowpass filter with a cutoff frequency $f_c$.

## 3. PROPAGATION OF ACOUSTIC WAVES THROUGH PIPELINES

The propagation of acoustic waves through a pipeline can be described by the wave equation :

$$\frac{\partial^2 \xi}{\partial t^2} = c^2 \nabla^2 \xi \qquad (3.1)$$

where $\xi$ is the particle displacement from its mean position, $c$ is the speed of sound in the pipeline and $\nabla$ is the Laplace operator. Solving this equation, however, is not easy. Pipeline geometry does not yield simplifications to (3.1). Furthermore, because the pipeline might be buried, possibly in wet ground, the characteristic acoustic impedances of the metal and the ground are relatively close in magnitude, and losses of acoustic power occur at the boundaries. In order to avoid solving equation (3.1) an acoustic transmission line model of the pipeline was utilized. This model is similar to the electric transmission line. The electric elements: $R$ the resistance--per--unit length, $L$ the inductance--per--unit length, $C$ the capacitance--per--unit length, and $G$ the leakage conductance--per--unit length are replaced with the appropriate mechanical constants: $R_m$ the damping due to friction--per--unit length, $M$ the mass--per--unit length, $C_m$ the compliance--per--unit length, and $G_m$ the loss at the boundaries--per--unit length, respectively.

Assuming that a force $F$ is acting at one end of the transmission line and the other end of the line is loaded with mechanical impedance $Z_r$, the force $F_m$ at an element $dx$, at a distance $x$ from the loaded end (Figure 3.2) will be [4]:

$$F_m = F_r \cosh(\gamma x) + \dot{\xi}_r Z_0 \sinh(\gamma x) \qquad (3.2)$$

where $F_r$ is the force at the loaded end of the line, $\dot{\xi}_r$ is the particle velocity at the loaded end, $\gamma = \alpha + j\beta$ is the propagation constant ($\alpha$ is the attenuation constant and $\beta$ is the phase constant) and $Z_0$ is the mechanical characteristic impedance of the line. Note that force, particle velocity and the propagation constant are all phasor quantities and thus are complex and depend on frequency.

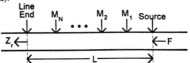

Figure 3.2: Mechanical Transmission Line

ts $M_1$–$M_N$ equation (3.2) becomes a system of equations which can be solved for the unknown transmission line parameters, $\alpha$, $\beta$ and the product $\xi'_r Z_0$. The sound source was produced by a steel ball, 1 inch in diameter, that was dropped on the pipeline from the height of 4 inches. This produced a sound impulse in the pipe that was then measured at a number of points along the pipeline. In our model, the length of the transmission line $L$ was set to 500 feet. The system of equations derived from (3.2) is non–linear and is difficult to solve, even if sophisticated numerical methods are used. Because the pipeline and the ground it is buried in are uniform throughout, $Z_0 = Z_r$. Using this equality, equation (3.2) can be greatly simplified to the form [4]:

$$F_m = F_r e^{\gamma x} \tag{3.3}$$

and taking logarithms of both sides gives:

$$\ln F_m = \ln F_r + \gamma x \tag{3.4}$$

Which is a linear relation in $\gamma$.

## 4.   EXPERIMENTAL RESULTS

A critical part of this project was to determine the sound signature generated by the leak signals. Because the pipeline on which the work was performed contained highly explosive gas, it was impractical to generate artificial leaks in the real pipeline for training. Furthermore, it was suspected that different leak shapes would generate different signatures. The alternative was to build a leak simulator from a section of the pipe. This simulator was built at the Texaco Bellare labs. The layout of this simulator is shown in Fig. (4.1). The hole shapes that can generally be encountered in the pipe are round holes, wide slits and narrow slits. Six different leak modules containing these hole shapes were constructed. The general leak collection strategy involved filling the simulator with nitrogen gas from a high pressure tank to the pressure that exists in the pipeline, opening the ball valve to release the gas through one of the installed leak modules, and recording the resulting acoustic signal.

### 4.1  The LPC Cepstrum Approach

Pipeline propagation experiments were performed on a Texaco ethylene carrying pipeline at Sour Lake, Texas. The section of the pipeline was 500 feet long and was buried in damp soil. A steel ball was used, as described in section 3 of this paper. The attenuation constant, $\alpha$ versus frequency was calculated using equation (3.4). The plot of $\alpha$ vs. frequency is shown in Fig. (4.2).

The phase constant, $\beta = \phi(\omega)$, was also calculated using equation (3.4). The result was randomly distributed with frequency, and uncorrelated. $\beta$ was, thus, modeled as a random process with Maxwell probability density function as shown in Fig. (4.3).

System evaluation was performed using simulations on a workstation, and field experiments. The scatter plot of cepstrum coefficients of leak sounds generated using the leak simulator in Fig. (4.1) is shown in Fig. (4.4). This plot shows that the cepstrum coefficients projected into the two best directions can be used not only to discriminate the leak from other sounds but also to identify the size and the shape of the leak.

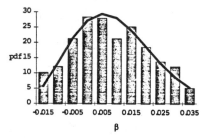

Figure 4.3: Probability density function of $\beta$

The system had no problems rejecting non–leak sounds generated at any distance from the receiver. In the worst case $n/N$ did not exceed 0.2 (e.g. at most 20 vectors out of 100 were misclassified as leaks). In addition the system had no problems recognizing leaks when the leak and the receiver were close. As expected, the performance degraded with distance. The recognition vs. distance results are summarized for various leaks in table (4.1):

| Distance (meters) | 1/8"x1/4" Slit $n/N$ | 1/16"x1/4" Slit $n/N$ |
|---|---|---|
| <260 | 1 | 1 |
| 280 | 0.89 | 0.79 |
| 300 | 0.68 | 0.61 |
| >320 | <0.14 | <0.40 |

Table 4.1

### 4.2 The Frequency Spectrum Approach

Let us observe for instance the Texaco gas pipeline at the Humble cite in Texas. The outer diameter of this pipeline is D = 6.625 in. and the thickness of the walls d, as shown in Fig. (4.5).

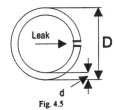

Fig. 4.5

The outer diameter in centimeters is D=6.625 in = 6.625*2.54=16.828 cm

Let us assume that there is a leak and observe the narrow segment of the pipe which includes the leak. Let us stretch this segment into a stripe with a thickens d, length l and width δ as shown in Fig. (4.6)

Fig. 4. 6

The length of the circumference of the pipeline is  l = D*3.14 = 16.8*3.14 = 52.75 cm

In order to investigate the propagation of the acoustic features of the leak along the pipeline, we created an artificial 1/16" leak on that pipeline. The measured dominant frequency ( with the highest peak) was 5,880 Hz as shown in Fig. (4.7). An additional peak at the frequency of 10, 280 Hz. can be seen as well. We believe that this peak represents the second harmonic of the dominant frequency component, and that the slightly incorrect position of that peak is due to a sampling error.

The dominant resonant frequency of the pipeline was calculated using the velocity of propagation of sound in steel  c = 585,000 cm/sec. The corresponding wavelength in steel  is  then

$$\lambda = c/f = 585,000/5,880 = 99.49 \text{ cm} \tag{4.1}$$

The ratio of the circumference to the wavelength is  l/λ = 52.75/99.49 = 0.53 ≈ .5

i.e.                             l = .5*λ

The conclusion is that the relationship between the half wavelength of the sound wave λ/2 and the length of the stripe shown in Fig. (4.6) looks like in Fig. (4.8). In other words the stripe acts as a "half-wave acoustic antenna" . The maximal displacement of the points along this stripe is at the hole and minimal displacement at the points A and B opposite the hole.

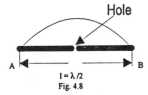

l = λ /2
Fig. 4.8

Points A and B are actually at the same location, A is on one side of the leak and B on the other. In general, the mechanical resonance will occur when

$$l = n*\lambda*/2 \quad \text{where n is  1, 2, 3,  etc.} \tag{4.2}$$

In our analysis we are considering two velocities of propagation. To find the resonant frequency of the pipeline we must use the velocity of sound in steel, however to analyze phenomena related to propagation we must use the velocity in gas. For our calculations we will use the velocity of propagation through steel given in tables at hand which is  c = 585,000 cm/sec

# THE LEAK SIMULATOR

### RPI Pipeline Leak Detection Project

### Leak Simulator

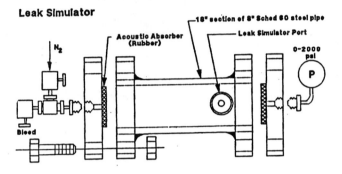

### RPI Pipeline Leak Detection Project

### Leak Modules (6 req'd)

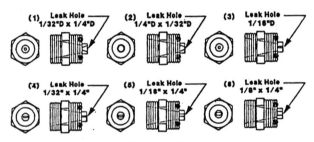

Fig. 4.1
The Leak Simulator

# $\alpha$ BELOW GROUND

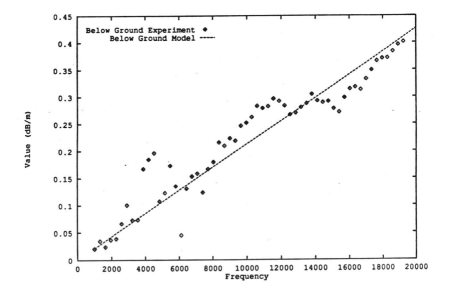

Fig. 4.2
Attenuation in terms of frequency of the acoustic signal propagating through an
underground pipeline

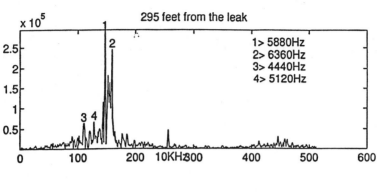
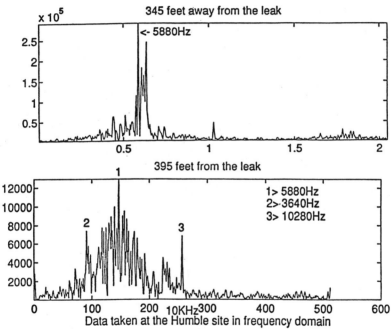

Fig. 4.7
Frequency spectra taken at the Humble cite at various distances from the leak.

# SCATTER PLOT OF LEAK SOUNDS

## CEPSTRUMS

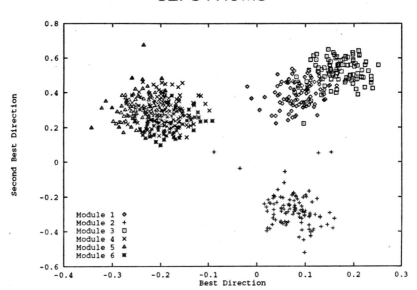

Fig. 4.4
Cepstrum coefficients of leaks with different hole sizes and shapes.
(Note that the size and the shape of the hole can be estimated from the diagram)

In case of the Humble cite the calculated fundamental resonant frequency  for  n = 1   will occur at     f = c/$\lambda$   so that   f = (585, 000)/(2*52.75)= 5,545 KHz. (4.3)

#### 4.2.1  Leak Detection

Instead of using the  LPC  coefficients to identify  the leak,  we can use the spectra of the leak as well. The frequency spectra of the leak signal that we recorded at the Humble cite at different distances  are shown in  Fig.  (4.7).  These spectra  indicate two characteristic peaks  one at  5.880 KHz   and  the other at  10.280 KHz. The first frequency is the fundamental resonant frequency, and the second is the second harmonic. The error of  5.7%  between the  calculated (5.545 KHz)  and  measured  (5.880 KHz)  resonant frequency is in all likelihood due to the difference in the actual velocity of  propagation through steel, and the velocity that we took from tables.

In summary a  leak can be detected by the presence of  characteristic harmonic peaks in the frequency spectrum. At the Humble cite these two peaks occur  at  5, 880 Hz  and at  10, 280 Hz These peaks can be detected in many ways such as by using digital signal processing, or by using some frequency detectors such as Phase Locked Loops.

### 5.   REFERENCES

[1]   W. C. Thompson and K. D. Skogman.  "The Application of Real Time Flow Modeling to          Pipeline Leak Detection"  In K. Chickering, editor, Pipeline Engineering Symposium, pp. 39-45. The American Society of Mechanical Engineers, 1983.

[2]   C. Sandberg etal.  "The Application of a Continuous Leak Detection System to Pipelines and          Associated Equipment," IEEE Transactions on Industry Applications, pp. 906--909, Sept.,          Oct. 1989.

[3]   S. Olafson, "An Alarm in Tulsa, Then Time Ran Out in Brenham," The Houston Post, pg. A1,          Sunday, Apr. 12, 1992.

[4]   L. V. Blake, Transmission Lines and Waveguides, John Wiley & Sons, 1969.

[5]   R. C. McMaster, editor.  Non Destructive Testing Handbook, Vol. 1:  Leak Testing. American Society of Metals, 1982.

[6]   M. I. Ribeiro and J. M. F. Moura, "LD$^2$--ARMA Identification Algorithm," IEEE Transactions on Signal Processing, pp. 1882-1835, Aug. 1991.

[7]   D. O'Shaughnessy, Speech Communication:  Human and Machine. Addison-Wesley, 1987.

[8]   I. Brodetsky, "Detection of Leaks in Underground Gas Pipelines", Ph.D. Thesis, Rensselaer Polytechnic Institute, 1993.

[9]   K. Fukunaga, Introduction to Statistical Pattern Recognition, Academic Press, INC., San Diego, CA, 2nd edition, 1990.

"TRUNK MOLE": LONG DISTANCE MICRO-TUNNELING
METHOD FOR GAS TRANSMISSION PIPELINES

MÉTHODE DE FORAGE LONGUE DISTANCE
DE TONNEL POUR GAZODUCS

S. Nagashima
M. Hayashi
M. Kurashina

Pipeline Engineering and Development Center
Tokyo Gas Co., Ltd

ABSTRACT

Tokyo Gas developed a sophisticated one-pass jacking gas transmission pipeline installation
technique called the "TRUNK MOLE". This method enables high-speed, high-precision and
long distance work to be carried in a single process. The drilling system can bore tunnels up to
600 meters long and hit the target precisely using an automatic steering technology. A single
process construction method was made possible by using the newly developed double steel
pipes in which the outer pipes slide over inner gas pipes.

RÉSUMÉ

La société Tokyo Gas a développé une technique d'installation de gazoduc en une opération
appelée "TRUNK MOLE". Cette méthode permet d'effectuer des travaux à grande vitesse, de
haute précision et à longue distance en un seul processus. Ce système de forage peut creuser
des tunnels d'une longueur maxi de 600 mètres et atteindre précisément l'objectif au moyen
d'une technique de contrôle et de commande automatique de l'orientation. Une méthode de
construction qu moyen d'un seul processus a été rendue possible grâce à l'utilisation des
tuyaux double en acier nouvellement mis au point, et caractérisés par le glissement du tuyau
extérieur sur le tuyau intérieur de gaz.

INTRODUCTION

   With the rapid increase in demand for city gas in the
metropolitan area in recent years, the situation has become such that
it will be necessary for Tokyo Gas to invest large funds for supply
facilities in the future. Of these, the weight rests heavily on trunk
line related facilities but construction plans for new high pressure
trunk lines are being advanced at a rapid pace towards the 21st
century.

   On one hand, since the major part of gas trunk line construction
is being conducted by the open cut method, construction time is
lengthening and becoming more difficult with costs increasing amidst
the heightening awareness of severe traffic congestions and protection
of the environment, particularly in the city area.

   With this type of background, Tokyo Gas is enthusiastically
engaged in technical development and introduction of gas trunk line
construction methods such as the trenchless construction method with
the objective of "reducing costs", "shortening the construction time"
and "preservation of the environment."
The TRUNK MOLE method is one of the methods developed with the
objective of laying high pressure trunk lines in the metropolitan
area.

   By using the newly developed double steel pipe, this new
construction method has now made direct thrusting of high pressure
main gas pipelines possible for long distances (max. of 600 m per
span), that was once not possible in the past.
The aim of the trenchless construction method is not only for
construction in special places such as in crossing rivers but also for
construction in sections where roads must be crossed.

PROBLEMS IN CONVENTIONAL TRENCHLESS CONSTRUCTION METHODS

   In the trenchless construction method used to date on high
pressure gas trunk lines, the humes were thrust in first and the gas
pipes were then pulled into the hume after being welded together in
the shaft. However, the following problems were encountered in this
method.

   Overall construction time is long since the two processes of
thrusting in the humes and pulling in the gas pipe is required.

   Excavation section is large since a humes with adequate bore is
required relative to the diameter of the gas pipe to enable pulling
the gas pipe in positively after thrusting in the hume.

   Intermediate thrusting jacks will be required to distribute the
thrusting force in laying long distance hume pipes of 100 m or over
since humes will not be able to withstand strong thrusting force, and
thus drastically reduces construction efficiency.

   Work environment is poor since measuring the advancing tip
position  and the work of injecting lubricant and backfill are manual
work for the thrusting pipe.

POINTS IN DEVELOPMENT OF TRUNK MOLE

The principal development items of TRUNK MOLE are explained below.

Double Steel Pipe

A construction method of simultaneous thrusting and piping was made possible with the use of double steel pipes in which the outer steel pipe slides over the gas main. The structure of the double steel pipe is shown in Figure 1. The principal features and functions of this double steel pipe are as follows.

Thrust Force Transmission. By applying all the thrusting force to the outer pipe, no load whatsoever is applied to the gas main during construction.
Furthermore, by using a thick outer piping capable of withstanding high thrusting force, extra long thrusting was made possible without the need of intermediate jacking equipment.

Protection of Gas Mains. When laying high pressure gas mains, protective steel plates are normally buried directly above the pipe to prevent harmful accidents from construction machinery used in various excavation work after laying the pipe. In the TRUNK MOLE method, the outer pipe serves as this protective steel plate. There is also no need to be concerned of damaging the outer coating of the gas main from friction with the earth when thrusting.

Housing Supplementary Piping. In line with laying the high pressure gas main, it is possible to install supplementary piping between the gas main and the outer protective pipe such as for optical fiber cables and for protection of cables against electrical corrosion, and also injection piping for lubricant and backfill that will be explained later.

Mechanical Joints of Outer Pipes. To prevent a drop in thrusting efficiency, mechanical joints were used to connect the outer protective piping. This also drastically reduces the coupling time.

Small Boring Section. By using an outer protective pipe with a diameter only slightly larger than the gas main, it was possible to make the boring cross section small and to produce the minimum amount of excavated earth.

Lubricant Injection and Backfilling System

This is a system of injecting lubricant while thrusting and backfilling after completing thrusting by means of an injecting system using an injecting pipe and double packer installed between the inner and outer pipes. (Figure 2) This system enables remote injection at optional points within the thrusting section without the need of workers in the pipe. There is also no need to open grout holes in the gas pipe.

Laser Theodolite for Long Distance

In the past, about 150 meters was the limit for measuring with a theodolite and workers actually entered the thrusting pipe to make measurements for longer distances. In this method, measurement work while thrusting was eliminated with the development of a long distance theodolite. (Figure 3)

Lead Drilling Machine

A high pressure liquid mud type shield machine was used for the lead drilling machine. (Photo. 1) This machine was equipped with a newly developed fully automatic direction control system linking the automatically controlled oscillating section with a laser target image processing system.

Back Jack

In this construction method, the length of the standard thrusting pipe is 6 meters. The back jacks used in the thrusting method generally matched the length of the hume pipe and were about 3 meters. By making the jack stroke 6 meters, it became possible to thrust one pipe length without the need of struts, thus improving thrusting efficiency. Also, by providing the high capacity of a maximum thrust of 1000 tons estimated as being required for a thrust of 600 meters, the need for a inter jack stations was eliminated.

GENERAL CONSTRUCTION PROCEDURE WITH THE TRUNK MOLE

As shown in Figure 4, piping is advanced by repeated thrusting and welding of the gas main. Laying of the gas main will be completed when thrusting is completed to the receiving shaft.

1.　The first double steel pipe is thrust in.

2.　As shown in the diagram, the double steel pipe is lowered. After setting, the gas pipe is shifted a little forward over the outer pipe.

3.　Gas main pipes are welded and joined together.

4.　After completing the welding, back jacking force is applied to the outer casing pipe to cause it to slide forward in order for it to join. If thrusting force is applied after joining the outer casing pipes, it will be transmitted to the front drilling machine and cause it to advance.

STATE OF INTRODUCTION AT ACTUAL CONSTRUCTION SITE

We are presently proceeding with construction of the Yokohama trunk line in Yokohama city. Since the route environment consists principally of urban and residential areas, use of the TRUNK MOLE method on 2.2 km of the overall length of 14.4 km was decided as a result of studies conducted on construction methods from various angles. The earth cover is 4 m to 17 m in view of the numerous buried conduits underground. A double steel pipe consisting of a 900 mm diameter gas main and a outer pipe with a diameter of 1,150 mm is being used at the site.

The first thrusting was commenced in the initial section from March 1994, and a span of 270 m was successfully completed in about 2 months.Next work started from July and finished in about 4 months, on the next span of 561 m which is the longest span of its kind to date. In these sections, all the processes went smoothly and the maximum deviation from the designed line was within 50 mm.
   Ground conditions are varied ranging from layers of mudstone or silt stone to fine sand where the mud stone is very stiff and showed the US of 3.5 Ma to 4.5 MPa.

Furthermore, according to estimated cost comparison with the open cut method, an estimated cost reduction of about 15% is anticipated in the section using the TRUNK MOLE method. It is scheduled that the remaining length to be pipejacked by the TRUNK MOLE method will be finished by March 1996.

CONCLUSIONS

1.   Tokyo Gas developed a sophisticated one-pass jacking gas transmission pipeline installation technique called the "TRUNK MOLE".

2.   This system is mainly composed of two elements. One is the newly developed unique double steel pipe as thrusting pipe and the other is the long distance drilling system.

3.   "TRUNK MOLE" has been applied to actual transmission pipeline construction works since 1994. According to this method, an estimated cost reduction of 15% is anticipated compared to conventional open-trench method.

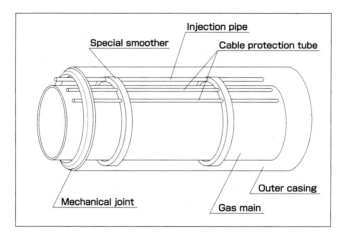

**Figure 1.  Double Steel Pipe**

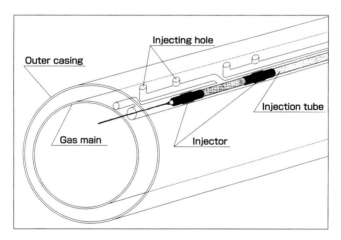

**Figure 2.  Lubricant Injection and Backfilling System**

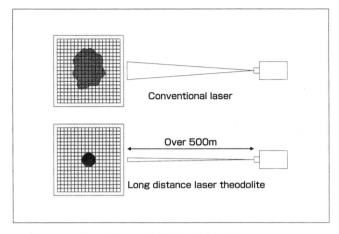

**Figure 3. Laser Theodolite for Long Distance**

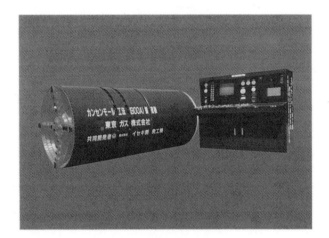

**Photo 1. Lead Drilling Machine**

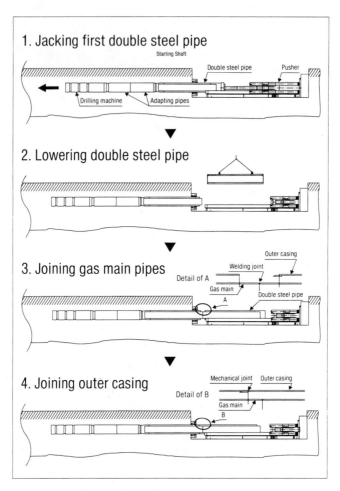

**Figure 4.  General Construction Procedure**

# TRANSIENT MODELING LEAK DETECTION

# MODELISATION DYNAMIQUE D'UN SYSTEM DE DETECTION DE FUITES

Author: Igor Poljanšek, Petrol Zemeljski plin, Ljubljana, SLOVENIA

## SUMMARY

The paper provides the insight of The Leak Detection and Line Break Valve Closure and Location System (LAVDAL), implemented as one of the functions of recently built Gas Control Modeling and Management System (GCMMS). The LAVDAL is embedded into the Modeling System (GMoS) of GCMMS. GMoS utilizes standard transport equations for real-time transient simulation of gas transmission. The results of numerical solution are on-line produced and compared with measured values from the field. The discrepancy of the two values are analyzed against the threshold. According to upstream and downstream pressure discrepancy the leak or line break valve closure alarm is issued and location established. The results are displayed on the dispatcher screen. The paper discuses the experiences in using the LAVDAL.


## RÉSUMÉ

La présentation éclaircit la connaissance des systèmes "La detection et la location des fuites et la fermeture de gazduc soupape de sûreté" (LAVDAL) lesquels étaient réalisés comme une fonction du cadre commun des systèmes récamment construits de "Gas conduire, modelage et ménager" (GCMMS). Le système LAVDAL est integré dans le "Système de modelage" de GCMMS. GMoS utilise équation standardisée pour une simulation transcendante d'un temps réél de la transmission du gas. Des résultats des solutions numeriques sont produit "on-line" à l'ordinateur et comparés avec des valeurs mesurées sur le terrain. La discordance entre les deux valeurs est analysée contre sa valeur seuile. Selon la discordance des pressions descendantes et montantes une alarme de fuite ou de "fermeture de soupape de sûreté" est delivrée et la location est établie. Des resultats sont presentes sur l'écran de distributeurs. L'experience d'utiliser le system LAVDAL est discutée dans la présentation.

## INTRODUCTION

The paper discuss the experiences on the Transient Modeling Leak and Line Break Valve Detection and Location System (LAVDAL), implemented as one of the functions of recently built Gas Control Modeling and Management System (GCMMS) on Slovenian pipeline.

The high pressure gas transmission network in Slovenia consists of 270 km long mainline running from the Austrian to Italian border and about 450 km of high pressure distribution lines. Gas of different quality and dynamics is supplied by both entries of the mainline and must meet the consumer requirements on mass (energy) flow rate and pressure. High environmental requirements in the European Alp region requires to install efficient Leak Detection and Location System. For minimizing the pipeline leak in the case of pipeline break 60 line break valves are installed (See Fig. 1): The line break valve closure may occur also in situations of high pressure oscillations caused by regulating the flow or sudden change of an offtake by big consumer. As the solution for the control, the company Petrol Natural Gas, the main natural gas supplier in Slovenia, decided for the installation of the LAVDAL. The method was selected on the base of minimal investment and operating costs.

The LAVDAL is embedded into the Modeling System (GMoS) of GCMMS. GMoS utilizes standard transport equations for real-time transient simulation of gas transmission. The results of numerical solution are on-line produced and compared with Scan and Data Acquisition System (SCADA) values. SCADA is a part of Gas Control System which transfers the measured values from the field to the GMoS. The discrepancy of the two values are analyzed against the threshold. If actual measurement discrepancy is established the alarm is issued. According to upstream and downstream pressure discrepancy the leak or line break valve closure and location is established and displayed on the dispatcher screen as presented on Fig: 1.

The LAVDAL is implemented for the first time on Slovenian pipeline system.

## LAVDAL FUNCTIONAL SPECIFICATION

The operation of the LAVDAL is presented in the following functional specifications:

- Detection and alarming the natural gas leak on pipeline grid based on volume balance and line pack change.
- Detection and location of the natural gas leak based on deviation between measured and modeled values

- Detection, location and alarming of sudden Line Break Valve closure based on deviation analyze.

For the operation the LAVDAL utilizes the capabilities of GCMoS. It can only work as a part of modeling software.

## GCMoS COMPOSITION

The GCMoS represents the integration of different models which enable the real time data calculation, pipeline load forecasting and pipeline system behavior prediction. A special part of modeling system integrated into Real Time Model is The Deviation Application Software. LAVDAL uses the calculated real time values and measured values from the field supplied by Scan And Data Acquisition System (SCADA). The Modeling System software composition is presented on Fig. 2.

### Real-Time Model

The Real-Time Model (RTM) in the Modeling System provides the current hydraulic state of the pipeline system. The Real- Time Model performs hydraulic calculations on a pipeline network configuration. The measurements from the physical instrumentation are used as an input for the simulation.

The RTM is based on numerical solution of following Hydraulic Equations (3):

1. Mass Balance Equation

$$(A\rho)_t + (A\rho v)_x = 0$$

$$0 \leq x \leq L; \ t \geq 0$$

2. Momentum Balance Equation

$$v_t + v v_x + \frac{p_x}{\rho} + \frac{(f)}{(2D_i)} v \, |v| = 0$$

$$0 \leq x \leq L; \ t \geq 0$$

3. Energy Balance Equation

$$\rho c_v (T_t - v T_x) = -T\{\frac{\partial p}{\partial T}\}_\rho v_x + \rho \frac{(f)}{2(D_i)} |v|^3 - \frac{(4U_n)}{(D)} (T - T_g)$$

Where:

$L$  =  length of the pipe, km

$x$ = position along the pipe, km
$t$ = time, sec
$A$ = cross-sectional area of the pipe, $m^2$
$\rho$ = density of the gas, $kg/m^3$
$p$ = pressure of the gas, bar
$v$ = velocity of the gas, m/sec
$h$ = elevation of the pipe, m
$g$ = acceleration due to gravity, $m/sec^2$
$f$ = Moody friction factor
$D_i$ = internal diameter of pipe, m
$T$ = temperature of the gas, °C
$Uw$ = overall heat transfer coefficient, kW/m°C
$Tg$ = ground temperature, °C
$c_v$ = heat capacity of the gas, kJ/kg °C

The output of the simulation consists of calculated pressure, flows, temperatures, and densities along the entire length of the pipeline system.

The Real-Time Model includes several applications that use the output of the hydraulic simulation to evaluate the operation of the pipeline system. These applications execute automatically following the completion each of step of the hydraulic simulation.

The trend diagram of measured and modeled flow for two critical point in pipeline grid is presented on Fig. 3.

**Load Forecaster**

The Load/Supply Forecaster (LSF) is the tool used to provide estimates of flow rates at supply/delivery points for the Predictive Models. The LSF combines load characteristic data with weather data, to establish the flows at each location for the forecast period. The LSF is used to generate forecast files for the Predictive and Look-Ahead Models.

**Predictive model**

The Predictive Model (PM)is used to predict the network behavior of the pipeline, starting from the current state generated by the Real-Time Model.

The PM simulates future pipeline profiles of pressure, temperature, flow rate, and quality. A Predictive Model simulation is accomplished by providing a set of starting conditions and scheduling all of the events planed in the future.

**Deviation application software**

The deviation application software is a part of RTM. It uses validated SCADA values in combination with the Real-Time Model current state values to identify, instrument operation, to size and locate pipeline leaks and to locate line break valve closures. Two independent techniques are used to analyze the incoming data:

- deviation between measured values and RTM calculated values

- an enhanced volume balance analysis

The combination of these two techniques allows detection sensitivity to be maximized while simultaneously minimizing the incidence of false alarms.

During the model operation, roughness and ambient temperature tuning is performed. Tuning adjusts the pressure loss calculation to improve the Real-Time Model simulation accuracy.

## LAVDAL TECHNIQUES

The LAVDAL detects the gas leak out line break closure on the pipe by two independent methods.

In the first method LAVDAL uses the imbalance, discrepancy and threshold values to identify the errors.

The imbalance is defined as:

$$IM_t \quad = \quad Vme_t - Vmo_t \ (\%)$$

$IM_t(\%)$ ...... imbalance in time t which is for one calculation period behind the current time

$Vme_t$... ....... measured value from SCADA and scanned by model

$Vmo_t$... ....... modeled value calculated from $Vme_{t-1}$ for time $t$

Discrepancy represent the difference between two consecutive imbalances:

$$DISC_t \ = \quad (Vme_t - Vmo_t) \ IM_{t-1}$$

$DISC_t$. ...... discrepancy in time $t$

The discrepancy values are compared against the threshold value. Threshold value calculation uses data known about the instrumentation along with real-time operating data to distinguish the predictable noise from real leak or line break closure event. The threshold value can be adjusted using a filter factor.

$$TR_t \quad = \quad C * TR_t - (1-C) * TR_t \ (\%)$$

$TR_t$ ..... ...... threshold in time t

$C$ ........ ...... filter factor

If discrepancy exceeds the threshold the vote is issued. According to direction of the discrepancy leak or value closure vote is issued. The prescribed number of votes are necessary to declare a leak or line break closure (Fig. 4).

In the location process LAVDAL simulations are performed, logically placing the leak at various positions in the simulated pipeline network. For Line break Closure location all the valves and their location are configured in the pipeline grid. The simulation only take place for this locations. The location with the best fit to the actual measurements is then selected and displayed to the pipeline operator.

The second method is an enhancement of the traditional volume (mass) balance technique used is SCADA systems. The different imbalance time windows may be adjusted for establishing a leak.


## PRACTICAL EXPERIENCES WITH LAVDAL

Both methods rely on the capability of the RTM to evaluate pipeline hydraulic variables to a high degree of accuracy. The RTM accuracy depends of:

- accuracy of pipeline network configuration
- accuracy and location of instruments
- percentage of total flow in the pipeline under telemetry control
- the flow load in the pipes
- SCADA data refresh
- frequency of RTM calculations

From the accuracy factors can be seen that computer power installed for the pipeline SCADA and modeling software has an influence on result accuracy. The number of elements in the configuration request more computer time for RTM calculation.

**Slovenian pipeline configuration**

The number of elements in the configured system are:

Number of equipment.............. 78
Number of legs ...................... 170
Number of nodes ................... 246
Number of external regulators . 82
Number of knots.................... 517
Number of gas qualities............. 3

The time for RTM execution is approximately one minute on SUN 360 server with 32 Mb of memory.

**Experiment results**

The line break closure experiment on Slovenian pipeline grid was executed. The flow in the main pipe in the experiment time was about 30% of the line capacity. The valve was closed for 15 minutes. The results of discrepancy exceeding threshold are shown on first downstream and upstream measured location are shown on Fig. 4 and Fig. 5.

The line Break Closure can be detected in the shortest time of 10 minutes. The accuracy for the valve location is 200 meters. The established location for the valves which are closer than 200 meters can differ for one valve.

The longest time for detection was 30 minutes and it depends of the pipe flow load where the valve is closed.

The leak on the pipeline system can be establish in values 10% of flow in the local pipe. In low load of the total pipeline system the false alarms may occur. They can be minimized if the leak alarming is connected to volume imbalances.

It is necessary to point out that LAVDAL can only work if all the configured instruments are working properly and are under the real operating conditions. This condition request frequent instruments checking. The maintenance works on the pipeline must be controlled  from the standpoint that all operating instruments are under real operating conditions. In this way the number of false alarms can be  minimized.

## BENEFITS

The LAVDAL enables the company to provide effective leak control of the pipeline grid and fast locating of closed line break valve. The function is included in existing dispatching center. Time for locate and open closed valve is shortened and allows the maintenance people to react in time and before the supply of the gas is interrupted. In comparison to the costs of the computer control installation on line break valve locations the saving exceeds 600.000 US$. The operating costs of the software are minimal. The system requires accurate instrumentation calibration and maintenance.

## CONCLUSIONS

The Transient Modeling Leak and Line Break Valve Closure Detection and Location System (LAVDAL) is implemented on high pressure gas transmission network in Slovenia.

The savings of 600.000US$ are achieved on instrument investments.

The first experiences showed that for effective usage of the LAVDAL the instrumentation maintenance work control must be improved.

## REFERENCES

[1]   Steven Pringle, The pipeline monitor: an overview of software based leak detection, Proc. PSIG annual meeting, Houston 1992.

[2]   Poljansek, I., and Zun, I., On line automation and management of high pressure gas transmission system, Proc. Modeling, identification and control, Grindelwald, 1994.

[3]   Scientific Software - Intercomp, INC, Pipeline & Facilities Division: Interact Version 1.4 Gas Keyword Reference, 1994.

[4]   Dal Molin Francesca: LBCLOS Line Break Closure Location Module, Rev 1.0 AFD, May 1992.

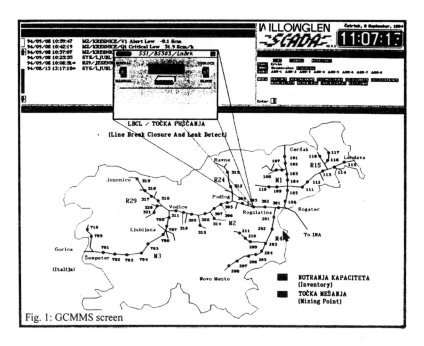

Fig. 1: GCMMS screen

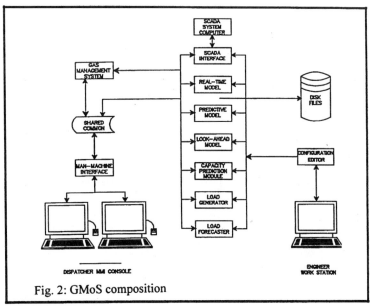

Fig. 2: GMoS composition

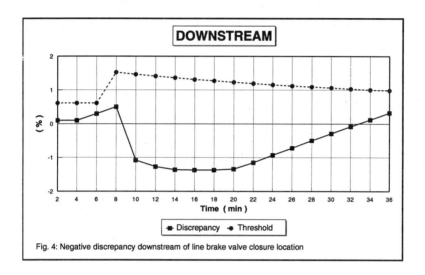

Fig. 4: Negative discrepancy downstream of line brake valve closure location

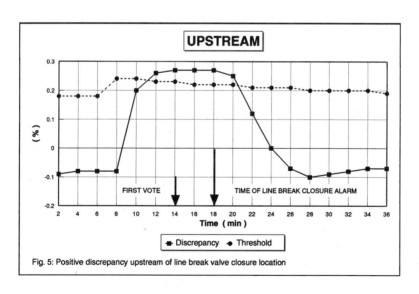

Fig. 5: Positive discrepancy upstream of line break valve closure location

# NEW MAINTENANCE PHILOSOPHY BASED ON A
# 100 KM PIPELINE COATING SURVEY

# NOUVELLE PHILOSOPHIE D' ENTRETIEN REPOSE SUR UNE
# 100 KM PIPE-LINE SURVEY DE COATING

A. Pijnacker Hordijk and B. van der Velde
N.V. Nederlandse Gasunie, The Netherlands

**ABSTRACT**

Although pipeline aging has not caused Gasunie significant problems in the past, the effects of ongoing degeneration of the pipeline coating have to be controlled. The attention of the Operation Department for corrosion prevention is focused on the cathodic protection of the pipeline system. Therefore, a lot of routine CP-measurements are performed at regular intervals, processed and corresponding corrective actions are taken. Coating surveys (Pearson technique) and excavations are carried out incidentally on random sections of pipeline, to check the actual quality of the coating. However, this approach is not capable to ascertain and control the actual condition of the total pipeline system (11,000 km). As a consequence, an increase in the total number of coating defects caused by degeneration or not reported (non failing) pipeline damages is not detected in this way. Metal loss might thus become a problem. Because the cp measurements cover only a relatively small amount of the overall pipeline system, the CP-system can therefore not be used as the only instrument to control the protection of exposed steel at coating defects.

It will be clear that Gasunie is interested in developing new maintenance and inspection philosophies for pipeline integrity. Therefore a project has been conducted in order to investigate the actual coating quality, to evaluate the coating defect measuring method, and to generate recommendations for an integral approach to implement a new technique into the existing maintenance program.

**RÉSUMÉ**

Bien que le vieullisement d' une pipe-linme n'il y a pas causé une problème dans le passé, il faut que l' effet de produit de degeneration d' une coating d'une pipe-line sera bien contrôlé. L'attention de departement d'entretien pour prevenir corrosion en pipe-lines est proportionné à la protection cathodique d' une systeme des pipe-lines. C' est pourquoi que beaucoup de mesurages routines mettent exécuté à un intervalle régulier, devenient transformé et les corrections assortissantes sont pris. Les surveuillances des coating (Pierson technique) et les déterrement seront exécuté "incidenteel" et à une section d'une pipe-line arbitraire pour controlé la qualité de la coating authentique. Pourtant ce façon sera reconnu comme qu' il y a insuffisante pour porté garant de controllement de la condition sincère de 11.000 km pipe-lines.

Si bien que l'agrandissement d'un grand total nombre de défaut dans la coating, sera causé par la dégéneration de la coating ou pas rapporté pipe-le\ine incidents, n'est pas découvert en cette méthode. La perte du métal porvoit un problème. Parce que les mesurages de la protection cathodique comprennent seul une quantité relatif peu des total pipe-lines. La système de la protection cathodique ne peut pas utilisé que l' instrument seulement pour controlé la protection du metal exposé avec les défauts de la coating.

Il y a évident que Gasunie est interessé dans le development d'une nouvelle philosophie d'entretien et d'inspection pour la intégrité des pipe-lines. Pour cette raison une project sera mis en le vérification de qualité authentique de coating, en l' évaluation de methodique en mesure de manque de la coating, et à développer récommendations pour implementer une nouvelle technique dans le programme entretien existant.

## INTRODUCTION

Gasunie operates and maintains approximately 11,000 km of gas transport pipelines in the Netherlands. The requirement is to guarantee a safe and reliable gas delivery to the customers. The gas transport system among others consists of high pressure natural gas buried pipelines, the majority of which is about twenty-five years old. The network is split into two systems :
o High pressure Transportation pipeLines (HTL) operating at pressures between 40 and 65 bar, with diameters in the range 18 to 48". The standard coating used is asphalt/bitumen. In certain cases sintered polyethylene is used although this is an exception for special circumstances. Since 1994 only polyethylene has been applied.
o Regional Transportation pipeLines (RTL) operating at pressures between 10 and 40 bar, with diameters in the range 2 to 24". More recent pipes (less than 20 years old with diameters less than 18") are coated with sintered polyethylene. Older pipelines are coated with asphalt/bitumen.

In order to guarantee the integrity of the transport system, the pipelines are protected against external corrosion. This protection is realized by a combination of two techniques, a protective coating (the "primary" corrosion-protection mechanism) and the cathodic protection (the "secondary" protection). The cathodic protection (CP) is a supportive technique, which is used to prevent external corrosion of buried pipelines at places with coating defects. Both the RTL and HTL systems are 100% cathodically protected and a range of electrical measurements are taken to evaluate the effectiveness of the CP.

The Pearson-technique has been used by the Maintenance Department to identify coating defects. Although the Pearson-technique is rather subjective, (it doesn't give a ranking of defects, doesn't predict the corrosion behaviour at a defect and is disturbed by stray current) it still gives more than an impression about the coating condition.

Because of the promising abilities of the DCVG-technique (see ref. [1]) it was decided to investigate if the DCVG-technique is capable to locate defects very accurately, to rank the coating defects and to give a prediction if a defect is corroding or not. Moreover, the amount of useful excavations can be truly justified and hopefully decreased, based on the predicting capability of the DCVG-technique. Therefore the Maintenance Department and the Gasunie Research Department decided to evaluate the DCVG-technique in practice (see ref. [2]).

After the completion of the evaluation project we started to develop a methodology in such a way that a structural top-down approach is possible to balance the maintenance resources between CP effectiveness measurements, coating surveys, useful excavations and the necessity of repair or rehabilitation.
By incorporating the DCVG methodology into the regular maintenance procedures we have an approach to balance first and second protection mechanisms with a minimum of extra investment. The need for such a balance is quite clear as indicated in reference [8].

## EXPERIMENTS

The coating survey was based on the Direct Current Voltage Gradient (DCVG) technique. The choice of the DCVG-technique was based on the following expected capabilities :

- it can be used in areas influenced by stray current;
- it will give a ranking of defects, because it combines the relative size of the defect with the flow of protective current at a
  defect;
- it shows the direction of the current at the coating defect (the
  corrosion behaviour);

The survey was carried out in the western part of the Netherlands over a thirty days period by the company Pipeline Integrity
Management (Burnley, UK) on parts of the RTL pipeline system.
Seven sections were randomly chosen based on a wide set of parameters. Some of the parameters were :
- 2 different types of coating (asphalt-bitumen and sintered
  polyethylene);
- several ages of pipelines (in some cases up to 30 years old);
- different amount of dc-traction interference;
- no pigging provisions;
- several types of environment (farmland, city streets and other
  complex areas);

The results presented in six volumes (see ref. [5]) were used to
evaluate if and when corrective actions are necessary. These
corrective actions, can for instance, consist of selective coating
rehabilitations or an increase in the flow of current by adjusting
the corresponding CP-rectifier.
This paper will give a summary of the results of the investigation, and will review the alternatives for Gasunie to implement
the technique as a key component in the pipeline maintenance
philosophy.

## RESULTS, DISCUSSION and PHILOSOPHY

### 100 km Survey Results

The survey resulted in identification of 3767 coating defects.
The coating defects divided over the seven sections (see table 1
in annex A) showed that only 1.4 % of all defects were found in PE
coated pipeline. The average distance between coating defects on
asphalt coated pipe was 19.2 metres and 362.7 metres on
polyethylene coated pipe. These figures cannot be universal
applied to other pipelines without considering additional parameters since we found considerable variation in coating quality ie:
a thirty years old asphalt coated pipeline was still in an excellent condition.
From table 2 in Annex A we see that less than 1% of all defects
were ranked as large or extra large. Table 3 showed that about 1%
of the defects are not protected. A part of the evaluation was
also the validation of the above ground observations against the
actual buried situation. Because of the infra structure in the
Netherlands and the corresponding high costs for an excavation
only twenty five excavations (see ref. [7]) were carried out.
These excavations proved that the size/importance of a defect did
correspond well with the above ground prediction and the location
of a defect was very accurate, within a few centimetres! Unfortunately the accuracy of the corrosion predicting capabilities of
the DCVG-technique was less than expected, 80% of the excavated
unprotected (anodic/anodic, a/a) defects showed no corrosion. In
many excavations cp-products were present indicating that the cp-
system had been working. Although the amount of excavations is too
small to prove statistically within 95% confidence limits we are
convinced that the DCVG-technique is very sensitive and accurate
to locate coating defects. The corrosion predicting capabilities
of the DCVG-technique however need more research.

Although there were 3767 defects found the amount of metal loss was virtually nil. Only <u>two</u> defects showed any significant corrosion! Therefore the Gasunie RTL pipelines are thought to be in an excellent condition. In order to keep this condition over many years, to eas coating degeneration problems and to postpone the onset for coating refurbishment or rehabilitation on a large scale, we want to implement the DCVG-technique into the existing maintenance program as discussed in the following section.

Discussion

To identify bad subsections of coating, measurements were made of the rate of decay of the amplitude of the DCVG pulsed signal with distance.The DCVG pulse signal strength was measured at test posts and is presented graphically to compare the attenuation of the measured potential between a sintered polyethylene and an asphalt/bitumen coated pipeline.

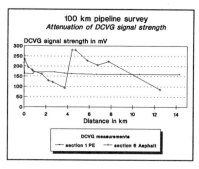

Figure 1

This has been done for section 1 and section 6. As given in table 1 in Annex A the ratio of the distribution of coating defects is 18.9 : 1. This means that an asphalt/ bitumen coated pipeline suffers about 20 times more defects per kilometre pipeline than a polyethylene coated pipeline. The behaviour of each section can be seen in figure 1.The attenuation of DCVG signal strength gives a gradient of the corresponding flow of current of a pipeline section between the test posts and consequently an indication of the relative quality of the pipeline coating. The derivation of the DCVG potential per meter of pipeline can be used as a trigger to schedule a coating survey of that specific section as shown in figure 2.

As indicated in reference [4] it is of the utmost importance that pipeline operators work along with a rehabilitation program. Such a program must consist of a test and measuring program to ascertain the condition of the pipelines together with a remedial action plan to determine the most cost effective rehabilitation option. After completion of the chosen necessary measures effectiveness must be certified with an assessment for the future. The referred paper gives a summary of several measuring techniques and a corrective action plan, but not an approach for a structural integrated program. After the evaluation of the 100 km coating survey project Gasunie started to develop an overall approach for corrosion protection. In this approach there is a balance between second and first protection mechanisms of pipe-

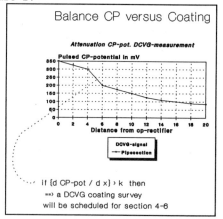

Figure 2

lines. This method requires criteria per item and general criteria to ensure efficient use of needed resources and estimated costs.

Philosophy

The following structural approach is given with the help of so called "measuring and control" schemes. First a short explanation is given on how to understand this scheme. As an example a flow control loop is given in figure 3. The appropriate measurement ($Y_m$) is evaluated against a setpoint R (=criterion, CRIT.) If the deviation (δ) exceeds certain preset control limits a correction will be carried out to ensure that the actual process values regain the desired criterion. The same control loop is given in figure 4 based upon the measurement and control drawing principles.

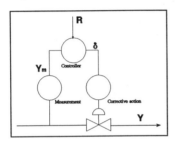

Figure 3

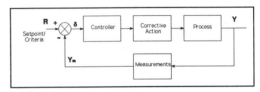

Figure 4

In the same manner we are going to describe the interacting processes of corrosion prevention :
- cp measurement and control process;
- coating degeneration process;
- corrosion process;
- incident control process;

Figure 5 gives an overview of the interaction and criteria of the above mentioned processes. Since this overview is rather global, the balance between cp measurement and control process versus the coating degeneration process is given in more detail in figure 6.

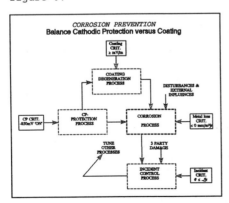

Figure 5

It is the intention of Gasunie to develop a pipeline integrity tool based upon this scheme. Therefore there is a need to describe all criteria (setpoints and preset control limits), physical processes, parameters and appropriate measurement techniques and corrective actions. Based upon the desired criterion it is then possible to tune the overall process in order to prevent pipelines from corroding in an efficient and effective way.

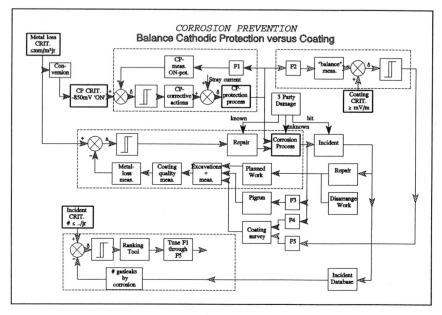

Figure 6

It will be quite impossible to give an explanation of all aspects in this scheme without going into more detail. To overcome this problem a simplistic chart (figure 7) has been drawn which shows the interaction between criteria and the "balance" between cp-measurement and control process and the coating degeneration process.

To gather data on coating and CP the DCVG-interrupter inserted into a Transformer/Rectifier, is switched on demand on and off from the test post location. Two types of measurements are made at the testpost:

1)    the normal on-potential will be measured for cp effectiveness as required by the today's company standard (F1);
2)    the DCVG interrupted cp-on / cp-off potential will be measured as an attenuation potential for coating degeneration control as an addition to the existing maintenance program. The interrupter must be triggered from remote at the test post location (F2).

The frequencies and the total amount of pipeline segments for measurements are controlled by F1 through F5 as indicated in figure 6. The balance measurements taken as a DCVG-measurement at a test post will give a small attenuation potential whereas a section with a large current consumption which has more coating defects will have a large potential attenuated. If these measurements are evaluated against coating quality criteria for instance given as K [mV/m] the corrective actions as in this case a coating survey will be scheduled (F5). In the same manner excavations will be carried out triggered by data from the coating survey database exceeding the specified criteria. Then corrective actions will be carried out to repair the coating and (if necessary) repair the metal loss at the excavated pipeline. To evaluate if this approach can be statistically justified annual surveys triggered from a ranking tool (see figure 7) will be carried out to verify if the sample taken at random by the balance measurement is within the normal confidence limits.

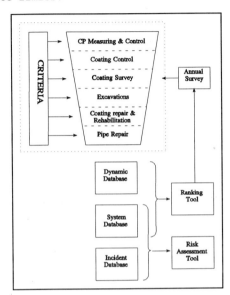

Figure 7

## CONCLUSIONS

Briefly, the evaluation of the results led to the following conclusions:

1) 3767 coating defects were found in 90.1 km pipelines. 93% of all faults were relatively small. Possible external corrosion was predicted for 44 defects (1%). Red rust was found only on a few defects, out of a number of selective excavations;
2) About twenty-five (25) excavations proved that the accuracy of locating the coating defect was within a few centimetres. Similarly, the predicted ranking of defects corresponded well with the findings from the excavations;
3) A lot of defects were caused by oil contamination, root ingrowth from trees and reeds or poor coating at field joints. Only two of the coating defects showed significant metal loss, one was due to an interference problem with a metal fence;
4) The actual visual corrosion behaviour at the coating defects did not correspond as well as was hoped with the predictive measurements. This was probably due to external interference effects through which the actual flow of current is hard to predict. This point needs more research;
5) The sintered polyethylene coating were relatively defect free. Asphalt coatings showed about 20 times more coating defects than the PE coatings. One thirty-year-old asphalt coating was still in an excellent condition;

**REFERENCES**

[1] Dr. J.M. Leeds and J. Grapiglia, The DC Voltage Gradient Method For Accurate Delineation Of Coating Defects On Buried Pipelines, UK Corrosion, October 1990

[2] Dr. R. Bilbé, Evaluation of Gasunie Approach For Monitoring The Performance Of Cathodic Protection On Buried Pipelines, Gasunie 11 September 1992

[3] Dr. J.M. Leeds, New Corrosion Detection Method For Buried Pipe Lines, Pipe Line Industry magazine, December 1992

[4] Herbert L. Fluharty, John W. Fluharty, Mears/CPG Inc., Rehabilitation Needs Assessment Procedures For Transmission Pipelines

[5] Dr. J.M. Leeds (PIM), Gasunie proj. nr. 742841 10 November 1993.
 - Volume 1,  DC Voltage Gradient Observations and Analysis of results;
 - Volume 2,  Detailed DC Voltage Gradient Observations;
 - Volume 3,  Excavations and Analysis of DC Voltage Gradient Coating Defect Locations;
 - Volume 4,  Interpretations of Defect Size\Importance Using %IR; Assessment;
 - Volume 5,  Pipeline Coating Repair After Exploratory Excavations,
 - Volume 6,  The Survey Data Base;

[6] Dr. R. Bilbé, Report of the 100 km Pipeline Coating Survey (dutch report), TR/T 94.R.2503 12 April 1994.

[7] Ir. D. Koster, Report of the Excavations of the 100 km Pipeline Coating Survey (dutch report including 96 coloured photographs), TR/T 94.R.2603 18 November 1994.

[8] Dr. J.M. Leeds, APRT, Bolton, Lancashire, CP Equipment Should Be Surveyed Along With Pipeline Coating, December 1994 Pipeline Industry.

6)   By interrupting the cp-current, the effective cp-rectifier
     influence area can be measured;
7)   An indication of the relative quality of the pipeline coating
     can be achieved by measuring the attenuation of DCVG signal
     strength at the regular CP test posts. A graph of DCVG signal
     strength against pipeline length will give a gradient of the
     corresponding flow of current of a section between the test
     posts;

The results of this study will contribute to a new structural
approach for the control of overall integrity of Gasunie's pipelines. Currently, Gasunie is developing a new maintenance philosophy related to pipeline integrity, which is to be ISO-9000 certified in the future. Examples of a few possibilities are :

The gradient of attenuation of the DCVG signal strength per unit
of length, measured at the cp test posts with an interrupting cp-
rectifier, can be used as a ranking for a coating survey of a
pipeline section. If the gradient is too high, the corresponding
section should be surveyed. As a surveying method, the DCVG technique can be used. The advantage of DCVG is that it will determine
a relative ranking (size/importance) of defects. The ranking
figure can thus be used to carry out immediately an excavation, to
postpone the excavation or to leave the defect unrepaired.

Another possibility is to apply a theoretical Ranking Tool,
which is now being developed within Gasunie Research. This tool
will select a pipeline to be surveyed from a set of approximately
thirty parameters, which derive beside the chance for a pipeline
to fail (depth of cover, wall thickness, etc.) also the external
corrosion process of a buried pipeline (for example pH-value, soil
resistance, type of soil, existence of Sulphate Reducing Bacteria
etc.).

A third alternative can be obtained by combining the above
mentioned alternatives. Here, the DCVG measuring program is based
on the results of the Ranking Tool.
The advantage of using the DCVG technique is that it will eventually result in a well balanced situation between the coating
survey and the cathodic protection technique. After repairing the
coating defects with the largest size/importance ratio, a better
and more effective distribution of cp current is achieved.

**ACKNOWLEDGMENT**

The support to this paper by Dr. John M. Leeds, APRT [1]) (Bolton,
Lancashire, UK) is gratefully acknowledged. Further the authors
like to thank as well as Dr. John Leeds as the company PIM [2]) in
Burnley UK, at which he was employed, for the 100 km coating
survey work they have performed for Gasunie through contract
742841.

Note [1])  :  Dr. John M. Leeds set up and worked for PIM, but started
             mid 1994 the company Advanced Pipeline Rehabilitation
             and Training Ltd.

Note [2])  :  PIM has been taken over by Cathodic Protection Services
             (CPS) since January 1995 and resides in the USA, UK and
             the Netherlands.

| Section | Section parameters | | |
|---------|---------------------|------------------------|-------------|
|         | Type of Coating | Pipelength (in km) | # of defects |
| 1 | PE | 14.55 | 48 |
| 2 | asphalt | 22.60 | 1297 |
| 3 | asphalt | 9.83 | 888 |
| 4 | asphalt | 8.25 | 418 |
| 5 | PE | 4.31 | 4 |
| 6 | asphalt | 17.93 | 788 |
| 7 | asphalt | 12.94 | 324 |
| TOTAL | | 90.07 | 3767 |

table 1 : The number of coating defects

| Section | Number of defects related to the relative size/importance of defects | | | |
|---------|-----------------|------------------|------------------|---------------------|
|         | Small 0 - 15 | Mean 16 - 35 | Large 36 -70 | Extra Large 71 - 100 |
| 1 | 43 | 3 | 2 | 0 |
| 2 | 1125 | 150 | 22 | 0 |
| 3 | 878 | 10 | 0 | 0 |
| 4 | 371 | 45 | 2 | 0 |
| 5 | 4 | 0 | 0 | 0 |
| 6 | 753 | 26 | 7 | 2 |
| 7 | 318 | 5 | 1 | 0 |
| TOTAL | 3492 92.7% | 239 6.3% | 34 0.9% | 2 0.05% |

table 2 : The number of coating defects related to
four categories of the relative size/importance of
a defect

| | Corrosion behaviour | | |
|---|---|---|---|
| | Not Protected | Protected | |
| Section | A / A | A / C | C /C |
| 1 | 0 | 0 | 48 |
| 2 | 11 | 71 | 1215 |
| 3 | 4 | 74 | 810 |
| 4 | 13 | 13 | 392 |
| 5 | 0 | 0 | 4 |
| 6 | 8 | 49 | 731 |
| 7 | 8 | 39 | 277 |
| TOTAL | 44 1.2% | 246 6.5% | 3477 92.3% |

table 3 : The number of coating defects related to three types of corrosion behaviour at a defect

| | | Excavation overview | | | | | |
|---|---|---|---|---|---|---|---|
| | Total | Divided over Defect size/importance | | | Divided over corrosion behaviour | | |
| Section | | Small | Mean | Large | A/A | A/C | C/C |
| 1 | - | - | - | - | - | - | - |
| 2 | 16 | 6 | 5 | 5 | 2 | 2 | 12 |
| 3 | 3 | 1 | 2 | - | - | 1 | 2 |
| 4 | 4 | 1 | 1 | 4 | 4 | - | - |
| 5 | - | - | - | - | - | - | - |
| 6 | 2 | 1 | - | 1 | 1 | - | 1 |
| 7 | - | - | - | - | - | - | - |
| TOTAL | 25 | 9 | 8 | 8 | 7 | 3 | 15 |

table 4 : Excavation overview

| | | Corrosion behaviour | | | | | |
|---|---|---|---|---|---|---|---|
| | | Not Protected | | Protected | | | |
| CP status | Measurement | A / A | | A / C | | C / C | |
| CP OFF | Current flow Anodic | A | | A | | | |
| | Current flow Cathodic | | | | | C | |
| CP ON | Current flow Anodic | | A | | | | |
| | Current flow Cathodic | | | | C | | C |

table 5 : Explanation of corrosion behaviour

AUTOMATIC INSPECTION ROBOT SURVEYING
PIPELINE FOR LOSS OF WALL THICKNESS


ROBOT D'INSPECTION AUTOMATIQUE DES PERTES D'EPAISSEUR DE CANALISATIONS

Y. Okajima
Trunkline Department, Osaka Gas Co., Ltd., JAPAN

ABSTRACT

Technology for diagnosing the soundness of pipelines at an early stage is important and essential to maintain safe operation and ensure safety of pipelines. To meet the needs for inspection and diagnosis of these pipelines, and to inspect pipelines more accurate than usual intelligent pigs, Osaka Gas Co., Ltd. has developed two types of automatically inspection robots as in the following:
(1) Automatic Inspection Robot For Loss Of Wall Thickness
     This robot detects corrosion and cracks in gas pipelines by using wheel type ultrasonic sensors.
(2) Automatic Inspection Robot For Dents
     This robot detects pipe deformations by using high-performance eddy current sensors.
In the development of these inspection robots, we also paid attention to the running performance so that the robots was able to run smoothly on 1.5DR bend pipes.
Furthermore, we applied these inspection robots to inspect and diagnose our high-pressure gas pipelines and confirmed that the robots were effective in inspecting deformations, corrosion and cracks in gas pipelines.


RÉSUMÉ

La technologie pour diagnostiquer la solidité de ces conduites ou pipelines au premier stade est donc importante et essentielle pour maintenir un fonctionnement sûr et assurer la sécurité de ces conduites. Pour répondre aux besoins concernant l'inspection et le diagnostic de ces conduites, la S.A. Osaka Gas a mis au point les deux types de robots de contrôle automatique suivants.
(1) Robot de contrôle automatique inspectant les conduites pour l'affaiblissement de l'epaisseur des parois.
     Ce robot permet de détecter la corrosion, les fissures et les craquelures dans les canalisations de gaz à grande distance en utilisant un palpeur à ultrasons de type à roue.
(2) Robot de contrôle automatique inspectant les conduites pour les bossellements.
     Ce robot détecte les déformation des conduites (bossellements et aplatissements) en utilisant un palpeur à courants de Foucault aux performances élevées.
Dans la mise au point de ces robots de contrôle, nous nous sommes penchés sur le comportement lors du parcours, de facon à ce que ces robots soient capables de se déplacer facilement dans des conduites cintrées d'un faible rayon de courbure (1.5DR), bien que chaque robot soit composé de jusqu'à cing éléments.
En outre, nous avons mis en pratique ces robots de contrôle pour inspecter et diagnostiquer nos canalisations de gaz à grande distance et nous avons pu vérifier que ces robots étaient efficaces lors de l'inspection de déformations, de corrosions et de fissures de telles conduites.

## INTRODUCTION

Pipelines have been used widely at various places in the world as means for safely transporting large amounts of oil, natural gas, etc. from production regions to consumption regions. Also in Japan, pipelines have been used to transport natural gas from LNG receiving bases to consumption regions, although the entire length of the pipelines is shorter than that of those used in Europe and America. Since starting the construction of the Kinki Eastern Trunkline I as the first high-pressure natural gas pipeline in 1967, Osaka Gas has constructed pipelines of about 500km in length, mainly composed of pipes of 600mm in diameter and rated at 4MPa in pressure. By using the pipelines, we safely transport gas of more than $5*10^9 Nm^3$ in a year.

Technology for diagnosing the soundness of pipelines at an early stage is important and essential to maintain safe operation and ensure safety of pipelines. In the U.S.A., DOT (Department of Transportation) is trying to legislate the application of intelligent pigs to inspection and diagnosis of pipelines as a measure to be taken for pipeline accidents.

To meet the needs for inspection and diagnosis of these pipelines, Osaka Gas has pursued the development of inspection robots since 1986 in cooperation with NKK.

In 1988, we developed the Automatic Inspection Robot For Dents (Photo.1) to detect pipe deformations (dents and oval) by using high-performance eddy current sensors. We have already used this robot to inspect our high-pressure gas pipelines of about 200km in length by running the robot through the pipelines.

We have recently developed the Automatic Inspection Robot For Loss Of Wall Thickness (Photo.2) to detect corrosion and cracks in high-pressure gas pipelines by using ultrasonic techniques. We will report the general descriptions of these inspection robots and the results of application of these robots to the inspection and diagnosis of our high-pressure gas pipelines.

## AUTOMATIC INSPECTION ROBOT FOR LOSS OF WALL THICKNESS

### Measurement Principle

Although intelligent pigs based on magnetic flux leakage technologies and eddy current technologies became practical to inspect and diagnose pipelines. However, they did not meet the needs of Osaka Gas in regard to defect detection accuracy and crack detection. Although intelligent pigs based on ultrasonic techniques became practical for oil pipelines, it was assumed difficult to apply such a pig to gas pipelines in which fluids to be transported through the pipelines were not able to be used as couplants in the ultrasonic techniques.

Osaka Gas has developed wheel type ultrasonic sensors which do not require any fluid couplants. By using a normal beam technique and an angle beam technique, the sensor can detect both corrosion and cracks.

The wheel type ultrasonic sensor is provided with ultrasonic probes at the center of its wheel to detect corrosion and cracks by using ultrasonic transmitted to and received from pipes via the wheel made of rubber. To select a proper material for the rubber wheel, more than ten kinds of rubber materials, such as natural rubber and urethane rubber, were subjected to tests for checking close contact performance to pipe walls and also subjected to ultrasonic transmission measurement tests. According to the results of the tests, we adopted butadiene rubber which had the highest ultrasonic transmission.

The wheel type ultrasonic sensor is classified into three types depending on the difference in the beam angle of ultrasonic. (Fig.1)

(1) V-Type Sensor: Detects corrosion on external surfaces by using a normal beam technique
(Used to measure pipe wall thickness.)

(2) F-Type Sensor: Detects cracks in the circumferential direction of the pipe by using an angle beam technique in the running direction of the inspection robot.

(3) S-Type Sensor: Detects cracks in the axial direction by using an angle beam technique in the circumferential direction of the pipe.

By mounting these three wheel type ultrasonic sensors on an inspection robot, corrosion and cracks in pipelines can be detected simultaneously by performing inspection once.

* Defect position detection accuracy
   This robot can detect a defect position at an accuracy of ±0.3m by using a
   combination of a rotary encoder and a weld detector.

   Applicable Pipelines.
* Pipe line diameter: 600mm or more
* Radius of curvature of bend pipe: 1.5DR or more
* Continuous measurement distance: Max. 100km

OFF-LINE TEST

Test Line Facility

   Unlike the pipelines installed in overseas countries, most of the pipelines
installed in Japan are buried under roads. Furthermore, since there are many
rivers and mountains in Japan, many pipelines are required to cross rivers and
harbors in relatively short distances.
   Therefore, bend pipes having a small radius of curvature (1.5DR) are used for
the pipelines. The inspection robot is required to smoothly run even in such
locations.
   Accordingly, we produced a test line comprising pipes of 600mm in diameter
and extending 100m in total length to confirm running and measurement
performance of the inspection robot. (Fig.5) In this test line, 1.5DR bend pipes
are combined complicatedly. By using flange connection, the combinations of bend
pipes can be changed and artificially defective pipes can be combined to confirm
measurement performance.

Running Performance Test

   Since the Automatic Inspection Robot For Loss Of Wall Thickness is composed
of up to five robot units, it was very difficult to make the robot units
smoothly run through complicated 1.5DR bend pipes. We improved the robot units
and repeated running tests at the test line. By putting some ideas into the
design of guide rollers (Photo.3), guide protectors, etc., the robot was able to
run through the complicated bend pipes smoothly and stably.

Measurement Performance Test

   Artificially defective pipes were built in the test line and the Automatic
Inspection Robot For Loss Of Wall Thickness and the Automatic Inspection Robot
For Dents were run through such pipes to confirm the measurement performance of
the robot.
   Fig.6 shows the artificially defective pipes used to confirm the corrosion
detection performance of the Automatic Inspection Robot For Loss Of Wall
Thickness and the results of the measurement tests. According to the test
results, it was found that the loss of wall thickness at circular and square
sections as well as the wall thickness at normal sections were measured with an
accuracy of ±1mm.
   Fig.7 shows the results of measurement tests conducted to confirm the
circumferential crack detection performance of the Automatic Inspection Robot
For Loss Of Wall Thickness. According to the test results, it was found that the
robot detected most of slit-shaped defects in the circumferential direction of
pipes.
   Fig.8 shows the results of the measurement tests conducted to confirm the
performance of the Automatic Inspection Robot For Dents. According to the test
results, it was found that the robot measured dents of 7mm in depth with an
accuracy of ±1mm.

ON-LINE TESTS AT GAS PIPELINES

Automatic Inspection Robot For Loss Of Wall Thickness

   In September, 1994, we conducted on-line tests at our actually-operating
pipeline by using the Automatic Inspection Robot For Loss Of Wall Thickness
completely developed by us.
   We inspected the pipeline extended between the Senboku Works I and the
Kawachi Station, 34km in total length, 600mm in diameter and 2MPa in maximum

## Structure

Three robot units are equipped with three types of sensors (16 sensors of each type in the circumferential direction of each robot unit). These robot units are connected when performing travel inspection. (Fig.2)
First robot unit : Memory robot..... equipped with IC memory and CPU
Second robot unit: Detector robot... equipped with an ultrasonic flaw detector
Third robot unit : Sensor robot..... equipped with 16 V-Type Sensors
Fourth robot unit: Sensor robot..... equipped with 16 S-Type Sensors
Fifth robot unit : Sensor robot..... equipped with 16 F-Type Sensors
During inspection running, data from 48 wheel type ultrasonic sensors in total are processed sequentially by the CPU and stored in the SRAM of the first robot unit. After inspection running, the robot is taken out from a pig receiver. Data are then transferred to a personal computer and processed by a data regeneration system. The results of the inspection are indicated on a visual color display.

## Performance

### Defect Detection Performance.
* External surface corrosion detection performance
  The robot detects external surface corrosion of 1.5mm or more in depth with an accuracy of ±1mm.
* Slit-shaped defect detection performance
  The robot detects cracks of 150mm or more in length.
* Defect position detection accuracy
  The robot can detect a defective position at an accuracy of ±0.3m by using a combination of a rotary encoder and a weld detector.

### Applicable Pipelines.
* Pipe line diameter: 600mm or more
* Radius of curvature of bend pipe: 1.5DR or more
* Continuous measurement distance: Max. 50km

## AUTOMATIC INSPECTION ROBOT FOR DENTS

### Measurement Principle

For pipeline deformation inspection, a mechanical measurement unit referred to as "caliper pig" has become practical. However, to measure the shapes and dimensions of dents at higher accuracy, we have developed a high-performance eddy current sensor. This sensor uses a sensor coil to detect a magnetic field formed by eddy current generated on a metal surface by a transmitter coil, thereby measuring the distance between the coil and the metal. (Fig.3)
This principle has been applied to an electromagnetic film thickness sensor used to measure nonconductor films, such as paint films of several millimeters in thickness coated on conductors. However, in the development of our inspection robot, we have developed a high-performance eddy current sensor capable of measuring a distance up to 60mm so that the deformation on pipe surface can be measured from the robot on running.

### Structure

The inspection robot is equipped with 18 eddy current sensors disposed at equal intervals on the external circumferential circle and measures dents and flats when the robot travels through pipelines.
The inspection robot is used as a single unit and equipped with IC memory for data storage, a battery, etc. inside the robot. (Fig.4)

### Performance

### Defect Detection Performance.
* Deformation detection performance
  This robot detects dents or swells of 3mm or more in depth or height with an accuracy of ±3mm.

operating pressure. In this pipeline, more than ten complicated pipe sections comprising 1.5DR bend pipes are included to cross rivers or the like. (Fig.9)

We inserted the robot into the pig launcher at the Senboku Works I and started the robot (Photo.4). Four hours after running the robot at an average speed of 2.4m/s, the robot arrived at the pig receiver of the Kawachi Station. The robot was then taken out and connected to a personal computer to analyze data.

According to the results, although data for the complicated pipe sections comprising continuous 1.5DR bend pipes could not be taken, measurement was performed at most sections other than the complicated pipe sections. It was confirmed that the pipeline was free from any defects (corrosion, cracks, etc.).

Automatic Inspection Robot For Dents

The Automatic Inspection Robot For Dents was actually used for inspection on our high-pressure gas pipeline extending about 200km since 1989. It was confirmed that the pipeline was free from any harmful dents or oval.

CONCLUSION

According to the results of the measurement performance tests at the test line and the results of the on-line tests of our pipeline, it was confirmed that the Automatic Inspection Robot For Loss Of Wall Thickness and the Automatic Inspection Robot For Dents are useful for diagnosing the soundness of gas pipelines.

In addition, according to the results of the online tests, it was also confirmed that the robots were reliable and durable in running of 1.5DR bend pipes and during long-distance continuous measurements.

In Japan, it is expected that the construction of gas pipelines will increase and be extended to wider areas in the future. Furthermore, the existing pipelines will deteriorate with time. In these circumferences, the needs for the diagnosis of soundness of pipelines will keep increasing.

Osaka Gas will progressively apply these inspection robots developed by us to the diagnosis of soundness of our pipelines and will positively engage in the development of new inspection systems.

Photo.2    Automatic Inspection Robot For Loss Of Wall Thickness

Photo.4    Launching of the Automatic Inspection Robot
For Loss of Wall Thickness

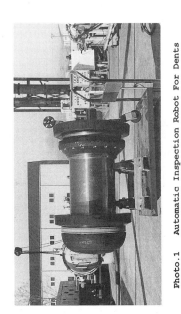

Photo.1    Automatic Inspection Robot For Dents

Photo.3    Guide Rollers

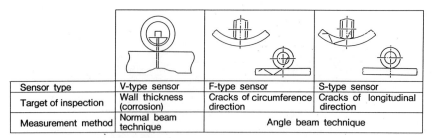

| Sensor type | V-type sensor | F-type sensor | S-type sensor |
|---|---|---|---|
| Target of inspection | Wall thickness (corrosion) | Cracks of circumference direction | Cracks of longitudinal direction |
| Measurement method | Normal beam technique | Angle beam technique | |

Fig.1    Three types of the Wheel Type Ultrasonic Sensor

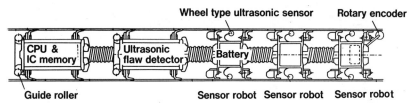

Fig.2    Structure of the Automatic Inspection Robot For Loss Of Wall Thickness

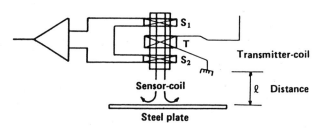

Fig.3    Eddy Current Sensor

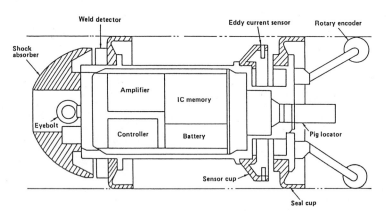

Fig.4    Structure of the Automatic Inspection Robot For Dents

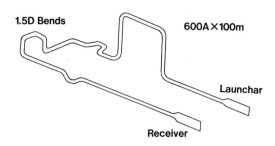

Fig.5    Test Line

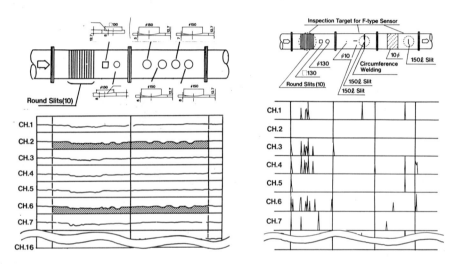

Fig.6    Measurement of Corrosion
at a Test Line

Fig.7    Measurement of Cracks
at a Test Line

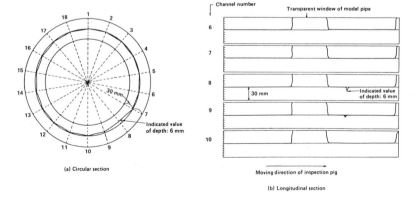

(a) Circular section

(b) Longitudinal section

Fig.8    Measurement of Dents at a Test Line

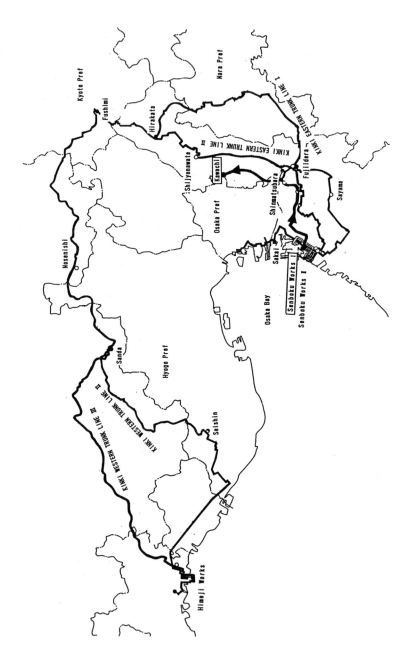

Fig. 9   High Pressure Gas Transmission Lines At Osaka Gas

# A NEW ACCURATE METHOD FOR CORRECTING THE VOS EFFECT ON VIBRATING GAS DENSITY TRANSDUCERS

## UNE NOUVELLE MÉTHODE EXACTE POUR CORRIGER LES EFFECTS DE LA CÉLÉRITÉ DU SON EN CONSIDÉRATION DE CAPTEURS OSCILLANTS

Dr. M. Jaeschke

Ruhrgas AG, Applied Physics Section, Germany

Dr.-Ing. X.Y. Guo, Dr.-Ing. R. Kleinrahm, Prof. Dr.-Ing. W. Wagner

Ruhr-Universität Bochum, Germany

## ABSTRACT

For the custody transfer of natural gas in pipelines the gas density is often measured using vibrating gas density transducers. However, due to the so-called velocity-of-sound (vos) effect and an additional viscosity effect, systematic errors of up to + 0.5 % can occur. For the accurate determination of these systematic transducer errors, six density transducers from three different producers have been comprehensively investigated with six pure gases and six natural gases over the last few years. Based on these very accurate results, a new method for correcting the vos and the viscosity effect is being developed in a current project. Corresponding to the present state of the development it is shown that the transducer errors for pure gases of up to about + 3 % can be reduced to less than ± 0.1 %. Considering this efficiency for pure gases, the accuracy for natural gases will most likely be better than the aspired accuracy of ± 0.05 %. The final purpose of the project is to achieve a total uncertainty of the density transducers (including calibration uncertainty etc.) of less than ± 0.1 % under field conditions. The development of the new correction method will be completed in autumn 1996.

## RÉSUMÉ

Pour le transfert de gaz naturel dans les pipelines, la densité du gaz est souvent mesurée avec des capteurs vibratoires de densité de gaz. Par contre, en considération des effets de la célérité du son et d'un effet supplémentaire de la viscosité, des erreurs systématiques augmentant jusqu'à + 0,5 % peuvent se produire. Pour la détermination exacte de ces erreurs systématiques concernant les capteurs de densité de gaz six capteurs de trois manufactures différentes ont été vérifiés d'une manière étendue avec six sortes de gaz naturel pendant les années précédentes. Basé sur ces résultats très exactes, une nouvelle méthode pour corriger les effets de la célérité du son et de la viscosité est développée dans un projet actuel. Conforme à l'état présent du développement il est illustré que les erreurs liés aux capteurs de densité pour de gaz pure qui augmentent à + 3 % peuvent être réduits à < ± 0,1 %. En considération de cette efficacité pour les gazes pures, la précision pour de gaz naturel sera certainement meilleur que la précision aspirée de ± 0,05 %. L'intention final de ce projet est d'achever une imprécision totale des capteurs de densité de < ± 0,1 % sous conditions opératoires (y inclus l'imprécision de calibrage etc.). Le développement de la nouvelle méthode corrective sera terminé en automne 1996.

## 1   INTRODUCTION

Very large quantities of natural gas are transferred by pipelines in numerous countries. For the custody transfer of this natural gas its density is often measured under pipeline conditions using vibrating gas density transducers. Due to the very large mass flows, the uncertainty of these density transducers should be less than $\pm$ 0.1 %. The sensor elements of these gas density transducers are vibrating thin-walled metal cylinders (Solartron) or vibrating forks (Bopp & Reuther; RMG-Meßtechnik); their natural frequency and their periodic time $\tau$, respectively, depend almost entirely upon the density of the gas surrounding the vibrating element. The relation between the periodic time $\tau$ and the gas density $\rho$ is described by the equation $\rho = K_0 + K_1 \cdot \tau + K_2 \cdot \tau^2$. The coefficients $K_0$, $K_1$, $K_2$ are individual transducer constants which are usually determined by calibrating the transducers with methane. However, when the density of natural gas is measured with such methane-calibrated transducers, systematic errors of up to + 0.5 % can occur. The main reason for this error is the difference in the velocity of sound of the calibration gas and the measuring gas at the same density (velocity-of-sound effect, abbreviated as vos effect). In addition to this main vos effect, measurements with the transducers can also be influenced by differences in further thermophysical properties of the calibration gas and the measuring gas, especially by differences in viscosity.

For the accurate experimental investigation of this "gas-specific" effect on the gas density transducers, a special apparatus was developed a few years ago; its design is briefly described in the next section. With this apparatus, six density transducers from three different producers have been comprehensively investigated over the last few years. Based on these very accurate results, a new accurate method for correcting the gas-specific effect is being developed in a current project. In this paper the present state of the development is presented.

## 2   BRIEF DESCRIPTION OF THE MEASURING APPARATUS

The measuring apparatus, used for the experimental investigation of the gas density transducers, consists of two coupled parts: a very accurate gas densitometer and a calibration unit for six gas density transducers. The calibration unit consists of a temperature-controlled liquid bath in which six density transducers from different manufacturers can be simultaneously investigated or calibrated with either pure gases or natural gases. In order to determine simultaneously the density of the gas with which the gas density transducers are tested, a special apparatus for accurate gas density measurements (densitometer) was developed. For the very accurate density measurements required, a "Two-Sinker-Method" is used which is based on the Archimedes' buoyancy principle but is applied in quite a new way as a compensation method. The specifications of the densitometer correspond to the special requirements of the gas industry; the apparatus covers a temperature range from 0 °C to 50 °C, a pressure range from 0.1 MPa to 12 MPa, and a density range from 1 kg/m³ to 1000 kg/m³. Its total uncertainty in density (including uncertainty of temperature and pressure) is less than $\pm$ 0.02 % for densities above 5 kg/m$^3$ and less than $\pm$ 0.04 % for densities of about 1 kg/m$^3$.

The gas densitometer and the calibration unit were presented at the IGRC 1992 in Orlando and more details about the design are given in reference [1]. A photo of the entire equipment is shown in figure 1.

**Figure 1:** Gas densitometer with calibration unit at Ruhrgas AG.

## 3  SYSTEMATIC ERRORS OF GAS DENSITY TRANSDUCERS DUE TO THE GAS-SPECIFIC EFFECT

By means of the described apparatus, six gas density transducers from three different producers (Solartron Transducers, Great Britain; Bopp & Reuther GmbH, Germany; RMG-Meßtechnik GmbH, Germany) were at first calibrated with methane and then comprehensively investigated with six pure gases ($N_2$, $CO_2$, $C_2H_6$, $C_2H_4$, Ar, Ne) and six natural gases. The measurements were usually carried out in the density range from 20 kg/m$^3$ to 80 kg/m$^3$ at the temperatures 0 °C, 10 °C, and 20 °C. A part of the results were already presented at the IGRC 1992 in Orlando [1]; the complete results are described in a final report for the Ruhrgas AG [2]. In the following some selected results of these experimental investigations have been reviewed because they form the basis required for the development of a new correction method.

Firstly, figure 2 shows the required calibration of three different gas density transducers (one from each producer) with methane. The transducer constants $K_0$, $K_1$, $K_2$ were determined by fitting the correlation equation given in section 1 to the densities measured with the gas densitometer for the 10 °C isotherm (marked by circles). To investigate the temperature dependence of the transducer, the 20 °C and the 0 °C isotherm were also measured. To check the stability of the vibrating elements, the 10 °C isotherm was measured once more three weeks after the first run.

As typical examples, figure 3 and 4 show the systematic error of the three transducers due to the gas-specific effect when such methane-calibrated transducers are used for density measurements of gases different from the calibration gas. In figure 3, the systematic errors for six pure test gases are presented on the 10 °C isotherm (calibration temperature) and figure 4 shows these errors for four natural gases. The transducer errors amount to about + 3 % for pure gases and up to about + 0.4 % for natural gases. The high accuracy of the new experimental results can clearly be recognized in figures 2 to 4. In the past, other laboratories which investigated vibrating gas density transducers on the whole obtained an accuracy not better than ± 0.1%.

In order to complete these existing experimental results, the systematic errors due to the gas-specific effect on the new Solartron transducer, type 7812, is being experimentally investigated in a current project with the apparatus described in section 2. The errors of this new transducer type amount up to about + 1.1 % for pure gases and up to about + 0.15 % for natural gases. These complementary measurements will probably be finished in summer 1995.

## 4 INVESTIGATION OF THE CURRENT VOS CORRECTION METHODS CONCERNING THEIR EFFICIENCY

After finishing the comprehensive experimental investigations on three various types of gas density transducers, the current vos correction methods, i.e. the Solartron correction method [3, 4], the correction method developed by Hinze and Jaeschke [5], and the correction method proposed by RMG-Meßtechnik [6], were investigated with respect to their efficiency [2]. The results show, however, that the currently known correction methods are not accurate enough with regard to the present requirements. The residual errors after applying the various correction methods to the measuring errors of the transducers amount to up to about ± 1 % for pure gases and up to about ± 0.2 % for natural gases depending on the correction method considered and the respective transducer type. The Solartron correction method applied to the Solartron transducers yields the best results. In this case, the residual errors are < ± 0.3 % for pure gases and < ± 0.1 % for natural gases. Especially in the case of vibrating forks used as density sensor elements it is clearly recognizable that, in addition to the vos effect, a significant part of the transducer error is caused by the difference in the viscosity of the calibration gas and the measuring gas (viscosity effect).

## 5 DEVELOPMENT OF A NEW CORRECTION METHOD FOR THE GAS-SPECIFIC EFFECT

Due to this present situation, a new accurate correction method for the gas-specific effect is being developed in a current project based on the new comprehensive experimental results and in consideration of the existing correction methods. Since the final purpose of the project is to achieve a total uncertainty of the gas density transducers (including calibration uncertainty, scattering of the measurements, small shifts of the transducer calibration curve, etc.) of less than $\pm$ 0.1 % under field conditions, the uncertainty of the new correction method should be less than $\pm$ 0.05 %. This means that the residual errors after applying the correction method to the measuring errors of the transducers should usually be less than $\pm$ 0.05 % for natural gases.

Corresponding to the present state of the development, figure 5 shows the residual density errors for pure gases after applying the new correction method to the systematic errors of the three selected density transducers presented in section 3. It can clearly be seen that the residual errors are mostly considerably less than $\pm$ 0.1 % for all three transducers. Hence, the transducer errors have been reduced from up to about + 3 % to less than $\pm$ 0.1 %. Nevertheless, it is conspicuous that the measurements on $CO_2$ show a considerable deviation of up to + 0.3 % for the Bopp & Reuther and the RMG transducers and a small but recognizeable deviation of about + 0.05 % for the Solartron transducer. The reason for this residual error is not the gas-specific effect but the extremely strong adsorption of $CO_2$ on the surface of the sensor elements. For all the other gases this effect is mostly negligibly small. Furthermore, it should be mentioned that the $N_2$ measurements of the Bopp & Reuther transducer have been omitted in figure 5 because the transducer yielded wrong oscillating measuring values for nitrogen (see figure 3).

Corresponding to the current correction methods, the new correction method also needs the velocity of sound of the calibration gas and the measuring gas as input values. Additionally, the viscosity of these two gases are needed. In comparison with the vos effect, which causes the main part of the gas-specific effect, the viscosity effect is smaller but, nevertheless, can cause errors up to + 1 % for pure gases depending on the measuring gas and the transducer type considered. Since the development is still in progress the equation of the correction method is not presented and discussed in this paper.

Considering the achieved accuracy of the new correction method for pure gases, the accuracy for natural gases will most likely be better than the aspired uncertainty of less than $\pm$ 0.05 %. However, the error reduction is not possible (and also not necessary) in the same ratio as for pure gases because the uncertainty of the input values needed for the correction method, namely the velocity of sound and the viscosity of natural gases, is greater than for pure gases. For the accurate calculation of the velocity of sound of natural gases in the temperature range from 0 °C to 50 °C and at densities up to 100 kg/m$^3$ a new simple equation has recently been developed which has a sufficiently small uncertainty of less than $\pm$ 0.5 %. Moreover, a new equation for the calculation of the viscosity of natural gases has been developed which also has a sufficient uncertainty of less than a few per cent.

The development of the new correction method will be completed in autum 1996.

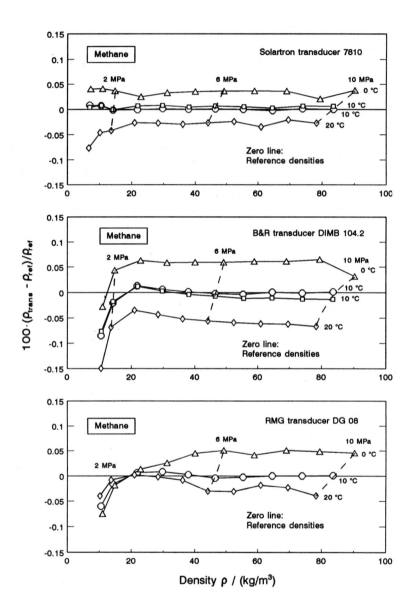

**Figure 2:** Calibration and investigation of three different gas density transducers with methane. Percentage deviations between densities measured by the transducers $\rho_{trans}$ and reference densities $\rho_{ref}$ measured by the densitometer. The transducers were calibrated with methane at 10 °C (-o-, calibration set).

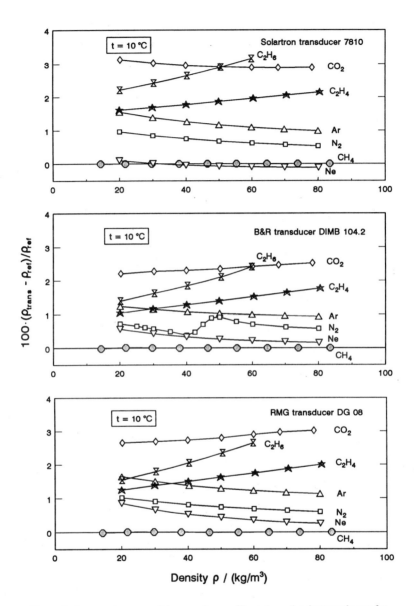

**Figure 3:** Systematic errors of three methane-calibrated gas density transducers for six pure gases. Percentage deviations between densities measured by the transducers $\rho_{trans}$ and reference densities $\rho_{ref}$ measured by the densitometer at 10 °C.

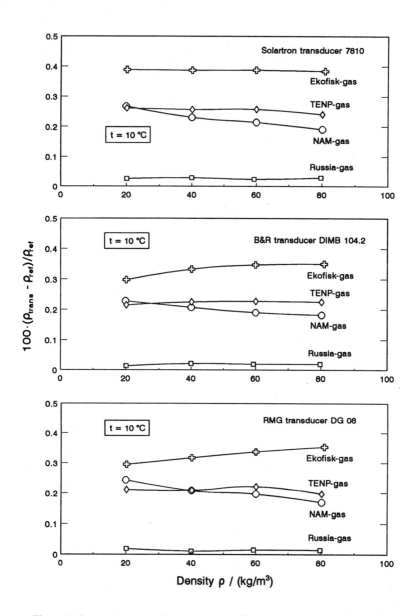

**Figure 4:** Systematic errors of three methane-calibrated gas density transducers for four natural gases. Percentage deviations between densities measured by the transducers $\rho_{trans}$ and reference densities $\rho_{ref}$ measured by the densitometer at 10 °C.

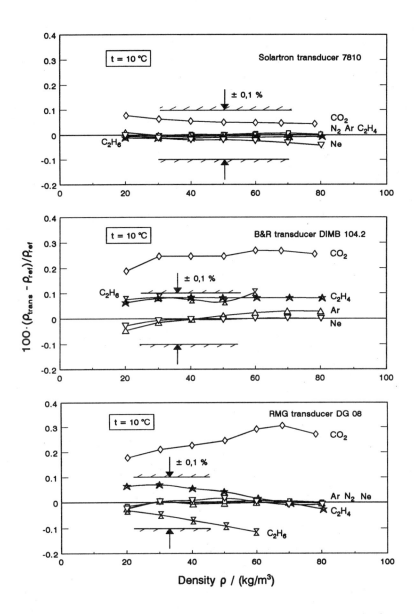

**Figure 5:** Residual errors of three methane-calibrated gas density transducers for six pure gases after correcting the vos and the viscosity effect applying the new correction method in its present state.

## References

[1]  Wagner, W.; Kleinrahm, R.; Guo, X.Y.; Olbricht, G.; Jaeschke, M.: Experimental investigation of the vos effect on gas density transducers for natural gas pipelines. Proc. of the Int. Gas Res. Conference, Orlando (Nov. 1992) 863-874. Gas Research Institute, Chicago, USA.

[2]  Guo, X.Y.; Kleinrahm, R.; Wagner, W.; Jaeschke, M.: Experimentelle Untersuchung der systematischen Meßfehler von Betriebsdichteaufnehmern für Erdgasmeßstrecken. Teil 1: Meßergebnisse für Stickstoff, Kohlendioxid, Argon, Neon, Ethan und Ethen (1992); Teil 2: Meßergebnisse für Erdgase (1993); Teil 3: Untersuchung der Güte der gebräuchlichen Verfahren zur Korrektur des Gasarteneinflusses (1993). Lehrstuhl für Thermodynamik, Ruhr-Universität Bochum .

[3]  Stansfeld, J.W.: VOS-Korrekturmethoden für Erdgasmessungen unter Verwendung von Solartron Dichte-Meßwertaufnehmern für den Bereich von 0 - 60 kg/m$^3$. Engineering Report DENS-01121, Ausgabe 2, 1986. Solartron Transducers, Farnborough, England.

[4]  Stansfeld, J. W.: Velocity of Sound Effect on Gas Density Transducers - The Theory, Measurement Results and Methods of Correction. North Sea Flow Metering Workshop, Glasgow, 7-9 October 1986, Paper 2.2. National Engineering Laboratory, Glasgow, U. K.

[5]  Hinze, H.M.; Jaeschke, M.: Messung der Dichte von Erdgasen nach der Wägemethode und mit Betriebsdichteaufnehmern. Fortschr.-Ber. VDI-Z., Reihe 6, Nr. 162, VDI-Verlag, Düsseldorf (1985).

[6]  VOS-Korrektur Vergleich. Technischer Bericht. RMG-Meßtechnik GmbH, Butzbach, 1987.

ANALYSIS OF METAL IMPURITIES IN NATURAL GAS: NEW METHODS OF TRAPPING

ANALYSES DES TRACES METALLIQUES PRESENTES DANS LE GAZ NATUREL: NOUVELLES METHODES DE PIEGEAGE.

Sylvie JADOUL, Frédérique MASSON

GAZ DE FRANCE, RESEARCH AND DEVELOPMENT DIVISION, FRANCE

## ABSTRACT

Environmental concerns over natural gas built up in aquifers layers have led Gaz de France to search for possible presence of pollutants in natural gas. In particular, heavy metals (Cr, Cu, Zn...) and metalloids were studied. This work presents different methods of trapping developed in order to evaluate the level of those pollutants in natural gas: - one involves trapping in a pressurised system with acid solutions ($HCl/HNO_3$). The latest modifications eliminate the flow-rate variations due to hydrates formation. The use of filters before the liquid system will separate the solid particle elements from the gaseous ones. - The other consists of using adsorbents. The adsorbents are initially selected on the basis of their purity. Tests on their efficiency are not made yet.Finally, we present the existing trapping method and its main characteristics.

## RESUME

Gaz de France s'intéresse très étroitement aux problèmes environnementaux liés au stockage de gaz naturel en nappes aquifères. La présence éventuelle de polluants pouvant diffuser dans les nappes phréatiques est largement étudiée. En particulier, le cas des métaux lourds (Cr, Cu, Zn ...) ou des métalloïdes toxiques a été soulevé. Ce travail présente la mise au point des différentes méthodes de piégeage et de dosage permettant d'estimer la quantité présente dans le gaz naturel. Deux méthodes de piégeage ont été testées : - La première consiste à piéger par barbotage dans une solution acide ($HCl/HNO_3$). Les dernières modifications apportées à ce système ont permis de supprimer les variations intempestives du débit dues à la formation d'hydrates. De plus, l'utilisation de filtres en amont du piège liquide devrait séparer les éléments sous forme de poussières de ceux présents sous forme gazeuse, - la seconde consiste à piéger ces composés sur un support solide. Une première sélection permet de choisir les adsorbants les moins pollués en composés métalliques. leur efficacité reste à tester.Enfin, la méthode mise au point et ses principales caractéristiques sont résumées.

INTRODUCTION

As environmental concerns increase, Gaz de France raises the issue of possible pollution of aquifers by trace compounds present in natural gas. In particular, the presence of heavy metals and toxic metalloids is studied to evaluate their contribution to underground water pollution.

Some of these elements may be naturally present in gas, like mercury, which exists in the form of metallic vapours. This problem has been widely studied due to the risk of corrosion on the cryogenic exchangers used to liquefy natural gas (3). To this end, Gaz de France has developed a special apparatus designed to trap and quantitatively analyse mercury in natural gas. American research notes the presence of arsenic, especially in the form of trimethylarsine, in certain natural gas deposit (4). Other elements are probably not naturally present in gas; they seem to be brought in during transport due to phenomena of erosion and corrosion of metal pipeline.

The study deals with the development of methods for trapping metallic and metalloïdic impurities in natural gas. Once trapped, the elements are analysed by inductively coupled plasma emission spectroscopy (ICP-AES) or inductively coupled plasma - mass spectroscopy (ICP-MS).

Two trapping methods are tested:
- The first method involves trapping in solution in a pressurised system in order to keep trapping time to a minimum. Tests are made on thermal regulation to avoid flow rate variations due to hydrates generation.
A system of dust filtration before entrapment is currently being studied. It will be used to separate, identify and quantify the elements present in the form of particles transported in the gas.
- The second method is based on selective adsorption on a solid support.
Finally, we give a description of the existing system and its main characteristics.

LIQUID TRAPPING METHOD

Principle.

The absorbent solution used is a 10% nitric acid / 10% hydrochloric acid mixture (1), (2). As we are looking for a very low level of impurities in gas, we need to trap a large volume of gas. Hence, we work under pressure to limit the trapping time. The gas pressure in the pipe is approximately 60 bar, our system works at 40 bar (5). The flow rate is 20 l/min for 7 days. The system is made of titanium to avoid pollution coming from corrosion (see figures 1 and 4).

Heating system improvement.

The device is fitted with an ADF heating cord, which is capable of maintaining a proper heat level adjustment, even in winter. Laboratory tests show a good flow rate and temperature regulation after a day's work (see figure 2). On site, we had the same temperature evolution. During the ten trapping days, the flow rate remained stable because there was no hydrate generation. At that pressure, hydrates start to be generated at 10°C (6) (see figure 3).

A day or two are required to let the temperature stabilise completely, before it can be ascertained that the flow rate will not fluctuate .

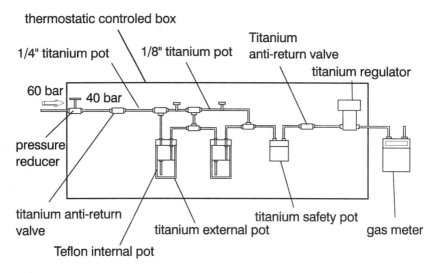

**Figure 1: liquid trapping system.**

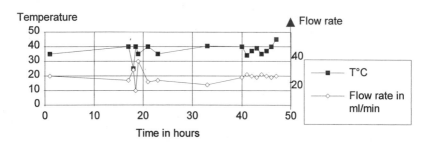

**Figure 2: Change in flow rate and temperature over time using the new temperature regulation system. This test was made at the Gaz de France Research Centre.**

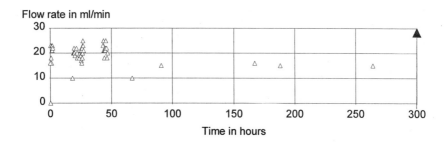

**Figure 3: Change in flow rate over time. Test made on site (Taisnières, North of France)**

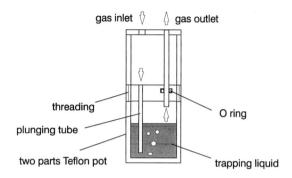

gas inlet     gas outlet

threading

plunging tube

two parts Teflon pot

O ring

trapping liquid

**figure 4: Teflon pot view**

DUST FILTRATION

The main advantage of this method is to separate the elements according to their physical form (solid or gaseous). We studied filters with pore diameter in the range of 0,4 to 0,8 µm in order to eliminate dust particles with size greater than 1 µm The choice of filters depends on three criteria:
- the metallic impurities naturally present in the filter, (7)
- their retention efficiency depending on the trapping flow rate and the particle size. (8)
- their ability to be analysed.

Choice of filters

| Filter type | porosity µm | company | mass in g | As | Cd | Sn | Pb | Bi | V | Cr | Cu | Zn | solubility |
|---|---|---|---|---|---|---|---|---|---|---|---|---|---|
| | | | | \multicolumn{9}{c}{Elements en µg/l     *} | |
| Cellulose acetate | 0.8 | Sartorius | 0.086 | <1 | <1 | <1 | <1 | <1 | <1 | <6 | 1 | <9 | complete |
| Cellulose nitrate | 0.8 | Sartorius | 0.075 | <1 | <1 | <1 | <1 | <1 | <1 | <6 | 1 | <9 | complete |
| Cellulose fibre | 0.8 | Whatman | 0.162 | <1 | <1 | <1 | <1 | <1 | <1 | <6 | 1 | <9 | complete |
| Cellulose ester | 0.8 | Millipore | 0.092 | <1 | <1 | <1 | <1 | <1 | <1 | <6 | 1 | 16 | complete |
| Cellulose ester | 0.8 | Gelman | 0.061 | <1 | <1 | <1 | <1 | <1 | <1 | 12 | 1 | <9 | complete |
| Polycarbonate | 0.45 | Millipore | 0.015 | <1 | <1 | <1 | <1 | <1 | <1 | <6 | 1 | <9 | complete |
| PVDF | 0.65 | Millipore | 0.133 | <1 | <1 | <1 | <1 | <1 | <1 | <6 | 1 | <9 | partial |
| PTFE | 0.45 | Sartorius | 0.08 | <1 | <1 | <1 | <1 | <1 | <1 | <6 | 1 | <9 | no sol. |
| Quartz fibre | / | Whatman | 0.153 | <1 | <1 | <1 | <1 | <1 | <1 | <6 | 1 | <9 | partial |
| Fibres with active charcoal | / | Whatman | 0.33 | | | | | | | | | 7500 | partial |
| Glass fibre | / | Whatman | 0.09 | | | | | | | | | 6500 | partial |
| Acid digestion blank | | | | <1 | <1 | <1 | <1 | <1 | <1 | <1 | 1 | 3 à 7 | / |

*Concentrations correspond to acid digestion of a filter ( mass is given) diluted in 50 ml de-ionized water.
PVDF: polyvinylidene difluoride; PTFE: polyethylene tetra fluoride

**table 1: impurity level in filters.**

Different type of filters can be used in this case: cellulose, PVC, Nylon, polypropylene, polyimide, polysulfone, PTFE membranes. We choose a large range of filters and make analytical tests in order to quantify their metallic content. Acid attack with nitric acid and then analysis by ICP-MS are performed on a selection of filters. Each type of filter is analysed twice. We observe a good agreement for the values. The average results are given in table 1.

In light of table 1, the cellulose filters from Sartorius and Whatman are interesting for their purity and their good solubility in nitric acid. The polycarbonate, PVDF, PTFE, quartz fibres filters, which solubility is not as good, will be tested for their efficiency because of their high purity. The others are eliminated because of their level of impurities.

Simulation of efficiency

Principle of ultrasonic nebulization. Figure 5 shows the flowchart for ultrasonic nebulization used in this studied. Samples flow drop-by-drop on the piezometric head, creating a thick fog. A nitrogen flux carries the small drops into a heating system (144°C) and then into a condenser(1°C). After this treatment, a large part of the water is condensed. The final particles, now almost dry, are carried to the filters.

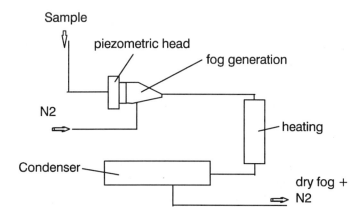

**Figure 5:  ultrasonic nebulization system**

Operating conditions. The multi-element solution used is a 5 mg/l solution in 2% nitric acid. The flow rate within the ultrasonic nebulization is 0.5 ml/min, the auxiliary flow rate is 14 ml/min. The solution is vaporised in the nebulizer for 20 min, and then is washed out with water for five minutes. The filters are analysed in the same way as in the purity tests. The flowchart for the assembly is given in figure 6.

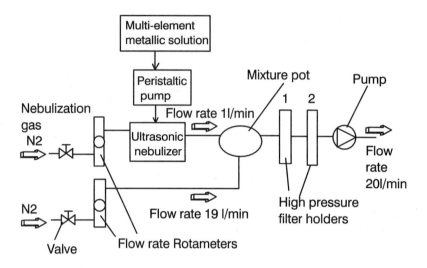

**Figure 6: Filtration simulation system assembly flowchart at a flow rate of 20 l/min.**

Results. A first experiment is made at 2 ml/min to test our simulation system using pure filters. After this test, all types of cellulose (except cellulose nitrate), PTFE and polycarbonate continue to be good enough for our work. The quartz filters are less efficient at this flow rate. The PVDF causes a major problem of solubility.

A second simulation is made at a flow rate of nearly 20 l/min in order to select the best one and to approximate as closely as possible actual site conditions. To be sure that the filtration is complete, a second filter of the same type is placed after the first one (table 2).

The filters have a comparable efficiency and we may note that the second filters do not contain any of the particles generated. The Teflon has a higher resistance to flow rate because of its lower porosity. The cellulose filters become brittle, so it is difficult to remove them from the filter holder.

Conclusion. Cellulose filters are advantageous for their good purity and good relative efficiency during the simulation and they are easy to dissolve in acid but they have poor mechanical resistance and stability.

Polycarbonate filters have good qualities of purity, mechanical resistance, and efficiency though they are partially dissolved in acids. Furthermore, polycarbonate filters are the easiest to use on site and give results comparable to the cellulose ones, so we will keep those filters for further work.

| type of filter | cellulose 0.8µm Sartorius | PTFE 0.45 µm Sartorius | polycarbonate 0.8 µm Millipore | cellulose same as filter 1 | PTFE same as filter 1 | polycarbonate same as filter 1 |
|---|---|---|---|---|---|---|
| position | 1 | 1 | 1 | 2 | 2 | 2 |
| elements in µg/l* | | | | | | |
| V | 40 | 41 | 39 | 0.3 | 0.2 | 1 |
| Cr | 41 | 40 | 40 | 2 | 1 | 2 |
| Cu | 38 | 37 | 35 | 2 | 1 | 0 |
| Zn | 45 | 34 | 28 | 0 | 0 | 0 |
| As | 40 | 41 | 39 | 0.4 | 0.3 | 1 |
| Cd | 38 | 39 | 36 | 0.2 | 0 | 0.5 |
| Sn | 39 | 43 | 42 | 0.5 | 0.2 | 1 |
| Pb | 40 | 40 | 39 | 0.4 | 0 | 1 |
| Bi | 39 | 40 | 39 | 0 | 0 | 1 |
| average of metallic elements collected on filters | 40 | 40 | 38 | 0.4 | 0 | 0.7 |
| relative standard deviation in % | 12 | 10 | 11 | 253 | 800 | 170 |
| filters aspect | brittle | good | good | brittle | good | good |
| average flow rate of simulation | 14 l/min | 9 l/min | 13 l/min | 15 l/min | 9 l/min | 14 l/min |

*The value in µg/l corresponds to a filter digestion in nitric acid diluted in 100 ml desionised water.
For each of the filters, two tests are made. Average and standard deviation are calculated from results of the two tests using the values measured for all elements.

**Table 2: filtration simulation with ultrasonic nebulization at a flow rate of 20 l/min.**

TRAPPING ON SOLID ADSORBENT

We choose a large range of adsorbents available on the market and make an initial selection based on their purity. Tenax, active charcoals, and Zeolithe are too polluted to be used for our application. The 20/45 molecular sieve is too reactive with acid, so we have to eliminate it from our potential adsorbents. 60/80 molecular sieves, 60/80 black graphited charcoal from supelco are pure enough for our application.

A Blank was made with the two chosen adsorbents to have an idea of their reaction in on site conditions. This test was made with high purity Argon (99,9997 %). This experiment shows that no extra pollution from the system appeared (see table 3).

We did not test the efficiency of the adsorbent but a major problem of trapping can appear. In each adsorption column we use 500 mg adsorbent. For a flow rate of 20 l/min, the filtration speed is 11 m/s, which leads to 1 ms contact time. In this case, the contact time is too short; 0.4 to 0.8 s is the time recommended in the references. We have examined two solutions:

- reduce the flow rate, which means increase the sampling time. That is not feasible.
- increase the quantity of adsorbent. In this case, we need to find a new means of desorption of our metallic impurities. By acid digestion, no more than 500 mg adsorbent can be used.

This sampling technique looks interesting but it needs more searching work to have good performance. For the moment, we decide to stop any complementary tests.

| test | blank | |
|---|---|---|
| volume in Nm3 | 72 | |
| trapping media | molecular sieve | black graphited charcoal |
| elements in µg/m3 | | |
| V | | |
| Cr | ≤ 0.009 | ≤ 0.009 |
| Cu | ≤ 0.005 | ≤ 0.005 |
| Zn | ≤ 0.004 | ≤ 0.004 |
| As | ≤0.004 | ≤0.004 |
| Cd | ≤0.06 | ≤0.06 |
| Sn | ≤0.004 | ≤0.004 |
| Pb | ≤0.05 | ≤0.05 |
| Bi | ≤0.004 | ≤0.004 |
| | ≤0.006 | ≤0.006 |

**Table 3: Results of the blanks for solid adsorbent.**

DESCRIPTION OF THE EXISTING METHOD

Operating conditions:

pressure: 40 bar
Flow rate: 20 l/min
temperature: 25°C
trapping time: 7 days
trapping volume: 200 Nm3
trapping solution : 10% HNO3, 10 % HCl

System assembly flowchart using filters for "on site" control:

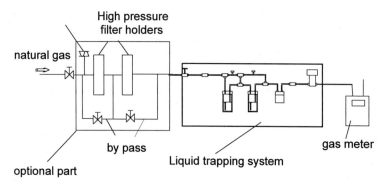

Detection limits of this method:

|  | particulate | gaseous compounds |
|---|---|---|
| elements in µg/m3 | | |
| V | ≤ 0.009 | ≤ 0.009 |
| Cr | ≤ 0.005 | ≤ 0.005 |
| Cu | ≤ 0.004 | ≤ 0.004 |
| Zn | ≤0.004 | ≤0.004 |
| As | ≤0.06 | ≤0.06 |
| Cd | ≤0.004 | ≤0.004 |
| Sn | ≤0.05 | ≤0.05 |
| Pb | ≤0.004 | ≤0.004 |
| Bi | ≤0.006 | ≤0.006 |

CONCLUSION.

In this work, solid and liquid trapping methods are tested, as well as dust filtration. An initial choice of filters and adsorbents is made.

A significant improvement is made in the liquid trapping system. By reinforcing the heating system, better regulation inside the sampling box is achieved, even in very cold weather. As hydrates are generated at this pressure at 10°C, we only need to keep the temperature at around 20 to 30°C to avoid flow rate blockage; it is also important to avoid temperatures above 50°C because of acid decomposition.

Filtration has to be used in pre-treating gas before liquid or solid trapping. To make a choice, a large range of filters is tested. Two parameters are taken in account:
- purity,
- efficiency.

Cellulose and polycarbonate filters are the purest and have the best filtration efficiency but cellulose becomes brittle after gas flows through it, so we choose polycarbonate filters, which, in addition, have the best mechanical resistance to high flow rate.

Before conducting any trapping test with solid adsorbents, we test the purity of a wide range of products. Only the molecular sieves and black graphited charcoal are pure enough for our purposes. We did not test their efficiency on volatile elements because the bibliography shows that the contact time was surely too short in our application to achieve a sufficient degree of efficiency.

The blanks made show that no additional pollution appeared coming from the system and that the filters resist well to pressure and high flow rates.

As yet, the selected method is the liquid trapping system. Now this technique is operational, and we have eliminated all causes of pollution of the apparatus and flow rate blockage. The detection limits for gaseous compounds of the studied elements, are in the range 0.004 - 0,06 µg/m3.

## REFERENCES

1.    W. LOMMERZHEIM
      Neuer untersuchungen über erdgasspurenelement.
      GWF GAS/ERDGAS,vol 117, NR 10, pp 430-432, 1976.

2.    R.A. ZINGARO
      Determination of arsenic and arsine compounds in natural gas samples.
      APPLIED ORGANOMETALLIC CHEMISTRY, VOL 5, pp 117-124, 1991.

3.    D.RATARD, M. PRZYSZWA.
      L'analyse du mercure dans le gaz naturel.
      Rapport GDF/ DETN, n° 68731, 1978.

4.    A. ATTARI
      Gas industry update on gas quality and related research activities at IGT.Paper
      presented at Gas Quality Measurement Symposium, Chicago, Illinois, June 10-12,
      1991.

5.    S. JADOUL
      Piégeage et analyse des métaux lourds dans le gaz naturel.
      International Gas Union Conference. 20-24 June 1994.

6.    A. ROJEY, B. DURAND, C. JAFFRET, S. JULLIAN, M. VALAIS.
      Le gaz naturel, production, traitement, transport. Publications de l'institut français du
      pétrole, Avril 1994.

7.    P.R. HARRISON.
      Monitoring for trace metals in the atmospheric environment: problems and needs.
      Cycling control metals, proc. environmental resources conferences, October 1972,
      Columbus Ohio.

8.    K. W. OLSON, W.J.HAAS, JR. VELMER, A. FASSEL.
      Analysis of airborne particulates and human urine by inductively coupled atomic
      emission spectroscopy.
      National Institute for Occupational Safety and Health. PB 297775 (1978).

# DEVELOPMENT OF CALORIE TRANSMITTER
## FOR QUICK RESPONSE CALORIFIC VALUE CONTROL

## DÉVELOPPEMENT D'UN ÉMETTEUR POUR CONTROLE
## À RÉACTION RAPIDE DU POUVOIR CALORIFIQUE

M. Seto
Tokyo Gas Co., Ltd. Japan

H. Muto and Y. Kajio
Yamatake-Honeywell Co., Ltd. Japan

## ABSTRACT

In order to improve control performance, there is a need for quicker response in calorimeters used in calorific value control for city gas. Instead of the combustion and gas density type calorimeters which have conventionally been used for this purpose, we have developed a calorimeter which works by measuring thermal conductivity. This calorie transmitter can be set up in the plant yard, and furthermore enables stable control at high speed. This report discusses this new technology for measuring thermal conductivity, and methods for calculating the calorific value of city gas.

## RÉSUMÉ

Dans le dessein d'améliorer les performances, les calorimètres utilisés pour la commande du pouvoir calorifique du gaz de ville doivent présenter une réponse plus rapide. Les auteurs ont mis au point un calorimètre à mesure de la conductivité thermique qui peut avantageusement remplacé les calorimètres à combustion et mesure de la densité du gaz, lesquels on été largement utilisés jusqu'à présent. Le transmetteur de calorie peut être installé dans l'usine et assure des commandes stables, même à grande vitesse. Cet article présente les nouvelles techniques employées pour mesurer la conductivité thermique et les méthodes de calcul du pouvoir calorifique du gaz de ville.

## INTRODUCTION

In recent years, recommendations have been made to Japanese domestic city gas utilities to switch to high calorie gas based on natural gas, and there has been an increasing need to develop a low-cost calorimeter with superior response time and stability. The calorific value of city gas in Japan is regulated within a fixed calorie range by the Gas Utility Industry Law. Therefore city gas sent out from a gas plant must constantly be adjusted to a fixed calorific value by mixing multiple gases with different calorific values. Thus calorie control is the most important point in city gas quality control. The equipment for mixing gas is called a calorie mixer. In order to control gas within the precise calorie range, it is critical for the calorimeter for controlling this equipment to have a sufficiently rapid response time. The following summarizes the features of the 3 types of calorimeters which have been used heretofore in calorie mixers.

Combustion Type Calorimeters. With this system, gas is combusted and the calorific value is measured by the rise in temperature of the combustion exhaust gas.

Gas Density Type Calorimeters. With this system, the gas density is measured by variation in frequency of a vibration tube, and this is converted to a calorific value.

Light Wave Interference Type Calorimeters. With this system, the calorific value is obtained by measuring the gas density from the brightness of interference fringes corresponding to differences in the refractory index of gas.

Combustion type calorimeters have slow response because they measure the difference in the temperature of air before and after combustion. This is a non explosion-proof type, and calorie mixers employing this type cannot be set up in a plant yard. Although gas density type calorimeters have a very good response time, their measurements become extremely unstable if there is variation in the external environment, so they must be set up in a thermostat tank. Light interference type calorimeters require a reference gas. They also need to be calibrated frequently due to their large output drift, and since measurement is impossible during calibration, they cannot be used for continuous control applications.

The goal of the current work was to overcome the disadvantages of conventional calorimeters. This was achieved by devising calorific value measurement technology based on the principle of thermal conductivity measurement, and thereby developing a calorimeter capable of measuring the calorific value of city gas. We call this instrument a "calorie transmitter". It has previously been known that there are correlations between the calorific value and thermal conductivity of city gas. However, technology has not been available for simply measuring the thermal conductivity of gas on an industrial level, and no calorimeters for city gas have been designed using the thermal conductivity system.

This system does not measure the difference in thermal conductivity between a measurement gas and comparison gas like a conventional thermal conductivity gauge. Rather its distinguishing feature is that it measures the absolute value of thermal conductivity. Therefore exploiting this principle makes it extremely simple to measure the calorific value of city gas. Also, considering response time from the standpoint of control, what is important is not just the performance of the calorimeter itself. It is also important to set up the calorimeter in the plant yard for the calorie mixer, and further reduce the time delay for gas sampling. With this system, the measurement principle and equipment structure ensure that external temperature variation has virtually no effect. Therefore the calorimeter can be set up under the severe environmental conditions in the plant yard, thereby minimizing the sampling time delay, and enabling stable calorific value control.

The following introduces the new technology for measuring thermal conductivity, and describes the method by which the calorific value of city gas is measured from the thermal conductivity.

BASIC STRUCTURE

Fig. 1 shows the composition of the calorie transmitter. As the drawing indicates, the structure is simple based around a μTCD in the flow path for gas measurement. The system does not measure the difference in thermal conductivity with a comparison gas; it directly measures the thermal conductivity, so a comparison gas flow path is unnecessary. This calorie transmitter is an application of two technological developments which differ from a conventional thermal conductivity gauge.

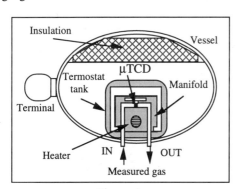

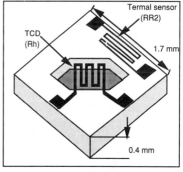

| Figure 1 | Figure 2 |
| Configuration of the calorie transmitter | μTCD |

Development 1 (μTCD)

The sensor section of the calorie transmitter employs a monocrystal silicon chip, fabricated via micro-machining. (Fig. 2) A μTCD (Micro Thermal Conductivity Detector) is incorporated into the extremely thin diaphragm section, and a temperature sensor (RR2) is built into the silicon base. The μTCD is thermally insulated from the silicon base, but this part is made of a thin-film resistor, and the area contacting the gas is extremely large so the sensor is highly sensitive. The temperature sensor is placed near the μTCD, at a position which is thermally insulated, and the thermal conductivity can be measured with the sensor chip temperature kept fixed.

Development 2 (Constant temperature driver circuit)

Fig. 3 shows the conventional method of measuring thermal conductivity. With this circuit, the measurement gas and comparison gas flow together, and the difference in temperature is detected by the platinum resistor of a Wheatstone bridge. The thermal conductivity is then calculated from the unbalanced voltage. The disadvantage of this method is that the TCD temperature varies when there is variation in the thermal conductivity of the measurement gas. Thermal conductivity follows a temperature function, but for that reason it is difficult to maintain a constant temperature with this method, and thus it is difficult to measure the absolute value of the thermal conductivity.

Fig. 4 shows the temperature control circuit for the calorie transmitter. The μTCD is always controlled to a constant temperature by a constant temperature driver circuit. The temperature inside the casing is also kept constant using a temperature sensor provided on this μTCD. As a result, the temperature gradient between the μTCD and temperature sensor is kept constantly fixed, thereby creating the conditions for measurement of thermal conductivity at a fixed temperature. The temperature inside the casing does not vary, so the temperature stabilization time is almost zero, and the μTCD responds at high speed. Furthermore, the μTCD is always kept at a constant temperature, so there is no thermal stress, and this is advantageous for both reliability and service life.

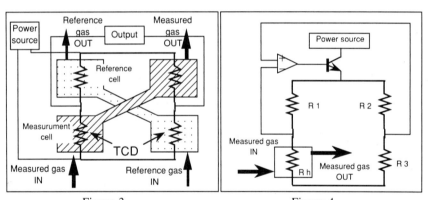

Figure 3
Conventional Thermal Analyzer

Figure 4
Thermal Conductivity Analyzer

MEASUREMENT PRINCIPLE

The following describes the principle by which the μTCD and constant temperature driver are used to measure the thermal conductivity of gas. The amount of heat $Q_T$ conducted to the outside from the TCD sensor is expressed as follows:

$$Q_T = Q_G + Q_S + Q_C + Q_R \quad \ldots \ldots \quad (1)$$

Where,
$Q_G$ : Heat conveyed to gas by conduction

$Q_S$ : Heat conveyed to the silicon substrate through membrane and resistor pattern

$Q_C$ : Heat conveyed to gas by forced or unforced convection

$Q_R$ : Heat conveyed to the silicon substrate and flow channel body by radiation

The temperature $T_{Rh}$ [°C] of the μTCD is driven to a constant value (constant resistance drive), so the supplied power increases and decreases with variation in the thermal conductivity of the measurement gas, thereby constantly maintaining a fixed temperature. The resistance value Rh for the TCD is given by the following formula. (Fig. 4)

$Rh = R1 \times R3 / R2 = $ constant

The temperature $T_{Rh}$ of the μTCD at this time is given by the following quadratic equation.

$Rh = Rh20 \times \{ 1 + ah20 \times (T_{Rh} - 20) + ßh20 \times (T_{Rh} - 20)^2 \}$

Where,
Rh : Rh resistance value [Ω]

$T_{Rh}$ : Temperature of Rh [°C]

Rh20 : Resistance value of Rh at 20°C [Ω]

ah20 : Primary resistance temperature coefficient of Rh at 20°C [°C$^{-1}$]

ßh20 : Secondary resistance temperature coefficient of Rh at 20°C [°C$^{-2}$]

Rh is obtained from the resistance values R1, R2 and R3, and this in turn determines the drive temperature $T_{Rh}$ of the μTCD. The inside of the casing is controlled to the constant temperature $T_{RR2}$, by taking the temperature sensor RR2 as a feedback signal and applying PID control to the supply power of the heater. Here, noting that almost all the power applied to Rh is changed to heat by Rh, $Q_T$ can be expressed as follows:

$Q_T = I^2 \times Rh = V^2 / Rh$

Where,
I : Current flowing through TCD (Rh) [A]

V : Voltage at both ends of TCD (Rh) [V]

$Q_G$ in formula (1) is a term which varies with changes in the thermal conductivity of the measurement gas.

$Q_G = (T_{Rh} - T_{RR2}) \times LA \times G$

Where,
LA : Average thermal conductivity of measurement gas [mW/m-K]

Thermal conductivity at average temperature TA of $T_{Rh}$ and $T_{RR2}$

$(T_{Rh} - T_{RR2})$ x $G = A =$ constant

$G =$ constant (equipment constant)

Furthermore, regarding $Q_S + Q_C + Q_R$ as a term which does not vary with changes in the composition of the measurement gas,
and assuming that $Q_S + Q_C + Q_R = B =$ constant, then formula (1) can be rewritten:

$Q_T = A$ x $LA + B$
$LA = V^2 / (Rh$ x $A) - B / A$ .......... (2)

Due to the constant temperature drive, the resistance value Rh of the μTCD is always fixed. Therefore, if the constants A and B are found beforehand, and the output voltage V is measured when a flow of measurement gas is provided, it is possible to determine the average thermal conductivity LA [mW/m-K] of the measurement gas by calculating with formula (2). Seven types of pure gas were actually measured using the calorie transmitter. Fig. 5 shows the relationship between the actual thermal conductivity and the square of the output voltage of the calorie transmitter ($V^2$). This relationship can be linearly approximated, and this is the reason why formula (2) holds. If, based on these results, we find the equipment constants A and B and calculate the thermal conductivity, the results are as shown in Table 1. As can be seen, the thermal conductivity of the measurement gas can be measured with satisfactory precision.

Table 1. Thermal conductivity measurement results

| Pure gas type | Actual thermal conductivity (TA : at 114 °C) [mW / m-K] | Measurement results [mW / m-K] |
|---|---|---|
| $H_2$ | 219.34 | 220.19 |
| He | 183.69 | 180.90 |
| $CH_4$ | 47.34 | 48.06 |
| $C_2H_6$ | 34.04 | 33.63 |
| $N_2$ | 31.76 | 32.56 |
| $C_3H_8$ | 28.71 | 28.82 |
| $CO_2$ | 23.34 | 22.83 |

The thermal conductivity of the pure gases was found as the average thermal conductivity at the average temperature TA. This was done using data in physical tables for fluids, and creating a quadratic approximation formula using the method of least squares in the range 0 to 200°C.

## MEASUREMENT OF THE CALORIFIC VALUE

With LNG based city gas [13A: Calorific value 11,000kcal/Nm3 (approx. = 46.2 MJ/Nm3], the gas is blend, based on methane, and containing hydrocarbons ranging from ethane to butane. Table 2 shows the calorific value, thermal conductivity and composition percentage range in ordinary city gas for each hydrocarbon component. The relationship between thermal conductivity and calorific value is as given in Fig. 5.

Table 2. Thermal conductivity and calorific value

| Component | Concentration range [%] | Thermal conductivity [mW / m-K] | Calorific value [MJ / Nm³] |
|---|---|---|---|
| $CH_4$ | 80 - 98 | 47.34 | 40.07 |
| $C_2H_6$ | 0 - 15 | 34.078 | 70.69 |
| $C_3H_8$ | 0 - 5 | 28.714 | 101.72 |
| $i-C_4H_{10}$ | 0 - 2 | 25.963 | 134.74 |
| $n-C_4H_{10}$ | 0 - 2 | 25.735 | 133.52 |

With pure gas, thermal conductivity and calorific value stand almost in an inverse proportional relationship. If the relationship between the thermal conductivity and calorific value of city gas is known, it becomes possible to determine the calorific value by measuring the thermal conductivity of the mixed gas. However, previously there has been no theoretical formula relating the composition of mixed gas with its thermal conductivity. Furthermore, there has been no experimental formula with satisfactory precision. For this reason, this relationship was determined by assuming a gas composition close to that of city gas.

As a result, it was found that the relationship is almost linear in the thermal conductivity range of 46.5 - 42.5mW/m-K, which corresponds to a city gas calorific value range of 42.0 - 50.4 MJ/Nm³ (10,000 - 12,000kcal/Nm³). So the following linear equation was obtained to express the relationship between thermal conductivity and calorific value.

$$H = -2.1693 \times L + 142.751$$

Where,
H : Calorific value [MJ/Nm³]
L : Thermal conductivity [mW/m-K] (at 114°C)

For Fig. 6, various mixed gases were blended with a calorific value of 42.0 - 50.4 MJ/Nm³ (10,000 - 12,000kcal/Nm³) and the calorific value calculated from the composition ratio found through gas chromatograph analysis was compared with the calorific value measured with the calorie transmitter. Satisfactory results were obtained, with the error between the two calorific values being at most ±210kJ/Nm³ (±50kcal/Nm³).

## PERFORMANCE COMPARISON OF CALORIMETERS

Combustion type calorimeters measure the amount of heat by actually combusting the gas, so they have the advantage that errors do no not arise even in the presence of non-flammable gases. However, these types can never be explosion-proof. Therefore it is difficult to set up this type near equipment at the site, and a large time delay arises due to the need to transport a sample to the set up location. An explosion-proof gas density calorimeter can be set up at the site, thereby improving response, but errors arise due to severe variation in air temperature at the set up location, and the mechanism is easily affected by changes in the temperature and pressure of the sampling gas. Therefore an insulating cover must be provided if the instrument is to be actually set up on-site, or the readings must be corrected by providing a pressure gauge.

In contrast to these existing calorimeters, the calorie transmitter discussed here has its detection sensor in a thermostat chamber controlled to a fixed temperature, and the effects of ambient temperature variation are minimal. Since the thermal conductivity of a gas changes very little even if the pressure varies, this calorie transmitter requires no special protection or correction even when set up near equipment on-site. Consequently the instrument can be set up on-site with a degree of construction work on a par with other industrial instrumentation. Fig. 7 shows the configuration of a system employing a calorie transmitter as the calorimeter installed on-site. Table 3 shows a comparison of performance with other calorimeters.

Table 3: Calorimeter performance comparison

| Calorimeter | Combustion type | Gas density type | Thermal conductivity type |
|---|---|---|---|
| Measurement accuracy [kJ / Nm$^3$] | ± 460 | ± 170 | ± 210 |
| Response time (Sample flow rate) | 30 - 90 sec (10NL/min) | 7 sec (10NL/min) | 5 sec (0.1NL/min) |
| Pressure characteristics [kJ/Nm$^3$ / kPa] | * | * | ± 43 |
| | Can be used only under conditions near atmospheric pressure | | |
| Temperature characteristics [kJ / Nm$^3$ / °C] | 25 | 5 | 2 |

CONCLUSION

The calorie transmitter discussed in this paper exploits two basic technologies -- a μTCD and a constant temperature drive circuit -- thereby achieving measurement of calorific value based on thermal conductivity, an impossibility with conventional calorimeters. As a result, it is now possible to employ the previously unfeasible construction technique of mounting a stanchion in the plant yard. This greatly reduces set up and construction costs, as well as minimizing the gas sampling delay, so the technique has the potential to greatly improve control performance. At present, local gas utility companies throughout Japan are changing or planning to change their calorific values to natural gas based high calorie gas. This calorie transmitter can be easily used by many gas utilities (who previously could not use calorimeters due to their high cost) to save labor and resources.

REFERENCES

1.  "Guides for Analyzers," Japan Analytical Instruments Manufacturers' Association. July 1983.

2.  JSME Data Book: Heat Transfer, 4th Edition. October 1986.

3.  M.Seto: "Development of a New Explosion-proof Calorimeter for Calorific Values." Proceedings of 42nd City Gas Simposium. Japan Gas Association.

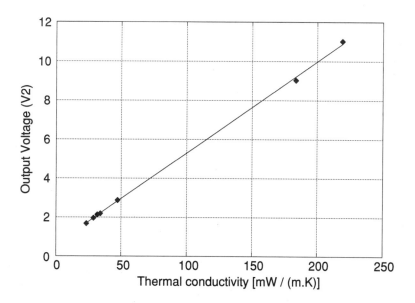

Figure 5
Output Voltage vs. Thermal Conductivity

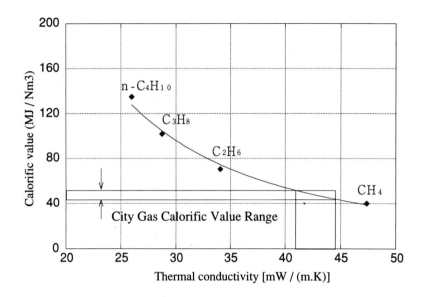

Figure 6
Thermal Conductivity vs. Calorific Value

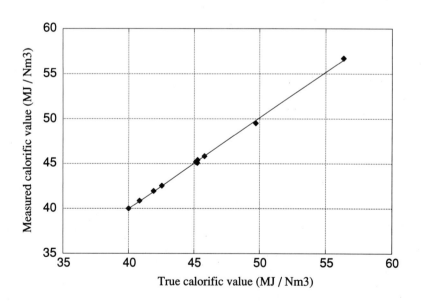

Figure 7
Basic Measurement Caracteristics of Calori Transmitter

## SIMULATION OF UNSTEADY FLOW, MASSIVE RELEASES AND BLOWDOWN OF LONG, HIGH-PRESSURE PIPELINES.

## SIMULATION D'ECOULEMENTS INSTATIONNAIRES DANS DE LONGS GAZODUCS A HAUTE PRESSION SUITE A DES RELACHEMENTS MASSIFS DE GAZ.

J.P. Kunsch
Swiss Fed. Inst. of Technology Zürich, Switzerland

K. Sjøen
Statoil A/S Stavanger, Norway

T.K. Fanneløp
Swiss Fed. Inst. of Technology Zürich, Switzerland

ABSTRACT.

Permits for new, high-pressure gas transportation systems require today detailed safety studies and proof of acceptable environmental impact. To this end a simulation model for 1D unsteady flow in pipelines, including a realistic model for a barrier valve and accounting for real gas effects, is presented. The technique for the treatment of the various boundary conditions, based on the method of characteristics, is discussed in detail. The model has been tested for a massive gas release due to pipeline rupture and it has been validated by comparison with results from a controlled pipeline blowdown through a valve. In the latter case, excellent agreement with data of the large scale field experiment has been achieved. In this context relevant parameters are identified and their respective influence estimated and discussed based on numerical experiments or sensitivity studies. It can be demonstrated that a precise knowledge of the friction coefficient and coefficients of loss in general is not required and also that mass-loss rates are rather insensitive to the exact geometric shape and contraction ratio of the break resulting from an accidental rupture.

RESUME.

Pour l'autorisation de nouveaux systèmes de transport de gaz sous haute pression, des études détaillées de sécurité ainsi que des preuves d'un impact négligeable sur l'environnement, sont requises. Dans ce mémoire est présenté un modèle établi à cette fin. Il permet la simulation numérique d'un écoulement monodimensionnel instationnaire, avec effets de gaz réel, et comprend un modèle réaliste d'une valve de fermeture. Une technique pour le traitement des différentes conditions aux limites, basée sur la méthode des caractéristiques, est présentée en détail. Le modèle a été testé pour un relâchement massif de gaz, suite à une rupture de gazoduc et a été validé également par comparaison avec des résultats d'essais à grande échelle obtenus lors d'une évacuation contrôlée par l'intermédiaire d'une valve.
Les paramètres importants ont été identifiés et leur influence respective a été évaluée et discutée à l'aide d'études paramétriques. Il a été constaté q'une connaissance précise du coefficient de frottement, et des coefficients de perte en général, n'est pas nécessaire. Il a été montré de même que les débits de perte sont peu sensibles au coefficient de contraction et à la forme exacte de la brèche provoquée par une rupture accidentelle.

## INTRODUCTION.

During the planning and licensing of offshore pipelines, the attention is focused increasingly on safety and the potential environmental impact of the whole system. In spite of considerable effort during design and operation to prevent accidental gas releases, experience shows that the gas leakage and even accidental rupture of the pipeline remains a potential threat. The design of new and advanced gas transportation systems, such as the gas pipelines from the Norwegian Continental Shelf, represents technological milestones, e.g. with regard to the operating pressures or lengths of the pipelines involved. Safety studies are therefore required that take the new and unique features of the system into account ( Sjøen ,1993 ).

In order to study the effects of uncontrolled gas releases, a model has been developed to estimate the corresponding mass-loss rates and to simulate the fluiddynamic transients caused by an accidental pipeline rupture or blowdown. The corresponding computer code presented herein, is applicable to dry gas pipelines.

## SIMULATION MODEL.

### Basic features of the model.

For offshore systems in the North Sea, it is typical not to have re-compression installed between endpoints. The lengths of pipelines in operation or under planning are of the order of several hundred kilometers. The longest pipeline in operation, which goes from the Sleipner riser platform to Zeebrugge in Belgium, has a length of 815 km. The combination of great length and high discharge pressure, requires upstream pressures exceeding 150 bars. This results in enormous gas inventories, a safety concern, as well as complications in the analysis due to the large and nonlinear variation in the variables of state.

Many general simulation models exist for flow calculations in natural gas pipeline systems. We will here state the basic requirements for a realistic model suitable for the safety engineer.

It will not be our task to add one more description of a simulation model for unsteady pipeline flow, but rather to define the basic requirements to a realistic simulation tool, which can be useful for the safety engineer. The basic requirements to the modelization of the various components of the system, but also to the numerical input for the corresponding computer code, can be formulated only after identification of the relevant parameters influencing the system. Physical reasoning, rough estimates and numerical experiments, including parametric sensitivity studies, will support most of our options and they will also allow a critical evaluation of similar prediction methods and tools. Many pipeline systems for scenarios of interest can be reduced to the basic technical configuration of Fig.1. It includes a reservoir upstream and downstream connected by a flowline, as well as flow control by a barrier valve. A constant boundary condition at the downstream end of the flowline (e.g. with respect to the static pressure) can be represented by a reservoir of very large volume.

Simplicity, rather than numerical accuracy or efficiency, motivates the choice of the explicit finite difference scheme implemented in the present computer code. The classic Kentzer scheme, used for the implementation of the boundary conditions, is chosen by virtue of its flexibility and reliability.

Basic equations and assumptions.

The basic one-dimensional equations, describing the unsteady flow with friction in a pipeline, can be written in conservative form as follows :

$$\rho_t + m_x = 0$$

$$m_t + \left( \frac{m^2}{\rho} + p \right)_x = -2 \frac{f}{D} \frac{m|m|}{\rho} \tag{1}$$

$$E_t + \left[ \frac{m}{\rho} (E + p) \right]_x = 0$$

with the dependent variables $\rho$, $m = \rho u$ and $E = \rho \left( e + \frac{1}{2} u^2 \right)$.

The equation of energy has been formulated for adiabatic flow. This choice is indicated for the estimate of the temperature drop of the expanding gas at a broken end, e.g. due to a guillotine rupture. For the large mass-flow rates considered, heat addition can usually be neglected, because heat transfer rates from the surroundings ( with limited heat capacity ) to the gas flow is found to be small. For ideal gases, in the case of a guillotine rupture of a pipeline, it has been shown that the assumption of isothermal flow yields approximately the same results as the adiabatic assumption, as far as the mass-flow rates are concerned ( Kunsch et al. , 1991).

Viscous effects are accounted for by means of a friction factor f, discussed below. It is evident that empirical values for f, obtained from steady flow tests, are of uncertain validity for transients dominated by inertial forces. The friction factor f will be adequate, most likely for the late-time regime of a massive gas release, when the flow is quasisteady and dominated by frictional forces.

Suitable equations of state are required to predict the thermal and the caloric properties of the gas mixtures in the high pressure gas transportation system, with pressures exceeding often 150 bars. The BWR equation of state, as adapted by Starling (1973), has been chosen for the present application. It is provided for mixtures including the most common hydrocarbons $C_1$ to $C_8$, as well as $H_2S$, $N_2$, $O_2$ and $CO_2$. The coefficients provided include the critical parameters and acentric factors $\omega_i$, which are needed for consistent thermodynamic property calculations. Although updated versions of this equation of state exist, including certain improvements, we will make use of the version of Starling (1973). It is felt that the overall influence of improved coefficients will be small in comparison with other uncertainties in the system.

The present investigations will be limited to the flow of dry gases. The separation of liquid components takes place prior to the gas entry into the large gas transportation systems piping the gas from Norway to the Continent.

The numerical scheme.

The integration is performed by means of the explicit finite difference scheme of MacCormack. It is a second order accurate, two step predictor-corrector scheme. A fine mesh size is imposed at the boundaries or interfaces of the various components of the pipeline system, in regions where the gradients of some flow variables are expected to become large. The mesh size is allowed to increase in a geometrical progression towards the centre of each pipeline segment, where generally small gradients occur.

The difference form of the equation of continuity is written below for illustration :

predictor
$$\overline{\rho_j^{n+1}} = \rho_j^n - \frac{2}{\varphi(1 + \varphi)} \frac{\Delta t}{\Delta x} \left[ m_{j+1}^n - m_j^n \right] \tag{2}$$

corrector
$$\rho_j^{n+1} = \frac{1}{2} \left\{ \rho_j^n + \overline{\rho_j^{n+1}} - \frac{2\varphi}{(1 + \varphi)} \frac{\Delta t}{\Delta x} \left[ \overline{m_j^{n+1}} - \overline{m_{j-1}^{n+1}} \right] \right\}$$

with a space increment $\Delta x_- = \Delta x$ on the left of a point j in a difference molecule and a space increment $\Delta x_+ = \varphi \Delta x$ on the right. For comparable accuracy, the mesh with equal grid spacing would require about 5 times more grid points than the refined mesh, with roughly the same grid size at the boundaries.

The same procedure is applied to the equation of momentum and the equation of energy, in order to obtain the new values of $\rho$, m and E after the time increment $\Delta t$ at time $t + \Delta t$. In case of the ideal gas assumption, the pressure can be deduced explicitly from the new conservative variables $p = (\gamma - 1) \left[ E - \frac{1}{2} \frac{m^2}{\rho} \right]$, owing to the simple forms of the equation of state $p/\rho = RT$ and the caloric equation of state $e = c_v T$. The general form of the equation of state is $p = p(\rho, T)$ and $e = e(\rho, T)$ for real gases ( Starling, 1973 ). The analytic calculation of the internal energy is straightforward : $e = \dfrac{E}{\rho} - \dfrac{1}{2}\left(\dfrac{m}{\rho}\right)^2$ , but an iterative algorithm is required for the computation of T from $e = e(\rho, T)$ and $\rho$ , T being an implicit function of e and $\rho$. The explicit computation of $p = p\,(\rho, T)$ is again straightforward. When the iteration is performed by means of a Newton algorithm, where the temperature of the preceding time step can be used as a starting value, usually no more than 2 iteration steps are required.

p and e in the basic equations could be linearized with respect to $\rho$ and T, in order to compute $\rho$, m and T in an explicit manner for each time step. Although iterations were eliminated, the computational gains were not significant and numerical instabilities appeared in some circumstances.

Simplicity, rather than computational efficiency, has motivated the choice of the present algorithm. The numerical accuracy can be checked by performing mass balancing at each time step, as well as globally for the overall process for a full simulation run (Kunsch et al., 1991). Introduction of an implicit numerical integration scheme could be a step towards improved computational efficiency. But considerable supplementary effort would be required for the implementation of the various boundary conditions and for the introduction of flow control devices such as valves etc. This is particularly true for spectral methods, where the simplicity of the boundary conditions is a prerequisite for the numerical efficiency of the scheme ( Lang, 1991).

**Treatment of the Boundaries.**

At the end of each pipeline segment, boundary conditions have to be imposed, e.g. the ambient pressure in case of an undercritical release at a broken end or a specified flow velocity ( speed of sound ) in case of choked flow.

A possible approach would be to integrate the basic equations at the boundaries, in the way it is performed at interior points of the flow field. In a subsequent step, the imposed values at the boundaries (boundary conditions) would replace the values obtained by means of the integration. A disadvantage of this method is that the other quantities obtained by integration, which are not affected by this resetting, would not be consistent with the boundary conditions.

Techniques, which are based on the method of characteristics and related to the physics of wave propagation, can cope with these shortcomings. Information on the flow field adjacent to the boundaries is carried towards them by means of waves. In mathematical terms, this information is provided by the solution of ordinary differential equations (or compatibility relations), which are valid along the waves or characteristic directions. The technique, as proposed by Kentzer, has been described in detail by Kunsch et al. (1991) for the ideal gas assumption. It will be summarized below.

The equations relative to the flow field can be written in matrix form :

$$U_t + \overline{A} \cdot U_x = B \qquad \text{with the Jacobian } \overline{A} \qquad\qquad (3)$$

and where $B : \left(0, \ -2\,\dfrac{f}{D}\,\dfrac{m|m|}{\rho}, \ 0\right)$ is related to friction and $U : (\rho, \ m, \ E)$ contains the conservative variables. The eigenvalues of the system, which are a measure of the speed of wave propagation, are :

$$\lambda_1 = \left.\frac{dx}{dt}\right|_1 = \frac{m}{\rho}, \qquad \lambda_2 = \left.\frac{dx}{dt}\right|_2 = \frac{m}{\rho} + c, \qquad \lambda_3 = \left.\frac{dx}{dt}\right|_3 = \frac{m}{\rho} - c \qquad (4a)$$

The compatibility equations, corresponding to the three waves, and characterized by their speed of propagation $\lambda_i$, can be written hence :

$$l_1^i \ \rho_{jt} + l_2^i \ m_{jt} + l_3^i \ E_{jt} = -\left[l_1^i \ \rho_{jx} + l_2^i \ m_{jx} + l_3^i \ E_{jx}\right]\lambda_i + l^{(i)} \cdot B \qquad (4b)$$

with the left eigenvectors $l^{(i)} : \left(l_1^i, \ l_2^i, \ l_3^i\right)$ associated to the Jacobian $\overline{A}$. The index i denotes the compatibility equation i corresponding to the eigenvalue $\lambda_i$, the index j = 1 is taken for right-running characteristics originating from the left side of the boundary to be considered and accordingly $j = 2$ is related to left-running characteristics. This technique, where the characteristics act as an interface between the boundaries (or system components) and the adjacent flow field, will be illustrated in the section discussing the valve.

**Representative System Components and Locations.**

Modeling of a valve.
    The flow in a valve presents fundamental similarities to the flow through an orifice plate. For a discussion of the basic physics of the flow within a valve, it is referred to the work of Miller (1990).

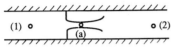

It is assumed that the flow is accelerated without losses from a location (1) upstream of the valve to the "vena contracta" (a), i.e. $p_a^\circ = p_1^\circ$, where the circles denote total conditions. Jet detachment and strong mixing contributes to the losses between (a) and (2). Valve characteristics are generally available only for steady state operating conditions. In the present study these characteristics (also called static characteristics) are also used during the closing and the other transient flow conditions in the valve, for lack of better information. Reality is adequately modeled for quasisteady conditions (small Strouhal-numbers, closing times large in comparison with flow times through the valves). The addition of dynamic, time dependent factors could otherwise yield an improvement.
    Typical closing times for valves, of the order of 20 to 60 s, are often very small compared to the characteristic time intervals ( e.g. blowdown times ) of the long pipelines considered in the present studies. Even large errors in the evaluation of the mass-flow rates during the closing time of a valve, would have a small influence on the total release of importance for the safety scenario. Static valve characteristics are adopted for consistency for all the operating conditions considered herein.
    The equation of continuity is formulated for any location between (1) and (a) :

$$\dot{m} = \rho \, u \, A = \rho_0 \, c_0 \left(1 + \frac{\gamma - 1}{2} M^2\right)^{-\frac{(\gamma+1)}{2(\gamma-1)}} M \, A \qquad (5)$$

where the circles denote total conditions.
In addition, an empirical relation provides the mass-flow rate through a valve :

$$\dot{m} = 0.0167 \, A_v C_1 Y \sqrt{\rho_1 \, p_1} \qquad (6)$$

with the incompressible flow coefficient $A_v$ obtained from water flow tests, the flow factor $C_1$ based on manufacturers tests with critical flow and the subcritical flow factor $Y$. For a variety of valves, $Y$ has the following form ( Benedict, 1980 ) :

$$Y = \sin\left(\frac{\pi}{180} \frac{3417}{C_1} \sqrt{\frac{\Delta p}{p_1}}\right) \qquad \text{( argument in rad. )} \qquad (7)$$

which covers the complete operating range from incompressible to critical flow. When (5) is applied to the "vena contracta" $A_a$, it follows from (5) and (6) :

$$A_a = 0.0167 A_v C_1 \frac{1}{\gamma} \left(\frac{\gamma+1}{2}\right)^{g(\gamma)} f(M_1)^{-g(\gamma)} F \qquad \text{with} \qquad f(M) = 1 + \frac{\gamma-1}{2} M^2;$$

$$\text{and} \qquad F = \frac{1}{M_a} f(M_a)^{g(\gamma)} \left(\frac{\gamma+1}{2}\right)^{-g(\gamma)} Y \; ; \qquad g(\gamma) = \frac{(\gamma+1)}{2(\gamma-1)} \qquad (8)$$

With the help of eq. (10) below, and the simplification because of $M_1 \ll 1$, it can be shown numerically that $F$ is equal to one (within $\pm 3\%$) for all operating conditions considered. It follows for $A_a$ :

$$A_a = 0.025 A_v C_1 \, f(M_1)^{-g(\gamma)} \qquad (8')$$

It can be demonstrated that the coefficient 0.025 depends only weakly on the isentropic coefficient $\gamma$. When equation (5) is applied to the "vena contracta", we obtain with $A = A_a$ :

$$M_1 f(M_a)^{g(\gamma)} = 0.025 \frac{A_v C_1}{A_1} M_a \tag{9}$$

In order to complete the set of equations describing a valve, an equation relative to the total pressure loss between location (1) and (2) is required :

$$p_1^o - p_2^o = K_a \left( p_1^o - p_a \right) \quad \text{with } K_a = 2 \left( \frac{A_a}{A_v} \right)^2 \text{ and } \quad p_a = p_1^o \, f(M_a)^{-\gamma/(\gamma-1)}$$
$$\tag{10}$$

Quasisteady adiabatic flow implies constant total enthalpy :
$$h_1^o = h_2^o \tag{11}$$

Mass conservation requires :
$$\dot{m}_1 = \dot{m}_2 \tag{12}$$

The system of equations (9) to (12) is formulated in terms of conservative variables and differentiated w.r.t. time
The resulting system is completed by the compatibility equations, which are valid along the characteristic directions. The compatibility equations, which represent an interface between the valve and the adjacent flow field, have the following form :

$$l_1^i \, \rho_{jt} + l_2^i \, m_{jt} + l_3^i \, E_{jt} = - \left[ l_1^i \, \rho_{jx} + l_2^i \, m_{jx} + l_3^i \, E_{jx} \right] \lambda_i \qquad (i = 1,2,3) \tag{13 i}$$

In case of positive flow direction (u > 0), two right-running characteristics or waves, with speed $\lambda_1 = u_1 + c_1$ and $\lambda_2 = u_1$, originate from the left flow field ( i.e. j = 1), and a left-running characteristic, with speed $\lambda_3 = u_3 - c_3$ , originates from the right flow field ( j = 2 ).
Equations ( 9), (10), (11), (12) and (13.i , i = 1, 2, 3) provide the time derivatives of $M_a$ and the conservative variables $\rho$, m and E on both sides of the valve (i.e. 7 unknowns). $M_a$ indicates whether sonic blockage occurs in the "vena contracta". Choking, i.e. $M_a = 1$ , requires a resetting of $M_1$ in equation (9). In order to obtain values at location (2), consistent with those at location (1), equations (10) to (12) can be used to reset all variables at location (2), in case of positive flow direction.

Reservoirs.
As the approach is similar for the reservoirs upstream and downstream, we shall concentrate the discussion on the reservoir upstream. The equations of continuity and energy for the reservoir are respectively :

$$V_1 \frac{d\rho_1}{dt} = -m_2 A_2 \tag{14a}$$
and
$$V_1 \frac{dE_1}{dt} = - \left( e + \frac{p}{\rho} + \frac{1}{2} u^2 \right) \Big|_2 m_2 A_2 \tag{14b}$$

The index 1 denotes the reservoir and the index 2 the inlet of the pipe connected to the reservoir.
The equations relative to the inlet are :

$$p_1^o - p_2^o = K_{o2} \left( p_2^o - p_2 \right) \qquad \text{( pressure loss )} \tag{14c}$$
$$h_1^o = h_2^o \qquad \qquad \text{( adiabatic flow )} \tag{14d}$$

During evacuation, with outflow velocity $u_2 > 0$, the compatibility equation, which is associated with the only leftrunning characteristic, can be used to complete the system for the time derivatives of $\rho_1$, $E_1$, $\rho_2$, $m_2$ and $E_2$.
Rough estimates and numerical experiments show that an accurate knowledge of the losses is not required, $K_{o2}$ being small in comparison with the overall losses in the pipeline characterized by f L/D.

The assumption of equal values for the variables of state (e.g. pressure) throughout the volume is crucial. Estimate show that the model is adequate for volumes $V_1$ which are relatively small (e.g. compared to the volume of the pipeline), and where the pressure equalizes faster than in the pipeline attached to it. This is not the case for large reservoirs or caverns. For long and slender geometries, the flow velocities are no longer negligible. In the limit, a reservoir can be compared to a pipeline of a large diameter, including viscous effects. A large, slender reservoir connected to a pipeline, can be modeled as two connected pipelines of different diameters. We mention here the work of Botros et al. (1989) who simulated a gas release from a long pipeline through a valve and compared the results to those obtained with the simplified "lumped volume" treatment, assuming equal pressures in the pipeline. This part of their study, which is mostly analytical, provides estimates of the "blowdown" rates and the corresponding durations.

Broken end.
        Problems relative to pipeline ruptures are of prime interest for the safety engineer, because the number of lives at risk and the potential environmental damage is related directly to the mass-flow rates of the gas released. A conservative approach, representing a worst case scenario, is to assume a guillotine rupture, with an unobstructed opening at the broken end equal to the pipeline cross section (Fannel\o{}p, 1994). Experience confirms that there never will be a neat cut, but rather a more or less pronounced contraction at the broken end. The shape of the contraction, which often exhibits sharp edges, is not well defined and will be accounted for by a pressure-loss coefficient :

$$p_2^\circ - p_c^\circ = K_{oc}\left(p_c^\circ - p_c\right) \text{ with } p_c \geq p_a \quad (\,a : \text{ambient}\,) \qquad (15)$$

The equations of continuity and energy : $\dot{m}_c = \dot{m}_2$ and $h_c^\circ = h_2^\circ$ respectively, complete the basic equations describing the flow at the broken end (see Fig. 2 for notation ). Choked flow is characterized by $u_c = c_c$ and the boundary condition for undercritical flow is $p_c = p_a$.
        It can be demonstrated by numerical experiments that the mass-flow rate is remarkably insensitive to variations of the pressure-loss coefficient and of the contraction ratio, within a wide range of values. It is clear that the influence of the pressure-loss coefficient, which predicts small losses compared to the overall pressure loss in the system, is rather week. The influence of the contraction ratio has been investigated by means of the configuration of Fig.2 , assuming critical, quasisteady flow in the smallest section. It can be shown that the critical Mach numbers at location (1) and (2) are related by the following formula (see e.g. Kunsch et al., 1991) :

$$\mathrm{Ln}\left(\frac{M_2^*}{M_1^*}\right) + \frac{1}{2}\left(\frac{1}{M_2^{*2}} - \frac{1}{M_1^{*2}}\right) = -\frac{4\gamma}{\gamma+1}\frac{fL}{D} \quad \text{with } M^* = \frac{u}{c^*} \qquad (16)$$

and the friction factor f.
It is reasonable furthermore to neglect the dissipative mechanisms of the flow accelerating to the contraction or "vena contracta" . The highly dissipative expansion of the free jet after section (c) is not relevant for the present estimates, as it occurs outside the region considered. Then $M_2^*$ follows from the implicit relation :

$$M_2^*\left[\frac{\gamma+1}{2} - \frac{\gamma-1}{2}M_2^{*2}\right]^{1/(\gamma-1)}\left(\frac{A_2}{A_c}\right) = 1 \qquad \text{with } M_c^* = 1 \qquad (17)$$

The corresponding dimensionless mass-flow rate $\dot{m}$ / $\dot{m}_{max}$ as a function of the contraction ratio $A_c/A_2$, with f L/D as a parameter, is shown in Fig. 2. It can be observed that the mass-flow rate is almost independent of the contraction ratio $A_c/A_2$, ( provided that $A_c/A_2 \geq 0.5$ ) for values of the  parameter f L/D, in excess of 20. It can be concluded that the simplifying assumption of a "guillotine rupture" with a free opening of the broken end, equal to the full cross-sectional area of the pipeline, appears adequate.

## APPLICATION AND RESULTS.

### Validation of the Model.

The capabilities of the model under consideration have been demonstrated for many different configurations. Two fundamentally different discharge processes are particularly relevant and will be considered as test cases :
1. massive release of gas after a guillotine rupture of a high-pressure pipeline.
2. blowdown of a pipeline with discharge through a blowdown valve.

In the first example, methane is transported through a pipeline, having a length of 145 km, an upstream pressure of 133 bar and a delivery pressure of 55 bar during steady state operation. At time t = 0, a guillotine rupture occurs on the high-pressure side, producing an extreme acceleration with sonic flow at the broken end. The mass-flow rate, as calculated with the present code, is documented in Fig. 3 (continuous line) and compared with that obtained by Flatt (1985) (circles), who implemented Martins' equation of state, which has a limited range of validity. Prior to the rupture, the flow enters the pipeline on the high pressure side (positive flow direction); flow reversal takes place after the rupture at the high pressure side (negative sign for the mass-flow rate $\dot{m}(t)$ in Fig. 3 ). The solution of Flatt (based on the method of characteristics) is probably more accurate than that obtained by means of the present method, for the inertia dominated early time regime, but the corresponding numerical scheme ( inverse marching method) is rather time consuming. In order to demonstrate the influence of real thermal behaviour, a calculation has been performed with the ideal gas assumption (Fig. 3). A non-negligible systematic underestimate of the mass-flow rate (depending on the absolute pressure level) results from this simplifying assumption.

The second case, dealing with a pipeline blowdown through a valve, is depicted in Fig.5. This case is particularly interesting as it corresponds to a large field test documented by Botros et al. (1989). A computer simulation has been performed with the parameters specified by Botros, e.g. a length of the pipeline of 25523 m, a diameter of 0.203 m and a discharge coefficient of the valve equal to $C_d = 0.75$. The corresponding pressure distribution over the length of the pipeline, with time as a parameter, is shown in Fig. 4. The time history of the pressure upstream of the valve is shown in Fig. 5. The agreement with the experimental results of the field test is excellent.

### Numerical experiments and sensitivity studies.

Numerical experiments have been performed in order to test the model and to demonstrate its capabilities and limitations.

Simultaneous rupture of the pipeline at two locations has been simulated in order to check the mass-balance as well globally for a specified duration, as for each time step. In the time of the simulation run, about half the initial mass-content is released. The corresponding pressure distributions between the two broken ends, are shown in Fig.6 for equal time intervals. They confirm the parabolic profile assumptions in the analytical Pohlhausen method, which predicts successfully the friction dominated late-time regime of the release process ( Fanneløp et al., 1982).

A further numerical experiment demonstrates the effect of the closing (closing time t = 20 s) of a barrier valve in a 30 km long pipeline, at a distance of 300 m from the downstream delivery point. The technical configuration corresponds to that of Fig.1. The numerical simulation starts with the process of pressure equalization of two reservoirs connected by a flowline with a fully opened barrier valve. The valve starts closing at time t = 40 s. The corresponding pressure profiles are shown in Fig.7 . The oscillation frequency of the mass-flow rate, as provided by the simulation (Fig.8), is equal to the eigenfrequency $\omega$ of an oscillating gas column. The eigenfrequency can be estimated by means of the analytical expression

$$\omega = \frac{\pi}{2} \frac{c_o}{L} ,$$ when the speed of sound $c_0$ is evaluated as a function of average pressure and density.

Frictional effects are accounted for by means of a friction factor depending on the pipewall roughness and the Reynolds number. The most commonly used correlations are those of Colebrook or Swamee & Jain (Benedict, 1980). Numerical experiments have demonstrated that the friction factor f can be reduced, with good approximation, to the American Gas Association (AGA) - formula :

$$1 / f^{1/2} = 4 \cdot \log_{10}(3.7 D / k_s)$$    with pipewall roughness height $k_S$

when the Re number dependence is neglected. Corrosion and other weathering processes alter the pipewall roughness considerably during the service life, so that precise correlations for f are of limited utility. A simulation run for massive release through a broken end, resulting from a guillotine rupture ( corresponding to the first test case ), shows that an increase of f of the order of 20% reduces the mass-flow rate only by about 5% .

## REFERENCES.

R.P. Benedict (1980)
  "Fundamentals of Pipe Flow"
  A Wiley-Interscience Publication, John Wiley & Sons (1980)
K.K. Botros, W.M. Jungowski, and M.H. Weiss (1989)
  "Models and Methods of Simulating Gas Pipeline Blowdown"
  The Canadian Journal of Chemical Engineering,
  Volume 67, August 1989
T.K. Fanneløp, I.L. Ryhming (1982)
  "Massive Release of Gas from Long Pipelines"
  AIAA Journal of Energy 6 (1982)
T.K. Fanneløp (1994)
  " Fluid Mechanics for Industrial Safety and Environmental Protection ",
  Elsevier
R. Flatt (1985)
  " Zur Anwendung numerischer Verfahren der Strömungslehre
  in der Realgasdynamik"
  Forschung im Ingenieurwesen Bd.51 (1985) Nr.2
J.P.Kunsch, K.Sjøen, and T.K.Fanneløp (1991)
  "Loss Control by Subsea Barrier Valve for Offshore Gas Pipeline"
  23rd Annual Offshore Technology Conference OTC
  in Houston, Texas, May 6-9, 1991
E. Lang (1991)
  "Gas Flow in Pipelines Following a Rupture Computed by a
  Spectral Method"
  Journal of Applied Mathematics and Physics (ZAMP)
  Vol. 42, March 1991
D.S. Miller (1990)
  "Internal Flow Systems" 2nd ed.
  BHRA (Information Services), Cranfield UK.
K. Sjøen (1993)
  "Present and Future Challenges in Gas Transport"
  Gas Transport Symposium
  Haugesund, Norway, Feb. 1-2, 1993
K.E. Starling (1973)
  "Fluid Thermodynamic Properties for Light Petroleum Systems"
  Gulf Publishing Company, Houston , 1973

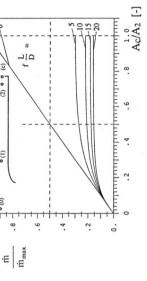

Fig. 2 : Dimensionless mass-flow rate $\dot{m}/\dot{m}_{max}$ versus contraction ratio $A_c/A_2$ ( f L/D is parameter )

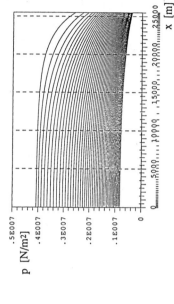

Fig. 4 : Pipeline blowdown through a valve ( see Fig. 5 ) : pressure distribution over the length of the pipeline ( time is parameter )

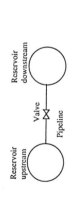

Fig. 1 : Basic configuration of the simulation model.

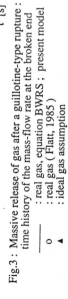

Fig.3 : Massive release of gas after a guillotine-type rupture : time history of the mass-flow rate at the broken end

——— : real gas, equation BWRS ;  present model
o  : real gas ( Flatt, 1985 )
◄  : ideal gas assumption

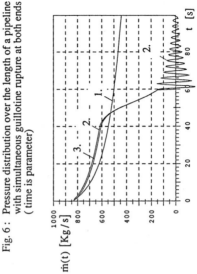

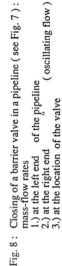

Fig. 6 : Pressure distribution over the length of a pipeline with simultaneous guillotine rupture at both ends ( time is parameter )

Fig. 8 : Closing of a barrier valve in a pipeline ( see Fig. 7 ) : mass-flow rates
1.) at the left end    of the pipeline
2.) at the right end ,,    ( oscillating flow )
3.) at the location  of the valve

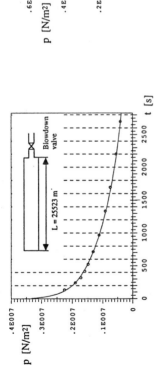

Fig. 5 : Pipeline blowdown through a valve :
time history of the pressure upstream of the valve
——— : present model    ( Botros, 1989 )
o    : field experiment

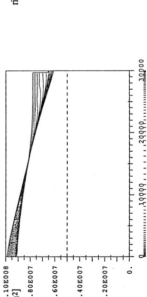

Fig. 7 : Closing of a barrier valve in a 30000 m long pipeline
( location of the valve : x = 29700 m )
pressure distribution over the length of the pipeline
( time is parameter )

NOUVELLE APPROCHE A L'ESTIMATION DES CONSEQUENCES
ECOLOGIQUES D'ACCIDENT AUX GAZODUCS


A NEW APPROACH TO ESTIMATING THE ENVIRONMENTAL CONSEQUENCES
OF GAS PIPELINE ACCIDENTS

A.I. GRITSENKO
ALL-RUSSIAN GAS RESEARCH INSTITUTE (VNIIGAS), RUSSIE


V.M. MAXIMOV
OIL & GAS RESEARCH INSTITUTE, RUSSIE


G.D. ROZENBERG, V.I.ISSAEV
STATE OIL & GAS ACADEMY, RUSSIE

RESUME


On propose une nouvelle approche à la simulation des processus inte-
nsifs qui se déroulent lors des accidents possibles sur les conduites à gaz et à gaz-condensat. Cela permet de prévoir la dynamique
d'écoulement d'un mélange biphasique dans l'endroit de rupture d'une
conduite et sa dispersion à l'atmosphère basse. Méthodes existantes
orientées sur les modèles stationnaires ne conviennent pas aux calculs de tels processus. L'exposé comprend l'analyse originale, solutions analytiques, algorithmes et applications numériques.


ABSTRACT


A new approach to simulation the intensive processes occuring during
the accidents on gas- and gas-condensat pipelines is proposed. It
permits to forecast the flow dynamics of 2-phase mixture at the
place of pipeline rupture and its dispersion in the lower atmosphere. The existing methods directed to the stationary models are not
suitable for the calculation of such processes. The paper contains
an original analysis, analytical solutions, algorithms and numerical
calculations.

## INTRODUCTION

La modélisation des consequences écologiques de la rupture d'une conduite à gaz-condensat consiste à la position et résolution de quatre problèmes liés entre eux: simulation de l'écoulement biphasique multicomposant dans une conduite (cet écoulement est essentiellement non stationnaire); le calcul des caractéristiques thermophysiques du mélange gaz-liquide; la formation du jet d'éruption dans l'atmosphère; la dispersion de gaz à l'atmosphère turbulente.

Cette simulation se traduit par le calcul en fonction du temps dans l'endroit de rupture et en tout point de l'atmosphère de grandeurs fondamentales telles que la pression, les débits en masse des phases, la masse d'éruption et la concentration d'impureté à l'atmosphère.

Pour illustrer cela nous allons considérer un exemple d'un gazoduc concret.

## SIMULATION DE L'ECOULEMENT BIPHASIQUE APRES LA RUPTURE D'UNE CONDUITE A GAS-CONDENSAT

### Modèle mathématique

On considère l'écoulement non permanent biphasique multicomposant dans une conduite circulaire compte tenu de l'échange de chaleur. Suppositions prises sont: l'écoulement est homogène, c'est-à-dire les vitesses des phases sont égales; les pressions $p$ et les températures $T$ des phases sont les mêmes et constantes dans une section; les conditions d'équilibre local thermodynamique sont accomplies dans chaque section. Alors les lois principales de conservation [1] amènent au système d'équations suivantes:

$$
\begin{aligned}
&\frac{\partial \rho}{\partial t} + v\,\frac{\partial \rho}{\partial x} + \rho\,\frac{\partial v}{\partial x} = 0 \\
&\rho\,\frac{\partial v}{\partial t} + \rho v\,\frac{\partial v}{\partial x} + \frac{\partial p}{\partial x} = -(A_1 + A_2), \\
&\rho v\,\frac{\partial v}{\partial t} + \rho v^2\,\frac{\partial v}{\partial x} + \rho\,\frac{\partial h}{\partial t} + \rho v\,\frac{\partial h}{\partial x} - \frac{\partial p}{\partial t} = -A_1 v + A_3,
\end{aligned} \tag{1}
$$

où

$$
A_1 = \rho \cdot g \cdot \sin\alpha, \quad A_2 = \lambda \rho\,\frac{|v|\,v}{2D}, \quad A_3 = \frac{4k(T_o - T)}{D};
$$

$$
\rho = \phi \cdot \rho_g + (1-\phi)\rho_l, \quad h = c \cdot h_g + (1-c)h_l; \tag{2}
$$

$$
\frac{1-\phi}{\phi} = \frac{1-c}{c} \cdot \frac{\rho_g}{\rho_l} \quad (\phi = \beta); \tag{3}
$$

$$
\lambda = \lambda(Re, \varepsilon), \quad Re = \frac{\rho v D}{\mu}, \quad \mu = \beta \cdot \mu_g + (1-\beta)\mu_l; \tag{4}
$$

$\rho$ et $h$ étant la masse spécifique et enthalpie du mélange gaz-liquide respectivement; $\phi$ et c est la concentration volumique et massique de gaz ($\beta$ est contenu en débit du gaz); $T_o$ est la température de l'environnement, $\alpha$ est l'angle d'inclinaison de l'axe de conduite.

Les paramètres des phases $\rho_i$, $h_i$, $\mu_i$ ($i = g,l$), $\phi$ et donc $\rho$ et h pour la mixture sont déterminés d'après l'équation d'état comme les fonctions de p et T. Pour les calculer on utilise le paquet spécial thermodynamique. C'est pourquoi, avec les équations (1) et relations (2)-(4), le problème devient bien posé. L'écoulement du gaz naturel après la rupture d'un gazoduc est un cas particulier du modèle cité ci-dessus.

Conditions aux limites sur les vannes de sécurité tiennent compte de la dynamique de leur fermeture. La condition aux limites dans l'endroit de rupture (x = 1) dépend du caractère d'écoulement du gaz:

$$p(1,t) = p_{at}, \quad T(1,t) = T_o \quad \text{si } v(1,t) < a,$$

ou bien $v(1,t) = a$, si l'écoulement est sonique,
a étant la vitesse du son.

La résolution numérique du système (1) - (4) est réalisé par la méthode des caractéristiques. Analyse des résultats permet d'obtenir les formules analytiques approchées appliquées lors du calcul pratique.

## Approximations des recherches numériques

On a élaboré la conséquence suivante de calculs approximatifs.

a). Les débits en masse à travers de la section de rupture (x = 1, fig.1) $Q_{m1}(t)$ et $Q_{m2}(t)$ des parties $0 < x < 1$ et $1 < x < L$ respectivement sont:

$$Q_{mi}(t) = Q_{mi}(0) \cdot \exp(-b_i t) \quad (i = 1,2),$$
$$Q_{m1}(0) = Q_{m2}(0) = Q_m = \mu S \sqrt{\gamma \rho_o p_o} \, (2/\gamma+1)^{\gamma+1/(\gamma-1)} \quad ,$$

où S est la surface de la section de conduite; $\gamma$ est l'indice d'adiabate; $p_o$ et $\rho_o$ est la pression et la masse spécifique avant la rupture; $\mu$ est le coefficient de débit.

b). Les masses du mélange $G_i(t)$ sorties à travers de la section x = 1 à l'instant de temps t sont:

$$G_i(t) = \int_o^t Q_{mi}(t)dt = \frac{Q_m}{b_i} [1 - \exp(-b_i t)] \quad (i = 1,2) \qquad (5)$$

c). La masse totale d'éruption est égale à

$$G = G_1 + G_2 = \sum_{k=1}^{4} M_k \qquad (6)$$

où $M_1 = \rho_1 1S$, $M_2 = \rho_2(L-1)S$; $M_j = k_j Q_m t_j$ (j = 3,4);

$$t_3 = t^* + 1/c_o, \quad t_4 = t^* + (L-1)/c_o; \quad c_c = \sqrt{\gamma p_o/\rho_o} \quad ,$$

$\rho_i$ (i = 1,2) étant la masse spécifique du mélange en partie $0 < x < 1$ et $1 < x < L$ respectivement; $t^*$ étant la durée de fermeture des vannes. Les valeurs numériques des coefficients $k_j = 3 \div 5$ (j = 3,4) dependent des characéristiques de conduite.

d). Il résulte des formules (5) et (6) que

$$b_1 = Q_m/(M_1 + M_3), \quad b_2 = Q_m/(M_2 + M_4).$$

e). Le temps d'éruption $t_i$ du mélange de partie $0 < x < 1$ et $1 < x < L$ respectivement est

$$t_i = - \ln(1-\alpha)/b_i \qquad (i = 1,2),$$

$\alpha = 0,98 - 0,99$ étant la fraction de masse d'éruption calculée par l'égalité (5).

CALCUL DES CARACTERISTIQUES THERMOPHYSIQUES DU MELANGE GAZ-LIQUIDE

Ce calcul est réalisé sous les suppositions suivantes:
- le composé du mélange est connu, et sa composition sommaire reste la même;
- la condition de l'équilibre local thermodynamique est accomplise;
- Pengue-Robinson équation d'état peut être utilisée.

L'algorithme du calcul des paramètres de l'équilibre vapeur-liquide est présenté à [2]. Après avoir fait les calculs thermodynamiques on obtient les concentrations en masse $X_g, X_l$ de phase gazière et liquide respectivement et les fractions molairs $\eta_i$ de chaque composante en fonction de temperature $T$ sous la pression atmosphérique. D'après l'analyse des résultats de calculs nombreux on a établit les approximations suivantes:

$$X_l = \frac{a_l + b_l T}{c_l + T}, \quad X_g = 1 - X_l,$$

où les coefficients $a_l$, $b_l$, $c_l$ dependent du composé de mélange d'éruption; ils sont constants pour le mélange d'un gisement donné. En particulier, pour Astrakhan gisement on a: $a_l = 6,6;$, $b_l = 0,028;$ $c_l = -200$.

Les grandeurs de masse d'éruption des phases sont déterminées d'après la formule $G_\alpha = X_\alpha G$ $(\alpha = 1,g)$, où $G$ est la masse sommaire d'éruption.

Sachant les fractions molaires $\eta_i$ et les masses moléculaires $M_i$ pour les conditions thermobariqus données, on trouve la masse d'une composante en chaque phase:

$$M_{\alpha i} = X_\alpha G \, \eta_i M_i / \Sigma \eta_i M_i \qquad (\alpha = 1,g).$$

MODELES DE DISPERSION DE GAS DANS L'ATMOSPHERE

L'écoulement de gaz après la rupture d'un gazoduc est un processus subit et de courte durée.

Dans ce cas là, pour évaluer la pollution de l'atmosphère, une approche de "scenario" est plus convenable. Elle consiste en calcul de versions nombreuses d'accidents pour les différentes conditions météorologiques. Telles météo-conditions typiques sont établies d'après l'analyse d'information statistique pour une région concrète.

Le calcul de dispersion des impuretés toxiques (ou bien du gaz naturel) est basé sur les solutions analytiques de l'équation non permanente demi-empirique de diffusion turbulente [3]. Ces solutions sont mises en correspondance avec le Gaussian modèle, avec les schémas de classification de la stabilité atmosphèrique et avec σ-courbes [4].

On propose deux approximations [5]:

1) Celle quasi-stationnaire (pour l'éruption prolongée), quand le débit en masse d'une composante de gaz $Q_{gi}(t)$ depend de temps et entre dans la relation à calculer la concentration $q_i(x,y,z,t)$ d'impureté:

$$q_i(x,y,z,t) = \frac{Q_{gi}(t-x/u)}{2\pi\sigma_x\sigma_y\sigma_z u} \exp\left( -\frac{y^2}{2\sigma_y^2} \right) F(z,x) \quad (x/u < t < t_k + x/u),$$

$$F(z,x) = \exp\left( -\frac{(z-H)^2}{2\sigma_z^2(z,x)} \right) + \exp\left( -\frac{(z+H)^2}{2\sigma_z^2(z,x)} \right) , \tag{7}$$

où u est la vitesse du vent dans la direction de l'axe x, H est la hauteur effective d'éruption, $t_k$ est la durée d'éruption. Si $t < x/u$ et $t > t_k + x/u$, on a $q_i = 0$.

2) Modèle non stationnaire de "nuage" si l'éruption du gaz est presque instantanée (c'est le cas de rupture entière de la conduite). Dans ce cas-là, la masse totale d'éruption $M_{gi}$ est utilisée pour le calcul des concentrations. On a:

$$q_i(x,y,z,t) = \frac{M_{gi}}{(2\pi)^{3/2}\sigma_x\sigma_y\sigma_z} \exp\left( -\frac{(x-ut)^2}{2\sigma_x^2} - \frac{y^2}{2\sigma_y^2} \right) F(z,x). \tag{8}$$

Les grandeurs de dispersions $\sigma_x^2, \sigma_y^2, \sigma_z^2$ sont calculées d'après la paramétrisation expérimentale choisie des états d'atmosphère [4,5].

Pour estimer les dimensions d'une zone dangereuse de pollution, on applique aussi un paramètre integral applé la dose toxique

$$D = \int_0^\infty q(x,y,z)dt$$

et le temps effectif d'exposition $T_{ef} = D/q_{max}$.

La valeur $q_{max}$ est déterminée d'après les relations (7) et (8) si l'on met x = ut. L'utilisation de cette valeur permet d'éviter l'analyse pénible de la dynamique des lignes de concentrations.

Ainsi, pour évaluer la pollution de l'atmosphère lors d'un accident sur une conduite il faut choisir les conditions météorologiques qui correspondent au scenario considéré, déterminer la classe de stabilité d'atmosphère, calouler les grandeurs de dispersion $\sigma^2$ et ensuite trouver les valeurs de concentrations maximales, des doses toxiques et de temps effectif d'exposition.

EXEMPLE D'UTILISATION

A titre d'exemple on considère les calculs des paramètres d'éruption du gaz et sa diffusion à l'atmosphère lors d'un accident hypothétique sur une conduite d'Astrakhan gisement à gaz-condensat (Russie) avec un grand pourcentage de $H_2S$ (jusqu'à 26%).

## Dynamique d'éruption et la dispersion dans l'atmosphére

Les données initiales sont (voir la fig.1): $L = 7.65$ km; $l_1 = l_2 = 850$ m; $D = 0,366$ m; $\Delta l = 1,7$ km (la distance entre deux vannes voisines); $Q_m^o = 85$ kg/s (le débit en masse avant la rupture); $p_1 = 7,543 \cdot 10^6$ Pa, $T_1 = 40 \div 41^o$ C; $p_L = 6,442 \cdot 10^6$ Pa, $T_L = 30 \div 36^o$ C; $t^* = 20$ s (le temps de fermeture de vanne).

Quelques résultats de calcul sont presentés sur les figures 2÷4. Selon le calcul, le temps d'éruption du mélange est 90 s; la table 1 représente des autres résultats sommaires (pour deux valeurs de température d'ambience correspondante aux conditions d'hiver et d'été).

Table 1

| Température d'ambience $T_o$ (en K) | Masse sommaire d'éruption | | Masse d'éruption de $H_2S$ | |
|---|---|---|---|---|
| | de gaz $M_g$ (en kg) | de condensat $M_l$ (en kg) | en phase gazière $M_{g,H2S}$ (en kg) | en phase liquide $M_{l,H2S}$ (en kg) |
| 263 | $31,75 \cdot 10^9$ | $8,95 \cdot 10^3$ | $9,8 \cdot 10^9$ | 39 |
| 283 | $33,58 \cdot 10^9$ | $7,22 \cdot 10^9$ | $10,3 \cdot 10^9$ | 19 |

Ces charactéristiques sont les conditions initiales à calouler la dispersion d'impureté. Les isolignes sur la fig.4 décrivent la dispersion d'hydrogène sulfuré dans l'atmosphère caloulée selon le modèle non stationnaire (8) ($z = 1,5$ m; $H = 5$ m) pour deux classes de stabilité de Pasquill-Gifford: B (non stable tempéré, fig.4 a) et D (neutre, fig.4 b). La première est propre à la période d'été en Astrakhan région, la deuxiéme est à l'hiver. Les domaines entre les lignes 1,2,3 sur la fig.4 correspondent respectivement à la zone mortèle (jusqu'à la ligne 1), à la zone de lésion grave pour la santé (jusqu'à la ligne 2) et à la zone de lésion légère (irritation des yeux, de respiration, etc.) -jusqu'à la ligne 3. La zone de sûreté est en dehors de la ligne 3.

## Remarques sur l'effet secondaire de pollution

L'abaissement du condensat sur la surface du sol exige une étude de pollution secondaire de l'ambience (son évaporation à l'atmosphère, la pollution du sol et de la flore).

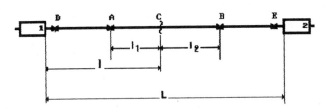

Fig.1. Le schema de rupture

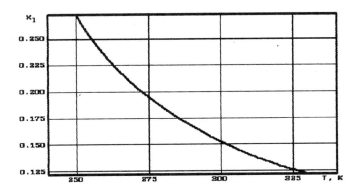

Fig.2. Concentration en masse $X_l$ de phase liquide en
fonction de temperature $T$ sous la pression
atmosphérique.

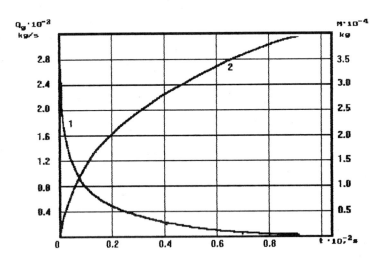

Fig.3. Variation du débit d'éruption $Q_g$ (courbe 1)
et de la masse M (courbe 2) dans le temps.

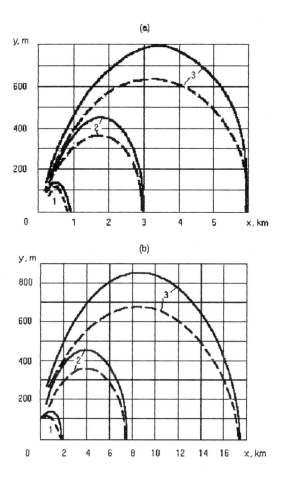

Fig.4. Lignes d'égales concentrations maximales ( —— )
et de dose toxiques (-----) dans le temps.

| Classe de stabilité d'atmosphère | Isoligne N° | Paramètre | | |
|---|---|---|---|---|
| | | $q_{max}$ en $\mu g/m^3$ | D en $gs/m^3$ | $T_{ef}$ en s |
| B(u=3,8 m/s) fig.4 a | 1 | 800 | 62 | 86 |
| | 2 | 29 | 8 | 276 |
| | 3 | 5,3 | 2,7 | 509 |
| D(u=4,5 m/s) fig.4 b | 1 | 800 | 62 | 77 |
| | 2 | 34 | 8 | 235 |
| | 3 | 5,6 | 2,7 | 482 |

Sur l'évaporation du condensat. Calculs présentés (voir la table 1) montrent que, pour le mélange d'Astrakhan gisement, la plupart d'hydrogène sulfuré est sortie dans l'atmosphère en phase gazière. Sa fraction en phase liquide par rapport à son contenu en phase gazière est de 0.39% en hiver et de 0,18% en été. Donc, dans ce cas-là la contribution de l'évaporation de composante liquide de H2S dès surface du sol à la pollution d'atmosphère est négligeable.

S'il faut en tenir compte (pour des autres gisements) on propose deux modèles de l'évaporation d'impureté [6]: a). l'évaporation dans l'atmosphère turbulente;  b). modèle d'évaporation diffusible au milieu immobile s'il y a une zone de vents faibles.

Pollution du sol par condensat. Ce processus est étudié à la base des écoulements biphasiques dans un milieu poreux [7]. On applique deux modèles de pénétration du condensat dans le sol: 1). modèle d'imbibition capillaire et de gravité qui tient compte du phénomène de mouillage, des forces capillaires et des forces de pésanteur; il est valable pour le milieu poreux sec (saturé par l'air); 2). modèle de système des capillaires verticaux (pour le sol inondé).

Au cas d'exemple considéré, le front de pollution par condensat pénètre à l'interieur du sol à la profondeur de 5 m dans 2 mois (pour le premier modèle) et dans 5 jours (pour le deuxième).

CONCLUSION

Estimation quantitative des conséquences de rupture d'un gazoduc comprend:

- détermination du temps d'éruption, de la pression $p(t)$, du débit $Q(t)$, de la masse des phases $M_g(t)$ et $M_l(t)$ dans l'endroit de rupture;

- calcul de la diffusion de nuage d'éruption (répartition des concentrations d'impureté dans l'espace et dans le temps, isolignes de concentration, doses toxiques, etc.);

- estimation de l'effet secondaire de pollution (évaporation du condensat à l'atmosphère, pollution du sol et des eaux souterrains par condensat).

Les résultats sont présentés sous la forme d'un software d'ingénieur.

Cette étude permet d'estimer les dimensions des zones de protection et les risques écologiques, de choisir mieux des mesures de précaution à éviter un accident et de se préparer aux travaux possibles de sauvetage.

Les auteurs remercient RAO "GAZPROM" pour le financement de cette recherche.

REFERENCES CITEES


1. Nigmatoulin R.I. "Dynamique des milieux polyphasiques", v.1.-
Moscou, "Naouka", 1987. - 464 p (en russe).

2. Walas S.M. "Phase equilibria in chemical engineering". - Butter-
worth Publishers, 1985.

3. Marchouk G.I. Simulation mathématique dans le problème de l'environnement. - Moscou, "Naouka", 1982. - 320 p. (en russe).

4."Handbook of air pollution technology". - New York,etc. 1986.

5. Maksimov V.M. and Limar E.E. "A new approach to estimating the
environmental consequences of gas-pipeline accidents". - Gas Industry, 1992, N 10, 22-24 pp (en russe).

6. Maksimov V.M., Rozenberg G.D., Issaev V.I. et al. "Calculation
method of atmospheric pollution after nonstable gas-condensat blowouts".- Moscow, 1993. - 71 p.

7. Basniev K.S., Kotchina I.N., Maksimov V.M. "Subterranean Hydrome-
chanics". - Moscow, "Nedra", 1993. - 414 p.

PROBABILISTIC HAZARDS ASSESSMENT
ON A NATURAL GAS COMPRESSOR STATION

ETUDE DE DANGERS PROBABILISTE
SUR UNE STATION DE COMPRESSION DE GAZ NATUREL

Géraldine BERNARD

GAZ DE FRANCE , Direction de la Recherche, Saint Denis, FRANCE

Rémi ARNAUD

GAZ DE FRANCE, Direction de la Production et du Transport, Paris, FRANCE

ABSTRACT

The safety studies carried out up to now, as part of request for authorisation to operate some installations of the natural gas transmission network, run by Gaz de France, have mostly been performed by using a determinist approach. Nevertheless, in order to quantify better the risk level related to compressor stations, Gaz de France decided to use reliability methods. It has carried out an experimental hazards assessment.

In this study, the methodology used is based upon a combination of various safety methods, deductive and inductive, in an effort to fine-tune the problem analysis.

The risks assessment has been done by combining the undesired events consequences with their occurrence probabilities. In order to discuss these risks, the step adopted by Electricité de France for its prevention against aircrash on nuclear plants has been used.

RESUME

Les études de dangers réalisées jusqu'à présent, dans le cadre de la demande d'autorisation d'exploiter certaines installations faisant partie du réseau de transport de gaz naturel, exploité par Gaz de France, ont été essentiellement menées en utilisant une approche déterministe. Toutefois, pour mieux quantifier le niveau de risque présenté par les stations de compression, Gaz de France a décidé d'utiliser des méthodes fiabilistes, et a réalisé une étude probabiliste expérimentale de dangers.

Dans cette étude, la méthodologie employée s'appuie sur une combinaison de différentes méthodes de sûreté de fonctionnement, déductives et inductives, afin d'affiner l'analyse du problème.

L'estimation des risques a été faite en associant les conséquences des événements redoutés à leurs probabilités d'occurrence. Pour situer ces risques, la démarche adoptée par EDF dans sa prévention contre les chutes d'avion sur les centrales nucléaires a été utilisée.

INTRODUCTION

In 1978, for the first time, a complete risk analysis was carried out on a non-nuclear unit by the United Kingdom Atomic Energy Commission (UKEA). Its purpose was to evaluate the risks inherent in the extension of the petrochemical complex at Canvey Island (1),(2).

In France, since the Seventies, reliability analysis methods have been used intensively in the nuclear field, both for military and civilian uses as well as in aeronautics field (for example, the Concorde (3)). Among oil companies, in 1982, the Elf-Aquitaine, Total C.F.P. and the French Petroleum Institute companies jointly launched a research project about oil systems safety and reliability.

As for Liquefied Petroleum Gas (LPG), three recent probability studies have been devoted to the BLEVE effect on tanks. These studies come from three different countries : France (4), the Netherlands (5) and the United Kingdom (6). These three countries have "risk" cultures which are quite different, especially in France, where the probability approach is not used to evaluate industrial risks.

Gaz de France has been operating natural gas facilities since 1946. During these years, it has given high priority to safety as shown by the very low number of incidents occurring in its facilities. Nevertheless, Gaz de France remains concerned about safety and environment. Even now, improving safety and contributing to environmental protection are among the strategic orientations chosen by Gaz de France.

The safety studies carried out up to now, as part of request for authorisation to operate some installations of the natural gas transmission network, run by Gaz de France, have mostly been performed by using a determinist approach. Nevertheless, in order to quantify better the risk level related to compressor stations, Gaz de France decided to use reliability methods. It has carried out an experimental hazards assessment that associates the consequences of an accident with its probability of occurrence. This study was realized in close collaboration with the french Ministry of Environment.

The study concerns the Voisines natural gas compressor station, which consists of the major equipment that can be found in other Gaz de France installations.

In this study, the methodology used is based upon a combination of various reliability methods. These methods could be independently used to perform this study. But, in order to fine-tune the problem analysis, it has been decided to combine deductive and inductive methods.

A preliminary hazards analysis (PHA), a functional analysis, a failure modes and effects analysis (FMEA), a fault tree analysis (FTA) have been used. All the steps of the used methodology are shown on the following graph.

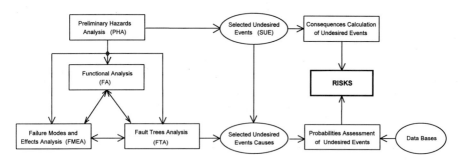

At every step of the methodology, each method is used in a specific objective. For example, the prelimary hazards analysis leads to the events that have to be studied but also need a consequences assessment, and so on.

STATION DESCRIPTION

Surroundings

The compressor station is surrounded by farmland and woods on the "plateau de Langres". Its natural surroundings as well as meteorological and seismic historical data do not show special characteristics. The population density, near the station, is very low. The near communication routes have a low traffic; however, it can be noticed that the station is located under a commercial airway and under a low altitude military training flights area.

Location in the transmission network

This station belongs to Gaz de France transmission installations. It allows to insure the interconnection and the required gas volumes transit, especially from the storage of Cerville to the Paris region or the Rhône valley.

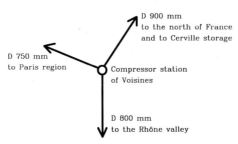

Compressor station

The station occupies a surface of 1,97 ha. It mainly includes :
• a gas dispatching on the transmission network which allows to insure distributions of gas according to 54 possible different configurations.
• 5 turbocompressor units of 4810 kW power each, and their auxiliaries.
• a remote driving and control system from the National Dispatching Center and from the Regional Control Center.

PRELIMINARY HAZARDS ANALYSIS

Principle

The aim of preliminary hazards analysis is to identify the compressor station hazards and their causes, and to assess potential incidents.

The units which present a potential risk are identified. They are associated with hazardous entities such as fuel, pressurised fluids, for example.

Every event which can lead to a hazardous situation are then listed. Then is undertaken the identification of additional events that transform the hazardous situation in potential accident.

This method is mainly based on a perfect knowledge of the station, on engineers experience and judgement.

The consequences are classified as following :
• class of severity 1 ⇔ minor consequences,
• class of severity 2 ⇔ significant consequences,
• class of severity 3 ⇔ critical consequences : prejudice to workers, significant damage to the system
• class of severity 4 ⇔ catastrophic   consequences : prejudice    to people out of the station and surroundings damage, system destruction.

The method results are shown in tabular form. The table headings are :

| system or function |
| --- |
| phase |
| hazardous entities |
| events causing a hazardous situation |
| hazardous situation |
| events causing a potential accident |
| potential accident |
| effects and consequences |
| classification by severity |

Selected undesired events

Among the counted hazards, events belonging to the class of severity 4, i.e. which have consequences that go beyond the station boundaries, have been selected. They have been divided into three scenarios :

**Scenario 1** : Unfed natural gas release with ignition at the station vents; this event corresponds to the purging of gas contained between the inlet and outlet valves of the station, followed by an ignition of the gas plume;

**Scenario 2** : Fed natural gas release with ignition at the station vents; this event corresponds to a rupture or untimely opening of a vent or of the safety valve, without closing the station inlet and outlet valves, followed by an ignition of the gas plume;

**Scenario 3** : Rupture of one of the main pipes followed by an ignition of the gas plume.

Plumes ignition

Notice that the alone vent opening or the alone ruptures quoted above do not represent the undesired hazards. It is the ignition of the plumes which transform these events into undesired hazards.

Natural gas plumes, created by the previous incidents, can be ignited in the inflammability limits, by hot surface which origins are various :
- turbine fire,
- low altitude military flight,
- woods fire,
- presence of a running vehicle in the station,
- lightning,
- electrostatic charge,
- aircrash which also induces gas releases.

FUNCTIONAL ANALYSIS

A functional analysis of the station has been performed. The station has been split in simple elements from principle diagrams and fluids circuits. These elements are such as, on the one hand, failures modes can be specified a priori and without ambiguity and, on the other hand, quantitative data are available, without splitting the element itself to make its own analysis.

In order to represent the running of the station, relationships between the different elements have been made. The following diagram shows the relationships between elements and their functions :

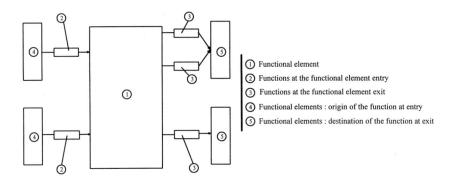

① Functional element

② Functions at the functional element entry

③ Functions at the functional element exit

④ Functional elements : origin of the function at entry

⑤ Functional elements : destination of the function at exit

FAILURE MODES AND EFFECTS ANALYSIS (FMEA)

The failure modes and effects analysis has been used to check and complete the functional analysis. This method consists in considering, systematically, one after the other, each of the elements of the compressor station and to analyse each of their failure modes, the possible causes being able to induce it, the consequences for the station and for the surroundings, and to list them as shown below.

| Element identification | Function, state | Failure modes | Possible failure causes | Effect on the system | Effects on outside |
|---|---|---|---|---|---|

FAULT TREES ANALYSIS (FTA)

The method of fault tree allows to determine the possible causes combinations that can induce a undesired event.

The results are presented in arborescent graph form, where the different events, which can happen during the compressor station running, are linked in a logical manner.

Each intermediate event is linked to lower level event by logical operators. The tree is thus built by a deductive manner, from the undesired event up to basic events.

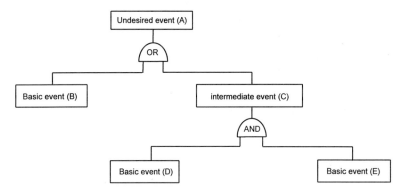

Basic events agree with three criteria :
• they are independent between them,
• their occurrence probabilities can be calculated or estimated,
• a split in simpler elements would bring no significant progress.

The basic events belong to two types :
• element failure, due to an intrinsic defect or to a command defect,
• element aggression by the surroundings.

When the fault tree is built, it is subjected to two processings :
• a qualitative processing that consists in determining, by the tree development, the various combinations of failures which can induce the undesired event. Then, by using the rules of BOOLE algebra, these combinations are simplified to minimum combinations called minimum cutsets (the repair of any failed element of the minimum cutsets allows the system to run again). These minimum cutsets can be classified according to the number of failures that they include. As generally, the double failures are less probable than the simple failure, that the triple failures are less probable than the double failures and so on, a hierarchic classification of minimum cutsets can be made. It then allows to determine the points to be improve at first. The minimum cutsets knowledge is thus interesting in the qualitative point of view.
• a quantitative processing : the occurrence probability associated with initiator events allows to obtain the undesired event occurrence probability.

PROBABILITIES ASSESSMENT OF UNDESIRED EVENTS

Failure rate

For a risk analysis of an installation, the ideal situation is to have reliable historical data of failure rate concerning an identical equipment used in the same application. Unfortunately, in most of cases, data specific to an installation are not available or can give a weak confidence level to be used without other data confirming them. This problem can be overcome by using generic data of failure rate. A large number of generic data exists. Nevertheless, it is necessary to be vigilant in the choice of these data. They must have a good level of confidence but also a good tolerance. The uncertainties on data can be reduced by analysing the manner whose these data have been obtained, especially the type, the conception and manufacture of the considered equipment, but also the manner whose it is requested and the maintenance it received as well as the failure modes occurred.

The failure rate of the compressor station equipment have been selected in the following data bases : the data base of the "Center for Chemical Process Safety" (CCPS) of the American Institute of CHemical Engineers (AICHE)[7], the OREDA[8] data base, Electricité de France data bases (for example (9)) as well as the IEEE-Std 500[10] data base.

For some element failures taken into account in this study, the rate have not been found in the previously quoted data bases. An estimated failure rate has been calculated by using one of the methods proposed for rare events, or never observed ones (11),(12),(13). It consists to calculate this estimated failure rate as the upper boundary of the unilateral confidence 50%. This value is such as the real value has the same probability (0.5) to be lower or higher. The estimated failure rate is given by the following expression :

$$\hat{\lambda} = \frac{\chi^2_{0.5}(2)}{2T} \approx \frac{0.7}{T}$$

The T value corresponds to the number of years of Gaz de France compressor units running, i.e. 844 years.

Calculation method

This type of calculation and probability theories associated are perfectly described in some reliability or safety books, for example (11). In this study, these methods are applied to minimum cutsets.

It is admitted that the undesired events probabilities are calculated by propagating elementary failure rate according to the fault tree BOOLE logic.

Results

**Scenario 1 :** The probability of unfed natural gas release with ignition at the station vents is 2 10^-5 / year.

**Scenario 2 :** The probability of fed natural gas release induce by rupture of a vent or of the safety valve followed by an ignition of the gas plume is 7,23 10^-9 / year.

The probability of fed natural gas release induce by an untimely opening of the vent station, without closing the station inlet and outlet valves is 6 $10^{-7}$ / year.

**Scenario 3** : The probability of the rupture of one of the main pipes followed by an ignition of the gas plume is $10^{-7}$ / year.

However, it is necessary to consider an aircrash on the compressor station. This catastrophic scenario have a probability of 1,3 $10^{-6}$ / year.

CONSEQUENCES CALCULATION OF UNDESIRED EVENTS

The selected undesired events are gas release in the atmosphere followed by ignition. Their consequences assessment lead to study the following phenomena :
- leakage flow rate,
- gas dispersion,
- overpressure at ignition,
- thermal radiation of the flame,
- radiation effects on people.

The corresponding calculations sequence is shown below :

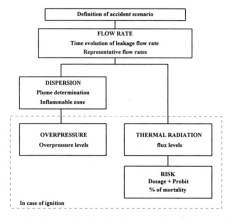

Each phenomenon is characterised by a variable calculated with a model and compared to reference values. The used models are typical of natural gas. They are validated by large scale experiments and integrated into the PERSEE software.

The most significant results are summarised in the following table. They are the distances reached by the 5 kW/m² thermal flux - reversible effects threshold (burns) for a 30 second exposure.

| Scenario | representative flow rate | Distance (m) reached by 5 kW/m² thermal flux |
|---|---|---|
| 1 | mean between 0-30 s | 175 |
| 2 | steady | 175 |
| 3 vertical | intermediate | 330 |
| 3 horizontal | intermediate | 540 |

RISKS

For risk assessment, the class of severity 4 has been sub-divided, taking into account criteria concerning thermal radiation which is the most important hazard. The following severities have been used :
- **severity 4.1** : the incident thermal radiation outside of the station, during the steady state is lower than the 5 kW/m² threshold;

- **severity 4.2** : the incident thermal radiation outside of the station, during the steady state, is greater than the 5 kW/m² threshold, at certain locations, but does not reach the nearest road;

- **severity 4.3** : the incident thermal radiation outside of the station, during the steady state, is greater than the 5 kW/m² threshold, at certain locations, including the nearest road;

The risk of the three studied scenarios can be present in the following manner. The X-axis represents the severity level of scenarios consequences and the Y-axis is the annual occurrence probability of the scenarios.

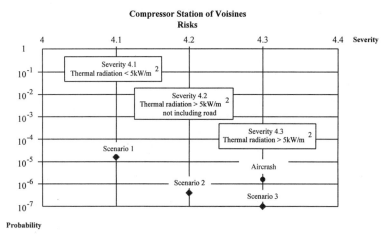

CONCLUSION

The hazard probability analysis of the compressor station of Voisines allowed to determine the three events whose consequences go beyond the station boundaries. The associated probability and the incurred risk based on the 5 kW/m² threshold incident thermal radiation have been assessed.

In order to discuss these risks, the step adopted by Electricité de France for its prevention against aircrash on nuclear plants has been used. For an impact probability greater than $10^{-7}$/year/unit, EDF has judged that it was necessary to realise particular protection. Taking to account the associated thresholds as references, it is possible to discuss the risks presented by the selected undesired scenarios for the station of Voisines :
- They have a severity very lower than a nuclear accident one (number of potential victims),

- the two most serious scenarios (scenarios 2 and 3) have probabilities of a few $10^{-7}$ near from the threshold taking to account in a nuclear plant dimensioning.

It is thus possible to conclude that the risks presented by the station of Voisines are very low and do not involve supplementary protective system.

REFERENCES

(1) - An investigation of potential hazards from operations in the Canvey Island Thurrock area, UK Health and Safety Executive, 1978.

(2) - A second report, A review of potential hazards from operations in the Canvey Island Thurrock area, three years after the publication of the Canvey Report,UK Health and Safety Executive, 1981.

(3) - C. Lievens, Sécurité des sytèmes, Cepadues Ed. , Collection Sup'Aéro, 1974.

(4) - Analyse des probabilités des événements indésirables dans une installation de GPL, CREMER et WARNER S.A., Juillet 1992, France. Etude réalisée pour le compte de Butagaz.

(5) - LPG a Study Main report, A comparative analysis of the risks inherent in the storage, transhipment, transport and use of LPG and motor Spirit, TNO, Mai 1983, Pays Bas.

(6) - The predicted BLEVE frequency of a selected 2000 m3 butane sphere on a refinery site. SAFETY AND RELIABILITY DIRECTORATE/HEALTH AND SAFETY EXECUTIVE (SRD/HSE), Rapport R492, 1988, Royaume Uni.

(7) - Center for Chemical Process Safety of the American Institute of CHemical Engineers, Guidelines for Process Equipment Reliability Data, with Data Tables, 1989

(8) - Det Norske Veritas Industri Norge As, OREDA Offshore Reliability Data Handbook 2nd edition, 1992

(9) - EDF GDF SERVICES, Technique Electricité, Atlas 1991, Pour un kWh de Qualité, 1993

(10) - IEEE Std 500 Reliability Data, IEEE Guide to the Collection and Presentation of Electrical, Electronic, Sensing Component, and Mechanical Equipement Reliability Data for Nuclear-Power Generating Stations, 1993

(11) - A. Villemeur, Sureté de fonctionnement des systèmes industriels, Collection de la Direction des Etudes et Recherches d'Electricité De France, Editions Eyrolles, 1988

(12) - A. Lannoy, Analyse des explosions air-hydrocarbure en milieux libre Etudes déterministe et probabiliste du scenario d'accident prévision des effets de surpression, 1984

(13) - NF-X-60-510, Techniques d'analyse de la fiabilité des systèmes, Procédure d'analyse des modes de défaillance et de leurs effets (AMDE), 1986

(14) - EDF, Service de la Protection Thermique, Memento de la sûreté nucléaire en exploitation, 1990

A PISTON PROVER AS PRIMARY STANDARD FOR GAS FLOW MEASUREMENT.

P.M.A. van der Kam, H. Bellinga and F.J. Delhez
N.V. Nederlandse Gasunie
Groningen, the Netherlands

ABSTRACT

A piston prover has been developed that should operate as primary high pressure flow standard in the flow rate range from 20 to 2000 m³/h. After preliminary tests to improve the performance of the prover, it has now been used for the first time in dircet conjunction with the "classical" bootstrapping method to calibrate the flow standard meters in the Netherlands. The first results obtainde look promising, but careful analysis of the data will have to prove if the aim of smaller uncertainties for the flow standard meters in the various test facilities can be reached.

INTRODUCTION.

In the total uncertainty of a flow measurement result the uncertainty in flow standards still plays a major role. High pressure test facilities typically estimate their uncertainty in the order of 0.2 to 0.3 %. Recent intercomparison campaigns have confirmed these figures [1]. Although primary standards in most cases have a much smaller uncertainty, it is the step to the working standards in which the uncertainty increases. This is caused by lack of basic knowledge of thermodynamic properties of natural gas is in most cases. When using sonic nozzles as transfer standards from the primary system, often a weighing vessel, highly accurate speed of sound data are needed. This is specifically required when the gas composition is varying or when primary calibrated nozzles are used in other facilities then the one where the primary system is installed. For volumetric methods very accurate data are needed on gas compressibility.

Therefore, Gasunie has been looking for a primary calibration method that avoids the need for this knowledge. From liquids measurement the use of pipe provers is a well known technique. It has been shown that pipe provers can also be used as primary standard in high pressure gas calibrations, only sofar on relatively small scale [2,3]. Gasunie has a direct interest in high presssure calibrations at large flow rates. The largest standard meters used are turbine meters with $Q_{max}$ = 4000 m³/h. To avoid bootstrapping of both flow rate and pressure as much as possible a piston prover has been developed that should have an operational range from 20 m³/h to 2000 m³/h at pressures from 8 to 65 bar. Using this piston prover almost all flow standard meters can be calibrated directly against a primary standard at their full flow rate range and at their operational pressures. In this way gas properties play only a second order role in the calibration and thus a smaller uncertainty should be obtained.

DESCRIPTION OF THE PISTON PROVER

The principle of the piston prover is the displacement of a known volume of gas by a piston. The piston is free floating and driven by a small pressure differential. The movement of the piston can be detected from the outside using proximity switches. The heart of the Gasunie piston prover is a 12 m long stainless steel cylinder with diameter of 584 mm. The measuring section is 5.22 m long with a volume of 1.4 m³. In order to stabilize the movement of the piston after it has been launched, normally a length of 4 m is available. As for high flow rates this tends to be somewhat short, the measuring section has been divided in two parts, allowing an increased starting length of about 6.5 m and consequently a smaller measuring section. The prover works unidirectionally. By a proper selection of valves and piping the gas flow is continuous and nearly undisturbed by the movement of the piston.

The prover is transportable so that standard meters in the various test facilities in the Netherlands can be calibrated in situ.

The volume of the measuring section has been determined by Netherlands Measurements Institute with static water draw and dynamically against a calibrated water meter. The result has been verified by geometrical measurement. The calibrated volume is specified to have an uncertainty of 0.03%.

Figure 1 shows a scheme of the setup of a meter calibration. For situation where large volumes are present between the piston prover and the standard meters to be calibrated it has been found that buffer effects can play an important role. This is specifically the case at low flow rates. To deal with this an auxiliary meter has been installed directly at the outlet of the prover. The auxiliary meter is then calibrated against the piston prover and this meter is subsequently used to calibrate the standard meter. It has been found that this can be done without a great loss of accuracy.

In 1992 and 1993 test scries have been carried out to assess the performance of the piston prover [4]. These resulted in further improvement of the instrumentation and control software and of the actual calibration procedure. Especially, unsteady flow problems at low flow rates had to be dealt with.

## INTRODUCTION INTO THE TRACEABILITY CHAIN

For the first time now the piston prover has been used in parallel to the procedure by which the high pressure flow standards have been calibrated for the last 20 years. Periodically, typically every 2 to 3 years the working standards get a full basic recalibration, starting from the Dutch national Kilogram [5]. In 1995 the "classical" procedure was followed immediately by the piston prover procedure. After calibration of the standards with the boots trapping method [5], the same standards were once again calibrated with the piston prover.

A first analysis has shov:n that the degree of agreement between both sets of data is of the same order of magnitude as during previous measurements with this prover and with the smaller provers at an earlier date. A typical result is shown in figure 2.
Full details of all results will be presented at the conference.

Eventually, the aim is that the piston prover will replace the long and tedious procedure by which the working standards are calibrated nowadays [5]. The aim is to reduce the uncertainty and to considerably save time. Careful analysis of all data obtained will have to prove that these aims can be reached. If the piston prover is introduced as primary high pressure flow standard this will be done in close cooperation with Netherlands Measurements Institute, the authority on weights and measures in the Netherlands.

## REFERENCES

1. Intercomparison exercise of high pressure test facilities within GERG, P.M.A. van der Kam (on behalf of the GERG working group), Flow Meas. in the mid 90's Conf, FLOME-KO 94, Glasgow, 1994.

2. Using a piston prover as a primary standard in high pressure gas metering, H. Bellinga, C.P. Hoeks, A. Kooi, F.A. van Laak, P.J. Orbons, 4th IMEKO Conf. on Flow Meas. FLOMEKO 85, Melbourne, 1985.

3. Erfahrungen mit de Rohrprüfstrecke als neues Urnormal de Bundesrepublik Deutschland zur Überprfung von Gaszählern unter Hochdruck, O. Brandt, G, Schmitz, J. Kämper, GWF Gas/Erdgas 133 (1992) 168-174

4. Experience with a high capacity piston prover as a primary standard for high pressure gas flow measurement, H. Bellinga, F.J. Delhez, Flow Meas. Instr. 4 (1993) 85-89.

5. Calibration facilities for industrial gas flow meters in the Netherlands, P.F.M. Jongerius, M.P. van der Beek, J.G.M. van der Grinten, Flow Meas. Instr. 4 (1993) 77-83.

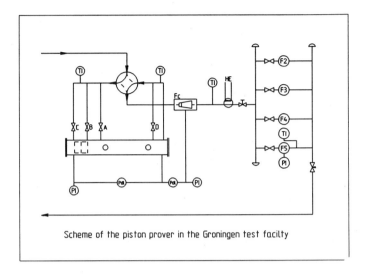

Scheme of the piston prover in the Groningen test facilty

Figure 1    Operation principle of the piston prover.
TI = temperature measurement, PI = pressure measurement
Fc = auxiliary meter, $F_{2-4}$ = standard meters to be calibrated.

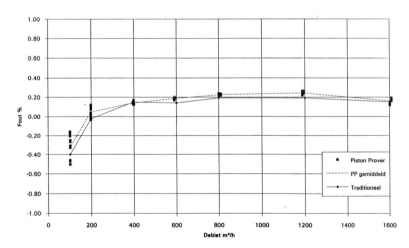

Figure 2    Typical calibration result with the classical method (♦) and the piston prover
(■).

IMPROVED FLOW CONDITIONERS FOR ORIFICE METERING

CONDITIONNEUR D'ECOULEMENT AMELIORE POUR LA PRISE DE MESURES
PAR RHEOMETRE A ORIFICE

Dr. Thomas B. Morrow
Southwest Research Institute, USA

Mr. John G. Gregor & Dr. Renny S. Norman
Gas Research Institute, USA

ABSTRACT

A comprehensive research program on orifice meter performance is ongoing at the Gas Research Institute (GRI) Metering Research Facility (MRF). The objective is to determine the flow conditioning specifications necessary for acceptable orifice metering performance in installations built to conform with existing standards. Previous research results focused on conventional tube-bundle flow conditioners or straighteners in piping configurations that are typical of field installations. While this has resulted in recommendations for better use of tube-bundle flow conditioners for orifice metering applications, their proper use is contingent on parameters such as the flow Reynolds number, orifice beta ($\beta$) ratio, pressure tap orientation, and inlet piping configuration. Therefore, the GRI program and other international flow research organizations are rigorously pursuing the test and development of alternate flow conditioners. This paper presents recent MRF results on the performance of flow conditioners used to minimize flow rate measurement errors in field installations of orifice meters.

RÉSUMÉ

Un vaste programme de recherche sur la performance des rhéomètres à orifice a lieu en permanence au sein de la Metering Research Facility (MRF, Département de recherche en · mesurage) du Gas Research Institute (GRI). L'objectif consiste à déterminer les spécifications de conditionnement d'écoulement nécessaires pour une performance acceptable de prise de mesures par rhéomètre à orifice dans des installations construites de manière conforme aux normes existantes. Les résultats de recherches antérieures se concentraient sur les conditionneurs d'écoulement conventionnels à faisceau tubulaire ou sur les configurations avec redresseurs dans les tuyaux qui sont typiques des installations sur le terrain. Alors que ceci a abouti en des recommandations pour une meilleure utilisation des conditionneurs d'écoulement à faisceau tubulaire pour les applications à rhéomètre à orifice, leur utilisation correcte dépend de paramètres tels que le nombre Reynolds de l'écoulement, le rapport bêta ($\beta$), l'orientation de la prise de mesure de pression et la configuration du tuyau d'arrivée. C'est pourquoi, le programme du GRI et d'autres organismes internationaux de recherche en écoulement poursuivent avec rigueur les tests et le développement de conditionneurs d'écoulement alternatifs. Cet exposé présente des résultats récents du MRF concernant la performance de conditionneurs d'écoulement utilisés pour minimiser les erreurs de mesure du débit d'écoulement dans des installations de rhéomètres à orifice sur le terrain.

INTRODUCTION

A comprehensive research program on orifice meter performance is ongoing at the Gas Research Institute (GRI) Metering Research Facility (MRF), which is located at Southwest Research Institute (SwRI). The objective is to determine the flow conditioning specifications necessary for acceptable orifice metering performance in installations built to conform with existing standards (1,2). Previous research results (3) have focused on the use of conventional tube-bundle flow conditioners or straighteners in piping configurations that are typical of field installations. While this has resulted in recommendations for better use of tube-bundle flow conditioners for orifice metering applications, their proper use is contingent on a number of operating parameters. These include the flow Reynolds number, orifice beta ($\beta$) ratio, pressure tap orientation, and inlet piping configuration. Therefore, the GRI program and other international flow research organizations are rigorously pursuing the test and development of alternate flow conditioners. The goal is to identify a flow conditioner design that can be universally used for all metering installation configurations with a minimum of straight pipe required between the conditioner and the orifice plate. In essence, a flow conditioner that isolates the meter from any and all upstream flow disturbances.

To date, several different flow conditioning devices have been tested at the MRF. These tests have been accomplished with nitrogen gas in a 102-mm (4-inch) diameter orifice meter tube at pressures of 0.72 MPa (105 psia) and primarily a Reynolds number of $9 \times 10^5$. The devices tested have consisted of alternate tube-bundle designs and perforated plate type conditioners. The test installation is configured so that the different flow conditioners can be easily installed in the meter tube and located at various positions for the collection of discharge coefficient ($C_d$) data. Because the existing U.S. gas industry standard (1) allows for the use of relatively short orifice meter configurations, the initial tests have involved a meter tube with an upstream length of 17 pipe diameters (D). ISO 5167 (2) specifies much longer minimum values of upstream and downstream length without flow conditioners, and specifies a minimum meter tube length of more than 40 D when a flow conditioner is used. Therefore, some tests have also been performed with an upstream meter tube length of 45 D.

GRI MRF ORIFICE METER INSTALLATION EFFECTS RESULTS

Experimental Arrangement

Tests were performed in the MRF Interim Low Pressure Loop (ILPL) flowing nitrogen. Two meter tube assemblies were used. The first was a three-section meter tube with orifice flanges and a meter tube diameter of 102.25 mm (4.0254 inches). The combined length of the two upstream sections was about 45 D. The long, 45 D meter tube was installed downstream of a tee as shown in Figure 1. Gas flowed from a "stagnation bottle" or header into a short 12 D long spool piece and into the central branch of a tee. The tee turned the flow by $90°$ into the meter tube. The piping attached to the other side branch of the tee was used when inserting and removing flow conditioners from the meter tube. The ball valve shown in Figure 1 was left open, and a rod connected to the flow conditioner was used to position the conditioner in the meter tube. Following a test, the conditioner was withdrawn through the valve into a short spool piece, and the valve was closed to avoid depressurizing the flow loop.

The meter tube with the long 45 D upstream length was also used in the baseline calibration tests when it was installed downstream of an oversized Sprenkle flow conditioner. Baseline calibrations were performed both before and after the installation effects tests. The "official" baseline calibration $C_d$ value was 0.60818 for $\beta = 0.67$ at a value of Reynolds number of $9 \times 10^5$. The baseline calibration repeated to within about 0.05%. The baseline calibration results are presented and discussed in reference (4).

The second meter tube used in these tests was a two-section meter tube with orifice flanges. The length of the upstream section was about 17 D, and the meter tube diameter was 102.3 mm (4.027 inches). Figure 2 is a photograph of the double out-of-plane $90°$ elbow arrangement used. In this installation configuration, the lower elbow was removed when flow conditioners were changed.

Both meter tubes have orifice flanges with four sets of flange pressure taps located at 90° intervals around the circumference. Research in short meter tubes with the conventional 19 tube-bundle (3) showed that orifice $C_d$ could vary significantly with pressure tap orientation. Three pairs of pressure taps were used in the sliding conditioner tests. Referring to Figure 1, these are tap 1 at 90° to the plane of the tee, tap 2 along the inside of the plane of the tee, and tap 3 along the outside of the plane of the tee. Smart differential pressure transducers were attached to these three sets of flange taps.

For the performance evaluation of different flow conditioner designs, an orifice plate with a $\beta = 0.67$ was installed. Sliding flow conditioner tests were performed at a single line pressure, 0.72 MPa (105 psia), and a single value of flowrate, 0.15 m$^3$/sec (320 acfm). The nitrogen flow rate was measured by a critical flow Venturi, checked by a reference 150 mm (6-inch) turbine meter. The calibration of the critical flow Venturi was checked daily against the MRF ILPL weigh tank. Values of orifice coefficient shift, $\Delta C_d$, were calculated as the percentage deviation from the baseline (reference) $C_d$ value measured for the long, 45 D upstream length meter tube installed downstream of an oversized Sprenkle flow conditioner. In the results and graphs presented in this paper, tap-to-tap variations in $C_d$ have been suppressed by calculating and reporting the average value of the three separate $C_d$ values. However, it should be noted that tap-to-tap variations can be significant in some cases (for certain flow conditioner designs when located near to a valve, elbow, or tee at the inlet of the meter tube).

Standard 19 Tube-Bundle Straightening Vane Flow Conditioner

The conventional 19 tube-bundle straightening vane is described in A.G.A. Report No. 3, Part 2.5.5 (1). For nominal 102-mm (4-inch) diameter pipe, the straightening vane has a length of 254 mm (10 inches). The straightening vane used in these tests had 19 tubes with an average internal diameter of 18 mm (0.710 inch) and an average outer diameter of 21.1 mm (0.830 inch). The tubes were arranged in an axi-symmetric pattern. References (3 - 5) contain the results of MRF ILPL orifice meter installation effects tests with a 19 tube-bundle straightening vane used as a flow conditioner.

Figure 3 compares the results obtained for the 19 tube-bundle for $\beta = 0.67$ in the long 45 D meter tube downstream of a tee, the short 17 D meter tube downstream of two out-of-plane elbows, and the short 17 D meter tube downstream of a tee. For all three installation configurations, the $\Delta C_d$ results appear to cross the $\Delta C_d = 0\%$ axis between x/D = 1 and x/D = 3, but the slope is very large, and placement of the tube-bundle this close to the orifice plate would not be practical. For the 17 D meter tube downstream of two out-of-plane elbows and for the 45 D meter tube downstream of a tee, there is another zero crossing between x/D = 11 and x/D = 13. For values of x/D in an interval from 3 to 11 or 13, $\Delta C_d$ is negative in the range from -1.0% to -0.1%. For values of x/D in the interval from 15 to 41, $\Delta C_d$ is positive, with values in a range from +0.10% to +0.25%.

Note that for the 17 D meter tube downstream of a tee, the $\Delta C_d$ data points reverse direction and turn downward for x/D greater than 10. A crossing of the $\Delta C_d = 0\%$ axis between x/D = 11 and x/D = 13 was not found for the combination of a 19 tube-bundle straightening vane and a 17 D meter tube installed downstream of a tee. Although the general features of the $\Delta C_d$ curves in Figure 3 are similar, there are significant differences for all three orifice meter installation configurations. It can be concluded that the standard 19 tube-bundle straightening vane doesn't perform well as an isolating flow conditioner, and doesn't give the proper velocity profile shape to minimize the variation of $\Delta C_d$ as a function of x/D for this value of $\beta = 0.67$.

Stuart E3 Tube-Bundle Straightening Vane Flow Conditioner

Stuart (6,7) described the development of a new flow conditioner design based upon the 19 tube-bundle straightening vane concept. Several different Stuart tube-bundle flow conditioner designs have been tested previously in the MRF ILPL for a short, 17 D meter tube downstream of either a 90° elbow or a tee used as an elbow (4,5).

This paper presents a comparison of test results for $\beta = 0.67$ for the Stuart E3 straightening vane design. Figure 4 compares E3 flow conditioner results for the 17 D meter tube downstream of a tee with the results for a 17 D meter tube downstream of two out-of-plane 90° elbows, and a 45 D meter tube downstream of a tee. The $\Delta C_d$ results for the 45 D meter tube downstream of a tee differ from the results obtained for the two short, 17 D meter tube installations downstream of either a tee or two out-of-plane 90° elbows. Note that the magnitude of variation of the installation error is reduced for the E3 flow conditioner (in comparison to the standard 19 tube-bundle design) to a range of $\Delta C_d$, from -0.10% to +0.30% for x/D values greater than 5.

The E3 flow conditioner performed well in both short, 17 D meter tube installations. This suggests that the tube-bundle arrangement does a good job of shaping the underdeveloped (flat) type of velocity profile with relatively thin boundary layers along the pipe wall that can occur in short meter tube lengths. When more pipeflow development length is available upstream of the tube-bundle, as in the 45 D meter tube downstream of a tee, the velocity profile entering the tube-bundle is more rounded by the development of thicker boundary layers along the pipe wall. The E3 tube-bundle flow conditioner design augments the flow along the pipe centerline and provides more profile shaping correction than is needed, resulting in a more peaked velocity profile and a positive shift to the discharge coefficient.

Gallagher Perforated Plate 21 Flow Conditioner

Gallagher et al (8) have discussed the development of the Gallagher flow conditioner. The conditioner was designed to isolate flow meters from piping-induced disturbances upstream of the conditioner, and to achieve "pseudo-fully developed" flow in a meter tube with respect to axial position. Several different Gallagher perforated plate designs have been tested before in the MRF ILPL, and the results are presented in references (4) and (5).

This paper presents the test results for $\beta = 0.67$ for a flow conditioner assembly consisting of a Gallagher conditioner plate 21 and a 0.5 D long segment of a 19 tube-bundle straightening vane. The straightening vane segment was located upstream of the conditioner plate, and was attached to the plate by four small-diameter rods that are 3 D in length. Figure 5 compares the plate 21 results for the 45 D meter tube downstream of a tee with results for the 17 D meter tube downstream of either a tee or two out-of-plane 90° elbows. The results for the 45 D meter tube and the 17 D meter tube downstream of a tee are very similar. In fact, for all three meter tube installations, $\Delta C_d$ for plate 21 varies in a range from -0.10% to -0.10% for flow conditioner locations in the interval from about x/D = 7 to 42.

Gallagher (9) recommends that a 3 D upstream length be provided between the downstream end of the disturbance (tee or elbow) and the inlet to the tube-bundle segment of the flow conditioner. This upstream length of bare pipe allows the secondary flow produced by the elbow or tee to begin redistributing the flow before reaching the flow conditioner. If this minimum upstream length requirement is applied to the results shown in Figure 5, it limits the maximum value of x/D to about 10.5 D in the short 17 D meter tube.

Nova Perforated Plate 50E Flow Conditioner

Karnik (10, 11) has reported on the development of a perforated plate flow conditioner design for isolating and conditioning the flow profiles in short meter tubes. Two different perforated plate designs, 50E (with a porosity of approximately 50%) and 60A (with a porosity of approximately 40%), were provided by Nova for inclusion in the sliding flow conditioner tests (4). Figure 6 shows the results for $\beta = 0.67$ for the Nova 50E perforated plate flow conditioner for the 17 D meter tube downstream of two out-of-plane elbows and the 45 D meter tube downstream of a tee. The results are very similar for x/D values in the interval from 1 to 5. Between x/D = 6 and x/D = 14, a small difference of $\Delta C_d = 0.15\%$ appears. Although small, this difference is double the amount that would be expected as a result of test-to-test variations. The magnitude of the difference is similar to that shown in Figure 5 for Gallagher plate 21 for these same two installations. For plate 50E in the short 17 D meter tube downstream of two out-of-plane $90^\circ$ elbows, $\Delta C_d$ varied in a range from -0.10% to +0.10% for an interval of x/D between 7 and 14.  For plate 50 E in the long 45 D meter tube downstream of a tee, $\Delta C_d$ varied in a range from -0.10% to +0.10% for an interval of x/D between 11 and 41 for this $\beta$ ratio.

Other Flow Conditioners

References (4) and (5) contain measured $\Delta C_d$ results for other alternative flow conditioner designs that could not be included in this paper.  These include a Stuart C3 tube-bundle, a Nova perforated plate 60A, a Laws perforated plate flow conditioner, a K-Lab Mark V flow conditioner, two versions of Vortab flow conditioners, and Gallagher perforated plate designs 10, 36, 37, and 38.

CONCLUSION

Tests with the conventional A.G.A. Report No. 3 (1) 19 tube-bundle and a $\beta$ ratio of 0.67 showed that orifice $C_d$ is strongly sensitive to the distance, x/D, between the orifice plate and the tube-bundle and to the type and location of the upstream disturbance.  For the tests with either a short 17 D meter tube downstream of two out-of-plane $90^\circ$ elbows, or a long 45 D meter tube downstream of a tee, the average value of $\Delta Cd$ (tap-to-tap variations are averaged out) increased from a minimum in the range from -0.75% to -1% at x/D = 3 to about +0.1% at x/D=14.  However, for the short 17 D meter tube downstream of a tee, no crossover point where $\Delta Cd$ = 0% was found.  While the 19 tube-bundle is effective in removing the swirl velocity component, it is not as good as a velocity profile shaping device for $\beta$ = 0.67.

The performance of the Stuart E3 tube-bundle was considerably improved over than that of the conventional 19 tube-bundle.  Values of $\Delta C_d$ with the Stuart E3 tube-bundle show much less sensitivity to x/D than the 19 tube-bundle.  However, the results from the long, 45D meter tube test and the short, 17 D meter tube downstream of two out-of-plane $90^\circ$ elbows are noticeably different.  This indicates that the present Stuart tube-bundle designs will probably work best in short meter tubes.  However, it might be possible to improve the isolation capability of a tube-bundle design by generating mixing upstream of the tube-bundle to smooth out the upstream profile distortion.

Both the Gallagher perforated plate 21 flow conditioner and the Nova perforated plate 50E flow conditioner displayed very good performance in both short and long meter tube installations.  Values of $\Delta C_d$ were generally within a range of ±0.1% when the distance from the conditioner plate to the orifice plate was at least 7 D.  Beyond x/D = 7, the $C_d$ values measured were relatively insensitive to the location of the flow conditioner in the meter tube.

ACKNOWLEDGMENTS

The MRF and the Upstream Effects Research Program are sponsored by the Gas Research Institute in Chicago, Illinois.  Thanks go to SwRI staff members including Dr. Joel Park, Mr. Bob McKee, Mr. Henry Frazier, Mr. Ken Nickel, Mr. Terry Grimley and Ms. Linda Montez for their assistance and participation in the flow conditioner tests.  Appreciation is also extended to gas industry repre-sentatives on the MRF Technical Advisory Committee, who provide valuable guidance to this program.

FUTURE RESEARCH PLANS

Additional MRF orifice meter installation effects tests are planned in 1995 and 1996.  These will be performed with natural gas in both the GRI MRF High Pressure Loop (HPL) and the Low Pressure Loop (LPL).  Tests are planned to confirm the scaling of flow conditioner performance results from 100 mm (4 inch) to 250 mm (10 inch) pipe diameters.  Further flow conditioner performance evalu-ations are planned for meter tube upstream lengths ranging from 10 D to 45 D, for orifice $\beta$ ratios from

0.2 to 0.75, and in meter tube diameters of 50 mm (2 inch), 100 mm (4 inch), and 250 mm (10 inch). These evaluations will be performed for flow conditions upstream of the meter tube ranging from good (fully developed pipe flow) to highly disturbed (asymmetry of the axial velocity profile coupled with swirl). A limited series of tests is also planned for bare meter tubes (without flow conditioners). The data from this research program are being made available to the organizations and groups responsible for maintaining and revising the standards for orifice flow measurement of natural gas.

REFERENCES

1. Concentric, Square-Edge Orifice Meters, Part 2 - Specification and Installation Requirements, A.G.A. Report No. 3 (3rd Edition), American Gas Association, Arlington, Virginia, February 1991.

2. Measurement of Fluid Flow by Means of Orifice Plates, Nozzles and Venturi Tubes Inserted in Circular Cross-Section Conduits Running Full, ISO 5167, International Organization for Standardization, Geneva, Switzerland, 1980.

3. Morrow, T. B. and J. T. Park, Metering Research Facility Program: Installation Effects on Orifice Meter Performance, Topical Report GRI-93/0054.1 and GRI-93/0054.2, Gas Research Institute, Chicago, Illinois, September, 1993.

4. Morrow, T. B., Orifice Meter Installation Effects: Alternative Flow Conditioner Designs Tested in 45 D Meter Tube Downstream of a Tee, and 17 D Meter Tube Downstream of Double Out-Of-Plane Elbows, Technical Memorandum MRF-UE-14, Gas Research Institute, Chicago, Illinois, August 1994.

5. Morrow, T. B., Orifice Meter Installation Effects: Sliding Vane Test With a 17 D Meter Tube and Alternative Flow Conditioner Designs Downstream of a Tee, Technical Memorandum MRF-UE-13, Gas Research Institute, Chicago, Illinois, May, 1994.

6. Stuart, J. W., "Improvements in Flow Conditioner Design for Orifice Metering," A.G.A. Distribution/Transmission Conference, Orlando, Florida, May 1993.

7. Stuart, J. W., Park, J. T. and T. B. Morrow, "Experimental Results of an Improved Tube-Bundle Flow Conditioner for Orifice Metering," FLOMEKO '94, Flow Measurement in the Mid 90's, National Engineering Laboratory, Glasgow, Scotland, June 13-17, 1994.

8. Gallagher, J. E., LaNasa, P. J. and R. E. Beaty, "Development of Gallagher Flow Conditioner," FLOMEKO '94, Flow Measurement in the Mid 90's, National Engineering Laboratory, Glasgow, Scotland, June 13-17, 1994.

9. Gallagher, J. E., private communication.

10. Karnik, U., "A Compact Orifice Meter/Flow Conditioner Package," 3rd International Symposium on Fluid Flow Measurement, San Antonio, Texas, March 19-22, 1995.

11. Karnik, U., "A Compact Orifice Meter/Flow Conditioner Package," 1995 A.G.A. Operations Conference, Las Vegas, Nevada, May 8-10, 1995.

12. Morrow, T. B., "Orifice Meter Installation Effects in the GRI MRF," 3rd International Symposium on Fluid Flow Measurement, San Antonio, Texas, March 19-22, 1995.

13. Morrow, T. B., "Orifice Meter Installation Effects in the GRI MRF," 1995 A.G.A. Operations Conference, Las Vegas, Nevada, May 8-10, 1995.

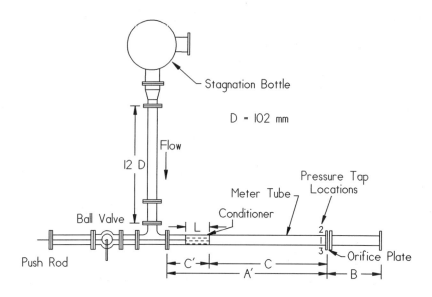

**Fig. 1   MRF test arrangement for orifice meter sliding flow conditioner tests
for 17 D and 45 D meter tubes downstream of a tee**

**Fig. 2   Photograph of piping arrangement for sliding conditioner tests
for a 17 D meter tube downstream of two 90° out-of-plane elbows**

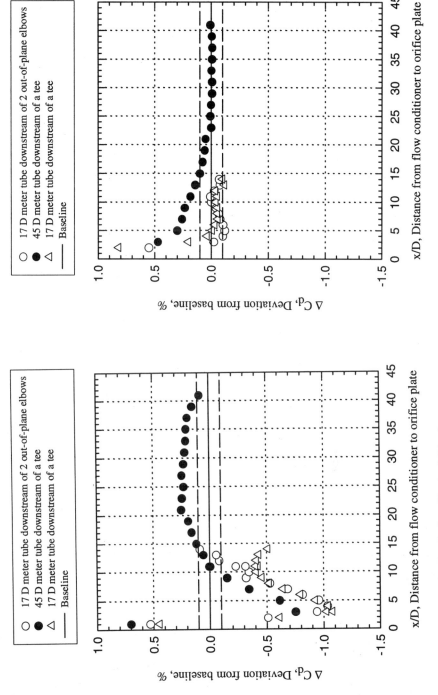

Fig. 4 Stuart E3 tube-bundle flow conditioner

Fig. 3 19 tube-bundle straightening vane

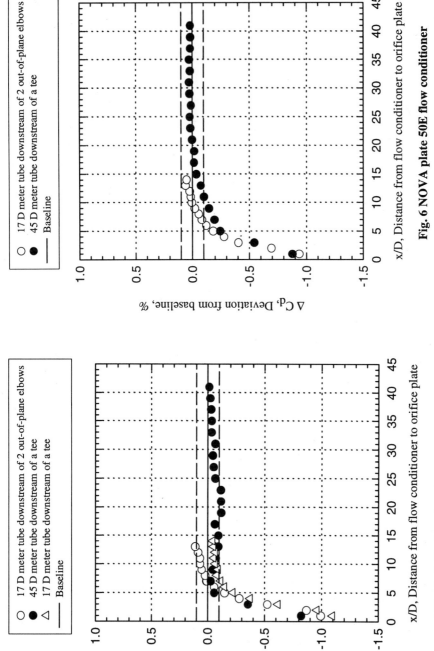

Fig. 6 NOVA plate 50E flow conditioner

Fig. 5 Gallagher plate 21 flow conditioner

# EFFECTS OF HEADER CONFIGURATIONS ON FLOW METERING

S. de Jong and P.M.A. van der Kam
N.V. Nederlandse Gasunie
Groningen, the Netherlands

## ABSTRACT

Multirun gas metering stations are usually built in a header configuration. This geometry is likely to produce swirling flow, one of the most persisting deviations from the ideal, fully developed velocity profile. For a set of metering stations with meterruns of D = 500 mm, the inlet velocity and swirl profiles have been determined. Based on that, the influence on the metering performance of gas turbine meters and of two types of multipath ultrasonic meters has been investigated. Turbine meters are found not significantly influenced. The effect on ultrasonic meters depends on the particular path geometry, but is found to be at maximum 0.8% and 0.4% resp.

## RÉSUMÉ

Postes de comptage de gaz sont construé généralement avec multiple tuyaux de mesure sortant d'un tuyau collectioneur. Cette géométrie peut creé un écoulement rotatif, un des deviation d'un profil ideal le plus persistant. Dans une nombre de postes de comptage avec tuyaux de mesure en D = 500 mm sont determiné les profils de vitesse et des angles du rotation. A base de cettes données, l'effet sur le comptage avec compteurs à turbine et avec deux types de compteurs à ultrasons est investigé. Les compteurs à turbine ne sont pas influencé significante. L'effet au compteur à ultrasons se depends au le geometrie du compteur; erreurs maximals obtenu sont 0,8 % resp. 0,4 %.

INTRODUCTION

The use of a socalled header geometry for gas metering stations is quite common. As the pipe lines are usually located underground and the metering station above ground this almost unavoidably leads to double bends out-of-plane. This is the typical geometry that creates swirling flow, a bulk rotation of the flow. From numerous experiments and theoretical considerations [e.g. 1] it is known that this type of deviation from a fully developed flow profile is the most persistent. It takes typically 50 to 100 D for swirl to decay to the generally accepted level of 2° or less at which flow metering is supposed to be no longer influenced (although this depends also on the type of flow meter).

Recently, a number of papers have been presented that studied the effect of header configurations on orifice plate performance [2,3,9]. To export gas to various West European countries Gasunie operates 6 large metering stations with as primary elements turbine meters and multipath ultrasonic meters [4]. These stations have all been built with underground headers and 4 to 7 meterruns, diameter 500 mm, per station. The straight lengths upstream of the meter are according to ISO 5167, as these stations were equiped originally with orifice plates as primary element. In the period 1990-1992 these stations have been renovated and have been equiped with modern instrumentation.

Given the geometry of the stations the question was raised if swirl would be present in the meterruns, and if so, what the influence would be on the meter performance.
A test program was initiated that consisted of 4 steps:
1.	Pitot tube profile measurements at 3 stations, coded A, B and C.
2.	Flow profile calculations to help explain the found phenomena.
3.	Experiments in the Bernoulli laboratory at Westerbork, where the station geometry was simulated.
4.	Tests to eliminate possible effects, i.e. use of flow conditioners.
This paper reports on the findings of the first 3 items. The flow conditioner tests will be reported later.

FLOW PROFILE MEASUREMENTS AT THE STATIONS.

Pitot tube

Gasunie has at its disposal a 3-hole pitot tube, see figure 1. The gas velocity can be measured by using holes P1 and P0, rotating the tube such that a maximum pressure difference is obtained. By rotating the tube such that the pressure difference between holes P1 and P2 is zero the local angle of the flow with respect to the pipe axis direction can be obtained. By measuring velocity and swirl angle at a number of radial locations, the velocity profile and swirl angle profile can be found.

The uncertainty in the measured velocity is estimated to be 2 % in the pipe centre and about 3 % near the pipe wall. As measurements took place in a live station, flow rate variations attributed some 5 % extra to the velocity uncertainty.

The uncertainty in the measured swirl angle is estimated to be 1° in the pipe centre and 3° near the pipe wall and in case of asymmetric velocity profiles.

Construction of the meterruns

Figure 3 shows the typical setup of the Gasunie stations. The headers have diameters of 750 mm (A), 900 mm (B) and 500 mm (C). The riser is welded perpendicular on the header and has a length of typically 4.5 D. The bends into the meterrun have a radius of 1.5 D. The length from the last bend to the ultrasonic meter position is 36 D. About 25 D further downstream the turbine meter is installed.

At about 6D from the riser a 2" vent valve could be used to install the Pitot assembly to measure the profiles at the inlet of the meterrun in the vertical direction (see fig.2). In station A the velocity and swirl profiles have also been measured at the position of the ultrasonic meter by replacing this with a special spoolpiece with 2" insertion pipes. Measurement were taken at +45° and -45° with respect to the vertical direction. Alltogether, velocity and swirl profiles have been obtained in 8 meterruns at 3 stations.

Velocity and swirl profiles

Some typical profiles obtained in station A, meterrun 1 are shown in figures 4 to 7. Contrary to the expectation the highest velocity was found in the lower part of the pipe ($x/R=1$). It soon develops to a more symmetric profile, as at the position of the ultrasonic meter the velocity profile is very close to a power law profile.

The maximum swirl angle is +10° at the lower pipe part and -15° in the upper pipe part. As expected from the geometry the flow rotates anti-clockwise. At the ultrasonic meter the swirl has decayed to about 5°. This is reasonably in line with the empirical exponential decay law for swirl $S = S_o \exp -C(x-x_o)$ [1,5]. Using as decay constant the value $C = 0.02$ the swirl angle should have decayed to 55%. The swirl angle appears to be independent from flow rate.

The very pronounced asymmetry at the beginning of meterrun A1 was not found in the other investigated runs. Figure 8 shows the inlet velocity profile of run A3 and figure 9 that of run C3.

Table 1 sums up the maximum swirl angles measured. The shape of the swirl angle profile was in all cases similar to the one presented in figure 7. In line with the geometry, station A had anti clockwise rotation and stations B and C clockwise rotation.

Some special attention is drawn to meterrun A3. Figure 10 shows measured swirl angle profiles at the ultrasonic meter position for various operation conditions of the station: more or less meterruns in operation. It shows that in some cases the swirl angle is near zero. No explanation is at hand.

Flow profile calculations.

The Dutch Institute for Environmental and Energy Technology TNO-IMET, has been asked to perform numerical calculations of the velocity and swirl profiles. TNO uses the CFD package TASCflow. Gasunie provided TNO with the geometry of station A. The calculation started from the outlet of the scrubber section and thus included the U-turn in the upstream header. The flow parameters were: pressure = 56 bar, density = 50 kg/m³, temperature = 283 K. The total flow rate through the station and the flow rate through a meterrun depend on the specified number of runs open. Flow profile data were kept from TNO until after the calculation results were obtained.

Not all data and comparisons with the measured profiles can be given here. Some typical results are shown. Figure 11 shows the calculated and measured velocity profile at the beginning of meterrun A1. At the lower pipe side the agreement is very good, at the upper pipe side an increasing discrepancy is seen. The profiles at the beginning of meterrun A3 show good agreement on the lower pipe side. But the calculation again gives an asymmetric profile with increasing velocities at the lower pipe side, whereas the measured profile is much more symmetric.

The swirl profile calculation for meterrun A1, figure 13, is remarkably good compared to the measured one, values and shape match excellent. For meterrun A2 this is less good, cf. figure 14. Also meterrun A3 is less good: figure 15 shows the swirl profile at the ultrasonic meter position in run A3. The variation in swirl angles found due to switching of other meterruns is not found in the calculation. Table 1 includes a review of the calculated swirl angles.

It was investigated if the numerical procedures influenced the results. The number of grid points was increased by 40%. The swirl angles found in that case at the 6 D position changed upwards by 1° to 3°. At the 36 D position the change was marginal. It indicates that in the more complicated situation at the begin of the meterrun, the data are not yet fully grid independent.

Alltogether, it can be stated that the CFD gave a qualitative view on what is happening inside the pipe.

EFFECTS ON METERS

Swirl generator

From the tests at the stations and from other work [1,5] it is clear that swirling flow develops towards a solid body type bulk rotation, regardless of the initial velocity and swirl profile. This allows the use of a simple device to study the effects of the header configuration on the meter involved. Figure 16 shows a swirl generator, consisting of 2 plates that can be oriented in the flow. Profile measurements have shown that a solid body rotation can be created with a swirl profile resembling the typical profile found in the meterrun and as measured by others [1,5].

As it is not possible to rebuild the station situation on the flow test facility of Gasunie at Westerbork, the Bernoulli laboratory, it was decided to simulate the situation with the use of the swirl generator.

Turbine meter

Figure 17 gives the mean shift in error of a turbine meter (D=500). Due to the inlet flow conditioner of the meter, consisting of 16 parallel vanes over a length of about 0.7 D, the meter is not significantly influenced - less that 0,03 % for anti-clockwise swirl, less than 0,08 % for clockwise swirl - given the repeatability of the turbine meter, which is in the order of 0.05 %. This was expected on the basis of previous experiments using the ISO 9951 perturbation test [6,8] and the results of the GERG project, presented at this conference [7].

There is a clear difference between the influence of clockwise and anti-clockwise swirl. This was also seen before [6,7], but is not yet fully understood.

Ultrasonic meter with 4 paths

A first set of tests was done on a meter with criss-cross arrangement of the four paths, see figure 18. Figure 19 gives the shift in meter error relative to the base line as function of clockwise and anti-clockwise swirl angle. An irregular pattern of shifts is found, that ranges from -0.2 % to 0.8 %. The reproducibility of the data points is about 0.1 %, thus the pattern is not caused by random variations.

The fact that the meter is swirl sensitive can be understood from the geometry of the paths. The change in axial velocity due to the swirl on an outer path is not fully compensated by the change in velocity on the neighbouring inner path that measures in the opposite direction: the outer path "sees" on average larger swirl angles than the inner one. The lower part of the meter is just reversed relative to the upper part, but there also the swirl direction is reversed, so that the same effect is obtained. For this rather general type of swirl, equal orientation of the outer paths on the one hand and of the inner paths on the other hand, would improve the swirl insensitivity.

Ultrasonic meter with 5 paths

A somewhat smaller set of tests has been performed on a meter with reflection type arrangement of five paths, see figure 20. The meter has 3 single reflection paths, used to measure axial velocity components and 2 double reflection paths, intended to detect and compensate for swirl. Figure 21 gives the error shift relative to the base line for clockwise swirl at 2 flow rates. Over the range up to 10° the error shift remains within +\- 0.4 %.

As the details on the method of processing the data from the various paths are not known, it is possible only in a fairly qualitative manner to provide an explanation for the encountered swirl dependency. The signal from the acoustic paths is used to recognize the type of flow profile, including asymmetry and swirl, from a library of profiles in the meter. The flow profiles encountered in practice are no doubt different from the profiles on which the meter "learned" its performance. Thereby, a fully correct calculation of the flow is not obtained and some influence of swirl remains.

Thus, even though the setup of the paths is such that a large part of the flow profile is covered, it cannot be excluded that in practical cases the meter performance is still somewhat dependent on the actual flow profile.

ELIMINATION OF HEADER EFFECTS

For turbine meters there is hardly any need to eliminate the swirl using flow conditio-ners. If some straight length can be allowed, say 10 to 15 D, and the meter has passed the typetest with the ISO 9951 perturbation unit, the influence of headers is negligible.

For ultrasonic meters to perform equally good, some flow conditioning appears necessary. Tests at Gasunie give very promising results for the new types of flow conditio-ners like the Laws and Gallagher conditioners. These data will be reported later.

CONCLUSIONS

*   Header configurations induce swirling flow, that decays only slowly in the meterrun, and thus is a disturbance to be taken into consideration when assessing the accuracy of measurement. The data show that velocity and swirl profile at the entrance of the meterrun are quite diverse for nominally equal geometries, and that the operational situation influences the actual profiles. However, if the flow is allowed to settle for some length it decays to a solid body like swirl with reasonably symmetrical velocity profile.

*   Turbine meters with effective inlet flow conditioning can be used without significant change in performance in the swirling flow conditions found in header configurations (less than 10°). The effectiveness of the inlet flow conditioning can be investigated with the ISO 9951 perturbation test [7,8].

*   Ultrasonic meters, that have no inlet conditioning at all, show a significant influence. The influence depends on the arrangement of ultrasonic paths. To obtain the robust-ness of gas turbine meters probably some inlet conditioning remain necessary. Preliminary data on the new "thick plate" conditioners look promising.

*   Numerical simulation has reached a point were some geometries can be predicted quite good. It can serve as a tool to understand the phenomena; the quantitative power needs further development.

REFERENCES

1. The decay of swirl in turbulent pipe flows, W. Steenbergen, J. Voskamp, K. Krishna Prasad, 7th Int. Conf. on Flow Meas. FLOMEKO, Glasgow, 1994.

2. The disturbance of flow through an orifice plate meterrun by the upstream header, B. Harbrink, W. Zirnig, H.H. Hassenpflug, W. Kerber, H. Zimmerman, 5th Int. IMEKO Conf. on Flow Meas. FLOMEKO, Düsseldorf, 1989.

3. Flow characteristics and orifice meter error caused by upstream headers in multi-run meter stations, I.D. Williamson, K.K. Botros, G.R. Price, 1993 ASME Forum on Fluid Meas. and Instr., Washington, 1993.

4. Gasunie selects turbine meters for renovated export metering stations, P.M.A. van der Kam, A.M. Dam, K. van Dellen, Oil & Gas Journal Dec. 24, 1990, 39-44

5. Effects of pipe elbows and tube bundles on selected types of flowmeters, G.E. Mattingly and T.T. Yeh, Flow Meas.Instr. 2 (1991), 4-13

6. Turbine meter performance under perturbed flow conditions, P.M.A. van der Kam, H. de Vries, S. de Jong, IGRC, Orlando, 1992.

7. Perturbation tests on turbine meters, B. Harbrink, W. Kerkmann, P.M.A. van der Kam, G.J. de Nobel, D. King, C. Trimel, J.L. de Schutter, V.M. Cannizzo, IGRC, Cannes, 1995.

8. Measurement of gas flow in closed conduits - Turbine meters, International Standard ISO 9951, 1993.

9. The use of flow conditioners to improve measurement accuracy downstream of headers, M.J. Reader-Harris, J.A. Sattary, E. Woodhead, 3rd Int. Symp. on Fluid Flow Meas., San Antonio Tx, 1995.

Table 1    Measured and calculated swirl angles. The first figures indicate the max. angle at the upper pipe side, the second the max angle at the lower pipe side.

| Station/ meterrun | Swirl orientation | Measured 6 D | Measured 36 D | Calculated 6 D | Calculated 36 D |
|---|---|---|---|---|---|
| A1 | ACW | -18 / +10 | -5  / +5 | -18 / +10 | -4  / +4 |
| A2 | ACW |  | -5  / +5 | -10 / +12 | -2  / +2 |
| A3 | ACW | -10 / +6 | -5 / +4 and -0 / +1 | -10 / +8 | -3  / +3 |
| B1 | CW | +5  / -7 |  |  |  |
| B3 | CW | +15 / -8 |  |  |  |
| B5 | CW | +17 / -7 |  |  |  |
| C1 | CW | +8  / -7 |  |  |  |
| C3 | CW | +7  / -12 |  |  |  |

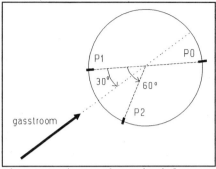

**Figure 1** Pitot tube principle

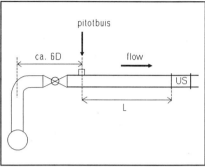

**Figure 2** Meterrun setup. L=30 D

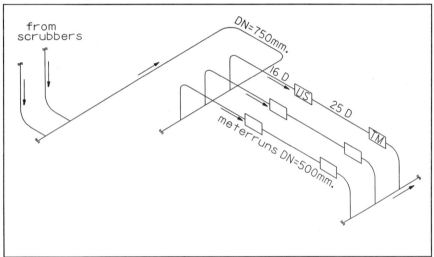

**Figure 3** Schematic layout of metering station

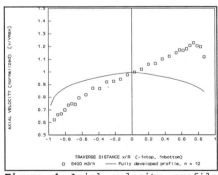

**Figure 4** Axial velocity profile at begin of meterrun A1

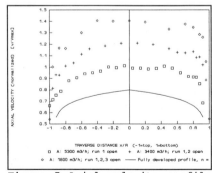

**Figure 5** Axial velocity profile at 36 D position, meterrun A1

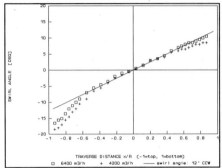

**Figure 6** Swirl angles at begin meterrun A1

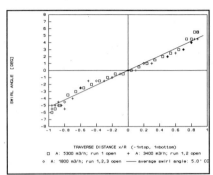

**Figure 7** Swirl angles at 36 D position, meterrun A1

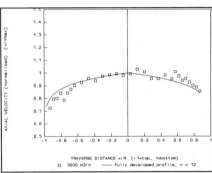

**Figure 8** Velocity profile begin meterrun A3

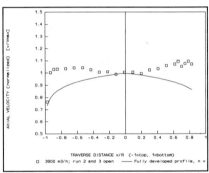

**Figure 9** Velocity profile begin meterrun C3

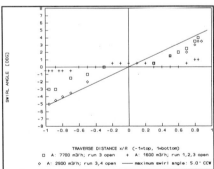

**Figure 10** Swirl angles at 36 D position meterrun A3

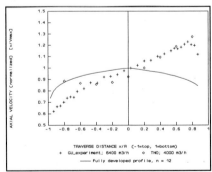

**Figure 11** CFD calculated velocity profile, compared with measured profile, meterrun A1

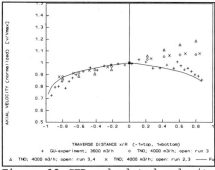

**Figure 12** CFD calculated velocity profile compared with measured profile, meterrun A3

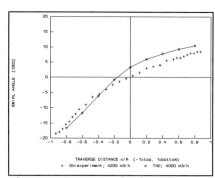

**Figure 13** CFD calculated swirl angles, compared with measured ones, meterrun A1

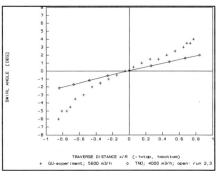

**Figure 14** As figure 13, at 36 D position, meterrun A2

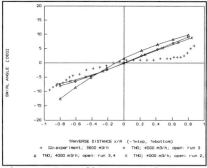

**Figure 15** As figure 13, for meterrun A3

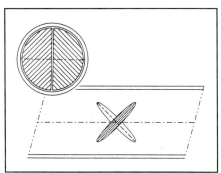

**Figure 16** The swirl generator

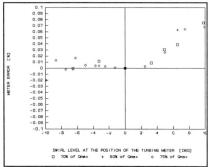

**Figure 17** Influence of swirl on a turbine meter, D = 500 mm.

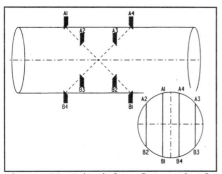

**Figure 18** Principle of 4-path ultrasonic meter

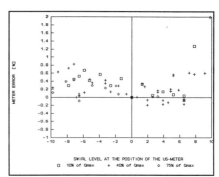

**Figure 19** Influence of swirl on 4-path ultrasonic meter,D=500mm

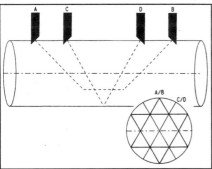

**Figure 20** Principle of 5-path ultrasonic meter

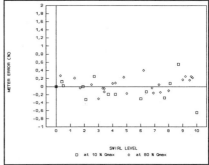

**Figure 21** Influence of swirl on 5-path ultrasonic meter,D=500mm

CARACTERISATION D'ONDES ACOUSTIQUES ET INFLUENCE
SUR LES COMPTEURS A TURBINE


CHARACTERIZATION OF ACOUSTIC WAVES AND THEIR
INFLUENCE ON TURBINE FLOWMETERS


Doris DONAT, Anne Claire DELBET, Vincent DE LAHARPE
GAZ DE FRANCE


**RESUME**

Gaz de France souhaite développer un outil de diagnostic des perturbations de l'écoulement dans les postes de détente-comptage et qui permette en particulier de prédire l'erreur d'un compteur à turbine soumis à des perturbations acoustiques.

Une étude théorique a débouché sur l'élaboration d'une procédure de caractérisation des ondes acoustiques et d'un modèle de comportement dynamique de compteur à turbine. Une série d'essais d'un compteur à turbine soumis à des pulsations acoustiques de fréquences et amplitudes diverses et à plusieurs débits, a permis de valider les résultats théoriques.

Après une rapide description des modèles de compteur et de propagation des ondes, cet exposé présente les essais, les outils de mesure développés et les résultats de l'étude. Ceux-ci permettent d'envisager de façon optimiste l'élaboration de l'outil de diagnostic sur site.


**ABSTRACT**

Gaz de France is seeking to develop a tool capable of diagnosing flow disturbances in pressure regulating and metering stations which would in particular make it possible to predict the degree of error of a turbine flowmeter subjected to acoustic pulsations.

A theoretical study has led to the drafting of a procedure for characterizing acoustic waves and a dynamic behaviour model for turbine flowmeters. A series of tests carried out on a turbine flowmeter subjected to acoustic pulsations at various frequencies and amplitudes and at several different flow rates then served to validate the theoretical results.

After a brief description of the meter and wave propagation models, this paper will present the tests, the measurement devices developed and the results of the study. The results give us every reason to be optimistic about being able to design an on-site diagnostic tool.

## CONTEXT

Under pressure from increasingly demanding standards and user requirements there is a growing need for accurate metering for reasons of cost, network optimization, energy saving and environmental protection. Meters are often used in disturbed flows downstream of bends, double bends, pressure regulators and other obstacles. For a long time the primary concern of researchers and operators has been to determine the optimum distance that has to be respected between the meter and the last obstacle to ensure accurate metering. In reality, this approach has its limits for unsteady disturbances which, unlike steady disturbances, persist over very long distances and are not removed by flow conditioners. Before we can consider to improve metering in stations it is essential that we find a method which lets us accurately characterize all steady and unsteady flow disturbances at the exact meter position.

In 1989, Gaz de France launched a major research programme on the subject of metering diagnosis looking to develop an industrial tool for on-site diagnosis of flow disturbances. One of the aims of this project is to develop a method for characterizing acoustic disturbances in order to predict the error in turbine flowmeters subjected to such disturbances. Turbine flowmeters are widely used on the GDF network. However, these meters are sensitive to unsteady conditions. It is therefore logical to concentrate our efforts on this technology. This paper presents the work done on characterizing acoustic waves and their influence on a turbine flowmeter.

## INTRODUCTION

Predicting the error of a turbine flowmeter due to acoustic disturbances is a complex problem. In general the energy of flow pulsations is not uniform along the whole length of the pipe. It is not sufficient to measure pulsation frequency and amplitude at one point of the pipe to determine pulsation energy at the meter. Only by knowing the pulsation energy at the meter (at the rotor in the case of a turbine flowmeter) can we predict the metering error. We also need a theoretical model of the dynamic behaviour of the turbine flowmeter validated by testing.

To determine the metering error of a turbine flowmeter subjected to pulsations, one method is to use the data obtained from the meter's HF output. This signal shows the effect of the pulsations on the turbine rotor by measuring the variations in blade rotation velocity. It is a simple method that can be used on site. However, such an approach is only effective at frequencies of just a few Hertz. For higher frequencies the rotor's inertia and the background noise render the signal unusable. In addition, it can only be used with turbine flowmeters in good working condition and equipped with a HF output.

To overcome these limitations, Gaz de France researchers opted instead for a different approach, using the data acquired directly from the flow and not from the meter. In order to do this it is necessary to characterize the pulsations (frequency, spatial distribution of the amplitude, etc.) using measurements taken in the flow. To find the longitudinal distribution of the amplitude of pulsations and their amplitude at the exact rotor position we need a theoretical wave propagation model. We also require a theoretical model of the turbine flowmeter which can use this data to calculate the additional error caused by the pulsations.

We studied the case of forced acoustic sinusoidal (single-frequency) waves. This choice was based on the concrete observation of what occurs in reality in pressure reducing stations. All periodic signals can be broken down into individual sinusoidal signals and very often, in practice, we see the disturbance energy being concentrated at a single frequency, the signal's fundamental frequency.

## THEORETICAL STUDY

### ACOUSTIC WAVE PROPAGATION

Modelling using plane waves.    The basic principle consists of considering that acoustic waves are propagated along the pipe in the form of plane waves. To represent pressure fluctuations caused by plane acoustic waves the following hypotheses have to be used:
- pressure fluctuations are small;
- velocity profile is uniform;
- average flow velocity is negligible compared to the velocity of sound;
- the resulting fluctuations caused are monodimensional.

Wave propagation assumes an upper frequency limit. This limit is the cut-off frequency of the pipe, the frequency at which the first transverse acoustic mode appears. Modelling using plane waves therefore consists in particular of pressure fluctuations occurring in the pipe that are uniform at any time and at any place. In this way, all the parameters may be represented as functions of a single spatial dimension. As well it is assumed that the wave propagation along the whole length of the pipe is not subjected to any attenuation, which is identical to considering that gas compression is purely adiabatic.

We can thus consider that any pressure fluctuation in the pipe results from the superposition of just two elementary plane waves:
- an incident wave p+ which propagates "from left to right";
- a reflected wave p- which propagates the other way, "from right to left".
These are usually represented in the following way:

$$p_+ = P_+ e^{j(\omega t - kx + \phi_+)} \qquad \text{and} \qquad p_- = P_- e^{j(\omega t + kx + \phi_-)} \tag{1}$$

p+ propagates in the direction of the positive x coordinates while p- propagates in the negative x direction. Both move at the velocity of sound $c = \omega/k = (dp)_S/(d\rho)_S$ where dp and $d\rho$ are the variations in pressure and density at constant entropy, i.e. during an adiabatic transformation. The fluctuation in acoustic pressure $P_a$ in a given section is represented by the real part of the sum of p+ and p-:

$$P_a = P_+ \cos(\omega t - kx + \phi_+) + P_- \cos(\omega t + kx + \phi_-) \tag{2}$$

At each point of the pipe, the variations in pressure and velocity cause by the passage of a wave are linked by the impedance relation:

$$p = (pc)v \tag{3}$$

and the fluctuation of the acoustic velocity in a given section is:

$$V_a = \frac{1}{\rho c}\left[P_+ \cos(\omega t - kx + \phi_+) - P_- \cos(\omega t + kx + \phi_-)\right] \tag{4}$$

## MODEL OF THE DYNAMIC BEHAVIOUR OF THE TURBINE FLOWMETER

The dynamic behaviour of turbine flowmeters has been studied on numerous occasions over the past 40 years. We chose the most commonly-used model shown by the following equation [4, 5 and 6]:

$$D_1 \frac{dF}{dt} = Q(Q - F) \tag{5}$$

This arises out of the principle of the conservation of momentum, assuming that there is neither aerodynamic nor solid friction. The torque on the rotor is equal to the rate of change in the angular momentum of the fluid going through the blades.

All the parameters of the equation are dimensionless. Q and F are respectively the real instantaneous volume flow rate, q(t), and the instantaneous volume flow rate indicated by the meter, f(t), standardized using the average flow rate q0. t is the time normalized by the pulsation period, and $D_1$ is the rotor response parameter. This parameter is proportional to the moment of inertia J of the rotor, the frequency v of the pulsations, inversely proportional to the mean quadratic radius $\bar{r}$ F of the blades, the density $\rho$ and the average flow rate q0.

$$D_1 = \frac{(1+\eta)Jv}{\bar{r}^2 \rho q_0} \tag{6}$$

Where $\eta$ is the deviation factor which depends on the shape of the rotor. It is an essentially constant value for any given meter [6]. The metering error is therefore given by the difference between the indicated flow rate F and the real flow rate Q. Expressed as a percentage of the real flow rate it is written:

$$E = \frac{f_0 - q_0}{q_0} = F_0 - 1 \tag{7}$$

Because equation (5) is non linear it is difficult to find an analytical solution. We therefore developed a numerical program for the prediction of the metering error. Figure 1 shows the numerical solutions obtained for flow rates of the type $q0[1+\alpha\cos(\omega t)]$ like those caused by the presence of single-frequency plane waves in an average flow. We can distinguish three zones:

- an initial zone where error is low for very small values of $D_1$;
- a second zone where the error increases with $D_1$;
- and a third zone where the error merely depends on the relative amplitude $\alpha$ of the pulsations for large values of $D_1$.

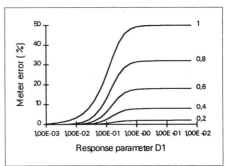

Figure 1 : Predicted turbine meter error versus the rotor response parameter, for several pulsation amplitudes.

In the first zone the rotor manages to follow the oscillations of the flow rate and the indication error remains low. In the third zone, however, it can no longer follow the pulsations and the error is positive and depends solely on the pulsation amplitude $\alpha$.

## TEST MEANS AND PROCEDURES

### DESCRIPTION OF THE TEST BENCH

The tests were carried out on a Gaz de France flowmetering test bench reserved exclusively for the study of installation conditions. This test bench is supplied with natural gas and makes it possible to test a maximum flow rate of 8,000 $m^3(n)/h$ at pressures of 20 mbar to 35 bar. A pressure regulator permits to regulate the pressure upstream of the two variable nozzles which are used as flow references. The gas flows along the test line before being expelled downstream of the test bench into a gasometer at the gasometric pressure of 20 mbar via a valve which allows to regulate the pressure in the working section downstream of the nozzle. Figure 2 shows a diagram of the test bench between the variable nozzle and the outlet. This can be divided into two zones:

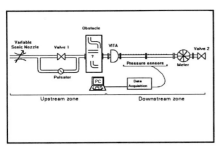

Figure 2 : diagram of the test bench

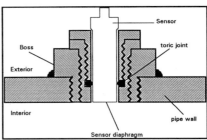

Figure 3 : flush piezo-electric dynamic pressure sensors

The upstream zone consists of:
- a source of acoustic waves which are generated by passing part of the gas stream through a butterfly valve whose rotation determines the pulsation frequency;
- a valve, marked 1, whose position determines the proportion of the total flow which passes through the pulsation generator and thus makes it possible to control the amplitude of the pulsations;
- an "obstacle" (bend, double bend, divergent and convergent ducts, and a straight-line section) which is used to modify the velocity profile.

The downstream zone consists of:
- "VITA", an automatic system for measuring the velocity profile. This device is based on the principle of a double hot wire probe which can be rotated and translated throughout the section to measure the average and fluctuating tangencial velocity and the average and fluctuating axial velocity at any point [8];
- two straight spool pieces equipped with a number of piezoelectric dynamic pressure sensors flush with the internal flow (see figure 3);
- a data acquisition terminal which receives, filters and samples the signals returned by the pressure sensors;
- a computer workstation running the software needed for signal processing, the calculation of the acoustic parameters and the calculation of the metering error;
- the turbine flowmeter that is being tested.

### DESCRIPTION OF THE TESTS AND THE PROCEDURE FOR CHARACTERIZING ACOUSTIC WAVES

Tests were carried out at a pressure of 1.3 bar with a G250 turbine flowmeter with a nominal diameter of 100 mm. We ran a series of tests during which the turbine flowmeter was subjected to sinusoidal-type acoustic pulsations. To assess the effect of the shape of the velocity profile on wave propagation, tests were repeated on different assembly configurations: straight line, downstream of a bend, two bends out of plane, a restriction and a diffuser.

Choice of test parameters . According to the theory the meter response depends only on the rotor response parameter $D_1$ and the amplitude of the flow pulsations. For a given wave shape and for constant pressure and temperature conditions, the meter error therefore depends only on the flow rate, the frequency and the amplitude of the pulsations. We therefore ran tests on each assembly configuration using several values in the meter's flow rate range, i.e. 400, 280, 100 and 40 m³/h. At each flow rate value we subjected the meter to high and low amplitude disturbances at 75, 180 and 250 Hz. Each test could therefore be characterized by:

- a frequency;
- an amplitude;
- a flow rate;
- an assembly configuration.

Measurement of the over-registration of the turbine flowmeter. In each test a reading was taken of the flow rate indicated by the meter and of the reference flow rate (which was not affected by the pulsations). The error shift due to the flow pulsations is obtained by comparison with the meter's calibration curve under ideal flow conditions.

Calculation of incident and reflected pressure waves p+ and p-. At the same time a reading was taken of the pressure signals measured by the piezoelectric sensors. These signals are then processed by the data acquisition terminal to determine, in accordance with the theoretical model, the frequency of the pulsations and their amplitude at all points along the pipe according to the following procedure:

For each pressure sensor the average quadratic pressure is calculated. According to the theory this value can easily be derived from equation (2). Since an arbitrary phase reference can be used, the following procedure adopts the convention whereby the phase of the incident wave is zero at all frequencies at point x=0 at t=0. Thus, the mean theoretical quadratic acoustic pressure can be written:

$$\overline{P_a^2} = \frac{1}{T}\int_{-\frac{T}{2}}^{+\frac{T}{2}} P_a^2 dt = \frac{P_+^2 + P_-^2}{2} + P_+P_-\cos(2kx + \phi) \tag{8}$$

This is a sinusoidal function of the position x along the pipe, which we call the amplitude modulation function of the pulsations. The heart of the characterization method consists of finding the amplitude modulation function by interpolating the mean quadratic pressures measured by the sensors by a sinusoidal function with four unknowns:

$$A + B\cos\left(\frac{4\pi v}{c}x + \psi\right) \tag{9}$$

Where v is the pulsation frequency measured using spectral analysis of the pressure signals. The four unknowns of the interpolation are therefore A, B, c and $\psi$. Once these parameters have been estimated using the least error squares method we can deduce the parameters of the acoustic field by identification of (8) and (9):

$$P_+ = 1/2\left(\sqrt{A+B} + \sqrt{A-B}\right)$$
$$P_- = 1/2\left(\sqrt{A+B} - \sqrt{A-B}\right)$$
$$\omega = 2\pi v$$
$$k = 2\pi v / c$$
$$\phi = \psi$$

(10)

Figure 4 gives an example of the interpolation of the mean quadratic pressures measured by the sensors; the average quadratic pressure has been plotted on the ordinate scale while the distance x from the first sensor is plotted on the x-axis. The continuous curve is the obtained interpolation curve. Using the equation (2) for the fluctuating velocity, we can then calculate the fluctuating volume flow rate at all points along the pipe and in particular at the rotor of the turbine flowmeter and in the VITA measurement section.

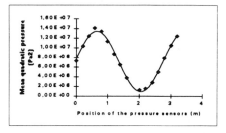

Figure 4 : Interpolation of the mean square acoustic pressures by a sinusoïdal function.

$$Q_a = \alpha \cos(\omega t) \quad \text{and}$$

$$\alpha = \left[\frac{A}{\rho c}\sqrt{P_+^2 + P_-^2 - 2P_+P_-\cos(2kx_m + \phi)}\right] \quad (11)$$

Amplitude of the flow pulsations.    The butterfly valve of the pulsation generator produces acoustic waves that are theoretically sinusoidal. The acoustic flow rate (the fluctuating component of the flow rate) is therefore written as shown in equation (11). The amplitude $\alpha$ depends first and foremost on the opening of valve 1. For each flow rate and each frequency, tests were carried out for one, two or three different valve positions, namely:

- valve closed;
- valve half-closed;
- valve open.

The amplitude $\alpha$ also depends on the frequency and the flow rate and as such it is a parameter that is difficult to control. The range covered by all the tests is 0.1 to 0.8.

Choosing the number and spacing of the sensors.    One of the difficulties consists of performing a correct spatial sampling of the function of the amplitude modulation of the acoustic pressure. Using a discrete set of measurements in space we have to find all the information we need, i.e. the parameters of the sinusoidal function which passes through these points. This is possible on condition that we satisfy the Shannon criterion, i.e. that we have at least two measuring points for each wavelength. We also need to take measurements over at least one half wavelength. The distance separating two successive sensors therefore determines the smallest measurable wavelength (or the highest frequency, since $\lambda = \pi/k = c/2f$), while the number of sensors determines the longest measurable wavelength (or the smallest frequency). We chose to install 16 sensors placed 20 cm apart (except sensors 9 and 10 which are 40 cm apart for reasons of the assembly configuration) on one generating line of the pipe. This assembly therefore makes it possible to measure the functions of amplitude modulation for frequencies between 34 Hz and 550 Hz in normal conditions of pressure and temperature (c = 440 m.s-1).

Calculation of the velocity of sound.    The velocity of sound is one of the four unknowns in the interpolation problem of the mean quadratic pressures. Comparing the calculated value with the measured one allows to validate the plane wave propagation model.

Measurement of the average and fluctuating velocity profiles.          The average and fluctuating velocity profiles are also measured using the VITA device. This makes it possible to directly measure the overflow (mean quadratic acoustic flow rate) in the VITA section. The comparison between this value and the one calculated by the characterization method from equation (11) permits to validate this method.

Prediction of the meter error.          The characterization method gives the frequency and the amplitude of the flow rate pulsations at the meter. Thus we can calculate by numerical simulation the extra error induced in the meter, using the model presented in the theoretical section above. To do this we need to calculate the rotor response parameter $D_1$ and therefore obtain the meter's geometric parameters $\eta$, J and F. Their measurement produced the following results:

$$\eta = 0.15$$
$$J = 7 .10^{-5} \text{ kg.m}^2$$
$$F = 42.3 .10^{-3} \text{ m}$$

The theoretical value of the error calculated in this way can then be compared to the error measured by taking the difference between the value shown on the meter and the value of the reference flow rate.

## RESULTS

### INFLUENCE OF THE VELOCITY PROFILE

One of the underlying hypotheses of the model is that the flow is uniform, i.e. the velocity is the same at any point along the section, so the waves remain plane throughout their propagation. A mathematical model devised by Gaz de France [3] has shown by numerical simulation that the distortion of plane waves in the presence of non-uniform, viscous and turbulent flows are negligible. The average and fluctuating velocity profile measurements taken by VITA confirm this hypothesis. They show that the amplitude of the pulsation velocity in a section is indeed uniform irrespective of the average velocity profile (figures 5.1 to 5.5). We also verified that this deformation of the velocity profile compared to the fully-developed profile had no effect on the turbine flowmeter.

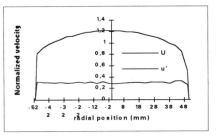

Figure 5.1 : Mean and fluctuating velocity profiles downstream of a straigh pipe.

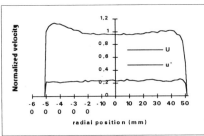

Figure 5.2 : Mean and fluctuating velocity profiles downstream of a bend.

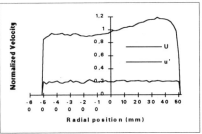

Figure 5.3 : Mean and fluctuating velocity profiles downstream of a double bend out of plane.

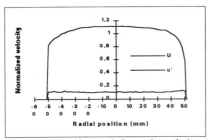

**Figure 5.4 : Mean and fluctuating velocity profiles downstream of a restriction.**

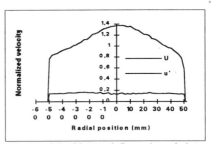

**Figure 5.5 : Mean and fluctuating velocity profiles downstream of a diffuser.**

**CHARACTERIZATION OF THE INCIDENT AND REFLECTED WAVES**

Calculation of the velocity of sound.        For all our tests (43 in all) the average deviation between the velocity of sound found by interpolation and the velocity of sound calculated on the basis of thermodynamic data is -0.26% for a standard deviation of 2.25%. This excellent result definitively validates the plane wave propagation model in the pipe for frequencies less than the cut-off frequency.

Accuracy of the interpolation.        For each test we measured the standard deviation between the measured mean quadratic pressure and the value obtained by interpolation.

This is an indicator of the accuracy with which the method is capable of predicting the acoustic intensity at any point. The results varied greatly according to the experimental conditions. Expressed as a percentage of the average pulsation value it varied between 2% and 37% depending on the test. This was partly due to the fact that the waves generated by the pulsation generator are not always sinusoidal. When this deviation exceeds 20% we can clearly see in the pressure signal frequency spectra a number of significant energy harmonics. In the example in figure 4, obtained for a frequency of 75 Hz, the spectrum consists only of the fundamental frequency and the interpolation is good. On the other hand, in the example of figure 6 obtained at a frequency of 250 Hz, the signal spectrum contains several harmonics, and the interpolation is accordingly slightly worse.

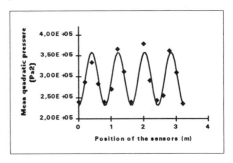

**Figure 6 : Interpolation of the mean square acoustic pressures for a frequency of 250 Hz.**

Comparison of predicted and measured overflows at VITA.

Presented in figure 7 are the results of the comparison between the predicted acoustic overflow (equation 5) and that measured by VITA, when the standard deviation of the interpolation residue is less than 20%. These results shown a fairly good agreement between the theory and the measurements. The average deviation is -0.8 dB for a standard deviation of 1.4 dB, which is quite satisfactory given the large number of measurements made and the sources of uncertainty.

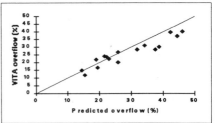

**Figure 7 : Comparison of the overflow measured by VITA and the predicted one.**

### CALCULATION OF THE METER ERROR - COMPARISON WITH EXPERIENCE

Figure 8 shows the predicted error as a function of the real error:
- between 0% and 10% the calculated and measured values tally well, with just a few exceptions, and with test bench uncertainty of $\pm 0.5\%$;
- above 10%, the calculated error is always greater than the real error but remains very close.

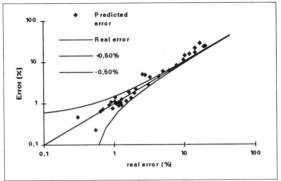

**Figure 8 : Over-registration error of a the turbine meter, for all the tests.**

Theory shows that the error depends only on $\alpha$ and $D_1$, while beyond a certain value of $D_1$, in the region of 1, (see figure 1) which is the case in our tests, the error depends only on $\alpha$. Our tests confirm this tendency (see figure 9). We then see that the limit of 10% beyond which the measurements and the calculations tally rather less well, corresponds to a level of pulsation amplitude of around 0.4. For amplitudes of more than 0.4 this model loses its accuracy.

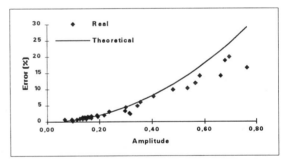

**Figure 9 : Comparison between the real and the predicted over-registration error of the turbine meter**

## CONCLUSION

This model must be adapted to measuring real disturbances and not purely sinusoidal ones. The characterization procedure is valid when there is one predominant frequency which contains most of the pulsation energy. This is the case for most of the phenomena observed in reality on operating stations. If this were not the case we would have to extend the model to process packets of waves.

The turbine flowmeter model is valid for all kinds of flow rate pulsations for relative amplitudes that are not excessively high. For amplitudes of less than 0.4 then the accuracy with which the calculation pinpoints the meter error is very good when you consider that in addition to the uncertainty factor for the flowmeter model there is also the uncertainty of the wave characterization method which supplies the input data to the former model. For amplitudes of more than 0.4 the model is less accurate. We would have to take into account the drag exerted on the blades by local turbulence, boundary layer and mechanical vibration phenomena. Nevertheless, the level of amplitude that is likely to be observed on site is generally less than this value.

For non-acoustic flow rate pulsations it is not enough to measure the fluctuating pressure. We also need to directly measure the velocity fluctuations.

This method for characterizing acoustic waves relies on a large number of pressure sensors. We purposely chose this solution because we had a long straight section and we needed measurement accuracy to validate the theoretical study. Moreover, these sensors are intrusive. Gaz de France is currently looking into optimizing the measurement system on the basis of the following criteria:

- non-intrusive sensors;
- fewer sensors;
- a short measurement distance.

## REFERENCES

[1]   **Ph. Grenier** - "Effects of unsteady flow phenomena on flow metering", Flow Measurement and Instrumentation, Vol. 2, no. 1, 1991.

[2]   **Ph. Grenier** - "Etude de la transmission des fluctuations de pression au sein de canalisations de gaz", Report M.CERMAP GRE/PG No. 88/I/633, Gaz de France, October 1988.

[3]   **A.C. Delbet** - "Définition et mise en oeuvre d'une méthode de caractérisation d'instationnarité d'écoulement gazeux en aval de postes de comptage", Doctorate Thesis for Paris University faculty VI, January 1994.

[4]   **A. Haaman** - "Pulsation errors on turbine flowmeters", Staatsmijen in Limburg, Holland Control Engineering, May 1965.

[5]   **H.H. Dijstelbergen** - "Dynamic response of turbine flowmeters", Gasunie, Instrument review, June 1966.

[6]   **W.F.Z. Lee & M.J. Kirik & J.A. Bonner** - "Gas turbine flowmeter measurement of pulsating flow", Journal of Engineering for power, Transactions of the ASME, October 1975.

[7]   **K.N. Atkinson** - "A software tool to calculate the over-registration error of a turbine meter in pulsating flow", Flow Measurement & Instrumentation, March 1992.

[8]   **D. King** - "Self-Acting Velocity Profile device for natural gas under pressure", Third International Fluid Flow Measurements Symposium, San Antonio, March 1994.

ANALYSE DE L'ECOULEMENT A L'AVAL D'UN DETENDEUR A PARTIR DE MESURES DE VITESSE ET
DE VISUALISATIONS D'ECOULEMENT


FLOW ANALYSIS DOWNSTREAM OF A PRESSURE REDUCER FROM VELOCITY MEASUREMENTS AND
FLOW VISUALISATIONS

A. Strzelecki[*], P.Gajan[*] L Malard[*], D. Donat[**], M. Bosch[***]
[*] ONERA/CERT/DERMES, 2 avenue Edouard Belin, 31055 Toulouse cedex, France
[**] Centre d'essai de Gaz de France, 3 chemin de villeneuve, 94140 Alforville, France
[***] Gaz du Sud Ouest, 49 avenue Dufau, B.P 522 64010 PAU cedex, France

**RESUME**

    Cette communication présente les résultats d'une analyse d'écoulement réalisée à l'aval d'un détendeur industriel utilisé sur un poste de détente/comptage de gaz naturel. Ces résultats montrent la complexité de ces écoulements qui peuvent présenter une forte dissymétrie couplée à un mouvement giratoire du fluide. Dans certains cas, des instabilités importantes peuvent être décelées. L'utilisation conjointe de mesures de vitesse et de visualisations d'écoulement permet d'expliquer et de quantifier les phénomènes. L'évolution de ces perturbations dans une conduite rectiligne est aussi étudiée.

**ABSTRACT**

    In this paper, a characterisation of the flow downstream of an indutrial pressure reducer used on a delivery station of natural gas is presented. These results point out the complexity of such flows which may combined non symetric distributions of the velocity with swirl. In some cases, high flow instabilities are detected. The use of flow visualisations in combinaison with velocity measurements give useful information about the origine and the magnitude of the phenomena. The axial attenuation of the flow perturbations is also analysed.

INTRODUCTION.

Le transport du gaz par gazoduc est réalisé à haute pression. Ensuite, le gaz est livré à plus basse pression pour des utilisations domestiques ou industrielles. Le plus souvent, le gaz est d'abord détendu puis compté à l'aide d'un débitmètre.ces deux fonctions sont généralement associées et forment ainsi un poste de détente/comptage. Pour réduire l'encombrement de ces postes, il est nécessaire d'optimiser la distance entre le détendeur et le compteur. Néanmoins, l'écoulement obtenu en sorti du détendeur est fortement perturbé et présente parfois un caractère instationnaire marqué. Ceci peut induire une erreur de comptage au niveau du débitmètre. Depuis cinq ans, Gaz de France (GDF), Gaz du Sud Ouest (GSO) et le Centre d'Etudes et de Recherches de Toulouse (CERT) mènent un programme de recherches sur l'analyse des écoulements à l'aval de détendeurs industriels.

Dans cette communication, seront présentés les résultats obtenus pour un type de détendeur et un taux de détente.

DESCRIPTION DU BANC ET DES TECHNIQUES DE MESURE

Géométrie du détendeur

Le détendeur testé correspond à une vanne de laminage industriel (sans fonction de régulation). (figure 1). Sur cette vanne, un comparateur a été placé afin de déterminer la distance h séparant le siège du clapet. Ce détendeur ayant un diamètre interne de sortie de 50mm, un divergent est placé à l'aval pour rattraper le diamètre de la conduite (100 mm). Tous les résultats présentés auront pour origine longitudinale le plan de sortie du divergent.

Banc d'essai

Les mesures ont été réalisées sur un banc aérodynamique (figure 2) fonctionnant à partir d'un réservoir en pression. Le débit massique est contrôlé à l'amont du détendeur, à l'aide d'un débitmètre col sonique à section variable mis au point par Gaz de France {1}. La manchette de mesures est placée à différentes positions l'aval du détendeur. Dans tout les cas, la pression aval est proche de la pression atmosphérique.

Paramètres d'essais

Deux paramètres d'essai sont pris en compte:
⇨ Le taux de détente $T_D$ qui est le rapport entre les pressions absolues obtenues respectivement à l'amont et à l'aval du détendeur.
⇨ Le débit volumique à l'aval du détendeur

Manchette de mesure

Les mesures de vitesse ont été réalisées par anémométrie fil chaud. Le principe de la mesure est détaillé dans Malard{2} et Malard et al {3}. Cette technique utilise une sonde à 1 fil montée sur un support droit. La mesure de l'angle local de la rotation est obtenue en faisant tourner la direction du fil autour de l'axe de la sonde (figure 3). et en repérant la position angulaire pour laquelle la tension de sortie de l'anémomètre passe par un minimum. La mesure du module de vitesse est ensuite effectuée en orientant le fil à 90° par rapport à la direction moyenne locale de l'écoulement.. Ces mesures sont corrigées des effets de blocage dus à la présence de la sonde (Malard{2} et Malard et al {3}). En chaque point de mesure on obtient ainsi la direction moyenne de la vitesse par rapport à l'axe de la conduite ($\alpha$), la valeur moyenne du module de la vitesse(V) et le taux de fluctuation du module ($\tau_t = \frac{\nu}{U_0}$ ). Dans cette expression $\nu$ est la valeur efficace de la fluctuation de vitesse et $U_0$ la vitesse débitante dans la section Les composantes axiale (U) et tangentielle (W) de la vitesse moyenne sont ensuite déduite par projection du module moyen.

En présence de phénomènes instationnaires, une analyse spectrale du signal de vitesse est également réalisée. On en déduit un coefficient de qualité du signal $C_Q$ identique à celui défini par Lanneville et al.[4]. Ce coefficient correspond au rapport entre l'énergie du signal dans une bande $\Delta f$ (RMS) centrée sur la fréquence d'instabilité $f_0$ sur l'énergie totale du signal (RMS$_{Total}$). On soustrait préalablement à l'énergie mesurée dans la bande d'analyse, le bruit équivalent estimé dans cette bande (RMS$_{bruit}$).

$$C_Q = \frac{\left[ RMS^2 - RMS^2_{bruit} \right]^{1/2} \Delta f}{RMS_{Total}}$$

En chaque section d'analyse, les scrutations sont effectuées sur 4 diamètres différents orientés à 45° les uns par rapport aux autres. L'orientation du diamètre de scrutation par rapport à la verticale est notée $\gamma$. On obtient ensuite par interpolation une représentation des champs mesurés. Les écoulements sont ensuite caractérisés à partir des nombres adimensionels suivants:

Nombre de swirl:

$$S = \frac{\int_0^R \rho U(rW) 2\pi r dr}{R \int_0^R \rho U^2 2\pi r dr}$$

Angle de swirl:

$$\alpha_s = arctg(\frac{3}{2} S)$$

Taux de dissymétrie du profil de vitesse axial

$$d = \frac{\left(Q_{r>0} - Q_{r<0}\right) \cdot 2}{Q_{r>0} + Q_{r<0}}$$

où $Q_{r>0}$ et $Q_{r<0}$ sont les valeurs respectives des débits obtenus par intégration des demi profils mesurés de part et d'autre de l'axe. Ces demi-profils sont repérés par $r > 0$ et $r < 0$.

Taux de turbulence moyen

$$|\tau| = \frac{1}{N} \sum_{i=1}^{N} \tau_{t_i}$$

<u>Techniques de visualisation</u>

Pour visualiser l'écoulement à l'aval du détendeur, deux méthodes ont été mises en oeuvre:

• Ensemencement globale de l'écoulement avec de la fumée injectée au niveau du divergent. Dans ce cas, la section droite étudiée est éclairée à l'aide d'une nappe de lumière Laser ou naturelle. Pour limiter les réflexions dues aux changements d'indice et faciliter l'observation perpendiculairement au plan d'éclairage, la section étudiée correspond au plan de sortie d'une manchette.

• Ensemencement locale par chauffage d'un fil métallique préalablement enduit d'huile. Cette technique permet de visualiser des filets de fumée donnant la répartition des angles de rotation locaux le long du fil métallique.

RESULTATS

La phase préliminaire de cette étude a consisté à établir l'influence des paramètres de réglage du détendeur sur le comportement d'un débitmètre à turbine. Ces essais présentés dans Malard[2] et Strzelecki et al {5} permettent de définir les points de fonctionnement pour lesquels une caractérisation fine de l'écoulement semble nécessaire.

Lors des premiers essais de caractérisation de l'écoulement à l'aval du détendeur, des résultats contradictoires ont été obtenus ne pouvant pas être attribués à un mauvais fonctionnement du système de mesure. Après examen de ces cas contradictoires, il ressort que ces observations peuvent s'expliquer par une modification des procédures suivies pour atteindre le taux de détente souhaité (phénomène d'hystérésis). Des règles d'essai trés strictes ont donc été mises en place permettant un bon recoupement des résultats. Nous présenterons dans cet article les tests réalisés pour deux points de fonctionnement du détendeur. Pour une de ces configurations ($T_D$ = 2 ; Q = 20 m$^3$/h), deux séries d'essais ont été effectuées en modifiant la procédure d'essai. Ceci permet de montrer l'existence d'un phénomène d'hystérésis.

<u>$T_D$ = 2 ; Q = 20 m$^3$/h; 1<sup>er</sup> mode d'obtention du taux de détente:</u>

Les mesures ont été réalisées à trois diamètres à l'aval du plan de sortie du divergent. Les répartitions de vitesse tangentielle, de vitesse axiale et de taux de fluctuation de la vitesse dans cette section sont présentées sur les figures 4, 5 et 6.

Les angles de rotation obtenus sont compris entre 0° et 13,7°. Le sens de rotation est négatif[1]. La visualisation de l'écoulement secondaire (figure 4), indique que cette rotation d'ensemble est légèrement

---

[1] La convention de signe suivie donne un angle positif pour les écoulement tournant dans le sens horaire lorsque l'on regarde fuir l'écoulement.

décentrée par rapport à l'axe de la conduite. Sur les iso-vitesses (figure 5) une légère dissymétrie est mise en évidence. Les taux de fluctuation de la vitesse (figure 6) sont relativement constants dans la section. Les valeurs mesurées ici (entre 20% de 26%) sont nettement supérieures à celles obtenues en écoulement établi (entre 4% sur l'axe à 13% prés de la paroi).

Les valeurs des paramètres caractéristiques moyens obtenus pour les quatre traversées dans cette section sont présentés dans le tableau suivant:

| $\gamma$ (°) | S | $\alpha_s$(°) | d(%) | $|\tau|$(%) |
|---|---|---|---|---|
| 0 | -0,069 | -5,92 | -0,41 | 22,05 |
| 45 | -0,071 | -6,09 | -7,63 | 22,4 |
| 90 | -0,079 | -6,78 | -7,93 | 22,62 |
| -45 | -0,069 | -5,88 | -6,91 | 22,06 |

Ces valeurs confirment l'analyse faite à partir des tracés précédents:
- Rotation faible dans le sens négatif (de l'ordre de 6° en moyenne)
- Écoulement faiblement dissymétrique
- Taux de turbulence homogène sur les 4 diamètres de l'ordre de 22%

Les analyses fréquentielles des signaux de vitesse n'ont pas révélé de fréquences caractéristiques dans l'écoulement.

$\underline{T_D =2 ; Q = 20 \text{ m}^3/\text{h}; 2^{ème} \text{ mode d'obtention du taux de détente:}}$

Une caractérisation complète de l'écoulement a été menée dans ce cas dans trois sections à proximité du détendeur (3D, 5D et 7D). Plus en aval, entre 7D et 38D, des mesures ont été réalisées sur un seul diamètre de conduite afin de suivre les évolutions longitudinales des paramètres d'ensemble utilisés pour caractériser ces écoulements.

Les analyses spectrales des signaux ayant montré dans ce cas l'existence d'instabilités à basses fréquences, une étude de ces phénomènes a été faite afin de connaître leur nature. Cette étude a mis en oeuvre différents outils que sont les visualisations d'écoulement et l'analyse spectrale.

### Caractéristiques moyennes de l'écoulement et évolutions longitudinales

Nous présenterons ici les caractéristiques de l'écoulement obtenues à proximité du détendeur et les évolutions des paramètres d'ensemble observées plus en aval.

#### Caractérisation de l'écoulement à x = 3D

Les résultats correspondants sont présentés sur les figures 7 à 9. Les angles de rotation, pouvant atteindre localement 60°, sont beaucoup plus importants que ceux mesurés précédemment. Contrairement au cas précédent, le sens de rotation est ici positif. Le tracé des vitesses tangentielles (figure 7) montre que cette rotation en bloc est en moyenne légèrement décentrée par rapport à l'axe de la conduite. Les tracés des vitesses axiales (figure 8) indiquent la forte dissymétrie de l'écoulement. Dans cette section, le maximum de vitesse est obtenu sur le rayon situé à 180°. Enfin la représentation des iso-taux de fluctuation de vitesse montre des niveaux très importants pouvant atteindre 45 % de la vitesse débitante. L'origine de ces fluctuations de vitesse sera étudiée par la suite.

Les caractéristiques d'ensemble de l'écoulement dans cette section sont répertoriées dans le tableau suivant:

| $\gamma$ (°) | S | $\alpha_s$(°) | d(%) | $|\tau|$ (%) |
|---|---|---|---|---|
| 0 | 0,4156 | 31,94 | -69,74 | 32,57 |
| 45 | 0,4656 | 34,93 | -50,24 | 34,41 |
| 90 | 0,4280 | 32,72 | -7,74 | 35,27 |
| -45 | 0,4080 | 31,47 | -51,58 | 32,85 |

Ce tableau permet de préciser les caractéristiques générales de cet écoulement:
- Rotation forte dans le sens positif (de l'ordre de 33° en moyenne)
- Écoulement fortement dissymétrique
- Taux de turbulence homogène sur les 4 diamètres de l'ordre de 33%

En comparant avec les résultats obtenus précédemment, on voit que ces deux écoulements sont très différents l'un de l'autre, bien que les conditions de réglage soient identiques. A ces différences, on doit ajouter l'existence dans le deuxième cas la présence d'instabilités basses fréquences qui seront étudiées par la suite.

#### x = 5D

Les résultats peuvent se résumer de la façon suivante:

- Les profils d'angle de rotation et de vitesse axiale ont des allures similaires à celles observées à 3D tout en ayant subi une rotation positive de 112°
- Les niveaux des perturbations diminuent. Ce dernier point est illustré plus nettement dans le tableau suivant:

| $\gamma$ (°) | S | $\alpha_s$(°) | d(%) | $|\tau|_l$(%) |
|---|---|---|---|---|
| 0 | 0,3835 | 29,91 | 26,83 | 23,55 |
| 45 | 0,3629 | 28,57 | -14,78 | 25,76 |
| 90 | 0,3680 | 28,89 | -45,83 | 25,82 |
| -45 | 0,3603 | 28,39 | 45,96 | 26,75 |

Le déplacement angulaire du maximum de vitesse est dû à un mouvement d'hélice engendré par le rotation d'écoulement. Ce déplacement angulaire $\Delta\theta$ peut être calculé à partir de la relation suivante faisant intervenir l'angle rotation local $\alpha$ au niveau du maximum de vitesse, la position radiale de ce maximum et de la distance séparant les deux sections:

$$\Delta\theta(°) = \frac{180}{\pi} \cdot \frac{\Delta x}{r_{max} \cdot tg\left(\frac{\pi}{2} - \alpha\right)}$$

Dans le cas étudié pour lequel $r_{max}$ est égal à 0,04 mètre, $\Delta x$ à 0,2 mètre et $\alpha$ à 23,5°, on obtient un déplacement angulaire théorique $\Delta\theta$ de 125° qui est proche de la valeur mesurée (112°). La rotation s'amortissant entre les deux sections considérées, nous avons pris une valeur moyenne pour $\alpha$.

$x = 7D$

Des conclusions identiques peuvent être tirées à partir des résultats obtenus à 7D et présentés dans le tableau suivant:

| $\gamma$ (°) | S | $\alpha_s$(°) | d(%) | $|\tau|_l$(%) |
|---|---|---|---|---|
| 0 | 0,3195 | 25,60 | 14,82 | 20,73 |
| 45 | 0,3210 | 25,71 | 39,34 | 20,52 |
| 90 | 0,3380 | 26,87 | 29,62 | 18,91 |
| -45 | 0,3100 | 24,93 | -13,19 | 18,48 |

Comme entre 3D et 5D, on observe entre 5D et 7D un déplacement angulaire du maximum de l'ordre de 112,5°. En effectuant le même calcul que précédemment, on trouve un déplacement théorique de 99°.

### Évolution longitudinale des paramètres d'ensemble

Pour compléter ces résultats une étude de l'évolution longitudinale de cet écoulement a été réalisée plus en aval. Afin de limiter le nombre des essais, les profils n'ont été mesurés que sur un seul diamètre ($\theta$=0°). Cette simplification se justifie par le fait que, dans les trois sections précédemment étudiées, les valeurs d'angle de swirl moyen et de taux de turbulence obtenues sur les différents diamètres sont comparables

Pour l'écoulement giratoire, on note une décroissance continue des paramètres caractéristiques. A 38 D l'angle de rotation moyen n'est plus que de 6°. Si l'on compare l'atténuation de cette rotation obtenue ici avec celles mesurée par différents auteurs, on obtient des résultats comparables[2]. En particulier en prenant une loi d'atténuation de type exponentiel:

$$A = A_0 \cdot Exp\left(-\lambda \cdot \frac{x}{D}\right)$$

où $A_0$ est la valeur initiale de A et $\lambda$ le coefficient d'atténuation, on obtient une valeur de $\lambda$ égale à 0,053 alors qu'en utilisant les travaux de Baker et Sayre[6], on trouve 0,0528.

### Etude des phénomène instationnaires

#### Visualisations:

Des visualisations ont été réalisées pour des distances situées respectivement à 6D et 16D du détendeur. Sur la figure 10, on observe nettement une rotation de l'écoulement décentrée par rapport à l'axe de la conduite.A 6 D du détendeur, l'analyse des bandes vidéo montre d'une part des mouvements importants du centre de rotation dans la conduite et d'autre part la disparition fréquente de cette rotation. En fait cette rotation n'apparaît que de façon intermittente. Plus en aval, à 16D on observe toujours un déplacement du centre de rotation mais avec des amplitudes plus faibles que précédemment. Dans ce cas l'écoulement est plus stable et les intermittences sont moins marquées.

*Analyse spectrale*

Ces traitements mettent en évidence en certains points, l'existence d'une fréquence caractéristique proche de 4 Hz. La répartition du coefficient de qualité $C_Q$ dans la conduite (figure 11) permet de constater que l'énergie de cette instabilité n'est pas homogène dans toute la section considérée ce qui exclue un phénomène de pulsation.

A 3D, la qualité du signal est maximale à proximité de l'axe ainsi que prés de la paroi sur le rayon situé à -90°. A 5D, on retrouve toujours un maximum prés de l'axe mais le deuxième maximum a tourné de 225°. Ce déplacement angulaire est bien plus important que celui observé sur le maximum de vitesse axiale. Néanmoins, en reprenant le précédent calcul avec un angle local de rotation égal à 40,15° et un rayon moyen de 0,035 m, on obtient un déplacement angulaire de 276,14°.

Entre ces deux sections on peut noter une augmentation de la qualité du signal qui peut être contradictoire avec les évolutions correspondantes du taux de fluctuation. Ceci peut s'expliquer par une diminution de l'intermittence et donc d'un accroissement de la qualité du signal.

A 7D on retrouve un maximum prés de l'axe. De nouveau on observe un déplacement du deuxième maximum avec une rotation de 120° et un rapprochement vers l'axe. Entre 5D et 7D, la qualité du signal diminue.

*Interprétation des résultats*

Les résultats obtenus indiquent que l'instabilité détectée à partir des signaux de vitesse est due au mouvement du centre de rotation de l'écoulement. A partir d'une analyse qualitative des visualisations, on voit en effet que ce centre tourne lui-même dans la conduite avec une fréquence de l'ordre 4Hz soit 12 à 13 images consécutives. A 6D, ce mouvement se produit entre 180° et 225°. Sur les représentations du coefficient de qualité, cette position est placée entre le maximum obtenu à 5D (135°) et celui obtenu à 7D (255°).

La rotation d'ensemble de l'écoulement n'étant pas stable, des phénomènes d'intermittence apparaissent.

$\underline{T_D = 2 ; Q = 200 \text{ m}^3/\text{h}}$

### *Caractéristiques moyennes de l'écoulement*

Les résultats obtenus pour ce point de fonctionnement du détendeur sont récapitulés dans les trois tableaux suivants:

- 3D

| $\gamma$ (°) | S | $\alpha_s$(°) | d(%) | $|\tau|_t$(%) |
|---|---|---|---|---|
| 0 | -0,0238 | -2,042 | -20,47 | 22,73 |
| 45 | -0,0247 | -2,123 | -15,98 | 23,14 |
| 90 | -0,024 | -2,060 | -3,32 | 23,82 |
| -45 | -0,0217 | -1,460 | -14,10 | 23,38 |

- 5D

| $\gamma$ (°) | S | $\alpha_s$(°) | d(%) | $|\tau|_t$(%) |
|---|---|---|---|---|
| 0 | -0,0159 | -1,39 | 2,71 | 15,68 |
| 45 | -0,0201 | -1,73 | 0,20 | 15,97 |
| 90 | -0,0178 | -1,51 | -2,73 | 16,05 |
| -45 | -0,0162 | -1,39 | -6,78 | 15,80 |

- 7D

| $\gamma$ (°) | S | $\alpha_s$(°) | d(%) | $|\tau|$(%) |
|---|---|---|---|---|
| 0 | -0,0236 | -2,03 | -0,32 | 12,06 |
| 45 | -0,0222 | -1,91 | -3,16 | 11,94 |
| 90 | -0,0242 | -2,08 | -5,78 | 11,93 |
| -45 | -0,0238 | -2,04 | -2,05 | 12,04 |

Pour ce point de fonctionnement, on peut observer que:
- La giration est très faible et qu'elle n'évolue pas de façon significative entre 3D et 7D.
- Les niveaux de fluctuation, forts en sortie du détendeur, décroissent rapidement
- Une faible dissymétrie est présente sur les profils de vitesse axiale. Celle-ci s'atténue entre 3D et 5D.

De plus, pour ce point de fonctionnement, aucune instabilité de l'écoulement n'a été observée.

CONCLUSIONS

Le travail présenté concerne l'étude de l'écoulement à l'aval d'un détendeur. On montre la complexité de cet 'écoulement qui combine une rotation du fluide avec une modification de la répartition de la vitesse dans la veine avec, dans certain cas la présence d'une instabilité basse vitesse. Les difficultés rencontrées lors du déroulement de cette étude indiquent le caractère très instable de ce détendeur, surtout à bas débit, avec dans certain cas l'apparition de phénomènes d'hystérésis.

Pour les trois conditions expérimentales présentées, une quantification de l'écoulement a été faite à partir de paramètres globaux décrivant la rotation, la dissymétrie et le niveau de turbulence.

Dans le premier cas ($T_D$ = 2 et Q = 20 m³/h), des angles de rotation et des niveaux de dissymétrie faibles sont obtenus. Néanmoins les niveaux de turbulence sont élevés.

Pour les mêmes conditions au niveau du détendeur ($T_D$ = 2 et Q = 20 m³/h) on voit apparaître, en modifiant la procédure d'obtention du taux de détente, un écoulement totalement différent présentant une forte rotation, une dissymétrie importante et la présence d'une instabilité. Lors de ces essais la rotation a changée de sens par rapport au premier cas traité. Les mesures réalisées dans trois sections montrent que la mise en rotation de l'écoulement entraîne un mouvement angulaire du maximum de vitesse. L'étude la propagation de cette perturbation à l'aval du détendeur montre son amortissement. Ainsi, entre 3D et 38D l'angle moyen de rotation passe de 32° à 6° et le niveau de turbulence de 32% à 11%. L'évolution de cette rotation est comparable à celle observée par d'autres auteurs étudiant l'évolution de rotations calibrées dans des conduites rectilignes. L'analyse de l'instabilité de l'écoulement révèle qu'elle est liée à un mouvement du centre de rotation dans la veine et qu'à proximité du détendeur, cette rotation présente des intermittences.

Le dernier cas traité correspond à un débit plus important ($T_D$ = 2 et Q = 200 m³/h). Dans ce cas la rotation et la dissymétrie sont faibles et aucune instabilité n'apparaît en sortie du détendeur.

Les résultats qui viennent d'être présentés sont une contribution à la connaissance des écoulements réels présents dans une canalisation industrielle. Néanmoins les caractéristiques d'ensemble de ces écoulements sont fortement dépendants de la géométrie du détendeur. Aussi, pour approfondir nos connaissances, il est nécessaire de tester d'autres détendeurs. Ceci fait l'objet d'un premier programme de recherche en cours de réalisation.

De plus, l'association entre le détendeur et le compteur se fait en général par l'intermédiaire d'un ensemble de coudes et de longueurs droites. Au passage de ces divers éléments, l'écoulement va être modifié. Il est donc nécessaire de connaître comment s'effectue cette propagation. Ceci fait l'objet d'un deuxième sujet de recherche lui aussi en cours d'exécution.

REFERENCES

1. Benzoni, Cornil, Etude et réalisation d'un appareil pour la régulation de pression et le comptage des gaz, Congrés ATG 1980.
2. Malard L, Contribution à l'étude expérimentale des écoulements giratoires en conduite. Influence d'une vanne de laminage sur différents débitmètres, Thése de doctorat de l'ENSAE, Toulouse, 1993.
3. Malard L, Heid G, Gajan P, Strzelecki A, Development of a self acting system in order to characterize hightly pertubed pipe flows, Flomeko'93, Seoul, Corea, October 1993.
4. Laneville A,, Strzelecki A, Gajan P, Hébrard P, On the signal quality of a vortex flowmeter exposed to swirling flows, Flow Measurement and Instrumentation, 1, PP 5-8,1989.
5. Strzelecki A, Gajan P, Malard L, Donat D, Bosch M, Investigation of the influence of a pressure reducer placed upstream of a turbine meter, 3rd International symposium on fluid flow measurement, San Antonio, USA, March 1995
6. Baker D.W, Sayre C L, Decay of swirling turbulent flow of incompressible fluids in long pipes. Flow its measurement and control in Science and Industry, 1, PP 301-312, 1974

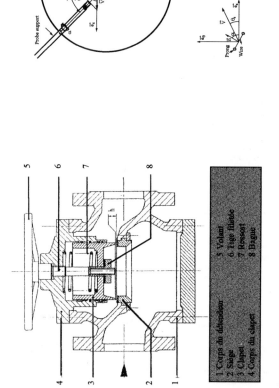

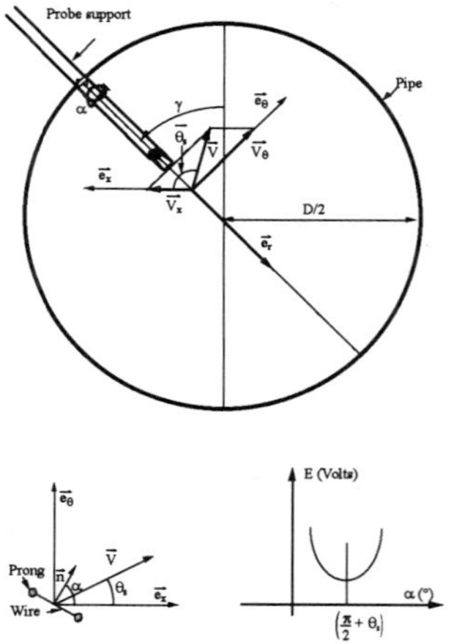

Figure 3: Principe de la mesure d'angle de rotation

Figure 1: Schéma de la vanne de laminage représentative du détendeur

1 Corps du détendeur    5 Volant
2 Siège                 6 Tige filetée
3 Clapet                7 Ressort
4 Corps du clapet       8 Bague

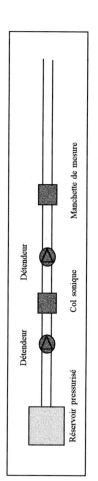

Figure 2: Schéma du banc

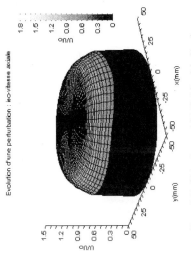

Evolution d'une perturbation : iso-vitesse axiale

Figure 5: Profil de vitesse axial à 3D à l'aval du détendeur
TD=2 ; Q = 20m³/h ; 1ère configuration d'essai

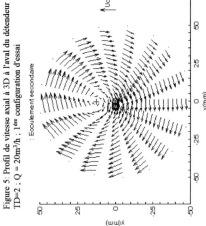

: Ecoulement secondaire

Figure 7: Ecoulement secondaire à 3D à l'aval du détendeur
TD=2 ; Q = 20m³/h ; 2ème configuration d'essai

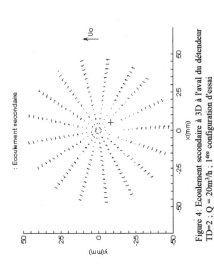

: Ecoulement secondaire

Figure 4: Ecoulement secondaire à 3D à l'aval du détendeur
TD=2 ; Q = 20m³/h ; 1ère configuration d'essai

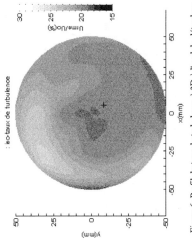

: iso-taux de turbulence

Figure 6: Profil de taux de turbulence à 3D à l'aval du détendeur
TD=2 ; Q = 20m³/h ; 1ère configuration d'essai

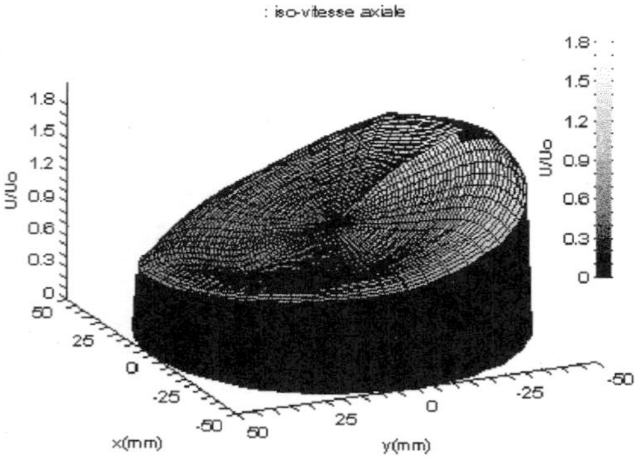

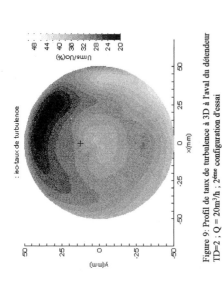

: iso-taux de turbulence

Figure 9: Profil de taux de turbulence à 3D à l'aval du détendeur
TD=2 ; Q = 20m³/h ; 2ème configuration d'essai

coefficient de qualité : iso-taux de turbulence

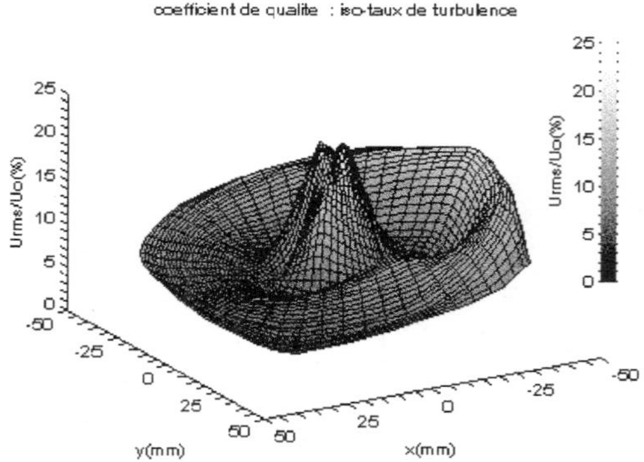

Figure 11: Coefficient de qualité à 3D à l'aval du détendeur
TD=2 ; Q = 20m³/h ; 2ème configuration d'essai

: iso-vitesse axiale

Figure 8: Profil de vitesse axial à 3D à l'aval du détendeur
TD=2 ; Q = 20m³/h ; 2ème configuration d'essai

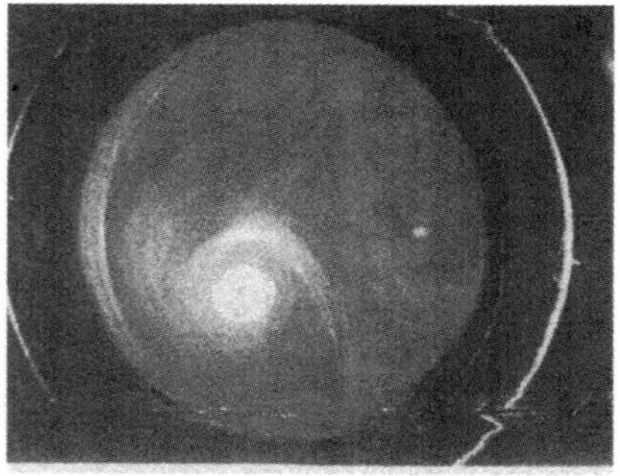

Figure 10: Visualisation d'écoulement à 3D à l'aval du détendeur
TD=2 ; Q = 20m³/h ; 2ème configuration d'essai

PERTURBATION TESTS ON TURBINE METERS

ESSAIS DE PERTURBATION AVEC DES COMPTEURS A TURBINE

Dr. B. Harbrink
Mr. W. Kerkmann
Ruhrgas AG, Germany

Dr. P. van der Kam
Mr. G. Nobel
Gasunie, The Netherlands

Ms. D. King
Ms. C. Trimel
Gaz de France, France

Mr. J.L. De Schutter
Distrigaz, Belgium

Dr. V.M. Cannizzo
Snam, Italy

ABSTRACT

The aim of the tests conducted as part of a GERG project was to eliminate uncertainties concerning the procedure for perturbation tests, in order to be able to set out more detailed requirements in ISO 9951. According to the results obtained, testing under only atmospheric conditions is adequate, provided that they are performed for both clockwise (CW) and counterclockwise (CCW) swirl. Also, the tests must be carried out on meters of different sizes. Apart from the bottom part of the measuring range of the meter, the high-level perturbation unit seems to cover the axial flow pressure reducer examined. This, however, must not be taken to apply to all types of pressure reducers. Further, the tests showed that the flow disturbance downstream of the high-level unit does not represent the worst of all flow disturbances found under operating conditions in the field.

RESUME

Les investigations effectuées dans le cadre d'un projet du GERG ont eu pour objectif de lever des incertitudes en ce qui concerne les essais de perturbation pour pouvoir rédiger de façon plus claire la partie de la norme ISO 9951 qui traite de ces essai. Les résultats obtenus montrent qu'il est suffisant de faire les essais à des conditions atmosphériques, mais qu'il est nécessaire de mesurer aussi bien dans les conditions où la torsion va dans le sens des aiguilles d'une montre que dans les conditions où la torsion va en sens inverse des aiguilles d'une montre. Il ne suffit pas non plus d'examiner un seul diamètre de compteur. Le détendeur de flux axial examiné est apparemment couvert par la perturbation à haut niveau, exception faite dans l'étendu inférieur de mesurage. Les résultat ne valent cependant pas pour tous les types de compteur, car la perturbation de l'écoulement en aval de l'unité de perturbation à haut niveau ne s'avérait pas comme le pire cas de toutes les perturbations rencontrées dans la pratique.

INTRODUCTION

Flow meters are calibrated under ideal inlet conditions, i.e. with a relatively long length of pipework upstream of the flow meter. These conditions are, however, often impossible to achieve in installations and it is therefore desirable to assess the extent of the measuring errors caused by the installation.

ISO 9951 on turbine flow meters describes a perturbation test for type approval testing, with which the length of the minimum straight upstream pipe section is to be defined. Observing this minimum length during operation is to ensure that the systematic deviations caused by the installation are always within one third of the maximum permissible error limits, irrespective of the type of perturbation used.

This makes it necessary for the type of perturbation unit to be used in accordance with the standard to represent the worst case conditions, i.e. must it cover all perturbations to be expected in a measuring station. By the time measurements started, there was still no absolute proof that this requirement had been met. Moreover, there were other questions surrounding the suitability of the perturbation tests described in the standard concerning the sensitivity of the meters for disturbed flows:

• The tests were performed with air at atmospheric pressure. Does this allow making assumptions for natural gas under higher pressures, or do the perturbation tests have to be performed at high pressures?

• Does the sensitivity change for different diameters?

• Because of their different designs and hence different flow mechanics, not all meter types react to a flow perturbation in the same way. How wide is the range of resulting deviations?

The aim of the measurements performed by GERG was therefore to determine the influence of flow perturbations produced by the ISO unit on downstream turbine flow metering also for higher pressures, for two different meter sizes and for several models. The objective was to check the standard in terms of its applicability under the above conditions. Testing also included a pressure reducer to examine to what extent the high level (HL) version of the ISO perturbation unit covers this very complex flow perturbation which causes steady and unsteady effects.

Where the tests cover all of the actual operating conditions of a measuring station as intended in ISO 9951, they are to be incorporated into the new standard as part of the type approval tests. Where the tests do not cover the actual operating conditions, they must be changed accordingly to include other perturbation units.

TEST PROGRAM

Testing included

• four different meter types of different manufacturers, tested for their sensitivity for disturbed flows downstream of the ISO perturbation unit,

• two diameters (DN150 and DN300) to establish whether it is sufficient to test only one meter size for type approval,

• three different pressures (atmospheric pressure, 10 bar and 25 bar) to determine possible differences in meter response,

• two distances (2 D and 5D),

• the four DN150 meter makes at a distance of 2D/5D downstream of the pressure reducer, to allow comparison of the results with the high-level perturbation; two different inlet/outlet pressure ratios were selected.

Apart from the meter behaviour, the velocity profiles for all installation positions and measuring conditions were to be determined using a hot-wire anemometer developed by Gaz de France for HP applications. By defining the inlet flow in this way, a relation between different meter behaviours and different meter inlet designs was to be determined. According to the standard, the perturbation unit consisted of

• a 5 x DN 1 long inlet pipe with a DN 1 diameter,

• two 90 ° bends arranged in different planes with DN 1 diameters and a bend radius of 1 x DN 1,

• a concentric diffuser (DN 1 to DN) with a length of DN.

For the DN150 meters, DN 1 equalled 100 mm; for the DN300 meters, DN 1 equalled 250 mm.

The high level (HL) perturbation differed from the low level (LL) perturbation in that it had an additional half pipe area plate installed between the two bends opening towards the outside radius of the first bend (Figure 1).

The pressure reducer was a RMG 512 pressure reducer without internal flow deflection.

The load points at which the error curves were to be plotted had been fixed in advance. Repeatability was determined from a total of 10 measuring points, each for minimum flow ($Q_{min}$ and 0.7 of the maximum flow ($Q_{max}$).

The locations of the traverse lines for the profile measurements in their horizontal and vertical positions and the 45°diagonals were also fixed. Measurements were performed at 29 positions on each traverse. In addition to the axial velocity, the swirl angle and a degree of turbulence (intensity) was also measured.

TEST PROCEDURE

Testing was divided between the GERG partners involved as follows:

- Gasunie examined the influence of the LL/HL ISO perturbation units on the DN150 meters.

- Ruhrgas performed the same tests on the DN300 meters.

- Gaz de France provided the flow profiles of the tests on both meter sizes at both distances and for both the LL and the HL unit.

- Distrigaz provided the ISO perturbation units for both meter sizes (two of each) and arranged transportation between the test sites. Two perturbation units of each size were required because both Ruhrgas and Gasunie had to bring the pipe moved sideways by the installation of the perturbation unit back in line with the rest of the piping and made use of this situation by testing another meter further downstream (Figures 2 and 3).

- Snam was the sponsor for the DN150 tests downstream of the pressure reducer. These tests were performed by Gasunie with regard to downstream meter behaviour, and by Gaz de France as regards measurement of the resulting velocity profiles.

The profile measurements performed by Gaz de France at 10 and 25 bar were conducted at the Ruhrgas test rig in Lintorf, while the 1 bar profile measurements were carried out on the Alfortville test rig. Gasunie used the test rig in Groningen. For the 1 bar measurements, Gasunie retained NMI (Nederlands Meetinstituut) while Ruhrgas commissioned PTB (Physikalisch-Technische Bundesanstalt).

For the tests, the meter manufacturers provided two models from their current production programmes. Only manufacturer I provided a new prototype fitted with an additional perforated inlet plate. The perturbation units and the 2 DN and 3 DN spool pieces used as minimum upstream straight lengths were produced by the same manufacturer to ANSI 600 RF SCH 40 (DN150) and to ANSI RF 600 XS (DN300). Gaz de France, on the other hand, had used ANSI 600 RF SCH 80 for fabrication of its flow profile spool piece (including the 2 DN spool piece). This resulted in the following diameter differences:

| Meter make | Internal diameter, $D_i$, of the meter inlet/the cartridge | |
|---|---|---|
| I | 152.4 mm | 286.0 mm |
| II | 148.5 mm | 300.0 mm |
| III | 151.7 mm | 299.5 mm |
| IV | 147.0 mm | 300.0 mm |
| | Internal diameter at outlet flange | |
| IPU | 154.8 mm | 297.3 mm |
| Profile measuring unit | 146.46 mm | 288.84 mm |

This meant that for the DN150 meters, the internal diameter immediately upstream of the meters always changed towards smaller diameters while for the DN300 meters it always changed towards larger internal diameters (with one exception). This source of additional influence on the meters can never be fully excluded during the perturbation tests and makes intercomparisons between the individual series of measurements more difficult.

For the DN300 profile measurements, the internal diameter difference was compensated by a ring, without this having any significant effect on the results of the measurements.

RESULTS FOR DN300 METERS

In its low-pressure tests, PTB examined the meters individually downstream of a unit, first installed to produce a clockwise and then a counterclockwise swirl. On the Ruhrgas test rig, meters II and III were installed downstream of unit I in the position 1, producing a counterclockwise swirl while meters I and IV were installed downstream of unit II in the position 2 (producing a clockwise swirl). Meters I and IV were subsequently also tested in position 1 (meter III only for the LL unit in the downstream position).

There is no real difference between the perturbation tests carried out at 1 bar and those performed at high pressures (10 and 25 bar). Meter behaviour is practically the same. The only difference is the following: at 10 and 25 bar, the deviations caused by the load are almost constant whereas under atmospheric conditions this only applies to meters I and III while on meters II and IV, deviations for clockwise swirl on the one hand and for counterclockwise swirl on the other drift further apart for increasing loads.

Meter I with the perforated plate in the inlet is by far the best meter, remaining within the $\pm0.33$ % tolerance under all test conditions. Meter II showed the poorest results, with deviations for the HL version at a distance of 2 DN of up to - 1.5 % for counterclockwise swirl and as much as 1.4 % for clockwise swirl.

With deviations in a band of $\pm0.33$ % to $\pm0.5$ %, the results obtained from meter III are only just acceptable. Other than that, the error curves recorded for meters II and III were as expected, i.e. with a negative shift for the counterclockwise swirl and a positive shift for the clockwise swirl, and with a higher total for the HL version than for the LL version. There was only one exception: at a distance of 2 DN, the HL curve of meter III for counterclockwise swirl showed a positive shift for all three test pressures.

The behaviour of meter IV was most strange: although the turbine wheel rotated in the clockwise direction, as do the other meters, it responded to a counterclockwise swirl with a positive shift; this was most pronounced at low pressure, while at 10 and 25 bar it could only clearly be observed for the HL version. For the clockwise swirl, only the 2 DN distance for the HL version does not produce a negative shift; again this applies to all test pressures (Figure 4).

Summary

While meter I met the $\pm0.33$ % criterion defined in ISO 9951 in all cases examined, meters III and IV met this requirement for only some configurations. Meter II failed altogether.

INSTALLATION OF PERTURBATION UNIT ON A TEST RIG

On the PTB test rig, the air is drawn into the pipe immediately upstream of the meter tested (suction mode). If the perturbation unit is not fitted with an additional straight inlet pipe, the velocity profile at the inlet of the first bend of the unit after 5 DN 1 has not fully developed. Additional tests with a second 13 DN 1 pipe spool and with a 9 DN spool piece and a reduction to DN 1 immediately upstream of the perturbation unit did not produce any different meter behaviour. Compared with the flow disturbance caused by the unit, this less-then-ideal inlet profile is negligible.

The standard also does not cover installation of the perturbation unit in a high-pressure test rig, particularly where two perturbation units are to be mounted in series. For the large diameter tests, the first unit was mounted downstream of a 27 DN 1 straight pipe with a Sprenkle flow straightener (DN 300) mounted at the inlet, while the second downstream unit was mounted on the outlet of a 33 DN1 straight pipe. A first alternative test configuration with the DN to DN 1 reducer immediately upstream of the first unit (same overall length of piping) resulted in only slight changes in meter behaviour. In a second alternative configuration, the length of the inlet pipe upstream of the second unit was reduced from 27 DN 1 to 0 DN 1 to examine possible effects on meter behaviour downstream of the second unit caused by inlet flow conditions not fully restored to ideal conditions. Meter I did not react to these overlapping disturbances while meter IV responded with a negative shift in the deviations, which could not be fully accounted for given the contrary behaviour when compared with that in position 1 downstream of unit I. Meter III mounted in position 2 downstream of unit II (and only subjected to the LL version) showed a deviation shift in the correct direction and also a slightly different behaviour, depending whether the LL or the HL version was installed at unit I or whether meter I or meter IV were installed downstream of unit I.

The tests thus showed that apart from the different diameters, a comparison of perturbation test results obtained on different test rigs must also take account of the installation differences. The standard must therefore include a more detailed specification for the installation.

## RESULTS FOR DN 150 METERS

The test configuration at Gasunie differed from that at Ruhrgas in that shorter inlet lengths upstream of the units were compensated by the use of flow straighteners. Apart from that, unit I again produced a counterclockwise swirl while unit II produced a clockwise swirl. In test series 1, the meters were mounted as for the Ruhrgas tests while in test series 2, the meters in positions 1 and 2 were swapped. At NMI, only one unit was used and installed for the individual meters tested as described for test series 1. On the NMI test rig operated on air, the fan is mounted at the test rig inlet pushing the air into the DN 1 meter run through a header. Again, there was the question of what inlet length to choose for the perturbation unit and thus the need for an additional test series.

Also in the small diameter range, meter I is the one least sensitive to the ISO perturbation. For all test conditions, deviations were within the ±0.33 % tolerance; the observed HP error curve gradient due to the pressure drop across the meter calls for improvement by the manufacturer. Meter II did far better than for the large diameter. Under counterclockwise swirl conditions, the deviation total is lower than for clockwise swirl conditions; in all, deviations were within a ±0.5 % tolerance band. The positive/negative systematic deviations were as expected.

For the small diameter, it was meter III that reacted to the counterclockwise swirl with a positive shift of up to 0.6 % (for all test pressures) and to the clockwise swirl with a negative shift of up to 0.4 %. The total of these deviations is greater or equals those of the DN300 tests.

This strange meter behaviour which runs contrary to expectations is not so pronounced for the smaller version of meter IV as it is for the DN300 meter or the DN150 version of meter III. With a positive shift of up to 0.8 %, this behaviour is clearly detectable for counterclockwise swirl under LL and HL conditions at a distance of 2 DN, and with a negative shift of up to 0.4 % it can be observed for a clockwise swirl only under HL conditions at a distance of 2 DN. All other deviations are within a narrow band of ±0.2 % (Figures 5 and 6).

The extra test with an additional 10 DN 1 spool piece upstream of the perturbation unit on the NMI test rig was performed with meter II in a counterclockwise position and meters III and IV in a clockwise position under both LL and HL conditions at a distance of 5 DN. Compared with the original 10 DN 1 inlet section upstream of the perturbation unit, no major differences were observed.

## Summary

In all cases examined, meter I was within the tolerance range of ±0.33 % stipulated by the standard, while meter IV fulfilled this requirement in part, the exception being the test configuration with the HL unit and the 2 DN distance. For meter III, the tolerance limit will have to be increased to ±0.4 % and for meter II to ±0.5 %, because the increase in distance from 2 DN to 5 DN did not result in any improvements. Meter II is within the newly defined tolerance range under all test conditions, while meter III meets the new requirements only in part (exception: HL, 2 DN distance and CCW swirl).

## CONCLUSIONS FROM METER TESTS

- It is not recommended to carry out the perturbation test with only one meter size, particularly when the meter is not fitted with a perforated plate or other flow straighteners in the inlet. Whether the different results obtained for the various sizes are actually due to the meter or the perturbation unit (there were different flow profiles, see Section on Flow Profile Measurements) still needs to be analysed in more detail.

- Counterclockwise swirl does not always mean a negative shift in the indication. Likewise, a clockwise swirl does not always mean a positive shift in the indication. Any such assumptions can already prove to be wrong for the same make with a different diameter. Deviations for CW and CCW swirl are not symmetrical. Examining only one bend configuration can therefore lead to wrong conclusions.

- There is a need to compare the internal inlet parameters of each meter type and size.

- It is sufficient to only perform the test at atmospheric conditions on an air test rig; the HP tests did not produce any significant differences in the results.

 The original test configurations of PTB (suction mode) and NMI (blowing mode) proved to be adequate, i.e. the standard can stipulate that where the suction mode is used, the 5 DN 1 straight length upstream of the first bend of the unit is adequate, while for the blowing mode it must be checked that there is no significantly disturbed profile at the inlet to this bend. In the present case, a straight length of 10 DN 1 upstream of the unit was sufficient.

- The test programme does not have to include the 2 DN distance for meters without a perforated plate/flow straightener in the inlet, if ±0.33 % continues to be the limit for permissible deviations.

FLOW PROFILE MEASUREMENTS

At distances of 2 DN and 5 DN, the velocity profiles were measured downstream of the LL and HL configurations at pressures of 1, 12 and 25 bar. With the exception of DN150 under atmospheric conditions, the unit used for profile measurements produced CCW swirl in all cases. The measurements were made at a flow of 70 % of $Q_{max}$ for DN 300 and of 40 % of $Q_{max}$ for DN 150.

The velocity profile was measured along four traverse lines (45 °, 90 °, 135 °, 180°). Along each traverse, a total of 29 measurements were performed.

At a distance of 2 DN, the mean swirl angles for both sizes are of the same magnitude, for HL conditions they are 50 % (for DN150) and 100 % (for DN300) larger than for LL conditions. At a distance of 5 DN, there is even a rise in the mean swirl angle. This is very pronounced under both LL and HL conditions for DN150, while for DN300 it can only be observed to a limited extent under HL conditions. This fact may have to do with the way the mean value is determined. Pressure does not have any significant influence (Figure 7).

The asymmetry rate, defined as

$$T_a = \frac{(Q)_{r>0} - (Q)_{r<0}}{Q_{tot}}$$ where $(Q)_{r>0}$ is the flow rate calculated for the positive radius,

provides meaningful results as a mean value for the measurements along the four traverse lines because the value drops by half for an increase in the distance from 2 DN to 5 DN (for DN150 and LL, it even drops to one quarter); this is for almost the same starting value at 2 DN for both LL and HL conditions - again irrespective of the pressure. The four asymmetry rates for each traverse indicate in which parts of the cross-section area the velocities are high (maximum values). In this respect, the two sizes behave very differently, both for the initial distribution for the 2 DN distance for both LL and HL, and for the change to the 5 DN distance. The axial flow velocity profiles for the two sizes have different shapes, with their maximum values in the cross-section turned into different positions (last column in Figure 7). This shows a certain dependence on pressure.

The changes in the axial velocity of time are characterised by the fluctuating rate (turbulence degree). This parameter is defined as follows:

$$T_f = \frac{u'}{\overline{u}}$$     where $\overline{u}$ is the mean and u' the fluctuating value (around the mean) of the local axial velocity.
     The same split can be made for the tangential velocity.

This value is reduced for the LL and HL versions and for both diameters by about 1/3 for the change in distance from 2 DN to 5 DN (except at DN300, LL). While for DN150, HL only causes a slightly higher fluctuation than LL, the difference for DN300 is considerable.

PRESSURE REDUCER TESTS

The profile measurements downstream of the RMG 512 axial flow pressure reducer (Figure 8) in the DN150 piping resulted both in a CW swirl and a CCW swirl. Whether the swirl angle has a positive or negative sign depends on the flow rate. For a selected pressure ratio of 1.2 across the reducer, there still was no significant mean swirl angle. At a pressure ratio of 3.0, however, it was (for 0.4 $Q_{max}$ = 400 m³/hr) +8° for a distance of 2 DN and +12° for a distance of 12 DN. At a flow rate of 80 m³/hr and for the same pressure ratio, the angle for 2 DN was -23° and for 20 DN it had still not ebbed. At the 0.4 $Q_{max}$ flow rate, the mean swirl angle for the pressure ratio of 3.0 was a little smaller than the values measured for the HL perturbation at 0.4 of the maximum flow rate. As regards the swirl increase and change of sign for a smaller flow rate, no tests with the perturbation unit have been made which could provide information on any dependence on the flow. Also, it is too early to comment on a dependence on the pressure ratio. Here, further analyses are necessary which must take account of existing flow profiles downstream of pressure reducers.

The asymmetry rates for these pressure reducer tests were smaller than (pressure ratio of 1.2) or comparable to (pressure ratio of 3.0) those for the HL tests. Irrespective of the flow rate and the pressure ratio, the fluctuating rate was slightly higher than in the HL tests. The maximum axial velocity values showed a different distribution across the cross-section than for the HL perturbation. These characteristic parameters for the disturbed flow also need to be examined further (Figure 9).

The response of the four DN150 meter makes to this disturbed pressure reducer flow was not in analogy to the behaviour downstream of the HL perturbation: For loads smaller than or equal to 0.15 $Q_{max}$, in one case for loads smaller than 0.1 $Q_{max}$, all four meters show a sudden rise in deviations (positive deviations), particularly for the 2 DN distance and a pressure ratio of 3.0. Quite interesting is the fact that a counterclockwise swirl was observed for this measuring range. Apart from this bottom measuring range, meter I proved to be more sensitive than meter II, with meter I being outside the ±0.33 %

tolerance at one load. The deviations for meter III as well as for meter II were within the band stipulated by ISO 9951, while for meter IV, the tolerance band needs to be expanded to $\pm0.5$ %.

Summary

- Apart from the measured peak in the deviation at 0.1 $Q_{max}$ (and 0.05 $Q_{max}$), the meter sensitivities observed downstream of the RMG 512 pressure reducer are comparable to those downstream of the HL perturbation. For higher flow rates, the HL perturbation unit apparently also covers this reducer. The analysis of the velocity profile will have to show why the abnormal deviations occur for smaller flow rates.

- Even the axial flow pressure reducer examined produced considerable swirl. Hence, there is an urgent need for more information on the pressure reducers used today and the flow disturbances they produce.

- The current status of investigations does not allow establishing a correlation between meter behaviour downstream of the HL unit and downstream of a pressure reducer.

ACKNOWLEDGEMENTS

The authors wish to thank all those who contributed to the success of this project, either by discussion or by performing work.

REFERENCES

ISO 9951 - Measurement of Gas Flow in Closed Conduits - Turbine Meters, 1993

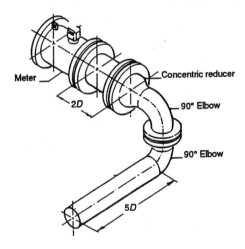

*ISO 9951 configuration for low level pertur-*
*bation tests*

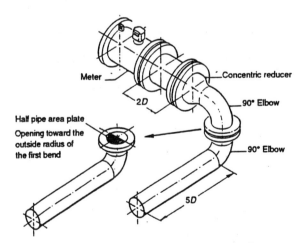

*ISO 9951 configuration for high level pertur-*
*bation tests*

# Fig. 1:        ISO Perturbation Unit

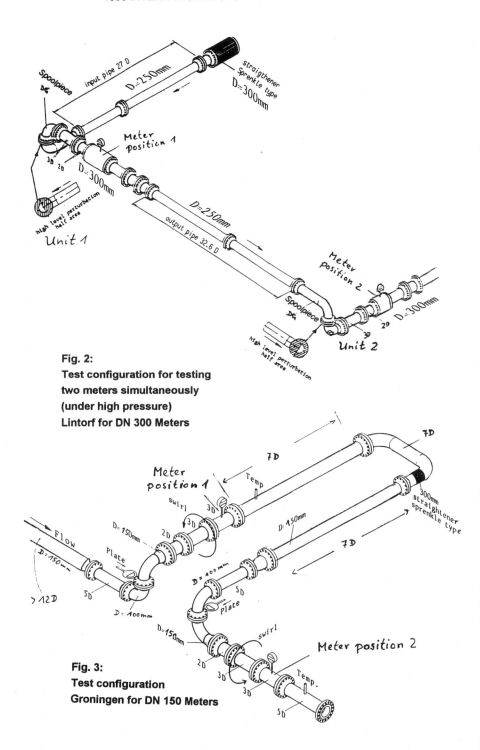

**Fig. 2:**
**Test configuration for testing**
**two meters simultaneously**
**(under high pressure)**
**Lintorf for DN 300 Meters**

**Fig. 3:**
**Test configuration**
**Groningen for DN 150 Meters**

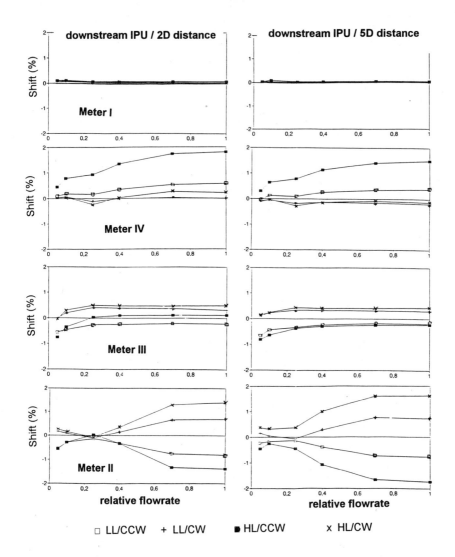

Fig. 4α :
DN 300 Meter behaviour downstream IPU
for atmospheric conditions

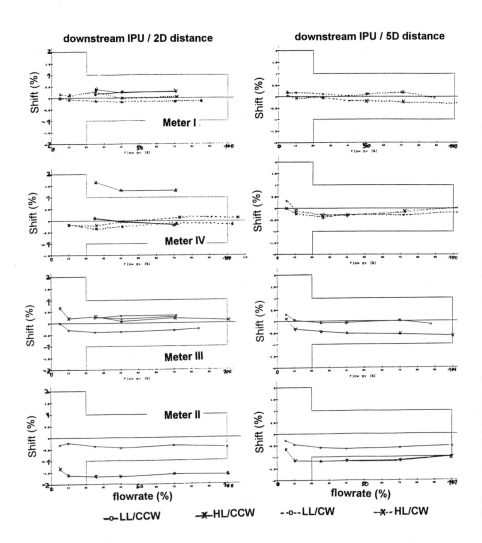

Fig. 4b :
DN 300 Meter behaviour downstream IPU
for 10 bar (as an example)

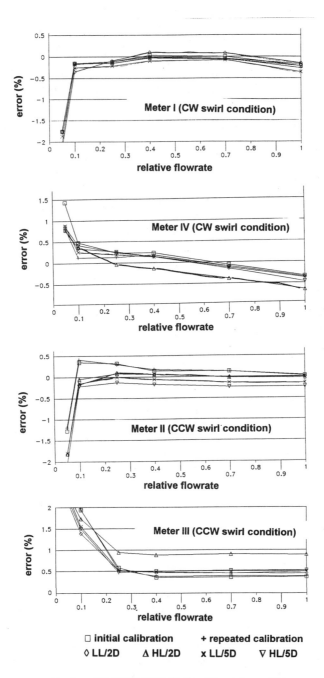

□ initial calibration    + repeated calibration
◊ LL/2D    Δ HL/2D    x LL/5D    ∇ HL/5D

Fig. 5:    DN 150 Meter behaviour downstream IPU
for atmospheric conditions

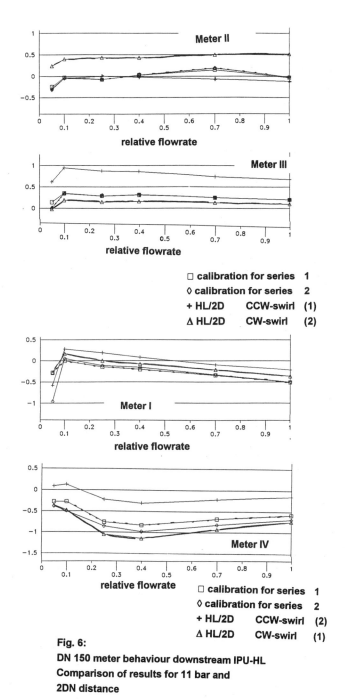

Fig. 6:

DN 150 meter behaviour downstream IPU-HL
Comparison of results for 11 bar and
2DN distance

| Config. | Distance | Direction | Pressure | Swirl (°) | Fluctuation Rate (%) | Asymmetry Rate (%) | Scheme |
|---|---|---|---|---|---|---|---|
| LL | 2D | CCW | LP | -6 | 18 | 21 | |
| LL | 2D | CCW | 12 | -6 | 18 | 23 | |
| LL | 2D | CCW | 25 | -6 | 18 | 22 | |
| LL | 5D | CCW | LP | -5 | 15 | 12 | |
| LL | 5D | CCW | 12 | -6 | 17 | 11 | |
| LL | 5D | CCW | 25 | -4 | 16 | 7 | |
| HL | 2D | CCW | LP | -11 | 31 | 23 | |
| HL | 2D | CCW | 12 | -12 | 29 | 29 | |
| HL | 2D | CCW | 25 | -11 | 34 | 25 | |
| HL | 5D | CCW | LP | -13 | 20 | 13 | |
| HL | 5D | CCW | 12 | -14 | 20 | 15 | |
| HL | 5D | CCW | 25 | -15 | 21 | 15 | |

Fig. 7b
Flow Profile Measurements in a DN 300 Pipe Downstream
of the Perturbation Unit

| Config. | Distance | Direction | Pressure | Swirl (°) | Fluctuation Rate (%) | Asymmetry Rate (%) | Scheme |
|---|---|---|---|---|---|---|---|
| LL | 2D | CW | LP | 6 | 28 | 27 | |
| LL | 2D | CCW | 12 | -8 | 31 | 28 | |
| LL | 2D | CCW | 25 | -7 | 30 | 27 | |
| LL | 5D | CW | LP | 7 | 18 | 7 | |
| LL | 5D | CCW | 12 | -10 | 20 | 7 | |
| LL | 5D | CCW | 25 | -10 | 20 | 7 | |
| HL | 2D | CW | LP | 9 | 33 | 25 | |
| HL | 2D | CCW | 12 | -12 | 34 | 24 | |
| HL | 2D | CCW | 25 | -11 | 32 | 24 | |
| HL | 5D | CW | LP | 14 | 21 | 14 | |
| HL | 5D | CCW | 12 | -16 | 22 | 13 | |
| HL | 5D | CCW | 25 | -16 | 21 | 17 | |

Fig. 7a
Flow Profile Measurements in a DN 150 Pipe Downstream
of the Perturbation Unit

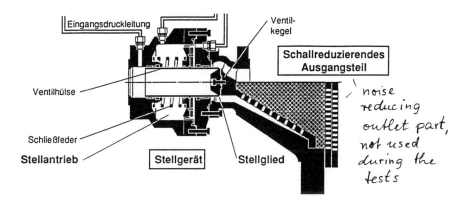

Eingangsdruckleitung

Ventilkegel

**Schallreduzierendes Ausgangsteil**

Ventilhülse

*noise reducing outlet part, not used during the tests*

Schließfeder

**Stellantrieb**     **Stellgerät**     Stellglied

**Fig. 8**
**Pressure Reducer RMG 512**

Q = 400 m³/h

| Config. | Distance | Pressure rate | Pressure | Swirl (°) | Fluctuation rate (%) | Asymmetry rate (%) | Scheme |
|---------|----------|---------------|----------|-----------|----------------------|--------------------|--------|
| REG | 2D | 1.2 | 12 | – 1 | 36 | 19 | |
| REG | 2D | 3.0 | 12 | + 8 | 37 | 29 | |
| REG | 5D | 1.2 | 12 | 0 | 22 | 5 | |
| REG | 5D | 3.0 | 12 | +12 | 25 | 13 | |

Q = 80 m³/h

| REG | 2D | 3.0 | 12 | – 23 | 36 | 26 | |
|-----|-----|-----|-----|------|-----|-----|---|
| REG | 20D | 3.0 | 12 | – 25 | 14 | 4 | |

Q = 400 m³/h

| REG | 20D | 3.0 | 12 | + 7 | 9 | 0 | |
|-----|-----|-----|-----|-----|---|---|---|

**Fig. 9:**     Flow Characterization Downstream of Reducer in DN150 Pipe

III. DISTRIBUTION

### EFFORTS DE RECHERCHE ASSOCIES SUR LA DUREE DE VIE EN SERVICE DES CANALISATIONS DE GAZ EN POLYETHYLENE

### COLLABORATIVE RESEARCH ON THE LONG-TERM SERVICE INTEGRITY OF POLYETHYLENE GAS PIPES

D. Gueugnaut, K. Boytard (Gaz de France) K. Dang Van, A. Ouâkka (Ecole Polytechnique)
M. M. Mamoun (Gas Research Institute)
M. F. Kanninen, C.J. Kuhlman, C.H. Popelar (Southwest Research Institute)
G. Bernardini (Italgas) R. Frassine, M. Rink (Polytecnico de Milano)
B. Berggren ( Vattenfall ), T. Tränkner (Studsvik Material AB)

RESUME

L'utilisation croissante du polyéthylène (PE) pour les réseaux de distribution de gaz, depuis le début des années 60 aux Etats-Unis et depuis la fin des années 70 en France, s'est traduit par la mise en place dans le sous-sol d'un patrimoine financier très important. Afin de rentabiliser au mieux ce patrimoine, il est primordial d'optimiser la gestion des installations en place. Ceci passe notamment par la prédiction de la durée de vie des canalisations en PE.

Une estimation fiable de la durée de vie constitue une aide à la décision en ce qui concerne la rénovation ou le renouvellement des canalisations . Ceci nécessite une connaissance approfondie des mécanismes de vieillissement des résines PE utilisées. Jusque très récemment, les prédictions de durée de vie des canalisations en PE s'appuyaient sur des approches semi-empiriques. Aussi, depuis quelques années, l'accent a été mis sur des recherches plus fondamentales visant à développer des modèles de prédiction plus précis afin d'affiner les pronostics établis antérieurement. Ceci s'est traduit à la fois par des améliorations notables de la fabrication des résines et par la mise en place de nouvelles méthodes analytiques pour les prédictions de durée de vie. De manière à accélérer ces recherches, le Gas Research Institute, Gaz de France, Italgas et Vattenfall ont engagé une collaboration en 1991 dont le but était de mettre en commun certains travaux concernant la prédiction de durée de vie du PE. Le projet "EVOPE" comprenait des échanges de données concernant la détermination des chargements imposés aux tubes enterrés, l'analyse des avaries de terrain, la résistance à la propagation rapide de fissure, le comportement rhéologique ainsi qu'un programme d'essais croisés relatif à la propagation lente de fissure. Cette communication passe en revue les différentes méthodologies développées par les partenaires pour prédire la durée de vie du PE, dans le cadre du projet "EVOPE".

ABSTRACT

The growing use of polyethylene (PE) in the gas distribution networks, initiated in the early 1960's in the United States and in the late 1970's in France, has resulted in the installation of an underground plant having a very important financial asset. To optimize this asset, the management of PE pipeline installations is of great importance. One aspect of pipeline management is the ability to predict reliably of PE pipe lifetimes.

Reliable estimates of gas pipe lifetimes permit making timely decisions about renovation and replacement. This requires an in-depth knowledge of the aging phenomena of the materials. Until recently, lifetime predictions of PE piping were based on semi-empirical approaches. However, in the last few years, emphasis has been put on more fundamental research that is aimed at developing more accurate predictive models and at the refinement of the former predictions. This has resulted both in improvements in the manufacturing of new materials and in the formulation of new analytical methods for pipe life predictions. To further advance this technology, the Gas Research Institute, Gaz de France, Italgas, and Vattenfall agreed in 1991 to conduct a cooperative program directed at sharing and exchanging their development on the lifetime prediction of PE piping. This project referred to as "EVOPE", includes exchanges of data and methodologies on field load determination, field failure examination, rapid crack propagation, rheological behavior, and slow crack growth (SCG) failures of PE gas pipes. This paper reviews the life forecasting methods for PE pipes developed by the participating "EVOPE" organizations.

## INTRODUCTION

Most of the PE gas piping systems are trouble-free, but some field failures occur due to abnormal loadings such as excessive bending, squeeze-off, and defects at fusion joints, or rock impingement. Other than third-party impact failures, PE gas pipe failures have occured after many years of service by a brittle, slow crack growth (SCG) mechanism. Under most operating conditions, SCG failures take place several years after the system has been placed into service. As a result of concern that exists for SCG failures, many different investigations have been conducted by the "EVOPE" partners. These investigations have the common aim of developing test procedures that will quantify SCG mechanisms. In this paper, we present methodologies that have evolved from a collaboration between GDF, GRI, Italgas and Vattenfall. The overall goal is to develop a validated methodology that can effectively forecast SCG failures that limit the life expectancy of PE gas pipes.

## METHODOLOGY

The SCG failures process is governed by the material resistance to SCG and the crack driving force that acts to initiate and propagate an initial defect to a critical size. The SCG resistance of a PE material must be experimentally established. The crack driving force is calculated from the knowledge of the defect size, pipe geometry and internal pipe stresses caused by gas pressure, soil load, settlement-induced bending, external forces, and from manufacturing induced residual stresses. The service life also is strongly influenced by the temperature of the pipe. All of these quantities must be included in a lifetime forecasting methodology. The procedure that has been developed combines laboratory tests, time-temperature shift factors, and a slow crack growth theoretical analysis model. In depth, details of the development including test methods, test data, formulations, analyses, and correlations are presented in several documents published elsewhere [1 - 7].

The two factors -SCG material resistance and crack driving force- need to be quantified in a fundamental fracture mechanics model to forecast the life expectancy of PE pipe.

The SCG characteristics of a PE is quantified using laboratory specimens taken from a pipe. Typically specimens are C-shaped, three or four point bend, Full Notch Creep Test ( F.N.C.T. ) specimen and tensile single edge notched specimens as shown in Figure 1. A constant or dead load is applied to the specimen, and the resulting deflection of the load point is measured and recorded as a function of time. For F.N.C.T. specimens an axial displacement gauge was used in order to record the local displacement right around the notch, and the profile of the opening notch has been evaluated by means of a camera. Furthermore, for CTL specimens a travelling microscope was used to measure deformations and crack length.

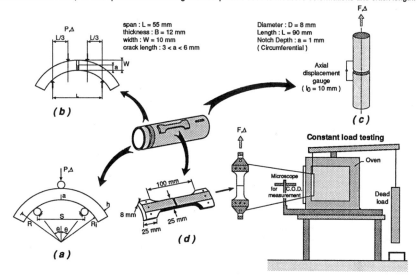

Figure 1 . SCG test specimen configurations used through the EVOPE project. GRI (a); Italgas (b); GDF (c); Vattenfall (d).

## RESULTS AND DISCUSSION

The measured displacement is the sum of the time-dependent creep deformation of the material and the deflection due to crack growth. Prior to crack growth initiation, the displacement is solely due to the time-dependent deformation of the sample. After this time, the displacement is due primarily to the increased compliance resulting from crack growth.

Figures 2 and 3 present some typical SCG curves obtained by means of the Full Notch Creep Test on the one hand and of

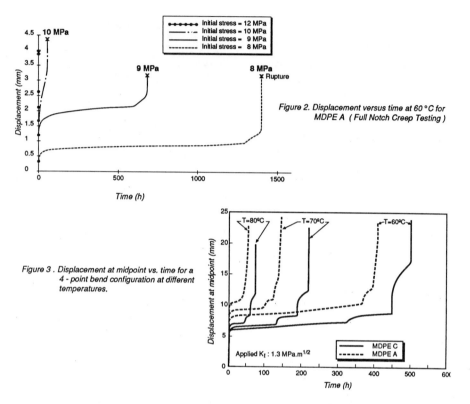

Figure 2. Displacement versus time at 60 °C for
MDPE A  ( Full Notch Creep Testing )

Figure 3 . Displacement at midpoint vs. time for a
4 - point bend configuration at different
temperatures.

the 4-point bend test on the other hand for 2 widespread gas MDPE. From the highest to the lowest initial stresses, fracture of the specimens passes from a ductile mode to a brittle one, representative of brittle field failures. SEM evaluation confirms this. In that way, it can be mentioned that F.N.C.T. leads to a ductile/brittle transition in the creep rupture diagram very similar to that obtained by means of hydrostatic pressure testing, as was already shown [8]. Moreover, the data show that the ranking of the materials tested remains whatever the testing temperature, in the range under study.

### GRI's Approach

Viscoelastic fracture mechanics theory is used to deduce the crack length history and the crack growth rate da/dt from the measured load point displacement record. The crack growth rate is correlated with the crack driving force as measured by the stress intensity factor.

A key element in this methodology arises because PE -like all polymeric materials- exhibits time-dependent behavior. This means that there is a direct connection between time and temperature in the deformation and failure processes that occur in these materials. It has now been established [9] [10] that properties of PE gas pipe materials can be related by universal time-temperature shift factors given by

$$a_T = \exp [ - 0.109 ( T - T_R ) ]$$

$$b_T = \exp [ - 0.0116 ( T - T_R ) ] \tag{1}$$

were temperature $T$ and the arbitrarily chosen reference temperature $T_R$ are expressed in degrees Celsius or Kelvin. Figure 4 shows the effectiveness of this approach by collapsing all the data obtained at different temperatures to that for an arbitrary reference temperature of 40°C. These results clearly show the veracity of these functions for quantifying the influence of temperature on the SCG process.

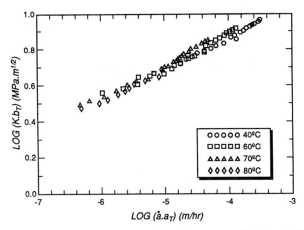

*Figure 4 . Crack Growth Data Collected at Various Temperatures and Shifted to 40°C Using Shift Functions*

It can be seen in Figure 4 that since the data are linear on a log-log plot, the crack growth relation

$$\frac{da}{dt} = AK^m \tag{2}$$

generally describes the relationship between $K$ and the crack growth rate. The constants $A$ and $m$, are determined from the data. Results from multiple SCG tests using the same type of specimen but different load levels ($K$) can be plotted in the form of time-to-initiation of crack growth

$$t_i = BK^n \tag{3}$$

where $B$ and $n$ are determined from a log-log plot. The material parameters required to quantify the initiation of crack growth and propagation are the constants $A$, $B$, $m$ and $n$.

The most obvious source of crack driving force arises from the gas pressure P. Other contributions to the crack driving force arise from residual stresses due to the pipe extrusion process and from soil loads. External forces from rock impingement or settlement can also occur. Based upon the particular service conditions of interest, stress intensity factors are determined for each type of load and are superimposed to arrive at the total $K$.

**Life forecasting model.** The total life time of a PE pipe can be expressed as the sum of the time spent initiating crack growth, which can be determined from Eq. (3), and the time spent in propagating a crack. The latter can be determined by rearranging and integrating Eq. (2). Incorporating the shift functions given by Eq. (1) allows the SCG constants $A$, $B$, $m$ and $n$ to be conveniently obtained at a high temperature (typically 80°C) to accelerate the process. The general form of the life prediction equation, which allows values to be determined at a temperature $T$ to forecast time to failure $t_f$ at a temperature $T_R$ is then

$$t_f = \frac{1}{a_T} \left[ \frac{1}{b_T^m A} \int_{a_0}^{h} \frac{da}{K^m} + b_T^n BK_0^n \right] \tag{4}$$

where $a$ is the crack length, $a_0$ is the initial defect size, $K_0$ is the initial stress intensity factor, and $h$ is the pipe wall thickness with other parameters as already defined. Note that this same methodology is applicable to butt heat fusion and electrofusion joints. Eq. (4) can be used to predict the life expectancy of a pipe for known operating conditions ans initial defect size. Conversely, for specified operating conditions and design life, Eq. (4) determines the size of acceptable initial flaw size for setting quality control standards. It can also be used to establish the derating of a pipe line if a flaw is detected.

**Lifetime forecast using lifespan.** The forecasting of the life expectancy consists of introducing the total stress intensity factor for the operating conditions into Eq. (4) and performing the integration. LIFESPAN software was developed by the Southwest Research Institute, San Antonio, TX as part of a program sponsored by the GRI to automate this integration. Life expectancy predictions can be developed for PE piping components such as pipes, butt fusion joints, and electrofusion joints that are subjected to typical service conditions. Also, it can be used to quantify safe operating lifetimes of gas piping systems subjected to damage resulting from abnormal loadings such as excessive squeeze-offs and rock impingements. The following is a typical example of lifetime prediction and interpretation.

**Effect of defect size.** The safe operating life expectancy of a PE gas pipe as a function of the initial crack length is shown in Figure 5. The total life expectancy is the sum of initiation life and propagation life.

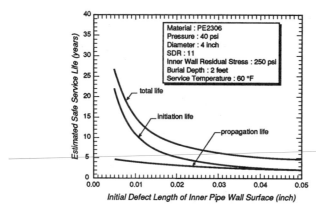

*Figure 5 . Sensitivity of Initial Crack Length on Estimated Pipe Lifetime*

Note that the time spent by the crack propagating through the pipe wall decreases modestly with increasing initial defect size. By contrast the time to initiate crack growth depends strongly upon the initial defect size. For relatively small initial defects, the initiation process dominates the life expectancy whereas for larger defects the time spent in initiation and growth are comparable.

### ITALGAS' Approach

**Rheological behavior.** The creep compliance of the materials, $D(t)$, was determined in uniaxial tension at temperatures between 23°C and 80°C, using compression moulded dumbell specimens 6 mm-thick, by at least one of the three methods :

- directly from creep experiments, $D(t) = \varepsilon(t) / \sigma_0$
- from the relaxation modulus, $E(t) = \sigma(t) / \varepsilon_0$ obtained in stress relaxation experiments,
- from the tangent modulus, $E(t) = d\sigma / d\varepsilon$ obtained from stress-strain curves at constant displacement rate.

From the modulus, $E(t)$, the creep compliance, $D(t)$ was obtained by applying the approximate relationship :

$$D(t) = \frac{\sin(nx)}{nx} \frac{1}{E(t)} \qquad (5)$$

in which n is the slope of the log $(E(t))$ vs. log $t$ curve.

For each material, creep compliance $D$ vs. time - isothermal curves covering 3 decades of time were obtained at small strains (approx. 1 % depending on temperature). By applying the time temperature superposition principle, the master curves and the relevant shift factors could be derived.

Figure 6 shows the master curves for the three materials examined at the reference temperature of 23°C.

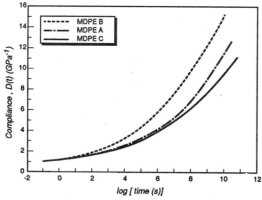

*Figure 6 . Compliance vs. log time for 3 MDPE resins currently used on the European gas market*

**Crack resistance behavior.** Testing was conducted in 4-point bending at three temperatures (60°C, 70°C and 80°C) with applied loads ranging from 4 to 16 kg, on slide-grooved notched specimen (see Fig. 1). From the applied load, the stress intensity factor, $K_I$, was calculated using the well known relationship :

$$K_I = \frac{PL}{BW^2} \, Y \sqrt{a\pi}$$

(6)

in which $P$ is the load, $L$ is the span, $a$ is the crack length, $B$ and $W$ are the specimen thickness and width respectively.

The shape factor, $Y$, was determined experimentally from a set of arc specimens with crack length ranging from 0 to 8 mm, made of aluminum.

Figure 7 shows, as an example, the applied stress intensity factor, $K_{I0}$ , as a function of time to initiate fracture for material A at three testing temperatures. Material MDPE C showed a similar behavior. The third material (MDPE B) is currently under testing and, after approximately 4 months, no crack growth could be detected at any testing temperature.

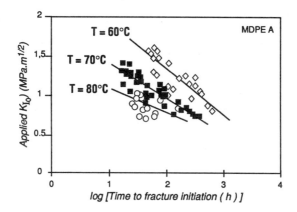

Figure 7 . Applied stress intensity factor vs. fracture initiation time  at different temperatures

$K_{I0}$ values show a linearly decreasing trend with increasing initiation time for the three temperatures examined. Lower $K_{I0}$ values with decreasing slope are also observed for increasing temperature. For material MDPE C slightly shorter initiation time were observed.

**Correlation with viscoelastic characteristics.** No direct correlation with compliance curves derived at small strains could be done. However, an analysis of the fracture results in the frame of viscoelastic fracture theories is currently in progress at Politecnico di Milano.

### GDF's approach.

Gaz de France has chosen to use non "classical" concepts regarding both rheological behavior and crack resistance of PE to approach life expectancy of PE pipes.

**Rheological behavior.** A 5-parameter model has been developed that allows one to describe accurately the visco-elasto-plastic behavior of the material [11] [12]. Figure 8 gives a schematic representation of the behaviorial model.

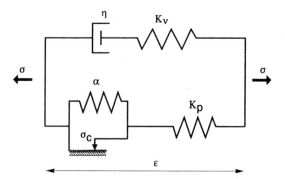

*Figure 8 . Rheological model proposed for PE. η is the viscosity, $K_p$ and $K_v$ the elastic moduli for the plastic and visquous branches, α a hardening parameter, $σ_c$ the threshold value of the stress for the friction block to be actived, σ the stress and ε the strain.*

A very simple 3-step test procedure (traction, relaxation, recovery) makes possible the determination of the 5-parameters set for each material under consideration. Moreover, temperature dependence of these parameters has been established for the range [- 10°C ; + 60°C]. The numerical tool developed on the basis of this methodology allows one to determine accurately the stress-strain state in the material, at any time and temperature.

**Fracture Analysis of the material under different sollicitations.** The achievement of the step described hereabove permits to determine the damage law of the material in relation with the 5-parameters set, on the basis of a "local approach" developed by De Langre, Bui et al. [13] [14]. The approach gives the possibility to relate the damage to the anelastic strain.

The rheological model developed makes it possible to define an anelastic parameter $ε^{ane}$ as follows

$$K : ε^{ane} = k_p : ε^p + K_v : ε^v \tag{7}$$

where $Kp$ and $Kv$ are the elastic moduli for the plastic and visquous mechanisms and $K$ is the sum of $Kp$ and $Kv$. $ε^{an}$ represents the accumulated damage and takes into account the irreversibility effects under sollicitation. The following criterium could be defined

$$Ø = \| ε^{ane} \| - ε_c \tag{8}$$

where $ε_c$ is a temperature-dependent critical value, characteristic of the material.

From the shape of the SCG curves obtained by means of the F.N.C.T., it is possible to define 3 domains corresponding to different processes in the material until rupture and to determine a critical time $t_c$ from which crack initiation occurs, as shown on Figure 9.

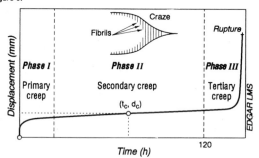

*Figure 9 . GDF's procedure for the quantitative evaluation of the critical values of displacement and time for crack initiation ( Full Notch Creep Test ). Phase I corresponds to the loading of the material. Phase II is characterized by a constant force and a constant strain rate; crack initiation is detected at time $t_c$ and corresponds to the displacement dc. Phase III is characterized by an increase of the strain rate until rupture occurs.*

Time $t_c$ corresponds to a critical value of the displacement, $d_c$ which, in turn, can be associated with the occurence of a damage well concentrated at the crack tip and the propagation of the crack until rupture.

The computer program associated with this procedure gives way to the calculation of the critical anelastic strain at the crack tip on the basis of a finite element modellization of the F.N.C.T. specimen (axisymmetrical calculation) as shown on Figure 10.

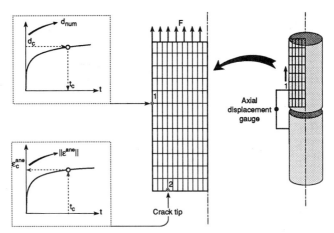

Figure 10 . GDF's procedure for the quantitative evaluation of the threshold of the equivalent anelastic strain at the crack tip ( Full Notch Creep Testing ). Positions 1 et 2 represent respectively the location of the axial displacement gauge and the point at the crack tip.

Work now in progress is devoted to the modellization of the other specimen geometries of the EVOPE collaboration in order to verify the intrinsic character of the critical value $\varepsilon_c$ and to simulate the crack propagation kinematic for different configurations.

### Vattenfall's approach

**SCG failure data :** Different fracture mechanical approaches were investigated for lifetime calculation [15]. As neither o these were easily applicable, due to the non-linear viscoelastic fracture behavior of modern PE resins, a phenomenologica approach was chosen to access the lifetime prediction of PE pipes, and CTL testing was compared with intensive hydrostatic pressure testing on unnotched and prenotched 110 mm - MDPE pipes, as described elsewhere [16].

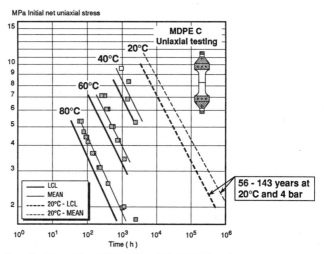

Figure 11 . Extrapolation of SCG data from Vattenfall' C.T.L. testing

The time to failure at different stress levels ( 1 to 10 MPa ) and temperatures ( 40°C, 60°C, 80°C ) were correlated with failure time using a 3-coefficient equation, as follows:

$$log\ t = A + \frac{B}{T} \cdot log\ \sigma + \frac{C}{T} \tag{9}$$

where $t$ is the failure time (h), $T$ is the temperature (K) and $\sigma$ is a constant applied stress ( MPa ). $A$, $B$ and $C$ are empirically calculated constants. The methodology is widely used for lifetime extrapolation of hydrostatic pressure testing data [17] [18]. By following the procedure as described in [17], it is possible to calculate the expective mean failure time and the lower confidence failure time limit at different temperatures and stresses. The results from testing of MDPE C is indicated in Fig. 11.

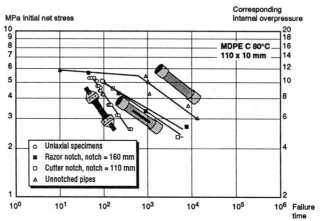

*Figure 12 . Comparison between uniaxial ( C.T.L. ) testing and hydrostatic pressure testing ( pipes )*

The extrapolated failure time at 20°C and 4 bar (which corresponds to a hoop stress of 2 MPa for a SDR 11 pipe ) was 56-143 years, as shown in Fig. 11. The range evaluated is very broad but the lower limit ( 56 years ) gives some safety assurance regarding the lifetime of the corresponding pipe free of any defects. When performing the extrapolation with MDPE C data according to [17], not all statistical requirements were fulfilled.

Slow crack growth testing is very useful for quality control and ranking of the SCG-resistance of different PE resins. In the CTL test by Vattenfall MDPE C showed the shortest failure time compared to MDPE A and MDPE B. Compared to notched pipes the failure time was 2-times faster and 15-times faster compared to unnotched pipes at 4 MPa / 80°C. Fig. 12 presents failure times for uniaxial specimens and pipes. CTL testing reveals to be a faster method to characterize stage II in a creep rupture diagram [6] [7].

## CONCLUSION

The different approaches chosen by the EVOPE participants to assess for lifetime of PE gas pipes lead to the evaluation of either an extrapolated predictive value or a calculated value.

Extrapolated values are obtained from series of SCG testing at elevated temperatures for several stress levels. The comparison of the lifetime of the SCG specimens with that of pipes under sustained pressure suggests a good reliability of the former pronostics made on the basis of hydrostatic pressure testing.

Calculated values of the lifetime are based on numerical models from both classical and non classical fracture mechanics. GRI's LIFESPAN and GDF's VIPLEF - PE-3D computer programs will be used to estimate the useful life of PE pipes and joints in service based on residual stresses, operating pressure and temperature, soil load, PE resin, pipe diameter and SDR.

At the time being GDF's numerical model is very promising as a valuation tool since it should permit to solve real operational problems.

This SCG life forecasting procedure is a very useful tool for the gas industry that will point renovation and replacement schedules to be developed appropriately.

The collaboration between Gaz de France, GRI, Italgas and Vattenfall has substancially contributed to the development of a technology that would benefit the entire gas industry.

**BIBLIOGRAPHY**

[1]     LIFESPAN PC Program for Life Integrity Forecasting of PE Gas Distribution Piping Systems, Version 1.0 (GRI-941-217)
[2]     Volume 2 : Applicability of the Slow Crack Growth Test Method for Polyethylene Gas Pipes, (GRI-9210480)
[3]     Volume 2 : Technical Reference for the Use of the Slow Crack Growth Test for Modeling and Predicting the Long-Term Performance of Polyethylene Gas Pipes, (GRI-9310106)
[4]     Life Prediction of Butt Test Fusion Joints in Polyethylene Gas Pipe Materials, (GRI-9110360)
[5]     EVOPE Project - Doc. EVOPE n° 1992-037, (Nov. 1992)
[6]     D. Gueugnaut, "Le Vieillissement des Matériaux Polymères : Application aux Tubes Gaz en Polyéthylène", 3ème Conférence Scientifique et Technique du CERSTA, GDF DETN (France), 19 Juin 1992
[7]     Studvik Material AB, "Fracture Mechanics. A tool for lifetime Prediction of Polyethylene Gas Pipes ?", Seminar at the Royal Institute of Technology, Stockholm (Sweden), 26 April 1993
[8]     N. Nishio and S. Iimura, " Full Notch Creep Test Method for Life Prediction and Quality Evaluation for Polyethylene Pipe". Technical report of the R&D Institute of Tokyo Gas Co., Ltd., Vol. 29,  pp. 25-37 ( 1984 )
[9]     Popelar C.H., Kenner V.H. and Wooster, J.P., Polymer Engineering and Science, **31**, 1693 (1991)
[10]    Popelar, C.H., Proceedings of the13 th International Plastic Fuel Gas Pipe Symposium,  pp. 151-161,  San Antonio, TX, November 1-4, 1993
[11]    J. Kichenin, "Comportement Thermomécanique du Polyéthylène. Application aux Structures Gazières". Thèse de l'Ecole Polytechnique, Janvier 1992
[12]    J. Kichenin, K. Dang Van, K. Boytard, Proceedings of the 13th International Plastic Fuel Gas Pipe Symposium, pp. 291-300, San Antonio, TX (USA),  November 1-4, 1993
[13]    E. de Langre, "Analyse de la Fissuration des Milieux Viscoplastiques. Application de la théorie de l'endommagement brutal". Thèse de l'Université de Paris VI, Juin 1984
[14]    H.D. Bui, K. Dang Van, E. de Langre, Nuclear Engineering and Design, n° 105, 147 (1987)
[15]    F. Nilsson, " Aspects on Criteria for Crack Growth in Polymers", EVOPE Project- Doc. EVOPE n°1992-033, (June 1992)
[16]    T. Tränkner, U.W.Gedde, Proceedings of the 13th International Plastic Fuel Gas Pipe Symposium, pp..316-325, San Antonio, TX (USA),  November 1-4, 1993
[17]    Standard ISO / TR 9080 : 1992 ( E )
[18]    M.Ifwarson, H.Leijström, Proceedings of Plastics Pipes VIII, The Netherlands pp. C1 / 1-16 , September 21-24, 1992

# ESTIMATION OF ACCEPTABLE BENDING RADIUS CURVATURES OF POLYETHYLENE PIPE IN CONSIDERATION OF STRESS RELAXATION

## CALCUL DU RAYON TOLÉRÉ DE COURBURE DES CONDUITES POLYETHYLENE TENANT COMPTE DE LA RELAXATION

Shin-ichi AKIYAMA
Tokyo Gas Co., Ltd.,

Yuichiro GOTO
KUBOTA Co.,

and

Kazuhiko IWATA
Mitsui Petrochemical Industries., Ltd.

## ABSTRACT

Polyethylene pipe was tested using a life expectancy prediction method under which constant strain conditions were applied with stress concentrated points. The tensile stresses at the fracture points of the specimens were calculated using numerical stress analyses that took into account of the true intrinsic stress. Fracture times predicted based on the calculated stresses agreed with experimental fracture times very well in the cases of the specimens given U- or V-shape notches. Based on this result, this method estimated the acceptable bending radius curvature of polyethylene piping system in terms of the view of creep rupture time.

## RÉSUMÉ

Une méthode de prédiction de la durabilité sous contrainte a été appliquée à un tuyau PE à points à contrainte concentrée. La contrainte aux points de fracture des spécimens a été calculée par analyse numérique tenant compte de la contrainte intrinsèque. Le temps de fracture par fluage des spécimens à entaille en U ou en V calculé à partir de la contrainte a bien correspondu au temps de fracture réel. Sur la base de ce résultat, le rayon de courbure acceptable du tuyau PE a été estimé du point de vue du temps de fracture par fluage.

## 1.0 INTRODUCTION

Reducing the acceptable bending radius curvature of polyethylene pipe is highly desirable from the point of view of adequately utilizing the flexibility of such pipe. The acceptable bending radius curvature should be determined based on the life expectancy of the bent pipe. Apart from chemical degradation, the life expectancy of the pipe is influenced by stress arising from continuous deformation.[1] Even if the level of such stress is low, it will cause creep rupture (slow crack growth) in the pipe material.

The present recommended acceptable bending radius curvature has been determined experimentally through various bending durability tests[2] not by using life prediction theory based on generated stress. If the bending radius curvature were to be determined using life prediction theory, the stress generated in the bent pipe would have to be known. Based on calculation of this stress, the life expectancy of the pipe until creep rupture occurs can be determined using many life prediction methods that have been proven effective in experiments.

Despite this, the stress generated in polyethylene pipe cannot be calculated simply on the basis of deformation. Owing to the viscoelastic and plastic characteristics of the pipe materials, a constant strain does not produce a uniform stress, thus it is impossible to obtain the flexibility coefficient examining deformation.

We therefore took on the task of calculating the acceptable bending radius curvature by conducting experimental research aimed at expanding the applicability of life prediction methods entailing constant strain conditions to include stress concentration. Having gained extremely useful practical knowledge regarding the calculation of acceptable bending radius curvature in pipes having joints or other stress concentration points, we have prepared this report.

## 2.0 THEORY

We previously proposed a method for predicting life expectancy under conditions of constant strain based on Nishio's formulae[3] for estimating for the period leading to brittle rupture of polyethylene pipe.[4] Our method assumed that the relaxing stress inherent in polyethylene causes a constant strain on intrinsic stress ($\sigma_{int}$) – which is nonlinear to strain and unaffected elapsed time – in other words act as a constant stress condition. Using this method, the life expectancy of materials until the onset of creep rupture can be predicted from the measured amount of strain. Nishio analyzed the mechanical behavior of polyethylene in a brittle rupture region applying the Maxwell model (Figure 1). Using the result of this analysis, he developed formulae that can be used to predict

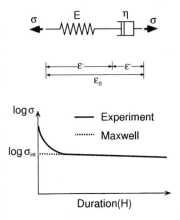

Figure 1. The Maxwell model behavior in the constant strain condition.

the lives of polyethylene both under constant strain conditions and under constant stress condition, utilizing the differential equations. He introduced the limit strain on the viscous element (see Figure 1) as a boundary condition to solve the equation. His prediction formulae are shown below.

For the brittle rupture due to constant strain conditions,

$$\ln t_f = (C_1 - C_2 \ln \sigma_{int})/T + C_3 + f(\varepsilon_0) \quad (1),$$
$$\sigma(t) = \sigma_{int} * \exp(-E't/\eta) \quad (2),$$

and for the brittle rupture due to constant stress conditions,

$$\ln t_f = (C_1 - C_2 \ln \sigma_{int})/T + C_3 \quad (3),$$

where,

$C_1 \sim C_3$ = material constant (experimental),

$f(\varepsilon_0) = \ln(1 + 0.500\xi + 0.333\xi^2 + 0.250\xi^3 + ..),$

$\quad \xi = \varepsilon_c/\varepsilon_0,$

$\varepsilon_0$ : total strain,

$\varepsilon_c$ : the limit of the $\varepsilon''$,

T  : temperature [K],

E  : elastic modulus( = E (T, $\varepsilon_0$) [MPa],

$\eta$  : viscosity( =$\eta$(T)),

$\sigma_{int}$: the initial stress (see Figure 1) [MPa],

$\sigma$  : stress [MPa],

t  : elapsed time [hour],

$t_f$  : time to rupture [hour].

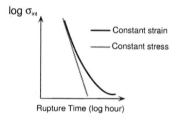

Figure 2. The relationship between of ruptures under the constant strain condition and under the constant stress condition.

The formulae for the two ruptures share some coefficients. Their relationship is shown in Figure 2. Nishio's formulae have subsequently, after some experimental study[4], been modified to describe nonlinear behavior and have been used to correctly estimate stress and accurately predict life expectancy for a specimen having no stress concentration point.

## 3.0 EXPERIMENT

Our basic concept involved;

    1) Using a finite element method (FEM) that employed intrinsic stress to make elast-plastic analyses of the materials'

    2) Comparing these results to the life expectancy curve to verify their effectiveness in evaluating the life expectancy of bent pipes with stress concentration points

In other words, we hope to find that this is a good method for calculating stress with a numerical analysis using strain that can be measured.

## 3.1 MATERIALS

For this study the resin used was one with low resistance to creep rupture. The choice of a resin was made in the interest of aiding experimental research only as this particular substance allowed researchers to obtain a substantial amount of useful data on rupture over a relatively short period. Although the material was polyethylene, it was not a type designed for use with gas. Table 1 shows the characteristics of the model resin (called CSX).

Table 1. Properties of the CSX

| | |
|---|---|
| Density [g/cm$^3$] | 0.954 |
| MFR [g/10min] | 0.80 |
| Yield Strength [MPa] | 25 |
| Break Strength [MPa] | 35 |
| Elongation [%] | >500 |
| ESCR [$F_{50}$,Hr] | 30 |
| Melting Point [K] | 404 |

## 3.2 TEST PIECES

The key to successful testing was creating specimens with specific stress concentration points, almost all brittle rupture starts from a stress concentration point and rupture time at such points is briefer than that at any other points not stress concentration points. We therefore manufactured specimens in two types with stress concentration points that, because of our object, were not joint shapes. The first type of specimen was round bar cut from pressed sheets of the resin notched in different ways. These notches served as stress concentration points (Figure 3). The other type of specimen was extruded pipe made from the resin and processed with a V-shaped stress concentration point (Figure 4).

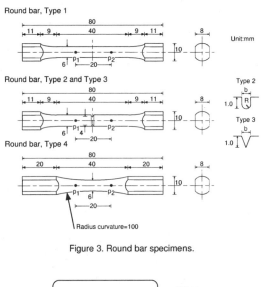

Figure 3. Round bar specimens.

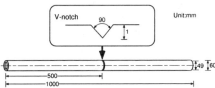

Figure 4. Pipe specimen

## 3.3 APPARATUSES AND EXPERIMENTAL PROCEDURES

**3.3.1 Tensile rupture tests under constant strain conditions.** The constant strain rupture test was carried out at constant tensile speed of 5mm/min with the test specimen (round bar) placed between the crossheads of the machine until the desired degree of deformation was attained. The testing temperature was 353K. The tension, strain and elapse time until ruptures were measured. In Figure 5 the apparatus for the tensile rupture test under constant strain conditions is shown. The true intrinsic stress – the logarithmic strain curve and Poisson's ratio of the resin were measured, especially for Type 1 specimens by plotting the relationship between the true intrinsic stress and logarithmic strain of based on test data from several specimens (see Figure 6 for the estimating procedure). These relationship curves were employed in elast-plastic analysis using the finite element method.

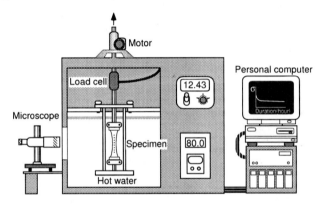

Figure 5. An apparatus of the tensile rupture test under constant strain conditions.

**3.3.2 Tensile rupture tests under constant stress conditions.** Tensile creep rupture testing of type 4 round bar specimen was carried out at temperature of 353K after preheating for over one hour. The time until rupture and stress were measured to obtain a creep rupture master curve for the resin to enable the for prediction of the creep rupture life expectancy under the for the desired stress using Nishio's formulae.

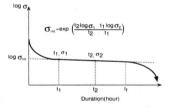

Figure 6. An estimation of $\sigma_{int}$ with a stress relaxation curve.

**3.3.3 Bending test for pipe specimens under constant strain conditions.** Bending creep rupture tests of a pipe with a V-shaped notch were carried out at temperature of 353K after preheating for over an hour. This test was aimed at determining the crude bending creep of actual pipe. In Figure 7 the apparatus for this bending test is shown. The time until rupture and stress were measured.

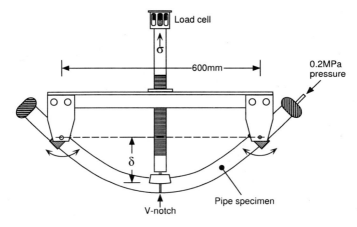

Figure 7. The apparatus for the bending rupture test.

## 3.4  FEM ANALYSES

3.4.2    Material Constant.    The true $\sigma_{int}$ – logarithmic strain curve obtained through the constant strain test is shown in Figure 8. It was found that the area of elasticity was limited to a very small strain level and the curve is largely nonlinear, in keeping with plastic mechanics.

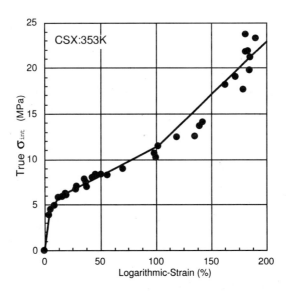

Figure 8. The true $\sigma_{int}$ –logarithmic strain curve of CSX at 353K.

3.4.1 FEM codes. The finite element methods (FEMs) used were ABAQUS ver. 4-8-5 and ANSYS-PC ver.5.0A. The rounded bar specimens and the actual pipe specimens used in the test were analyzed using the true $\sigma_{int}$ − logarithmic strain curve. Used were two element types, an 8-node 2-dimensional large strain isoparametrical element in axisymmetrical condition for the round bar specimen and an 8-node 3-dimensional large strain isoparametrical element for the pipe specimen.

## 4.0  RESULTS AND DISCUSSIONS

The testing conditions and parameters are shown in Table 2 and Table 3. An example of the meshing conditions for the FEM is shown in Figure 9 (Type 3 round bar specimen), and an example of the result of FEM analyses(Type 3, No.2) is shown in Figure 10.

Table 2. The tensile test conditions and parameters for the round bar specimens. (T=353K)

| Unit:mm | Type 2 | | | Type 3 | | | | | Type 4 | | | |
|---|---|---|---|---|---|---|---|---|---|---|---|---|
| ID. No. | No. 1 | No. 2 | No. 3 | No. 1 | No. 2 | No. 3 | No. 4 | No. 5 | No. 1 | No. 2 | No. 3 | No. 4 |
| b | 2 | | | 1 | | | 2 | | - | | | |
| R | 1 | | | - | | | | | - | | | |
| $\Delta(p_1 \sim p_2)$ | 1.47 | 0.83 | 0.46 | 0.34 | 0.79 | 2.41 | 0.38 | 0.68 | 1.02 | 1.77 | 2.79 | 3.76 |

Table 3. The bending test conditions and parameters for the pipe specimens. (T=353K)

| Unit:mm | No. 1 | No. 2 | No. 3 | No. 4 | No. 5 | No. 6 |
|---|---|---|---|---|---|---|
| $\delta$ | 50mm (bending radius curvature 15D) | | | 40mm (bending radius curvature 20D) | | |
| Reaction force | Measured | - | - | Measured | - | - |
| Rupture time | Measured (by nitrogen gas leak under internal pressurized (0.2Mpa) ) | | | | | |

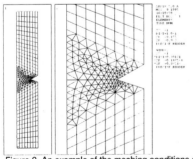
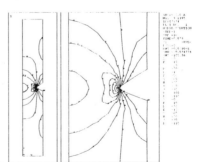

Figure 9. An example of the meshing conditions of round bar specimens (Type 3).

Figure 10. An example of the results of FEM analyses  (Type 3, No.2).

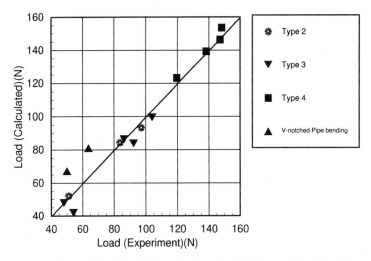

Figure 11. A comparison of analytical reaction force (load) with the experimental reaction force of various specimens types.

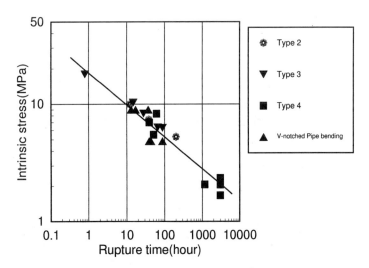

Figure 12. The relationship between $\sigma_{int}$ and rupture time at 353K.

All experimental data are given in Figure 11 and Figure 12. The data for tension generated on both ends of the rounded bar specimens when constant strain was applied and the reaction forces monitored in the bent pipes agreed closely with our analytical calculations (Figure 11). This shows that using the $\sigma_{int}$ – logarithmic strain curve in the FEM analyses is very effective.

By plotting the constant strain rupture data conducted on Types 2,3 and 4 specimens and the pipe specimens and the levels of $\sigma_{int}$ at stress concentration points calculated using the FEMs (Figure 12), we determined a single master curve. This result indicates that the slow crack growth depends on the magnitude of the surrounding stress and can be calculated using FEM at the rupture point. We can thus predict the rupture time for pipe with a stress concentration point, such as a joint, under constant strain conditions such as bending. So, it is confirmed that stress analyses are effective in predicting the life expectancy of polyethylene piping from the point of view of slow crack growth.

Usually, life evaluation tests of polyethylene pipe are carried out under such conditions of constant stress as an internal pressure test in hot water. Therefore, there is already a large amount of data on ruptures and many life prediction curves based on experiment made under these conditions. Through this measuring of the deformation of pipe using the $\sigma_{int}$ method we can associate these rupture data with actual rupture data under constant strain condition.

In Japan, the acceptable bending radius curvatures are 15D for straight pipe and 75D for some joints (where D represent a diameter of the pipe). We are now carrying out bending tests on these radius curvatures with the purpose of obtaining additional data on actual resin and pipe in which the resistance to slow crack growth is very strong. We will present these results in this meeting.

## 5.0 CONCLUSION

From the above results, it appears nearly certain that, by comparing the $\sigma_{int}$-logarithmic strain curve with the finite element method, the method for predicting life expectancy under conditions of constant strain may be applied to stress concentration points. Therefore, this method is valid for analyzing stress in polyethylene pipe, and we believe that it will enable the acceptable bending radius curvature for polyethylene pipe to be revised from the standpoint of life prediction based on revealed stress.

## 6.0 ACKNOWLEDGMENT

This study is drawn from results obtained by the joint research work conducted by three city gas companies (Tokyo Gas, Osaka Gas and Toho Gas) and eight PE pipe and resin manufacturers (Showa Denko K.K., Sekisui Chemical Co.,Ltd., Mitsui Petrochemical Industries,Ltd., Mitsubishi Plastics Industries Ltd., Kubota Corp., Hitachi Metals, Ltd., Nippon Petrochemical Co., and NKK Corp.) in Japan. The authors thank the researchers in these companies for their useful discussions. The author wishes to express his sincere appreciation to Dr. Nishio for his many helpful suggestions.

## 7.0 REFERENCES

1. A. Lustiger, 'Analysis of Field Failures Caused by Slow Crack Growth', Proc. 8th Plastic Fuel Gas Pipe Symposium (1983), pp.176.

2. For example, C.G.Bragaw, 'Crack Stability under Load and the Bending Resistance of MDPE Piping Systems',Proc. 6th Plastic Fuel Gas Pipe Symposium(1978), pp.38.

3. N. Nishio, 'A Theory on Stress- and Temperature-Dependance of the Life of Polyethylene', Proc. 8th Plastic Fuel Gas Pipe Symposium (1983), pp.30.

4. S. Akiyama et al., 'A Method for Life Prediction of PE under the Constant Strain Condition', Proc. 12th Plastic Fuel Gas Pipe Symposium (1991), pp.170.

A TECHNIQUE OF ELASTO-PLASTIC STRESS ANALYSIS
FOR BURIED PIPELINE

UNE TECHNIQUE D'ANALYSE CONTRAINTE ELASTOPLASTIQUE
POUR DES CONDUITES SOUTERRAINES

Kenji Shimizu
Distribution Engineering Center
Osaka Gas Co., Ltd.

ABSTRACT

Buried pipelines are affected by external loads. For example, it is considered that a differential ground settlement in a reclaimed land provides pipelines with extra force. It is important for gas company to ensure goodness of pipelines in order to keep safely gas supply. This technique is developed in order to analyze deformation, stress and strain of pipelines with high accuracy by a computer. The computation with the finite elements method (FEM) by a shell-spring elements model has been used. The shell-spring elements model is a model that pipelines are modeled by collective of shell and soil around the pipelines are modeld by spring. It is possible to analyze strss or strain distribution of pipelines under the situation of large pipelines deformation with a pipe section flattening. This technique contributes to maintenace of pipelines and safely gas supply.

RESUME

Les conduites de gaz enterrées subissent, selon leur environnement d'utilisation et d'enterrement, diverses forces extérieures, pressions interne et externe, changement de température, etc. Dans l'industrie du gaz, il est important d'examiner is santé métallurgique des conduites afin d'assurer la sécurité et la stabilité de la distribution de gaz. La technique que nous avons mise au point permet d'analyser les efforts engendré sur les conduites enterrées. Elle consiste à utiliser un modéle coque-ressort, qui simule les conduites au moyen d'élémentes coque et la sol au moyen de ressorts. cette technique de modélisation permet également d'étudier la déformation transeversale ainsi que les creux locaux produits sur les conduites. Cette technique contribuera a saisir la réalité des conduites et à assurer la distribution de gaz.

**INTRODUCTION**

Buried pipelines are affected by external loads. For example, it is considered that a differential ground settlement in a reclaimed land provides pipelines with extra force. It is important for gas company to ensure goodness of pipelines in order to keep safely gas supply.

This technique is developed in order to analyze deformation, stress and strain of pipelines with high accuracy by a computer. This technique contributes to maintenace of pipelines and safely gas supply.

Some experiments and computer simulations were carried out for the development of this technique. In this paper, the technique itself and the process of developmentare are described.

**FEATURES OF TECHNIQUE**

The computation with the finite elements method(FEM) has been used for an analysis of pipelines affected external loads. Generally, the beam-spring elements model, which is a model that pipelines are modeled by beam and soil around pipelines is modeled by spring, is used for a computation with FEM in order to analyze deformation, stress and strain of pipelines.

By the computaion with the beam-spring elementsut, it is impossible to analyze strss or strain distribution of pipelines under the situation of large pipelines deformation with a pipe section flattening . Furthermore, it is impossible to analyze stress or strain distribution around a partial dimple of pipelines.

In order to solve above problems, the computation with shell-spring elements model has been developed. The shell-spring elements model is a model that pipelines are modeled by collective of shell elements, and soil around the pipelines are modeld by spring. The difference between the beam-spring elements model and the shell-spring elements model is shown in Figure 1.

It is possible to analyze deformation and stress or strain distribution of pipelines with high accuracy by the computation with shell-spring elements model.

The features of the developed computaion with the shell-spring elements model are follows;

1) It is possible to analyze stress or strain distribution of pipelines with consideration of pipe section flattening. It is effective in analysis for large-diameter pipelines which are easy to be flattened.

2) It is possible to analyze stress or strain distribution around a partial dimple of pipelines, which is generated by a surport.

3) It is possible to analyze stress or strain of pipelines in a wide range, from elastic range to plastic range. The elasto-plastic relation of the shell elements enables to analyze large deformation of pipelines with high ccuracy.

4) The pipe/soil interaction is considered by the spring elements. Soil around pipelines are modeled by nonlinear spring elements. The property of spring elements depend on some full-scale experiments and computer simulations.

5) The external loads from soil to pipelines are modeled. The distribution of soil pressure around pipelines is considered by the radiation of spring elements.

**VALIDITY OF TECHNIQUE**

In order to validate the developed stress analysis technique, the comparison between the full-scale experiment of settlement and the simulation of the experiment by the developed stress analysis technique.

The outline of the full-scale experiment is shown in Figure 2. A pipe, whose specification was API-5L-X52 and diameter was 60.96cm, was buried in a large moval pit without internal pressure. The central part of the pit, whose length was 24m, wassettled untill 20cm. The stress-strain of the pipe were measured.

The comparison between the experiment and tne simulation is shown in Figure 3. This figure shows the distribution of the pipe-axial stress at the pipe top at the stage of the 20cm settlement of the pit. The circles show the results of the experiment, and the continuos line shows the result of computer simulation by the technique.

It is clear that the computer simulation by the shell-spring elements model coincides with the result of the experiment even under the situation that large ground settlement occurred.

## EXPERIMENT FOR DEVELOPMENT OF TECHNIQUE

It is very difficult to model the pipe/soil interaction. In order to clarify the distribution of soil pressure around a pipe and to model the pipe/soil interaction, full-scale experiments were carried out.

The full-scale experiments were carried out in order to clarify the soil pressure on a pipe surface during soil around a pipe settles vertically. Figure 4 shows a schematic diagram of the full-scale experiment. The test pipe was consisted of three 60cm straight pipes connected in line. The test pipe was buried in a moval pit. The test pipe was suspended by 6 steel rods from the fixed beam. Figure 5 shows a schematic diagram of test pipe. The soil was compacted at every 30cm depth by a rammer. In order to observe a sliding surface, white quartz sand was laid every 10cm in the ground. The cases of the experiments are shown in Table 1.

Figures 6 and 7 show the results of experiments. Figure 6 shows the relation between the amount of moval pit settlement and the sum of the load mesured by load cell L3 and L4. Figure 7 shows the schetch of the sliding surface after the experiment finished.

Three hypothesis are set in consideration with the results of experiments.

1) The sliding surface is circular.
2) The total load acting on pipe is sum of the weight of soil above the pipe and the friction along the sliding surface.
3) The friction occurring along the sliding surface decreases as the moval pit settles.

Figure 8 illustrates the above hypothesis called circular sliding surface model.

## ANALYSIS OF DISTRIBUTION OF SOIL PRESSURE

In order to validate the above hypothesis, 2-dimensional analysis of distribution of soil pressure around a pipe by computation with FEM is carrid out. The full-scale experiment of case 4 was simulated. Figure 9 shows mesh for FEM analysis.

Figures 10 and 11 show the comparison between the experiment and the computer simulation. Figure 10 shows the relation between the amount of moval pit settlement and the load at the load cell L3 and L4. Figure 11 shows the relation between the angle from the top of the pipe and normal soil pressure acting on the pipe.

The results of computer simulation coincides with the result of the experiment. The circular sliding surface model is validated. It is effective to caluculate the distribution of soil pressure around a pipe by this circular sliding surface model.

## CONCLUSIONS

Some experiments and computer simulations were carried out in order to clarify the pipe/soil interaction. And based on their result, the technique ofelasto-plasticstress analysis for buried pipeline has been developed.

## ACKNOWLEDGEMENTS

Thanks to GAZ DE FRACNCE for significant collaboration.

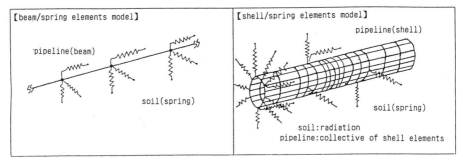

Figure 1. difference between beam/spring elements and shell/spring elements

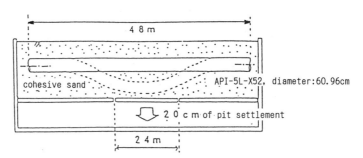

Figure 2. Outline of the full-scale experiment

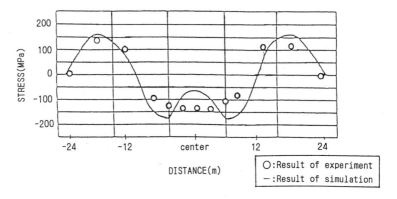

Figure 3. Comparison between the experiment and the simulation
Distribution of pipe-axial stress at the top of pipe

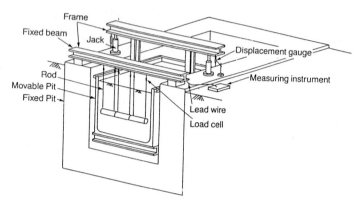

Figure 4. Schematic diagram of the full-scale experiment

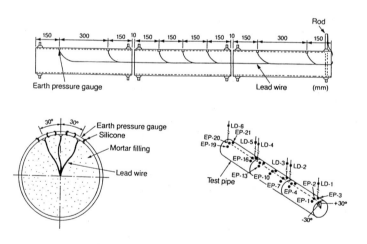

Figure 5. Schmatic diagram of test pipe

Table 1. Cases of the experiments

| | case 1 | case 2 | case 3 | case 4 | case 5 | case 6 | case 7 |
|---|---|---|---|---|---|---|---|
| Soil | river sand | | | | | | cohesive sand |
| Compacting condition | loose | loose | dense | dense | loose | dense | dense |
| Depth of cover (cm) | 60 | 120 | 60 | 120 | 120 | 120 | 60 |
| Pipe diameter (cm) | 16.52 | 16.52 | 16.52 | 16.52 | 31.85 | 31.85 | 16.52 |

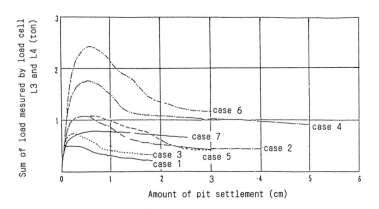

Figure 6. Relation between the amount of pit settlement and the sum of load mesured by load cell L3 and L4

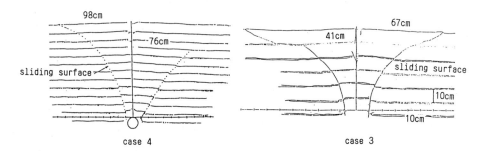

case 4                                    case 3

Figure 7. Schetch of sliding surface after experiment

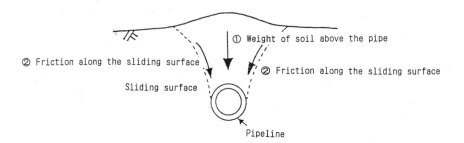

Total load acting on pipe = ① Weight of soil above the pipe
                          +② Friction along the sliding surface

Figure 8. Hypothesis called circular sliding surface model

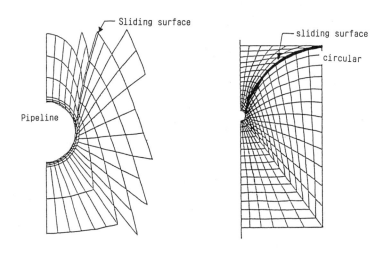

Figure 9. Mesh for FEM analysis

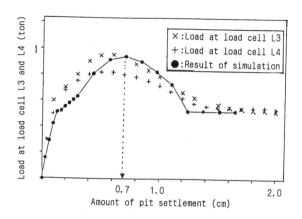

Figure 10. Relation between the amount of pit settlement
and load at load cell L3 and L4

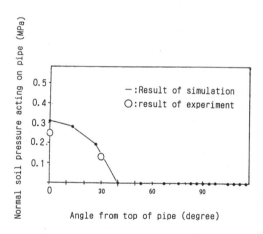

Figure 11. Relation between angle from top of pipe
and normal soil pressure acting on pipe
⟨Amount of pit settlement:0.7(cm)⟩'

DEVELOPMENT AND TESTING OF A NEW GAS METER FOR
DOMESTIC AND COMMERCIAL APPLICATIONS


MISE AU POINT ET ESSAI D'UN NOUVEAU COMPTEUR A GAZ POUR
LES APPLICATIONS DOMESTIQUES ET TERTIAIRES

Jacob Klimstra and Bert Hoven
N.V. Nederlandse Gasunie, NL
Leo Wolters
Deltec Fuel Systems, NL

ABSTRACT

An intrinsically simple gas meter, based on a pressure reduction
valve, and using the simultaneous measurement of the valve stem
position and the pressure drop, appeared to provide sufficient
accuracy. The flow range is suitable for domestic and commercial
applications.
The advantage of combining the pressure reduction and metering
function is the small range in pressure drop over the system.
The valve opening will be automatically adapted to the required
flow. It has an exponential characteristic to provide sufficient
accuracy in the lower part of the flow range. The very important
accurate determination of the valve stem position has been
accomplished by using a capacitive displacement technique. All
measured quantities are being processed and stored by a micro
computer, which allows an electronic read out of the meter. The
paper describes in detail the principle of the meter as well as
the measured accuracy.

RESUME

Un compteur à gaz de concept simple, basée sur une vanne de
détente et combinant la mesure de la position de la tige de la
vanne et de perte de charge, semble donner une précision
suffisante. Le domaine de débit accessible est adapté à des
usages domestiques et tertiaires.
L'avantage de combiner mesure de la position et perte de charge
est que la perte de charge globale du système reste réduite.
L'ouverture de la vanne est automatiquement adaptée au débit
demandé. Le compteur a une caractéristique exponentielle qui
permet une précision suffisante pout les débits les moins
importants. La détermination trè précise de la position de la
tige de la vanne a été réaliséc grâce à un capteur de
déplacement capacitif. Toutes les données mesurées ont été
traitées et stockées sur un micro-ordinateur, qui permet un
affichage électronique de compteur. Le papier décrit en détail
le principe du compteur ainsi que la précision mesurée.

INTRODUCTION

A new, intrinsically simple, gas meter as a replacement for the current generation of domestic and commercial meters has been developed and tested. Electronic meter read out and a high accuracy are reasons that gas companies are introducing alternatives, such as ultrasonic and vortex meters, for the common positive displacement meters. The new meter is based on the measurement of the pressure difference across a reducer valve, the stem position in the valve being a reliable indicator of the opening of the valve. The primary advantage is that the often applied reducer valve upstream of the meter and the meter itself have been combined. Another advantage is that the opening of the valve is automatically adapted to the required flow so that the range in which the pressure difference across the valve will be measured is limited. Further, if the Wobbe index of the gas remains constant, the meter is automatically an energy flow meter irrespective of changes in gas composition.

The paper will give the results of measurements, initially carried out with laboratory equipment of high resolution and requiring high investments. The initial results were very encouraging, giving a high accuracy in a wide range of flows. When using a restriction as a gas meter, it is necessary to measure the pressure drop. It is relatively easy in that case to measure also the absolute pressure and the temperature of the gas, and to correct the measured gas throughput for that.

The next step was the conversion to low-cost transducers, in order to transform the concept into an economically acceptable meter. From the automotive technologies, pressure and temperature transducers of sufficiently high accuracy could be used. A major problem remained the accurate determination of the instantaneous position of the valve stem. Induction methods appeared to be insufficiently accurate and multi-slot stems with a digital read out appeared to be too expensive. Eventually, a carburettor system based on a valve, recently developed by Deltec Fuel Systems, and using a capacitive method to determine the opening of the valve, offered perspectives. In close co-operation with Deltec, Gasunie Research has tested the possibility to use this valve as a combined gas meter and reducer.

The results with the Deltec valve were very successful. Apart from a small, soluble, problem in the low flow range, sufficient accuracy was found in a wide range of operating conditions. For the tests, a special test rig was used having wet positive displacement meters as a reference. All measured quantities were stored and processed with digital measurement equipment. The paper will show the relationship between valve opening and flow, for a number of process conditions. The results had an excellent repeatability which means that the properties of each individual meter can be attained and fixed during calibration. The valve can be equipped with a pneumatic dome to control the downstream pressure. In case an electric actuator is used, a permanent connection with the mains is required. That however allows for remote shut-off possibilities which can be advantageous for safety and billing.

THE ORIGIN OF THE IDEA

In some cases, processes using natural gas are instable because of an oscillatory gas supply. The pressure reducing system often present between the gas-supply pipe and the user is basically a control system using feedback, which can become instable: a humming reducer valve. In order to find solutions for such problems, Gasunie Research has carried out investigations into the mechanisms causing instability of reducer valves. During tests for determining the

transfer function of a reducer valve used for domestic purposes, a
very reproducible relationship between the position of the valve stem
and the volume flow was found, for a given pressure drop and gas
temperature. To accurately measure the valve stem position, an eddy-
current displacement transducer, intended for determining the shaft
position in tilting-pad bearings (Dymac 600), was used. To complete
the use of the reducer valve for flow measurement, transducers were
added for measurement of the absolute gas pressure, the pressure drop
and the gas temperature. The traditional combination of a reducer
valve with a displacement-type gas meter could then be replaced by a
space-saving, flow-measuring, reducer valve.

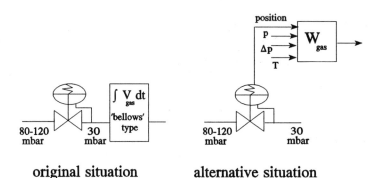

Figure 1: The traditional combination of reducer valve and gas meter
replaced by a measuring reducer valve.


      Traditional methods based on pressure drop across orifices of a
fixed opening to measure the volume flow of gas to domestic and
commercial users have failed because of the large variation in flow
to such customers. A typical flow range for a domestic user is
between 20 l/h (a pilot flame) and 5000 l/h. Since the pressure drop
varies with the square of the flow over a restriction, this would
mean a variation in pressure drop of a factor 62,500. It is
impossible to find pressure transducers which are accurate in such a
wide range. Until recently, the so-called Manhattan gas meter was
being advertized, having a number of orifices with different
openings. A motor-driven system could make available the proper
orifice for creating a suitable pressure drop for the given flow. The
Manhattan design still needed very accurate pressure transducers, it
had a complicated orifice-manipulating system and it still required
the installation of the traditional reducer valve.

      In a typical domestic situation in The Netherlands, the gauge
pressure of the gas grid near the homes has a setpoint of 100 mbar,
while in the home a pressure of 25 mbar is required. Because of
control inaccuracies and pressure-drop effects, the supply pressure
can vary between 120 mbar and 80 mbar. This means that the pressure
drop across the reducer valve will range between 55 and 95 mbar. This
has the advantage of a very limited range compared to the
specifications of modern pressure transducers. Currently, most
domestic gas meters have not been provided with a correction for gas
temperature. The reason for that is the difficulty to correct the
mechanical volume counter. The temperature of the gas entering the
home is generally close to 15 °C, with, in theory, possible

excursions between -20 °C and 30 °C. Not including the gas
temperature can introduce substantial errors in the flow measurement.
The temperature range given can easily be accomodated by modern
transducers. For the read-out of the stem position of the valve and
the pressure drop across the valve, electronic data acquisition is
required anyhow. So, the addition of a temperature sensor will not
cause any problems. The electronic data acquisition also allows an
automatic read out of the meter.

An advantage of using the measurement of the pressure drop
across a flow restriction, as in case of the suggested reducer valve,
is that the measurement system measures the energy flow as long as
the Wobbe index of the gas remains constant. By definition, the Wobbe
index of the gas is an indicator of the - chemically stored - energy
flow past a flow restriction for a given pressure drop. If the Wobbe
index of a gas remains constant, the heating value of the gas may
vary without affecting the energy flow and the requirement of
combustion air. Displacement-type gas meters need a correction if the
heating value of the gas varies for a constant Wobbe index.

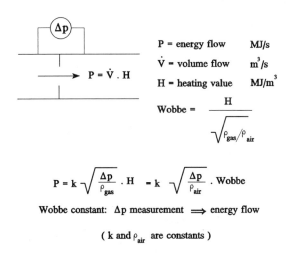

$P$ = energy flow      MJ/s

$\dot{V}$ = volume flow      $m^3/s$

$H$ = heating value      $MJ/m^3$

$$\text{Wobbe} = \frac{H}{\sqrt{\rho_{gas}/\rho_{air}}}$$

$$P = k \sqrt{\frac{\Delta p}{\rho_{gas}}} \cdot H = k \sqrt{\frac{\Delta p}{\rho_{air}}} \cdot \text{Wobbe}$$

Wobbe constant: $\Delta p$ measurement $\Longrightarrow$ energy flow

( $k$ and $\rho_{air}$ are constants )

Figure 2: The energy flow depending on the delta p for a constant
Wobbe index.

However, problems arose restricting a quick conversion of
reducer valves into gas meters. Soon after the successful tests with
the domestic reducer valve, it appeared that the type of valve tested
was being replaced by a smaller type, having less proper guidance of
the valve stem and a deformable seat. Both the reduced construction
space and the non-reproducible relationship between valve position
and valve opening hampered the measurement of the valve opening.
Moreover, it appeared that the Dymac transducer used for the initial
measurements was not available in a low-cost version. Its current
price of US$ 1500 is unacceptable for domestic gas meters.

THE DELTEC TECJET

In parallel to the developments by Gasunie Research, Deltec Fuel
Systems had designed a special valve intended for accurate and rapid
gas metering for natural-gas-fueled engines. The valve has an
exponentially increasing opening, resulting in a larger stem travel
in the lower flow range. This greatly improved the resolution and
consequently the accuracy in the lower flow range. The opening of the
valve is measured with a capacitive system. Deltec has included a
pressure transducer, a pressure-drop transducer and a temperature
sensor in the valve. Instead of having a dome connected to the valve
stem, as is the case with reducer valves, the TECJET uses an electric
motor to set its position. Basically, this electric motor can be
replaced by a dome with membrane, controlled by the downstream
pressure. In that case, the TECJET can perform the pressure-
regulation function as a traditional reducer valve. Naturally, this
can also be done by using the built-in electric motor, although that
requires a heavy power supply. Each fully assembled TECJET can be
calibrated individually, including the various sensors. The
dimensions of the smallest standard TECJET, the TECJET 15 with a
maximum flow of 30 $m^3$/h, are 135*70*70 mm.

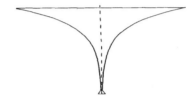

Figure 3: Shape of the valve opening of the TECJET.

The TECJET 15 was subsequently tested by Gasunie Research on its
accuracy. The various sensors of the TECJET have a read out in
counts. The resolution of the transducers is always better than
0.05 % of the span, so that the readout does not put any restrictions
to the attainable accuracy. Table 1 gives an overview of the
calibration values and the resolution of the transducers present.

Table 1: Sensor data of the TECJET.

| QUANTITY | Counts | | Calibration values | | 1 count = | Resolu-tion |
|---|---|---|---|---|---|---|
| | "zero" | "span" | "zero" | "span" | | |
| Vn *) | 0 | 4095 | 0.0 (l/s) | 5.0 (l/s) | 0.00121 (l/s) | 0.024 % |
| $\Delta p$ | 2 | 2500 | 0 mbar | 120 mbar | 0.048 mbar | 0.04 % |
| p_abs | 1695 | 1910 | 1013 mbar | 1133 mbar | 0.558 mbar | 0.05 % |
| T | 1312 | 4095 | 0 °C | 144 °C | 0.052 °C | 0.036 % |
| valve position | 797 | 2986 | 0.0 mm | 16.0 mm | 0.00731 mm | 0.05 % |

*)   Vn = normal flow registrated by TECJET

MEASUREMENT ARRANGEMENT.

To investigate the accuracy and reproducibility of the TECJET as a gas meter, a test arrangement was built using three calibrated wet gas meters as a reference (Schlumberger types 1, 5 and 15 with maximum flows of viz. 0.7 $m^3/h$, 3 $m^3/h$ and 8 $m^3/h$). This allowed an accurate flow measurement in a wide range. The natural gas used for the tests was Groningen-quality gas. The gas was supplied by an 8 bar system and reduced to the domestic-grid pressure of 100 mbar. It was possible to adjust the pressure between 120 mbar and 80 mbar, to simulate the pressure variations in practice. High-quality transducers for pressure, pressure drop and temperature were installed to check the sensors of the TECJET. Hewlett Packard data-acquisition equipment (HP-3497A) was used in combination with a HP 9000 computer. Figure 4 gives a schematic overview of the measurement arrangement.

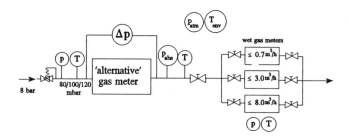

Figure 4: The measurement arrangement.

During the measurements, the pressure downstream of the TECJET was adjusted using a manual valve. The position of the valve opening was set with the built-in electric motor using an external power supply.

MEASUREMENT RESULTS

The first measurements with the TECJET were intended for generating a so-called calibration line, relating the valve position with the normalized flow. The next step was the determination of the deviation from the calibration line in the full flow range. Finally, the TECJET was checked on its repeatability.

The calibration line

The TECJET has been tested in a flow range up to 5 $m^3/h$, corresponding to the required range for a domestic gas meter. Roughly 15 valve opening positions have been set, for the three upstream pressures of 120, 100 and 80 mbar. For each setting, the downstream pressure was adjusted manually to 30 mbar. The full set of data has been measured in one day, with an approximately constant atmospheric pressure and temperature. Initially, flows lower than 400 l/h could not be realised, because of a preprogrammed limitation in the lowest possible flow. This lowest possible flow is required for the start-up process of engines. Further, a fixed opening has been deliberately machined in the TECJET by DELTEC to help in attaining the minimum flow. For the use of the TECJET as a domestic gas meter, these limitations are not necessary. During the tests, it appeared possible

to overrule the preprogrammed minimum flow. In that case, a minimum
flow of 90 l/h could be reached for an upstream pressure of 100 mbar.
For domestic purposes, the gas meter should be able to accurately
measure flows exceeding roughly 25 l/h.

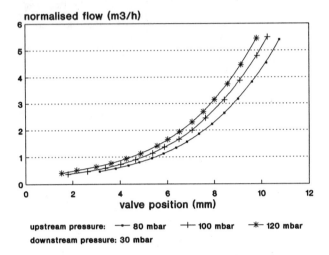

Figure 5: The normalised flow versus valve position.

    Figure 5 shows the relationship between the normalized flow,
i.e. the volume flow conditions converted to 1013 mbar and 0 °C, and
the valve position. It is obvious that the flow increases with
increasing pressure drop across the valve, for a given opening. All
three lines have a similar, smooth, shape. From the data indicated in
figure 5, a valve coefficient $k_v$ has been determined. The coefficient
$k_v$ relates the normalized flow $V_n$ with the process conditions:

$$V_n = k_v \sqrt{\frac{\Delta p\, p}{T}}$$

in which p and T are the absolute pressure and the absolute
temperature and $\Delta p$ indicates the pressure drop. The so-called
calibration line gives the relationship between the valve position
and the valve coefficient. Figure 6 illustrates that the calibration
line is identical for all three different pressure drops tested. The
calibration line is approximated by a polynomial least-squares fit.
This calibration line can be stored in a microcomputer to calculate
the flow from the measured valve position and the process conditions
provided by the various built-in sensors.

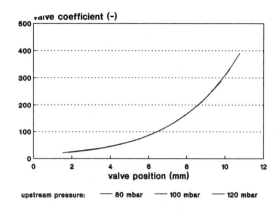

Figure 6: The calibration line of the TECJET.


Accuracy

The accuracy of the flow measurement of the TECJET using the previously determined calibration curve has been expressed in an error curve based on the formula given in Figure 7.

In this formula, V is the normalized flow measured with the wet gas meters and flow_calc is the flow according to the TECJET. Within the flow range between 1 and 5 $m^3/h$, the error is less than 1% of the given flow. For flows lower than 0.5 $m^3/h$, the small fixed opening in the valve was the cause of larger deviations between the real flow and the flow 'measured' by the TECJET. One week after the initial tests, the test series have been repeated. The error remained well within the initial 1.5% in the flow range between 0.5 and 5 $m^3/h$. In the flow range between 90 l/h and 500 l/h, the error was less than 5%. It is expected that the removal of the fixed opening will improve the accuracy in the lower flow range.

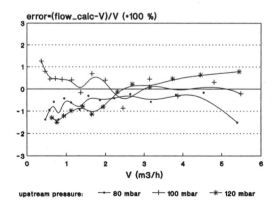

Figure 7: The error curve of the TECJET.

CONCLUSIONS

*    A specially designed reducer valve can be used as a gas meter
with sufficient accuracy in a wide flow range. The required
electronic readout of the necessary sensors allows the use of
elctronic meter read out.

*    For the reducer valve tested, the TECJET 15, the error in the
flow range between 0.5 $m^3$/h and 5.0 $m^3$/h was less than 1.5% of the
indicated flow. In the flow range between 90 l/h and 500 l/h, the
error was less than 5%, but this can probably be improved by a small
change in the valve design.

*    The sensors of the TECJET for valve displacement, pressure,
pressure drop and temperature proved to have a resolution better than
0.05% of the span resulting in a sufficient accuracy.

*    The costs of the components and the manufacturing costs of the
TECJET offer possiblities for an economic, large-scale, use as a gas
meter for domestic or commercial applications.

RESULTS OF THE MTI COMPACT ELECTRONIC METER
TEST PROGRAM

RESULTATS DU PROGRAMME D'ESSAI DU COMPTEUR
ELECTRONIQUE COMPACT MTI

Eugene L. O'Rourke
Measurement Technology International, USA

ABSTRACT

MTI has completed an extensive test program to ensure a new compact electronic gas
meter meets all specifications and standards customarily employed by the U.S. gas
industry.   Thirty (30) test plans were developed to cover the American National
Standards Institute (ANSI) and other performance requirements.

- The prototype meters have met or exceeded the ANSI B109.1 standards
- The prototype meters have demonstrated the feasibility of GRI's decision to seek a
  compact meter for early market entry.
- Leading U.S. utilities have participated in sponsoring the project and have expressed
  keen interest in field testing the compact meter.
- The meter generates the necessary electronic output for either telephonic or radio
  based automatic meter reading (AMR).

Meters for the U.S. and overseas markets have been manufactured by AMC.  Four hundred
units are or will be installed at twenty or more utilities and tested for a period of up
to one year.

RÉSUMÉ

MTI a conduit un programme d'essais trés large pour garantir la conformité du nouveau
compteur de gaz, electronique et compact, aux spécifications et normes couramment
utilisees dans l'industrie du gaz aux Etats-Unis.  Trente (30) types d'essais ont été
réalisés pour couvrir les spécifications de l'ANSI et d'autres exigences de
performances.

- Les prototypes répondent aux exigences de la norme ANSI B109.1 ou parfois les
  dépassent.
- Les prototypes répondent an besoin exprimé par le GRI de disposer d'un compteur
  compact pour entrer au plus tot sur le marché américain.
- Les sociétés de distribution leaders aux Etats-Unis ont sponsorisé le projet et se
  sont montrées trés intéressées pour mener des essais sur le site.
- Le compteur dispose des sorties électroniques nécessaires pour faire de la reléve
  automatique a distance par téléphone ou par radio.

Les compteurs pour les Etats-Unis ou d'autres pays ont été fabriqués par AMC.  Quatre
cents compteurs scront installés dans au moins vingt sociétés de distribution pour une
durée de un an.

## INTRODUCTION

The United States natural gas industry has expressed a strong need for a smaller, more aesthetic gas meter. This need has been emphatically voiced by marketing professionals across the nation. The void frequently has been a deterrent to persuading architects, developers and customers to utilize clean burning natural gas in multi-family, single family attached and "zero" lot line residential and small commercial projects.

The space required for a multiple meter installation dictates the gas meters being installed in a driveway or side yard. In a driveway or parking area the meters are subject to vehicular damage and represent a potential hazard. Side yard area may not be available or may be needed for other purposes. The unattractive appearance of current gas meters is also a disadvantage. A compact gas meter would minimize these obstacles and make natural gas a more acceptable alternative in these highly competitive markets.

The Gas Research Institute (GRI) responded to the need for a compact gas meter by issuing a request for proposal (RFP) No. 91-271-0383, Compact Gas Meter for Early Entry Market on July 20, 1990. Select Corporation (Select) responded to the RFP on September 21, 1990. Select is a California corporation formed to commercialize and market a new technology for gaseous fluid flow metering. In April 1991, Select was awarded GRI Contract No. 5091-271-2150 to conduct a test and development program prior to initiating full-scale utility field tests. The GRI contract was subsequently amended to include additional testing.

Measurement Technology International (MTI) is a joint venture formed by Select and American Meter Company (AMC). As you may know, AMC is the predominant gas meter manufacturer in the United States. AMC is owned by Ruhrgas of Germany. Ruhrgas also owns Elster and Kromschroeder, prominent meter manufacturers in Europe. MTI's mission is to continue testing and development of the compact meter until production meters are available in the marketplace.

### Metering Principle

The MTI meter employs a new technique for measuring gas flow. The sensor contains an undulating flexible membrane. The membrane traps discrete volumes of gas which move through the flow chamber in pulses as shown in Figure 1. Each

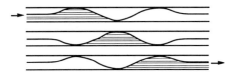

Figure 1. Sensor Action

pulse creates a signal by means of a piezo electric element. The signal is amplified, digitized and recorded in real time. A micro-processor and software convert the signal into volumetric flow, which is added incrementally to previous volumes. The cumulative volume is stored in the memory and displayed on a liquid crystal display (LCD). Certain features of the device are disclosed in U.S. Patents No. 4,920,794 issued May 1, 1990, No. 5,069,067 issued December 3, 1991, No. 5,347,862 issued September 20, 1994 and No. 5,390,542 issued February 21, 1995.

While the technique is new, the principle of positive displacement has been retained. Positive displacement has been the only measurement approach which can measure volume accurately over the wide range (1000:1) of flow rates required for a residential gas meter. Other concepts for gas measurement are dependent upon small velocity or pressure differentials. Thus the size or geometry of other techniques and gas quality inherently constrain their accurate range.

Features And Specifications

The meter is small and light weight.  The smallest residential gas meters are about 20 cm high, 15 cm wide and 12 cm deep -about 3600 cm³.  The MTI meter is 15 cm high, 9 cm wide and 5 cm deep -less than 675 cm³.  The meter weighs about 1 kg.   It fits easily inside a stud wall.  The preferred configuration has a  bottom  inlet and  top  outlet  as  show  in  Figure 2.  A  conventional

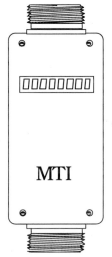

Figure 2.  THE MTI Meter

arrangement  with both inlet and outlet at the top can be provided easily.  The design specifications for the meter are summarized in Table 1.

Table 1.    Design Specifications

| | |
|---|---|
| Physical Size | 675 cm³ - 15 cm H x 9 cm W x 5 cm D |
| Weight | 1 kg |
| Totalizing Accuracy | ±1.0% from 0.007 to 7 m³/h |
| Piping Orientation | Bottom inlet, top outlet |
| Pressure Drop @ 7 m³/h | 125 Pa |
| Pressure Rating | 0.69 bar |
| Temperature Compensation | Optional |
| Fixed Factor Pressure Compensation | Optional |
| Accuracy Retention | ±2% over 20 years (projected) |
| Service Life | 20+ years |
| Remote Reading | Optional |
| Cumulative Readout Resolution | 1 liter |
| Easily Adaptable to Automatic Meter Reading | |
| Insensitive to Orientation, Particulates and Electrical Noise | |
| Tamper Resistance | Equal to existing meters |

TEST RESULTS

MTI developed a test program which included thirty (30) individual test plans to ensure the new compact electronic meter would meet or exceed American National Standards Institute (ANSI) B109.1 performance requirements as well as other specifications and standards customarily utilized by the U.S. gas industry. Many of the ANSI standards are directed at the design and construction of the outer meter case. The prototype meter cases were subjected to these tests as a matter of interest and some discrepancies were encountered. The results are summarized in Table 2. These shortcomings would be quickly

Table 2.    Meter Case Tests

| ANSI Requirement | Brief Description | Comments |
|---|---|---|
| 2.9.1 | Accelerated Weathering Test | 14 days of 2 hr. UV and water spray cycles - some chalking and discoloration on AMC coating, none on So Cal's coating. |
| 2.9.2 | Salt Spray Test | 24 hr. salt spray test - no blistering, corrosion or deterioration of the surface. |
| 2.9.3 | Chemical Resistance Test | 30 minute immersion produced no discernible effects. |
| 2.10 | METER INDEX WINDOW IMPACT TEST | Window itself not damaged, but mounting epoxy failed. |
| 2.11 | METER INDEX WINDOW CLEARNESS TEST | Normal operating conditions did not affect window clarity. |
| 2.12.1 | Temperature Resistance | No visible effects on case. |
| 2.13 | STRENGTH OF METER CONNECTIONS | Case and connections passed, but sealing epoxy cracked during torsion test. |
| 3.4.1 | Internal pressure of 10 psig minimum or 1.5 MAOP | No leakage in one minute. |

corrected by any experienced meter manufacturer. As these tests are simply mechanical requirements and unrelated to any particular measurement technology, further discussion of them has been omitted for brevity.

Accuracy

The primary function of any gas meter is, of course, to measure the volume of gas consumed by the customer accurately over the entire range of usage rates from pilot load to maximum rated capacity. The relevant ANSI standards are 3.3.1, 3.3.2 and 3.3.3. In addition the meter must measure volume accurately under conditions of varying density, pressure and temperature and be provided with internal compensation for these conditions where desired by the gas utility. The accuracy tests conducted and the results are summarized in Table 3.

Table 3.    Accuracy Tests

| ANSI or Test Number | Brief Description | Results |
|---|---|---|
| 3.3.1 | Initial Accuracy | Meter demonstrated excellent repeatability. Electronic calibration ensures accuracy. |
| 3.3.2 | Sustained Accuracy | Accuracy tests have not revealed any loss of accuracy after long-term durability tests. A formal sustained accuracy test of 10 meters is currently underway at AMC. |

| 3.3.3 | Accelerated Life Test | Ten meters at So Cal operated an average of 34 thousand m³ (4800 x) and eight meters at American Meter Company operated an average of 23 thousand m³ (3200 x) without appreciable effect. |
|-------|----------------------|---------|
| SS-17 | Accuracy at Various Temperatures | Operated satisfactorily from -40° to +140°F. |
| SS-20 | Accuracy at Varying Pressures | Accuracy was not affected by varying bell prover pressures. |
| SS-21 | Accuracy at Varying Densities | Gas mixtures of air and helium were used for determining the effect of gas density on meter operation. Mixtures of 0.526, 0.569, 0.612, 0.655, 0.698 and 0.741 specific gravity were utilized in addition to air. A 40% change in gas density produced a 7% change in meter registration. |

The meter is designed with two operational modes. The proof mode is calibrated with air to facilitate conventional proof testing. The operating mode is calibrated for natural gas to ensure accurate registration during normal service. The calibrations are electronic and can be easily adjusted for any natural gas density. The meter also incorporates temperature compensation if the user so desires.

Prototypes of the meter were tested for accuracy at Southern California Gas Company's (So Cal) meter shop. The results were excellent. Repeatability, a key test of the concept, was 99.9%. Accuracy was within ±0.5% at both high and moderate flow rates as shown in Table 4.

Table 4.    Bell Prover Runs

|  | Open Flow = 4.1 m³/h | Check Flow = 1.4 m³/h |
|---|---|---|
| NO. of TESTS | 14 | 13 |
| PROVER VOLUME (m³) | 0.0566 | 0.0566 |
| AVERAGE TEST VOLUME (m³) | 0.0566 | 0.0566 |
| LARGEST VARIATION (%) | +0.25/ -0.3 | ±0.2 |

Low flow accuracy was equally good. The accuracy of current meters sometimes deteriorates at low flow rates. The MTI meter was accurate within ±0.5% at flow rates as low as 0.015 m³/hr as shown in Table 5.

Table 5.    Low Flow Tests

| NO. of TESTS | 8 | 20 | 20 |
|---|---|---|---|
| TEST FLOW RATE (m³/h) | 0.0144 | 0.0600 | 0.2758 |
| TEST AVERAGE (m³/h) | 0.0144 | 0.0600 | 0.2758 |
| LARGEST VARIATION (%) | +0.43/ -0.37 | +0.54/ -0.52 | +0.29/ -0.28 |

Durability

In the United States, gas meters are expected to operate dependably for 20 years or more before they are repaired or replaced. Thus long-term reliability is an important criteria for evaluating gas meter acceptability

An early prototype of the meter was run for more that two years on So Cal's meter test rack at an accelerated flow rate. The meter accumulated a volume of more than 78,000 cubic meters, the equivalent of about 40 years of normal usage in a moderate climate such as southern California. There were no indications of significant wear or deterioration. This was a strong indication of the meter's long term durability.

Moreover, gas meters operate in a variety of climates, from frigid arctic blizzards to sizzling sun-drenched deserts. MTI (or its predecessor Select) performed several temperature tests to ensure the new measurement technology was equal to the challenges that extreme temperatures can pose. Table 6 summarizes

Table 6.    Temperature Tests

| ANSI or Test Number | Brief Description | Results |
|---|---|---|
| 2.12 | TEMPERATURE AND THERMAL SHOCK RESISTANCE | Meter operated well between -40° and +140°F (20°F higher and 10° lower than ANSI requirement). Meter was repeatedly started and stopped at the lower temperatures without any indication of problems. |
| SS-25 | Prolonged Temperature | A 30 day exposure to prolonged temperatures between -5° and +140°F had no apparent affect on the meter. |
| SS-26 | Extreme Temperature | Operated satisfactorily from -40° to +140°F. |
| SS-29 | High Temperature Aging | Meter operated at 150°F for 30 days - no significant effect on accuracy. |

the results of the tests and amply demonstrates the new meter's ability to function in extreme temperatures.

Resistance to Corrosion and Chemical Attack

Paragraph 2.8 of the ANSI B109.1 Construction Requirements states that internal parts and surfaces of the meter shall be resistant to corrosion or chemical attack that would adversely affect the operation of the meter. Three different techniques were utilized to determine the effects of a variety of substances on the sensor and its components - 1) direct immersion, 2) periodic exposure and 3) continuous exposure. The substances employed were pipeline condensates from SoCal, Oklahoma Natural and the Columbia Gas system, water, oil, transmission fluid, brake fluid, antifreeze, windshield cleaner, leaded and unleaded gasoline, kerosene, diesel fuel, alcohol, acetone, glycol and brine solutions, weak sulfuric acid, ammonia, ammonium hydroxide and SoCal's standard test solution.

• The direct immersion test involved submerging one sensor and one sample of each of the components in the individual substances continuously for a period of 30 days, except for the SoCal standard test solution. Another sensor and set of components was submerged continuously for a period of 90 days. For the SoCal standard solution a sensor was subjected to a 60 day soaking test. The samples were microscopically examined for surface irregularities and porosity at the commencement and the conclusion of each test period. The thickness of the samples was measured with a digimatic indicator accurate to one micron at the commencement and conclusion of each test period. Similarly, the weight of the samples was measured with an electronic balance accurate to one milligram.

• The periodic exposure test utilized eleven of the above substances in individual sensors - SoCal condensate, SoCal's standard solution, gasoline, acetone, alcohol, water, kerosene, diesel fuel, Jet HIB 349, Oklahoma Natural (ON) pipeline liquids and an ON glycol/oil mixture. Each sensor was connected to test piping flowing at 50 cfh. A liquid was continuously atomized into the air stream for one hour each day. The test was repeated for fourteen consecutive days. The sensors were examined for fluid absorption or deterioration as described above at the commencement and conclusion of the test.

• The continuous exposure test utilized the same substances as above.    An essentially saturated vapor/air mixture (condensed liquid was always present in the bottom of the lines) was continuously recirculated through the sensor for 28 days.   The sensors were examined for any deterioration or absorption as described above.

Only one substance, acetone, produced any discernible effect on the interior parts or surfaces of the sensor.   Acetone damaged the protective insulation coating on the piezo electric element.   Although acetone is not normally found in a gas distribution system, a more durable and chemically resistant coating will be specified for production meters.

Meter Class Test

Paragraph 3.2.2.2 of the ANSI standards for residential meters specifies that the rated capacity of the meter shall be determined on a bell prover with air supplied at exactly 125 Pa pressure differential across the meter.   The observed volumetric flow rate is subsequently adjusted for natural gas at an assumed specific gravity of 0.60 as well as temperature and barometric pressure. The calculated volumetric flow rate determines the meter class (rating).   Based upon this procedure the MTI meter has a meter class rating of approximately 7.9 $m^3$/hour.

Electronic Reliability

The ANSI standard does not currently include performance requirements for the electronic elements in residential gas meters.   Yet electronics are the heart and soul of the newly emerging technologies.   Electronics which are durable and reliable are essential to the viability of these developments. Moreover, low power consumption is vital to avoid frequent battery changes and added costs for the gas distribution utility.   MTI's predecessor Select, devised several tests for the electronics to monitor power consumption, tolerance to moisture, extreme temperatures, magnetic interference and radio frequency interference.   Table 7 summarizes the test results observed.

Table 7.    Electronic Reliability Tests

| Test Number | Brief Description | Results |
|---|---|---|
| SS-16 | Power Consumption | Results indicated a 10 year battery life will be readily achievable with an ASIC |
| SS-23 | Temperature Tolerance | Electronics tested between -40° and +140°F without any discernible effect |
| SS-24 | Moisture Tolerance | Electrical shorts occurred on early tests - additional conformal coating cured shorts |
| SS-27 | Magnetic Interference | No discernible effects from a very strong magnet placed on the meter case |
| SS-30 | Radio Frequency Interference | No discernible effects from high gain radio frequencies at the meter case |

MAJOR ACHIEVEMENTS OF THE PROJECT

• Prototype meters have undergone an extensive and intensive testing program to demonstrate the viability of the technology.

• The prototype meters have met or exceeded the ANSI B109.1 standards.

• The prototype meters have demonstrated the feasibility of GRI's decision to seek a compact meter for early market entry.

• So Cal, the largest United States gas utility has been intimately involved with the project and has participated in the testing.

- Several other leading U.S. utilities have participated in sponsoring the project and have expressed keen interest in field testing pre-production meters.

- American Meter Company, the predominant U.S. meter manufacturer, has participated in the sponsorship and testing of the compact meter and has formed a joint venture with Select to bring the meter to the U.S. and world-wide marketplace.

## FUTURE PLANS

Field tests at U.S. utilities have already begun. Three hundred units are or will be installed at ten to fifteen utilities and tested for a period of up to one year. This will permit natural gas distribution companies to specify the meter in bid packages for meter deliveries next year. One hundred units have been manufactured for overseas testing. These units will be allocated to prominent gas utilities in Europe, Asia and other major natural gas markets for testing and evaluation.

## SPONSORS

The testing and commercialization program has enjoyed the direct support of several prominent sponsors including:

| | |
|---|---|
| Gas Research Institute | Southern California Gas Company |
| Pacific Gas and Electric Company | The Brooklyn Union Gas Company |
| Consolidated Edison Co. of New York | American Meter Company |

## CONCLUSIONS

- The results of the testing program demonstrate that GRI's objective to develop and test a smaller, more aesthetic gas meter and to make the new meter available to natural gas utilities was feasible and has been attained.

- The compact meter concept need not compromise well accepted ANSI B109.1 standards for gas meters under 500 cfh capacity.

- The MTI compact electronic meter technology is sufficiently proven for a competent U.S. manufacturer to manufacture pre-production meters for a geographically dispersed field test program in the United States and overseas.

- The MTI meter generates an electronic output which lends itself perfectly to rapidly emerging AMR technology, either telephone or radio based.

Thank you.

ULTRASONIC DOMESTIC METERS - EXPERIENCE AND ENHANCEMENTS

COMPTEURS À GAZ DOMESTIQUES ULTRASONIQUES - EXPÉRIENCE
ET PERFECTIONNEMENTS

N.R.Chapman and D.W.Etheridge
British Gas plc, U.K.

ABSTRACT

The paper covers experience with the new ultrasonic domestic gas meters (E6), both in the laboratory and in the field, and enhancements to the basic meter design. Laboratory experience focuses on two particular difficulties faced by any novel meter, namely the unsteady nature of domestic flows and the presence of small quantities of contaminants in the gas. The reasoning behind the test procedures developed to ensure that these difficulties are overcome is discussed. Operational experience with the production versions of the meter is illustrated with results from field trials in the U.K. and in Canada.

Enhancements to the basic meters include the diagnostic data reader which has been developed to take advantage of the extensive diagnostic information available from the meters. Possible future enhancements which are under development are temperature compensation, an intelligent valve and remote meter reading.

RESUME

La communication traite de l'expérience pratique dans le domaine des nouveaux compteurs à gaz domestiques ultrasoniques (E6), à la fois dans le laboratoire et sur le terrain, et des perfectionnements apportés à la conception de base du compteur. L'expérience en laboratoire met en évidence deux difficultés spécifiques auxquelles tout nouveau compteur est confronté, à savoir la nature instable des débits domestiques et la présence de petites quantités de polluants dans le gaz. Le raisonnement derrière les procédures d'essai mises au point pour assurer que ces difficultés sont surmontées est examiné. L'expérience opérationnelle des versions de série du compteur est illustré par des résultats d'essais pratiques au RU et au Canada.

Des perfectionnements apportés au compteur de base comprennent le lecteur des données de diagnostic qui a été mis au point pour tirer profit de vaste informations de diagnostic fournies par le compteur. De possibles perfectionnements futurs, qui sont encore en phase de mise au point, comprennent la compensation en température, une valve programmable et un relevé du compteur à distance.

## INTRODUCTION

Two new types of ultrasonic domestic meters (known as E6 meters to distinguish them from the U6 diaphragm meter) are now being installed by British Gas. One is manufactured by Siemens Measurements Ltd. (see Figure 1) and the other by Eurometers Ltd. (shown in Figure 2). Both were developed under a new meter development programme pursued by British Gas. The history of this programme up to the commencement of initial production is given in Reference 1. Since that time more field experience has been gained and enhancements to the basic meters have been progressed. These aspects are covered in the latter part of the paper. The first part of the paper deals with two particular areas of laboratory testing (unsteady flows and contaminants). Experience to be gained from laboratory testing is a key element in meter development, and indeed in meter approval.

## LABORATORY TESTS - UNSTEADY FLOWS

One of the novel features of the E6 meters which tends to be overshadowed by the ultrasonic technology is that the meters are sampling devices. The decision to accept sampling meters was a major one and required considerable thought at the outset of the development programme. The main priority was to ensure that any errors due to sampling would be negligible in practical terms. Sampling only leads to errors with unsteady flows. Domestic gas flows are unsteady, but usually in the sense that the flow rate steps from one value to another.

Errors can be classified under two headings - random and systematic. Random errors have the characteristic that they reduce to zero when averaged over long time periods, whereas systematic errors do not. The major source of random error with a sampling meter is the numerical integration of discrete measurements with time to obtain the volume of gas consumed. This is referred to here as the sampling error. It is one of the few aspects of the meter development which is amenable to theoretical treatment. (There are other potential contributors to the variance e.g. errors in the measured flow rate and buffer delays but these should be relatively small). The systematic error due to sampling is referred to here as bias. This is not amenable to theoretical treatment and has to be obtained from measurement.

In order that there should be no correlation between samples and flow unsteadiness it was necessary to specify that the sampling should take place at random intervals. This also has the benefit of eliminating a possible fraud mechanism. Having taken this decision it was necessary to specify a maximum basic sampling interval. This was chosen by taking a worst case scenario (namely a minimal gas consumption consisting of a large number of short bursts of flow) and specifying that the sampling error should be negligible (typically less than 0.15 % i.e. one tenth of the permissible error). Theoretical calculations were then carried out and these led to the conclusion that a mean sample period of 2 seconds is adequate. The basis of the calculations can be found in Reference 2, for the case of a trapezoidal integration procedure. Subsequent test results from the unsteady flow rig confirmed that the statistical properties of the random errors were very close to the theoretical values. This implies that other sources of random errors are negligible compared to sampling errors. Support for this was also obtained from the initial field trial (see Reference 1).

Derivation of test procedure

A test procedure was required to confirm firstly that the random errors were of acceptable magnitude and secondly that there was no significant bias. It was decided to subject the meters to a square wave flow profile over a range of on/off frequencies and to obtain the errors by reference to three diaphragm meters. At the passage of each cubic foot registered by one of the reference meters, readings of actual volume are taken from the test meter and the other two reference meters. For each frequency a statistical analysis is carried out on the data to determine the variance of the error in each cubic foot (the "instantaneous" error). Three values of the time-mean error are obtained, corresponding to the three reference meters.

The choice of three reference meters was deliberate. It gives intrinsic repeatability checking and the failure of one reference meter is immediately apparent.

Results

Some results are shown in Figures 3 and 4. Figure 3 illustrates the magnitude and the random nature of the instantaneous error for the severe case with a stepping frequency of 0.25 Hz and a flow rate of 2.3 $m^3/h$ (80 $ft^3/h$). Figure 4 shows how the time-mean error varies with stepping frequency. Ideally the error should be independent of frequency and equal to the steady flow value i.e. zero bias. It can be seen that this is effectively the case, the dependence on frequency being very small. The high frequency case (0.25 Hz) has very much faster switching than that encountered with gas appliances and it was chosen to give an extreme point for the comparison with theory. It is of course possible that the reference meters are affected by such a high stepping frequency.

It is relevant to note here that sampling can be the cause of spurious errors when testing meters in the conventional way on steady flow rigs. If the flow is not completely steady, sampling errors will occur and these can be significant when the volume used for the test is small (a few cubic feet). To minimise this problem the British Gas Specification requires that the meter be operable in fast sampling mode for laboratory testing. A frequency of about 5 Hz is recommended. Even so it is important to check that the flow rate is sufficiently steady and in our experience the ultrasonic meter itself is a very good device for doing that.

LABORATORY TESTS - CONTAMINANTS

Derivation of test procedure

It is known that distributed natural gas contains small quantities of contaminants, notably dust and glycol, and any inferential meter needs to be tested to ensure that its performance is not affected by such substances. The main problem is to quantify the exposure of meters in a form suitable for test purposes. Glycol exposure is relatively easy to deal with, because it is deliberately introduced into the distribution network at known sites for the purpose of preventing leakage from old parts of the network. Those meters which are very close to these sites could experience gas which is saturated with glycol and this can be taken as the test criterion.

Dust is much more difficult to deal with. At the outset of the new meter development programme the conventional wisdom was that meters could be subjected to high dust loads (of the order of 100 g) as a result of occasional dust "storms". The original dust test was based on this expectation and the new meters were developed to cope with this level of load. A description of the contaminants test rig can be found in Reference 2.

Since a major source of dust is corrosion of old cast-iron pipes and these are being replaced by plastic pipes, two new surveys were carried out. These looked respectively at the amounts of dust found in the current diaphragm meter and in meter governor filters. It was concluded that a typical dust load is very small (typically 20 g in 20 years). Only on very rare occasions is a meter likely to encounter large dust loads. As a result it was decided to reduce the amount of dust used in the contaminants test rig to 20 g for approval purposes.

In the contaminants test rig the dust is introduced relatively rapidly, compared to a dust load of 20 g in 20 years which corresponds to a concentration of approximately $35 \mu g/m^3$. Simulating such concentrations for approval testing is not feasible, and it is very difficult for any type of test. However it has been achieved in our reliability rig (see Reference 2) by adapting a dust injection system developed for testing filters for motor vehicle engines.

Laboratory tests have shown that the transducers do need to be protected from dust build-up. There are various ways of achieving this. For example, each transducer can be protected locally by means of a filter, or the filter can be placed upstream of both transducers so as to prevent dust passing through the meter.

FIELD EXPERIENCE

Two field trials of production meters are currently being carried out. In the U.K. the original British Gas trial with prototype meters (known as the initial field trial (IFT)) is being continued under the title of the extended field trial (EFT). In Canada Consumers Gas are carrying out their own trial in collaboration with British Gas. Each trial uses the same basic arrangement and equipment, namely two ultrasonic meters in series with a diaphragm meter and a data logger specially developed by British Gas. Every 24 hours the diagnostic data from the E6 meters are logged as well as the daily volumes of gas consumption indicated by each meter. The volume data can be analysed in a variety of ways. One way is simply to plot the ratios of the daily volumes against time. There are however likely to be significant discretisation effects apparent, because the diaphragm meter volume is obtained from a pulse counter. In the U.K. trials this counter only resolves to $0.028 m^3$ ($1.0 ft^3$), such that when the volume consumed is small the daily error can be large ($\pm 1 \%$ for a consumption of $2.83 m^3$ ($100 ft^3$)). The variance which this causes in the daily error is however predictable and it can be eliminated from statistical analyses. At the other extreme, the ratio between the cumulative volumes can be plotted against time. This has practical relevance, because it relates directly to billing differences. Lying between these two extremes is the process of taking a moving average in order to determine long-term drift (i.e. very low frequency variations in the error). Examples of each of these analyses are illustrated with data from the three field trials.

U.K. field trial results

Early results from the initial field trial can be found in Reference 1. All three meter types were found to perform very well, but statistical analysis showed that the random component of the error was slightly larger for the diaphragm meter than for the ultrasonic meters. This was believed to be partly due to a small but measurable drift in the calibration of the diaphragm meters, which are known to be prone to this in their early life.

Statistical analysis by the same independent consultants (Reference 3) has now been carried out using a Kalman Filter technique to investigate long-term drift on those sites with the longest periods of continuous data (16 sites, 48 meters). The average drift over the test periods was found to be -0.2 % and zero for the two ultrasonic meters which is considerably less than that for the diaphragm meters, although in the latter case there was evidence that the drifts were decreasing at the end of the periods. Interestingly the analysis revealed summer/winter drifts with each of the meter types, with the greatest average (0.5 %) being found with the ultrasonic meter with zero long-term drift. This could simply be a reflection of lower flow rates during the summer correlating with a non-linear calibration curve. It could also be a genuine temperature effect.

Extended Field Trial

The geometries of the production E6 meters differs considerably from those of the prototype meters used for the IFT and it proved impossible to install both production meters in the meter box (in the U.K. external meters are placed in purpose-designed boxes). Each installation therefore consists of a diaphragm meter (U6), a Gill IFT meter and one type of production meter.

Although there are gaps in the data, the results presented in Figures 5 and 6 have been selected, because they are from a test site with a very extreme consumption profile and they show clearly the effect of the daily consumption on the daily volume ratios. The first Figure shows the variation of daily volume with time and it can be seen that there is a long period in the summer with consumptions of order 0.28 m$^3$ (10 ft$^3$) per day and two short periods with much higher consumptions.

Figure 6 shows the corresponding ratios between the daily volumes (the diaphragm meter and the two ultrasonic meters are denoted by U6, IFT and E6 respectively). The discretisation errors in the two ratios involving the U6 meter are clearly apparent in the summer period. These errors are of course not important. However it can also be seen that the average of the U6 ratios lies 2 or 3 % above the average of the ratio between the two ultrasonic meters. This indicates that at this particular site, the diaphragm meter reads 2 or 3 % lower than the ultrasonic meters at the very low flow rates associated with pilot lights.

Canadian field trial

The Consumers Gas trial was initiated in early 1994 with early production meters (see Reference 4). There are more than 20 sites and at most of them the meters are external and fully exposed to the rigours of the Ontario weather (i.e. the meters are not in boxes).

Perhaps not surprisingly, some problems have been encountered with the early meters, but the results which have been obtained are very encouraging. The trial is particularly important because the external sites allow both production E6 meters to be used, and the operating temperatures experienced cover a wider range than those encountered in the U.K. (70 °C rather than 45 °C). The Canadian diaphragm meter is temperature compensated and this can be compared directly with one of the E6 meters which records both temperature compensated and uncompensated volumes.

Figure 7 is an example of results expressed in terms of the ratios between the cumulative volumes recorded by the meters. The lower curve corresponds to the temperature compensated meters (the diaphragm meter and one of the E6 meters). Apart from the expected initial variation, the curve is virtually flat, indicating very good agreement between the two meters. The upper curve shows the ratio between uncompensated volumes (the two E6 meters). Even with this presentation there is some evidence of a seasonal variation (approximately 0.3 %). This could simply be a reflection of the fact that the volumes are not compensated, because a 1 °C difference between the gas temperatures would give rise to a difference of 0.3 %.

## ENHANCEMENTS

Several features of the E6 meters makes them particularly suitable for enhancements, namely the intelligence of the on-board microprocessor, the built-in interfaces and the integral battery. The enhancements described in the following paragraphs are in various stages of active development.

### The Diagnostic Data Reader (DDR)

The DDR forms the basis of a support system which has been specially developed by British Gas for dealing with diagnostic data from the meters. It is a specially programmed "palm top" computer equipped with an optical communications head (see Figure 2). The optical head is placed over the optical port of the meter and the diagnostic data held in the memory of the meter can then be transmitted to the DDR. This data can then be downloaded to a PC and stored for subsequent analysis.

### Temperature Compensation

Temperature compensation offers significant improvements in operational accuracy even in the relatively mild climate of the U.K. and it is relatively easy to incorporate in the E6 meter. In fact both meter designs were developed with temperature compensation although it is not currently activated. Work is now in progress to obtain type approval for compensated versions of the meters. This is not as straightforward as it may seem, because the procedures for approving such meters have yet to be established. However it is anticipated that both meter designs will be approved by early 1996. The subsequent introduction of the meters into the U.K. market will of course depend on several factors, but gaining type approval is seen as important simply in terms of overseas applications.

### Automatic Meter Reading (AMR)

By virtue of its built-in interfaces and integral battery, it is relatively easy and inexpensive (compared to a mechanical meter) to adapt an E6 meter for a radio form of AMR. The technical feasibility has been demonstrated both with an integral unit and with a retrofit unit. Figure 8 shows an example of the latter developed at the Gas Research Centre for the Eurometers meter. Either or both of these versions of the E6 could form the basis of a full AMR system, but whether such a system will be introduced in the U.K. depends on many factors other than purely technical ones.

### Intelligent Valve

The intelligence of the on-board microprocessor can be put to use for the operation of a gas shut-off valve to satisfy a number of requirements. Interest in an integral or bolt-on valve has been expressed by several utilities throughout the world for a wide variety of reasons.

The outputs from separate detectors (e.g. smoke, methane, carbon monoxide) could in principle be fed to the meter in some way, such that the valve would be activated when a safety hazard was detected. A temperature compensated version of the meter could itself act as a fire detector and shut the valve when necessary. Similarly the basic meter could be programmed to close the valve if an exceptionally large flow rate of gas were recorded.

Another possible application is earthquake protection. This could take the form of a meter equipped with some form of motion detector which leads to closure of the valve when certain parameters are exceeded.

Perhaps the most obvious application of an intelligent valve is prepayment metering. In fact this is probably the most demanding application, because the valve has to be opened as well as closed by the meter. This has implications on battery life and places stringent demands on the software in that there should be negligible risk of the valve being opened at the wrong time. (For all the other applications mentioned above it is probably adequate for the valve to be opened manually at the discretion of the customer.)

CONCLUDING REMARKS

The E6 meters are very innovative devices which have required new testing procedures to be developed. A good example of this, which has been discussed in some detail here, is the sampling nature of the meter. The need to demonstrate that sampling errors are negligible in practice was recognised at the outset of the development programme to be fundamental to the success of the meters. Fortunately this is one of the areas where a theoretical approach is useful.

Field trial experience of the meters, both in the U.K. and in Canada, has continued to demonstrate that the E6 meters have a metrological performance which is as good as, and in some respects better than, conventional diaphragm meters.

Enhancements to the basic meters are now being developed to take advantage of their special features.

REFERENCES

1.    Chapman, N.R., Etheridge, D.W. and Sussex, A.D. Ultrasonic domestic gas meters - from concept to realisation. Communication 1527, Inst. of Gas Engineers, Proc. of 130th Annual General Meeting and Spring Conference, May 1993.

2.    Etheridge, D.W. and Gaskell, M.C. Testing Novel Domestic Gas Meters. Proc. of "Flow Measurement in the mid-90's", National Engineering Laboratory, East Kilbride, June 1994.

3.    Gent, C. and Bruce, D. Internal reports from EDS Defence Ltd. under contract to British Gas.

4.    Eagleson, D. Ultrasonic meter trial at Consumers Gas. Proc. of 34th Annual CGA Measurement School, Toronto, Canada, May 1995.

ACKNOWLEDGEMENTS

The permission of British Gas to present this paper is gratefully acknowledged. So too are the contributions to the E6 project of many colleagues in British Gas and elsewhere in the gas industry, both in the U.K. and in Canada.

Figure 1. The Siemens Measurements meter.

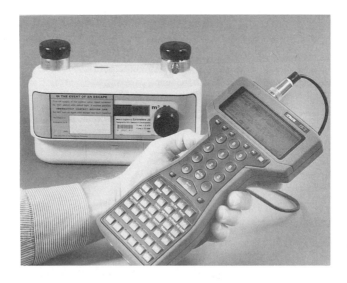

Figure 2. The Eurometers meter and the diagnostic data reader.

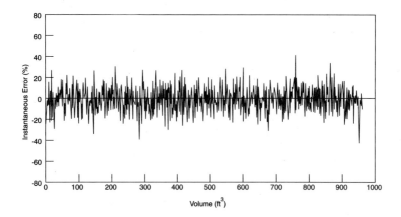

Figure 3. Instantaneous errors observed on the unsteady flow test rig at an extreme
stepping frequency of 0.25 Hz.

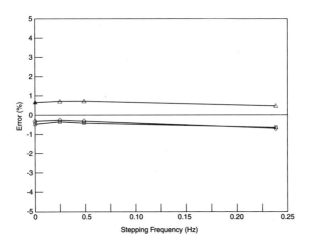

Figure 4. Measured error of E6 relative to three reference meters as a function of
stepping frequency, illustrating very low bias.

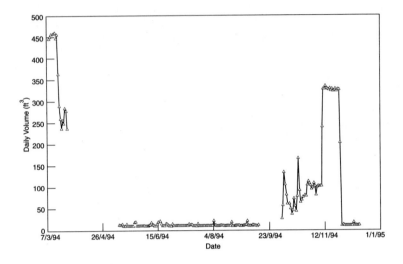

Figure 5. Example of an extreme variation of daily consumption profile.

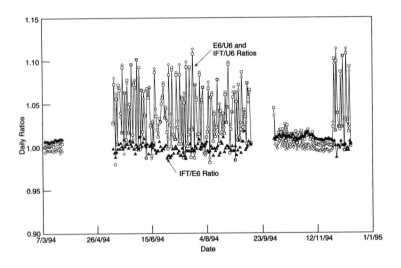

Figure 6. Ratios between the daily volumes recorded by the three meters (U6, IFT and E6 denote diaphragm meter, initial field trial  meter and production meter respectively).

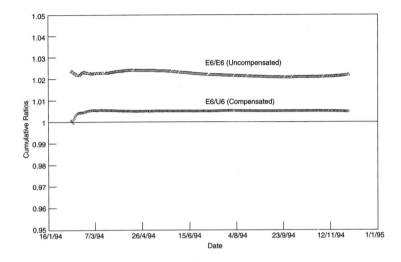

Figure 7. Ratios between the cumulative volumes recorded at a test site in Canada .
Upper curve is for the uncompensated readings from the two E6 meters.
Lower curve is for temperature compensated readings from the diaphragm
meter and one of the E6 meters.

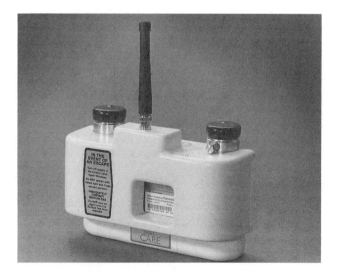

Figure 8. Eurometers meter equipped with a prototype bolt-on AMR system.

OPTICAL SENSORS IMPROVE LEAK
DETECTION AND LOCATION

LES CAPTEUR OPTIQUES AMÉLIORENT
LA DÉTECTION ET LE LOCALISATION DES GAZ

S.C. Murray
British Gas plc, Research & Technology, UK

Mr L.L. (Tom) Altpeter
Gas Research Institute, USA

Mr T. Pichery
Gaz de France, France

ABSTRACT

The detection and location of natural gas leaks is important to ensure the safety of the public and minimise the loss of product. This paper outlines the development of three, optical, gas (methane) detection systems, each aimed at a different market sector, based upon the absorption of infra-red radiation. Following a review of current techniques, the paper outlines the development of a high sensitivity, field portable, gas detector, a laser based domestic methane sensor and a patrol survey mounted optical leak detection system.

RÉSUMÉ

La détection et la localisation des fuites de gaz naturel ont d'une importance vitale pour garantir la sécurité du public et minimiser les pertes de produit. Cet article présente le dveloppement de trois systémes de détection optique du gaz (méthane), basés sur l'absorption des rayons infra-rouges, qui visent chacun un secteur différent du marché. Suite à l'examen des techniques actuelles, l'article présente le développement d'un détecteur de gaz portatif de haute sensibilité, d'un détecteur de méthane domestique à laser et d'un systéme de détection optiques des fuites monté sur un véhicule de brigade de surveillance.

INTRODUCTION

The detection and location of natural gas leaks is an important everyday activity of gas engineers around the world. Preserving the safety of the public and minimising the loss of product are the two most important considerations. To accomplish these goals, a number of different detection scenarios must be addressed and suitable instruments developed.

Most leaks are identified, initially, by the public, via the odouriser content of the gas, but a precise location of the leak site is not generally possible. Historically, a number of different instrument types have been used, depending upon environmental constraints and the required detection sensitivity, to identify the magnitude and location of leaks. Widely used instruments for the detection of methane in air are based on either flame ionisation detection (FID) or catalytic oxidation methods. Neither technique is specific to the detection of methane, and care has to be taken when using these instruments in the presence of other combustible gases or, when using catalytic detectors, in oxygen deficient atmospheres. The need for improved methods of gas detection and measurement has led to the development of novel optical detection methods which are specific, sensitive and accurate.

In recent years, the dynamic progress made in fibre optic telecommunications has yielded a ready supply of optical sources and detectors in the infra-red portion of the electromagnetic spectrum. Availability of these devices has led to a rapid growth in the development of gas detection techniques based upon absorption spectroscopy.

Like many other gases, methane exhibits a unique, characteristic, absorption spectrum in the near and mid infra-red portion of the electromagnetic spectrum. The position, spacing and number of absorption bands is determined by the quantum mechanical nature of the molecule. When illuminated with a broadband optical source, a gas will, in general, absorb a small portion of this radiation at specific wavelengths determined by the quantum mechanical nature of the gas molecule. The absorption is directly related to the amount of gas contained within the optical path, enabling the concentration of the gas to be determined. This mechanism is the principle upon which all spectroscopic detection techniques are based. The amount the optical source is absorbed is related to the concentration of the gas via the Beer-Lambert Law;

$$I(\upsilon) = I_o(\upsilon)\exp[-\alpha(\upsilon)\ P_{gas}\ L] \qquad\qquad \text{Eqn 1.1}$$

where $I_o(\upsilon)$ and $I(\upsilon)$ represent, respectively, the intensity of the radiation, of frequency $\upsilon$, before and after passing through the gas, $P_{gas}$ is the partial pressure of the gas, L is the optical pathlength containing gas and $\alpha(\upsilon)$ is the absorption coefficient of the gas at frequency $\upsilon$ measured in $atm^{-1}cm^{-1}$.

Methane has a fundamental absorption band in the mid infra-red portion of the electromagnetic spectrum (3.3 micrometers) and a number of overtone and combination bands in the near infra-red (1.666 and 1.331 micrometers respectively).

This paper reviews the development of three optical detection systems, based upon the above principle, each aimed at a different application area, and outlines the performance benefits achievable over current technology.

The first section of this paper deals with the development of a reliable, high sensitivity, hand-held, optical instrument designed to address the walking survey and industrial/domestic leak assessment markets. A limited number of optical instruments, based upon tungsten source technology, are currently used to measure methane. They do not have, however, the sensitivity, resolution or stability needed to detect low levels of gas leakage. Instruments currently being developed by AMG Systems Ltd., based upon 3.3 micrometer, semiconductor source technology, should provide a background -limited detection capability suitable for these application areas.

The detection of natural gas in domestic premises is a technologically challenging area. Semiconductor sensors, which have marginal market penetration in this area, are costly, require permanent main power and can suffer from false alarms. A prototype, optical device has been developed by EPREST (Electronic Eastern Professional), in collaboration with Gaz de France, which utilises a scanning 1.331 micrometer laser diode. Detectors based upon this technology, which is discussed in section two, are highly selective to natural gas and can provide low maintenance, drift free operation.

Optical absorption spectroscopy is not limited to the point detection of combustible and toxic gases, but can be utilised in an open-path configuration where the path length integral gas concentration is measured between two separate points. The Westinghouse Science and Technology Centre (WSTC) have demonstrated an open-path, optical instrument which can be mounted across the front bumper of a patrol survey vehicle. This vehicular mounted instrument uses a spectral correlation technique which is capable of determining small leaks at vehicle speeds of up to 20 m.p.h.. Instruments of this type obtain their high sensitivity by integrating the signal obtained over many absorption lines simultaneously. A small on-board computer, or data logger, can record the data including the exact roadside location of the leak. This technology is discussed in section three.

HIGH SENSITIVITY METHANE DETECTION USING LED SOURCES

Introduction

The ability to detect, selectively, low levels of methane using portable instrumentation is of interest to a number of gas utilities. Currently, low levels of methane, down to 50 ppm, are measured using special, high sensitivity catalytic detectors while concentration levels below this are measured using flame ionisation detectors (FID's).

High sensitivity catalytic detectors suffer from a number of technological problems which limit their performance;

*   Response times limited to approximately 10 s.
*   Relatively large, short term drift, typically +/- 10% of full scale deflection
*   Variable accuracy, +/- 15 to 50% of actual gas value.
*   Prone to poisoning, although poison tolerant sensors now available.
*   Environmental conditions can effect accuracy and resolution.

Although intrinsically safe FID's are now available, they are prohibitively expensive and respond to a number of gases. Optical sensors, on the other hand, cannot be poisoned (although optical obscuration is a problem), have rapid response times (typically less than 2 seconds) and have a higher sensitivity and better accuracy than catalytic sensors over a range of environmental conditions.

This section details the development of a portable, high sensitivity, methane specific optical detection instrument based upon the gas correlation technique and using mid infra-red emitting LED's. AMG Systems of Biggleswade, England have, with the support of British Gas plc and the Gas Research Institute, demonstrated this technique as a possible alternative to the currently used Pellistor and flame ionisation detectors. A battery powered, light weight (less than 1.5 kgs), hand held instrument with a detection capability of better than 5 ppm should be available within the next two years.

The Detection Technique

Infra-red radiation from the a light-emitting-diode, LED 1, Fig.1, passes through a small gas cell containing methane. The methane contained within this cell absorbs specific wavelengths of the incident radiation and produces a filtered LED spectrum, deficient in these absorbed wavelengths, at its output. Radiation from the filtered LED (the reference beam) and LED 2, which does not have the above wavelength components removed, are combined using the beamsplitter, passed through the gas sampling area and focused onto a detector. The two LED's are modulated at different frequencies and a lock-in detection technique is employed to measure the light intensity signals from both the sources simultaneously.

As the target gas, methane, is introduced into the gas sampling area, the intensity of the sample beam is reduced due to optical absorption by the gas. The intensity of the reference beam is unaffected by the target gas because the reference cell has removed the light at the wavelengths that the target gas absorb. Obscuration of the optics will effect both beam intensities by the same amount so that, whilst the received intensity reduces, the calibration for the target gas is unaffected. If another combustible gas is present within the sampling beam then, unless there is a high correlation between the absorption spectra of reference gas and the gas in the sampling area, a similar reduction in both beam intensities is observed. This technique is, therefore, highly specific to the detection of gases showing a good spectral correlation with the gas contained within the reference cell. The sensor assembly is calibrated for detector response as a function of target gas concentration and uses both analogue stabilisation techniques and digital signal processing to remove any LED signal drift.

If suitable optical sources, emitting in an appropriate part of the electromagnetic spectrum, are available this technique can be applied to a number of gases, vapours or gas mixtures. To maximise detection sensitivity, and minimise the sample and reference cell path length requirements, source and detection components optimised for the 3.4 micrometer region were chosen.

The 3.3 Micrometer LED Source

The above detection scheme relies upon a mid infra-red optical source which emits in the 3.3 micrometer region, corresponding to the fundamental C-H absorption band of methane. This was not commercially available. AMG Systems Ltd. in collaboration with DERA Malvern, the UK's leading Laboratory for semiconductor material and device R&D, have developed a 3.3 micrometer LED source for this application.

The aim of this joint venture was to develop LED sources emitting in the 3.3 micrometer region with a maximum drive current of 50 mA and having room temperature operation. Additionally, an LED structure was required which would give a polar output radiation pattern, required to produce effective light coupling from the source through the optical system. Calculations have indicated that a 10 ppm detection sensitivity could be achieved with a LED output power of 1 microwatt launched into f/4 optics. This 1 microwatt refers to the power at the methane absorption wavelengths not the total LED output power, which would cover a wider spectral band and hence contain more energy.

These LED's were fabricated in the InGaAsSb III-V alloy system with alloy compositions chosen to give the required emission wavelength. Epitaxial material was grown using the MBE (molecular beam epitaxy) process and pn junctions grown-in during the epitaxial deposition. Burrus structure LED chips were fabricated with 100 micron diameter emission areas. This small emission area was chosen to maximise the LED to detector coupling efficiency. A typical output spectrum is shown in Fig.2. Usable power output of 3.5 microwatts into a 40 ° acceptance angle have been achieved.

Detection Sensitivity

The instrument response was measured, as a function of methane concentration, for an sample pathlength of 330 mm. Both commercially available PbSe photoconductive detectors and InAs photovoltaic detectors, fabricated by AMG/DERA, were used to conduct these measurements. The LED was driven using a 50 mA 1:1 duty cycle signal at 1 kHz.. Typical results can be seen in Fig.3. The PbSe detector had an active area of 1mm square whilst the InAs detector has a diameter of 0.25 mm and a zero bias slope impedance of 500 Ohms. It can be seen from the results that a noise limited methane detection sensitivity of 5 ppm was possible using this configuration.

Instrument Design

A prototype instrument has been designed by AMG Systems Ltd. consisting of a compact optical bench assembly, onto which the optical components and the gas reference cells are mounted, and a number of electronic, signal processing boards. The optical bench assembly was used to evaluate a number of different optical configurations before the final design is chosen. This optical arrangement has also been used to construct a further compact optical bench assembly capable of measuring the total hydrocarbon content (THC) of a gas with a 1% LEL resolution in a package size 50 mm in diameter by 70 mm long.

DOMESTIC DETECTION OF METHANE

Introduction

Gaz de France, in collaboration with EPREST (Electronic Eastern Professional), is currently involved in the development of a low cost, reliable, fast response, methane selective detector for domestic environments. The development programme known as AMELIE (Alert to Methane by Infra-red Laser - Explosimeter), which is technically co-ordinated by EPREST, was started in June 1993 and is part funded by the Ministry of Industry. The project will finish in June 1995, when a prototype detector should be available.

The aim of project AMELIE is to develop and manufacturer a reliable methane sensor in accordance with draft European Standard (prEN50194) . To meet this standard, the following detector requirements were agreed upon by Gaz de France and EPREST;

- Selective detection of methane in the presence of other contaminant gases
- Sensitive detection, %LEL detection capability
- Mechanically robust
- Stable optical and electrical operation
- Battery life of approximately 1 year.
- Competitively priced, less than 500 Francs.

Although some detectors are available, based upon physio-chemical techniques, they are not very sensitive, have large zero drifts and respond to a number of different gases and vapours. This section deals with the development of an optical methane sensor based upon low cost semiconductor laser diodes.

The development programme was split into three phases, a six month feasibility study, a ten month sensor development programme and a final product engineering stage, due for completion this year. The initial six month feasibility was concerned with evaluating the most suitable technology and providing recommendations for phase two of the project. A second phase entitled "Theoretical Validation of the Sensor" was undertaken in December 1993 with the objective of producing a laboratory demonstrator based upon the technique identified in Phase 1. A laboratory demonstrator was produced which had a detection capability of 1% v/v methane (1% methane in air) for an optical pathlength of 10 cm. The final product engineering phase, which started in October 1994, was devoted to the development of a small, battery operated version of the gas sensor which met the requirements of the European Standard.

The Detection Technique

High quality optical sources, semiconductor laser diodes, are available in the 1.331 micrometer region, a part of the em spectrum used extensively in fibre optic communications systems. Moreover, few other gases have absorption lines in this region of the spectrum, thereby ensuring that 1.33 micrometer based detection schemes have few cross sensitivity problems.

Near infra-red radiation from a semiconductor laser diode, Fig.4, was collimated using a 60 mm focal length lens and passed through an optical interference filter and a beamsplitter. The interference filter has a bandpass characteristic corresponding with the 1.33 micrometer methane absorption line. The laser diode module, which is mounted upon a temperature controlled Peltier element, can be spectrally tuned so that it's emission spectrum coincides with the transmission properties of the interference filter. At the beamsplitter, 50% of the radiation passing through the optical interference filter is focused onto detector 1 (the reference measurement) and the remaining passed through the gas sampling area and focused onto detector 2 (the signal measurement).

When methane is introduced into the sampling area, the amount of radiation reaching detector 2 is reduced while the amount reaching detector 1 is unaffected. Processing both detector signals eliminates the effect of optical source variations and transmitter noise upon the gas concentration measurement.

Detection Sensitivity

At present, this instrument has a noise limited performance of 2% methane over a 10 cm optical path. This, according to Eqn 1.1, corresponds to a minimum measurable signal variation of 0.4%. Lowering the detector noise from 0.4% to 0.2% will half the minimum methane concentration (1% (20% LEL)) which can be measured.

Application Areas

When coupled to the new domestic gas meter, DIALOGAZ, it will be possible to reduce the inlet gas pressure when an abnormally high level of methane gas is measured in the surrounding atmosphere.This technology can also be used to address the detection requirements of an number of application areas, e.g. air quality control and environmental protection.

DEVELOPMENT OF A NEW, IMPROVED, GAS LEAK DETECTOR FOR LEAK SURVEY VEHICLES

Introduction

The Westinghouse Science & Technology Centre (WSTC), funded by the Gas Research Institute (GRI), has demonstrated a new, improved, technique for leak surveying by vehicle based upon the infra-red absorption of methane gas. Conventional leak survey vehicles are equipped with a flame ionisation detector (FID) in which vehicle speeds are limited to 3-10 k.p.h. (2-7 m.p.h.). With the WSTC approach, vehicle speeds of 30-40 k.p.h. (20-30 m.p.h.) or greater are possible. Productivity of survey operations can be improved by 20-50%.

Early in the programme, when Westinghouse had developed its first conceptual evaluation unit (CEU), a series of experiments were performed in which a leak survey vehicle, equipped with a state-of-the-art (SOA) flame ionisation detector, was compared directly with the CEU. As part of these experiments, a simulated ground leak site was created from which a set of controlled leaks, covering a wide range of leak rates, could be produced. Each vehicle was driven over the leak site at speeds which included 0, 3, 6, 10 and 13 k.p.h. (5, 10, 15 and 20 m.p.h.) An overall comparison of the vehicles' responses is shown in Fig.7. The horizontal axis refers to the vehicle speed. The vertical axis indicates the percent response of a survey vehicle to the full range of leaks presented at each tested speed. It can be seen that, as the vehicle speed increased, the overall percent response of the SOA vehicle drops off. No measurements were taken with the SOA vehicle at 20 mph.

The Detection Technique

From the CEU, WSTC developed an engineering prototype gas leak detector, based on the absorption of 3.34 micrometer radiation by methane gas. The engineering prototype unit (EPU) is shown in Photograph 1. The detector is mounted on the front bumper of a vehicle. An infra-red light source sends a beam of light across the front of the vehicle to a detector on the other side. An electro-optic filter in front of the detector limits the response of the system to methane only. The EPU makes thousands of measurements per second, permitting an instant response to any methane over a wide range of vehicle speeds.

When a leak is encountered, a signal is sent to a readout device mounted inside the vehicle, Photograph 2.. The readout provides a number of useful pieces of information. First, an audio alarm will signal the detection of a leak to the survey crew. Then, the strength and extent of the leak is shown in two ways;

- a continuous 60 second analogue trace of the detector output,
- continuously updated digital readings describe the background level of methane, the most recent maximum reading (e.g. from the detected leak), and the prevailing threshold level.

The latter is controllable by the operator. Should the background level begin to climb, due to local sources of methane, the THRESHOLD Control allows the operator to "zero out" the background. The calibration of the detector is easily checked with the front panel "CALIBRATE" switch. When the switch is thrown, a small transparent cell of methane, fixed in concentration and located in the detector compartment, is swung into the beam in front of the detector. A detector response of known predictable level appears as an analogue trace and a MAXIMUM level digital reading, Fig.5. The CALIBRATE function is particularly useful for easy alignment of the light source and the detector during initial mounting of the detector.

EPU Field Trials

Field trials of the EPU were held during 1994-95 to demonstrate it's feasibility. A total of 10-12 gas utilities participated, using the EPU for periods ranging from several days to 3-4 weeks. Weather extremes from -23 to +30 ° C (-10 to +85 °F) in snow and rain were experienced by the EPU. The feedback from the users was uniformly positive. Features that were appreciated included the ability to survey at traffic speeds, instant response to a leak, good sensitivity, elimination of the need for hydrogen gas (FID), ease of handling and assembly, and the ability to operate in wet weather. Selectivity for methane was an advantage relative to the FID, which response to all combustible substances. Nevertheless, the EPU could not distinguish sewer gas from natural gas; and in certain traffic situations, such as starting from a traffic light with other vehicles or following vehicles with smoky exhaust, the EPU could detect the emission of methane from auto exhausts. However, traffic-based false alarms were relatively infrequent and easily diagnosed.

The leak detector could be easily stored in a carrying case until needed. Mounting on the vehicle was a relatively simple matter, requiring only several hours. When not required, it could be easily removed and repackaged in it's case.

A commercialisation partner has been chosen by GRI and WSTC for the final phase of the product development. A final design of the gas leak detector will be developed by this consortium and, following a final field test, should become commercially available in late 1996-97.

Photograph 1. Prototype Natural Gas Leak Detector mounted on the front of a survey vehicle.
(Light source in the background, towards the right, photooptical detector package in the forground
and to the left)

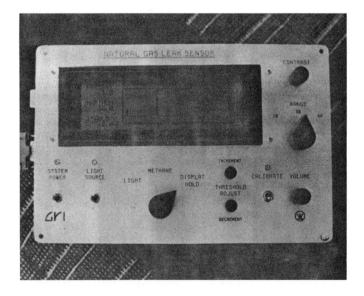

Photograph 2. Display panel (within the vehicle) for the output signals from the photooptical detector.

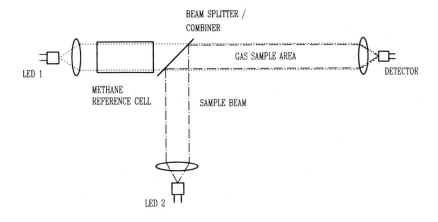

Fig.1 SCHEMATIC LAYOUT OF THE OPTICAL DETECTION TECHNIQUE

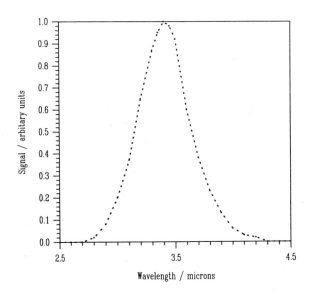

FIG.2 OUPUT SPECTRUM OF THE 3.4 MICROMETRE LED

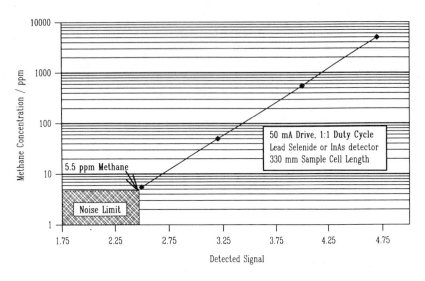

Fig.3 DETECTED SIGNAL AS A FUNCTION OF METHANE CONCENTRATION

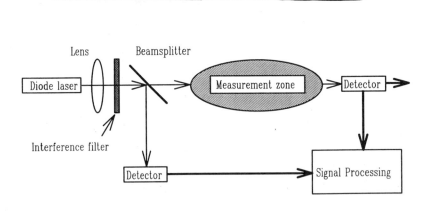

Fig.4 DOMESTIC METHANE DETECTOR; OPERATIONAL SCHEMATIC

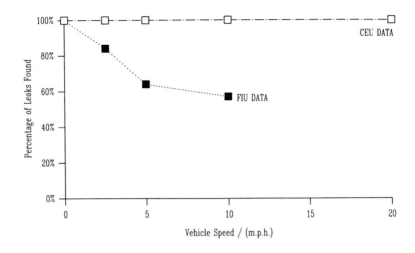

Fig.5 Direct Comparison of Performance Between a Leak Survey Vehicle Equipped with a Westinghouse Concept Evaluation Unit (Initially Developed by Westinghouse) and a Survey Vehicle Equipped with a State-of-the-Art Flame Ionisation Detector (Operated by the Local Gas Utility). Overall Percentage of Detectable Responses at Each Vehicle Speed to a Broad Range of Controlled Leak Rates.

Flammable Gas Imaging System Using Infrared Absorption

Systéme Imageur de Gaz Inflammable Utilisant l'Absorption Infrarouge

Toshihide kanagawa
Hirofumi Ueda
Kohichi Sumida
Takeshi Nishio

Osaka Gas Co., Ltd, JAPAN

ABSTRACT

We are currently developing visualization technologies for flammable gas leaks as a new, more efficient means of monitoring such leaks over a wide area. This method uses real-time imaging of flammable gas not normally visible with the naked eye together with real-time images of the surrounding landscape. The goal is to create a device better suited to on-site applications through the use of motion pictures taken simultaneously of flammable gas and the surrounding landscape, rather than using complicated measuring instruments that simply extract gas.

We selected a visualization method that uses the infrared absorption characteristics of a hydrocarbon-based gas to begin basic studies. When simulations indicated that methane, propane and butane could be visualized simultaneously, we began demonstration experiments on visualization using infrared cameras and light sources to see whether leaking gas could be imaged under controlled environmental conditions. The next step in this line of research will be to develop a device suitable for industrialization.

RÉSUMÉ

Des technologies de visualisation des fuites de gaz inflammables sont actuellement en cours de développement en vue de fournir un nouveau moyen de détection plus efficace de ce type de fuites sur une vaste échelle. Cette méthode utilise la représentation visuelle en temps réel des gaz inflammables qui ne sont pas normalement visible à l'œil nu ainsi que des images en temps réel des sites environnants. L'objectif est de créer un système mieux adapté aux applications locales en utilisant des images du gaz inflammable et des sites environnants filmées simultanément, plutôt que d'utiliser des instruments de mesure complexes qui ne font qu'extraire le gaz.

Pour commencer les recherches élémentaires, nous avons sélectionné une méthode de visualisation utilisant les caractéristiques d'absorption des infrarouges des gaz à base d'hydrocarbures. Des simulations ayant montré qu'il était possible de visualiser simultanément le méthane, le propane et le butane, nous avons procédé à des essais de démonstration concernant la faisabilité d'une représentation visuelle des fuites de gaz à l'aide de caméras infrarouges et de sources lumineuses dans un environnement contrôlé.Le développement d'un dispositif adapté à l'industrie sera la prochaine étape de cette ligne de recherches.

INTRODUCTION

Strict attention is paid to protective and disaster prevention equipment at LNG terminals because of the large quantities of flammable gas handled there. Within this context, gas detectors play an important role in discovering gas leaks at an early stage in the rare event of a leak, and in gathering information for appropriate measures. Storage and production equipment like LNG / LPG tanks and vaporizers are currently equipped primarily with point-type gas detectors, but extensive monitoring, like wide-area gas leak monitoring, requires many sensors and much labor for maintenance control and other work. To overcome this problem, Osaka Gas has focused on developing even larger area detection and monitoring devices, such as systems for measuring methane gas concentration on the optical path using He-Ne laser.

The present research is related to developing a new method for monitoring flammable gas leaks in which the surrounding landscape as well as methane, propane and butane leak conditions are displayed in real-time on a TV monitor. Designated leak action that normally requires gas detection from multiple locations using conventional point-type gas detectors can be taken immediately after a leak is viewed on screen, and operators can accurately appraise the rapidly changing dispersion and holding behavior of leaking gas using this method. (See Fig. 1.)

The present report focuses on the operating principle, simulation evaluations on visualization performance as well as results from demonstration experiments for a visualization method based on the infrared absorption characteristics of flammable gas.

OPERATING PRINCIPLE OF VISUALIZATION METHODS

Since flammable gas has certain absorption characteristics at specific wavelengths as shown in Fig. 2, we can tell that flammable gas is present by measuring infrared ray propagation at that wavelength. Measuring methods are classified as either active or passive, depending on whether the infrared rays measured are supplied by a special external light source, or from infrared rays radiating from the surrounding landscape. (See Fig. 3.) By the same token, evaluation methods for visualization performance vary even within the active method because evaluations are based on the type of light source. The operating principles for active and passive visualization methods are outlined below.

Neither method is suitable facing skyward from the ground because a background that reflects or radiates infrared rays is an essential condition for operation.

Active Method Using An He-Ne Laser

When laser light is absorbed by gas on its optical path, the relationship between Io, the intensity of light incidental to the gas, and I, the intensity of light that has passed through the gas, is generally expressed with the Lambert-Beer equation shown below.

$$I = Io \ exp(-k_\lambda \ l \ c) \tag{1}$$

Here, $k_\lambda$ is the absorption coefficient at wavelength $\lambda$ of the subject gas, l is the gas and light working length, and c is the gas concentration.

We can evaluate the amount of light absorbed if we use the equation to find the absorption coefficient $k_\lambda$ for flammable gas targeted for detection. The He-Ne laser has been used for some time now as a light source for measuring methane gas by the infrared absorption method because one of the oscillating wavelengths of the laser conforms to the $\nu 3$ line of the methane absorption spectrum. In the present study, white cells were also used on propane and butane - targeted for visualization - in order to measure their respective absorption coefficients. The results, shown in Table 1, confirmed that a 3.39-μm He-Ne laser can detect methane, propane and butane simultaneously.

A method that expands laser beams via an optical system was used with the laser described above to irradiate an area targeted for monitoring. The method improves the reliability and lowers the cost of devices because it lacks movable parts like those used in the beam scan method.

In order to visualize flammable gas with this device configuration, the amount of light absorbed by gases must exceed the detectable level of the infrared image sensor. The following equation is used to express visualization conditions when the area irradiated by laser is sufficiently large, the area is irradiated at a constant Io intensity, and thermal radiation effects from the background are minimized by a cold filter on the front of the image sensor.

$$\gamma Io \ \{1 - \exp(-2 \ k\lambda \ l \ c)\} > Isd \tag{2}$$

Here, $\gamma$ is the reflectance ratio for the background. Isd is a light intensity differential that is used to distinguish differences in concentration when viewing a visualized image, and that is determined experimentally according to the type of infrared image sensor used.

The equation for visualization conditions indicates that even a low-concentration gas cloud can be visualized when identical infrared image sensors are used as long as the reflectance ratio of the background as well as the intensity of laser irradiance are both relatively large.

## Passive Method Using Background Thermal Radiation

The passive method is comprised as shown in Fig. 3 of an infrared camera and a background that radiates infrared rays. Here the background and flammable gas present between the background and the camera are imaged simultaneously.

In terms of the absorption wavelengths for flammable gases given in Fig. 2, gas components in the atmosphere, such as $H_2O$ and $CO_2$, have such a small "atmospheric window" for absorption that there is little absorption and dispersion within a range of several tens of meters. Here the transmission of infrared rays propagated through the atmosphere is expressed by the equation below.

$$\frac{dIv}{dx} = -k\lambda \ \rho \ ( \ Iv - B \ ) \tag{3}$$

Here, Iv is the radiation intensity, x is the length of the medium, $k\lambda$ is the absorption coefficient of flammable gas at wavelength $\lambda$, $\rho$ is the concentration of the absorbed medium (flammable gas) and B is the Planck's equation of thermal radiation.

Assuming that the background is a gray body with a emissivity of $\varepsilon$, and that flammable gas is uniformly distributed from the background to the infrared camera, then if we define $T_{back}$ the background temperature and $T_{gas}$ the gas temperature, we can use the following equation to express radiation intensity in wavelength range $\lambda 1 \sim \lambda 2$ detected by the infrared sensor.

$$Iv = \varepsilon \int_{\lambda_1}^{\lambda_2} B(\lambda, T_{back}) \exp(-k_\lambda \ c \ x) d\lambda$$
$$+ \int_{\lambda_1}^{\lambda_2} B(\lambda, T_{gas})\{1 - \exp(-k_\lambda \ c \ x)\} d\lambda \tag{4}$$

The first term on the right side of the equation represents the transmission of background radiation, while the second term represents the radiation and absorption of the absorbed medium. If the background is a black body and the background and flammable gas temperatures are the same, then thermal radiation from the background will not be absorbed by the gas. However, the propagation of background thermal radiation will be altered by the presence of flammable gas because the atmospheric temperature will always be slightly different from the background temperature and black body backgrounds are rarely found in outdoor environments where the device is actually used.

The equation below is used to express visualization conditions when Io is the intensity of radiation detected by the infrared camera with no flammable gas present.

$$| \text{Iv} - \text{Io} | > \text{Isd} \qquad (5)$$

Just as with the active method, Isd is a light intensity differential that is used to distinguish differences in concentration when viewing a visualized image, and that is determined experimentally according to the type of infrared image sensor used.

Infrared camera sensitivity and the transmit wavelength of the infrared bandpass filter mounted on the camera determine detection sensitivity with this method. As the transmit band of the filter narrows to match the absorption peak within the transmit band as shown in Fig. 2, the SN ratio increases. However the amount of transmitted light tends to decrease at the same time, and imaging is more difficult. There exists preferable band width of the filter that provides well balance of the SN ratio and the amount of transmitted light. For this reason, a bandpass filter that can be varied for the background conditions of the desired visualization area as well as for gas absorption characteristics is highly desirable.

Active Method Using A White Light Source

An He-Ne laser that oscillates at a wavelength of 3.39 μm is large in size relative to its output, so the device must be enlarged to monitor gas leaks over a wide area. With that in mind, we devised a visualization device that uses a relatively small and inexpensive white light source. The light source used here is a globar lamp of sintered silicon carbide (SiC). Because the globar lamp is a conductor, it can be heated directly by current flow. Emissivity for the globar lamp ranges from 0.7 to 0.8 at wavelengths ranging from 3 to 4 μm, and its radiated infrared spectrum conforms to Planck's law of thermal radiation. Globar lamps are simply structured and readily provide a large output, so they feature relatively easy device operation, and they eliminate the need for detecting faint infrared rays in the border area of sensor sensitivity as is often the case with a passive method and an active one with a laser.

Like the passive method, visualization with a globar lamp requires gas absorption and radiation evaluations using wavelength integration rather than visualization performance evaluations based on the Lambert-Beer equation used for lasers. Here, performance evaluations are extremely complex because simulations are performed with new parameters like light source output and convergence performance as well as background reflectance that are appended to the passive method.

VISUALIZATION PERFORMANCE SIMULATION USING THE PASSIVE METHOD

Because so many parameters affect visualization performance with the passive method, the most efficient means of evaluating performance is through simulation calculations. The following results were calculated using propane as an example.

The graph in Fig. 4-a represents variations in infrared ray intensity, Iv-Io in equation (5), caused by both propane's absorption and radiation when the concentration of the gas was varied. In case the temperature of propane is lower enough than that of the background, the quantity of the absorbed infrared ray exceeds that of the radiation. In this situation the variation, the value of vertical axis, becomes negative, and the gas is visualized darker on a TV monitor.

Here the temperature difference between the background and the gas was varied from 0°C to 8°C, and background emissivity was fixed at 0.9. Here infrared intensity corresponding to a detection level of the infrared camera whose noise equivalent temperature differential (NETD) is 0.1°C was set at 1. Generally the greater the temperature differential, the greater the differential between flammable gas

absorption and radiation, so the differential intensity of infrared
rays reaching the sensor varies tremendously. We know, however, that
gas temperature, which is extremely difficult to detect is not the same
as the background temperature because of background emissivity.
     Fig. 4-b shows the variations in infrared ray intensity as well as
Fig. 4-a when the temperature differential between the background and
propane gas is fixed at 2°C. In this case background emissivity is
varied from 0.8 to 1.0. From this we know that the higher the
emissivity, the greater the attenuation due to the gas, and that a
emissivity of +0.1 causes variations very close to 2°C in the
temperature differential between the background and gas.
     These variations in the temperature differential between
background and gas as well as in background emissivity cause infrared
ray intensity - an indicator of visualization performance - to vary
dramatically. When visualization performance studies were conducted by
varying parameters for methane and butane gas as well, we found that
butane exhibited the same absorption tendencies as propane.
     Visualization by the passive method using commercially available
cameras is limited at this time to methane, propane and butane.
Considering technical trends indicating regular improvements in the
sensitivity of infrared cameras, however, we anticipate that this
method is the future of flammable gas visualization technology because
of features like the size and simplicity of device structures, power
consumption, as well as remote and wide-area monitoring capability.

VISUALIZATION EXPERIMENTS USING MODELED GAS LEAKS

     Visualization experiments using modeled flammable gas leaks were
conducted in order to confirm just how an actual flammable gas leak is
imaged based on our understanding of the infrared absorption
characteristics of gases, evaluations on infrared camera performance
and the results of studies, such as performance evaluation simulations.

Experimental Condition

     The behavior of outdoor gas leakage from cylinders and tubes of
flammable gas at a maximum rate of 3 liters per minute was videotaped
with a visualization device installed several meters away from the
release site. Fig. 5 shows the device structure. The amount of
leaking gas was adjusted by a mass flow controller that maintained a
constant mass flow rate. The visualized images were gray-scale images
shot in NTSC format, and were stored on a video tape recorder (VTR).
     With the active method, a screen made of styrene was installed in
the background to maintain consistent background reflectance
conditions, both to maintain an adequate amount of reflected light and
to confirm reflection conditions for the leaking gas. The background
screen, light source and camera were installed in positions which
prevented the mirror reflection. The light sources were an He-Ne laser
and globar lamps, and visualized images for both sources were recorded.
     With the passive method, the background consisted of ground
surface and surrounding landscape made of concrete.
     The characteristics of the bandpass filter mounted on the infrared
camera for the passive method were different from those for the active
method. Because the intensity of infrared rays in the active method is
much greater than that of the passive method, the bandwidth of the
filter for the active one can be narrower to obtain better SN ratio.

Experimental Results

     Active and passive method images recorded on VTR are shown in
Figs. 6 and 7, respectively. Fig. 6 shows propane leaking at a flow
rate of 3 liters per minute from a 9-mm (diameter) rubber tube
positioned in the center of the monitor screen. The styrene screen is
positioned in the background, and the distances between the background
and the rubber tube as well as between the rubber tube and the
visualization device were 0.5 m and 3 m, respectively. Fig. 7 shows a

visualized image videotaped under direct sunlight 5 meters away from a leaking of butane gas container.  The following summarizes the results.
(1)   Methane, propane and butane could all be visualized with the same device in the active method using an He-Ne laser and a globar lamp as light sources.
(2)   Propane and butane could both be visualized with a commercially available infrared camera using the passive method as long as an adequate amount of radiated background light could be maintained.  (Visualization performance was improved with strong sunlight, but the overall effect was essentially the same as with the active method using a white light source.)
(3)   Monitor screen concentration variations due to gas absorption as well as concentration variations due to background conditions were easily distinguishable if flammable gas was visualized together with the background in real time.
(4)   The frame rate of a TV monitor was found to play an important role like sensor sensitivity in order for observers to ascertain a gas leak from the visualized image.
(5)   Gas leaking from the surface was videotaped when a modeled underground flammable gas leak was observed at ground level by the visualization device.

CONCLUSION

We focused on a flammable gas visualization method that uses the infrared absorption characteristics of hydrocarbon-based gas as a method for monitoring flammable gas leaks over a wide area, and we conducted studies on active and passive methods using He-Ne lasers as well as an active method using a white light source.  A visualization device was set up for performance evaluations, and videotaping experiments were conducted on methane, propane and butane.  The results are given below.
(1)   Methane, propane and butane were simultaneously detected with the active method.
(2)   Propane and butane were visualized by the passive method using a commercially available infrared camera when environmental conditions, such as background temperature, were controlled.
(3)   Visualizing flammable gas and the background in real time not only provides a simple mechanism, but also facilitates the ability to visualize the situation of gas leaks.
(4)   The visualization device set above ground has the possibilities to detect gas leaks from buried pipes.
(5)   As a result of the experiments, the flammable gas imaging together with surrounding landscape is confirmed a very effective measure to find leak locations and to observe the behavior of leaking gas.

ACKNOWLEDGMENTS

We would like to thank the Industrial Supplies & Equipment Division of Nikon Corporation for kindly providing an equipment package containing an infrared camera with cold filters and imaging equipment used in the present visualization demonstration experiments.

REFERENCES

1.   Infrared Engineering Society : Infrared Technology, OHM publishing/Tokyo, 1991
2.   Y. Yamasaki, et al. : Development of methane detecting system utilizing He-Ne laser, Instrumentation Vol.34     No7, 1991
3.   K. Gannbo, M. Tanaka, T. Tokioka : Atmospheric Environment (Atmospheric Sciences Lectures),Tokyo University Publishing, 1982
4.   T. Kannno et al. : Infrared sensors(II) IRCCD focal plane arrays sensitive in the 3 to 5 $\mu$m range, Technical report, Technical research and development institution, Japan defense agency, 1987

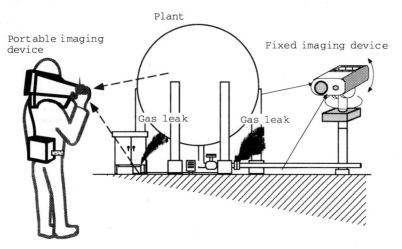

**Figure 1     Image of the gas leakage monitoring system based on gas imaging**

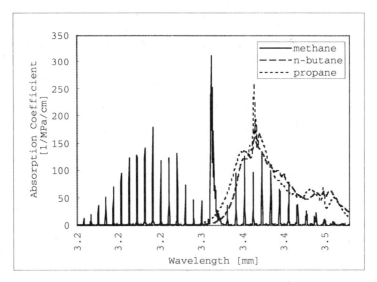

**Figure 2     Infrared absorption spectrum of flammable gases**

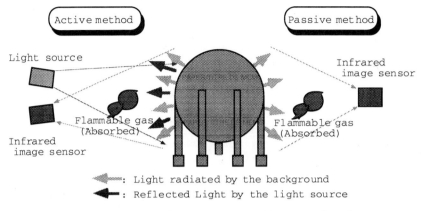

Figure 3    Principle of flammable gas imaging

Table 1    Absorption characteristics of subject gases
(He-Ne laser)

| Type of gas | Absorption coefficient [MPa$^{-1}$cm$^{-1}$] |
|---|---|
| Methane | 8.9 x 10 |
| Propane | 8.3 x 10 |
| n-Butane | 1.2 x 10$^2$ |
| i-Butane | 1.2 x 10$^2$ |

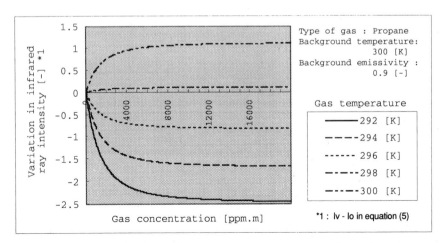

Figure 4-a    Variations in gas concentration and infrared ray
intensity (Background gas temperature differential)

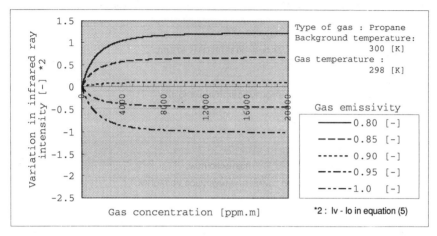

**Figure 4-b     Variations in gas concentration and infrared ray intensity (Background emissivity)**

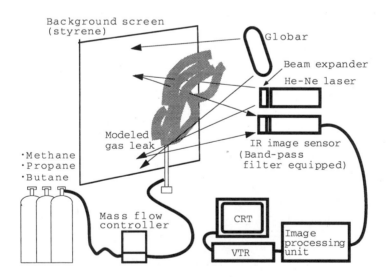

**Figure 5     Configuration of the active method test device**

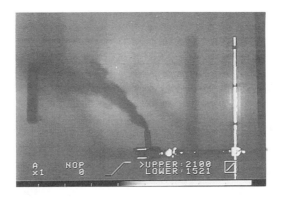

Figure 6    Visualized image using the active method (Propane)

Figure 7    Visualized image using the passive method (Butane)

METHODS TO MEASURE METHANE LOSSES
FROM DISTRIBUTION GRIDS

METHODES DE MESURE POUR DETERMINER
LES PERTES DANS DE RESEAUX DE DISTRIBUTION DE GAZ NATUREL

L. van Heyden
Ruhrgas AG, Germany

W. Weßing
Ruhrgas AG, Germany

ABSTRACT

In view of the political challenges associated with the anthropogenic greenhouse effect, there is a general need to quantify gas and in particular methane losses from local distribution systems. Suitable measuring methods are necessary for this work. This paper describes two methods which can be used without interrupting the gas supply. One uses a suction method to determine the leakage rates at individual leaks found during above-ground surveys without exposing the pipeline. The second method is an improved version of the long-known grid pressure variation method used during periods of low demand. This paper outlines the main results and experience gained from tests with the suction method on artificial leaks at trial sites as well as results and experience from field tests gained with both methods. The work was performed as part of a GERG project (European Gas Research Group).

RESUME

Devant le débat politique concernant l'effet de serre provoqué par des émissions anthropiques la nécessité est née de déterminer la quantité de pertes de méthane respectivement de gaz dans de réseaux de distribution. Ceci nécessite de disposer des méthodes de mesure appropriées. La présente communication se propose de décrire deux méthodes qui peuvent être appliquées sans interruption de l'approvisionnement en gaz. La première vise à déterminer la quantité des pertes détectées par la recherche des fuites à la surface par aspiration sans dégager la conduite. La deuxième constitue l'évolution d'une méthode de mesure connue depuis longtemps, celle de la variation de pression dans les réseaux pendant les périodes de faible débit. Les résultats obtenus par la méthode d'aspiration sur site avec des fuites artificielles et les expériences acquises par l'application des deux méthodes sont présentés. Les investigations menées faisaient partie d'un projet dans le cadre du Groupe Européen de Recherches gazières (GERG).

INTRODUCTION

In 1989, the Battelle Institute in Frankfurt carried out a study on methane/gas losses from distribution systems in the Federal Republic of Germany (at that time not yet including eastern Germany) /1/ concluding that about 0.7 % of gas sendout (reference year: 1987) is lost, mainly through leaks in older gas distribution systems. A general aim should be to improve the data sets used so far by carrying out gas loss measurements on selected grids. In this way, the gas distribution companies can be provided with suitable data to evaluate their own distribution networks with regard to the probability of losses through leaks and, if necessary, to use this information as an orientation tool for decisions on rehabilitation work.

The suitability of measuring methods depends on whether they can be used at reasonable cost and without interrupting gas supplies. For customers can only be expected to put up with interruptions in supply in exceptional cases. The aim of the project was to develop and test two measuring methods which meet these requirements. The work performed by Ruhrgas AG was part of the GERG project "Methods to Measure Methane Losses from Distribution Grids", which was performed by British Gas, Gaz de France and Ruhrgas with the GERG members Dänisches Gastechnologie-zentrum, Gasunie, Ocigas, SNAM, Italgas and Gastec making financial contributions.

SUCTION METHOD FOR MEASURING LEAKAGE RATES AT INDIVIDUAL LEAKS

Principle

The dotted lines in Figure 1 depict the unimpaired flow of leakage gas from a damaged pipeline. As the density of the natural gas is less than that of the soil air, it flows upwards in the shape of a funnel. Given the prevailing pressure ranges of the gas distribution systems in Germany (low pressure up to 100 mbar, medium pressure up to 1 bar), the leakage rate is largely governed by the flow resistance of the soil under the conditions encountered in practice. Therefore, the boundary conditions of the leakage gas flow into the atmosphere must not be disturbed to any appreciable extent if the leakage gas rate measurements are to be sufficiently reliable.

Therefore, the original concept of the suction method was to cover the surface leakage area with a sheet and to extract the leakage gas at as low a negative pressure as possible from the centre while allowing a controlled flow of ambient air from the edges of the sheet to the point of extraction. The leakage gas rate can be determined by measuring the $CH_4$ concentration in the measured flow of extracted gas. However, tests at a trial site with an artificial leak and a known leakage rate revealed the following disadvantages:

- failure to detect a substantial amount of leakage gas owing to biological degradation in the soil,

- impairment of the results through wind influences,

- practical applications limited to leaks under freely accessible surfaces and with defined surface leakage areas.

These disadvantages can be avoided if probes are inserted into the soil to extract the leakage gas as shown in Figure 1. First of all, the leakage gas present in the soil has to be extracted until an equilibrium is reached where there is only a small amount of leakage gas still in the soil and the gas leaking from the pipeline flows directly to the tips of the probes. The leakage gas still mixes with a much larger amount of soil air.

In order to minimise the time required for surveying a leakage site, as high a negative pressure as possible must be acting on the probe tips which, however, generally affects the leakage gas rate at least on low-pressure grids, consequently making correction necessary. Therefore, the leakage gas should be "completely" extracted from the leakage area at as high a negative pressure as possible before the actual leakage gas rate is determined at a lower extraction rate. A reliable check of complete extraction of the leakage gas in the soil is that soon after commencement of extraction until completion of extraction no escape of gas can be detected on the surface.

Trials of the Suction Method on Test Sites With Artificial Leaks

The tests were performed at a Ruhrgas test site in Dorsten and at two Gaz de France test sites in Paris. The test site at Dorsten measured 10 m x 10 m and was in the open air. The soil was removed to a depth of 1 m and then the area refilled in three layers and compressed in layers as prescribed for pedestrian areas (80 cm building sand/15 cm ballast/5 cm stone chippings). Before the hole was filled in, a thin copper pipe was laid from outside to the middle from which natural gas could be released as an artificial leak at a depth of 95 cm. The first site in Paris was a round test site, 8 m in diameter, in the open air, made up of compacted sand with a covering of gravel and the second site was a covered larger area with a clayey soil and a sand covering several centimetres thick. In both fields, the pipe to act as a leakage point was installed at a depth of 0.8 m.

Figure 2 shows the results of the test. The leakage gas flow rate is shown on the x-axis and the ratio of measured to released amount of leakage gas in percent is shown on the y-axis. The results obtained using sheeting are shown on the far left. It can be seen that, at leakage rates of approx. 50 litres per hour, only 70 - 80 % of the leakage gas is collected, even when the edge of the sheeting is weighted down. By measuring the $CO_2$ in the extracted gas, it was possible to demonstrate that $CO_2$ starts to form after the natural gas is released in the soil. Whilst without extraction, the unconverted natural gas gradually disperses after the gas stops leaking, the $CO_2$, owing to its higher density, remains in the soil and can later be extracted. Therefore, it is not generally possible to convert CO concentrations into equivalent $CH_4$ concentrations. If the results with improved covering at the edge of the sheeting are taken as a basis, it can be estimated that approx. 15 to 40 litres of gas per hour were biologically degraded during the tests with sheeting.

Considerably better results overall were achieved with suction probes. In Dorsten, the artificial leakage gas rate (Figure 2/b) was between 175 and nearly 185 litres per hour. The tests took place at intervals of 3 to 11 days which meant that a more or less undisturbed leakage gas flow field could form in the soil as the flow of leakage gas was never interrupted. With these conditions prevailing, it took between 8 and 28 hours before a new equilibrium as shown in Figure 1 was established. The shortest measuring time was achieved in dry weather, the longest on days with high rainfall. Apart from measuring errors, the deviations from the 100 % line are most likely explained by the fact that complete equilibrium had not yet been achieved or that biological degradation processes may still play a role although the residence period of the leakage gas in the soil is considerably shortened when the suction method is used.

In Paris, owing to initial technical problems, there was not the time to determine the time required for transition from unimpaired leakage gas flow in the soil to the establishment of an equilibrium for measurement with the suction method (Figure 1). However, it is most remarkable that, after equilibrium had been reached, it was possible to measure changes in the amount of leakage gas in the soil after only a few minutes, with only a few percent deviation from the amounts of leakage gas released, even if there was a great change in the amount of leakage gas. During tests with the round test site filled with sand, in which only one of the probes in place was used, it only took, for example, 109 minutes after equilibrium had been reached to completely divert an unchanged leakage gas flow from one probe to an adjacent probe. The two probes were 1.1 m away from the leakage point and 1.55 m away from each other in the horizontal plane.

Technical Equipment Required for the Suction Method

The suction probes consist of 1.5 mm thick stainless steel tubes. On the suction end of a probe is a piece of pipe, 15 cm long and 23 mm in diameter. It is sealed at the tip and has perforations over the first 10 cm with a total aperture surface of 15 cm². This thinner piece of suction pipe is connected to a pipe with a 28 mm diameter. The probes can be inserted into the soil up to a depth of 55 cm.

The probes are connected to a collector via commercially available rubber hoses (20 mm x 3 mm) and connected to the extractor fan via a dust filter. The fan is a so-called side channel fan which is particularly suitable owing to its compact design, low weight and comparatively high negative pressures. The characteristic line of the type used (230 V; 1.1 kW) can be characterised by the following two points: 115 mbar negative pressure compared with a suction flow of 25 m³ per hour as well as 55 mbar negative pressure at 80 m³ per hour (both $Q_n$). On the discharge side of the fan was a turbine flow meter, a pressure and temperature measuring device for converting to $Q_n$ as well as the withdrawal point for measuring the $CH_4$ concentration in the flow of extracted gas. The $CH_4$ concentration was measured using an FID.

Results of the Field Tests of the Suction Method

Figure 3 and Table 1 show the results of the field tests which were performed in collaboration with the two LDCs, Vereinigte Elektrizitätswerke Westfalen AG in Dortmund and Stadtwerke Gelsenkirchen. The leakage rates determined are very different. It was only possible to give an approximate figure for the smallest amount of leakage gas detected (No. 1). However, the aboveground survey performed on different days clearly showed that gas was definitely escaping at the point under investigation. At the point where the largest amount of leakage gas was detected (No. 7) the surface results suggest that there are several leaks on just a few meters of gas pipeline. It always took 24 hours to survey a leakage point. The team arrived at the site around mid-day and had set up the equipment by the afternoon. The leakage gas was extracted and measurements taken with a computer-aided measuring data acquisition system until the next morning. In the morning, the results were evaluated to make sure the state of equilibrium had been reached and, if necessary, measurements were continued for a certain period. As long as no hitches had been encountered during measuring, the equipment was dismantled and transported to the next measuring point. In all cases nine probes were used, the arrangement of which is shown in Figure 4.

The leakage gas rates given are those actually measured, i.e. without allowing for any influence of the negative pressure produced in the soil on the leakage gas rate. It was only possible to deal with the question of the negative pressures produced in the soil to a limited extent (see next paragraph). In all field tests, gas detectors were used to ascertain whether traces of gas could be detected on the surface during the time in which extraction was being performed. This was not the case.

Negative Pressures Measured in the Soil as a Result of the Suction Effect. The results are shown in Figure 4, the left-hand graph referring to results from the test site in Dorsten and the middle and right-hand graphs referring to results from field tests No. 5 and 6 with clayey soils. The measurement and probe positions are shown above the graphs. In the two field tests, one suction probe was disconnected from the extractor fan and only used as a measuring line. The other probes remained in full operation. At the test site in Dorsten, a steel pipe (10 m x 1 mm) was driven into the soil at the marked points. Or the leakage gas injection point was used as the measuring line.

The results suggest that negative pressures in the soil depend greatly on the type of soil. A sandy soil is comparable to a rather even fine-pored structure whilst a clayey soil whose water content varies according to the time of the year has a differing fine structure and consists of more or less gas-tight areas and between them gaps. Sand layers ensure relatively even flow and pressure distribution in the soil and therefore lead automatically to rapid reduction of negative pressure and flow rates at a distance from the probe tip. In clayey soils, the effect of gaps and cracks obviously leads to a generally lower and less even reduction of negative pressure and flow rates at a distance from the probe tip. The negative pressures measured in the soil during extraction in the immediate vicinity of probe entry into the soil were between 16 and 22 mbars.

The maximum pressure loss due to suction measured at the sand test field in Paris on an artificial leak was 2 mbar. At the clayey test field, where the soil had dried out more, there was a negative pressure at the artificial leak of up to 28 mbar given a suction volume flow rate of 104 m³/h.

Allowing for the Influence of the Suction Effect on the Leakage Gas Rate by Approximation. In view of the negative pressures measured, it is only necessary to allow for the influence of the suction effect on the leakage gas rate with leaks on low-pressure pipelines where the leakage gas rates are known to rise approximately proportionally to the pipeline overpressure (cf. grid pressure variation method). If the pressure field in the gas-filled pore space near a leak is reduced by the suction effect, the $\Delta p$ between the pipeline overpressure and the surrounding area determining the leakage gas rate rises by approx. the same amount. With a pipeline pressure of , for example, 50 mbar and a pressure reduction of 10 mbar, the $\Delta p$ acting during the measurement is 60 mbar. The leakage gas rate measured would therefore have to be reduced by a ratio of 50 to 60. It can only be estimated that the $\Delta p$'s were increased by 5 to 15 mbar in the field tests with clayey soils and that the measured leakage gas rates would have to be corrected.

Conclusions

- The negative pressures of only 16 - 22 mbar measured in the soil at the probe tips show that most of the negative pressure generated by the extractor fan is lost on the way to the probes. The dust filter had only a small pressure loss. Therefore, the dimensions of the connecting hoses and connections for further applications must be much bigger. The extraction rate - at least during the initial phase of extraction (to achieve equilibrium) - can be considerably increased. It should be possible to considerably reduce the time required for surveying a site and/or the number of probes required could be reduced.

- The negative pressure generated in the soil must be checked particularly with low-pressure gas pipelines so that the leakage gas rate can be corrected, if necessary. Two to three thin measuring probes should be installed as near as possible to the gas pipeline at the suspected leak site so that the pressure can be measured with and without suction.

GRID PRESSURE VARIATION METHOD

Principle

This is a measuring method which was primarily used on low-pressure grids after conversion to natural gas. With this method gas losses of entire grid sections equipped with service governors can be determined on warm summer nights. The method makes use of the fact that changes in grid pressure only affect leakage gas flow but not gas offtake by the customer. Originally, it was only possible to use this method if the gas offtake by the customer was very low and nearly constant. Then it was possible to deduce the gas losses by using the changes in the gas supply in the grid system with comparatively few pressure changes having to be made at the district pressure regulator station. Such conditions are no longer found today. The work which is reported on in this paper is designed to make the method suitable for present-day gas offtake conditions by allowing a maximum number of fully automatic pressure changes to be performed in a minimum time.

Figure 5 shows the interrelationships. On the left variations in the gas feed rate at the district pressure regulator station are taken which are very favourable for the grid pressure variation method. It is clear that a sufficient number of measurements of feed rate at sufficiently close intervals must be made for both grid pressures to be able to plot an interpolating curve reflecting gas feed rates at high and low grid pressures. The vertical difference between the two plotted curves corresponds to the leakage gas increase during a change from low to high grid pressure. It would also be possible to integrate the area under the two curve lines for a certain operating time to determine the difference in feed rate. Or the grid pressure could be alternated between high and low and all measurements taken over a certain period of time could be grouped into high and low pressure measurements, then added together in these groups and the average taken. The difference between the average figures corresponds to the increase in gas leakage provided the time span selected is sufficiently long and many measurements are taken.

It is known that with low-pressure gas pipelines there is a linear relationship between gas loss and grid pressure /2/3/. This is due to the fact that, with the usual size of leak, the flow resistance of the soil dominates and the laminar flow character prevails. It is very easy to calculate the specific gas loss per mbar of grid pressure or at x mbar from a measured increase in gas loss due to an increase in grid pressure from, for example, 30 to 50 mbars. If this method were to be used on medium-pressure pipelines, the functional relationship between gas losses and grid pressure would have to be determined before grid losses at certain grid pressures could be given.

Present-Day Conditions for Using the Method. The field tests conducted and the subsequent consumption model calculations with assumed customer structures show that gas supply at district pressure regulator stations with average service areas varies much more than had been assumed in the left-hand graph in Figure 5. The right-hand graph shows a small section of the actual feed variations measured. It is a low-pressure grid section with 5.8 km of supply lines, 2.4 km of service pipes and 376 residential and commercial consumers, who, on the summer night when the measurements were conducted, were only supplied by one district regulator station. From this short but typical measurement log, it is obvious that there is no discernible regularity in the relationship between the amounts of gas supplied at the higher and lower pressures.

In order to achieve a useful result in the form of a sufficiently reliable difference in supply - if there is a gas loss -, a large number of pressure changes must be performed. This is the critical precondition for using the method with today's gas purchase conditions. Statistical procedures with complex technical measuring series have to be used to determine the losses. The most suitable method of evaluation is to form differences between all successive gas supply results at alternating grid pressures and to put the following signs before each of these differences: If the gas feed increases when the grid pressure is increased, the sign must be positive and if the gas feed decreases, the sign must be negative. If the gas feed decreases when the grid pressure is decreased, the sign must be positive and if the gas feed increases the sign must be negative.

Assuming that the probability distribution of the figures of all feed differences in practice corresponds to the normal distribution, the following applies: the feed difference which leads to the calculation of the real gas loss in the grid section under investigation lies within the confidence limits, the centre of which corresponding to the arithmetical mean of all individual results:

$$x = \bar{x} \pm CL$$

x = gas feed difference, e.g. in m³/h
$\bar{x}$ = arithmetical mean of all differences
CL = confidence limits

For 90 % confidence limits:

$$x = \bar{x} \pm \frac{1.65}{\sqrt{n}} \cdot s$$

n = No. of feed differences measured
s = standard deviation of feed differences

A result for x lies with a 90 % degree of probability within the confidence limits to be calculated. Small confidence limits are only achieved with comparatively low relative standard deviations and/or with a comparatively large number of measured values.

Results of Field Tests and Critical Assessment

For this purpose, an automatic pressure-change demonstration plant including measuring data acquisition and storage facilities was built and tested for proper functioning on a grid simulation test rig with artificial leaks. However, the simulated gas feed variations were much smaller than when it was actually used in practice at a district pressure regulator station of the Vereinigte Elektrizitätswerke Westfalen AG. The grid lengths and customers of the grid, which was supplied during the trials solely by this particular district station, have already been described previously in this paper. The average length of each period at a certain pressure was 10 min to achieve sufficiently steady conditions. The grid pressure was varied between 30 and 53 mbar.

Over a period of 7 nights, 347 pressure changes were performed and 346 gas feed differences determined. To list all the results would go beyond the bounds of this paper. At this point, it is sufficient to show the cumulative frequency distribution in the uniformly divided probability grid to examine them for normal distribution (Figure 6). They are grouped more or less around a straight line (precondition for normal distribution) so that the above-mentioned evaluation formula can be applied. Figure 6 shows the results. The average gas feed during the measuring period was 14.51 $m^3/h(Q_n)$ and between min. 5.8 and max. 46.8 $m^3/h$. The standard deviation was 6.7 $m^3/h$.

The arithmetical mean of all feed differences is nearly exactly zero $m^3/h$. Thus the gas loss would also be zero, not allowing for the confidence limits. It should also be mentioned that during preparations for the field tests several leaks requiring immediate repair were found on the grid section used during the trials so that the grid could be regarded as gas tight at the time the measurements took place. However, as far as the statistical assessment of the results is concerned, it is a coincidence that the arithmetical mean is almost exactly zero. A 90 % confidence region can only be interpreted as positive here because it is not possible to "gain" gas through leaks. If the above formula is applied, the gas loss is less than 0.501 $m^3/h$ with a degree of probability of 90 %. For the grid section under investigation this means that the annual gas loss is less than approx. 0.4 % of gas sendout.

The modelling of the consumption behaviour of the 376 customers over a period of time showed that the measured standard deviation, mainly due to the fact that most customers now get their domestic hot water from storage tanks, is more or less typical for 376 customers. To increase the number of customers on the grid under investigation would lead to more constant gas supply but the standard deviation is only reduced by the square root of the relative increase in the number of customers. It should be possible to double the number of pressure changes which can be performed per time unit by optimising the pressure variation method. So, in field tests on a grid with five times as many customers it would be possible to reduce the above-mentioned confidence limits by 75 %, relatively speaking. If the same gas sendout per customer as in the field tests is assumed, the annual gas loss could be given to within confidence limits of ± 0.1 percentage points.

Conclusions

•   The grid pressure variation method only produces satisfactory results if grids with at least 2,000 residential and commercial customers can be examined and no gas is supplied to contract customers during the measuring period.

•   The field tests show that the grid presssure has to be repeatedly changed over a period of at least 100 hours during the summer when demand is low.

LITERATURE

/1/   Schneider-Fresenius, W. et al.: Ermittlung der Methan-Freisetzung durch Stoffverluste bei der Erdgasversorgung der Bundesrepublik Deutschland. Studie des Battelle-Instituts, Frankfurt, August 1989

/2/   Schneider, A.: Messen von Gasverlusten in Niederdrucknetzen und Folgerungen für den Betrieb. Neue DELIWA-Zeitschrift (1976), No. 11, pp. 421/423

/3/   Wilmsmann, W.: Gasverluste - ungemessenes Gas, gwf-Gas/Erdgas 121 (1980) Heft 3, pp. 115/118.

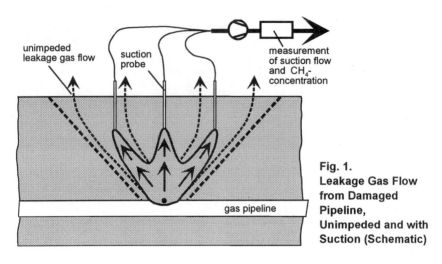

**Fig. 1.**
**Leakage Gas Flow**
**from Damaged**
**Pipeline,**
**Unimpeded and with**
**Suction (Schematic)**

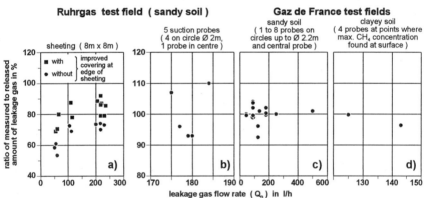

**Fig. 2. Results of the Suction Method at Test Fields with Artificial Leaks**

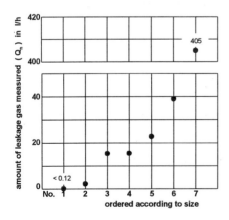

TABT / 3_678_03 / S 01 / 12.05.95

**Fig. 3.**
**Practical Results with the Suction**
**Method ( 7 Leaks )**

| leakage point | leakage flow rate ($Q_n$) l/h | max. $CH_4$ concentration found in bore holes | gas pipeline (only steel) | location (position / surface) | type of soil |
|---|---|---|---|---|---|
| 1 | ≤ 0.12 | 100 Vol.-ppm | DN 150 50 mbar | pavement, paving stones, trees in vicinity | predominantly clayey soil |
| 2 | 2.2 | 3 Vol-% | DN 150 50 mbar | pavement, paving stones | |
| 3 | 15.4 | 68 Vol-% | DN 100 45 mbar | street parking line, old tar surface | |
| 4 | 15.5 | 48 Vol-% | DN 100 45 mbar | | |
| 5 | 22.8 | 50 Vol-% | DN 100 45 mbar | pavement, old tar surface | predominantly clay and loam soil |
| 6 | 39.0 | 60 Vol-% | DN 150 45 mbar | | |
| 7 | 404.9* | 55 Vol-% | DN 80 50 mbar | pavement, paving stones | predominantly sandy soil |

*From the results of the leak search conducted above ground it can be assumed that there are several adjacent leaks*

**Table 1. Details of the Leakage Points Surveyed Using the Suction Method**

TABT / 3_678_03 / S 02 / 12.05.95

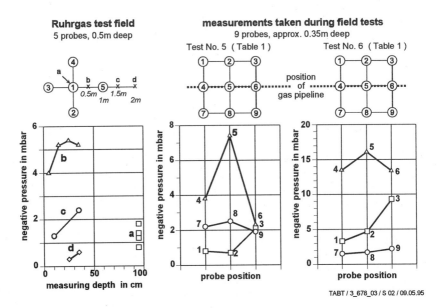

**Fig. 4.**
**Negative Pressure Measured in Soil as a Result of the Suction Effect of the Probes**

TABT / 3_678_03 / S 02 / 09.05.95

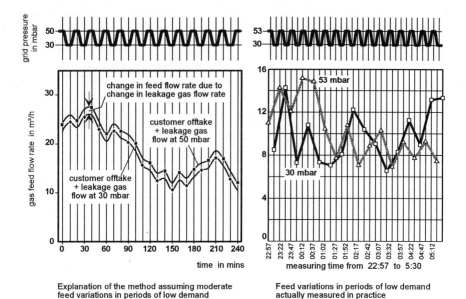

Explanation of the method assuming moderate feed variations in periods of low demand

Feed variations in periods of low demand actually measured in practice

**Fig. 5. Application of the Grid Pressure Variation Method with Fluctuating Gas Feed in Grid Sections under Investigation**

TABT / 3_678_03 / S 03 / 12.05.95

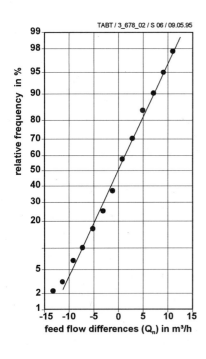

TABT / 3_678_02 / S 06 / 09.05.95

| No. of feed differences measured (at pressures 30 mbar/ 53 mbar, Fig.5) : | 346 |
|---|---|
| Arithmetical mean of all differences : | 0.00041 m³/h |
| Standard deviation : | 5.70 m³/h |
| Greatest increase in feed flow after change in pressure : | 18.54 m³/h |
| Greatest decrease in feed flow after change in pressure : | -23.54 m³/h |
| Average gas feed flow rate : | 14.51 m³/h |

**Fig. 6.**
**Cumulative Curve of all Gas Feed Differences Measured in a Field Test of the Pressure Variation Method**

Gas Load Center: A Value-Added Advantage for Interior Gas Piping
Systems

Centralisation des consommations:  Une valeur ajoutée pour la
gestion des systémes de réseaux gaz intérieurs

Renny S. Norman
Gas Research Institute

Robert Torbin
Foster-Miller, Inc.

## ABSTRACT

The Gas Research Institute (GRI) has been developing new products for
effectively delivering natural gas within single family and multifamily residences
for over ten years.  Following the introduction of corrugated stainless steel tubing
into the gas energy marketplace in 1990 in the United States, a quick
connect/disconnect gas outlet was introduced in 1993.  The most recent
product, a Gas Load Center (GLC) is now available as a third enhancement to
interior gas distribution.  The GLC is described here with respect to its overall
applications and specific hardware functions.  This unit is being used as a control
center for interior gas distribution piping as it is divided into individual gas
appliance runs from the main, street gas supply.  The GLC provides the
homeowner increased flexibility for gas energy use and improved control of
individual gas lines.

The Gas Load Center (GLC) is a prefabricated piping assembly and enclosure box shown in Figure 1. The plastic enclosure is designed to be installed either between two standard wall studs or on a wall surface. When fully installed, the box includes a service shut-off valve, drip leg, Maxitrol regulator, piping union (to facilitate regulator replacement), inspector test port, and multi-port welded steel manifold with mounting bracket and clamps. The entire manifold assembly can be removed from the enclosure to facilitate the mounting of the box between the studs. The front door panel is also removable which permits greater access during the tubing installation. The enclosure is provided with knock-outs for five tubing runs, and can be oriented for tubing runs entering/exiting the GLC from above or below.

Although the manifold is designed with a standard four port configuration, it can be customized in terms of the number and size of the ports.

An optional two tier horizontal configuration has been designed for upscale, single family homes where many gas appliances are typical. However, the single tier, four port configuration fits in a much smaller enclosure. If more ports are required to accommodate additional appliances, a second load center can be installed at the same or other locations within the house.

All manifold components can be assembled at the plumbing contractor's shop prior to field installation. Once assembled, the entire Gas Load Center can be shop inspected and tested for leakage. After the enclosure is installed in a house, the field operation is reduced to installing the meter and appliance tubing runs, and completing the assembly of the fittings. As an option, shut-off valves can be installed at each manifold port to facilitate the servicing of the appliances and any future piping system modifications. The

a)

b)

**Figure 1. Gas Load Center with Door Closed (a) and Door Opened (b)**

GLC also provides the consumer with other safety features. Each port can be numbered and recorded on a log sheet attached to the door, so that each appliance connection can be easily identified. Safety information, system sizing data, and important telephone numbers can also be listed on a notice located on the door panel.

Although the primary benefit of the Gas Load Center is to reduce the installation cost of the piping system, it can also be a major factor for increasing the natural gas load. The GLC is a visible and attractive feature (heretofore totally lacking in conventional steel piping systems) which focuses consumer attention on the enhanced use options available with this new distribution product. These use options include the ability to add more gas appliances (spare ports on the manifold) without any major re-plumbing of the existing piping system; the use of individual appliance shut-off valves conveniently located inside the Gas Load Center; and the ability to incorporate home monitoring technology (i.e. smoke and CO detectors) into the gas distribution network through the use of electrically operated shut-off valves. The GLC coupled with a 2 psi system will provide the LDC with the option of obtaining the gas load either at the time of initial construction or after occupancy as add-on appliances. The potential for load growth, in fact, *may be much larger with the existing customer base* than with new construction.

The GLC is manufactured by R. W. Lyall & Company, Inc. Several production units are currently being installed in residential applications as part of a GRI sponsored field evaluation and demonstration. Typical initial applications have included large upscale single family homes where many gas appliances are being installed. For example:

- Topeka, KS: two 4-port GLCs with 8 connected appliances: total load 400 CFH

- Gardenerville, NV: one 4-port and one 8-port GLC with 10 connected appliances: total load 550 CFH

- Colleyville, TX: two 4-port and one 8-port GLC with 16 connected appliances: total load 1,500 CFH

ENVIRONMENTAL LIFE CYCLE ASSESSMENT OF GAS DISTRIBUTION SYSTEMS

ANALYSE DIACHRONIQUE DES EFFETS ECOLOGIQUES ATTRIBUABLES
AUX RESEAUX DE DISTRIBUTION

J.B.W. Wikkerink[1], J.J.G.S.A. Willems[1], H.C.L.M. Kraak[2] and G. Huppes[2]

[1] GASTEC NV, Dutch Centre of Gas Technology, Apeldoorn, The Netherlands
[2] Centre of Environmental Science, Leiden University, The Netherlands

ABSTRACT

Environmental aspects tend to be increasingly important in designing gas distribution
systems and in selecting gas distribution materials. Therefore the environmental aspects
of various materials options for gas distribution networks were analyzed by means of a
quantitative life cycle assessment. This paper describes the methodology used and
presents provisional quantitative results to indicate the potential environmental effects
caused by the various materials options. In general fairly small differences were found
between the individual networks analyzed in this study. Over the full life cycle, gas
leakages in the user stage might turn out to be a major element in the environmental
profile.

RESUME

Les considérations d'ordre écologique sont en train de devenir de plus en plus décisives
lors de la conception des réseaux de distribution et de la sélection des matériaux de
distribution du gaz. C'est pourquoi les effets écologiques de plusieurs matériaux utilisés
pour la construction de réseaux de distribution ont fait l'objet d'une analyse
quantitative couvrant l'ensemble de leur cycle de vie. Le présent mémoire décrit la
méthodologie adoptée et présente, à titre provisoire, des résultats quantitatifs illustrant
les éventuels effets écologiques liés à l'utilisation de chacun des matériaux.
Généralement parlant, les différences constatées entre les réseaux examinés sont plutôt
faibles. En outre, les effets des fuites de gaz se produisant durant le cycle de vie d'un
réseau pourraient s'avérer considérables au niveau du profil écologique.

## INTRODUCTION

Energy utilities invest a lot in their gas distribution networks. Cost-effectiveness, safety and operational reliability all play a major role in designing gas distribution networks and in selecting gas distribution materials. Environmental considerations, too, tend to be increasingly important. As part of the overall evaluation of various alternatives, the energy utilities in the Netherlands needed a quantitative environmental tool to support the design of gas distribution networks. In making a well balanced choice of materials to be used in a gas distribution network, all environmental impacts should be taken into account 'from the cradle to the grave'. In formulating a responsible environmental policy, life cycle assessment (LCA) of distribution networks has proved to be a valuable tool for supplying environmental information.

In 1993 GASTEC started an LCA study on piping systems for gas distribution, under the authority of the Netherlands energy utilities. In performing the LCA, GASTEC chose to cooperate with CML, the Centre of Environmental Science of the Leiden University. GASTEC has been aiming at a quantitative assessment of the total environmental load caused by the various materials options for natural gas distribution networks in the Netherlands. The study aims to provide environmental information capable of helping decisions on gas distribution networks, and ultimately aims to improve the environmental performance of the energy utilities. The study involved materials such as modified polyvinyl chloride (PVC), polythene (PE) and cross-linked polythene (PEX), steel and ductile iron.

This paper describes the methodology used and presents provisional quantitative results to indicate the total environmental load caused by the various materials. The results are provisional as the data needed for the assessment of some predominant processes are incomplete at present. Further research will be done to establish the exact characteristics of these processes, and to draw more definitive conclusions.

The provisional results might be relevant for other distribution networks, e.g. for water distribution and sewage, although direct transposition of the conclusions would be inappropriate.

## THE LCA METHODOLOGY

Life cycle assessment (LCA) is an environmental load analysis taking into account all life stages of a product, resulting in an environmental profile or ecobalance. In the EU LCAs are considered to be the official basis for eco-labelling. LCA is the most suitable way to analyze and evaluate the environmental aspects of a product during its entire lifespan. In 1992 CML published a general method for conducting LCAs[1]. Developed to analyze the total life chain of a product 'from the cradle to the grave', it has been a de facto standard since in the Netherlands. All the environmental interventions, originating from the extraction of resources, the production of materials, the production of components, transmission, the use of a product and finally the disposal of that product, should be accounted for. This method has also been used for the present study.

Five individual components can be distinguished in LCA: goal definition, inventory analysis, classification, evaluation and improvement analysis. Each component in turn can be subdivided in several steps necessary to operationalize an LCA. In the sections to follow, these components are described separately, since each component is essential in establishing the final results of this study.

## GOAL DEFINITION

The purpose of this study was to gain insight into the environmental aspects of various materials options for gas distribution networks by conducting a quantitative LCA. All stages in the life cycle of a network are included in this study, from the extraction of basic resources to the final disposal of the used materials. This study has been restricted to the 4 - 8 bar feeder

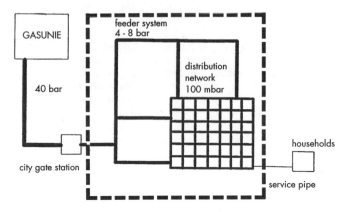

*Figure 1: The definition of the analyzed gas distribution networks.*

systems and the 100 mbar distribution networks operated by the energy utilities. Not included in this study are the high pressure transmission grids (i.e. 40 bar grids) and city gate and distribution regulator stations. Also the service pipes and all gas utilization equipment in households like central heating have been excluded. In figure 1 a schematic view of the boundaries of the gas distribution networks analyzed is given.

An overview of the environmental aspects of the various options makes it possible to draw a rational picture of the environmental impacts associated with the use of these materials. Such a picture would be helpful in answering the following questions:
– What are the main characteristics of various gas distribution systems in relation to the environment?
– Which option is presently preferred from an environmental point of view?

Because of the unique history of gas distribution in the Netherlands, the choice of materials used in gas distribution networks is wider than in most countries. The total length of these gas distribution networks amounted to 102,600 km on a total area of 34,000 $km^2$ in the year 1992. The networks may be divided into a number of subsystems based on the internal pressure class and the materials used. In the high pressure section of the network, here referred to as the 'feeder system', steel (8  bar) and PE (4 bar) are most widely used. In the low pressure section of the system, referred to as the 'distribution network', rigid PVC (until the early 70's) and impact-modified PVC (100 mbar) are dominantly used, in total 56,500 km, and also some ductile iron and PE.
In principle all currently installed pipe materials in the Netherlands were included in this LCA study. Furthermore PEX has been included as a potential new material in the near future.
The various gas piping materials which were compared in this study are therefore:
– For the 8 bar subsystem: steel, polythene PE-100, polythene PE-80 (4 bar) and cross-linked PE (PEX),
– For the 100 mbar subsystem; ductile iron, modified PVC, and polythene PE-80.

To structure the analysis the alternatives were compared on the basis of a functional unit, which is kept constant for each type of network under consideration. The functional unit is defined as the annual supply of 20 million $m^3$ natural gas to clients, from a city gate station to 10,000 services. This definition is based on the following considerations. A typical Dutch household consumes 2,000 $m^3$ gas annually. Furthermore the maximum capacity of this gas distribution network is based on a peak load of 1.5 $m^3$ gas per household per hour, i.e. 15,000 $m^3$ gas per hour for all branches. The gas distribution networks compared consist of

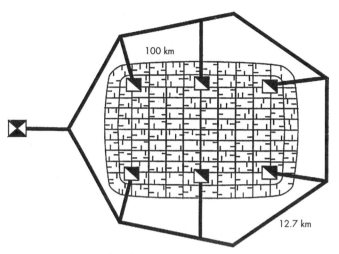

*Figure 2: The standardized system.*

a high pressure feeder subsystem (4 or 8 bar) and a low pressure distribution subsystem
(100 mbar). Together they make up the gas distribution networks considered. The total length
of the feeder subsystem is 12.7 km, and the total length of the 100 mbar distribution subsystem
is 100 km. In figure 2 a schematic view of the standardized system is given.

All networks analyzed in this study are defined specifying all components, their required
numbers and their weights in kg. A distribution network has many different components,
whereas a feeder system is mainly straight pipeline. A distribution network contains numerous
bends and joints, because all 10,000 households have to be connected to this system.
The pipes for the standardized feeder subsystems come in 2 or 3 different diameters. For the
standardized distribution subsystems, pipes of 4 different diameters have been used. For each
type of network involved a lifespan of 70 years is assumed.

INVENTORY ANALYSIS

In general an inventory analysis comprises four different steps: drawing up the process
trees, entering of the process data, application of the allocation rules and the creation of an
inventory table, i.e. a list of all environmental interventions associated with the fulfilment of the
functional unit. The life cycles of the networks selected consist of a number economic processes,
which are directly linked together: each input into a process is either an output from other
economic production, consumption or waste processes or an environmental resource. All these
economic production, consumption and waste processes concern the production of raw
materials (oil, gas, coal, iron ore, rock salt), the production of materials (raw iron, steel, PE,
chlorine and PVC), the production of components (pipes, elbows, T-pieces), the construction of
a network, the use of the network and finally its disposal. In addition to the economic processes
directly related to the life cycle of a network, all kinds of additional support processes are
required concerning electricity, transportation, capital goods and all other possible ancillaries.
All these economic processes produce certain products or services. These services are the
inputs to other economic processes in the life cycle of a network, which cause environmental
interventions. Examples of these environmental interventions are emissions to air, water and
soil, space used, resources used and radiation. Based on these environmental interventions,
inventory tables have been generated, listing all environmental interventions caused by the
fulfilment of the functional unit.

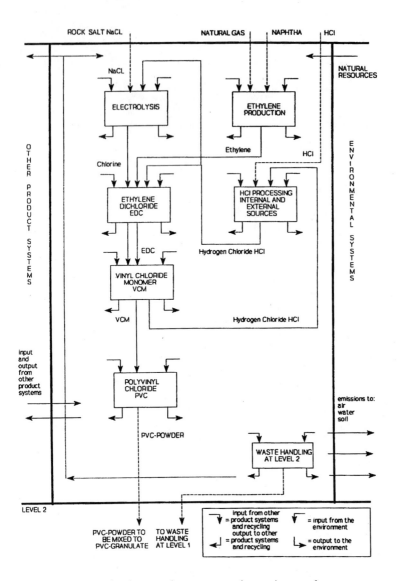

*Figure 3: An example of a partial process tree: the production of PVC powder in the Netherlands.*

For allocation purposes all environmental interventions have been quantified as input and output products from economic production, consumption and waste processes by drawing up process tree flow sheets. Process trees are hierarchically structured. The high level summary process tree consists of a large number of interconnected technical production, consumption and waste processes. From this overview it is possible to zoom in on each high-level process, which will then reveal a partial process tree. An example of a partial process tree is given in figure 3. In turn, it is possible to zoom in yet another time to get an even more detailed view of each of the individual processes.

On the basis of these process trees the life cycles of the various networks were quantified. To do this a special data format was used, constructed to quantify all the economic inputs and outputs and all environmental interventions of all the processes determining the life cycle of a network. Originally, company specific data were preferred. However only for PVC, where company specific data from the Netherlands were used, this turned out to be possible. If no company specific data were available, process data were taken from the database published by ETH, Eidgenössische Technische Hochschule, Zürich: 'Environmental Life Cycle Inventories for Energy Systems'[2]. In general this has been the case for all other materials examined. Some other processes involved data from CML databases and other sources. The ETH database is mainly concerned with the modelling of different energy systems in an unaggregated transparent and consistent 'cradle to grave' approach.

At the end of the life cycle of the various networks three different outputs can be identified:
- the transported gas during its use,
- reusable scrap or regranulate,
- possible energy recovered from waste incineration.

It is not correct to allocate all the environmental impacts to the transport function of the gas networks only, so for the purpose of this study a calculation was made of the allocation factors. These are used to divide the economic inputs and environmental interventions of the network under investigation among the co-products. In this study a multiple output is considered to be a co-product when it is clear that it has a positive economic value in society. The allocation factors distribute the environmental interventions of the multiple outputs among the gas transport function of the network in question and other product systems, using scrap, regranulate or secondary energy from the discarded network material. Similarly, the environmental burden caused by the network under investigation should be attributed to more than one product system. Converserly, if a multiple output has a negative economic value it is considered to be waste, and the additional environmental interventions and economic inputs originating from the processing of these outputs should be added to the original network under investigation. For instance PEX pipes had to be considered as waste, because materials recycling of PEX is not possible at the moment, apart from energy recovery.

Because the transportation service cannot be measured in terms of the mass of the system, mass based allocation factors could not be used. The only common unit capable of expressing the relative usefulness of these multiple outputs was their relative economic value. In calculating the allocation factors the economic value of the processed regranulates and scrap materials was estimated at Dfl. 0.50 per kg. The net economic value of the service delivered by the network was estimated at Dfl. 5.75 per 1,000 m$^3$ gas transported. The allocation factors were calculated by dividing the revenues of the various products by the total value of the multiple outputs of the networks.

The environmental interventions caused by all processes necessary to fulfil the predefined functional unit are listed in inventory tables for the various networks. These lists provide quantitative overviews of all resources used and substances emitted to air, water and soil originating from the fulfilment of the functional unit as modelled in this study. These inventory tables are based on the allocation factors explained above and represent the quantified environmental interventions of 20 million m$^3$ natural gas transported by the various networks analyzed.

CLASSIFICATION

In the classification stage, the environmental inventory table is classified, with the aid of models, according to nine environmental effect scores. These models link the environmental interventions mentioned in the inventory table to their potential environmental effects. These models enable an analysis of the contribution of a functional unit network to these environmental effects. In this study the environmental profile used to compare the various product alternatives distinguishes between the following nine environmental problem types:

– Global Warming Potential (GWP)
– Ozone Depletion Potential (ODP)
– Photochemical Oxidant Creation Potential (POCP)
– Acidification Potential (AP)
– Nutrification Potential (NP)
– Ecotoxicity Aquatic (ECA)
– Human Toxicity Potential (HTP)
– Abiotic Depletion Potential (ADP)
– Odour Threshold Limit (OLT)

This is a fairly complete set of well defined environmental effects that may result from the existence and use of the various networks. However, environmental effects such as noise, waste heat, depletion of biotic resources, number of victims of accidents, terrestrial ecotoxicity and damage to landscapes are not included.

By normalizing the effect scores, the contribution made by a given network to an environmental effect is linked to the contribution made by a given community to the same problem over a given period of time. In this study the world annual effect scores[3] were used to normalize the specific effect scores related to the functional unit. The ratio between each effect score and the global contribution to that effect score over a year provided the normalized environmental profile consisting of normalized effect scores, all of which were expressed in years.

The classification produces a list of all environmental effects in which the networks plays a part, either itself or in fulfilment of its function. The environmental profile was subjected to sensitivity analysis on reliability and validity of the results. In this study, the environmental profile is the basic environmental indicator on which the various product alternatives were compared, all equally capable of fulfilling the same function in society.

EVALUATION AND IMPROVEMENT ANALYSIS

The product assessment was executed by evaluating the environmental profiles. This means that the environmental profiles of the various types of networks and materials were compared. Ideally the scores for the various environmental effects of which these environmental profiles consists, should be weighted and combined into a single environmental index. Considerations about the actual importance of these environmental effects depend on subjective, personal opinions, which may benefit from a public discussion. Since objectively constructed weighting factors are not available at present, the elaboration of an environmental index will be one of the future developments.

The insights obtained in performing this LCA study may be suitable inputs for an improvement analysis. Actually, the knowledge gained will allow to identify areas where technical change would be most desirable from an environmental point of view. Conducting an improvement analysis of the main problem areas over the total life cycle of a network would pinpoint the most likely candidates for effective reductions in environmental loads. Reliable environmental information may also be helpful to authorities dealing with national and international standards, rules and regulations for gas pipes.

PROVISIONAL RESULTS PER SUBSYSTEM

Figure 4 and table 1 present the provisional normalized environmental profiles of the 4 - 8 bar feeder subsystems. In general the differences between the feeder subsystems analyzed are small, meaning that none of these networks is scoring significantly better or worse in the whole range of effects.

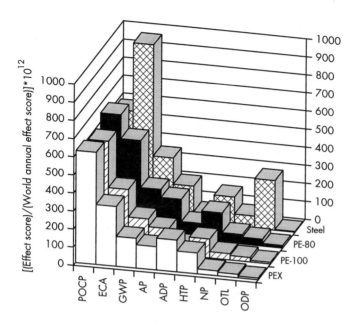

Figure 4: Provisional normalized environmental profiles for the feeder subsystems.

| Subsystem | POCP | ECA | GWP | AP | ADP | HTP | NP | OTL | ODP |
|-----------|------|-----|-----|----|----|-----|----|-----|-----|
| Steel | 5.82E-10 | 9.61E-10 | 3.45E-10 | 2.00E-10 | 5.89E-11 | 1.62E-10 | 6.79E-11 | 2.75E-10 | 4.12E-12 |
| PE-80 | 6.50E-10 | 5.19E-10 | 2.59E-10 | 2.15E-10 | 9.17E-11 | 1.61E-10 | 5.22E-11 | 3.79E-11 | 1.39E-11 |
| PE-100 | 5.93E-10 | 3.36E-10 | 1.84E-10 | 1.40E-10 | 5.93E-11 | 1.04E-10 | 3.42E-11 | 2.46E-11 | 8.99E-12 |
| PEX | 6.19E-10 | 3.30E-10 | 1.64E-10 | 1.28E-10 | 1.75E-10 | 1.15E-10 | 2.70E-11 | 1.91E-11 | 9.40E-12 |

Table 1: Provisional normalized environmental profiles for the feeder subsystems:
[(Effect score)/(World annual effect score)].

One should bear in mind that since no evaluation has been made stating the relative importance of the individual effect scores, no ranking of the feeder subsystems involved can be given based on the results presented here. Indeed, some effect scores may be judged less important than others, and without the proper normative weighting factors making an environmental index is just impossible.

The scores for a 4 bar PE-80 network are in general slightly higher than those for a 8 bar PE-100 network. This is because both networks are modelled in an identical way, except that a PE-80 network uses more material inputs because of the larger construction diameters due to the lower pressure capacity. The additional environmental interventions caused by this higher material use are not outweighed by the lower allocation factor applied, which reflects the larger quantity of reusable regranulate at the end of the life cycle.

Figure 5 and table 2 contain the provisional normalized environmental profiles of the 100 mbar distribution subsystems. The results for the distribution subsystems tend to be more divergent than for the feeder subsystems. However, some serious doubts exist about the correctness of the results found for a ductile iron distribution network. These results seem to differ by a factor of ten from those of the PE-80 and PVC subsystems analyzed. In trying to explain the

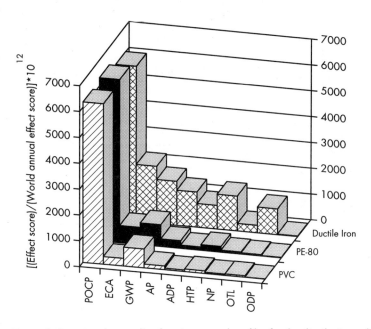

*Figure 5: Provisional normalized environmental profiles for the distribution subsystems.*

| Subsystem | POCP | ECA | GWP | AP | ADP | HTP | NP | OTL | ODP |
|---|---|---|---|---|---|---|---|---|---|
| Ductile iron | 6.01E-09 | 2.21E-09 | 1.70E-09 | 1.36E-09 | 9.17E-10 | 1.35E-09 | 2.89E-10 | 1.00E-09 | 2.47E-11 |
| PE-80 | 6.32E-09 | 6.73E-10 | 8.45E-10 | 2.93E-10 | 1.23E-10 | 2.16E-10 | 7.79E-11 | 4.92E-11 | 1.81E-11 |
| PVC | 6.20E-09 | 2.92E-10 | 7.25E-10 | 1.43E-10 | 5.99E-11 | 9.89E-11 | 4.67E-11 | 5.71E-11 | 7.60E-12 |

*Table 2: Provisional normalized environmental profiles for the distribution subsystems: [(Effect score)/(World annual effect score)].*

difference it was found that imperfections in the specification of the scrap iron casting process, involving the energy inputs and their underlying technical production processes, were responsible for the unfavourable outcome shown above. Given the facts that recycled cast iron may make up 80 % of such a system and that the weight of a cast iron network is about 15 times that of a PVC system, this production process is likely to have a major impact on the results found so far. Still, the uncertainty of the results should not be underestimated, since the process involved was constructed using several contradicting sources. Therefore, the only conclusion possible at this stage ought to be that further research should establish a more reliable specification of this process.

Compared to the other normalized effect scores in figures 4 and 5, the effect scores for photochemical oxidant creation potential (POCP) are the highest. These high effect scores are mainly caused by emissions of methane, ethane etc. 90 % or more of these alkane emissions are due to gas leakages occurring during the use of the networks. It has proved to be extremely difficult to establish the average amount of gas leaking from the various networks through the soil into the atmosphere, because of the parameters involved and the lack of hard empirical figures. In general, three major influencing factors may be identified: the materials used (mainly through the number of connections and the connection technique applied), the soil conditions in which the network is located and the age of the networks involved. It should be noted that the gas leakages discussed here are of very small magnitude and do not affect the safety of the networks.

The substances causing most of the aquatic ecotoxicity (ECA) effect score for steel and ductile iron are phenol, Pb, Cd and $Cu^{2+}$. For steel also Cu, and for ductile iron also fats and oils are responsible for this effect score. The phenol for steel and ductile iron is for 50 % or more generated by the production of raw iron. For plastics materials, the major causes of ECA are also phenol and the category fats and oils, through transportation of crude oil by trans-oceanic tanker and through refinery. After all, crude oil is the feedstock for plastics materials.

For the global warming potential (GWP), the most important substances behind the effect score are $CO_2$ and $CH_4$. $CO_2$ emissions are caused by a large number of processes throughout the life cycle of the various gas networks analyzed, usually involving the combustion of energy carriers. For the steel network, the production of raw iron contributes most to the emission of $CO_2$. For ductile iron the energy inputs (and their underlying processes) into the casting process of scrap iron are responsible for this outcome, but then again the specification of these processes is questionable as mentioned before. For the other materials, the oil and gas refinery and power plant processes contribute more to this emission. The $CH_4$ emissions are basically caused by gas leakages as mentioned before.

$SO_2$ and $NO_x$ are mainly responsible for the effect scores for acidification potential (AP) and human toxicity air emissions (HTA). Both substances originate from a large number of processes over the total life cycle of the various networks, in particular materials production and transportation.

The slightly higher effect score for abiotic depletion potential (ADP) for PEX is caused by the brass connection pieces, consisting of a mix of copper and zinc inputs, which might however be replaced by less depletable resources.

Because for certain materials no classification factors have been developed yet, the score for ADP in general should be considered very incomplete at this time. The high ADP score on zinc for ductile iron is unmistakeably caused by the use of a protective layer of metallic zinc sprayed onto the pipes.

The effect scores on human toxicity water emissions (HWT) and one for air emissions (HTA) combined yield the total effect score for human toxicity potential (HTP). The HWT scores originate mainly from the hard coal tailings in landfills.

The effect score on nutrification potential (NP) is mainly caused by two emissions, $NO_x$ to air and P to water. The emissions of P into water are again caused mainly by the hard coal tailings in landfill, a waste process linked to the extraction of coal used in electricity generation and cokes production.

The relatively high effect score for odour threshold limit (OLT) for steel and ductile iron is solely caused by the emission of $H_2S$ during the production of coal cokes.

The effect score on ozone depletion (ODP) is nearly exclusively based on the emissions of halon-1301, being emitted during crude oil production and transoceanic tanker transport.

## CONCLUSIONS

In general only small differences are found between the individual networks analyzed in this study. None of the networks can be said to score significantly better or worse on all environmental effect scores than the other networks analyzed. The results are provisional as the data needed for the assessment of some predominant processes in the inventory analysis are incomplete at this moment. GASTEC will continue this LCA of gas distribution networks to establish more detailed data for these processes.

Regarding ductile iron distribution subsystems, any conclusions would be premature because the results are biased by just one incompletely specified process. Further research will be undertaken to establish more detailed process data on the casting process of scrap iron.

An interesting result is the fact that gas leakages during the user stage dominate the photochemical oxidant creation potential (POCP) and the global warming potential (GWP) scores, making these effect scores very sensitive to changes in the actual amount of gas leaking in that stage. This is a somewhat surprising result, since at the outset of this study, the user stage of a distribution network was not expected to have a considerable impact on the potential environmental effects analyzed. Further research will be undertaken to gather more reliable and recent data on gas leakages from the various distribution networks during the user stage.

Since no evaluation of the relative importance of the individual effect scores in the environmental profiles has been made yet, it would be inappropriate to draw conclusions on the absolute ranking of the networks analyzed in terms of 'better or worse to the environment'. GASTEC will continue this LCA of gas distribution networks to enable more definitive conclusions to be drawn. In a second phase, an extensive sensitivity and reliability analysis will be made of all dominant processes in the life cycles of the various distribution networks. Additionally, new sensitivity analyses will be made concerning the more important underlying assumptions in order to quantify their relative weight. Better or additional classification factors may also be developed. Similar attention will be given to the normalisation factors, bearing in mind especially their influence on the relative height of the normalized effect scores.

LITERATURE

1.    Heijungs R. (final editor) (1992), 'Environmental life cycle assessments of products, Guide & Backgrounds', Centre of Environmental Science Leiden (CML), Netherlands.

2.    Laboratorium für Energiesysteme, ETH Zürich/PSI Villigen (1993), 'Ökoinventare für Energiesysteme, Grundlagen für den ökologischen Vergleich von Energiesystemen und den Einbezug von Energiesystemen in Ökobilanzen für die Schweiz', Frischknecht R., Hofstetter P., Knoepfel I., Walder E. (Eidgenossische Technische Hochschule ETH, Zürich), Dones R., Zollinger E. (Paul Scherrer Institut PSI, Villingen/Würenlingen).

3.    Guinée J. (1993), 'Data for the Normalisation Step within Life Cycle Assessment of Products', Centre of Environmental Science Leiden (CML), CML paper no. 14, Netherlands.

'STATION24' CENTER COMPUTER SYSTEM

- Implementing a 'Holonic System' -

SYSTÉME INFORMATIQUE DU CENTRE 'STATION24'

Aki KOYANAGI

Station 24
Pipeline and Facilities Engineering Dept.
TOKYO GAS CO., LTD. (Japan)

ABSTRACT

Tokyo Gas has succeeded in developing a non-stop, highly flexible, easy-to-operate, high cost-performance computer system. Using this system, we aim to monitor the safety of gas usage around-the-clock for approximately one million customers and provide remote meter-reading services for approximately ten million customers in the near future. We were able to find solutions for a number of issues faced by our company through the introduction of the 'Holon' concept. We at Tokyo Gas were the first in Japan to succeed in constructing an autonomous distributed processing system offering total EWS(Engineering Work Station) and LAN(Local Area Network) redundancy, as well as in introducing the 'Holon' concept for the development of a computer system. We believe this makes ours unique among all such systems in Japan.

RÉSUMÉ

Tokyo Gas a réussi le développement d'un système informatique 24 heures sur 24, très flexible, facile à opérer et à rapport coût/performance élevé. Avec ce système, nous avons l'intention de surveiller la sécurité de l'utilisation du gaz 24 heures sur 24 pour environ 1 million de consommateurs et d'assurer des services de lecture de compteur à distance pour environ 10 millions d'utilisateurs dans un proche avenir. Nous avons pu trouver des solutions à un certain nombre de problèmes auxquels notre entreprise était confrontée par l'introduction du conception 'Holon'. Chez Tokyo Gas, nous sommes les premiers au Japon à réussir la construction d'un système de traitement réparti autonome à redondance EWS et LAN, ainsi que l'introduction du concept 'Holon' pour le développement d'un système informatique. Nous considérons que cela rend notre système unique parmi tous les systèmes de ce genre au Japon.

INTRODUCTION

    Through the supply of energy and development of various
gas equipment, the Tokyo Gas Co., Ltd. seeks to assist its
customers in the process of comfortable living.  The concept of
'Intelligent Services' assists these efforts from the aspect of
'peace of mind.'

    'Intelligent services' are achieved when computer and
communication technologies are combined to build a communication
network system linking a gas company and its customers.  If we
think of the gas company as a living organism, the existing gas
lines would correspond to blood vessels and the communication
network system to a central nervous system.  Just as highly evolved
life forms have such a nerve network, so Tokyo Gas must offer fully
'Intelligent Services' in order to fulfill customer desires for a
higher quality of life.(1)

    The company's 24-hour-a-day monitoring center, named
'STATION24', plays a key role in these services, acting like a
brain and controlling the entire 'nervous system'.  STATION24
currently serves customers through major three systems :(5)

    - Remote monitoring systems for gas facilities such as GEHP
      (Gas Engine Heat Pump system), HEATS (Housing hEAting Total
      System, a collective boiler system for apartment houses),
      boilers for commercial use and co-generation systems.

    - A home security and home automation system

    - Automatic warning service systems, which provide automatic
      warning service that advice customers of abnormal gas use,
      remote shut-off service that shuts off the gas remotely in
      cases where the customer has forgotten to turn off the gas
      before leaving the house and automatic remote meter reading
      service.(2)(3)(4)

    (See Fig. 1 for a view of the overall network system.)

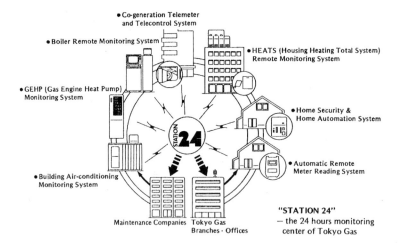

Fig. 1 Intelligent Service System

COMPUTER SYSTEM DEVELOPMENT NEEDS

As of the end of May 1994, the widely used automatic warning service system had about 165,000 users (about 2% of all Tokyo Gas customers), and it is expected that this number will exceed 300,000 by the end of 1995. Since the supercomputer being used in existing STATION24 center computer system can handle a maximum load of about 200,000 customers, its limits will soon be reached. Requirements for refined and extended services further suggest that the current STATION24 center computer system now needs to be updated.

A study on the characteristics of STATION24 concluded that the new STATION24 center computer system must be equipped with the following functions.

- 'Non-stop' design allowing 24-hour-a-day operations. The greatest selling point of these 'Intelligent Services' for customers is that Tokyo Gas will be able to carefully monitor the level of safety for gas usage. Therefore, our goal is to develop a computer system capable of providing 'Non-stop' services.

- Extendibility. Tokyo Gas must improve the competitive position by providing a higher level of service via the information network. Therefore, the system should be able to flexibly accommodate new services and new customers.

- High cost-performance. The system should be able to provide both automatic warning service for 10% of all customers and remote meter reading service for all customers by 2010 while it keeps the basic construction.

- Integration of separate service systems and increased operability.

- Ability to evolve. The system should be able to incorporate rapidly developing new computer technologies.

DEVELOPMENT CONCEPT

To meet these difficult requirements simultaneously, a completely new development concept is required. To do so, the new concept of 'Holon' is being employed in system development for the first time. The word 'holon' is an artificial compound word which is a combination of 'Holos', a Greek word meaning 'whole', and 'on', Greek for 'individual' or 'part', and thus translates as 'holistic individual'.

A 'Holonic System' refers to a flexible and autonomous system which simultaneously performs both the functions of a part which exists within a whole as well as functioning as a whole made up on various smaller parts. Therefore, a 'holonic system' has both holistic and individual functions, and these functions are harmonized to allow flexible control of the entire system. Tokyo Gas judges that establishment of such a system will solve the problems listed above.

FEATURES OF THE NEW SYSTEM

Fig. 2 shows the specific system configuration of the new STATION24 center computer system. The ready-made sub-systems are utilized for the inter-server communication sub-system (DT; Data Trade) and the data management sub-system (RDB; Relational DataBase).

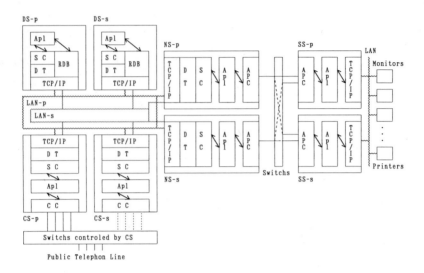

Abbreviations of EWS and LAN        Abbreviations of Subsystems and Programs

CS:Communication Server            CC :Communication Control sub-system
DS:Date Server                     SC :Server Contorol and network monitoring sub-system
NS:Network Server                  DT :inter-server communication sub-system (Data Trade)
SS:Station24 monitoring Server     RDB:data management sub-system (Relational DataBase)
-p:primary server or LAN           Apl:Application program
-s:secondary server or LAN         APC:inter-APplication program Communication sub-system

Fig . 2 The New STATION24 Center Coumpter System


A High Cost-Performance, Highly Extendable System

The new system can execute distributed processing on
server-by-server basis.  This means the system has the potential to
accommodate new services and accept additional customer
registrations.  To describe its functions concretely:

- Communication server (CS)
  Thanks to the communication control sub-system (CC), this
  server establishes communications between STATION24 and gas
  facilities and automatic warning service system terminals or
  security information devices that have several different
  communication protocols.

- Data server (DS)
  Controls information about customers and gas facilities and
  meter-monitoring systems, and maintains a history of
  monitoring status information.

- Network server (NS)
  Monitors each component for trouble, and performs an
  automatic exchange in such cases and establishes
  communications with CIS (Customer Information System) of
  our host computer.

- STATION24 monitoring Server (SS)
  Provides applications, e.g., MMI (man-machine interface); to
  execute remote monitoring for STATION24 operators.

This distributed processing system has two types of the servers for the same function. One is the 'Primary Server' and another is the 'Secondary Server'. The primary server executes the original part of the distributed processing at some moment and the secondary server stands-by for the case that the correspond primary fails while it does nearly equal processing with its primary.

The new STATION24 center coumpter system is compact by using EWS (Engineering Work Station) and LAN (Local Area Network), and a large-capacity computer system equivalent in performance to a large FTC (Fault-Tolerant Computer) can be built at about 1/5 hardware cost by taking account of function below.

This system is high cost-performance system which succeeds in so-called down-sizing and right-sizing. If the processing load of any server reaches to the maximam throughput, this system can esaily rise the total throughput by installing more servers of the bottle-neck.

A System with Constant Availability

Thanks to the network monitoring function, the new system offers highly trouble-free performance. The network monitoring function monitors troubles on the full duplex EWS, LAN and components such as communication lines, and automatically selects only trouble-free components. If a component fails, STATION24 uses this function to automatically detect the failure and replace the component within several seconds. This allows the STATION24 to operate 24 hours a day throughout the year, without any downtime for system expansion, software replacement or hardware maintenance.

An Integrated System

In the new system, existing computer systems providing intelligent services for each gas facility are integrated into a single system to establish a compatible MMI for STATION24 operaters. This leads to enhanced system operability.

Future Evolution

The new system uses the UNIX operating system thereby configuring an open system capable of future development.

DETAILS OF THE NETWORK MONITORING FUNCTION

The new STATION24 center computer system can offer highly trouble-free performance from the network monitoring function which is executed by SC (Server Control and network monitoring sub-system) on each server, and SC can execute the performance by using the heartbeat.

Heartbeat

Introducing the 'Holon' concept, this system execute autonomous detection of troubles on the system components and continuation of the service from the existence information packet which is sent and recieved between servers. This packet is called 'Heartbeat'. A heartbeat is sent from one primary server or one secondly server to another server and NS via LAN-p and LAN-s every second. Fig. 3 and Fig. 4 show examples of the heartbeat from DS-p.

SC of DS-p broadcasts a heartbeat via LAN-p every second. SC of DS-s always monitors the heartbeat from DS-p via LAN-p and checks recieving the new heartbeat within 3 seconds since recieving the last heartbeat. Each SC of NS-p and NS-s is similar to monitor and check the heartbeat from DS-p via LAN-p. (see Fig. 3)

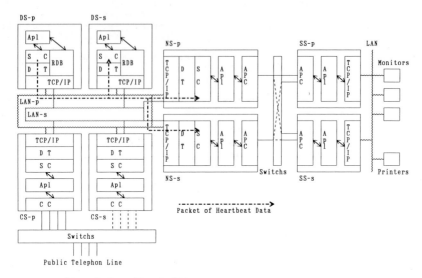

Fig. 3 Heartbeat (1)

Similarly, SC of DS-p bloadcasts a heartbeat via LAN-s every second and DS-s and both NS monitor and check the heartbeat (see Fig. 4) and these arrangements are continuously repeated.

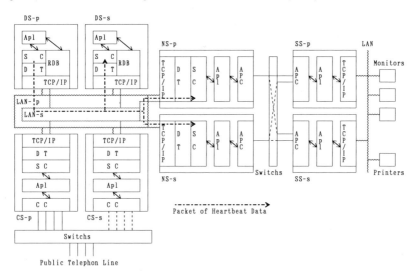

Fig. 4 Heartbeat (2)

In this way, for example, if DS-s can't check the new heartbeat from DS-p via LAN-p and LAN-s within 3 seconds, SC of DS-s can find out the trouble of DS-p, and, for example, NS-p can't check the heartbeats from every server via only LAN-p, SC of NS-p can find out the trouble of LAN-p.

An Example of the Network Monitoring Function

        If DS-p fails, how SC of each sever can fulfill the network
monitoring function by using heartbeat is explained below.

        If DS-p fails, SC of DS-p can't sends a heartbeat and SC of
DS-s decides that any trouble is happened on DS-p since SC of DS-s
can't check recieving the new heartbeats from DS-p via LAN-p and
LAN-s within 3 seconds, and DS-s quickly changes the part to the
primary server and provide the service without any downtime.
Similarly, the SC of NS-p decides the trouble of DS-p and the
information packet about the failure of DS-p and DS-s changes the
part to the new primary server is sent to SS-p. This information
is displayed on the monitor in the STATION24 monitoring room and
the STATION24 opetator contacts with the system mentenance section.
(see Fig. 5)

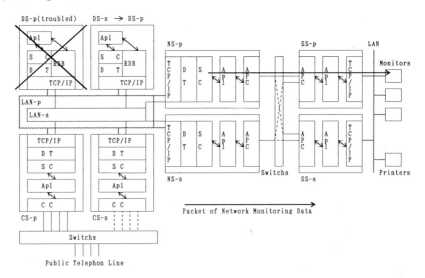

Fig. 5 The Network Monitoring Function (1)

        If troubled DS is restored, it plays the part to the new
secondary server and re-starts to broadcast the heartbeat as same
as ever. New DS-p and NS-p check recieving the new heartbeats from
new DS-s via LAN-p and LAN-s ,and decide that new DS-s is
restored. And NS-p sends the information packet about restored
DS-s to SS-p and the information is displayed on the monitor in the
STATION24 monitoring room. (see Fig. 6)

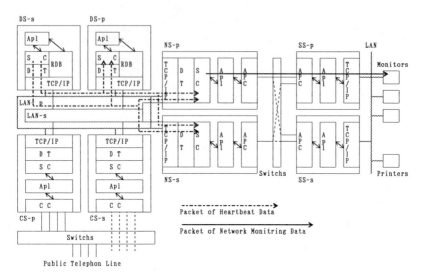

Fig. 6 The Network Monitoring Function (2)

New DS-p sends the recovery datas which are new RDB datas written into RDB of new DS-p since previous DS-p (new DS-s) failed to new DS-s. (see Fig. 7)

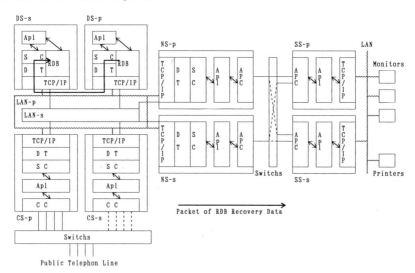

Fig. 7 The Network Monitoring Function (3)

In this way, the perfect dual system with EWS and LAN is autonomously re-constructed without any downtime.

CONCLUSION

The new STATION24 computer system is now equipped with the following advanced functions.

- Constant availability, derived from network-control function

- High flexibility and extendability, from distributed processing

- High cost performance, from down and right sizing

- Increased operability, from system integration

- Ensured future evolution, from introduction of UNIX system

At present, the new STATION24 center computer system is providing three types of intelligent services as before. Tokyo Gas is planning to integrate other system, e.g., total management service which manages and monitors all facilities of business buildings and apartment houses and so on, area management service which manages and monitors the whole of a local community, automatic remote meter reading service for other utility company and home shopping and reservation service; into the STATION24 center computer system to develop a network linking customers to STATION24.

The basic contrivance of this system can be easily utilized for general purpose, and application for the field of other information services or communication enterprise are now under review.

REFERENCES

1.  H. Watanabe, 'Application of Information Technology in the Gas
    Indusutry', Preprints of IGT's ASIAN NATURAL GAS II FOR A
    BRIGHTER '90, Singapore, April 1989

2.  N. Itakura and T. Rachi, 'Development of Automatic Meter
    Reading system', Preprints of the 1989 International Gas
    Research Conference, Volume 1, Nov. 1989

3.  N. Itakura and Y. Yamazaki, 'Automatic Meter communication
    system', Preprints of 18th IGU WGC, Berlin, July 1991

4.  M. Suzuki, 'Development of Automatic Meter Reading system at
    Tokyo Gas', Preprints of The 4th Automatic Meter Reading
    Association symposium '91, Boston, Sept. 1991

5.  N. Itakura, Y. Yamazaki and K. Katayama, 'Communication
    Network Sysytem between Customers and a Gas Company',
    Preprints of III World Symposium on Computing in the Gas
    Industry, Germany, April 1993

THE RANGE EXTENDER - AN APPLICATION OF
SONIC NOZZLES TO PRACTICAL METERING

L'ETENDEUR DE GAMME - UNE APPLICATION DE
TUYERES SONIQUES EN COMPTAGE PRATIQUE

Dr. H. H. Dijstelbergen
Instromet International, BELGIUM

## ABSTRACT

By installing a sonic nozzle downstream of a meter in a metering and regulating station, the effective range of both turbine meters and rotary piston meters can be extended considerably. This makes it possible to use smaller meters at a significant cost advantage. The operation of the station is described in the paper giving the pressure ratio over the nozzle and actual flow at different locations. The benefits of the construction in terms of meter size, range, flow limiting possibilities and built-in calibration facility are highlighted.

## RESUME

Le montage d'une tuyère sonique en aval de, soit un compteur à turbine, soit un compteur à pistons rotatifs dans un poste de détente et de comptage, permet de réaliser un élargissement important de la gamme de mesure effective du compteur. Ceci permet de faire des économies considérables. Le fonctionnement du poste est décrit dans cette communication, qui indique le quotient de la pression en amont et en aval de la tuyère sonique et les débits actuels à des positions différentes. Les avantages de ce poste sont accentués en termes de taille du compteur, gamme de mesure, possibilité de limiter le débit et méthode d'étalonnage incorporée.

## INTRODUCTION

Most turbine and positive displacement meters are installed downstream of a regulator. The supply pressure to the customer is roughly constant and limited to a safe value. The customer's installation can be designed for a lower pressure rating than the supplying distribution system.

Meters are sized for the maximum throughput. The minimum flow rate is determined by the size of the meter and the operating pressure.

Especially for straightforward spring loaded regulators the variations in pressure can be significant and may preclude the use of a constant pressure factor. Automatic volume correctors can then be used to correct for the pressure variations remaining downstream of the regulator. Alternatively the pressure can be assumed to be constant. For sophisticated pilot operated regulators this may suffice.

In some cases meters have been installed upstream of the regulator. If the pressure upstream of the regulator is sufficiently high, the meter can be of a smaller size and of a lower cost for the same maximum load. However, a higher pressure rating may negate this price advantage. For these types of installations, as pressure is uncontrolled, an automatic volume corrector is of course a necessity .

In modern distribution systems with PE piping, the pressure would typically be 4 bar (gauge). As a general rule, pipeline systems are never run to pressures less than 60% of absolute inlet pressure. At this pressure less than 20% of transport capacity remains. Even at the extremities of the system and on peak days, the pressure would not be allowed to drop below 2 bar (gauge). With the meter installed upstream of the regulator, the automatic volume corrector would have to operate accurately over the pressure range from 2 to 4 bar.

## MINIMUM FLOW RATE

The operating pressure of the meter has an effect on the minimum flow rate that can be accurately measured. For turbine meters and for rotary piston meters the influence of operating pressure on minimum flow rate is different.

Volumetric flow meters, such as turbine meters and rotary piston meters, have an output signal that is, in the first approximation, proportional to flow rate. The calibration or error curve of the meter gives the difference of the indicated value from the actual value of the flow rate. OIML recommends an acceptable band of +/- 2% at the lower end of the range. Both turbine and rotary piston meters need a certain flow rate to start operating at all and initially the error will be negative. The flow rate above which the error is within the acceptable error brackets, is the minimum flow rate $Q_{min}$.

The value of $Q_{min}$ for turbine meters is dependent on the density of the gas. At higher pressures more momentum is available to drive the rotor and thus the balance with friction forces occurs at a lower flow rate. The minimum flow rate for a turbine meter is therefore inversely proportional to the square root of the gas density (ref. 1)

$$Q_{min} = q\sqrt{\rho_o/\rho},$$

with $\rho$ the density of the fluid and $\rho_o$ the density of the fluid at reference conditions. Similarly $Q_{min}$ and q are the minimum flow rate at operating conditions and the minimum flow rate at reference conditions. For atmospheric pressure the measuring range of turbine meters is in the order of 1:20. For 9 bar (absolute) the range becomes 1:60.

For rotary piston meters the minimum flow rate is determined by the leakage around the pistons. This leakage is proportional to the dynamic viscosity $\mu$ and the pressure differential. The value of the viscosity is only very slightly dependent on pressure and, as the pressure differential serves mainly to overcome the (constant) friction, the leakage will be independent of pressure. As a result $Q_{min}$ is also independent of pressure. For conventional rotary piston meters the measuring range is around 1:50. In the Instromet IRM Infinity series leakage has been reduced significantly to give a range of 1:150 or more, independent of pressure.

## SONIC NOZZLES

Sonic nozzles are at present predominantly used as reference flow standards for testing meters. For a well designed and manufactured sonic nozzle, the flow in the throat becomes sonic if the pressure drop over the nozzle exceeds 5% of the (absolute) inlet pressure $P_m$. A further reduction of the downstream pressure $P_o$ does not increase the throughput of the nozzle. This is illustrated in figure 1.

If the inlet pressure is increased, while keeping the downstream pressure at least 5% lower than the inlet pressure, the volumetric flow rate at line conditions, upstream of the nozzle will still remain the same. However in terms of volumetric flow rate at standard conditions (or mass flow rate), the flow rate will increase proportional to the absolute pressure.

Sonic velocity is dependent on the gas composition and on the temperature. The flow rate under sonic conditions can in first approximation be expressed as:

$$Q = C * A * Z * \sqrt{T/d}$$

where C is a constant, A the surface area of the throat of the nozzle, Z the compressibility, T the absolute temperature and d the relative density (ref. 2). Most gases presently distributed in Europe have relative densities between 0.59 and 0.65. If we consider for the moment pressures up to 5 bar (absolute), we find that the variation in Z is in the order of +/- 2%. Temperatures would be between 0 and 30 °C. Within a few % the sonic flow rate is therefore independent of gas composition or temperature and solely determined by the area of the throat.

## THE RANGE EXTENDER

In figure 2, the schematic diagram of the "Range Extender" is given. Gas is supplied to the meter/regulator station at an inlet pressure $P_{in}$ which is in excess of a specific value $P_i$. The pressure is reduced in the regulator to a value $P_m$, which represents the meter pressure. After passing the meter, the gas flows through the sonic nozzle where it expands to the delivery pressure $P_o$.

The operation is as follows: For very small flow rates the sonic nozzle does not pose any significant obstruction. Flow is subsonic and there is no or very little pressure drop over the nozzle. When flow rate increases, the pressure drop over the nozzle increases. The meter pressure increases but the delivery pressure remains the same, as the sensing point for the regulator is downstream of the nozzle. When the absolute value of the meter pressure exceeds the absolute outlet pressure by more than 5%, velocity in the throat of the nozzle is sonic. The size of the nozzle is chosen to match the maximum flow rate of the meter. Any further increase in demand will not increase the gas velocity in the nozzle. Only the meter pressure will increase with the meter indicating the same flow rate. The volumetric flow rate at the outlet increases only as a result of higher meter pressure (see figure 1).

As the meter pressure varies considerably, an automatic volume corrector has to be used to calculate the standard volume.

A complete skid mounted station for a maximum capacity of 300 m³ (std)/h at 100 mbar and a minimum inlet pressure of 2 bar (gauge) is shown in figure 3. The rangeability, using an Instromet IRM Infinity G65 is 1:500 with a maximum error of -2%, occurring at the low end. For an inlet pressure of 4 bar (gauge) the capacity of the same station increases to 500 m³(std)/h.

## COMPARISON OF A RANGE EXTENDER WITH CONVENTIONAL INSTALLATIONS

The range extender configuration has a different effect on meter range for turbine meters and for rotary piston meters. This is because the minimum flow rate of these meter types behaves differently as a function of pressure.

In table 1 a comparison is made between three types of installations : One conventional design, one with the meter upstream of the regulator and a range extender arrangement.

The basic principle of the three designs is given in figure 4. Both a rotary piston meter and a turbine meter are considered.

The capacity of the station is calculated at a minimum inlet pressure $P_i$. For sake of simplicity, the pressure drop over filters, heat exchangers etc. is neglected.

Examples are given in the table for two different types of stations: A station with low outlet pressure supplied from a 4 bar (gauge) distribution system and an 8 bar (gauge) outlet pressure station supplied from a 40 bar (gauge) transmission system. These stations are representative for, for example, an industrial metering station and for a city gate station.

It is clear from the table that the range extender has a considerably larger range than either the conventional station or the one with the meter installed upstream of the regulator. The minimum station capacity remains the same as in the conventional design but the maximum capacity increases to the same value as achieved when the meter is installed upstream of the regulator.

Alternatively, for the same capacity, a smaller meter can be used. In example 1 the meter can be chosen at least 2 steps lower in the G series. In example 2, at least one downward step can be made in the G series.

In the range extender the pressure downstream of the regulator can be limited by an arrangement as in figure 5. The pressure rating of the meter can then be fully exploited. For example 2, ANSI 150 suffices for the range extender, whereas for the meter upstream of the regulator it is necessary to use ANSI 300.

It is clear that the range extender is most effective if the ratio of minimum absolute inlet pressure to outlet pressure is highest. Modern distribution systems in PE often use 4 bar (gauge) as the nominal distribution pressure. In practice a minimum pressure of less than 2 bar (gauge) anywhere in the system would not be tolerated and the minimum operating pressure can be assumed to be 2 bar.

## FLOW/PRESSURE LIMITER

The range extender's prime advantages are to reduce the meter size while increasing the rangeability. One of the additional benefits is a simple facility to limit the maximum flow rate that the customer is able to take.

Contracts in many cases stipulate a maximum take-off related to a demand charge. For higher maximum demands a higher demand charge would have to be paid. Policing would normally involve the installation of automatic registration equipment and the checking of those records.

By installing a back pressure regulator as indicated in figure 5 the pressure at the meter, and consequently the maximum flow rate, can be limited to a predetermined value. For pressures in excess of its set point the back pressure regulator will open. Further endeavours to increase the flow rate will only serve to lower the outlet pressure as the back pressure regulator overrules. The value to which the back pressure regulator should be adjusted can be estimated quite simply.

If the maximum meter capacity is equal to Q and the capacity to which the installation should be limited is $Q_{o\,max}$, then the maximum meter pressure should be limited to

$$P_{limit} = (Q_{o\,max}/Q)^*\ P_{base}$$

with both pressures in absolute terms.

As was pointed out in the preceding section, the pressure may also be limited to be able to restrict the pressure rating of the meter, e.g. to ANSI 150.

OVERSPEED PROTECTION

Another additional benefit of the range extender is an automatic protection from meter overspeed. As the absolute velocity in the nozzle is limited to the speed of sound, the maximum flow rate is limited by the size of the nozzle. The size of the nozzle is chosen to match meter capacity and it is therefore impossible to overspeed the meter.

Though this would eliminate most causes of overcharging the meter, very fast opening of valves could still result in very large accelerating forces that could damage the meter.

CALIBRATION

As mentioned earlier, sonic nozzles are presently mostly used for calibration purposes. Being a simple, passive device, the sonic nozzle is an excellent reference device. Indeed, some transmission and distribution companies use sonic nozzles to prove meters in the field, either venting the gas to atmosphere or by manipulating the take-off to achieve the proper flow rate.

The range extender allows for automatic checking of the meter, at least at maximum flow rate, in a simple and straightforward way. The flow rate has to be at a level where the nozzle is operating in sonic mode. This is the case when the upstream (meter) pressure is 5% or more above the downstream pressure.

Pressure and temperature at the meter have to be measured and for an accurate check the gas composition also needs to be known.

THE ELECTRONIC VOLUME CORRECTOR

Most electronic volume correctors are only used over a fairly narrow range of pressures, fundamentally determined by the accuracy and stability of the pressure regulator. For the range extender this is not the case. In example 1 the range in absolute pressure is 1:5; in example 2 it is 1:2.

Traditionally the accuracy of pressure transducers is given in terms of a percentage of span. For a range of 1:4, even a 0.5% transducer has an accuracy of only 2% at the end of scale.

Gasmeters and correctors on the contrary have their accuracies expressed in terms of percentage of actual value. The range extender needs, therefore, pressure transducers that have an accuracy of a few tenths of a percent over a reasonable range.

The main problem is temperature dependence. Pressure transducers with built-in temperature compensation display the desired characteristics and are presently readily available.

Examples of the error as a function of temperature for a pressure transducer incorporated in a compact, moderately priced corrector, are given in figure 6 and 7.

## CONCLUSION

- Application of the range extender in a meter and regulator station can give appreciable savings in investment. It also gives the possibility to limit the flow to a predetermined value in a simple manner. It reduces the risk of meter damage due to operation faults and provides a facility to perform an easy way to check a meter in the field.

## REFERENCES

1. V.E. Eujen, "Untersuchungen über die Meßeigenschaften von Hochdruckgaszählern, II. Teilbericht: Messungen an Schraubenradgaszählern, G.W.F. 105. Jahrgang, Heft 43, 23. Okt. 1964.

2. ISO 9300, "Measurement of gas flow by means of critical flow venturi nozzles", International Organisation for Standardisation, 1989.

| Flow rates: | | Example 1 | Example 2 |
|---|---|---|---|
| Maximum meter flow rate: | Q | Q | Q |
| Minimum meter flow rate (gas, atmospheric): | q | q | q |

| Pressures: | | | |
|---|---|---|---|
| Maximum inlet pressure Pin (bar abs.): | Pmax | 9 | 41 |
| Minimum inlet pressure Pin (bar abs.): | Pi | 3 | 19 |
| Outlet pressure Pout (bar abs.): | Po | 1 | 9 |
| Base (reference) pressure (bar abs.): | Pb | 1 | 1 |

| Meter ranges for gas @ Pb assumed for examples: | |
|---|---|
| Rotary piston meter | 1:150 |
| Turbine meter | 1:20 |

| | Rotary piston meter | | | Turbine meter | | |
|---|---|---|---|---|---|---|
| | Equation | Example1 | Example2 | Equation | Example1 | Example2 |
| **CONVENTIONAL STATION** | | | | | | |
| Station maximum capacity (m³/h @ base cond.) | (Po/Pb)Q | Q | 9Q | (Po/Pb)Q | Q | 9Q |
| Station minimum capacity (m³/h @ base cond.) | (Po/Pb)q | Q/150 | Q/16.7 | (Po/Pb)$^{0.5}$q | Q/20 | Q/6.67 |
| Station range | Q/q | 150 | 150 | (Po/Pb)$^{0.5}$(Q/q) | 20 | 60 |
| Pressure rating meter: | Po | 1 | 9 | Po | 1 | 9 |
| | | | | | | |
| **METER UPSTREAM OF REGULATOR** | | | | | | |
| Station maximum capacity for Pin = Pi (m³/h @ base c.) | (Pi/Pb)Q | 3Q | 19Q | (Pi/Pb)Q | 3Q | 19Q |
| Station minimum capacity for Pin = Pi (m³/h @ base c.) | (Pi/Pb)q | Q/50 | Q/7.89 | (Pi/Pb)$^{0.5}$q | Q/11.55 | Q/4.59 |
| Station range | Q/q | 150 | 150 | (Pi/Pb)$^{0.5}$(Q/q) | 34.6 | 87.2 |
| Pressure rating meter: | Pmax | 9 | 41 | Pmax | 9 | 41 |
| | | | | | | |
| **RANGE EXTENDER** | | | | | | |
| Station maximum capacity for Pin = Pi (m³/h @ base c.) | (Pi/Pb)Q | 3Q | 19Q | (Pi/Pb)Q | 3Q | 19Q |
| Station minimum capacity (m³/h @ base c.) | (Po/Pb)q | Q/150 | Q/16.67 | (Po/Pb)$^{0.5}$q | Q/20 | Q/6.67 |
| Station range | (Pi/Po)(Q/q) | 450 | 317 | Pi(PoPb)$^{-0.5}$(Q/q) | 60 | 127 |
| Pressure rating meter: | Pi | 3 | 19* | Pi | 3 | 19* |

* The pressure is limited to 19 bar using an arrangement as in figure 5.

**Table1. Comparison of the properties of a "range extender" with a conventional regulator station design and with a design where the meter is located upstream of the regulator.**

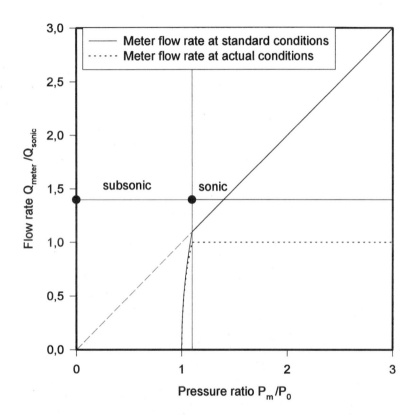

**Figure 1. The ratio of meter flow rate at actual and at standard conditions to sonic flow rate, both as a function of the ratio of the inlet to outlet nozzle pressure**

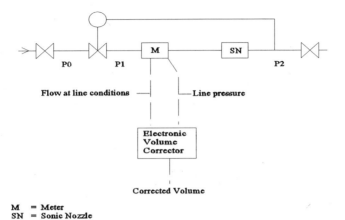

M  = Meter
SN = Sonic Nozzle

**Figure 2. Schematic diagram of the Range Extender**

**Figure 3. A skid mounted station equipped with a Range Extender.**
**Outlet pressure         :        100 bar**
**Meter                    :        Instromet IRM Infinity G65**
**Minimum flow rate  :        0.73m³(std)/h**
**Maximum flow rate @ 2 bar (gauge) inlet pressure  :   300m³(std)/h**
**Maximum flow rate @ 4 bar (gauge) inlet pressure  :   500m³(std)/h**

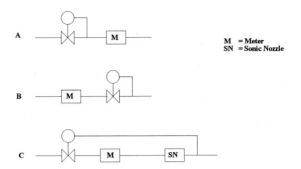

**Figure 4. The three types of installations compared in table 1**

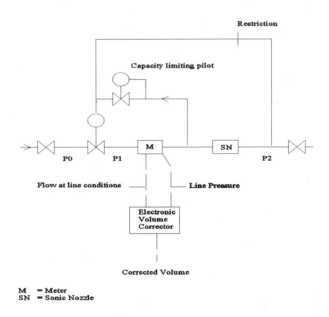

**Figure 5. The Range Extender equipped with a capacity/pressure limiting back pressure regulator**

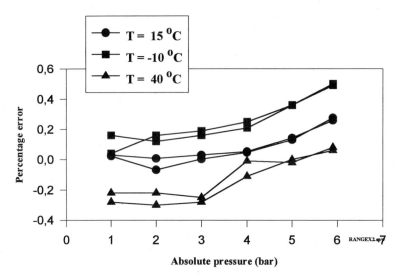

Figure 6. Pressure gauge error (of indicated value) as a function
of pressure for different temperatures for a 1 to 6 bar (abs)
Electronic Volume Corrector type INSTROMET 510 N

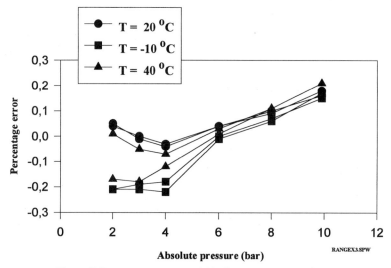

Figure 7. Pressure gauge error (of indicated value) as a function
of pressure for different temperatures for a 2 to 10 bar (abs)
Electronic Volume Corrector type INSTROMET 510 N

AN ANALYSIS OF RESIDENTIAL GAS CONSUMPTION USING
LOAD SURVEY TECHNIQUE


ANALYSE DE LA CONSOMMATION DOMESTIQUE DU GAZ PAR
LA TECHNIQUE DES COURBES DE CHARGE

Shin Yamagami, Shin-ich Sasayama and Hajime Nakamura
Tokyo Gas Co., Ltd, JAPAN

## ABSTRACT

We have succeeded in developing a new technique to analyze final
gas consumption: waterheating, spaceheating and cooking, by
monitoring the continuous gas flow through the meter. Since the
fluctuation of the flow has strong relation with the control
characteristics of appliances, we can identify appliances in use
at each moment. The load survey approach has two benefits
compared with the former macroscopic approaches such as
multivariate analysis. First, more accurate estimation of the
demands is attained and secondly, the load curve of each final
demand can also be estimated. For this purpose, a decomposition
technique of the gas flow is used. This technique is applied to
some 600 samples and the final demands are investigated. The
result shows a strong evidence that our methods eventually works
and the obtained information seems to be applicable to various
purposes.

## RÉSUMÉ

Nous avons réussi à développer une nouvelle technique permettant
d'analyser la consommation de gaz finale: chauffage d'eau,
chauffage d'espace et cuisine en surveillant le flux de gaz
continu au compteur. La fluctuation du flux étant en relation
étroite avec les caractéristiques de contrôle des appareils, on
peut identifier les appareils utilisés à tout moment. L'approche
par étude de charge présente deux avantages, comparée aux
approches macroscopiques antérieures, telles que l'analyse à
plusieurs variables. Premièrement, l'obtention d'une estimation
plus précise et deuxièmement, la possibilité d'estimer la courbe
de charge de chaque demande finale. A cet effet, on a utilisé la
technique de décomposition du flux de gaz. Elle a été appliquée
à quelque 600 échantillons pour rechercher les demandes finales.
Le résultat obtenu montre clairement que nos méthodes
fonctionnent en fin de compte, et les informations obtenues
semblent applicables à des usages variés.

INTRODUCTION

For a gas company, it is important to know how much gas is consumed as the final demands: waterheating, spaceheating and cooking. We had been making efforts at investigating this problem for a long time without making it sure how accurate the estimations were. Recently, we have succeeded in developing a new technique to analyze gas consumption of each final demand mentioned above through monitoring the gas flow using the smart gas meter which was originally developed for securing the safety of the residential usage.

Except for the load monitoring information, the only available data are the monthly meter-readings of each household. Typically some old techniques estimate the final demands by regressing them on the appliances it holds. The new technique uses the information of control characteristics and input level of appliances to decompose the total gas consumption of a household at each moment into the three categories. The new technique makes it possible to avoid the inherent problem of macroscopic techniques that prevents us from accurate estimation of the final demands. The similar technique are studied by chance in the electronic power field (1).

In the following, we briefly review the traditional estimation schemes. Then we explain the new method and compare it with the old methods. Further we report the results of the proposed method applied to the data of some 600 samples in Tokyo Gas distribution area. Finally we show some perspectives of this load survey data on various analyses such as forecasting the future demand.

REVIEW OF THE TRADITIONAL ESTIMATION SCHEMES

As is mentioned, the monthly meter-readings and appliance holding information  are the only available data before the new technique is developed. Most of the traditional methods are based on statistical inference in some way and they defer only in the underlying assumptions. In the following we briefly review two typical models: (1)appliance group analysis and (2)multiple regression.

Appliance Group Analysis

We divide the customers into three clusters depending on the combination of appliances they hold; cluster 1: those that use gas only for cooking, cluster 2: both for cooking and waterheating, but not for spaceheating, cluster 3: for all of three final demands. Assuming no interaction, we estimate the final demand from the difference among the mean consumption values (one way layout). Interaction, however, obviously does exist, and hence we can't make sure that how accurate the estimations are.

Multiple Regression

This technique is very similar to the appliance group analysis. Gas consumption per appliance is estimated as coefficients by regressing monthly meter reading of a household on the appliances it holds. The problems here lies again in the interaction of the appliances (that is the linear model is no longer correct.)

THE LOAD SURVEY TECHNIQUE

Load Survey Data

The load data was originally used to analyze the capacity of the pipeline network. The data is usually an accumulation of gas consumption in certain time period, e.g., fifteen minutes or an hour (fixed-time method).

This time, however, in order to decompose the gas usage into three final demands, the time interval needs to be much less than 1 minute, say 5 seconds. Unfortunately, the flow in 5 second-interval is not measurable with the conventional gas meter since the flow may be far less than the minimal distinguishable unit. The smart gas meter measures the time duration of each $0.90\times10^{-3}m^3$ (for the other purpose) and we take benefit of this measuring characteristics. That is, we log the time interval for a fixed amount of flow (fixed-volume method). We describe this point a little more than in detail in the following.

Monitoring Method

The gas meter used in Japan changes the movement of the diaphragm into a cyclic crank rotation. The smart gas meter has a sensor which detects rotation of a magnet attached to the crank and submits an electric pulse every crank cycle. Between two pulses, $0.9\times10^{-3}m^3$ of gas flows through a standard size meter, $1.74\times10^{-3}m^3$ through a large size meter and $0.6\times10^{-3}m^3$ through a small size meter. From these pulses, we can calculate the flow velocity (Table 1 and Figure 1). The relation among inputs, intervals and corresponding appliances are shown in Table 2. The data logger measures the time intervals and write them into a memory after data compression to avoid redundancy. The number of data is about 600 (= 1.2 Kbyte) a day on average since the logger doesn't write all intervals but only the first one of a sequence of almost the same intervals and the number. The stored data are easily downloaded into IC memory cards.

The Analysis Technology of Accumulated Data

The analysis technology of accumulated data mainly consists of two parts. One is the decomposition algorithm: we decompose the aggregated gas flow into individual consumption, and the other is the estimation method: we identify each consumption with the appliance.

Decomposition Algorithms. We assume not more than one appliance either turn on or turn off simultaneously. Figure 2 shows an example of the decomposition when 2 appliances are used. We can apply a similar algorithm for decomposition when more than 2 appliances are used (See Figure 3).

Estimation Method. Heuristic rules are applied to identify the appliance used. Especially we look at (a) input level (b) duration time. Each final demand gas the following characteristics.
Waterheating: a high but a short flow
Spaceheating: a stable, long flow or periodical flow
Cooking: a low, short flow

COMPARISONS OF THE ESTIMATION METHODS

We compare the proposed load survey technique with those in the past (Table 3). The load survey technique is more accurate but requires more detailed and expensive information than the other conventional estimation schemes which are as follows.

RESULTS

About 600 household monitors have been set from our customers. Figure 4 shows that the proposed algorithm works fairly well. The results of the analysis are shown in Table 4. Statistical theory shows that sufficient samples guarantee certain confidence level of the estimation and we plan to extend up to 1,000 samples.

Figure 5. shows a load curve of each demand of a typical day. These analyses could not be realized by the traditional methods.

We list several examples of the application of the results by the proposed method.

Application

Gas Consumption By Each Appliance. Obviously, the main purpose of the new method is to investigate each appliance's annual demand. Further with the customer audit, we find various reason that causes the variance of the consumption. For example, the gas demand of households with only gas space heater is $6.3 \times 10^9$ [J] a year larger than that of a household with electric heat pumps. This information is used in sales promotion strategy for the appliances.

Meteorological Effect. The influence of meteorological effect on each final demand is separately analyzed. We verify existence of a linear relationship between the waterheating demand and the temperature too.

Development of a Low NOx Water Furnace. The NOx emitted by the water furnace is an environmental problem. Since the furnace may not always be used at its maximum output level, we see the distribution of the input gas level from the load survey data. And this information helps us to design the burner that minimizes the annual total emission.

Rate Making of the Gas Tariff. We refer to the demand data to design a special rate table for the air-conditioning tariff.

New Facility Designing. Load curve suggests the hourly maximum demand of each house and the aggregated demand of a condominium complex and so on. We use this information in designing the gas supplying facility with minimum costs.

Trend Analysis. The accumulation of the surveyed data will support the time series analysis of the demand structure. For example, the effect of the decreasing size of a family, age of the family, or the effect of the economy will be dynamically investigated.

Demand Forecasting. Gas demand can be decomposed into the three factors described by the following equation.

$$G = N \times P \times C \qquad (1)$$

where,
- G: gas demand
- N: number of households
- P: diffusion of gas appliances
- C: consumption per appliance

To forecast the future final gas demands, we have developed a forecasting model of the population and the number of households and are now developing a diffusion model of appliances considering the competition with other fuels such as electricity, kerosene and so on. Through these analyses and other studies we are researching the residential demand structure.

FUTURE PROBLEM

We are now launching the same kind of load monitoring survey of the electricity demands. First, we need to establish the analyzing algorithm. Then, we combine both result to investigate the domestic energy demand structure and further problems.

Also, the current estimation algorithm seems to have 95% accuracy. With the help of the electricity load monitoring, we need to enhance the reliability of the decomposition algorithm.

CONCLUSION

We have succeeded in developing a new load survey technique to investigate the  final demand. This technique is superior to the other conventional techniques in the following points: we can obtain (a) reliable and robust estimation, (b) the change of the final demand at the time of day.

We could also make sure that our technique is effective in analyzing the final demands by the field-test results.

We intend to apply the results to various researches synthesized in the analysis of residential demand structure.

REFERENCES

1.    Hart, G. W., "Nonintrusive Appliance Load Monitoring," Proceedings of the IEEE, Vol. 80, No. 12, pp. 1870-1891, December 1992.

2.    Shin, Yamagami Shin-ichi, Sasayama Hajime, Nakamura, "Residential Load Survey (in Japanese)",City Gas Symposium, June 1993.

Table 1 An example of pulse data

| DD/MM | HH/MM/SS | gas flow (W) | interval (s) | pulse count |
|-------|----------|--------------|--------------|-------------|
| 24/01 | 06/23/10 | 3095 | 25.89 | 1 |
| 24/01 | 06/23/36 | 3039 | 52.72 | 2 |
| 24/01 | 06/24/29 | 4230 | 18.94 | 1 |
| 24/01 | 06/24/48 | 38706 | 2.07 | 1 |
| 24/01 | 06/24/50 | 46179 | 3.47 | 2 |
| 24/01 | 06/24/53 | 44266 | 1.81 | 1 |
| 24/01 | 06/24/55 | 41088 | 1.95 | 1 |

Table 2 Relation among inputs, intervals and corresponding appliances

| input | small size meter | standard size meter | large size meter | appliances corresponding to inputs |
|-------|------------------|---------------------|------------------|-----------------------------------|
| (W) | $0.6 \times 10^{-3}$ $m^3$/pulse | $0.9 \times 10^{-3}$ $m^3$/pulse | $1.74 \times 10^{-3}$ $m^3$/pulse | |
| 500 | 40.9 | 61.3 | 118.5 | |
| 1000 | 20.5 | 30.6 | 59.3 | rice cooker |
| 2000 | 10.2 | 15.3 | 29.7 | cooking stove dryer |
| 3000 | 6.8 | 10.2 | 19.8 | room heater |
| 5000 | 4.1 | 6.1 | 11.9 | oven |
| 10000 | 2.1 | 3.1 | 5.9 | bath heater instantaneous water heater (small) |
| 30000 | 0.7 | 1.0 | 2.0 | instantaneous water heater (large) |

Table 3 Comparison among the estimation techniques

| | information | accuracy |
|---|-------------|----------|
| Appliance group analysis | monthly gas consumption data appliance holdings | Δ |
| Muliple regression | same as above | Δ |
| Load survey | instantaneous gas consumption data input of appliances | O |

Table 4 Final demand (MJ / day)

| (MJ) | waterheating | spaceheating | cooking | total |
|------|--------------|--------------|---------|-------|
| Feb., 1994 | 75 | 25 | ·10 | 110 |
| Aug., 1994 | 22 | 0 | 7 | 29 |

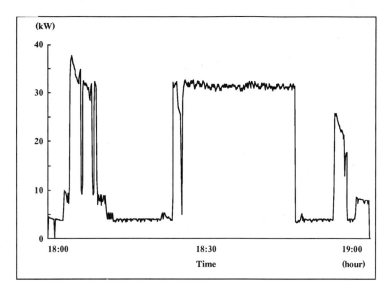

**Figure 1 An example of load data**

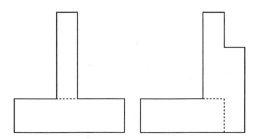

**Figure 2 Decomposition algorithm in two appliances' case**

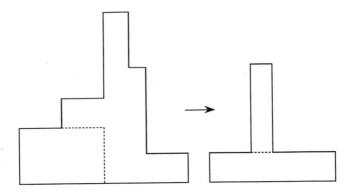

**Figure 3 Decomposition algorithm in more than two appliances' case**

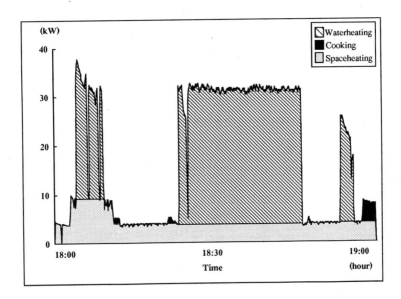

**Figure 4 An example of decomposition**

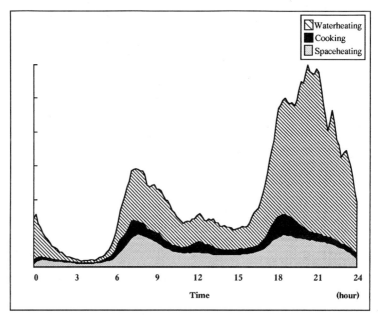

**Figure 5 A load curve of each demand**

NUMERICAL ANALYSIS OF FLUIDIC OSCILLATION
APPLIED TO THE FLUIDIC GAS METER

APPLICATION DE L' ANALYSE NUMÉRIQUE DE L'
OSCILLATION FLUIDIQUE AU COMPTEUR FLUIDIQUE

Shiniti.Sato and Kazumitsu Nukui
Tokyo Gas CO.,LTD,JAPAN

Seiichi Ito
Osaka Gas CO.,LTD,JAPAN

Yukio Kimura
Toho Gas CO.,LTD,JAPAN

ABSTRACT

Fluidic gas meter is utilizing fluidic oscillation generated by fluidic element (here after " FD element" ). The simulation method of numerical analysis ( here after simulation ) was adopted to analyze the fluidic oscillation. At the first step simulation was carried out to verify " coincidence of simulation result and experimental result,". At this step the numbers of mesh divisions and time division, the simulation parameter, were optimized. This parameter was then used to simulate the effect of shape variation of FD element on the fluidic oscillation. The obtained analysis data was found to be almost equivalent to the experimental fluidic oscillation, proving that the simulation could be used for evaluating the performance of FD element. We are, therefore, planing to use the simulation for the development of future gas meters.

RÉSUMÉ

Le compteur á gaz fluidique, est un compteur á gaz utilisant les vibrations d' un fluide par les éléments fluidiques(ci-aprés désignés par FD). Afin d' analyser la vibration du fluidie, nous avons recouru á la mét hode de simulation par analyse numé rique(ci-aprés designée par "la simulation"). Au départ, nous avons procédé á une vérification visant á ét ablir la mesure dans laquelle il était possible d' obtenir, par simulation, des valeurs proches des valeurs expérimentales. Ensuite, nous avons pratiqu é l' optimisation duchiffre de résolution de temps, le chiffre de rés olution de maille, qui est un paramétre de la simulation.Utilisant ce param étre, nous avons fait changer l' aspect des éléments FD et nous avons procéd é á une analyse des vibration du fluide. Nous avons obtenu pour résultat une valeur sensiblement égale á celle des vibrations de fluide. Nous avons ainsi obtenu la preuve qu'il était possible d'utiliser cette simulation pour l'appréciation de la performance des éléments FD. En conséquence de quoi, nous envisageons dans l'avenir d'utiliser la simuration pour la viabilisation de ce compteur.

INTRODUCTION

     Tokyo Gas Co., Ltd., Osaka Gas Co., Ltd. and Toho Gas Co.,
Ltd. are making joint efforts   in developing the Fluidic gas meter
with a view to making the gas meter more compact and more
intelligent. Because of the complicated shape of the FD element,
the conventional development has been done only by the method
involved a large number of trial-manufactures and experiments. We
would like to report here that the new simulation has been proved
an effective means for the development of FD element.

PURPOSE

     The Fluidic gas meter measures the flow rate by means of the
fluidic oscillation which is generated when the gas flows through
the FD element, so that the shape of FD element is an important
factor for the precise measurement of the flow rate. It is,
therefore,evaluated that the application possibility of the
simulation to developing the FD element shape.

DETAILS OF THE DEVELOPMENT OF FUIDIC GAS METER

     1983:   A joint development program was commenced Tokyo Gas
             Co.,Ltd., Osaka Gas Co., Ltd. and Toho Gas Co., Ltd.

     1989:   Trial-manufacture started before putting into practical
             use

     1993:   Trial-manufacture of the meter for field test started
             before putting into commercial test

Same year:   The simulation of FD element fluidic oscillation
             started in order to make final confirmation of the
             element shape.

     1995:   The simulation is currently carried out by changing the
             FD element shape to study on the improvement of the
             element shape.

PRINCIPLE OF FLOW MEASUREMENT BY FLUIDIC GAS METER

     The principle of fluidic oscillation is given in Fig.1, and
the composition of fluidic gas meter in Fig.2. The gas, fed through
the nozzle, has its flow oscillated regularly inside the meter in
the left and right directions, with the fluidic oscillation
frequency getting increased in proportion to the flow rate through
the nozzle as shown in Fig. 3.   Thus the gas flow rate can be
obtained by measuring the fluidic oscillation frequency.
Furthermore, the integrating flow volume can be obtained by
counting the number of cycles since the gas flow rate per cycle is
constant from the relationship shown in Fig. 3.   The fluidic
oscillation pulse of FD element is detected by means of the
differential pressure cycle between pressures  P1 and P2, obtained
from the 2 pieces of pressure propagating pipes installed against
the center line of FD elements.

SIMULATION ANALYSIS METHOD

     The performances required of an FD element are:

A: stable fluidic oscillation
B: strong fluidic oscillation
C: fluidic oscillation starting flow rate
D: measuring range

Evaluation has been made on the item A and B by means of the
simulation.  As for the analysis method, the flow inside the
element is calculated by using NavierStokes'equation and the
equation of continuity.

Equation-1  Navier-Stokes' equation: $\frac{\partial u}{\partial t} + (u \cdot \mathrm{grad})u = -\frac{1}{\rho}\mathrm{grad}\,p + \nu\Delta u + K$

Equation-2  Equation of continuity : $\frac{\partial \rho}{\partial t} + \mathrm{div}(\rho u) = 0$

The data, obtained through calculation, are expressed in two forms
given below.

  a: Evaluation of the frequency, strength, and stability of
     fluidic oscillation by plotting the graph of the time series
     variation of the differential pressure between two points in
     FD element

  b: Overall expression of the flow in FD element through animation
     of the flow vector and pressure distribution.  (See Fig. 4)

The analysis of the obtained data enables improvement of the FD
element.  The items of analysis, analysis conditions, physical
constants, etc., used in the measurement, are given below.

  (1)Items of analysis
     Flow rate :  300  1/hr
     FD element:  Model 1, 2, 3 (See Fig. 5 for shape and size)

  (2)Analysis conditions

|            | Conputer name | Analysis method |
|------------|---------------|-----------------|
| Tokyo Gas  | CRAY-YMP      | Hawell Flow3D   |
| Osaka Gas  | TITAN-Ⅲ       | $\alpha$-Flow   |
| Toho Gas   | VP2600/10     | $\alpha$-Flow   |

  Assumption of flow:Two-dimensional unsteady and incompressible
                     fluid,laminar flow
  Number of mesh divisions:9,888 (See Fig. 6), 3,650, 3,640,
                           1,015

  (3)Physical constants
     Gas:  Air( 0℃ 1 atmospheric pressure)
     Density:  1.293  kg/m³
     Coefficient of viscosity:  $1.71\times10^{-5}$  kg/ms

EVALUATION OF ANALYSIS RESULT

Result of Simulation and Comparison with Experimental data

     The experimental data of the fluidic shape (model 1:mesh 9888)
is given in Fig. 7, and the analysis (simulation) result in Fig. 8,
with (a) indicating the pressure waveform and (b) the Fourier
spectrum, showing excellent correspondence in waveform and spectrum
peak rising between the experimental data and the analysis result.
This proves that the evaluation of the flow due to simulation is
equivalent to that due to experiment.

Comparison of Analysis Methods (Softwares)

     The Harwell-Flow 3D and the $\alpha$-Flow are compared in the
fluidic shape (model 1), with the results shown in Table-1, and the
waveform and spectrum given in Figs.8 and 9 respectively.

It has been found through comparison that there is little difference between the analysis methods, and it is considered that the two methods can yield exactly same results in the future by tuning the parameter of mesh, etc. Furthermore, the comparison with the experimental data also show excellent correspondence in waveform and spectrum shape. It can, therefore, be concluded that there is no difference between the two analysis methods.

Influence of The Number of Mesh Divisions of FD Element Shape and Time Divisions on Calculated Data

In order to examine the influence of the number of mesh divisions on the calculation, calculation was carried out in the fluidic path (model 1) by varying the calculation accuracy. The frequency of the fluidic oscillation and calculate condition are shown in Table-2.

Aforesaid results and Table-2 show that the finer the mesh, the closer the calculated data to the experimental data. However, when the mesh exceeds 10000,the calculation time gets sharply increased. With the mesh at 10000 level, the calculated data is quite close to the experimental data in terms of waveform and spectrum shape. Thus, the 10000-mesh seems to be appropriate in practical sense.

Influence due to The Variation in Fluidic Element Shape

It has been found, through the developments and experiments so far made, that the fluid oscillation frequency and strength of FD element largely depend on the target, of its size, shape, etc.

Calculation was, therefore, made by varying the target shapes of FD element (models 2 and 3), with the target shape and size given in Fig. 5 and the calculated data in Table-3.

The delicate variation in target shape causes the fluidic oscillation frequency and differential pressure to change, which is conspicuously reflected in the simulation result. This proves that the target shape, size, etc. greatly influence the fluidic oscillation of FD element.

FUTURE PLANS

The result of simulation has been found to correspond substantially with the experimental data. In future the following items are planned by using the simulation.

I : Study on the improvement of FD element shape with low starting flow rate of the fluidic oscillation for the wide measurement range

II : Study on the improvement of FD element shape capable of producing large differential pressure due to the fluidic oscillation

III : Study on the improvement of FD shape with fine linearity

IV : Clarification of linearity influenced by the element to observing the animation of the fluidic oscillation

CONCLUSION

The simulations have clarified the following points. We are
planning to proceed further developments in FD element by carrying
out simulations.

I : The result of simulation shows excellent correspondence with
the analysis result, and, therefore, simulation is effective
in the development of FD element.

II : It is possible, through simulation, to evaluate FD elements
performance differing delicately in shape.

III : The correspondence between two analysis methods proves the
validity of the simulation.

IV : The simulations have confirmed that the target shape largely
influences the performance of FD element, which has been
known only through experience.

REFERENCE

1.   T.Tatsumi "Ryutai rikigaku (Fluid mechanics)" Baifuukan.,co,ltd
octorber 1990

2.   H.Yasuda, K.Sakai, M.Okabayashi "Debelopment of small-sized
fluidic gas flowmeter" international gas research conference
November 6-9, 1989

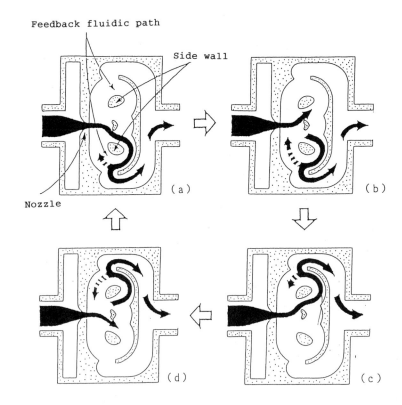

Fig. 1:  Principle of Fluidic Oscillation

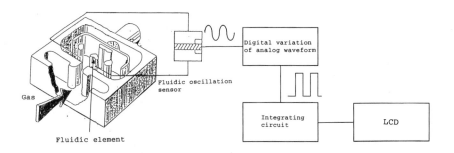

Fig. 2:  Components of Fluidic Gas Meter

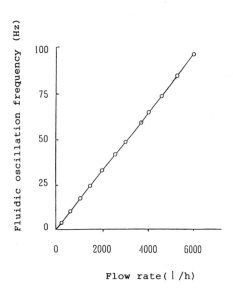

Fig. 3:   Relation between Flow Rate and Frequency

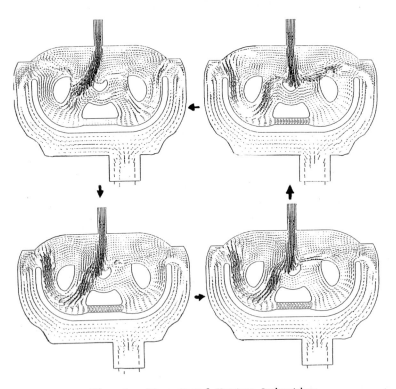

Fig. 4:   Flow Speed Vector Animation

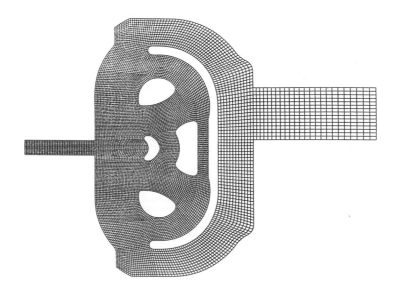

Fig. 6:  Mesh Design

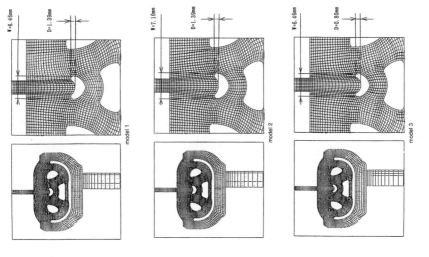

Fig. 5:  Element Shape and Size

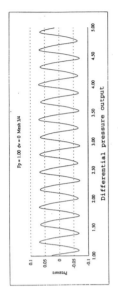

Fig. 9 : Simulation result ($\alpha$ -Flow)

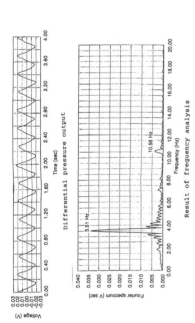

Fig. 7 : Experimental Data (Result) :

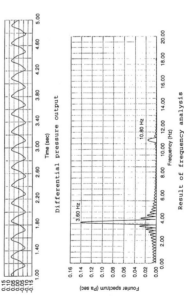

Fig. 8 : Simulation Result (Harwell-Flow 3D) :

| Analysis method | Oscillation frequency | Oscillation differential pressure |
|---|---|---|
| Harwell-Flow3D | 3.60 Hz | 0.15 Pa |
| $\alpha$ -Flow | 3.48 Hz | 0.14 Pa |
| Experimental result | 3.51 Hz | |

Table-1 Difference due to analysis method

| Mesh | Number of mesh division | Time division | Oscillation frequency | Calculated time |
|---|---|---|---|---|
| Medium | 1015 | 400 | 2.45 Hz | 0.5 hr |
| Coarse | 3650 | 600 | 3.28 Hz | 4 hr |
| Fine | 9888 | 900 | 3.58 Hz | 20 hr |
| Experimental result | | | 3.60 Hz | |

Table-2 Difference due to number of mesh divisions
and the comparison with experimental result

| Model | Features | Oscillaton frequency | Oscillation differential pressure |
|---|---|---|---|
| Model 1 | Standard | 3.30 Hz | 0.16 Pa |
| Model 2 | Large width | 3.26 Hz | 0.14 Pa |
| Model 3 | Deep indentation | 3.10 Hz | 0.17 Pa |

(Mesh is set to 3650)

Table-3 Difference due to target shape

Optical fibre gas detection

La détection de gaz par fibre optique

by T. Pichery, N. Katcharov

Gaz de France - R&D Division, Saint Denis, France

## ABSTRACT

This document describes the project of Gaz de France which aims at demonstrating the technical feasibility of a system of distributed detection of natural gas. The former has to operate in intrinsic security and therefore to be able to make remote measurement in explosive zones. The device studied in this project is a bus system of sensors supporting a finite number (between 20 and 100) of distributed points of measurement on distances of more than ten kilometres. This bus system of sensors is questioned by OTDR (Optical Time Domain Reflectometry) allowing to localise points of measure with a resolution of a few meters. Most of the elements constituting the system are standard products developed for telecommunication applications. Aimed applications are the supervision of gas pipes in confined or semi-confined space.

## RESUME

Ce document décrit le projet du Gaz de France visant à démontrer la faisabilité technique d'un système de détection distribué de gaz naturel. Celui-ci doit fonctionner en sécurité intrinsèque et être donc à même de faire de la mesure déportée dans des zones explosibles. Le dispositif étudié dans le cadre de ce projet est un "réseau bus" de capteurs supportant un nombre fini de points de mesure répartis sur des distances de plusieurs dizaines de kilomètres. Ce "réseau bus" de capteurs est interrogé par réflectométrie temporelle permettant de localiser les points de mesure avec une résolution de l'ordre du mètre. La plupart des éléments du système sont des produits standards développés pour les applications de télécommunication. Les applications visées sont la surveillance de canalisation de gaz en espace confiné ou semi-confiné.

## The gas detection by optical fibre

1.THE CONTEXT

Gaz de France has initiated by 1990 a project which aims at demonstrating the technical feasibility of a system of distributed detection of natural gas. This study was done in collaboration with the Laboratoire de Physique Chimie des Interfaces in Lyons, the Laboratoire de Traitement du Signal et Intrumentation in Saint Etienne, the Laboratoire d'Electronique et MicroOnde in Grenoble, the Institut de Recherche sur les Communication Optique et Microonde in Limoges and with the Ecole Supérieure de Physique Chimie Industrielle in Paris

The system had to operate in intrinsic security and must be therefore able to make remote measurements in explosive zones. This system had also to support a finite number of points of measure distributed on distances of more than tens kilometres. Constitutive elements of system (i.e. the optical fibre and optoelectronic components) will be to the extent of possible standard products developed for telecommunication applications.

A first study shows that commercialised point detectors do not allow to satisfy the functional specifications the Research Division of Gaz de France. On the one hand because these sensors are designed originally to function in an autonomous manner, the electronics of the signal processing is notably integrated, this complicates their utilisation in networks. On the other hand these sensors (pellistors, semiconductors) use technologies that do not allow them to function in intrinsic safety.

2.OPTICAL FIBRE SENSORS NETWORKS (RCFO).

RCFO seems therefore to be the best candidates for the distributed detection of natural gas. They draw the advantage to be both little cumbersome, light, insensitive to electromagnetic perturbations, relatively easy to put in network, and finally to offer intrinsic security and a good galvanic insulation. Furthermore techniques of interrogation by OTDR (Optical Time Delay Reflectometry) (figure 1) allow already to examine individually or collectively points of measure with spatial resolutions less than ten meters. This technology based on the analyse of the back propagated light by the optical fibre allow to know the state of the fibre anywhere on the network. Applied to RCFO, OTDR allows to question each sensor but also connections and defaults.

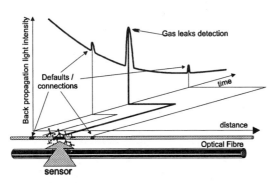

Figure 1 : Interrogation RCFO by OTDR. On this e the reflectance peak sho presence of methane.

Furthermore RCFO offer the advantage to regroup the electronics of signal processing for the totality of sensors in one point, the former being able to be situated in non explosive atmosphere.

**3.**THE RCFO MARKET.

From optical fibre caracteristics it appears clearly that the RCFO of gas sensors are destined preferentially to the supervision of gas pipes crossing confined spaces to the extent that these configurations are limited in number and in length (slip lined pipe, technical galleries). This measure can be realised continuously; the signal processing device is then situated in a control room or connected to telecommunication network through the French Minitel (device which allow to consult database by using telecommunication network). The measure can equally be made punctually with a portable acquisition device. The RCFO is then installed near the installation to be supervised.

The systematic use of this product for the supervision of buried gases transportation or distribution systems seems a priori inappropriate because of the discontinuous nature of the measure and of finite number of sensors. Indeed the buried piping supervision would necessitate a length of system, a number and a density of points of measure incompatible with RCFO possibilities. Calculations show indeed that the number of points of measure can difficulty exceed the hundred on optical fibre with a maximal length of sixty kilometres.

**4.**THE NATURAL GAS OPTICAL SENSOR.

The achievement of RCFO needs to focus on optical transducer and Gaz de France has launch since 1991 the study of reliable and sensitive sensors suitable for network use.

Sensor #1 :

The first results have been obtained with an optical fibre strongly multimodes of six hundred micrometers where only modes of higher order were excited. The optical sheath of this fibre was locally and partially replaced by a material of the heteropolysiloxan (HPS) family sensitive to methane (figure 2). The diminution of the indication of refraction of HPS after absorption of gas yield a variation of intensity of the output light. This first sensor has allowed to detect concentrations of methane of about eight per cent. Although potentially very sensitive the insertion in network of the former remained difficult and its interrogation by OTDR impossible.

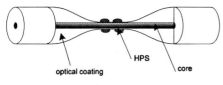

Figure 2 : Optical fibre intrinsic sensor (central view in section)

HPS

optical coating        core

Sensor #2 :

So as to palliate to these defaults the multimode optical fibre was replaced by a single mode optical fibre. This solution allowed to simplify its installation in network and to make possible its interrogation by OTDR. More an improvement of processing of signal based on a temporal differential measure has allowed to reduce the influence of the temperature and thus to lower the sensitivity down to one per cent. However the selectivity of sensor to methane is insufficient (figure 3), the reproducibility of sensor remains uncertain and its consumption in energy relatively important. Calculations based on results obtained by the demonstrator (figure 4) show that the number of sensors on the bus system cannot exceed about twenty.

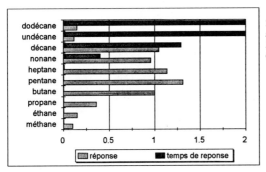

Figure 1 : Detection of saturated hydrocarbon by the laboratory prototype compared to butane.

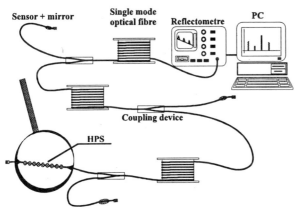

Figure 4 : GAZ DE FRANCE Experimental device understanding 5 sensors distributed on a fibre of 1500 m long.

So as to solve problems linked to luminous energy losses of the sensors GAZ DE FRANCE has initiated the study of more effective transducers. Today the two ways susceptible to give better results notably in term of number and density points of measurement on an optical fibre are Bragg Grating sensors and couplers.

Sensor #3 :

In the first case a low reflection Bragg Grating is made by photo-induction in the optical fibre core. Then as for the transducers showed on figure 2 the optical coating of this fibre is locally and partially replaced by a material sensitive to methane. Variations of refractive index of this new optical coating are going this time to act on the resonance wavelength on the one hand and on the reflectivity of the Bragg grating on the other hand. It has been demonstrated that this type of sensors can be questioned by OTDR. Their better sensitivity would allow to decrease the consumption in energy and therefore to increase the number of points of measure. Finally the utilisation of tuneable light sources wavelength will allow the wavelength multiplexing of sensors, this yields an increase of the density of sensors inserted on a same optical fibre. Tuneable light sources wavelength begin to appear on the market but remain expensive (350 kFF) and a reliability that remains again to prove.

Sensor #4 :

In the second case a coupler with low coupling rate is covered by the material sensitive to methane. Variations of refractive index of this new optical coating are going this time to act on the coupling rate. This coupler, represented on figure 5 by the drawing on the bottom, would allow to take on the main line a low quantity of light only in the presence of gas. In theory this solution presents therefore the advantage on the demonstrator represented on figure 4, to optimise the consumption in light of the transducers. Non active sensors penalise no longer the power consumption of the RCFO allowing thus to insert a large number of points of measure on the optical fibre.

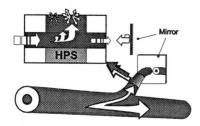

Figure 5 : The sensor with variable and permanent coupling ratio.
The drawing on top shows the sensor of experimental device represented on the figure 4 contained couplers with permanent coupling ratio. The light intensity in the upper branch reflected against the mirror is linked to the refractive index of HPS (i.e to methane content).

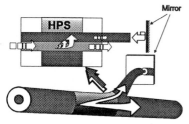

The bottom one presents the new transducer based on a coupler with variable coupling ratio. The light intensity in the upper optical fibre core reflected against the mirror is linked to the refractive index of HPS (i.e to methane content).

5.CONCLUSION

GAZ DE FRANCE in collaboration with several laboratory has demonstrated the technical feasibility of a system of distributed detection of natural gas capable to make measures in explosive atmosphere. Satisfactory solutions allow notably to reach a sensitivity of approximately a per cent in methane with sensor #2 (i.e. twenty per cent of the inferior limit of explosivity). More innovative processes based on systems of Bragg grating and variable couplers will make possible the insertion of approximately fifty points of measure. GAZ DE FRANCE is now studying the association of these two techniques in different configurations witch would allow to go beyond this last limitation. Nevertheless sensitivity to temperature and selectivity remain problems that have not yet been solved in a satisfactory way but will have to be imperatively solved before starting the final phase which aims at realising an industrial demonstrator in collaboration with industrial partners.

The application of DIAL remote sensing technology to safety and environmental monitoring

La technologie DIAL de détection à distance appliquée aux contrôles de sécurité et de protection de

l'environnement

H.L. Walmsley
Shell Research Ltd., UK


D.R. Brown and S. Bullman
British Gas plc, UK

Abstract

An infra-red Differential Absorption LIDAR (DIAL) system has been used to measure methane emission plumes to the atmosphere. The calibration of the system is discussed and site measurements are presented. Comparisons are made with emission rate estimates from other remote sensing techniques and with point sensor measurements. With careful tuning and calibration, the accuracy of DIAL emission rate measurements is comparable to, or better than, that of both receptor-based point-sensing methods and other remote sensing techniques. All these techniques are significantly more accurate than source-based point-sensor methods. A key advantage of DIAL is that measurements can be made in two or three dimensions over large areas and on sources that are inaccessible to the other techniques. Because of this improved coverage, DIAL is less likely than other techniques to underestimate emission rates by missing potential emission sources.

Resume

Description de l'utilisation du systéme DIAL à infrarouge pour mesurer les panaches d'émissions de gaz méthane dans l'atmosphère. Discussion sur l'étalonnage du système et présentation de prises de mesures sur le terrain. Des comparaisons sont effectuées avec des estimations de taux d'émission au moyen d'autres techniques de détection à distance et avec des mesures par détecteurs ponctuels. Moyennant un ajustement et un calibrage soigneux, on constate que la précision des mesures des taux d'émissions avec DIAL est comparable ou meilleure que celle obtenue par les méthodes de détection ponctuelles par récepteurs et que celle obtenue par d'autres techniques de détection à distance. Toutes ces techniques sont sensiblement plus précises que les méthodes basées sur la détection ponctuelle par capteurs à la source. Un avantage-clé de DIAL réside dans le fait que les mesures peuvent être effectuées en deux ou trois dimensions dans de vastes zones et que l'on peut mesurer des sources d'émissions qui sont inaccessibles par d'autres techniques. Grâce à cette meilleure couverture, le système DIAL sera moins sujet que d'autres à sous-estimer les taux d'émission en ne prenant pas en compte certaines sources potentielles d'émission.

## INTRODUCTION

DIAL (Differential Absorption Lidar)[*] is one of the most powerful tools yet devised for mapping extended atmospheric emissions plumes. A DIAL system has recently been acquired jointly by Shell Research Ltd, British Gas plc and Siemens Environmental Systems Ltd. Shell and British Gas have many common aims for DIAL applications and therefore, to maximise the benefits to each company from this powerful but expensive technology, they are combining some of their DIAL access time in a joint programme addressing topics of common interest.

This paper describes:

(a)     Calibration work done on behalf of the joint venture partners by the United Kingdom National Physical Laboratory (NPL) as part of the system construction contract. This work was carried out using the NPL National Calibration Facility.

(b)     Work carried out as part of the Shell/British Gas joint programme to compare DIAL with other techniques under field conditions.

---

[*] DIAL - Differential Absorption Lidar, LIDAR - Light Detection And Ranging

(c)      Initial field measurements that clearly demonstrate the benefit of DIAL in permitting the measurement of emissions from inaccessible sources.

## OTHER EMISSION MEASUREMENT TECHNIQUES

Before considering DIAL, we briefly outline the capabilities of other techniques for comparison.

We begin with fixed beam remote-sensing methods of which the principle examples, for methane, are Fourier Transform Infra-red Radiometry (FTIR) and Hawk. Both these methods measure the path integral of the target gas concentration along one or more fixed lines of sight. The path integral concentration is normally reported directly (often as a mean concentration along the sight line) but, after the input of wind velocity data and the application of a dispersion model, it is possible to derive an emission rate. Typical detection limits are 10 to 100 ppm m and, in favourable conditions (i.e. absence of interfering species, simple air flow patterns and emissions that come close to the ground at the beam location), our current research indicates that it is possible to measure emission rates to an accuracy of 50% or better.

Emission rates may also be measured by point sensors, usually flame ionisation devices (FIDs). This can be done in two ways which we will call source-based monitoring and receptor-based monitoring respectively.

Source-based monitoring uses point sensors to determine gas concentrations around potential leak sources such as valves and flanges and applies published factors or correlations to convert the results for each component into an emission rate.[1] This approach is subject to statistical uncertainties which are at least a factor of three and may often be much larger. The method can also systematically underestimate emissions if a potential source is omitted from the measurements programme because, for example, it was inaccessible or simply not identified as a potential leak point.

Receptor-based monitoring involves moving a mobile point sensor around an area which is exposed to the emitted gas and measuring the concentration at or near ground level as a function of position. If the measurements are far enough from the source, it is possible to use dispersion models such as UK ADMS[2] to assess the emission rate from the measured concentrations. On-going research indicates that this method can give an accuracy of 15% to 40%, but the conditions necessary for reliable application of the dispersion model cannot be met around complex or congested plant structures and then the uncertainties may rise to a factor of two or more. It can be difficult to assess when the requirements for model validity are met and to evaluate emissions from multiple sources. At some sites, receptor-based monitoring is not possible at all because the region where useful measurements can be made is inaccessible to the test equipment.

## DIAL LIDAR

LIDAR (Light Detection and Ranging) works by sending out a pulsed light beam from a laser and detecting the signals scattered or reflected back to the source. When the beam is reflected from solid targets, it can be used for range finding, when it is scattered from atmospheric aerosols or particulates, it can indicate particulate concentration.

The variant known as DIAL[3] (Differential Absorption Lidar) measures gas concentrations using the atmospheric scattering LIDAR signals at two slightly different wavelengths. The wavelengths are selected so that one, the measurement wavelength, is absorbed by the target gas and the other, the reference wavelength, is not. The gas concentration is derived from the ratio of the signals at the two wavelengths. Because light is scattered from all points along the beam path, DIAL measurements give the gas concentration as a function of distance. DIAL needs no reflector so the line of sight can be varied at will and hence, by scanning, 2-D or 3-D maps of gas concentrations within plumes can be generated.

DIAL is a complex and expensive technique requiring powerful lasers and fast, sensitive detectors but it is extremely effective and likely to play a significant role in atmospheric emission measurements. Consequently, Shell Research Limited, British Gas plc and Siemens Environmental Systems Ltd commissioned the construction of the DIAL LIDAR system shown in Plate 1 and arranged to share its use. The system was constructed by Siemens using technology developed by NPL. The unit is completely self-contained, with its own diesel generator and air conditioned laboratory. As it is mounted in a standard 40 foot ISO shipping container, it may be transported by road, rail or sea to the measurement site.

The system operates in the infra-red (wavelengths from 2 to 4.5 μm) and can measure the concentration of any gas or vapour that absorbs radiation in this waveband. Measurable species include the alkanes, ethylene, methyl chloride and, of particular importance to the present audience, methane. The detection limits for methane and the alkanes can be at sub ppm levels.

DIAL measurements can be made from a minimum range of 50 m out to a maximum of 600 m to 1.5 km depending on atmospheric conditions and the species concerned. The extended range and free choice of beam direction greatly reduce the accessibility problems that can be encountered with other techniques (particularly point sensors). The benefits of this freedom will be demonstrated later.

Measured concentrations are stored immediately on a computer. The data for each line of sight are displayed in real time as they are acquired and sets of data from multiple lines can be displayed in a 3-D representation within a few minutes of data capture using the IBM Data Explorer data visualisation package. This software also allows the superposition of the measured data onto site plans or simplified 3-D site models and the derivation of emission rates from the measured concentration data using imported wind data.

## DIAL CALIBRATION

We have taken great care to verify that our DIAL system is correctly set up and calibrated. The basic approach has been to generate target gas samples outdoors and measure the gas content with both DIAL and one or more other measurement techniques such as fixed-beam open-path methods or point sensors which are used to transfer calibrations from gravimetric standard laboratory gas samples. We have carried out or commissioned three categories of DIAL calibration test which differ in the way the target gas is supplied. These are as follows:

(a)     External cell tests in which the DIAL beam is directed through large cells (10 m long by 1 m diameter) containing predetermined quantities of gas (see Figure 1). These tests provide better control of the gas sample than other calibration techniques and therefore give the most accurate calibration data but they are expensive and time consuming.

(b)     Controlled release tests in which a target gas is released freely into the atmosphere at a known rate. These tests offer less control over the gas concentration than the cell tests, but they are cheaper and can therefore be done more frequently. They can also be used to check the accuracy of emission rate (flux) measurements.

(c)     Cross-calibrations in which the target gas from an uncontrolled source or the normal atmospheric background is measured both with the DIAL and another reference instrument. This approach is particularly useful for methane because of its presence as an atmospheric background.

The DIAL system has undergone external cell calibrations for both propane and methane at the NPL National Calibration Facility. Both FID instruments and Hawk open-path monitors were used as transfer standards. These tests confirmed the accuracy of the DIAL concentration calibration to within 10%.

To date we have carried out a large number of controlled releases in three separate trials. Figure 2 shows a Data Explorer image of the methane concentrations measured by DIAL during one such test. Each DIAL measurement point is marked by a symbol ("glyph") whose grey level indicates the measured local concentration (the results are in colour but have been reduced to grey scale for reproduction here). The release point is marked by the vertical cylinder. The ratio of measured to known release rate for the first 12 such releases is shown in Figure 3. The mean ratio of 0.75± 0.1 (95% confidence levels) indicates that there has been a slight systematic underestimate of the emission rate. The standard deviation of the ratio about the mean is ± 0.18.

The systematic underestimate is now known to be partly associated with laser tuning difficulties which gave rise to frequency fluctuations (mode hopping) and increased line width. These led in turn to a variable reduction in the absorption coefficient and a corresponding underestimate of the gas concentration. Now it has been recognised, this condition can be eliminated or allowed for.

A further contribution to the systematic underestimate of flux arises from the fact that the measurements were made on small gas plumes whose concentrations are always subject to strong fluctuations. With a fluctuating plume, the signal averaging procedure inevitably introduces a systematic underestimate.[3] The magnitude of this contribution is still being investigated but appears likely to be at least 10%.

The spatially extensive plumes associated with fugitive emissions from industrial plant are normally subject to much lower levels of fluctuation than the small plumes we have investigated. Therefore, in a real measurement situation, the errors introduced by plume fluctuation will be smaller than those in our calibration trials. We believe that our system will now provide a flux measurement accuracy of better than 25% in a steady plume and with accurate tuning.

We have compared the methane backgrounds measured by DIAL with FTIR, HAWK and canister-sampled FID data. Before the importance of careful tuning was realised, the DIAL measurements were 20% lower than corresponding FTIR data. With careful tuning, DIAL measurements were within 5% of both HAWK and canister-sampled FID data.

## DIAL FIELD MEASUREMENTS

### Comparison with Source-Based Monitoring By Point Sensors

The power of the DIAL technique compared to source-based monitoring by point sensors is revealed by some work that was done to measure ethylene emissions rates from a polyethylene plant using both DIAL data and FID point sensor data analysed according to US Environmental Protection Agency protocols. (The DIAL measurements for this comparison were carried out by NPL using a similar system to the one referred to above). Although the measurements relate to a chemical plant rather than to gas handling, the lessons are general and relevant to the choice of emission measurement techniques for a gas plant.

A key feature of the polyethylene plant was the existence of numerous process vents which could not be accessed by the FID point sensors. These vents accounted for 90% of the total emissions from the site. Thus, at this site, source-based point sensors were inherently incapable of giving the required measurement. These circumstances are not unique and it is quite common for sources that are difficult to estimate accurately from industry-wide factors or point sensor measurements to contribute a significant proportion of the emissions from a site. In this case it can beneficial to use techniques, such as DIAL or other remote-sensing methods, that can respond to all emissions.

Even for the 10% of emissions that could be measured by the source-based point-sensor approach, the uncertainties in the point-sensor emission rate estimates were about a factor of five either side of the best estimate. This level of error is inherent in the statistics of the method and could not have been improved. The DIAL measurements, on the other hand, were subject to errors of only about 15%.

**Comparison with Source- and Receptor-Based Monitoring by Point Sensors: Compressor Turbine Vent Measurements**

Measurements at a gas terminal have demonstrated the value of DIAL remote sensing compared to the use of point sensors in both source-based and receptor-based monitoring modes.    At the terminal there were high level process vents and turbine exhausts that were completely inaccessible to point sensors for source-based monitoring. The emissions from these components were easily measured by DIAL.

As an example, Figure 4 shows an overlay of the methane concentrations measured in the exhaust plume of a turbine-driven gas compressor and a simplified, but dimensionally accurate, perspective view of the site. Plate 2 is a photograph of the plant which indicates the degree of simplification in the graphical representation. Several compressor housings (the buildings that consist of two rectangular blocks) can be seen in both Figure 4 and Plate 2. The compressor that produced the measured plume was in the third housing from the right on the Figure. The other compressors were inactive. The exhaust emerged from the top of the housing which was 20 m above the ground and 140 m from the DIAL system. The methane flux calculated from the concentrations in Figure 4 (after subtraction of the measured background) using wind velocities measured by anemometers on a nearby 15 m mast, was 6.5 kg h$^{-1}$.

At this site, the prevailing winds and proximity of adjacent sites were such that, from the outset, it was doubtful whether it would be possible to measure methane emission rates using point sensors in receptor-based monitoring mode. The DIAL measurements confirmed these initial doubts by showing that many emission sources gave gas plumes that were elevated above ground level in the area accessible to the mobile point sensors. (It is a fundamental requirement of the point-sensor receptor-based monitoring analysis that the plumes should not be elevated.)   By using the DIAL data to indicate the plume location, it would be possible to amend the point-sensor analysis to take into account the elevated plumes, but in the absence of the DIAL data there would have been no way of knowing what the correction should be.

**Vent Stack Plume**

As an example of measurements on a highly inaccessible source, we used DIAL to measure the emissions from an 80 m high methane vent at a gas terminal. The plume from this stack did not come to ground anywhere accessible to point sensor measurement. The concentration profiles measured by DIAL approximately 50 m from the vent outlet are shown in Figure 5. The corresponding flux estimate is 180 kg h$^{-1}$.

**DISCUSSION**

Apart from DIAL, the other remote sensing techniques for estimating emission rates rely on path-integral concentrations, measured along a single line, or at most a small number of lines. These methods all then utilise some form of dispersion modelling to estimate the plume height as part of the emission rate calculation. Because DIAL measures the gas concentration over the entire cross-section of a plume, the plume height is measured rather than estimated. Because no dispersion model is used, differences between actual conditions and model assumptions cannot influence the results. DIAL emission rate measurements are therefore considerably more robust than those obtained with other remote sensing techniques.

If reliable flux measurements are to be made by receptor-based point sensors, it is necessary for the gas plumes from each relevant source to have reached the ground before arriving at the monitoring location. This cannot always be ensured in congested areas or where there is limited access downwind of a plant. If plumes do not reach the ground, accurate emission rate measurements are not possible. The gas could be missed completely and even where it is detected, attempts to estimate the flux using standard models will underestimate emissions. DIAL is particularly well suited to measurements on elevated plumes.

Because DIAL measurements give detailed information on concentration profiles, they are potentially capable of supplying measured values for the plume parameters in dispersion models. These models may then be used to derive emission rates from measurements made with other techniques, such as receptor-based sensing or fixed-beam, open-path measurements. At present, model parameters are usually assigned standard values. DIAL offers the possibility of measuring local parameters relevant to given weather conditions at the actual site concerned, thus providing more accurate site-specific flux determination models. This makes effective use of DIAL time because the fixed beam or point sensors can be left to monitor continuously whilst the relatively complex and expensive DIAL system is free to make measurements at new sites.

## CONCLUSIONS

1.    The DIAL remote sensing system has been satisfactorily commissioned and used to determine emission rates from controlled releases and real gas handling plant.

2.    Remote sensing techniques in general are more likely than point-sensor methods to pick up all emissions from a site. In particular, point-sensor methods may miss elevated plumes. Of the remote sensing methods, DIAL is the most likely to pick up all emissions because it is not restricted as to where the beam can be directed. With fixed path methods, it can be difficult to mount the necessary light sources or reflectors high enough to include the most elevated plumes.

3.    DIAL measurements must be carefully calibrated. This can be done by cross-calibration exercises involving point or fixed-beam measurements with external gas cells, controlled gas releases or background gas.

4.    The emission rate measurement errors associated with DIAL in small-scale controlled releases have been in the range 0 to -50%. A variable systematic error of around -15% has been ascribed to tuning problems that have now been eliminated. A further systematic error has been identified with an interaction between plume fluctuations and the signal averaging process. We therefore believe that with a steady plume and careful tuning, overall errors will be less than 25%. This is comparable to or smaller than the errors associated both with other remote sensing techniques and with receptor-based point sensor measurements. It is significantly better than the errors associated with source-based point sensing measurements, which have uncertainties of a least a factor of three.

5.    DIAL flux measurement estimates are significantly more robust than those obtained from fixed beam or point sensors because they do not require dispersion modelling and therefore eliminate the assumptions embedded in the models. Also, DIAL is much more versatile as it can deal with fluxes from inaccessible plumes in relatively congested areas.

## REFERENCES

1.    Radian Corporation, "Protocol for equipment leak emission estimates" Research Triangle Park NC 1993

2.    D.J. Carruthers et al, "UK ADMS: A new approach to dispersion modelling in the earth's atmospheric boundary layer" J. Wind Engng and Industrial Aerodynamics, **52**, 139-153, (1994).

3.    R.M. Measures, "Fundamentals of laser remote sensing", Ch. 1 of "Laser remote chemical analysis", R.M. Measures (Ed) Wiley Interscience (1988).

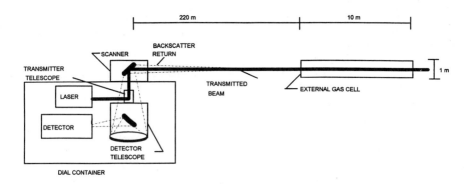

FIG. 1 - Schematic of external cell tests

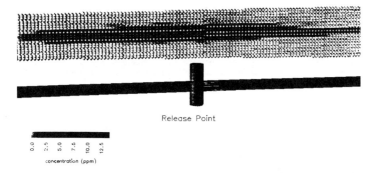

FIG. 2 - The methane plume registered in a small-scale controlled release experiment (background = 1.8 ppm, emission rate = 1.9 g/s)

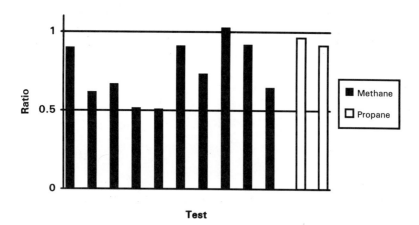

FIG. 3 - Ratio of measured to known emission rate in controlled release experiments

Mean background = 1.67 ppm
Emission rate = 0.0018 kg/s

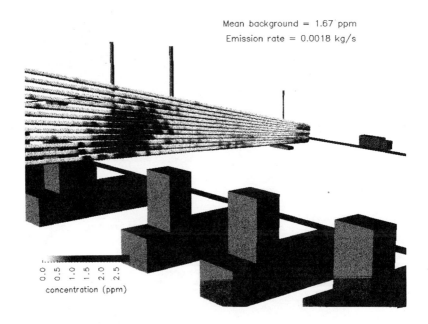

concentration (ppm)

FIG. 4 - Methane plume from one of the gas compressors in Plate 2

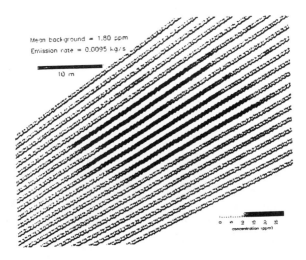

FIG. 5 - Methane plume from an 80 m high vent

PLATE 1  The DIAL system

PLATE 2 - The compressor housings represented schematically in Figure 3

**Using Acoustic Methods**
**To Pinpoint Gas Leaks**

**Localisation de fuites de gaz**
**par des méthodes acoustiques**

by V. Delarue, M. Chamant*

Gaz de France - R&D Division, Saint Denis, France
(*) METRAVIB RDS, Lyons, France

ABSTRACT

Inserting polyethylene pipes into old cast iron and steel pipes is a well-known rehabilitation technique used in France for more than 10 years.

In order to detect any leak, which should occur in a slip-lined network, the standard techniques, could prove to be cumbersome. It was therefore worthwhile for Gaz de France to have a method that filled this need and which could possibly be used on systems placed in the ground as a complement to standard pinpointing techniques.

After assessing the limitations of the acoustic methods used for a while by water companies, we present in this paper a new method addressing most of the problems encountered. In particular, it is now possible to pinpoint a leak in the presence of gas consumption on a pressure reducing valve. These results can be profitably used for the localisation of leaks of fluids other than natural gas.

RESUME

La rénovation des anciennes canalisations en fonte et en acier par tubage de tubes en polyéthylène est une technique bien connue et est utilisée en France depuis plus de dix ans.

Les techniques classiques de détection, si une fuite survenait, pourraient se révéler lourdes à mettre en oeuvre. Il était donc intéressant pour Gaz de France de disposer d'une méthode répondant d'abord à ce besoin, et étant éventuellement utilisable sur les réseaux posés en terre en complément des méthodes de localisation traditionnelles

Après avoir évalué les limites des méthodes acoustiques utilisées couramment par les compagnies des eaux, on présente une nouvelle méthode répondant à la plupart des problèmes rencontrés. En particulier, il est maintenant possible de localiser une fuite en présence d'une consommation à un détendeur. Les résultats obtenus sont de plus valorisables pour la localisation de fuites d'autres fluides que le gaz naturel.

1-PREAMBLE.

Inserting polyethylene pipes into old cast iron and steel pipes is a well-known rehabilitation technique used in France for more than 10 years. Up to now, this technique has made possible to renew more than 5000km of networks, to which are added each year some 500 additional kilometres.

In order to detect any leak, which should occur in a slip-lined network, the standard techniques, could prove to be cumbersome. It was therefore worthwhile for Gaz de France to have a method that filled this need and which could possibly be used on systems placed in the ground as a complement to standard pinpointing techniques.

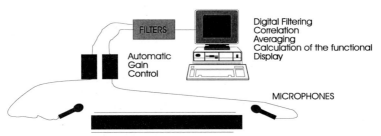

**Figure 1. Diagram of principle**

The acoustic waves produced by a leak are propagated at a known speed. They are therefore well adapted to the development of a method which pinpoints the leak from the extremities of the leaky sections. The techniques of acoustic correlation developed for a french water distribution company in the middle of the 70s by METRAVIB have thus been evaluated.

2-LIMIT OF EXISTING METHODS.

With these acoustic correlation methods, good results are obtained whenever the microphones are placed in the ring space between the old and new plumbing, but it is necessary to make sure that nothing obstructs this space, which could disturb the trajectory of the acoustic wave. Since it is difficult on site to be certain about the integrity of the ring space and since it is not always easy to access (necessity to dig excavations, or to install permanent equipment with vents), it is desirable to have a method which can eliminate this uncertainty.

The same methods which gave good results in the previous case have therefore been tested by installing microphones on the customer connections and listening to the gas pipes. The results obtained from a simulated leak facility were less good than previous results but remained usable. Test campaigns on operations on urban gas networks have nonetheless shown that these methods were very sensitive to parasite noises, especially to the noise produced at a precise location by user pressure relief valves situated between the two microphones. To overcome these problems it would also be possible to interrupt the feeding of the disturbing connections, but when these connections feed into collective buildings, the inconvenience to customers is deemed to be too much.

These tests have also shown that the information picked up by the microphones contained the leak signal even in the presence of loud parasite noise, but that the processing of the signal undertaken by the correlation was not able to extract it. Indeed, the correlation is an operation which is based only on the difference of phase between the two signals; it cannot therefore distinguish between two sources of noise which emit on the same frequency range if one is too dominant in relation to the other.

3-NEW DEVELOPMENTS.

A collaboration between Gaz de France and METRAVIB RDS has been created in an effort to overcome these difficulties. In a first phase, theoretical studies have been carried out to come up with a method especially designed to solve this problem by using the characteristics of the acoustic waves produced by a gas leak more thoroughly. Of course, in the case of the microphones being in the ring space, the improvement brought by these developments are often superfluous.

The results obtained with this method allow the location of up to two noise sources transmitting into a pipe between two microphones. In particular, it is possible to pinpoint a leak in the presence of gas consumption on a pressure reducing valve. More generally, leak detection with this method is less sensitive to ambient noise.

The signal analysis is carried out by computerised mathematical processing, which allows the localisation of the revealed leak(s). The processing is made up of two phases. The first phase consists of recording the signals generated by the two sensors through an analog to digital converter, the sensors are installed on both sides of the zone where the leak(s) can be found; The useful variables (autocorrelation and intercorrelation) are then computed. The correlation is a simple mathematical function whose formula is:

$$\Gamma_{xy}(k) = \frac{1}{2N+1} \sum_{n=-N}^{N} x(n) \cdot y(n+k)$$

where, in the case of the acoustic leak location, x and y are the digitised signals picked up by the two microphones and 2N+1 the number of samples. The maximum of $\Gamma$ gives the leak position.

In a second phase, detailed below, these variables are used by software which calculates a functional whose minimum is characteristic of the leaks' position. Exploitation of those results can be made out of the indications provided by the software or by analysing the results displayed in the form of a picture.

The method that has been developed consists of minimising an estimator ($f_\tau$) of the intercorrelation function between signal $S_1$ and $S_2$ generated by zero, one or two noise sources. In other words, it means, to calculate a linear combination of the autocorrelation and intercorrelation functions of the signals picked up by the two sensors $s_1$ and $s_2$ (intercorrelation matrix). This method proves to be particularly interesting due to its improved performances as compared to a simple calculation of the intercorrelation function (between the two signals $s_1$ and $s_2$). The minimum of $f_\tau$ gives the leak(s) position.

3.1-Theoretical developments

Supposing that there are at most two sources of noise $S_1$ and $S_2$, it follows:

$$s_1(t) = S_1(t-\tau_{11}) + S_2(t-\tau_{21})$$
$$s_2(t) = S_1(t-\tau_{12}) + S_2(t-\tau_{22})$$

[1]

where $\tau_{ij}$ is the delay of the signal emitted by the source $S_i$ to reach the sensor j.

Taking into account that the two sound sources are independent, the intercorrelation function between $S_1$ and $S_2$ is ideally nil. Therefore to find the leak(s) we must, in function of the position of the sources $x_1$ and $x_2$, which are simply linked to the delays $\tau_{ij}$, minimise an estimator of this correlation function. By transposing it to the Fourier domain, the equation system [1] gives:

$$\hat{s}_1(\omega) = e^{-j\omega\tau_{11}}.\hat{S}_1(\omega) + e^{-j\omega\tau_{21}}.\hat{S}_2(\omega)$$
$$\hat{s}_2(\omega) = e^{-j\omega\tau_{12}}.\hat{S}_1(\omega) + e^{-j\omega\tau_{22}}.\hat{S}_2(\omega)$$

[2]

where $\omega$ is the pulsation and $\hat{s}(\omega)$ is the Fourier transform of $s(t)$.

From the equation system [2], we can deduce:

$$\hat{S}_1(\omega) = \frac{e^{-j\omega\tau_{22}}.\hat{s}_1(\omega) - e^{-j\omega\tau_{21}}.\hat{s}_2(\omega)}{e^{-j\omega(\tau_{11}+\tau_{22})} - e^{-j\omega(\tau_{12}+\tau_{21})}}$$

$$\hat{S}_2(\omega) = \frac{e^{-j\omega\tau_{11}}.\hat{s}_2(\omega) - e^{-j\omega\tau_{12}}.\hat{s}_1(\omega)}{e^{-j\omega(\tau_{11}+\tau_{22})} - e^{-j\omega(\tau_{12}+\tau_{21})}}$$

We write the correlation function of $\hat{S}_1(\omega)$ and $\hat{S}_2(\omega)$ and we derive the functional to minimise where $\Gamma$ is the correlation function. Once the formula is simplified, we get:

$$f_\tau(x_1,x_2) = \Gamma_{s_1s_1}(\tau+\frac{x_2-x_1}{C})+\Gamma_{s_2s_2}(\tau+\frac{x_1-x_2}{C})-\Gamma_{s_1s_2}(\tau+\frac{x_2+x_1-D}{C})-\Gamma_{s_2s_1}(\tau+\frac{D-x_1-x_2}{C})$$

where C is the speed of sound in the considered pipeline, $x_1$ (respectively $x_2$) is the distance covered by the sound during the time $\tau_{11}$ (respectively $\tau_{21}$) and D the total length between the two sensors.

3.2-Results on simulated data

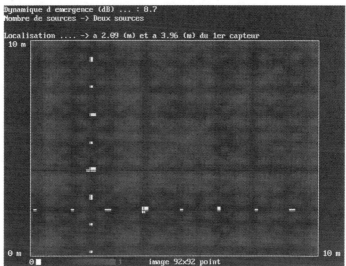

FIGURE 2. Results of a pinpointing for a leak at 2m
and an other at 4m

The method was tested by computer simulation. The leaks were simulated by noises with different distribution laws, and up to three noise sources. The effect of the bandwidth of the leak signal was also estimated.

In all of these cases the results were better than what was obtained with the simple correlation. The method was especially good at coping with "leaks" which were very narrow-band and for which the correlation is badly suited.

4-FIELD TRIAL.

This new method has been tested on data that had been previously recorded during some of the test campaigns made on a small network of Gaz de France Research Department. For the data that were processed, the results were satisfying even in some cases where the correlation had not been able to localise the leak.

To confirm the performances of this method, tests have been carried out on different types of networks in larger Gaz de France facilities. These systems have been built in the same manner as the Gaz de France PE networks and were filled by a pressure of 4bar relative of air. Different leaks, holes of approximately a millimetre in diameter, have been made and the method was tested without knowing where they were. All leaks have been located within one meter.

The method has also been tested on a low-pressure, leaky pipeline on which agents are taught how to use the standard methods of leak pinpointing. The largest of the two leaks has been localised. This leak corresponds, in term of debit, to a breakage of cast iron.

5-CONCLUSIONS.

The finalised project to develop a leakage localisation method for inserted pipes has made it possible to significantly improve the method of acoustic localisation. Its field of application has been widened to pinpointing leaks without making probe holes on pipes placed in the ground, the only condition being that there must be access to the gas (for example, service connection on both sides of the leak). The results obtained can be profitably used for the localisation of leaks of fluids other than natural gas. The water companies who are major users of correlators for monitoring their pipelines, could be interested in these results.

Nevertheless, the method such as it has been developed currently necessitates a minimum technical knowledge. It is currently used by the Research Department of Gaz de France whose teams can be called by the operationals to find every kind of tricky leak. Complementary developments, essentially to automate the choice of parameters, would be necessary to make that method usable by operational people.

REFERENCES.


1.    "Techniques et méthodes de recherche et de détection des fuites dans les réseaux d'adduction d'eau", les cahiers techniques de la fondation de l'eau, #2, 1986

2.    A.Grimaud, O.Pascal, "Automatic leak detection system on large diameter pipes", American Water Works Association 1990 Annual Conference Proceedings, Cincinnati, 17-21 juin 1990, part 2, pp. 1981-1986

3.    H.V.Fuchs, R.Riehle, "Ten Years of Experience with Leak Detection by Acoustic Signal Analysis", Applied Acoustics, #33, 1991, pp. 1-19

4.    F.Cagnon, "Localisation des fuites de gaz par une méthode acoustique", Gaz d'aujourd'hui, #5, pp. 1-4, 1991

5.    Kajiro WATANABE, Hiroshi KOYAMA, "Location and Estimation of a Pipeline Leak", Electrical Engineering in Japan, Vol. 110, #7, 1990.

6.    K.Watanabe, H.Koyama, H.Tanoguchi, T.Ohma, D.M.Himmelblau, "Location of Pinholes in a Pipeline", Computers Chemical Engineering, Vol. 17, #1, pp.61-70, 1993.

7.    J.Millet, "Localisation des fuites de gaz dans les réseaux tubés moyenne pression -nouvelles approches-, phase 1 : développement théorique de deux méthodes de localisation", METRAVIB R.D.S.

8.    J.Millet, "Localisation des fuites de gaz dans les réseaux tubés moyenne pression , phase 2 : analyse des signaux expérimentaux -méthode utilisant deux capteurs-", METRAVIB R.D.S.

9.    V.Delarue, G.Liffraud, "Essais de localisation acoustique de fuites au Centre de Formation de Gennevilliers", GDF Report M.CERSTA #95.438

FIELD TRIAL RESULTS OF A DIGITAL SONIC LEAK PINPOINTER

LE PROCES-VERBAL D'ESSAI SUR LE TERRAIN DU DUARD SONIQUE
DIGITAL POUR LA DETECTION DES FUITES

J. E. Huebler and C. J. Ziolkowski
Institute of Gas Technology, USA

## ABSTRACT

A method of locating a leak in the first 0.9 by 1.2-meter excavation is a very important need for day-to-day operations of the gas distribution industry. Pinpointing difficulties arise when gas migrates away from the leak, when the soil is saturated with gas or water over a large area, or when there are multiple leaks in the area. Detecting the sound created by gas escaping from the pipe provides an alternative method of leak pinpointing, one that does not depend on the detection of the gas itself. The Digital Sonic Leak Pinpointer pinpoints leaks from gas distribution operating pressures of 1 bar (14.7 psig) and higher by using state-of-the-art sensors and the digital signal processing technique of adaptive filtering to minimize the effects of background noise. This paper describes this new instrument and its initial field trial results.

## RÉSUMÉ

La méthode qui permet de détecter exactement une fuite dans l'excavation primaire de 0m,9 sur 1m,2 s'avère essentielle lors des travaux quotidiens exécutés par l'industrie de distribution du gaz. La détection exacte devient difficile lorsque le gaz migre au-delà de la fuite-même, lorsque le sol est saturé par le gaz ou l'eau sur une grande étendue, ou lorsque plusieurs fuites se produisent à cet endroit. Détecter le son produit par le gaz qui s'échappe de la canalisation offre une méthode alternative de localisation des fuites, méthode qui, de plus, n'exige pas la détection du gaz en lui-même. Le Duard Sonique Digital pour la détection des Fuites localise ces fuites à des pressions opératoires de distribution du gaz de 1 bar (14,7 psig) ou plus, à l'aide de détecteurs les plus récents et en appliquant la technique de signalisation digitale par filtrage adaptif afin de réduire à un minimum les bruits de fond. Le présent document décrit cet instrument tout nouveau et fournit le procés-verbal des premiers essais exécutés sur le terrain.

## INTRODUCTION

This paper describes the Digital Sonic Leak Pinpointer and the results of the first field trials. This new instrument is capable of accurately detecting and pinpointing gas leaks emanating from the buried pipes of natural gas distribution systems with operating pressures of 1 bar (14.7 psig) and higher. The first field trials were performed in the spring and summer of 1995.

## IMPROVEMENT IN LEAK PINPOINTING IS NEEDED

Improved leak pinpointing is a very important need to reduce the cost of day-to-day operations of the gas distribution industry. Combustible gas indicators and hydrogen flame ionization units are commonly used to detect leaks from natural gas piping. They are also used to pinpoint the location at which to dig. Pinpointing difficulties arise when the gas has migrated away from the leak (for example, along the pipe, under pavement or frozen ground, or in a sewer); when the soil is saturated with gas over a large area; when a heavy rain has saturated the soil with water, displacing the air and gas; or when there are multiple leaks in the area. Incorrect leak pinpointing results in enlarged or extended holes, the excavation of one or more dry holes (no leak present) and, in extreme cases, the exposing of substantial pipe lengths before the leak is found. Although delays in pinpointing a leak can result in a safety hazard, the issue is one of economics rather than safety because the leak repair crews are very persistent in finding and repairing leaks. In such cases, an additional method of leak pinpointing is required, one that does not depend on the detection of the gas itself.

An instrument that effectively pinpoints leaks could save a typical U. S. gas distribution utility $50,000 per leak repair crew each year. Approximately 900,000 gas leaks are repaired in the U. S. every year. These leaks are normally repaired by digging a 0.9 by 1.2-meter (3 by 4-foot) hole over the suspected leak location. A recent study (1) determined that first excavations at leak sites result in a dry hole 10% to 20% of the time and that an average of 1.2 holes are made to clear a leak. Excavation costs per hole range from $500 to over $1500, depending on local labor costs and the amount of pavement that must be repaired. Assuming an average of $1000 per dry hole and 10% extra excavations, an efficient pinpointer would save the U. S. gas distribution industry over $90 million annually. Viewed another way, if a crew pinpointed and repaired 10 leaks per week, making one dry hole each week, there is a potential annual savings of $50,000 per leak repair crew. Therefore, the payback period can be very short for an instrument that could substantially reduce the number of extra excavations.

## LEAKS CAN BE PINPOINTED ACOUSTICALLY

The sound created by gas escaping from a leak in buried natural gas piping can be used to detect and pinpoint the leak. An acoustic approach has long been considered promising because, in the repair process, natural gas leaks are often heard before all of the soil is removed from around the leak. In addition, acoustic detection of water leaks has been a standard tool for decades. In water leak location, the operator listens to the acoustic signals to interpret the location of the leaks. In contrast, gas utilities desire the elimination of operator "art" in leak pinpointing.

Acoustic detection and pinpointing of gas leaks is much more difficult because gas leaks generate substantially less sound than water leaks. Because of the relatively weak acoustic signals, sonic leak pinpointing of gas leaks is also more susceptible to background noises, such as those caused by passing automobiles and trucks, buried electrical cables, etc. Practical acoustic detection and pinpointing of natural gas leaks required the development of high-sensitivity sensors and effective methods to minimize the effects of background noise.

Improvements in technology have been made with the development of very high-sensitivity accelerometers, very low-thermal noise solid state electronics, and low-cost digital signal processors capable of performing adaptive filtering in the field. The resulting improvement in sonic leak pinpointing technology can be seen by comparing the Digital Sonic Leak Pinpointer described in this paper with what is now referred to as the Analog Sonic Leak Pinpointer. The latter instrument was reported on at the IGRC held in London in 1983 (2).

The Analog Sonic Leak Pinpointer was evaluated in field testing at six utilities by IGT and Heath Consultants, Inc. Thirty-four leak sites were investigated (3). The combined use of the Analog Sonic Leak Pinpointer and the combustible gas indicator correctly predicted the location of 91% of the leaks (31 of 34) compared to 74% (25 of 34) when only the combustible gas indicator was used. In spite of this success, it was decided that the Analog Sonic Leak Pinpointer needed improvements in sensitivity and background-noise minimization to be acceptable to the industry. In particular, it was desired to increase typical spacing between sensor positions from 0.6 to 1.5 meters (2 feet to 5 feet). Also, a method of handling the 60-Hz acoustic hum from buried electrical cables and the continuous background noise that occurs at many leak sites was needed.

To make these improvements in background noise rejection, the Analog Sonic Leak Pinpointer was completely redesigned. The resulting Digital Sonic Leak Pinpointer utilizes digital signal processing technology. In analog processing the continuous electrical signal from the sensor is conditioned or processed with electronic components, such as, resistors, capacitors, operational amplifiers, etc. In digital signal processing, the signals from a sensor are periodically digitized, converting the sensor output into a series of numbers. The resulting data are mathematically processed to eliminate or enhance specific features. This mathematical filtering typically uses a set of predetermined coefficients. An important aspect of digital signal processing is to determine the appropriate coefficients for the task at hand. One advantage of digital signal processing is the result can be changed simply by changing the coefficients rather than replacing components.

In the past, digital signal processing was performed on mainframe computers. Recently, inexpensive microprocessors specifically designed to perform digital signal processing have been commercialized. These enable the use of sophisticated signal analysis and processing techniques in field instruments, including those applicable to the needs of the natural gas distribution industry. One familiar application of digital signal processing is in noise rejection in digital cellular telephones. However, in cellular telephones, the desired signal is voice and the background noise is static (white noise). Much work has been done to develop techniques for eliminating white noise from signals. In acoustic leak detection, the desired leak signal is very similar to white noise. Thus, we are enhancing a signal type most applications eliminate.

The Digital Sonic Leak Pinpointer uses two methods to greatly reduce the effects of background noise on the detection of the acoustic leak signal: signal gating and adaptive filtering. The combination of these two techniques is very effective in dealing with background noise, making passive sonic leak pinpointing feasible on almost all leak sites. Signal gating is technique that interrupts data collection whenever the background noise level at the leak site exceeds a preset value. Two or more sensors are required; one sensor to listen for the leak, the others to monitor background signals. Most leak sites have periods (sometimes only for a few seconds, as between passing cars) where the background noise is low enough to allow detection of the acoustic leak signal. Part of the time the background noise overwhelms any leak signal present. Such noise is eliminated by simply stopping data collection (gating the signal on and off) until the background noise subsides to a workable value. Because the transient-noise level at a site can be very loud, signal gating reduces the affect of background noise by orders of magnitude.

An additional noise suppression technique is required when the background noise is continuous rather than transient. Adaptive filtering, enabled by digital signal processing, is used to increase the noise-rejection capabilities of the Digital Sonic Leak Pinpointer. In adaptive filtering, the appropriate coefficients are not selected beforehand. Rather, the filter coefficients are determined in real time in the field based on the actual background noise present. Two or more sensors are required; one sensor for the leak, the others for common background noise to be removed. This approach is advantageous for sonic leak pinpointing because the background noise is not the same at each site. In fact, the background noise at any given site varies with time. The adaptive filtering determines the best coefficients to minimize the effect of background noise present at that time. The hardware and software used in the Digital Sonic Leak Pinpointer is fast enough to adjust as the background noise changes occur in the field.

In practice, three (two to four sensors can be used with the current hardware) sensors are used to collect data. The sensors are placed on probes along the pipe in the area of the suspected leak. One sensor is used as the leak sensor and the other sensors are used to monitor the background noise. One of the sensors will be closer to the leak than the others. The signal from the sensor closest to the leak is composed of acoustic leak signal and background noise. The signals from the other sensors are composed of the acoustic background noise. Adaptive filtering uses signals from the monitor sensors to determine the background noise common to all the sensors. These signals are used to determine the filter coefficients needed to eliminate the common background noise portion of the signal detected by the leak sensor. After elimination of the common noise, what remains is the leak signal. Of course, when the sensors are initially placed, it is not known which sensor is closest to the leak or if the leak is even there. Thus, the instrument automatically assigns each sensor, in rotation, as the leak sensor and the other two as monitors. The sensors are moved only after each has served as the leak sensor. Software in the Digital Sonic Leak Pinpointer interprets the processed signals and provides the operator with the sonic reading.

The adaptive filtering employed in the Digital Sonic Leak Pinpointer can reduce the affects of background noise by a factor of 300. It has the practical effect of permitting meaningful data collection as vehicles approach (because the common signal is eliminated) and permits the signal gating threshold to be set higher.

The Digital Sonic Leak Pinpointer is being developed in steps. First, a breadboard instrument was constructed with the digital signal processor and several laboratory instruments. An indoor test facility with simulated leaks was constructed to provide a controlled test bed (4) for documenting sensitivity improvements. The adaptive filtering software was written, tested, and revised. Coincident with the electronic improvements provided by the adaptive filtering, accelerometers of improved sensitivity became available. This was also an enabling factor in attaining the desired improvements. Tests in the indoor facility demonstrated the substantial improvements of the breadboard instrument in sensitivity and its ability to minimize background noise compared to the analog sonic leak pinpointer. For example, it was demonstrated that the breadboard Digital Sonic Leak Pinpointer could detect a leak with 1.5-meter (5-foot) spacing between the sensors, whereas the Analog Sonic Leak Pinpointer required a sensor spacing of 0.6-meter (2 feet) to be able to detect the same leak. The adaptive filtering technique was also proven to be very effective in reducing the effect on leak pinpointing of background noise from 60-Hz and harmonic hum from power lines and from truck and automotive traffic near the indoor facility.

The next step was to replace the laboratory instrumentation in the breadboard instrument with commercially available printed circuit boards, packaging them and the digital signal processor and software into a compact and easy-to-carry instrument. Figure 1 is a photograph of the resulting instrument. At present, the instrument requires a trained operator to use. The instrument will be made simple to use after the field trials prove successful enough to justify the expense of simplifying the interface. Field trials and refinement of the instrument are being performed in the spring and summer of 1995.

HOW IS THE DIGITAL SONIC LEAK PINPOINTER USED?

The Digital Sonic Leak Pinpointer is used to pinpoint a leak in a manner very similar to leak pinpointing with a combustible gas indicator. First the location of the pipe is determined. In the area of the suspected leak, a series of probes are driven into the ground with a modified barhole driver. A commercially available barhole driver was modified so that the upper portion of the driver can be detached from the probe, permitting the probe to remain in the ground (Figure 2). Each probe is 0.94 meters (37 inches) long and 12.4 millimeters (0.5 inch) in diameter. As shown in Figure 3, a sensor is magnetically attached to the top of the probe. A shield is placed over the sensor to minimize the effect of airborne sound. Two, three, or four sensors are used to collect data. (Part of the field trials are to determine the optimum number of sensors.) Software in the Digital Sonic Leak Pinpointer interprets the processed signals and informs the operator of the sonic reading for each probe location. The strongest meter reading is over the leak. Once the leak is detected, closer sensor spacing will more precisely pinpoint the leak prior to excavation. The use of additional sensor locations to more precisely locate the leak is similar to the practice presently used in pinpointing with the combustible gas indicator.

It should be emphasized that the Digital Sonic Leak Pinpointer is not intended as a replacement for instruments that sense natural gas, such as the combustible gas indicator. Gas-sensing instruments are required to determine if natural gas exists in potentially hazardous locations, such as at a building foundation. Because the ground attenuates acoustic leak signals within a few meters, the acoustic leak signal cannot migrate. However, gas can migrate, thus, an instrument like the combustible gas indicator is needed to identify potential safety hazards.

Although a few leaks on low-pressure 1.5-kPa (6 inches of water column) systems have been detected with a sonic leak pinpointer, all attempts to hear a low-pressure cast iron joint leak have been unsuccessful. The lengthy path through the packing in the joint may prevent the turbulent flow required to generate sound. To date, the Digital Sonic Leak Pinpointer has not been used on broken low-pressure cast iron mains; however, we expect it to work in such situations. Tests on cast iron joints operating at higher pressures (around 1 bar) have not been made.

FIELD TRIAL RESULTS

A typical field trial is conducted as follows: First, the host utility identifies the general location of the leak and determines the location of the pipe. If necessary, holes are drilled in the pavement in the same manner as for combustible gas indicator readings. Then IGT personnel drive the sonic probes into the ground, take readings with the Digital Sonic Leak Pinpointer, and predict the location of the leak(s) based on the sonic readings. Next, the probes are removed and combustible gas indicator readings are taken by utility personnel in the same barholes used for the acoustic sensors. These same utility personnel use the combustible gas indicator readings to predict the location of the leak. The readings and predictions of both instruments are recorded. The site is excavated to determined the actual location of the leak. If the predictions differ, both predicted locations are excavated to determine the cause of the reading. A leak is considered to be accurately pinpointed if it was in the initial 0.6 by 1.2-meter (2 by 4-foot) excavation. This would mean the leak is found in the first excavation.

The initial tests of the Digital Sonic Leak Pinpointer have been to assess the efficacy of the noise suppression techniques and make minor adjustments that were not possible in the indoor leak facility. The signal gating and adaptive filtering are working well in the initial tests. We have also been able to use 1.5-meter (5-foot) spacing between sensors to detect leaks. As of the date when this preprint was being prepared (early May), too few leak sites have been surveyed to draw any definite conclusions. Field trials will continue into spring and summer. The final version of the paper will be updated to include those results.

FUTURE PLANS

The commercialization strategy for the Digital Sonic Leak Pinpointer is to use a commercially available personal computer in a rugged, field-worthy chassis with plug-in boards to perform the specialized signal processing. Such hardware has recently become available. This approach has two benefits: First, the cost of development and commercialization of the specialized boards is borne by another market, rather than that of the Digital Sonic Leak Pinpointer alone. Market forces are continually improving these products and reducing their cost. Second, this approach reduces the cost and risk to the manufacturer/marketer of the Digital Sonic Leak Pinpointer because they do not need to expend substantial capital to produce a commercial product.

ACKNOWLEDGMENTS

The authors would like to thank IGT's Sustaining Membership Program, the Gas Research Institute, and the Southern California Gas Company for sponsoring this work. We would also like to thank Northern Illinois Gas Company for permitting access to leak sites and making their repair crews available during the testing of the Digital Sonic Leak Pinpointer.

REFERENCES

1.     J. A. Kinast, J. H. Kostro, J. E. Huebler, and V. Tamosaitis, "Natural Gas Distribution System Leak Pinpointing Survey," Final Report to Gas Research Institute, GRI-95/0026, March 1995.

2.     J. E. Huebler, C. J. Ziolkowski and J. M. Craig "Development of a Medium and High-Pressure Sonic Leak Pinpointer,". Paper presented at the 1983 International Gas Research Conference, London, June 13-16, 1983.

3.     J. E. Huebler, C. J. Ziolkowski and N. C. Saha, "Fabrication and Field Testing of a Prototype Sonic Leak Pinpointer for Medium and High-Pressure Gas Pipelines," Final Report to the Gas Research Institute, GRI-86/0044, March 1986.

4.     J. E. Huebler and C. J. Ziolkowski, "Efforts to Develop an Improved Sonic Leak Pinpointer," Draft Topical Report to the Gas Research Institute, July 1994.

Figure 1. Photograph of the Digital Sonic Leak Pinpointer

Figure 2. A Probe is Driven into the Ground to Provide Good Coupling Between
the Leak Sensor and the Soil Surrounding the Leak

Figure 3. The Leak Sensor is Magnetically Attached to the Top of the Probe

NEW TECHNOLOGY FOR FINDING AND MEASURING GAS LEAKS


NOUVELLES TECHNOLOGIES POUR DETECTER ET EVALUER
L'IMPORTANCE DES FUITES DE GAZ

R D Pride, J D Allen, H Hill
British Gas Research & Technology

## ABSTRACT

Portable hand held electronic instruments suitable for
the service engineer have been developed for   detecting
and quantifying the size of gas leaks from domestic
installations.  Classical  leak  detection  uses  leak
tracing solutions, stop-watches and U-Gauges, but    the
need  for  faster,  more  accurate  and  environmentally
acceptable approaches has been recognised.  The gas leak
tracer utilises semiconducting oxide gas sensors    for
detecting ppm gas leakage levels, whilst a traditional
technique has been combined with a pressure    transducer
and  microprocessor  to  provide  absolute  leak  rate
measurements.  The paper details the requirements for
these instruments, the practical hardware realisations,
and the results of laboratory and field trials.

## RESUME

Un instrument portatif électronique pouvant être   utilisé
par le réparateur a été mis au point pour la détection
et l'évaluation quantitative des fuites de  gas provenant
des  installations  domestiques.  Les  dispositifs  de
détection des fuites classiques empoient des déceleurs
de fuites sous forme de solutions, des chronomètres et
des manomètres en U mais le besoin d'une approche plus
rapide,   plus   précise   et   plus   acceptable   pour
l'environnement a été reconnue.  Le déceleur de fuites
de  gaz  utilise  des  senseurs  de  gas  à  oxyde  semi-
conducteur pour détecter les niveaux de fuites de gaz
ppm.  En  outre,  une  technique  traditionnelle  a  été
combinée à un capteur de pression et un microprocesseur
pour offrir une  mesure absolue du flux de la fuite.  La
communication   expose en détail les conditions requises
pour  ces  instruments,  les  réalisations  partiques
accomplies  grâce au matériel et les résultats des essais
en laboratoire et des essais sur le terrain.

## INTRODUCTION

British Gas (BG), as the prime gas supplier in the UK, is obliged to respond to all emergency call outs where gas leaks are suspected. With over 18 million users it is estimated that this amounts to in excess of two million calls per year - although many of these are found subsequently to be due to other reasons. BG engineers on emergency service use a catalytic, pellistor based quantitative gas leak detection instrument, (the Gascoseeker), to assess major gas leakage hazards and this instrument needs regular calibration checks. On arriving at the premises of the suspected leak, assuming no major gas concentrations are identified, it is normal practice to isolate the system at the meter control valve and perform a pressure drop test over two minutes using a U-gauge manometer and stop watch. If a predetermined maximum acceptable drop is exceeded, then a search for the leak is conducted that may include the use of soap solution brushed onto suspected leakage points.

## NEW DEVELOPMENTS

BG Research and Technology has developed two hand-held, battery operated instruments. The first is designed to trace the source of gas leaks and the second to measure absolute volumetric leak rate from a domestic or commercial gas pipework system. The gas leak tracer has been tested in the field and shown to significantly reduce the time taken to locate gas leaks compared with conventional methods using leak tracing fluids. The gas leak rate monitor uses a design principle previously described as a manual operation within existing BG industrial operational procedures[1]. The new feature is the automation of the operational sequence to produce a portable instrument which is easy to use and gives a rapid, accurate display of the absolute gas leak rate without prior knowledge, or any estimate, of the system volume. The gas leak rate monitor can also be used to measure system gas pressures.

### Leak Tracing

The BG Gascoseeker, used extensively by emergency teams, is primarily a safety tool for assessing explosion hazards and its accuracy must be closely maintained. It can be poisoned by solvents and aerosol vapours found in domestic premises. The new requirement is for a small hand-held instrument which is robust and sensitive enough (to 10ppm methane) for leak tracing and which does not need frequent calibration. A specification was drawn up for a battery powered instrument (Table 1) and an examination of commercially available gas leak tracers showed that none met all of the requirements, a prime one being cost. As a result a prototype instrument was developed, using a low-cost semiconducting metal oxide gas sensor (the Figaro TGS 842), an internal sample pump and rechargeable batteries, with a target price below £100. Changes in sensor resistance, in response to changes in gas concentration, are signalled to the user by change in audible and visual pulse rate, that can be offset by the user to give a slow pulse rate for background air.

Following successful field trials of 65 prototype instruments, a design and performance specification was produced and commercial instruments are now being manufactured to meet this specification. The paper discusses the testing of units in the laboratory and the field trial results.

**Leak Rate Measurement**

Domestic gas pipework installations in the UK have traditionally been tested for leaks by measuring the pressure drop in an isolated system, usually over a period of two minutes. For existing systems, if a predetermined maximum acceptable pressure drop is not exceeded then the soundness, or integrity, of the system is considered to be satisfactory. The disadvantage of this method is that it assumes that all domestic gas pipework systems have the same total volume. In the past this was a valid assumption since the volume of the positive displacement meter (7 litres) was the dominant factor in the total system volume (typically 10 litres) and variations due to small pipework lengths could be ignored. However, the introduction of smaller volume ultrasonic gas meters (typical volume 1.5 litres) means that variations in pipework volume have a more significant effect on the total system volume. Further, for a constant sized leak rate, the system pressure drop will be different for meters that have significantly different volume capacities. These features are displayed in Figure 1. Additionally, since methane is a "greenhouse" gas, it is desirable to be able to quantify leaks at an absolute level in order to ensure that undue leakages are not allowed to remain.

The principle used in the gas leak rate monitor is similar to that employed in the testing of industrial installations. The system is pressurised and isolated and the time (T1) for a predetermined pressure drop, if any, is recorded. After repressurising, a small, known leak is introduced to the system via a calibrated orifice, and the time for the same pressure drop is measured (T2). The system leak rate can then be calculated as:

$$\text{Leak Rate} = \frac{C \times T2}{(T1 - T2)} \quad \dots\dots\dots\dots\dots \quad (1)$$

where C is the known flow rate through the calibrated orifice (for a given pressure differential). It is therefore not necessary to know the system volume in order to calculate the absolute leak rate. The instrument also provides conventional pressure measurements from the sensitive pressure transducer. An instrument employing these principles has been designed and built and following evaluation on laboratory test rigs eight models were built for field testing. However, the target price of below £100 could not be met with this design and a further simplified instrument was subsequently built. This paper describes the design and testing of these instruments.

## GAS LEAK TRACER

**Evaluation of Commercial Products**

Four models were evaluated for sensitivity, response time, sensor stability and battery performance. Sensitivity was measured at three control settings in air containing methane concentrations up to 12000ppm and saturated with water vapour, and although not found to be linear all products responded to <50ppm at ~10% of full scale output. A fast response time is important for leak tracing and this was assessed as the 10-90% response time for a 1000ppm step change of methane in air. Response times of the various products ranged from 1-5 seconds and decay times of 1-9 seconds. Short term stability is essential for consistent readings and tests were performed at a 50% sensitivity setting by exposing the instruments to 2 minute pulses of 200ppm methane in air. The stability was defined as the percentage deviation in ten readings of the output taken at 10 second intervals and all products were found to be

better than ±4%. Although most performance requirements were
achieved in many cases, a cost target below £100 was not, and this
warrented an investigation to develop a device to meet the
specification at the right price.

## Prototype Development

A prototype instrument, shown in Figure 2, was made from
off-the-shelf components according to the target specification,
given in Table 1, and the instrument was found to meet the basic
requirements. Figure 3 shows the response characteristic of the
final unit.

## Results from Field Trial

65 units were produced and distributed to BG service engineers
across the country, together with questionnaires to assess the
usefulness of the instrument compared with conventional methods.
From 453 returned questionnaires the following points were of note;
89% of the jobs related to emergency call outs and 95% were in
domestic premises and interestingly, 54% were traced to appliance
connections. Table 2 shows that for just under 50% of the jobs
undertaken, the time taken to locate a leak and the precision in
locating the site of the leak with the instrument, was better than
current practice. The opinions were also very favourable with
regard to sensitivity, cleanliness and customer image. The
engineers were also asked to assess the design features of the unit,
also shown in Table 2, and the main criticism was the noise level of
the sample pump. This was overcome in the commercial product by
selecting a different pump unit. There was also some indication
from the replies that the unit was too sensitive and that it
responded to newly applied jointing compound. The latter is a
disadvantage of this TGS842 sensor which has subsequently been
overcome by selecting an alternative gas sensor for the commercial
product. A manufacturer has now taken the product specification
through to a commercially available product.

## LEAK RATE MONITOR

## Prototype Development

A schematic diagram of the instrument is shown in Figure 4. The
gas leak rate monitor consists primarily of a pressure transducer,
with bridge amplifier, a latching solenoid valve with calibrated
orifice, an alphanumeric display and a microcontroller to control
the sequence of operations and carry out the calculations. Power is
provided by a rechargeable battery. With this hand-held device the
measurement is fully automated which ensures accuracy in the timing
of pressure drops. Coupled with accurate pressure measurements this
enables pressure drops to be calculated from much reduced
measurement times (typically 20 seconds) compared with traditional
methods. It has also been possible to avoid the need to
repressurise the system in order to undertake the second pressure
drop measurement which includes the artificial leak. The two
pressure decays occur one after the other, with the calibrated leak
added in automatically (see Figure 5). A modified form of equation
(1) was then required to improve the correlation which includes a
proportionality factor and a fractional reduction in the second
pressure drop measurement. The procedure for using the instrument
is very simple and rapid, with an accurate leak rate being
calculated and displayed within 1 minute. Soundness testing of the
meter control valve may also carried out as part of the initial one
minute stabilisation period.

**Laboratory Tests**

Laboratory tests were conducted using the test rig shown in Figure 6, where a series of simulated domestic gas pipework systems can be created by a) varying the length of pipework b) introducing different types of gas meter and c) adding different sized leaks through calibrated orifices. The instrument is programmed to measure the time interval for the first predetermined pressure drop.

The time to repeat an equivalent pressure drop is then measured with the artificial leak introduced to the system. However, in the case of small leaks, the pressure drop recorded over a predetermined time interval is measured and this differential pressure is used as the pressure drop in the subsequent measurement with the additional leak introduced. Figure 7 shows that leak flow rates as measured by the leak rate monitor and a bubble flow meter were within ±3% error for leak rates less than 200ml/min. Measurements conducted in an environmental test chamber over the temperature range 0-40°C showed that errors of ±0.6 mbar could result in the measured zero pressure relative to that at 25°C. However, the instrument redefines zero pressure at ambient temperature each time it is switched on and so only ambient temperature changes during the measuring operation would cause such errors. Several solutions to this problem are possible if necessary, such as some form of on-line temperature compensation, via built-in thermistors.

A number of refinements were introduced following the laboratory tests. Domestic governors are designed to lock-up at 27.5 mbar, and this can lead to a pressure release into the system pipework if measurements are conducted above and/or through this pressure, leading to incorrect leak rate calculations. Therefore the software ensures that the pressure at the start of a measurement is below 20 mbar before a leak rate measurement can commence. To ensure that this is achieved rapidly, the solenoid valve is opened allowing gas to escape through the artificial leak. In new systems, checked with air alone, air will flow through both the real and known leaks, but for existing systems, since air and gas leaks will have different discharge coefficients this modification has the further advantage that the instrument pipework is filled with natural gas rather than air, ensuring that it is gas that flows through the calibrated orifice.

**Field Trial Results**

Ten units were initially prepared for field trial and the leak rates measured by each unit compared with a bubble flow meter for a range of four leak sizes (13 - 340 ml/min) and two meter sizes. These results, shown in Figure 8, showed a response distribution of ±15% of reading for all instruments over all conditions, which was considered sufficient for the field trial. Further consideration is being given to software/hardware improvements to reduce these errors. Several prototype units have now been issued to service engineers who are completing questionnaires on the usefulness of the instrument. If such an instrument were adopted as a standard service tool then an acceptable leak rate would need to declared for existing pipework systems. The current standard of a 4 mbar pressure drop in 2 minutes, equates to a leak rate of 28ml/min for a system volume of 10 litres.

**Lower Cost Design**

Following preliminary field trials of the instrument, a number of improvements were introduced. These included a more sensitive pressure transducer and a back-lit display for use under poor light conditions. A review of the microcontroller and associated electronics has also been undertaken in order to meet the target

small volume production price of less than £100.  Design features
that have been changed include the message display, which has been
dispensed with, and a low cost RISC processor that has replaced the
microcontroller.  A low powered magnetically latching solenoid valve
was used in the first prototypes in order to reduce power
consumption.  However, in order to ensure that intrinsic safety
requirements would be fully met without recourse to potting all the
gas paths within the instrument, this valve has now been replaced by
a conventional low powered solenoid valve.  It is anticipated that
future units may be able to use micromachined valves that are now
coming onto the market.  A manufacturer and a distributer have been
identified to produce and market the final product.

**BENEFITS**

The greatest benefit of both the gas leak tracer and the new
gas leak rate monitor instrument is the saving in time.  The service
engineer is given accurate identification of leak source and
magnitude and, following leak repairs, a pass/fail indication of
pipework soundness.  There is no requirement to know or estimate the
pipework or total system volume and an accurate measurement of the
gas leak rate can also be displayed if required.  A patent
application has been made for the gas leak rate monitor.

**CONCLUSIONS**

A hand held gas leak tracer and a gas leak rate monitor have
been developed and field trialled and shown to significantly reduce
the time taken to find leaks and prove the soundness of gas pipework
systems.  The instruments and the operational techniques have been
shown to have satisfactory accuracy on a wide range of systems.
These low cost portable instruments also have potential uses in
commercial, as well as domestic, servicing operations.

**ACKNOWLEDGEMENTS**

The authors wish to thank British Gas Research and Technology
for permission to publish this paper.

**REFERENCES**

1. Soundness Testing Procedures for Industrial and Commercial Gas
Installations.  BG publication IM/5, Third Edition, Dec. 1989

| PARAMETER | SPECIFICATION | PARAMETER | SPECIFICATION |
|---|---|---|---|
| Dimensions (mm) | 200x100x50 (max.) | Rise Time (Secs) | 3 max. |
| Weight (g) | 400 (max.) | Decay Time (Secs) | 3 max. |
| Battery Life (hrs) | 2.0 (min.) Rechargable | Warm-up Time (Secs) | < 60 max |
| Max.Sensitivity | <50ppm | Response Stability | $< \pm 20\%$ |
| Min. Sensitivity | 5000ppm | Output Signal (dBA) | >70 at 300mm+ LED |
| Flow Rate (l/hr) | >10 | Safety | Intrinsic in gas path |
| Temp.Range (C) | -10 to 40 | User controls | On/off & threshold |

## TABLE 1

## SPECIFICATION FOR HAND HELD GAS LEAK TRACER

| PARAMETER | % OF RESPONSES | | | FEATURE | % OF RESPONSES | | |
|---|---|---|---|---|---|---|---|
| | Better | Same | Worse | | Increase | OK | Reduce |
| Time to locate leak | 47.5 | 39.9 | 12.6 | Warm-up time | 7.1 | 62.5 | 30.4 |
| Precision of site | 45.3 | 41.5 | 13.2 | Battery capacity | 25.6 | 74.4 | 0 |
| Sensitivity | 51.2 | 45.3 | 3.5 | Response speed | 9.3 | 90.7 | 0 |
| Cleanliness | 43.5 | 56.5 | | Pump noise | 1.7 | 40.4 | 57.9 |
| Customer Image | 63.6 | 36.4 | | Sensitivity | 11.1 | 66.7 | 22.2 |
| | | | | Response range | 25.4 | 69.1 | 22.2 |

## TABLE 2

## RESULTS FROM GAS LEAK TRACER FIELD TRIAL

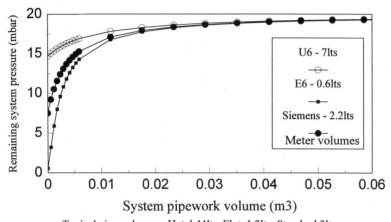

Typical pipe volumes:- Hotel:44lts; Flat: 1.2lts; Standard:3lts

Figure 1. Remaining system pressure for a range of pipe & meter
volumes following a 2 minute pressure drop from 20mbar

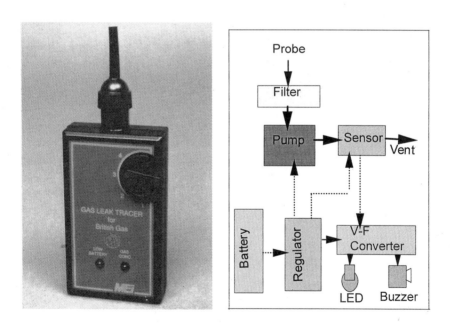

Figure 2. Photograph & schematic of Leak Tracer

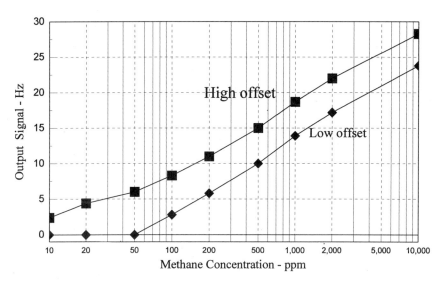

Figure 3. Response Characteristic of prototype
Leak Tracer to methane gas.

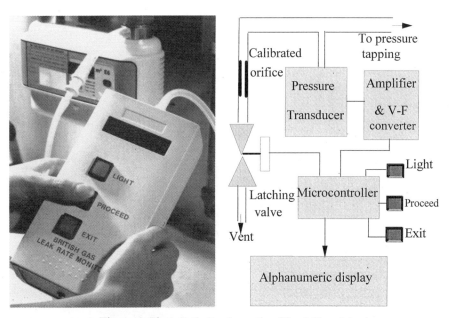

Figure 4. Photgraph & schematic of Leak Rate Monitor

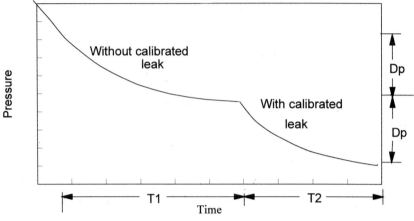

Figure 5.   Principle of single pressurisation and
introduction of a calibrated leak

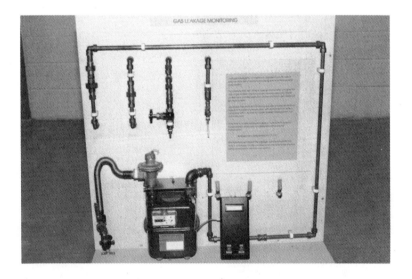

Figure 6. Prototype leak rate monitor & laboratory simulated domestic carcass

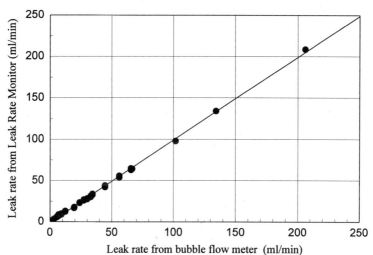

Figure 7. Comparison of leak rate measurements
from the Leak Rate Monitor & a bubble flow meter

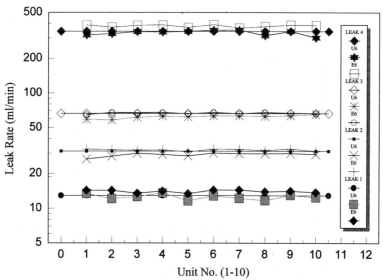

Figure 8. Leak rates measured by 10 field trail units
compared with a bubble flow meter.

## DEVELOPMENT OF A NOVEL VALVE INSTALLATION METHOD
## FOR PLASTIC GAS SYSTEMS

## DEVELOPPEMENT D'UNE NOUVELLE METHODE D'INSTALLATION DE
## VALVES A L'INTENTION DES RESEAUX GAZIERS EN PLASTIQUE

**Chi M. Lei and N. C. Saha**
**Institute of Gas Technology, USA**

**G. K. Ching**
**Southern California Gas Company, USA**

ABSTRACT

Southern California Gas Company is interested in a cost-effective method of installing isolation valves in its existing PE pipeline system. The current method is costly and time consuming because it requires a large excavation, two squeeze-offs, construction of bypass(es), and use of multiple fusion fittings and hot-taps. The Institute of Gas Technology developed a valve installation system that can install commercial PE valves into live mains without gas blowing, squeeze-offs, and flow interruptions. The system basically consists of two symmetrical enclosures, each comprised of split shells and seals to allow assembly around the main. Each enclosure contains its own cutter assembly, an electrofusion coupler positioning and joining provision, and a sliding mechanism for travel relative to the main. Prototype hardware for 100 mm pipe was fabricated, and testing at 4 bar was successful, although some areas of improvement were identified. The next step is the development of a preproduction prototype by a commercial partner.


RÉSUMÉ

La Southern California Gas Company désire sectionner son réseau PE existant en installant un plus grand nombre de valves. La méthode actuelle ultilisée est coûteuse et elle exige également un temps considérable, car elle a recours à une excavation étendue, à deux compressions, à la construction d'une ou plusieurs dérivations, et à l'utilisation d'accessoires à fusion multiple et de piquages sur conduite en charge. L'Institute of Gas Technology a développé une méthode qui permet d'installer des valves PE commerciales sur des conduites en charge sans échappement de gaz, sans compressions ou interruptions de dèbit. Il s'agit fondametalement d'installer deux enveloppes symétriques, comprenant chacune un machon endeux pièces et des joints étanches, qu'on enrobe autour de la conduite. Chaque eveloppe contient son propre coupe-tube, un dispositif pour positionner et ajuster l'accouplement d'électrofusion, et un mécanisme de glissement qui se fait le long de la conduite. On fabriqua les éléments du prototype pour un tuyau de 100 mm. Des essais à 4 bar furent exécutés avec succès, tout en révélant la nécessité de certains perfectionnements. L'étape qui suit verra le développement par un partenaire commercial d'un prototype devançant la production.

INTRODUCTION

The need for retrofitting existing gas distribution systems with pressure control devices to be used for system sectionalization or isolation has been long recognized by Southern California Gas Company (SoCalGas). The primary intent is to enhance the gas utility's capability of stopping the flow of gas into a specified area of the system quickly and effectively. The essential requirements of a preferred method of pressure control are quick response capability, safe and reliable performance; and low-cost installation and operation. This need for SoCalGas' steel system has been satisfactorily met with the Institute of Gas Technology (IGT)-developed Hot-Tap Sectionalizing Valve being manufactured by T. D. Williamson, Inc. (TDW). The Hot-Tap Valve, whose body is actually a steel nipple welded onto the gas main at the required location, uses existing SoCalGas hot tap procedures and equipment to install the internal mechanism which basically consists of a non-rising lead-screw and a cylindrical elastomeric plug. A previous near-term effort to develop a similar hot-tap valve for PE system was unsuccessful, largely due to the fact that suitable commercial electrofusion saddles were not available.

SoCalGas' need to incorporate a large number of isolation valves in the PE system has continued. The traditional method for adding commercial PE valves into an existing system is by squeeze-off. If a flow shutdown is unacceptable, the operation requires a large excavation (1.25 x 3.75-meters, or 4 x 12-feet) and a setup of bypass(es) consisting of multiple fusion fittings and hot-taps. Excessive labor, time, and material costs make this approach unacceptable. Additionally, many gas utility personnel feel that squeezing may affect the long-term strength of PE pipe and is potentially a safety hazard due to static electricity.

SOLUTIONS

In this project sponsored by SoCalGas, IGT set out to develop a no-blow enclosure to address the need for the PE system. The concept originally consisted of a single mechanical enclosure with several attached mechanisms. The mechanisms would perform the cutting of a section of the PE main, replacing of the cut pipe with a new pipe section containing a commercial valve on it, positioning of electrofusion couplers over pipe ends, and joining by electrofusion. The operation would be done live in a small excavation without blowing gas, flow interruption, and bypassing. A review of this enclosure concept led to the plan to extend its uses to an improved method of live repair of PE mains by replacing damaged pipe sections with new. The current practice uses squeeze-offs and has the same disadvantages as noted above for valve installation. After further evaluation of its usage, in addition to valve installation, a two-enclosure concept emerged and was pursued. As illustrated in Figures 1, 2, 3, and 4, this system basically consists of two symmetrical enclosures, each comprised of split shells and seals to allow assembly around the main. Each enclosure contains its own cutter assembly comprised of a perforated blade, an electrofusion coupler positioning and joining provision, and a stationary end plate with a sliding mechanism for moving each enclosure relative to the main. The entire operation is performed under a no-blow condition from the outside of the enclosures using common hand tools.

The enclosure system is not limited to valve installation, it also will find widespread use as a valuable tool for PE systems. As the two enclosures can be spaced at will, the system is very flexible and can be used for adding any valves and branch tees, and replacing any lengths of damaged, leaking, or gouged mains, but without gas blowing, flow interruption, and bypasses. Since it avoids the need to use squeeze-off, the related safety concerns are eliminated. In addition, for valve installation and typical short-length pipe replacement, the method requires only a small pit 1.25 x 1.25-meters (4 x 4-feet) versus a 1.25 x 3.75-meters (4 x 12-feet) excavation for the current practice. The overall savings in time, labor, and materials are very substantial.

TECHNICAL APPROACH

Following the extensive evaluation of concepts and the selection of the two-enclosure concept, a very detailed design was initiated. This design utilized a multitude of preliminary proof-of-feasibility tests, a 3-D modeling design, a preliminary Finite Element Analysis (FEA), and finally a detailed 2-D engineering design suitable for the prototype fabrication as well as the future manufacture of the system. For the proof-of-feasibility and prototype hardware demonstration, a complete system for 100 mm (4-inch) pipe was the primary focus of this project. During the design evaluation, valuable input from SoCalGas and a participating manufacturer was incorporated. Parts were then constructed by workshops contracted by the participating manufacturer. After several trials and modifications, the prototype hardware was finally tested and the concept of live insertion of PE valve and live replacement of PE pipe was proven feasible.

Design of the Concept

The detailed design task was broken down into several sub tasks:

- Cutter Assembly Design
- Sliding Seal Design, and
- Enclosure Design with its Attachments.

The design exercises took into consideration not only the wide choice of applicable materials, but also their design and construction for low-cost, near-term availability. To be an efficient, portable tool, the parts should be as light as possible. High-strength aluminum was therefore selected for the enclosure body. Since the casting of enclosures and molding of seals would have been expensive and time-consuming, they were postponed until the manufacturing phase. Fabrication of the prototype by extensive cutting and welding of parts was pursued, which required great care because of aluminum's sensitivity to heat. Since the structure of the enclosure is complex and 3-D, Computerized Numerical Control (CNC) machining was used to ensure the enclosures were made accurately. The sealing grooves on the enclosure walls were carefully designed, allowing enough space for the compressed seals to expand. At this proof-of-concept stage, the seals were just handmade from ordinary stock elastomer. Special care was given to the sealing of split shells and sliding surfaces. Steel was the material of choice for the components involved in power transmission. Off-the-shelf items like square seals, collars, bearings etc. were used as often as possible.

To make it a user-friendly tool, operations are designed to be executed with ease by one person. However, the sliding of the enclosures is best accomplished by two operators. Regular bolts and nuts on flanges are used for the assembly of top and bottom shells. An easy-clamping means would be preferred, but was left for inclusion in the future. To provide a visual check inside the enclosures, two viewports were attached on each top shell. The pipe cutting, enclosure sliding, and electrofusion-coupler positioning processes utilized a non-rising lead-screw design. Stops were provided at the end except for the enclosure sliding where it was found useful to have the extra movement for better alignment. The viewports are used to confirm the final alignment. With regard to the operating tools and equipment, the approach was to make use of standard hardware as much as possible. No special tool is required for the operations.

Before the detailed design could be finalized, a number of preliminary proof-of-feasibility tests were conducted. After the critical questions on the performance were answered by various functional tests, the rest of the design became straight forward. In order to determine the optimum profile and thickness of the blade for the cutter assembly design, a series of blades were tested. The blade was perforated so that the flow would only be partially interrupted during the cutting process. A full-scale setup was made for testing different designs of the sliding seal. The results of these tests were then incorporated in the enclosure design. With the basic dimensions of the enclosures determined, a preliminary FEA was run to ensure the structural integrity of the enclosure.

The enclosure was fabricated by cutting, welding, and machining of selected stocks of high-strength aluminum. Each enclosure consisted of a top and bottom shell, weighing 19 kg (42 lbs) and 10 kg (22 lbs) respectively. The housing for the cutter assembly and two viewports were welded to the top shell. Also, flanges were welded to each shell that facilitated the bolting of the top and bottom shells. The weight of the whole enclosure assembly is about 29 kg (64 lbs).

Testing of the Concept

Blade Cutting Testing. A hydraulic setup and a Kerotest pipe cutter were used for the preliminary blade testing. The initial profile of the blades was chosen to be the same as that of the Kerotest pipe cutter for a reasonable start. Blades with a sharp pilot angle were also tested. The blade thicknesses of 1.59 and 3.18 mm (1/16 and 1/8 inches) were tested.

Testing revealed important points relating to the blade geometry. As expected, the 1.59 mm blade required less force to cut the pipe and caused less out-of-roundness. However, this blade was not rigid enough to produce a squared cut surface and was thus abandoned. The 3.18 mm blade was then tested. This thicker blade produced more out of roundness. Full-encirclement supports were used to try to reduce this undesirable effect. Roundness of the pipe is very important for proper coupler insertion and electrofusion. Excessive out-of-roundness can not be tolerated. Using the Kerotest pipe cutter, the full encirclement supports appeared to reduce the out-of-roundness. Therefore, the use of full-encirclement support was included in the final enclosure design. As blades, both with and without a sharp pilot angle made good cuts, the blade without the sharp pilot angle, as shown in Figure 5, was selected due to lower manufacturing cost.

Sliding-Seal Testing. One of the critical questions needed to be certain was whether the enclosures could move while the gas-tight seal was maintained. A great amount of force is required to overcome the friction generated by the seal in compression. A critical set of tests were made on the sliding seal with a full-scale setup. Three different sliding arrangements were tested. These included a linear movement device with sliding contact between the bolts and end plate, the same device with rollers added between the bolts and end plate for reduced friction, and a radial movement device with sliding contact between the bolts and end plate. This last device utilized a 760 mm (30 inches) lever arm for overcoming the friction forces. The tests were designed to mimic the actual conditions by maintaining the required amount of force to simulate the compression in the seal and allowing for relative movement to simulate sliding. An attempt was made to move the linear setup by hand and, as expected, this was not possible. However, moving the setup became easy when a C-clamp was adapted. Adding rollers between the bolts and end plate did not improve the sliding performance significantly. However, it appeared also to make sense because most of the friction was created on the other side of the end plate due to the compression of the seal. As a result of these tests, all arrangements would successfully move the "enclosure" at full seal compression. It meant that the sliding seal problem could be solved and the final enclosure design would have a lead-screw driven linear device without rollers for the reasons of simplicity, ease of operation and low manufacturing cost. However, a light grease film was used to ensure a smooth reliable movement of the seal in those tests. Since a greasy seal was undesirable because it could collect dirt in the field, this greasy lubrication film was then replaced with a dry coated surface called Magnaplate, which provides a low coefficient of friction. The sliding test was resumed and it revealed that the lubrication provided by the plating was sufficient for the proper operation of the sliding seal. As a result, the feature of using Magnaplate as the dry lubrication would be included in the enclosure design.

Enclosure Testing. Careful dimensional analysis inclusive of manufacturing tolerances is important in this complex, 3-D design of the enclosure. For instance, after assembly of the top and bottom shells, a perfect continuous line-seal for providing a gas-tight enclosure has to be formed. Also, the enclosure surfaces, which are to be in contact with the stationary end plates, have to be perfectly flat because these surfaces are the sliding surfaces of the enclosures against the stationary end plates. After an extensive amount of refinement work conducted, all parts of the enclosure assemblies fitted together and all mechanisms tended to function properly.

The initial cutting tests were disappointing because the pipe support, which was provided to prevent the PE pipe from deformation during cutting, caused non-squared cutting. Since the pipe support, which could only be provided on one side within each enclosure, restrained any pipe material from moving during the cutting process; it in turn generated an unbalanced force and deflected the blade away from the pipe support. (In the preliminary proof-of-feasibility tests, the pipe supports were in place on both sides of the Kerotest pipe cutter and forces were in balance). Several modifications of the blades were attempted to preserve the pipe support. However, further testing showed that the blade deflection still remained. Since the deformation of the PE pipe without this extra pipe support was found inexcessive after the cutting, the pipe support was then finally abandoned. A redesign moved the pipe support away from the cutting plane, which now functions as a pipe clamp to aid the initial assembly of the enclosure.

A series of pressure containment tests using water and air as the pressurized mediums followed. However, the water pressure test for structural integrity of the enclosure to 150 percent of rate pressure was not possible due to the limitations in the test setup. For leak tests, air pressures up to 4.1 bar (60 psig) were used. IGT did not attain a bubble-tight seal though a significant effort was made. Since the seals are split-type, and at several places there are seals merging to the same spot and being compressed twice in two different directions, it was difficult to make a perfect matching seal by hand without some good guides. The split circumferential seals on the top shells, which provides sealing to the PE pipe, were the most troublesome. Even so, IGT believes that a bubble-tight seal is achievable on this prototype and much more readily on future production parts. With a set of good guides in cutting and grinding to achieve the desired seal length and end profile, and in addition, using glue to fix the seal in place, a bubble-tight seal should be achieved. Without these improvements, the best result was a leak rate of 0.19 standard m3/h (6.9 scf/h) corrected at a pressure of 4.3 bar (63 psig).

As the seal will be molded and fabricated in a totally different way in the commercial product, IGT did not spend an excessive amount of efforts in fixing the leaks at this proof-of-concept stage. Allowing leakages not exceeding 0.28 standard m3/h indicated (10 scf/h indicated) from the enclosure system, several performance tests at 4.1 bar (60 psig) air-pressure environment were conducted. The performance was satisfactory. The prototype system repeatedly made good cuts on the pipe, performed sliding of the enclosures with respect to the stationary end plates, enabled proper positioning of the electrofusion couplers over the cut pipe sections, and provided good looking, leak-proof electrofusion joints. Also, using the prototype, an electrofusion test in a natural gas environment was successfully conducted; however, standard American Society for Testing and Materials (ASTM) tests will be required to substantiate the integrity of fusion. A picture showing the enclosures system on the test stand is shown in Figure 6.

ACCOMPLISHMENTS

The project achieved the following results:

- The concept of installing new valves or replacing damaged PE pipe sections without gas blowing, bypass, and flow interruption was successfully proven.
- The best leakage flow rate was 0.19 standard m3/h (6.9 scf/h) corrected at air pressure of 4.3 bar (63 psig). Bubble-tight operation is achievable, and safe, reliable performance is demonstrated.

- The enclosure system for 100-mm (4-inch) PE pipe should work in a standard pit, about 1.25 x 1.25 meters (4 x 4 feet) in size.

- The electrofusion joining being done by this method in a natural gas environment would be satisfactory.

- The assembly process, requiring only hand wrenches, is easy and friendly. A quick-clamping feature can be added to further save time.

- The enclosure system is basically manually-operated. The operations involving cutting of the PE pipe, sliding of the enclosures, and moving of the electrofusion couplers are wrench-operated. Except for the sliding of the enclosures, the entire operation can be handled by one operator.

- The heaviest single part weighs no more than 19 kg (42 lbs) and thus easily handled.

- The enclosure system is basically a portable tool not exposed to the gas stream for long periods. Therefore, the corresponding long-term exposure effects, like elastomer property changes, plastic deformation or creep, and corrosion, are of little concern.

- The enclosure system is believed to be free of static electricity hazards. Although no test was conducted, the static electricity can be effectively eliminated by grounding the cutter assembly as currently practiced by SoCalGas.

FUTURE WORK

The following is the future plan:

- To test and evaluate the prototype system and to determine what changes and improvements, if any, would be desired by the SoCalGas operating personnel.

- To commission a participating manufacturer and commercial partner.

- To begin the preproduction prototype development and commercialization.

ACKNOWLEDGMENT

The authors acknowledge the valuable contribution and support of T. D. Williamson, Inc., Tulsa, Oklahoma, USA for their participation in the prototype fabrication. In particular, acknowledgment is to Mr. Joe Welch of TDW for his valuable inputs on the engineering design of the prototype system.

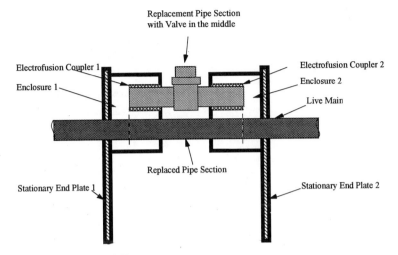

Figure 1. Operational Procedures Sequence 1

- Each enclosure makes a leak tight seal around the live main and replacement pipe section.
- After the enclosures are purged, the live main is cut along the two dotted lines.
- The replacement pipe section can include a braching tee, or contain gouges or leaks that need replacement.

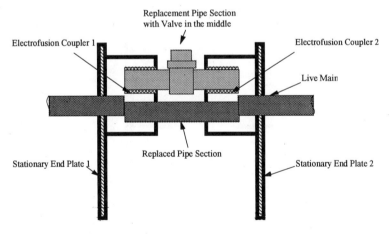

Figure 2. Operational Procedures Sequence 2

- The two enclosures are moved in unison to slide the replacement pipe in line with the live main.
- The live main and replacement section form a bypass during this process.

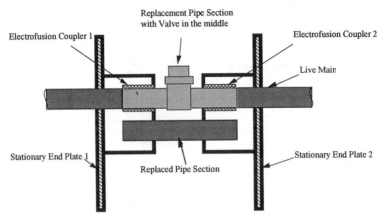

Figure 3.  Operational Procedures Sequence 3

❏     The replacement pipe section is in line with the live main .

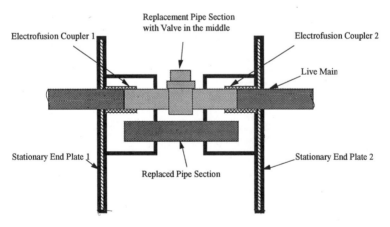

Figure 4.  Operational Procedures Sequence 4

❏     The electrofusion couplings are positioned to join the live main and
       replacement section.

❏     The hardware is removed and used on the next job site.

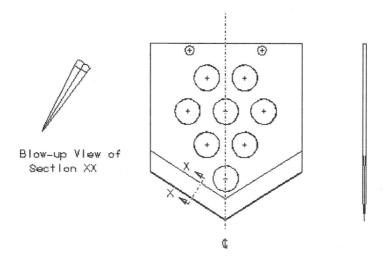

Blow-up View of
Section XX

Figure 5. The Design of the Cutting Blade

Figure 6. The Enclosures System on the Test

**L'ABOUTISSEMENT D'UNE RECHERCHE PERMETTANT D'AMELIORER
LA FIABILITE DES JONCTIONS ENTRE TUBES PE : LE FILET CHAUFFANT.**

**THE  FRUIT OF RESEARCH AIMED AT IMPROVING
THE RELIABILITY OF PE PIPING JOINTS : THE HEATING NET.**

by D. Dufour, Gaz de France Research Division, Saint Denis, France

**RESUME**

Suite à une étude comparative de différentes techniques d'assemblage des tubes en PE (bout à bout, électrosoudage, soudage dans l'emboîture), Gaz de France a choisi l'électrosoudage pour sa fiabilité et sa simplicité.
Le retour d'expérience confirme la fiabilité de cette technique. En effet, le taux d'avaries est très faible, cependant de nombreuses non-qualités sont dues à des dérives dans la mise en oeuvre sur chantier.
De 1985 à 1990, la Direction de la Recherche de Gaz de France a entrepris, en partenariat avec des industriels, des recherches et des développements avec pour objectif d'automatiser le déroulement du cycle de soudage afin de réduire les avaries ayant pour origine un mauvais réglage du poste de soudage.
Après 1990, les recherches ont été reconduites dans l'optique cette fois de développer des principes favorisant l'émergence d'une gamme de raccords électrosoudables encore plus fiables. Cette nouvelle génération de raccords doit permettre:
- un contrôle de l'énergie de soudage au moins aussi performant que celui des raccords de dernière génération,
- la détection de certaines dérives de mise en oeuvre qui, par la modification des transferts thermiques du raccord vers le tube, altèrent la qualité du soudage,
- le renforcement de la qualité du soudage notamment dans le cas d'une préparation imparfaite de la surface du tube (grattage, nettoyage).

Les études réalisées par la Direction de la Recherche de Gaz de France mettent en évidence que l'innovation " filet chauffant " qui consiste à remplacer l'actuel élément chauffant des raccords électrosoudables par un fil tricoté revêtu présentant des caractéristiques bien définies s'avère être une solution technologique prometteuse.

**ABSTRACT**

After a comparative study of different techniques for joining PE pipes (butt fusion, electrofusion, socket fusion), Gaz de France chose electrofusion for its reliability and simplicity.
The feedback from the field  confirms the reliability of this technique.  Indeed, the defect rate is very low. However many quality shortfalls are due to deviations in field installation.
From 1985 to 1990, the Research Division of Gaz de France undertook research and development work, in collaboration with manufacturers, aimed at automating the fusion cycle in order to cut back the number of defects caused by incorrect settings of the electrofusion system.
After 1990, the research was continued and geared this time toward developing design principles promoting the emergence of a range of yet more reliable electrofusion fittings.  This new generation of fittings is expected to allow:
- control of the fusion energy that is at least as effective as that of the latest generation of fittings,
- detection of certain deviations in joint implementation which, thanks to the modification of the heat transfers from the fitting to the pipe, alter the joint quality,
- enhancement of joint quality, in particular in the case of less-than-perfect preparation (scraping and cleaning)of the pipe surface.

The research carried out by the Gaz de France Research Division makes it clear that the "heating net" innovation, which consists in replacing the present heating element in electrofusion fittings by a knitted, coated wire with well-defined characteristics is a promising technological alternative.

## I) INTRODUCTION

In the nineteen seventies, Gaz de France began to use polyethylene (PE) for the extension and renewal of its distribution networks.

Today, out of the 126,000 km of the distribution network, 52,000 km are made of polyethylene, to which are added the service branches for connecting customers. We estimate that there are currently over 7,000,000 electrofusion fittings in operation, of which nearly 5,000,000 are used for joining pipes and 2,000,000 as tapping tees. To all of these must be added about 110,000 repair saddles used to reinforce pipes that have been squeezed.

Gaz de France has chosen a joining technique characterized by all of the following:
- high reliability,
- simplicity of field installation,
- suitability for building a distribution network made up of tubes packaged in great lengths, with numerous tapping tees, and operated at four bar.

The choice of such a technique was based on research and development work which culminated in the drafting of simple guidelines for using PE materials. Among the products of this research, are the study of the physico-chemical and thermal mechanisms operating at the fusion interface between two polyethylene parts (Ref. 1), the design study of electrofusion fittings (Ref. 2) and the study of the mechanisms at work in the evolution over time of fused materials and assemblies (Ref. 3). Besides this research, Gaz de France collaborated with manufacturers to develop various procedures for automating the electrofusion (EF) cycle (Ref. 4). Also, actions have been undertaken to implement EF joint inspection or auto-control procedures (Ref. 5).

Moreover, the choice of electrofusion is not economically disadvantageous for two reasons. Firstly, the pipes used for distribution networks are operated at a pressure of four bar and, due to this fact, always have a diameter of less than 200 mm; in this range of diameters, the price of the fittings remains reasonable. Secondly, the packaging of PE pipes in great lengths (hundreds of meters) up to dia. 160 mm considerably reduces the number of joints to be made. For pipes 200 mm in diameter packaged as straight bars, Gaz de France has over the last few years been using the so-called "butt- fusion" technique.

The technique of assembling PE pipes with EF fittings has, for several years, been used very extensively by the other European gas companies and is spreading rapidly in Japan. It is as yet not very widespread in North America but research is underway and this is expected to promote its spread in the long run.

## II) THE LIMITATIONS OF ELECTROFUSION

### II.1) Economic limitations

The techniques of electrofusion fitting manufacture entail substantial production costs. In fact, making an electrofusion fitting first requires implanting a heating coil consisting of a metal wire, generally wound around an injection-molded PE insert. The winding techniques are relatively complex. They require continuous control and hence, the presence of an operator.

The heating implant is then encapsulated by the injection method, which requires a substantial investment for the fabrication of a mold. The capital cost of the mold is very high for small production runs, which partly explains the high cost of large diameter fittings.

### II.2) Technical limitations

An analysis of flawed EF fittings over a five-year period (Ref. 6) highlights the following patterns:

- 60% of the flaws (having been the subject of a damage analysis) were due to a manufacturing defect or a design defect of the fitting,

- the main deviations in installation were errors in setting the electrofusion machine (14%), followed by incorrect preparation (scraping and cleaning) of the tubes (10%), deviations in the assembling and positioning of the "pipe-fitting" assembly (10%) and the remainder were due to multiple causes.

Depending on their origin, the different defects do not have the same impact on safety. For example, over-heating a coupling sleeve due to incorrect setting of the electrofusion system will be immediately identified by heavy smoke and will lead to dismantling of the defective assembly prior to charging the network. This type of defect does not present a major hazard in the long run.

Conversely, making a joint on an unscraped pipe or making an error in the fusion parameters leading to a shortfall of fusion energy can produce a joint that is tight enough for the acceptance test but that may become leaky under more substantial mechanical loading. This type of defect, being more difficult to detect, is of significantly more cause for concern than the previous one.

Gaz de France continued its research on electrofusion with the goal of inducing the development of a new generation of fittings, more tolerant of manufacturing and installation deviations and costing substantially less in order to facilitate industrial production of such fittings.

The analysis shows that this new generation of electrofusion fittings can be built by taking into account the following:

- control of the fusion energy,

- obtaining mechanical strength of the fusion plane that is less sensitive to certain deviations in the installation procedure (such as less-than-perfect pipe preparation),

- detecting in the course of the melting cycle certain deviations of joining which alter the quality of fusion by modifying the heat transfers from the fitting to the pipe.

## III) SEARCH FOR DIRECTIONS OF TECHNOLOGICAL IMPROVEMENT

The search for technological solutions allowing detailed development of the new range of fittings to progress was based on past knowledge acquired in three fields:

- the change in weldability as a function of the aging of the PE pipes,
- the behavior of the fittings' electric coil during heating,
- the heat transfers in the course of an electrofusion operation.

### III.1) Change in weldability as a function of the aging of the PE pipes

The current installation procedures for electrofusion fittings require to scrape the pipe outside surface to achieve a sound joint. This operation consists in removing a film of plastic about 0.2 mm thick from the outside of the pipe.

Other laboratories (7, 8) have likewise established the incidence of oxidation or surface contamination on the mechanical strength of assemblies.

**III.1.1) Tests made on real parts :** Tests made in the laboratory show that tapping tees from three different suppliers, fused onto unscraped pipes stored outdoors for 9 months lead to assemblies of inadequate mechanical strength.

The results given in Table 1 are the failure times found for assemblies subjected to a hydrostatic pressure test at 9.2 bar in water at 80°C. This type of test makes it possible to quickly determine the long-term strength of the joint at 20°C.

The specifications call for the time-to-failure under these conditions to be more than 170 hours. As can be seen, the failure times determined on unscraped pipes are very clearly shorter than the specified values, irrespective of the source of the tee.

| Type of tapping tee | Pipe surface preparation | Failure time ( hour ) |
|---------------------|--------------------------|-----------------------|
| A | No scraping | 0 |
| B | No scraping | 1,9 |
| C | No scraping | 0 |

Table 1 : Failure times for joints made on unscraped pipes, under the hydraulic pressure test.
A, B, C : Tapping tees from three different manufacturers.

**III.1.2) Tests made on laboratory test pieces (Ref. 1) :** These tests consist in fusion-joining 0.4 mm thick micro-specimens and then characterizing the mechanical strength of the fusion plane by a peeling test.

Application of this method to the study of the fusion joining behavior of PE test pieces having been subjected to aging has shown that pipe surfaces, after eight months of natural aging, had a minimum good bonding temperature about 55°C higher than the sound surface (for a heating rate of 200°C/mn). After 14 months, the minimum good bonding temperature goes up by about 70 to 90°C.

These test results for laboratory micro-specimens confirm that there is a significant reduction of the weldability of oxidized surfaces. However, they tend to indicate that the parts can still be joined, provided the temperature at the interface during the heating operation is significantly increased.

Note : The minimum good bonding temperature serves to characterize the thermal conditions of heating that make it possible to obtain sufficient mechanical strength of the two micro-specimen assembly.

#### III.2) The heat transfers around the wires

Modelling the heat transfers involved during an electrofusion operation allows to quantify the very substantial temperature gradients in the heated zone. By way of example, Figure 1 represents the temperature change calculated in the vicinity of the wire of a 63 mm coupling sleeve at the end of the heating cycle. According to these calculations, near the wire, the temperature gradients are about 100°C per millimeter.

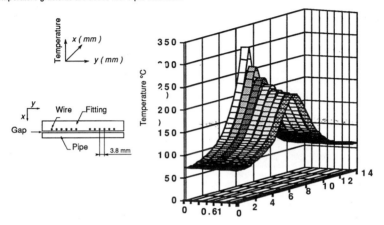

Figure 1 : Temperature profile near the wire

This result helps to better appreciate the difficulties faced during the detailed design of an electrofusion fitting. Indeed, the heating element of these fittings is generally made up of an electric wire helically coiled and positioned near the inside wall of the fitting.

From a purely thermal standpoint, the ideal location for the wire would be as close as possible to the inside wall of the fitting, such as to achieve high temperatures at the fusion interface without thermally degrading the PE around it. However, from a practical standpoint, that configuration is not desirable because it presents a large risk of the wire moving and being pulled out when the pipe is pushed into the socket.

Likewise, in order to limit the thermal gradient between the turns of the coil, it seems wise to reduce the winding pitch. Here again, practical experience shows that this orientation has limits. In fact, turns too closely spaced favor the occurrence of short circuits, which cause the electrical resistance to decrease and, due to this, the heat output to increase, resulting in overheating of the fitting.

Such short circuits, generally caused by movements of molten matter, are favored by an increase of the mechanical stress in the fusion zone. For example, certain installation deviations, such as a pipe positioning defect, favor their occurrence.

In conclusion, the usual techniques (wire winding) currently used to make the electrical implants in electrofusion fittings themselves bring about technical limitations.

#### III.3) Description of the innovation proposed by the Research Division of Gaz de France

This innovation consists in modifying the way the heating implant of electrofusion fittings is made, such as to:

- increase the temperature of the fusion interface whilst avoiding thermal degradation of the PE near the electric wire,
- prevent or detect short circuits between the turns of the wire coil.

To achieve this, a meshed network (net) replaces the heating implant, which allows the heating energy per unit area to be increased without thermal degradation of the PE material, thanks to a better distribution of heat.

To prevent short circuits between the meshes of the net, the metal wire is coated with an insulating varnish of well-defined characteristics. The melting temperature of this varnish lies between the good bonding temperature of the parts to be joined and the thermal degradation temperature of the PE. Thus, the wires are insulated from each other where they cross, up to the temperature at which the varnish melts; beyond that point, short circuits can occur. Yet these shorts, which cause the overall electrical resistance of the fitting to change, can be used either as an indicator of flaws, or to trip the cessation of heating.

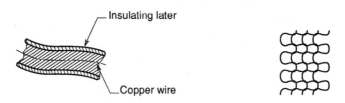

*Figure 2 : Diagram of a net and an enamelled wire*

## IV) EVALUATIONS OF PROTOTYPE PARTS INCORPORATING A HEATING NET

A test program was carried out by Gaz de France Research to:
- define the characteristics of nets suitable for the manufacture of fittings,
- assess the industrial feasibility of such nets,
- produce prototype fittings using these nets and evaluate their performance both in relation to the current specifications and in respect special installation conditions.

### IV.1) Feasibility study of heating implants made with nets

The feasibility study consisted in identifying a metal wire (wire type, diameter, insulating varnish) and defining the geometry of the mesh to produce a heating net able to be used as heating implant in an electrofusion fitting. The fitting was required to be fusible at a voltage of about 38 V.

Two types of fitting were investigated: a 110 mm tapping tee and a 63 mm coupling. As an example, the main characteristics of the net used in the tees are given in Table 2.

| Rectangular Net geometry | 75 x 82 mm |
|---|---|
| Mesh geometry | 3 x 5,5 mm |
| Wire material | Copper |
| Fusion temperature of insulating varnish | > 350 °C |
| Initial resistivity | 3,7 < R < 4,1 ohm |

*Table 2 : Main characteristics of the net used in the tapping tees*

### IV.2) Net manufacture

The enamelled copper wires (wires electrically insulated by varnish) are products commonly used to make electric motors; their procurement is therefore not a problem.

Similarly, wire knitting is used in various manufacturing sectors and in particular in the cable industry where it is used as protection against electromagnetic interference. Various knitting methods can be used, the most conventional and widespread being the one employing a circular loom that makes it possible to create a net of one or more wires shaped like a sock. To create more complex shapes, it is necessary to use looms known as a double-bed tricot machines, which are far less common.

All of the nets made as part of our study were formed on circular or "hose" knitting machines. Our experiments showed that this type of product did not present any particular manufacturing problems. The existing tools of the trade can be used without modification, needing only a few adaptations to meet the production specifications. For example, it is essential to do away with the wire lubrication to preclude problems during pipe joining, and to adapt the mechanical stresses imparted to the wire during knitting to prevent local damage to the insulation as knitting proceeds.

### IV.3) Fabrication of prototype fittings

**IV.3.1) Creation of 110 mm tapping tees :** We created two types of tee prototypes, which differ by the geometry of the heating implant made in both cases from a section of tubular netting.

A first series of tapping tees was made by laying down flat a tubular net (see photos in annex ) and embedding it in the inside wall of the fitting by preheating (at 38 Volts for 45 seconds) the net placed between the tee and a "conformator" cooling fixture.

This technique turned out to be particularly simple and repeatable for the production of more than 200 prototype fittings. Nevertheless, we evaluated a second technique allowing a heating implant to be created with an unheated center area to make it easier to perforate when charging the branch with gas.

To make the second series, the tubular net was worked into the shape of a washer (see Figure 3). This disk-shaped part is then embedded into the inside wall of the fitting in the same way as before.

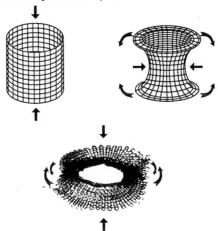

*Figure 3 : Shaping of a tubular net to obtain a washer*

**IV.3.1) Creation of couplings :** Prototype couplings 63 mm in diameter were created by embedding a heating net in the inside wall of a coupling designed for the socket fusion technique. The shortness of these couplings did not allow us to create a cold center zone.

### IV.4) Assessment of the performance of the prototype fittings

A series of tests were made to check that the fittings complied with the applicable French standards, NFT54079 and NFT54066. In this context, the following tests were carried out:
- upper safety factor (over-heating),
- lower safety factor (energy shortfall),
- fusion joining at different temperatures (-10°C, 0°C, 23°C, 45°C),
- determination of the pull-out resistance after bonding,
- hydraulic pressure of 9.2 bar at 80°C.

### IV.4.1) Assessment of tapping tees made with a "rectangle" net

**Determination of the upper and lower safety factor :** Determination of the upper safety factor consists in determining the heating time at the end of which an abnormal effect appears. The abnormality may be complete melting of the fitting, smoking, breaking of the electrical resistance and so on.

Table 3 summarizes the results obtained at different temperatures. For the fittings with a heating net, over-heating is characterized by melting of the electric wire, which translates visually into a very small emission of smoke. Contrarily to fittings made with a coiled wire, no projection of melted polyethylene was observed. Such sprays could burn the operator. The fitting equipped with a heating net is therefore safer than a conventional electrofusion fitting from the standpoint of this hazard.

In addition, it can be seen, by examining the results given in Table 3, that the over heating is preceded, approximately 10 seconds before it occurs, by the appearance of short circuits between the meshes that may be indicated by melting of the insulating varnish. This observation demonstrates the value of the principle of a heating net, which with a carefully selected varnish, allows the supplied heating energy to be checked.

| Sample | Over-heating time | First short-circuit time | Initial resistivity | Initial temperature |
|---|---|---|---|---|
| CYX11RE339 | 253 | 245 | 3.7 | -10 |
| CYX12RE340 | 240 | 216 | 3.71 | -10 |
| CYX13RE341 | 252 | 234 | 3.68 | -10 |
| CYX14RE343 | 210 | 197 | 3.7 | 0 |
| CYX15RE346 | 203 | 190 | 3.61 | 0 |
| CYX16RE345 | 215 | 200 | 3.6 | 0 |
| CYX01RE324 | 210 | 200 | 4.01 | 23 |
| CYX02RE325 | 271 | 245 | 4.36 | 23 |
| CYX03RE326 | 243 | 215 | 3.96 | 23 |
| CYX04RE327 | 200 | 185 | 3.89 | 23 |
| CYX08RE332 | 205 | 200 | 3.9 | 45 |
| CYX09RE333 | 217 | 210 | 3.9 | 45 |
| CYXR10E334 | 180 | 162 | 3.9 | 45 |

Table 3

*Table 3 : Results of the over-heating tests on "rectangle" type tapping tees*

For these prototype tapping tees, the nominal heating times are respectively 91, 100 and 113 seconds for initial temperatures of 10, 23 and 45°C. The upper safety factor, which corresponds to the ratio of the over-heating time to the nominal heating time, is therefore always greater than 2 and hence broadly greater than the specified value of 1.5.

The lower safety factor, which corresponds to the ratio of the nominal heating time to the minimum time required to obtain a joint of satisfactory quality, is always greater than 1.25. So far, no value has been specified for this safety coefficient. Nevertheless, experience shows that a fitting is less sensitive to certain deviations of installation when this coefficient is close to, or better still, higher than, 1.25.

**Fusion-joining at different temperatures and pull-out test :** The results of the tests of fusion-joints made at different temperatures between -10°C and +45°C meet the French standard.

The pull-out tests revealed a good bonding of the tee to the pipe; the results on the whole meet the standard. The fracture surfaces are not smooth; we find that the fitting material remains attached to the pipe after the test ( see photo in annex ).

**Hydraulic pressure test :** The prototype fittings performed according to the standard in all the tests made. For a pressure of 9.2 bar at 80°C, the time-to-failure must be more than 170 hours; the three specimens tested had failure times better than 3500 hours.

## IV.4.2) Assessment of tapping tees with a washer-shaped net

Comparable tests were made on prototype tapping tees with a washer-shaped net. The results were as follows:
- upper safety factor >1.5,
- lower safety factor >1.25
- no problem with fusion joints made at -10°C, 23°C and 45°C,
- no failures in the fusion plane of joints made at -10°C, 23°C and 45°C,
- time-to-failure at 9.2 bar and 80°C >6900 hours.

The prototype fittings of this configuration performed according to the standard in all the tests made. However, analysis of the test results allows us to observe that the operating range — the difference between the minimum bonding time and the over-heating time — is narrower than for the rectangular configuration.

## IV.4.3) Assessment of net-equipped couplings

The assessment of these couplings served to verify that they were compliant with Standard NFT 54066, except for the lack of a center cold zone that allows heating to be limited to the center portion of the inside wall of the sleeve, where the two pipe ends are located.

## IV.5) Additional tests

**Joining of unscraped pipes :** Tests additional to those prescribed in the standard were made on the tapping tees. These were designed to assess the long-term mechanical strength of joints made on unscraped pipes.

The tubes used for the test were stored for three years, exposed to natural weather conditions. The long-term mechanical strength was measured by the test which we currently consider to be the most discriminating test for tapping tees: the hydraulic pressure test at 9.2 bar, 80°C.

The results obtained with tapping tees currently on the market as well as those obtained on prototype tees incorporating a heating net are reproduced in Table 4.

| Type of tapping tee | Pipe surface preparation | Failure time ( hour ) |
|---|---|---|
| A | No scraping | 0 |
| B | No scraping | 1,9 |
| C | No scraping | 0 |
| Rectangular net | No scraping | 866 |
| Washer - shaped net | No scraping | 1 to 12 |

*Table 4 : Results of a comparative study of the mechanical strength of tapping tees fused onto unscraped tubes.*

It can be observed that the results obtained with tees equipped with a net implanted in the form of a rectangle are very clearly better than those obtained with the other fittings.

The results obtained with the prototypes equipped with a washer-shaped net are clearly not as good and are in fact below specification (170 hours). Their times-to-failure however are better than those obtained with the conventional fittings.

**Time to appearance of short circuits :** Other additional tests made it apparent that the time to appearance of short circuits was inversely proportional to the fusion temperature. It will therefore be possible to interrupt the fusion joining when short circuits arise and thus to regulate the fusion energy according to the fusion temperature.

Furthermore, we found that too shallow an insertion significantly reduced the time to appearance of short circuits. This behavior can be explained by a reduction of the heat transfers from the fitting to the pipe, which causes premature melting of the insulating varnish. Even if the appearance of short circuits is not exploited to control the heating energy, it will be able to serve in detecting inadequate pipe insertion.

## V) CONCLUSIONS AND PROSPECTS

The assessment of prototype fittings having a heating implant consisting of a coated, knitted wire, with well-defined characteristics, shows that they afford the following advantages:

- The heating net offers additional security. Indeed, each intersection of two wires plays the role of a sensor capable of detecting any over-heating: when the varnish melting temperature is reached, the intersection of two wires becomes the seat of a detectable short circuit, thus preventing any risk of local damage to the material of the fitting. This characteristic specific to the "heating net" technology can be used, for example, to detect inadequate insertion of the pipe in the coupling sleeve or other deviations in installation workmanship inducing a significant modification of the heat transfers from the fitting to the pipe.

- The introduction of a heating net near the fusion plane allows to supply a much greater electrical energy per unit area than that supplied by a single coiled wire. Thanks to this, the quality of fusion joining is improved.

In terms of volume production, the manufacturing of the net is based on a fully mastered technology. The fabrication of prototype fittings equipped with nets allows us to envisage, in the context of volume production, the possibility of doing away with the specific steps of injecting an insert and winding the wire, thus providing a cost advantage and enhanced product reliability. It will also be possible to make knitted heating elements in a variety of shapes. It will be possible to capitalize upon this feature to develop new electrofusion products that would be difficult to create by the usual techniques.

The R&D work on this "heating net" technology applied to electrofusion fittings is continuing, in the prospect of pre-industrialization. To this end, it is first of all desirable to have heating nets produced with which a center cold zone in couplings and a still more even distribution of energy in the washer-rings used in tapping tees can be obtained. Thereafter, it will be necessary to tackle the detailed design of a volume production process for implanting the heating net in the fitting. This pre-industrialization work is expected to be completed by the end of 1995.

## REFERENCES:

(1)     D. Gueugnaut, M.Nussbaum Caractérisation des mécanismes du soudage par fusion du polyéthylène. Application à l'électrosoudage. Congrès IGRC 1989.
(2)     D. Dufour, E. Meister Electrosoudage du polyéthylène: modèle de prévision de la qualité d'un soudage. Congrès IGRC 1989.
(3)     D. Gueugnaut, ...Influence des conditions de viellissement du PE sur son comportement au soudage.
(4)     J.C. Hugueny,D. Dufour, Y. Demonchy Fiabilisation des jonctions des tubes en polyéthylène avec des raccords électrosoudables: l'autorégulation.
(5)     D. Dufour, J-C. Hugueny : Un outil pour l'assurance qualité des ouvrages en polyéthylène: le guide de l'électrosoudage.
(6)     T. Picard, ... rapport interne.
(7)     N. Misaka, H. Nishimura: Effect of pipe surface conditions on weld strength for electrofusion fittings.
(8)     Scholten, Rouwenhorst: Electrofusion of PE Pipes, the necessity of a proper surface treatment.

# Annex

**Prototype tapping tee made with a "rectangular" net**

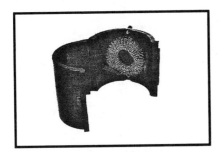
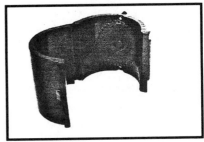

**Prototype tapping tee made with a "washer-like" net**

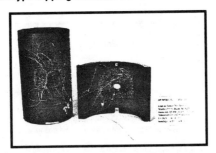

**Fracture surface after a pull-out test**

INSPECTION OF GAS DISTRIBUTION MAINS


L'INSPECTION DES CANAUX
DE DISTRIBUTION D'ESSENCE

Karl F. Kiefer

Invocon, Inc., USA


Dr. Kiran Kothari
Gas Research Institute, USA

ABSTRACT

The U.S. gas distribution industry spends approximately a billion dollars annually forthe replacement of pipes deteriorating as a result of corrosion.  Substantial economic advantages exist in the ability to differentiate between pipe which has an appreciable remaining service life and pipe which requires replacement due to corrosion damage.  Current R & D efforts have demonstrated the feasibility of an ultrasonic inspection imaging system which provides accurate numerical and graphical representations of wall shape, wall thickness and wall defects in buried gas mains.  The inspection system, titled "SIGHT" (Site Inspection of Gas Mains by Helical Tomography), gathers information from the inside of gas mains still in service.  It is composed of an in-pipe imaging unit and an uphole processing/display computer which forms three-dimensional tomogram images of the pipe wall.  Prototype hardware has demonstrated precise resolution and works on all materials used for gas main pipe.  The system control display consists of an easy-to-interpret, interactive graphical user interface which readily alerts the operator to wall thicknesses that are outside acceptable tolerances.

RESUME

L'industrie de la distribution de l'essence des U.S.A. dépense environ un milliare de dollars par ans au remplacement des tuyaux déteriorés à cause de la corrosion.  Des avantages economique considérables existent en la possibilité de differencier un tuyau ayant une duré de vie causé par la corrosion.  Les efforts courrente des Researche et Development ont démontré la possibilité d'un système d'inspection, imagé, ultrasonic qui fournirait des représentations numérique et graphique de la forme de mur, l'épessure du mur et des défauts du mur d'une conduite maîtresse enterré.  Le système d'inspection, "SIGHT" (l'inspection de canalisation d'essence avec Tomographie Helical), rassemble de l'information de l'intérieur de canaux encore en service.  Il est composé d'un appareil pour reproduire, à travess d'un ordinateur à procès/exposition, des images trois-dimensionelles tomogromique du mur du tuyau.  "Prototype Hardware" a démontré des travaux et des résolutions précise sur tout le matérielle utillisé les conduite maîtresse du tuyau d'essence.  Le système de control exposition consiste d'un facile à comprendre, d'un interface graphique interactife qui alerte l'opérateur imédiatement d'une épessure en dehors de la tolérance acceptable du mur.

BACKGROUND

The U.S. gas distribution industry spends approximately a billion dollars every year for replacement of damaged or deteriorating pipes within its complex of some 1,280,000 km [800,000 miles] of distribution mains. Next to third-party damage, the most common causes of main replacement consist of joint leakage in cast iron pipe and corrosion in cast iron and steel pipes. Leak surveillance, statistical data bases, and excavation comprise the traditional approaches for locating, repairing, and replacing leaking pipes.

The industry needs a reliable, cost-effective inspection technology which can operate on in-service gas mains. Ideally, the system should function within the environmental constraints of gas distribution systems and result in the following benefits:

*      reduction in the costs of locating and repairing potential leaks;
*      identification of pipe replacement needs with minimal excavation; and
*      prevention of the replacement of pipe with considerable service life remaining.

TECHNICAL CHALLENGE - GAS MAIN INSPECTION WITH ULTRASONICS

The "SIGHT" sensor consists of a complex system of ultrasonics, digital processing electronics, graphical display processing, and mechanical assemblies. Ultrasonic technology has been used for many non-destructive testing applications for the measurement of wall thickness and flaw detection. In virtually all applications, the surfaces of the materials to be tested are either consistently smooth by nature or are prepared prior to the test so that the surface finish is sufficiently smooth to enhance the coupling of the ultrasonic transducers to the material-under-test (MUT). Further, in conventional applications, fluids are used to provide a low impedance path for transferring the ultrasonic signals from the transducer to the MUT. Since the inside surface of gas main pipe is not smooth and the introduction of fluids into an active gas main is unacceptable, the application of this technology to the measurement of natural gas pipe presented a major coupling challenge.

This problem was first addressed in a small exploratory research project that focused on materials and their ability to couple and pass ultrasonic energy. Several commercially available materials were tested. These included various forms of rubber that were formed into tires for use in continuous ultrasonic scanning operations. Although effective when used with couplent liquids, these materials were not acceptable in dry coupling situations.

The application required a material that had almost fluid characteristics but which could hold a specific shape and resist abrasion. It also had to be non-toxic to humans and non-corrosive to various metals that would be used to fabricate scanning mechanisms. A polymer material was identified that could be molded into complex shapes and had unique physical characteristics that allowed it to mechanically comply with uneven surfaces of material-under-test. The material demonstrated a unique mechanical pass-band that presented a very low impedance to 5 megahertz ultrasonic energy. Dry coupling and transmissivity tests were run on the polymer material and compared to dry coupling tests of commercial materials. The summary results of the comparison tests of dry coupling capability between commercial couplent material and the newly defined polymer couplent are shown in Figures 1a, 1b, and 1c.

Figure 1a

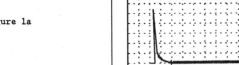

TRAVEL TIME THROUGH RUBBER     TRAVEL TIME THROUGH TEST BLOCK

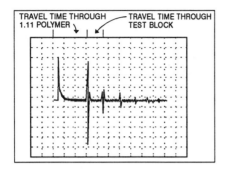

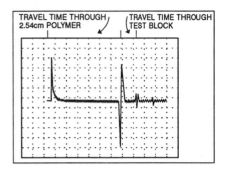

Figure 1b.                                          Figure 1c.

Figure 1a was a test of conventional rubber material that was the best commercially available at the time. The material was effective when used with fluids or greases, but when used dry, it was almost an insulator. The narrow pulse at the left of the trace is the travel time through a rubber sample with a thickness of 0.191 cm (0.075 inches). Thicker samples were tested but would not allow any signal return when forced to couple without fluids. Further, in order to get the return in Figure 2a, twenty pounds per square inch of normal force was required to maintain any coupling at all. The small "dimple" in the waveform (shown by the arrow) is the backwall return from the test block. This is not a useful signal.

Figure 1b is a test of the same block and transducer combination but with a polymer couplent. The couplent sample was 1.111 cm (0.438 inches thick). The peak to the far left is the interface pulse between the transducer and the couplent material. The second peak is the interface between the couplent and the material-under-test. The travel time indicated by this portion of the waveform is the time necessary for the pulse to travel through the couplent material. The next peak is the backwall reflection return from the MUT. The time difference between the second pulse and the third pulse multiplied by the rate of energy travel in the medium is the thickness of the material. Notice the dramatic improvement in signal-to-noise ratio using the polymer couplent.

Figure 1c is another test of polymer couplent. This case used a 2.54 cm (1 inch) thickness of polymer. Note that the increase in thickness resulted in a 38% reduction in amplitude of the backwall signal. However, the signal is still quite useful and would be easily converted and decoded by digital electronics.

In Figures 1b and 1c, the pulses following the first backwall reflection pulse are reverberation pulses from energy trapped in the material-under-test. Each time the input pulse reflects back and forth from the surface to the backwall of the material-under-test, a small portion of this energy escapes and is detected by the transducer. The data shows the efficiency of the coupling material used in a dry environment over the best commercial products available at that time.

To achieve moving scans, a tire assembly was designed that used transducers imbedded into the wheel axle and coupled to the polymer material in the tire by the same dry coupling that would be used between the tire and the material-under-test. Figure 2 shows the tire assembly and the combination of physical compliance and mobile plasticizer that actually makes the material "work" as an ultra-sonic coupling.

The structure of the polymer uses plasticizers to form the rotational bonds that connect the mers and allow them to "rotate." 
This rotation property gives the material the ability to conform to

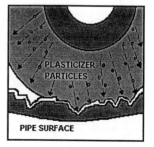

Figure 2. Polymer molded into a tire shape showing "free" plasticizer used to complete the coupling process.

irregular surfaces with very little pressure.  The formulation also provides for an
excess of plasticizer far beyond the amount that can be molecularly bonded into the
polymer matrix.  This plasticizer remains mobile in the material and continues to
appear on the surface as an almost imperceptible film.  This film completes the
coupling process initiated by the physical compliance of the material with the
surface of the material-under-test by filling small interstices that cannot be
filled by the compliant polymer.  Minute quantities of the plasticizer are always
available to "fill in" the small void areas where even the high compliance of the
material cannot provide a complete coupling.

      The combination of high compliance and plasticizer film has provided an
acceptable ultrasonic coupling even on unprepared surfaces.  For use in this
application, the material has been formed into a miniature tire structure that
provides the coupling of the ultrasonic transducer with the material-under-test.
The transducer is housed inside the tire and rides lightly on the inside surface of
the tire.

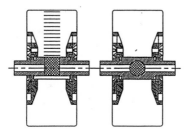

Figure 3.  Mechanical drawing of the tire
showing the location of the transducer
mounted on the axle assembly.

      The outside of the tire is placed lightly on the surface of the material-
under-test and is rolled along.  The tire provides a constant coupling as it moves
over the surface and allows a continual flow of reflection data to be recorded.
Successive passes of the tire over a regular coordinate pattern provides the
ability to create a three-dimensional map of the material-under-test.

      Figure 4 is a composite
of a photograph of the wheel
as it scans a sample section
of used pipe.  For purposes of
tests, a small saw cut was
placed in the cast-iron pipe
on the outside diameter (OD).

      This saw cut is shown
with a mechanical pencil
pointing to the cut both to
identify its location and
provide a comparison of
physical size.
      Along with the photo
of the scan wheel in motion
is a oscilloscope trace of
the rectified analog data
being received at the instant
that the scanning wheel
passed over the saw cut.
As annotated in the figure,
the returns clearly indicate
the backwall of the pipe
sample and the bottom of
the saw cut.  This representative data demonstrated that
it was possible to use the
polymer couplent to scan actual gas mains while moving
and still retain sufficient
signal-to-noise margin to
support automatic detection
and processing.

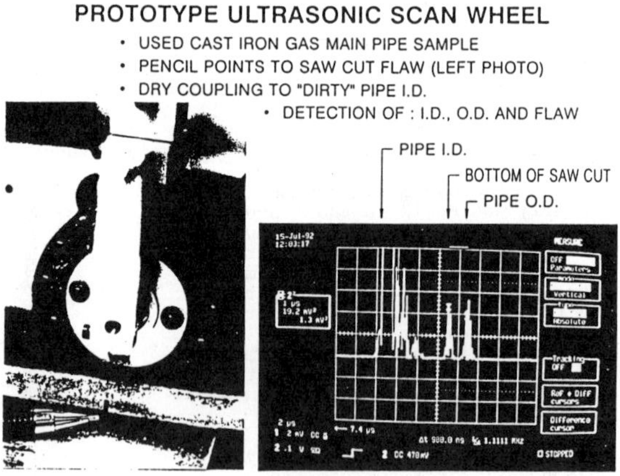

### PROTOTYPE ULTRASONIC SCAN WHEEL

- USED CAST IRON GAS MAIN PIPE SAMPLE
- PENCIL POINTS TO SAW CUT FLAW (LEFT PHOTO)
- DRY COUPLING TO "DIRTY" PIPE I.D.
  - DETECTION OF : I.D., O.D. AND FLAW

Figure 4.  Tire assembly scanning an
actual sample of "used" cast iron pipe.

DEVELOPMENT OF THE TECHNOLOGY

The SIGHT system is a specialized electro-mechanical package that is inserted into working gas mains to collect measurements and graphical images of the condition of the pipe. Designated as "SIGHT" (Site Investigation of Gas Mains by Helical Tomography), the system is composed of two items of equipment: the Down-Hole tool (DHT) and the Operator Display/Control Unit (ODCU). The DHT is inserted into the gas main to be surveyed while the ODCU remains on the surface in the support vehicle. Propulsion in the pipe is provided by an operator-controlled push rod system under development by PLS International.

Three-dimensional images (tomograms) are presented on the ODCU (Operator Display and Control Unit) computer screen showing the inside diameter (ID), outside diameter (OD), and corrosive flaws within the pipe wall. The tomogram image is derived from the measurements taken from the attenuation of focused non-destructive energy. The process can be implemented by separate transmitters and receivers or by transmitting and receiving reflected energy. The energy is passed through the material-under-test in a specific pattern with rotational redundancy. The image of the material can then be reconstructed by computerized manipulation of the successive sets of attenuation data. These techniques are common in medical CAT scans and precision measurement of aircraft engine components.

The presentations to the operator are an oblique side-view of the pipe, a cross-sectional view, and several composite scans of the pipe surface that can be rotated for convenient viewing. As the scan is being collected down-hole, it is processed and then appears on the screen, in near real time, as a thin multi-colored tape that is wound in a helical pattern across the screen to form the oblique image of the pipe. The colored sections of the tape and the subsequent pipe image on the screen are visual codes that specify the actual thickness of the pipe wall at a given location. (Reference Figure 5. Colors appear as a grey scale here since the reproduction format is restricted to black and white.) Simultaneously, a cross-sectional view of the pipe is drawn to scale that shows the actual wall thickness of the pipe at the scan location.

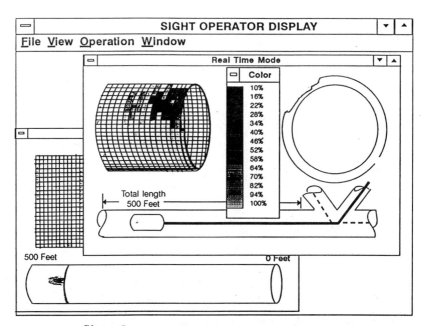

Figure 5. An example ODCU Screen showing both
the display of the oblique view tomogram, the
cross-sectional view of the wall thickness,
and the "Windows" format that provides
mouse control over the DHT.

The down-hole tool sends survey data to the up-hole operator display/control unit (ODCU). The operator hardware then forms tomogram and video images of the inside and outside of the pipe wall. The example screen in Figure 5 shows the tomogram portion of the tool output during a survey. Ultrasonic transducers mounted in the center rotating assembly of the DHT, shoot beams of ultrasonic energy into the pipe wall as the unit moves forward through the pipe. The resultant scanning pattern is helical. The reflected energy from the outside diameter (OD) of the pipe is captured, encoded, and routed to the up-hole operator unit. The encoded energy is then mathematically processed to form graphical images of the pipe wall that are both spatially and numerically correct. Engineering model hardware has demonstrated thickness resolutions of <0.025 cm [0.01 inches].

Measurements that are used to form the tomogram are made from time-of-flight (TOF) data of ultrasonic pulses. The pulses are placed into the pipe wall at high frequency and in a regular pattern. The down-hole computers measure the time necessary for the pulse to enter the pipe wall, reflect off of the OD of the pipe and return to the transducer. Since the speed of sound in the material is known precision values of wall thickness can be calculated from TOF data.

The technique will operate on all materials used in the construction of gas main pipe: cast iron, steel and plastic. The display is easy to interpret and performs audio and visual alerts for the operator when wall thicknesses that are outside acceptable tolerances are encountered by the survey. The display also provides the control format and the human interface for the tool. Operator commands to the tool such as "go," "stop," "scan," "re-run," etc. are all performed from the screen with a mouse device.

## PRECISION MEASUREMENT VS VIDEO INSPECTION?

Alternative technical approaches to gas main inspection were addressed at the outset of the R&D program. One of the most intently debated questions was whether or not real-time video would ultimately be acceptable as a single sensor inspection technique. The issue mainly concerned new high technology CATV systems that can recover video images of the inside of gas mains with a miniature camera mounted on the end of a push rod. The operational tradeoffs indicated that the SIGHT technology and the video imaging are complementary because they report very different information. No duplication exists because the CATV cannot "see" through the pipe walls and provide estimates of the degrading forces at work on the outside diameter (OD) of the pipe. Conversely, ultrasonics cannot generate real-time pictures of the internal pipe environment. Both types of information make significant contributions to the inspection process and both capabilities are designed into the tool. Video provides quick visual inspection of the interior of the pipe while the SIGHT technology looks through the wall of the pipe and provides precision wall thickness data from which remaining service life can be extrapolated.

Proper inspection of the pipe must include scrutiny of the outside surface. It is not uncommon for gas mains to have a severely decomposed outside diameter while the inside surface remains virtually free of flaws. A high percentage methane environment with no free oxygen protects the internal pipe walls from most corrosion processes. Conversely, environmental processes (both natural and man-made) can cause the outside of the pipe to degrade more rapidly than the inside. The CATV sees only the inside of the pipe where age damage to the main is least likely. The unprotected exterior of the pipe is exposed to all the corrosion and oxidation mechanisms that nature has to offer. Therefore if the remaining service life of the pipe is to be determined, precision measurement of the pipe OD is required.

The SIGHT technology fulfills this need by measuring and mapping the wall thickness to tolerances within 0.0254 cm [0.01 inches]. (Measurements of 0.00254 cm [0.001 inch] have routinely been achieved in laboratory simulations. Operational precision has yet to be determined.)

## SYSTEM DESCRIPTION

As previously mentioned, two major items of hardware comprise the SIGHT system: the down-hole tool and the surface display unit. The down-hole tool (DHT) is responsible for all data acquisition and data transmission to the surface. The ODCU (operator display and control unit) handles all data communications from the DHT, data processing, data base storage, operator commands, and generation of pipe wall images for immediate viewing of the section under inspection. Data from the down-hole unit will be returned to the surface using conductors located in the push rod assembly.

The DHT is the transportation mechanism for the sensors and electronics. It

provides the support mechanisms required for the unit to remain centered in the
pipe, to transit the pipe, and for the rotational movement of the scanning wheels.
The mechanical hardware also provides the roller couplent (polymer tire) that forms
the compliant interface for coupling the imaging energy from the ultrasonic
transducer into the pipe and from the pipe back to the transducer with sufficient
strength for detection.

Imaging transducers and position sensors make up the sensor suite. The
position sensors allow the system to maintain a constant reference in space for
accurately matching the "pictures" to the location of the pipe in the ground.
Also, environmental sensors such as a temperature, humidity, pressure, gravity, and
noise are included for reference.

The information from the imaging transducers is passed to the DSP module
where it is buffered, processed, and compressed. The compressed data is then
transferred to the surface via the communications electronics. These electronics
also perform all data formatting and EDC (error detection and correction). The EDC
function insures that only error-free data will be received by the ODCU. The
imaging function, within the ODCU computer, resolves the raw image data and
positional data so that a reconstructed "picture" of the pipe appears as clear and
dimensionally accurate as possible. The image processing also filters incoming
data and assigns identification tags that will allow the system manager to display
multicolored images of the pipe and the flaws it contains. In addition, actual
numerical dimension data is stored and can be recalled in numerical or graphical
form for each scan interval.

## THE Operator Display and Control Unit (ODCU)

The ODCU main processor will be a RISC (Reduced Instruction Set Computer)
with a custom video processing capability attached to the high speed local bus.
The RISC is required because of the processing speed needed for the complex real-
time video display. The commercialized system will use "industrial strength"
computer assemblies due to the mobile environment of the SIGHT support vehicles.
This same industrial specification would also be placed on the video recording
equipment that will be in support of the scanning operation.

Total operator control of the system is through a "mouse" or mouse-related
device. The operator will be prompted by direct interaction with the display
screens as well as the video presentation. Using visual cues from both these
media, the operator will guide the tool into the pipe and then begin the scanning
operation upon withdrawal. All operator interaction with the ODCU will be through
the Windows operating system visual and manual protocols. Both keyboard control or
complete mouse control or any combination of both will be available to the
operator. Help menus will be available at all times as well as the prompt menus
that can be used for normal operation. As in all other Windows control
applications, the prompt menus can be bypassed as the operator becomes more highly
skilled in the operation of the system.

The physical location of the operator and the ODCU will be inside a support
vehicle. This protected location will dramatically reduce the development costs of
the ODCU electronics and the video equipment because it removes the immersion proof
specifications needed if electrical equipment is required to operate unprotected.
The support vehicle will also house and transport the coiled push rod insertion
equipment as well as the mechanical injection head that pushes and pulls the rod
into and out of the gas main.

## Down-Hole tool (DHT)

A mechanical drawing of the DHT developmental engineering model is pictured in
Figure 6. Small wheels are placed on spring loaded whiskers on both ends of the
carrier to maintain the down-hole unit in the center of the pipe. The wheels are
coupled to rotation sensors that track the exact axial movement of the unit as it
travels down the pipe. This positional data is used by the Scan Data processing
module to correct the longitudinal position of the scan data. The wheels also
negate the torque effects of the scan rollers. This prevents the DHT from
"corkscrewing" in the pipe as it moves.

In the center section of the tool are the scan wheels. Each scan wheel
contains the ultrasonic transducer that transmits and receives the sound pulses
that are used to measure the pipe walls. The tires for the wheel are made of the
compliant polymer (couplent) developed in the early stages of the project. The
transducers are mounted in the hub of the wheel and therefore do not rotate with
the tire assembly. This assures that the transducer is always directed at the ID
of the pipe at the proper angle. Figure 3 shows the mechanical drawing of the
wheel, transducer, and tire.

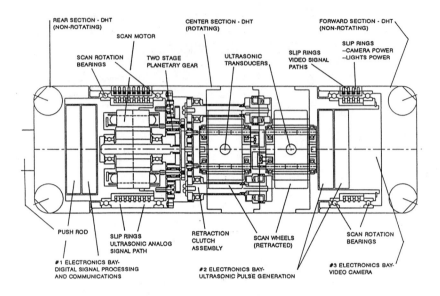

**Figure 6.  SIGHT - DHT (Down-Hole tool)**

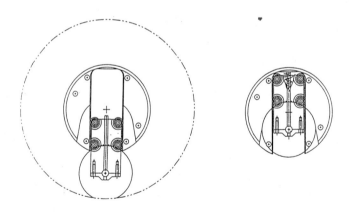

**Figure 7.  Scan Wheels shown on the extension
tracks that provide extension and retraction.
One wheel is shown in the extended position
and the other wheel is shown retracted.**

Figure 7 shows the scanning wheels mounted on the extension forks.  These
forks hold the wheels against the ID of the pipe wall when the tool is in
operation.  The wheels are withdrawn into protected recesses in the side of the DHT
when the tool is quickly slewed to a new location in the pipe.  This retraction
command function can be done by the operator at any time.  The extension tracks
that guide the extension forks are located within the rotating section of the tool.
This section is in the center and is rotated by the motor and planetary gear train.

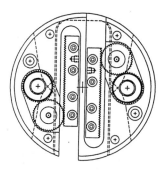

Figure 8.  The section of the DHT
that houses the rack-and-pinion
gearing that provides the extension
and retraction of the ultrasonic
scan wheel assemblies.

Figure 8 shows the extension and retraction rack-and-pinion gearing.  These gears are turned through a uni-directional clutch that slips in the extension position and locks in the retraction position. This provides the retraction drive when the motor is reversed.  As the center section is rotated, the scan wheels are extended into contact with the ID of the pipe.  They are then rotated by friction with the wall and thereby provide a moving ultrasonic coupling between the pipe wall and the transducer.

The mounts of the extension arms must be precise so as to preclude any movement of the arm when extended.  Movement of this sort could cause misalignment of the transducer relative to the pipe wall.  Radial pressure on the wheel to consistently contact the ID of the pipe is provided by rotational energy from the scan motor.  The rotation energy is converted to a radial vector by means of the retraction slip clutch assembly located in the pinion gear of the rack-and-pinion assembly.  The tighter the setting of the clutch, the more radial extension force is placed on the scan wheels.

The scan motor is a low voltage, electrically commutated DC motor located in the rear section of the DHT.  (See Figure 6.)  The scan motor can be reversed at any time under operator control.  It is a very efficient device that produces a lot of power from a very small space.  It manages this by use of high technology magnets and by operating at a high RPM (7,000 RPM nominal speed).  Since this is much too high for the scanning wheels that are designed to operate at less than 200 RPM, the speed of the motor must be reduced by a gearbox.  The gear train that does this job is a two-stage planetary and is also used to drive the slip clutches that convert scan rotation to radial force to pre-load the scan wheels.  (See Figure 9.) The scan motor speed is controlled by a pulse width modulator that effectively limits the current to the motor while allowing conduction to occur at the rated voltage.

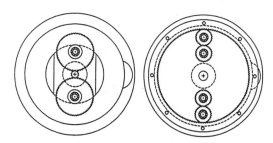

Figure 9.  The two-stage planetary gear speed
reduction mechanism.

The OD of the scan wheel tire is pressed against the ID of the pipe with force from the slip clutch assembly that converts motor torque to consistent radial pressure through the rack-and-pinion extension mechanism.  The rotary motion for this function is provided from a gear interconnect located in the planetary gear box.  Two short, low speed shafts transfer the low RPM rotation directly to the clutch and wheel extension mechanism.  The constant drag of the clutch insures a constant contact between the pipe wall and the scan wheel.

As previously stated, counter-rotation of the complete down-hole assembly due to the torque of the scan wheel section of the tool is prevented by the friction of the axial position centering wheels on the end of the "whiskers." When it is necessary to retract the wheels for rapid movement down the pipe, the scan motor is reversed for a few revolutions. This action pulls in the scan wheels to their protected location. When rotation is again reversed, the wheels will deploy to their working positions against the pipe wall.

The scan motor power supply is also a speed and torque controller. The circuitry is located up-hole as a part of the ODCU. It is capable of modulating the input drive current to the motor to change the speed output as well as providing the change in input voltage polarity that reverses the direction of rotation of the scan motor. Further, the controller is a closed loop speed control device. Since a constant RPM must be maintained to keep the scan data spatially consistent the controller must sense changes in the scan speed. For example, if the scan wheels encounter increasing resistance to movement, the motor rpm will be reduced unless the input drive current is increased. Thus the controller must monitor motor speed and vary drive current as necessary to maintain constant RPM. If the controller determines that the speed reduction in the motor is beyond compensation, it must alert the processor that a problem exists that must be corrected by the operator. This capability in the motor control circuits relieves the DHT control computer from the speed control responsibility.

The down-hole tool contains three electronics bays. (See Figure 6.) One is for digital data processing. It is located at the rear of the tool where there is easy wiring access to the push rod interface. The second is for housing and shielding the high voltage pulse generation for the ultrasonic transmitter. Electrically speaking, generating pulses of 450 volts that only last for 70 nanoseconds is a noisy operation. The rapid voltage changes radiate wide band RF energy quite efficiently. This is not a desirable condition and thus the area in the #2 bay is a shielded compartment for the pulse generators. To simplify the interconnection of the high voltage pulses from the electronics to the transducers, the electronics in the #2 bay rotate with the scan wheels. The receiver data is amplified and sent to the #1 bay via slip rings designed into the housing. The #3 bay is the extreme forward section of the down-hole unit. It contains the CATV and its support electronics. This section of the DHT does not rotate so the camera remains stable.

Data and process control management are directed by a multiprocessor control architecture resident in the DHT. The subsystem is made up of a high speed digital signal processor (DSP) and a conventional microprocessor. The DSP handles all the high speed data flow from the ultrasonic receiver as it is converted from analog to digital. The microprocessor manages the communications and the control decoding and implementation. The DSP high speed processing is used to minimize the data rates on the communications link from the DHT to the ODCU. The DSP is slaved to the microprocessor and the operating system is always executed from the microprocessor.

## THE PROJECTED COMMERCIAL ROLE OF THE SENSOR IN PRACTICAL USE

Leak history data shows that the pipe degradation processes that ultimately result in leaks strongly correlate with local conditions of contamination, electrochemical, or physical stress processes. When a leak occurs, historical evidence indicates that the degradation processes causing the leak do not cover long lengths of pipe, nor are they evenly distributed. Instead, the leak-producing mechanisms are most often restricted to a few meters.

The data that supports this premise has been collected by another GRI program aimed at the study of recovered pipe. The amount of available data in comparison to the amount of pipe in the ground is so small that there is no assurance that a statistically sound sample data set exists. However, data gathered to date seems to agree with the statistical data in utility "leak" database files. In an attempt to gather statistically significant data, GRI continues to support a project that carefully excavates used pipe to determine the nature and condition of mains that have been in service for long periods of time. Further, there are studies in place that use the exhumed pipe to evaluate various degradation mechanisms.

Currently, leak history database procedures are the only mechanism to predict whether the degradation mechanism causing the leak is localized or widespread. The "first" leak in a large run of pipe has no predictive value. Many leaks must accrue to indicate a problem. Visual inspection can only be done when the leak is excavated for remedial action. Even after excavation, only 1 to 3 meters of pipe is usually uncovered. This limited exposure provides very little information on the condition of the pipe within 100 meters or so on either side of the leak.

When leaks due to external corrosion occur, the probability that another leak will occur in that same vicinity within a short period of time in the same local area is a serious concern.

Pipe examples from the pipe recovery project indicate that degradation appears in localized areas. In several samples, severe corrosion had attacked localized areas ranging from 15 to 60 m [50 to 200 feet] in length. Pipe recovered from areas adjacent to the badly damaged sections was virtually flawless even after forty years of service. In several areas, corrosion had removed the total wall resulting in crater-shaped leaks. Within the local "group" area of degradation, other crater-shaped flaws existed that would become leaks within a very short period of time.

At least one scenario for the use of the SIGHT technology consists of using the tool for surveys in conjunction with the excavation and repair of "first" leaks. These areas would be defined as leak locations where a "leak history" database does not show multiple occurrences in a localized area. In this case, no evidence exists on which to formulate an educated plan of action for simple repair of the single leak or replacement of a potential problem area.

When a known leak requires excavation to repair, the SIGHT tool would be used to determine the condition of the pipe for 150 m [500 feet] in both directions. This would establish whether a single local repair would suffice or whether many more leaks are imminent. If the condition of the pipe for some distance in each direction from the leak is badly degraded, then replacement of the entire area would be prudent. If the area adjacent to the leak was in good condition, a single repair procedure would insure many more years of trouble-free service from the area. In this way, the SIGHT system would provide the following operational and cost advantages:

1) Leak repair activities provide "free" entry points for the acquisition of valuable information. If the survey is conducted using the same entry hole as the repair excavation, no excavation cost is assigned to the survey because the hole was already necessitated by the leak.

2) Some sort of a sleeve device is usually installed on the pipe to repair the leak. Since the SIGHT tool entry hardware uses a sleeve, part of the entry hardware can be retained after the survey as a permanent leak repair. Thus, the cost of the permanently installed section of the entry tool is reduced by the cost of a "standard" leak repair fixture.

3) Procedural surveys of leak areas where decision making information is unavailable insures that use of the tool occurs where the need is great and the relative value of the survey information is the highest.

PROJECT STATUS

The work accomplished to date has demonstrated the feasibility of an ultrasonic/video inspection imaging system to provide accurate, numerical data and graphical representations of wall shape, wall thickness and wall defects in buried gas mains. The information can be taken from the inside gas mains without interruption of service to customers.

The first engineering prototype of the DHT was mechanically completed in April 1995. This prototype has been installed in a test fixture that has the ability to accept many different samples of pipe that have been excavated after being retired from service. The engineering tool is the in-house development platform for software that will reside and operate down-hole. After software development is complete in October of 1995, the tool will be modified for runs in long sections of excavated pipe. It will then be integrated with an insertion and propulsion system in preparation for the first field experiments.

REFERENCES

1.    Invocon, Inc. and Maurer Engineering, Inc. *Final Report - Site Inspection of Gas Mains by Helical Tomography (SIGHT) Phase 0*. Chicago:  Gas Research Institute, 1994.

2.    Invocon, Inc. and Maurer Engineering, Inc. *Final Report - Site Inspection of Gas Mains by Helical Tomography (SIGHT) Phase 1*. Chicago:  Gas Research Institute, 1994.

DEVELOPMENT OF A PIPE RENEWAL SYSTEM
FOR HIGH PRESSURE GAS LINES


DEVELOPPEMENT D'UN SYSTEME DE RENOUVELLEMENT DE TUYAUX
POUR CANALISATIONS DE GAZ A HAUTE PRESSION

Franklin T. Driver
Paltem Systems, Inc.

Steven Gauthier
Gas Research Institute

Steven Lawrence
Pacific Gas & Electric

## ABSTRACT

Many high pressure feeder mains have been in the ground 30 to 40 years, or longer, and are in need of rehabilitation or replacement. Currently, the only viable method of rehabilitation/replacement is by open-cut excavation to replace the old pipe with new. This paper details the development of a pipe renewal system that adds structural integrity to existing high pressure gas lines, extending their useful life, as well as adding the capability to withstand significant stress caused by earthquakes and other outside forces without suffering a major rupture in the line. This system is a cured-in-place flexible high strength liner that will be installed using the liner inversion process, similar to the Pal-Liner process, which was developed for gas distribution lines. It was developed for gas pipes up to 610 mm (24 inches) in diameter with operating pressures up to 30 bar (450 psig).


## RÉSUMÉ

La plupart des canalisations de gaz à haute pression ont été sous terre pendant 30 à 40 ans ou davantage et nécessitent d'être rénovées ou remplacées. Actuellement, la seule méthode de rénovation/remplacement viable est par la méthode d'excavation à ciel ouvert pour remplacer les anciens tuyaux par des nouveaux. Cet exposé décrit en détail le développement d'un système de renouvellement de tuyaux qui apporte une intégrité structurelle aux canalisations de gaz à haute pression existantes, afin de prolonger leur durée de vie utile. Ce système apporte également une capacité de résistance supplémentaire aux importantes contraintes causées par des tremblements de terre ou par d'autres forces extérieures sans que les tuyaux ne souffrent de rupture majeure. Ce système consiste en un tubage de revêtement flexible extrêmement résistant durci en place et installé à l'aide du procédé d'inversion de tubage, similaire au procédé Pal-Liner, qui a été développé spécialement pour les canalisations de distribution de gaz. Ce système a été développé pour les tuyaux à gaz d'un diamètre maximum de 610 mm avec des pressions de fonctionnement pouvant atteindre jusqu' à 450 psig.

## BACKGROUND

Pacific Gas and Electric Company (PG&E), GRI, and Paltem Systems, Inc. (PSI) have been involved, with Ashimori Industries Company, Ltd., in the development and testing of a cured-in-place-pipe renewal product for use in natural gas applications at up to 28 bar (400 psig). Other GRI member gas companies, notably Consolidated Edison of New York (Con Ed), Public Service Electric and Gas Company of New Jersey (PSE&G), and Brooklyn Union have also contributed input to the functional specification for this product.

Pacific Gas and Electric Company, one of the US's largest investor owned utilities, serves gas to 3.5 million customers in northern and central California. The widespread service territory varies from open desert to rich agricultural lands to densely populated cities of the San Francisco Bay Area, and is covered by approximately 8,047 kilometers (5,000 miles) of transmission pipelines and 53,107 kilometers (33,000 miles) of distribution mains.

In 1985, PG&E started a 25-year program to replace or revitalize approximately 4,023 kilometers (2,500 miles) of aging gas mains and lines throughout its service territory in order to maintain a safe and reliable gas system. The initial program called for replacement of all cast iron distribution mains, most steel mains installed prior to 1931, and many older transmission lines which have outdated girth welds or girth joining methods which could be subject to damage in the event of earthquake, earth settling or movement, or other high-stress conditions.

Most of the replacement work, naturally, is in the older urban areas such as the Bay Area of San Francisco. In these areas open-cut replacement is not only very costly, but also results in a very high adverse impact on the community (gas industry customers) due to street closures, traffic congestion, loss of business, construction noise, and the deterioration to street surfaces.

The potential market for trenchless renewal systems is very large. For instance, at the present time, less than half of PG&E's originally planned replacement work has been completed, leaving an estimated $1.6 billion of pipe replacement to be completed over the next 15 years, or $100 million per year. Trenching, backfilling, and repaving represent the major costs in the projected work, if open-cut methods are used.

## TRENCHLESS RENOVATION AT PG&E

PG&E has successfully used trenchless construction/renovation methods for many years. Since the early 70's, one principal method of replacing low-pressure gas mains has been by sliplining with polyethylene plastic and upgrading the system pressures to maintain flow capacity. Since the beginning of its replacement program PG&E has also experimented with pipe-bursting methods, live-insertion methods, and sliplining with steel-in-steel for transmission line replacement.

These methods have proven very useful and have saved considerable expense compared to open-cut replacement. However, these methods have limitations which make their use impractical in many jobs. Other methods, including cured-in-place liners, close-fit polyethylene liners, internal welding, etc., appear to also have significant potential to reduce the costs and impacts of replacement.

As PG&E searched for practical trenchless solutions for pipeline replacement or revitalization, through various contacts and conferences, including national and international No-Dig conferences, it became clear that several other gas companies were also looking for trenchless solutions. In 1992, representatives of five gas companies (PG&E, Brooklyn Union, Con Ed, PSE&G, and Southern California Gas Company) met in San Francisco and formulated a consensus agenda of trenchless technology issues. In subsequent meetings of these five gas companies with GRI, at a GRI Project Advisory Group meeting and at the 1992 No-Dig Conference, GRI's present program in trenchless technology development efforts was formulated.

GRI has facilitated and sponsored test installations of various trenchless gas main renovation methods with ten member companies, as well as testing and development of liner materials, service tapping and connection methods and fittings, internal inspection methods and tools, and gas service pipe relining and renovation methods.

PG&E is actively pursuing such trenchless renovation methods as sliplining with both plastic and steel (depending on the operating pressure of the line), relining with cured-in-place pipe and with close-fit polyethylene pipe, gas service relining and renovation, and internal weld repair. Some of these are in regular use, while others are in the initial demonstration stage, and others such as service relining are being evaluated to resolve technical and other issues.

## TRANSMISSION PRESSURE LINERS

At PG&E, major transmission trunklines bring gas into its service territory from its principal sources in Canada and the US Southwest, and from its storage fields, at pressures ranging from 55 bar (800 psig) to 149 bar (2160 psig). The gas is moved from principal terminals to the many communities and load centers in PG&E's territory in intermediate-pressure feeder lines at pressures ranging from just over 7 bar (100 psig) to 50 bar (720 psig).

PG&E designates pressures over the 4 bar (60 psig) standard distribution "high pressure" as transmission pressures. This designation is not universal, and many gas companies classify pressures in the neighborhood of 7 to 10 bar (100 or 150 psig) and often higher as distribution feeder pressures.

Many of the older transmission and distribution feeder pipelines in the PG&E system, as well as nationwide, were built in the years between the early use of natural gas (as opposed to manufactured or "town" gas), or in the late 20's or early 30's to World War II. These lines are typically fairly new, large diameter, 406 to 762 mm (16 to 30-inch), and range in pressures from around 10 bar (150 psig) to about 31 bar (450 psig). A high percentage of the older pipelines designated for replacement in PG&E's pipeline replacement program fall into this category. Many of these lines are also now located in built-up urban and suburban areas, where construction costs are quite high and environmental impacts of cut-and-cover construction are high. For this reason, development of methods to revitalize pipelines for operation at up to about 28 bar (400 psig) is a high priority.

## COMPETITION AND THE CHANGING UTILITY WORLD

Another major factor playing a role in the market for renovation methods in the gas industry is competition. There has been much discussion recently about competition in the utility industry. In the decision to replace or renovate gas mains and pipelines, competition does not represent just a theoretical discussion, but has a real and fundamental role.

Under the old regulated utility or "rate-base economics" paradigm in the utility industry, capital investment was good. Investment programs like pipeline or other plant-replacement programs were not only good to assure that the infrastructure was kept fairly new, fully serviceable, and as safe as technologically possible; they also "renewed" the capital plant rate base periodically and helped maintain earnings. In other words, when you are allowed to set your rates based on earning some return on the total capital value of your rate base, spending money to put new pipe in the ground not only increases the safety and reliability of your system, it increases your profits too.

The world is now changing. Over several years, Federal and State regulatory actions have opened the gas business to competition. Where once a gas distribution company bought, transported, and distributed gas to all of "their" customers, and had a monopoly franchise and obligation to do so, it now often only transports someone else's gas to their customers. And competitors now want to build pipelines and compete for the right to transport that gas too.

Under these conditions, price becomes an object, and maybe the most important object, to the person who is making the purchasing decision. In such a world, it does not pay to add capital plant, increase the rate base, and thus increase the price. The desirable condition is, rather, to keep the pipeline system viable and safe at the least practical cost, thus keeping the transport price low and competitive.

## SPECIFICATION DEVELOPMENT

In PG&E's search for renovation methods, it became obvious very early on that they needed to clearly define what was meant by renovation, or what a sufficient renovation product must do. While the result of a replacement program is very clearly and simply a new pipe, the product of a renovation program or revitalization program must be defined in terms of performance.

To do this, PG&E put together a cross-functional task group within the company, with representatives from R&D, Engineering, and Construction. The task group looked at various pipe relining technologies, in order to identify issues which might be common to all, or peculiar to only one, or to one type. They also wrote a test specification for internal liners, to define and quantify the properties that they wanted the renovated line to have, or more importantly, the tests which they wanted the liner to pass.

Although it was not considered practical at this time to propose this as an industry-wide specification, the draft was circulated to the "five companies" and GRI for comments, and their comments were considered in formulation of the specifications as stands at this time.

Basically, this specification requires three things: strength adequate to safely carry the design operating pressure of the pipeline even if the body of the pipeline is partially deteriorated; flexibility to allow the liner to maintain the gas-tight integrity of the pipeline at maximum operating pressure in spite of potential failures due to settling or ground movement; and the ability to withstand aging or chemical factors such as pipeline liquids, etc., without serious deterioration.

The basic tests to determine if a pipe lining system meets these specifications are as follows:

Strength. The liner will be installed in a test segment which has one 100 mm (4-inch) diameter hole (to represent a large pit) and a 50 mm (2-inch) full-circumference gap. The liner is then required to not fail when tested to a pressure two (2) times the MAOP (Maximum Allowable Operating Pressure) of the pipe for a period of one hour. For a liner to qualify for use in a 28 bar (400-psig) pipeline, it must withstand 55 bar (800 psig) for one hour.

Flexibility. The liner is installed in a test piece consisting of two pieces of pipe butted together at the center. The test piece is then blind-flanged, and pressured to the full MAOP of the line. The liner must hold that pressure while the two pieces are pulled apart so as to be separated by 50 mm (2-inches), or are bent at the center to an angle of about 5-degrees. The liner must hold the pressure without failing for an extended period of time (originally set at 24 hours).

Chemical Resistance and Life. The liner must be shown to not deteriorate when subjected to various petroleum and other liquids which may be encountered in gas pipelines.

## DEVELOPMENT OF A 28 BAR (400-PSIG) LINER

During the 1993 No-Dig International Conference in England, a paper was presented on the testing of a Paltem liner for service at about 28 bar (400-psig) in a water system in France. The possibility of developing such a product for gas use was discussed by the PG&E and Con Ed representatives at the conference, and discussions with Paltem Systems in the US were begun.

GRI, working with PG&E and other gas utilities, in the Spring of 1994 asked PSI for a proposal for the Development of a High Pressure Hose Lining Material for Natural Gas Pipelines to be based upon the inversion lining technique utilized by the Paltem reverse lining process (figure 1).

On September 29, 1994, Paltem Systems, Inc. submitted a proposal to GRI for Material Development and Testing of a Hose Lining System for High Pressure Gas Pipelines. The proposed hose lining material was developed as a trenchless technology system for the renewal of gas distribution pipelines operating at pressures up to 31 bar (450 psig). The hose lining material was designed to seal pipes against internal corrosion, stop existing leaks and reduce the risk of future leaks. In addition, the hose lining material was designed to prevent leaks in gas lines subject to earth movements. This specially circular woven hose jacket was designed to withstand both circumferential and axial forces on the hose line due to holes and gaps in the pipeline walls as well as pipeline movements. The circular woven hose jacket is coated with an elastomeric skin which is compatible with the intended use.

## A GENERAL STATEMENT OF THE MATERIAL TESTING & DEVELOPMENT PROGRAM DEVELOPMENT BY ASHIMORI

Ashimori Industry Company Limited (AICL), and Ashimori Europe International Limited, in cooperation with PSI, has designed, developed and fabricated a liner system to rehabilitate natural gas transmission pipelines with a MAOP of 31 bar (450 psig), in diameters up to 610 mm (24-inches).

## TESTING BY ASHIMORI IN JAPAN

AICL performed product tests to demonstrate material strength on August 24, 1994, at their Osaka facility. This test involved testing the high pressure liner at 62 bar (900 psig) in a not fully deteriorated pipe.

## TESTING BY PALTEM SYSTEMS, INC.

PSI has demonstrated the durability and flexibility of the liner as installed in steel pipe by performing bending and tensile tests while the liner was pressurized to the maximum allowable operating pressures.

## THIRD PARTY LABORATORY TESTING

Under a separate contract with Battelle, testing will be performed to determine the long term performance and life expectancy of the liner.

## PRODUCT TESTING SCHEDULI

Ashimori, at their facility in Osaka, Japan, conducted a pressure test to demonstrate the strength of liner material. The test was conducted on a 610 mm (24-inch) diameter partially deteriorated pipe. To simulate partially deteriorated pipe a test section was made which contained a 50 mm (2-inch) gap between two pipe segments and a 100 mm (4-inch) diameter hole in the pipe body. The material was tested at 62 bar (900 psig) for a period of 1 hour without leaking.

Paltem Systems, Inc., at their facilities in Chesterfield, has performed both a bend test and a tensile test. The purpose of these tests were to demonstrate the flexibility of the liner as installed in steel pipe. The tests were performed while the pipe system was pressurized.

The flexibility testing consists of two tests. One a bend test and the other a tensile test. In the bend test, two continuous steel pipe segments, 3 m (10-feet) in length with a liner installed, were to be bent to form a minimum deflection angle of 10 degrees without leaking. The fully deflected pipe was to be held for a period of 24 hours. In the tensile test two continuous steel pipe segments, each 3 m (10-feet) in length with a liner installed, were to be pulled in tension until there was a minimum separation of 50 mm (2-inches) between the steel pipe segments without leaking for a minimum of 24 hours.

The first materials were received by Paltem Systems, Inc., in October, 1994. In order to perform flexibility tests Paltem Systems, Inc., designed and built a test apparatus. The test apparatus was approximately 9 m (30-feet) in length and 4 m (14-feet) tall and was equipped with six hydraulic cylinders.

The test segments consisted of two 3 m (10-foot) sections of 610 mm (24-inches) diameter plain end and flanged end steel pipe. The 3 m (10-foot) sections of pipe were held together for lining by steel clips welded to the plain ends of the steel pipe. After lining the two test segments, end seals were installed at each of the flanged ends. Prior to placing the test segment in the apparatus specially prepared end flanges were attached to each end of the two test pipe segments.

The steel clips which held the pipe segments together during movement and placement into the test apparatus were cut free prior to the start of the test. In order to bend it to a total deflection angle of 10 degrees, two hydraulic cylinders were attached at the top of the pipe near the plain ends of the pipe. Two additional hydraulic cylinders were placed 180 degrees from the cylinders on the top. The specially prepared end flanges had steel slotted frames which allowed the two pipe segments to pivot around each end of the test frame. The test sections were first brought up to test pressure and then deflected upwards at the center in half inch increments. After each vertical deflection the total deflection angle was calculated as well as the gap at the top of the pipe plain end.

In the tensile test, the pipe test segments were again placed in the test rig and the metal clips removed. Prior to placing the test segment into the test rig the two upper hydraulic cylinders were removed from the test apparatus. Once in the test apparatus the two hydraulic cylinders at the one pivot end were energized to prevent the pipe from separating when pressurized. In the bending tests, both pivot points were pinned to the test frame. In the tensile test, the one pivot point was unpinned and its movement controlled by actuation of two horizontal hydraulic cylinders.

It was initially thought that the internal pressure would cause the pipes to separate to the required 50 mm (2-inch) gap. During the initial test the pipe separated about 19 mm (3/4-inch) and stopped. Although the hydraulic cylinders were backed completely off the end of the flanges, the gap did not grow. The test was stopped and the slotted flanged end frame was welded to the pivot point. This permitted us to apply longitudinal pull on the pipes while they were under pressure. We then continued separating the pipe sections up to the 50 mm (2-inch) separation in 13 mm (1/2-inch) increments.

The original high pressure liners, Pre-Pal-Liner and Pal-Liner GHT, received in October 1994 from AICL did not meet the specifications set forth in the "Proposal for Development of High Pressure Hose Lining Material for Natural Gas Pipelines" submitted to GRI, September 29, 1994.

New material was manufactured by AICL and sent to PSI for testing in January of 1995. This material showed great improvement in performance over the previously tested materials.

An initial bend test at 31 bar (450 psig) failed at a total gap of 51 mm (2.01-inches) and equivalent angle of 4.80°; below the requirements of our proposal to GRI.

Two further tests at 28 bar (400 psig) demonstrated ability to pass the 50 mm (2-inch) gap in a bend configuration although neither pipe was allowed to stay at the 50 mm (2-inch) gap for the full 24 hours. We believe the tests indicate the Pal-liners ability to meet this requirement. Failure of both pipes occurred at total gap greater than 75 mm (3-inch) and equivalent angles greater than 7°.

Bend tests at a reduced pressure of 19 bar (275 psig) showed almost a linear improvement in gap and equivalent angle; i.e.:

28 bar (400 psig): 80 mm (3.15 inch) gap; versus, 19 bar (275 psig): 121 mm (4.78 inches) gap, and 28 bar (400 psig): 7.51°deflection angle; versus, 19 bar (275 psig): 11.44° deflection angle.

At present we believe the existing material qualifies for 21 bar (300 psig), and is very close to qualifying for 28 bar (400 psig) installations. New material has been received at Paltem System's facility in Chesterfield, Missouri, and is scheduled for testing. We believe these new materials will be successfully tested at up to the 31 bar (450 psig) range.

**PROJECT IMPLICATIONS:**

There is substantial network of high pressure gas lines in service with the U.S. gas industry, whether they are called feeder lines, trunk lines or transmission lines. These lines are a vital part of the overall gas distribution system that brings natural gas service to over fifty million gas customers. Many of these pipes are reaching the end of their useful service life, having been in service for as much as 50-60 years, and will have to be renovated or replaced. Due to the age of these pipes they are often now located in built-up urban or suburban areas that represent very high open-cut replacement costs. The cost of pavement cutting and replacement, excavation, shoring, new pipe installation, permitting fees, site restoration, as well as the public ill will resulting from traffic congestion and construction noise, has provided an opportunity to pursue the development, testing and commercialization of the High Pressure Gas Pipe Renewal System.

To evaluate the technical viability and economic savings of this pipe renewal technology field tests are being planned for 1995. Plans are currently being developed to test this system on a 3 kilometer (2 mile) section of 660 mm (26-inch) diameter transmission line, operated by PG&E, which is scheduled to be replaced in 1995. This line was built in 1932 with oxyacetylene welds and bell-bell and chill ring joint configurations. The line is located within a major street in San Francisco in a commercial and residential neighborhood. The road has been recently repaved which would cause additional ill will with the neighborhood, as well as with the city government, if the street were again torn up and traffic disrupted for an extended period of time to replace this pipe. This line is an ideal candidate and a good example of a pipe renewal project that could be quickly and economically addressed through the use of the High Pressure Gas Pipe Renewal System.

The benefits to the gas industry resulting from the development of the High Pressure Gas Pipe Renewal Systems could be substantial. Using as a benchmark the recently completed GRI/Gas Industry technical and economic field evaluations of trenchless pipe renewal systems for gas distribution mains, we can get a feel for the potential cost savings. In this program nine gas utilities evaluated six different pipe renewal systems for gas distribution mains. These evaluations demonstrated cost savings over open-cut replacement of up to fifty-five percent. If similar savings are achievable, which we believe they are, through the use of the High Pressure Gas Pipe Renewal System, the overall cost reduction for O&M and pipe replacement activities for an individual gas utility will be great.

GRI is currently soliciting the participation of additional gas utilities to test and evaluate the High Pressure Gas Pipe Renewal System under field operating conditions.

# HIGH PRESSURE PIPE LINER

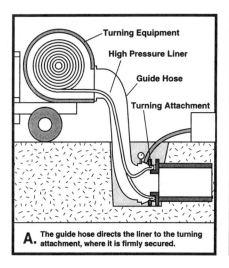

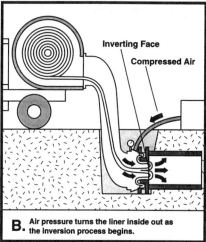

A. The guide hose directs the liner to the turning attachment, where it is firmly secured.

B. Air pressure turns the liner inside out as the inversion process begins.

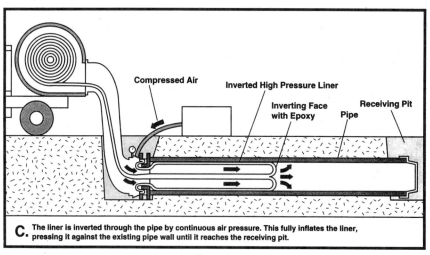

C. The liner is inverted through the pipe by continuous air pressure. This fully inflates the liner, pressing it against the existing pipe wall until it reaches the receiving pit.

Figure 1

INTERNAL SEALING OF CAST IRON MAINS

ETANCHEITE INTERNE DES CANALISATIONS PRINCIPALE EN FONTE

Donald Eagleson

Consumers Gas Company, Canada

## ABSTRACT

Consumers Gas has been using anaerobic sealant to seal leaking cast iron joints since 1987. This process requires that the joint be excavated to allow drilling into the bell and injecting anaerobic sealant into the jute. The anaerobic procedure has a success rate above 90% in terms of leak stoppage and is more cost effective than clamping or encapsulating leaking joints. In 1992 Consumers Gas began working with the Robotics and Automation Laboratory at The University of Toronto, and Engineering Services Incorporated (ESI) to develop a tool that will perform the same repair procedure from the inside of the live gas main. This paper describes many of the design features being designed into the robot.

## RESUME

Consumers Gas utilise un produit anaerobie pour étanché les fuite de gaz provenant des joints dans les canalisation on fonte depuis 1987. Pour sa il faux creuser un trou jusqu'aux joint pour pouvoir percer un trou dan la cloche du joint et introduire le produit anaerobie dans le jute. Se procédé a un succès de 90% en terme d'arrêté la fuite a un coût moins élevé que le système d'agrafage ou d'encapculer. En 1992 Consumer Gas a commence des démarche avec le Département d' Automation et d'Automate de l'Université de Toronto et Engineering Services Incorporated (ESI) pour développé un outil qui pourrai faire les réparation par l'interne sur ligne de gaz vive. Ce papier décrie les caractéristiques du dessein de cette automate.

INTRODUCTION

Consumers Gas attempted a field trial of internally sprayed anaerobic sealants during 1991. The trial had limited success in sealing leaks at the joints and caused problems with anaerobic sealant lodging on the valves of several meters immediately downstream trial site. After the trial, Consumers felt that internally sealing cast iron joints was an approach that had potential but needed further development. The potential to seal several joints from a single excavation while keeping the main in service would reduce our repair costs significantly. Consumers approached ESI and requested their assistance in developing a tool to seal several joints from a single excavation. ESI reviewed the anaerobic sealant procedures and recommended the development of a robot. Inside the live gas main the robot would locate each joint, drill into the jute and inject the sealant from the inside of a live main directly into the jute packing. This approach had a great deal of appeal to Consumers because it duplicates the repair steps being performed during an external repair and reduces the number of excavations.

REQUIREMENTS FOR ANAEROBIC SEALING SYSTEM

During the initial phases of development it was decided that all of the following criteria were important to ensure success.
1. The first robot developed would be for NPS 6 Cast Iron
2. The system must be inserted easily into the cast iron piping system. The tap hole into the main must be less than 80 mm.
3. The robot head must be positioned precisely at the joint.
4. The system must maintain an effective seal between the injection head and the cast iron main. Anaerobic sealant must not be spilled into the gas main.
5. The robot head must be capable of being inserted into the main at least 45 metres.
6. The robot must be capable of being launched in either direction from the tap hole in the main.
7. The gas main will remain live during the repair procedure.
8. The robot must easily cleaned.
9. The drill bit must drill a minimum of 15 joints before exchange.
10. Wherever possible the tool is to be automated.
11. The final product must be easy to operate.

PROTOTYPE TESTING

During April 1994 a prototype tool was tested for proof of concept. This testing while not a complete success did indicate that the concept had considerable merit. The problems, solutions and successes were:
1. Rust and drilling debris accumulated on the top of the robot head and prevented an effective seal during the injection phase. The accumulation of this debris and sealant leakage made each successive joint that the robot attempted more prone to sealant leakage.

2. The video image of the robot head next to the pipe joint was not sufficiently effective to position the robot accurately.

3. The total overall height of the robot was slightly larger than the internal diameter of some sections of cast iron. The height of the robot has been has been reduced to allow for larger variances in the internal diameter of cast iron mains.

4. The position of the video camera did not allow the operator to see the full circumference of the main. The camera position has been changed and a special lens has been incorporated to give a full view of the inside of the main.

5. The sealant set up prematurly restricting the length of operation.

6. The insertion of the robot into the main was a complete success. Consumers was able to insert the robot approximately 40 metres into an abandoned NPS 6 main. This main was installed on an incline that increased in height approximately 3 metres. The robot drilled the main at this point without problem.

7. The umbilical cable delivery system operated according to the design with no problems.

CURRENT PROJECT STATUS

The components of the redesigned tool head are currently being machined. Delivery of the components is expected in June 1995. Field trials will begin shortly thereafter.

TOOL OPERATION

The basic operation of the tool begins with installing a special tapping saddle over the main then tapping a 76 mm hole at a 45 degree angle into a live NPS 6 cast iron main. This tapping saddle has been designed to work a with Mueller R Drilling and Tapping machine. The robot head is inserted through the tap, the support arms are extended and the umbilical cable pushes the robot into the main. The tool is operated remotely using a control box and video monitor. The operator locates the joint, positions the robot at the joint. The drill head is then raised into position to drill into the joint. The drill bit has been designed to allow it to penetrate the spigot pipe wall but not be long enough to penetrate the bell pipe wall. The drill bit is shaped to prepare a chamfer on the hole. This chamfer provides a smooth clean surface for the sealant head gasket. The thrust actuator lowers the robot head but keeps the entire assembly firmly in place. The sealant head is then rotated into position and the thrust actuator is engaged to firmly press the sealant head against the main. A measured amount of sealant is injected into the joint. The thrust actuator is fully lowered and the robot head is rotated parallel to the main. The unit is then moved to the next joint. Once the robot has repaired all joints in one direction it is removed. If repairs are being completed in both directions from the tap hole then the main is drilled to allow the robot to be inserted in the second direction. Typically twenty-four joints can be repaired from a single excavation.

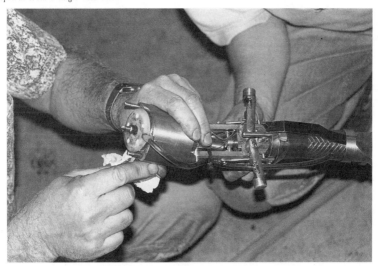

Picture # 1
Prototype Anaerobic Sealant Robot
Note: Description does not match picture

The major components of the robot are:
1. Sled Assembly: The robot is mounted on a rigid sled assembly that allows the robot to be pushed or pulled easily inside the live main. The sled has two parallel runners spaced to ensure the robot remains stable when the drill head is raised into drilling position. Mounted on the sled are the following components:

Support Arms: These expandable arms stabilise the robot when it is operated inside the main. These arms are controlled by the support arms actuator.

Tool Orientation Actuator: The tool orientation actuator folds or unfolds the drill head / sealant injection nozzle. The robot must be unfolded for insertion or moving in the main. The robot is folded 90 degrees into an upright position to seal the joint.

Thrust Actuator: The thrust actuator raises or lowers the drill / injection nozzle after they are in the upright position.

Drill Head: The drill head contains a small low voltage high torque motor capable of powering the unit to drill into the cast iron joint. The drill selection is critical to ensure that it has sufficient torque to perform its intended task while being a small as possible. The combination drill bit / chamfering tool is made of carbide for longer life.

Sealant Injection Nozzle: The sealant injection nozzle is used to inject the sealant into the joint. It is non metallic to ensure that the sealant does not set. O rings are used to ensure a complete seal against the drill chamfer.

Tool Selection Actuator: The tool selection actuator is used to position either the drill head or the injection head into position.

Video Camera: The video camera and monitor allow the operator to observe the robot positioning and sealant injection. This camera gives the operator a full view of the joint If sealant leakage should occur the operator is able to observe this fact and stop the injection process..

Umbilical Cable: The umbilical cable is 54 metres in length. This cable is composed of an outer clear polyethylene hose. Inside this hose are the various hydraulic, electrical and video lines required to operate the tool.

The tool components that support the operation of the robot but remain outside the main are:

Picture # 2 Umbilical Cable Storage Turret

Umbilical Cable Storage Turret: The umbilical cable storage turret system is used to store the umbilical cable. The cable is stored in a ring shaped channel approximately 2 metres in diameter. The turret also stores the hydraulic components and anaerobic sealant tanks.

Power Insertion and Power Storage Units: These power units are synchronised to ensure that the umbilical cable length between the insertion point and the cable turret is kept constant. The power insertion unit either pushes the umbilical cable into the main or pulls it out of the main. The power storage unit loads or unloads the umbilical cable.

<u>Control Panel</u>:  The control panel allows the operator to control the entire system. From this panel he is able to perform the following:
1. Activate the lighting system
2. Activate the tool delivery system in either forward or reverse
3. Operate the support arms actuator
4. Fold or unfold the tool
5. Switch position of the drill head and injection head
6. Operate the drill
7  Operate the injection pumps
8. Raise or lower the robot head assembly.

Consumers and ESI are currently working on phase 4 of this project to produce a field production unit. The forecast completion date for this phase of the project is the mid 1995. Field trials of this tool will be documented in the presentation.
The robot being developed is for NPS 6 Cast Iron.  Consumers has a significant quantity of NPS 6. Scaling this tool up for larger sizes has been discussed and will depend on the success of the NPS 6 robot. Scaling the robot down for NPS 4 mains will be more difficult but it might be possible. Robots for larger sizes may include multiple heads or the ability to have the robot rotate to allow multiple injections at various positions of the same joint.

ACKNOWLEDGEMENTS
Consumers Gas wishes to acknowledge the creative design, innovation and adaptability of Dr. Andrew Goldenberg, Pawel Kuzan, Jacek Wiercienski and Daniel Meidan of ESI.

REVOLUTIONARY PIPE REHABILITATION TECHNIQUE
- PVC FIT PIPING METHOD -


TECHNIQUE REVOLUTIONAIRE DE RENOVATION DES TUYAUX
- METHOD D'AJUSTEMENT PVC POUR TUYAUTERIE -

Tomoyoshi Nakao and Yuji Higuchi
Osaka Gas Co. Ltd., JAPAN

Masanori Akita and Takayuki Kurobe
Toho Gas Co., Ltd., JAPAN

ABSTRACT

Maintenance and management of pipelines are indispensable to safe and stable gas supply. In Osaka Gas and Toho Gas, some pipelines such as gray cast-iron need to be reinforced or renewed. As there are many bends in gas pipelines and many earthquakes in Japan, we want a new rehabilitation techniques for mains which is applicable to a pipeline with 90° elbows, effective against pipe cracking, earthquake resistant and little in the decrease of gas carrying ability of the pipe. Under these circumstances, we have developed PVC Fit Piping Method as a revolutionary cost effective technique which satisfies the requirement mentioned above. The rehabilitation cost of this method is 10% to 60% of the replacement method. This method has been jointly developed by Osaka Gas Co., Toho Gas Co., and Osaka Bousui Construction Co.

RÉSUMÉ

L'exploitation et l'entretien des gazoducs sont indispensables à une distribution sûre et stable de gaz. A Osaka Gas et Toho Gas, certains gazoducs comme ceux en fonte grise doivent être renforcés ou remplacés. Comme il y a de nombreux coudes dans les gazoducs et de nombreux tremblements de terre au Japon, nous avons besoin de nouvelles techniques de rénovation pour les canalisations qui soient applicables à un gazoduc ayant des coudes de 90, efficaces contre la fissuration des tuyaux, garantissant une résistance aux tremblements de terre et une faible diminution de la capacité de transport de gaz des tuyaux. Nous avons donc mis au point une méthode d'ajustment PVC pour tuyauterie comme technique rentable révolutionnaire qui répond aux conditions requises mentionées ci-dessus. Le coût de rénovation de cette méthode est de 10% à 60% de celui de la méthode de replacement. Cette méthode a été mise au point conjointement par Osaka Gas Co., Toho Gas Co. et Osaka Bousui Construction Co.

OUTLINE OF PVC FIT PIPING METHOD

A conceptual diagram of this method is shown in Figure 1.  The basic concept of the method is to insert a special polyvinyl chloride pipe (PVC pipe) into an existing pipeline.  The PVC pipe itself has high internal pressure resistance and good shape retention against external pressure.

Since the PVC pipe does not bond with the inner wall of the existing pipe, it is necessary for the both ends of the PVC pipe to be mechanically sealed with rubber ring and stainless seal rings, as shown in Figure 2.  A small manually operated jack is used to expand the stainless steel ring to ensure an airtight seal.  We have confirmed the long-term reliability of this mechanical seal with pressure tests on the rubber ring.

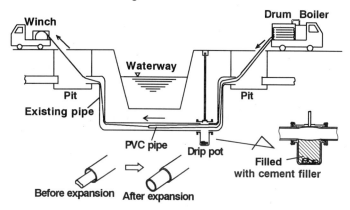

Figure 1   Conceptual Diagram

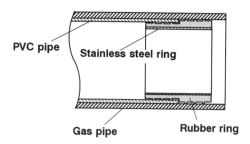

Figure 2   Mechanical Seal at Pipe End

AIR TIGHT TREATMENT OF SERVICE PIPE JUNCTIONS

Where services branches from the rehabilitated pipe, the services and the PVC pipe should be jointed not to cause any leak from that joint.  We have developed the airtight seal joint as shown in Figure 3.  The procedure is as follows.

(1) A saddle or a clamp is attached to the rehabilitated pipe.
(2) A hole is drilled on the pipe.
(3) The special joint is fixed installed at the junction.
(4) The joint is fixed by tightening a lock nut.
(5) By turning a tightening device, a rubber ring is compressed making an airtight seal between the existing pipe and PVC the pipe.
(6) A resin is injected between the existing pipe and the PVC pipe for ensuring the airtight seal at the junction.


SCOPE OF APPLICATION

The scope of application of PVC Fit Piping Method is shown in Table 1.  The scope of application of Hose Lining Technique, which is now being replaced with PVC Fit Piping Method, is also shown in Table 1.

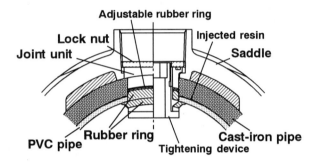

Figure 3  Airtight Seal Joint at Service Junction

Table 1    The scope of application

|  | PVC Fit Piping Method | Hose Lining Technique |
|---|---|---|
| Applicable pipes | Steel and cast–iron pipes | Steel and cast–iron pipes |
| Pressure resistance | 0.294 MPa internal pressure 0.294 MPa external pressure | 0.294 MPa internal pressure 0.034 MPa external pressure |
| Pipe diameter | 75 ～ 400 mm | 100 ～ 750 mm |
| Workable range | Up to 200 m, Applicable to a pipeline four 90° elbows | Up to 300 m, Applicable to a pipeline four 90° elbows |
| Extension of material | 150 % | 10 % |
| Workability | One day for one span | Four days for one span |


PROCEDURE OF PVC FIT PIPING METHOD

(1) Both ends of an existing pipeline section to be rehabilitated are cut off.
(2) A wire with a brush is inserted and the inner wall of the pipeline is roughly cleaned.
(3) A PVC pipe is heated and softened on the ground and is inserted into the pipeline (Photo 1).
(4) If there is a drip pot, the riser pipe of in the drip pot is cut off.
(5) The PVC pipe is expanded by heating and pressurizing with steam so that it will fit the inner wall of the pipe line.

(6) Air is then blown inside the PVC pipe to cool and harden it.
(7) Both ends of the pipeline are mechanically sealed with rubber rings and stainless steel rings.
(8) If there are service pipes, special joints are installed to make
(9) The rehabilitated section of the pipeline is reconnected.

Photo 1  Overview of Insertion

CHARACTERISTICS OF PVC PIPE

Physical properties of PVC pipe. The physical properties of the PVC for this method shown in Table 2 with the PVC for water pipes and polyethylene for gas pipes.

Table 2   The physical properties of the PVC pipe

|  | PVC for this method | PVC for water pipe | PE |
|---|---|---|---|
| Pyrolysis temperature [ ℃ ] | 230 | 210 | 120 |
| Glass transition temperature [ ℃ ] | 80.5 | 82.0 | 120 |
| Brittle temperature [ ℃ ] | − 25 | − 9 | − 80 |
| Density [g/ cuf ] | 1.43 | 1.43 | 0.94 |
| Hardness [R] | 105 | 115 | 60 |
| Tensile strength [kgf/ cuf ] | 515 | 530 | 200 |
| Extension [%] | 150 | 10 ∼ 80 | 650 |
| Charpy impact resistance [kgf·cm/ cuf ] | 17 | 5 | 22 |

In order to improve the qualities of the PVC pipe in its extensibility, resistance against shock and low-temperature brittleness, the composition of the polyvinyl chloride resin was slightly changed. Especially the resistance against shock of PVC pipe improved to be 80% of PE pipe.

Long-term performance of PVC pipe. As PVC pipe is high-molecular material like PE pipe, it has high creep resistance. The fracture strength of PVC pipe with long-term stress has been evaluated by the stress rupture tests. The experimental result is shown in Figure 4. The PVC pipe does not show the brittle fracture region in

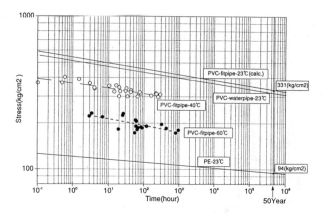

Figure 4  Stress Rupture Diagram

our experiment at 40°C and 60°C.  The creep curve at 23°C was calculated by Larson-Miller method[1] using the data at 40°C and 60°C.
This method is used to estimate the creep fracture strength of PE
for gas pipe.  The 50-year strength of PVC pipes is more than three
times as PE pipes.

 Evaluation of earthquake resistance.  In order to evaluate
earthquake resistance of the rehabilitated pipe, bending tests are
carried out.  As shown in Photo 2, the PVC pipe was not broken even
if the existing pipe was broken.

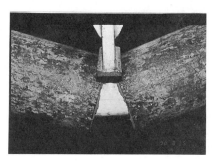

Photo 2  Bending Test

FEATURE OF PVC FIT PIPING METHOD

(1) The  earthquake  resistance of this method is much  better  than
    that of Hose Lining Technique.
(2) Effective for preventive maintenance against corrosion, cracking
    and joint leakage.
(3) Applicable to a pipeline with 90° elbows, sleeves, and
    dressers.
(4) No wrinkling, even at pipe bends (Photo 3).
(5) Easy  pipe cleaning since no adhesive is used (only one  day  is
    required for lining).
(6) Lower in cost than pipe replacement.
(7) If  there is a drip pot in the pipeline section to be  rehabili-
    tated,  it is possible to cut off the riser in the drip  pot  by
    internal cutter from ground level without excavation.

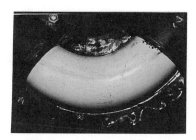

Photo 3   PVC Pipe at Pipe Bend

PRESENT AND FUTURE PLANES

This method is effective especially in preventive maintenance of pipelines under special environment conditions, such as deeply buried pipelines under a water way, a railroad or a main road because it is difficult to repair these pipelines.  As field tests yielded positive results, this method has been in actual use since 1992 at Osaka Gas and Toho Gas.  About two thousands meter of the existing pipelines have been rehabilitated at thirty work sites.  In the future, being used at twenty to forty work sites per year, this maintenance and management of gas pipelines.

In addition, Osaka Gas introduced this method as a breakage prevention technique for gray cast-iron pipelines instead of conventional pipe replacement methods this year.  About eight kilometers of gray cast-iron pipelines will be rehabilitated annually.

REFFRERENCES

[1] F.R.Larson and J.Miller : Trans., ASME 74, 765,1952

# THE DEVELOPMENT OF THE LIVE - JOINT - SEAL PROCESS

## LE DEVELOPPEMENT DU PROCEDE DE SOUTENEMENT A JOINTS ACTIFS

Masanori.Akita and Takayuki.Kurobe
Toho Gas Co.,Ltd , Japan

Yoji.Mori and Hirosuke.Matsui
Osaka Gas Co.,Ltd , Japan

ABSTRACT

As a new method to eliminate leaks from joints in superannuated low pressure cast-iron pipelines, the live joint seal process was developed. This can detect and seal joints from inside a pipe while gas flow is maintained. At the work site, a hole is drilled in the subject low pressure main to a diameter of 1/2 the pipe diameter. An internal unit called "Packer" is inserted through the hole into the pipeline under no blow condition (i.e., with no release of gas). When a joint is detected, a sealer is coated from the packer over the yarn in the joint clearance. By thus sealing the joint, any leaks are repaired and prevented. The new method improves work efficiency and reduces cost for leak prevention and repair of low pressure cast-iron pipelines.

RÉSUMÉ

Pour parer au problème des fuites de gaz au niveau des joints des vieilles canalisations en fonte à basse pression, nous avons mis au point une méthode dite "méthode d'étanchéification des joints vif" qui consiste à détecter les joints et à les rendre étanches de l'intérieur de la canalisation, sans couper le gaz. En pratique, l'on perce un trou dans la canalisation, le diamètre du trou étant égal à la moitié du diamètre de la canalisation et, sans laisser fuir le gaz, l'on insère un dispositif "Packer" dans la canalisation par ce trou. L'on détecte ensuite le joint et l'on commande au dispositif Packer d'injecter du mastic d'étanchéité dans les fibres (en lin) du joint pour le rendre étanche. Cette méthode permet d'éviter et d'arrêter les fuites de gaz au niveau des canalisations en fonte à basse pression d'une manière efficace et économique.

## INTRODUCTION

In low pressure cast iron mains using yarn a joint seals, leaks may result from loosened joints, depending on the burial site. In addition, yarn dryness and shrinkage due to the conversion to near moisture free LNG may increase the frequency of leakage.

As a remedy for leaks at joints, interior lining, encapsulation, and like measures have been taken. However, the interior lining needs excavation at both ends of the work section, requiring gas supply stoppage and cutting the gas pipeline. Although the encapsulation process does not require stopping the gas supply or cutting the pipeline, excavation is needed at every leaking joint. This increases the working period and costs.

Taking into account the above, the live joint seal method, capable of sealing joints with the pipeline kept live, has been developed to permit repair and prevention of leaks at joints regardless of the type of yarn; cement or lead yarn.

## DESCRIPTION OF THE LIVE JOINT SEAL METHOD

### Operating Principle

In this method a special clamp is attached to the gas pipeline, and a hole of about half the pipe bore is drilled. The injection packer incorporating the joint sensor is introduced through the hole into the piping. After the joint position is detected, the packer is expanded using pressurized town gas, the sealer injected into the yarn at the joint. Work for preventing leaks of cast iron pipes can thus be completed under no blow with the pipeline kept live.

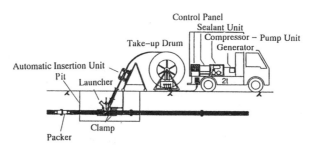

Fig. 1   Conceptual Diagram

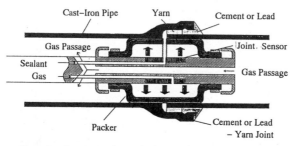

Fig. 2   Construction of the Sealer Injection Packer

Scope of Application

| Pressure | low (up to 1 kg/cm) |
|---|---|
| Type of pipe | low pressure cast iron mains with cement or lead – yarn joints |
| Bore | 75 to 300 mm |
| Working conditions | on live pipeline under no blow |
| Working length | up to 100 m (50 m on each side) |
| Bend passing | capable of passing a maximum of four 45° bends |

Working Equipment

●Packer
       This is the key to the present method.  Stops and expands at the joint to be repaired, injects acrylic resin into the joint.
       The through-hole provided along the center axis of the packer ensures gas flow even during expansion of the bag.
       A joint sensor is incorporated at the center of the packer. The sensor can accurately detect the joint position.  When a joint position is detected, the sensor causes the packer to expand with town gas, injecting sealer from the nozzle into the yarn in the joint clearance.

●Tube Pulley
       This is used to store the PE tube used to introduce the packer into the pipeline.  Incorporates a pressure sensor to measure the gas pressure in front of and behind the packer whenever needed and a flow meter to measure the amount of gas supply into the packer.

●Driving Power Unit
       This is provided with a compressor and vacuum pump to contract and expand the packer. Incorporates an oxygen concentration meter to monitor the inclusion of oxygen in the packer expansion and contraction line.

●Injection Unit
    This feeds the sealer to the
packer. The sealer is fed by a
gear pump from the sealer tank to
the packer.
    Feed rate can be varied by
adjusting the motor speed and is
thus be kept constant.

●Pusher
    This introduces the PE tube
into the pipeline and also
withdraws it. The moving rate can
be switched between either high or
low.
    Is provided with a distance
meter to measure the length of PE
tube introduced and a load meter
to measure the load during
introduction and withdrawal.

●Operation Panel
    This is branched from the
control panel. Centralizes all
necessary controls near the
excavation. Only one operator
needed.

●Launcher
    Used to insert the packer
into and remove same from the pipe
while attached to the shutter
plate. Operation is carried out
under no blow with the pipeline
kept live.

●Shutter Plate
    Cuts off gas to permit live
work under no blow, while the
pipeline is kept alive.  Attached
to the clamp when installing or
removing the units.

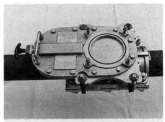

●Drilling Jig and Hole Saw
    drills a hole of about half
the size of the subject pipeline.
Operation is carried out under no
blow with the pipeline kept live.

WORK PROCESS

Work Flow

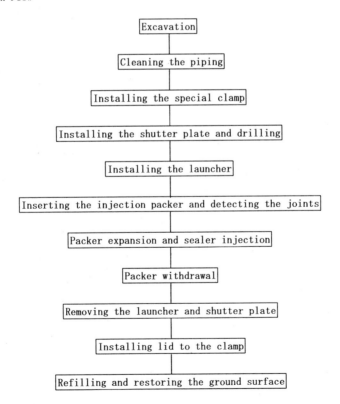

Work Procedures

     Details as presented in follows.

(1) Preparation
    Excavate a section at an appropriate location for work on the
    line.
    Connect units and make initial adjustments.

(2) Install the special clamp.
    Clean the pipe surface and attach the clamp.
    Carry out clamp airtightness test (1000 mmAq).

(3) Install the shutter plate and drill.
    Fasten the shutter plate to the clamp using bolts.
    Carry out shutter airtightness test.
    Set the drill in place and commence drilling.
    Set the non-blow bag in place and clean the pipe interior,
     removing chips etc.

(4) Install the launcher.
    Set the live pipe insertion launcher in place and connect to
    units involved for gas feed.  Purge the unit interior with air.
    Set the guide tube on the launcher.  Open the shutter plate.
    Insert the packer into the pipeline using the pusher.

(5) Introduce the packer into the pipeline and detect joints.
    Feeding the packer at high rate until it reaches the end of
    the work section, detecting joints.

(6) Draw back and expand the packer. Inject the sealer.
    Draw back the packer and stop at the joint detected.
    After fine adjustment of the position, expand the packer.
    Inject the sealer into the joint.
    Contract the packer.

    Repeat procedure (6) for all joints.

(7) Change of direction.
    Withdraw the packer into the launcher and close the shutter
    plate.
    Turn the launcher 180° and fasten.
    Repeat procedures (5) and (6) in the reverse direction.

(8) Withdraw the packer.
    Upon completion of work in both directions, withdraw the
    packer into the launcher.
    Making sure that the packer is accommodated in the launcher,
    close the shutter plate.

(9) Gas-purge
    Purge unit interior with gas.

(10) Clean
    Wash off the sealer adhering to the packer and other units.
    Remove the launcher.  After fastening the flange to the clamp
    hole using bolts, check for airtightness and apply corrosion
    preventive measures.

(11) Refill and restore ground surface.
    Refill the excavation and restore ground surface.  This
    terminates the work.

DESCRIPTION OF DEVELOPMENT

Time Course

April     1987: Development initiated
October   1989: Field tests commenced with prototype equipment
December  1990: Commercial equipment completed; monitor
                installation begun
October   1991: Field use initiated


Focuses of Development

     Development of the resin injection packer.  For the packer to
be inserted and removed through a hole of about half the subject
pipe diameter, the packer diameter must be smaller than 1/2 the
diameter of the pipe to be worked.  To permit work on live pipelines
a through hole must be provided along the center axis of the packer
so that gas flow rate is assured even during packer expansion.

     Although a sufficient gas flow rate can be assured even if gas
feed is monolateral, the expanded packer may possibly decrease the
gas feed pressure either in front or behind.  The packer design,
therefore, must be such that, should this occur, the continuous
automatic monitoring of gas feed pressure in front and behind the
packer using pressure sensors prevents likely problems.

     The double construction consisting of the folding parasol bag
and the bag cover tightly against to the pipe wall must be compact
when contracted and have high sealing performance when expanded.

     To allow working in pipes with bends, the packer must be
flexible to the extent that it can pass beyond 45°  .  The sensor
that detects joints must accurately detect them via changes in the
induction current.  The design of the sensor incorporated in the
packer provides very high injection precision, since expansion and
injection can be accomplished immediately a joint is detected.

     The sealer injection process should be taken in two stages to
enable the sealer to quickly reach the joint from top to bottom.  At
the first stage the primary injection is performed in liquid form,
and at the subsequent stage the secondary injection is provided as
foam.  In this method the system can be constructed so that the
sealer spreads around the entire periphery of the joint.

     Packer expansion must not hinder gas supply, even if the packer
is broken or burst in the pipeline.  In addition, to minimize the
gas pressure needed for expansion, the packer expansion member has
been made of fabric-reinforced vinyl sheet formed into a parasol
shape.


     Development of The Pusher.  The pusher must be capable of
accommodating the various tubes needed to feed the sealer and
expansion gas, joint sensor cables, and so on, and also be flexible
so as to introduce the packer into the pipeline, allowing it to pass
beyond bends, and yet rigid enough for to travel over a long
distance.  To meet this, the PE pipe for gas works was applied.

     An automatic pusher was developed with the capabilities of
pushing and pulling the tubes at a given rate via remote control.
The pusher can also detect passing load and automatically stops
under excessive load.


     Development of the sealing method.  For the sealing of leaks at
joints to be maintained over a long period; at least 30 years, the
sealer must be such that elasticity is kept intact after setting to
cope with long-term traffic load.  To meet this requirement, using
acrylic resin emulsion type sealer was developed.

The new sealing method was evaluated by repeating the bending test 1.4 × 10⁶ times (equivalent to 30 years of heavy traffic; P = 250 mmAq; N = 8 pcs). The fact that the method passed the test indicates that leaks will be prevented over a long period under general type burial.

Development of The Cast Iron Pipe Reinforcement Clamp. This was designed exclusively to serve two purposes: reinforcing the drilled part (hole diameter: about half the pipe diameter) and to provide a base to install the non-blow launcher that assists in packer insertion.

Development of One-Man-Operated Control System. All necessary functions, such as inserting the packer into the pipeline, sensing joints, expanding the packer, and injecting the sealer, are integrated in a single operation panel. The automatic control needs only one operator.

Packer expansion, injection, feed pressure in the pipeline, packer expansion gas concentration, and so on can be monitored on the operation panel.

Miniaturizing The Units. Efforts were made to reduce the size and weight of all units. Since the entire system can be loaded on a single 2-ton truck, its application is not too restricted by field conditions and therefore the system is superior in mobility.

## FEATURES

Working on Live Pipeline Under No Blow

Since work can be accomplished without stopping the gas supply, customers are not inconvenienced.
Since gas can flow even during packer expansion, work can be accomplished even if the gas feed is monolateral (gas passing rate: approx. 40 m³/h at 150 A and approx. 100 m³/h at 200 A).
The packer is expanded with town gas. Therefore, should accident occur, safety remains intact.
Gas feed pressure in front of and behind the packer can be continuously monitored even during packer expansion, which ensures stable gas supply.

Drastic Reduction in Work Time And Costs

It is not necessary to cut or connect gas pipes. Excavation at a site provides preventive maintenance of joints at 10 to 30 places. Cost is thus greatly reduced.

Applicable to A Wide Variety of Piping Shapes

The present method can work in live pipelines, bypass work is not needed even at branches where tees, cross joints and the like are used.

Space saving

The working system (excluding excavation equipment) is compact and can be loaded on a 2-ton truck and thus occupies only a small area at the site.

REMARKS

Field tests have been carried out for 75 mm- , 100 mm- and 150 mm-diameter pipes by Toho Gas and for 200 mm- and 300 mm-diameter pipes by Osaka Gas. This process was introduced fully at work sites from 1992 and total work experience amounts to approx. 300 km.

According to the results to of field tests and on-site tests, this process is considered the best method for repairing joint leaks and preventing leakage. We intend to make the most of this process as an effective measure against leakage.

LIVE, INTERNAL SEALING SYSTEM FOR
CAST IRON DISTRIBUTION MAINS

SYSTÈME INTERNE DE FERMETURE (SCELLEMENT) EN ETAT D'UTILISATION,
POUR LES CONDUITS DE DISTRIBUTION EN MOULE DE FER

Allan T. Fisk and David I. Freed
Foster-Miller, Inc., USA

Kiran M. Kothari
Gas Research Institute, USA

ABSTRACT

Under development is an internal sealing system to repair leaking bell and spigot joints in cast iron gas distribution mains. The system is a "no-dig technology" capable of sealing multiple joints from a single entry point, thus saving excavation and restoration costs. A snake-like sealing device is inserted into and pushed down the main a distance of up to 45 m (150 ft) each way from the entry point, enough to treat 24 joints. The system uses a sealed entry into live mains in the 100 to 300 mm (4 -12 in.) size range through a 43 mm taphole (1.5 in. NPT). The joint sealing approach is unique in that it mechanically applies a thick, compliant sealant which fills and overlays the gap at the joint. The specially formulated sealant is self supporting, bonds to corroded pipe, and seals without dependence on the type or quality of packing material (jute/lead/mortar) in the joint.

RESUMÉ

Sous développement est un système interne de scellement pour reparer les cloches fuyantes et les jointures (charnières) en fausset dans les conduits de distribution du gas en moule de fer. Le système est une "technologie sans tranchées" capable de sceller les jointures multiples d'un point d'entrée unique, en economisant les prix d'excavation et de restoration. Un instrument de scellement en forme de serpent est introduit et poussé dans le conduit à une distance qui peu aller jusqu' à 45 metres (150 pieds) dans chaque direction à partir du point d'entrée, assez de quoi traiter 24 jointures. Le système presente une entrée sans gas dans les conduits en état d'utilisation dans l'ordre de taille de 100-300mm (4-12 inch), a travers un trou dans le tuyau de gas de 43mm (1.5 inch NPT). La methode de scellement est unique dans la mesure ou elle applique mecaniquement un sceau epais, flexible qui remplit et couvre l'ouverture à la jointure. Ce sceau specialement crée se maintient tout seul, s'assemble aux tuyaux en état de corrosion et ferme dans las jointure sans dependre de las qualité du materiel d'emballage (Jute, plomb, mortier).

## INTRODUCTION

As buried cast iron gas mains age, the need for maintenance to repair leaks usually increases. Leaks commonly occur at the bell and spigot type joints which, in the United States (U.S.), may have been joined with lead and jute, jute and mortar, or lead and yarn. Traditional methods of leak repair involve mechanically clamping an external seal to the joint, or applying an adhesive urethane sealant to encapsulate the face of the joint, or by drilling into the joint from the outside and injecting an anaerobic sealant into the joint space. These methods are very expensive in an urban environment because an excavation is required (possibly with shoring) at each joint. In addition, the required joint surface preparation and cleaning are difficult and time consuming, and reinstatement costs are very high. U.S. cast iron joint repair costs can range from $300 per joint for a small joint at a suburban utility to $1500 or more for a large joint at an urban utility.

If the joint repair could be performed internally instead of externally, and multiple joint repairs could be done from a single point of entry, then the repair cost per joint could be minimized by amortizing the high excavation and reinstatement costs over more joints. There are two such systems currently in use, one in the UK and U.S. and another in Japan. Neither is thought to be highly effective in the extremely variable conditions found in the U.S. Consequently this research program, conducted by Foster-Miller, Inc. for the Gas Research Institute (GRI), seeks to develop an alternative internal sealing capability.

## BACKGROUND AND HISTORY

The British Gas-developed internal sealing system is called Mainspray™ and is marketed in the U.S. by ALH Systems, Ltd. Mainspray utilizes a spray head on the end of a plastic snake, combined with an electromagnetic joint locator device. This snake enters the main through a taphole via a drilling and tapping fixture and is pushed down the main a distance of up to 60 m (200 ft) in each direction. The spray head sprays a low viscosity anaerobic sealant onto each joint. The sealant is wicked into and absorbed by the jute (if jute is present) and it climbs by capillary action into the minute leak paths. The anaerobic material is destabilized by the presence of metal, so if the sealant makes its way into the leak paths it subsequently cures in the absence of oxygen, thus sealing the joint. A cross section of a typical cast iron lead and jute joint is shown in Figure 1.

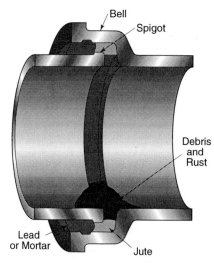

**Figure 1. Cross section of a lead/jute cast iron joint**

The Mainspray system is very simple and has been found to be cost effective in certain high cost urban scenarios because it saves considerable excavation and restoration cost and it does reduce leakage, usually by a substantial amount. However, laboratory and field tests conducted earlier in this research program[1] have determined that its effectiveness in the U.S. is often limited because of highly variable joint conditions. Reductions in individual joint leakage rates varied widely from site to site, from negligible to near 100 percent, but on average were typically about 75 percent. Older U.S. mains often are loaded with considerable scale and debris, as well as with the remnants of decades of rejuvenation and sealing treatments. The jute is not always in good shape, and is often "petrified" by absorbed hydrocarbons. Random spraying of sealant plus capillary climb seems less than 100 percent effective in overcoming gravity, particularly if the leak is on the top of the joint. These conditions no doubt account for much of the variability in field results.

Another internal sealing system developed by Osaka Gas and its partners is currently in use in Japan. Called Live Joint Seal, the format is similar to Mainspray in that the sealing head is on the end of a snake launched through a taphole and mechanically pushed down the main. But there the similarity ends. The sealing head consists of a hollow inflatable packer, or bladder. The snake and bladder deliver a thin, latex-type sealant which is forced under pressure into the jute and the rest of the joint. The injection pressure is slightly above the pressure in the main. The hollow bladder must contain the injection pressure by sealing on the walls of the pipe on either side of the joint. Large amounts of loose debris can interfere with this seal. As with Mainspray, the Live Joint Seal system contains an electromagnetic joint location sensor. The acrylic-latex sealant cures by loss of moisture over time. The fact that it is a water based material is of little concern in Japan where freezing ambient conditions are rare.

Osaka Gas has found their system to be very effective when pipe and joint conditions are relatively good. That tends to be the case in Japan since, compared to U.S. mains, Japanese cast iron mains are far newer than U.S. mains. Discussions are underway related to testing the Osaka Gas sealant and bladder in actual joints as part of the curent GRI research program.

Earlier phases of this program concentrated on evaluating new, and commercially available or modified sealants for applicability in U.S. conditions. Sprayable sealants were first evaluated and some were tested with the Mainspray system. Some of these compounds peformed resonably well, and are still in use with the Mainspray system, but no new sprayable material was found that could deliver a large improvement to the performance of the basic internal spray concept. Thus it was concluded that sealing concepts which relied on the sealant wicking into the joint would not be sufficiently effective in a high percentage of the joints found in the U.S. to meet GRI program goals.

Non-sprayable sealants were also evaluated for possible use with other, as yet undetermined application schemes. Some of these materials showed promise, but they required different delivery and applicator methods than a simple spray head. Ultimately, an alternative approach was developed for sealing the joint internally, one which does not depend on the jute as a key element in the sealing process.

PROGRAM GOALS

The GRI research and development program currently underway at Foster-Miller is focused on the development of an internal sealing system which would inexpensively seal multiple joints from a single excavation, and be highly effective in the conditions found in the U.S. The goal of the program is to develop a system which would completely seal (100 percent leak reduction) at least 90 percent of all joints attempted, at a cost which is only one-fifth that of the traditional encapsulation method.

The conceptual approach is basically to not rely upon the packing materials in the joint, and also not to rely on the inner walls of the pipe to build a dam, or form, in order to pressure-inject a sealant. Instead, a viscous, adhesive sealant is mechanically applied to fill the gap in the joint (between the tip of the spigot and the heel of the bell) under live conditions. The approach is more like a caulking operation than an injection, but since the sealant is applied at pipe-ambient pressure, the gas pressure is available to help force the sealant into the leak path.

A major benefit of this approach is that the sealed joint can be left to cure slowly while the sealing device moves on to another joint. Time/motion study indicates that this benefit is pivotal in making the productivity and hence the economic targets.

The mechanical applicator also applies an overlay of sealant onto the pipe walls for a short distance on each side of the joint. This covers over and seals any porous or encrusted scale which cannot be simply pushed away from the joint area. A joint sealed with this approach is shown in Figure 2. The sealant will remain pliable over its lifetime in order to accomodate future joint movement that occurs in all cast iron joints.

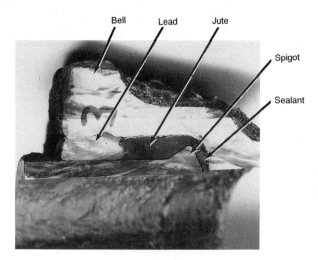

**Figure 2.  Sealant filling the gap of a cast iron joint**

Several sealants are currently being considered and tested for this program.  The sealant must bond to rusty cast iron in a pure methane environment, be thin enough to pump through small diameter tubing yet thick enough to remain inside the gap at the top of the joint.  It must also be elastic so it can resist the normal joint movements due to seasonal ground temperature variations.  The sealant must resist water and any other chemicals found inside a gas main, and not be harmful to the worker, the environment or the distribution system.

FEATURES OF THE INTERNAL JOINT SEALANT SYSTEM

The sealant system being developed has many features which enable reliable, inexpensive sealing of live gas mains.  The system is launched into the main through a standard service tap hole and is pushed down the main to seal multiple joints.  A sealed fitting is used on the hole to prevent the escape of gas while the head is launched and during the sealing operation.  The system is run by two people.  The first person operates the system and the second oversees the uphole equipment.  The sealing process is quick and the system can be moved to the next joint as soon as the sealant is finished being applied.

Once the sealing head is launched, it is pushed down the main its full range.  The program plan includes development of two separate systems.  The first system will have a 15 m (50 ft) range in either direction from the entrance point, and the second system will have a 45 m (150 ft) range in either direction.  Thus either 8 or 24 joints could be sealed from a single excavation with the two systems.

After the system is pushed to its maximum range, the sealing head is pulled back to the launch point, and stops at each joint to clean and seal it.  A vision system allows the operator to locate the joint and watch the sealing operation.  The joint will require a minor cleaning to push the loose scale and debris away from the joint area.  When the head is in position, it takes approximately 3 to 4 minutes to seal each joint.  After the system comes back to the launch point, it is withdrawn into the launch fitting, and the operation is repeated in the other direction.

The 50-foot system will be launched through a 43 mm diameter tapped hole (1.5 in. NPT).  Because the hole is so small, no reinforcement fitting will be required on mains 150 mm (6 inch) diameter and larger.  It uses a fiber optic video system, and a methane-powered gas motor so that there are no electronic devices inside the gas main.  A more detailed description of the 15 m (50 ft) system is given below.

SYSTEM DESCRIPTION - 50 FT SYSTEM

A schematic of the 50-ft range system is shown in Figure 3. The sealing head and centralizer are the downhole components which apply the sealant to the gap between the pipes at a cast iron joint. The head is connected to the end of a snake, which is comprised of a plastic pipe housing the conduits that supply the head, the fiber optic bundles, and a fiberglass structural member. The snake is used to push the head up and down the main. At the entrance point in the main is a sealed launch fitting, incorporating the ALH Control Gas™ hot tap system.

On the far end of the snake is the rear snake termination. The snake termination contains the interfaces to the uphole components (video camera, sealant pump, methane supply), and also contains the actuation mechanism for the centralizer. The electronics enclosure is attached to the snake termination. It contains the video camera and a light source for the fiber optic system. The system also contains a sealant pump and a gas supply, which supply the head with sealant and power for the motor.

Sealant Head and Centralizer

Figure 4 is a drawing of the sealant head and centralizer. The head applies sealant to the joint while the centralizer keeps the head in the center of the pipe so it can function properly. The head contains retractable flappers, a gas motor, the end of the fiber optic vision system, and sealant supply tubes.

The flappers are spun by a miniature gas-powered motor. The gas motor is powered by compressed natural gas, so that the exhaust from the motor can be emptied straight into the gas main. The flappers are retractable as shown in Figure 4. This feature allows the head to fit through a small opening while it is launched or retrieved from the main.

The first step in the sealing operation is to clean the loose scale and debris from the area. This is done by spinning the flappers and moving the head back and forth across the joint area. While this will not

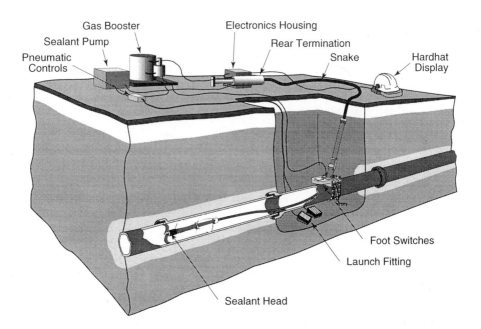

**Figure 3. Overall view of the 50-ft range system**

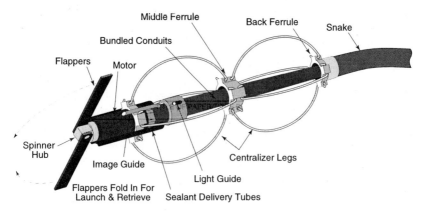

**Figure 4. Diagram of the sealant head and snake.**

scrape away any bonded scale, it will push aside the loose debris. The bonded scale is covered over and sealed by the sealant.

In sealing the joint, sealant flows from the sealant supply tubes onto the spinning flappers. The sealant is then centrifugally spun out to the end of the flappers and onto the pipe. Figure 5 shows an end view of the flappers. The flappers can trowel a wave of sealant back and forth a short distance axially along the pipe and push the sealant into the gap between the pipes.

The fiber optic vision system is somewhat similar to those used in other applications such as remote inspection and arthroscopic surgery, but consists of separate light supply and image return guides. The light supply guides provide illumination to the pipe, while the image guide returns an image to an uphole video camera. In the sealant head the light supply bundle is located a few centimeters (inches) behind the image bundle. This results in shadows being generated by the joint features and better image quality.

The centralizer is a double-bow design. The double bows keep the head centered when the centralizer is deployed, yet retract to a very small diameter so the head can fit through a small launch hole. The centralizer is actuated by pulling on the bundled conduits inside the snake, which draws the head closer to the end of the snake and expands the legs. The centralizer is retracted by pushing the head away from the snake. This push/pull action is accomplished from the far end of the snake at the rear snake termination. Thus it can be performed with the head far away from the launch point.

"No-Blow" Launch Fitting

The system is designed so that the entire sealing operation, including drilling and tapping the main, and launching and retrieving the snake can be performed with almost no escape of gas from the main. The launch fitting is the device which seals the main during the operation. It is built around the commercially-available ALH Control Gas™ "hot tap" equipment. Figure 6 shows the launch fitting prior to launching the head into the main, while a photograph of the fitting itself is shown in Figure 7.

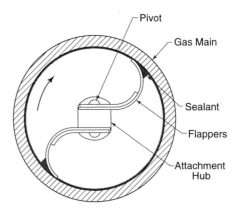

**Figure 5. End view of the flappers in operation.**

The only nonstandard launch hardware is the launch tube assembly shown in Figure 6. Once the main has been drilled and tapped, the launch tube assembly is attached to the hot tap fitting. The gate valve is then opened and the inner tube slid down so that the tongue fits inside the tapped hole. The tongue guides the head and protects it from the edges of the pipe as it is pushed into and withdrawn from the main. The centralizer legs are then opened by pulling the snake innards from the rear termination of the snake.

Push Snake

The push snake is the backbone of the system, connecting the sealing head to the uphole equipment. The snake is also the means of transporting the head, for it is the component that the operator pushes or pulls to move the head up and down the main. There are many conflicting requirements on the snake. It must be stiff enough to push the head the required distance, yet flexible enough to enter the main at an angle and bend to run along the main. It must also be small in diameter so it can enter the main through a small tap hole, yet large enough to contain all the necessary conduits contained inside. The outer material must also be durable, and have low friction inside the gas main.

For the 15 m (50 ft) sealant system an IPS size high density polyethylene gas service pipe is used. This is commonly available to U.S. utilities and is thus easily replaceable when it wears out.

The snake houses many components. A cross section of the snake is shown in Figure 8. The snake contains tubing for carrying sealant to the head. It also contains a fiberglass tension member used to pull the head to deploy the centralizer. There are fiber optic guides for the vision system. A single image guide and three light guides are contained within the snake. All of the tubes within the snake are contained within a shrink-wrapped exterior skin.

The annular space between the shrink wrap and the inner diameter of the outer pipe is used to transport compressed natural gas to the motor in the head. Thus even this "empty" space in the snake is put to good use, which allows the snake to be as compact as possible. The ends of the snake are sealed to prevent the escape of gas from the annular space. At the uphole end of the snake is the rear termination. This is where the conduits which run through the snake are terminated and interface to the uphole components. It is also where the centralizer is actuated.

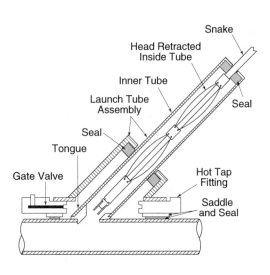

**Figure 6. Schematic of launch fitting**

**Figure 7. Photograph of launch fitting**

Uphole Components

There are other components of the system which remain outside the gas main in addition to the rear termination of the snake. These uphole components include the sealant supply, compressed gas supply, light supply, and video electronics.

The sealant pump supplies sealant to the head through a conduit in the snake. The sealant is currently packaged in disposable 500 ml (16 oz) cartridges, which contain enough sealant for 2 to 4 joints. The cartridges are an easy, clean and economical way to supply sealant. Almost no sealant is wasted when the cartridge is empty, and there is no risk of contaminating the sealant as it is installed into the pump. The pump mechanism is an air-operated mechanical ram. This arrangement supplies a constant volume of sealant with each stroke of the actuator, and allows fine metering of the sealant.

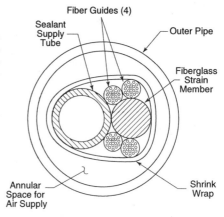

**Figure 8. Cross section of the push snake**

The gas supply system provides compressed natural gas to the downhole motor. Methane or natural gas is used to allow the motor to exhaust inside the gas main. The system is currently configured to withdraw gas from the main, compress it and store it in an accumulator. The output of the accumulator is regulated down to 4 bar (60 psi) and fed to the motor. An alternate supply configuration could employ compressed natural gas supplied in standard high-pressure cylinders.

Both the sealant pump and the gas supply are controlled by two pneumatic foot switches located near the operator. Using foot switches allows the operator to use his hands to push and pull on the snake while the system is in operation. Pressing the first switch turns the motor on, while pressing the second switch turns the motor on and simultaneously supplies sealant to the head. Only one switch needs to be pressed for any stage of the operation. Releasing the switches turns off the controls.

The fiberscope in the snake is connected to the video camera and light source. The video camera is connected to a display, which is used by the operator to monitor the sealant operation. The system uses a unique hard-hat mounted video display monitor. This commercially available unit is compact enough to fit under the brim of a hard hat, yet has resolution fine enough to see small details inside the pipe. The main advantage is that it eliminates the glare and washout normally associated with outdoor viewing of video monitors and is "hands-free". The hard-hat display also allows "up-close" viewing of the monitor from anywhere in the trench. This results in higher productivity, and better performance of the system. Figure 9 is a photograph of the hard-hat video display unit.

THE 45 m (150 FT.) LONG-RANGE SYSTEM

After the 15 m (50 ft) system is tested and debugged, a long-range system capable of 45 m reach from the launch point will be developed. This will minimize the cost per joint sealed. The 45 m (150 ft) range system will be functionally similar to the 15 m (50 ft) system, but many of the components will differ due to technical and economic reasons. For instance, fiber optics may no longer be economically desirable at this range and a downhole camera may be used. Design of this system will commence following testing of the 15 m (50 ft) system.

ECONOMIC ANALYSIS OF THE INTERNAL JOINT SEALANT SYSTEM

An economic analysis was performed to compare the cost of using the internal sealing system with the cost of traditional encapsulation. Since one of the biggest cost components in joint repair is the excavation and restoration cost, the cost per joint will vary depending on how many joints are sealed from a single excavation. Figure 10 is a graph of the estimated per joint repair cost versus the number of joints sealed from an excavation. The cost of encapsulation is relatively fixed on a per joint basis and does not vary appreciably when multiple joints are sealed.

Notice that as more joints are sealed from a single excavation, the costs per joint are reduced. This is because the fixed excavation costs are spread over more joints. The curve flattens out as more joints are sealed, however, since the variable costs per joint (i.e. labor, sealant material) are not reduced as more joints are sealed from a single hole. It is estimated that the two products to be developed in this program will meet the desired goal of an 80 percent reduction in the cost to seal each joint when used at their maximum ranges.

**Figure 9. Hard-hat mounted video display unit.**

There is a cost discontinuity at the 15 m (50 ft) range due to a technological discontinuity, namely, the fact that the longer ranges can only be achieved with a more complex and expensive system, and increased labor requirements. If the graph were extended beyond 45 m (150 ft) there would be another cost/technology discontinuity at approximately the 45 m (150 ft) range, indicating the use of even more costly equipment and procedures. This, plus the generic flatness of the cost curve at this range, probably argues against any economic benefit for a system having still longer range.

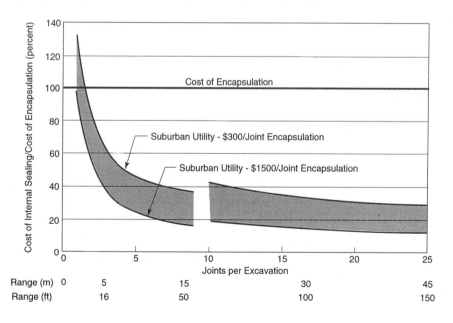

**Figure 10. Cost of sealing a joint with internal system compared to cost of encapsulation**

On the other side of the graph, notice that the systems need not be pushed to their maximum ranges to provide substantial cost savings. For instance, if only three joints per excavation are sealed (on average), the cost per joint will be approximately half that of encapsulation.

TESTING OF THE SEALANT SYSTEM

The main focus of the testing so far has been an evaluation of currently available sealant products and their ability to seal cast iron joints. All types of adhesives and sealant were considered. An initial sweep eliminated those which had problems curing in methane, posed health, handling or ecological problems, released volatile materials when curing, or were not compatible with the delivery or other system requirements. Laboratory testing is being performed on the remaining candidates to select the preferred sealant for this application.

Testing has also been performed with early breadboard-quality applicators to gauge the performance of the concept before committing to the overall approach. These tests included sealing actual leaking joints. Testing to date show that the applicator concept is very reliable and effective at sealing joints. The flappers work well at distributing sealant around and along the pipe and forcing it into the joint.

The sealing system and the joints sealed will undergo extensive testing to verify not only the performance of the sealing system, but also the integrity of the sealed joints and the safety of the sealant material. Testing of the system will include laboratory and field tests. The sealant material is undergoing many tests to prove it is a safe, durable material. Accelerated aging and thermal cycling tests will determine whether the sealant will have long-term durability in the joint. Other tests will ascertain any potential hazard for workers, the environment (soil, groundwater), and the gas system itself (regulators, meters, appliances).

Joints sealed with the internal sealant system will also be tested to assure long leak-free performance. The joints will be subjected to cyclical axial pullout similar to those which are normally experienced due to seasonal changes in the ground temperature. Recent studies[2] have shown that these cyclical thermal joint movements can be as much as 1.25 mm (0.050 in.), and one-time movements of 2.5 mm (0.100 in.) are also possible. The joints will be tested with these movements while being continuously monitored for leaks.

PROGRAM SUMMARY AND CONCLUSIONS

A new system for internally sealing cast iron joints is being developed by Foster-Miller, Inc. for GRI. This system will work better than existing internal sealing systems because it is more tolerant of dirty pipe and deteriorated jute. It is launched through a single tapped hole and can seal joints in each direction. Several different sealant formulations are currently being evaluated and once the sealant itself is finalized, development of the applicator and the rest of the system will continue. System testing is expected to be in 1996 with commercialization to follow.

REFERENCES

1. Fisk, et. al., "Investigation of Sprayable Anaerobic Sealants for Internally Sealing Cast Iron Joints in Gas Distribution Mains." GRI Report Number GRI-94/0428, Gas Research Institute, Chicago, IL, USA, 1995.
2. T.D. O'Rourke and A.N. Netravali. *Evaluating Service Life of Anaerobic Joint Sealing Compounds*, Industry Advisors' Meeting, Cornell University, Ithaca, New York, August 1995.

THE USE OF CROSS-LINKED POLYETHYLENE PIPE FOR LINING GAS
DISTRIBUTION MAINS.

L'UTILISATION DE TUYAUX EN POLYETHYLENE RETICULE
POUR REVETIR INTERIEUREMENT LES CANALISATIONS DE
DISTRIBUTION DU GAZ

L. Maine and J.A. Greig
British Gas Engineering Research Station, U.K.

## ABSTRACT

Existing methods for close fit lining gas distribution mains require plugs
and offset joints to be removed. This causes disruption, time delays and
additional excavation and reinstatement costs. British Gas is developing
a renovation technique, using cross linked polyethylene (PE-X), a shape
memory material with excellent stress crack resistance, which can be
used when the protruding plugs are left in place. The reduced diameter
pipe is inserted using slip lining methods then heated above its melt
crystallisation temperature to cause recovery and pipe expansion. The
high toughness PE-X deforms around the plugs when it is in the 'molten'
state.

## RÉSUMÉ

Les méthodes actuelles pour revêtir interieurement, avec ajustement sans
jeu, les canalisations de distribution de gaz nécessitent le retrait des
obturateurs et des raccords coudés. Ceci entraîne des interruptions du
service, des retards, des travaux de creusement et des coûts de
rétablissement. British Gas met au point actuellement une technique de
rénovation qui utilise le polyéthylène réticule (PE-X), un matériau à
mémoire plastique avec une résistance aux criques de fatigue excellente.
Ce dernier peut être utilisé quand les obturateurs saillants sont laissés sur
place. Le tuyau au diamètre réduit est inséré en utilisant des méthodes
de revêtement intérieur avec ajustage doux. Il est ensuite chauffé
au-dessus de sa température de cristallisation par fusion afin de
provoquer une récupération et une dilation du tuyau. Ce PE-X très
résistant se déforme autour des obturateurs quand il est en 'fusion'.

## INTRODUCTION

Grey cast iron mains (pit and spun cast) are normally replaced to maintain or improve levels of safety. Replacement tends to be concentrated in environments where there is a high density of buildings in close proximity to the mains and a predominance of paved surfaces. Such environments usually imply high excavation and reinstatement costs, and disruption to road users and pedestrians as the work on the mains is carried out. The use of trenchless techniques for mains replacement is therefore especially attractive.

A number of trenchless methods already exist, the simplest being slip lining, where a fully pressure rated, flexible polyethylene (PE) pipe is inserted into the existing main. To ensure satisfactory insertion there must be a clearance between the existing and lining pipeline. This clearance results in a reduction in the flow capacity of the pipeline; unless the pressure can be increased, which is not always possible due to the condition of the network to which the lined pipe is connected. Where little or no reduction in capacity can be tolerated, close fit lining techniques are available, eg. Swagelining (1), which achieves a close fit by temporarily reducing the diameter of an oversized PE pipe as it is pulled through a die, while simultaneously pulling it into the old cast iron main. After insertion of the PE pipe, the pulling load is removed, and the pipe reverts back towards its original diameter, achieving the close fit with the host main. In this operation the insertion clearance is relatively small, and additional excavations to remove plugs and service connections which protrude into the bore of the main are required to avoid damage to the PE lining.

To minimise the disruption to the customer, the lining and transfer of existing services on low pressure gas distribution mains is usually carried out under tight time constraints, with up to 20 consumers being disconnected from the iron main and reconnected to the inserted PE main within one working day. Location of unexpected plugs (eg old gas lamp connections or abandoned services) and additional excavations can cause extensive delays and inconvenience.

This paper outlines the use of cross-linked polyethylene (PE-X) pipes for the close fit renovation of cast iron mains without removal of the protruding plugs. Cross-linked PE is a shape memory material, which can be deformed from its original shape and when heated above its crystalline melt temperature it will return to its original shape, without any loss in performance. These recovery properties have been extensively used for heat shrink repair systems, applied externally to leaking joints. The material has a very high resistance to stress cracking, and a series of tests has been carried out to evaluate the long term performance of PE-X pipes which have been reduced in diameter after manufacture, then heated to cause recovery to their original diameter. The evaluation included recovery of the pipes in the location of protruding plugs, which can penetrate up to 20mm into the cast iron main.  The PE-X pipe, in its molten state, deforms around these protrusions.

## PROPERTIES OF CROSS-LINKED POLYETHYLENE.

Polyethylene has a carbon chain backbone surrounded by covalently bonded hydrogen atoms.  The conventional 'gas' grade of medium density polyethylene (MDPE) has short, regularly spaced side branches attached to the main chain.  The branching is controlled by the addition of a co-monomer during the polymerisation stage and produces the optimum level of crystallinity to give the required combination of strength, stiffness and long term performance.

In a cross-linked polymer the branches of the chain structure are chemically joined together with primary covalent bonds to form a three dimensional network.  This can be achieved in several ways, including radiation bombardment or chemical decomposition of a peroxide, by heating, to produce free radicals which remove hydrogen atoms from the polyethylene chain and form the tie points.  In cross linked polyethylene the chains are prevented from sliding past each other and 'flow' is not possible without rupture of the covalent bonds.  However, between the cross linked sites, the molecular segments remain flexible, and the degree of cross linking determines the flexibility of the structure.  Once the specimen has been cross linked, its shape is fixed.  However, it can be temporarily deformed at temperature and cooled to lock in a new shape.  If the specimen is then reheated above its crystalline melt temperature (approx. 140°C), it will revert to its original shape.

Cross-linked polyethylene does not behave like traditional thermoplastics when heated above its 'melting' point, the crystal structure is destroyed, but the material does not flow (ie the melt flow rate of PE-X is zero).  This is the limiting factor in the fusion jointing of PE-X, which has been a restriction to the wider spread use of the material in pipe form.  In its molten state the PE-X pipe maintains its form, but behaves like an elastomeric material, with a very low modulus.

PE-X pipe is widely used for hot water pipes, but its use in the gas industry, to date, has been limited.  In October 1994 an ISO working group (2) was set up to prepare a performance specification for PE-X pipes carrying gaseous fuels.

## PIPE PRODUCTION AND INSTALLATION METHOD.

The proposed method of installation requires the PE-X pipe to be produced at a diameter which gives a close fit inside the cast iron main.  Then, whilst still hot, it is factory deformed to a suitable shape/ dimension which would allow easy insertion into a cleaned main without removing the protruding plugs or bends, up to 22.5°. With the plugs remaining in the main it was felt that the preferred pipe profile would be circular, as the recovery, on reheating, would be by radial growth and fairly uniform, thus, eliminating the risk of scouring, or tearing, the liner in its softened condition. As the required PE-X pipe is not commercially available at present, British Gas is working jointly with Uponor UK to develop the close fit lining system. The PE-X pipe used in the evaluation was produced by Wirsbo, part of the Uponor organisation, using the Engel Process (3), in which a powder form of high density polyethylene is mixed with a measured quantity of peroxide before being introduced into the extruder. The material is heated and then forced through the extruder die head and extruded over a heated mandrel where the cross-linking process is completed. A haul-off unit pulls the pipe through the calibration die and into the cooling baths. The dimensions achieved during the cross-linking process become the preferred shape of the product and any distortions after this time are recoverable by heating the material above its crystalline melt temperature of approximately 140°C. Wirsbo have been able to produce a 110 mm PE-X pipe reduced, during production, to a stable diameter of 78 mm, with minimal elongation.

Insertion of the PE-X pipe into the cast iron main is essentially a slip lining process. Excavations are only required at the positions where existing services have to be transferred from the old main to the newly inserted main. At these positions, a section of the cast iron main has to be removed, to allow connections to be made to the recovered PE-X pipe. Once inserted, the pipe has to be heated above its melt temperature to recover its original shape giving a close fit lining inside the original main. In its 'molten' condition the material deforms around the protruding plugs. On cooling, thermal contraction causes the PE-X pipe to shrink slightly, away from the sharp edges of the plug. The materials inherent high stress crack resistance minimises the likelihood of failure by slow crack growth at these points. Results of plug indentation test are given in a later Section.

British Gas has produced an initial guideline specification (Appendix 1) for a close fit lining system using PE-X pipe. The specification is for the renovation of 4" and 6" cast iron mains.

To establish the power requirements to raise the pipe temperature above its reformation temperature, the thermal properties have been determined and are given in Table 1. Using these values, the energy required to raise 100 metres of 110mm SDR17.6 PE-X pipe to 160 °C is around 100 MJ or 14 kW per hour. This assumes the heating is 100% efficient; in reality higher energy levels will have to be delivered to recover the pipe. Various methods to recover the deformed PE-X pipe to its original shape are currently being evaluated, including hot gasses, steam and infra red radiation. Polyethylene is an insulating material and heating by conduction or convection would be inefficient.

The PE-X pipe, being evaluated, is translucent and therefore it absorbs and transmits infrared radiation at different frequencies. To determine the most efficient method of heating the translucent plastic material, the absorption characteristics were identified using a Fourier transform infrared (FTIR) spectrometer. Measurements were taken in the infra red wavelength range 1.65 to 24 microns and are shown in Figure 1. The Figure shows a fundamental absorption line between 3.4 and 3.5 microns, relating to the C-H bond stretching mode. Further strong absorptions can be seen at 6.8 microns (C-H bending) and 13.7 microns (C-H rocking). It is common practise in vacuum forming processing to use infrared heat sources, where the radiant source peak wavelength matches the primary absorption wavelength of the polymer. The radiant heat energy is primarily absorbed at the surface of the PE-X pipe, within the first few millimetres, and this raises the temperature of the remaining material by conduction.

| | |
|---|---|
| Specific heat (Cp solid < 130°C) | 2.68 kJ kg-1 K-1 |
| Specific heat (Cp melt ) | 2.16 kJ kg-1 K-1 |
| Latent heat of fusion | 145 kJ kg-1 |

**Table 1. Thermal properties of PE-X pipe.**

Infrared heat lamps were initially used to demonstrate the recovery of the PE-X pipe, however it was felt that these would not be robust enough for field applications, so current investigations are examining the use of 3 metre long flexible electrical heating ropes, wound around an articulated carriage (Figure 2). The heater train is 45 mm diameter, giving 20 mm clearance inside the PE-X pipe. The power to the heaters are controlled by thermocouples monitoring the bore temperature of the PE-X pipe. Figure 3 shows the electrical heater being pulled through the PE-X pipe. One problem to be overcome with this system is the hot convection gasses rise to the top of the pipe and char the inner surface. Air movement has been introduced to try and circulate the air inside the pipe, but it tends to cause the heating elements to overheat and fail. An alternative energy source also being studied is a gas heated infrared source, where a pre-mixed gas-air mixture is supplied to a number of burners built into a 3 metre long flexible carriage, which is pulled through the pipe. Combustion products, from the burners, are used to preheat the un-recovered section of pipe.

To meet the operational constraints, and the draft British Gas specification, the heater carriage has to be pulled, by a speed controlled winch, through the pipe at a minimum speed of 0.83 m/min (50m/hr). Recovering the pipe from one end allows services to be transferred from the old main to the newly installed PE-X pipe, once the heater has passed the section and the pipe has recovered and cooled.

PIPE STRENGTH TESTS

The PE-X pipe is designed to be fully pressure rated.  If plugs are to be left in position, the pipe will be deformed as it flows around the protrusion in its molten state.  A series of tests has been carried out on 110 mm SDR11 and SDR33 PE-X pipe to assess the long term performance of the material when deformed around plugs.  Tests were carried out at 80°C, using stainless steel rings fitted over the PE-X pipe, with an M24 bolt fitted to give a penetration of 20mm into the recovered PE-X pipe.  A 110 mm diameter ring was used to simulate a tight fitting liner at a plug position (ie the test pressure stress was unable to deform the PE-X pipe) and a 125 mm diameter ring used to simulate where the liner was free to further expand around the protrusion.  To achieve the necessary deformation, the PE-X pipe was heated above its recovery temperature of 140°C and placed centrally in the stainless steel ring.  The M24 bolt was then screwed into the 'molten' pipe until the required 20mm deformation was achieved.

The test geometry is shown schematically in Figure 4.

The most common flow stopping  method used in British Gas distribution activities is by squeeze off.  To determine the effects of this operation on recovered PE-X pipe, a series of tests were carried out using SDR 11 and SDR17.6 pipe.   Using proprietary equipment and squeezing the pipe at -5°C, there was no measurable let-by leakage at 75 mbar, and only 0.015 m3/hr at 2 bar pressure.

The results of the penetration and squeeze off tests are given in Table 2.

| Test | SDR | Time on test (hrs) | Comments |
|------|-----|--------------------|----------|
| Penetration of M24 bolt, 20mm into the XLPE pipe to simulate recovery around protruding plug. | 11 11 33 33 | 4800 7158 1000+ 1000+ | Pipe in 125mm collar Pipe in 110mm collar Pipe in 125mm collar Pipe in 110mm collar |
| Squeeze off test | 11 17.6 | 3500 3500 | |

Notes:  All samples tested at 80°C and a nominal hoop stress of 4MPa.
          All samples removed from test without failure.
          Minimum specification time for plain PE pipe is 1000 hours.

**Table 2: Test results on deformed cross linked polyethylene pipes.**

The results show that the PE-X pipes are capable of withstanding a penetration of 20 mm by a plug of nominally 24 mm diameter, without affecting the long term integrity of the pipeline.

FITTING EVALUATION.

It is not possible to fusion join two PE-X pipes together, normally mechanical compression fittings are used for this purpose. Tests by British Gas have shown that PE-X pipes can be fusion jointed using proprietary MDPE electrofusion fittings, without special procedures. Various geometries of fittings including service saddle connections (tapping tees) and in-line socket fittings have been evaluated. In British Gas operations, electrofusion tapping tees are installed by applying a constant load to the fitting stack. It was found necessary, when fusing these fittings to SDR 33 pipe, to support the pipe either side of the fitting to prevent ovalisation during the fusion operation. Only a slight distortion of the pipe bore occurred during the fusion operation. In some circumstances the PE-X pipe may not fully recover to its original size ( eg when restricted by the host main) and during subsequent fusion operations the residual recovery may affect the quality of the fusion joint; this has been evaluated by fusing 110 x 32mm tapping tees onto PE-X pipe, reduced to 95 mm. The results show the performance of all fusion joints evaluated, when tested at a nominal pipe stress of 4MPa, exceeded the minimum 80°C test time of 1000 hours by at least a factor of two, without failure.

CONCLUDING REMARKS

*   This close fit lining system offers many benefits including maximising flow capacity, savings in excavation and reinstatement cost, minimising the inconvenience to the general public by having a number of excavations open at any time and having a material which is very tolerant of defects. The main development work outstanding is the optimisation of the heat recovery tool.

REFERENCES

1.    Maine. L and Ross. J  'Swagelining - A pipeline renovation technique' Plastics Pipe VIII, 21-24 September, 1992, Netherlands

2.    ISO /TC138 /SC4 'Cross linked PE pipe systems for the transport of gaseous fuels. AHG 'Cross linked polyethylene'

3.    Harget. D C, Skarelius. J and Imgram.F  ' Crosslinked polyethylene - Extending the limits of pressure pipe system performance.

4.    Plastics Pipe III, 21-24 September, 1992, Netherlands.

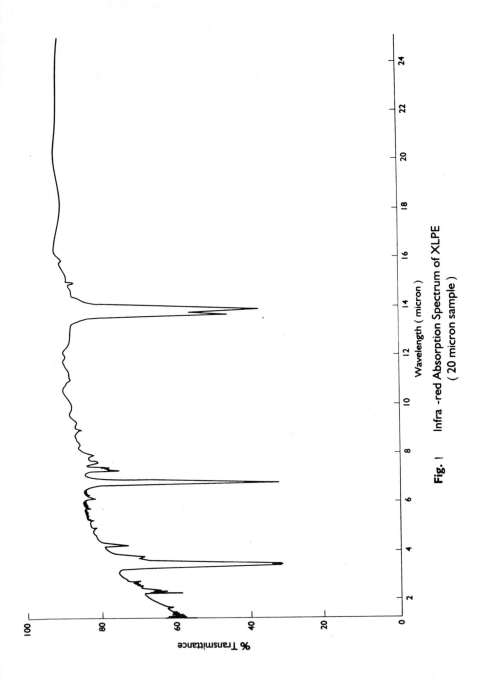

**Fig. I**    Infra -red Absorption Spectrum of XLPE
( 20 micron sample )

Figure 2          Articulated electric heater train

Figure 3          Heater train being pulled through PE-X pipe

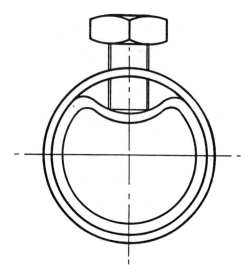

a) Tight Fit Liner with Plug Penetration

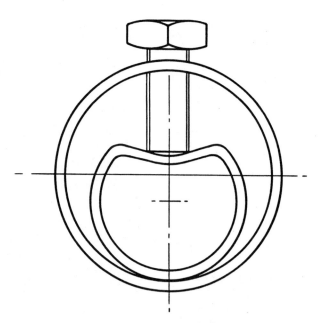

b) Loose Fit Liner with Plug Penetration

Figure 4     Plug Penetration Tests

**ROBOTICS - THE FINAL LINK!**


**ROBOTISATION - LE MAILLON FINAL!**


**Derek Stoves**
**British Gas plc**
**Research & Technology, UK**


## ABSTRACT

Much of the 230,000 km of British Gas low pressure pipe
network has been in place for many decades. Maintenance and
replacement activities are therefore continuously underway.
Economic and environmental pressures to minimise excavation
have encouraged much innovation. Mains can be replaced using
methods such as swagelining, and service pipe can be lined by
insertion; yet there is an excavation required on average every
9 metres to connect the inserted service to the lined main. A
development has been outlined aimed at enabling this task in
particular, and many related activities, to be carried out
with minimum excavation by using a remote controlled or
semi-autonomous robotic system. The system concept is
presented, prototype equipment described and future potential
indicated.

## RÉSUMÉ

Une grande partie des 230,000 km du réseau British Gas de
tuyautage basse pression est en service depuis maintes décades.
Des activités d'entretien et d'échanges sont donc en route sans
cesse. Des contraintes économiques et environnementales pour
minimiser l'excavation ont stimulé de grandes innovations. Des
réseaux peuvent être remplacés en se servant de méthodes telles
que le revêtement par l'emboutissage, tandis que les tuyaux
d'abonnés peuvent être revêtés par l'insertion. Toutefois ceci
nécessite une excavation en moyenne toutes les neuf mètres pour
lier le service inséré au réseau revêté. Une évolution est
résumé qui vise à permettre d'exécuter ce travail en
particulier et beaucoup d'activités associées avec excavation
minimale en se servant d'une système de robotisation
demi-automatique ou commandée à distance. La conception de la
système et des installations prototype sont décrites et les
possibilités futures sont indiquées.

BACKGROUND - MAINS REPLACEMENT

The British Gas distribution system has been developed over a period of more than a hundred years. It comprises approximately 420,000 km of low pressure mains and service pipe. Around 230,000 km of this is classified as low pressure distribution main, of which over 60% is cast iron.

Active policies have been pursued to replace those pipes which, in the event of failure, would have the worst consequences, and as a result iron pipe has been selectively replaced at around 2500 km per year.

Economic and environmental pressures to minimise excavation whilst replacing the pipe have encouraged considerable innovation, particularly in the use of polyethylene pipe (Ref 1). The British Gas Swagelining system for pulling polyethylene pipe into the old cast iron main is a typical example (Ref 2). Using this technique lengths of several hundred metres of pipe can be pulled in with no intermediate excavations. In addition, methods have been developed for inserting a polyethylene pipe into the old service pipe, from the customer's premises up to the connection on the main. But the inserted pipe stops short of the old tee or elbow which connects the original service to the main, leaving a gap to be closed. An excavation is therefore required to complete every connection on the main (fig 1), normally by removal of a section of main along with the old service tee, so that a polyethylene saddle connector can be electrofusion welded onto the polyethylene main (fig 1 insert).

NO-DIG OPTIONS FOR THE FINAL CONNECTION

There is no available sub-surface method to complete the process of mains and service replacement, by closing the gap between the two and making a suitable connection. The main features required of a process to achieve this are:

- Bore through the PE mains liner to open into the service

- Provide a closure element between the inserted service and the main

- Connect the closure element to the inserted service and the main

The routes to a solution are:

a)   Access through a small bore hole from the ground surface - but this will require accurate location of the tee from above ground and it does not eliminate excavation.

b)   Access through the service pipe - typically 25mm bore and 14m long with at least one bend prior to the tee.

c)   Remote access from within the main - preferably down to 150mm pipe or less.

As a result of exploring the possibilities associated with these modes of access and the feasibility of specific ideas, a system concept was developed based upon (b) and (c) above. This involved development of the service insertion process and development of an in-pipe robotic system to provide remote access from within the main. In the context of the original connection on the main the worst case of a tee was assumed as the connection to be negotiated. A swept bend is substantially less severe, and an elbow slightly less difficult to negotiate.

THE ROBOTICS CONCEPT

The concept envisaged (fig 2) to provide this final link in the process of sub-surface replacement, comprised a remote controlled in-pipe vehicle to locate the old tee connection and drill through the PE liner into the tee. Service insertion would require developing to enable negotiation of the tee, such that the lead end will enter the hole drilled in the main. Then the inserted service would be joined, preferably fusion welded to the main, probably via tooling on the in-pipe vehicle.

Access distances of around 100 metres are necessary to enable a typical street of homes to be connected without intermediate excavations, and pipes down to 150mm bore and preferably less were the target because of their predominance. Hydraulic drives and the associated heavy umbilicals, such as those employed by KA-TE with their sewer repair system (Ref 3) are inappropriate because of their weight and the associated drag. The only practial alternative is electrical power, and this must ideally be on board to avoid the drag from a long umbilical. Electrically actuated vehicles such as the GRI Mouse (Ref 4) have been developed for application in small pipes, but they are generally targeted on inspection only. Space is very limited for carrying, manipulating and powering tools such as milling or drilling machines.

Tele-robotic operation is commonly used in the remote control of vehicles and tooling, but the limited space and the repetitive operation targeted (up to fifteen connections per access) merit a semi-autonomous approach with operator override.

DEVELOPMENT STATUS

Service Insertion

A method of enabling a service liner to be inserted fully around the old tee connector, into a predrilled hole in the PE mains liner, has been developed to prototype level in parallel with exploring the means of making a fusion connection between the two.

Most, and possibly all service tees are close to top dead centre of the main, hence gravity can be used to assist the insertion process. Using this approach a guide wire has been developed with a specially constructed lead end (fig 3), to enable negotiation of the tee. The guide wire comprises a flexible lead end which is guided into the tee by the dead weight on the lead end. A more rigid section of the wire then provides a guide for the service liner, which is inserted over the wire.

There are three elements to the service liner; a lead component which will easily fit into the drilled hole and can preferably be fused to the main, a flexible element to bend around the tee with minimum effort and whilst maintaining its internal flow area, the remainder being less flexible to withstand the axial insertion force.

The lead component was developed from cross linked polyethylene (PE) which can be expanded into the hole and fused to the main using a locally placed heating element on board the in-pipe machine. Convoluted PE tubing was employed as the flexible element and standard 20mm medium density PE service tubing was used in the prototype system for the remainder. The three elements were able to be fusion welded together (fig 4).

Joint Fusion

The lead component on the inserted service liner was developed from cross linked PE, because of its "memory" properties. It was cold formed from 20mm tube to produce a tapered lead end and a reduced lead diameter, to facilitate negotiation of the tee and location of the hole in the main. A new technique has been developed and patented for producing a fused joint remotely between this component and the main. Heat is applied via a radiant element, raising the temperature to the crystalline melt stage, at which the component expands and simultaneously fuses to the main (fig 5).

Laboratory experiments have shown that a low powered radiant heating element is adequate. Work to date indicates that a satisfactory level of fusion should be achieved with this process, but further development of the process and the components is required to ensure reliable and repeatable results.

In-Pipe Vehicle

General. A prototype vehicle has been designed for operation in polyethylene lined 150 mm bore cast iron pipe. It is of modular form and it incorporates the basic features required for the above application, whilst providing the flexibility to be adapted for a wide range of other potential applications.

A view of the prototype is shown in fig 6. The machine comprises a number of units; there is a traction unit, power pack, manipulator and end effectors, which are virtually independent operational modules such as a geometric sensor, a drill and a fusion module.

Analysis of bend passing capability, with particular regard to the maximum expected 11.5 degree "kick joint" in iron mains provided dimensional limitations which were applied to rigid module bodies. Because of severe limitations on module size the suspension was designed as a stand alone unit, flexibly connected to the rigid operational modules.

Traction. A Traction drive has been produced to accommodate significant variations in pipe diameter by employing an adjustable lever mechanism to drive the wheels out against the pipe wall.

Both driven and idler wheels carry sensors to detect motion, thus the unit is able to detect slippage of the drive wheels and compensate by increasing the traction load via adjusting a ball screw and the lever arm position.

A small geared electric motor rotates the drive wheels, and another controls the transverse load via the ball screw and lever arms. Feedback from transducers on the wheels and gearing provides information from which movement, direction and slippage can be estimated by on-board software. Although the performance is not yet optimised the current traction unit will provide a tow force of up to 80N, and a speed of 30 mm/s.

Manipulator. Rotational manipulation of on-board tools or sensors can either be carried out locally within the appropriate module or "globally" by a module designed specifically to provide movement to several adjacent modules simultaneously. Although local manipulation is required for some movements such as rotating a drill bit, there is an advantage in global movement for operations which have the same datum. For example the geometric sensor must locate the old service tee, then the drill is to be centred under the same location and subsequently the service sensor placed in the same site.

A rotational manipulator has been designed to provide rotation in two 180° arcs, whilst the body of the unit is clamped against the pipe wall. To avoid slip rings and resulting interference with the transmission of digital information along the vehicle train, a spiral cable is employed within the manipulator. There are two drives on board the unit – one to produce the clamping action and the other to provide rotation.

Geometric Sensor. The sensing system for locating the service through the PE liner is based on a variable reluctance magnetic circuit, containing a Hall effect magnetic flux detector. The presence (or absence) of ferromagnetic material, the pipe in this case, over the sensor will cause a change in the magnetic field measured. There is a correlation between the field level and the amount of material which can be detected at some distance from the inner wall. An offtake will, in all cases, have a hole in the centre; this corresponds to a large loss of material locally. The response at the centre of the hole will be a maximum and it is the identification of this maximum which allows the offtake position to be determined as indicated by the characteristic in fig 6 (insert top left).

Drill Module. It has been found that a hole of approximately 16 mm diameter is required in the mains liner to enable successful service insertion through a 25 mm tee, and to provide for interference during the fusion process. The drill module is required to produce this hole, machining the polyethylene with a minimum of power and with sufficient travel to pierce the wall of the PE liner. A unit has been developed to produce the required torque with minimum of power consumption and avoiding leaving a ring or disc of liner material in the tee. Drill bit profile, drive systems and support clamps have all been developed and prototype tests are promising.

Service Sensor and Heating Element. It appears feasible to carry the heating element on the same module as a sensor to detect the presence of the guide wire and inserted service liner, utilising the same drive mechanism for two purposes and minimising the space required. The module simply needs to be rotated through 180° to carry out the two different operations. Development of this module is in its early stages. Nevertheless, work on the initial prototype has provided confidence in the approach.

Suspension Unit. A variety of suspension options have been considered, a major criterion being to maintain the operational modules concentric with the pipe, within a few millimetres. Since the vehicle must be able to pass around slight bends in the pipe, the suspension was not connected rigidly to each module because this would increase the module length or diameter. A separate suspension module was introduced and connected flexibly to the rigid modules on either side.

The suspension units are provided with common mechanical and electrical connections; support is through six spring loaded lever arms each carrying a wheel. In order to avoid the use of a highly preloaded suspension spring, the three level arms at one end of each unit are interconnected via a slider. Thus when the body of the suspension unit is depressed below the pipe centre line the wheels at the top will be pulled away from the pipe wall providing no resistance to the upward centralising force. Friction forces in this type of mechanism can be high and development is progressing to minimise this. Low friction wheels were chosen to minimise the

resistance to their transverse motion relative to the pipe wall as in
the work of Okada and Kanade (Ref 5), thus to facilitate the required
centering action.

A central shaft through each suspension unit is free to rotate
relative to the body. Communications and power harnessing also pass
through the suspension units to link the "intelligent" modules.

Control & Electronics. The control strategy is based on a
hierarchical modular control and monitor processes operating on
independent communicating modules. A number of connected modules act
as a single entity under the control of a Master controller, which
can also communicate with an off-board user interface. The Master
will interrogate the other modules in the train at power-up to
determine the module configuration, hence the required task. A
control unit within each module in the vehicle train carries out low
level control of the module, acting under high level control from the
Master. An internal communications protocol is employed to handle
message routing, multiplexing messages for return to the Master and
fielding commands from slave modules. Link-driver processes are
incorporated to detect communications failure and transmit an
internal alarm signal.

Each module is fitted with a control board, sensors and
actuators to provide the required control function. The majority of
the modules share a common design of the electronics control board,
which can be set up to support a number of different modes of
operation under software control.

All the control boards are transputer based, which provide a
Risc processor CPU, internal RAM and a set of inter-processor
communication links. This allows optimisation of functional
requirements within economic limitations, and provides a standard
high speed data link between modules.

The common control board (fig 6 insert bottom right), based on
the T225 transputer, includes a programmable peripheral device which
combines handling of multi-channel pulse inputs and outputs, switch
inputs and outputs and multi-channel analogue to digital conversion,
all under software control. Motor drivers are included to provide
both single-ended and bridge outputs, and support devices include
volatile and non-volatile memory. Non-standard board designs cater
for high speed, high resolution multi-channel analogue inputs, large
memory requirements, and power switching.

Board construction is multi-layer PCB, with the majority of
components in surface mount form in order to meet the constraints of
severely limited space.

Power Pack. The power for the vehicle train is carried on-board
and is presently in the form of a high capacity nickel-cadmium
rechargeable battery. This battery consists of two series connected
'pancakes', each 'pancake' comprising a number of series connected
cells; the pair of 'pancakes' located within a module chassis.
Battery control includes a multi-battery operation capability, with
intelligent switching between battery units under supervision of the
Master controller. The control board includes multi-channel analogue
inputs and MOSFET power switching output to allow monitoring of
output voltage, current and capacity.

Wireless Telemetry Link. A wireless telemetry link is being
developed to provide communication between the in-pipe machine and
the user interface. This link uses a pair of data transceivers, one

fitted to the end of the robot, the other to be inserted into the
open end of the pipe.

The communications link is to operate at a nominal frequency of
1.394 GHz, largely determined by international agreement on frequency
allocations, with the additional constraint imposed by the ability of
the pipeline to propagate the transmitted signal with low loss.
Within a 150 mm pipeline frequencies below approximately 1.1 GHz
suffer very high attenuation and cannot be used.  The pipeline acts
as a waveguide for the transmitted signal, achieving a relatively low
loss transmission path at the operating frequency.  A transputer link
adapter will provide the interface between the telemetry module and
the Master controller.

This system will be capable of enhancement to provide a video
transmission channel if required.

CONCLUSION

·   This development demonstrates the feasibility of remote in pipe
    robotic operations down to less than 150 mm bore.

·   The methodology provides the final link in enabling PE
    replacement of old iron mains without the need for multiple
    excavations in the road or path.

·   The approach provides the basis for a modular in-pipe
    maintenance system with the potential flexibility to undertake a
    range of tasks remotely.

·   There is the potential for such a machine to "live" in the pipe
    and recharge via a plug-in connection.

·   Development of a single design to operate over a range of pipe
    sizes will provide significant advantages.

·   Application of the concept to smaller pipes, down to 75mm bore,
    is of particular interest, since there is a large population of
    pipe which would benefit.

·   Development of smaller high output, rechargeable power packs
    will increase the potential range of applications.

REFERENCES

1.   L. Maine, "The Renovation of Gas Mains Using Polyethylene Pipes,
     International Symposium on Relining", 6 October 1994, Ghent.

2.   L. Behenna, K. Hicks, "Swagelining – The ERS Experience: Died,
     Buried and Forgotten", North of England Gas Association Meeting,
     12 May 1992, Killingworth.

3.   D.J. Green, "The Multi-Faceted Use of Robots in Sewer Repair",
     North American NO-DIG '93, 4 May 1993, San Jose, CA.

4.   M. Wilkey, R. Wiesman, G. Hazelden, "GRI's Internal Inspection
     System for Gas Distribution Mains", AGA Operating Section
     Proceeding, 1991.

5.   T. Okada, T. Kanade, "A Three-Wheeled Self-Adjusting Vehicle in
     a Pipe, FERRET-1", The International Journal of Robotics
     Research, Vol 6, No 4, Winter 1987.

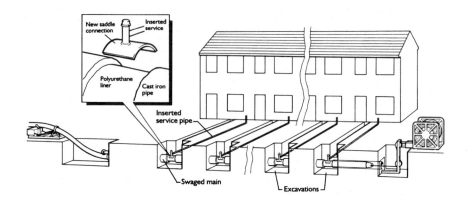

**Fig.1**  Current practice - multiple excavations

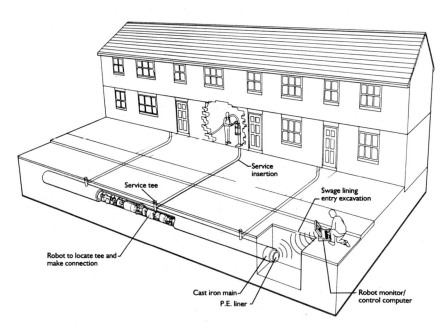

**Fig.2**  Proposed concept - no intermediate excavations

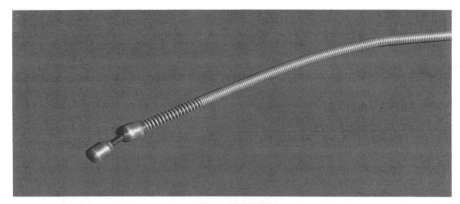

**Fig.3** Guide wire

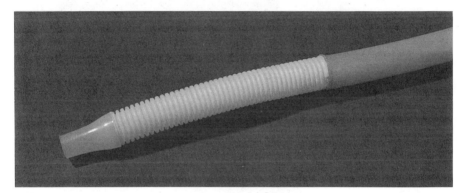

**Fig.4** Service lead end

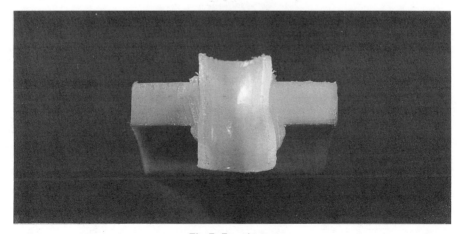

**Fig.5** Fused joint

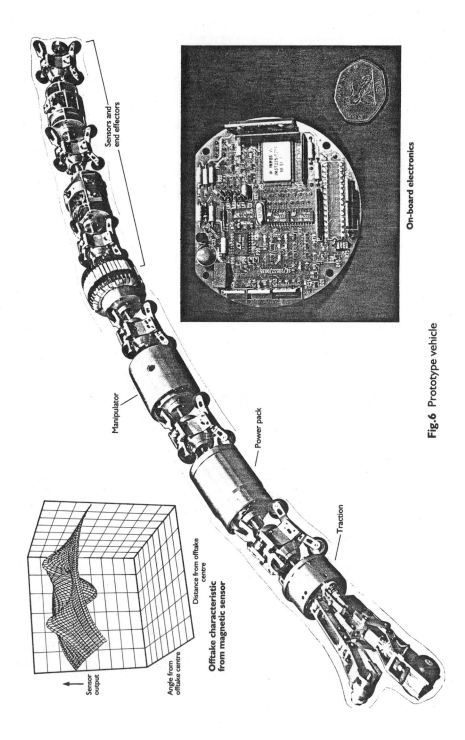

**Fig.6** Prototype vehicle

DEVELOPMENT OF STEERABLE PNEUMATIC IMPACT MOLE

DÉVELOPPEMENT D'UNE MOLE (instrument de percage) D'IMPACT, DIRIGEABLE, PNEUMATIQUE

Allan T. Fisk and David I. Freed
Foster-Miller, Inc., USA

Steven Gauthier
Gas Research Institute, USA

ABSTRACT

More than 1.2 million gas services are installed annually in the United States, as well as 27,000 km (17,000 miles) of gas distribution mains. Almost all of this pipe is polyethylene (PE) and the majority is smaller than 100 mm (4 in.) diameter. This paper describes the development of a new guided boring tool (a trenchless technology) designed to address this segment of the gas industry. The new device is based on the familiar pneumatic piercing tool, or impact mole, and includes the ability to track and steer the mole from launch point to destination pit. A simple steering head is combined with electromagnetic locating technology, resulting in a very economical guided boring capability.


RESUMÉ

Plus d'un 1.2 millions de services de gas sont installés annuellement aux Etats Unis aussi bien que 27000 km (17000 miles) de conduites de distribution du gas. Presque tout ce tuyau est du polyèthylene (PE) et la majorité est plus petite que 100 mm (4 in.) de diamètre. Ce papier decrit le développement d'un nouvel outil de perçage dirigé (une technologie sans tranchèes) destiné à addresser cette partie de l'industrie du gas. Ce nouvel instrument est basé sur le familier outil pneumatique de perçage, ou môle d'impact et inclus l'habilité de suivre et diriger le mole à partir du point de lançée à la fosse de destination. Une simple tête de direction est combinée avec une technologie electromagnetique de placement, resultant dans une très economique capacité de perçage dirigé.

## INTRODUCTION

Gas utilities have long sought the least expensive methods to install new underground gas services and mains. In today's climate of high surface values and even higher restoration costs, there is increased pressure on utilities to avoid as much excavation as possible when performing these installations. As a result, there is heightened interest in what has come to be known as no-dig, or trenchless construction methods. But for gas utilities, the need is for a very simple and economical tool; one that provides only moderate range, but with the ability to be set up very quickly and operated with no more than a two-man crew.

Until recently the only tool available to meet this mission was the familiar, unguided impact mole. An impact mole is a percussive tool, classified as a piercing tool, which creates a borehole using the compaction principle. Pneumatic impact moles are simple and relatively low in cost, but suffer from an infamous inability to be kept on course when soil conditions are even mildly challenging. The only alternative to date has been to utilize one of the mini-directional drilling rigs developed over the last few years. Unfortunately, even the smallest and simplest drilling rigs are much larger and more costly than an impact mole.

Foster-Miller has succeeded in developing a prototype of a steerable pneumatic impact mole. The tool incorporates several familiar technologies with a novel steering mechanism that is inexpensive and simple to operate. The result is a low cost capability to install gas services and small mains exactly on course.

## BACKGROUND

The early R&D effort on this new tool was funded internally by Foster-Miller and then jointly with U.S. utility Consolidated Edison Co. of New York. Later, the Gas Research Institute and U.S. utility Pacific Gas & Electric joined the program as sponsor and participant, respectively, as the focus of the effort shifted to developing a rugged, fieldable end product. Hardware support was provided by Charles Machine Works, makers of the Ditch Witch® line of products which includes Pierce Airrow® piercing tools. Foster-Miller selected the Pierce Airrow tool as the basis for the initial full-scale unit (for reasons explained later).

Pre-production models of the guided mole are currently being developed by Foster-Miller with funding from the Gas Research Institute and support from all of the above named parties. The chosen tool size is 65 mm (2.5 in.), primarily for use installing gas services to homes and apartments and for small diameter mains. Con Edison and Pacific Gas & Electric are participating in the utility field trials, and additional utilities will likely be added.

Both past and current efforts to steer piercing tools have been based on much the same principle as mini-directional drilling tools. That is, the tools all utilize a slant faced head which has a constant and permanent tendency to steer. In order to bore straight ahead these tools are made to rotate (to spiral through the ground) as they advance, thereby negating the steering tendency. Spiralling of a piercing tool has historically been accomplished by external soil-engaging fins which spin the entire tool about its axis. The fins are remotely actuated to enable/disable the spiralling action. In order to execute a turn these tools must be brought to the desired toolface angle (the slant head roll orientation) and allowed to advance without rotation. That is accomplished by coordinating the advance of the tool with its spiralling action so that the desired toolface angle is attained at the planned point of turning. The Foster-Miller guided mole program sought to avoid spiralling as the basis for straight boring.

## FOSTER-MILLER GUIDED MOLE CONCEPT: SIMILAR BUT DIFFERENT

The Foster-Miller guided mole is based on two simple concepts, one for steering and the other for tracking and guidance. The overall system schematic is shown in Figure 1. A detailed discussion of the principles of operation follows an overview of the major system elements.

The tool uses a novel, bistable steering head on an otherwise standard piercing tool. The term "bistable" means that the steering head has two operator-selectable configurations, one of which is symmetrical for boring straight ahead, and another which is asymmetrical for executing turns or steering corrections. By using this approach no external soil-engaging fins are needed to spiral the tool through the soil when boring a straight hole. When the steering mode is selected the entire tool, including its asymmetrical head, is rolled to the desired toolface angle at the beginning of the turn.

The second fundamental of the guided mole concept involves guidance and tracking. Walkover tracking has become a well-known standard of the mini-directional drilling industry. Onboard transmitters (sometimes called beacons or sondes) and handheld electromagnetic locators are now available from a

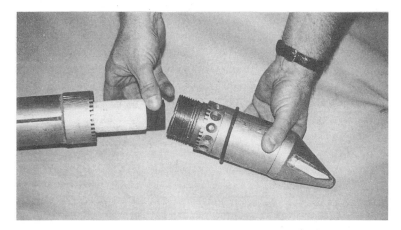

**Figure 2. Removable steering head and locator beacon**

The steerable head design is very simple, having only one moving part. It operates in two modes, one for straight and one for turning. Figures 3 and 4 show several views of the steering head in its two configurations. The nose on the steering head is rotatable about an axis that is skewed relative to the axis of the tool. The range of rotation is 180 deg between two bistable stops. In the first position the head is symmetrical, which directs the mole in a straight path. In the second position the head is asymmetrical, presenting a somewhat slanted face to the soil. In this asymmetric configuration the mole tends to steer in the direction of the toolface angle.

Shifting the head from the straight position to the steering position (and vice versa) is accomplished by a 180 deg relative rotation (CW or CCW) between the nose and the tool body. In practice, it is the piercing tool body that is rotated in the ground while the nose is restrained in place by the soil. That relative rotation is accomplished by applying a torque to the air hose, from the surface, while the tool is running. Once the steering head has been shifted to the steered position, additional tool rotation is performed to bring the toolface angle to the desired direction. End-of-travel stops in the head keep the nose in the steered position as the tool is brought to the correct toolface angle. Opposite hose torque shifts the head back to the straight configuration.

Tail Assembly

Attached to the back of the mole is a sensor housing which contains the pitch and roll sensors. The air which powers the tool and the direction control air line both pass through this sensor housing. Behind the sensor housing is a "hose whip," which is a flexible section which connects the surge valve to the tool.

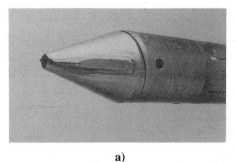

a)                              b)

**Figure 3. Steering head in straight configuration**

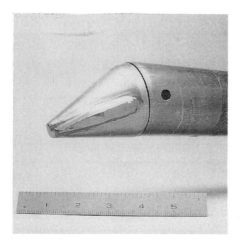

**Figure 4.  Steering head in steering configuration**

The orientation sensors measure the pitch and roll angles of the mole body. Power to, and signals from the pitch/roll sensors are transmitted to the surface over wires inside the air supply hose. The surge valve (sometimes called a shock valve) is required for reliable starting of the piercing tool when operating on long lengths of hose. The surge valve remains closed until pressure builds in the air supply hose to a preset value. It then snaps open and starts the mole quickly with a big "surge" of air. The surge valve design is based on a GRI-patented concept developed in an earlier R&D program.

Air Supply and Control

The guided mole is supplied air through an oversized hose. The fiber reinforced hose design is selected for light weight, flexibility, collapse resistance and high torsional stiffness. It is provided in 20m (60-ft) modular sections to facilitate ease of transport and a variety of job lengths. The hose sections are connected using custom-designed, bi-directional quick-connect couplings shown in Figure 5. The couplings transmit bi-directional torque through the joint, and are makeable/breakable without tools.

The air supply hose originates at an air supply skid. This skid is designed to slide along the ground with the air hose as the guided mole travels through the ground. The skid contains electrically-operated on/off and forward/reverse valves, two hose swivels, and an in-line air lubricator. The swivels allow the air hose to rotate relative to the skid as the guided mole is steered.

Guidance and Control Unit

The control display unit is used by the operator to monitor the attitude of the mole and to control its operation. In addition to an LCD display, the unit contains on/off and forward/reverse switches. It also contains a microprocessor-based data acquisition and display board which reads the pitch/roll sensors, performs the necessary calculations, filters and displays the output to the operator. The display format is intuitive; 24 clockface positions for roll angle and percent grade (up/down) for pitch. The electronics allow accurate pitch/roll readings to be taken while the tool is in operation. This saves considerable time, as stoppages are not required to survey the progress of the tool. Figure 6 shows the prototype guidance and control display unit.

PRINCIPLES OF OPERATION

Crew Makeup and Duties

The guided mole system can be operated by a two-man crew. The first crew member is the tracker who uses the walkover locator to determine and mark the location and depth of the tool as it advances. The procedure is identical to mini-directional drilling and so is the equipment. The second crew member is the operator. He monitors and controls the attitude of the mole and executes steering maneuvers, not unlike a directional drill operator. A layout of a typical residential gas service installation is shown in Figure 7.

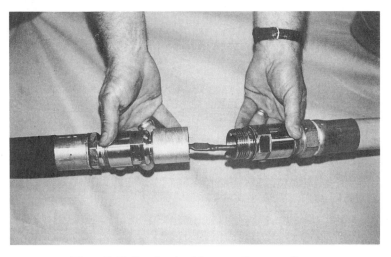

Figure 5.  Bi-directional quick-connect hose couplings

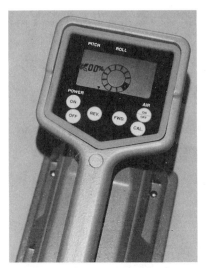

Figure 6.  Prototype guidance control display unit

**Figure 7. Typical installation of residential gas service**

In this case the guided mole was surface launched to pass through the small starting pit at depth, and then guided to the gas main in the street. Surface launching, shown in Figure 8, allows the user more options in planning and executing a job, and helps limit the size of launching and receiving pits.

The tracker detects azimuth deviations (left/right) from the planned path and communicates needed course corrections to the operator. The tracker can also detect unplanned fluctuations in depth (pitch), but by the time he recognizes these departures the tool has already begun to climb or sink more than a little. The operator (at the launch point) is in a better position to detect the onset of pitch deviations because he has a continuous display of the pitch angle on his control unit, and the resolution of the pitch sensor is much better than that of changing surface depth measurements. If the operator sees a need to make a pitch correction he can do so immediately. Of course, the tracker may also call for a pitch (depth) correction based on desired trajectory or topography.

Executing a Steering Correction

When a steering correction is called for the operator must first shift the steerable head to the steering configuration by rotating the guided mole body 180 deg relative to the nose. This is accomplished by applying an appropriate torque to the torsionally stiff air hose near the point of entry into the bore. The notion of rolling a piercing tool by twisting on an air hose was at least bold and probably radical at the outset. But it does work. The hose torque is felt at the back of the tool.

Soil friction on the tool body is overcome by applying the torque while the tool is running. With each blow of the piston (at several hundred blows per minute) the tool body rotates slightly in the soil while the nose, which remains engaged with the soil, does not rotate. The head is therefore shifted when 180 deg or more of relative rotation has taken place. The operator monitors the rotation by observing the roll angle (toolface angle) display.

Normally the mole will advance a few feet, depending on soil properties, during this 180 deg roll shift. But a quicker transition has been found to be effective and efficient. While applying the torque to the hose the operator momentarily jogs the piercing tool back and forth between the forward and reverse directions. This frees up the nose a little from the soil and allows it to nutate (to wobble) around, relative to the rotating head and tool body, to the new position. Using this technique the roll shift occurs much more quickly and virtually in place.

**Figure 8.  Surface lauching the guided mole**

Once the roll shift has been executed the operator must bring the now-asymmetric head to the desired toolface angle. This is accomplished by simply continuing the tool rotation (the hose torque) in the same direction until the desired toolface angle is achieved. Because the nose is against an internal top in the head, it is carried around with the tool body. Again, setting the toolface angle is done with the tool running and using the quick-reverse jogging feature to speed the process.

Hose torque is applied to the hose at the launch point, which is in the middle of the hose most of the time. A swivel at the trailing end of the hose (at the control valve and oiler) allows the entire hose to rotate freely on the ground.  Figure 9 shows a steering correction being implemented with the hose torquer during an early field test.

Resumption of Straight Boring

The tracker and the operator decide when a sufficient course correction has been completed using location, depth, and pitch data. When they are satisfied it is time to revert to straight moling, the operator does this by simply reversing the roll shift process. The hose is torqued in the opposite direction to produce at least a 180 deg tool body rotation, thereby shifting the nose back to its former stop which defines a symmetrical head configuration. The reverse roll shift is also done in place with the tool running.

Holding the Bistable Nose Positions

There are several features in the steerable head which help maintain the nose in each of its two positions. The 180 deg rotational stops have already been described. In addition there are bistable control surfaces built into the nose which keep the nose against the desired stop.  The reader is referred back to Figures 3 and 4 for an illustration of these features.

Two wings are positioned on the front of the nose within the cross-sectional profile of the tool. The wings are bevel-biased so that when the head is in the symmetrical position and boring straight, a slight clockwise torque is generated on the nose as soil passes over the nose. This torque keeps the nose rotated against the straight position stop, even if temporarily bumped off the stop by rocks in the soil. These clockwise biases are small, and when the nose is in the asymmetric or steered position they are shadowed and do not generate any torque.

However, when the head is in the steered position there are other features which come into play. The two wings are on opposite sides of the nose and have unequal areas. While this has no effect in the

**Figure 9.  Steering correction made by torquing the air hose**

straight mode, it causes a counterclockwise torque to be generated when the head is moving through the soil in the steered configuration. This keeps the nose against the steered stop when executing a turn.  Thus there are no detents or actuators in the steerable head assembly. Two-position, bistable operation is entirely passive, as the soil does the work. There is also plenty of room in the head for a very simple and robust nose bearing with proper lubrication.

FEATURES AND BENEFITS OF GUIDED MOLE

Many of the positive features of this new guided boring device (and some of the drawbacks) are the direct result of the underlying piercing tool technology. Others are more attributable to the simplicity and execution of the concept. As a generic compaction tool, the guided mole offers features not available in mini-directional drilling rigs, including:

- No drill cuttings.
- No drilling fluids.
- No mud pumps.
- No drill string.
- No hydraulic power unit.
- Common power source (standard compressor).
- Flexible air supply hose.
- Easy storage/transport.
- Very quick setup.

Of course, there are also generic limitations. Performance is dependent on soil conditions. Piercing tools are not for use in solid rock, or even in boulder fields, very hard soils, or completely unstable formations. Borehole size and range are also limited relative to mini-directional rigs. Fifty to 150 mm (2 to 6 in.) diameter guided piercing tools are practical.  Usable piercing tool range is enhanced by having a steerable feature, but maximum range will not match that of mini-directional drill rigs in comparable soils. The predicted usable range of the guided mole is 50 to 100m (150 to 300 ft) again, depending on soil conditions and borehole size.

Compared to previous developments in the area of steerable piercing tools, the Foster-Miller guided mole achieves its objectives with some distinct differences:

- Steering is accomplished with no increase in tool cross-sectional area over that of the underlying piercing tool. A 65mm tool makes a 65mm hole. Limited available impact energy is not wasted. Productivity is not impaired.
- No external soil-engaging mechanisms are dragged through the soil. This keeps the impact energy going into making hole, and is a reliability benefit.
- Integrated tool body construction is strong, durable.

- Simple steering concept with integrated body construction is compact, with very little increase in total tool length or parasitic weight, both of which would impair piercing tool performance.

Compared to traditional unguided piercing tools the guided mole offers the following advantages:

- Surface launch and retrieval is practical.
- Curved borehole trajectories are practical.
- Straight bores can be kept straight.
- The usable range of piercing tools is extended, filling a need below that of mini-directional rigs.
- The range of soil types amenable to piercing tools is broadened significantly by the ability to make steering corrections.
- Jobs not previously possible with piercing tools become practical, at a cost closer to that of unguided moles than to that of mini-directional drill rigs.

## GAS INDUSTRY AND ALTERNATIVE APPLICATIONS

Of the 1.2 million polyethylene pipe gas services installed annually in the United States about two-thirds, or 800,000 per year are new services (the rest are replacements and most of those are inserted with PE). Approximately 95 percent of these new services are presently installed by direct burial methods, and the average service length is about 21m (70 ft), although that length is increasing each year. Ninety-nine percent of these new PE services are 51mm (2.0 in.) diameter or smaller. This clearly makes the gas service market a prime candidate to benefit from the availability of a low cost guided mole. Guided moles of 65 and 76 mm (2.5 and 3.0 in.)[1] diameter would address this need.

In the United States, polyethylene is also the material of choice for most new and replacement gas mains. About 27,000 km (17,000 miles) of PE mains are installed each year. Seventy-two percent of these mains are 51mm (2.0 in.) or smaller, and 95 percent are 102 mm (4.0 in.) or smaller. At the present time between two-thirds and three-quarters of these mains are still installed by direct burial methods (the rest are by insertion, boring, pipe splitting and plowing) and most are placed under pavement in municipal rights of way[1]. The guided mole offers a trenchless opportunity to significantly reduce the cost of installing such mains. Guided moles of 76 and 152 mm (3.0 and 6.0 in.) diameter would address this need.

A guided mole would be a valuable asset in any contractor's or utility's arsenal of trenchless technologies, not only for gas lines but also for, elecric, water, phone, fiber and cable services. Innovative contractors will undoubtedly see other uses as well. For instance, piercing tools can and have been used to pull a liner into the borehole. In fact, with the Foster-Miller guided mole it is perfectly feasible to use the liner as the air hose to the tool. These possibilities open up a number of non-utility applications for guided piercing tools in the environmental area. Among them would be surface-to-surface horizontal boreholes at hazardous waste sites for the installation of environmental wells. These wells would then be used for site characterization, monitoring and remediation. The ability to do these bores dry, with no fluid contamination into or out of the borehole, would be a valuable asset in such scenarios.

## REFERENCE

1. GRI Distributiuon Cost Components Database, 1994-95; T. Joyce Assoc., Inc.

DEVELOPMENT OF A NEW TOOL FOR NON-DESTRUCTIVE
TESTING OF ROADS AND PAVEMENTS

P. Ward and P. McGonnell
British Gas Plc, UK

ABSTRACT

This paper describes the development of an instrument which uses impulse radar to measure the thickness of the surface
layers of roads and pavements. In the UK, several organisations use Ground Probing Radar (GPR) to inspect roads but the
systems are expensive. In addition, they are complex to set up and use, difficult to interpret, not easily portable and must
be calibrated for the material to be inspected by use of on site core samples. The new instrument developed by British Gas
is designed to be a simple tool for use by staff with no technical expertise in GPR, which provides accurate and reliable
measurement data for on the spot decision making. The paper outlines the major features of the design, and quotes
performance results obtained from laboratory and field testing of the instrument. Finally, the potential for application of
this technology to other engineering problems is explored, particularly the non-destructive investigation of concrete
structures and bridges.


RÉSUMÉ

Cet article décrit le développement d'un instrument qui utilise un radar à impulsions pour mesurer l'épaisseur des couches
superficielles des routes et des chaussées. Au Royaume-Uni, plusieurs entreprises utilisent des radars pour inspecter les
routes mais ces systèmes sont coûteux. En outre, ils sont complexes à installer et à utiliser, difficiles à interpréter, peu
faciles à transporter et ils doivent être étalonnés en fonction du matériau à inspecter en relevant des échantillons sur place.
Le nouvel instrument devéloppé par British Gas est un outil de conception simple destiné à être utilisé par un personnel
qui n'a acune connaissance technique des radars. Il fournit des mesures précises et fiables des données permettant au
personnel de prendre des décisions immédiates. L'article décrit les principales caractéristiques de conception et présente
les résultats des essais de laboratoire et in-situ de l'instrument. Enfin, il explore le potentiel d'application de cette
technologie dans le cadre d'autres secteurs techniques, en particulier l'examen non destructif des ouvrages en béton et des
ponts.

## INTRODUCTION

Excavation and reinstatement of roads and pavements are an everyday problem for engineers in Utility companies world-wide. For excavations in roads and pavements, the largest part of the cost is to reinstate the excavation, to an engineering standard suitable for withstanding the normal traffic usage for the road. Local arrangements for specifying the quality of the reinstatement and for carrying out the work will vary but inevitably the utility bears the cost of carrying out the temporary and permanent reinstatements and often the cost of subsequent failures within a defined guarantee period.

In the UK, the regulatory framework for carrying out streetworks underwent a major revision in 1991, with the introduction of the New Roads and Street Works Act, under which utilities were empowered to reinstate their own excavations to an agreed standard. British Gas was determined to take advantage of this situation by increasing the first time permanent reinstatement, and by implementing improved quality control procedures, to reduce the occurrence of failures within the guarantee period and to reduce the cost of the job. One of the major factors that affects the load bearing capability of a road is the thickness of the bound material at the surface. Unfortunately, this is one of the most difficult parameters to check without destroying the integrity of the surface. The conventional method of checking the thickness of a bituminous or concrete surface is to take a core sample which is impractical for small area excavations and for larger excavations provides only a spot sample. A requirement was therefore identified for a Non-Destructive, Quality Control Tool, which was capable of measuring the thickness of the surface layers of a road in a non-invasive manner.

## CURRENT INSPECTION METHOD

The conventional method of checking the thickness of a bituminous or concrete surface is to take a core sample using a hydraulically driven rotary drill. There are a number of drawbacks to using core sampling to check reinstatements:

- Bituminous road base materials typically have an aggregate size of 20mm so that it is necessary to use a core size of at least 80mm (4inch) diameter to obtain a representative sample.

- The equipment required to carry out a coring operation is bulky, comprising generator, hydraulic power pack, drill and water.

- The time taken to set up the equipment and drill a core is at least 20 minutes.

- Coring is impractical for small area excavations as in the UK core diameters greater than 50mm must be reinstated using the agreed procedures.

- A core sample provides only a spot check which may not be representative of the general condition of the reinstatement.

A requirement was therefore identified for a Non-Destructive, Quality Control Tool, which was capable of measuring the thickness of the surface layers of a road in a non-invasive manner. The major points of the Instrument Specification are reproduced below:

## INSTRUMENT SPECIFICATION

- The instrument should measure the total thickness of 2 or 3 layered bituminous surfaces.

- The instrument should be capable of operation on all types of hot laid and cold laid materials.

- The interface to the bituminous layers will normally be unbound crushed rock, concrete or excavated rubble.

- The measurement range should be between 60mm to 300mm.

- The accuracy of reading should be +/- 10mm.

- The instrument should give a real time display of the layers in the ground and a numerical indication of layer thickness.

- The equipment should be self contained and hand portable, weather proof and usable over a temperature range of -5C to 30C.

- It should be possible to survey a 10m long trench in under 10 minutes.

- Cost of the equipment should be under £10K.

EVALUATION OF GROUND PROBING RADAR

The principle of operation of Ground Probing Radar (GPR) is that a microwave antenna placed on the ground directs an impulse of electromagnetic energy into the ground. The impulse is reflected from interfaces between layers of material with different conductivity and permeability, the strength of the reflection being dependent on the difference in electrical parameters between the materials. The reflected impulses from the sub-surface layers are detected by a receive antenna placed on the surface. The time taken for the signal to make the round trip from the transmitter through the material and back to the receiver is related to the depth or thickness of the sample. If the propagation time of the signal can be measured and the velocity of the signal in the material is known, the depth can be calculated.

In the UK, several organisations use GPR to inspect roads. These systems use impulse radar to acquire information on the structure of the road surface and sub-surface layers. The Radar antenna is scanned across the surface and the operator is presented with a 'picture' of the ground. However, the current ranges of proprietary GPR systems are complex to set up and use, difficult to interpret, not easily portable and cost in the region of £25K to £40K. Another significant drawback is that the radar must be calibrated for the material to be inspected by use of on site core samples. Clearly this is not practical for small reinstatements and the technique is therefore only used on large construction projects.

Commercially available GPR equipment was used initially to determine whether reliable reflections of the radar signal could be obtained from the interface between the bituminous and the unbound materials and to investigate the use of time of flight measurements for calculation of layer thickness. The equipment used was a GSSI SIR8 system. This system generates an electromagnetic impulse with a centre frequency of about 1GHz, which is injected into the ground using a microwave antenna. The reflected impulses from the sub-surface layers are detected by a receive antenna placed on the surface. An RF sampler is used to convert the received high frequency signals into lower frequency 'audio' signals which can be processed using more conventional electronics. The data is typically stored on a computer and processed before display.

A test facility, containing a range of road constructions with accurately known thickness and material properties, was therefore created at the British Gas Engineering Research Station, for the purpose of evaluating the GPR equipment under controlled conditions.

The results of this work indicated that the boundary between the bituminous and unbound layers usually provides good reflection characteristics for the radar signals. However, there were a number of problems with the technique:

- The resolution of the information from the GPR system was poor with accuracy of measurement of a 100mm layer being no better than +/- 20mm.

- The method of measurement was to store the data on computer then print the data onto a graph paper and then measure the layer thickness using a ruler.

- The time of flight calculations for different bituminous materials were used to estimate velocity variations in each of the materials. These variations were significant and it was concluded that a method of compensating for velocity differences would be required if the instrument were to be viable.

A typical plot from a GPR survey is shown in Figure 1. The plot shows a 2m long survey over two test patches, one 300mm thick and the other 100mm thick. The black bands on the plot are the peaks of the signals reflected from interfaces. A considerable degree of expertise is required to interpret the plots and recognise the boundary layers. Accurate measurements are clearly impractical.

From this initial work, it was clear that the information was present in the reflected microwave signals but the commercially available GPR systems were unsuitable for use as a measurement tool. It was decided to develop a prototype tool specifically for the purpose of measuring the thickness of the surface layers. We were to call this the Concept Demonstrator. The major features that were to be incorporated into the Concept Demonstrator were:

- A custom design microwave sub-system with one transmit antenna and one receive antenna, higher frequency operation and improved timing accuracy.

- A suite of on-line signal processing algorithms to provide a real time measurement capability.

- Velocity Independent measurement

- A simplified operator interface with numerical depth read-out and a real time picture of the surface layers.

DEVELOPMENT OF THE CONCEPT DEMONSTRATOR

The Demonstrator comprises three sub-systems, the RF sub-system, the Base Station and a 486 Personal Computer. A photograph of the Concept Demonstrator in use is shown in Photograph 1. The photograph shows the hand held RF unit with the antennas resting on the ground. The umbilical is connected to the Base Station and the system is being controlled by a laptop P.C. sitting on top of the Base Station.

RF Sub-System

A key requirement for the design of the Concept Demonstrator was to improve the resolution of the time measurements. This was achieved by increasing the centre frequency of the impulse generator to 2.5GHz and designing the RF sampling system with higher stability for more accurate measurements. The RF sub-system is packaged into a portable unit with a handle for use when scanning the surface. The antennas are mounted on the bottom of the housing in a replaceable shoe which sits directly on the road surface. In the RF sub-system, the high frequency microwave signals are converted to low frequency 'audio' signals which are then transmitted up a 30m umbilical to the Base Station.

Base Station

The Base Station contains the rechargeable batteries, a DAT (Digital Audio Tape) recorder and a processing module (TRAM). The rechargeable batteries supply power to the Base Station and the RF sub system. The DAT is used for recording and storing data from field trials for further analysis and for development of new algorithms. The TRAM processing module is a high performance Digital Signal unit that contains software to operate on the Radar signals from the RF sub-assembly in real time. The processed signals are then passed to the Personal Computer.

Personal Computer

The system is controlled by a 486 Personal Computer (P.C.). A user friendly interface was designed which was intended to simulate a custom designed keypad and display. An example of the user interface is shown in Figure 3. A mouse is used to place the cursor on the required button and that function is selected by clicking the mouse. Information is displayed on the screen in real time and the operator can see the layer structure under the antenna as he scans across the surface. The P.C. also contains the algorithm for calculation of depth from the time data. This information is displayed in the box on the lower left hand of the screen.

Signal Processing Algorithms

One of the drawbacks of commercially available GPR systems was considered to be the poor graphical display of the sub-surface features. The reason for this is that the systems are only capable of displaying 'raw' data which inevitably is cluttered and difficult to interpret (Figure 1). The quality of the displayed data can be improved by post processing but the relationship between the location of the antenna and the picture is then lost.

A major objective of this development was to provide a real time display of depth and a picture of the sub-surface layers, which was uncluttered and easy to interpret, as the instrument was scanned over the surface.

A number of processing algorithms were developed to simplify the measurement task for the operator including automatic scaling and peak detection. Other algorithms were intended to 'clean up' the signals coming from the Radar and these included Temporal Averaging, Time Varying Gain and Pulse Compression. Figure 3 shows a cleaned-up trace of a survey. The ground surface is between the two narrow grey bands near the surface and the strong black line is the reflection from the bottom of the bituminous layer. The use of the Pulse Compression technique also assisted with improvement of the measurement accuracy of the system.

Velocity Independent Measurement

Testing on the purpose built field test facility with early prototypes, revealed that the velocity of the EM waves in bituminous and concrete surfacing materials can vary by as much as 100% depending on the material content and composition. Clearly, such variations affect the calculation of depth directly. Further development therefore took place to eliminate the velocity component in the estimation of depth, by use of two receive antennas.

A simplified diagram showing the physical arrangement of the antennas is shown in Figure 2. From this diagram it is possible to perform a geometrical analysis and deduce an expression that relates the bulk thickness 'd' to the antenna separation 'x' and the signal propagation time 't'. The velocity term 'v' is removed by virtue of the analysis and renders the depth of the sample independent of velocity.

The expression for depth is stated as:

$$d = \sqrt{\frac{(t_1 x_2)^2 - (t_2 x_1)^2}{4(t_2^2 - t_1^2)}}$$

where $x_1$ = Tx to $Rx_1$ separation distance
  $x_2$ = Tx to $Rx_2$ separation distance
  $t_1$ = time of receive pulse at $Rx_1$
  $t_2$ = time of receive pulse at $Rx_2$
  $d$ = depth of layer
  $h$ = assumed transmission path through layer
  $v$ = signal velocity

The expression obtained is a first approximation model, and assumes the following:

- The measured boundary is parallel to the surface

- The measured layer is homogeneous - constant velocity

- Constant velocity and no refraction in multiple layers

## TESTING AND CALIBRATION

### Calibration Facilities

A test area was created containing 15 representative reinstated trenches and square patches which were constructed to the standards laid down in the National Reinstatement Specification for the New Roads and Street Works Act.    Three bituminous materials were used for the bound layers; Hot Rolled Asphalt, Dense Bituminous Macadam, and cold laid Bitumen Emulsion Macadam, with each material having a depth range of 50mm to 400mm.  Surveying techniques were used in the construction to determine the depth of each layer to within +/- 1mm.

### Performance Of The Demonstrator

Extensive testing of the Demonstrator on the purpose built field test facility provided an estimate of the accuracy of measurement which was achievable.  Measurement accuracy's of better than +/- 10mm were achieved for depths of 50mm to 200mm, for the three types of material tested.  However, at depths of 300mm and 400mm the measurement accuracy reduced significantly with a corresponding increase in the scatter of results.  Further testing at depths of 300mm and 400mm suggested that the cause of the reduction in accuracy at the greater depths was the close spacing of the antennas and that for accurate measurement at these depths a larger antenna spacing would be required.

## FIELD TRIALS

A number of field trial sites were selected in British Gas Northern Region, at locations where excavation and permanent reinstatement had been carried out over the last 6 months.  The reinstatements had been produced using Hot Rolled Asphalt or Dense Bitumen Macadam with a road base of loose granular or foamed concrete material.  Both rectangular and trench type of reinstatements were examined.  The nominal depth of the bituminous material was 100mm, comprising 35mm wearing course on the surface with a 65mm base course.

Each reinstatement was examined by scanning the antennas across the surface along the length and across the width of the reinstated area.  The accuracy of the measurements was then checked by taking a core sample at selected points.

Figure 3 shows the results of a survey along an 8m trench, with a nominal bituminous layer depth of 150mm. The start of the survey is on the left and the end of the survey is on the right. The bold black line shows the profile of the bottom layer of the reinstatement over the 8m length. The ground surface is located between the two narrow grey lines near the surface. In this case the reinstatement had been carried out to a high standard and the depth of the bituminous layer varied over a narrow range of 155mm to 168mm. The numerical depth read-out displays the instantaneous depth value at the leading edge of the trace. The trace shown in Figure 3 also includes the weaker reflections from other features in the ground. Further processing can be applied to remove these weaker signals as shown in figure 4.

PRODUCT DEVELOPMENT

Development of the Concept Demonstrator had shown that a tool could be produced to measure the layer thickness of bituminous road surfaces. However, it was clear that further engineering development was necessary to meet the ergonomic requirements of size and portability, to survive the environmental conditions in field use and to enable the instrument to be produced for the target price of under £10K. An illustration of the proposed design of the production unit is shown in Figure 4.

RF Sub-System

In the construction of the concept demonstrator maximum use was made of commercially available modules to simplify design and construction. The costs associated with this approach are unacceptable for a commercial product.
Peter Ward
A number of the most expensive modules have therefore been re-designed for low cost manufacture. Further cost benefits and reductions in size and weight are being achieved by integration of the bulk of the RF circuits onto a pcb and design of the control circuit into a Gate Array device.

Computing and Processing Sub-System

A custom microprocessor card capable of carrying out real time processing of the signals and controlling the keypad and display has been designed to replace the functionality of the personal Computer and the TRAM processing module. The design uses two 32bit, 25 MHz, T805 Transputers. By using a custom design it is possible to minimise the unit cost, optimise the size of the processing unit and minimise power consumption.

Operator Display And Controls

The display used for the product design is a liquid crystal display (LCD) module, and was selected for its lightweight, low power consumption and its ability to generate a high contrast display in outdoor conditions and in bright sunlight.

The operator communicates with the instrument through a 16 button keypad. There are five multi-function soft keys which are placed directly under the display, a cluster of four keys which control the direction of the display cursor and a cluster of six keys which control the recording and replay of data. The legends on these keys are the same as those found on a standard video recorder, but instead of recording on video tape data is recorded in solid state memory.

OTHER APPLICATIONS

The surface thickness radar has been developed to measure the bulk thickness of bituminous layers in road constructions. The unique combination of a high resolution measurement radar with the real time display of material thickness and layer profiles raises the prospect of using the system for a range of other Civil Engineering applications. Some initial work has been carried out on the use of the system for inspection of concrete structures. Typical applications would be:

- Inspection of the structure and properties of the granular road base materials

- The inspection of concrete cladding on buildings

- Examination of reinforcement bars in concrete structures and bridges

- Location of cracks in concrete roads

- Detection and measurement of the depth of electricity cables in concrete structures and infill before excavation

CONCLUSIONS

British Gas has developed an instrument for measurement of the thickness of the load bearing bituminous or concrete road structures. The instrument uses Impulse Radar to obtain accurate measurement of the layer depths using time-of-flight measurement of the reflected Radar pulses. The instrument has been extensively tested on a purpose built field test facility to determine the performance. Measurement accuracy of better than +/-5mm was achieved at 100mm depth and better than +/-10mm at 200mm depth. Modifications to the instrument will be required to achieve the required accuracy of +/- 10mm at depths greater than 200mm.

The design of a production instrument for use by supervisors and craftsmen is now underway. The production design is compact and fully portable, with real time display of the profile of the surface layers and a simple numerical read-out of thickness. The compact design is achieved by replacing the Personal Computer and signal processing electronics with custom designed microprocessor circuitry. The design also contains an integral keyboard and a graphic liquid crystal display. The use of this technology coupled with development of low cost RF components will enable us to reduce unit manufacturing costs compared to other GPR systems, which is expected to result in a selling price within the reach of utility companies.

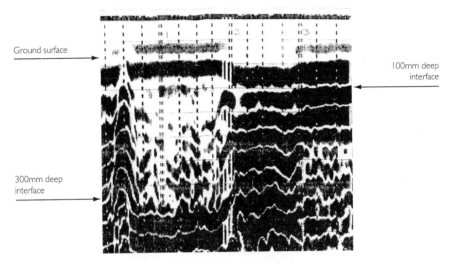

Ground surface

100mm deep interface

300mm deep interface

**Fig 1** Radar scan of test patches using GSSI equipment

**Photograph 1** The concept demonstrator

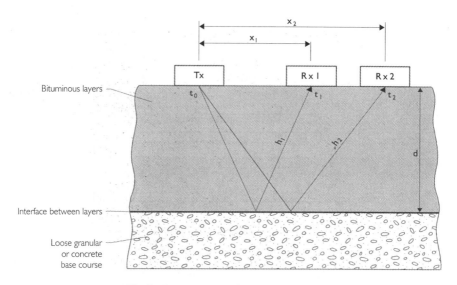

**Fig.2** Arrangement of antennas for velocity independent measurement

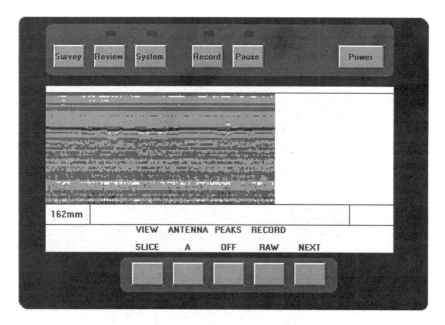

**Fig.3** Demonstrator display - reinstatement depth profile and numerical read-out

**Fig.4** Production design concept

RESEARCH AND DEVELOPMENT OF RADAR LOCATOR AT OSAKA GAS

RECHERCHES ET MISES AU POINT D'UN DETECTEUR A RADAR A OSAKA GAS

Y. Manabe and H. Matsui
Distribution Engineering Center, Osaka Gas Co., Ltd. JAPAN

M. Tsunasaki
Research and Development Center, Osaka Gas Co., Ltd. JAPAN

ABSTRACT

It is very important for the gas utility industry to develop techniques to locate various underground structures without excavation. Osaka Gas undertook the research of the radar locator as a device to locate various underground structures including gas pipes without excavation in 1979. As the fruit of years of research, field tests, and improvements, we developed a radar locator called the RADARMAN. We introduced it for on−site use in 1990. We are now using 18 RADARMANs. In 1993, we developed a small and light radar locator called the RADAR MINI with good locating performance for shallow−buried pipes in order to extend the application of radar locators. We introduced it for on−site use in 1994, and we are now using 68 RADAR MINIs. Now we are carrying out the development of an advanced radar locator. It is to have a greater maximum locating depth than the RADARMAN's and an image processing capability.

RÉSUMÉ

Pour les opérateurs de gaz, la mise au point de techniques d'exploration des objects enterrés sans excavation des rues est d'un enjeu majeur. La compagnie Osaka Gas Co., Ltd. s'est lancée en 1979 dans la recherche−développement d'un localisateur à radar permettant de détecter, sans excavation et donc à partir de la surface du sol, la position de n'importe quel objet enterré, notamment des canalisations de gaz. Après toute une série d'éssais sur place et d'améliorations, Osaka Gas est finalement parvenue à mettre au point un localisateur à radar monobloc à haute définition appelé "RADARMAN" qu'elle a commencé à utiliser dans la pratique en 1988. Pour faciliter et donc propager l'utilisation des localisateurs à radar, des"RADAR MINI" ont été mis au point en 1993 en coopération avec les compagnies Tokyo Gas Co., Ltd. et Toho Gas Co., Ltd. La profondeur d'exploration de ces derniers localisateurs est inférieure à celle des "RADARMAN" mais leur taille de même que leur poids sont plus réduits et ils permettent un déchiffrement de l'image plus facile. Nous travaillons actuellement à la mise au point d'un "localisateur à radar de la prochaine génération" (appellation évidemment provisoire) d'une profondeur d'exploration supérieure à celle du "RADARMAN" et doté d'une fonction de traitement de l'image facilitant le déchiffrement des images.

## INTRODUCTION

Electromagnetic-induction type locators were used for locating gas pipes by the gas utility industry. They could reduce excavation area and prevent damage to gas pipes by third-party construction. However, they could locate only electrically conductive gas pipes and could not locate non-metallic pipes, such as polyethylene pipes, or pipes connected with insulated joints. If the pipes to be located are not our gas pipes, they cannot be electrified, even if they are electrically conductive.

Under these circumstances, Osaka Gas undertook the research of the radar locator as a device to locate various underground structures including gas pipes without excavation in 1979. As the fruit of years of research, field tests, and improvements, we developed a radar locator called the RADARMAN. We introduced it for on-site use in 1990. We are now using 18 RADARMANs. In 1993, we developed a small and light radar locator called the RADAR MINI with good locating performance for shallow-buried pipes in order to extend the application of radar locators. It weighs only about 19.5 kg, which is one-third of the weight of the RADARMAN. We introduced it for on-site use in 1994, and we are now using 68 RADAR MINIs. Now we are carrying out the development of an advanced radar locator. It is to have a greater maximum locating depth than the RADARMAN's and an image processing capability. In this paper, the technical characteristics and performance of the RADARMAN and the RADAR MINI are described, and then an outline of the advanced radar locator is given.

## OPERATING PRINCIPLE

The radar locator is used to locate underground structures(pipelines, cables, cavities and so on) by means of pulse waves. Figure 1 shows its operating principle, and Figure 2 shows its construction. It is composed of antennas, a controller, a display, and an operation unit. Pulse waves are generated by supplying pulse currents with very short time intervals to the transmission antenna. The generated pulse waves propagate underground and are reflected by a buried object. The reception antenna receives those reflected waves and the depth of the object is obtained from the time(T) elapsed between the transmission and reception of the pulse waves. To locate a buried pipe, transmission and reception of pulse waves are repeated continuously as the locator is being moved across the ground surface as shown in Figure 1. Then the reflected waves are processed to produce a crescent-shaped image. The peak(point D) of the crescent indicates the position just above the pipe, and the depth of the pipe can be calculated from the vertical distance at this position by the following equation.

$$H = VT / 2 \quad [ V = V_0 / \sqrt{\varepsilon_r} ]$$

where
$V$ :underground propagation speed of pulse waves (m/s)
$V_0$ :speed of pulse waves in vacuum ($3 \times 10^8$ m/s)
$\varepsilon_r$ :dielectric constant of earth (5 to 40)
$H$ :depth of pipe(m)
$T$ :time difference(s)

## RADARMAN

The RADARMAN is a radar locator developed by Osaka Gas in 1988. Photo 1 shows the appearance of the RADARMAN. Figure 3 shows an example of images of located objects. Table 1 shows its specifications.

## Technical Characteristics of RADARMAN

The technical characteristics of the RADARMAN are as follows.

1. Being equipped with a three-dimensional tower-shaped antenna, it can emit pulse radar waves into the ground at high efficiency. Accordingly, we can locate, with high accuracy, underground structures buried less than 1.5 m deep. (The maximum locating depth is about 2.5 m where the soil is sandy.)

2. Being equipped with STC (sensitivity timing control), a high-frequency signal amplification unit, it can amplify signals at the best magnification for a given depth. Accordingly, we can obtain high locating sensitivity for non-metal pipes such as polyethylene pipes as well as metal pipes.

3. With the electronic circuits, the CRT display, memories, and the operating unit mounted together on the antenna housing, the system is very compact and can be operated by one person.

## Results of Field Tests

Osaka Gas has performed field tests for 3 years, during which period evaluation was made in respect of the unit's applicability to on-site use. The results of the tests are described below.

Locating Rate for Underground Objects  Defining the ratio between the number of underground objects confirmed by excavation and the number of underground objects located by the RADARMAN as the "locating rate," locating was conducted at work sites of various soil types. As a result, a locating rate of approximately 80 % was obtained for 593 excavated objects in total. In addition, the locating rate when the soil consisted of clay was approximately 50 %, indicating a lower value. This was because clay has a higher electric conductivity and a larger electric wave attenuation factor. Also, the survey revealed that there was a considerable amount of dispersion in the locating rate, depending on the depths of the buried objects. Figure 4 shows the locating rate by depth. When the depth is less than 1.5 m, it generally indicates locating rates better than the mean locating rate (approximately 80 %) and when in particular the depth is 0.6 to 0.9 m, it indicates a locating rate as good as 95 %. However, it is shown that when the depth is more than 1.5 m, the locating rate decreases because the pulse waves emitted into the ground rapidly attenuate with depth, considerably reducing the signal level. Strangely, it is noted that the locating rate for underground objects less than 0.3 m deep is somewhat lower. It is because, in some cases, a strong multiple image due to the reflection of pulse waves by the surface of an asphalt pavement is superimposed on the image of the buried object.

For 82 % of the buried objects located during this investigation, the error in the horizontal direction was within ±20 cm. Further, the rate of successful reading of an image with an error in the vertical direction of ±2 0 cm was 74 %.

## Use of RADARMAN

As the field test results were very good, we introduced this system for on-site use in 1990. We have already obtained good results in various underground surveys. We are using it mainly for the following surveying work.

(1)Investigation of buried pipes prior to pipeline design and construction
The RADARMAN can be used to locate any buried object. Investigation prior to pipeline design and construction is primarily for checking if sufficient underground space exists, thereby providing reference data for trial excavation and site selection. The RADARMAN is particularly useful at sites where excavation is restricted owing to road conditions.

(2)Indication of gas pipe location for third-party work
If the RADARMAN is used for indicating the location of gas pipes for which the electromagnetic-induction type pipe locator cannot be used, it will be very effective for the safety of third-party work.

(3)Investigation of missing gas pipes
The RADARMAN is particularly effective in locating missing gas pipes which are difficult to locate with the electromagnetic-induction type pipe locator or by trial excavation. The RADARMAN can be used to determine trial excavation sites or to correct unreliable drawings and ledgers.

(4)Investigation of cavities
Now 18 RADARMANs are at work.

## RADAR MINI

Using the knowledge acquired through the development of the RADARMAN, Osaka Gas completed the development of the RADAR MINI in March 1994 jointly with Tokyo Gas and Toho Gas. Although its maximum locating depth is less than that of the RADARMAN, it has a better locating performance for shallow-buried pipes and is smaller and lighter than the RADARMAN.(The maximum locating depth of the RADAR MINI is about 1.2 m where the soil is sandy.) Photo 2 shows the appearance of the RADAR MINI. Figure 5 shows an example of images of located objects. Table 2 shows its specifications.

### Technical Characteristics Of RADAR MINI

The technical characteristics of the RADAR MINI are as follows.

(1)High-frequency pulse waves are used for the purpose of displaying clear images of shallow-buried pipes.

(2)The best STC curve is used to amplify signals at the best magnification for given soil quality and pipe depth.

(3)An image processing technique is used to reduce double reflection images due to the reflected signals from the ground surface.

### Results of Field Tests

Locating Rate for Underground Objects  On our test field, the RADAR MINI successfully located 60 pipes out of 63 pipes buried down to a depth of 0.6 m. The 3 pipes that the RADAR MINI failed to locate were a polyethylene pipe with a diameter of 25 mm buried at a depth of 0.5 m in clay, a steel pipe with a diameter of 25 mm buried at a depth of 0.6 m in clay, and a vinyl pipe with a diameter of 20 mm buried at a depth of 0.5 m. Therefore, the RADAR MINI's locating rate is approximately 95 %. Table 3 shows the locating rate by depth. When in particular the depth is less than $0.4$ m, it boasts a locating rate of $100$ %. Accordingly, the RADAR MINI has a better locating performance for shallow-buried pipes.

The RADAR MINI's horizontal accuracy is $\pm 20$ cm and the vertical accuracy is $\pm 30$ cm.

## Use of RADAR MINI

Osaka Gas has been using $68$ RADAR MINIs since May $1994$ to prevent the damage to shallow-buried pipes caused by pavement cutters during gas pipeline works. From now on, we are going to extend the application of the RADAR MINI in order to make gas pipeline work safer.

## ADVANCED RADAR LOCATOR

We have been working on the research and development of an advanced radar locator, which is to be much more advanced compared with the existing radar locators, since $1990$. We have set the targets as shown in Table $4$.

So far, the maximum locating depth has been improved by improving the antenna and the electronic circuits, and the image processing technique has made both accurate locating and easy reading of located images possible. Figure $6$ shows an example of the image processing technique. The step (pre-processing) reduces the horizontal stripes across the image. The second step ($2$D inverse Fourier transform) pinpoints the peaks of crescents. The final step draws circles to indicate buried objects. Thus we expect that we will be achieving the goal in two to three years. With the advanced radar locator, the following will be realized.
($1$)Accurate advance design of gas pipelines
($2$)Reduction of excavation for locating buried third-party objects
($3$)Promotion of trenchless techniques such as jacking method

## CONCLUSION

We have been working on the research and development of the radar locator for a long time. We have already introduced $18$ RADARMANs and $68$ RADAR MINIs to decrease excavation and to ensure safety. We are now developing an advanced radar locator for pipes buried deeper than those which the RADARMAN can locate. We will continue our endeavors to achieve a comprehensive radar locating system for gas pipeline and other pipeline works.

## REFERENCES

$1$. I. Sugimoto, T. Kikuta, Y. Hayashi and M. Takagi, "COMPACT UNDERGROUND RADAR SYSTEM", the $6$th Scandinavian Conference on Image Analysis, Oulu, Finland, June $19$ $22,1989$

$2$. J. Koyabu, "THE DEVELOPMENT OF THE 'RADARMAN'-- A compact underground radar system--" INTERNATIONAL CONFERENCE NO-DIG $92$, PARIS

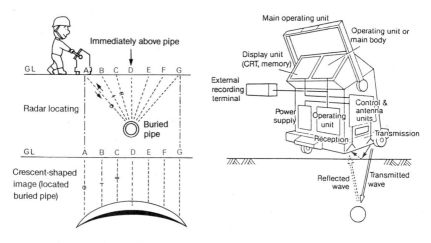

Fig.1 Locating principle          Fig.2 Construction of radar locator

Photo1 "RADARMAN"

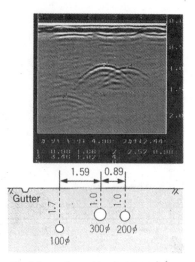

Fig.3 Image located by "RADARMAN"

Table1 Specifications of "RADARMAN"

| Weight | 60kg |
|---|---|
| Dimensions | 660mm(L)×636mm(W)×892mm(H) |
| Locating depth | 0 to 1.5m (0 to 2.5m where the soil is sandy) |
| Display | Monochromatic CRT with 256 color tones |
| Image processing | None |
| Scanning speed | Max 4.5km/h |
| Power Supply | Battery(one hour continuous use) |

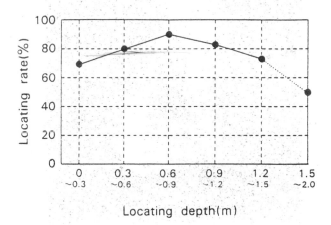

Fig.4 Locating rate of "RADARMAN" by the depth

Photo2 "RADAR MINI"

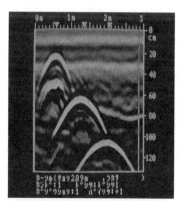

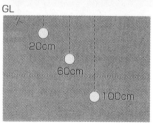

Fig.5 Image located by "RADAR MINI"

Table2 Specifications of "RADAR MINI"

| Weight | 19.5kg |
|---|---|
| Dimensions | 560mm(L)×350mm(W)×640mm(H) |
| Locating depth | 0 to 0.6m (0 to 1.2m where the soil is sandy) |
| Display | Monochromatic CRT with 16 color tones |
| Image processing | Reduction of reflected images from ground surface |
| Scanning speed | Max 4.5km/h |
| Power Supply | Battery(1.5 hour continuous use) |

Table3 Locating rate of "RADAR MINI" by the depth

| Depth of buried object | 0~0.4m | 0.4~0.6m |
|---|---|---|
| Locating rate | 100%(36/36) | 90%(24/27) |

Table4 Development targets of "Advanced radar locator"

| | Advanced radar locator | RADARMAN |
|---|---|---|
| Locating depth | 1.5 m (100% accuracy) | 1.5 m (80% accuracy) |
| | 2.0 m (80% accuracy) | 2.0 m (Less than 50% accuracy) |
| Accuracy:Horizontal | ±10 cm | ± 20 cm |
| Vertical | ±10% | ± 20% |

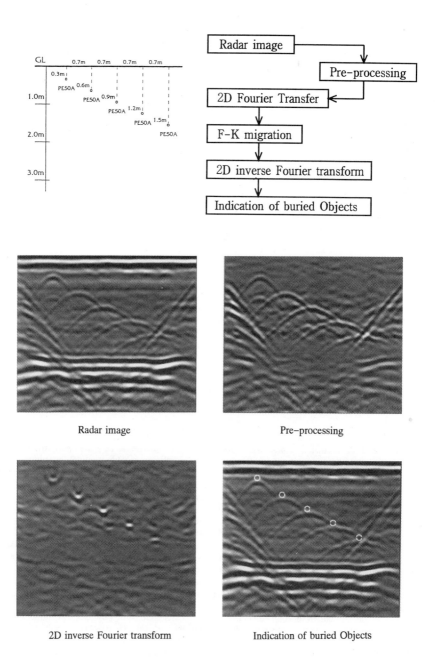

Fig.6 An example of the image processing technique of "Advanced radar locator"

# FLOW SHUT-OFF AND DAMAGE
## IN POLYETHYLENE GAS PIPING DURING SQUEEZE-OFF

## ARRÊT DE COULÉE ET DOMMAGES DANS LES CONDUITES
## DE GAZ EN POLYÉTHYLÈNE PENDANT LA COMPRESSION

S. M. Pimputkar, B. Leis, J. A. Stets and D. R. Stephens
Battelle, USA

M. M. Mamoun
Gas Research Institute, USA

## ABSTRACT

Polyethylene (PE) piping constitutes the vast majority of new gas distribution piping installed in the United States today. Squeeze-off is a procedure that is routinely used to stop gas flow in PE gas distribution pipes in order to effect repairs or maintenance downstream of the squeeze-off point. During the process of squeeze-off, the pipe undergoes a change in shape and deformation of the pipe wall. The objective of this investigation was to develop field-usable guidelines to safely and effectively stop the flow of gas using squeeze tools, without inducing damage, under different conditions for different PE gas pipe materials and for a broad range of pipe sizes and squeeze conditions. Based on current practice, three medium-density PE materials and one high-density PE material were evaluated for different diameters, wall thicknesses, and squeeze tool geometries and sizes. The test setup consisted of the pipe to be squeezed with a source of adjustable, constant pressure upstream and flowmeters downstream. Trends were determined as a function of pipe diameter, wall thickness, squeeze bar geometry, and squeeze bar size.

## RÉSUMÉ

Arrêt de circulation et dommages survenant dans les tuyauteries de gaz en polyéthylène au cours de l'écrasement par compression Les tuyauteries en polyéthylène (PE) constituent la plus grande majorité des nouveaux réseaux de tuyauterie de distribution de gaz récemment installés aux Etats-Unis. La procédure d'écrasement par compression est employée couramment pour arrêter la circulation de gaz dans les tuyauteries de distribution en PE lorsqu'on souhaite effectuer des réparations ou des opérations de maintenance en aval du point d'écrasement. Au cours du procédé d'écrasement par compression, le tuyau subit un changement de forme et sa paroi se déforme. L'objet de la présente enquête consistait à mettre au point des directives utilisables sur le site pour arrêter la circulation de gaz en toute sécurité et de manière efficace, à l'aide d'outils écrase-tube, sans causer de dommages, dans des conditions variant en fonction des différences de matériaux en PE utilisés dans les tuyauteries de gaz, d'une gamme de dimensions de tuyauterie étendue et des conditions de compression. Compte tenu des pratiques courantes, on a évalué trois matériaux en PE de densité moyenne et un matériau en PE de haute densité, pour en étudier le comportement en fonction de diamètres et d'épaisseurs de paroi variés, et de configurations diverses d'outils écrase-tube de différentes tailles. L'aménagement des essais a été le suivant : les tuyaux ont été écrasés sous une pression dont la source, située en amont du point de compression, était réglable et constante, avec des débitmètres situés en aval. Les tendances ont été calculées en fonction du diamètre de tuyau, de l'épaisseur de paroi, de la configuration et de la dimension de la barre de compression.

## INTRODUCTION

Polyethylene (PE) piping constitutes the vast majority of new gas distribution piping installed today. Squeeze-off is a procedure that is routinely and widely used to control gas flow in PE gas distribution pipes in order to effect repairs or maintenance downstream of the squeeze-off point. The pipe is compressed between two (or more) bars until flow effectively ceases. After the downstream repairs are completed, the bars are released, and the pipe tries to regain its former circular shape. The practice of squeeze-off has evolved primarily through experience and few systematic studies are available.

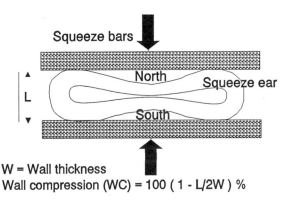

Figure 1. Schematic representation of squeeze procedure

As compression of the pipe begins (in the North-South direction, looking along the flow direction as shown in Figure 1), the circular cross-section becomes elliptical (with the North-South axis becoming smaller) and the cross-sectional area available for flow decreases. When the inner walls touch at the North-South axis, there are drop-shaped areas still available for flow near the West and East points of the inner wall. These are termed the "ears" of the squeeze. To reduce the flow further, compression of the PE pipe walls is necessary. A measure of the extent of squeeze is the amount of wall compression. This is formally defined as

$$W_c = (1 - \frac{L}{2W}) * 100$$

where $W_c$ is the wall compression in percent, L is the distance between the squeeze bars at the North-South axis, and W is the average wall thickness of the unsqueezed pipe. The physical interpretation of $W_c$ is intuitive. If the wall compression is negative, the inside walls of the pipe are not in contact. When the wall compression is zero, the inside walls of the pipe have just touched, but the pipe wall thickness has not been reduced. At values of wall compression between zero and 100 percent, the pipe walls along the North-South axis have been compressed from their original value. At a wall compression of 100 percent, the squeeze bars touch and the pipe has been severed.

During the process of squeeze-off, the pipe undergoes a drastic change in shape and the pipe walls undergo substantial deformation. Field failures have been observed because of improper squeeze-offs. Because of this, and because squeeze-off is widely used, it is desirable to evaluate the conditions under which the pipe may be damaged and to evaluate the factors that influence the effectiveness of squeeze-off.

There are two limits to the squeeze-off procedure. The lower limit is determined by the effective stoppage of flow. The upper limit is determined by the onset of damage to the PE pipe. Between these two limits is the usable range for squeeze-off operations as shown in Figure 2.

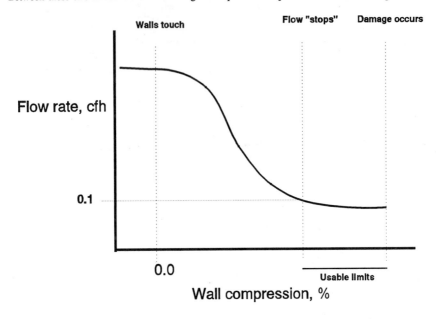

**Figure 2. Desirable usable range for squeeze-off in terms of wall compression**

The practically usable, or "safe," range of wall compressions is smaller than the theoretically usable range because of field effects that are not considered when developing the theoretically usable range. In field practice, it is expected that the stops on the squeeze tool will be located in such a way that flow ceases without damage to the pipe.

Gas Research Institute funded a multi-year project at Battelle to study both the upper and lower limits to squeeze-off (References 1 to 3). The data and analyses demonstrate the effect of the following variables on the squeeze process: pipe material, extent of squeeze, wall thickness, pipe diameter, squeeze-off tool size, squeeze-off tool geometry, upstream pressure, temperature, rate of compression, duration of squeeze, rate of release, rerounding, post-squeeze-off reinforcement.

The results on flow shut-off are presented first, followed by the results on damage occurrence. Finally, the implications of these results for the practice of squeeze-off and for the design of squeeze tools are discussed. The results are based on measured data supported by a theoretical understanding and explanation. However, because the squeeze-off process is strongly dependent on material properties, the conclusions may not apply to the same extent to other materials.

**FLOW SHUT-OFF**

Squeeze-off is practiced to provide flow control and effective flow stoppage in the field. The objective of this investigation was to develop field-usable guidelines to safely and effectively stop the flow of gas using squeeze tools, without inducing damage, under different conditions, for different PE gas pipe materials, for a broad range of pipe sizes and squeeze conditions.

Based on current practice, two medium-density PE materials and one high-density PE material were selected for evaluation for different diameters, wall thicknesses, and squeeze tool geometries and sizes. The diameters ranged from 50 mm (2 inches) to 300 mm (12 inches). As many wall thicknesses were tested for each diameter as were commercially available. The squeeze was undertaken at upstream pressures of 4 bars (60 psi), 2.75 bars (40 psi), and 1.4 bars (20 psi). The following squeeze bars were used: 25-mm (1-inch) round bar, 50-mm (2-inch) round bar, 100-mm (4-inch) round bar, double (adjacent) 50-mm (2-inch) round bars, and 100-mm (4-inch) flat bar with rounded edges.

The test setup consisted of the pipe to be squeezed with a source of adjustable, constant pressure upstream as shown schematically in Figure 3. The pressure was measured upstream and

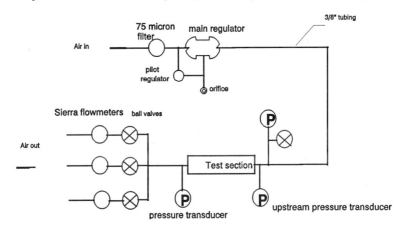

**Figure 3.** Schematic of experimental setup

downstream of the test section using pressure transducers. The flow rate through the squeezed section was measured by a set of flowmeters that collectively spanned a range greater than that which could be measured by only one flowmeter. The amount of squeeze and flow rate were measured with the upstream pressure held constant. The squeeze was undertaken in steps so that the flow rate stabilized before the squeeze was continued. The squeeze was terminated when the flow rate dropped below $2.8*10^{-3}$ m$^3$/hr (0.1 ft$^3$/hr), or when the wall compression exceeded 35 percent. A typical set of data for three upstream pressures, with all other parameters remaining the same, is shown in Figure 4. The data were analyzed to determine the trends as a function of pipe diameter, wall thickness, squeeze bar geometry, and squeeze bar size.

**Results and Discussion**

Effect of Rate of Compression

- The progressive reduction in flow rate is directly proportional to the cross-sectional area available for flow at the squeeze location.

- The flow rate in the final stages of closure is somewhat random because of the random nature of the wrinkle formation in the ear of the squeeze.

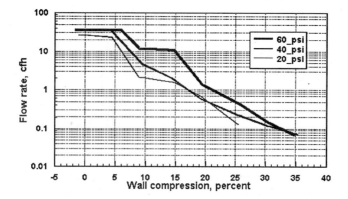

**Figure 4.** Typical data showing flow rate as a function of wall compression with upstream pressure as a parameter

- The rate at which the pipe is squeezed marginally affects the instantaneous cross-sectional area available for flow because of the viscoelastic nature of the polyethylene pipe material.

- If the pipe is squeezed quickly (2 mm/s (5 inches/min)) and the squeeze is paused, the flow tends to increase somewhat after the material has relaxed.

Effect of Upstream Pressure

- As the upstream pressure is increased, the flow at a given wall compression (all else remaining the same) generally increases.

- The highest upstream pressure that was tested was 4 bars (60 psi). At this pressure, with the downstream pressure being atmospheric, the flow is sonic at the squeeze location. Further increase of upstream pressure will not change the flow rate because the flow is "choked."

- If the flow in the last stages of squeeze is modeled as a sharp-edged venturi flowmeter, it can be shown that for a flow rate of $2.8*10^{-3} m^3/hr$ (0.1 $ft^3/hr$), the flow area is about $3.23*10^{-6} mm^2$ (0.005 $mil^2$) at 1.4 bars (20 psi) upstream pressure, and $0.84*10^{-6} mm^2$ (0.0013 $mil^2$) at an upstream pressure of 4 bars (60 psi). These areas are equivalent to circular hole diameters of 0.03 mm (1 mil) and 0.08 mm (3 mils), respectively.

Effect of Pipe Size and Material

- As the pipe diameter increases, a greater wall compression is necessary to stop the flow. This is because pipe walls first touch and continue to be compressed along the North-South axis even though the flow openings are located at the East-West ends (see Figure 1).

- Because the point of effective flow shut-off is defined as a numerical value, $2.8*10^{-3} m^3/hr$ (0.1 $ft^3/hr$), in this study and because with increasing diameter a greater wall compression is necessary to stop the flow, the usable range for squeeze decreases as the diameter increases.

- As wall thickness increases, a greater wall compression is needed for flow shut-off.

- For small-diameter pipe, there was little observed difference between materials.

- For large-diameter pipe, there appeared to be some difference in material behavior but the amount of data was inadequate to derive firm conclusions.

## Effect of Squeeze-Bar Size and Shape

- As the squeeze-bar size increases (with the shape remaining constant), a lesser value of wall compression is needed for flow shut-off.

- As the squeeze-bar size decreases with respect to the pipe diameter, the flow may not stop before the suggested damage occurrence limit of 30-percent wall compression is reached.

- Two 50-mm (2-inch) bars behave very similarly to one 100-mm (4-inch) bar.

- Flatter squeeze bars are more effective in shutting off gas than round bars (but flat bars also require a greater driving force and are more likely to cause damage depending on the edge curvature).

## DAMAGE OCCURRENCE

In practice, a poorly squeezed pipe fails by a slow crack growth (SCG) mechanism. Damage is induced primarily by excessive wall compression, but the term "excessive" depends on other squeeze process parameters. SCG is characterized by relatively low stresses, little deformation, and long times to failure. SCG-resistant materials are defined as those which, when subjected to the standard SCG test, show great resistance to crack initiation and crack propagation. Typically, materials manufactured after 1985 are much more SCG-resistant than those made earlier. A more extensive discussion of SCG-resistant materials is given in Reference 2.

With regard to damage occurrence, the objectives were to identify the mechanisms and parameters controlling squeeze-off damage in PE pipe and to recommend modified squeeze-off procedures and/or tool designs that avoid or mitigate damage and enhance long-term serviceability.

The technical approach consisted of

- Performing squeeze-offs while parametrically varying parameters that included pipe material, tool size and geometry, wall thickness, and pipe diameter

- Examining the squeezed-off pipe for damage in the proximity of the squeeze ears

- Formulating a phenomenological model to explain the experimental results.

The intent was to

- Define conditions that initiate damage during the squeeze-off process

- Evaluate conditions under which a defect could initiate and grow to failure after squeeze-off if damage was prevented during the process itself.

This investigation relied heavily on the understanding of fundamental damage mechanisms in PE obtained in slow crack growth (SCG) research.

Five materials (PE2306I, PE2406IX, PE3408I, PE3408II, PE3306III) and three pipe sizes (50-mm (2-inch) Standard Dimension Ratio (SDR) 11, 150-mm (6-inch) SDR 11.5, 150-mm (6-inch) SDR 21) were tested at two temperatures (24 C (75 F), -29 C (-20 F)) for a variety of squeeze bar types (single round bar, double round bars, and single flat bar). Micrographic examination of squeeze-off-induced field failures suggested that damage nucleation and growth in squeeze-off is similar to that found in SCG. Laboratory squeeze-off experiments were performed to confirm that essentially the same PE damage sequence controls the formation and growth of squeeze-off damage. The phenomenological model indicated that the damage could initiate below the surface. Fundamental to the model is the hypothesis that void formation occurs only under triaxial tensile stresses and that these stresses are induced during release of the squeeze-off. No evidence was found that defects form during the squeeze or compression phase of the squeeze-off process. In most of the pipe sections examined, the subsurface defects grew sufficiently during the release process to break through the pipe surface. In one case, a defect was found entirely below the surface. These results imply that the basic mechanisms are consistent with the phenomenological model, which is based on fundamental fracture mechanics observations.

## Results and Discussion

The results showed that immediate damage occurs during the early stages of release if wall compression is excessive. If immediate damage does occur, the growth rate of the crack is significantly slower in SCG-resistant materials than in non-SCG-resistant materials. If damage can be avoided during the squeeze-off and release process, damage is unlikely to subsequently begin and grow to failure in SCG-resistant materials. While the primary mechanisms of squeeze-off-induced damage are understood, the state of the art for three-dimensional stress analysis of large-deflection constitutive models for PE to characterize damage formation is not adequately developed. Therefore, where concern exists, for example when using new materials, new tools, or new procedures, validation should be undertaken through a qualification test such as that described in Reference 2. Long-term field experience demonstrating the acceptability of current procedures is adequate proof for existing materials and procedures.

The primary variables that were observed to control the stress field (and therefore the damage) during squeeze-off and release were wall compression, pipe wall thickness, tool diameter, and pipe material. Temperature and strain (displacement) rate effects on squeeze-off were found to be important in materials whose stiffness is increased significantly over the practical range of these two parameters. The effects of other variables, such as time held in compression, were sufficiently small that their influence could not be discerned.

### Effect of Wall Compression

Wall compression governs both the amount of applied load and the area of pipe under compression. Battelle data and experience indicate that wall compression levels greater than 30 percent significantly increase the likelihood of damage in SCG-resistant materials. Damage may be induced in non SCG resistant materials at lower levels of wall compression.

Pipe should be compressed no more than necessary to control flow up to a maximum of 30-percent wall compression. Stops to prevent wall compression beyond 30 percent are essential to minimize the likelihood of damage.

### Effect of Release Rate

The tensile stresses that induce damage occur during release. Release rate is an important variable and is more important than compression rate. The critical portion of the release is the initial portion as the ear begins to open. The pipe should not be permitted to spring open without restriction. The pipe should be released as slowly as is practical and safe.

While not exhaustive, Battelle data indicate that release rates of up to 0.2 mm/s (0.5 inch per minute) do not increase the likelihood of damage and are therefore acceptable. Release rates on mechanical, screw-driven, tools are not likely to cause problems. Some hydraulic tools can open quite rapidly when released. Measures should be taken to limit the rate of opening of hydraulic tools.

## Effect of Pipe Diameter, Wall Thickness, and SDR

There are three dimensions of relevance in squeeze-off: pipe diameter, wall thickness, and tool size. If pipe diameter and SDR vary so that wall thickness is unchanged, the likelihood of damage formation is unchanged if the same tool is used. If the wall thickness and the diameter vary, the effect of changing wall thickness dominates the effect of changing diameter for the same tool size.

## Effect of Tool Design

Single small-diameter bars tend to concentrate stresses in a small region during squeeze-off, reducing the effectiveness in controlling flow and increasing the likelihood of damage. Smaller diameter tools also require less force to achieve a fixed amount of wall compression. The advantage of lower forces may have prompted the early use of smaller-diameter bars with the disadvantage of a higher likelihood for damage. This is consistent with field experience, which suggests that small-diameter squeeze-off tools without limit stops, as sometimes found in "home-made" tools, may be a significant cause of over-squeeze and squeeze-off-induced failures.

Experiments indicate that sufficiently large single, double, and flat bars with radiused edges all can be used for squeeze-off without damaging PE pipe. Battelle experience suggests that, for pipe diameters equal to or greater than 50 mm (2 inches), tools whose total width is greater than or equal to four times the maximum wall thickness of the pipe and have a minimum radius of 25 mm (1 inch) are unlikely to induce damage in SCG-resistant materials when they are squeezed to less than 30-percent wall compression. For larger diameter pipes, the curvature of the tool should also be increased.

## Effect of Material

Squeeze-off performance is material-dependent; however, long-term behavior is consistent across SCG-resistant materials. PE pipe materials which are not as SCG-resistant may still be subjected to squeeze-off as long as the degree of wall compression does not induce immediate damage.

## Effect of Temperature

The effects of temperature on inducing squeeze-off damage depend upon the material being squeezed. Temperature was found to be important in inducing squeeze-off damage in materials whose stiffness changes significantly as the temperature is varied. If there are no available data or experience to indicate the behavior of a material, then a qualification test should be performed at the temperature in question to confirm that damage is not induced.

## Effect of Compression Rate

Compression rate, like temperature, is important in materials whose stiffness changes significantly with variations in loading rate. Pipe should be compressed as slowly as is practical and safe. While an exhaustive evaluation of squeeze-rate effects has not been conducted, Battelle experience indicates that compression rates of 0.85 mm/s (2 inches per minute) or less are appropriate.

## Effect of Time Compressed

The length of time the pipe is compressed is of secondary importance when considering the likelihood of inducing damage. Time-dependent stresses decay rapidly after the wall compression is completed; they change relatively little with the length of time held in the compressed position. Consequently, no limitations are necessary on the length of time the pipe is compressed.

## Effect of Reround

Rerounding can result in beneficial compressive stresses on the inside of the squeeze ear in materials undamaged during the squeeze and release process. However, there may be little or no practical benefit achieved from rerounding in undamaged materials because times-to-failure for current materials are well beyond practical levels even without reround.

In the reround process of inducing compressive residual stresses, a large tensile stress is applied briefly on the inside of the ear. If the squeeze ear has been damaged and defects are present, this tensile stress is likely to induce rapid growth of the defects. Hence, the benefits of reround depend upon whether damage (voids) has been induced in the squeeze-off ear as well as other factors.

Rerounding in SCG-resistant materials is an option for the improvement of gas flow or concerns other than damage mitigation. However, when rerounding is undertaken it should be done slowly enough so that any existing damage is less likely to be propagated.

## Effect of Post-Squeeze-Off Reinforcement

Sometimes, reinforcement sleeves are installed around the pipe after squeeze-off on the assumption that compression of the pipe wall will prevent any defects from growing. Field experience with PE3306III, a pipe material known to perform poorly following squeeze-off, has demonstrated that squeeze-off defects will grow underneath a reinforcement clamp. This suggests that a reinforcement clamp may not be able to generate enough compressive stress to limit defect growth. While this argument is not conclusive, no direct evidence has been found of any long-term benefit derived from post-squeeze-off reinforcement. Note, in regard to discussion of rerounding, that materials with poor SCG performance may be left with a tensile residual stress due to the rerounding, which can promote crack growth. It is feasible that this was the cause for the above noted crack growth underneath the reinforcement clamp.

## GUIDELINES

- The exact wall compression at which the flow effectively stops is situation-specific because of the randomness of final closure.

- If the damage-occurrence limit for SCG-resistant materials (most modern materials) is taken to be 30-percent wall compression, it is desirable to stop flow at 20-percent wall compression or less in order to maintain a safe usable range.

- As pipe diameter increases, wall thickness also typically increases, and the usable range of wall compression decreases.

- Flatter bar shapes (or multiple bars) are more effective but require a greater applied force and should be adequately curved (cross-sectionally) to avoid damage.

- It is crucial that the squeeze tool have stops that are set to the proper specifications. Excessive wall compression is the main cause of potential pipe damage.

- Damage initiates below the inside wall surface at the squeeze-off ear due to "excessive" wall compression compounded by rapid release. The level of wall compression that is "excessive" depends primarily on the pipe material, pipe dimensions, and the tool size and design.

- If immediate damage occurs, it occurs at the beginning of the release and is more likely to occur when releasing rapidly. The release should always be controlled and the pipe should never be allowed to spring back rapidly. Release rates less than 0.2 mm/s (0.5 inches/minute) do not appear to increase the likelihood of damage.

- For SCG-resistant materials, a wall compression of 30 percent is unlikely to induce damage and should not be exceeded.

- For non-SCG-resistant materials, past practice or a suitable qualification procedure should be used to determine the maximum allowable wall compression.

- If immediate damage does not occur, damage is unlikely to initiate subsequently. If immediate damage does occur, the growth of the damage will generally be much faster in non-SCG-resistant materials than in SCG-resistant materials.

- As pipe diameter and SDR change, the tendency to damage formation does not change as long as the tool size is unchanged and large compared with pipe wall thickness and diameter.

- As pipe wall thickness increases significantly, the tool diameter should be increased proportionately.

- Typically, for a pipe diameter greater than 50 mm (2 inches), the tool width should be greater than four times the wall thickness (minimum tool size of 1 inch) and wall compression should be less than 30 percent.

- Flat tools should have a radius of curvature at least four times the wall thickness.

- Small tool sizes (compared with pipe wall thickness or diameter) tend to damage the pipe.

- The effect of temperature depends on the pipe material. If the stiffness of the pipe material increases significantly with change in temperature, damage is more likely to be induced.

- The duration of squeeze-off is of secondary importance and is unlikely to influence damage.

- Rerounding provides no practical benefits from the point of view of damage formation. However, it may be performed for other reasons, such as increasing the flow area to maintain a high flow rate.

- There is no evidence that post-squeeze-off reinforcements are beneficial.

- The rate of compression changes the rate of closure because of the viscoelastic nature of PE but does not significantly affect the wall compression at which the flow stops. Compression rate affects the squeeze-off process if stiffness increases significantly with increasing compression rate. Compression rates of less than or equal to 0.85 mm/s (2 inches/minute) do not appear to increase the likelihood of damage.

## REFERENCES

1. Stephens, D.R., B.N. Leis, R.B. Francini, and M.J. Cassady, *Volume 1: User's Guide on Squeeze-Off of Polyethylene Gas Pipes*, GRI Topical Report No. GRI-92/0147.1, Oct. 1992.

2. Stephens, D.R., B.N. Leis, R.B. Francini, and M.J. Cassady, *Volume 2: Technical Reference on Squeeze-Off of Polyethylene Gas Pipes*, GRI Topical Report No. GRI-92/0147.2, Oct. 1992.

3. Pimputkar, S.M., and J.A. Stets, *Guidelines and Technical Reference on Gas Flow Shut-Off in Polyethylene Pipes Using Squeeze Tools*, GRI Topical Report No. GRI-94/0205, June 1994.

DEVELOPMENT OF THE INSPECTION SYSTEM FOR GAS MAINS

DÉVELOPPEMENT D'UN SYSTÈME D'INSPECTION POUR CANALISATION

Kiichi Suyama and Yasuharu Hosohara
Tokyo Gas Co., Ltd., Japan
Akira Kinoshita
Osaka Gas Co., Ltd., Japan
Kenichiro Hayashi
Toho Gas Co., Ltd., Japan

ABSTRACT

Tokyo Gas Co., Ltd., Osaka Gas Co., Ltd. and Toho Gas Co., Ltd. have jointly developed an inspection system for gas mains capable of detecting thinning of external walls from corrosion by inserting a sensor into the buried gas mains. At the present stage, final evaluations and improvements are being carried out through field tests. This system has extremely high wall thinning estimating accuracy which enables accurate grasping of the state of corrosion of the line. This will make further planned and effective preventive maintenance possible and also greatly reduce maintenance costs. This paper explains the principle of measuring the thinning of walls from corrosion, equipment specifications, methods of inspection and results of field tests.

RESUME

Tokyo Gas Co., Ltd., Osaka Gas Co., Ltd. et Toho Gas Co., Ltd. ont développé conjointement un dispositif d'inspection de la canalisation principale de gaz capable de détecter l'amincissement des parois externes par la corrosion, uniquement en introduisant un capteur dans l'extension de la canalisation. A l'heure actuelle, des évaluations définitives et des améliorations sont effectuées par le biais d'essais en site. Ce système procure une précision extrêmement élevée non seulement en matière d'estimation de l'amincissement des parois mais également en ce qui concerne la position qui permet de connaître avec exactitude l'état de corrosion de la canalisation. Cet équipement permettra de procéder une maintenance préventive plus efficace et de réduire les coûts d'entretien et de contrôle. Le pr'ésent document explique les principes de mesure de l'amincissement des parois par la corrosion et indique en outre les spécifications de l'équipement, la méthode de construction et les résultats des essais en site.

**FOREWORD**

**Background of Development**

Maintenance of gas mains in their proper state is one of the most important duties of city gas companies. It is also necessary for this to be carried out efficiently. Tokyo Gas Co., Ltd. has an overall pipe length of about 43,000 km of which gas mains compose about one half or 20,000 km. Furthermore, it is practically impossible to evaluate the state of the gas mains directly since practically all of the line is buried under the road. Excavating is therefore essential to inspect gas mains but its cost commands the greatest percentage of the overall costs. Furthermore, with the increasing volume of traffic and sophisticated paving, excavating is becoming increasingly costly.

From these points, development of methods and equipment for rational maintenance of the gas mains with minimum excavation is therefore desired.

**Object of Development**

From this state of affairs, Tokyo Gas Co., Ltd., Osaka Gas Co., Ltd. and Toho Gas Co., Ltd. jointly developed an inspection system for gas mains capable of evaluating the state of external wall thinning from corrosion and also specifying the place by simply inserting the sensor into the buried main. The object in developing this device is to reduce maintenance cost of the gas mains and improve safety levels from the corrosion information obtained.

If accurate information can be obtained on the state of corrosion of the line, it will be possible to implement appropriate measures such as replacing or repairing the mains requiring maintenance at suitable periods before a leakage occurs. A more planned and effective preventive maintenance will become possible by grasping the state of corrosion of the line in this manner and it will also be effective from the aspect of reducing maintenance costs.

At present, the line is excavated at several places to check the state of corrosion and, after exposing part of the pipe, the state of the overall line is estimated by examining the surface of the exposed portion. However, a problem here is that diagnosis will not necessarily be accurate since the entire system is judged based on a few portions. By using this device, accurate inspection of the entire line will be possible with minimum excavation.

**PRINCIPLE**

**Requirements**

The requirements to attain the objective of this development are as shown below.

* Accurate measurement of depth shall be possible of outer surface corrosion thinning of buried pipes to determine the state of corrosion.
* Inspection shall be possible even if there is some dirt, dust,

water or burrs in the pipe.
* Time required for inspection and possible inspection distance
  shall be appropriate.
* It shall be of a shape and softness enabling passing through
  bends in the pipe.
* Since low pressure pipes make up the bulk of the piping system,
  inspection shall be comparatively simple without the need of
  pressure.

The 100A to 200A cast iron and steel pipes that compose the major
percentage of gas mains were also made the target of development at
this time.

## Comparison of Various Systems

In relation to these demands, various test methods relative to
internal inspection techniques of gas pipes such as the remote field
eddy current test, ultrasonic test, magnetic flux leakage method and
eddy current test were compared and the results are shown below.

The ultrasonic test has the merits of the possibility of
measuring wall thickness with comparatively high accuracy and the
comparatively low sensor traction force required. The previous problem
of the need for contact liquid between the sensor and pipe and the
need for adequate precleaning since inspection will not be possible if
there is dust in the pipe     are being resolved with the development
of the dry coupler wheel. However, we believe that application of the
dry coupler wheel will not be possible since it is basically for crack
detection and cannot detect holes that penetrate through the pipe, has
insufficient resolution to detect pits and its inspection speed is
slow compared to other means.
Although detecting performance of corrosion thinning of wall  is
excellent in the magnetic flux leakage method, application was judged
to be difficult because of the large and rugged structure of the
sensor module due to the need of a magnet, the difficulty of passing
through mechanical joint sections and bends, and the excessive
traction force for use in low pressure pipelines. In the case of eddy
current tests, adequate results cannot be anticipated in the current
objective since measurement of the state of corrosion of the outer
surface of the pipe is not possible from the inside.

In relation to this, the remote field eddy current test has the
merits of using light and flexible sensor modules with small traction
force. We are already using a practical remote field eddy current test
for inspection of branch pipelines (small gas mains: steel pipes 50A -
00A) and have obtained excellent inspection results. Although the low
sensor signal level is believed to be the only point that is inferior
compared to other methods, much technology has already been
accumulated relative to this signal processing which is now at a
practical level. The remote field eddy current method is therefore
being used for the sensor in this system for the foregoing reasons.

## Principle

The principle of RFEC (Remote Field Eddy Current) method is shown
in Fig. 1. The sensor section is composed of one transmitting coil and

multiple receiving coils. The distance between the transmitting coil and receiving coil is over twice the inner diameter of the pipe. Electromagnetic energy generated in the transmission coil is propagated in two forms consisting of those propagated directly through the inside of the pipe and those propagated indirectly through the wall of the pipe. When the exciting frequency is comparatively low (30 Hz in this device), indirect transmission becomes dominant if the distance between the sending and receiving coil is about twice the diameter of the inside of the pipe since indirect propagation dampens more slowly compared to direct transmission. In indirect propagation, it is qualitatively understood that the electro-magnetic waves from the transmitting coil penetrate the pipe wall and, after reaching the outer wall of the pipe, they are propagated along the surface of the pipe and penetrate the pipe wall again and are caught by the receiving coil. For this reason, the amplitude and phase of the receiving signal contains information on wall thickness near the receiving coil and this is expressed quantitatively with the following equation.

$$\theta = kd \sqrt{\pi\mu\sigma f}$$

$$A = A_0 \ exp \ (-d \ \sqrt{\pi\mu\sigma f})$$

$\theta$   Phase difference between sending and receiving signals
$A$   Amplitude of receiving signal
$k$   Proportional constant
$d$   Wall thickness of pipe
$f$   Frequency
$\mu$   Permeability
$\sigma$   Electrical conductivity

In this manner, the phase difference between signals transmitted and received is proportional to the thickness of the pipe wall. Measuring the pipe wall thickness by detecting this signal is the principle of this method.

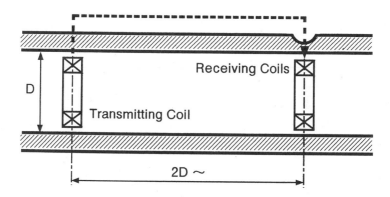

**Figure 1. Principle of the Remote Field Eddy Current Method**

## SYSTEM OUTLINE

### System Composition

An external view of the system developed is shown in Photo 1. The basic composition of this system consists of the sensor to be inserted in the pipe, cable drum, flaw detector and data processing unit. The unit shown at the front is the 150A sensor and the unit at the back is the 200A sensor. The flaw detector processes the sensor signal and the data processing unit outputs the results. Since the sensor signal is extremely weak in the remote field eddy current method, noise countermeasures and high precision signal processing techniques become extremely important development problems.

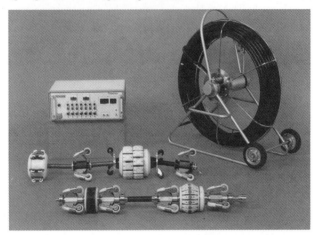

**Photo 1.  External View of the Inspection System**

### System Specifications

Specifications of the system are shown in Table 1.

**Table 1.  Sensor System Specifications**

| Items | Sensor Specifications |
| --- | --- |
| Applicable bore | 100A, 150A and 200A |
| Applicable type of pipe | Cast iron and steel pipe |
| Detection performance<br>    (Wall thinning all around) | Over 30% |
| (Surface pit) | $\phi$10mm Over 50% |
| (Holes that penetrate through the pipe) | Detectable |
| Circumferential inspection area | 100% (all around pipe) |
| Place of inspection | Pipe wall excluding joints and bends |

**Sensor Module**

Sensors used for inspecting branch pipes differ in that the receiving coils are wound vertically relative to the axial direction of the pipe. This was changed to a more advantageous type for detecting since adequate signal level could not be obtained with conventional types of receiving coils because of the thickness of cast iron pipes. The receiving coil is also flexible in the radial direction of the pipe to enable it to cope flexibly with projections in the pipe and with bent parts to enable it to pass through the pipe.

When estimating wall thinning depth, changes in pit opening (flaw volume) and magnetic characteristics of the pipe (permeability, electrical conductivity) become error factors. We have corrected these effects and have established a method for accurate estimation of flaw depth.

**Qualification Test Results (Output example)**

A typical output data relative to an artificial flaw (pit) is shown in Fig. 2. The test piece in this output example is a 150A ductile cast iron pipe. The upper part shows the state of the artificial flaw and the lower part shows the output signal $A\sin\theta$ [A:Amplitude, $\theta$:Phase lag]. This shows that it has adequate performance.

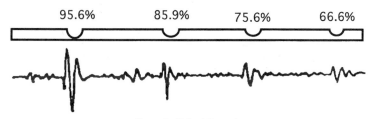

95.6%    85.9%    75.6%    66.6%

**Figure 2. Output Example**

Multiple receiving coils are connected in series in this unit to realize practical output channels. However, this worsens S/N and reduces its primary detecting performance. On the contrary, detecting performance can be improved by reducing the number of channels to be connected. When one coil is used per channel, 30% detection is possible with a $\phi$10 aperture.

**METHOD OF INSPECTION**

The following three methods of inspection are now being developed to respond to the various demands relative to inspection on site.

**Insertion method under live conditions**

An image of the insertion method under live conditions (insertion method) is shown in Fig. 3. Excavate the road at one place and cut the gas main after assembling a bypass pipe. Insert the sensor from the cut part with no-blow and inspect the pipeline by moving the sensor back and forth with the cable. At present, we are at the stage of improvement to increase the inspection length.

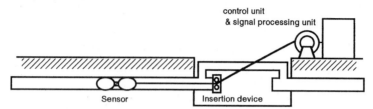

**Figure 3.  Insertion Method Under Live Conditions**

Traction method using a winch

An image of the traction method using a winch (traction method) is shown in Fig. 4. The road is excavated in two places and the gas main cut. A wire attached to the front of the sensor is passed through the pipe and inspection of the pipe carried out by pulling the wire with a winch.

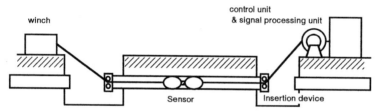

**Figure 4.  Traction Method Using a Winch**

Robot method

The image of the robot method is shown in Fig. 5. The road is excavated in two places and the gas main cut. Inspection of the pipe wall is then carried out by causing a robot with sensor mounted to pass through the pipe. 100A robots of a type that operate in air environments have already been developed and field tests conducted with excellent results obtained.

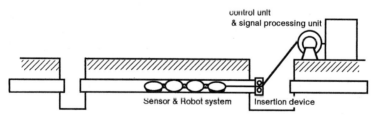

**Figure 5.  Robot Method**

## Method of inspection

Comparison of the various systems is shown in Table 2. At present, inspection is planned mostly using the traction method. In cases where live pipe inspection must be carried out because of special conditions of the inspection site such as where excavation is possible on one side only since it crosses a trunk road, the policy is to cope with the insertion method. A 150A cableless robot of a type that can be driven in live pipe conditions is now being developed as a pipe traveling robot. This robot is shown in Photo 2. At the same time, since it is cableless, it is believed that long distance inspection will be possible without being affected by the number of bends.

**Table 2. Comparison of Methods of Execution**

| Method of inspection | Inspection conditions | Passability of bends | Inspection length |
|---|---|---|---|
| Insertion method | Live pipe | Not possible | 50m |
| Traction method | Purge required | 45° elbow possable | 100m |
| Robot method | Purge required (Live pipe possible in future) | 45° elbow possable | 100m |

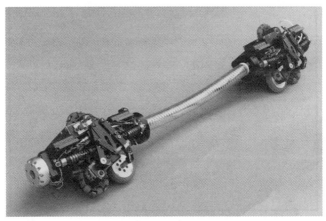

**Photo 2. Cableless Robot**

## FIELD TEST RESULTS

### Field test outline

Field tests are presently being carried out mainly using the traction method. Visual inspection is initially carried out with an internal pipe inspection camera unit for existence of abnormality relative to the piping and the state of the interior. Inspection of the pipe is then basically conducted without cleaning. This has been implemented at nine sites up till now for a total of 670 m and excellent results have been obtained. The record of achievement is shown in Table 3.

**Table 3  Field Test Implementation Results**

| No. | Pipe specifications | Inspected distance | Method of inspection |
|-----|---------------------|--------------------|----------------------|
| 1 | 150A, Cast iron pipe | 43m | Traction method |
| 2 | 150A, Cast iron pipe | 39m | Traction method |
| 3 | 150A, Cast iron pipe | 37.5m | Traction method |
| 4 | 100A, Steel pipe | 320m | Robot method |
| 5 | 200A, Steel pipe | 20m | Insertion method |
| 6 | 200A, Cast iron pipe | 60m | Traction method |
| 7 | 150A, Cast iron pipe | 30.2m | Traction method |
| 8 | 200A, Cast iron pipe | 38.1m | Traction method |
| 9 | 200A, Cast iron pipe | 81.7m | Traction method |

**Example of field test evaluation**

The sensor data signal in the No. 7 field test site is shown in Fig. 6. It may be judged that point A, where all channels change in the same manner, is a joint. Point B, which is large in Channel 6 and with some variation in Channel 1, may be judged as corrosion extending from Channels 1 to 6. This part of the pipe excavated is shown in Photos 3 and 4. Photo 3 is the overall view which shows corrosion in the three places a, b and c. Of these points, corrosion at point a is shown in Photo 4. The area was 100 X 62.5 mm and maximum depth 3.3 mm (about 34.7%T).

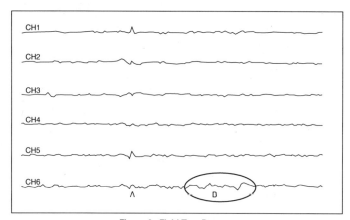

**Figure 6.  Field Test Data**

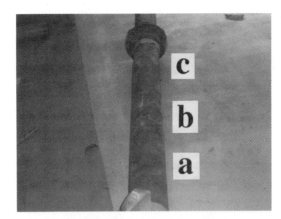

**Photo 3.  Overall View of Excavated Pipe**

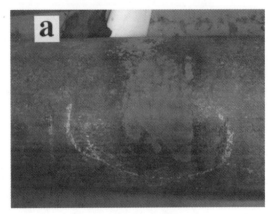

**Photo 4  Corrosion at Point A**

CONCLUSION

A gas main inspection device was developed. It was confirmed that the necessary specifications such as detecting performance and ease of inspection were thoroughly satisfied through various performance tests and field tests. Future plans are to focus on  the robot method.

SOIL COMPACTION METER

LE COMPTEUR POUR LA COMPACTION DE LA TERRE

Robert Torbin and Frank Heirtzler
Foster-Miller, Inc., USA

Michael Lukasiewicz
Gas Research Institute, USA

Thomas Artzberger
M-B-W Inc., USA

ABSTRACT

Improper densification of soil in an excavation often requires a crew to return to the site and re-move and properly compact the backfill. Since U.S. gas utilities excavate more than 2 million bellholes annually, the cost of this process is substantial. The Compaction Meter is a low cost, easy-to-use, compact instrument that helps utility crews optimize backfill compaction. The meter consists of a small sensor (placed at the bottom of an excavation), a connecting wire, and an elec-tronic readout box. It operates on a principle that compaction tool impact energy transmitted through soil is a function of fill density. As each layer of fill becomes more compacted, energy transmitted to the sensor increases. When each layer is sufficiently compacted, the readout box alerts the operator to stop, without interrupting the backfilling process. Utilities have demonstrated the unit's performance in field trials and a manufacturer is readying the technology for commercialization.

RESUMÉ

Le mauvais compactage de la terre pendant l'excavation oblige souvent l'equipe à retourner au site et à déplacer et compacter convenablement la terre (le materiel utilisé pour remplir l'excavation). Puisque les compagnies de gas des Etats Unis creusent plus de deux millions de trous dans les rues chaque anneè, le prix de ce procédé est substantiel. Le compteur de compactage est un instrument de compactage peu coûteux, facile a utiliser qui aide l'equipe a réaliser le meilleur compactage de la terre possible. Le compteur consiste d'un petit mecanisme sensible, (placé au fond de l'excavation), d'un fil de cuivre connecteur et d'une boîte indicatrice électronique. Il opère à partir du principe que l'energie d'impact de l'instrument de compactage transmise a travers la terre est une fonction de la densité de la terre. A mesure que chaque niveau de la terre devient plus compacte, l'energie transmise au mecanisme sensible, augmente. Quand chaque niveau est suffisamment compacte, la boite indicatrice alerte l'operateur de s'arrêter, sans interrompre le procès de remplissage de l'excavation. Les exploitants ont demontré la performance du compteur dans les champs d'experimentation et le fabricant est en train de preparer la technologie pour le commerce.

## BACKGROUND

Repairs made on underground utilities (natural gas, water, sewer, electricity) normally require that the street pavement be cut and removed, and the ground excavated down to the particular utility service line. Utility crews backfill the excavation (whether a trench or a bellhole) with excavated material or special imported material. Each layer of soil, or lift, is compacted before the addition of the next lift of backfill. If the backfill material is not properly compacted, or if unsuitable backfill material is used, the completed backfill may subside. If this subsidence is excessive, the roadway itself may fail, requiring a costly call-back to the construction contractor or utility.

There are many reasons why the compaction of the backfill material leads to failure of the restored roadbed. The backfill material may not have the desired cohesiveness or its moisture level may be too high or too low to achieve proper compaction. The lift thicknesses may exceed the utility's specifications for acceptable backfilling practices. The compaction tool may not have adequate impact force for the job; the air pressure may be too low; the tool itself could be improperly used or maintained; or the tamper operator may not be adequately trained.

The cost associated with returning to a single site to repair a failed street can be as high as $800. To control costs, and maintain goodwill with the public, many utilities have comprehensive training and operating procedures for restoring pavement cuts. The industry accepted best backfilling practices include measurements, which when compared with accepted standards, assure a quality restoration.

## CURRENT QUALITY ASSURANCE TOOLS

To address these possible shortcomings in the compaction process, quality assurance tools/instruments are available to monitor the backfilling process. Two of the most commonly used devices are the nuclear densitometer and the Dynamic Cone Penetrometer (DCP). These devices have many advantages as well as disadvantages. The nuclear densitometer uses radioactive materials and directs gamma and neutron rays through the soil. The radioactive sources are contained within a slim cylindrical probe which must be inserted into the ground a typical distance of 15 to 20 cm at each test point. Once the probe is inserted, the instrument counts the amount of radiation transmitted through the soil. The sampling time is a minimum of 60 seconds, but can be several minutes in some situations. Because of its radioactive sources, the densitometer must be operated by a certified technician, requires an annual federal licensing fee, and must be periodically checked for radiation leakage. Consequently, most densitometers are maintained by private service contractors, are relatively expensive to employ, and require close coordination with the construction contractor whenever they are used to monitor backfilling operations. Typical per hole cost of a nuclear densitometer is $250.

The Dynamic Cone Penetrometer device uses a cone-shaped element that is pushed into the soil using a slide hammer, which imparts a consistent impact energy with each hit. The distance the cone penetrates the soil is an indication of the soil "density." Field DCP procedures typically require the cone to be struck a minimum of 15 times before a penetration threshold is exceeded. With certain soil types, this number of blows can be much higher. The accuracy of the measurement is affected by the consistency of the operator to make identical blows with the slide hammer. Like the nuclear densitometer, the DCP must be set up and implemented with each lift if the entire depth of backfill is to be checked, increasing the time to complete the overall backfilling.

The procedures for operating the nuclear densitometer or the DCP must be followed closely to obtain a proper indication of the density of the backfill compaction. If one of these devices is only used on the last lift, the reading only indicates the density of approximately the top 15 cm of soil. The acceptability of the entire excavation is very uncertain based on this single measurement. To get truly comprehensive readings of backfill quality, the field crew must stop at every lift, and take the 3 to 5 minutes required to set up, measure and remove either instrument.

SOIL COMPACTION METER DESCRIPTION

Foster-Miller, Inc. and M-B-W Inc. have developed a Soil Compaction Meter to give utility crews information that ensures a quality backfill, while overcoming the disadvantages of current quality assurance tools. The Soil Compaction Meter is a small, hand-held, battery operated, electronic device which indicates to the tamper operator when maximum compaction has been achieved for a given soil lift. Gas Research Institute (GRI) has sponsored research to develop the technology on which the Soil Compaction Meter is based. M-B-W Inc. is currently working to design and commercialize a production version of the device. Use of the Soil Compaction Meter by utility and private contractor field crews holds the promise of improving the quality of backfill compaction, reducing the number of callbacks, and minimizing the time required to adequately compact each soil lift.

The Soil Compaction Meter consists of a small, rugged control box, as shown in Figure 1, and an inexpensive disk shaped disposable sensor which is connected to the meter by a wire. A polymer-based piezoelectric element is bonded to the inside of the top surface of the disposable sensor. A single sensor is used in small pit type excavations, and a series of sensors is used for long trenches. As individual soil lifts are compacted, signals from the sensor are interpreted by the meter electronics. As each soil lift becomes more dense, the compaction energy transmitted through the soil to the sensor increases. A mathematical algorithm programmed into the electronics filters and manipulates successive energy pulse readings to determine when compaction is optimized. The field crew is notified by a visual signal from the meter box that the lift has been completed. The device can also be configured to log excavation data in memory for subsequent downloading by the crew supervisor.

**Figure 1. Soil compaction meter and disposable sensor**

The specific operating procedure is straightforward, requiring very little training, and is understandable by everyone in the field crew. Before starting the backfilling, a single sensor is placed at the bottom of the excavation and its connecting wire is plugged into the compaction meter. Referring to Figure 2, the meter is energized by simply pressing the ON-OFF switch to the ON position. The red POWER light will turn on, indicating that the unit is operational. The SENSOR OK/START light will also come on indicating that the sensor and cable are functioning, and is used as the OK signal to begin the backfilling and compaction process. At this time, the tamper operator begins compacting following the utility's approved procedures. Once the compaction process is started, the PROCESSING light on the meter is activated. This light will flash each time valid data is received by the meter. After an initial 30 seconds or so of data processing and compacting, the green lights (above the PROCESSING light) come on sequentially to indicate the approximate stage of the compaction process. The compaction continues until the STOP light comes on, indicating that the optimal degree of compaction has been achieved. To reset the the meter prior to the start of the next lift, simply turn the ON-OFF switch to the OFF position and then back to the ON position.

Following completion of the final lift, the operator disconnects the sensor wire from the meter. If good compaction procedures are followed, soil moisture content is within a reasonable range, and the compaction equipment is in good repair, the meter's final stop signals assure the utility of a high quality backfill.

THEORY OF OPERATION

Peak Detect Algorithm

The following text describes how the Soil Compaction Meter determines when compaction has reached its maximum achievable level for a given soil condition. It explains the mathematical procedure, referred to as the Peak Detect Algorithm, that calculates maximum achievable compaction. Two United States patents have been issued covering the general compaction monitoring approach and related techni-

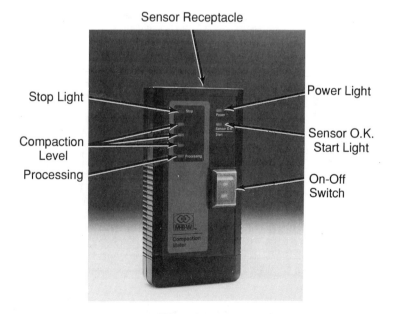

Figure 2. Meter Indicator lights and switches

cal developments (U.S. Patent Nos. 5,105,650 and 5,402,667). There is currently a United States patent pending on the Peak Detect Algorithm itself.

The enclosed piezoelectric (Kynar™) sensor placed at the bottom of the hole produces a voltage in response to pressure waves transmitted through the soil from the tamper. The voltage level is proportional to the amplitude of the pressure wave reaching the sensor and is dependent on several factors (moisture, soil type, etc.). The most important factor for the peak detect technique is soil density. When backfill material is first shoveled into the hole, it is uncompacted and at a relatively low density. The efficiency of transmission of pressure pulses through the soil is low. Thus, the voltage generated by the sensor is also small. As the soil becomes more compact, the transmission efficiency increases and the voltage produced by the sensor similarly increases. Eventually, the soil reaches maximum achievable compaction and the voltage increases level off. The concept that the density and the signal voltage level off to some asymptotic value is crucial to determining when to stop compaction.

Figure 3 shows the voltage output of the sensor during compaction for a typical lift. Note that the discrete nature of the signals is due to the finite sampling frequency of the meter. The signal passes into a peak detect circuit which holds the maximum value during the sampling period. The peak value is then stored at 1 second intervals. The huge variations in the signal are due to the changing distance between the sensor and the compaction tool as the operator moves about the surface of the excavation. The signal is small at the periphery of the hole and is a maximum directly over the sensor. For large holes, signals near the periphery approach the noise threshold of the meter and are ignored. This is accomplished by setting a low level threshold.

In order to see the asymptotic nature of the time trace, the gross variations need to be smoothed out. This is performed in two steps. First, the logarithm of the raw data is taken to reduce the dynamic range. Second, a rectangular moving window digital filter is applied. The raw data shown in Figure 3 are smoothed in this manner to produce the curve shown in Figure 4. This curve can be approximated by the expression:

$$y = \frac{t}{b + mt}$$

where **b** and **m** are constants (**y** is signal magnitude and **t** is time). Employing an appropriate choice of coordinate transformation:

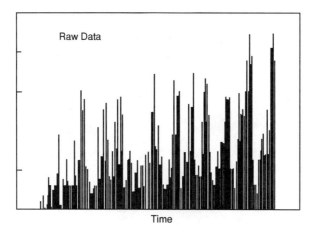

Time

**Figure 3. Voltage signals from dynamic pressure sensitive
sensor during soil compaction**

$$y' = \frac{t}{y}$$

produces the linear expression:

$$y' = b + mt$$

The result of this linearization on the data from our example is shown in Figure 5. The transformed data can then be processed with a weighted linear regression scheme to find the constants **b** and **m**. The regression equation is given by:

$$R = \sum_{n=1}^{N} w_n \left( y'_n - (b + mt_n) \right)^2$$

where **w** is a weighting factor chosen to reduce the scatter in the data over the time area of interest (when the compaction is expected to be completed), and can be optimized for the range of hole sizes for which the meter is expected to be used. If **N** is interpreted as the number of data points collected up to a particular time, the regression can then be applied in real time. The regression constants **b** and **m** are updated with each new point added. The original smoothed curve may then be reconstructed using the current regression constants:

$$y^* = \frac{t}{b + mt}$$

The curve above approaches an asymptotic value (for sufficiently large **t**) of **1/m**. This value for **y*** represents the maximum possible compaction given the existing conditions. Since this is an asymptotic value, and, thus, achievable only after an infinite time, a cut-off criteria was chosen as a percentage of this maximum to be reached in a finite time:

$$\text{cutoff} = \frac{K}{m}$$

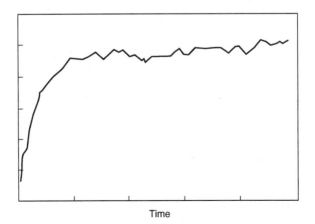

Time

**Figure 4. Compaction data after temporal filtering techniques are applied**

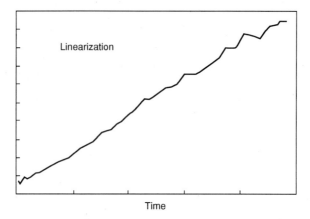

**Figure 5. Compaction data after linearization transformations**

Figure 6 shows the final result for our example. The bottom curve is the reconstructed data **y\*** calculated at each time step with the current regression constants. The top curve is the cut-off criteria found from the asymptotic value which is being updated with each step. When the two curves meet, compaction has reached **K** (generally in the 0.90 to 0.98 range) of the theoretical maximum.

Testing has shown that the Soil Compaction Meter reliably indicates maximum achievable compaction for a variety of compaction tools and any tamping pattern, including random movement of the tool. Figure 7 shows the correlation between the conditioned signal from the Soil Compaction Meter and actual successive density measurements (using a nuclear densitometer) for a typical soil lift.

Technology Capabilities and Future Device Options

The current version of the Soil Compaction Meter is a simple, low cost way to ensure good backfill compaction. The technology built into the device provides opportunities for a number of future refine-

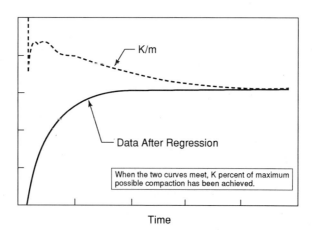

**Figure 6. Compaction completion criteria**

INSPECTION OF EXTERNAL CORROSION OF STEEL PIPES
WITH BENDS BY EDDY CURRENT

INSPECTION DES CORROSIONS EXTERNES DES COUDES
EN ACIER PAR COURANT DE FOUCAULT

Hideki FURUKAWA, Kiwamu SUZUKI, Mitunori KOMAKI
Tokyo Gas Co., Ltd., JAPAN

ABSTRACT

The electromagnetic measurement method called remote-field eddy-current method was adapted to develop a new inspection system that is not only able to detect external corrosion of small gas pipes from the inside, but is also able to pass through bent pipes using an innovative rotating sensor. The prototype for this sensor was developed after conducting research on various sensor shapes and methods of signal processing to reduce noise caused by sensor rotation. Preliminary tests on the prototype produced satisfactory results regarding its passing ability and inspection performance.

RÉSUMÉ

Il existe une méthode de mesure électromagnétique appelée méthode d'inspection par courant de Foucault (créant un champs magnétique éloigné), permettant d'évaluer de l'intérieur des conduites en acier de faible diamètre, l'importance des corrosions externes. A partir de cette méthode, nous avons conçu un système d'inspection pour ces types de conduites, utilisant un détecteur rotatif. En se basant sur la recherche d'une forme de détecteur qui soit capable de circuler dans les coudes avec plus de facilité, et d'un traitement de signaux éliminant les bruits parasites provenant des mouvements de rotation, un prototype de système d'inspection a été crée. Les premiers tests sur conduites d'essai ont donné des résultats satisfaisants quant à sa capacité d'infiltration et d'inspection.

## INTRODUCTION

Gas pipes in the supply area of Tokyo Gas Co., Ltd. are classified into two types: 1) pipes that are owned by customers and located on their property; and 2) pipes that are owned by Tokyo Gas and located on public property such as on public roads. Customer-owned pipes laid after 1973 are either polyethylene-coated steel pipes or polyethylene pipes. However, those laid before 1973 are zinc-plated steel pipes. For these pipes, poor soil condition causes corrosion that accelerates with time and in some cases causes gas leakage. When gas leakage is discovered, the corroded part of pipe is either replaced by corrosion-proof polyethylene pipes or the inner surface of pipe is coated with resin without replacement.

Since the degree of corrosion varies depending on the environment where the pipe is laid, it cannot be evaluated only by the number of years passed. Therefore, for pipes whose degree of corrosion is expected to be intense, some kind of inspection method is required to determine what preventive measures to take. In addition to such basic conditions as low inspection costs and ease of operation, it is also desirable to minimize excavation work, to allow inspection of bent pipes, and to make gas purging unnecessary.

Several corrosion inspection methods are available: remote-field eddy-current method, eddy-current method, leakage magnetic flux method, supersonic method and mechanical impedance method. To satisfy the needs mentioned above, we have developed an inspection system based on the remote-field eddy-current method combined with a traction equipment for the rotating sensor.

## SPECIFICATIONS

In consideration of the actual pipe positioning and of the ease of operation, the following specifications were adapted to the inspection system:

Diameter of pipe:      50mm
Inspection Length:     15m
Number of bends:       6
Speed of inspection:   1m/min
Performance of detecting defects:
                       More than 90% reduction of wall thickness and
                       through-hole can be detected
Gas supply:            On line
Inspection method:     Remote-field eddy-current method
Insertion method:      Rotation of sensor and spring

The remote-field eddy-current method was selected because it is able to inspect the external corrosion from inside of steel pipes without stopping gas supply to customers.

It was also decided that a sensor would be inserted by spinning a spring connected to the sensor using a traction equipment. This method has the following advantages when compared to a method which uses a robot to pull the sensor:
- Low costs
- Good operability
- Applicable to small diameter pipes (25mm - 50mm)

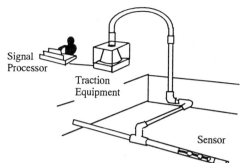

Figure 1. A Conceptual Diagram of An On-Site Operation

PRINCIPLE OF REMOTE-FIELD EDDY-CURRENT METHOD

The sensor for the remote-field eddy-current method is composed of an exciter coil to transmit an electromagnetic wave and a receiver coil to receive an electromagnetic wave (Figure 2). The electromagnetic wave, which is generated by placing an alternating current of low frequency (35Hz in this system) to the exciter coil, penetrates the steel pipe wall by the skin effect, passes along the steel pipe surface as eddy-current, penetrates the steel pipe wall again, and is received by the receiver coil. The propagation speed of the electromagnetic wave inside the pipe wall is much slower than the speed along the pipe surface. Therefore, the thickness of the pipe wall can be measured by the total propagation time of the electromagnetic wave. Because the propagation time from the exciter coil to the receiver coil is expressed in phase difference between the transmitted signal and the received signal, external corrosion and through-hole of steel pipe can be detected by obtaining this phase difference.

The electromagnetic wave from the exciter coil also propagates along the pipe in an axial direction directly to the receiver coil. However, as the attenuation rate of this direct wave is bigger than that of the surface wave, its influence can be almost eliminated by keeping the distance between the two coils two or three times the length of pipe diameter.

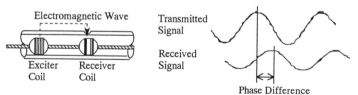

Figure 2. Principle of Remote-Field Eddy-Current Method

PASSAGE PERFORMANCE

In order to realize the effective utilization of the sensor in bent pipes, the "rotating sensor" method was adopted. The first step was to determine the appropriate sensor shape with minimal resistance when passing through bent pipes. During the tests, when the sensor received a resistance force, the load of the motor spinning the spring increases and its current increases. Therefore, the change in the motor current was employed to quantitatively evaluate the  passage performance of the sensor. The motor current

was measured as the sensor passed the bends in the test
configuration and its magnitude of change was calculated in the
following manner:
1) Cut a section containing three bends
2) Calculate a mean value(m) of the current in the cut section
3) Find a peak value(p) which is farthest from the mean
4) Calculate the magnitude of the change in the current by d= | p-m |

Shape Of Sensor

   To evaluate the passage performance according to sensor shape,
two dummy sensors without coils, a globe type and a streamline
type(Figure 3), were tested. The sensors were composed of three
"balls" connected at 160mm intervals. As shown in Figure 3, the
magnitude of the current change for the streamline sensor was larger
than that for the globe sensor. It was considered that large
friction resistance was generated with the streamline sensor as the
movement of both ends were restricted when passing bends. Therefore,
it was concluded that the sensor length should be as short as
possible.

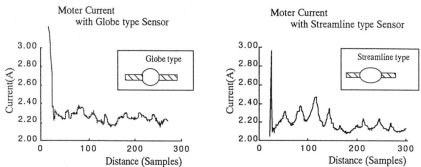

Figure 3. Comparison of Motor Current of Two Sensor Types

Sensor Guide

   We observed in past experiments that the edge of the "ball" at
times prevented smooth movement of a pulled sensor. Thus it was
thought necessary to introduce sensor guides to reduce the change in
outside diameter of a sensor. We tested the following two kinds of
sensor guide(Figure 4):
1) Maximum diameter: 25mm, Length: 25mm
2) Maximum diameter: 25mm, Length: 40mm

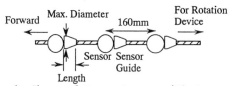

Figure 4. Shape of Dummy Sensor with Sensor Guide

   We compared the passage performance of a 42mm diameter dummy
sensor with and without sensor guides. The results showed that the
sensor guides improved the passage performance. However, although
the change in motor current for the 40mm-guide was smaller than that
for the 25mm-guide, in some cases, the sensors with the longer
40mm-guide was unable to pass bends.

From the results of the experiments, sensor specifications were determined as follows:
Shape of sensor: sphere or sphere-like, short length
Sensor guide:      25mm in length

NOISE REDUCTION

In the already commercialized straight pipe inspection system using the remote-field eddy-current method, a signal from a corrosion part is magnified by employing differential connection of receiver coil and by incorporating a compensation circuit to reduce the effect of induction between transmitter and receiver cables. These measures are sufficient when a sensor does not rotate. However, for rotating sensors we anticipated a possible noise problem. As the second step of this development process, we built a test system to determine the various noises that would be generated by rotation and to examine the measures to eliminate them.

Configuration Of Test System

Inspection Device. The schematic circuit of the inspection device is shown in Figure 5. An alternating current signal of 35Hz from a signal generator is transmitted to the exciter coil through a cable. The signal from the receiver coil passes through an amplifier and an induction compensator to a phase detector that converts phase difference to voltage.

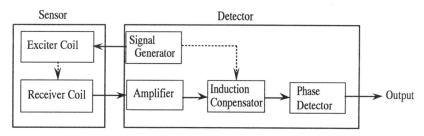

Figure 5. Schematic Circuit of Inspection Device

Sensor. (Figure 6)
Exciter coil:      0.4mm-diameter wire, 500 turns
Receiver coil:     Winding 1: 0.07mm-diameter wire, 3600 turns
                   Winding 2: 0.07mm-diameter wire, 3300 turns
                   Distance between Winding 1 and Winding 2: 10mm
Diameter of coils: 42mm
Distance between exciter coil and receiver coil: 160mm

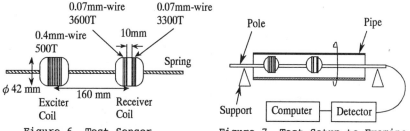

Figure 6. Test Sensor          Figure 7. Test Setup to Examine
                                         Rotational Noise

Influence Of Rotational Noise

     In order to examine the influence of rotation on an
electromagnetic field, the sensor was fixed at the center of a steel
test pipe and the output signal from the phase detector was observed
while rotating the pipe(Figure 7). The test pipe included
artificially defective areas and non-defective areas. At the
non-defective areas, the output signal was hardly affected by
rotation. However, at the defective areas, the fluctuation of the
output signal increased as the rotational speed increased(Figure 8).

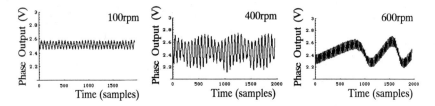

Figure 8. Influence of Rotation at Defective Areas

     These fluctuations were considered to appear because the
electromagnetic field was affected by the existence of relative
revolutional speed between pipe and sensor. From the results of the
experiments, it was concluded that the maximum rotational speed
should be kept at 200rpm to achieve good inspection results (Figure
9).

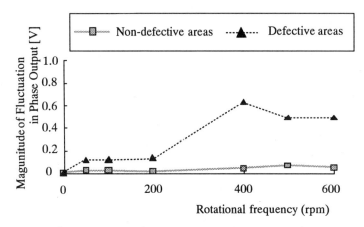

Figure 9. Relation between Phase Fluctuation
and Rotational Frequency

Influence Of Vibrational Noise

     During actual inspection, a sensor vibrates as it rotates and
comes in contact with the inner surface of the pipe. To evaluate the
noise caused by vibration, we removed the sensor support of the test
system, and observed the phase output as the sensor was pushed at a
speed of 2m/min through a rotating test pipe. Furthermore, we
examined three methods of signal processing to reduce vibrational
noise: cumulative average, FFT filter, and moving average.

Cumulative Average. The cumulative average is taken to reduce the random noise component by averaging data collected from multiple inspections. Figure 10 shows that the change in the signal level at at the defective area can be magnified by adding two inspection data. Since this method requires repeated inspection of the same defect, it is inevitably time-consuming.

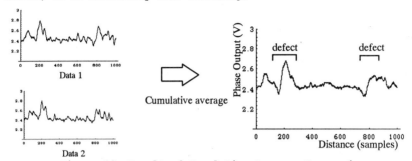

Figure 10. Result of Cumulative Average Processing

FFT Filter. By converting measured data into a frequency domain by FFT, excluding a component over a cut-off frequency, and then converting into a time domain by inverse FFT, we can realize a low-pass filter. Figure 11 shows that the defective area becomes more recognizable by FFT filter with a cut-off frequency of 1Hz.

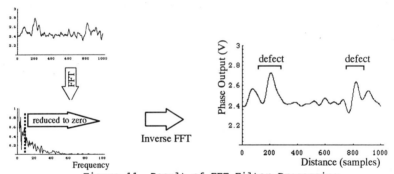

Figure 11. Result of FFT Filter Processing

Moving Average. The moving average is a method of averaging the measurements from shifting windows of a certain width. Figure 12 shows the moving average of windows (width: 20 samples).

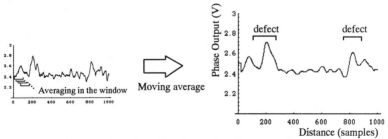

Figure 12. Result of Moving Average Processing

Although all three methods showed good potential for noise reduction, we finally employed the moving average method for further experiments. Since the cumulative average method required multiple inspections and large data storage, and the FFT filter required much calculation and also large data storage, both were eliminated.

EXPERIMENT ON SIMULATED PIPING

To examine the inspection performance under the conditions close to actual use, we placed a test pipe with defects within a simulated piping configuration that matched the specifications previously set, and observed the output signal while rotating a sensor through the pipe. As shown in Figure 13, the test pipe in this experiment had four defects, different in circumferential sizes(15-90mm) but equal in axial size(15mm) and depth(60% of pipe thickness). The position of the defects were set either at the upper or lower part of the pipe. Reference data were also obtained without rotating the sensor.

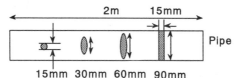

15mm 30mm 60mm 90mm
Figure 13. Dimension of Defect on Test Pipe

Table 1 summarizes the result of the experiment. It was proved that a defect with 30mm in diameter and 60% reduction in thickness could be detected, satisfying the specifications. According to the principle of the remote-field eddy-current method that the magnitude of the change in output signal corresponds to the volume of a defect, it is predicted that a defect with an even smaller diameter can be detected even if its depth is larger.

It was observed that the sensor rotation deteriorated the inspection performance to some level. This phenomenon was caused by the increase of vibrational noise from the irregularity of sensor rotation whose magnitude was varied by the length of the spring from the rotation drum to the sensor and the number of bends passed.

Table 1. Result of Experiment on Simulated Piping

| Pipe Length | No. of Bends | Rotation | Location of Defect | Size of Defect | | | |
|---|---|---|---|---|---|---|---|
| | | | | 15mm | 30mm | 60mm | 90mm |
| 13m | 6 | NO | Upper | △ | ○ | ○ | ○ |
| | | | Lower | ○ | ○ | ○ | ○ |
| 10.5m | 6 | YES | Upper | × | △ | ○ | ○ |
| | | | Lower | △ | ○ | ○ | ○ |
| 13m | 6 | YES | Upper | × | × | ○ | ○ |
| | | | Lower | × | ○ | ○ | ○ |

Detection Level : ○ - Clear   △ - Weak   × - None

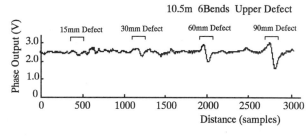

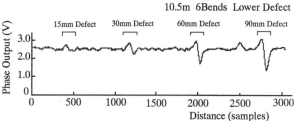

Figure 14. Output Signals of Experiments on Simulated Piping

In order to pass bends, the diameter of a sensor must be smaller than the inner diameter of a pipe to be inspected. This means that the sensor comes in contact with only the lower part of a pipe. Accordingly, the electromagnetic wave from the upper surface of a pipe to the sensor diminishes, resulting in a smaller change in the output signal for a defect at the upper part than for the same defect at the lower part.

CONCLUSION

In order to develop an inspection system for external corrosion of bent steel pipes using the remote-field eddy-current method, we achieved the following:
1) Designed shape of sensor and sensor guide to adapt the "rotating sensor" method
2) Selected signal processing method to reduce noise accompanied by sensor rotation
3) Evaluated inspection performance under practical conditions

As a result, it was confirmed that this method satisfies our inspection requirement for small diameter gas pipes. Further development activities for commercialization are scheduled including the improvement of performance and operability and a series of field demonstration.

REFERENCE

1. Y. Hosohara, T. Yamagishi, K. Yasui, "TECHNIQUES FOR DIAGNOSING EXTERNAL SURFACE CORROSION ON SMALL-DIAMETER STEEL PIPES", International Gas Research conference, Vol. I , 1989, pp199-207.

2. T. Kikuta, T. yamagishi, Y. Hosohara, I. Yamada, "DESIGN OF REMOTE FIELD EDDY CURRENT PROBE FOR GAS PIPES", J. of JSNDI, Vol. 41, No. 2, 1992, pp81-89

3. K. Koyama, H. Hoshikawa, "INSTANTANEOUS ELECTOROMAGNETIC ENERGY FLOW IN REMOTE-FIELD EDDY CURRENT TESTING", J. of JSNDI, Vol. 42, No. 11, 1993, pp610-616

DESIGN AND EVALUATION METHODS FOR ELECTROFUSION JOINTS OF
POLYETHYLENE PIPES FOR GAS DISTRIBUTION

MÉTHODES DES DESSIN ET ÉVALUATION SUR LES JOINTS PAR L'ÉLECTROFUSION DES
POLYÉTHYLÈNE PIPES POUR LA DISTRIBUTION GAZIÈRE

Hiroyuki Nishimura
Masami Suyama
Fumio Inoue

Gas Distribution Technology Team
Research & Development Center

and

Tetsuo Ishikawa

Piping System & Construction Team
Distribution Engineering Center

Osaka Gas Co., Ltd.

ABSTRACT

Electrofusion (EF) joints have been widely used as easy-to-fuse and high-quality joints for joining polyethylene (PE) pipes. As Osaka Gas has introduced EF joints 100 mm or less in diameter since January 1992, it has been designing EF joints 150 mm and 200 mm in diameter.

The quantity of trial construction and experimental tests to evaluate electrofusion strength for small-diameter joints was large, it is too difficult to design large-diameter joints due to time-consuming and costly experiments.

A computer program "EPOK" that simulates the electrofusion process of an EF joint and a pipe has been developed. It was verified that the simulation results calculated by the EPOK agreed well with the experimental results for small-diameter EF joints in practical use now. We have obtained much useful information concerning the design and evaluation of EF joints from the simulation and experimental results. It has been become possible to reduce the number of trial construction and experimental tests to evaluate electrofusion strength. Since the EPOK was highly evaluated by EF joint manufactures, it has already been transplanted to three such manufactures' computers.

The present authors attempted a determination of the fusion conditions of EF joints and investigated the effect of various design factors on fusion parameters and fusion strength.

RÉSUMÉ

Les joints à électrofusion (EF) sont largement utilisés comme joints de haute qualité et faciles à fondre pour raccorder les conduites en polyéthylène (PE). Osaka Gas a introduit des joints EF de 100 mm ou moins de diamètre depuis janvier 1992 et étudie des joints EF de 150 mm et 200 mm de diamètre.

La quantité d'essais de construction expérimentale pour évaluer la résistance à l'électrofusion des joints à petit diamètre a été importante; la conception de joints à grand diamètre est trop difficile du fait des expériences qui prennent beaucoup de temps et sont très coûteuses.

Un programme informatique "EPOK" qui simule le procédé d'électrofusion d'un joint EF et d'une conduite a été mis au point. Il a été vérifié que les résultats de la simulation calculés par "EPOK" correspondaient bien aux résultats d'expériences pour les joints EF à petit diamètre actuellement utilisés. Nous avons obtenu des informations très utiles concernant la conception et l'évaluation des joints EF à partir des résultats de simulation et d'expériences. Il est devenu possible de réduire le nombre d'essais de construction expérimentale pour évaluer la résistance à l'électrofusion. L'évaluation du programme EPOK par les fabricants de joints EF ayant été très positive, il a déjà été installé dans les ordinateurs de trois de ces fabricants.

Les auteurs de ce document ont essayé de déterminer les conditions de fusion des joints EF et ont étudié l'effet de divers facteurs de conception sur les paramètres de fusion et la résistance à la fusion.

CALCULATION METHOD

    With respect to the numerical calculation method, a nonlinear unsteady heat transfer analysis was carried out first to obtain the thermal profile. When a gap between an EF joint and a pipe existed, the heat flux was transmitted from the EF joint to the pipe by heat conduction and radiation in the air. When the gap was closed, the heat flux was transmitted by heat conduction in the polyethylene. Next, the mechanical material properties were input to obtain the displacement, strain, stress profile. The gap width was updated continuously during the gap closing process. This calculation process was then repeated as shown in Fig. 1.

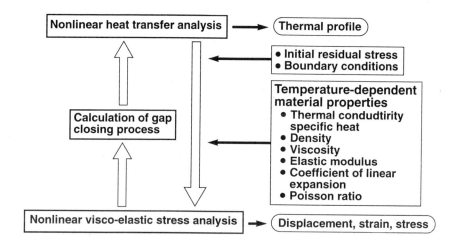

**Fig. 1 Numerical Repetitive Calculation Method**

The new computer program "EPOK" has the following five features:

(i)   Unsteady state analysis is precisely possible.
      Numerical analysis can be precisely conducted on the temperature profile and gap closing process between an EF joint and a pipe by combining heat transfer analysis and stress analysis for every step (minimum time for unsteady state analysis).

(ii)  Non-linear analysis is possible.
      Various physical properties can be determined in relation to temperature and time.

(iii) Calculation time is short.
      Analysis of phase change from solid phase to liquid phase using the enthalpy method permits the setting of a large time step; the calculation time for heat transfer analysis is 80 times shorter than that by a general-purpose program.

(iv)  Parametric studies of EF joining are easy.
      Parametric studies can be easily conducted by changing parameters; EF joint and pipe shape, wire pitch, wire resistance, wire diameter, wire length, gap width, voltage, heating time, ambient temperature, and initial residual stress in the EF joint and pipe.

(v)   Program capacity is small.
      Since this program was developed specifically for EF process analysis, the program capacity is as small as 1 MB.

Fig. 2 shows the calculated temperature contours of the fusion joining part at 50 s, 100 s, 200 s (power supply stopped) using the EPOK.

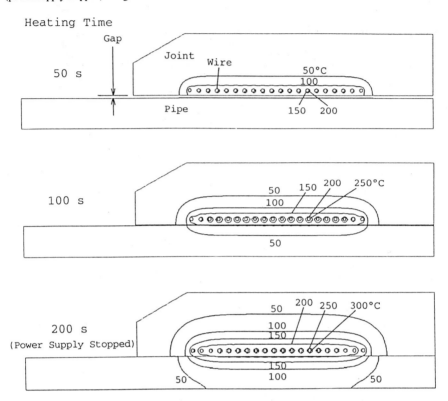

Temperature Contours (Diameter 100 mm:    Gap 1.18 mm)

**Fig. 2  Temperature Contours Using "EPOK"**

EXPERIMENTAL METHOD

In order to verify the calculated results through experiments, the temperature and displacement were measured as shown in Fig. 3. The temperature was measured using a thermocouple at the joint's outer surface, joint's fusion interface, pipe's fusion interface, and pipe's inner surface. To measure the displacement, the joints's outer diameter and thickness between joint's outer and pipe's inner were measured. We verified the simulation results agreed well with the experimental results as shown in Fig. 4 and Fig. 5.

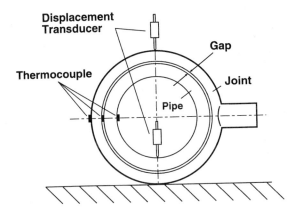

Fig. 3 Experimental Measurement of Temperature and Displacement

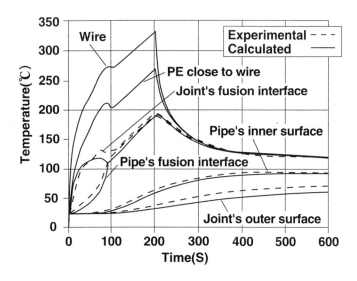

Fig. 4 Comparison of Relation between Temperature and Time

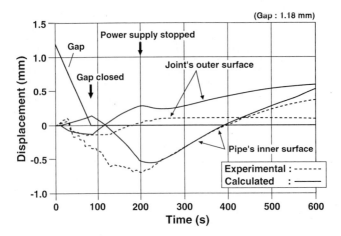

**Fig. 5 Comparison of Relation between Displacement and Time**

The melted layer of the fusion zone was measured from photographs taken through a polarizing microscope. A thin film was cut from the EF joint after a constant voltage was applied for a given time. The film was observed and photographed through a polarizing microscope. Then, the thickness of the melted layer was measured at the fusion zone as shown in Fig. 6.

Heating Time: 110 s

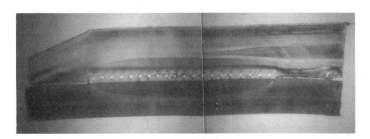

**Experimental value**    Thickness of melted layer: 5.9 mm

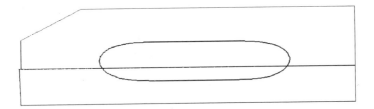

**Calculated value**    Thickness of melted layer: 5.8 mm

**Fig. 6 Comparison of the Thickness of Melted Layer (Diameter 50 mm)**

A square bar specimen (9 mm wide) cut out from an EF joint fully notched to a depth of 1.5 mm was fused to an extension bar for a tensile test and a tensile creep test, as shown in Fig. 7. The tensile test was conducted at a tensile speed of 200 mm/min at 23°C, and the failure strength at the fusion interface or close to the wire was obtained. The time to failure was also obtained at 3.9 MPa applied stress and at 80°C by a tensile creep test.

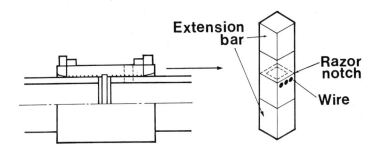

**Extension bar**

**Razor notch**

**Wire**

## Test specimen cut out from an electrofusion joint

**Fig. 7 Geometry of Test Specimen for Tensile Test and Tensile Creep Test**

The heating conditions needed to maximize fusion strength in a tensile test and a tensile creep test were investigated. Fig. 8 shows the supplied power per unit area against heating time with temperature and mechanical strength as parameters. The curves that represent four fusion strengths in the electrofusion process are shown in Fig. 8. The first curve from the left indicates the line at which the tensile strength was 80% of the maximum tensile strength in the tensile test and the time to failure was 100 hour or more in the tensile creep test. Therefore, this curve is regarded as the minimum allowable line of fusion strength. As regards the second curve from the left, the time to failure was maximum value in the tensile creep test. The heating time of 110 s, denoted by the solid mark, is specified as the standard fusion condition of this EF joint. The third curve from the left indicates the line at which the time to failure was 100 hour or less in the tensile creep test. Therefore, this curve means that fusion strength declines again. The dotted curve indicates the line at which the failure began to occur at the wire because of the thermal degration of the resin close to the wire in the tensile test, although a razor notch was made at the fusion interface for stress concentration. The wire temperature, calculated on the basis of the wire resistance value, was approximately 350°C, and the resin temperature close to the wire was slightly lower than 350°C. The resin temperature close to the wire was 322 to 339°C in the simulation. As regards the three curves on the left side, for several supplied powers per unit area during the electrofusion, the experimental fusion interface temperature values agreed well with the calculated values at the heating times on the three curves.

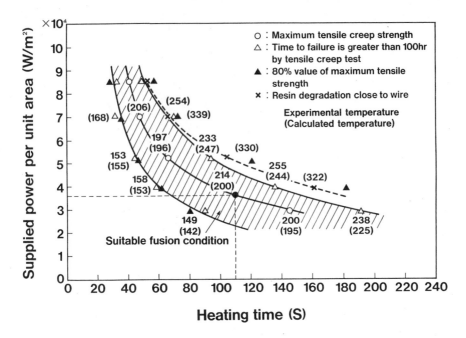

**Fig. 8   Relation between Supplied Power per Unit Area and Heating Time with Temperature and Mechanical Strength as Parameters**

## EVALUATION OF EFFECTS OF MANY PARAMETERS ON THE EF PROCESS

We have evaluated the effects of many parameters on the EF process using the simulation. We have already studied with respect to the following parameters;

- Pipe and joint thickness
- Voltage and heating time
- Initial and ambient temperatures
- Cooling, by fan, dry ice, and water
- Time needed to start backfilling
- Wire pitch
- Embedded wire depth
- Embedded wire length in the longitudinal direction

Among them, we explain the evaluation results on, for example, relation between cooling time and pipe or joint thickness. We conducted a study on four cases as shown in Fig. 9.

| Pipe thickness / Joint thickness | 8.5mm | 6.8mm |
|---|---|---|
| 16.4mm | Case 1 | Case 2 |
| 10.0mm | Case 3 | Case 4 |

**Fig. 9  Joint and Pipe Thickness as Parameters**

Fig. 10 shows the fusion interface temperature changes with time, calculated when 100 mm EF joints were used with a gap of 1.18 mm in cases 1 through 4, as shown in Fig. 9.

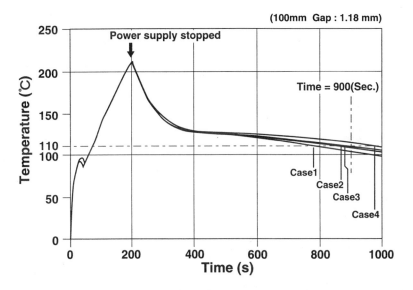

**Fig. 10  Fusion Interface Temperature Changes with Time in Cases 1 through 4**

After 200 s of heating, the pipe and joint were cooled. For up to 240 s, there was no significant difference in temperature change among the 4 cases. After 240 s, the cooling process differed depending on the pipe and joint thickness. If the total duration from the start of heating until the cooling of the pipe-joint fusion interface temperature down to 110°C or less is defined as the time needed to start backfill (Tf), the Tf for each of the four cases is estimated as follows:

Case 1: Tf=13.0 min
Case 2: Tf=14.5 min
Case 3: Tf=14.7 min
Case 4: Tf=16.4 min

We found that Tf for cooling tended to increase with decreasing pipe and joint thickness. Tf is the most important factor to shorten cooling time and improve workability at work site.

Fig. 11 shows the temperature contours of the fusion joining part at 900 s (15 min) in cases 1 through 4. We can see, only in case 4, a temperature zone exceeding 110°C remained.

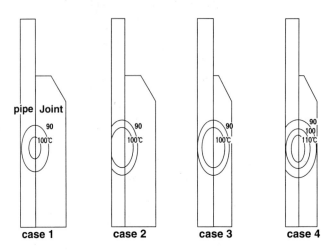

**Fig. 11  Temperature Contours at 900 s (15 min) in cases 1 through 4**

CONCLUSIONS

Simulation results using the developed program "EPOK" agreed well with the experimental results on temperature, displacement profile and thickness of melted layer.  Fusion simulation is applicable for designing electrofusion conditions and evaluating fusion parameters.  Therefore, decisions can be made earlier and at lower cost using fusion simulation with respect to high-quality joints specification and suitable fusion conditions.

REFERENCES

1.  L. Ewing and L. Maine, Proc. Eighth Plastic Fuel Gas Pipe Symp., 102 (1983).

2.  D. Usclat, Proc. Ninth Plastic Fuel Gas Pipe Symp., 57 (1985).

3.  J.J. Cheron and J. Chevrand, Proc. 1986 Int. Gas Research Conf., 88 , Toronto (1986).

4.  J.P. Jouary and M. Nussbaum, Proc. Tenth Plastic Fuel Gas Pipe Symp., 75 (1987).

5.  A. Nakashiba, H. Nishimura, F. Inoue, T. Nakagawa, K. Homma, and H. Nakazato, Polym. Eng. Sci., 33, 1146 (1993).

6.  H. Nishimura, M. Nakakura, T. Shishido, A. Masaki, H. Shibano, and F. Nagatani, Proc. Eleventh Plastic Fuel Gas Pipe Symp., 99 (1989).

7.  H. Nishimura, M. Suyama, M. Nakakura, A. Masaki, H. Shibano, and F. Nagatani, J. Japan Soc. Polym. Processing, 2 (1), 73 (1990).

8.  M.S. Welling, Injection Moulding Technology, VDI-Verlag (1981).

9.  D. Saint Royre, D. Gueugnaut, and D. Reveret. J. Appl. Polym. Sci., 38, 147 (1989).

10.  M. Nussbaum, D. Dufour, and D. Gueugnaut, Proc. Twelfth Plastic Fuel Gas Pipe Symp., 324 (1991).

Development of a small earthquake acceleration sensor

Développement d'un détecteur d'accélération miniaturisé pour phénomènes sismiques

Ken-ichi NAKAMURA
FTRI, Tokyo Gas Co., Ltd.

Hiroshi ISHIO
R&D Dept.2, Japan Resistor Mfg. Co.,Ltd.

Abstract

Since several major earthquakes have occurred in Japan during the last few years, many countermeasures have been made in order to minimize the damage. Among them  the Spectral Intensity (SI) sensor previously developed is now in use in all regulator stations and shuts down the distribution of natural gas in case of a major earthquake. However, the system used at present is still very expensive and its large dimensions prevent its widespread use. This paper presents a new earthquake sensor of small dimensions for the measurement of SI values. The 3-axial acceleration sensor was adapted for earthquake detection and measured seismic accelerations effectively and precisely. A SI value with enhanced accuracy was calculated from numeric treatment.  The improvements of the efficiency of this small SI sensor will be made in a near future.

Résumé

Depuis quelques années, un nombre important de tremblements de terre d'intensité majeure ont eu lieu au Japon. Aussi, des mesures de détection et de prévention sont-elles prises de manière à minimiser les dégats. Parmi les moyens utilisés, un détecteur d'Intensité Spectrale (SI) mis au point et actuellement installé sur toutes les stations de régulation, permet la coupure de la distribution de gaz naturel en cas de séisme important. Ce type de détecteur reste cependant très cher et de grandes dimensions. Dans cet article, nous présentons un nouveau détecteur de petite taille pour la mesure des valeurs d'Intensité Spectrale. Ce détecteur[1] d'accélération triaxiale a été adapté au cas des secousses sismiques et a permis la détection effective et précise d'accélérations sismiques. Les valeurs d'Intensite Spectrale ont été calculées par traitement numérique. Les performances de ce détecteur seront améliorées dans un futur proche.

## INTRODUCTION

City gas companies think that countermeasures against earthquake are the utmost importance and continue to make great efforts to minimize the effects of serious disasters. However, because of the Hanshin Earthquake, we must reconsider the countermeasures currently being used.

For example, two independent seismic shut-off devices are in use in the service area of Tokyo Gas now. One is the microcomputer-controlled gas meter with simple seismic sensor. This meter can detect vibrations when the seismic intensity scale(JMA) is more than 5 and shuts off the distributed gas automatically. More than 90% of consumers use this type of gas meter. The other is the low-pressure regulator with the SI(Spectral Intensity) earthquake sensor. The SI value is thought the most appropriate value when assessing the damage of structures during earthquakes. The SI earthquake sensor was developed by Tokyo Gas about ten years ago. There are more than 3500 low-pressure regulators in our service area. Each regulator has a SI earthquake sensor and shut-off function. When the SI value exceeds a standard value, which is decided as the critical point of serious disaster, low-pressure regulators immediately stop the distribution of gas in order not to expand the disaster.

Fortunately, after Tokyo Gas developed this SI earthquake sensor and installed in our service area, there has been no serious earthquake around the Tokyo metropolitan area. We positively believe our countermeasures are effective and useful. We continue to research more effective SI sensors and better shut-off systems.

There are two problems in the widespread use of SI sensors. One is that the cost of system is expensive and other is that the size is large. If such problems are solved, we expect the use of these SI earthquake sensors to become widespread ensuring safe consumption of gas. In this paper, we present the development of a novel, small earthquake sensor especially for SI value measurement system using the 3-axial acceleration sensor which was originally developed for auto mobiles.

## SI VALUE

In general, it seems that the SI value is most suitable in showing expected seismic disasters. SI values are mutually related with disaster level. This value was proposed by Prof.G.W.Housner in 1958(1). In fact, Fig.1 shows the relation between the SI value and the effect of an earthquake(2). The white circles show the earthquake which damaged structures and the white triangles show no damage. This data shows that the damages to structures depend on the SI value and not on the acceleration magnitude. Serious disasters occur when the SI value is over 30cm/sec.

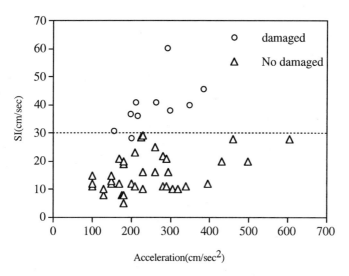

Fig.1 The relation between the SI value and the effect of an earthquake

From ref.(1), SI value is calculated as follow.
Newton's equation of motion for the systems is

$$m\frac{d^2}{dt^2}(y+z) = -ky - c\frac{dy}{dt} \tag{1}$$

The displacement of the structure y is given by

$$y = -\frac{1}{\omega}\int_0^t \ddot{z}(\tau)e^{-n(t-\tau)}\sin\omega(t-\tau)d\tau \tag{2}$$

where $\quad \omega = \sqrt{p^2 + n^2}$ = circular frequency

$p = \sqrt{\dfrac{k}{m}}$ = undamped circular frequency of vibration

t = time at which y is evaluated

$\ddot{z}$ = base acceleration

$n = \dfrac{c}{2m}$ = damping factor

$\dfrac{n}{p}$ = fraction of critical damping

The maximum response of the structures is characterized by the value of Sv which is
written

$$Sv = \left[\int_0^t \ddot{z}e^{-n(t-\tau)}\sin\omega(t-\tau)d\tau\right]_{max} \tag{3}$$

The spectrum intensity(SI)  is defined to be the average of the area under the curve between 0.1 and 2.5 seconds period:

$$SI = \frac{1}{2.4} \int_{0.1}^{2.5} Sv(n=0.2,T)dT \qquad (4)$$

In this expression n indicates the amount of damping and n=0.20 is suitable to express the influence of the earthquake(3). As a result, to calculate the SI value from input acceleration data, it is necessary to measure the acceleration whose frequency region is at least between 0.4 Hz and 10Hz.

## ACCELERATION SENSOR

To detect earthquake vibrations, three independent acceleration sensors are usually needed. That causes the cost of system become higher. Several kinds of acceleration sensors have already been developed and are using. However, most acceleration sensors can detect only one direction of vibration. To reduce the cost and the size, we can choose the 3-axial acceleration sensor.

Fig.2 shows the schematic cross-section view of the 3-axial acceleration sensor. This sensor can detect 3-directional acceleration independently. In this sensor, the piezo-ceramic element is stuck on the thin diaphragm which has the cylindrical mass in the center. On both sides of the piezo-ceramic element, the electrodes are equipped separately by microfabricating method as Fig.3(a). A total of 16 electrode sets are made on the sensor. Each electrode is connected with the same polarity. Fig.3(b) shows the electric circuit for X-direction acceleration. To detect the horizontal acceleration in one direction, connecting four electrode sets together as Fig.3(b) give us good channel separation.

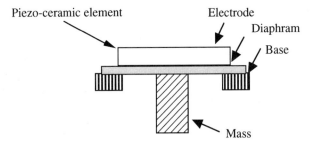

**Fig. 2 "3-axial acceleration sensor" schematic cross-section view**

Fig.4 shows the principle for 3-axial acceleration detection. The strain occurs on the piezo-ceramic element through the thin diaphragm when the mass is shaken by earthquake movement. The voltage on the electrode is proportional to the magnitude of earthquake acceleration and the sign depends either on the compressive stress or the tension stress. Fig.4(a) shows the schematic figure when the vibration in X or Y direction occurs. If horizontal acceleration happens, the mass is moved like a pendulum by the inertial force. That movement occurs the piezo-electric voltage on the piezo-ceramic element as in Fig.4(a). One of the method of electrode connection, shown in Fig.3(b), only X-voltage can be generated. When perpendicular acceleration occurs, the behavior of this sensor becomes as shown in Fig.4(b). In this case, Z-voltage can be detected but not X or Y.

Three independent electrode units generate the piezo-electronic voltage corresponding to the X, Y and Z axis of the seismic acceleration respectively.

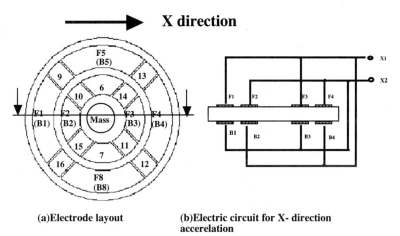

(a)Electrode layout    (b)Electric circuit for X- direction accerelation

**Figure 3. Schematic view of electric circuit**

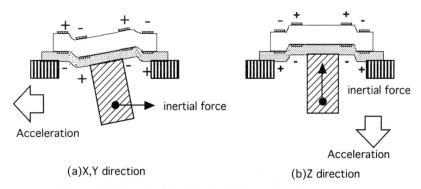

(a)X,Y direction    (b)Z direction

**Figure 4. The principle for 3-axial acceleration**

AMPLITUDE CIRCUIT

The inner resistance of the piezo-ceramic element is so large that it does not allow the use of a commercial amplitude circuit because of the low sensitivity below 10Hz. We have developed an electronic circuit that can amplify the signals corresponding to earthquake acceleration between 0.1Hz and 100Hz using analog circuit simulation techniques. Fig.5 shows the amplitude circuit. The input resistance R1 which is extremely high makes the frequency characteristic of this amplitude circuit expand to 0.1Hz. The signal of this acceleration sensor is so small that we must assemble the sensor and the circuit in the same package to increase S/N level. As a result, the acceleration sensor size is only 40mm(W) x 20mm(L) x 16mm(H), including the amplitude circuit.

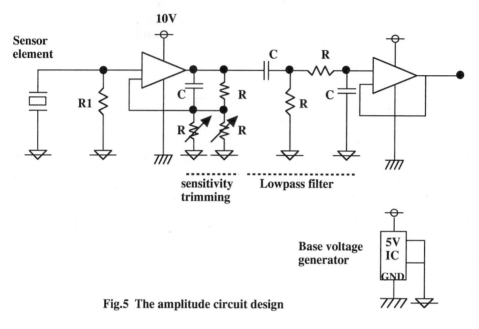

Fig.5  The amplitude circuit design

MEASUREMENT SYSTEM

Fig.6 shows the vibration measurement system. The large shaking table was used for vibration measurement. This table is controlled by a personal computer and can move in a sine wave and real earthquake motion but only in the X-direction. The acceleration signal inputs into A/D converter. Personal computer is used to collect the data and calculate the SI value from the acceleration data followed by equation(3) and (4).

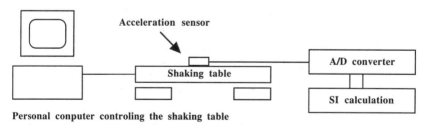

**Fig.6  Vibration measurement system**

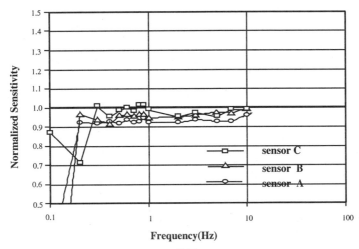

**Figure 7. Measured Frequency response**

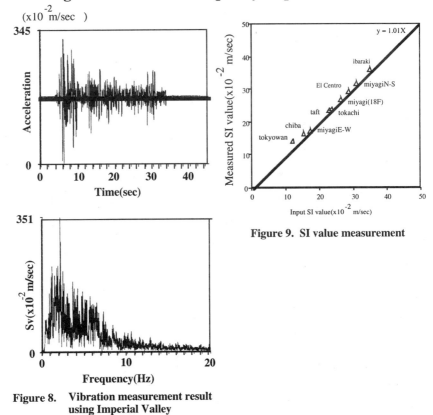

**Figure 9. SI value measurement**

Figure 8. **Vibration measurement result using Imperial Valley earthquake data**

## VIBRATED TEST RESULTS

To measure the frequency characteristic of this sensor, the sine wave between 0.1Hz -10Hz is used. Fig.7 shows the frequency characteristic measurement results of sensor A,B and C. The X axis shows the input vibration frequency(Hz) and Y axis shows the sensitivities normalized by correct input acceleration magnitude. As a result, we confirmed that the frequency characteristic of this sensor is flat in the frequency region between 0.2Hz-10Hz.

Fig.8 shows the results of vibration test using the seismic wave date of the Imperial valley Earthquake in U.S.A. in 1940. The upper figure shows the acceleration characteristic. The other is the Sv curve calculated from acceleration data. We measured the SI characteristic response by using nine kinds of typical earthquakes as Fig.9. The X axis shows the input SI value calculated PC and the Y axis shows the measured SI value calculated by PC. Note that the input vibration magnitude is different from earthquakes because of the limit of the shaking table. This figure shows that the measured SI values are simply proportionate to the input SI values but not depend on the kind of earthquakes.

## CONCLUSIONS

The 3-axial acceleration sensor is adapted for the earthquake and proved that this sensor can measure seismic acceleration accurately. Also we are able to achieve correct SI values by using the calculating system on a personal computer. In the near future, we will develop a small sized SI sensor to estimate seismic disasters more correctly.

## ACKNOWLEDGMENTS

The authors thank Ground Engineering Team at Fundamental Technology Research Laboratory, Tokyo Gas for cooperating with vibration measurement and thank Center for supply control and disaster management for valuable discussions about earthquake.

## REFERENCE

1. G.W.Housner, Proceedings of the American Society of Civil Engineers,New York, October 1958

2. Sato, Katayama, Proceeding of the 18th seismology conference, July 1985

3. G.W.Housner " Vibration of Structures Induced by Seismic Waves" (Shoch and Vibration Handbook by C.M.Harris & C.E.Crede),1961,pp.50.10-32

DELIVERY AND CAPTURE OF ELECTRONIC
INFORMATION AT THE WORKPLACE

MISE A DISPOSITION ET SAISE DE L'INFORMATION
ELECTRONIQUE SUR LE LIEU DE TRAVAIL

M E Morey
British Gas PLC

## ABSTRACT

Operational field staff in a public utility (British Gas) have increasing requirements for access to accurate and relevant technical data, maps and documents in order to do their work. In addition, many utilities are attempting to reduce costs by reducing staff levels and the number of support offices, this makes it increasingly inefficient for gathered at the workplace. Radio communication and traditional sources, such as microfiche, can assist in making the field worker self supporting, but recently, new mass storage and IT technologies such as portable operational staff to have to return to the office to collect information, receive training, or to deliver documents computers and CD-ROMs, have emerged. British Gas has a series of initiatives using new field information technology, some of which are discussed here.

## RESUME

Les membres du personnel d'exploitation d'un service public (British Gas) intervenant en clientele ont de plus en plus besoin d'avoir acces aux donnees techniques necessaires et precises, aux plans et aux documents afin d'acomplier leur travail. Par ailleurs, de nombreux services essayant de reduire les frais en limitant a la fois les niveaux de personnel et le nombre des bureaux d'assistance, ces conditions etant de moins en moins performantes pour le personnel d'exploitation devant retourner ou fournir des documents regroupes sur le lieu de travail. Les radiocommunications et les sources traditionnelles du genre microfiche peuvent contribuer a rendre independant le technicien d'entretien en clientele, mais recemment, de nouvelles technologies et informatique et disques compacts_ROM sont apparues. British Gas a pris plusieurs initatives faisant appel a de nouveaux moyens informatiques en clientele, et certaines sont examinees ici.

## INTRODUCTION

Traditionally, IT (Information Technology) has been seen by utilities as providing major business benefits in the office. For the purpose of this paper, I will assume that the function of the 'office' in a utility is to support front line activities, such as excavating the street, laying or repairing pipelines, erecting plant, installing and repairing the customers appliances. The 'workplace' is therefore defined here as the place where front line activities take place. Best overall business efficiency is likely to be achieved when all central and office facilities are minimised, and front line workforce are empowered with all the facilities of the office, in their vehicle. In this paper I will use the terms 'field' and 'workplace' to describe front line locations, and IT (Information Technology) to imply the use of computers and other electronic means to deliver, or capture, information. PC is an abbreviation for Personal Computer. Where I use the term 'Company' I am refering to British Gas.

It is very difficult to achieve a large scale introduction of IT in the workplace in one step, furthermore, because the technology itself is changing rapidly, it is almost impossible to have a complete field IT system conceived, designed and committed at one point in time. A step by step approach to the introduction of field technology is therefore often the most practical.

Radio systems are an exception to the evolutionary approach, because they have to be planned with a large amount of costly infrastructure. Once a radio system is designed it will always have a finite capacity, and generally represent a large capital investment.

Here, I will describe systems to deliver documents, maps, and databases to field users by laptop PC computers, I will explain why a substantial amount of the field data must be stored on a CD-ROM or similar mass storage device in the field. I consider how trunk radio data systems and local mass data storage are complementary technologies. I will cover two applications of electronic data collection and illustrate these from examples of systems that are now either under trial, or commencing full field service. None of the examples mentioned here could have followed their evolutionary path without the vision, and financial commitment of my end users within British Gas

## INFORMATION AND SUPPORT NEEDED AT THE WORKPLACE

### Maps

British Gas is fortunate in that it has adopted a strategy whereby all of its distribution, and many of its transmission maps were to be digitised against a background of (usually 1:1250 scale) UK Ordnance Survey vector map geography. This Digital Records System(DRS) is nearing completion of data take-on and, by the end of 1995, all the UK low pressure gas distribution system will have been captured. Initially, it was assumed that the DRS would output its maps to a microfiche system where all maps would be shown as 1 kilometre square tiles. (An operational district would typically have some 600 such tiles). This map detail becomes valuable at both the planning and the excavation stages of any field work, and has particular benefit to staff who are responding to an emergency a long way from their normal operating base. In addition to Gas maps, it is also useful to have access to the plans and maps of other utilities to avoid damage to their plant when we are digging. Maps from another utility may often be held by British Gas as microfilm. In the many districts, Electricity cable microfilm is available on the Company emergency team vehicle. Otherwise, in order to verify the location of electric, telephone, of water plant, a journey to a district office is often necessary which will often disrupt and delay work. (1)

### Documents and Procedures

Efficient and safe working is achieved by giving staff appropriate training, and then by supporting them with technical reference documents. As procedures become more complex, and legal requirements increase, there is an increasing need for documents to be held in the field vehicle. These documents come from a variety of sources, and, despite efforts to provide summaries of the more lengthy documents, there remains a major document storage and maintenance problem.

### Databases

For many years, the Company has maintained databases of useful information. Hazardous chemicals are one particular example where access to a database of safety and handling information is vital. Health and Safety legislation now requires that staff have access to the relevant information on substances they are handling, here again, a simple office database has hitherto had to be converted to a book in order to supply it to field staff, loosing all the benefits of a searchable database.

Expert Systems

As the workplace becomes increasingly complex a whole series of diagnostic tools become useful. Model based, rule based, and neural systems all have the potential to help in the diagnosis of a complex fault. Modern systems that have redundancy and safety interlocks are very difficult to fault find on, and especially so, if they are to remain in service.

Training

Training is an essential element in achieving efficiency and safety, but it is expensive. It has traditionally been done off the job, with a loss of staff time. New techniques can allow staff to study in spare time, and, if a field PC is available to them they can learn ,interactively, on the job.

THE MEANS OF DELIVERY

Traditional Methods

In the case of maps it has been necessary, to supply users with small battery powered microfilm viewers. Unfortunately, these have proved to be of limited use, and consequently, there has been general dissatisfaction with such methods of distribution.

Books, which have been abridged and reduced to a small format, can be a successful method of providing field procedures. British Gas has, on occasions, created special sets of books for the field staff, but keeping these up to date, or providing a suitable index and retrieval systems have proved difficult, also paper, although having the virtue of simplicity, does not have a long life. Training books, video tapes, and audio tapes have all been used to provide training to the remote worker, the most traditional and costly method, of course, is to withdraw them from the work place to the classroom.

Radio Data Transmission

Some attempts have been made to identify the amount of data that a typical field worker might need access to if he or she had no office to visit for reference. Early estimates from work done within Rank Xerox indicated that their field workers might each need access to as much as 9Gb (equivalent to 7000 computer floppy disks) of data. Although it is possible to provide access to office main frame computer systems over radio data links, it is not an efficient way to use expensive radio air time. Present utility, voice based, PMR (Private Mobile Radio) systems typically can be used to carry between 100 and 1000 characters per second. Recent work within British Gas to digitise our appliance service manuals resulted in data amounting to 1.3 gigabytes (after it had been compressed).(2) If we were to consider this in relationship to a PMR data channel we can show that it represents the equivalent of some three months of continuous radio transmission. (A user is unlikely to request a complete down load of such data, however, even when browsing, such as when locating a difficult part or procedure, would consume many minutes of air time). It is, therefore, best that radio data channels are reserved for messages and urgent information, and bulk field data are provided by other means.

Portable Computers (Field PCs)

The key to accessing field data is to use portable computers. We can now have a powerful computer packaged in to a small lap-top unit at modest cost. Until recently, the needs of the utilities has been neglected by the computer manufacturers, who were focused on selling these devices to the executive market. Pressure from utilities, and service organisations, is set to change this, with rugged lap top devices emerging. In trials, we have used a range of computers including those with pens to replace the mouse function, and we have the following observations:-

- The robustness of the computer should be carefully assessed, particularly where the screen is concerned as this is a very fragile and costly item.
- Performance over a range of temperatures should be verified
- Users much preferred colour screens both for clarity and contrast of image.
- Weight and battery life are very important to users who are required to take the computer in to customer's houses.
- Users liked a pen interface, but were unhappy with handwriting recognition, so they also favoured a keyboard.
- If a pen was not available, then a track ball was acceptable, the 'accupoint' button devices were not liked.
- A large screen (10" Diagonal) is essential if technical drawings and manuals are to be viewed.
- Sound facilities are valuable if multi-media training is to be delivered.
- If the Floppy Disk drive usually provided with a lap-top computer is replaced with additional batteries the system run time can be improved and the chances of unauthorised software being introduced can be reduced.

The pen computer seems to be a natural choice for use in the field, and there are some systems, particularly those for surveying described later, that are dependant on the pen interface. Unfortunately, as the volume of sales in the pen market is small they remain a specialist item.

Mass Data Storage (and CD-ROM)

From a review of field information requirements and the limited capacity of our radio systems, it became apparent that some local mass data storage would be needed in the field if we were to have comprehensive field information systems based on a portable PC. If the information store is not sufficient to cover most eventualities it would mean that staff will continue to make journeys to the district office. A significant element of the cost justification for any field information system is that it saves travel and the associated delay in starting work.

From 1989 onwards British Gas Research and Technology has monitored developments in mass data storage systems that were likely to be useful in the field. As new devices became available, we tested them under simulated field conditions of vibration and temperature. Early CD-ROM drives were slow, and not tolerant of vibration or use away from the horizontal plane; laptop computers were heavy and costly, however recently CD-ROM drives have improved in robustness and performance, and the price of CD replication has fallen to very attractive levels. Laptop computer design has improved considerably in the past three years.

In 1993, co-operative work, between British Gas, BT, and Rank Xerox lead to a consultative document being offered to the makers of portable PCs that asked for a CD-ROM drive to be made integral to the laptop. (1) It also addressed the need for some protection for the CD-ROM disk itself as the disks are to be changed in a dirty environment. Work at British Gas has shown that an un- protected disk, being changed regularly by a service engineer (usually five times per working day) will have only a disk life of one month. Systems adopted by British Gas, for the use of field CD disks, require a three month (or longer) life, and hence the Company has adopted a stance of requiring CD drives that have some means of disk protection. Unfortunately the desire for cost reduction has led many manufacturers to ignore this requirement. CD-ROM disks conform to a series or standards that ensures their interchangeability. The capacity is some 680 megabytes, and although there are developments that would allow greater capacity, this would require a change of standard, and many drive systems would become obsolete. CDW (Compact Disk Write) disks present a very useful means of providing data to small user groups. As the CD can be written by a user, but can-not be erased,and because its data can be validated by date and encrypted it also presents a very secure way of disseminating Company data.

Hard Disk technology has made remarkable strides in terms of capacity and size, and some very small disk systems are now available, these suit field applications that require the storage of large field files such as images. The PCMCIA (Portable Computer Manufacturers Card Interface Association) have defined the interface for a series of credit card devices that can be plugged in to portable computers. These include GPS (Global Positioning Systems), Disks, and Modems, Presently, some 260 Megabytes of data can be accommodate on one card disk, a little more than 10 Millimetres thick. These devices are suited to field use, but are costly. The PCMCIA connector originally appeared as though it would be too fragile for the field, however trials to date have shown no connector problems, and second generation disk units now prove reliable and some survive being dropped. Solid state memory cards remain expensive and of low capacity, and in many cases actually work more slowly than their mechanical disk competitors.

Data Delivery Software

In order to present the information to the user we must have display software. In the office, a high level of sophistication is often required, and office software, whether in the form of Hypertext document retrieval, or GIS (Geographic Information Systems) is frequently complex. In the office, we expect the user to have a variety of uses for information, and to need the tools to carry out analysis, and modification of information. In the field, the need is different, and software display tools that appear simple, and are focused on reading only the relevant information, are essential. It is not necessarily the case that the field software is simple, it is just that it must appear so.

For those not familiar with some of the terms, it may help to explain two of them: GIS and Hypertext.

GIS (Geographical Information Systems) have some superficial similarity to draughting or drawing display programmes. These allow the display of geographic data (usually maps). The distinctive feature of true GIS is the ability to deal with different features of the map not only as a picture, but also as attribute entries in a database. The database approach allows the user (usually in the office) to carry out sophisticated analysis of the map data, for instance in marketing, to, for example, calculate how many objects with the attribute 'house' on the map are not connected to the series of objects with the attribute 'gas pipe' thus enabling a market penetration survey to be carried out. If a GIS were programmed to export only the relevant map, pipeline, and gazetteer (Street and Address index) information, and perhaps write this to a CD-ROM, then we would have the basis for a simplified field (read only) database. This simplified extract is the basis for the British Gas field map display systems.

Hypertext is the technique that allows rapid access to textual documents and their associated illustrations. In order to create hypertext you need to convert the document(s) in to electronic form, (as computer characters, not as an image) and then arrange mark up at points where the document has signposts and branches The mark-up should conform to SGML (Standardised Generalised Markup Language) and will contain pointers to help the reader jump to his required destination. For instance, where a reference in a document stated 'see fig 12' a hidden code would be attached to the words 'see fig 12' which would point to the figure image file. When read by the user, a mouse click on the highlighted words ' see fig 12' would bring the figure to the screen. Similar jumps and branches can happen throughout the text. Our field experience has shown that a simple Hypertext user programme is acceptable to a wide range of field staff and ability levels, the only drawback is the need to convert the original paper document to computer text, and then perform the mark up. Fortunately there are bureaus who specialise in outsourcing this type of work.

INFORMATION  COLLECTION REQUIREMENTS

Billing and Management

Timesheets and details of chargeable work done are necessary to manage work and recover costs. Requests for follow on tasks, such as the reinstatement of a roadway are also relevant, as is the data on new plant fitted at a particular location. Much of this information is not to be stored locally, but is to be transmitted by radio or telephone link to a supervisor within the day so that the necessary actions can be approved and initiated. Local copies of documents are needed simply by way of 'carbon copies' as a convienience to the field worker.

Maps and Geographic

This area of work presents a challenge to the IT system developer in that the quality of any data gathered is paramount. In a utility with a large inventory of underground plant, it is important that accurate records are taken before reinstatement. It has been practice in British Gas to have record clerks who visit sites and make records of high quality. It now seems desirable to allow records to be updated by those actually performing the streetwork. The difficulty in allowing 'self recording' is that there is no independant verification of accuarcy, and a real risk of cumulative errors creeping in to the map database un-detected.

INFORMATION DELIVERY EXAMPLES

The following examples represent a series of views from applications currently under trial or in full scale field use within British Gas. For brevity only the main functions are illustrated.

Document Delivery System using Hypertext (see Fig 1.)

Hypertext document retrieval systems are in use in both the service company of British Gas (BG Service) and the gas transport business (TransCo). The example shown here is from TransCo and illustrates the retrieval, on the field system, of a  technical document using a proprietary hypertext reader called DRUID. Here we have used a split screen to show a section of text and an associated diagram. (The screen layout, and hence readability, is under control of the user). In BG Service some 7500 field users are using similar software to retrieve all the appliance service data in the customers home.

Map Delivery System (See Fig 2.)

The map display system shown on is that used by British Gas in offices where 'view only' facilities are needed. The geography is divided in to 1 kilometre file sections however the display can pan continuously across the terrain. The view shows a zoom to full magnification, and a section of street and gas pipeline displayed. The inset box allows the precise grid location of any point on the map to be found and stored for later use. The same stored grid location can be used to locate a position on a corresponding map from another utility. To select the map a full street gazetteer is used, the user simply typing in the street name. Trials of this system in Thornaby on Tees and in Bristol give users access to both Gas and Electricity maps as separate views.

Diagnostics Expert system

Having developed a system to make the field worker self sufficient, we have to consider what happens when a particularly difficult problem is encountered. In the servicing of gas appliances such problems are encountered on complex, sealed, central heating systems. Previous practice in such events was to call on the help of a skilled technician and arrange a series of customer visits. Conventional technical manuals delivered in Hypertext as shown above may not

be sufficient when difficult faults occur, and BG Service has shown that it is useful to have available a model based diagnostic system. Here, the user describes the manifestation of the fault to the field computer, and it then models the appliance and proposes likely faults. The benefit of model based systems is that they do not need a body of knowledge to be built up before they are used. The disadvantage is that the model is costly to write as is has to be a coded description of the function of the appliance. It has been proved that such diagnostic systems are a help with fault diagnosis on complex appliances, but,  that due to the high diagnostic model development cost, are only warranted on the most complex devices.

Training Delivery System

Traditional classroom training for operational staff, is costly, and requires substantial logistical planning. In some cases the availability of a CD-ROM containing training materials is valuable. Video for windows provides the facility to supplement normal interactive computer learning packages with video footage and sound. In both TransCo and BG Service full multi media training is being delivered successfully on field portable PC systems. the technical requirements for such a PC are high, and are described in the MPC2 (MultimediaPC) specificaton (4) . TFT (Thin Film Transistor) colour screens and sound facilities are needed. The additional cost of the PC hardware is however offset by the savings in training use.

Database Delivery System (See Fig 3.)

In the example, I show the retrieval of local database information on chemical substances hazardous to health. UK health and safety legislation requires that workers have access to the handling information on substances that may be hazardous. Here a word search has taken a few seconds to retrieve information from the British Gas CHOIR (hazardous chemicals handling information) database on a hazardous substance. This system allows for a rapid and accurate response to incidents relating to chemical injury, and also places the approved chemical handling information at the users disposal.

INFORMATION COLLECTION EXAMPLES

Geographic data

British Gas now has a trial where digital cameras are used to collect photographs of sites during construction and maintenance work, and to collect simple dimensional information. The photographs, and other supporting data, are then used by a draughtsman, later, to update the digital map. (See below) An alternative, also under trial, is the use of surveying software separate to the field map delivery system. Proprietary systems such as those from Sokkia(Locator) and Leica(PenMap) are typical of these surveyors tools. In the hands of a trained records clerk they are effective. GPS (Global Positioning System) trials have also been carried out with a view to positioning plant simply by recording its 'Global Position'. The difficulty here is that, to obtain the accuracy needed for UK streetworks, a differential system must be used. This involves setting up two GPS systems. In addition (the UK) map data is not necessarily 'true' to GPS, so errors have to be reconciled. In the practical application of strectworks, relative measurements to local landmarks or map construct points are presently seen as the most useful sources of dimensions.

Photographs (See Fig 4.)

Photographs now seem likely to form an important method of record collection. They have several advantages. The are easy to take, and the technique is familiar to most people. They show the street works in relationship to other street furniture and landmarks; they can provide some dimensional information; they can be annotated with dimensions taken on site, and lastly they can be filed in a computer for use as an aide memoir as well as a source of verification data for a cartographer. The figure shows a retrieval screen and view from a field trial where we are using colour cameras, pen computers and PCMCIA disk storage to take, annotate and transfer photographs from site. Early indications from the trial are of high user acceptance, and potential cost savings when compared with paper records. Users have insisted on colour images, but have been prepared to accept a '300 line image as a minimum standard. This quality level is lower than is obtained from conventional colour prints which can be scanned and digitised, and allows low cost cameras, such as the 'Canon Ion' to be used. Presently fixed focus lenses are used, this has the advantage that each view has a a consistent perspective. Due to the large image file size we have no plans to transmit the images by radio.

Forms and Management Information (See Fig 5.)

Here we show an example of a prototype form that could be used to collect job details following the connection of a service pipe to a customer. Such forms can be used under Pen Windows or normal Windows operating systems, where Pen Windows is used, then handwriting recognition is possible. Early experiences with handwriting recognition have not been good, users preferring keyboard entry, or selection from drop down menu. The data from the form is placed in a local database on the field computer, before being forwarded by radio or telephone modem to the office.

Elsewhere, non graphical menu based 'form' applications have been used successfully within the Company. However in this example we make use of the graphical interface that is available on a 'Windows' field PC. Windows has in this case been selected as the operating system to facilitate the graphics, maps, video, and hypertext displays.

A VIEW OF FUTURE DEVELOPMENTS

Several trends are important to the future of information in the workplace. Firstly, the rapid growth in public digital telephone and data networks such as GSM (Global digital celular telephone system). The data rates promised begin to allow the possibility of delivering whole documents over the air. This will change the balance of the decision of when to use local field mass data storage and its associated maintenance costs versus the costs of on-line communication. The World Wide Web on Internet has developed the concept of Hypertext over wide area networks. Experience of the practical issues in delivering complex document structures over non-ideal links is growing, This knowledge will become relevant to the field data 'problem'. Mass Storage technology is continuing to grow at a rate where a doubling in capacity, or a halving in price, occurs every 18 months. Predictions from the learned institutions are that magnetic recording (only one of the mass storage methods) has, approximately, two orders of magnitude growth in capacity per unit area before any fundamental physical limits are approached. If mass storage continues to be the technology of choice for field data, then its size and cost will soon become a minor issue. Semiconductor technology may, in the end, produce the ideal solid state memory, but for now the most important semiconductor developments are in the reduction of power consumption and increase in speed of the computer itself. The issues that will remain will be the ones of the user interface, and of maintaining the data itself. User interface issues will continue to be dominated by the need for maximum screen sizes, keyboards, 'pens', equipment strength, power, and weight

CONCLUSION

My view is that IT systems are frequently overcomplicated and over specified. The applications described here have been developed in close co-operation with users, and by a process of demonstration and trial. Detailed specifications are developed through the development cycle and are needed when roll out to a large number of users is planned. It is useful to consider how field IT systems may eventually interconnect, but not to effect that interconnection until it is needed, this avoids project elements becoming too large, and un-manageable, at the design stage.

British Gas has shown the advantages of technology demonstration, and of user field trials, it is now beginning to gain the benefits of its investments in IT across many of its operations, supporting front line staff with electronic information.

REFERENCES

1. PCMIG "Portable Computers for Field Force Applications - a discussion document" issue 2 November 1993

2. G F Whitbread and M E Morey "Fiche and Chips" Institution of Gas Engineers, Communication 1511 November 1992

3. M E Morey and G Littlehales "Pac-a-Map" Institution of Gas Engineers, Midland Section 10th May 1994

4. Multimedia Personal Computer MPC(2) specification - Multimedia PC Corp.

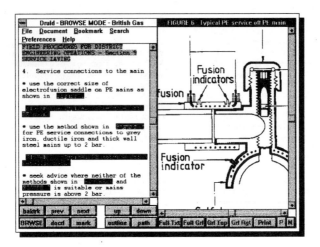

Figure 1. Document delivery using Hypertext

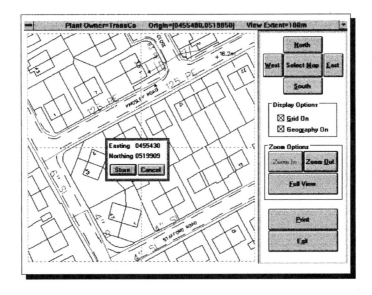

Figure 2. Map display system

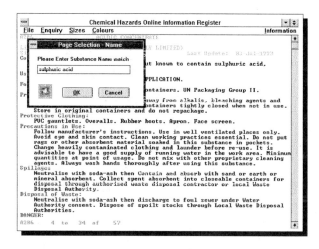

Figure 3. Chemical database query display

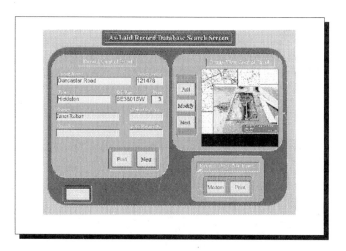

Figure 4. Photographic database query

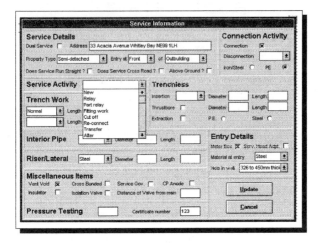

Figure 5. Electronic form to capture job details

OPTIMAL CONTROL OF COMPRESSORS
FOR GAS DISTRIBUTION NETWORKS

CONTROLE OPTIMAL DES COMPRESSEURS
POUR RESEAU DE DISTRIBUTION DE GAZ

Guansan Tian
Shandong Architectural and Civil Engineering Institute, P. R. CHINA

Zhigang Jin
Tianjin University, P. R. China

ABSTRACT

In this paper an overall research is made into the main problems related to the optimal control of compressors for gas distribution networks. A macroscopic model is developed to simulate the operation of gas networks, which has overcome the limits of the gas network analysis. The compressor performance curves are introduced into the macroscopic model. In this way the simulations of gas distribution networks can be used for analysis of the operation of gas distribution systems. Aiming at minimizing power consumption, the optimal control models of compressors for gas networks are established and the corresponding algorithms are given. The calculation results have indicated that the models are practical for engineering applications.

RESUME

Le project recherche profondement la modelisation aux condition de measure de reseau de gaz et commande optimale de compresseur, etablit des modeles, surmonte le limite d'analyse de reseau, introduit caracteristiques de compresseur au modelisation, pour que la modelisation peut etre employe au commande de distribution de gaz . Visant au econome de l'electricite,au condition d'assurer le volume et pressure de gaz,les modeles mathematique est etabli et le methode de calcul est introduit.

INTRODUCTION

Manufactured gas distribution systems generally have compressor stations which are in distribution stations and gas plants. Gas produced in gas plants and held in distribution stations is pumped to medium or high pressure distribution networks by compressors in gas plants or distribution stations. As the gas demand is changeable in the process of gas supply, the gas delivery and the number of operating compressors varies with the variation of gas demand during the operating process, i.e. inlet pressures of distribution networks vary with the pressures of compressor stations. The power consumption of compressors is affected by the outlet pressures of compressor stations. The higher the outlet pressure is, the more power they consume.

Under the condition of adequate gas supply and adequate pressure to customers at all time, simulations of distribution networks are made from time to time to determine the operating combination of compressors which made the outlet pressures of compressor stations at the lowest point. Compressor operators control the operating states of compressors according to the simulation results, to ensure lowest electricity consumption.

COMPRESSOR OPERATING ENVELOPE

Optimizing the operations of compressors involve two consideration: (1) the compressor operating characteristics; (2) electricity consumption. The compressor operating characteristics are a function of the outlet pressure and the gas flow, while its electricity consumption relates to the outlet pressures, flow, efficiency and operating time of compressor. Both problems can be calculated theoretically, but the results are not satisfactory in accuracy. In this paper statistical regression is used to simulate the compressor operating characteristics and to calculate the power consumption according to the latest operating data of compressors. In this paper the compressor operating characteristics envelope is called the P-Q curve.

P-Q Curve Model: $$\bar{p}_{i,k} = A_{0,i} + A_{1,i}q_{i,k} + A_{2,i}q_{i,k}^2$$

Electricity Consumption Equation: $$Z_{i,k} = \alpha_i p_{i,k}^\beta q_{i,k}$$

in which :
$\bar{p}_{i,k}$ = outlet pressure of the i-th compressor station at k time;
$q_{i,k}$ = flow of the i-th compressor station at k time;
$A_{0,i}; A_{1,i}; A_{2,i}; \alpha_i; \beta$ = regression coefficients;
$Z_{i,k}$ = electricity consumption per hour of the i-th compressor station at k time .

According to the operating data of Shanghai gas company, Table 1 is the calculation results about two kind compressors and two electricity consumption calculation equations established by least square method. The equation are as follows:

For the Roots compressor, $Z = 27.95p^{1.08}q$, $Q$ = 0.0116, S.D.= 0.0408, R = 0.9979

For the piston compressor, $Z = 29.01p^{0.82}q$, $Q$ = 0.0048, S.D.= 0.0283, R = 0.9842

in which:
Q = quadratic sum of deviation;
S.D. = standard deviation;
R = relation coefficient.

In this way the calculation results agreed with the actual operations much better than the traditional theoretical calculation procedures.

MACROSCOPIC MODELS

The optimal control of compressors is based on the accurate simulations of the operations of gas distribution networks. There are two methods to simulate the distribution network operations: network analysis and macroscopic model.

All methods of network analyses depend on the correct number of nodes, the number of links, demand at the nodes, the lengths, diameters, friction factors of all the links [1]. The flow at each node varies with the customer demand. It is difficult to determine the accurate flow at every node accurately. Tars, naphalene, and dust deposit on the pipe inner surface, reduces the pipe inside diameters and changes the link friction factors. The change of diameters and friction factors can not be determined accurately, so that the results of network analyses usually do not agree with the actual operation of gas distribution networks with compressors. Such results can not be used in gas supply dispatching.

The flows and pressures at most nodes are not important to gas supply dispatching. Only the outlet flow and pressure of every gas plant or distribution station and each control node pressure which have the lowest pressures are important to gas supply dispatching. These variables may be simulated accurately by macroscopic models [2]. Macroscopic models are based upon such macroscopic variables as the total projected gas demand, the outlet flow and pressure of every gas plant or distribution station, and allowable minimum pressure of each control node etc. Statistic regression is used for the establishment of regression equations of the macroscopic variables.

The macroscopic models do not include the those microcosmic variables such as the diameter and friction factor of each link, and the flow at every node. Through combining the system theories, the macroscopic model describes the functions involving the outlet

flow and pressure of each gas plant, outlet flow and pressure of
each gas distribution station, each control node pressure, and
telemetering pressures of measuring points which have relation to
the gas supply dispatching. This method overcomes the shortcomings
of network analysis. The general form of macroscopic models is:

$$P_{i,k+1} = a_{i,0} + a_{i,1}q_{k+1} + \sum_{j=1}^{m1} b_{i,j}q_{j,k+1} + \sum_{l=1}^{m1+m2} c_{i,l}P_{l,k}$$

$$i = 1, 2, \ldots\ldots, m_1 + m_2; \quad k = 1, 2, \ldots, 24$$

in which:

$m_1$ = number of compressor station in distribution stations and gas
plants;

$m_2$ = number of typical pressure test points (control points);

$P_{i,k+1}$ = outlet pressure of the i-th compressor station or pressure of
the i-th typical pressure test point at k+1 time;

$q_{k+1}$ = total projected gas demand at k+1 time;

$q_{j,k+1}$ = projected gas delivery of the j-th compressor station at k+1
time;

$p_{l,k}$ = outlet pressure of l-th compressor station or telemetering
pressure of the first typical pressure test point at k time;

$a_{i,0}, a_{i,1}, b_{i,j}, c_{i,l}$ = regression coefficients, obtained by the least square
method and renewed continually according to new operating data.

Figures 1 and 2 are the calculation results about two gas
distributions station of Shanghai gas distribution system. The
differences between the modeling results and the actual measurements
are very low, and it shows the applicability of the model to
practical engineering systems.

MODELS FOR OPTIMAL CONTROL

In this paper, the optimal control of compressors for gas
distribution networks refers to controlling the operating state of
each compressor according to projected gas demand at different gas
supply time. Basically, a distribution system has more than two
compressor stations, there would be many operation schemes of
compressors that could meet the gas supply demands. The different
operation schemes result in different electricity consumption [3].
Aiming at minimizing electricity consumption, the objective function
of optimal control of compressors for gas networks is established.
The constraints include the outlet flow of each compressor station
constraints, customer per-hour-demand constraints, network pressure
constraints etc.

Objective Function

The objective function describing the total electricity
consumption of gas distribution system for an hour can be written as

$$Z_{k+1} = \sum_{i=1}^{ml} \alpha_i P_{i,k+1}^{\beta} q_i$$

Constraints

The outlet flow of each compressor station is equal to algebraic sum of all outlet flow of compressors on operating in parallel in the compressor station, i.e.

$$\sum_{j=1}^{ki} q_{i,j} x_{i,j} = q_i \qquad (i=1,2,\ldots,m_1) \qquad (1)$$

The variables $q_{i,j}$ are determined by the P-Q cures.

The sum of outlet flow of all compressor stations is equal to the total projected gas demand at each gas supply time period (one hour is a gas supply time period)

$$\sum_{i=1}^{ml} q_i = q_{k+1} \qquad (k=1,2,\ldots,24) \qquad (2)$$

The outlet flow of each compressor station must be within the limits of the allowable maximum and minimum flow of the gas plant or distribution station, i.e.

$$Q_{i,min} \le q_i \le Q_{i,max} \qquad (i=1, 2,\ldots, m_1) \qquad (3)$$

The outlet pressure of each compressor station should agree with the P-Q cure model and calculation result of macroscopic model, i.e.

$$\overline{P}_{i,k+1} = P_{i,k+1} \qquad (i=1, 2,\ldots,m_1; \ k=1, 2,\ldots24) \qquad (4)$$

The control node pressure must be adequate for the allowable minimum pressure, i.e.

$$P_{i,k+1} \ge P_{i,min} \qquad (i = 1, 2,\ldots, m_1+m_2; \ k=1, 2,\ldots,24) \qquad (5)$$

$x_{i,j} =$    if the i-th compressor is on;
$x_{i,j} = 0$    if the i-th compressor is off.

in which :
$Z_{k+1}=$ total electricity consumption at the k+1 time;
$q_i=$ outlet flow of the i-th compressor station at k+1 time (variable);
$q_{i,j}=$ outlet flow of the j-th compressor of the i-th compressor station;
$k_i=$ number of compressors of the i-th compressor station;
$x_{i,j}=$ variables;
$Q_{i,max}, Q_{i,min}=$ allowable maximum and minimum flow of the i-th compressor station, respectively;

$P_{i,min}$ = allowable minimum pressure of the i-th node.

The optimal control models are constrained mixed discrete nonlinear programming. It is difficult to find the solution of the optimal control models by general mathematical methods. Taking the actual operations of gas distribution systems into consideration, it is decided to adopt a direct search procedure to look for all feasible solutions according to constraints (1), (2) and (3). Then, with the optimal control models the feasible solutions are dealt with and the optimal solution can be found, whose total power consumption is the lowest.

The authors have designed and debugged programs corresponding to each procedures. The examples have been calculated on the computer and the results have indicated that using this method to control compressors for gas distribution networks can reduce the electricity consumption by 2% to 7%.

CONCLUSIONS

The electricity consumption associated with gas compressors can be minimized by application of the optimal control models established in this paper. Compressor operators control the compressors according to the solutions of the models can save 2% to 7% electricity consumption and raise gas supply quality.

The accuracy of the optimal control models depends on the quality of data available about the present operating state of the distribution system, so the data to be used for the model fitting should be complete and accurate.

The deviation of solutions for the peak day of festival is greater.

REFERENCES

1. G. S. Tian "Network analysis of gas distribution networks with compressors" Journal of Shandong Architectural and Civil Engineering Institute, **6**(4), 69-73, 1991
2. G. S. Tian, Z. G. Jin "Macroscopic analysis of gas distribution networks" Gas & Heat, **14**(4), 34-37, 1991
3. M. C. Herr "POGAL: Prognosis and optimization in gas supply system", Gas Abstract, Sept., 1988

Table 1. Calculation Results of Two Kind Compressors

| outlet pressure (MP$_a$) | 0.03 | 0.05 | 0.07 | 0.09 | 0.10 |
|---|---|---|---|---|---|
| outlet flow of piston ( m$^3$ / h ) | 5940 | 5860 | 5770 | 5700 | 5670 |
| outlet flow of roots ( m$^3$ / h ) | 9820 | 9770 | 9680 | 9580 | 9540 |

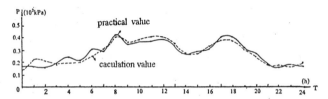

Figure 1. Outlet of the First Compressors Station

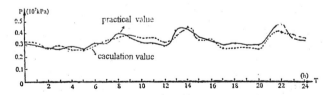

Figure 2.    Outlet of the Second  Compressors Station